JD EDWARDS

J.D. Edwards® OneWorld™: The Complete Reference

J.D. Edwards® OneWorld™: The Complete Reference

Joseph E. Miller, Allen D. Jacot, John A. Stern

Osborne/**McGraw-Hill**

Berkeley New York St. Louis San Francisco
Auckland Bogotá Hamburg London Madrid
Mexico City Milan Montreal New Delhi Panama City
Paris São Paulo Singapore Sydney Tokyo Toronto

Osborne/**McGraw-Hill**
2600 Tenth Street
Berkeley, California 94710
U.S.A.

For information on translations or book distributors outside the U.S.A., or to arrange bulk purchase discounts for sales promotions, premiums, or fund-raisers, please contact Osborne/**McGraw-Hill** at the above address.

J.D. Edwards® OneWorld™: The Complete Reference

1234567890 DOC DOC 01987654321

ISBN 0-07-212510-1

Publisher Brandon A. Nordin	**Copy Editors** Lunaea Weatherstone, Nancy Crumpton
Vice President and Associate Publisher Scott Rogers	**Proofreader** Susie Elkind
Editorial Director Gareth Hancock	**Indexer** Jack Lewis
Project Editor Jody McKenzie	**Computer Designers** Roberta Steele, Dick Schwartz, Tara Davis
Acquisitions Coordinator Jessica Wilson	**Illustrator** Peter Hancik
Development Editor Karen Riner	**Series Design** Roberta Steele
Technical Editor Kyle Kinder	**Cover Series Design** Ted Halladay
J.D. Edwards Publishing Liaisons Ben Martin, Cathy Robbins	

This book was composed with Corel VENTURA™ Publisher.

The authors would like to dedicate this book to our families who have supported us over the last year. Their willingness (and in some cases joy) in temporarily losing touch with their husbands, sons, and fathers who were busily devoted to working on this book while simultaneously managing multiple OneWorld implementations have made this publication possible more than any other single thing (with the possible exception of the OneWorld Magic 8-Ball used in all crucial technology decisions).

About the Authors

Joe Miller has worked on more than 35 OneWorld implementations and is the National Practice Leader for OneWorld technology at Deloitte & Touche. He was also Area Technology Services Manager for J.D. Edwards and has worked with OneWorld since the product's first release.

Allen Jacot is a OneWorld Certified CNC Specialist with J.D. Edwards, and has worked with OneWorld since its original beta release in 1996. He has supported numerous OneWorld implementations and has worked within J.D. Edwards, developing and leading the J.D. Edwards' OneWorld NT Technical Customer Support team.

John A. Stern, participating in more than 30 OneWorld implementations, is the Technology Manager for Deloitte & Touche's National ERP eEnablement Competency Center, and provides global leadership around the CNC practice.

Contents at a Glance

PART III
Appendix

Contents

PART II

System Administration and Troubleshooting

PART III
Appendix

Foreword

J.D. Edwards OneWorld is making a surge in the e-business arena; and its stable foundation gives you, the user, some comfort in the ever-changing, unpredictable technology world. Many Quest members are coexisting between WorldSoftware and OneWorld, while others are taking the OneWorld plunge. Whether you are coexisting or moving straight into a OneWorld implementation, *J.D. Edwards OneWorld: The Complete Reference* brings important and helpful technical information to the J.D. Edwards community.

J.D. Edwards recognizes that technology must be able to evolve in order to suit your changing business needs; and OneWorld was designed with this firmly in mind. It is the first network-centric solution that separates business rules from the underlying technology, allowing businesses to capitalize on new functionality without disrupting ongoing business. This comprehensive guide shows J.D. Edwards' commitment to providing practical information to both new and experienced OneWorld developers.

Similarly, Quest strives to help its members gain the most from their J.D. Edwards investments; and our support of this publishing project demonstrates our continued backing of J.D. Edwards' effort to communicate useful technical information to users. The partnership between J.D. Edwards and Osborne/McGraw-Hill that created J.D. Edwards Press is very much in tune with Quest's mission to provide information to its user community. Without this communication and support, those implementing OneWorld, or coexisting between WorldSoftware and OneWorld, would not have the information needed to implement it successfully nor gain the most from their software investment. *J.D. Edwards OneWorld: The Complete Reference* delves deep into the technology of OneWorld, giving users the "ins and outs" of the software while focusing on application development and customization.

As the e-business world changes at phenomenal speeds, technology must rapidly adapt to keep pace. Here is your chance, as a current or prospective OneWorld developer, to delve into information specifically aimed at helping your organization successfully develop and modify OneWorld applications to get the most out of its J.D. Edwards investment.

The technology world will keep changing. J.D. Edwards Press will help you keep up.

Robert A. Rosati

Robert A. Rosati
President, Quest J.D. Edwards User Group

Acknowledgments

There are a number of people we need to acknowledge with regard to this book. Some of them provided intellectual capital, while others merely provided support and the occasional inspiration (such as, if you don't get this finished, you're fired). Although we don't have enough room to list each contribution separately, we want to at least list their names to express our gratitude for their contributions.

Jeff Plewa
Mike Guerra
Killi Jones
Michael Jacot
Steve Spilker
Masood Khan
J.D. Edwards World Solutions Company
The entire support staff at Osborne/McGraw-Hill

Gareth Hancock
Craig Ledonne
Clayton Seeley
Mark Chaney
Chris Papineua
Jody Mckenzie

Jeff Michaels
Joe Litney
Sydney Nurse
DeRay Scholz
Sandra Holms
Deloitte & Touche

Introduction

Greetings, fellow travelers along the quest we call OneWorld. It is a pleasure to see that you are on this journey, are contemplating this journey, or are just plain bored and thought this book would interest you. It was almost a year in the making and we hope our efforts have produced a book that will interest you, entertain you, and provide you with deeper insight into the J.D.Edwards' OneWorld ERP suite of products. It has been a pleasure for us to bring it to you.

The combined experience of the authors includes ten years of OneWorld technology and implementation experience. We've pushed ourselves to show both the good and the bad, and though we have occasionally disagreed on specific content, we are all in agreement that this book will benefit every organization that is in the process, has completed this process, or is contemplating the process of implementing OneWorld.

One of our specific goals has been to ensure that the novice and experienced practitioner alike can read, understand, and get something out of these pages. We have it on good authority (and yes, we did test it) that it will benefit you and your organization. So much so, we recommend you buy as many copies as your company can afford. We even had one company suggest (and we blushed at the comment) that they should buy a copy for every user. Naturally, we, as the authors, agree. Still, joking aside, this book will benefit anyone who wants to understand the OneWorld product in detail.

Also, be sure to visit the J.D. Edwards Press Web site at **http://www.jdedwardspress.com** for additional OneWorld information that enhances the material covered in this book.

How to Use This Book

This section was difficult for the authors to agree on because there are simply a huge number of ways to use this book. One author recommended the best method of using this book was to read a page and throw the book away. Then buy a new copy, read the second page and throw it away too. Repeat the above process until you've completely read the book. Another author thought it would make an excellent paperweight, doorstop, or combustion fuel on really cold days. The third author had this to say on the subject: This book is specifically designed to be a user-friendly guide appealing to the inexperienced and experienced user alike. It can either be read cover to cover or as a true reference manual where you pick and choose the topics of interest.

Sections Within a Chapter

We've added several unique sections into the layout of each chapter. All chapters start with an introduction (some are humorous and some simply attempt it). At the end of the introduction, you will see a bulleted list of the topics covered in the chapter. We won't list every topic, just the main threads of discussion.

The Law of the West   You will see sections titled "The Law of the West." These sections contain information on how to quickly accomplish certain tasks by using methods other than J.D. Edwards OneWorld approved methods. As a caveat, the authors highly recommend that you back up tables and files that could be affected prior to following the steps listed in "The Law of the West." Additionally, the authors take no responsibility for your choosing to use the information provided in these special sections. If you are not comfortable using this information, we strongly advise that you do not apply the Law of the West recommendations to your production systems. As your company gains more experience with the product, you will be more comfortable with the information provided in these specialized, advanced discussions.

How did we come up with the name "The Law of the West"? As you work with the OneWorld product or attend OneWorld training, you might hear the term "cowboy" referring to a type of activity that is other than standard (for example, when you ask why you can't just perform a quick transactional SQL statement against the database instead of going through the GUI interface). This will be termed a cowboy maneuver. As such, this section is called "The Law of the West" to maintain the spirit of the activity.

Notes, Definitions, and Tables   You will also see a variety of notes, definitions, tables, and other special sections where we pull information from different sources to add to your overall understanding of the topics we are presenting. Additionally, we have added as many screen shots from the actual product and different supported platforms as we can. These screen shots have been picked not necessarily as duplicates of the examples provided (that is, the same information), but rather to assist you in understanding how the applications look and feel within the product.

Parts of the Book   The chapters in the book can be broken into two primary pieces: an in-depth section with very technical concepts illustrating how the product works (especially under the GUI), and a section on administering, configuring, and manipulating the system to your company's requirements. How you read the book is up to you, but we think that all of it is both informative and useful.

Writing Style   This book is written with an interactive style. Often, you will feel as if the authors are talking directly to you (or at least that is the feel we've been shooting for). We have tried to anticipate your questions. Many times, we actually write what we think you will be asking yourself while reading it. If we miss our mark, we hope our questions will address something you didn't think to ask but wish you had.

As mentioned, this book is the best compilation of the combined experiences of the authors' ten years of working with OneWorld technology. We have tried to provide real examples wherever possible to help with your learning curve. We have changed the names of companies and other pertinent information, but the vast majority of the work comes from our personal experiences working with and implementing the OneWorld product at real client sites. And again, we hope that you will find it both useful and educational.

Going forward, we thought that it would help if you understood some of the background of the company bringing you the OneWorld product and the history of that product itself. Take a couple of minutes and read through these pages to gain a better understanding of the company and where it came from.

A Little Company on the Prairie

If you have worked with J.D. Edwards for any amount of time, you will probably hear it referred to as "the little software company on the prairie". This company really did start out as a little software company. Three people with a vision came together to create J.D. Edwards: Jack Thompson, Dan Gregory, and Ed McVaney. Each of these founders lent a small part of their names to create J.D. Edwards.

When the company was first started, it designed custom business software for small and medium-sized companies. Eventually, J.D. Edwards focused on the IBM System/38 and began creating business application suites. It was this focus that allowed J.D. Edwards to create their CASE software development and design tool. This design tool gave the company consistency across the range of their integrated applications.

As the company rolled through the 1980s, it began to really grow. This is when J.D. Edwards started to open branch offices around the country. In the late 1980s, the decision was made to start concentrating on international expansion. To kick off this international growth, the company opened a European headquarters in Belgium (the European headquarters was later moved to the United Kingdom) and soon followed with a series of offices around the world to now encompass North America, South America, Europe, and Asia.

It soon became apparent from the company's incredible growth that it would either need to remain a small software company on the prairie servicing customers on an individual basis or it would need to break out as an industry leader, providing a software package that would meet the needs of many different companies. This is how the WorldSoftware suite was born. This software helped J.D. Edwards become recognized as an industry-leading supplier of applications software for the IBM AS/400.

J.D. Edwards has enjoyed great success with the WorldSoftware suite. However, this is a company that is use to being an industry leader. So as the industry started to move to client/server solutions, J.D. Edwards responded. In August 1996, OneWorld was brought to the market. This software again allowed the company to achieve a technological breakthrough. J.D. Edwards was not interested in just meeting industry standards—it wanted to go beyond them and remain an industry leader in the enterprise software market.

OneWorld has allowed the company to do this. This software is highly configurable and runs on a variety of different platforms. It also has an integrated toolset that gives J.D. Edwards' customers the ability to modify the software to meet their business needs. As customers' business needs change, the OneWorld software is flexible enough to change with them. After all, this is what J.D. Edwards does best: meet its clients' business needs. In fact, Ed McVaney, one of the company's founders and its current CEO, has been quoted as saying, "We believe our first job is to solve your business problems. Nothing else counts if we don't solve your business problems."

J.D. Edwards did not stop with just meeting its customers' business needs at the product level. J.D. Edwards realizes that to meet its customers' business needs it is imperative to attract and retain the best talent in the industry. Thus the J.D. Edwards' culture was born. This culture truly makes J.D. Edwards a unique company with whom to do business and with whom to work. The founders of this company created a workplace environment in which they would want to work. As a result, J.D. Edwards has attracted people with the highest personal and professional ideals. This culture helps guide employees in decision making. It concentrates on making a fair profit and having a heart for its employees. This is what has attracted and retained many loyal customers and employees. It has also allowed J.D. Edwards to concentrate on building relationships with its clients. The goal of this company is not only to do business with its clients today, but also to build relationships with its clients in order to conduct business over the years to come.

If you have been watching J.D. Edwards, you know that its business has boomed. The company has grown at an incredible pace over the last 23 years. Over most of this time, it has maintained a revenue growth rate of 50 percent and better. This growth has shown in the technology and solutions the company can offer its clients. The OneWorld software suite continues to grow and offer even more cutting-edge technology, such as e-business solutions.

J.D. Edwards has more than 5,000 corporate customers who do business in more than 100 countries. The company also now has nearly 6,000 employees in 48 offices worldwide.

As you can see, the little company on the prairie has grown to become an industry leader. It has moved from providing enterprise resource planning software to providing e-business solutions. It continues to search for new ways to provide highly configurable solutions to its customers. Keep in mind as you read this book something that Ed McVaney is fond of saying: "You ain't seen nothing yet!" As OneWorld continues to grow and expand into the e-business world to provide business-to-business solutions as well as business-to-customer solutions, all the authors can say is, Ed is right—you ain't seen nothing yet!

PART I

OneWorld Explained— Inside and Out

## CHAPTER 1

OneWorld Architectural Theory and Configurations

From Objects to Enterprise: Flexibility in
   Meeting Your Business Needs

Configurations Defined

Determining Which Architecture Best Fits
   Your Business

Standard Out-of-the-Box Configurations

OneWorld architecture is about one thing, and one thing only. It is about a software that is so flexible it becomes part of the solution instead of the problem. How many other ERP software packages can say the same? The OneWorld architecture allows you to pick and choose hardware and software solutions that meet your immediate needs while still providing the flexibility and forethought to allow you to change those decisions. If you outgrow your solution, or when new architectures become available or desirable, you can bet that with the OneWorld product it's easy for your organization to exploit those changes while not throwing away the investment you've already made.

This chapter covers the various architectures available to the OneWorld product in the following sections:

- From Objects to enterprise: Flexibility in meeting business needs

- Configurations defined: two-tier, three-tier, and N-tier

- Determining which architecture fits your business needs

- Standard "out-of-the-box" configurations

From Objects to Enterprise: Flexibility in Meeting Your Business Needs

The OneWorld product is a robust software package with unparalleled flexibility and scalability. Although many people have questioned this statement, we think that this chapter proves the flexibility of this product. Once you understand the options that are available in OneWorld, we think you'll agree that this product is easily one of the most powerful on the market.

OneWorld is an object-based product. To understand its flexibility, it helps to understand its base architecture. When you look at a OneWorld screen, just about everything you see is an object—including the OneWorld Explorer, the application, and the database tables.

A OneWorld object is any reusable entity based on the OneWorld toolset. We use a rule of thumb when trying to decide what is and what isn't an object: Everything other than business data is an object.

All objects start on the deployment server. They may not stay there, but we initially put them there. In most companies using OneWorld, the true "master" objects never leave this location. (For more information about the deployment server, refer to Chapter 5.)

Logic objects are deployed throughout the enterprise using compiled software packages. They show up as replicated objects on application servers and workstations. Because of the OneWorld toolset, developers are insulated against platform-specific programming. That means if you develop a piece of logic (maybe a business function designed to verify customer data in a custom EDI cross-reference table), you can transfer and compile this logic on the AS/400 and Windows NT Intel machines, a UNIX box, or a workstation without having to modify the code, providing both power and flexibility to meet your business needs.

In addition, OneWorld specifically uses an architecture designed to allow your organization the ability to decide where data resides and where to process logic. You'll be pleased to encounter the Object Configuration Manager (OCM). This product enables the OneWorld architecture to leap-frog ahead of its competition. Let's take an absolutely crazy scenario; suppose you wanted to dedicate an entire server to each table within the production environment. By using the OCM, not only could you do so, but the user really wouldn't realize that you'd done this. As far as the user is concerned, the product would continue to work as it normally did. (Refer to Chapter 2 for more information on the OCM.)

Though the phrase is no longer used by J.D. Edwards personnel, we refer to the previously described process as *masking complexity*. Masking complexity means that the user doesn't know where the logic is processed or where the data is stored. You can even mix and match hardware and database platforms without bothering the production user with the details. This allows you to leverage existing hardware and software and still not be tied to it. Consequently, you can continue to use the latest in technology advances. You also can leverage existing IT experience as well as any experience you might acquire. And the benefits of masking complexity don't stop there.

Suppose your users are continually launching huge, resource sucking universal batch engines (UBEs), which are OneWorld reports, on your production server. You know the type we mean—those 500-page detailed reports that they claim they read. What can you do architecturally to solve this problem?

Using ActivEra, you can add a departmental server for this particular group. Based on their business reporting requirements, you can even set up a special reporting environment using replicated data and a separate network segment to fully isolate the network traffic, database requirements, and processing time. How is that for an architectural solution?

Flexibility to Scale

As you can see from the preceding discussion, OneWorld quickly scales to meet your company's processing and data requirements. OneWorld is able to work with most new technologies including network disk arrays, clustering technologies, and Windows Terminal Server capabilities. Your organization can utilize fully redundant systems, LANs, WANs, virtual private networks (VPNs), and so on for communication purposes. It really is that simple. Let's look again at the solution of adding a departmental logic processing server (also referred to as an *application server*, see Chapter 5) to offload some UBE processing. Can you believe that the process of offloading some UBE processes can take less than a day? That's about what it should take to install and begin using a new application server.

N O T E

The preceding time estimate assumes the server's hardware, OS, and any database requirements are already installed and configured. It also assumes that the Configurable Network Computing (CNC) personnel are experienced.

Configurations Defined

To better understand the possible configurations, we need to define a number of terms:

- **Server**   A machine that processes service requests. These requests can be for data, logic processing, data replication, or even security.

- **Workstation**   A machine within the OneWorld system that makes requests for services. It acts as the primary interface between the end user and the application.

- **Client/server architecture**   A system design that specifically uses both servers and workstations to optimally spread workload requirements, utilizing each machine type to perform specific functions they are most suited to accomplish.

- **Two-tier architecture**   An enterprise design where a primary logic server works directly with the client workstations.

- **Three-tier architecture**   An enterprise design using two servers for data and processing functionality in addition to workstations. Each machine provides specific logic functionality.

- **N-tier architecture**   An enterprise solution using three or more logic processing servers in conjunction with workstations to run a specific application. In essence, the architecture allows you to continue adding servers until the desired performance level is achieved.

- **Virtual three-tier architecture**   A souped-up two-tier architecture with selected application logic running on the server. Although the term has only recently been coined, configurability for this solution has been around since 1997 and supported by J.D. Edwards since 1998.

Now that we have defined some basic terms, let's go into detail on the actual architectural designs. For information on how to set up these configurations, refer to other chapters in this book or in the documentation provided by J.D. Edwards.

Two-Tier Architecture

The majority of small implementations utilize this basic configuration. It is shown in Figure 1-1. Notice that a single, primary logic/data server directly works in conjunction with workstations.

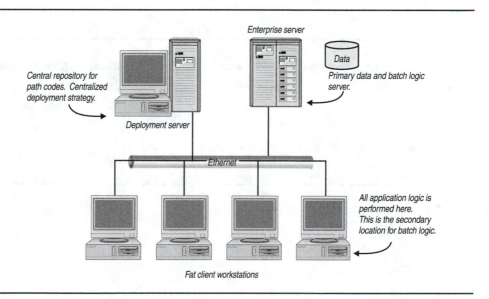

FIGURE 1-1.   The two-tier architecture, a typical configuration

In a two-tier configuration, the workstation performs all interactive application logic and provides database functionality for a total of six tables. These tables include user-defined code (UDCs) and menus. Workstations also have the ability to run batch application logic by overriding the submission location at the time of the UBE submission. The server provides the primary database functionality (the B733.2 version includes over 1,600 business data tables, over 100 system tables, over 20 central object tables, and over 40 control tables). This server provides data replication, software packaging, and security services. It is also the primary UBE batch logic process server (refer to Table 1-1).

In the third quarter of 1998, J.D. Edwards announced support for Microsoft Windows Terminal Server (as of B732.1 SP 9). This new technology allows multiple users to run remote Windows sessions from local workstations on the same server. It provides fast connections and centralized administration, but most people assume adding one of these servers automatically provides a three-tier architecture. Actually, unless specifically configured, just adding Terminal Servers is really no different from a traditional two-tier configuration using new technologies. When you run the OneWorld suite on a Terminal Server, that Terminal Server is actually the workstation, and the server is still the primary data and logic server on the enterprise, as shown in Figure 1-2.

	Application Logic	Batch Logic	Database Services	Other Services
Server	None	Primary location	Primary location	Security Replication Packages
Workstation	Primary location	Secondary location	Secondary (replicated only)	None

TABLE 1-1.   Logic Services

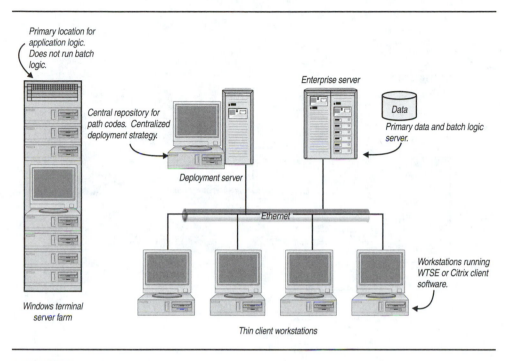

Primary location for application logic. Does not run batch logic.

Enterprise server

Central repository for path codes. Centralized deployment strategy.

Data

Primary data and batch logic server.

Deployment server

Ethernet

Windows terminal server farm

Workstations running WTSE or Citrix client software.

Thin client workstations

FIGURE 1-2.   Windows Terminal Server two-tier architecture

Three-Tier Architecture

The use of the Windows Terminal Server popularized both three-tier and N-tier architectures. In essence, a three-tier architectural design has more than one server providing logic services, as shown in Figure 1-3. People implementing OneWorld with a Windows Terminal Server quickly determined that offloading certain interactive application logic enables cost-effective hardware, system, and user configurations. Applications run faster, and the companies achieved a higher user-to-server ratio.

This same configuration is usable without Terminal Servers. However, unless you can justify the purchase of an application server by increased user performance, it is rarely

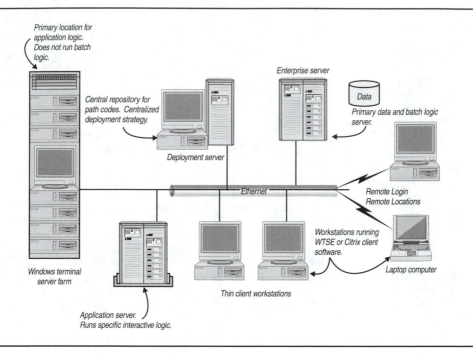

Primary location for
application logic.
Does not run batch
logic.

Central repository for
path codes. Centralized
deployment strategy.

Enterprise server

Data

Primary data and batch logic
server.

Deployment server

Ethernet

Remote Login
Remote Locations

Windows terminal
server farm

Workstations running
WTSE or Citrix client
software.

Laptop computer

Thin client workstations

Application server.
Runs specific interactive logic.

FIGURE 1-3.   Three-tier Terminal Server solution

worthwhile. Instead, three-tier architectures are deployed more often to offload nightly processing and specific departmental or location requirements when Terminal Servers are not in use (see Figure 1-4 and Table 1-2).

Virtual Three-Tier Solutions

We've recently seen virtual three-tier solutions advertised. They are actually two-tier solutions with distributed interactive application processing (refer to Table 1-3). This configuration can substantially increase the speed of workstations. If your enterprise server is beefy enough to support the additional logic processing requirements, we highly recommend it. Any of the supported server configurations can function in this capacity. However, you need to carefully decide which business functions (BSFNs) to run on the server. Data corruption problems can occur if you don't include everything you're suppose to. Additionally, some logic is designed to work on workstations only.

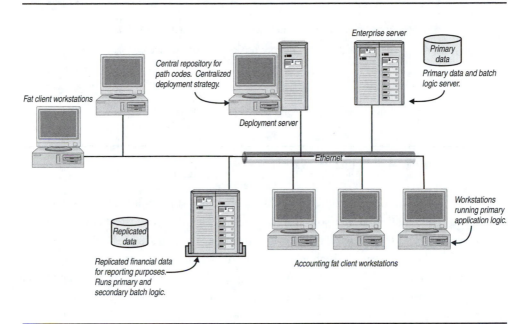

FIGURE 1-4.   Three-tier departmental architecture

	Application Logic	Batch Logic	Database Services	Other Services
Enterprise Server	None	Primary location	Primary location	Security Replication Packages
Workstation	Default location	Tertiary location	Secondary (replicated only)	None
Application server	Selected logic	Secondary location		
Database server	None	None	Secondary (real or replicated)	None

TABLE 1-2.   Three-Tier Software Configurations

Inside and Out

	Application Logic	Batch Logic	Database Services	Other Services
Enterprise server	Selected logic	Primary location	Primary location	Security Replication Packages
Workstation	Default location	Secondary location	Secondary (replicated only)	None

TABLE 1-3.   Virtual three-tier software setup

You may be wondering why you would want (or need) to look at an architecture similar to the virtual three-tier solution (see Figure 1-5). It is the fastest configuration currently designed for use with OneWorld. The closer the logic is to the data, the faster the logic can be performed, which is especially true when you can run at BUS speed with minimal latency as opposed to LAN or WAN speed. OneWorld has message-based communications. These are substantially faster when performed on the enterprise server. The logic request is made locally, the data is provided locally, the logic is

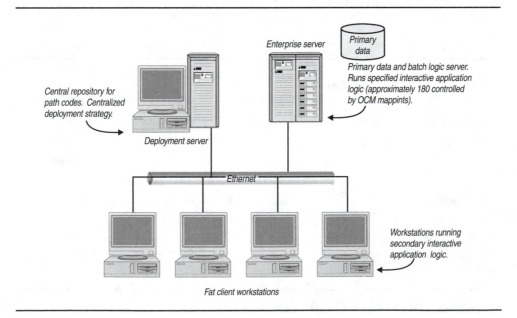

FIGURE 1-5.   Virtual three-tier architecture

performed locally, and results are posted locally. The only external requirement is a screen refresh with the results.

N-Tier Solution

Based on your business requirements, you can configure and distribute logic and data processing throughout your enterprise solution. The OneWorld product masks the complexity caused by differences between hardware platforms and database formats. This allows full functionality and scalability in designing and implementing your enterprise architecture.

N-tier solutions combine workstations, any number of logic servers, and any number of database servers into a single solution (see Table 1-4). As your company's needs grow through merger, acquisition, and other changes, you will be able to move data and logic processing at will, providing superior functionality and speed to the user.

Thin-Client Architecture

Thin clients are traditional file allocation table (FAT) client workstations or actual WinTerm devices that run the Windows Terminal Server software. The Terminal Server software enables multiple users to share the same application, running on the same server. Zero clients, on the other hand, are clients workstations that have a Web browser and access the OneWorld product through HTML and Java applications (refer to Figure 1-6 for an example of multiple architectural configurations).

	Application Logic	Batch Logic	Database Services	Other Services
Enterprise server	None	Primary location	Primary location	Security Replication Packages
Workstation	Default location	Tertiary location	Secondary (replicated only)	None
Application server	Selected logic	Secondary location		
Database server	None	None	Secondary (real or replicated)	None

TABLE 1-4. N-Tier Software Setup

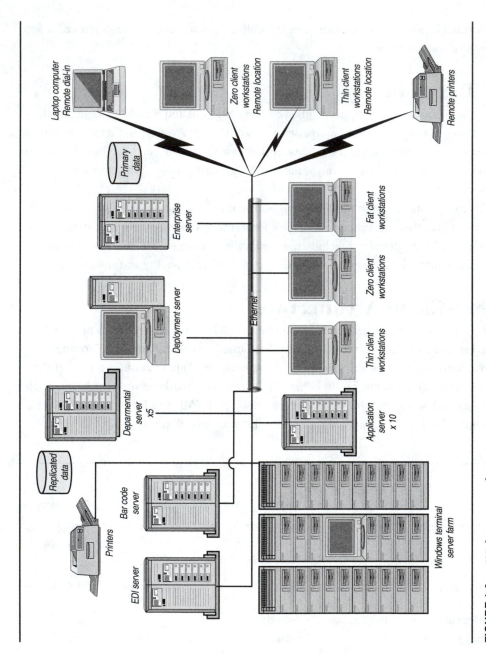

FIGURE 1-6. Wide-open architecture

Determining Which Architecture Best Fits Your Business

Every company is unique, and thus, it is almost impossible to determine in a book exactly what your company's architecture should be. In addition, because of the rapid rate of technological growth, you may start with one architectural design and end up with an entirely different one. This consideration is important, especially if you are in either the sales cycle or the initial scoping and planning phase of an implementation.

The fact that you may not end up with the same architecture that you start with indicates the power of the J.D. Edwards OneWorld enterprise resource planning (ERP) suite. OneWorld supports many different architectures and is continually improving to support more. As new technologies are introduced to the marketplace, OneWorld adjusts to embrace them as well. OneWorld's architectural diversity enables your organization to grow without being bound by the technology supporting it. OneWorld is specifically designed to allow rapid changes even after go-live, which is the premise of ActivEra.

Many different questions must be answered prior to deciding exactly what architecture best suits your organization.

Are You Running J.D. Edwards World Product?

The use of the World product gives rise to questions about coexistence and hardware/software platforms. If you are running World, your data conversion efforts should be significantly decreased. If you decide to run coexistence, then there are no conversions required. In addition, the fact that you are running the World product means that either you have in-house AS/400 experience or you have an existing service arrangement with someone who does. You have the option of using other platforms either with or in lieu of the AS/400 platform. You can start with AS/400 running in a coexistence strategy, then migrate to an AS/400 database server solution, and eventually end up without AS/400 entirely.

Inside and Out

DEFINITION

Coexistence: Coexistence is the ability of the J.D. Edwards OneWorld and World software products to share business data. If you make a change to data in the World software, you can see this change in the OneWorld software, and vice versa.

NOTE

World and OneWorld have several modules that are not coexistent, including accounts receivable, human resources, and the real estate module. Other items that are not coexistent include security, users, data dictionary, and development.

Is Your Organization Global?

If you work for a global organization, speed at remote sites is a significant consideration. Using data replication can solve some WAN speed issues. However, data replication cannot address this problem nearly as well as either thin clients with Microsoft Terminal Server or an HTML/Java zero client. If you have remote sites that do significant volumes of work (for example, sales order entry), you should consider methods of either distributing the data or centralizing the processing.

Do You Support Double-Byte Languages?

Although double-byte languages are supported by J.D. Edwards, they may ultimately accommodate different architectural solutions over organizations supporting single-byte languages. The greater the number of double-byte languages supported, the greater the architectural diversity within the system. Using the B733.2 version of OneWorld, you can support only a single double-byte language per database. In addition, although single-byte data and double-byte data can be maintained in the same database, data corruption could result if the records were updated by nonlike systems. If this is the case, you might decide to separate the systems geographically as well as separating the hardware. Centralized and decentralized configurations provide different user support options.

What Is Your Current IT Staff's Skill Set?

The skill level of your IT staff is important not only for hardware selection but also for diversification in location and support options. For example, an organization that implements a decentralized database solution has remote locations set up with data replication and location servers. If the remote site has a SQL DBA, it encourages them to use SQL Server as that location's database. If the home office has an Oracle DBA, however, it encourages them to use Oracle as the primary solution. You may be wondering how an architecture like this could work. Data replication within OneWorld uses a unique set of tables that are not platform specific, which means your IT staff's current skill set will be sufficient.

The level of your current IT skill set may also determine the platforms you choose. An organization we're acquainted with initially used Windows NT with Oracle even though their DBA was an UNIX/Oracle DBA. The Windows NT/Oracle side of their system was not set up well, and after a few unpleasant episodes, the organization changed its hardware platform. If they had considered their staff's skills in the first place, they could have avoided both the problems and the change.

Are You Going to Buy the Skills or Grow the Skills?

The level of complexity that you can achieve in your architectural design is based on the skills of your IT staff. Organizations that are self-reliant (that is, they don't outsource their setup and maintenance to third-party implementers) should probably look for relatively simple solutions. This is especially the case if your organization has decided to grow its skill set rather than buy it on the open market.

Although not many highly skilled JDE Technology consultants are available, some are in the marketplace. If they are talented, they will cost your company $120,000 to $175,000 per year, assuming you don't have to relocate them. If you do relocate them, you can expect to pay in excess of $200,000 the first year, which is definitely not a cheap proposition. If your implementation is large, these individuals can be the difference between being successful and failing.

What Are the Details of Your Development?

First, not all implementations perform customization of the software for business objectives. Second, if your organization chooses to engage in specific application development, you won't necessarily change your architectural design. Finally, depending on your organizational layout, the requirement for remote development can change your overall near- and far-term architecture. Managing this entire system is important and can make a difference in overall performance, as well as time-to-completion.

If you are developing, testing, and finalizing application customizations and system integration remotely, significant time can be wasted if the development path code is located across a WAN. It is far better to define local path codes and environments in decentralized development architectures. Over one and a half hours can be spent checking a single application into remotely located path code within the continental United States. If your development efforts extend beyond those boundaries, you can encounter additional difficulties based on international considerations.

The versatility and ability of the OneWorld product to support multiple architectural configurations doesn't stop with the hardware and software design, configuration, and deployment. Rather, the philosophy that the OneWorld product is part of your solution—and not your problem—is embodied throughout its design. Because many organizations have specific business requirements not addressed by the application suite, J.D. Edwards incorporates a robust development toolset designed to facilitate easy, quick modifications that can migrate with the multiple releases of the product itself. This value-added ability allows organizations to receive a rapid return on their investment.

What Is Your Organizational Requirement for Time Online, Redundancy, and Failover?

Based on your company's uptime requirements (24x7, 12x5, and so on), you may need to change your architectural design. You might also have to design redundant systems at remote locations, which, while it isn't a difficult task, is something that should be taken into consideration. In addition, uptime requirements and backup criteria may add additional hardware and software needs. The only limitation to what you are able to do in this arena is money.

Making Sense of It All

Let's try to gain some answers out of the questions we've just reviewed. If you are running J.D. Edwards World product, you should seriously consider coexistence. Although this solution isn't appropriate for all companies, you should consider both the advantages and disadvantages of this particular strategy. This decision will push you toward the AS/400 and will limit the amount of data you need to convert. Understanding languages, globalization, and IT skill sets enables you to decide about centralized and decentralized processing, data, and support. Understanding your current systems and infrastructure help in making this decision. If you know the scope of your implementation and the system requirements up front, you can plan your systems with much greater authority. If you have questions on the best methods of designing your OneWorld architecture, we recommend that you research the product (and the fact that you are reading this book is the first step) and contact a consulting organization with proven experience in this area. It is better to spend the money getting the experience on loan than trying to figure it out on your own.

Standard Out-of-the-Box Configurations

Some people laugh when they hear that there is such a thing as a standard configuration. With a product as versatile and flexible as OneWorld, not many clients retain the standard configuration; however, understanding a *typical* configuration is useful. The more you document and understand the changes to your system, the greater the opportunity you will have to determine the source when a problem arises. To help you solve potential problems, the following sections describe what OneWorld looks like straight out of the box. Our discussion will focus on the simplest of configurations with absolutely no architectural oddities.

More Details and Definitions

Many of the specific OneWorld topics covered in this and the following sections are described in detail throughout various chapters in this book. We understand that the information in the following sections may be overwhelming, so we recommend that you come back to this chapter as often as you'd like. Here are some very brief definitions that pertain to our discussion:

- **Data source**   A pointer to specific data or specific machines that performs logic processing in OneWorld.

- **Path code**   A combination of central object specifications and a directory structure containing application C code.

- **OCM**   The Object Configuration Manager is a utility within the OneWorld system that enables you to specify where data resides or where to process logic.

- **Environment**   A combination of path code and OCM mappings indicating where to find data and logic processing machines.

Inside and Out

As explained earlier, the OneWorld product has a two-tier architecture under a typical or standard installation. The installation itself contains elements including a deployment server, an enterprise server, and client workstations. Refer to the grid in Figure 1-7 for a graphic representation of data sources, environments, and path codes associated with the typical configuration.

SQL Database	Data Source Type	Data Source	Owner	Path Code	Environment
Environment Specific Data					
JDE_CRP	DB	Busiess Data - CRP	crpdta		
JDE_CRP	DB	Control Tables - CRP	crpctl		
					CRP733
JDE_CRPB733	DB	Central Objects - CRPB733	crpb733		
JDE_CRPB733	DB	Versions - CRPB733	crpb733	CRPB733	
JDEB7.MDB	DB	OneWorld Local - CRPB733	N/A		
					TST733
JDE_Development	DB	Business Data - TEST	testdta		
JDE_Development	DB	Control Tables - Test	testctl		
					DEV733
JDE_DEVB733	DB	Central Objects - DEVB733	devb733		
JDE_DEVB733	DB	Versions - DEVB733	devb733	DEVB733	
JDEB7.MDB	DB	OneWorld Local - DEVB733	N/A		
JDE_Production	DB	Business Data - PROD	proddta		
JDE_Production	DB	Control Tables - Prod	prodctl		
JDE_PRODB733	DB	Central Objects - PRODB733	prodb733		PRD733
JDE_PRODB733	DB	Versions - PRODB733	prodb733	PRODB733	
JDEB7.MDB	DB	OneWorld Local - PRODB733	N/A		
JDE_PRISTINE	DB	Business Data - JDE	pristdta		
JDE_PRISTB733	DB	Central Objects - PRISTB733	pristb733		PRT733
JDE_PRISTB733	DB	Versions - PRISTB733	pristb733	PRISTB733	
JDEB7.MDB	DB	OneWorld Local - PRISTB733	N/A		
Shared Data					
JDEB733	DB	System - B733	sysb733		
JDEB733	DB	Object Librarian - B733	objb733		
JDEB733	DB	Data Dictionary - B733	ddb733		
JDEB733	DB	machine name - B733 Server Map	svmb733		
JDEB733	DB	machine name - Logic	svmb733		
JDEB733	SVR	machine name	svmb733		
JDEB7.MDB	SVR	LOCAL	N/A		

* Using Oracle, the typical setup includes a single database called JDE.
* Using the AS/400, the library names will vary based on World

FIGURE 1-7. Typical OneWorld data sources

Making Sense of a Typical Configuration

The information provided in the grid in Figure 1-7 includes interesting architectural information in addition to showing you the actual setup and naming conventions. There are some peculiarities to the naming conventions. Let's take the PRD733 (production) environment as an example of a typical environment. Five data sources are uniquely associated with this environment:

- Business Data – PROD

- Control Tables – Prod

- Central Objects – PRODB733

- Versions – PRODB733

- OneWorld Local – PRODB733

Notice the case used in the preceding list. While databases should be configured in such a way as to make them case insensitive, the OneWorld data source names are both case and space sensitive, and the typical naming convention is exact. In the business data, data source, there are 1,616 environment-specific tables; the control tables include 47, the central objects have 23, versions have 1, and OneWorld local has 6. Most environment configurations follow this lead.

NOTE

A typical customer configuration is what would be installed straight out of the J.D. Edwards package with no CNC modifications.

Pristine

The greatest exception to the naming convention rules is the pristine environment. PRT733 doesn't have an associated control tables data source. This situation will be rectified in OneWorld Xe (formerly B733.3), which has the data source Control Tables – JDE. These tables are wrapped into the business data in earlier versions of the software. Another abnormality is that the business data, data source doesn't follow the standard naming convention. One would normally anticipate that this data source would have a name such as "Business Data – PRIST." Instead, the name for this data is "Business Data – JDE" to clearly indicate that PRT733 has JDE demonstration data instead of being populated with customer-specific information. Having both business data and control tables in the same data source also means you have the same number of tables as production's data sources combined—1,676.

What About CRP733, TST733, and DEV733?

Take another quick look through the list of typical data sources shown in Figure 1-7. You don't see either a Business Data – DEV or a Central Objects – TESTB733. J.D. Edwards intentionally put all of the elements necessary to work with their development methodology in the typical customer configuration. The development environment uses test's business data. The test environment is associated with the CRPB733 path code. This enables customers to develop objects in the development environment, transfer them to the CRP path code, and then test them in the TST733 environment.

One of the most important pieces of this development methodology is that the development and testing environments share the same business data and control tables. This minimizes perceived errors in developed code based on data alone. If errors exist, these errors must be based in the object's path code promotion (that is, you forgot to transfer necessary objects or you didn't have sufficient rights to the target directory), the package building processes (a method of deploying software throughout the enterprise), or in the code itself (your developer just didn't do it right).

Data Sources, Path Codes, and Environments—Oh My!

Under a typical configuration, J.D. Edwards delivers four path codes: PRODB733, CRPB733, DEVB733, and PRISTB733. These path codes deliver five environments: PRD733, CRP733, DEV733, TST733, and PRT733.

NOTE

In a typical customer installation, J.D. Edwards actually delivers seven environments. They include the previously listed five plus the DEPB733 and JDEPLAN environments. These other two environments, however, are used only when installing or configuring the OneWorld product. These environments are usable only on the deployment server and do not have deployment packages associated with them.

What About the AS/400?

The AS/400 in a typical customer configuration adds additional data sources, but there isn't any difference in the setup of the architecture, the path codes, or the environments themselves. The additional data sources are based on the requirement of the AS/400 for translation and not translating into and out of its native EBCDIC format. These data sources usually have a " – DNT" after the normal naming convention (for example, "System – B733 – DNT"). This data source does not translate from EBCDIC whereas its corresponding System - B733 data source does. Although the names of the data sources differ, there isn't a difference in how the OneWorld data sources themselves are set up. What makes these data sources different is their corresponding Open Database Connectivity (ODBC) setup. When setting up Client Access ODBC, you have the option of translating the data.

NOTE

If you incorrectly configure an AS/400 data source for translation, OneWorld provides a nice little error indicating that the data source was not properly set up the first time that the data source was used to extract data from AS/400.

Summary

We've described the various architectures available in OneWorld. We've provided enough information so that, as your experience grows with the product, you can creatively use it as you need to. We've even discussed some considerations that will determine the architecture and configurations you should employ. Other chapters that will increase your ability to understand and work with the overall architecture include Chapters 2, 4, and 5. When you combine those chapters with what you've learned here, you will begin to see not only the power of the OneWorld product but how it can solve your business requirements.

Inside and Out

CHAPTER 2

OneWorld Building Blocks

Date Sources

Path Codes

Environments

Object Configuration Manager

J.D. Edwards OneWorld Middleware

How does OneWorld work? This is one of the most frequently asked questions by both the new OneWorld initiate and the seasoned OneWorld professional. Unless you understand the building blocks that make OneWorld work, there seems to be a mystery to the entire product. In this chapter, we will go into enough detail to give you what you need to understand the OneWorld product from the ground up.

We will start with the simple data source and try to get an understanding of how the system finds data and machines that process logic. We will then move on to path codes and how applications are maintained within the OneWorld system. After that, we will talk about how we can define instances of OneWorld by using the building blocks we covered in the previous two sections. We will also discuss the power behind the OneWorld system: the Object Configuration Manager. We will then go into detail concerning J. D. Edwards middleware and see how that software helps you with all OneWorld activity. Finally, we will end with a quick discussion about asynchronous and synchronous processing.

Data Sources

In this section, we will go into detail concerning what data sources are, how many are required for a system, how to modify and maintain them, including why you might add and modify these elusive little devils. Below are some of the topics in this chapter that will help remove some of the mystery of OneWorld:

- Database differences

- Data source definitions

- Components that make up a data source

- The number and types of data sources

- Data source application P986115

- Special uses for data sources

- Data source law of the west actions

Some Information Necessary to Understand Data Sources

Before we jump directly into data sources, which we think is one of the most important topics in this book, we need to talk about the relational database management systems

(RDBMSs) supported by the OneWorld ERP product. There are four basic RDBMSs used by OneWorld. Depending on your implementation, you probably use two or three of these systems; however, you could use them all if it made business sense. OneWorld supports Oracle, Microsoft's SQL Server, DB2 on the AS/400, and Microsoft Access. Although many people don't count Access as a part of their business solution, in reality, it is the one database that is common among all of the OneWorld solutions.

We want to spend a couple of minutes going over the RDBMSs supported by the OneWorld solution because these systems will hold the tables you define using the OneWorld data sources. These systems are different, and these differences show up in how you configure your data sources and why. This may seem somewhat ambiguous, so let us get a little more detailed.

Oracle

Oracle maintains tables within table spaces (see Figure 2-1). These table spaces can have a specific owner and are maintained on separate data files. Consequently, if you were looking for F0101 (Address Book Master) for production, it would be in a different table space within the same database as F0101 for the CRP environment. Currently, J.D. Edwards ships OneWorld on Oracle with a single J.D. Edwards database defined. Breaking up this master database can yield superior performance, additional configurability, and flexibility to your OneWorld enterprise solution.

Oracle uses a custom communication software package called SQL*Net to communicate between the database itself and other machines trying to reach the data within the tables. Your Oracle database administrator (DBA) will define a connect string (in essence, a series of parameters that tell the client machines how to connect with the Oracle database) for the OneWorld database. If you decide to create several different databases, or if you implement a distributed data architecture, you will have several different connect strings. All the connect string data will be contained in a file called TNSNAMES.ORA under the Oracle path on each client machine.

SQL Server

SQL Server, on the other hand, can have all the tables within a single data file (called a device). The only difference between the tables is the owner of the tables. This is not to say that the data within the tables is identical, but that the tables themselves can be maintained in the same physical file. In the early releases of OneWorld, all the tables necessary to support all instances of OneWorld were maintained in the same database and consequently the same device. Many people who worked in the field noticed that this architecture, while easy to maintain, was certainly not the most efficient for speed or performance. Some began experimenting with breaking up

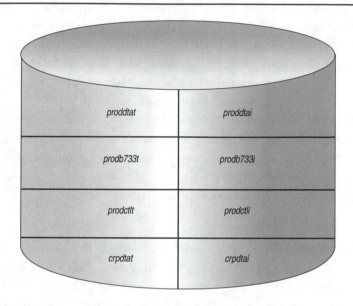

The traditional OneWorld Oracle database is
represented as a single instance of the Oracle
database system. This instance has multiple table
spaces (some designed for tables, some designed for
indexes) that can be designed from single or
multiple data file devices

FIGURE 2-1.   Oracle Database Cross-Section

the J.D. Edwards database into multiple databases maintaining fewer tables in smaller, more efficient devices. There was a marked increase in performance, and the B733 version of OneWorld shipped with multiple databases instead of a single master database. J.D. Edwards also uses multiple SQL Server databases to enhance performance and to make backups easier in the OneWorld system. This database instance configuration in shown in Figure 2-2.

AS/400

The AS/400 uses its integrated version of DB2 to accommodate OneWorld's table requirements (tables are referred to as files on the AS/400). These tables are maintained in libraries (the equivalent of directories or databases in UNIX and on NT). The AS/400 does not support table/file owners. Because of this, you can't have two identically named tables in the same library. What this means to the person installing or maintaining OneWorld is that you will have multiple libraries for your OneWorld solution. This setup is similar to Oracle's table spaces discussed earlier.

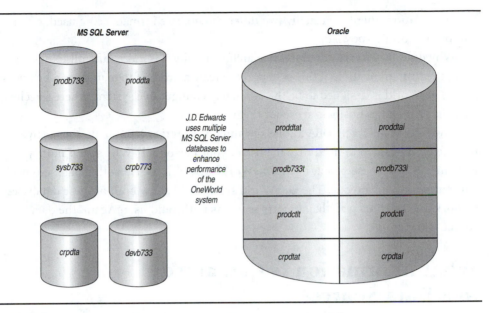

FIGURE 2-2.   Similarities between MS SQL Server 7 and Oracle

What Is a Data Source?

Before we can adequately answer this question, we have to ask what the underlying piece of any ERP software application is: the data. After all, in the end, it all comes back to the data that is stored, manipulated, and ultimately provides organizations with the return on their system's investment. Rather than have to hard code a data link to provide users with multi-system functionality, the J.D. Edwards software engineers came up with the data source.

In the simplest terms, a data source is nothing more than a pointer to where data resides or to a machine that will process logic. These pointers are then used by the OneWorld software itself to determine where the data resides and in what format.

When we talk about data pointers, we are really talking about a table or sets of tables that can be identified by either a common table owner or a common data location. Data sources always point out whole tables, not rows or sets of rows within a table. The data source is not used as a method of separating data within a table; transactional SQL statements will extract actual subsets of data as required by the specific OneWorld application.

Because OneWorld uses data sources, a client can use any one of four different databases (Oracle, SQL Server, DB2, or Microsoft Access) with equal ease and in multiple combinations designed to allow the user a freedom of choice. Even in a base installation, there are usually two different database formats being used, often without the user's knowledge.

Why did J.D. Edwards do this when architecturally it is more difficult to design? Well, the firm foundation of this system is to create a product that answers a business need. OneWorld is designed to be the ultimately configurable system, where the client decides what makes business sense for them.

If you have an Oracle DBA at one site and a SQL Server DBA at another, why not use both of them to maximize the use of your personnel? Why spend money retraining any of these people? The OneWorld answer is to use both database types without retraining anyone. The OneWorld system will allow both of these databases to work together in a way that appears seamless to the end user. Again, the data source is the answer.

What Information Is Contained in a Data Source?

The data source accomplishes its job by combining a series of information, including:

- **Data source type**   This indicates if you are using the data source to define tables within an RDBMS or a server that is performing OneWorld logic. Accepted values are DB and SVR.

- **Data source name**   This name can be up to 30 characters in length and will be used whenever you need to reference the tables defined by this data source.

- **Database type**   This will be SQL, Oracle, Client Access, or Access.

- **Table owner**   The table owner is only used with Microsoft SQL Server and Oracle. It indicates the database table owner.

N O T E

Only two of the four supported RDBMSs support table owners (SQL Server and Oracle). In essence, these databases allow you to have tables with identical names within the same database differentiated by the user who created them. Use of this system allows you to keep multiple copies of some tables (such as F986101 OCM) in the exact same location. This may simplify system maintenance when you have multiple application servers.

- **Library name**   This is for AS/400 data source only; it will contain the actual AS/400 library name where the tables reside.

- **Library list name**   This is for AS/400 data source only; it will contain the AS/400 server name.

- **Middleware translator**   This is the OneWorld dll, sl, or program name that performs the middleware function or JDEBase conversion. Refer to the section "J.D. Edwards OneWorld Middleware" for more information concerning the acceptable values for this field.

- **ODBC data source name or Oracle connect string**   This is called the database name on the OneWorld form, but it truly needs to be either the ODBC data source name or the Oracle connect string. This field is both case and space sensitive.

- **Server**   This is the name of the server that holds the database or performs the OneWorld logic. This can be case sensitive, depending on platform; UNIX servers differentiate between "machine" and "MACHINE."

- **Platform**   This field tells the software what type of platform you are running; accepted values are AS400, NTSVR, HP9000, ALPHA, LOCAL, RISC400, RS6000, and SUN.

Data sources also contain a series of flags and supplemental data, including:

- **Use Table Owner**   This flag tells the system to use the object owner ID listed in the data source and should only be used with an RDBMS that supports table owners (Microsoft SQL Server and Oracle).

- **Use Julian dates**   All RDBMSs supported by OneWorld with the exception of Microsoft Access should have this flag checked.

- **Use Decimal Shift**   This is used for OneWorld tables within data sources. It indicates that the OneWorld data dictionary will determine the number of decimal places displayed. All database formats except Microsoft Access should have this flag checked.

- **Support For Updates**   This flag indicates if the database supports row level locking. All database formats except Microsoft Access should have this flag checked.

- **OCM Data Source**   This flag tells the software that these data sources will have, at a minimum, the F98611 and F986101 tables. Examples include the

Inside and Out

system data source and any server map data sources. When this flag is checked, the data source will appear as an option when the user goes into the OCM or data source application.

- **AS/400 BLOB data source** This is self-explanatory. The AS/400 handles binary large object (BLOB) formats differently than the other supported databases.

There is also software-linked data source information contained in the F986115 table that regulates if the data source can have automatic table creation and whether data can be copied from the table. (Complete definitions and examples are provided in the section "Object Configuration Manager)." Although by default, the automatic table creation is on, by J.D. Edwards default, the copy table information is off. We generally recommend, however, that clients turn both of these on. It makes modifying the system easier.

```
Revise Table and Data Source Overrides                    _ □ ✕

 ✓      ✕      👓     📓     Links  ▼ Displ...  📄 OLE ...   📄 Internet
 OK    Can... Dis... Abo

 Release              9733

 Data Source          Business Data - PROD

 Object Name          DEFAULT


 Copy Data (Y/N)      Y

 Create Tables(1/0)   1            Automatically create tables


                                                    🌐
```

T I P

When you create a custom data source, automatic table creation is off by default. You will want to ensure that you turn this feature on. All J.D. Edwards' shipped data sources have this option turned on.

How Many Data Sources Do I Need?

We wish that we could say the answer to this was simple. It is really dependent on what type of implementation your company has chosen to perform and whether you have made custom changes that require additional data sources. Let's first go over the types of data sources and then we can move on to which ones you may need and why. Finally, we will discuss adding additional data sources to the system to meet your special requirements.

There are 12 primary types of data sources that can be configured with OneWorld. Remember, a data source is nothing more than a pointer to tables or logic within the system. These tables are usually identified either by owner or by a specific location and server.

Data Sources and Their Types

There are two categories of data sources that can be defined on the OneWorld system. One category points to data within the enterprise. This data source is the one that most people can quickly understand and deal with, and the majority of this section is dedicated to explaining it. This data source variety is identified by DB in the P986115 data source application and in the OMOCM1 column of the F98611 data source table.

The second data source type defines a machine running OneWorld services that can be accessed by other machines in the enterprise. By programmatic default, OneWorld automatically runs all applications and batch programs locally. To offload some of this processing time to a server (either the enterprise server or an application server) instead of taking up valuable workstation processing time, you have to define the server that you want to perform the job. This data source is designated by SVR in the OMOCM1 column of F98611, the data source master table.

Business Data

This DB (database) data source points out the OneWorld tables that are specific to business applications. Where it can be, and often is, shared between multiple environments in the OneWorld enterprise, it is a defining characteristic of an environment. There are more than 1,400 tables within a normal installation of OneWorld (B733 series) that qualify as business data. Does this mean you need 1,400 data sources? No. Rather, a single data source can point to all these tables provided they have a single owner or are in a single library. There are times when it might make good business sense to separate selected tables to different data sources (for example, if you were implementing HR/payroll and wanted to place database security on these tables in addition to regular security), but this will be discussed in more detail later in the book. Business data tables are most commonly used after you have logged in on a client workstation. The standard naming convention is Business Data – XXX. The XXX is specific to the business data being defined, such as TEST, CRP, PROD, and so on.

Control Tables

This DB data source identifies control tables, including user defined codes (UDCs), menus, and next numbers. These tables go hand in hand with the business data source described above and function strictly as controlling information for the OneWorld product. For more information on what tables are identified by this data source, see the appendix tables within OneWorld. Control tables can be used at any time during a OneWorld application session. The standard naming convention is Control Tables – XXX. The XXX is specific to the control tables being defined, such as TEST, CRP, PROD, and so on.

DEFINITION

User defined code (UDC): *These are sets of values that display in the OneWorld applications. These values can be modified by the end user so that they display in a way that is meaningful. An example of a UDC would be a search type in your address book, such as searching by vendors, employees, or other values the system administrator adds.*

Central Objects

This DB data source points to data necessary for running the actual OneWorld applications. These tables contain processing options for applications and universal batch engines (UBEs), template data, business view data, and a host of other information required to run the applications (both interactive and batch). Central objects often contain binary large objects (BLOBs) within the tables themselves. Under various RDBMS, you might see these described as long raw data. The information is in binary format and can range from 1 byte to multiple megabytes. The central object tables, consequently, are very large—up to 6GB on some RDBMSs (for instance, F98741 takes more than 950MB in Microsoft SQL Server version 7.0). Central objects can be hit at any time OneWorld is in use; however, they are most commonly updated during development or when processing options are changed for specific interactive and batch applications. The standard naming convention is Central Objects – XXXB733. The XXX is path code specific. The name is major release level specific, such as B732, B733, and so on.

Versions

The versions data source separates the F983051 table from other central object tables. This table maintains information on all the versions interactive and batch applications for each path code. This data source is database oriented. In earlier versions of OneWorld, this data source also pointed to F98306; however, this changed in the B733 series. The standard naming convention is Versions –XXXB733. The XXX is path code specific. This name is major release specific, such as B732, B733, and so on.

OneWorld Local

This database-oriented data source points to the jdeb7.mdb database loaded on the local client. It is often referred to as locally replicated data. This is a Microsoft Access database format, but you do not need Microsoft Access loaded on your local machine for OneWorld to run correctly. Rather, for various system security reasons, we recommend that you only have Access on those machines that actually need it (for example, a developer's machine or the system administrator's machine). This database traditionally contains six tables (F0004, F0005, F0082, F00821, F0083, and F0084); however, it can contain more, especially when used with data replication. The OneWorld Local data source is hit continuously during OneWorld client operations. The standard naming convention is OneWorld Local – XXXB733. The XXX represents the path code name. The name represents major release versions such as B732, B733, and so on. This data source does not exist for application/logic servers.

System

The system data source identifies tables that are common to the entire OneWorld implementation and are not environment or path code specific. These shared tables include information such as the data source tables themselves, the Object Configuration Manager, and printers, in addition to a range of other global settings. Many of the tables used in the system data source are cached to the client workstation at runtime and changes to them are only realized when the client logs off OneWorld and then back on. A good example of this is the security table (F00950). You can look in the appendix tables in OneWorld for all the tables that are associated with this data source. These tables can be accessed any time during a session of OneWorld; however, they are most heavily used during the initial client log on to OneWorld. The standard naming convention is System – B733. This data source is named according to major release level, such as B732, B733, and so on. It is a DB data source.

Server Map

This DB data source provides access to a special subset of the system tables maintained exclusively for use by enterprise and application servers. Because of special requirements of application servers, there may be times when data used by workstations is different. The only way of maintaining these differences is to have an identical set of tables maintained for this purpose. A good example of data that could be different between the server and the workstation is data sources themselves. Some servers use a different set of J.D. Edwards OneWorld middleware to acquire data. There are seven tables in a typical server map. The standard naming convention is *machinename* – B733 Server Map. The *machinename* is the name as defined in the logic data source; it is usually the same as the actual machine name on the LAN/WAN. This data source is named according to the major release level, such as B733.

Object Librarian

The object librarian data source contains five tables (the F986x series) that define every object in the OneWorld system. When we refer to an object in the OneWorld system, this includes applications, business views, UBEs, processing option templates, and so forth. The tables in this data source define every non-data object. These tables are integral in all object modifications. The standard naming convention is Object Librarian – B733. This name is major release level specific, such as B732, B733, and so on. This data source is a DB data source pointing to data with a relational database.

Data Dictionary

This DB data source describes a set of tables (the F92xx series). These tables provide a series of functions in the OneWorld enterprise that include defining all columns in the system, all error messaging, and how many decimal places are displayed. The master data dictionary tables are maintained in an RDBMS on the enterprise server. Workstations and servers use replicated copies of these tables copied to table access management (TAM) files. The standard naming convention is Data Dictionary – B733. This name is major release level specific, such as B732, B733, and so on.

Server

The server data source usually is annotated as the enterprise server's name, but is also a required data source for every enterprise or application server on the system. Depending on the hardware platform, this data source can be case sensitive. This is particularly true with the UNIX platforms. Its primary use is to indicate to OneWorld where it needs to process logic within the enterprise. Remember that J.D. Edwards' OneWorld product has a programmatic default to process all logic and applications locally. The only time OneWorld will process items anywhere other than locally will be instances where there is an Object Configuration Manager (OCM) override forcing a different location. By installation default (as opposed to programmatic), UBEs will process on the enterprise server. However, you can use the server data source to override where batch applications or business functions run. You can do this on the

fly when launching a UBE or by OCM mappings. The standard naming convention is
machinename. This is usually the name the computer is known by on the LAN/WAN.
This name is not release specific.

Server – Logic

This is a relatively new data source introduced in the B733 series and is primarily
used for server-to-server data replication. Similar to the server data source, this
data source can also be case sensitive and for the same reasons. It enables you
to perform data replication to data servers. It is a logic data source and will be
automatically set up when using the installation wizards. The standard naming
convention is *machinename* – Logic. This name is not release specific.

Local

The local data source defines the machine running OneWorld itself. It is generally used
to define a workstation to ensure that business functions are run locally or to run batch
applications on the local workstation rather than on the enterprise server or an application
server. The standard naming convention is LOCAL. This name is not release specific.

AS/400 Data Sources (DNT)

The do not translate (DNT) data sources are a series of data sources specific to the AS/400.
These data sources are for specific tables within the OneWorld implementation that
contains BLOBs. When you set up the ODBC data sources for these data sources,
you set it to not translate. Examples of DNT data sources include System – B733 – DNT
(because of the F98DRLOG, F98DRPCN, F98OWSEC tables), Business Data – PROD –
DNT (because of the F98811 table), and Versions – PRODB733 – DNT (because of the
F983051 table). Depending on your version of OneWorld, you may have additional DNT
data sources.

Now Back to the Question

How many OneWorld data sources do you need? Well, you could get by with as few
as one (if you are running the OneWorld standalone version), or as many as you can
define (this depends on how many application servers, DNT data sources, and so on
you may have). An average OneWorld installation (assuming PRD733, DEV733,
CRP733, PRT733, and TST733 environments) will either have around 25 (a
non-AS/400 installation) or over 38 (an AS/400 installation).

Inside and Out

How Do You Set Up and Configure Data Sources?

The following section is essential to understanding and being able to configure data sources. Various OneWorld guides produced by J.D. Edwards have information related to this topic. We have added more information with the hope of providing a deeper understanding of the application.

There are two basic methods used to set up data sources. During an installation, update, or upgrade, there are automated wizards that will set up the standard accepted data sources. For more detailed instructions on how to set these up during the installation process, we recommend that you review the installation manuals for whichever platform you are installing. During this part of this chapter, however, we do want to take you through a basic setup of a data source from scratch. If you understand how to set up a data source, you will have what you need to troubleshoot data source related issues. You will also be able to configure OneWorld to best suit your business needs and provide the fastest return on your ERP investment.

To understand how to manually set up a data source, you have to understand the architecture of the data source window. The program used is the P986115, and the place most OneWorld administrators will find it is the GH9011 menu. The method for setting up both logic and database data sources is similar. We will start with the database data sources and then look at the differences in setup for the logic data source.

When you first select the P986115 (Database Data Sources) application, you will see a form similar to Figure 2-3 (Machine Search_Select). This window is designed to allow you to choose which OCM data sources you want to configure. To change data sources used by workstations (both fat and thin clients), you need to choose the system data source in this window. If you want to work with the data sources for a specific enterprise or application server, choose the machine name – B733 server map associated with the server you want to modify.

N O T E

Earlier in this chapter, we discussed the flag that designates whether a data source is an OCM data source; that is, if it contains the F98611 and F986101 tables. The Machine Search_Select form automatically searches all the data sources in the system F98611 table for this flag and lists them on the form.

Once you select a specific data source to work with on the Machine Search_Select form, the Work With Data Sources Window form will automatically launch on your machine. This form will allow you to do the following:

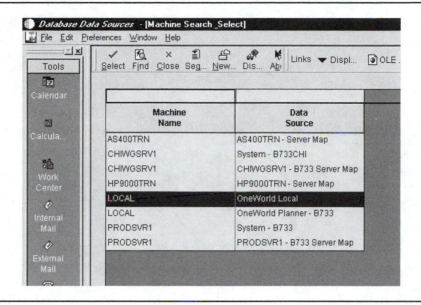

FIGURE 2-3.   Machine search and select

- Find any or all of the data sources defined for that specific machine

- Work with the data source database parameters

- Set up ODBC data sources (associated with OneWorld data sources, this will also add the information into the ODBCDataSource.inf used, which is read to automatically set up ODBC workstations during a client installation)

Architecture of the Data Source Revisions Window

This window, shown in Figure 2-4, is key to a system administrator, as it allows them to easily change the existing data sources or add new data sources to the system. Remember that a data source is just a pointer to your data.

1. The Data Source Use field indicates if you are defining tables within a database or a machine that processes OneWorld logic. Accepted values for this field are DB and SVR. When working with a database data source, this field will automatically fill in a DB to indicate the type of data source you are creating. This information, once saved, cannot be revised for a specific data source. If you set up a DB data source and meant to set up a logic (SVR) data source, you will have to delete the DB data source and set up a new data source for the SVR.

Inside and Out

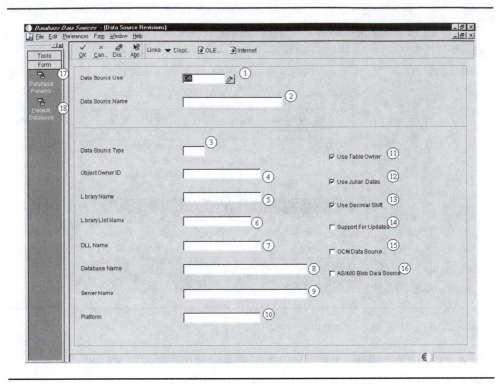

FIGURE 2-4.   Data source revisions window

2. The Data Source Name field can be any name up to 30 characters in length. It is usually recommended, especially in custom data sources, that you choose a name that will make sense to you and other users on the system. There is a standard naming convention for data sources. Examples of the naming conventions are provided in the descriptions of the data source types in previous sections.

3. The Data Source Type field indicates the type of RDBMS being defined by the data source. This is a required field for this form. If you are defining a logic data source, by convention, you would indicate the same RDBMS as in the logic's associated server map data source. For example, when defining an NT application server that has its server map in a Microsoft SQL Server database, you would put an **S** in the Data Source Type field for the server map and the machinename data source.

4. The Object Owner ID field indicates the table owner for that specific data source. You can have multiple data sources with identical table owners, depending on your

specific setup. This field is used when OneWorld structures the SQL statements that return data to the OneWorld applications. For example, if you where to perform a find in the Address Book Master for a specific customer with customer number 1234, OneWorld might automatically create the following SQL statement: select * from crpdta.f0101 where aban8='1234'. In this example, crpdta is a table owner and is used to differentiate the F0101 table associated with the crp data from the production, test, or pristine data.

5. The Library Name field is used for data source tables on the AS/400 only. This field tells OneWorld exactly which library contains the tables defined by the database data source.

6. The Library List Name field is generally the server name of the AS/400 itself and is only used on AS/400 data sources.

7. The DLL Name field is actually looking for the JDEBase DLL, SL, or program name used by OneWorld to create the proper SQL statement, manage the database connection, and produce an optimized fetch algorithm for the data. The information for this field is specific for both the machine and database in use. You can use the information shown here to assist in determining the proper file to enter into the DLL Name field. (This information was taken directly from pages 5-19 of the J.D. Edwards OneWorld: CNC Implementation Guide for B7331.)

- AS/400 to DB2/400 = DBDR
- AS/400 to any other server DBMS = JDBNET
- HP9000 to DB2/400 = libjdbnet.sl
- HP9000 to Microsoft SQL Server = libjdbnet.sl
- HP9000 to Oracle (Version 8.0) UNIX = libora80.sl
- RS6000 to DB2/400 = libjdbnet.so
- RS6000 to Microsoft SQL Server = libjdbnet.so
- RS6000 to Oracle (Version 8.0) UNIX = libora80.so
- Intel to AS/400 = jdbodbc.dll
- Intel to Oracle (Version 8.0) NT = jdboci80.dll
- Intel to SQL Server NT = jdbodbc.dll
- Digital Alpha to AS/400 = jdbnet.dll
- Digital Alpha to Oracle (Version 8.0) NT = jdboci80.dll
- Digital Alpha to SQL Server NT = jdbodbc.dll

Inside and Out

8. The Database Name field is actually looking for database connectivity information. In the case of a data source that uses ODBC as the third-party communication software (for example, Microsoft SQL Server, the DB2/400, and Microsoft Access), you should put in the exact ODBC name. Although this ODBC name does not have to be the same as the OneWorld data source name, for simplicity and as a standard it is usually configured as such. It is both case and space sensitive. In the case of data sources that are configured for Oracle, enter the connect string for the database holding the tables you are defining. The connect string is usually set up by the Oracle DBA, and in a traditional OneWorld setup, would be the same for all the data sources.

NOTE

For non-Oracle installs, we suggest the Database Name field be the same as the Data Source Name field to avoid confusion and potential problems if JDBNet is used. For JDBNet to work, the Data Source Name field and the Database Name field have to be the same.

DEFINITION

JDBNet: *JDBNet is a middleware product that was coded by J.D. Edwards to handle the communication between platforms where no middleware products exist.*

9. The Server Name field holds the network name of the server containing the database or the actual name of the logic server. Although its case sensitivity is dependent on the platform being hit, it is safest to assume that all information in the Data Source Revisions form is case and space sensitive. This is much easier than trying to figure out when case sensitivity is important.

10. The Platform field allows you to specify the server type. Accepted values include ALPHA, AS400, HP9000, LOCAL, NTSVR, RISC400, RS6000, SUN, and SYS390.

11. The Use Table Owner flag is used in conjunction with the Object Owner ID field. It must be checked in order for the information in the Object Owner ID field to be used in the SQL statements generated by OneWorld applications. Filling in that field by itself is not enough.

12. The Use Julian Dates flag indicates whether the database supports Julian dates. This flag should be set for all supported RDBMS types with the exception of Microsoft Access.

13. The Use Decimal Shift flag indicates that the tables within the data sources will use the data dictionary to determine the number of decimals displayed per item type. If this box is checked, OneWorld will automatically shift the information input into the database to account for decimal places and will automatically display the appropriate number of decimals when retrieved. (For example, you can define inventory to have four decimal places, while currency may only have two.) This flag should be used for all supported RDBMS types with the exception of Microsoft Access.

14. The Support For Updates flag determines if JDEBase should use row-level locking with this data source. It is used on all RDBMS data sources with the exception of Microsoft Access.

15. We've already talked about the OCM Data Source flag. It indicates that the data source contains, at the minimum, the F98611 and F986101 tables. The system and all server map data sources use this flag. This flag determines if the data source is shown in the Machine Search_Select form of the P986115 application.

16. The AS/400 Blob Data Source flag tells the OneWorld application that at least some tables within the data source contain binary large objects (BLOBs) on the AS/400. A good example of a data source that has this flag checked is Versions – XXXB733. The table defined by this data source is the F983051 (Versions List) table, which contains information in a BLOB format. You can also house the central objects data sources on the AS/400. If you choose to do this, these data sources would also have the AS/400 Blob Data Source flag checked.

17. The Database Params form hyperlink launches the P9861151 application. This program populates the F986115 table and is discussed in detail in the section "Object Configuration Manager."

18. The Default Database form hyperlink also launches the P9861151 application and is also discussed in detail in the section "Object Configuration Manager."

Now let's move on to something a little more fun.

Special Uses for Data Sources

You now know what data sources are and how you would configure them, but you might be wondering why you need to know so much about them, especially considering that wizards are going to set up all the basic data sources during the installation of the OneWorld product. There are several times during the life cycle of the OneWorld product

Inside and Out

where you might set up special data sources to perform legacy data conversions, to download and upload OneWorld tables, or to add additional environments, for example.

To accomplish some of the special uses for data sources, you have to understand which data sources are required for what you are trying to achieve. We will go over some of the more common system customizations so you will be able to continue on your own.

Adding an Application Server (from the Data Sources' Point of View)

There are three data sources that should be set up for a new OneWorld application server (that is, a server that performs OneWorld logic). Of these three, one is required and the other two are optional, based on what you are trying to accomplish with the application server and how you want to configure it. To determine which data sources are required, think back to the 12 types of data sources. Of those data sources, the one you must have is the server data source. This logic data source defines a machine that performs OneWorld logic (in other words, that has the OneWorld application loaded on it).

Many people would immediately argue that you have to have a server map. Though we would agree most of the time, this is not a required data source for an application server. If you have another server set up that is of the same machine type, same database type, and performs the same function, you can actually have the servers share server maps. Why would you want to do this, you ask? Well, let's take the example of the application server used to offload business functions from a Windows terminal server. If you have multiple application servers, you can have a single server map, which makes modifying the data sources and OCM tables much easier. Rather than have to modify each server separately, this would make a single modification universal (this is a two-edged sword; if you make a mistake, you made the mistake to all your servers at the same time).

The third data source associated with an application server is the server – logic data source. If you are not using OneWorld data replication, however, you will not have a need for this data source. If your application server is acting as a data replication server and is replicating to data-only servers, you will need to set this data source up.

What About Custom Environments?

Another reason you would add additional data sources centers around adding environments. As you will see in the "Environments" section of this chapter, OneWorld by default comes pre-configured with five environments. Though they meet the needs of most clients, these environments may not meet your specific business needs. When you add new environments, you will often have to define new data sources. Is there a hard rule as to how many? No, it all depends on what you are doing and exactly how you want these environments to interact with each other.

To gain a prospective on the possible data sources used by a single environment, let's assume you want this environment to be completely independent of the pre-configured environments. What this means is that you will configure the data sources necessary for a completely new environment, including business data, a path code, and control tables. For the sake of this set of questions, let's say you want to create a training environment. We will use the term TRAIN for most of the data sources we add, and we will follow the J.D. Edwards standard naming convention for these data sources.

How Many and Which Data Sources Do You Need?   Would you say three new data sources? Or do you think that four, five, six, or even twelve data sources are needed? If you answered five you would be correct. So, which data sources should you add? You need all the following data sources before you can add this new environment. Adding any new data sources is the first step to adding a new environment or path code.

- Business Data – TRAIN

- Control Tables – TRAIN

- Central Objects – TRAINB733

- Versions – TRAINB733

- OneWorld Local – TRAINB733

Would you need to add new data dictionary, object librarian, system, server, server map, local, or logic data sources? No. These data sources are all shared data sources throughout the OneWorld enterprise. Because of this, under a normal OneWorld configuration, these data sources contain data that is shared between all the environments.

Are there other reasons for adding data sources? Sure! What about data conversions? There are several different methods of getting legacy data into OneWorld, and if you are performing conversions from non-OneWorld tables, you often have to add a data source. Although data sources can be named anything, PROD Conversions – B733 or CRP Conversions – B733 would be a good start. The specific data source setup information for these data sources is dependent on what type of database holds the data you are trying to convert.

Do You Want to Be a Cowboy?

This is always one of our favorite sections in OneWorld. J.D. Edwards' OneWorld staff (especially during training) often refer to someone as being a cowboy. What is a cowboy? A cowboy is someone who is manipulating OneWorld either directly through a back door (that is, direct database access using the SQL language or a database tool) or who is using the OneWorld applications and tools in a manner not traditionally supported by J.D. Edwards' development and support staff. We will refer to this type of activity throughout this book as the Law of the West, since cowboys do need to follow at least frontier type rules!

Is being a cowboy wrong? That really is a matter of opinion. There is a saying within the OneWorld community that it isn't "cowboy" if you know what you are doing. It is only cowboy when you don't. To give you a better example of what this means, let's think about it this way. If you want to directly manipulate information used by OneWorld, you can often type SQL commands directly, affecting the data within the database faster than using a OneWorld toolset.

For example, you could turn hundreds of OCM entries on and off with a single statement. This is faster than starting OneWorld, entering the OCM application, choosing the data source, finding the records to manipulate, and then clicking change status button (after that, of course, you would have to log out of OneWorld and back in so that you could see the changes you'd just made).

Is this cowboy? Yes and no. If you didn't know what table was being affected, didn't know all associated tables, didn't understand exactly which fields to query against and finally modify, yes, this would have been cowboy. In this hypothetical example, however, you knew exactly what tables to modify and exactly what fields to query and update to quickly effect the changes you wanted to effect. It comes down to knowing what you are doing and how that affects the OneWorld environment.

The best advice concerning the law of the west is that if you aren't completely comfortable with what you are doing, don't do it. Even when the experienced perform maneuvers, they can be surprised, so you should always have a method of getting yourself out of trouble. This might be a recently performed backup or performing the maneuver in a testing environment first. Finally, if you are thinking of manipulating OneWorld directly through non-OneWorld methods, remember that J.D. Edwards may not support your efforts.

Law of the West

If there is such potential risk to law of the west activities, why do it? First, it is much faster for those who are experienced. Second, there are occasions where it is simply the only way to get the work done. These creative workarounds can be invaluable. Because of the potential gains, performing law of the west activities is worth consideration.

Data sources lend themselves to law of the west operations because they only use a few tables. Here is some information that you will need to perform data source manipulations:

- The F98611 and F986115 tables contain all the information defining a OneWorld data source.

- The F986101 OCM table uses data sources for all its work. If you change a data source, be sure it is not going to affect this table.

- There are multiple sets of F98611 and F986101 tables. There is only one copy of the F986115 table. When you make changes to the F98611 table, be sure you are changing the correct one for the desired effect. Many times, changes to one table need to be replicated to the other tables. For example, if you change the name of a data source in F98611, you must change the data source name in all the corresponding records in the F986101.

- Data sources are one of the most important definitions in OneWorld. If you are going to directly manipulate them, be sure you know what you are doing.

Using the guidelines above, you can quickly make changes to your system. An example of this is when an Oracle DBA changes the connect string's name for access to the JDE database. You could open every one of the data sources and manually change this information, or you could effect the same change by entering a SQL statement like this one:

```
update sysb733.f98611 set omdatb='JDE1' where omdatb='JDE';
```

This would quickly change every connect string currently defined as JDE to JDE1. The only thing to consider on this particular change is that it did not change the server map F98611 or the actual TNSNAMES.ORA. Your DBA would have to ensure that the TNSNAMES.ORA file was changed on all workstations and servers before they could correctly access OneWorld again.

Another quick cowboy maneuver that can help is creating a new F98611 table for an application server. You can copy F98611 from an existing source to the new machine's server map database and use SQL to modify the differences—for example, copy the F98611 from a UNIX server map to an NT machine (don't forget to change the omdllname from libora80.sl to jdboci80.dll). If you know what you are doing, this can be done faster than copying the table using a UBE. As with most cowboy operations, it comes down to quickly and efficiently making changes based on specific user requirements.

Path Codes

In this section, we will discuss what OneWorld path codes are, how they fit into the system, and how path codes meet business needs. A path code can be thought of as the specifications for OneWorld objects. These specifications can be in two different formats: TAM or a relational database format. Some of the topics covered in this section include:

- Path Codes: Overview

- Definition of path code

- Which tables are used

- Adding a path code

- When to add a custom path code

- Copying a path code

- Modifying the F9861 table

- Deleting a path code

Path Codes: Overview

A path code is really OneWorld's window to the world. This is because a path code contains all the information the system needs to run its objects. J.D. Edwards ships several "canned" path codes. These include pristine, Conference Room Pilot (CRP), development, and production path codes. The reason J.D. Edwards chose to ship these path codes is to allow their clients the ability to have a pristine set of specifications, which they can always use in troubleshooting as a benchmark comparison. The CRP path code is meant to be a testing ground. This path code allows users of OneWorld to test their changes to shipped J.D. Edwards objects or their custom objects before moving them into their production environment. Nothing should go into the production path code before being completely tested. This will help ensure the stability of the objects your production users are using. The development path code is meant for just that, development. This is the area where your developers can modify objects or add custom objects to meet your business needs. The entire purpose of this path code is to have an area where developers can code and ready their objects.

It is important to use the path codes in a correct manner. Development should be done in the development path code, then transferred to the CRP path code. The objects should then be tested in the CRP path code, which should point at a copy of the production data. This way you know that your objects are safe to move into the production path code, which is the final step of the process. This process will be discussed more in Chapter 10, which is about packages and their delivery.

Definition of a Path Code

A path code is how OneWorld finds the specifications necessary to run its applications, business functions, and reports. This is because a path code is also the storage area for these applications, business functions, and reports. When dealing with a path code, you need to ask yourself what area of the path code are you interested in at that time. The directory structure contains TAM specification files on clients and enterprise servers. TAM (table access management) is a proprietary J.D. Edwards file format that allows database specification files to be portable. OneWorld runs on a client machine and an enterprise server by using these TAM specification files. There are also the central objects of a path code. The central objects of a path code are a series of relational database files that store the specifications for OneWorld objects. These tables are very good at storing the information, but access to them is slow, which is why TAM files are used when OneWorld runs on a client or enterprise server. TAM files are created during a package build. Package builds will be discussed later in this book in the packages and their delivery chapter; for now, just think of a package build as a snapshot in time of the information contained in the central object tables. Finally, a path code tells OneWorld where to find its check-in location. Not all objects can be converted into a relational database format; these are the source and header files of OneWorld. When you check these objects in, OneWorld looks at the path code to determine where to store them.

Which Tables Are Used

In OneWorld, the F00942 table, which is contained in the system data source, is used to store path code information. This table contains several key pieces of information:

- The name of the path code.

- The description of the path code.

- The name of the machine that contains your path code's source and header files. This is normally your deployment server.

- Your server share path. This will be explained in more detail later.

- The status code of the path code.

- The merge option.

- The release level of the path code. This is important because you can apply an update to one path code—for example, the development path code—but not others. This means this path code would be at a different level than the other path codes.

- Deployment data source. This tells OneWorld where to find the central object tables.

- The UNC flag setting of your path code.

This table is read every time a client workstation logs on to the system. The system then looks to see if the client machine has the proper directory structure for each path code assigned to an environment. If this structure does not exist, the environment will not be displayed to the end user, even if their user profile has been assigned this environment. This is because there would be no specifications for OneWorld to run its applications on that client workstation.

Adding a Path Code

If you need to add a path code, an experienced OneWorld system administrator or someone who has read this book can accomplish this in a relatively short amount of time.

NOTE

The only time you really need to add a new path code is if you have an environment that needs its own specific set of OneWorld objects. In the authors' experience, you should only add a custom path code when it meets a business need, otherwise all the path code does is add overhead to the system and complicate the administration of the system.

There are several steps to adding a path code correctly:

- The path code information must be added into the F00942 table.

- The central object tables will need to be created or copied.

- The check-in location will need to be created and the path code created on the enterprise or application server.

Adding Information to the F00942 Path Code Master Table

To add path code information into the F00942 table, log on to a client workstation and go to menu GH9053 Environments. Double-click on the path code master program P980042. You will be presented with the Work With Path Codes screen, shown in Figure 2-5.

Click the Add button on the toolbar. This will take you to the Path Code Revisions screen, shown in Figure 2-6. This screen is very important. If the fields in this screen

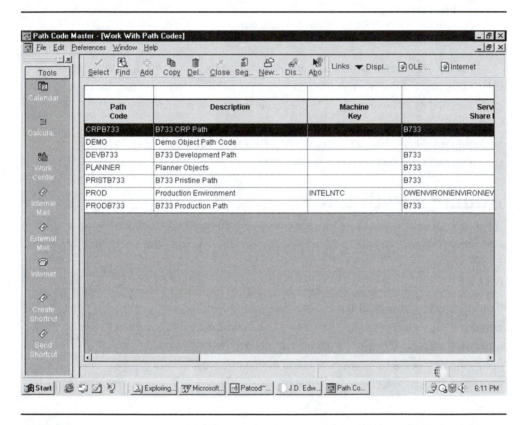

FIGURE 2-5. Work With Path Codes screen

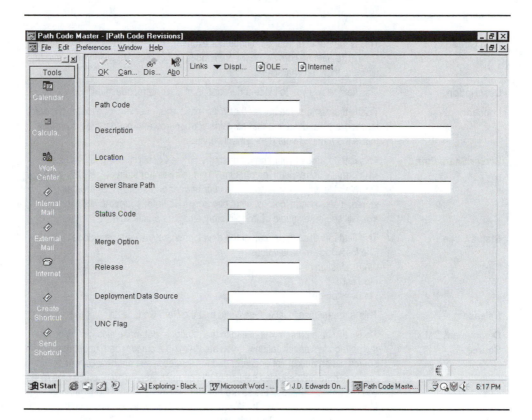

FIGURE 2-6. Path Code Revisions screen

are not populated correctly, you will have problems with check-in/check-out of objects, package builds, and package deployments. Table 2-1 lists the fields on this screen, explaining the use of each one and how they affect the OneWorld system.

Once you have filled in these fields, click OK. This will write the information to the F00942 table.

Path Code	This is the name of your path code (for example, PRODB733). Note: The naming convention for path codes is that they are all in uppercase and no more then ten characters.
Description	This field allows you to place a description of your path code into the system.
Location	This is the name of the server that will contain your check-in location. A check-in location is a set of folders that contains your source and header files. Normally this is the name of your deployment server.
Server Share Path	This is the name of your shared directory on the Location machine. This share will normally correspond to your OneWorld release (for example, B733). When OneWorld finds the machine where your header and source files are being stored, it also needs to know what directory to look for your path code in. You will see an example of this directory structure a little later.
Status Code	This field identifies the status of the development cycle your path code is in. The following are valid values: In Production In Test In Development
Release	This is the release level of OneWorld that the Path Code is on.
Deployment Data Source	This is the data source that points to the relational database files, which contain the path code's specifications. If you are defining a custom path code, this data source may not exist yet and will need to be added; see the how do you set up and configure data sources section of this chapter. As you start to use OneWorld, you will notice that these tables are not mapped in the Object Configuration Manager. This is because OneWorld knows to look for these tables in the data source listed here. The only exception to this is the F983051 table, which contains version header records for UBEs and interactive applications.
UNC Flag	This field tells OneWorld to use or not use the Universal Naming Convention. When this flag is set to Y, OneWorld will automatically look for the machine name and the share path, similar to when you map a drive in Windows Explorer (for example, \\LOCATION MACHINE\SERVER SHARE PATH). If this flag is set to N, you will have to not only give OneWorld the machine name in the location field, but indicate the back slashes to tell the system to look on the network for their machine. This field should always be set to Y.

TABLE 2-1.   Path Code Revision Screen Values

T I P

If you are ever unsure of what table an application is hitting, here is a simple trick to find the answer. In the JDE.INI file, which is located in the WINNT or Windows directory, set the output=file under the debug section of the INI file. This turns on the JDEDEBUG.LOG. Once you have done this, log on to OneWorld and go to the desired application. Open the JDEDEBUG.LOG; place your initials at the bottom of it so you can find where you entered the application. Enter the desired application and click Find. Now open the JDEDEBUG.LOG and find your initials. You should now see calls to the tables that were hit when you entered the application.

Central Objects

The next step in adding a path code is to either create or copy the central object tables. We will go over the procedure of creating these tables first. You will need to modify a script that J.D. Edwards ships with the OneWorld software. You will find this script on your deployment server under the database directory. When you open this directory, choose the directory that fits your database, such as Oracle or SQL Server. You will then see a series of bat files. Open the file named JDESET.BAT. This file will need to be modified to correctly create the central object tables. This file contains the name of your databases and the database users who will own the tables. Change the user and database to the correct name—this will be for one path code, such as PRODB733. The reason for this is that the files that actually do the work are named LOADXXXX.BAT, where XXX is the name of the path code (for example, LOADPRIST.BAT). This file takes the parameters from jdeset.bat and creates the central object tables. Table 2-2 describes the settings in the JDESET.BAT file. This file can be found on the deployment server under database\export\SQLsrvr (or Oracle\NT or UNIX).

Now, using the method described previously, pick a particular set of central objects and modify both the JDESET.BAT and the actual LOADXXXX.BAT for the new path code you are adding. If, for example, you want to add a path code for training, you might decide to call it TRAINB733. You could pick the PRODB733 path code as a baseline and modify its LOADPROD.BAT to call the TRAINB733 user and table space, which you would have added into the JDESET.BAT file.

Inside and Out

JDEDBA_USER	This is a data administrative user, which you should have set up with appropriate privileges when you prepared your database for OneWorld.
JDEDBA_PSSWD	Enter the password for the user JDEDBA.
PROD_SPEC_DB	This is the name of your database, which will contain the central object tables for your production path code. The standard for SQL Server is JDE_PRODB733. (If you are using Oracle, this field should be set to your connect string.)
PROD_SPEC_USER	This is the user that will own your production central object tables. If you follow J.D. Edwards' standards, this will be the user PRODB733.
PROD_SPEC_PSSWD	This is the password for the user PRODB733.
PRIST_SPEC_DB	This is the name of the SQL Server database that will contain the central object tables for the pristine path code. The standard name for this database is PRISTB733 for SQL Server installations. (If you are using Oracle, this field should be set to your connect string.)
PRIST_SPEC_USER	This is the name of the user that will own your central object tables for the pristine path code. The J.D. Edwards' standard is PRISTB733
PRIST_SPEC_PSSWD	This is the password for the prist_spec_user.
DEV_SPEC_DB	This is the name of the database where your development central object tables will be created. The standard for SQL Server is to name this database JDE_DEVB733. (If you are using Oracle, this field should be set to your connect string.)
DEV_SPEC_USER	This is the name of the user that will own your central object tables for the development path code. The J.D. Edwards' standard is DEVB733.
DEV_SPEC_PSSWD	This is the password for the dev_spec_user.
CRP_SPEC_DB	This is the name of the database that will contain your CRP path code central object tables. The standard for SQL Server is JDE_CRPB733. (If you are using Oracle, this field should be set to your connect string.)
CRP_SPEC_USER	This is the name of the user that will own your central object tables for the CRP path code. The standard is to use CRPB733.
CRP_SPEC_PSSWD	This is the password for the crp_spec_user.
JDE_DTA	This is the path to the import files that are used to create the central object tables. Normally this will be one directory structure back. The value you should have in this field is two periods/dots (..).
JDE_LOG	This path indicates where your log files will be written. It is important to check these log files and ensure that your central object tables were loaded correctly. The standard value is one period/dot (.), which will place the log files in the same directory as the jdeset.bat file.
JDE_ERR	This path specifics where error information will be stored. The standard value is one period/dot (.), which will place the log files in the same directory as the jdeset.bat file.
SQLVERSION	This variable is used to indicate if you are using SQL Server 6.5 or 7.0. If you are using 7.0, the correct value is 7. If you are using 6.5, the correct value is 6.
JDE_SVR	This is the name of the machine where your databases reside.

TABLE 2-2. JDESET.BAT File Settings

N O T E

The user you specify will need to already exist in your database with sufficient privileges to create tables or this procedure will fail. You will also have to ensure that the table spaces, if you are using Oracle, exist. This can be done by modifying and running the CRTABSP script. This script is located in the database directory on your deployment server.

N O T E

You need to be sure you modify the JDESET.BAT file correctly and execute the correct bat file. If you do not, you could overlay your existing central objects. Carefully review the example JDESET.BAT file described previously!

After you have modified this file, save and close the file. Double-click on the appropriate bat file, which would depend on the values you entered into your JDESET.BAT file—the LOADPRIST.BAT file would be one example of this type of file. This will create and populate almost all of your central object tables. This job creates and populates the following tables:

- F98306

- F98710

- F98711

- F98712

- F98713

- F98720

- F98740

- F98741

- F98743

- F98745

- F98750

- F98751

- F98752

Inside and Out

- F98753

- F98760

- F98761

- F98762

Once this process is finished, you still need to create one more central object table. That table is F983051; this table is normally loaded during the environment workbench. However, since you are only adding a path code, you are not going to execute the environment workbench. To create this table, use the following procedure:

1. Log on to the deployment server in the planner environment.

2. Open the object librarian application. You can run this application by typing OL in the fast path.

3. Type **F983051** in the Query By Example line and click Find.

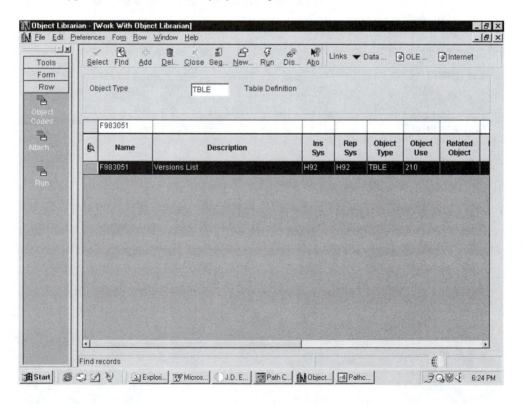

DEFINITION

Query By Example (QBE) Line: *This line represents the yellow boxes that appear on top of the column descriptions in the grid of an application. You can narrow your search down by typing information into this line. So if you were in address book searching for a specific address book number, you could place this address book number in the yellow box above the address book number column. You will then only be presented with the information you where looking for. This column will allow you to use wild cards (*), but it is case sensitive.*

4. Select the F983051 table. You will now see the Table Design Aid form.

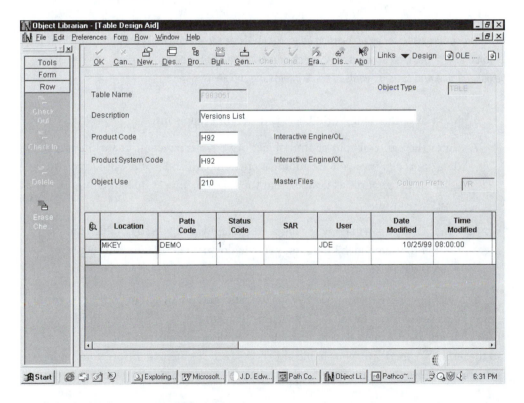

5. Go to the form exit and choose copy table.

Copy Table window showing:

- Table Name: F983051
- Source — Data Source: OneWorld Local
- Destination — Data Source: (blank)
- Object Owner ID: (blank)
- Password: (blank)

NOTE

This procedure will overlay an existing table. You will need to ensure that your source and target data sources are correct, otherwise you risk overlaying an existing table and causing yourself some interesting problems.

6. Make sure that OneWorld Local is the source data source.

7. Enter the name of your central object or versions data source for the target data source. Since you are adding a custom path code, you would have to add this data source as described in the how do you set up and configure data sources section.

8. Click OK. This will copy the shipped J.D. Edwards F983051 table from the Planner\data\jdeb7.mdb, on your deployment server, to your central objects database.

You will now have the shipped F983051 created and populated in your new central objects data source. You must now update this file with a SQL statement to reflect your path code and deployment server's name. Use the following select and update statement. In the authors' experience, you should always do a select statement before your update statement to ensure you are actually updating the records you think you are updating.

```
select * from XXXX.F983051 where VRENHV = 'PATH CODE' and VRMKEY = 'SERVER';
```

The XXXX is the user that you set up to own your central object tables. Now that you know what records you are going to update, you can perform the following update statement:

```
update XXXX.F983051 set VRENVH = 'YOURPATH CODENAME' and VRMKEY =
'DEPLOYMENT SERVER NAME' where VRENVH = 'PATH CODE' and VRMKEY = 'SERVER';
```

You have now created your custom central object tables. These tables will contain all of the shipped J.D. Edwards' objects. Now let's go over how you would copy an existing set of central object tables. You would do this when you want your new path code to match the source path code. OneWorld contains a utility to copy an existing set of central object tables. This utility is UBE R98403, version XJDE0019. You can get to this report by typing **BV** in the fast path or going to menu GH9011 and double-clicking on P98305 Batch Versions.

Highlight the XJDE0019 and go to form processing options. These processing options are very important, as R98403 is a utility that will copy tables between different data sources in OneWorld. Yes, that means you can copy a table between different types of databases as well as copying the tables between different owners in the same database. This utility is J.D. Edwards' recommended way of moving large amounts of data.

Inside and Out

Enter the following processing options, which you will see on the R98403, to copy your source path code into your new custom path code.

On the Environment tab, enter the following information:

Processing Option	Description of Processing Option Values
1. Enter the environment the database is created for. (If this report is called from another process, the environment will be passed in.)	You can enter the name of the environment to which you are copying the information. When this field is filled in, the report uses OCM mappings to find the target data source. The other process that would call this report is the environment workbench, as J.D. Edwards uses this utility to create OneWorld tables during an installation or upgrade.
2. Or enter the data source the database is created for.	Unless you are copying tables that exist in more than one data source, you should use this option in R98403. Place the name of your custom central objects data source in this field. Either processing option 1 or processing option **2** needs to be filled in, not both.
3. Enter a **1** to load production data or a **2** to load demonstration data. The default is to load production data. (If the report is called from another process, this flag will be passed in.)	This setting often confuses users. If you choose 1 to load production data, the report will create all the tables blank, except the ones necessary to run OneWorld. In this instance, you will need to choose **2** so that the contents of your source path code tables will be copied into your target path code.
4. Enter the data source for loading data. (If the report is called from another process, this value will be passed in.)	Fill this field with the name of your central objects data source (for example, Central Objects – CRPB733).
5. Enter the environment the database is created for. (If this report is called from another process, the environment will be passed in.)	You can enter the name of the environment you are copying the information from. When this field is filled in, the report uses OCM mappings to find the target data source. The other process that would call this report is the environment workbench, as J.D. Edwards uses this utility to create OneWorld tables during an installation or upgrade. Again, **4** and **5** are either/or, not both.

On the Update tab, enter the following values:

6. Enter a **1** for proof or a **2** to create the environment database.	If the job is run in proof mode, it will not copy tables, it will just show what it would have done. It is generally a good idea to run the job in proof mode first to verify it is affecting the tables that you want it to hit.
7. Enter an **A** to re-create existing tables in data sources that allow automatic table creation. The default is not to re-create tables.	For the purposes of copying an existing set of central object tables, this value should be set to A. Note: Any existing tables will be overwritten, so be sure that your processing options are correct before running this report in update mode.
8. Enter a **1** to only copy tables that exist in the target data source.	When this value is set to **1**, the UBE will only copy the tables that exist in the target data source. This value should be blank to copy your path code tables.
9. Enter a **Y** to add records without clearing the target table. This is used for language tables.	When this is set to **Y**, the UBE will amend to the table. Leave this field blank for the purposes of creating new central object tables.

Accept the defaults on the Print And Licensing tab. The default values for these tabs are blank. Click OK to save your processing options. You will now be back at the Work With Batch Versions screen. Highlight XJDE0019 and press Select. You will then be presented with the Version Prompting screen, shown in Figure 2-7. Go to form advanced; this will take you into the Advanced Version Prompting screen, shown here.

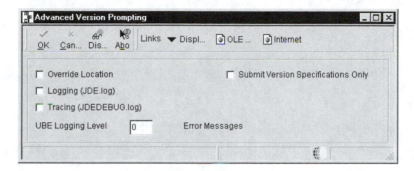

Check the Override Location box and click OK. You will now be back at the Version Prompting screen. Click Submit, select the local data source, select the output to be displayed onscreen, and the job will start running. This job will then copy the central object tables from your source path code to your new path code's central object data source. If you have problems with this report, look at the JDE.LOG, which will normally be located on the root of your C drive. You can also look for a JDECPY.LOG on the C root of your machine. This log will tell you what tables are copied and how many records succeeded and how many failed.

A benefit of running R98403 to copy an existing central object path code is that this tool will copy the F983051 table and update the table with the name of your deployment server and path code name. However, just to be safe, you should confirm that these values are correct after your job completes.

NOTE

You do not want to use SQL Server or Oracle's built-in bulk copy functionality to copy these tables, as padding issues have been encountered when this type of copy is used. However, what you can do is export your tables off to a dump file and then restore them to a new owner. This is a quick way of copying tables, but when you use this method, you will have to update the F983051 table to reflect your deployment server and path code name. This method should only be used when you have a database administrator or if you possess the database skills necessary to perform this operation.

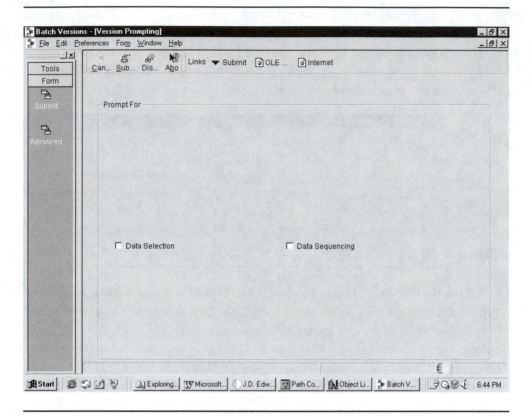

FIGURE 2-7. Version Prompting screen

Creating the Check-in Location

The final part of adding a path code is to create the check-in location and create the path code on the enterprise server.

Before we cover the actual process of creating the check-in location, we should go over exactly what a check-in location is, in reference to OneWorld. When you entered the path code information into the path code master application, you entered the name of a server in the Location field. This is how OneWorld knows where to copy the source and header files when objects are checked in. Some examples of objects that have source and header files are business functions and tables. These files are not stored in a relational database format, so they need to be stored in a directory structure.

TIP

A common problem for developers checking in objects is receiving the error "Cannot copy file." This error normally means the user does not have the permissions to copy a source or header file into the check-in location or OneWorld cannot find the check-in location due to an incorrect setup.

You can create the check-in location in two ways: by manually copying the directory structure through Windows Explorer or by running a report. To create it manually, open Windows Explorer on your deployment server and create a folder with the same name as your custom path code under OneWorld\B733. Copy the contents of the PRISTB733 directory into this new folder, if you are creating your custom path code from scratch. If you are copying an existing path code, you will need to copy that path code's directory structure. If your new path code was named TESTB733, for example, you would copy the contents of PRISTB733 or another path code into TESTB733. This is because you need to move the source and header records that match your central object tables.

If you do not want to do this process manually, you can run a report to copy these directory structures. This report is R9800942. To run this report, type **BV** in the fast path. You will now be in the Batch Versions screen. Type **R9800942** in the Batch Application field. Highlight the ZJDE0001 version and click Select to submit the job. Be sure to run the job locally by going to form advanced option on the Version Prompting screen and checking Override Location. When you submit the report, you will be prompted to enter some processing options.

Processing Options	Description of Processing Option Values
Source Path Code	This is the path code that you are copying—in our example, PRISTB733.
Destination Path Code	This is your target path code. In our example, this would be TESTB733.
Copy Package	Enter a **Y** if you want to copy the packages that currently exist in your source path code. Normally, you would enter a Y so you could deploy a package immediately, thus allowing your end users to work, and build a package later to test the new path code.
Load Specification	Enter a **Y** to copy the F9861 records or follow the procedures outlined below.

You will also need to change some filenames to match the new path code. After you have copied the directory structure into your new path code—for example, TESTB733—you need to rename the packages in the TESTB733\packages directory.

Inside and Out

Rename these from PRISTXXXFA to TESTXXX.FA. You will also have to perform this step on your enterprise server.

Once you have renamed the package names themselves, you will need to modify the package inf files to reflect your new path code. To do this, open the Package_INF directory located under J.D. Edwards OneWorld\B733. In this folder, you will find several inf files, such as PRISTB733FA.INF. These files are key to the client installation process. Copy the appropriate package inf files (in our example, PRISTB733FA.INF) and name your new file TESTB733FA.INF, where TESTB733 is your new path code. You then need to open the inf files and replace all occurrences of PRIST with TEST.

Creating the Path Code on the Enterprise Server

Unfortunately, the only way to get a path code onto the enterprise server is by manually making a manual copy. When you perform this manual copy operation, be sure the host services are stopped. Then all you have to do is copy the directory structure. You may also have to rename the package under the path code directory on the enterprise server. The concept of a packages directory on the enterprise server will be explained in Chapter 10. For now, let's say you are copying the PRODB733 path code. You copy this directory structure and then open it. You will find a folder called Packages under B7xx, where xx is your release of OneWorld; open this folder. There will be a package name there. You will need to rename this package to the name of a full package existing in your new path code. This means you will need to be able to find the package in the package assembly program, B733.1 and beyond. The program P9601 exists on menu GH9083; the functionality of this program will be discussed in detail in Chapter 10.

CAUTION

When you do this, be sure your host services are stopped or you could corrupt your specifications.

Modifying the F9861 Table

You now have a path code master definition in the F00942 table, you have your central object tables, and you have your check-in location created. The only thing you have left to do is modify your F9861 object librarian detail table. (This only needs to be done if you did not set the Y parameter when you ran R9800942 before.) This table will need to reflect your deployment server name and your new path code name; this is so that your developers can check out objects and work on them. To update this table, you can use SQL statements or you can run R989861 (Update/Write F9861).

If you are not familiar with SQL statements, you will want to run the R989861 report. To accomplish this, log on to a client workstation. The environment does not matter as all environments use the same object librarian. Type **BV** in the fast path and press enter. You will now be on the Work With Batch Versions screen. Highlight the XJDE0001 version and click Row Processing Options.

Enter the source path code you want to copy records from. If you created your path code from scratch, you will want to copy a pristine path code that does not have custom objects in it. This is because the UBE will place a record in the F9861 object librarian detail table for every entry of the source path code. If you have custom objects in this source path code, but have created your central object tables from scratch, it would appear that this custom object existed in the new path code even though it did not. So when your developers go to check this object out, they would receive an error. OneWorld would not be able to find the object in the central object tables, although the object would appear as if it existed in that path code in the object librarian.

If you copied an existing path code's central object files and check-in location, use that path code as your source path code. The target path code will be the name of your new path code. Click OK to save your processing option changes. You are now back in the Work With Batch Versions screen; highlight XJDE0001 and click Select. Go to form advanced and check the Override Location box, then click OK. You are now back at the Version Prompting screen. Click the Submit button. You will be prompted for your processing options again; just confirm they are correct and click OK. OneWorld will then ask you where you want to run the job. Choose LOCAL; this will cause the job to run on your local workstation. This job cannot be run on the enterprise server. The job will then enter your new path code into the F9861 table. To check the job after its completion, go into the object librarian application, click Find, select a shipped J.D. Edwards object, and click Select. You should now see your path code in the check-out line in the Design Aid screen.

The second way to update the F9861 table is by using a SQL statement to create a temporary table. Update this table and copy the records from it into your original F9861 table. Use the following SQL statements:

Create the temporary environment:

```
Create table temp.f9861 as select * from objb733.f98761 where SIMKEY =
'DEPLOYMENTSERVERNAME' and SIPATHCD = 'PRODB733';
```

If you are using Oracle, remember to perform a commit statement:

```
select count(*) from temp.f9861;
select count(*) from f9861 where SIMKEY = 'DEPLOYMENTSERVERNAME' and
SIPATHCD = 'PRODB733';
```

You now will need to update your F9861 temporary table so it contains the correct information and then copy the contents back into your original F9861 table:

```
update temp.f9861 set SIPATHCD = 'TESTB733';
```

If you are using Oracle, be sure to run a commit statement:

```
commit;
insert into objb733.f9861 select * from tempF9861;
```

Once you confirm that your new path code is in the F9861 table, you can drop this table by using the following statement:

```
drop table temp.f9861;
```

Deleting a Path Code

To delete a path code, you must perform several steps:

1. Remove the path code record from the F00942 table.

2. Delete the central object tables.

3. Manually delete the check-in location and path code directory on the enterprise server.

To delete the path code record from the F00942 table, from the client workstation, or on the deployment server in the deployment environment, go to menu GH9053 and double-click on the Path Code Master P980042. You will now be in the Work With Path Codes application. Press find, highlight the desired path code, and press delete. This will remove the path code record from F00942. This does not delete the central object tables or remove the path code's directory structure from the deployment or enterprise server. Have your database administrator drop the appropriate central object tables; he or she can do this by searching for the owner of these tables and then dropping all tables that are owned by that owner. Next you will need to delete the data sources associated with this path code. This can be done through the database data source application on menu Gh9611. Finally, from Windows Explorer on the deployment server, highlight the path code directory under OneWorld\B733 and press Delete. You will also have to delete the directory structure for your path code off your enterprise server. This procedure will vary a bit depending on your platform. However, no matter what platform you are on, you will need to ensure that your host services are down when you remove the path code's directory structure from the enterprise server.

Now that you have seen how to find the data and define the applications that are used in OneWorld, let's look at how you combine the applications with the data to create an instance of the OneWorld product. The tool used to do this is environments.

Environments

This section goes into detail about how OneWorld environments work. It describes what an environment is and how this feature of OneWorld ties into the entire system. An environment can be described as the framework on which the system rests. This framework is made up of object configuration mappings and a path code. These are what tell OneWorld where to find the data and specification files needed for its applications to run. We have just gone over what a path code is in detail in the last section. In this section, we will cover the following:

- Definition of an environment

- Tables used for environments

- Adding an environment

- Copying an environment

- Deleting an environment

- When to create a custom environment

Definition of an Environment

An environment is the framework on which your business runs. This framework is how OneWorld finds the company's business data. It also allows OneWorld to find other objects, such as a business function; this helps run the system more efficiently. To keep what a OneWorld environment is straight in your mind, just remember that an environment consists of object configuration mappings and a path code.

Tables Used for Environments

OneWorld touches or uses several tables to keep track of environment information. These tables are system files, meaning they are contained in the OneWorld system data source.

- F0093 – Library List Control

- F0094 – Library List Master

- F00941 – Environment Detail

- F986101 – Object Configuration Manager

- F98611 – Data Source Master

- F00942 – Path Code Master

The F0093 library list control table contains a list of the environments users are authorized to gain access to. This file is used in World software and OneWorld software. This table is read when a user logs on to OneWorld; the software then displays the environments they can log on to.

The F0094 library list master file basically contains the header record information for an environment. You can find the environment name and its description in this table. More detailed information is contained in the F00941 environment detail table.

The F00941 environment detail file contains information on the name of an environment, the path code it is associated with, if just-in-time installation is turned on or off for the environment, and the release level of the environment.

The F986101 is the object configuration manager table and act like the traffic cop of OneWorld. This table contains mappings, which tell the system what data source the data is stored in.

The F98611 is the data source master table. Once the system finds a mapping, in the F986101, it then has a data source name. It needs to read that data source in order to determine what type of database the business data is contained in, what machine these tables reside on, and how to connect to that database. All of this information is contained in the data source master table.

The F00942 path code master file contains information on the path code an environment is associated with. A path code tells OneWorld where to find the specifications it needs to run its applications and where the check-in location is located on the system.

Adding an Environment

Adding an environment is actually a simple process. If you are in OneWorld, you can add an environment from the Environment Master program (P0094), located on the Environments menu (GH9053). When you double-click on this program, you will be taken to the Work With Environments screen.

Inside and Out

Environment Name	Description	Path Code	Release	Just In Time Installation
ACT733	Accounting Environment	PRODB733	B733	Y
CHICRP733	B733 CRP Environment	CRPB733	B733	Y
CHIDEV733	B733 Development Environment	DEVB733	B733	N
CHIPRD733	B733 Production Environment	PRODB733	B733	Y
CHIPRT733	B733 Pristine Environment	PRISTB733	B733	Y
CHITST733	B733 Test Environment	CRPB733	B733	Y
CODECHANGE	Internet Code Change Env	PLANNER	B733	Y
CRP733	B733 CRP Environment	CRPB733	B733	Y

On this screen you will see the Display Only OneWorld Environments check box. If this box is not checked and you are a co-existent customer, you will see all your World environments as well as OneWorld. You can add an environment by clicking the Add button to bring up the Environments Revisions screen, shown in Figure 2-8.

This screen has several important fields:

- **Environment Name**   Place the name of your environment in this field—for example, JDE733.

- **Description**   Enter a description of the environment, such as "Atlanta's production environment."

- **Path Code**   This is the path code associated with the environment. The path code is the way OneWorld finds the specifications it needs to run its applications. These are contained in the central object tables or TAM specification files, depending on what area of OneWorld you are trying to use.

- **Release**   This is the release level of software you are on.

- **Just In Time Installation**   This field can be used to enable or disable just-in-time installation of applications to workstations in the environment. If you set this to N, your clients with partial packages will not be able to pull down applications. This is why you should use caution when setting this feature of OneWorld.

- **Developer**   This is a future use field.

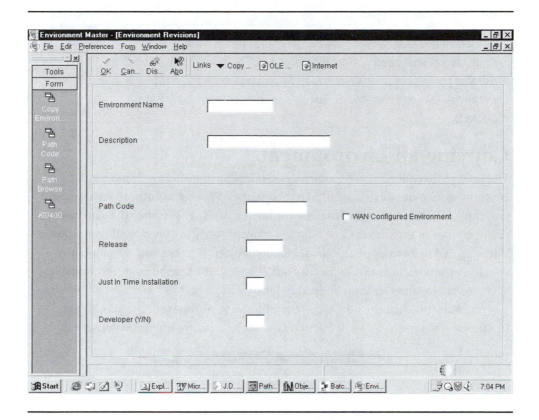

FIGURE 2-8. Environment Revisions screen

- **WAN Configured Environment** This check box is used to tell OneWorld if the environment is going to be used for a WAN. If this box is checked, it will affect the object configuration mappings.

N O T E

You must ensure that your environment is associated with a path code. If it is not, the software will not be able to find you check-in location or your central object tables. This means that you will have problems with package builds and the check-in/out process.

TIP

*It is important to realize that when you add an environment you will have to
manually add all your object configuration mappings. This is why in the authors'
experience you will almost never want to add an environment from scratch. It is
much simpler to copy a shipped J.D. Edwards environment and modify it to suit
your needs.*

Copying an Environment

The feature that allows you to copy an environment is one you will use more than
anything else in the Environment Master program. When you copy an environment,
you can copy the mappings of the environment as well. This is useful, as many of
the mappings in the Object Configuration Manager are the same for all environments.
These shared mappings are to data dictionary, object librarian, and system tables. If
you add an environment, you must manually add all the mappings to certain tables,
such as system tables, that are necessary for the OneWorld software to run. To copy
an environment, click the Row Copy Environments button from the Work With
Environments screen. You will be presented with the Copy Environment screen.

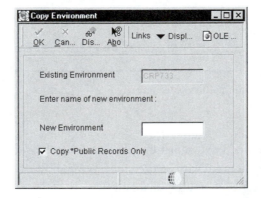

Enter the desired name of your new environment in the New Environment field. Be
sure to note the check box labeled Copy *Public Records Only. When this box is checked,
you will only copy the Object Configuration Manager mappings for *PUBLIC. This means
that mappings for individual users would not be copied. In most circumstances, you will
want this box checked. When you click OK, OneWorld will write to the F0094, F00941,
and F986101 tables. What about the path code? When you copy an environment, the new
environment is associated with the copied environment's path code. One path code can
have many environments assigned to it, but each environment can only be assigned to
one path code. What this really means is that OneWorld environments can share the

specifications for applications. So you can have two environments that have the same application functionality but point to different business data. This is useful when you have a company with different departments that need the same functionality, but also need their own business data.

Deleting an Environment

When you are in the Environment Master program, P0094, highlight an environment and click the Delete button on the toolbar. This will remove the records for the environment from F0093, F0094, F00941, and F986101.

NOTE

When you delete an environment, you are not automatically deleting the data sources and business data associated with that environment. This will need to be done as a separate step.

When to Create a Custom Environment

When do you need a custom environment and when is it just extra overhead? This is a question that faces a lot of OneWorld system administrators. Each custom environment should have a business purpose. One good example would be two departments that both need to use the same custom applications, but also need to have their own business data, menus, or user-defined codes. We cannot stress enough that the system is only there to meet the business's needs, so any environment that does not address a business need is extra overhead and should not be in the system.

Object Configuration Manager

In this section, we will discuss one of the nerve centers of a OneWorld system, the Object Configuration Manager (OCM). The OCM program is truly the nerve center of OneWorld, the application that tells the system in what data source data resides. If there are incorrect entries in this program, OneWorld will not function correctly. To avoid this, we will go over several areas of the Object Configuration Manager, including:

- The definition of the Object Configuration Manager
- Tables that are used
- What really happens when a workstation requests data or logic

- What happens when a workstation runs a UBE

- How to add OCM mappings

- How to copy OCM mappings

- How to delete OCM mappings

- The difference between system and server map

- Changing the mappings for object librarian tables

- Changing Oracle parameters that OneWorld uses

- Advanced Object Configuration Manager operations

Definition of the Object Configuration Manager

The Object Configuration Manager is key to a OneWorld system. It allows separate environments to access data on a variety of machines and databases. Think of this program as the nerve center of OneWorld where you can configure and guide the system. The program allows you to configure OneWorld in almost unlimited ways. Using this program, you can tell the system on what machines and databases business data resides, where to run reports, and where to run business functions.

You will always have two types of OCM mappings. These are system mappings and server map mappings. The system mappings are used to direct client workstations to business data tables, business functions, and to tell them where to run UBEs. Once a mapping is found, OneWorld determines what data source is to be used from the mapping and passes the information in that data source to JDEBase. JDEBase is the kernel software of OneWorld that will make the call to the database; it can determine how to construct the SQL statements based on the platform and the type of database being used.

The server map mappings, or OCM, are used once a UBE is run on an enterprise server. The report then looks at the server map OCM tables to find the necessary tables to run. Since this application is so powerful, we recommend that only system administrators have access to this program. You can restrict the use of this program through OneWorld security.

Tables that Are Used

The Object Configuration Manager mainly uses the F986101 object configuration master table. This table contains the environment names, user, objects, object status, and primary data source value (see Table 2-3). This information makes up an OCM mapping. The environment value is just an environment name. The user can be a specific user such as JDE, a user group, or *PUBLIC. The primary data source value contains a data source; this data source is what gives the system the final information on where the relational database tables, which the software is looking for, reside.

There can be many copies of this table on a OneWorld system. The workstations will use one copy, in the system data source, to find their data. The enterprise and logic servers have their own copy of this table, which is used when a report is run on an enterprise or logic server.

The F986101 table really only consists of what is called OCM mappings. These mappings tell the system what data source the table resides in, where to run its business functions, and how to process its reports.

What Really Happens When a Workstation Requests Data or Logic

When a workstation requests data or logic, it must use the F986101 object configuration master table as a guide. The workstation will poll this table looking for certain information. It will look for the environment that is needed, the user who is logged on, and the object that has been requested. How this works will become clear after we go through an example of a workstation's request for data. When a workstation requests data, it will read F986101 in a particular manner. The system will pass select statements using F986101's primary keys. It will look for the environment, an object name, a user, and a primary data source. The system will also only look for mappings that have a status of AV, for active. Below is an example of an OCM mapping.

Environment	Object Name	Object Type	Primary Data Source	User
PROD733	F0002	TBLE	Control Tables - Production	*PUBLIC
Object Status	**Data Source Mode**	**Secondary Data Source**	**Allow QBE**	
AV	P		Y	

TABLE 2-3.   Example of an Entry in the F986101 Table

This mapping is what is going to tell OneWorld in what data source the table that the system is looking for resides. We will discuss each individual part of this mapping later in this section; for now, let's take a look at how OneWorld reads mappings. The system reads the F986101 using the following logic:

1. The system knows you are logged in to the PROD733 environment and you are looking for an object of type TBLE, since that is what the application you are running tells the system.

2. The system will then poll F986101 for an environment—in this case PROD733— a status of AV, a type of TBLE, the object name, and the user who is logged on to the system.

3. If these are not found, OneWorld will look to see if there is a record for the environment, a status of AV, a type of TBLE, the object name, and a user group that the user logged on to the system belongs to.

4. Next, it will look for a record for the environment, a status of AV, a type of TBLE, the object name, and the user *PUBLIC. If you used the F986101 entry in the table above as an example, the system would have found a mapping for F0002.

5. If OneWorld still does not find the mapping, it will poll F986101 for a record with the environment, a status of AV, a type of TBLE, an object name of DEFAULT, and the user who is signed in to OneWorld. This object name of DEFAULT is used so that the F986101 does not need a record for every object. This helps improve performance.

6. If this does not return a mapping, the system will then look for a record with the environment, a status of AV, a type of TBLE, an object name of DEFAULT, and a user group.

7. Finally, OneWorld will poll F986101 for a record with the environment, a status of AV, a type of TBLE, an object name of DEFAULT, and the user *PUBLIC.

T I P

If you turn on your JDEDEBUG.LOG, you can see some of these calls to F986101. However, you will not see all of them. Instead of the full call, you will see a reset select to F986101, and instead of the values the system is looking for, you will see question marks. The only time you will see the actual values is in the first select statement passed to F986101. We feel this is a tedious process and hope the logging will be changed to include the values at all times. Until then, you will just have to find the first select statement.

Once OneWorld has found the mapping, it uses the data source contained in that mapping to determine what type of database to connect to, what machine, and what owner or library. It passes this information to JDEBase, which knows how to construct calls to these databases and platforms.

What Happens When a Workstation Runs a UBE

When a workstation attempts to run a UBE, the logic that OneWorld follows to determine where this report should be run is similar to how the system polls F986101 for data. The process is also the same for business functions. Let's step through the logic one more time, this time for a report being run from a client workstation.

1. The system knows you are logged on to the PROD733 environment and you are looking for an object of type UBE, since that is what the report you are running tells the system.

2. The system will then poll F986101 for an environment—in this case PROD733— a status of AV, a type of UBE, the object name, and the user who is logged on to the system.

3. If this is not found, OneWorld will look to see if there is a record for the environment, a status of AV, a type of UBE, the object name, and a user group that the user logged on to the system belongs to.

4. Next, it will look for a record for the environment, a status of AV, a type of UBE, the object name, and the user *PUBLIC.

5. If OneWorld still does not find the mapping, it will poll F986101 for a record with the environment, a status of AV, a type of UBE, an object name of DEFAULT, and the user who is logged in to OneWorld. This object name of DEFAULT is used so that F986101 does not need a record for every object. This helps improve the performance of the system.

6. If this does not return a mapping, the system will then look for a record with the environment, a status of AV, a type of UBE, the object name of DEFAULT, and a user group.

7. Next, OneWorld will poll F986101 for a record with the environment, a status of AV, a type of UBE, an object name of DEFAULT, and the user *PUBLIC.

If a record is found, OneWorld sends JDENET the proper information. JDENET is the area of OneWorld that handles sending messages between servers and clients. These messages are not database calls. This is how the enterprise server knows what report, version, and data selection to run, because the information is passed to it from JDENET. Once the enterprise or logic server receives the request, it responds by processing the UBE.

N O T E

The only call to F986101 in this example was to find out where to process the logic. Once the server starts to process the report, it will read F986101 in the server map data source to find the data required by the UBE. The logic behind this process is the same as the one described in the what happens when a workstation runs a UBE.

Some people ask, why have multiple OCMs at all? Why not just read one and be done with it? Well, there are several reasons for having a server map F986101. The main one is that the enterprise servers cannot read a data source that is pointing to an Access database, and J.D. Edwards ships its control tables mapped to an Access data source for the client machine's control tables. Another reason is performance and configurability. Your enterprise server may be across a WAN and you do not want to have it make calls across the WAN to find its data, as this could slow your system down.

How to Add OCM Mappings

You will only need to add a new OCM mapping when you need a specific user, group, or environment to look for its data, business functions, or where to process its UBEs in a different spot. Say you have 20 people in accounting, but only one runs your payroll checks. You want all this person's reports to run on one specific machine, and you want this person to look for his tables in a certain database. You can handle all this by adding OCM mappings for type UBE for this user's reports and of type TBLE for the tables that he needs to find in a different location than other users. These OCM mappings allow you to configure the system to run in a way that supports your business operations.

To add an OCM mapping, log on to a client machine. The reason you are logging on to a client machine is that it will update the system F986101. When you log on to the deployment server in the planner environment, it will change the F986101 contained in the jdeplan.mdb Access database. Since this is not the database accessed by your end users for mappings, you normally do not want to change your mappings in this database. Once you have logged on to the client machine, type **OCM** in the fast path or go to menu GH9611 (Advanced Operations) and double-click on P986110, Object Configuration Manager. You will then be prompted with the Object Configuration Manager Machine Search And Select screen. This screen allows you to modify either a server map F986101 table or the system F986101 table.

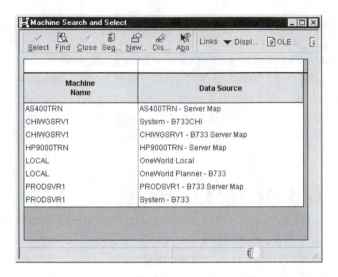

Normally you will choose a system to change a mapping for your client workstations. However, when you change these mappings you should always ask yourself, does this mapping need to be changed in the server map F986101 as well? If you change the mappings for your users in the system data source, but not the server map data source, you may see different results when running reports locally compared to reports run on the server.

You will now be on the Object Configuration Manage Work With Object Mappings screen. Click the Add button located on the toolbar. This will take you into the Object Mapping Revisions screen, shown in Figure 2-9.

The Object Mappings Revision screen contains the following fields:

- **Environment Name**   Enter the name of the environment that you want OCM mapping to affect.

- **Object Name**   Enter the name of the object the mapping is for. If you want the mapping to affect all non-mapped object names of a certain object type, enter **DEFAULT**.

- **Primary Data Source**   This is the data source in which OneWorld will look for your object. If you are mapping a business function or a UBE, the data source must be a logical data source. If you are mapping a table, the data source must be a database data source.

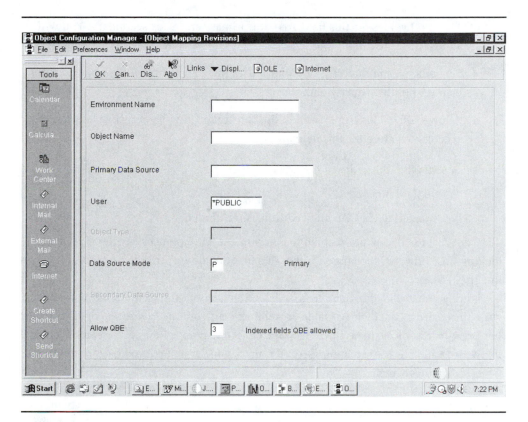

FIGURE 2-9.   Object Mappings Revision screen

- **User**   Enter the user you want this mapping to affect. You can enter a specific user, such as JDE, a user group, or *PUBLIC.

- **Object Type**   This is the type of object you are mapping. This field is grayed out and will default based on the Object Name field. However, if the object name is DEFAULT, you will be allowed to choose your object type. OneWorld allows you to map UBEs, tables, generic text (object type of GT), and business functions (object type of BSFN).

- **Data Source Mode**   This indicates if OneWorld should use the data source specified in the primary data source field or the secondary data source field.

The valid values for this field are P for primary and S for secondary. You will almost never use S.

- **Secondary Data Source**   OneWorld uses this data source if the object cannot be found in the primary data source.

- **Allow QBE**   This flag is used to turn on and off row-level record locking. The acceptable values for this field are:

  - All QBE allowed

  - No QBE allowed

  - Indexed fields QBE allowed (this is recommended)

OneWorld will look at this field to determine if JDEBase uses row-level record locking. J.D. Edwards recommends that this functionality be turned on to prevent data integrity issues.

Once you have filled in these fields, click OK to commit the record. OneWorld will write the record to the F986101 table. It will then blank out the Environment Name field, but keep the rest of the fields filled in on the Object Mappings Revision screen. If you do not want to add any more mappings, click Cancel, which will take you back to the Work Object Mappings screen.

N O T E

You may receive a warning on this screen if the table does not exist in the data source your mapping points to. This warns you that you are creating a mapping that points to a location where the table does not reside. You can set a processing option for the Object Configuration Manager to have this appear as an error or a warning. Go to menu GH9011, System Administration Tools, and right-click on the Object Configuration Manager program. Choose Prompt For Values. You will be allowed to enter a 1 to have the Object Configuration Manager produce a hard error when a mapping points to a location where the table does not exist. The other option is to leave this value blank and only a warning will be issued. OneWorld is shipped with this value set so that you will only be presented with a warning and not a hard error.

Now that we have added a new mapping, we must activate it. When a mapping is added to OneWorld, the status is set to NA (not active). OneWorld will ignore the mapping until the status is set to AV (active). To set your mapping to AV, enter the object name in the QBE line and click Find. Highlight your mapping and go to Row Change Status. This will change the status of the mapping from NA to AV.

	F0004					
Environment	**Object Name**	**Object Type**	**Primary Data Source**	**User**	**Object Status**	
ACT733	F0004	TBLE	OneWorld Local - PRODB733	*PUBLIC	AV	
CHICRP733	F0004	TBLE	OneWorld Local - CRPB733	*PUBLIC	AV	
CHIDEV733	F0004	TBLE	OneWorld Local - DEVB733	*PUBLIC	AV	
CHIPRD733	F0004	TBLE	OneWorld Local - PRODB733	*PUBLIC	AV	
CHIPRT733	F0004	TBLE	OneWorld Local - PRISTB733	*PUBLIC	AV	
CHITST733	F0004	TBLE	Control Tables - Test	*PUBLIC	AV	
CRP733	F0004	TBLE	OneWorld Local - CRPB733	*PUBLIC	AV	

TIP

You may want to click Find to refresh your screen and ensure that the status of your mapping has changed.

NOTE

The F986101 table is cached upon logon, so your client machines will have to log out and back into OneWorld to use the mapping change.

How to Copy OCM Mappings

You will often need to set up a mapping for the same object in several environments. Copying an OCM mapping can save you some time and typing. To copy an Object Configuration manager mapping, from the Work With Object Mappings screen, highlight the mapping you want to copy and click the Copy button on the toolbar. You will now be on the Object Mapping Revisions screen, like when you added a mapping. However, this time all the fields will be filled in for you, as shown in Figure 2-10, with the information from the mapping that you are copying.

You can now modify the mapping as necessary. This feature saves time when you are mapping several objects to the same data source. Remember that once you click OK to commit the record to F986101, you will also have to activate the mapping.

Inside and Out

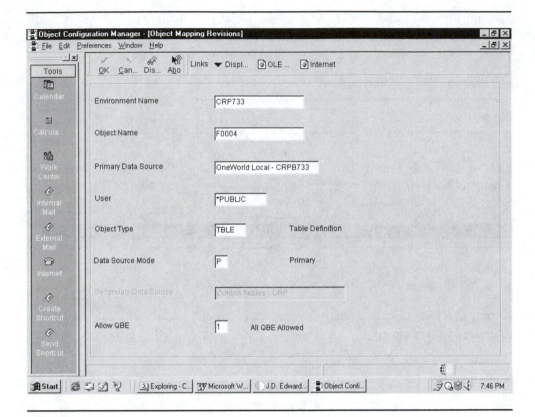

FIGURE 2-10.   Object Mapping Revisions screen

Deleting an OCM Mapping

Deleting an OCM mapping is a simple process. When you are on the Work With Object
Mappings screen, highlight the desired OCM record and click the Delete button on the
toolbar. This will remove this record from the F986101 table. Remember that if you
remove a mapping from the system data source, your client machines will need to log out
and back into OneWorld before they will be able to see the change. If you change a server
map F986101 entry, you will need to stop and start your host services to ensure that the
mapping takes effect.

The Difference Between System and Server Map

We have skirted the differences between the system and server map OCM mappings throughout this section. However, we will now address them head-on. The Object Configuration Manager is truly the nerve center of OneWorld. The system F986101 table tells client workstations where they need to look for their data, process their UBEs, and run their business functions. So any changes to this table will directly affect the client workstations. The server map F986101 table is used once a UBE starts to run on the enterprise or logic server. The UBE will read this table to determine where it needs to find its data, and business functions.

Changing the Mappings for Object Librarian Tables

This procedure will go through changing the OCM mappings for object librarian tables. Before you even think about attempting this procedure, you need to understand what changing the mappings for the object librarian tables truly means. It means your OneWorld system will have multiple object librarian data sources. The object librarian is how OneWorld keeps track of the objects in the system. This is what ensures that you do not have more than one object with the same name. However, if you add another mapping for the object librarian tables, you will have two object librarians. That means you could have two objects named the same in the OneWorld system. So if you performed an object transfer between the two path codes with which the environments are associated, you would overlay one of the objects. The other thing to keep in mind is that in all the authors' experience, we have not set up a system in this manner. This process should only be attempted by someone with advanced Configurable Network Computing (CNC) knowledge, as the possibility of introducing problems into the system exists.

DEFINITION

Configurable Network Computing (CNC): *This is a term used by J.D. Edwards to describe their software's ability to be easily configured to meet business needs. This describes the ability of the software to run on multiple platforms against different types of databases.*

To re-map the object librarian tables to a new object librarian data source, you need to do the following:

1. Log on to a client workstation and go to the Object Configuration Manager program. You can find this program on the GH9611 menu or by typing **OCM** in the fast path.

2. You will be prompted to select either the system or server map on the Machine Search And Select screen. Select your system data source.

3. You will now be on the Work With Object Mappings screen.

4. Go to Form Revise OL Data Source.

5. You will then be prompted for the path code and OL data source. The reason you are being prompted for a path code and not an environment is that the object librarian is used to keep track of objects in path codes and each environment is associated with a path code. So when you enter a path code on this screen, OneWorld will remap the object librarian tables for all the environments associated with this path code.

6. After you have entered the path code and your new object librarian data source, which must contain all the object librarian tables, click OK.

7. You will now be back on the Work With Object Mappings screen. Your client workstations will need to log out and back in to see this change.

CAUTION

Although this procedure is documented and any package builds should find the new object librarian mappings, the support line will probably caution you against using this functionality, due to the added complexity of system maintenance with two object librarians and the opportunity for introducing errors into the system.

Changing Oracle Parameters that OneWorld Uses

If you are using Oracle with OneWorld, you will need to pay attention to the Oracle parameter values that can be set within the system. If you use the standard J.D. Edwards shipped environments and data sources, you will not need to worry about these settings.

However, if you add a custom data source or do not follow the standard J.D. Edwards naming conventions, you will want to look at these settings. You can use these settings to control certain things within OneWorld, such as what Oracle table space and index space your data sources use. You can also control certain Oracle settings on specific tables within OneWorld for Oracle parameters. The system stores all the values we are about to discuss in the F986115 table (Table and Data Source Sizing). This table is a system table, meaning it is located in the OneWorld system data source.

To set the Oracle parameters, go to menu GH9011 and double-click on Object Configuration manager or type **OCM** in the fast path. Select the system data source when prompted on the Machine Search And Select form. You will now be on the Work With Object Mappings screen. From this screen, go to Row Oracle Params. You will now be on the Work With Table And Data Source Sizing screen, shown in Figure 2-11. Enter an

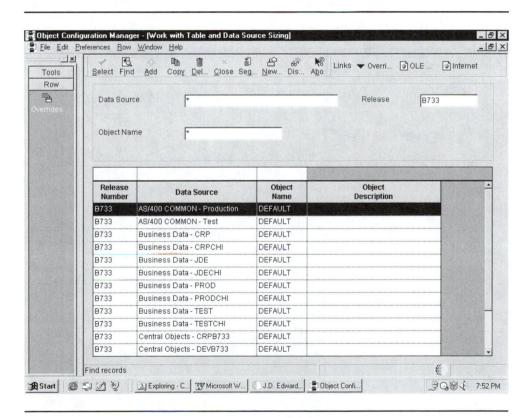

FIGURE 2-11.   Find the DEFAULT records in the Work With Table And Data Source Sizing screen

asterisk (*) in the Data Source field and click Find. This will show you the DEFAULT records for all your data sources.

Select one of these records; you will now be on the Revise Table And Data Source Sizing screen. This screen has a couple of important fields. You can define the Oracle table space and index space you want OneWorld to use when the system tries to find an object in this data source. In Figure 2-12, the system would attempt to use the crpdtat table space and crpdtai index space when it tries to locate a table using this data source. If you add a custom data source, you will need to use this screen to tell OneWorld what table space and index space to use in Oracle.

OneWorld also gives you the ability to affect Oracle parameters on individual tables within a table space. OneWorld is shipped with only the Oracle table space and index space defined for J.D. Edwards standard data sources. J.D. Edwards does not ship

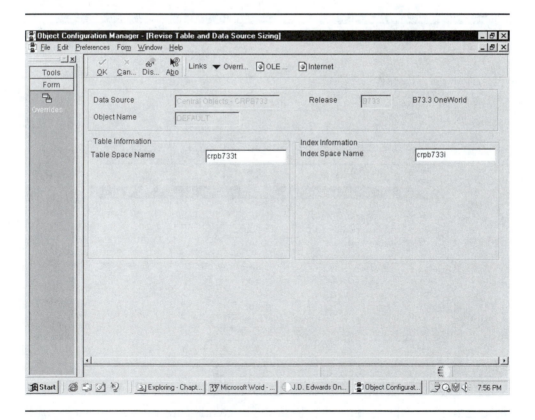

FIGURE 2-12. Revise Table And Data Source Sizing screen

Oracle settings for specific tables. If you want to use this feature, click Add from the Work With Table And Data Sizing screen. You will then be prompted with the new form, labeled Revise Table And Data Source Sizing, shown in Figure 2-13.

This screen allows you to set some specific table and index information for Oracle on individual tables. You can also leave the Data Source field blank, which asks OneWorld to use the specified settings for this table in all data sources, or you can specify a specific table and data source. You can also only specify a data source and ask Oracle to use the parameters on all tables within that data source. That being said, let's take a look at what Oracle settings you can specify from within OneWorld.

NOTE

These settings don't currently work, they are scheduled for an upcoming release of OneWorld.

FIGURE 2-13. Revise Table And Data Source Sizing form

On the lower half of this screen, you can specify table and index information. The system will allow you to specify the following Oracle parameters:

- Table/Index Initial Storage

- Table/Index Next Storage

- Table/Index Percent Increase Storage

- Table/Index Minimum Extent

- Table/Index Maximum Extent

Your Oracle database administrator should be the person who sets this screen up. You may also want to run with these settings only defined in Oracle and not OneWorld. That is an option, as setting the table information and index information in OneWorld is not a mandatory procedure. Setting up the table space and index space that a custom OneWorld data source will use (as described earlier), however, is a mandatory procedure.

Revise Table and Data Source Overrides Screen

There is one final setting that can be changed from the Work With Table And Data Source Sizing screen. This setting applies to *all* types of databases, not just Oracle. If you highlight a data source in the grid and go to Row Overrides, you will be taken to the Revise Table And Data Source Overrides screen.

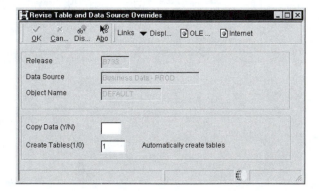

This screen will default in the Release, Data Source, and Object Name fields (if applicable). The only two fields you are allowed to modify on this screen are Copy Data and Create Tables. It is very important that these fields be set correctly for your data sources, as these values are used by R98403 to determine if tables should be created and if data should be copied.

- **Copy Data**   Currently this field is not used. However, if you add a custom data source, set this value to Y.

- **Create Tables**   This setting will accept either a 0 or a 1 as a valid value. If the field is blank, OneWorld considers it to be a 0 value. When this field is set to 1, OneWorld will automatically create the tables in this data source during the environment workbench, so any tables mapped to this data source will be created. If this field is set to 0 or is blank, the environment workbench and R98403 will not create tables in this data source. This means you would have to create them by hand. If you add a custom data source, set this value to a 1.

T I P

For further information on the environment workbench and the R98403 report, which loads the data tables into a OneWorld system during the environment workbench, check the J.D. Edwards web page at www.jdedwards.com. The company has written some good white papers on this topic.

Advanced Object Configuration Manager Operations

There are several reports that are useful when administrating mappings on a OneWorld system. These reports can be found on the GH9012 menu, Advance Operations. You can also get there by choosing the Advanced Operations folder on the GH9011 menu, System Administration Tools. These reports give you the ability to administer and add to your OCM mappings. Since the processing options of these reports may change from release to release, we only want to call your attention to the reports. If you want detailed instructions on how to use these reports, please refer to a current J.D. Edwards CNC Implementation manual.

J.D. Edwards OneWorld Middleware

Any chapter on OneWorld building blocks would not be complete without a section on the J.D. Edwards OneWorld middleware. In this section, we will discuss the following:

- The definition of middleware

- Functions of JDEBase and JDENet middleware

- OneWorld middleware processes

- Synchronous versus asynchronous processing

So, what is middleware? Is it hardware or software? Or maybe, as one of our clients thought, it is a mysterious black box that is required as part of the OneWorld solution? This client just wanted to know how much this black box was going to cost and what location would be the best place for it.

First, let's dispel this myth. Middleware is not a black box. Nor is it that mysterious. It doesn't cost extra, and you don't need special hardware to run it. As for its location, it is on every machine that runs the OneWorld product. Is it a requirement? Yes!

Middleware is software designed to perform two primary functions. As such, it comes in two distinctly different types: database middleware and communication middleware. They are also often referred to as JDEBase and JDENet, and they are the glue that keeps the OneWorld product working. They facilitate all computer-to-computer communications as well as structure each and every SQL statement generated by the system.

Types of Middleware

OneWorld has two different types of middleware that help perform all the work between machines (servers and workstations) and databases. JDENet is a network communication middleware that performs network communications workstation-to-server and server-to-server. It also ensures messaging for distributed requests (for example, when a two-phase commit is required between two different databases on two different servers). You might hear JDENet referred to as a "peer-to-peer, message-based, socket-based, multiprocess communication middleware solution."

What does that mean, you may ask? Well, most people who hear it assume that a marketing person had one too many drinks with a technical person and wrote this in a slightly blurry evening of deep discussions. But in reality, the phrase speaks volumes about the OneWorld product. This is because JDENet handles an immense amount of communication between the OneWorld servers and workstations. A server is a machine that responds to a request for information or services. A workstation is a machine on the network that initiates a call for information or services.

OneWorld is a message-based system. All communication goes through messages. To improve performance, OneWorld limits the size of the messages coming to your machine. A good example of this is when you click Find on an application within OneWorld. You come back with a certain amount of information. As you begin to scroll down the list of returned information, you will occasionally have a brief pause in scrolling (there is a little icon of a policeman blowing a whistle in the lower-right portion of the window telling you to wait). This happens when the OneWorld product is retrieving the next set of rows from the data set as derived from your initial query.

OneWorld is socket-based. OneWorld uses Win-Sockets to ensure data communication between servers and workstations. These sockets provide a duplex communication channel and are specifically set up in the JDE.INI on both the workstation and the servers. Servers and workstations must be set up on the same socket to communicate. The sockets used most frequently on different installations of OneWorld include 6003, 6006, and 6007. However, any socket specified can be used for this purpose (we've seen some clients use 10004 and 10005).

OneWorld has a process-based design and supports multiple processes. Although a client installation of OneWorld can only run a single instance at any one time, a server installation can support multiple requests from multiple machines. These service and data requests range from security to UBE to logic. We've seen up to 100 OneWorld kernels running on a single server supporting 20,000 business function requests.

JDENET_N, JDENET_K, and JDEQUEUE

On a server running the OneWorld runtime services, you can see a series of OneWorld processes. Let's take a minute or two to explore these processes to get a better understanding of exactly what role each of them plays in the OneWorld product.

First, though, let's talk about how requests are split up among the available processes. If you have ten JDENET_n processes defined in the JDE.INI, the first one would be the master process and would launch the other nine as needed. As network communication requests come in, each one is given to a separate JDENET_n until all nine are in use. At that time, the eleventh request for network connectivity would be processed by the first JDENET_n. This process continues evenly, splitting the load among the available processes. This is an example of OneWorld load balancing.

Inside and Out

JDENET_n is a network communication process. Its job is to determine what type of request is being made by the workstation. Once that determination is made, JDENET_n automatically routes the request to the appropriate server process to handle the request. Each type of request has a specified range of values used to determine the type of job being processed. The JDENET_n process offloads logic processing requests to JDENET_k processes.

The JDENET_k process ensures that requests for logic processing reach the appropriate server job and that the results are passed back to the JDENET_n job for the return route to the workstation. There are 11 defined kernel processes in OneWorld. They are identified by function and range in the JDE.INI.

JDEQUEUE is a UBE process that is set up to run batch logic requests. The OneWorld administrator can determine the number of JDEQUEUEs on any particular server. Generally, a server is only limited in the number of JDEQUEUEs based on system resources. We have seen in excess of 18 batch queues defined on a specific machine. Up to 18 UBEs could be run on that machine concurrently.

JDEBase Middleware

The JDENet middleware deals with communications (in particular, requests for logic services). The JDEBase middleware deals with database connectivity and communication. Its functions include interpreting API, converting SQL into the appropriate format for each machine and database, managing optimized fetch algorithms, and database transaction monitoring. Needless to say, you can't work with OneWorld without using JDEBase.

As described earlier, there are four different databases supported in the OneWorld solution and most implementations use at least two of them. Although this provides great flexibility for companies using OneWorld, it creates a certain amount of complexity for the developers of this ERP product. Why? Because each of these database types are different and support different SQL conventions. Let's look at one of the simplest SQL statements and see how it differs from one database to the next:

- SQL Server:

```
SELECT * FROM PRODDTA.F4201 WHERE SHAN8='123456'
```

- Oracle:

```
SELECT * FROM PRODDTA.F4201 WHERE SHAN8='123456';
```

- DB2 on the AS/400:

```
SELECT * FROM PRODDTA/F4201 WHERE SHAN8='123456'
```

- Microsoft Access:

```
SELECT * FROM F4201 WHERE SHAN8='123456'
```

The differences above are very quick examples of RDBMS requirements in SQL conventions. Note that the Oracle statement has to have a semicolon at the end of it; DB2/400 has to have a slash indicating a different library because it does not support table ownership; and Microsoft Access doesn't use a table owner at all—it just skips that part, relying on an Open Database Connectivity (ODBC) connection to point it to the correct database. Though these differences seem minor, there are other, more important, differences as well. Does the RDBMS support table owners? SQL Server and Oracle do; DB2/400 and Microsoft Access do not. Does the RDBMS support an explicit or implicit commit? Oracle supports explicit; SQL Server, DB2/400, and Microsoft Access support implicit. How does the RDBMS handle rollbacks—automatically or only when requested? What about indices? There are a slew of differences between each of the RDBMS vendors, each with their own pros and cons.

While these differences aren't great on the larger software scale, they do make a difference and must be reflected in the software. So, the next question you might ask yourself is, how could the architects of OneWorld handle these differences? Would it be best to code all four statements into the software? If so, how would an application know to use one type of SQL statement over the other? How would you upgrade this type of application to support changes in the database conventions that accompany RDBMS upgrades? These questions and many more like them went through the minds of the original OneWorld architects and their solution was JDEBase middleware.

When you set up a data source, you define to the OneWorld system the type of RDBMS used by that data source. This information, when combined with the DLL name (also defined in the data source), allows OneWorld to properly handle the differences between RDBMS conventions. The JDEBase middleware is a part of the foundation code of OneWorld and cannot be modified by clients.

Synchronous versus Asynchronous Processing

Though some of the sections of this chapter seem tedious and long, other sections will be quite blissfully short—such as this section. Really, it is little more than a note or an aside, but it contains an important issue to discuss and understand: What is synchronous as opposed to asynchronous processing?

Synchronous processing can be defined as logic processing that requires the application/client/user to wait until results are tendered (the logic event completed) before continuing to other processing. An example of synchronous processing will help you understand this better.

When you click the OK button on a sales order, certain business functions are launched which check inventory, customer credit limits, and so on. Before you can print a pick slip or add a new order, these business functions must run and return without user-defined errors. If the business functions bring back an error (such as the customer being over their credit limit), the application will either automatically initiate a new workflow procedure or it will prompt the user for an action. All this occurs before the user can enter the next sales order. The user waits until the processing completes with results before continuing.

This is called synchronous processing. In effect, the user must wait until the logic is processed before continuing to the next step. Some OneWorld applications are designed so that you can turn their processing to synchronous or asynchronous modes. With this in mind, what is asynchronous processing?

Asynchronous processing is logic that can be performed while other logic processing occurs. One of the simplest examples of asynchronous processing is a universal batch engine (UBE). This can be a basic report or a complicated posting job. The key is that it can be launched on either a client workstation or an application server, and the user doesn't have to wait for it to complete its work before continuing with other work. Considering that some of these UBEs can take days to complete, this is probably a good thing.

We mentioned that some applications can be set to run in either a synchronous or asynchronous mode. When you decide to use asynchronous mode, you are telling the application to run ahead of itself. This will often speed up data entry, but there could be some issues with this style of processing (memory overwrites and data corruption quickly come to mind as possible pitfalls). The best advice is to research these options before you decide to implement them. Your local OneWorld application consultant can often help you decide which mode of processing will best fit your business needs.

Summary

In this chapter, we have gone over the true building blocks of OneWorld: data sources, path codes, environments, Object Configuration Manager, middleware, and synchronous and asynchronous processing. A user or system administrator needs to understand these concepts to truly understand the OneWorld system.

The data source is a pointer to a set of tables within a database or to a specific machine that is running OneWorld logic. It is housed in two tables (F98611 and F986115) and is the first building block of OneWorld. We have talked about configuring data sources and when you might modify or add additional data sources. We have also discussed at length the data source's importance to the OneWorld enterprise system.

Another important piece to the OneWorld puzzle is path codes. We have stated that a path code consists of central object tables, a directory structure, and an entry in the F00942 table. We have also discussed how to add a custom path code and delete a path code. It is vital that you understand how a path code affects the OneWorld system, as these path codes contain all the specifications that OneWorld needs in order to run. Basically these path codes are storage areas for your specifications. To configure a OneWorld system correctly, you need to have a true understanding of what a path code is.

We also went over adding, copying, and deleting environments. The discussion of these important topics not only covered the mechanics of how to maintain OneWorld environments, but also why you would want to add additional environments and the impact this operation could have on your system. The technology is great, but don't lose sight of your business needs for the sake of the technology.

After we discussed OneWorld environments, we moved on to talk about the three most powerful letters in OneWorld, OCM (Object Configuration Manager). OneWorld uses the Object Configuration Manager to find its data, run logic, and run business functions. We have gone over the difference between the server map F986101 and the system F986101. The reasons why you would add a mapping and how to add OCM mappings were discussed. It is very important that you understand this chapter before moving on, as the Object Configuration Manager truly is one of OneWorld's building blocks.

Finally, in this chapter we covered the OneWorld middleware. The OneWorld middleware is an important piece of the product and one that greatly enhances the functionality of this ERP package. It is easily the butter on the bread of this software, allowing all database connectivity, machine-to-machine communication, multiple database and hardware independence, ease of use, guaranteed communications, transactional processing, and more.

With this knowledge at your finger tips, you are ready to move into the more advanced topics covered later in this book. Always remember that these topics are truly the building blocks to OneWorld and you will need to understand them before you can grasp more advanced topics.

Inside and Out

CHAPTER 3

OneWorld Explorer

Basic OneWorld Navigation

How Menus Interact with OneWorld

Logging In to OneWorld: What Happens
Under the Covers

OneWorld provides an easy interface for users to navigate through. This interface is very similar to a Windows Explorer tree structure interface, and it allows users to easily find and execute their programs. In OneWorld, there is a toolbar that allows users to change the look of their interface. In this chapter, we will look at how your users can interact with the OneWorld interface, including:

- Basic OneWorld navigation

- The window structure explained

- How menus interact with the explorer

- Logging in to OneWorld: what happens under the covers

Basic OneWorld Navigation

We'll start this chapter by discussing the basics of how to navigate in OneWorld. The first thing that a user sees when running a OneWorld session is the menu structure. This menu structure closely resembles the Windows Explorer directory structure, with a two-pane display. Just like Windows Explorer, the left pane displays directories and the right pane lists the files, subdirectories, and programs contained in the directories displayed in the left pane. The OneWorld interface was designed this way so users would quickly feel comfortable using it. Generally, the first thing a user sees when they sign on is the main menu, as shown in Figure 3-1. This menu can be specified in the User Profile application. How to do this is covered in Chapter 13.

Main Menu - Left Pane

The directory structure has a familiar look and feel for users who have had experience with Microsoft's Windows Explorer. When you sign on, you are taken to the default menu, which is usually the main menu, Master Directory (G). This menu is show in Figure 3-1. As you can see, each directory has a plus sign (+) next to it. You can expand the menu directory by double-clicking on the directory name or by clicking once on the + symbol. When you expand the directory, the subdirectories appear on the left-hand side of the window, and the programs for the menu that you selected will appear on the right-hand side. It is important to remember that the left-hand side of your screen represents directories and subdirectories, not the actual programs to execute. This split-screen interface allows you to easily navigate through the OneWorld application.

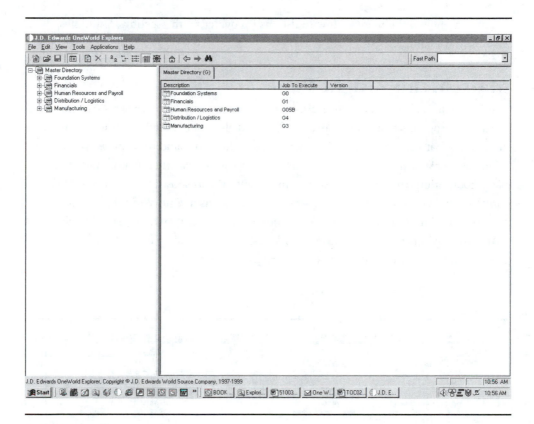

FIGURE 3-1. The main menu

NOTE

If your initial menu is anything but G, you will not see the entire directory structure of OneWorld; you will only see the directories available from that menu. This allows you to lock users out of certain menus, when the Fast Path is also disabled. Disabling the Fast Path is discussed in Chapter 13.

You will notice that each of the main menu directories represents a J.D. Edwards application suite. For example, if you expand the Financials directory, you will find menus containing the programs for the financial suite. This allows you to easily navigate to the programs that you use daily. This easy-to-use interface should help to reduce your training costs. It is also important to note that this menu is configurable, so the look may differ a little from site to site. This means that the users can customize the appearance of the menus. How to do this is covered in the section "Windows Structure Explained."

Main Menu - Right Pane

Now let's take a closer look at the right-hand side of the user interface. This pane displays the actual programs that your users can execute. It also contains subdirectories, if there are any, so that your users can drill down deeper. The right-hand pane allows your users to access OneWorld interactive programs, batch applications, other menus, and third-party applications that can be "hooked" into OneWorld, as shown in Figure 3-2. Users can also run World software applications from the menus in OneWorld through a WorldVision interface. World software is the software suite offered by J.D. Edwards that runs only on an AS400 platform; WorldVision is a software package that allows users to run this software through a graphical user interface.

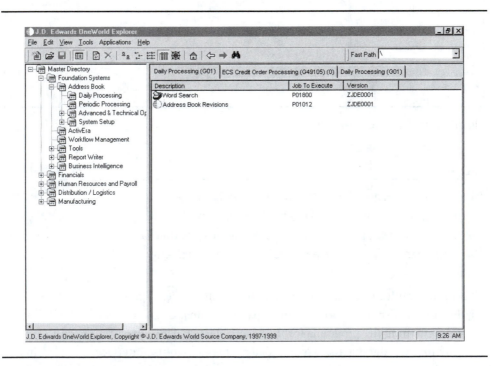

FIGURE 3-2.   Right Pane of Menu Structure

NOTE

When the system is initially set up, there is no security restricting users from accessing applications, so users can go anywhere and run any application they please. How to secure the system is covered in Chapter 13. Once security is added, there are entire applications that will not appear on users' menus if they are secured out of the application. It is also important to note that the initial menu may be different from system to system. This is because the system administrator can specify what each user's initial menu is and can even specify a custom menu.

Windows Structure Explained

You will notice that there is a menu bar across the top of the interface.

This menu bar gives your users several options:

- File
- Edit
- View
- Tools
- Applications
- Help

We will go though the selections on this menu bar one by one, from left to right.

File

The options on the File menu are:

- New Tab
- Open
- Save Settings on Exit

- Save Object As

- Exit

The New Tab option allows your users to create a custom tab for themselves. When you select File | New Tab, you are presented with a screen, as shown here, that allows you to choose which kind of tab to create: a menu tab, an object tab, or a Web tab.

A menu tab is exactly what it sounds like. It will appear on the right-hand windowpane, displaying a menu of your choice. If you choose to add a menu tab, you are taken to a screen that allows you to choose which menu will be displayed on this tab. This allows users to highly customize their interface.

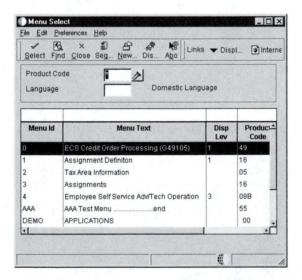

For example, financials users who know that they consistently use programs on three different menus can set up three different tabs for the appropriate menus. This allows the user to quickly and easily access the programs that they need. Instead of drilling down through the menus or using the Fast Path, you simply choose the tab you want. (We will discuss the Fast Path functionality in the section "Toolbar. ")

N O T E

Tabs are held in the registry of the local machine. Users that create a tab for themselves will only see it on the machine on which they created the tab. Also, tabs are user-specific, so if someone signs on to the machine with a different user ID, they will not see the custom tabs.

The next new tab option available is to add an object. This allows you to add a tab with an imbedded object. When you choose this option, you will be prompted to select the type of object you wish to imbed into a tab. You can choose to imbed an object from an existing file, or you can choose to imbed a new object. One of the most common uses for this is to place an Excel spreadsheet or a Microsoft Word document on the tab for easy reference and use, as shown in Figure 3-3. This type of functionality allows your users to access this type of data within OneWorld instead of needing to have another application running in the background and then switching between OneWorld and that application. In the example below, the user has imbedded an Excel worksheet.

The final new tab option is the Web option. This option allows you to imbed a Web page onto the tab. This means that users who need to access the Internet for information frequently can have their favorite Web site set up on a tab within OneWorld. The only down side to this option is that it will keep the connection to the Web site open while you are in OneWorld, which is similar to pulling up a Web site and then minimizing the Web browser. If your company is being charged per minute for Internet access, you may not want to allow your users the ability to add a Web tab. This functionality can be secured from your end users through OneWorld security, which is discussed in Chapter 13.

The next option under File on the menu bar is Open. This option allows you to change the menu that appears on the tab. The user will be shown a menu Search and Select screen and can then choose a menu that they wish to appear in their tab on the right-hand side of the interface. This means that a user does not have to delete and add a tab every time they want a different menu to appear on the tab.

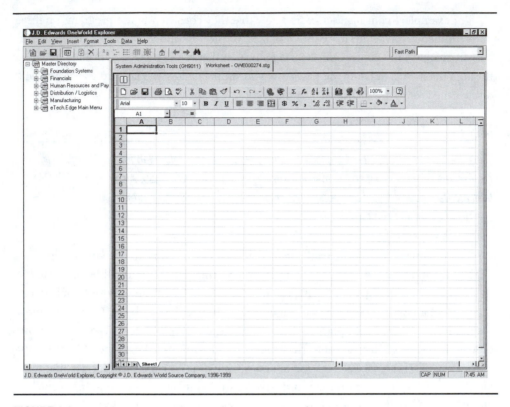

FIGURE 3-3. Adding an Excel Spreadsheet onto a tab

Save Settings on Exit is the next option under File on the menu bar. When a check mark appears next to this option, OneWorld will save any changes that your users have made to their interface during the current session. If the user does not check off this option, their settings will be lost when they exit the OneWorld program.

N O T E

These settings are saved in the workstation's registry under HKEY_CURRENT_USER\Software\JDEdwards\YourUser name. You can see how these settings are stored in the illustration shown next. This means that if users go to a different workstation, they will not see their tabs on that workstation. It also means if you remove or destroy these registry entries, end users will lose their tabs and will have to set them up again.

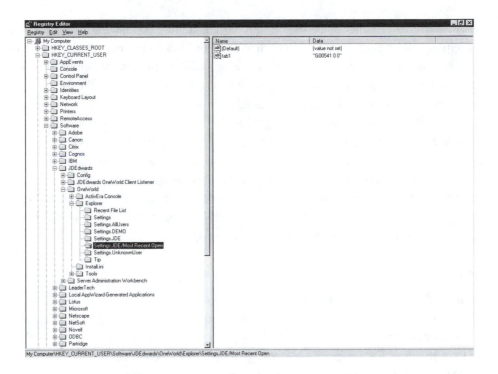

The next two options under File are Save Object As and Exit. The Save Object As option allows you to save objects that you have inserted onto an object type tab. This means that if you insert an Excel worksheet onto a tab, you can save your worksheet by going to File | Save Object As. This will save the object under the media queue that is defined in the Media Object Queues program on the System Administration Tools menu GH9011. The Media Object Queues program allows you to set up queues that hold information specific to verticals or, in this case, OLE objects. These queues are normally set up on a server so that the users of the system can share documents, that is, if one user saves an Excel spreadsheet, another user can access it.

The Exit option is self-explanatory: it allows you to exit out of the OneWorld program. Now let's move on to the Edit option on the menu bar.

Edit

The options on the Edit menu are

- Remove Tab

- Prompt for Values

- Prompt for Version

The Remove Tab option allows you to remove a tab that you have added. However, this option will be grayed out when you have only one tab on the right-hand side. The Prompt for Values option allows you to review and edit the processing option values for reports and interactive applications. All you need to do is highlight the report or application you are interested in and go to Edit | Prompt for Values. The processing options for that report or application are then displayed. Processing options allow you the ability to take advantage of different functionalities offered by a report or application so that, for example, you can specify whether or not to give a user a hard error or a warning when a certain action is taken. Processing options can also tell a report to run in proof mode instead of update mode, which allows you to check their work before committing records to the system. This option will be grayed out if the report or application does not have any processing options.

CAUTION

Processing Options are an important part of configuring your OneWorld system. Once these are set up, you will want to lock your users out of these processing options for certain applications and reports. Failure to do so may cause problems with the system later. For example, if a user changes the processing options on your some of your financial reports/applications, you may get unexpected results. Chapter 13 discusses how to secure processing options.

The next selection is Prompt for Versions. This option allows you to choose the version of a report or interactive application that you want to run. Users can set up different versions for reports and applications that allow them to specify, for example, different processing options or data selection. Instead of having to set the data selection up again and again, they can simply select a version with the desired data selection or processing options. This means that your users can easily run a version that suits your needs and then just as easily change to another version. However, it is important to note that not all applications or reports will have a version associated with them.

The next selection on the menu bar is View. Obviously, the prompt for values and prompt for versions are options that you may not want your users accessing. OneWorld does allow you to secure these options from your end users.

View

The options on the View menu are

- Tree
- Toolbar
- Toolbar Text
- Status Bar
- Split
- Large Icons
- Small Icons
- List Details
- Web
- Arrange
- User Options
- Refresh

The Tree option allows you to hide the left-hand window pane and be presented with your tabs, which show applications, subdirectories, and reports to run. When the Tree option is chosen, you will see the contents of the right-hand window pane, which displays directories, files, and applications but without the + symbol that the left-hand pane displays. The default is to have this option turned on so that your users have the tree structure to navigate through on the left-hand side of their screen.

The Toolbar option allows you to show or hide the OneWorld toolbar. This toolbar is displayed at the top of the screen and has buttons on it that allow users to easily access some menu bar options at the click of a single button. (We will discuss the toolbar in more detail a little later in this chapter. Hiding the toolbar is shown in the following illustration.)

The Toolbar Text option lets you see a text description under the buttons on the toolbar. This causes the buttons on the toolbar to become larger so that the text can fit on the buttons; it also causes the Fast Path text box to be moved down below the buttons and expanded.

When you choose the Status Bar option, the status bar shows up on the bottom of the OneWorld Explorer screen. This status bar shows the name of the software and the copyright date and, in the lower right-hand corner, it will display the time and if the caps lock feature is turned on. The clock and caps lock displays are probably the most handy features of this option.

The Split option is something that you will never use; this button is always grayed out, meaning you cannot access it.

The next option is Large Icons. This changes the display of the interactive and batch application icons to larger icons on the right-hand pane. This is very similar to the large icons display option in Windows Explorer. Similarly, the Small Icons option changes the applications and reports to smaller icons.

The List Details option will display details about the programs and reports listed on the menu. Some of these details are the job or program to execute and the version, if any, to be run.

The Web option displays the applications and reports in a Weblike manner. This is very similar to the Web view in Windows Explorer.

The Arrange option arranges the menu selections in your tab, if necessary. This option is normally grayed out, which means that the option is unavailable for use.

The next option is User Options. When you select this option, a screen is displayed that allows you to access several programs.

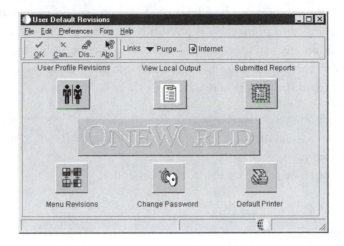

You can access the OneWorld user profiles, go into the menu revisions program, view local output, view server jobs, change your password, or change your default printer within OneWorld. These options are covered in more detail throughout this book, but here's a brief rundown of them:

- **User Profiles Revisions**   This application allows you to add, copy, and revise users and groups. It is covered in greater detail in Chapter 13.

- **Menu Revisions**   This program allows the user or system administrator to create custom menus or modify existing menus.

- **View Local Output**   When a report or UBE is run, it can be run on the server or locally on the workstation. When the report is run on the workstation, the output of the report is saved in the B7/printqueue directory on the local workstation. This option will allow you to view these jobs through OneWorld.

- **Change Password**   If you set up OneWorld sign-on security, each OneWorld user will be required to have their own password. This option allows users to change their own passwords. However, this option will not allow the users to change the passwords of other users or give themselves more authority on the system.

- **Submitted Reports**   This options allows you to view reports that have been run on your enterprise servers.

- **Default Printer**   OneWorld allows you to set up printers so that users can print reports on a printer that is physically near them. However, users may move around the building, so OneWorld gives you the ability to easily change the default printer for your users. The user can also manually change printers when running or printing a report.

The final option, under the view exit, is Refresh, which allows your users to refresh their view of the menus. This is very similar to a refresh button in a Web browser application.

The next option on the menu bar is the Tools option.

Tools

The options on the Tool menu are as follows:

- Report Design Aid

- Report Versions

- Calendar

- Calculator

- Internet

The Report Design Aid option is more for developers then normal production users. In fact, the authors recommend that you use OneWorld security to lock everyone but necessary users out of this option.

NOTE

In order to accomplish a full lock-out of your users from this application, you also have to place security on the Object Librarian application. This application also calls the Report Design Aid program.

The Report Design Aid program allows you to either customize the J.D. Edwards reports or create custom reports that suit the needs of your business. Only trained developers should use this tool, which can also be accessed through the Object Librarian application, as the incorrect use of this tool can corrupt reports.

The next option on the Tools menu is Report Versions. This option allows you to easily find and run batch applications or reports by taking your user into the Batch Versions program that allows you to find and run UBEs (Universal Batch Engine), which really are reports.

DEFINITION

UBE (Universal Batch Engine): *These are the reports that you can run in OneWorld. An example of this is a report that lists all of your customers.*

The Calendar is the next option. This is exactly what it sounds like, an online calendar. The users can also choose the Calculator option to bring up an online calculator when needed.

The final option is Internet. This option will just bring up the computer's default Web browser; for OneWorld clients, J.D. Edwards recommends that Microsoft's Internet Explorer be the default browser.

Applications

The next choice on the menu bar is Applications. This option simply shows you the applications that you currently have open in OneWorld and allows you to maximize them when you click on them.

Help

The Help option can give you just that, help. This option can lead you to help on specific topics or even information on the system itself, including:

- Contents
- About J.D. Edwards OneWorld
- Tip of the Day
- J.D. Edwards on the Web

The Contents option brings up a browser that shows you your online help files. These will only come up if you deployed them to the workstation or set your installation up so that your workstations know where to find these files.

The About J.D. Edwards OneWorld option gives you information on the OneWorld installation installed on the client machine. This option will tell you the release of OneWorld, service pack level, package installed on the client, and environment name.

The Tip of the Day option shows you the tip of the day and allows you to turn the tip on and off. Tips of the day are customizable and held in a relational database table.

The final option is J.D. Edwards on the Web. This option allows you to e-mail J.D. Edwards if e-mail is set up on your machine. It will also connect you to the J.D. Edward's home page, solution center, training page, and users group Web page. However, it is important to note that this will only work if your computer is set up with Internet access, a Web browser, and e-mail.

Toolbar

Now that we have discussed the menu bar, let's talk about the toolbar, the series of buttons across the top of the OneWorld interface. These buttons call up functionalities that we have already discussed in the menu bar. We will start from the left and move to the right.

New Tab

This button will add a new tab. The concept of tabs was discussed at the beginning of this chapter.

Open

The next button will open a menu to appear on a tab.

Save

This button will save an object that a user has imbedded into a tab.

Show/Hide Menu Tree

The next button allows you to hide or show the left-hand pane of your OneWorld Explorer menu. Remember, the left-hand side is the side of the menus that shows a directory structure.

Refresh

This button will refresh the user's view of the menus.

Delete

Following the Refresh button is the Delete button. This button allows you to delete any custom tabs you added.

Large Icons

The next button sets your application icons to a large size.

Small Icons

This button sets the icons to a small size.

List

This button adjusts how the items on the left-hand side of the interface are displayed. This button will show the applications in a list; from the top, the screen descends toward the bottom, in the right pane of the display.

Details

This button adjusts how the items on the left-hand side of the interface are displayed. It will display the applications, the job to execute, and the version to execute on the right-hand side.

Web

This button will change the right-hand side of your users screen to a Weblike view.

Home

This button will take your user back to their home or default menu.

Left/Right Arrows

The next two buttons are arrows pointing to the left and the right that are similar to the back and forward buttons on a Web browser. They will take you back to the first set of menus and allow you to move through them, just as a Web browser will allow you to "surf" through recent Web pages.

Menu Word Search

The final button allows you to search on key words and gives you the menus where these words appear. This tool is very useful, but this program only queries a relational database table F91013, which is located in your system data source. This table is shipped unpopulated, so you will need to populate the table by running a UBE on the A/P Advanced Technical Operations menu (G0131). The UBE is named Word Search Build; in B733.1, this UBE was the R01800.

CAUTION

One thing to remember when you build the word search information is that the job needs to run locally. You should build the table one system code at a time by setting up data selection on the UBE. The authors have found that if this job is run any other way, it will not complete correctly. There have been reports of this job taking up to 36 hours, so be sure that the workstation you are using can be dedicated to this task.

Fast Path

The final part of the toolbar that we should discuss is the Fast Path. The Fast Path allows you to go to menus or execute programs quickly. For example, if you type **GH9011** in the Fast Path, you would be taken to the to the system administration menu. You can also run programs from the Fast Path; for example, type **BV** and you will be taken into batch versions. Users or system administrators can add their own custom Fast Path values. This can be done through the Menu Design program P0082, which is located on the System Administration Tools menu GH9011. This is a powerful functionality, so you may want to lock most of your users out of the Fast Path.

TIP

The Fast Path application reads the User Defined Code tables to determine if a value is acceptable.

How Menus Interact with OneWorld

Menus are an integral part of the OneWorld Explorer. OneWorld is shipped with the menus mapped to the OneWorld Local-*Path Code*, where *Path Code* is the name of your path code, such as CRPB733. The menu tables can also be mapped directly to the Control Tables data source; this data source points to tables on your enterprise server. Data sources are covered in detail in Chapter 2.

The menus are contained in F0082, the Menu Master file; F00821, the Menu Selections file; F0083, the Menu Text Override; and table F0084, the Menu Path file. When you navigate through OneWorld, you are actually making calls to these menu tables. These tables control what you see as you navigate through OneWorld. They also control what applications or jobs are run with each menu selection. In other words, when a user logs onto a session, they see the menus as they do because of how the data is returned from the menu files.

N O T E

In the authors' experience, if you are running on a local area network, it is more efficient to map to the control tables for your menus. This means that all your users are pointing the same relational database tables, so if a change is made they can see it immediately and you do not have to set up replication. This configuration usually does not impact your system's performance at all.

You can control what is in these menu files through the interactive application P0082, Menu Design. This application is on menu GH9011, System Administration Tools. When you double-click on P0082, you will be taken into the Work with Menus screen (see Figure 3-4). This application allows you to customize the look and feel of

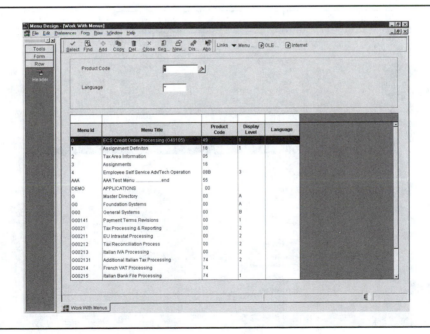

FIGURE 3-4.   Work with Menus screen

Inside and Out

OneWorld. First, let's look at customizing an existing menu. We will then move on to adding a custom menu, and finally, we will look at adding values to the Fast Path.

Customizing an Existing Menu

Let's start with customizing an existing menu. From the Work with Menu screen, find the menu you wish to customize. You can search by product code or the actual menu itself by using the Query by Example line (the yellow line above the grid). Once you have found the menu you wish to customize, highlight it and click on Select. This will take you into the Work with Menu Selections screen, as shown in Figure 3-5. This screen allows you to customize your menu in multiple ways. You can renumber the menu selections by going to Form Renumber, as shown on the left side of Figure 3-5. To modify an existing selection, highlight the selection and click on Select on the toolbar at the top of the screen.

This will take you into the Menu Selections Revisions screen (see Figure 3-6).

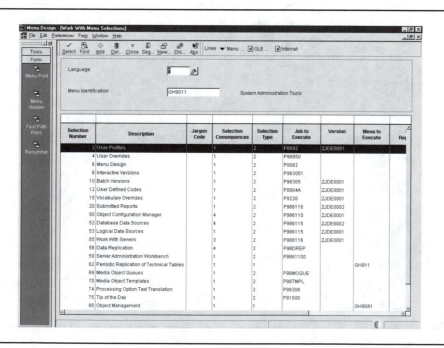

FIGURE 3-5. Customizing an Existing Menu

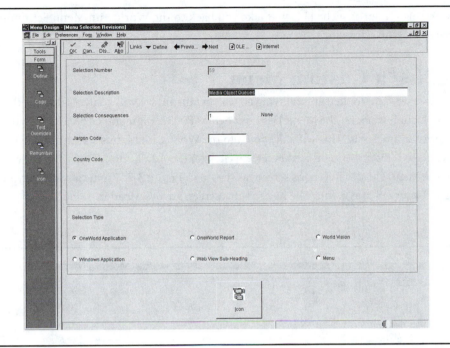

FIGURE 3-6. Modifying a menu selection

From this screen you can add a OneWorld Application, OneWorld Report, World Vision application, Windows Application, Web View Sub-Heading, or Menu to the menu you have selected. You can also choose the icon that you wish to have displayed on the menu.

To change the description and program that is called from a menu selection, first change the menu description in the Selection Description field on the Menu Selection Revisions screen. Then, on the left-hand side of the screen under Form, click on the Define icon; this will take you into the OneWorld Application screen. On this screen, you can enter the program that you want to run in the Object Name field. If you do not know the name of your application, go to Form and click on Application. This will take you into the Search and Select screen, where you can search for your application. You can also go to Form | Version to search for the version of the application that you wish to run when applicable.

In the example, you are going to change the object name to P0101 Address Book. Click on OK; this will take you back to the Menu Selection Revisions screen. Click on

OK on this screen as well. This will take you back to the Work with Menu Selections screen; click on Close.

Adding a Custom Menu

Now that we have looked at modifying an existing menu, we will go over adding a custom menu. Double-click on the Menu Design program P0082, on menu GH9011, System Administration Tools. This will take you into the Work with Menus screen as shown previously in Figure 3-4. From this screen, click on the Add button. This will take you into the Menu Header Revisions screen, as shown in Figure 3-7. From this screen, you can add your custom menu. The fields in this screen are described in Table 3-1.

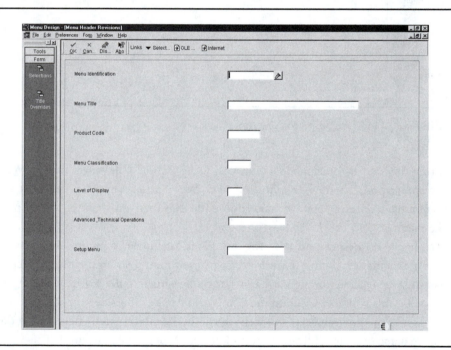

FIGURE 3-7.   Adding a Menu

Menu Identification	The Menu Identification number. When adding a custom menu, it is wise to prefix the menu ID with a 55, for example, GH5501.
Menu Title	The title of your menu
Product Code	This should be 55-59, as J.D. Edwards reserves these system codes for their customers. This means that an update or an upgrade will not overlay these system codes.
Menu Classification	This field indicates the type of menu that you are adding. The values that can be in this field are 　JDE Master 　Company Master 　Personal 　JDE Rumba 　Custom Explorer
Level of Display	This field contains a number or a letter that indicates the level at which menus and processing options are displayed. The values for this field are 　" " Display All (Default value) 　Daily Operations 　Periodic Operations 　Adv/Tech Operations 　Setup Operations 　Programmers 　Sr Programmers 　In Development 　A - Major Product Directories 　B - Product Groups 　P - Display, no changes allowed
Advanced_Technical Operations	This field directs you to another menu, which contains the programs to set up advanced operations.
Setup Menu	This field directs you to a setup menu, which you then have to set up. These last two fields do not normally need to be set up.

TABLE 3-1.　Values for Work with Menus Program

Once you have entered the proper values into these fields, go to Form Selections. This will take you to the Work with Menu Selections screen, shown in Figure 3-8.

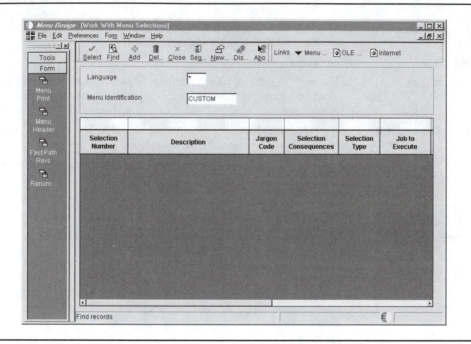

FIGURE 3-8. Adding Menu Selections

From this screen, you can add the selections and programs that you want to appear on your menu.

If you click on the Add button, you will see the Menu Selection Revisions screen, as shown earlier. Adding a new menu application is almost the same as changing one—simply fill in the Selection Description field on the Menu Selection Revisions screen.

Then go to Form | Define; this will take you into the OneWorld Application screen. On this screen, you can enter the program that you want to run in the Object Name field. If you do not know the name of your application, go to Form | Application. This will take you into a Search and Select screen, where you can search for your application. You can also go to Form | Version to search for the version of the application that you wish to run.

In the case of our example, you are going to add the object P01012 Address Book. Click on OK; this will take you back to the Menu Selection Revisions screen. Click on OK on this screen as well. This will take you back to the Work with Menu Selections screen, shown in Figure 3-9. Once you have finished adding all of your menu selections, click on Close. You should now be able to see your new custom menu change.

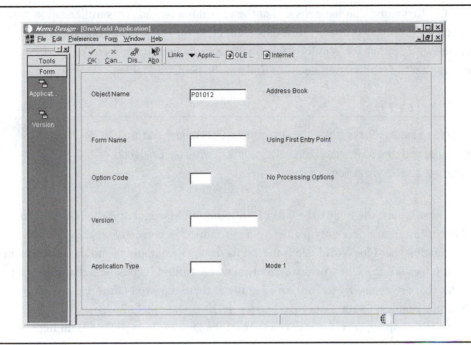

FIGURE 3-9. Adding Menu Selections

This section is not meant to go into detail on adding and maintaining menus. However, these examples should give you an idea of how menus interact with the OneWorld Explorer. Remember that when adding, changing, and administering menus, it's best to keep it simple. The easier it is for your users to reach their programs, the easier it is for them to do their jobs.

Logging In to OneWorld: What Happens Under the Covers

Have you ever wondered what really happens when you log on to a OneWorld client? Well, we are going to go over what happens when you successfully log on to a OneWorld workstation. This knowledge is useful when you attempt to troubleshoot a problem workstation.

The first thing that happens is that the jde.ini file is read. This initialization file, which will be located under the WINNT directory for NT Workstations and the Windows directory for Windows 95 and 98 users, is used upon startup. The first things that the workstation needs to find are the bootstrap tables.

DEFINITION

Bootstrap tables: *These tables are necessary for OneWorld to find its OCM mappings and data source definitions. Without this information, OneWorld would not be able to function.*

These tables, the F986101 Object Configuration Manager and the F98611 Data Source Master, are necessary for the system to function correctly, as they contain the information that OneWorld needs to find its data. The mappings and data sources in these tables tell the OneWorld workstation where to find its business data and other tables that are necessary to run. An example of these required tables are the data dictionary tables: F9200 Data Item Master, F92001 Data Field Specifications, F9201 Data Field Display Text, F9203 Data Item Alpha Descriptions, F9204 Data Item Aliases, F9205 Data Dictionary - Error Message Program ID, F9207 Data Dictionary Error Message Information, F9210 Data Field Specifications (OneWorld), and F9211 Data Dictionary - Smart Fields.

When the jde.ini file is read, OneWorld goes right to the DB System Settings section, an example of which is shown here:

```
[DB SYSTEM SETTINGS]
Version=43
Default User=JDE
Default Env=CRP733
Default PathCode=CRPB733
Base Datasource=System - B733
Object Owner=SYSB733
Server=OWCUSTS4
Database=System - B733
Load Library=JDBODBC.DLL
Decimal Shift =Y
Julian Dates=Y
Use Owner=Y
Secured=Y
Type=S
Library List=
```

When a user signs onto the workstation, the first thing the system looks for is the default environment value of the DB System Settings section. This value is used when the system passes a select statement to the F986101 table. The system will then look at the Object Owner, Server, Database, Load Library, Decimal Shift, Julian Dates, Use Owner, Secured, and Type fields. The system uses these settings to construct SQL statements against certain tables. The first is the F986101, which is the Object Configuration Master. Let's take a look at how the system uses these fields.

The system uses the Object Owner field to pass the correct owner in the select statement and the server to find the correct machine. The Database field has different uses. If you are using SQL Server or Client Access, this will be the name of an ODBC data source in your Control Panel's 32-bit ODBC program. This is the ODBC that OneWorld will look for in order to connect to the database; it will be looking for an exact match in case and space. If it does not find one, your jde.log file, which is located in the C: root directory of your workstation, will tell you that it could not find the ODBC data source specified. This is a common problem that can cause your end users grief. If you are using an Oracle database, this field will be the connect string to your database. The system uses this connect string in conjunction with the client workstation's tnsnames file (which is why the Oracle client software is necessary).

The next field that the system looks at is Load Library. This field contains a DLL that indicates what database the F986101 resides in; it will be JDBODBC.DLL for SQL Server, JDBOCI73.DLL for Oracle 7.0, or JDBOCI80.DLL for Oracle 8.0. These DLLs are created in Denver by J.D. Edwards development. These DLLs hook into the kernel code of OneWorld, which is how the system determines what type of select statements to pass, depending on the database. This is why OneWorld can have one data source reading data off an AS400 and another from an Oracle database.

The next field that is looked at is Decimal Shift. This field is a value that will allow the automatic shift of decimal places based on the OneWorld data dictionary.

The next field is Use Julian Dates. This field tells the system if the data source uses Julian dates (an Access database does not). The next field, Use Owner, tells the system whether or not to pass an owner with the select statement. If you are hitting an Access database, it does not use owners. An AS400 also does not use an owner since the AS400 uses libraries.

The next field is Secured, which is used to turn on row level record locking. The next field is the Type field, which tells the system what type of database it is hitting; for instance, if it is going against an Oracle or SQL database.

System Tables Selected upon Login

Once all of this information is read, the system knows what machine your database is on, what owner to use (if one is required), and what type of database you are attempting to access. With this information, the workstation makes several select statements.

- The first select will be against the F986101, using the environment that is stated in the Default Env field. The F986101 is the nerve center of OneWorld; it tells it what data sources the tables are contained in.

- The system then does a select from the F98611, the Data Source Master table. This table tells the system where to find its data (that is, in what database with what user). Once the system has made selects across these tables, it caches this information for performance reasons.

- The next table that the system looks at is the F0092, the Library Lists user table. This table contains your OneWorld users and will be polled for the user who signed on. For example, if you signed on as JDE, this table would be polled for the user JDE.

- The system then polls F00921, User Display Preferences. This table contains information about your user's display preferences. Remember that at this point in the process your user has already entered their user ID, password, and environment.

- OneWorld then does a select statement over F00941, the Environment Detail Table. The system will pass a select statement looking for the environment that your user specified during the logon process.

At this point, OneWorld has already connected to the database and gained enough information from the jde.ini file to display a sign-on screen.

After the user enters the user ID, password, and environment into the sign-on screen, OneWorld will look for the environment you have specified before continuing:

- If the environment name is found, the system will then look for the path code that the environment is associated with, in F00942, the Path Code Master table. The system will poll this table for information on the path code.

- The system will then poll F00945, the Release Master table, for the release of OneWorld that it found in the environment and path code master table. The system will then poll F0093, the Library List Control table. This table contains the information about what environments are assigned to your users, and the system will look to see if your user has this environment assigned to it.

- The next table that the system hits is F00960, the Machine Identification table. This table contains information on what machines have installed OneWorld.

- The next table that the system hits is F9650, the Machine Master table. This table also contains information on the machines running OneWorld.

- OneWorld then checks to see if it can hit your business data source by selecting from the F0009 and F0010 tables.

Checking for Replication

The system will then check to see if you are using replication by doing selects over F98DRPUB and F98DRSUB. These are the Replication Publisher and Subscriber tables. If you have replication set up, the system will look for data to replicate and, if necessary, will replicate the data.

Security Check

The system will then do a select over F00950, the Security Workbench table. This table contains security information such as if you have locked users out of running applications or if you have set up row or column security. This information is then cached. The next table that the system hits is F98613, the Business View Environmental table. The system will then hit several business data tables, which are not as important as the system tables.

Menu Tables

Finally, the system will move on to the Menu tables F0082, F00821, F0083, and F0084. These tables contain the OneWorld menus that your users see when logging on to the system.

Final Tables Hit upon Login

Once the system has gone through the menus, it finishes with F98101, Imaging Constants; F98950, the User Overrides table; F91500, Application Header for the Tip of the Day; and finally, F91510, the Detail Table for the Tip of the Day.

Sign-on Security Check

If sign-on security is set up, another table that will be hit upon login is F98OWSEC. OneWorld knows to look for this table by reading the Security section of the jde.ini file. The following is an example of the jde.ini file:

```
[SECURITY]
SecurityServer=OWCUSTS4
DataSource=System - B733
DefaultEnvironment=CRP733
```

OneWorld will read the security server field to determine what the machine name is that provides your OneWorld sign-on security. The system will then poll the F98OWSEC table using the Data Source field. This table contains the OneWorld users and passwords and the system user and passwords, the latter of which is a database user and password. Sign-on security allows you to have a different user and password sent to the database that your end users do not know about. This means that you do not have to maintain user accounts in OneWorld and your database. Sign-on security also allows you to set up a single user in your database that multiple OneWorld users can use to connect to the database. This can be done by setting up system users and passwords for the OneWorld users. Sign-on security is covered in more detail in Chapter 13.

Summary

This chapter has covered the details about the way OneWorld Explorer works, including basic OneWorld navigation using the Windows directory structure, Fast Path navigation, menus, and what happens when a user logs in to a OneWorld workstation. This information should assist you in administering and troubleshooting your users' client workstation issues.

CHAPTER 4

Flexibility and the Client

As you have seen and will see throughout this book, OneWorld architecture is designed to be as flexible as Nadia Comaneci. OneWorld, as a leading enterprise resource planning (ERP) system, is designed to allow businesses to quickly and easily adjust the system to meet business needs. The components of flexibility are inherent in the system. That flexibility is further enhanced by the plethora of client interfaces offered by J.D. Edwards. This chapter covers the following topics pertaining to clients:

- The "client" defined

- Types of OneWorld clients

- OneWorld client requirements

- Client architecture

- Deploying the client

- Clients and data

- Clients and logic

- Choosing a client strategy

The Client Defined

The definition of a "client" shifts as we move from a host-centric application, such as J.D. Edwards World, to a network-centric application, such as OneWorld. In a host-centric application, the work is actually performed on the host mid- or main frame. The "client" is either of the following:

- A dumb terminal connected to an AS/400 mid-frame.

- A PC-based session emulator (a.k.a. screen scrape or green screen), such as Client Access running a 5250 emulation, Rumba, or a quasi-GUI WorldVision interface. The World interface is a screen scrape with the application's performance dependent on the mid-frame server rather than the client PC hosting the interface.

In a host-centric ERP application, the client emulator is truly a simple user interface that provides a window to the applications and transmits user requests as a series of keystrokes back to the Host for processing. Application-level processing does not occur on the client in this case.

However, in a network environment, the definition of a "client" shifts to a component that is a decentralized, fully integrated component capable of processing data received from a server as well as commands received from a variety of IO devices, such as keyboards and CD-ROMS. The client executes user requests and sends network requests to servers as well. The client enables the user to get work done by typically performing several important tasks on a network, including:

- Executing user applications

- Providing a user interface to the network

- Providing the network connection

The client interfaces with either local resources or communicates with network resources to send requests to a server or servers which respond by delivering or "serving" what the client requests.

The client is capable of performing this work because it is composed of two main attributes:

- Hardware: A CPU for processing power, memory (RAM and ROM), and hard disk space. The hardware is the physical attribute.

- Software: The "client" software portion of a networked application sends requests to the server software portion of a network application. The software is the logic attribute.

We will discuss the hardware and software requirements of OneWorld clients later in this chapter.

OneWorld Clients

In many ERP systems, the client has traditionally been nothing more than a screen scrape. The World client is certainly just that. However, J.D. Edwards, in a dramatic 180-degree shift from World, initially delivered four clients as part of its network-centric OneWorld architecture. Further enhancing its technology leadership in the network-centric arena, J.D. Edwards broke from the stodgy client/server definition of a client by providing "Activators." Activators are a suite of tools within OneWorld that provide granular control over ERP operations to the Configurable Network Computing (CNC) administrator. In other words, the CNC Administrator can control both the degree to which the client executes applications as well as the location from where the client obtains its data for processing.

Initial Clients

The initial clients offered by J.D. Edwards are the following:

- **Fat client**　A Pentium-class, Windows-based machine loaded with OneWorld logic and data. This client contains a full set of OneWorld objects and thus consumes considerable hard disk space.

- **Development client**　This client is a fat client loaded with OneWorld development objects. C++ must be installed in order to include the development objects upon deployment.

- **Partial client**　Also a Pentium-class, Windows-based machine but loaded with a subset of OneWorld logic and data (a fat client with a partial lobotomy). This client provides certain security benefits and lowers the overall disk space requirements.

- **The store-and-forward client**　Again, a Pentium-class, Windows-based machine loaded with either a subset or full set of OneWorld logic but housing a more complete set of OneWorld data (a fat client that knows too much). This client is useful for users who are not connected continually to the network and need to use OneWorld even when not connected .

Thin Client

These initial clients, while providing excellent LAN-based OneWorld access (the fat, development, partial clients) and sporadic network access (store-and-forward client), do not address several issues facing system administrators, including ease of maintenance and real-time WAN access. For such requirements, J.D. Edwards released the thin client, a multiuser OneWorld client running on Microsoft's Windows Terminal Server and preferably employing Citrix's WAN protocol, Independent Computing Architecture (ICA). This protocol separates application logic from the user interface, allowing the application to run 100 percent on the server itself. In other words, Windows Terminal Server and Citrix present a multiuser Windows, GUI emulation for the OneWorld client.

In 1998, J.D. Edwards provided the very popular OneWorld thin client with release B732.1 SP9 in addition to the previously described four clients.

Microsoft's Windows Terminal Server is Microsoft's answer to host-centric computing. Many users feel Windows Terminal Server presents an ironic twist in the saga of computing's evolution from host-centric to client/server and now back to host-centric. The difference implied between the name Windows Terminal *Server* and the function that it performs, which confuses people, is that Windows Terminal Server does not offer OneWorld services as per a normal OneWorld server, such as an Enterprise or Deployment box within the OneWorld architecture. The service the Terminal Server offers is strictly multiuser client sessions. These clients still rely on OneWorld Enterprise servers and Deployment servers.

Browser-based Clients

As if five clients were not enough, J.D. Edwards has released the ActivEra Explorer client as of B733.2. This is a custom J.D. Edwards Internet browser that also allows users to access locally installed OneWorld applications via a series of HTML indexes on the deployment server. This client is not truly a zero client (a 100 percent host-based application processing) because the set of applications to be used must reside on the client PC.

J.D. Edwards continues forward by fine-tuning the JAVA and HTML clients. The HTML client has been available since B732.1, but neither of these clients is fully functional in B733.2. The authors do not expect these clients to be fully functional until after OneWorld Xe (formerly B733.3) is released.

N O T E

We are seeing an increase in the use of OneWorld-enabled PDA devices, which expands the client options. There is no particular standard from J.D. Edwards at this time.

Client Requirements

Because of the variety of clients available, understanding client requirements is not easy. However, we can simplify things by understanding that the software requirements are firm; the hardware requirements per J.D. Edwards' installation documentation are understated from a performance perspective.

You can find client requirements in the J.D. Edwards Installation Guides under Customer Preparation, OneWorld Hardware and Software Requirements, and OneWorld Disk Space Requirements. You can also find updated documentation on the J.D. Edwards Knowledge Garden.

After J.D. Edwards cuts the General Availability CD with the installation documentation, updates to client-side requirements are posted on the Knowledge Garden. We recommend that you periodically check this site for updates. If J.D. Edwards has not published support of the software version you intend to load on your client, do not assume that the software has been tested or that J.D. Edwards will support it.

Software Requirements

OneWorld will run on Windows 95, Windows 98, Windows NT 4.0, Windows Terminal Server, and Windows 2000. Pay special attention to required service pack levels as they are certified by J.D. Edwards.

Client connectivity software requirements vary depending on the nature of the database. Oracle databases require the Oracle client. SQL databases require SQL Open Database Connectivity (ODBC). AS/400 databases require Client Access (Express preferred) and either SQL ODBC or Oracle Client, depending on whether the central objects are being maintained on AS/400, in SQL, or in Oracle.

Other variations in software requirements depend on whether or not the client is to be used for development. Traditional development clients require Windows NT 4.0 Workstation with Microsoft Visual C++ v6.0 + SP3. Web development workstations also require MS Java ++ 1.1 and Netscape's IFC class libraries.

NOTE

OneWorld client deployment autodetects whether the client has a Web browser, Internet Explorer v4.01, and Adobe Acrobat 4.0 loaded. If not, it prompts the installer as to whether it should install the third-party software.

ODBC Defined

Open Database Connectivity (ODBC), according to Microsoft, is a C-level application programming interface (API) for SQL-based data. OneWorld middleware drivers installed on the client make calls to the ODBC API, which in turn translate the calls to SQL statements for the backend databases.

ODBC is based on SQL as a standard for accessing data, and its consistent interface provides a high level of interoperability. A single application such as OneWorld can access different database management systems (DBMSs) through a common set of ODBC codes.

This consistent interface makes it more convenient for OneWorld programming to multiple relational DBMSs (RDBMSs). ODBC enables a OneWorld developer to build and distribute a client/server application without targeting a specific DBMS or having to know the details of various backend data stores. When a OneWorld application needs get data from a data store, the application sends a SQL statement to the ODBC Driver Manager, which then loads the ODBC drivers required to talk to the data. The driver then translates the SQL sent by the application into the SQL used by the DBMS and sends it to the backend database. The DBMS retrieves the data and passes it back to the application through the driver and the Driver Manager.

According to Microsoft, ODBC has been the data access standard since 1992 and has played an important role in enabling client/server applications. More than 170 ODBC drivers are available. However, OneWorld clients operate using only the following:

- Microsoft SQL 6.5 or 7.0
- Client Access or Client Access Express
- Oracle Client
- Microsoft Access

N O T E

These DLL versions are subject to change with Microsoft service packs. Contact J.D. Edwards to verify whether the DLL version you have installed is appropriate for your OneWorld version or service pack level.

Configuring ODBC

It is important to understand how to manually configure OneWorld ODBC data sources. The installation requires it, and when performing CNC work, you may be required to demonstrate such knowledge. Adequate documentation for the process may be found in J.D. Edwards' Installation Documentation under Installation Utilities, Creating 3rd Party ODBC Data Sources, which is why we will not walk you through the steps here. However, we do want to draw your attention to ODBCDataSource.inf and Registry settings.

ODBCDataSource.inf   This file can be found on the deployment server in \JDEdwardsOneWorld\B733\Client subdirectory. When you open the file, you will notice that it looks much like a registry entry. During the OneWorld client installation process, the ODBCDataSource.inf is used to create the appropriate third-party data sources. These same entries can be found within the ODBC 32-bit Manager in the Control Panel as well as within the registry.

During installation, the ODBCDataSource.inf is created with the records the CNC administrator enters from the OneWorld Data Source definition component of the

Planner. If the administrator later adds data sources from an administrator's workstation, it may be necessary to manually update the file for the ODBC value to be created on subsequent workstations. This is easy to do because the file is a text file that can be easily edited in Notepad.

Registry Settings   The entries from the ODBCDataSource.inf are written to the registry under HKEY Local Machine\Software\ODBC\ODBC.INI. Also, some entries can be written to HKEY CURRENT USER\Software\ODBC\ODBC.INI. If you are having a difficult time with OneWorld on a particular PC, delete the OneWorld-relevant ODBC registry entries under ODBC.INI in both registry keys prior to reinstalling OneWorld. However, be careful not to delete other entries.

Hardware Requirements

In order to determine the client architecture that best enables you to meet your business needs, your organization can undergo a series of events and exercises that can help you better define the necessary hardware requirements. Due to the tremendous flexibility that J.D. Edwards presents in your client architecture and the overwhelming variety of corporate IT infrastructures, no one standard applies to every situation.

Companies with numerous remote sites all over the globe clearly cannot run with a fat client architecture. Thin client or zero client architectures are more appropriate for such companies. However, companies with small user bases might find the thin client and zero client architectures are too expensive due to the backend server technologies required. Having said all that, we find that a hybrid roll out—that is, some fat, some partial, some thin, and some zero client architectures– is the most general configuration.

As we said earlier, the J.D. Edwards published requirements for clients (which can be found in the J.D. Edwards Installation Documentation under Customer Preparation, OneWorld Hardware and Software Requirements) are best thought of as minimum requirements. However, even with the minimum requirements, OneWorld does include a tool set that enables you to tune performance by making better use of the entire system. As stated previously, updated information can be found on the J.D. Edwards Knowledge Garden at https://knowledge.jdedwards.com. Hardware requirements change based on cumulative level and release level, so whenever you are preparing for an update or an upgrade, be sure to consult these resources. We provide a summary of B733.2 fat and partial client requirements in Table 4-1.

Hardware	Requirements	Notes
CPU	Intel Pentium 120 (minimum)	Pentium 166 (recommended)
RAM	64MB (minimum)	96MB (recommended)
Hard drive	450MB–2.1GB free space	450MB—partial package without development objects
		1.34GB—full package without development objects
		1.65GB—full package with development objects
		2.1GB—standalone with development objects
Display colors	256 colors—8 color panes (minimum)	65,536 colors—16 color panes (recommended)
Screen resolution	800 × 600 pixels (minimum)	
Printer support	PostScript, PCL, or line	

TABLE 4-1. Client Hardware Requirements

Architecture

Simply deploy a client, and you will see the components that load on the client. You'll notice that a client looks like an abbreviated path code when development objects are not loaded, and just like a path code when development objects are loaded. OneWorld installs to B7, a directory off the root drive (for instance C or D). Underneath \B7, you will find a path code name, for instance "CRPB733."

Figure 4-1 illustrates the client directory structure and provides a brief description of some of the more salient objects as well as their size. The sizes shown here are based on a fresh B733.2 client installation. Although the sizes may vary somewhat, they provide a guide for your understanding.

Deploying OneWorld

To install OneWorld on a client, you must go through a process called "deploying a package to a workstation." A base OneWorld installation provides two sets of full packages and two sets of partial packages, which can be seen using the Package

B7   This is the default directory to which OneWorld loads.

CRPB733   The name of the path code.

BIN32   The master DLLs of the business functions.

CAEC.DLL	772KB	CMFGBASE.DLL	2,964KB
CALLBSFN.DLL	2,312KB	COBJLIB.DLL	300KB
CBUSPART.DLL	20KB	COBLIB.DLL	20KB
CCONVERT.DLL	408KB	COPBASE.DLL	2,164KB
CCORE.DLL	36KB	CRES.DLL	332KB
CCRIN.DLL	1,468KB	CRUNTIME.DLL	288KB
CDBASE.DLL	108KB	CSALES.DLL	488KB
CDDICT.DLL	136KB	CTOOL.DLL	296KB
CDESIGN.DLL	36KB	CTRAN.DLL	664KB
CDIST.DLL	3,288KB	CTRANS.DLL	148KB
CFIN.DLL	4,020KB	CWARE.DLL	996KB
CHRM.DLL	4,152KB	CWRKFLOW.DLL	168KB
CINSTALL.DLL	1,224KB	JDBTRG1.DLL	136KB
CINV.DLL	224KB	JDBTRG2.DLL	176KB
CLOC.DLL	920KB	JDBTRG3.DLL	36KB
CLOG.DLL	2,540KB	JDBTRG4.DLL	20KB
CMFG.DLL	3,232KB	SETUP.INF	
CMFG1.DLL	20KB		

DATA

JDEB7.MDB

STORFWD.MDB

RES   Contains 741 image objects not including the following subdirectories:

AVI files	Contains eight AVI files.
Form lines	Contains 38 BMPs.
Icons	Contains 18 icon DLLs.
Images	Contains 10 GIFs.
Tree BMPs	Contains 120 BMPs.

FIGURE 4-1.   OneWorld Client Components

Spec	This directory contains the replicated central objects in the form of TAM files (which are specification files).					
	ASVRDTL.DDB	493KB		FDASPEC.DDB	71,031KB	
	ASVRDTL.XDB	273KB		FDASPEC.XDB	19,342KB	
	ASVRHDR.DDB	290KB		FDATEXT.DDB	5,063KB	
	ASVRHDR.XDB	39KB		FDATEXT.XDB	5944KB	
	BOBSPEC.DDB	8,831KB		GBRLINK.DDB	5,645KB	
	BOBSPEC.XDB	431KB		GBRLINK.XDB	6,491KB	
	DDCLMN.DDB	8,820KB		GBRSPEC.DDB	622,070KB	
	DDCLMN.XDB	6,482KB		GBRSPEC.XDB	128,180KB	
	DDICT.DDB	0KB	*Will grow with JITI	GLBLTBL.DDB	0KB	*Will grow with JITI
	DDICT.XDB	3KB	*Will grow with JITI	GLBLTBL.XDB	2KB	*Will grow with JITI
	DDPKEYD.DDB	518KB		JDEBLC.DDB	2,244KB	
	DDPKEYD.XDB	2,466KB		JDEBLC.XDB	2,049KB	
	DDPKEYH.DDB	203KB		POTEXT.DDB	11,223KB	
	DDPKEYH.XDB	112KB		POTEXT.XDB	979KB	
	DDTABLE.DDB	358KB		RDASPEC.DDB	68,475KB	
	DDTABLE.XDB	366KB		RDASPEC.XDB	25,792KB	
	DDTEXT.DDB	0KB	*Will grow with JITI	RDATEXT.DDB	7,342KB	
	DDTEXT.XDB	2KB	*Will grow with JITI	RDATEXT.XDB	9,768KB	
	DSTMPL.DDB	12,615KB		SMRTTMPL.DDB	307KB	
	DSTMPL.XDB	359KB		SMRTTMPL.XDB	5KB	
				SETUP.INF		
System						
	bin32	Contains 231objects used at runtime, including the JDE kernel (jdekrnl), EXEs, DLLs, COMs, and/or external applications.				
	include					
	includeV					

FIGURE 4-1.   OneWorld Client Components (*continued*)

System

    lib32

    libV32

    locale

    models

FIGURE 4-1. OneWorld Client Components (*continued*)

Assembly program (P9601) on the Package and Deployment Tools menu GH9083. (Note: The 96 UDC series is called "Computer Operations.") This program shows typical package definitions after a base installation, as shown in Figure 4-2.

The Package Assembly program pulls information from the software package header file (F9603) found in the OneWorld System database:

```
SELECT  *  FROM SYSB733.F9603  ORDER BY PHPKGNAME ASC,PHPATHCD ASC;
```

At the point of the base installation, there is no difference at the code level between the various packages which install under each path code. Each package contains the exact same copy of code at this point in time. For more on packages, refer to Chapter 10.

There are several ways to deploy a package to a client:

- Pull deployment using the Workstation Installation program

- Push deployment using the Package Deployment application

- CD deployment

- Multitiered deployment

We will cover only pull deployment here because it is the most comonly used. See Chapter 16 for in-depth coverage of CD and multitiered deployment.

Pull Deployment

Pull deployment of a workstation package is accomplished using the OneWorld Workstation Installation program. There are two types of pull deployment: interactive and silent.

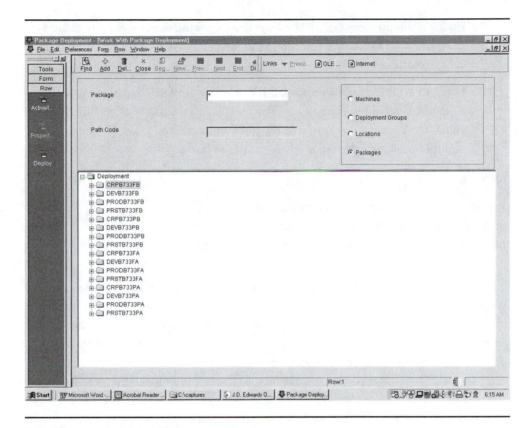

FIGURE 4-2. Package selections

To begin a pull deployment, you must map a drive to the B733 share on the deployment server. If the client is a Windows 95 client, you can easily start the installation by skipping the next three points and moving right into SETUP.EXE, However, if the client is an NT client, then you either need to log on locally to the Workstation as the local administrator, skip the next three steps, and move to SETUP.EXE as described next, or verify and enable disk and registry access for your NT user account prior to the OneWorld package deployment as per the following three steps:

1. Create an empty file at the root of the C drive called JDEINST.LOG and grant Windows NT Full Control security to you, the package installer.

2. Create a subdirectory called B7 on the drive on which the OneWorld client is to be installed and assign yourself Windows NT Full Control to B7 and its subdirectories.

3. Using REGEDT32, add a key called JDEdwards (capitalized as shown) with a blank Class field to the Software key on HKEY_LOCAL_MACHINE on the client. On Registry Key Permissions, add your name and grant Full Control with permissions to be replaced on existing subkeys.

N O T E

We realize that many administrators do not like to do direct registry edits, but the alternative is to give each user the local administrator's sign-on and password so they can perform package installations themselves.

To ease administration pains, export the key, copy the export from workstation to workstation, and by double-clicking the export on each workstation, the key is imported.

After completing this process, the CNC administrator double-clicks on the SETUP.EXE program found within mapped drive \B733\System\client installation\. This program initiates the client deployment.

When the Deployment director opens on the client, the administrator picks from a series of packages. It is possible and quite common to deploy more than one full package to a workstation provided the packages are in separate path codes. For instance, both CRP and DEV packages might be deployed to a single client workstation simultaneously. Clearly, there must be sufficient disk space on the target machine to host both package-delivered path codes.

After choosing the packages, the Deployment director calculates available disk space and notifies the administrator whether sufficient disk space is available. This methodology replaces the Network Checker service previously offered to OneWorld users.

A pull package deployment copies to the client from the deployment server or deployment location a series of CAB files as of release B733.1. These CAB files are the same package subdirectories/files from the deployment server, which have been compressed during the package build.

After the files are copied to the workstation, OneWorld goes through a process of exploding these files onto the hard drive and initializing the program. This process is a hands-free process for the CNC administrator and takes anywhere from 15 to 40 minutes, depending on network speed, client hardware, and the package chosen.

For the thin client, the deployment is two-fold. The thin client must be deployed to a client. For example, a Citrix metaframe client must be installed on a PC, and connectivity to the Terminal Server must be configured. And a OneWorld package must be deployed to the Terminal Server with use of the Add/Remove Programs applet in the Control Panel or by typing "user /install" at a command prompt.

Verifying Deployment

After deploying a client for the first time, the administrator should verify that it actually works. Such verification acts as a check on system integrity as well.

Directory Structure

A client should contain the appropriate directory structure for the package type and deployed client type as shown previously in Figure 4-1. It is worthwhile to become familiar with the directory structure because the structure serves as an excellent means to confirm that OneWorld deployed correctly.

Additional Files

After a package finishes deploying, the administrator can find the following files on the C drive. It is precisely because these files programmatically load to the C drive that a C drive (either real or mapped) is required for WinTerm installations. This requirement is of concern to Windows NT administrators everywhere due to Microsoft's suggestion that you do not deploy WinTerm with a C drive.

- JDEAUTH.DDA

- JDESEC.DDS

- JDEMOD.DDM

- JDEAPP.DDP

The J.D. Edwards Windows-level files also load, including drivers for ODBC. The administrator can peek at these on the deployment server under the Client\ ODBC directory.

Inside and Out

Signing on

Signing on is excellent verification of successful workstation deployment. Out of the box, OneWorld enables the administrator to sign on with the user JDE.

Sign-on prerequisites are that a user must be defined in OneWorld using the User Profile program P0092. The prerequisite to entering a user in the P0092 program is that the username must first exist in the Address Book program P01012 so that the user can be assigned a unique address book number.

Prior to B733, it was possible to add a "0" in the Address Book number field via the P0092 program. Although a "0" in place for multiple users leads to nonunique address book numbers, thereby causing workflow messaging issues, at least the administrator could quickly verify system operability. As of B733, however, OneWorld requires that a unique, nonzero number be assigned prior to P0092 entry. This requirement is both a good and a bad thing. Here's why.

As stated previously, OneWorld uses the address book number assigned to a user profile to process workflow messages. But why is there only one User Profile table (F0092), whereas each environment maintains its own set of address book tables? The problem becomes evident when switching environments and watching workflow error messages fail to be delivered. The user might see this message in the JDE.LOG: "User Profile Not Found." We hope that J.D. Edwards will change the location of user profiles, which is currently System – B733 or base workflow on the System entry rather than address book. Of course, using OneWorld's Object Configuration Manager (OCM), you could manually reposition the F0092 set of tables so that they are environment specific.

Additional Tools

Additional tools to verify proper client deployments include the following:

- Running the application NETMON.EXE found in B7\System\Bin32

- Running the application NETTEST.EXE found in B7\System\Bin32

- Launching a UBE both locally and against the enterprise server

- Launching a package build, both full and update

Client and Data

You have now deployed your OneWorld client and have run through some basic steps to verify the deployment. To see what is going on behind the scenes, turn on OneWorld debug and take a look. JDEdebug may be turned on by signing off OneWorld, finding the JDE.INI (on c:\winnt or, for a thin client configuration on WinTerm, c:\userprofile\ windows), and then turning on switches as per the following:

```
[DEBUG]
TAMMultiUserOn=0
Output=file
ServerLog=1
LEVEL=BSFN,EVENTS,SF_CONTROL,SF_GRID,SF_PARENT_CHILD,SF_GENERAL,
SF_MESSAGING,SF_WORKFLOW,SF_WORKFLOW_ADMIN,SF_MEDIA_OBJ
DebugFile=c:\jdedebug.log
JobFile=c:\jde.log
Frequency=10000
RepTrace=0Xxxxx
```

Here you see that OneWorld sends the log information to a file. It sends error information and debug information to JDE.LOG and JDEDEBUG.LOG, respectively, on the C drive. You can change the location of these logs. Simply log off OneWorld, edit JDE.INI, and then sign on to OneWorld.

Signing on initially to OneWorld shows that the tables as shown in Table 4-2 are being hit.

In Table 4-2, you can see that OneWorld is reading security information, OCM information, Environment master information, and Path Code master information. Some of these tables are interpretive—that is, OneWorld will read them again from a particular database. However, some are stored in the memory cache and are dynamically updated only when a user signs off/signs on.

Type of Table	Table Name	Description	Action
Business data	F0006	Business Unit Master	Open/close
Business data	F0007	Work Day Calendar	Open/close
Business data	F0008	Date Fiscal Patterns	Open/close
Business data	F0009	General Constants	Select—read only
Business data	F0010	Company Constants	Select—read only
Business data	F0012	Automatic Accounting Instructions Master	Open/close
Business data	F0013	Currency Codes	Open/close
Business data	F0014	Payment Terms	Open/close
Business data	F0015	Currency Exchange Rates	Open/close
Business data	F0022	Tax Rules	Open/close
Business data	F0025	Ledger Type Master File	Open/close
Business data	F0026	Job Cost Constants	Open/close
Business data	F069116	Payroll Transaction Constants	Open/close
Business data	F08320	Benefits Plan Master	Open/close
Business data	F083202	Plan Additional Options	Open/close
Business data	F08320B	Plan/Plan Option Tag Table	Open/close
Business data	F08350	Categories within Benefit Groups	Open/close
Business data	F08351	Plans within Benefit Categories	Open/close
Business data	F0901	Account Master	Open/close
Business data	F1200	Fixed Asset Constants	Open/close
Business data	F3009	Job Shop Manufacturing Constants	Open/close
Business data	F40070	Preference Master File	Open/close
Business data	F40073	Preference Hierarchy File	Open/close
Business data	F4008	Tax Areas	Open/close
Business data	F4009	Distribution/Manufacturing Constants	Select—read only
Business data	F40095	Default Locations/Printers	Open/close
Business data	F40203	Order Activity Rules	Open/close
Business data	F40205	Line Type Control Constants File	Open/close
Business data	F4070	Price Adjustment Schedule	Open/close
Business data	F4071	Price Adjustment Type	Open/close
Business data	F41001	Inventory Constants	Open/close
Business data	F41002	Item Units of Measure Conversion Factors	Open/close

TABLE 4-2.   OneWorld Tables Touched at Login

Type of Table	Table Name	Description	Action
Business data	F41003	Unit of Measure Standard Conversion	Open/close
Business data	F49002	Transportation Constants	Open/close
Business data	F49003	Load Type Constants	Open/close
Business data	F49004	Mode of Transport Constants	Open/close
Business data	F4950	Routing Entries	Open/close
Business data	F4951	Carrier Zone Definitions	Open/close
Business data	F4953	Routing Hierarchy	Open/close
Business data	F4970	Freight Rate Schedule	Open/close
Business data	F4971	Freight Rate Definition	Open/close
Business data	F4973	Rate Structure Definition	Open/close
Business data	F4978	Charge Code Definitions	Open/close
Business data	F7306	Quantum Sales and Use Tax Constants	Select—read only
Business data	F7308	Quantum Database Connection	Select—read only
Control tables	F0004	User-Defined Code Types	Open/close
Control tables	F0005	User-Defined Codes	Open/close
Control tables	F0082	Menu Master File	Select—read only
Control tables	F00821	Menu Selections File	Select—read only
Control tables	F0083	Menu Text Override File	Select—read only
Control tables	F0084	Menu Path File	Select—read only
System	F0092	Library Lists—User	Select—read only
System	F00921	User Display Preferences	Select—read only
System	F00925	User Access Definition	Select—read only
System	F0093	Library List Control	Select—read only
System	F00941	Environment Detail—OneWorld	Select—read only
System	F00942	Object Path Master file	Select—read only
System	F00945	Release Master	Select—read only
System	F00950	Security Workbench Table	Select—read only
System	F00960	Machine/Group Identification	Select/update
System	F91500	Application Header for Tip of the Day	Select—read only
System	F91510	Tip Details for Tip of the Day	Select—read only
System	F9650	Machine Master	Select/update
System	F98101	Imaging Constants	Select—read only

TABLE 4-2. OneWorld Tables Touched at Login (*continued*)

Inside and Out

Type of Table	Table Name	Description	Action
System	F986101	Object Configuration Master	Select—read only
System	F98611	Data Source Master	Select—read only
System	F98613	Business View Environmental Server	Select—read only
System	F98825	Package Deployment Scheduling	Select—read only
System	F98950	User Overrides Table	Select—read only
System	F98980	Font Override by Language	Select—read only
System	F98DRENV	Data Replication Environment Mapping Table	Select—read only
System	F98DRLOG	Data Replication Change Log	Select—read only
System	F98DRPUB	Data Replication Publisher	Select—read only
System	F98DRSUB	Data Replication Subscribers	Select—read only

TABLE 4-2.   OneWorld Tables Touched at Login *(continued)*

At the start of sign-on, you will see the following:

```
KERNEL type = KERNEL_MDA
Feb 14 19:40:33 ** 4294461499/4294464363 Entering JDB_InitEnv
Feb 14 19:40:33 ** 4294461499/4294464363 Entering JDB_SetEnv
Feb 14 19:40:34 ** 4294461499/4294464363 Entering JDB_InitUser with commit mode 0.
Feb 14 19:40:35 ** 4294461499/4294464363 Entering JDB_BeginTransaction
Feb 14 19:40:35 ** 4294461499/4294464363 Entering JDB_InitUser with commit mode 0.
Feb 14 19:40:35 ** 4294461499/4294464363 Entering JDB_BeginTransaction
Feb 14 19:40:36 ** 4294461499/4294464363 Entering JDB_FreeUser
Feb 14 19:40:36 ** 4294461499/4294464363 Entering GetUserProfileCache
Feb 14 19:40:36 ** 4294461499/4294464363 GetUserProfileCache returns
system/default value
Feb 14 19:40:41 ** 4294461499/4294464363 Entering JDB_InitUser with commit mode 0.
Feb 14 19:40:41 ** 4294461499/4294464363 Entering JDB_BeginTransaction
Feb 14 19:40:42 ** 4294461499/4294464363 Entering JDB_OpenTable( Table = F986101)
Feb 14 19:40:42 ** 4294461499/4294464363 Entering JDB_OpenTable( Table = F986101)
```

The J.D. Edwards runtime kernel in conjunction with JDE.INI is in control at
this point, initializing the environment, initializing the user, and caching user profile
information. Because it is happening at the kernel level, this process cannot be modified
without access to OneWorld kernel source code. If you could modify the process,
basic OneWorld security would be greatly impaired. However, by editing the JDE.INI
file, you can modify the location where the OneWorld client grabs this information.

After OneWorld confirms the ODBC base data source middleware as defined in
the JDE.INI section [DB SYSTEM SETTINGS], Load Library=, OneWorld generates the
following SQL statement:

```
        Feb 14 19:40:48 ** 4294461499/4294464363 SELECT OMENHV,
OMAPPLID, OMOBNM, OMDATP, OMDATS, OMUGRP, OMOAPP, OMDATM, OMOVRE, OMSY,
OMSTSO, OMFUNO, OMOCM2 FROM F986101  WHERE  ( OMENHV = 'DEMOB73' AND OMSTSO
= 'AV' )  ORDER BY OMSTSO ASC,OMAPPLID ASC
```

This statement indicates that OCM data has already been cached and is now being
read from local memory. The reason you know this is because you do not see a table
prefix to the F986101 table, such as SYSB733.F986101 or SYSB733/F986101.

There are pros and cons to caching this information. On the dark side, Luke, even
if you make changes to OCM, the only way for the client to receive these changes is to
either do a purge cache or sign-off/sign-on. On the other hand, the benefit to caching
such information is clearly response time.

Does the fact that this information is cached mean that the information must reside
in only one predefined location? Again, the kernel at sign-on reads the JDE.INI section
[DB SYSTEM SETTINGS], which tells OneWorld where to find system tables such as
User Profiles and OCM. We do not recommend lightly changing the location of your
system files without first thoroughly considering and planning the overall CNC
consequences of doing so.

OneWorld also caches tables from business data. This data, however, is reread
from the central database at various points of operation. Beyond performance reasons,
OneWorld caches business data because this information is integral to OneWorld's
more fully integrated security system and enterprise resourcing system.

For instance, by assigning users to branch plants, the application team can make
sure they perform transactions, operations, and so on only over relevant business data

Inside and Out

sets while still maintaining a global Item master, a global Customer master, and so forth. These issues are more application-side issues and further discussions belong in another book altogether.

Flexible Data

Through combined ODBC and OneWorld Activator OCM, OneWorld enables the flexible deployment of data across the enterprise and even across multiple, diverse database engines. You could, for instance, point one data source to SQL for central objects, one data source to DB2 for business data, and one to Access for control tables. In fact, such a configuration is completely normal in an AS/400 OneWorld installation.

We can easily imagine a wide variety of combinations but caution that proper and careful planning is necessary when moving beyond the standard data set combinations. The point, though, is that the client caches OCM, data source, user profile, and environment information that acts as pointers indicating where the OneWorld client can and should read its data.

NOTE

Out of the box, OneWorld UDC tables (F0004 and F0005) as well as Menu tables (F0082, F00821, F0083, F0084) are mapped locally. We advise changing the mappings to point to the server database during the pilot phase of a project so that all users have immediate access to the UDCs and menus, and to avoid the loss of changes.

Client and Distributed Logic

Perhaps one of the most interesting features of OneWorld is its ability to configure logic in a tiered network environment. In traditional systems, the programming logic runs on either the host, the client, or on both the client and server. These choices are traditionally not manageable. Rather, they are hard-coded and not changeable.

However, J.D. Edwards breaks with such a stodgy model, leap-frogging over it with OneWorld's OCM Activator. OneWorld through OCM has built-in functionality that allows you, as a CNC strategist, to granularly control the locations for logic processing of both interactive and batch process applications.

The default canned OneWorld approach from the client perspective is to have C business functions process locally along with batch versions. However, the default is not the optimal solution in many cases.

Distributed Batch Applications

Consider batch processes. In System OCM, UBEs are set to run locally by default. Accordingly, all batches a user launches from the menu process by default locally on the PC. The problem comes with UBEs that are:

- Data-manipulative (Update, Insert, Delete)

- Extremely long-running, whether data-manipulative (Update, Insert, Delete) or reporting only (Select)

Suppose a user launches a UBE locally that manipulates data across the network on the enterprise server, and the network connection is spotty. Then, suppose the user accidentally unplugs the PC power cord. Data corruption would most likely result with recovery being potentially very difficult.

Extremely long-running reports also cause productivity issues for the user whose PC is dedicated to the running of the report. Security issues arise as well if the user leaves without signing off, enabling the UBE to run to completion. Additionally, the flow of data across the network might have an impact on bandwidth-challenged campuses.

Because UBEs can run on any server in the implementation where OneWorld services are running, the solution is to creatively use OCM to tell OneWorld which UBEs will run locally and which will run on servers. By doing so, the CNC administrator can:

- Take a network-centric approach to load-balancing processing using distributed logic

- Further enhance and ensure data integrity

In essence, you could have an infinitely scalable, network-centric system approaching Cray supercomputer capabilities using this methodology.

Inside and Out

We recommend a structured approach during the pilot phase of an implementation to identify UBE candidates for distribution. The candidates for local PC processing have the following traits:

- Reporting only (Select), no data manipulation (Insert, Update, Delete)

- Short (range of 5 to 10 minutes or less)

To understand how OneWorld enables you to define versions that run in distinct processing job queues on the servers, see Chapter 21. That chapter addresses OS400 job queue definitions, required UDC entries, operating system definitional requirements, and the choice of the job queue within the report specifications.

Distributed C++ Business Functions

In addition to UBE process distribution, business functions can be distributed as well. However, the capacity for business function distribution is relatively immature compared to UBE distribution. Whereas almost every UBE (with the exception of a relatively minor few) can be distributed within a OneWorld N-tier architecture, only 190 out of 2,409 business functions per path code can be granularly controlled by OCM. Still the ability to do so is exciting (are we geeks or what?!), and we hope it will progress with future versions of OneWorld.

The benefit of mapping business functions to servers is not readily seen within the financial suite of OneWorld applications; however, it becomes quite apparent with other modules especially Sales Order Management.

Consider the Sales Order Management master business function, which requires approximately 40MB RAM to process. Multiply that number by 40 users on a thin client, and just one business function requires 1.6GB RAM. When system requirements for all of the other business functions, kernel operations, and OS are included, you can see how great the detrimental impact this one business function would have on thin client performance.

You could map this business function to any server running OneWorld logic, thereby offloading what would otherwise be a major system drain on the thin client.

An Approach for Choosing a Client Strategy

With so many clients available, what approach should your implementation take with regard to client strategy: Java clients, HTML clients, all fat clients, all thin clients?

As we said earlier, most implementations require a hybrid approach with various degrees of FAT development, FAT nondevelopment, thin client, and soon zero client.

The larger the implementation, the more important careful planning is to avoid having to make additional budgeting requests. However, even the smallest implementations need to consider the pros and cons of the various client strategies as they progress in their implementation.

Table 4-3 is a mini-mini decision-making matrix; actually, it's more a rule of thumb to keep in mind as you plan.

The fat client is clearly restricted to LAN-based implementations relevant to its access to data due to its large footprint and high-bandwidth requirements. The thin client is an excellent approach to WAN-based implementations due to its low-bandwidth requirements.

Summary

The purpose of this chapter is to present a review of OneWorld client architectures. We started with a high-level overview of the client definition and role within client/server technology and then moved quickly to the definition of a OneWorld client and the various types, from fat to zero clients.

We then briefly touched on software and hardware requirements, indicating the decisions that must be made during an implementation. In some ways, the remainder of the chapter is designed to help you understand how the clients exist in a OneWorld enterprise system architecture so that when you go through a planning strategy session, you will have better understanding of what is involved.

Client Type	Footprint	Bandwidth	Centralized Administration	Development	Planning Complexity
Fat	Large	High	Getting There	Yes	Low
Partial	Medium	High	Getting There	No	Low
Thin	Medium	Low	YES!	Cowboys only	High

TABLE 4-3.   Client Choice Matrix

Following the discussion of requirements, we went into an in-depth review of client components. We addressed the expected directory structures and even defined the master DLLs within the client.

We then addressed OneWorld client installations and focused on the pull deployment methodology. We discussed a method and data to use to verify your client deployments.

Next, we discussed OneWorld clients relative to OneWorld data and logic. We looked at some of the tools relevant to managing OneWorld performance and implications from a client perspective. Finally, we came full circle to discussing at a 50,000-foot level an approach for defining your client architecture. We presented a matrix of high-level key points for various client types that should be considered in every planning strategy.

CHAPTER 5

OneWorld Servers

Does the Platform Matter?

The OneWorld Deployment Server

Data Servers

Application Servers

Enterprise Servers

Windows Terminal Server

Web Servers

As you continue learning about the basics of the OneWorld system—what the building blocks are and do, how to successfully implement the system and what types of topics to keep in mind before, during, and after an implementation—we need to take time out to talk about the underpinnings of the system itself (both hardware and software). Though we certainly don't want to minimize the other topics we have discussed thus far, or the topics we will discuss later, we would be remiss in our duties as OneWorld tour guides if we didn't spend an inordinate amount of time on servers and the options surrounding them.

One of the topics that inevitably comes up on every OneWorld implementation is hardware. After all, this is one of the largest single expenditures you will make (right next to the software itself). In truth, having a good understanding for the various types of servers and their functionality might enable a company to rapidly receive a return on their OneWorld investment.

Does the Platform Matter?

Although the OneWorld ERP package does not support all platforms, it does support a wide range of hardware platforms. Will OneWorld work on the AS/400? Yes! The HP9000? Yes! A WinTel (Windows NT/Intel) solution, such as Gateway, Compaq, or Dell? Yes! The RS6000? Yes! The Sun Solaris? Yes! Can you mix and match servers and databases? Yes, within the limits of the hardware and databases themselves.

We would be lying to you if we said that all of the platforms (both hardware and software) were created equal. However, we can honestly say that there are pros and cons to all of them. There is no one single best solution. Rather, there is a best solution per set of circumstances—yours may not be the same as other companies that are implementing this product. This chapter is devoted to the options available to the OneWorld architect, rather than on what hardware and software to implement (though we go into that too). We will go into detail on the following:

- The deployment server
- The data server
- The application server
- The enterprise server
- The Microsoft Windows terminal server
- The Web server

The OneWorld Deployment Server

What better way to start a chapter dedicated to servers and hardware than with the good, old-fashioned deployment server. To assist you in this, we will discuss the following:

- Exactly what is the deployment server?

- Why do we have it?

- Can it be used for other functions?

A deployment server is an integral part of the OneWorld system and is always mentioned as part of the enterprise. So much so that you will notice that the simplest architectural models have one. Figure 5-1 shows a standard "out of the box" OneWorld configuration.

In the least of terms, a deployment server is an Intel (and yes, it does have to be based on the Intel chipset) server running Microsoft Windows NT. Some companies try to get clever and substitute a different chipset. Do not try this—you will run into problems and J.D. Edwards' customer support will not be able to help you.

NOTE

Your deployment server can exist on the AS/400 because IBM offers an Intel NT chip that uses the AS/400's disk space. When you use this chip, your deployment server can then exist on the AS/400.

Depending on your specific environment, the deployment server may perform several different functions.

Deployment Server Basics

The deployment server acts as a primary deployment location in a centralized software deployment model. It is the primary location for all path codes in the system and maintains the actual C code that comprises the OneWorld ERP system. It maintains the system's license security and can build packages for both clients and application servers. It houses packages for deployment to workstations, Windows terminal servers, or other deployment locations.

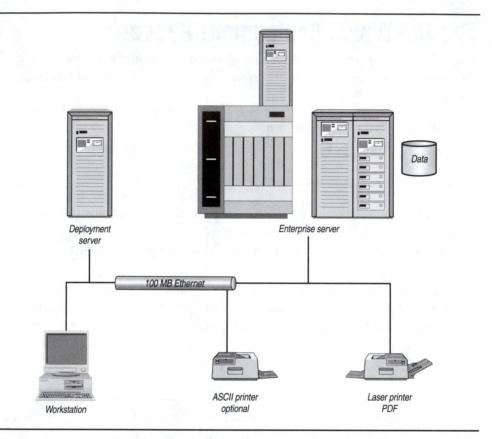

FIGURE 5-1. Simple OneWorld architecture

Although the B7331 series of OneWorld (and higher) allows you to house central objects on the AS/400, due to space requirements (6.8GB per path code—a total of almost 28GB in a typical installation of OneWorld using the AS/400) and speed (the central objects are much slower in DB2/400 than in Microsoft SQL Server or Oracle), many companies with AS/400s tend to use the deployment server to house these as well. Instead of the 6.8GB per path code, both SQL Server 7.0 and Oracle get by with less than 2.2GB of space. This savings in disk space, as well as the performance boost, is substantial.

Inside and Out

TIP

The speed of accessing central objects on the AS/400 is getting better with time. So do not rule this solution out, just be sure to research the speed you can expect and the disk space requirements compared to having the central objects on the deployment server in SQL Server or Oracle.

Does the Deployment Server Have to Do All That?

No! There are many circumstances where the deployment server functionality would be better decentralized. However, you won't see all this functionality dispersed even on a highly decentralized architectural model. Many of these functions make sense and are logically located where they do the most good.

The deployment server is where OneWorld is first introduced to your enterprise. The CDs shipped by J.D. Edwards get installed here, the OneWorld system is defined here through the installation process, and packages are dispersed from this location. More importantly, however, this server contains the Table Access Manager files, or TAM, that track OneWorld licenses on the system.

DEFINITION

Table Access Manager (TAM): *The Table Access Manager can be thought of as a miniature database. TAM is used to locally store design specifications for applications (for example, screen layouts or event rules).*

Off with Its Power

Many companies have asked if the deployment server can be shut off. Most of these companies do so because they are Novell, UNIX, or AS/400 shops and the introduction of NT is neither wanted nor tolerable to the existing system staff. Unfortunately, on some platforms (and depending on your specific configurations), you simply shouldn't shut this system down.

Now, we know there is a base premise which states you should never tell a client no, and we certainly don't want to violate that concept. Rather, we would ask why an Intel/NT machine couldn't reside on the system. It doesn't require a huge amount of maintenance, it is a very easy operating system to support, and has cheap hardware. Why not let it live? Let's think again about what this system does for your organization:

- Provides an initial point of installation, update, and upgrade

- Maintains OneWorld license security

- Maintains C code for all path codes (under typical configuration)

- May contain a series of databases housing the central objects

- Can be used for building software deployment packages

- Houses all software packages for deployment throughout the OneWorld enterprise

Rules for Turning the System Off

With all these functions, we think you should simply leave the system on; however, there are some rules for turning the system off. First, because it may contain databases that house central objects, you should never turn the deployment server off for a prolonged period of time. The system will not work correctly if you do.

NOTE

The deployment server should be backed up regularly to ensure disaster recovery capability.

Second, since this system does house the OneWorld license security in TAM files, you can turn the deployment server off; however, you need to turn it back on when it is time to renew the license for a workstation and the system security. Third, when you are building either OneWorld workstation or server software packages, this server must be on. Fourth, though you can turn this system off, depending on your software configuration, you may experience difficulty checking items into or out of the path code.

NOTE

Many users do not recognize when they have successfully checked modified objects into or out of their OneWorld system. There will often be an error stating that the system could not access a file. Do not ignore these error messages. Instead, look at the JDE.LOG and find out why you got the message in the first place. We have seen companies ignore this type of error and fail to have their modifications carry forward to the next release of OneWorld.

Finally, and yes, this reiterates the above rules, if you plan to perform a lot of development, package deployments, or future upgrades and have not implemented multi-tier deployment or some other modification, it is not advisable to turn this system off for more than routine maintenance.

Rolling the Deployment Server into a Configuration

Concerning the information already provided, we never recommend the particular WinTel solution to implement. Whatever platform you are comfortable with works for the deployment server. Now we'll get specific about the actual hardware configuration for this machine. It all comes down to what your company's objectives are when implementing this ERP package. Let's look at a couple of different scenarios under consideration.

OneWorld and the AS/400

In this particular case, we are going to make the following assumptions:

- There is no special development for the implementation of this software.

- The central objects are going to be housed in an RDBMS on the deployment server.

- You are implementing B7331 and plan on upgrading to B9 when available.

Now come the fun questions: What types of hardware do we need? Should we have system redundancy? What is the best configuration?

Concerning hardware, you will need approximately 25 gigabytes just in OneWorld hard drive space. When you consider the upgrade, you will minimally add another 35GB of required space (updates, prior to OneWorld Xe, formerly B733.3, require significantly less). Because you are housing a relational database, you might consider configuring these drives to maximize the database throughput; however, since your development is minimal, your optimizations can be also.

N O T E

If you perform some basic optimization procedures on both hardware and software configurations, you will decrease the time required to install or upgrade OneWorld. Whenever possible, try to separate the data files and the archive/redo/log files onto separate physical and logical disks. This separation will improve your database read/write capabilities. If you have multiple controller cards in your server, separating the data and logs on these will also improve performance.

The system described above is a mission-critical piece of the enterprise system. As such, system redundancy is highly recommended. This redundancy could be as little as using RAID (we, of course, prefer hardware RAID with a 0/1 configuration for the RDBMS) or as much as having a real-time hot backup system. Your company must decide how important OneWorld's being online is against your internal ability to support this solution. It comes down to how long OneWorld can be down. In this system, we would also recommend nightly backups (either full or incremental) with offsite storage.

Depending on your hardware solution, go with either a 9 or 18GB system drive. This will be used for the operating system, a paging file, and the database log files. Then add a 54GB data drive (obviously several drives combined using some RAID technology) to house the OneWorld directory structure and the RDBMS data files. This would provide enough space to grow. You will minimally want a Pentium III 500 (let's face it, the additional cost just isn't that much) or a duel processor system (you could go with a quad for future functionality, but most companies won't go for it, and it is overkill both now and in the immediate future). On the memory side, we recommend a minimum of 512MB on this system and encourage a full gigabyte of RAM because of the multi-functionality requirements of this system—most databases like their memory.

Now, all this sounds like an expensive trip for a server that many people want to turn off. Still, under this scenario, you don't want to bet your ERP solution on something under-powered and in continual need of upgrade. Most companies have problems with the actual disk storage requirements of this system, and we know of several companies that are continually running out of disk space. Let's look at a cheaper solution in our second scenario.

OneWorld and the Minimalist Deployment Server

If you are using OneWorld with UNIX or NT (or for that matter, the AS/400) and have configured the central objects to reside on a different server, you can get by with much less of a deployment server. Let's assume for this configuration that you have a UNIX based system and plan on keeping the central objects on the enterprise server. In this scenario, you will not be doing heavy development—rather, you will be trying to apply as few changes as possible to the system.

Now, from the previous information provided, we know what type of server you can come up with, but do you need that server for this type of solution? No, the deployment server in this scenario can be as little as a workstation PC with quite a bit of associated hard drive. Let's go into the details of what you actually need.

Considerations   The first consideration for this machine is whether the deployment server is a system-critical piece of hardware. To this we would argue yes, but only at specific times. Similar to our earlier discussions on whether you should turn the deployment server off, it could be argued that most of the time this server is simply not a requirement for the system as a whole. It is required during any development that may occur. It is required when you are building OneWorld software deployment packages. It is required during deployment of these OneWorld packages. It is even required when you are initially installing or update/upgrading OneWorld. However—and this is a *big* however—it is not required during normal day-to-day activities or for running your business. Consequently, this is one of those scenarios where a company could turn the server off for months at a time, turning it back on for very short periods.

Inside and Out

CAUTION

Although turning the deployment server off for long periods of time is technically possible, it is not recommended as it adds to the complexity of maintaining the system, such as determining when you turn it back on. We merely present you with the option so you can make informed decisions.

As a non-mission-critical piece of hardware, the redundancy, backup, and administration of this particular system takes a much lower priority and provides opportunity for system savings. You don't need to do nightly backups unless you are doing a lot of development work, which includes business functions or tables. Is there a high requirement for basic system redundancy? No! Is this really a PC with a large disk drive? Yes!

The second consideration for this machine is the actual hardware required to make it work. Visit the J.D. Edwards Web site, www.jdedwards.com, to find the minimum requirements necessary to run the system. In this scenario, you could get by with those requirements.

Data Servers

We are dedicating an entire section of this book to data servers for a number of reasons. First, because the data server is a legitimate OneWorld server. Although they are not prevalent in many of the existing installations, we think you will see a marked increase in their use. Second, in a chapter dedicated to OneWorld servers, we could not honestly call this a complete reference without it. Finally, the more we talk about the virtues of the data server, when and why you would use one, and how easy they are to implement, the more likely you are to start using them and quickly gain the return on your investment.

Data Servers Defined

In its simplest terms, a data server is defined on OneWorld through data sources only (see Chapter 2 for more details on OneWorld data sources). It can be any type of server that can run a OneWorld supported database. A data server does not contain OneWorld logic. Because this server never has J.D. Edwards OneWorld application code installed, it can neither run OneWorld services nor does it take up a software license. Consequently, this server is nearly undefined to the OneWorld suite of applications. You will not find entries in the F9650 series tables as you would for application or enterprise servers or even workstations.

A data server contains an RDBMS (Oracle, Microsoft SQL Server, DB2/400, or Microsoft Access) that houses OneWorld tables. These tables can either be "master" tables or replicated tables. Basically, a data server is a server that provides OneWorld access to data through a database. Pretty simple, isn't it?

Why You Would Implement a Data Server

Although many people, even the ones who know OneWorld well, don't have much use for data servers (after all, there is the hardware expense, the configuration, the support, and so on), we personally find multiple uses for them. Many times, you can vastly improve OneWorld's performance by their use. Let's take a look at specific reasons why.

No Enterprise Server

There is an argument, among the various platforms, that states you cannot optimize a server to act as both a data server and an application server. Though we certainly think that any of the supported hardware platforms can run as both, we've seen firsthand the increase and raw performance gain of implementing two separate systems. UNIX and NT both reap tremendous benefits from that separation.

UNIX: An Example   When you are optimizing a UNIX server, you can increase the speed of your database by decreasing the UNIX kernel time slice. Depending on your UNIX server, a kernel time slice of 3 or 4 would certainly not be unreasonable. When optimizing your UNIX server for the OneWorld application, it would not be unreasonable to have a time slice of 15 to 20. Finally, when trying to optimize a UNIX server for both, you will actually leave the box from 10 (which is the software default) to 14. As you can quickly determine, however, this is not optimal for either the database or OneWorld. Consequently, this server, when fulfilling both roles, is not doing well for either one. A substantial gain is realized when you put two servers in place even if those systems have fewer raw resources than a single giant one. NT is similar, though you don't have as much control of the operating system kernel.

Remote Development

There are many ways to implement remote development, including creating a distributed path code. It really is very simple. Take a server and load either Microsoft SQL Server or Oracle on it. Add a new path code and during the process define the new server's database as the repository for the central objects. Add the directories associated with the new path code on the same machine (this assumes the machine is an NT server). You will then need to update the path code master to reflect the new server's name; this is how OneWorld

Inside and Out

determines where your check-in location is. Then move the new server to the location you want to develop at. If you want to speed this system up even more, you can make a copy of the business data and control tables, so all development and initial testing can be done at the remote site. When the development is completed (on an object-by-object basis), you can transfer these objects to a consolidated space (CRPB733 could be used).

NOTE

In order for this configuration to work, you need an in-depth understanding of OneWorld and the remote site will need to have network connectivity to your original site.

CAUTION

J.D. Edwards' support will not assist you in setting up a distributed path code solution. They consider this a custom implementation approach and will refer you to either their field consulting arm or a business partner to implement this. This also means that if you run into problems with a distributed path code you will not be able to easily obtain assistance from customer support. Keep this in mind if you are planning on implementing this configuration.

Departmental Servers

There are two types of departmental servers (or three if you combine these options). One is a data server that houses either static or transactional data. This machine allows the department to hit its data without having the entire organization hitting the same box. A quick and useful example of this would be moving personnel/payroll data to a departmental server. You could much more effectively control this very sensitive data in this manner. A second type of departmental server is an application server. This server is discussed in more detail in the section "Application Servers." Finally, you can add a new enterprise server for a specific department. This is discussed in more detail in the section "Enterprise Servers."

TIP

If you are implementing a departmental server at multiple sites, you will either need staff to maintain those servers at these sites or provide remote support. This might drive up the cost of maintaining your system.

Data Replication

Another good reason for installing a data server is data replication. Using data servers in a wide area network (WAN) environment with OneWorld client workstations running full packages (shown in Figure 5-2), you can decrease logon times by 80 percent across a 56KB line. By replicating other static data, you can also achieve significant increases in other applications. You can learn more about data replication in Chapter 15.

How to Implement the Data Server Solution

Explaining the implementation of the data server could be very quick, or we could go into more detail. With what you've read of this book so far, which route do you think we took? We will spend some time in this chapter discussing why and where you put this solution in place, and we also discuss the overall system architecture in more detail in Chapter 11.

The Mechanics

The mechanics of actually adding a data server are quite simple. Acquire a server and configure it with the appropriate amount of disk, RAM, and processor resources.

N O T E

We know that merely stating the configuration should have the appropriate amount of resources is frustrating; however, it is almost impossible to predetermine what you need without making some very specific determinations as to what you are using the system for.

1. Optimize this server for the database you will be using. Your DBA should have some very specific changes to implement.

2. Add the RDBMS software. Set it up for optimal use based on what the data server will be used for. Will this database be a primary read/write or read only? The configuration is different for each.

3. Create the appropriate data files, databases, table owners, and log/rollback segments. For Oracle, define a new connect string. For DB2/400, Microsoft Access, or Microsoft SQL Server, set up new ODBC data sources.

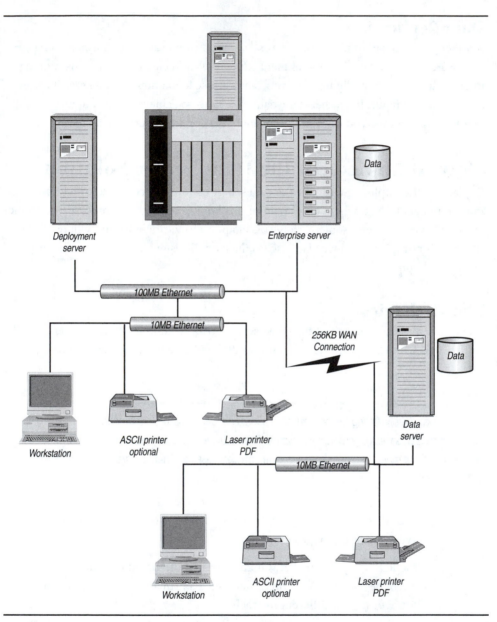

FIGURE 5-2. WAN environment with data replication

NOTE

If this server is going to be used for replicated or departmental data, we recommend that you use a table owner (on Oracle or SQL Server only) that is different than the primary for the environment being hit. This makes troubleshooting some problems easier.

4. Set up new OneWorld data sources for the new data server, as shown in Figure 5-3. (This is only required if you are not implementing a single enterprise server solution, such as data replication, departmental server, and so on.)

5. Copy or generate the new tables using the RDBMS or R98403 (shown in Figure 5-4; more information on this UBE can be found in Chapter 7).

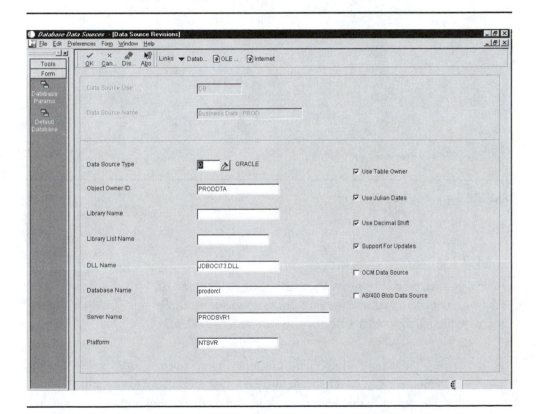

FIGURE 5-3.   Data source setup screen

Inside and Out

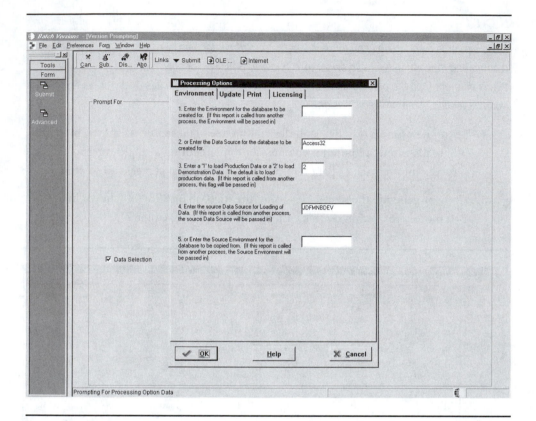

FIGURE 5-4.   R98403 initial screen

CAUTION

There were difficulties copying central objects using SQL Server version 6.5, which often resulted in data corruption. If you are still using this version of SQL Server, it is required that you copy this data using OneWorld instead of the RDBMS.

6. Change OCM to point users, groups, or everyone to the new data server being implemented. You could alternatively set up a special environment pointing to this data server, if this server is an addition to an existing implementation and is not replacing the enterprise server for data storage requirements. For more information on OCM or setting up environments, refer to Chapter 2.

Application Servers

The application server (also commonly called an app server) has become a fashionable addition to any enterprise solution because it allows what is called an N-tier architecture. You've heard of 2-tier architecture and already know the benefits of a 3-tier solution. But the N-tier solution means you add as many application servers as you need to adequately fill your data processing needs. In this section, you will find the following information:

- App servers defined
- App servers pros and cons
- How to implement app servers

App Servers Defined

An application server is a supported hardware platform server running OneWorld server code. Is there a difference in server code as opposed to workstation code? Yes! Server code runs OneWorld services, including security, data replication, time stamp, distributed processing, and UBE. The app server can perform many functions, including logic services (both BSFN and UBE), security, and data replication. Currently supported hardware includes the following: AS/400, HP9000, RS6000, Sun, WinTel, and the Alpha.

The primary difference between an application server and an enterprise server is that the enterprise server is also the primary database server. An application server (including the enterprise server) must have two data sources associated with it: one logic data source and one server map.

N O T E

What was once known as DEC Alpha, then Digital Alpha, and finally Compaq Alpha, will lose its status as a supported hardware platform during 2000. As of OneWorld Xe, the Compaq Alpha will no longer be a supported platform for OneWorld. If your enterprise is currently using this platform, we would recommend you replace it as soon as it is feasible.

Uses for App Servers

In a generic form, the OneWorld application server can be an add-on to an enterprise designed to improve system performance, or it can be part of the original solution.

Inside and Out

When initially designing your enterprise, you should consider the addition of
OneWorld application servers. This will allow a reasonable budgetary process for
your implementation.

There are several uses for the OneWorld application server and, although they are
not a required part of the OneWorld solution, they are in almost all implementations.
Running OneWorld stand-alone is an example of when you don't have an application
server. In a traditional OneWorld implementation, however, you will minimally have one
application server (the enterprise server). This application server will provide basic
OneWorld services (such as batch, security, and transaction processing).

App Servers for the Microsoft Windows Terminal Solution

If you are designing or re-designing your OneWorld solution to include MS
Windows Terminal Server Edition and what is known as a OneWorld thin client, it
is recommended that you minimally implement a 3-tier solution (as shown in Figure
5-5) and very possibly an N-tier solution. What this means in layman's terms is that
you will enhance performance and cost effectiveness by offloading specific logic
processing from the terminal server to application servers within the enterprise. The
more terminal servers in use, the more application servers required for the solution.

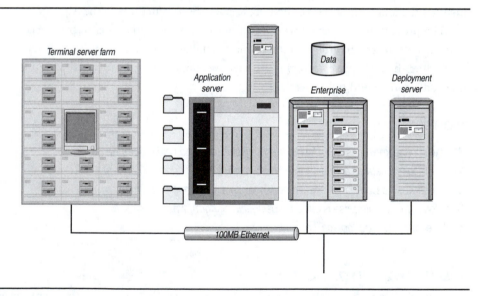

FIGURE 5-5.   3-tier architecture

App Servers for Nightly Processing

When determining your nightly or end-of-day reporting requirements, you will often find occasions where you simply don't have enough time to get everything done. This can be remedied in many scenarios by adding application servers to offload certain processes. This is especially true in multinational accounts where the official end-of-day is a predetermined time and not a true time when business has ended.

App Servers for a Specific Department

Similar to the data server, application servers can be specifically defined for a department. This could be done for security purposes or to offload processing from a specific group of people.

N O T E

Do not add an application server to the far side of a WAN setup (that is, away from the data). This does not buy you any performance gain and could actually decrease your performance.

App Servers in a Distributed Environment

It is possible and often useful to implement OneWorld with separate application and data servers. This solution is discussed in more detail in the section titled "Data Servers." If you implement this particular solution, you will obviously have a true application server setup.

App Servers Pros and Cons

We've just gone over the reasons you would add an application server. Are there other benefits to the application server, and what about the downside to this hardware solution? Let's discuss both of these in a little detail.

Pros

Other than the obvious—the four reasons for implementing them that we've already gone over—there are some advantages to having multiple logic servers. For one thing, an app server's OS can be optimally configured for the OneWorld application. Another advantage to multiple application servers is their scalability. To a very large extent, additional processing requirements can be effectively resolved by this simple addition. This allows the OneWorld enterprise architect to optimally configure OneWorld so as to maximize their configuration. This is especially true in cases where the company has implemented a distributed data architecture.

Another benefit of application servers is that they can be added to your overall version control strategy. The ability of taking one of these servers offline to test ESUs, custom reports and modifications, and updates/upgrades is well worth the effort of maintaining one.

Cons

As with any good solution, there has to be a downside, right? We've compiled a few of what we consider disadvantages to adding application servers. They include maintenance, maintenance, and more maintenance.

OneWorld Maintenance   The biggest problem with the app server is the OneWorld maintenance. Does this mean they are difficult to maintain? Not really, but the more you add to the mix, the more complicated it becomes. Each of the application servers maintains its own unique set of OneWorld code. If you change this code by implementing a new software action request (SAR) or by adding a new UBE, you have to build and deploy a OneWorld software package to each of the application servers. This can become much more difficult when you implement servers for specific functions—which servers need what changes? Once you begin adding multiple servers, we highly recommend that you closely monitor your version control. Failure to do this can result in unpredictable results or data corruption. (Hmmm…how is that for a disadvantage?)

N O T E

One of the safest methods of version control is to ensure that all packages are applied to all application servers rather that trying to determine what functionality is required on each. This will also provide greater system redundancy (all servers will be able to serve all required functionality).

Another possible disadvantage to adding application servers involves maintaining OneWorld system changes. Each application server has a server map (you can share the server map between multiple servers of the same platform). Different server types require different server maps and, depending on what functions you have designed, the additional application servers may require unique server maps as well. The problem with more server maps is that OCM, data sources, and replication setup changes must be preformed to each of the servers affected by the change.

OneWorld Maintenance: Update/Upgrade Don't forget that multiple application servers require that you upgrade multiple sets of code. Luckily, with the addition of B7331, you are able to perform full server package builds. This will enhance your ability to keep these servers in line; however, the greater the number of servers, the longer it will take to fully upgrade the system.

System Maintenance Multiple application servers also create more administration in hardware, third-party software, and general OS maintenance. Depending on the number of servers, you might need to increase your IT support personnel.

Application Server Elements

Rather than go through the mechanics of adding an application server in detail (the actual steps can be found in the J.D. Edwards OneWorld Installation Guides), we want to ensure that you understand all the elements associated with application servers. Once you have a good feel for what is required for the application server, you can either follow the standard installation procedure or get creative in how you install these servers. Once the server is up and operational, it is very simple to quickly put it to use in your enterprise.

The elements required for an application server to function properly are as follows:

- Two data sources associated with an application server

- The actual OneWorld host code (the base version of this ships on separate CDs with the OneWorld software)

- OneWorld services

- The server map tables themselves

- Entries in the F9650, F9651, F9652, F9653, and F9654 tables. These tables contain information on your application server

- Actually using the server

Two Data Sources

If you add an application server using the OneWorld installation planner, it will automatically configure two data sources for you. It will be simpler to explain if we use an example server scenario. Let's assume you are adding an NT application server on an NT system using Microsoft SQL Server.

Server Map   The first data source is a database data source that points to a server map. If the server you are adding is named APP01, the data source would be named APP01 – B733 Server Map. It would be set up similarly to all the other database data sources (refer to Chapter 2 for additional information on data sources), but it would need the OCM flag checked so that a system administrator could effectively administer both data sources (F98611) and OCM (F986101) entries in the server map tables.

Server   The second data source, and the only required one, would be a logic data source defining the server to OneWorld. This data source would be named APP01. When adding a data source from scratch, there are certain required fields, including Database Type and Database Name, that simply have to have something entered into them. We're often asked what information should be put in these fields when there is no database associated with a logic data source. We recommend that you put the same information you entered for the server map data source (this is of course why we mentioned the server map data source first). This is actually a holdover from B73.1 when the database name for the server name data source (in this case, APP01) was Server Name instead of Server Map as it is now. Therefore, when a client submitted a UBE on a SQL Server or AS/400, it would look for F986110 in the Server Name ODBC data source. This data source would have to be configured to point to the location of F986110. Hence, in later releases J.D. Edwards changed the database name for the server name data source to be the server map data source.

Server Codes and the Services Run by Them

As mentioned earlier, the code that resides on a server is different from the code that workstations use. Server code runs a series of services that do not run on a workstation, including network, security, replication, UBE, and logic. Additionally, as you could well imagine, the code for the different hardware platforms is also different from each other (think about it—the code that drives an AS/400 is very different from the code that drives an HP9000).

Making the Application Server Work for You

Now that the application server is up and operating, you want to know how to put it to work as quickly as possible. There are two basic ways to start using an application server in the OneWorld enterprise. This server can be accessed by users who override the location when launching their UBEs. It can also be put into service by using OCM to automatically map workstation or other server logic to the new application server. These mappings can be set up for your environments by individual or group, and will take effect when people log on to the OneWorld environment. You can also schedule nightly jobs to run on these servers. In fact, these servers can act as the schedule server.

Enterprise Servers

After reading this section, you will have an understanding of what an enterprise server is and how to set one up. You will also have an understanding of what types of platforms are considered enterprise servers. In this section, we'll cover:

- Definition of an enterprise server

- Types of enterprise servers

- How to add an enterprise server

- When you would add an enterprise server

Definition of an Enterprise Server

An enterprise server can be defined as a server that contains a database and can process logic. This means that your business data, for at least one environment, is located in a database on this enterprise server. You can take advantage of this server's processing power to run UBEs or reports on this enterprise server.

The fact that you can place data specific to environments on these servers is very important. This means that you can set up a production enterprise server and a development enterprise server. We will discuss the benefits of adding enterprise servers later in this section.

Types of Enterprise Servers

One of the advantages of a OneWorld system is that it is not platform dependent. The currently supported platforms for a OneWorld system are:

- HP9000

- RS6000

- Sun Solaris

- Intel NT

- Compaq Alpha

- AS/400

You can log on to one client machine and retrieve data stored on any of these platforms or run reports on any of these platforms. This configurability is very important today, as your sites may all have different types of hardware. With the OneWorld system, you do not have to adopt a new platform for each site or department. You just need to set OneWorld up to run on each type of server.

How to Add an Enterprise Server

Your first enterprise server will be configured as part of the installation plan for your OneWorld system. However, business needs change, and you may have to add another enterprise server later. This section assumes that you already have a OneWorld system installed and running. You have now decided that you need another enterprise server.

To add an enterprise server, log on to a client machine and type **GH9611** in the fast path. You will now be on the advanced operations menu. From this menu, double-click on Machine Identifications, P9654A. You will now be at the Work With Machine Identification screen. Click Find on this screen to show your locations. Expand your location and you will now see folders for your workstations, deployment servers, enterprise servers, data servers, Java application servers (JAS), Windows terminal servers, and remote locations. Expand the enterprise server section. You will see your enterprise server in the window, as shown here.

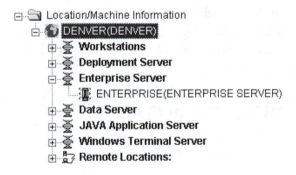

Click the Add button, which will take you to the Enterprise Server Revisions screen, shown in Figure 5-6. It is from this screen that you can tell the system about your new enterprise server. When you add an enterprise server, the information will be stored in the F9650 machine master and F9651 machine detail tables. Let's go

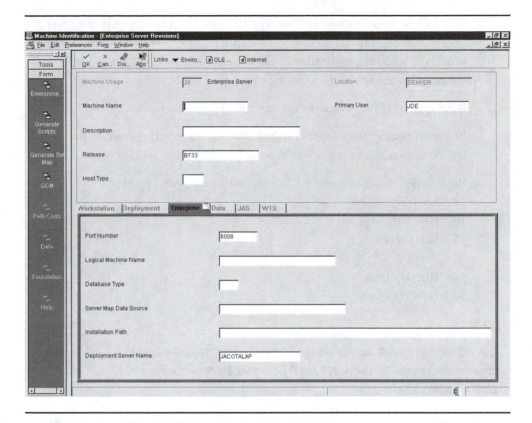

FIGURE 5-6. Adding an enterprise server

over the specific fields you will need to populate to add an enterprise server into
the system.

- **Machine Usage** This field will be filled in automatically, since you highlighted
  the enterprise server directory before clicking Add. If this field is not filled in,
  enter **20** in the field, for enterprise server. This field is used to tell the system
  what the machine's function will be.

- **Machine Name** Enter the name of the machine that is going to be your new
  enterprise server in this field. If you are adding an enterprise server that uses

a UNIX operating system, you need to place the machine name in the correct case in this field. If you do not, you will not be able to see your jobs in the Work With Servers application because OneWorld will poll tables for the machine name using the wrong case.

- **Description**   Enter a description of your enterprise server.

- **Release**   Specify the release of OneWorld that the enterprise server has loaded onto it. An example would be B733.2 for release B733 level 2.

- **Host Type**   Enter one of the following values for your host type:
  - 10   AS400
  - 20   HP9000
  - 25   Sun Solaris
  - 30   RS6000
  - 40   Digital Alpha
  - 50   Intel NT

N O T E

Since you can add records for workstations from this screen, you will also see entries for client machines running NT and Windows 95. Do not use these when adding an enterprise server.

- **Location**   This field contains the name of the location where you are adding your enterprise server—for example, you could have a location named corporate for your headquarters' machines.

- **Primary User**   This is the primary user for this machine. Enter **JDE** in this field.

- **Port Number**   This is the port OneWorld will use when listening for requests from client machines. This port number will default in depending on your release of OneWorld. Only change this port number if you are running multiple releases of OneWorld in parallel.

- **Logical Machine Name**   This is a logical name for your machine. If you are running multiple releases of OneWorld on the same server, you will need to have different logical names and port numbers so the OneWorld system can keep track of what release you are trying to use. For example, if your enterprise server is named FINANCIAL, you could call the second release of OneWorld on the server FINB733.

- **Database Type**   This field contains the type of database you are using. The acceptable values for this field are:
  - A   Access
  - D   DB/2
  - I   Client Access
  - O   Oracle
  - S   SQL Server

- **Server Map Data Source**   This is the name of the data source that will contain tables necessary to run UBEs on a server. Some of these tables are F986101 and F98611. These tables tell OneWorld where to find its data when you submit a UBE to the server. See the section regarding environments and OCM in Chapter 2 for further explanation.

- **Installation Path**   This is where the OneWorld host code is installed on your enterprise server. If your server is an AS/400, this will be a library name. If your enterprise server is running NT, this will be a drive and a directory structure.

- **Deployment Server Name**   This is the name of your deployment server. This field is necessary because OneWorld will generate an INI file on this deployment server. This INI file will then be copied to your enterprise server when you install your host code.

Now that you have filled in these fields, click Form Environments. You will be on the Machine Environment Revisions screen. Click in the grid under the Environments column and you will be given a visual assist. Click the visual assist and choose the environments you would like to be able to run reports for on this enterprise server.

Inside and Out

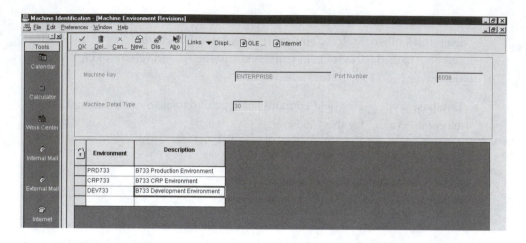

Click OK and you will be back on the Enterprise Server Revisions screen. From this screen, click OK; you will now be on the Data Source Setup screen, where you can add your data server map data source. Most of the screens will default in, as you can see in the next illustration.

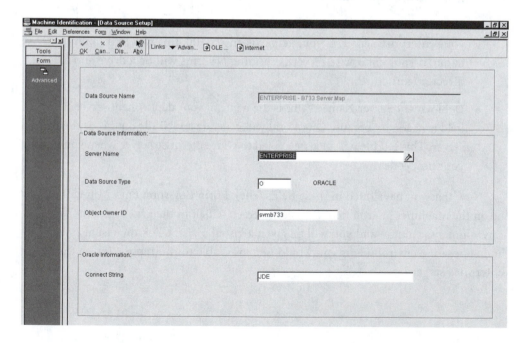

You will only need to verify most of this screen. The data source name, server name, data source type, and object owner ID will all fill in automatically. The only fields you will normally have to change on this screen are Connect String, if you are adding an Oracle data source, and Object Owner ID. You change the Object Owner ID so you do not overlay current server map tables.

N O T E

B73.3.1 does not allow two server map data sources to have the same owner even if they were on two different machines and databases. This is part of the design of the software.

If you are adding a new Oracle data source, click Form Advanced to go to the Data Source Revisions screen. Then click Form Default Database; this will take you to the Revise Table And Data Source Sizing screen. Enter the names of your table space and index space. The index and table space can either be an existing index and table space or you can add new ones. This would be up to your database administrator, as the number of table spaces and index spaces affects how they administer the database.

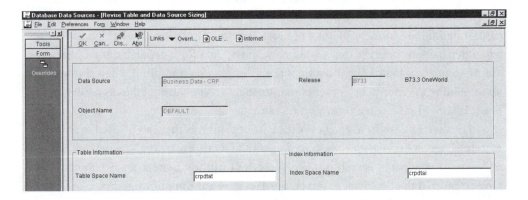

Click OK to return to the Data Source Revision screen. Click OK again to return to the Data Source Setup screen. Click OK. This will take you back to the Work With Locations And Machines screen. You have now told the system about your new enterprise server, but you are not done yet. You still need to generate an INI file for this server, and you will need to create the server map tables, which the enterprise server needs to run UBEs. To accomplish this, from the Work With Locations And Machines screen, click Find. Expand the enterprise server directory and highlight the name of your new enterprise server. Click Select; this will take you to the Revise Enterprise Server screen. Click Form Generate Scripts. This will generate the INI file for your new enterprise server. This file will be located on your deployment server in the \B733\HOSTS*PLATFORM\MACHINENAME* directory. This INI file will later be copied to the enterprise server when you install your host code.

Once the process of generating the scripts completes, click Form Generate Server Map. This will actually generate RDB tables in your new server map data source. Don't forget to have your database user, Client Access, or Microsoft ODBC data sources or Oracle connect string created before this step is run. Once this process completes, you only have one thing left to do to complete adding your new enterprise server: installing your host code. The host code is the OneWorld software that runs on the enterprise server. To install the host code, put your host code CD in your enterprise server's drive and answer the questions you will be prompted for on the screen.

When to Add an Enterprise Server

The only time to add an enterprise server is when you have a true business need. One example of when you would add a new enterprise server is if your current server cannot handle the number of current users. Another reason would be if you want to add a departmental server that would contain the data for a department and have the ability to process logic. The most important thing to keep in mind when thinking about adding an enterprise server is that the new server should address a business need. It should give you a return on investment.

In this section, we have gone over the type of platforms that can be used as an enterprise server and what needs to be done to add a new enterprise server. This process will become invaluable as your business grows and you add more users. So now that we have completed the deployment server, the data server, the application server, and the enterprise server, surely that's all you need to know concerning servers and OneWorld, right? No! There are specialty servers that perform a host of functions to add additional functionality and system configurability. One of these specialty servers uses Microsoft Windows Terminal Server Edition and is often referred to as a terminal server.

Windows Terminal Server

In this section, we discuss how a Windows terminal server solution may be able to assist your company in meeting the needs of your users. Windows terminal server, like the Web server, is a powerful tool for companies that have remote locations or traveling users. We have had several clients who have set this up, and their administrators can perform such tasks as monitoring the system, updating user passwords, and setting up security, all from a remote location. This means your administrator may not have to drive into work at three in the morning! In this section, we will cover the following:

- Windows terminal server defined
- Configuration
- Special considerations

Windows Terminal Server Defined

Windows terminal server (WTS) is software Microsoft brought to the market that allows multiple users to use applications running on one server. They can use that server's processing power to complete their work. The OneWorld system has been written so it can take advantage of the Windows terminal server functionality. The basic idea behind a OneWorld Windows terminal server is that it is a single FAT OneWorld client installation on a system running WTS. The system is coded so that multiple users can use the same client installation, meaning that these users are using the same application specifications. We will go into detail about this TAM sharing a little later. OneWorld also has special WTS environments that you can set up. Since you have multiple users hitting this single machine, you want to maximize its performance. These special WTS environments map business functions to run on your enterprise server so your WTS server has to do less processing and is faster for your users.

Configuration

It is important to remember that you are really just setting up a FAT OneWorld client installation to run on Microsoft's Windows terminal server software. However, since you are setting up the client installation on a different operating system than Windows NT or Windows 95/98, you will need to follow a slightly different procedure for installing the OneWorld software. In this section, we discuss what a Windows terminal server can do for your business, when you would want to use a WTS, how to set one up, and special considerations for Windows terminal servers.

Let's first take a look at what a WTS configuration can do for your business. WTS systems are most commonly added to provide service to remote production users. These users are normally the users who enter your sales orders, invoices, pick slips, and other day-to-day functions of your company. These users are also normally located in a remote

Inside and Out

location. One example might be a company that has two sites, one main location where their enterprise server is located and one remote location where their users are located. The remote users would then be hitting the WTS server in the main location. The WTS server is what does the actual processing, so users are only passing commands and screens across the network, not database calls. The Windows terminal server is what actually makes the calls to the database. This means that users do not use that much of the WAN's bandwidth. A good rule of thumb is that every user connecting to a Windows terminal server will use 24KB of your WAN's bandwidth. This figure may go up or down a little bit depending on your users. To emphasis this point, let's take a look at Figure 5-7.

The example shows a typical reason to set up a Windows terminal server. Your company's main location, which is where your enterprise server is located, is in Denver. Atlanta is your second location, where you have some users. In the past, you might have set up an actual enterprise server for the Atlanta location. We encourage you not to do this unless you have a very specific need for a full enterprise server in your remote location. By installing a Windows terminal server, you do not need to have system administrators in both locations, you get more bang for your buck on hardware, and you do not have to pay for and administer two databases. This is because your database and your Windows terminal server are all located in Denver, so administration of the system is much easier and less expensive. The hardware costs are normally less as well, since your users in Atlanta do not need machines as powerful as those of your users in Denver who are using fat clients.

As you can see, the users in Atlanta are only sending screens and commands over the WAN. The actual processing of their requests is handled in Denver. This is because the Windows terminal server is the machine that actually makes the database calls. Since this machine is on the same LAN as your enterprise server, these requests are handled much faster. It is also important to note that all of the Atlanta user's logic or UBE requests are being sent by the Windows terminal server to your enterprise server. This means your enterprise server is actually processing all the reports out of Atlanta. This is because when you set up a Windows terminal server environment in OneWorld, you will not be allowed to run UBEs locally. Running a UBE locally would mean that the Windows terminal server in Denver would actually be responsible for processing that UBE. The software does not allow this, since running reports can be processor-intensive and you have multiple users hitting this machine requesting their data. If you ran a report locally on your WTS machine, your end users would see serious performance degradation.

Another feature of the OneWorld Windows terminal server environments is that your business functions will be mapped to run on the enterprise server. What this means in a

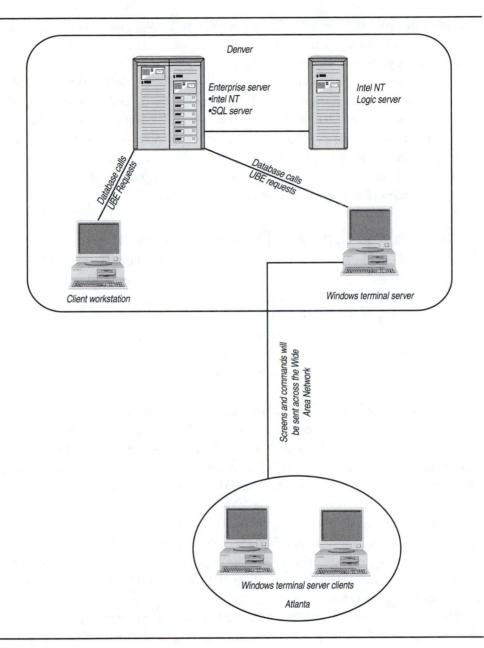

FIGURE 5-7.   Multiple site architecture

nutshell is that you are taking any process that will slow the WTS server down and running it on your enterprise server instead. This helps reduce the load on the WTS machine and it performs better.

The final point that needs to be made on this diagram is that the logic server has been added. If you add logic servers, which will take some processing load off your enterprise server, you can maximize your Windows terminal server. The reasoning behind this is that you can map an entire environment to the logic server and this will then take some load off your enterprise server. The only downside to this configuration is that you have to maintain one more server, and your logic server will need to make calls to your enterprise to retrieve data for reports run on the logic server.

Installing Windows Terminal Server

Now that we have discussed a common configuration for a Windows terminal server, let's go into some detail on how to actually install it. We'll cover this section in a fairly detailed manner as we do not feel that the subject is currently well documented. We will assume that you already have the Windows terminal server operating system, the correct MDAC levels, and the correct Windows terminal server service packs applied. This information constantly changes, so when you're installing a WTS be sure to visit J.D. Edwards' Web site for the most current recommendations on service pack and MDAC levels.

The first thing to realize is that you are going to be installing a normal OneWorld client on a Windows terminal server machine. The only things that will be different on this client as opposed to a normal client installation is that multiple users will be able to share OneWorld's specification or TAM files, and your environment for WTS will have UBEs and business functions mapped to run on your enterprise server.

To start your installation, log on to the Windows terminal server machine as a user with administrative privileges. This is important since the installation process needs to update the registry, and this can only be done by users with administrative privileges on the machine. Once you have logged on to your WTS, go to Start | Settings | Control Panel. Double-click on Add/Remove Programs. You will be at the Add/Remove Programs dialog box, as shown in Figure 5-8.

On the Install/Uninstall tab, click the Install button. You will be prompted to insert the floppy disk or CD for the product. Ignore this message and click the Next button. Your drive will be checked, so be sure it is empty. You will be on a screen that informs

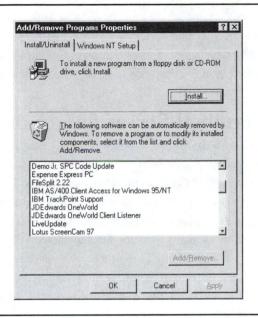

FIGURE 5-8.   Add/Remove Programs dialog box

you that Windows was unable to locate your program and asks if you would like to find it yourself. Click the Browse button to find your program through the Windows Explorer interface. Connect to your deployment server and find the Install Manager.exe program, which is located under the OneWorld client install directory, for B733.1 and above. Choose this program, and the client installation will look like a "normal" client installation, meaning you will be prompted to select a package.

The reason you are installing OneWorld through Add/Remove Programs is so that all your users can run the software. If the software is installed outside the Add/Remove Programs screen, only the user who installed the software will be able to use it. This is because when OneWorld is installed correctly on a WTS machine, each new user who logs on to the WTS machine will get his or her own directory structure, which will contain a OneWorld INI file for that user. If the software is not installed correctly, this INI file will not be created for your users, and only the user who installed the OneWorld client will be able to use the system. Once the client installation is complete, you should be able to log on to the system.

Inside and Out

NOTE

If you have not set up a WTS environment you may want to set up a WTS environment to improve the performance of your WTS server. See the section "Environments" in Chapter 2 for more information on adding an environment.

Windows Terminal Server Environment

Once you have set up a WTS environment, you will need to ensure that this environment is known by your enterprise and logic servers. If you remember from our discussions of enterprise servers and the Object Configuration Manager, you will need OCM mappings in the server map for any environment you want to install on your enterprise server. To verify that these mappings exist, log on to a client and type **GH9611** in the fast path. You will now be at the Advanced Operations menu. Double-click on the Object Configuration Manager P986110. You will be prompted to select the system or server map data source; choose the server map data source for the enterprise or logic server you are interested in. This will take you to the Work With Object Mappings screen. Type the name of your WTS environment in the yellow grid line above Environments and click Find, or use the visual assist to select your environment. If you see mappings for this environment, all you need to do is assign this environment to your users. If you do not see this environment, you need to ensure that it is added into your server map. This is covered in detail in the section "How to Add an Enterprise Server" earlier in this chapter.

TIP

If you follow J.D. Edwards' standards, all Windows terminal server environments will start with a W.

You now have a Windows terminal server installed and a WTS environment set up. The only thing that has not happened is that OneWorld does not know about this WTS for the machine identification program. The fact that this machine doesn't appear will not affect its functionality. However, if you want this machine to show up so you can see what machines are on your system at a glance, you can do this through the Machine Identification program on menu GH9611, Advanced Operations. Go to this menu and double-click on the Machine Identification program. This will take you to the Work With Locations And Machines screen. Click Find and expand your location. You will see directories for workstations, deployment servers, enterprise servers, data servers, Java servers, Windows terminal servers, and remote locations.

Highlight the Windows Terminal Server directory and click the Add button. You will now be on the WTS Server Revisions screen, shown in Figure 5-9. Most of this screen will be filled in for you. You only need to fill in a couple of fields.

- **Machine Usage**   This field should be set to 35 for Windows terminal server. This field tells OneWorld what the machine's function is going to be.

- **Location**   This is the name of your location. A location can be set up to describe your installation for geographic areas, such as Denver in our earlier example.

- **Primary User**   This is the primary user of the machine. Enter **JDE** in this field.

- **Machine Name**   Enter the name of your Windows terminal server in this field.

- **Description**   The description of the server; for example, Windows terminal server for Atlanta.

- **Release**   The release of the software running on the WTS machine.

- **Host Type**   This will default in as 50 for Intel NT. This is because Windows terminal server runs on the Intel platform.

- **Installation Path**   This is the actual location of the OneWorld client installation on your WTS machine. For example, if you installed the client software to your C drive, the value would be C:\b7.

Once you have entered the information on this last field, click OK. This will save the information so you can easily see how your system is configured from the Machine Identification program.

Special Considerations

For this section to be complete, we must address some special considerations to take into account when using a Windows terminal server solution. WTS is a great solution for many businesses that have remote users or users who travel. However, it does have some limitations: all UBEs must be run on an enterprise server, you cannot do any type of development work on Windows terminal server, and you must deploy packages to this machine in a specific manner.

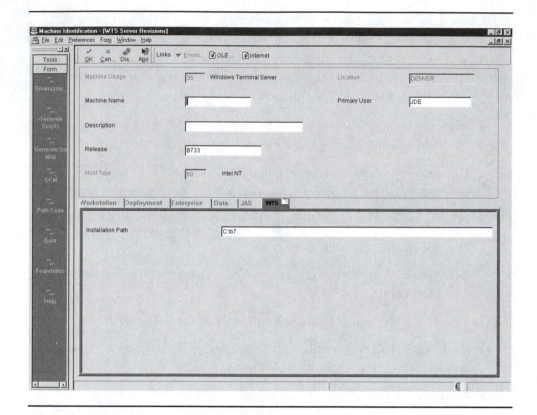

FIGURE 5-9. WTS Server Revisions screen

N O T E

In OneWorld Xe you will be allowed to create custom reports and versions on a Windows terminal server. This is a brand new feature with this release of the software. However, it's the only type of development work that you will be allowed to perform on Windows terminal servers.

UBEs

Windows terminal server environments are mapped to run UBEs on enterprise servers, because if you run a job locally on a WTS machine, your users will see performance issues. This is why J.D. Edwards ships its WTS environments with UBEs mapped to enterprise servers. What this means is that if your enterprise server cannot run jobs for some reason, your remote users will not be able to process any UBEs. This is different from a normal client machine, which can run UBEs locally. If you install a WTS server, you will need to first ensure that your administrator can keep the host services running correctly on your enterprise server.

Development

Another special consideration for a WTS machine is that you cannot develop on this machine. This means that the WTS machine can only be used by production users. Production users are end users who only enter data and run reports; they do not develop any custom applications or reports. The reason that you cannot perform development on a WTS machine is that you would be modifying specification files that other users would be attempting to use at the same time. This would cause your specification or TAM files to become corrupt.

TAM Files

This sharing of the TAM files is what can cause another issue. The issue has been called recursive versions. An example of what would happen in this case is where two users launch the same version of the same UBE report. User 1 physically completes the data selection and processing options first. However, prior to clicking OK on the Printer Select screen, this user answers the phone. While User 1 is busy, User 2 starts the same version of the same UBE and makes a different data select, then completes the UBE submission, including clicking OK on the Printer Select screen. User 2 gets the report and is very happy with the results. User 1, in the meantime, completes the phone call and clicks OK to submit his UBE to the server. When User 1 gets the report, he finds that he actually got User 2's data selection and processing options. This is because on versions of OneWorld prior to B7332, the UBE submission process waited until the very end to pick up the processing options and data selection from the local TAM files. This is why User 1 got the wrong report. During his initial process, he updated the terminal server's TAM files. Unfortunately, User 2 provided a more recent update before User 1 completed the submission. Ugly, isn't it? Take heart—this issue is addressed in B733.2.

Deploying Packages

Deploying packages to a Windows terminal server is also something that must be taken into consideration. Once the initial OneWorld installation has been performed on a WTS machine, most clients will assign packages to be deployed to their machines. (See Chapter 10 for further details on assigning packages.) This can cause a problem with WTS machines. When you deploy a package, you are updating the specification files on the WTS machine—the same specification files your users are accessing. To avoid corrupting these specification files, you deploy the package to your WTS machine when only one user is logged on. To do this, use the Windows terminal server operating system to ensure that all your users are logged off the system. Once your users are logged off the system, log on to the WTS machine as your administrative user. This is because your user will need privileges to update the registry. Sign on to OneWorld and you will see the package you set up to deploy to your WTS machine. Select the package and it will install. Once the installation is complete, you can allow your other users to log in. If you are a 24-hour shop, you would need to schedule a time to take the WTS server offline to deploy your packages. This should not take a lot of time, and it is absolutely necessary that you deploy your modifications and code changes to your WTS users.

The final special consideration we will discuss is using a third-party software called Citrix. Citrix gives you additional functionality for your WTS end users. You may or may not want to purchase Citrix, since it can be expensive depending on the number of users for whom you need to obtain a license. If you are considering Citrix, you should see if the functionality is worth the price tag.

In this section, we have discussed what a Windows terminal server can do for your business. We have gone over a common configuration of this system. We have also discussed that a Windows terminal server is just a client installation on a WTS machine. The details of installing OneWorld onto this type of platform have been discussed. Finally, the special considerations that apply to a Windows terminal server implementation were covered. These considerations must be taken into account when you are thinking about rolling a Windows terminal server into your configuration. There is only one other type of server that we want to go into detail about: the Web server, another method of making a very thin client (and in this case, we call it a zero client).

Web Servers

A Web server, also called a Java server, allows you to run OneWorld over a WAN without severe performance degradation. The idea behind the Web server is to allow your users to connect to the system no matter where they are, through a Web browser. This section will cover:

- Definition of a Web server
- Configuration

- Setting up a Web server

- Special considerations

Definition of a Web Server

Once you set up a Web server, your users can connect to your system from anywhere in the world through a Web browser. This is a very powerful tool for your business if you have isolated users on a WAN or if some of your users travel and need to dial in to the system. It also can assist you in keeping your maintenance costs low, as the Web server is located in one spot. Thus you do not need to have your support personnel spread all over the country or the world. They can maintain the system from one central location.

A OneWorld Web server can be set up for HTML or Java scripts, depending on your preference. Currently, Web servers can only be set up on a Intel NT box. However, it seems that J.D. Edwards is moving to allow users to run their Web server on multiple platforms, such as the AS/400. There has been talk of J.D. Edwards testing their Web server software with Apache. Apache allows you to have more platforms than just an Intel NT server as your Web server—the prime example would be an AS/400. The e-business solution is definitely having an effect on the market, and J.D. Edwards is trying to respond to this demand. This means their current Web software will be changing and adding functionality quickly over the next couple of years. Keep your eye on this solution— if it does not meet your current needs, it may in the future.

Configuration

When you are thinking about setting up a Web server you should be asking yourself a few questions. Will this server help my users meet their business needs? Do I have a server large enough to handle my users' requests? What kind of resources will it take to support this type of server?

These questions will help you set up your Web server correctly. The first thing to do is ensure that this server will address a business need. The most common need that Web servers or Windows terminal servers are used to address is WAN users. A Web server will allow your remote users to connect at a higher speed than if they had installed a full client. Web servers also help reduce maintenance costs, as your server will be in your main location, so you don't have to have an IT staff at every one of your locations across the country or around the world. We will address this type of configuration in detail a little later.

Inside and Out

Next, you must ensure that your server meets the minimum technical requirements. These requirements change from release to release, so check J.D. Edwards' Web site for current requirements. If your machine only has the minimum requirements, it will be able to function as a Web server, but may not deliver the performance you want. Remember, when you see "minimum requirements" they really do mean minimum requirements needed to merely run the system, not necessarily run it well.

After you have ensured that you have meet the machine requirements, you will need to train your administrator in the use of Web servers. The technology is advancing very quickly, so this administrator will need to constantly be looking for new information on the subject. This will help ensure that your company is in a position to take advantage of any new functionality.

Figure 5-10 shows a typical Web server configuration.

In this example, the majority of your system is located in Denver, with a few remote users in Atlanta. Let's first take a close look at Denver. Your enterprise server is an HP9000 with an Oracle database. This is where your business's data is being stored. The clients' machines in Denver, which are fat clients, are making direct calls to this database, since they are going over a LAN. However, making a call from a fat client in Atlanta would be incredibly slow, so you have installed a Web server in Denver to serve your users at the Atlanta location. The Web server in Denver acts like a fat client. It passes the requests to the database for the users in Atlanta. The users in Atlanta only send a minimal amount of data across the WAN.

It is also important to note that there is not a server or a database located in Atlanta. This means you would not need a system administrator in Atlanta, since the clients from this site are only using Web browsers to connect. Your support staff can remain located in Denver, which helps reduce your cost of maintaining the system.

Now that we have discussed the high-level aspects of using a Web server, let's dig a little deeper into how you would actually set up the server. Please note that because of the pace at which this technology is changing, you will need to obtain complete, current installation documentation (see J.D. Edwards' Web site).

Setting Up a Web Server

The following is a brief checklist to help ensure your success when installing a Web server. We will address each of these points in more detail later.

- Make sure your enterprise server meets the minimum technical requirements published by J.D. Edwards.

- Confirm that your enterprise server is running correctly.

- Verify that you have Microsoft IIS installed.

- Make sure WebSphere is installed on your Web server.

- Confirm that a OneWorld client is installed on your Web server. (This step is now optional, but it can aid in troubleshooting.)

- Install the Web server product from the CD.

- Make sure you have an environment for your Web server.

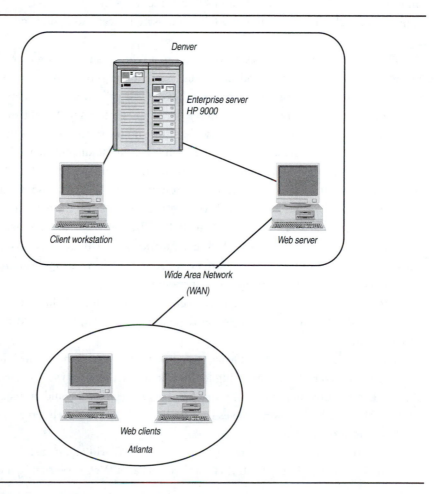

FIGURE 5-10.   Typical Web server configuration

The first point in the checklist is to verify that the machine you have chosen for your Web server meets the minimum technical requirements. You can find these published on J.D. Edwards' Web site, since they change from release to release. If you meet only the minimum, you may not see the performance you would like. Ask yourself not only how many users are going to be using this server today, but also how many users may be hitting this server in the future. This will help ensure that your Web server is properly sized.

The second point in the checklist is to confirm that your enterprise server is functioning correctly. The reason this is important is that a Web server is similar to a Windows terminal server configuration. This means that all logic or UBEs will process on the enterprise server. Since you have multiple users hitting the Web server, you cannot run UBEs locally, as this is a CPU-intensive process and your end users would see performance issues.

The other way that a Web server is similar to a Windows terminal server is that when a user makes a request for data very little is sent across the WAN. The Web server is where the actual processing is done, and the database call is then made across a LAN. If you refer back to Figure 5-10 you will see that your end users in Atlanta are calling the Web server in Denver. The Web server is sitting on the same LAN as your enterprise server. So when a call to the database is made, it is quicker than going across the WAN. The only thing that goes across the WAN is the results of the search, and these would be displayed in HTML or Java on the end user's browser. This is why it is so important that your enterprise server is functioning. If you cannot run UBEs on the enterprise server, none of your remote users can run UBE at all. It is also important to note that you can add an application server to process business functions and UBEs for your Web users. This will take some of the load off your enterprise server. Using an application server may help increase the performance of your system.

The third point in the checklist is to verify that IIS is installed on your Web server. OneWorld and your Web server depend on this software from Microsoft to function correctly.

The fourth point on the checklist is to make sure that WebSphere is installed correctly on your Web server. We are not going to document exactly how to set up WebSphere in this book. Currently, in release B773.1 and earlier, a Web server could only be an Intel server. J.D. Edwards is making moves to allow you to have your Web server on a variety of platforms, including the AS/400.

The fifth point is to confirm that you have a OneWorld client installation installed on your Web server. In the past, this was because all a Web server really boils down to is a OneWorld client installation that can be hit through a Web browser. Every user hitting the Web server, similar to a Windows terminal server configuration, uses the specifications or TAM files for that OneWorld client installation. The main difference is that instead of using a product like Windows terminal server, your end users are logging in through a normal Web browser. However, J.D. Edwards now offers a solution that is pure Java. This means you do not have to have a client workstation installed for the Web server to aid in troubleshooting, although this is still recommended if you are on a Windows NT platform.

But where do HTML and Java fit in, you ask? When you install a Web server, there are some special tables—F989999 and F989998 files—that need to be loaded. These tables contain the specifications for your applications to run in HTML or Java format. If you want to use P0101, for example, you will need to move those specifications from your client installation into these tables. This is done by running an executable, the APPGEN.EXE file. This file will be located under B7\system\bin32 on the JAS server, if you have installed a client on the Web server. If not, this can be accessed through a fat client workstation. This file will convert your objects into a format the Web server can use. This is done by the batch file process placing information into the F989998 and F989999 tables, which are used by the OneWorld Web server software.

T I P
_____

Currently, the F98998 and F989999 tables can only reside in an Oracle or SQL Server database. Due to issues with BLOB (binary large object) fields, they currently cannot reside on the AS/400.

The next step is to confirm that the Web server software is installed on your machine. To do this, put the Web or Java server CD into your server's CD-ROM drive. You will then be prompted with the OneWorld Installation Manager screen. Follow the steps to install the JAS server software

The final step in this checklist is to make sure your Web or JAS server has an environment set up. The Web server is very similar to the Windows terminal server in that it needs a special environment to function correctly. This environment will have business functions and UBEs mapped to run on the enterprise server. You want to take processing load off your Web server so that it can serve your end users more efficiently.

To ensure that the Web server's environment is set up correctly in OneWorld, log on to a client machine (the environment will not matter). Go to menu GH9053 and double-click on the environment master program, P0094. This will take you to the Work With Environments screen (see Figure 5-11). Click Find and you will see the current environments that have been installed on your OneWorld system. If you have followed the J.D. Edwards standards for environments, a J will precede all Web or JAS server environments (for example, JPRD733). If you do not see a Web server environment, you can add one.

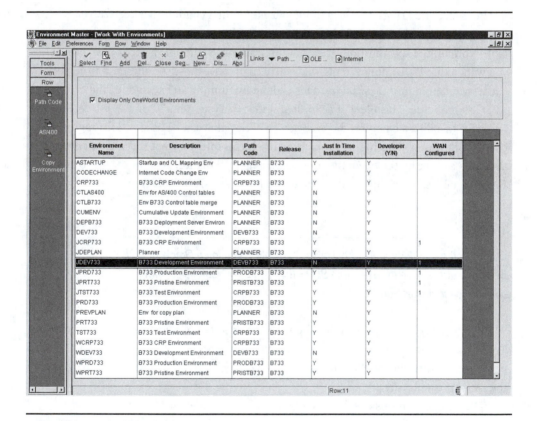

Environment Name	Description	Path Code	Release	Just In Time Installation	Developer (Y/N)	WAN Configured
ASTARTUP	Startup and OL Mapping Env	PLANNER	B733	Y	Y	
CODECHANGE	Internet Code Change Env	PLANNER	B733	Y	Y	
CRP733	B733 CRP Environment	CRPB733	B733	Y	Y	
CTLAS400	Env for AS/400 Control tables	PLANNER	B733	N	Y	
CTLB733	Env B733 Control table merge	PLANNER	B733	N	Y	
CUMENV	Cumulative Update Environment	PLANNER	B733	N	Y	
DEPB733	B733 Deployment Server Environ	PLANNER	B733	N	Y	
DEV733	B733 Development Environment	DEVB733	B733	N	Y	
JCRP733	B733 CRP Environment	CRPB733	B733	Y	Y	1
JDEPLAN	Planner	PLANNER	B733	Y	Y	
JDEV733	B733 Development Environment	DEVB733	B733	N	Y	1
JPRD733	B733 Production Environment	PRODB733	B733	Y	Y	1
JPRT733	B733 Pristine Environment	PRISTB733	B733	Y	Y	1
JTST733	B733 Test Environment	CRPB733	B733	Y	Y	1
PRD733	B733 Production Environment	PRODB733	B733	Y	Y	
PREVPLAN	Env for copy plan	PLANNER	B733	N	Y	
PRT733	B733 Pristine Environment	PRISTB733	B733	Y	Y	
TST733	B733 Test Environment	CRPB733	B733	Y	Y	
WCRP733	B733 CRP Environment	CRPB733	B733	Y	Y	
WDEV733	B733 Development Environment	DEVB733	B733	N	Y	
WPRD733	B733 Production Environment	PRODB733	B733	Y	Y	
WPRT733	B733 Pristine Environment	PRISTB733	B733	Y	Y	

FIGURE 5-11. Work With Environments screen

To add a Web server environment, copy an environment that is pointing to the business data you want your users to see. So if you want your users to hit your production data, for example, copy the environment pointing to your production data, usually the PRD733 environment. However, when you copy this environment you will need to specify that it is a WAN-enabled environment. We will briefly discuss how to copy the environment for the purpose of creating a Web server environment; for more information on OneWorld environments see the section "Environments" in Chapter 2.

Highlight the environment you want to copy and click Row Copy Environment. You will now be at the Copy Environment screen. Enter the name of your new environment and make sure the Copy Only *PUBLIC Records check box is checked. This will copy the environment and all the *PUBLIC OCM mappings. Once you have copied the environment, you will be back at the Environment Master screen. Select your new environment and you will be at the Revise Environment screen. On the right side of this screen is a check box labeled WAN Configured Environment. Make sure this box is checked. Click OK and you have added a Web server environment to your OneWorld system.

Now you need to ensure that your enterprise server knows about this environment. Client machines find their data from reading the F986101 table in the system data source, and UBEs running on an enterprise server find their data by reading the F986101 table in the server map data source. To make sure this environment exists in your enterprise server's server map, type **OCM** in the fast path or go to the GH9011 menu and double-click on the Object Configuration Manager program. When prompted to select a data source, select the server map data source. Place your Web server environment in the yellow QBE line above the Environment column. If you see records for your environment, you have mapping for the environment. If not, you will need to create these mappings in your server map.

To create the mappings in your server map for your new Web server environment, from a client machine, type **GH9611** in the fast path. You will now be at the Advanced Operations menu: double-click on the Machine Identification program. Click Find and expand your location. You will be presented with directories for workstations, deployment servers, enterprise servers, data servers, Java application servers (Web

Inside and Out

servers), and Windows terminal server. Expand the Enterprise Server directory, highlight the name of your enterprise server, and click Select. You will now be at the Enterprise Server Revisions screen. Click Form Environments and you will be presented with the Machine Environments Revisions screen, shown in Figure 5-12. This is a list of the environments you have set up to be able to run logic or UBEs on the enterprise server. Place your cursor in the blank line under the Environment column. You will be presented with a visual assist. Click the visual assist and you will be taken to the Work With Environments screen. Select your Web server environment. Click OK; this will save your change and take you back to the Enterprise Server Revisions screen.

The next step should be done after-hours, since it will change mapping on your enterprise server and you do not want to disrupt your production users. Click Form

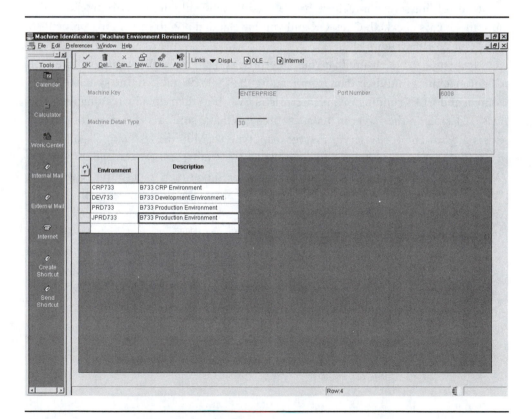

FIGURE 5-12. Machine Environment Revisions Screen

Generate Server Map. This will generate the mappings in the F986101 table in your server map data source.

N O T E

You will want to perform a "porttest" against this new environment on your enterprise server, and you should bring your host services down and back up again before using the new environment. This is because the F986101 table is cached upon startup.

You now have an environment to which you can assign your users. The last check you perform is to ensure OneWorld knows about your Web server. To do this, run the Machine Identification program located on menu GH9011, click Find, expand your location, and expand the Java Application Server directory. If you see the name of your Web server, you are set; if not, highlight the Java Application Server directory and click Select. You will now be at the JAS Server Revisions screen.

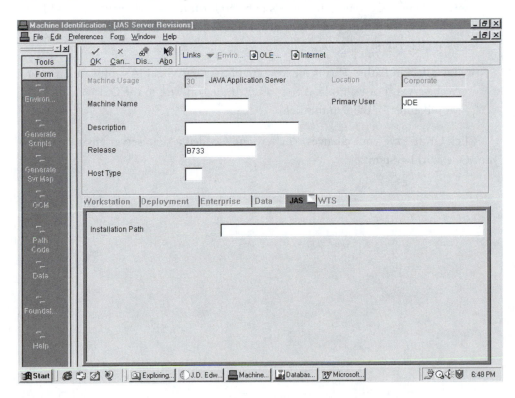

The JAS Server Revisions screen contains the following fields:

- **Machine Usage**   This should be set to 30 for Java Application server. This field tells OneWorld what the machine's purpose is.

- **Location**   This is the location where the machine is located. Locations are logical names, such as Denver, which can be set up to show your system's configuration.

- **Machine Name**   This is the name of your Web server.

- **Primary User**   This is the primary user of the machine. Enter **JDE** in this field.

- **Description**   Enter a description that is meaningful to you—for example, Dallas Web server.

- **Release**   This is the release of OneWorld that is running on the Web server, such as B7331.

- **Host Type**   Currently, this needs to be 50 for Intel NT. However, this will change in the future as J.D. Edwards is moving to allow other platforms to act as Web servers.

- **Installation Path**   This is the location of the OneWorld JAS software on your Web server. For example, if you installed the software to the D drive, you would enter D:\B7*xx* in this field.

Click OK to save your changes. You have now added a Web server environment to your OneWorld system.

Law of the West

Possible Issues with Mapping Master Business Functions to a Server for Performance

We have talked about setting business functions for a Web server to run on your enterprise server. This will increase your performance on the Web server. However, prior to OneWorld Xe there is a problem you may run into when attempting this configuration.

Certain business functions are coded to only run locally on a workstation. That is a problem if you are going to use a UNIX or AS/400 system as your enterprise server. What you can do is build all of your type 2 business functions on your enterprise server (a type 2 business function can run either on the enterprise server or the client workstation). You can determine a business function's type by looking at it in the object librarian application.

Building these business functions can be accomplished by specifying them in a server package build. This process has been more successful when done on Windows NT servers. If you are running a UNIX or AS/400 implementation, you may want to add an NT applications server and map your Web server's master business functions to it. This still leaves about 140 business functions that will not run on the enterprise server prior to OneWorld Xe.

If you run across one of these client-only business functions, you have two choices. One is to have someone familiar with the business function and the Web product come out and modify the business function to run on the enterprise server. This is accomplished by cutting out the code that is specific to the client workstation. The second choice is not to run the application that calls the client-only business function on your Web server until OneWorld Xe, where the issue has been addressed.

Special Considerations

As with a Windows terminal server configuration, there are some special considerations to take into account when setting up a Web server. One of these special considerations is security. If your Web server is inside your firewall, you will want to ensure that only your users can access the server. How to set up a firewall and complete security for a Web server is outside the scope of this book. However, we feel it's necessary to bring this consideration to your attention.

Finally, we need to address the hot topic of e-business. Currently, with release B733.2 and below, J.D. Edwards is not shipping a ready-made electronic storefront. However, they are shipping the tools to create this storefront. As the features and functionality of this piece of OneWorld are changing so rapidly, we will not go into how to set up an electronic storefront. If this is something you are interested in, obtain current documentation on the process from J.D. Edwards.

Summary

In this chapter, we have discussed what the different types of OneWorld servers can do for you. We have discussed the deployment, data, application, enterprise, Windows terminal, and Web servers. We have touched on the uses of these types of servers and why they are important to your business.

The deployment server is used for administering the system and deploying the OneWorld software out to your enterprise. Data servers are used to store your business's data. As we discussed, certain businesses may need them more than others. It all depends on how you need to configure your system to meet your business needs.

Application servers are a great way to offload some of your processing from the enterprise server or your client workstations. These servers can be set up to be workhorses for your enterprise and can deliver serious performance gains.

The enterprise server allows you to store all your data and run reports on the server. This is by far one of the most commonly used server types within OneWorld.

The Windows terminal server offers a great WAN solution. These machines allow users to access OneWorld across networks without an outlandish amount of bandwidth being required. They also allow you to consolidate users onto one machine, which can help cut your costs since you are only paying for one large machine and the rest are smaller.

A Web server can do incredible things for your business. This type of solution, like the Windows terminal server solution, lets you keep your support staff in one location and have users all over the country or world. These users can access the OneWorld system by simply using a Web browser. This allows any of your remote locations and users easy access to your system. It also allows you to set up an electronic storefront.

The intention of this chapter was not to take you through every step of setting up these servers. It was to give you a good feel for what is available for you to consider. Some of these solutions may not meet your business needs; others may be perfect. It is these varied choices and options that will keep you ahead of your competition.

Inside and Out

CHAPTER 6

Coexistence: The Best of Both Worlds

Coexistence Rationalized

Database Objects Defined

Files that Are and Are Not Coexistent

Data Structures

Applications and Coexistence

Coexistence Administration
   and Maintenance Issues

OneWorld and World running together, sharing the same AS/400 with the same data, is called coexistence. Why would a company create two separate ERP systems and then have them share the same data sets? Wouldn't one system be enough? Some people might argue that coexistence adds unnecessary complexity. However, we disagree. We think coexistence makes sense from a business perspective for both J.D. Edwards and J.D. Edwards' Clients. While it is true that coexistence forces some additional technology-related maintenance requirements, it is also a bridge technology for many companies on World who would like to move into the client/server realm.

J.D. Edwards clearly holds the lion's share of the midrange AS/400 ERP market with approximately 4,000 clients on World. World is a 20-year-old AS/400-based host-centric ERP suite of applications accessible via an emulation program such as Client Access (commonly referred to as green screen access or a screen scrape). Following the rise of client/server technology, J.D. Edwards wisely decided to adapt to this dramatically growing market as well and so, developed OneWorld.

Even more wisely, J.D. Edwards decided to offer a migration path from World to OneWorld for their considerable market base. Coexistence allows World users to "seamlessly" migrate their enterprise solution without having to convert their data or adapt to a new hardware platform entirely.

A coexistent implementation is a unique animal. In this chapter, we will discuss the following in an attempt to help demystify coexistence and shed some light on how to best manage the challenges presented to the system administrator by this implementation approach:

- Coexistence rationalized

- Coexistence database objects defined

- Data that is and is not coexistent

- Applications that are and are not coexistent

- Coexistence administration and maintenance issues

Coexistence Rationalized

Many of the system administrators we meet who are about to face coexistence ask the same thing, "Why change?" Such administrators might feel better by examining the pros and cons of each system in the first place. Such an examination will yield an understanding of how these two ERP systems complement each other.

World Pros

- **Faster application execution in general than OneWorld**   World is written in RPG, a native programming language on the AS/400. All processing is on the AS/400 and all data resides on the AS/400. OneWorld, on the other hand, is written in C (both ILE and C++) and J.D. Edwards proprietary interpretive coding defined in object specifications (which is obviously not the issue). The issue is that OneWorld has logic components running over a network, and data goes through translation as it is handed off from J.D. Edwards middleware to Client Access middleware. Additionally, OneWorld performs field-level data verification rather than page-level verification as per World; hence, there is a high degree of network chatter in OneWorld.

- **HR/payroll**   World's got it; OneWorld did not have it until B733.2.

- **Stability**   Let's face it, World has been around a lot longer than OneWorld. More of the "Gotchas" have been worked out of World. Even though J.D. Edwards still releases new versions of World, it is arguably a more stable platform.

- **Ease of maintenance**   Because World has been around for as long as it has, there are many more people who are familiar with maintaining World. Support personnel for OneWorld are fewer and far between at this point, although we do see growth in the resource pool. Also, World is, generally speaking, a single box implementation and that one box must be an AS/400. The client side can be as simple as a dumb terminal or as complex as a screen-scrape running on a PC. OneWorld is not that simple.

World Cons

- **Soon to be discontinued**   At Focus 2000, J.D. Edwards agreed to extend World support for five more years. If World is not going to be around for that much longer anyway, it makes sense to start considering coexistence as a migration path to OneWorld.

Inside and Out

- **Inflexible**   World is in many ways less complex than OneWorld. Less complexity often means inflexibility. For instance, World is strictly AS/400 dependent. If a company were to acquire another company and wanted to bring up that company's data on the World platform, that company's data would need to be formatted and outfitted for DB/2 (notwithstanding, data conversions would have to occur in OneWorld as well, but the likelihood that the RDBMS would need to change would be lower). Additionally, the ability to perform Store and Forward processing does not exist in a World implementation. Coexistence introduces flexibility into your ERP implementations.

- **Interoperability and lack of third-party add-on modules**   Because World is on its way out, there are not as many vendors writing software for World at this point. Most of the development work taking place is for OneWorld.

OneWorld Pros

- **Flexibility**   OneWorld is truly the epitome of flexibility within the ERP community. It is the realization of the promise of client/server. OneWorld can run on numerous platforms, including AS/400, UNIX, and NT, *simultaneously*. OneWorld will also run on various database engines, including DB2, Oracle, SQL 7, and even Access, *simultaneously*. OneWorld includes fat clients, partial clients, store and forward clients, thin clients, and even zero clients as in the Java and HTML clients.

- **Continuing support from J.D. Edwards**   J.D. Edwards is phasing out World in support of OneWorld. In other words, J.D. Edwards' intention is to bring all their clients over to OneWorld anyway. Coexistence provides a pathway to the target ERP package, OneWorld.

- **Highly scalable**   Whereas World is clearly robust, OneWorld is robust and scalable. With its N-tier solution, your organization can easily realize the computing power equivalent of a Cray supercomputer. Perhaps this is an overstatement, but perhaps it is not. OneWorld can have infinite processing locations due to its client/server architecture. OneWorld can also have a multitude of data sources from which to draw data.

- **Availability of all World modules and new modules in the future**   As of B733.2, almost all of the modules found in World can be found in OneWorld as well. Additional modules will be added in OneWorld, but we cannot say with certainty that these same additional modules will be added in World.

- **Interoperability**   Beyond the modules found in OneWorld, a key component of J.D. Edwards' strategy for OneWorld is interoperability with competitive third-party products. Due to a very large and growing strategic alliance base, J.D. Edwards is building a powerful offering in the Internet marketplace for ERP, ASP, and now, second-phase ERP packages such as Active Supply Chain (ASC), Customer Relation Management (CRM), and other enabling technologies. Key interfaces at this point include Numetrix (which J.D. Edwards has purchased and integrated into OneWorld as Active Supply Chain), Siebel, BizTalk/Commerce Server, Net.Commerce, and others, with many exciting adapters to come.

- **Web integration**   OneWorld is keeping up with the Business Internet (Internet-related software) by offering not only the above interfaces but also a powerful development toolset to create Internet-based modifications, customizations, and full-blown development work. The OneWorld Java development toolset should provide the ease of a page development platform with the functionality of application server model development tools.

OneWorld Cons

- **Complexity**   All these great features come at a cost. One of the costs is the complexity involved in maintaining such a flexible system. Given that there are so many parts to OneWorld, and given that you have so much control over the where, when, and how of those components, it becomes easy to see how much attention must be paid to the internal OneWorld system maintenance as well as the architecture on which it runs. To achieve an N-tier solution in OneWorld, additional hardware, setup, and configuration is necessary. A 1,000-user WAN-based implementation is going to cost you a little more money than a 1,000-user WAN-based implementation of World. Keep in mind, though, World is not designed to accommodate that size user base without substantial modification.

- **Slower return of data request due to ODBC translation**   Although great progress is being made to increase the performance of OneWorld on AS/400, it is still not as fast as World due to the ODBC middleware translation that occurs and the network logic calls. However, with the release of V4R4, Client Access Express, and some of the new technologies being included in the AS/400, we would be surprised if performance were not actually equivalent to World or better. J.D. Edwards has demonstrated sub-second response time in simulated environments for well over 1,000 OneWorld users.

Conclusion

Two of the key factors that we see in favor of OneWorld are interoperability and J.D. Edwards' intention to phase out World. If the move is going to occur, the migration path called coexistence provides an easy step toward the direction of OneWorld without committing fully to OneWorld right from the start. Coexistence mitigates training issues, allows you to phase in OneWorld by module, and gives you the best of both worlds (so to speak).

Database Objects Defined

OneWorld runs on various database platforms, and terminology can become somewhat confusing. So we think it is best to define our terms prior to engaging in a full-blown discussion of coexistence.

Although it supports Interactive SQL and SQL Manager, AS/400 is still a list-processing system. On the other hand, MS SQL Server and Oracle are SQL engines rather than list-processing systems. The commonality can be seen in that these three systems are each based on the relational model as fathered by IBM's E.F. Cobb, who defined relational database theory. Cobb defined the following three basic terms: relation, attribute, and tuple. Table 6-1 identifies how the engines for AS/400, MS SQL Server, and Oracle refer to these elements:

When talking about coexistence, we will refer to database objects based on this chart. It is also important to remember that on AS/400 there are both physical and logical database files. Physical files contain data. Logical files are in the MS SQL/Oracle SQL vernacular, indexes, and as such contain pointers to data.

Relational Model	AS/400 List-Processing System	MS SQL/Oracle SQL Language
Relation	File	Table
Attribute	Field	Column
Tuple	Record	Row

TABLE 6-1.   Database Objects Defined

By definition, a file is an object with object type *File on the AS/400. A physical file is an object with the PF attribute. A logical file is an object with the LF attribute. Files are stored in libraries and each file has a set of file descriptions associated with it.

File descriptions describe the characteristics of the file and can be displayed with the Display File Descriptions command, which is written at the command line as **DSPFD FILE(**_filename_**)**. You can also type **DSPFD** on the command line and prompt the command by hitting F4.

Files that Are and Are Not Coexistent

Perhaps the best way to approach an understanding of coexistence is to understand the data sets on the AS/400 which are accessible by both World and OneWorld and those that are not. Generally World is installed before OneWorld. Both applications have an address book, both have system tables for user profiles, security, and so on, but in actuality they share fewer data sets than you might think. The two applications are not mirror images of each other, as Table 6-2 shows.

As you can see, from a shared data perspective coexistence is not a terribly complex concept. OneWorld and World can share UDCs, which are control tables, next numbers, which are also control tables, and business data.

Perhaps it is more telling to know the data sets that OneWorld and World do not share. You'll find these differences shown in Table 6-3.

Clearly, there is more that is not coexistent than there is that is coexistent. Yes, both OneWorld and World have data dictionaries, but they are not shared between the two applications. Also, the structure for the system data sets is so significantly different between OneWorld and World that these tables are not shared. There is no server map in

Inside and Out

OneWorld Data Source	Filename	File Description	World Library
AS400 Common	F0004	User-defined code types	XXXCOM
AS400 Common	F0005	User-defined codes	XXXCOM
AS400 Common	F0002	Next numbers – automatic	XXXCOM
AS400 Common	F00021	Next numbers by company/fiscal year – automatic	XXXCOM
Business Data	All business data files (other than those in the applications not coexistent, as shown in Table 6-4)	Are you kidding? No way are we going to list all 1,972 of them here.	XXXDTA

TABLE 6-2.   Coexistent Files

OneWorld Data Source	Filename	File Description	World Equivalent
Data dictionary	F9200 series	Provides description of all data elements in OneWorld files	F9200 series, including F00165. Generally found in XXXSEC library.
Object librarian	F9860 series	Maintains list of all objects in OneWorld	JDFOBJ
Central objects	F987* series and some others	Maintains binary large object specification data for OneWorld proprietary coding	JDFOBJ/JDFSRC
Server map	Replication tables, OCM, Data source Master, Process Master F986101, F98611, F986110, F986111, F986113	Provides system-level information in data from a server perspective	NA
System	Various	Provides system level information and data from a user perspective	XXXSEC

TABLE 6-3.   Non-Coexistent Files

OneWorld Data Source	Filename	File Description	World Equivalent
Control Tables	Menus (F0082, F00821, F0083, and F0084) are not shared	Menus and control table information other than UDCS.	XXXCOM
Versions	F983051 and F98306	Maintains data selection sequencing, data selection, processing options, processing option text for batch and interactive applications	

TABLE 6-3. Non-Coexistent Files*(continued)*

World. Central objects do not exist. No object librarian exists for World either. Are you starting to get the sense that there is a strong need for dual system maintenance with coexistence?

One other important point at this juncture: there are even limitations on the types of files that can be shared between World and OneWorld. Let's look at these limitations, move on to applications, and then come back to issues of administration and maintenance.

For more information, please refer to J.D. Edwards Knowledge Garden. Under the Product category, there is a link regarding migrating to OneWorld. This link points you to a page that has more information on coexistence.

Data Structures

Within the physical and logical database files that are coexistent, the data structure of the file is restricted on the World side. World tables are created in data description specification (DDS) format. OneWorld tables are created in SQL format. While OneWorld can read DDS, World cannot read SQL.

DDS is actually source code that defines record layout. A DDS file is called an externally described file because it is created by compiling the DDS source; therefore, the detailed descriptions of the file exist outside the program and are associated with the file itself. In the DDS, the record format is the logical description of the physical record; it describes how the group of fields are organized into the record. The following shows DDS for a file:

```
SEQNBR*...+... 1 ...+... 2...+... 3 ...+... 4...+... 5 ...+... 6...+... 7 ...+
100    A              R RCDFMT              TEXT('THE MASTER FILE')
200    A                CUSNUM    6   0       TEXT('CUSTOMER NAME')
.......
              ***********END OF SOURCE*************
```

There are of course other ways to create files on AS/400. The method used in OneWorld is called SQL. The SQL method is to use the SQL Create Table command to create the database files. The following demonstrates the SQL Create Table command:

```
Create table_name (column_name data type)
```

When you consider that OneWorld supports multiple database engines, it becomes clear why OneWorld creates tables using SQL. The SQL Create Table command on AS/400 is for all practical purposes equivalent to the SQL Create Table command for MS SQL and Oracle. Hence, duplication of development effort at J.D. Edwards is reduced.

Issues with Data Formats

Because OneWorld accesses AS/400 data via ODBC SQL-calls, OneWorld can read DDS tables. However, the problem with creating SQL tables on AS/400 in a coexistence environment is that World programs are compiled to look for DDS-formatted tables.

World programs do not access the data via ODBC-issued SQL calls. Rather, World accesses the data directly. When World programs try to read the SQL-created tables, you will get level checks and the World programs will not run.

How can you tell whether a table was created in DDS format or SQL? You can do a DSPFD *Library/Filename* to determine the format. In the case of a SQL-formatted file,

```
                        Display Spooled File
File  . . . . . :   QPDSPFD                    Page/Line   1/1
Control . . . . .        _____              Columns    1 - 78
Find  . . . . . .      _____
*...+....1....+....2....+....3....+....4....+....5....+....6....+....7....+...
   4/02/00                  Display File Description
DSPFD Command Input
   File  . . . . . . . . . . . . . . . . . . . :  FILE      F0002
      Library . . . . . . . . . . . . . . . . :            TESTCTL
   Type of information . . . . . . . . . . . :  TYPE      *ALL
   File attributes . . . . . . . . . . . . . :  FILEATR   *ALL
   System  . . . . . . . . . . . . . . . . . :  SYSTEM    *LCL
File Description Header
   File  . . . . . . . . . . . . . . . . . . . :  FILE      F0002
   Library . . . . . . . . . . . . . . . . . :            TESTCTL
   Type of file  . . . . . . . . . . . . . . :            Physical
   File type . . . . . . . . . . . . . . . . :  FILETYPE  *DATA
   Auxiliary storage pool ID . . . . . . . . :            01
Data Base File Attributes
   Externally described file . . . . . . . . :            Yes
   SQL file type . . . . . . . . . . . . . . :            TABLE
                                                          More...
```

FIGURE 6-1.   SQL Format File Definition

you will see under database file attributes a line saying "SQL file type… Table" as shown in Figure 6-1 (look at the bottom line of this figure).

In the case of a DDS-formatted file, you would see a "file level identifier" rather than SQL file type, as shown in Figure 6-2.

Coexistence Upgrade Points of Caution

The problem becomes particularly painful and evident with coexistence upgrades and updates. Coexistence upgrades and updates are prone to re-creating some control tables as SQL-created files. In particular, menu files can be overwritten. Also, although

```
                        Display Spooled File
 File . . . . . . :    QPDSPFD                    Page/Line    1/1
 Control . . . . .     _____                   Columns      1 - 78
 Find . . . . . .      _____
 *...+....1....+....2....+....3....+....4....+....5....+....6....+....7....+...
    4/02/00                  Display File Description
  DSPFD Command Input
     File . . . . . . . . . . . . . . . . . . : FILE       F0002
        Library . . . . . . . . . . . . . . . :            JDFDATA
     Type of information . . . . . . . . . . . : TYPE       *ALL
     File attributes . . . . . . . . . . . . . : FILEATR    *ALL
     System  . . . . . . . . . . . . . . . . . : SYSTEM     *LCL
  File Description Header
     File . . . . . . . . . . . . . . . . . . : FILE       F0002
     Library . . . . . . . . . . . . . . . . . :            JDFDATA
     Type of file  . . . . . . . . . . . . . . :            Physical
     File type . . . . . . . . . . . . . . . . : FILETYPE   *DATA
     Auxiliary storage pool ID . . . . . . . . :            01
  Data Base File Attributes
     Externally described file . . . . . . . . :            Yes
     File level identifier . . . . . . . . . . :            0960501211402
                                                              More...
```

FIGURE 6-2.   DDS Format File Definition

rare, at times some business data files which World accesses can be converted during the OneWorld table conversion process of the upgrade to SQL files. However, there are several ways to protect yourself from this problem created during a coexistence update/upgrade:

- It is important to make sure that OneWorld OCM mappings for menu files do not point to the libraries on AS/400 that house the World menu files.

- Identify each table that will go through some form of table conversion during the OneWorld portion of the coexistence upgrade. Then review all tables that are shared between World and OneWorld.

- Following a OneWorld upgrade/update process, examine each table that went through some form of table conversion during the OneWorld upgrade/update process to verify that its format has not been rendered unusable to World programs. The key will be to use the DSPFD command and verify that the files used by World are still in DDS format.

Applications and Coexistence

We have looked from the database level at coexistence and its restrictions and points of confluence. But to really understand the business impact of coexistence, it is important to examine coexistence from an application viewpoint. Key questions to ask are, "Are there any business application limitations?" and "Are there any business applications that can be run either from World or OneWorld simultaneously?"

Applications that Are Not Coexistent

One striking limitation of coexistence is the inability to run every application from both World and OneWorld. In other words, there are certain applications you must run as either World or OneWorld, but not both, as shown in Table 6-4.

Applications that Are Coexistent

Beyond these applications and not including the interoperability targets mentioned earlier, the base suite of applications offered by World and OneWorld are coexistent. Keep in mind, though, that application modifications made on one side of the fence are not recognized on the other side. Dual development is required in these cases.

Application Changes and Coexistence

World development objects are stored in JDFOBJ. The applications are a combination of RPG programs and CL programs. OneWorld development objects are stored in

Module	Application	Coexistent
Financials	Accounts receivable	Not coexistent – can only be World or OneWorld
Financials	Property management	Not fully coexistent – planned to be fully coexistent by B733.3
Human Resources	Benefits	Not fully coexistent
Human Resources	Payroll	Not coexistent

TABLE 6-4.   Non-coexistent applications

Inside and Out

Central Objects as proprietary runtime interpretive code in binary large object format and as business functions in C code. In other words, development objects are not shared between World and OneWorld.

Any application modifications that are made need to be made in both systems if the programs are to be coexistent.

The same holds true for files that are created in either system. If a program is modified in World to use a custom table, the same file definition must be entered in OneWorld specifications in order for OneWorld to recognize it. That file needs to be generated by World in order for World to use it, but the specification definition must exist in OneWorld for OneWorld to know about the table.

Coexistence Administration and Maintenance Issues

It would be nice and convenient if there were one central location to manage both of these ERP suites of applications simultaneously. However, given that such a toolset does not exist yet even in the case of coexistence, it is important to understand administration and maintenance issues in order to have a successful implementation. Considerable maintenance requirements exist for the coexistent organization. Even though most of the business data and relevant control data are shared between the two systems, the internal system architecture is unique and separate. Furthermore, the requirements from an O/S and third-party software perspective are different even though both systems exist on the same AS/400. We will examine the following topics in the following sections and will provide some best practices in managing the issues discussed:

- Library refresh, which includes *SQL package maintenance and file maintenance

- Data Dictionary maintenance

- AS/400 database security

- Dual system maintenance, which includes user administration and disk maintenance

Library Refresh

Both World and OneWorld can have multiple environments. Generic implementations will include production, CRP (or Prototype with OneWorld Xe, formerly B733.3), test, development, and pristine in both systems. During the pilot phase of an implementation, business process staging requires significant use of multiple environments. The more modules being implemented, the more data conversion to be performed, the more sites to be brought online, the more development work taking place, and the more users to be trained there are, the more there will be a need for multiple environments.

The use of multiple environments requires that libraries are periodically refreshed with "good" data. For instance, a training environment is prone to data corruption as users learn to work their way through the applications. To keep the training environment useful and meaningful, we recommend that you copy the data from the pilot phase setup environment, usually CRP. Or, perhaps you are converting data from your legacy system to your coexistent system. Typically, the data conversion would occur in the CRP environment and then be migrated forward to production. The method used to move that data into production is significantly different in a coexistent environment than it would be in a strict OneWorld or World implementation on AS/400.

In a OneWorld-only implementation, it is possible to copy entire data sets using OneWorld's R98403 Environment Database Creation program. The problem here is that this program deletes files, re-creates them in SQL format rather than DDS, and then copies the data (depending on Processing Option selection). World will not be able to read these tables.

Key points to keep in mind are that in order to refresh business data, you must also refresh next numbers (F0002) and possibly UDCs (F0004 and F0005) as well. The steps are as follows:

1. Notify users and schedule several hours for the data refresh. Users cannot be on the system working on either the source or the target environments during the refresh. If users are on the system, or if OneWorld services are running, the chance of a file lock is high and the file will copy over without the data or will fail to copy altogether.

Inside and Out

2. Identify libraries: It is critical that you verify both the World and the OneWorld libraries that are being shared for the source and target libraries. In OneWorld, you need to perform the following steps:

   a. Check OneWorld OCM: Look to see where OCM is directing users for business data and control tables, especially next numbers and UDCs for both the source and target environments. In a coexistent implementation, usually next numbers and UDCs will be in an AS/400 common data source rather than in a control table data source. You might also find that next numbers are also in business data if you are following an older World model.

   b. Verify OneWorld Data source: Verify the libraries maintained in the OneWorld data source definition as indicated by OCM for business data, next numbers, and UDCs for both the source and target environments.

   c. Verify ODBC DSN: As a final safety check, verify the libraries maintained in the ODBC definition on the client by looking at the ODBC definition for the business data, next number, and UDC data sources.

3. Stop OneWorld services: Prior to refreshing, issue an ENDNET command to stop OneWorld services. (The library containing the ENDNET program—B7332SYS in B733.2, for example—must be in your library list.)

   a. AS/400 – B733 and later: Sign on as OneWorld or whoever has B7332SYS in lib list. Set message display for OneWorld.

   b. Enter B7332SYS/A98OWMNU in the command line to bring up the OneWorld menu.

   c. Select Opt.17 which is the equivalent to WRKACTJOB to determine whether any batches are running.

   d. On a OneWorld client, go to b7\system\bin32 and run NETMON.EXE to verify signed-on users. Send them a message that OneWorld services are coming down.

   e. On the AS/400, select 13, ENDNET to kill OneWorld processes. ENDNET is a J.D. Edwards supplied command in B7332SYS. This command ends the OneWorld services JDESNET and JDEQUEUE, which are kernel-defined services.

   f. Select 17 to verify OneWorld services are down.

g. Select14 for CLRIPC. CLRIPC is a J.D. Edwards supplied command found in B7332SYS. IPC stands for interprocess communications. CLRIPC removes IPC structures. If ENDNET does not adequately clear these structures, STRNET will not perform properly when restarting services.

4. Back up current libraries: Prior to actually refreshing the target libraries, we highly recommend doing a full backup of the target libraries. We also recommend making an online backup of next numbers and UDC files for easy retrieval if necessary.

5. Clean up *SQL packages: OneWorld through ODBC creates *SQL packages which are records of paths to data. The Client Access ODBC definition indicates in which libraries the *SQL packages will be created. In order to avoid copying these objects, delete them. Don't worry, they are dynamic and will be re-created following the library copy when users access the data via ODBC again.

   a. Enter **WRKOBJ *ALL / *ALL *SQLPKG** on the command line.

   b. Erase all SQL PACKAGES other than those beginning with Q (the ones beginning with a Q are IBM-supplied system SQL packages and should never be deleted: QZDAPKG, QSQLPKG2, QSQXDPKG). If you do delete the *SQLPKGs that begin with a Q, OneWorld services will fail and you will not be able to utilize AS/400 as an enterprise server. If you delete these packages, you can reinstall them from tape. (For one client who inadvertently deleted them during an environment refresh, we created save files of these objects from a different AS/400 on the same OS release, FTPed them to a PC, e-mailed them to the client, who then FTPed them back to their AS/400 and did a restore object (RSTOBJ) on them.)

6. Do a WRKLIBPDM on the target library and then do a rename.

7. Enter **SBMJOB** on the command line, press F4, and type **CPYLIB**, then press F4.

8. Fill in blanks designating source (existing library) and target libraries (new library), and indicate whether to create the new library or not (Create Library Yes/No).

9. Press ENTER and then ENTER again to submit the job to batch.

10. Enter **WRKACTJOB** on the command line and increase resources applied to the job. For instance, type **2**, and on the command line type **TIMESLICE(9999)** to increase processing power supplied to the job.

11. While the job is running in batch, delete OneWorld global tables from the server path code spec folder in IFS by doing the following:

    a. Type **WRKLNK** *PATHCODE NAME*, type 5 to go to the specfile folder, then type 5 again to go to the specfiles.

    b. Type 4 (meaning delete/remove) next to glbl.ddb/xdb files. These files will rebuild dynamically when OneWorld services are started again.

12. After the job completes, verify that all the tables are available and contain data. You can use the following steps from 13 to 18.

13. Build two tables on the AS/400 containing a list of all tables in the new library and the source library by entering **DSPFD** on the command line, pressing F4, and filling in the relevant data. The key is to output the data to a file so that you can then run a SQL query against the data.

```
                      Display File Description (DSPFD)

     Type choices, press Enter.

     File . . . . . . . . . . . . . . > *ALL        Name, generic*, *ALL
        Library . . . . . . . . . . > CRPCTL      Name, *LIBL, *CURLIB...
     Type of information  . . . . . . > *MBRLIST    *ALL, *BASATR, *ATR...
                   + for more values
     Output . . . . . . . . . . . . . > *OUTFILE    *, *PRINT, *OUTFILE
     File attributes  . . . . . . . .   *ALL        *ALL, *DSPF, *PRTF, *DKTF...
                   + for more values
     File to receive output . . . . .   myfile      Name
        Library . . . . . . . . . . .   jassav      Name, *LIBL, *CURLIB
     Output member options:
        Member to receive output  . . . *FIRST      Name, *FIRST
        Replace or add records . . . .  *REPLACE    *REPLACE, *ADD




                                                                     Bottom
     F3=Exit   F4=Prompt   F5=Refresh   F10=Additional parameters   F12=Cancel
     F13=How to use this display      F24=More keys
```

14. Run an exception join to determine which records from the first table do not have a match in the second table. To do so, enter **STRQRY** on the command line, press SHIFT-F1 to change the session attributes to write the results to yet another file.

```
                         Change Session Attributes

    Type choices, press Enter.

       Statement processing . . . . .    *RUN        *RUN, *VLD, *SYN
       SELECT output  . . . . . . . .    3           1=Display, 2=Printer
                                                     3=File
       Output file:
         File . . . . . . . . . . . .    mycompare   Name
           Library  . . . . . . . . .    jassav      Name
         Member . . . . . . . . . . .    *FILE       Name, *FILE, *FIRST
         Option . . . . . . . . . . .    1           1=Create file
                                                     2=Replace file
                                                     3=Create member
                                                     4=Replace member
                                                     5=Add to member

       Authority  . . . . . . . . .      *LIBCRTAUT  Authorization list name
                                                     *LIBCRTAUT, *CHANGE, *ALL
                                                     *EXCLUDE, *USE

       Text . . . . . . . . . . . .      _____

    ___                                                           More...

    F3=Exit   F4=Prompt   F5=Refresh   F12=Cancel
```

15. Then run the following query:

```
select a.odlbnm, a.odobnm from jassav/olddev a exception join
jassav/newdev b on a.odobnm=b.odobnm.
```

You can then reset the attributes on the session and query the results table you just created to verify whether all the tables made it to the target library. Or, you could copy that file to a workstation or print the file.

16. To copy the file to your workstation, go to the 32bit ODBC administrator applet, and add a System DSN data source pointing to your AS/400 savelibrary. Configure the format tab to SQL naming convention. Open Microsoft Access, create a new database or use an existing one, then select import table. Under import, go to Files of Type and select ODBC Databases(). Then select Machine Data Source with the correct DSN name, highlight the library and file combination and click OK. Then you can easily print out the table from Microsoft Access.

17. Investigate the list to determine how to add tables—that is, do you have any files without logicals? If so, and if the missing indices are OneWorld generated (end in _1, and so on), it is best to regenerate indices using OneWorld Object Librarian Index Generation. If the missing logicals follow the World naming convention (_LA, and so on), we recommend you use World.

18. To create logicals for World other than using World (let's use F46021 as an example), you can do the following:

a. Enter **STRPDM** on the command line. Choose option 3, Work With Members.

b. At the prompts, use file JDESRC, library JDFSRC, and member F4602l_LA

c. Press SHIFT +F4 with file QAUOOPT library QGPL and MEMBER QAUOOPT

d. Use Option C Call&0/&N and Copy to Name LF Option LF

e. Run the command CRTLF File(SDGDEVDTA/&N) Srcfile (JDFSRC/JDESRC)

f. Press ENTER, type **LF**, then press SHIFT-F1 to copy down the list. Press ENTER.

g. Verify logicals created correctly within the target library.

```
              Work with User-Defined Options                PGRTJDE

File . . . . . . . :   QAUOOPT      Member . . . . . . :   QAUOOPT
   Library  . . . . :     QGPL      Position to  . . . :   ____

Type options, press Enter.
  2=Change          3=Copy          4=Delete          5=Display

Opt  Option  Command
 _     GO    GO &L/&N
 _     IM    IMPPART ??OBJ(&L/&F) ??OBJTYPE(*FILE) ??MBR(&N) ??PART(&N) ??LANC
 _     IO    IMPPART ??OBJ(&L/&N) ??OBJTYPE(&T) ??PRJ() ??GRP() ??TYPE(&S) ??F
 _     JL    DSPJOBLOG
 _     LF    CRTLF FILE(PGRCRPCOM/&N) SRCFILE(JDFSRC/JDESRC)
 _     PL    WRKPARTPDM  PRJ(&ZP) GRP(&ZG) TYPE(*ALL) PART(*ALL) LANG(*ALL) PF
 _     RP    RMVPRJLIBL
 _     RQ    runqry qryfile(&l/&n)
 _     SL    SBMJOB ??CMD(SAVLIB LIB(&N))
                                                            More...
Command
===> _____
F3=Exit          F4=Prompt        F5=Refresh       F6=Create
F9=Retrieve      F10=Command entry                 F24=More keys
```

NOTE

*If a file needs to be regenerated, then use the AS/400 **CRTDUPOBJ** command. Do not use OneWorld to regenerate the file because World would not be able to read it. However, if the file is a custom one designed with only OneWorld in mind, then you can generate the file using OneWorld.*

NOTE

Remember to perform many of the same procedures for next number and UDC files as well.

Data Dictionary Maintenance

In addition to library refresh, another area of concern is data dictionary maintenance for both World and OneWorld, specifically synchronization.

OneWorld and World data dictionary tables are not the same, or more accurately, they are not shared. However, it is imperative that the data dictionaries be synchronized between World and OneWorld. If a data dictionary item is changed without synchronizing the two data dictionaries, data being placed in the same coexistent file may not be accurately recognized by one of the two systems.

A limitation in synchronization of World and OneWorld data dictionary is that you cannot synchronize from OneWorld to World software other than by manually entering the change. Of course you could write a custom program to do this, but one is not provided by J.D. Edwards. On the other hand, J.D. Edwards does provide a method to synchronize World software to OneWorld using the World application P99800.

The J.D. Edwards synchronization process compares World software data items to OneWorld data items as follows:

- If an item is in the World software data dictionary and not in OneWorld, the synchronization process adds the item to OneWorld.

- If an item is in OneWorld and not in World, the process prints the information on an exception report and the administrator must either add the item to World or delete the item from OneWorld.

- The synchronization process replaces the glossary information row and column headings in OneWorld with information from World. This means you must carefully determine which items you have changed in the OneWorld data dictionary prior to allowing the process to actually update the tables. It is very important to run this process in proof mode the first time!

- Item specifications that both World and OneWorld use, such as data item size, system code, and decimal places, are overwritten in OneWorld with information from World.

Inside and Out

J.D. Edwards publishes a helpful step-by-step guide for the synchronization process, which can be found on the Knowledge Garden site. (Once there, select the following menus on left side of the page: Product, Publications\Translations, View\Download Guides, OneWorld, B733.2, and English. Then on the right side, click the following: Technical and Application Coexistence. Go to pages 21–26.) And again, you may want to visit the new migration home page on the Knowledge Garden as mentioned previously.

AS/400 Database Security

Perhaps the biggest concern in coexistence is the gaping security hole opened by allowing users to have direct green-screen access to the AS/400. J.D. Edwards has created a program called SECAUT to help the database administrator close this gap.

The security model provided by SECAUT addresses non-coexistent, non-system libraries; coexistent, non-system libraries; and OneWorld system libraries.

- **Non-coexistent, non-system libraries**   The JDE user profile owns data path libraries, and the OneWorld user profile owns the object libraries. *Public has *All authority to these objects. JDE or OneWorld owns the objects. Library authority to create objects is wide open.

- **Coexistent, non-system libraries**   All libraries are the same as in a non-coexistent environment except an additional profile such as JDEGRP secures data path libraries. This profile has *USE authority to the library. For World the SBMJOB command requires *USE authority to all the libraries in the library list to function properly. The JDE user profile for table objects owns all of these objects.

- OneWorld system library   The OneWorld user profile owns the OneWorld system library and the *Public authority is OWADMINL. All objects associated with OneWorld server administration are secured with the *AUTL OWADMINL authorization list. All other objects are secured by the *AUTL ONEWORLD. Administrative programs such as CLRIPC, STRNET, ENDNET, and PORTTEST, among others, are set to adopt the authority of the owner.

The four main steps to completing this security model involve the following:

- Set up IPCS

- Set up AS/400 OneWorld database security

- Add additional administrators as necessary

- Remove administrative authority from user profiles to complete the lockdown

J.D. Edwards has made available a very nice document containing about 28 pages describing the steps to go through to run SECAUT. It is available through the Knowledge Garden on the J.D. Edwards Web site.

Dual System Maintenance

One irony about coexistence is that yes, the business application users will benefit because their applications run in both World and OneWorld. The enterprise benefits with a phased implementation approach. However, system administrators now have more work.

User Administration

Specifically, World and OneWorld user profile environments and application security settings are not shared in the coexistence manner. Both systems have their own method of user administration and security. Additionally, the methods are not mirror images in functionality either. For instance, to add new users to World, you must go through the World G94 series of menus. In OneWorld, you must go through the OneWorld GH9011 menu with application P0092. You will see some shops share the user table (F0092) between World and OneWorld. However, this is not a J.D. Edwards supported architecture and there is no guarantee that the user table will be capable of being shared in the future.

Some organizations will employ two system administrators—one for World and one for OneWorld—due to the difference in the systems and the work involved in maintaining both. However, the work of these two administrative positions must be coordinated. Coexistent applications that are not properly secured in one of the two systems are wide-open invitations for problems. Changes in personnel would mean changes in both systems and so forth.

Disk Maintenance

Another element that becomes more complex to administer is disk maintenance.

Libraries   As we have shown, not all libraries are shared between World and OneWorld. The system administrator must have a clear understanding of each library, its contents, and its maintenance requirements. Keeping a constant list of libraries being used in both World and OneWorld environments is an important task to prevent deletion of libraries which the administrator mistakenly assumes are not in play.

Logs   World and OneWorld logs are not maintained in the same location. OneWorld logs are stored in IFS under the JDEB733X directory as streamfiles. World logs are usually stored in the output queue QEZJOBLOG and are stored as job logs under QDFTJOBLOG. To clean up OneWorld logs, you must delete them from the directory structure. For World, logs must be deleted from the library.

Reports   World and OneWorld reports are not stored in the same locations either. OneWorld reports are stored in the Printqueue member. To clear out members from the Printqueue file, you can do a WRKMBRPDM FILE(B7332SYS/PRINTQUEUE)* and then select option 4 next to each member you want to delete. To clear out World reports, delete them by using the WRKSPLF command.

As you can see, there are some additional system administration and maintenance difficulties inherent in running a coexistence shop. However, understanding these issues—and making sure management is aware of them as well—will go a long way in easing these difficulties.

Summary

In this chapter, we discussed coexistence—a migration strategy from World to OneWorld that J.D. Edwards developed to help ease their client base over to the client/server world. We looked at the pros and cons of World versus OneWorld, and used these findings in support of coexistence as a migration strategy.

Following that exercise, we examined some of the fundamental differences between World and OneWorld. In doing so, we identified potential trouble spots for coexistence and provided some ways to manage those solutions.

We looked at differences in object management between World and OneWorld, which files and applications are and are not coexistent (we even looked at the type of files within shared files that can be coexistent), and what to do in case of application modifications. We then moved on with some very detailed instructions around best practices for system administration and maintenance in a coexistence enterprise.

We hope this chapter provides some useful information around key issues within coexistence for World and OneWorld and will help those who must maintain such an enterprise do so more successfully.

CHAPTER 7

OneWorld Tables

E arlier in this book, we asked what the most important part of any enterprise resource planning (ERP) package was, and we (being the authors) agreed the data was the single most important part. After all, the applications, the processes, everything revolves around acquiring and manipulating data. We also discussed in Chapter 2 how we find where tables are held within the OneWorld Enterprise. One would suppose, however, that an explanation of how the tables are structured would be helpful when trying to fully explain a product like OneWorld.

In this chapter, we will quickly explore how OneWorld tables are defined, what tables reside in what data source, and how you can make modifications to enhance your OneWorld table performance. We will discuss the following:

- Tables and their architecture

- Table breakdown by data source

- The OneWorld Table Design Aid

- How to modify and add tables to OneWorld

- OneWorld shortcuts

Table Names and Some Simple Naming Conventions

Most people, when first introduced to OneWorld tables, look at them and wonder why J.D. Edwards came up with the table and column names. They don't seem to have either a rhyme or a reason, and they certainly aren't descriptive. Indeed, they don't provide a single hint to what they do or an indication as to what they are. What? You don't believe us? Then you obviously haven't looked at an actual description of a OneWorld table. Let's take a quick look to provide you with some basic understanding of what we're talking about.

The address book's master table (one of our favorite examples because everyone uses it regardless of what modules they are implementing) is named F0101. Other address book tables include F0111, F0115, F0116, and F0117. When you first glance at the table names, you immediately see that the tables were not actually given names. Instead, they were given numbers. It makes perfect sense when you remember that the OneWorld product's origin is the J.D. Edwards World product. These two systems, though totally different in functionality and software design, can coexist (that is, they can share the same set of data). The naming convention for the tables fits design specifications supported by the AS/400 in its earliest incarnation.

You might think this is nice but that J.D. Edwards, with a world-class product of the 1990s, ought to come up to speed on the naming convention for its tables. We would normally agree with you. After all, we love the leading-edge (up to and including bleeding-edge) technology. However, when you look closer at OneWorld's table naming convention, you will see that it is logical and still very useful today—so much so that we are willing to argue the naming convention's merits.

First, you will notice that all tables start with the letter F. Why is this? On an AS/400, these tables are referred to as files. Where this is obviously a holdover from the World days, it makes sense. Second, in the examples listed earlier, you will notice that each of the tables starts with the numbers 01. This will be a constant with all the direct address book tables. These two numbers are known as a system code. 01 is the address book's system code. Once you learn system codes, you will be able to quickly determine which table belongs to which module of the OneWorld product. The remaining numbers are used to make the table/file names unique. Notice that the address book master table is F0101, indicating that it is the first table of the address book.

Table naming has a couple of other conventions that will help you identify how the table is used. If you see a Z in the name (for example, F0101Z1), this usually indicates that the table is a work file for mass loading of data. When companies implement OneWorld, they often load Z files and run specialized universal batch engines (UBEs) to properly populate the OneWorld tables with their legacy data. You might also notice that there are many tables with UI in them (such as F42UI800). These tables are often used by OneWorld applications as temporary work files. Information is written into these tables, manipulated, and the results copied back to the original tables. If the applications successfully update these fields, the temporary table is then cleared for its next use.

Column Naming Convention

Now that you can easily see that the table naming convention really works, do you still think that column names make no sense? What if we told you that the address book number assigned to each person within the address book application was maintained in a column named ABAN8? Would that make sense to you? If so, you have either worked with J.D. Edwards products before, are reading this chapter for the second time, or just find the writing boring and are looking for an excuse to move to the next section. You can either move on or strap yourself in for another exciting section on naming conventions.

Column naming conventions are similar to table conventions in that there is a normally prescribed method in use. The first two letters are used to indicate a specific table. The example we want to use here deals with Sales Order Entry (the F42 series tables). When you add a new sales order, you populate the F4201 table (the sales order header table) and the F4211 table (the sales detail table). These records are linked using a sales order document number. In the F4201 table, this number is maintained in the SHDOCO column. In the F4211 table, it is kept in the SDDOCO column. You can quickly see the OneWorld column naming conventions with the example.

The first two letters of a column name are table-specific. For the most part (and yes, there are some exceptions, such as the F98611 and the F986101 tables), each table within OneWorld will have a unique two-letter identifier. The F4201 table uses SH for sales headers. The F4211 table uses SD for sales detail. After the table-specific identifier, column names are actually the alias name.

Aliases as Part of a Column Name

So, what is an alias? Aliases are shortened names for objects as defined in the data dictionary. Within the data dictionary, you might define an object called DocumentOrderInvoiceE. That column name only has 21 characters, but can you imagine coding a SQL statement with 20 columns that length? It would take forever and would make OneWorld's code even fatter than it already is. Now imagine the code with 100 columns. You get the idea.

Instead, within the OneWorld data dictionary, J.D. Edwards defines an alias to make the naming convention much shorter: DOCO. Heck, that's only four letters. Even the typing of it is easier. Now, when you combine the two-letter table identifiers with the alias, you get a column name of SHDOCO. This is much better than a column named SalesHeaderDocumentOrderInvoiceE.

There are ways to find out what the alias is for a specific field within a OneWorld application. You could find the tables being populated by turning JDEDEBUG.LOG on in JDE.INI, then make a change to an application and search for the update statement in the resulting log file. Or you could do the following:

1. On the workstation, open the JDE.INI file (it is located in the Windows or WinNT directory) using Microsoft Windows Notepad or another text editor.

2. Find the section called [EVEREST].

3. Modify the ShowAlias variable to 1:

```
[EVEREST]
ColorScheme=1
ShowAlias=1
ServerHelpPath=\B7\helps
```

4. Save, and then exit the text editor.

5. Start OneWorld and go to the application with the field which interests you.

6. Right-click the field you want and look at the pop-up menu. You will notice it specifies the alias of that field.

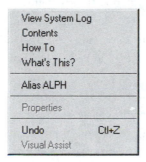

For more specific information on any one alias, go to the data dictionary application and look it up. The data dictionary will contain more information concerning the object, including its number of characters, whether it is numeric or text, a basic description, and the help field-level data. If you want more information on the data dictionary application, see Chapter 9. Now, back to tables.

Indices and Their Naming Conventions

To speed up data selection in a relational database, indices are added to tables. These indices are subsets of data with specific columns from the OneWorld tables. All the relational database management system (RDBMS) platforms supported by J.D. Edwards support table indexing to some degree. A single table can, and usually does, have multiple indices associated with it. Consequently, the naming convention is quite simple. Indices are given numbers (such as 1, 2, 3, and so on). These numbers are automatically created in a sequential order by the OneWorld toolset. In order to differentiate the index names for different tables, the table name is used in front of the index number. The resulting name looks something like this: F0101_1. This would be the first defined index of the address book master table. It is just that simple.

Indices, as a function of the RDBMS, must follow certain rules. Unfortunately, these rules vary from database platform to database platform. Indices can be unique. A unique index can be comprised of one or multiple columns. The information in this (these) columns cannot be duplicated elsewhere in the same tables (hence the unique part). A good example of this is the F986101_9 index. It is unique and contains the columns OMENHV, OMOBNM, OMUGRP, and OMDATP. What this means to the administrator of OneWorld is that you can't have two OCM record mappings for the same object in the same environment for the same user or group of users with different data sources. This is, of course, a good thing—right?

Indices can be defined with ascending order, descending order, or some combination thereof. If you had three columns in an index, the first and third columns could be ascending, and the second column could be descending.

NOTE

Although the Oracle database supports ascending and descending columns within an index, it will not support two indices with the same columns in the same order. This has been known to cause some indices to fail during installations and upgrades involving Oracle.

Table Design Aid (TDA)

As we've mentioned before, OneWorld was specifically designed to enable companies to meet their business objectives by producing a rich suite of applications that could be modified as necessary to meet those needs. To ensure this, the architects of J.D. Edwards OneWorld created and continue to enhance a robust set of tools specifically designed to enable customization of the software while protecting a company's ability to upgrade to future releases of the software. One of those tools is the table design aid (TDA). This application was designed to enable customers to modify, enhance, or add new tables to the OneWorld ERP package for use with existing or new applications.

Why Would You Want to Modify an Existing Table?

One of the more common reasons for modifying an existing OneWorld table is to add indices. Though OneWorld ships with a standard set of indices, customers are often able to enhance the performance of this software package by the judicious addition of indices based on the client's usage of OneWorld. We will go into more detail about how to determine if you should add additional indices to existing OneWorld tables in Chapter 19, which deals with optimizing your system.

Another reason for changing an existing table would be to add additional functionality to a specific application. Often, you will either add additional tables or modify the tables already in use by J.D. Edwards to accomplish these changes. During an upgrade or update of your OneWorld system, you may launch multiple table conversions. One of the changes these table conversions could be making is adding additional columns to existing tables (in a B732 to B733 upgrade, for example, one table has more than 140 columns added to it during the upgrade process). For now, however, let's concentrate on what we need to do to add these indices.

Okay, I Agree I Need to Change Tables; Now, How Do I Do It?

There are several ways to start the TDA, however, most people use the Object Librarian to find, select, and check out the specifications of a table to their local development workstation. This application can also be started directly from the Cross Application Development Tools menu (GH902). The program is the Object Librarian application (P9860) version ZJDE0009 (Table Design). Because of the nature of development in the OneWorld product, users are able to modify table specifications locally and test these changes without adversely affecting other users. Once those changes are tested, users are able to check these changes into the deployment server and generate them on the enterprise server. For this specific example, let's add an index to the F986110 table for the columns JCEXEHOST, JCJOBQUE, JCJOBSTS, and JCENHV (this will speed up the performance of UBEs on the server).

1. Start the TDA by highlighting your checked-out copy of the F986110 table and clicking Design on the Object Librarian application (P9860). This will launch the table design aid, shown in Figure 7-1.

2. From the primary TDA window (J.D. Edwards Table Design – Job Control Status Master, shown in Figure 7-2), arrange your two table windows (columns and indices) side by side. You will not need the data dictionary browser open for this particular example.

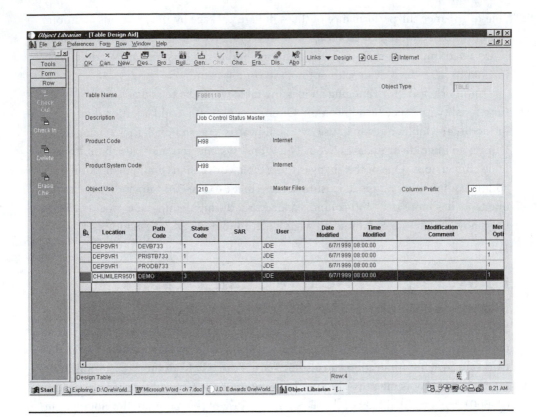

FIGURE 7-1.   Table Design Aid

3. Right-click in the Indices window and select Add New from the shortcut menu, shown here, to add a new index. Name this index F986110_M1. This name is in the TDA only; it will not be viewable in the database.

N O T E

Personally, we find that adding a letter in front of the index number helps to identify custom indices. By traditional naming conventions within OneWorld, the index is given a description in the TDA. Once generated, however, the index is automatically assigned the next numeric value for its name.

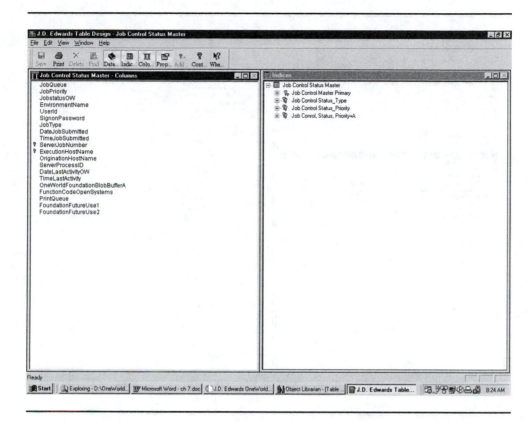

FIGURE 7-2. J.D. Edwards Table Design – Job Control Status Master window

4. Select the first column on the Columns window for the index you are creating (JCEXEHOST is the column name; ExecutionHostName is the data item name; JC is the 2 character table identifier; EXEHOST is the alias name) and drag it to the new index. Drop the column on your new index to place that in the index, as shown in Figure 7-3.

5. Repeat steps 3 and 4 until all of the columns have been properly added to the new index, as shown in Figure 7-4.

6. Save your changes and exit from the TDA.

Inside and Out

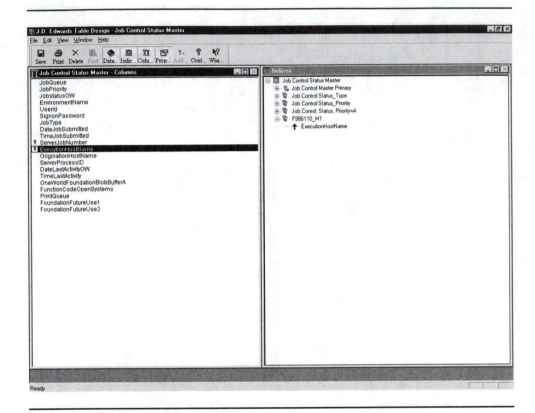

FIGURE 7-3.   Adding columns to the index

At this Point, Do You Have a New Index in Your Environment?

No, development is done locally on the workstation. Consequently, although you have made a change to your local specifications, you haven't updated any actual tables on the system. To do this, you would need to check your changes into the deployment server and then generate the indices using the Object Librarian application. For more information on the Object Librarian, refer to Chapter 9 of this book or reference *J.D. Edwards OneWorld: Developers Guide* (Osborne/McGraw-Hill, J.D. Edwards Press, 2000).

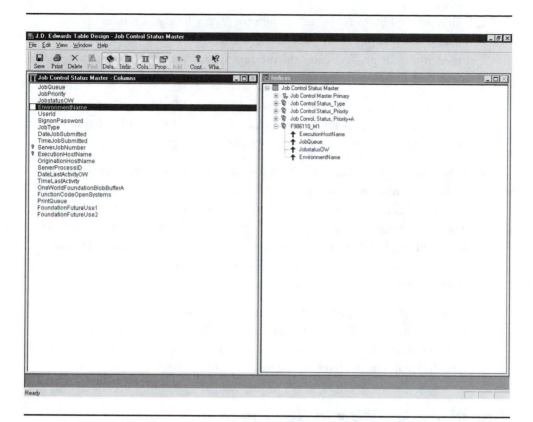

FIGURE 7-4. Multiple columns in the index

Adding Tables Using the TDA

Using the table design aid, you are able to create custom tables within OneWorld. These tables can be used as custom interfaces to legacy systems or to add additional functionality to the existing OneWorld product. You use both the data dictionary and the Object Librarian programs in addition to the TDA to create new tables in OneWorld. We could go into excruciating detail regarding exactly how to add tables to OneWorld, with cool pictures and quite a bit of advice, but our publisher told us we shouldn't steal the developer's thunder. Consequently, we'll cut this one short.

In truth, there is no science or mystery to adding a table in OneWorld:

1. Go to the Object Librarian and choose TBLE for the object type.

Inside and Out

2. Click the Add button. This will bring up a form where you can set up the header information for the table itself, including: the table name, the table description, the product code, the product system code, the two-character table identifier, and an optional SAR number.

3. Once you've filled in the information and clicked OK, this application enters a row in the F9860 table and allows you to design your new table. Highlight your table in the Table Design Aid window and click Design.

4. When the J.D. Edwards Table Design window comes up, you can use the data dictionary browser to find and select fields that are already defined within the OneWorld table. Simply drag and drop the selected field onto the Columns window. If the field you want to add to your table is not in the data dictionary, you need to add it before you start this procedure. After you have added all of the fields you want to your new OneWorld table, you should also add indices as appropriate, using the techniques listed in the previous section.

5. When you have completed designing your table, save and exit out of the J.D. Edwards Table Design window. As with other changes to tables, these changes are not complete until you activate them. The table should be checked into the deployment server and generated in the appropriate data source.

Copying OneWorld Tables

With early releases of the OneWorld product, J.D. Edwards included a program called Copy Table (CPYTBLE.EXE). It was located in the B7\SYSTEM\BIN32 directory of OneWorld workstations. This utility was a very versatile tool designed to copy tables from one data source to the next. It used scripts located at the root of C:\ on the local workstation (CPYSCRIPT.DAT). By using this tool, the OneWorld installer, CNC administrator, or DBA was able to copy tables and data or even append tables within OneWorld. Of course, that was then. In the base release of OneWorld B733, J.D. Edwards quit shipping this tool with the product.

We know what many of you are thinking: why would J.D. Edwards get rid of such a versatile, useful tool? Simply put, they have replaced this utility with a UBE that contains much of the same functionality as the original product plus several added benefits, including a report indicating exactly what changes have occurred. As of the B733.1 version of this product, clients can reliably copy data using variables including environments, data sources, the Object Librarian, and so on. You can create tables that are empty or populated from the source. There are variables that can be set to ensure you don't accidentally overwrite tables that already exist. And yes, OneWorld comes with a series of predefined versions for performing certain tasks such as refreshing CRP business data from production and refreshing locally replicated data. With this version of OneWorld, this UBE works extremely well.

The R98403 Copy Table UBE

The R98403 UBE, designed as the Copy Table replacement, first debuted in the B732 version of OneWorld; however, as with many new applications, it lacked the full functionality and robustness of Copy Table. Still, it is one of two ways of copying tables within OneWorld (the other is using the Object Librarian copy table utility). Using and customizing this application is very simple:

1. To start this batch application, start the batch version program (P98305). You can do this by double-clicking the application on the GH9011 menu, by typing **BV** in the fast path, or by typing **P90305** in the fast path.

2. Type **R98403** in the Batch Application field and click the Find button (pressing the ENTER key will have the same effect). This will bring up a list of the versions of this UBE that are defined in your path code (see Figure 7-5).

3. Double-click the version you need. This could be a predefined version shipped by J.D. Edwards or it could be a version you added. For this example, let's use version XJDE0505. It is designed to refresh locally replicated data (F0004, F0005, F0082, F00821, F0083, and F0084). When you double-click the

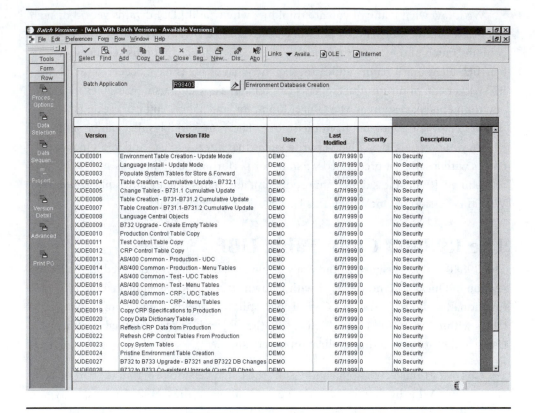

FIGURE 7-5. Versions of R98403

version, it will automatically submit the version you selected. You could also click the version once (highlighting it) and then press the Select button on the tool bar. (See Figure 7-6).

4. Click the Advanced button on the exit bar or choose Advanced from the Row menu. This will launch the advanced options form (see Figure 7-7). Check Override Location (the first option) and click OK.

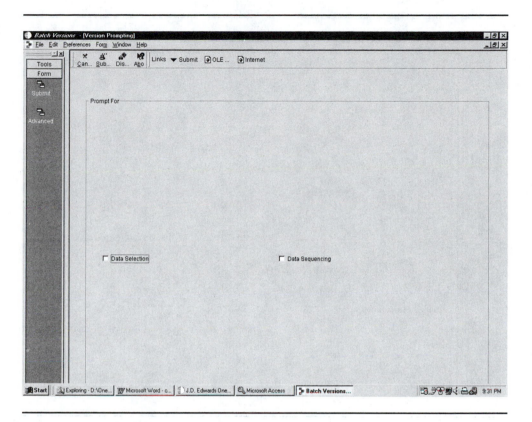

FIGURE 7-6.   Submit Form

5. If you want to see the data selection, check the Data Selection box (as shown
    in Figure 7-6) and then click Submit. This will launch a form called Batch
    Versions – JDE Data Sources, which will display all of the data sources
    associated with SVR (or server) machines.

6. Choose LOCAL as the machine you want to run the UBE on and click Select
    (see Figure 7-8).

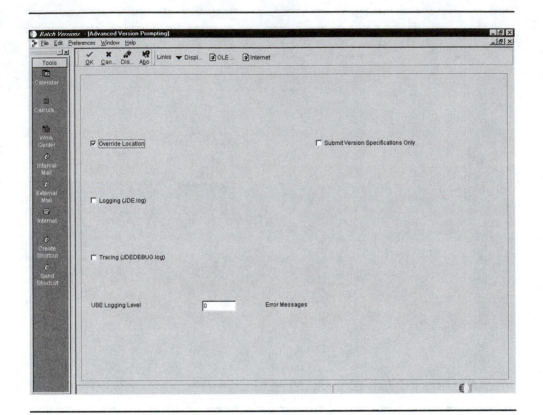

FIGURE 7-7. Advanced options

NOTE

The R98403 must be run on a local workstation or the deployment server. It will not work if run on a server (UNIX, AS/400, or NT).

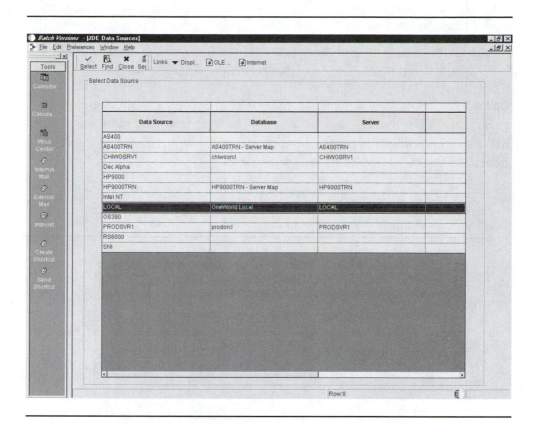

FIGURE 7-8. Override location LOCAL

7. The data selection (if you chose it) will come up. You will notice that the tables being copied have been predefined with the statement as listed in the Right Operand (see Figure 7-9).

Operator	Left Operand	Comparison	Right Operand
Where	BC Object Type (F9860)	is equal to	GT, TBLE'
And	BC Object Name (F9860)	is equal to	F0002, F00021, F0004, F0004D,

Inside and Out

Click the OK button.

8. The Processing Options dialog box will come up, shown in Figure 7-10. At this point, you can make some adjustments to fit your specific needs.

Option 1 Choose the environment for the tables to be copied to (the target environment). If you use this option, tables will be copied into data sources as defined in the environment's OCM entries. This option is good when you are copying tables from multiple data sources to multiple data sources.

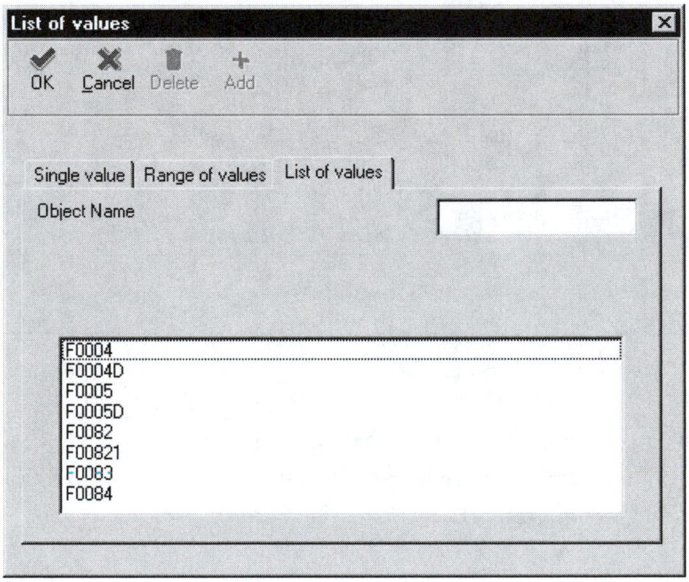

FIGURE 7-9. R98403 Data Selection

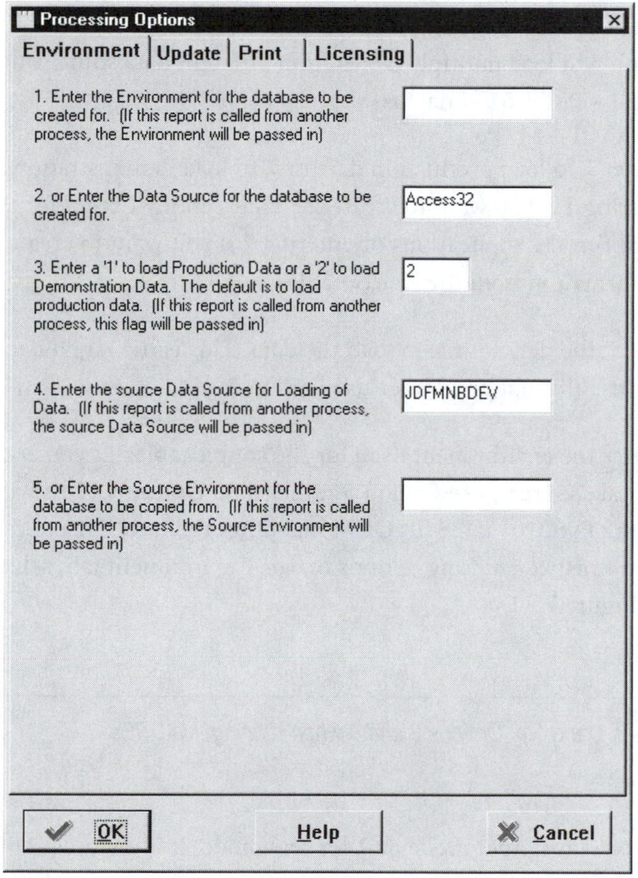

FIGURE 7-10. Processing Options dialog box

Option 2   Choose the data source for the tables to be copied to (the target data source). If you use this option, all the tables will be copied into the same data source regardless of their normal definition. This comes in handy when you are intentionally

Inside and Out

loading tables from one specific data source to another, or when you are making custom changes (if, for example, you want to enable store and forward processing—you will load multiple tables from different data sources to a single OneWorld Local – PRODB733 database).

Option 3   Enter 1 to load production data or 2 to load demonstration data. This equates to entering 1 if you want to create the tables empty except for the minimally required data to run the applications or entering 2 if you want to create the tables and copy all the information from the source tables.

Option 4   Enter the data source to load the data. This is the target data source as it is defined. If you use this option, do not use Option 5.

Option 5   Enter the environment used for the source tables. If you are loading tables from multiple data sources, use Option 5 rather than Option 4. This will instruct the UBE to check the F986101 table for OCM mappings to locate the tables being copied. When you have finished entering options on the Environment tab, select the Update tab, shown in Figure 7-11.

N O T E

Either use Options 1 and 5 or Options 2 and 4 when running this UBE.

Option 6   Enter 1 for proof mode or 2 for real mode. It is always best to run the UBE in proof mode to validate your process. Although you have to run the UBE twice if you run it in proof mode first, you will often catch errors this way. Proof mode will create a PDF suitable for making sure you are doing what you intend prior to actually doing it.

Option 7   Entering A re-creates existing tables. Leaving the field blank doesn't allow existing tables to be dropped and then re-created. Again, it depends on what you are trying to achieve. If you're replacing an existing table in its entirety, use this option. The UBE will actually drop the table, re-create it, and then copy the data you want.

Option 8   Enter 1 if you only want tables that already exist copied into the target data source. A prime use for this would be if you are using this UBE to refresh an existing data source from another data source (such as refreshing CRP data from Production).

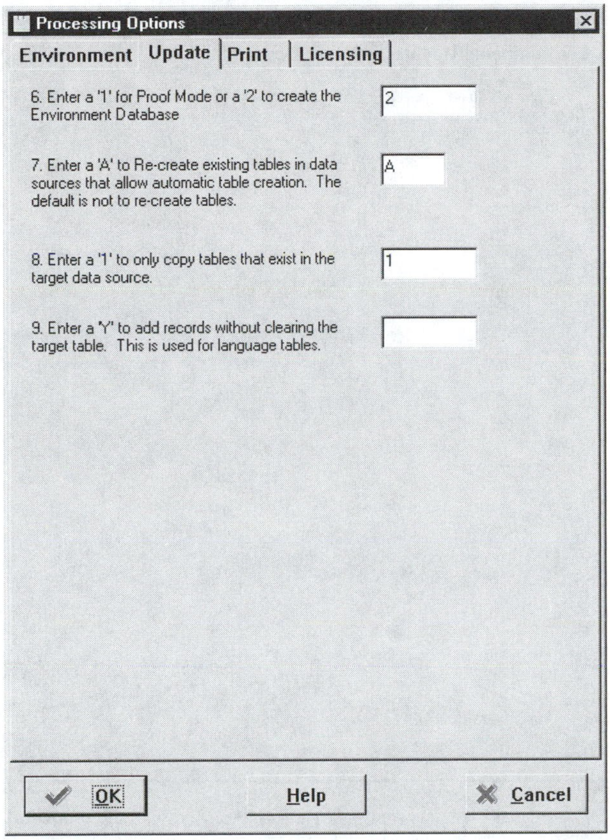

FIGURE 7-11. Update tab

Option 9 Although this processing option describes use with language tables, this variable is actually the most useful for making OneWorld append data to the tables. If you enter a Y in Option 9 and leave Option 6 blank, the UBE will append the source data table to an existing table. This report will not, however, violate table indices when run. In other words, you will not be able to input data that violates an index—this allows the good data to be added and avoids errors on the data that would cause issues. When you have finished entering options on the Update tab, select the Print tab, shown in Figure 7-12.

Option 10 Enter 1 if you want the report to print exceptions only. This is very useful when your UBE will result in a large report. Rather than 41 pages, you can get a 1-page report. Next, select the Licensing tab, shown in Figure 7-13.

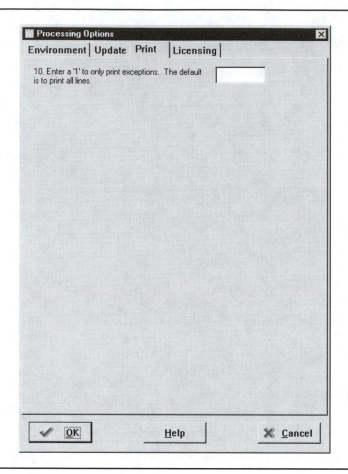

FIGURE 7-12.   Print tab

Option 11   Enter **Y** to create all tables or **N** to create licensed tables only. Most of the time, you are going to want to create all the tables you selected in your data selection, so you would either want to enter **Y** or leave it blank.

Option 12   Enter **Y** to print all tables or **N** to print licensed tables only. Keep a consistency to your processing options—if you entered **Y** on Option 11, do likewise on Option 12. When you have finished selecting all options, click OK to close the Processing Options dialog box.

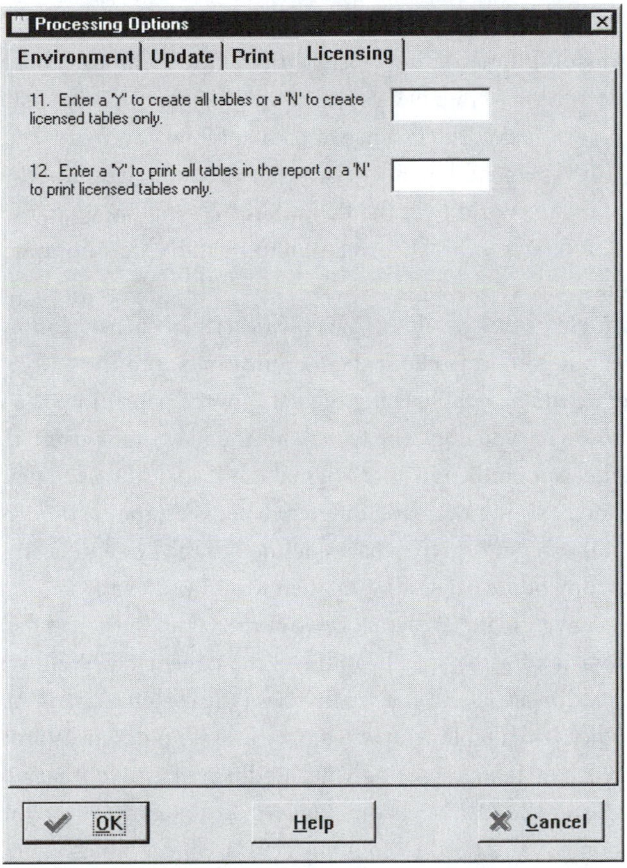

FIGURE 7-13. Licensing tab

OneWorld Shortcuts

There are many ways you can modify OneWorld tables without using the OneWorld toolset; however, each of those methods will have limitations. Where we see the greatest opportunity for the use of tables is in their manipulation using the RDBMS itself. Often, you will do everything in a single instance of OneWorld and want to replicate it to other environments within the OneWorld system.

One of the quickest shortcuts available when using OneWorld is copying a table directly from one data source to the next. Other than table ownership, the OneWorld system has no way of differentiating tables with identical names. Consequently, using the RDBMS is a very effective way of rapidly replicating information across environments. Now, OneWorld also has tools that allow you to do this, so which is better? This is 100 percent dependent on what you are trying to achieve. The advantage of using OneWorld over the RDBMS is that you are guaranteed that the table created will have a direct correlation to the table definition within the Object Librarian.

A prime example of this would be the case described earlier: you modify a table by adding an index, but you don't check the modifications into the path code. When you attempt to generate the new table using the data source definition, the new index will be missing. If, however, you copy the table with the new index using the RDBMS, it will have the same exact indices as the original table, including the new index.

This immediately shows the basic difference between the methods. Using the OneWorld toolset, you get exactly what is defined in the system. Using the RDBMS, you get an exact copy of the original. Why then would you ever want to use OneWorld? After all, it doesn't even make an actual copy of the table. Rather, it uses the definition in the Object Librarian for the specifications of the table itself. Well, what about when you test a table modification and it actually slows the system down? After all, if you put too many indices on a table, you will slow the system down. Wouldn't it be nice to re-create or copy a new table replacing your modifications? Another possible reason for using OneWorld over the RDBMS is that OneWorld copies work. If you used the MS SQL Server version 6.5 and tried to copy the central object tables, it could corrupt the resulting data. OneWorld, however, copies these tables very well. Finally, there are predefined scripts in OneWorld for copying tables. If you used the RDBMS, you would have to create your own jobs to identify, copy, and re-index tables by the data sources.

Summary

We've come to the end of another chapter in the adventure known as *J.D. Edwards OneWorld: The Complete Reference*. We've briefly discussed tables, how they are defined in OneWorld, and why you would add or modify them. We've also provided a list of every table associated with each of the data sources that point to databases. Tables and the data within them are the jewels of OneWorld. Understanding them, their naming conventions, and how to modify them is essential to understanding OneWorld itself. Although the naming conventions used seem archaic, they have both rhyme and reason and ultimately play the OneWorld song.

CHAPTER 8

Interactive and Batch Applications Defined

Applications Defined

Interactive Applications

Batch Application Definition

Versions

The name OneWorld is apropos. Within the OneWorld Explorer you will find a large suite of integrated applications—4,239 of them as of B733.2, to be exact—presented through a common user interface. These applications are presented in OneWorld Explorer menus and are accessed by double-clicking on them from the menu.

Generally, the applications have versions associated with them. Versions provide certain runtime parameters that the user base can manipulate if the Configurable Network Computing (CNC) administrator allows within his or her security plan. Versions can be assigned to individual users and various job queues. There are 5,506 versions out of the box with B733.2.

This chapter will thoroughly analyze each and every one of these applications and versions in a really, really small font. Actually, this chapter will examine the two main classes of applications at the top of the OneWorld object hierarchy. We will also break down the food chain of OneWorld objects with regard to applications.

Notice we did not say "programs." OneWorld does utilize a series of programs, such as BusBuild.exe, Netmon.exe, and others; however, they are not considered applications, as they are not directly maintained by the OneWorld object librarian application.

OneWorld Explorer programs are maintained in the \B7\System\bin32 subdirectory on each client. Because these programs are precompiled and J.D. Edwards does not provide the source code for further manipulation, we suggest it is sufficient that the CNC administrator make him/herself aware of them without our further exploration. Rather, in this chapter, we will focus on the following:

- Applications defined
- Interactive applications
- Batch applications
- Versions

We will look at subcomponents, processing, and development at a high level for both interactive and batch applications (however, to better understand version control, we refer you to Appendix A). We also address how versions extend OneWorld flexibility in the enterprise and discuss security issues which arise due to this flexibility.

Applications Defined

We struggled with the definition of the word "application" and have arrived at a definition which is less than satisfying: an application is a collection of objects that perform a specific task. In this sense, a single .c file could be considered an application, or OneWorld could be considered a single application. When it comes down to it, the philosophical nature of this question could take us in a direction we do not need to go. At what level is a human being more than a collection of atoms?

Luckily, we can take an easy way out and say if you are a OneWorld user and if you are not a CNC practitioner or developer, a OneWorld object can be considered an application if its OneWorld name begins with the letter P or R. We are hesitant to apply this same logic to defining human beings, and not just because there are a lot of people out there whose names do not begin with P or R.

The word "application" might bring to mind a precompiled, Windows-based executable such as Word or Excel. While it is true that OneWorld has some precompiled executables that it runs, OneWorld interactive and batch applications are not as singular in nature. These applications are actually a combination of various types of logic containers designed in a form-based interactive presentation or as a series of instructions to be executed in batch. The logic is contained within C-based business functions and specification files whose instructions are interpreted by the OneWorld engine at runtime. Interactive application names usually begin with a P and the batch applications usually begin with an R. Interactive applications are often referred to as IV, and batch applications are referred to as UBEs (universal batch engines).

N O T E

OneWorld applications—both report and interactive—are a combination of compiled C code and interpretive code known as "application specifications." OneWorld runtime application specifications are stored in a J.D. Edwards proprietary format called Table Access Management (TAM), found in the path codes stored on both the OneWorld client and logic servers. TAM stands for Table Access Management. Ignoring Data Dictionary relevant TAM files for the moment, TAM files are essentially a series of flat files that simulate the relational database structure of Central Objects. Each application specification relevant TAM file correlates to a specific Central Object specification table, and each also has an associated index TAM file, which correlates to the indices found on the Central Objects specification table. (See Chapter 10 for more information on Central Object tables.)

Inside and Out

Logic Interfaces

Beyond the functional difference of these two applications, the way users interact with them is different as well. The batch application, called a UBE, represents bundled code the user can call and have run without further user intervention. In other words, the application runs "asynchronously" of the user or generally of the event that called the batch job.

On the other hand, the interactive application is more of a task master, requiring constant feedback from the user, who must type data into the form and then wait for validation. This type of application typically processes in a "synchronous" mode.

Naming Conventions

J.D. Edwards OneWorld groups functional modules together with system codes. Some examples of system codes are:

- 00 Foundation Environment

- 01 Address Book

- 03 Accounts Receivable

- 04 Accounts Payable

- 07 Payroll

- 08 Human Resources

- 09 General Accounting

In keeping with our first definition of a OneWorld application, you can quickly see that an application with the name R00xx would be a Foundation Environment batch application and P04XX would be some type of Accounts Payable interactive application.

Although OneWorld comes out of the box with more than 4,000 applications, perhaps your organization will still have reason to add more functionality to the system by developing new applications or modifying existing ones. While we will not stand in the way of your development efforts, we will mention that J.D. Edwards designates development standards. We strongly encourage you to become familiar with and to follow these rules if you are going to undertake a OneWorld development program. Of immense importance is that you maintain the convention of using system codes 55 through 59, which are reserved for client development.

The hand-off of long-term application maintenance from developer to developer can be greatly complicated if these standards are not followed. Additionally, the custom application code faces grave danger in the case of OneWorld updates/ upgrades if the standards are not followed. So we suggest that you at least follow naming convention rules.

When developing any type of object, from the subcomponents that make up the high-level business applications to the high-level business applications themselves, you will need to provide a name for the object. The first letter should be a P for interactive (obviously) and an R for UBE (again, obviously). You will then be asked for a system code. These system codes are used by OneWorld to group applications within functional modules, as already mentioned.

Again, J.D. Edwards has designated a series of system codes—55 through 59—that are reserved for the identification of client objects by clients. By using these system codes for your customized objects, you will have ensured the first line of protection for your hard-earned custom work from the threat of destruction posed by a OneWorld upgrade/update.

N O T E

Even though your code will be intact by following this naming convention, your custom applications still may not function correctly following the upgrade/update. The objects with which these applications interact might change and so the original logic may no longer be valid. The process called "retrofitting mods" following an upgrade/update is a necessity.

Application Design

One of the best ways to understand OneWorld applications is to examine their components. Application Design is the entry point to several tools for creating, generating, running, maintaining, and securing applications. Application Design includes Form Design Aid for creating forms and Event Rules Design for attaching business logic through event rules. Use Application Design to:

- Access Forms Design for creating forms

- Define processing options

- Run an application

- Access BrowsER

- Create text overrides

- Browse forms in an application

You can use the OneWorld toolset to create applications in different client modes, including:

- Windows client

- Java client

- HTML client

Taking a Peek Inside Applications

Whether the developer is designing a new form or batch application or modifying an existing object, he or she must start with the object librarian. The object librarian is the central point where objects can be accessed. The object librarian will also show the developer if someone else has the object checked out or not. The object librarian will be discussed further in Chapter 9.

Interactive Applications

We will first examine the structure of interactive applications.

Forms: An Overview

The total number of interactive applications on a fresh install of OneWorld B733.2 is 1,830. There is a certain similar appearance to each one of these applications in that there are only seven types of forms used in the OneWorld system. These forms are:

- Find/Browse

- Fix Inspect

- Header Detail

- Headerless Detail

- Parent/Child

- Message

- Search & Select

Each form has a specific purpose and function that will be reviewed in the sections that follow.

Find/Browse Form

The Find/Browse form is one of the most used forms in the system. It is the entry point into most applications, including the Object Librarian as shown in Figure 8-1.

The Find/Browse form consists of a header section and a grid where the data will be displayed. The header section consists of key fields for the specific application. The grid section will display the detail data. It is also possible for the user to use the grid to search. On the grid, the top line is a section where you can search under each

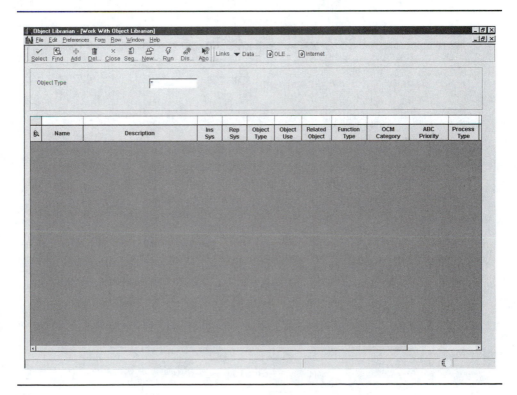

FIGURE 8-1.   Find/Browse form

individual column. This line is the Query By Example (QBE) line. If it is enabled, you can type search items in that section, although not all lines are always enabled to perform this task. An item for which the QBE is grayed out is either not a business view column, has QBE functionality turned off in the data dictionary for that particular field, or is not enabled in the OCM definition.

This form, if called from a menu, doesn't automatically preload. If this type of form is called from a different application, however, it can preload the form with the appropriate data.

Fix Inspect

The Fix Inspect form as shown in Figure 8-2 does exactly what you expect. It lets users look at their data and make the necessary changes where they are needed. It also lets the users add a new record where needed. This form has two buttons that perform specific actions when used. The first is the OK button. When this button is clicked, it will update

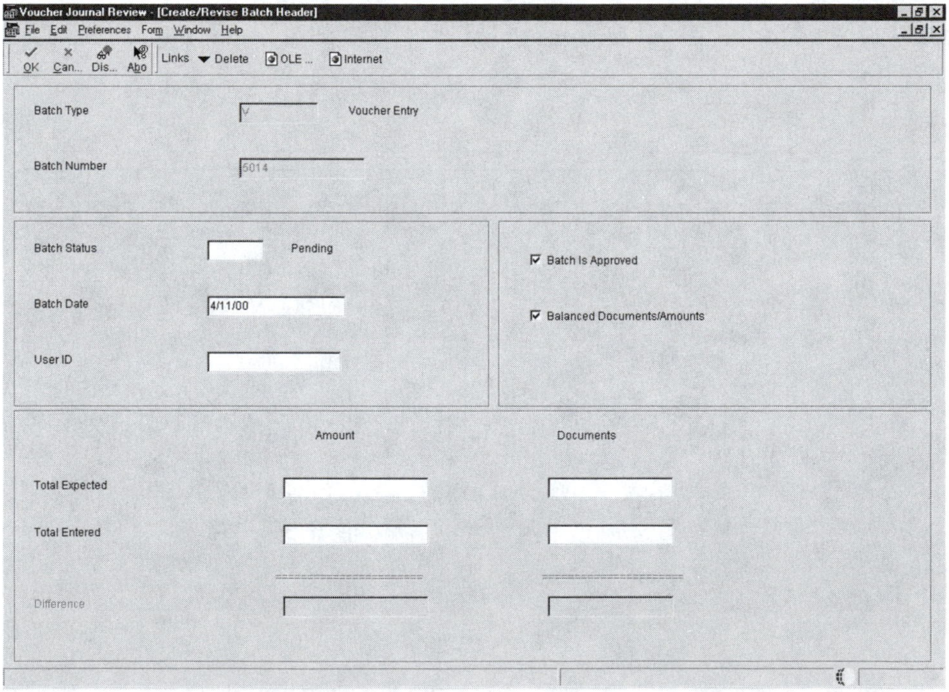

FIGURE 8-2. A Fix Inspect form

or write the specific information that you have changed or added to the appropriate table. The other button is the Cancel button. When it is clicked, the form will ignore all changes that were made and no updates or additions to the database will be made.

Since this form only allows you to edit or add one record at a time, there is no grid record associated with this form. This form is usually accessed from another form and the detail information is brought into the Fix Inspect form for editing purposes.

Header Detail

The Header Detail form in Figure 8-3 gives you the ability to update or add records to two separate tables at one time. The top portion of this form is used to add or update the header records of data. The bottom half or grid portion of this form lets you add or update multiple detail records associated with the particular header record. This unique form lets you attach two business views to one form. A business view can be attached to the header portion of the form, and a separate business view can be added to the detail section.

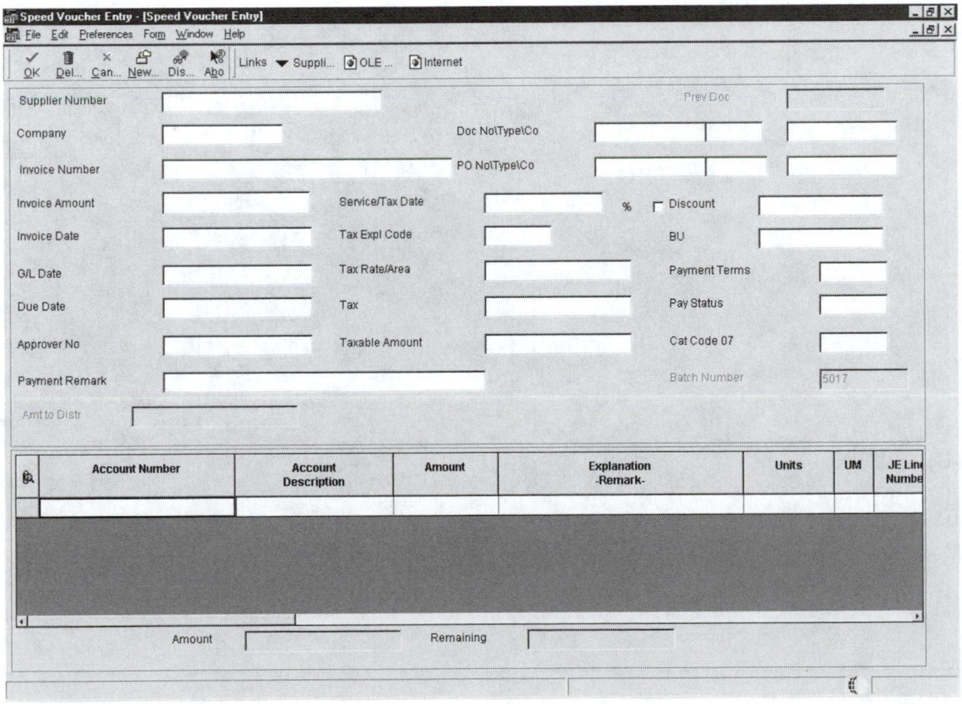

FIGURE 8-3. A Header Detail form

Headerless Detail

This type of form is very similar to the Header Detail form as shown in Figure 8-4, but it can only display information that is associated to one table. Therefore only one business view can be attached to this form, and both the header and detail come from that view.

Parent/Child

This form, as shown in Figure 8-5, is laid out differently than the previous forms that have been described. The top portion of the form still has the header records that some of the other forms showed. The bottom right half of the form is a grid section used to display the detail records of the child section of the tree. The bottom left half of the form is a graphical representation of the relationship between the parent and child.

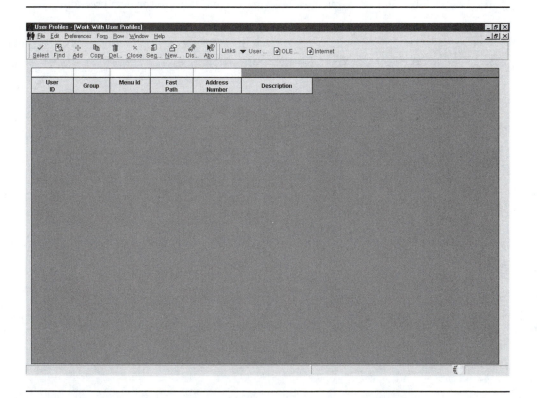

FIGURE 8-4.   A Headerless Detail form

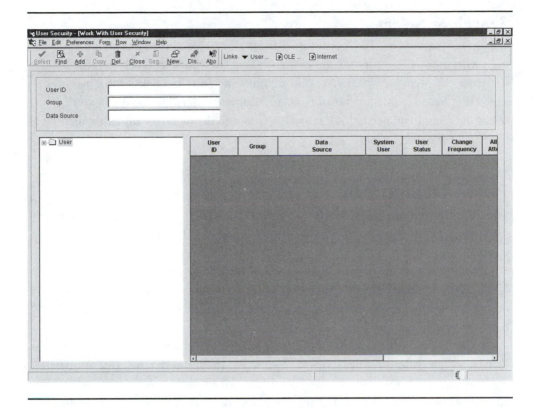

FIGURE 8-5.   A Parent/Child form

Message

This is a typical form that can be seen with most software packages and operating systems (shown here). It is a pop-up box where the user is warned about possible problems or informed about actions that have been completed. This form can only be composed of static text and push buttons. This type of form doesn't perform any database changes or inquiries of any type.

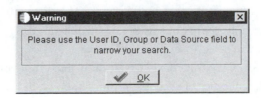

Inside and Out

Search & Select

This type of form is used to return values to specific fields. It is most commonly used with the visual assist function of the system. These forms must be attached to the specific item for which you are searching. The Search & Select form includes a grid that has the same functionality as the Headerless Detail form. When you select the record you need, this form will return it to the field that initially called the Search & Select form.

Form Design Aid

The Form Design Aid (FDA) is where programmers will go to modify and create new forms. Unlike the Report Design Aids Director, the FDA doesn't have a wizard-type program.

Creating new forms begins with the object librarian. Once in the main screen of the object librarian (as shown earlier in Figure 8-1), you can query on any of the objects in the system. This can be done by any of the specific object types on any of the QBE capable columns.

To add a new form, type **APPL** in the Object Type field and click the Add button. (This also works for the other types of objects that are in the systems: UBE for batch applications, TBLE for tables, BSVW for business views, and so on). After you have chosen the object type, you will be prompted for additional information that pertains to it. In Figure 8-6, you can see the screen for the additional information that needs to be entered in for an interactive application.

Once the form is completed, you will be routed into the object librarian's Application Design Aid. From this form, you will see a Design button on the toolbar which will launch the actual Form Design Aid (FDA).

Initially this screen just comes up blank. This is because each new form must be started from scratch.

Creating a new form does take some planning before the hands-on programming begins. First, you must decide the purpose of the form. This is important since it will determine what type of form construct will be used. Also, a very important part of the setup process is determining what business views will be used. The business views determine what data will be accessed from the form.

To create a new form, choose Form | Create, at which point you will be prompted with a list of the different types of available forms, as shown in Figure 8-7.

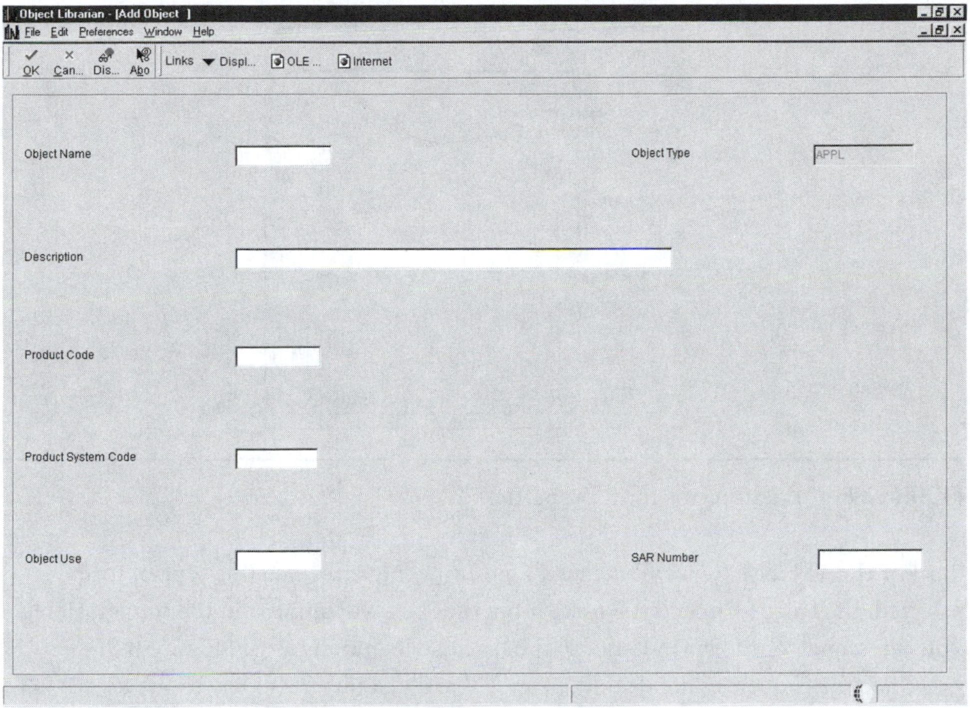

FIGURE 8-6. Adding information to an interactive application

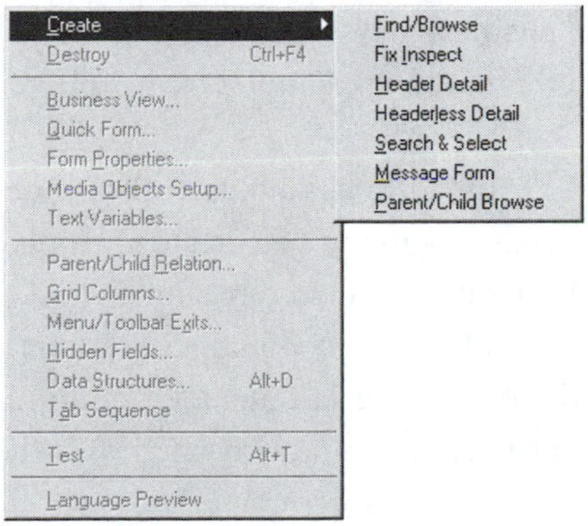

FIGURE 8-7. Form prompting

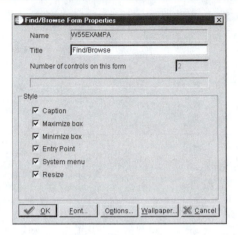

FIGURE 8-8.   Find/Browse form properties

For this exercise, you will create a Find/Browse form. Once this type of form is selected, the basic form and the form properties box will appear on the screen. Here you can name your form and choose the listed style options as per Figure 8-8.

Once the properties are decided, you will assign a business view to the form. Choose Form | Business View from the menu bar. This, in turn, will display a form (as seen in Figure 8-9) where the QBE (query by example, a SQL select generating tool) line can be used to select the desired business view.

Once the business view is selected, you can start adding fields to the form. Not only can you add the business view fields, but additional fields can be added and coding can be put behind them. A few examples of the different types of items are shown in Figure 8-10.

As shown in Figure 8-11, the form has a blue outline box in the upper-left corner. This box is a guide only; it ensures that if you create multiple forms, they are the same size and the placement of the different fields are similar.

To enter a business view column, you would go to Insert | Business View Field in the exit bar. This will display the Select Database Column For Controls window. This window lists all the business columns associated with the business view (as seen in Figure 8-12).

To enter one of these fields on the top portion of the Find/Browse form, double-click on the field you need or highlight it and click OK. From here, the field can be placed anywhere on the screen. To place one of the columns in the grid section of the form, the grid must first be selected before you insert any columns. Once a

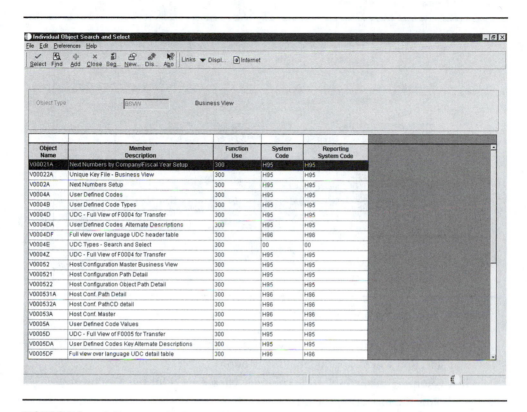

FIGURE 8-9. Selecting a Business View

FIGURE 8-10. Adding items to a form

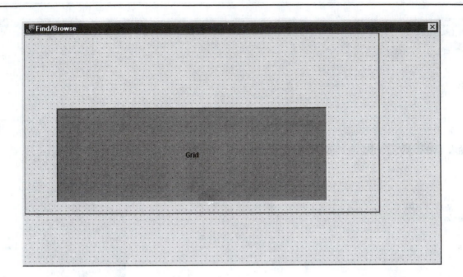

FIGURE 8-11. Outline Box for form creation

column is selected from the window, it will automatically appear in the grid section. Then that selection will disappear from the window.

When you have finished selecting columns, click Cancel for the window to disappear. Now the formatting can begin with the form.

To move a field in the upper portion of the form, the only step needed is to click the field. To move multiple fields at one time, right-click and hold the mouse button in, then drag the gray box to surround the fields you want to move. Once they are completely surrounded, release the mouse button and the gray box around the field

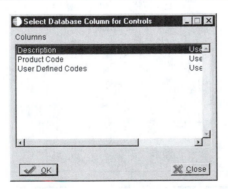

FIGURE 8-12. Select Database Columns

will stay in place showing a grouping of the fields. Now, click anywhere in the box and drag the fields to their desired location.

Moving fields in the grid is a little different. With grids, all the fields are automatically placed in the top portion of the box. To align fields in the proper order, click on the field you want to move. This will present that field in an inverse manner to show that it is the selected field. To move that field to the left or right, press and hold the CRTL key and use the arrow keys to place the field in its desired spot.

To add event rules to any of the fields, right-click on the field and choose Event Rules. This will display the event rule design section. Here you can manipulate the data fields in a different way using the different sections (see Figure 8-13), depending on when the code to be entered needs to be executed.

This is just an overview of the Form Design Aid. This tool is very powerful and can be used to give end users particular views of the data they might need. Using this same tool, the developer can also modify any existing form to add fields or modify the layout to fit a particular need. Furthermore, developers can further extend the flexibility of interactive processing by assigning versions, but we will look at that topic later in this chapter.

Batch Application Definition

As an alternative to interactive applications, batch applications can also help your user base perform a large variety of business-related functions. Batch applications more

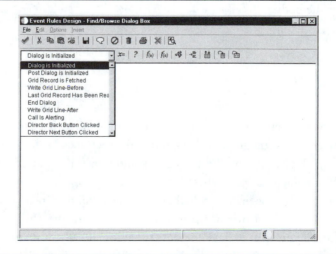

FIGURE 8-13.   Event Rules design

fully utilize the power of CNC with scheduling and batch mapping to servers (see Chapter 9 regarding Object Configuration Manager).

Batch applications are extremely powerful tools for massive data manipulation and output. UBEs can read data from tables within OneWorld for informational purposes, and they can perform data conversions to read and manipulate data within the system. Reports can print viewable data or produce files that are needed for systems that are integrated into the OneWorld application.

Out of the box, OneWorld comes with 2,409 different types of batch applications that are ready for use. If these applications do not meet your business needs, however, the Report Design Aid will assist in the creation of applications that will accommodate your requirements.

Walkthrough of Report Design Aid (RDA)

This section will walk you through the basic screens in the Report Design Aid Director, a wizard-like tool that assists you in setting up a basic report. Additional code must be added to the report for further functionality or custom requirements.

The first screen of the Report Design Director, as shown in Figure 8-14, provides the initial setup of the report. This is where the developer must make decisions about the three main sections of the report. The first section is the header section, where the name of the company or other information can be placed. In addition to a page header, a report header can be selected if necessary.

The next section is the body of the report. There are three types of layouts that can be selected for the body:

- Column

- Group

- Table

A column type of report will give the report a look similar to a listing and will place the selected fields straight across the top of the section. The group format, as the name suggests, will give you the ability to group and move the selected fields around. The table format will give a spreadsheet look to your report.

The final decision to be made is whether the report will require a page footer or a report footer. If you decide to put a page header into the report, the Report Design Director will ask if you want to have the director automatically or manually lay out the page header. If the automatic option is chosen, as shown in Figure 8-15, the Report

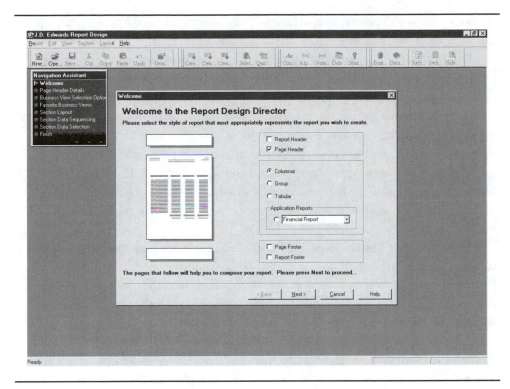

FIGURE 8-14.   Report Design Director

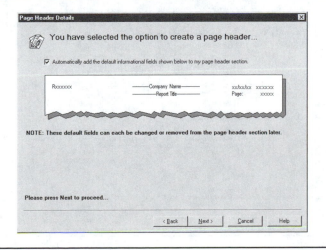

FIGURE 8-15.   Automatic Page Header

Design Director will place the report name, the company name, the report title, a page number, and a date and time stamp on the header of the report.

The next step in the process is to decide which business view will be assigned to the report, as shown in Figure 16. Here you can choose whether to have the system give you a list of business views or to have the program choose the business view. Generally, it is easier to have the program choose the business view. When first laying out the information needed for a report, the developer should initially know which business views are out there or create one for the specific purpose of the report.

Choose the business view you will use, as shown in Figure 8-17. Here, via the QBE utility, you can choose the business view by supplying either a description or the name of the business view. After finding the appropriate business view, highlight it and click the Next button.

After choosing a business view, the Report Design Director leads you to choose which columns are needed for the report or the section layout screen, as shown in Figure 8-18. On the left side of this screen are all of the columns that are in the chosen business view, and on the right side are the columns that have been chosen for the report. To add or subtract the columns, you can highlight them and click the arrows on the bottom of the screen, or just double-click and drag them. After choosing the columns to be displayed, you can align their order by highlighting them and using the up and down arrows until they are in their desired order on the right side of the display.

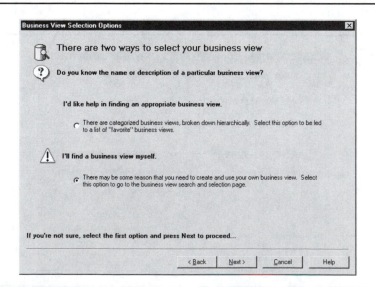

FIGURE 8-16.　Selecting a Business View

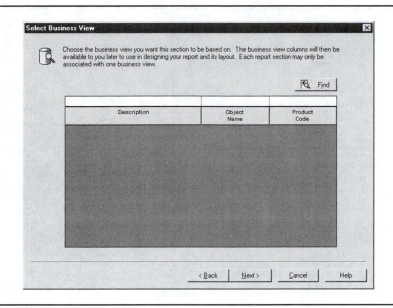

FIGURE 8-17. Choose Business View

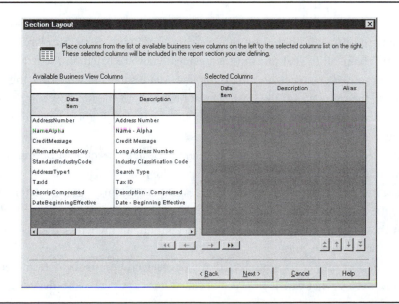

FIGURE 8-18. Columns/Section Layout

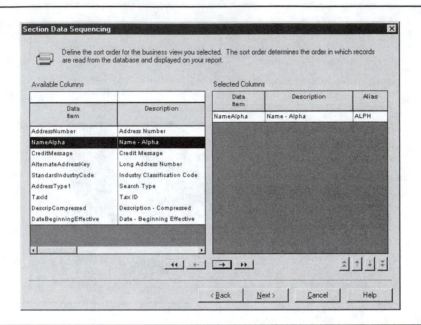

FIGURE 8-19. Section Data Sequencing

After completing this portion, the Report Design Director will help you with sequencing the data within the columns, as shown in Figure 8-19. Similar to the layout screen, all the columns in the business view are listed on the left side and the data is sequenced on the right side. Make sure that when placing columns on the right side of the form they are listed from the top down in the sort order you want, starting with the top field being the first or highest level for the data sequencing.

After the sort order is determined, the Report Design Director will bring the columns that were selected into the next step of the process. This is where the actual sort properties are determined, as shown in Figure 8-20. Here it can be determined whether the sort order for each column should be ascending or descending order, whether there is a level break needed for each column, and whether there should be a page break after each column.

After the sort properties are selected, the data selection must be determined. Here you can be decide what data from the associated business view is needed, as shown in Figure 8-21.

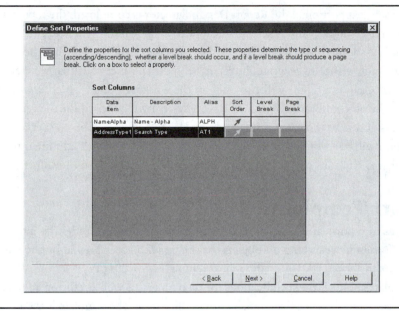

FIGURE 8-20.   Define Sort Properties

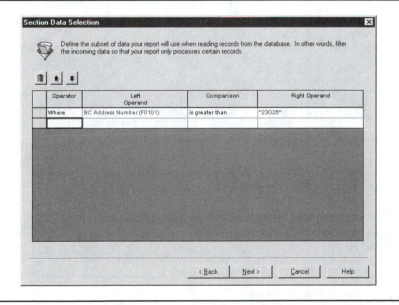

FIGURE 8-21.   Section Data Selection

After this last portion of the Report Design Director is completed, the report is finished, and a congratulations screen will appear, as shown in Figure 8-22. This is the final screen associated with the Report Design Director. Click the Finish button, and the system will automatically generate the report with the specifications that were entered.

At this point, the report will run only on the workstation on which it was created, although the object librarian will now have a system-wide record for the report. To give others access to the batch application and/or to have it run on the server, the application will need to be "packaged" and deployed by the CNC administrator to the other workstations and servers (see Chapter 10 for package build information).

Report Templates

Templates in reports are the engines behind the scenes. You can identify a template in object librarian by searching on objects that begin with a T followed by the name of the report. For instance, T0010P is the report template for R0010P.

Templates hold all the specifications for each report, as well as storing all the business function calls and the code that actually drives the report. The template is the basis of the

FIGURE 8-22. Finish Notification

report and gives the initial layout, format, data selection, and sequencing. After the template is laid out, it serves as the starting block for each version of the report.

Report Versions

Each report is based on the template, but a version is required for the report to run. A version can be created automatically when the report is initially made.

Consider the following example. Say you have a report that shows sales orders by business unit. The version would allow you to specify sales orders for a subset of data, such as only one business unit rather than all business units. Let's look at versions in more detail for both reports and interactive applications.

Versions

Versions are a stroke of development genius. They are a set of dynamic specifications that the user can manipulate to customize either batch or interactive applications. With versions, the integrity of the report or interactive engine is preserved while still allowing for very quick, on-the-fly data-manipulation modifications by the user base. The user does not have to change the code to change the operation of the code. Rather, versions allow the user to stipulate a variety of possible options. Versions let you extend OneWorld functionality beyond your application developers out to the people who should know the business better than anyone: power users.

CAUTION

Even though versions extend flexibility to the power user base, it is important that any changes being considered go through a very tightly controlled change management plan. Changes in processing in one module of an integrated enterprise system may have unintended effects on other modules. Your implementation partner can best help you design a change management plan that will suit your organization's business requirements. The CNC administrator needs to have an understanding of application security (see Chapter 13) and version security (see below) to help maintain system integrity with the change management plan.

Through the use of data selection and processing options, the user can easily modify the scope of the report versions. These versions inherit the characteristics of the parent or template application, but can be modified for specific purposes. Each application can have any number of versions associated with it, and each version can perform different functions depending on its characteristics. There are three main characteristics that can be changed by each version:

- Data selection

- Data sequencing

- Processing options

Data Selection

Data selection is used to narrow down or limit the amount of data that the application will process. For instance, the user might want to pull specific business units for a trial balance report. Without requiring any knowledge of SQL, data selection is the mechanism that allows the user to specify the specific business unit. The data items—such as business units—that these data selections can be processed against have to be associated to the batch or interactive applications through the business view.

Data Sequencing

Data sequencing is another way of formatting and specifying the display order for your data. For instance, data sequencing within a report allows you to put business units in ascending order and then sort each object in descending order. The columns to be sorted must be associated to the business view of the application.

Processing Options

Processing options are powerful tools that can change the functionality of the report just by changing a flag on the processing option screen. For instance, a processing option flag allows you to set a report to clear data after the report is run or keep the data in the tables to be erased later. Processing options are similar to data selection in that they specify subsets or qualified data for the application to process. For example, processing options allow you to specify ledger types. Other processing option flags allow the user to decide whether a report should commit records to the database or just run in proof mode (this option is very handy in cases of data manipulation such as updates, inserts, and deletes).

Batch Versions versus Interactive Versions

In One World, every batch application has an associated version connected to it. However, not every interactive application has a connecting version. Overrides can also be placed on a report version through the design tools. With these overrides, a programmer can actually change the report to fit a specific need while still keeping the template intact. This can be done for batch applications through the object librarian. The version must be checked out in the same fashion as the template of a report.

Interactive applications are handled in a much different manner. The Work With Interactive Versions application (P983051) is a separate application that handles all of these versions. With interactive versions, you do not have as much freedom to manipulate the application. The main use for interactive versions is to modify the processing options for that particular application.

Commonalities

When creating new versions—interactive or batch—there are some common items that must be filled out by the user: prompting option and version security.

Prompting option

Applications called from the OneWorld Explorer menu will behave in one of three ways with regard to prompting versions for the user to manipulate, depending on the following settings:

- **Blank (no processing options)** This option states that there are no processing options associated with this application.

- **1 (blind execution)** This option indicates that this version has processing options that are not displayed when the application is run.

- **2 (prompt for values)**   This option specifies that every time this version is run, the user is prompted for processing options.

Version Security

The next important option is the security level assigned to the version. There are four different levels of security that can be applied to versions:

- **0 (no security)**   This is the default value and will let all users design, change processing options, change detail values, check in, check out, install, transfer, copy, delete, or run the versions.

- **1 (medium security)**   This level will allow only the "Last Modified By" user to have access to design, change processing options, change detail values, check in, check out, or delete the version. It will allow other users to install, copy, transfer, or run the version.

- **2 (medium to full security)**   This level allows all users to install or copy the version, but lets only the "Last Modified By" user complete all the tasks.

- **3 (full security)**   This level allows only the "Last Modified By" user to do anything, including run the application.

What is happening behind the scenes is the following. Version security is a UDC called H98:EX which correlates to the data dictionary item called EXCL. Possible UDC values are 0, 1, 2, or 3, as listed above. When you create a new version and assign the security level, the security value is stored in the F983051 table as VREXCL, with the user as VRUSR0. When the user does a Find against versions on the UBE, OneWorld does a Select against F983051 as well as against the UDC tables. Then, when the user selects a version to run, the business function VersionListCheckVersion validates whether the user has access against all the various cached data.

This type of security is different than security as described in Chapter 13. Application security provides or prevents access for users running a particular version and still gives them access to the report or application. In some cases, you may create multiple versions that you want to make accessible to your user base for their selection, although within that series of versions you might want to make one particular version available to only one particular user.

Summary

In this chapter, we have taken a look at what defines an application and the two main types of OneWorld applications: the batch application and the interactive application. We also briefly covered some development standards and the development process for the applications. We discussed the different ways that batch and interactive applications enable users to interface with the data stored in OneWorld. Interactive applications are field-level, tab-validation forms with which the user interacts. Reports can be initiated by the system or scheduled to run with no further user intervention.

We then presented the steps necessary to develop both interactive and batch applications so that the CNC administrator can better understand what developers are doing. This step-by-step explanation will help CNC practitioners in their troubleshooting function.

Finally, we explored the subject of versions, which we feel is the key to J.D. Edwards OneWorld flexibility and the element that enables the power of ERP to be extended throughout the enterprise. We discussed how data selection, data sequencing, and processing options allow users to flexibly address data without altering code. But with flexibility comes danger, so we discussed version security and indicated the difference between application and version security.

Our intention with this chapter was not to make you a developer, but to provide the CNC administrator with a more in-depth understanding of applications in OneWorld.

Inside and Out

## CHAPTER 9

OneWorld Specialty Applications

Object Librarian

Data Dictionary

System Tables

Server Map

Control Tables

Welcome to a chapter totally dedicated to some of the most important topics related to OneWorld. These topics, in addition to being essential to the product, are also unique in how they operate and in what they do. There are tables and applications that don't fit the traditional modes discussed in this book to date. Though some of them are addressed in other books produced by the J.D. Edwards Press, we would be remiss in our duties if we didn't mention them here. Some of the topics covered include:

- The Object Librarian

- The Data Dictionary

- System Tables and Their Tools

- The Server Map and Its Tools

- The Control Tables

Object Librarian

OneWorld, as discussed in other chapters, is an object-based product (even if not actually object oriented). As such, one of the tasks the original architects of OneWorld had to come up with was a method of keeping track of all of the objects. In many different products, there is no central repository for all objects defined by the system. In this section, we'll go into detail about the object librarian and its tools.

The Object Librarian Defined

When we talk about an object-based product, we refer to applications that are a compilation of one or more objects. By J.D. Edwards' standard, an object is any reusable entity created by the OneWorld tool set. Is a table an object? Yes! Is an application an object? Yes again—though applications are generally a compilation of several different objects defined as a single object (such as forms, business views, templates, and BSFNs). Is a UBE an object? Of course—it is similar to the interactive application in that it is usually several objects combined into a single working entity. Other than the data in the OneWorld tables, pretty much everything in OneWorld is an object. To get a better understanding of this, look at Table   , which shows the raw number of objects maintained by the object librarian.

Object Type	Abbreviation	Number of Objects – B733.1	Number of Objects – B733.2	Number of Objects – Xe (B733.3)
Interactive Applications	APPL	1785	1830	2023
Business Libraries (DLL)	BL	33	35	38
Business Functions	BSFN	4530	4699	5251
Business Views	BSVW	3165	3275	3930
Data Structures	DSTR	7343	7739	9318
Media Object Data Structure	GT	205	212	255
Tables	TBLE	1836	1972	2290
Batch Applications	UBE	2136	2409	3083
Application Forms		4190	4313	5230

TABLE 9-1.   OneWorld Object Counts

Inside and Out

N O T E

The numbers listed in Table 9-1 come from OneWorld stand-alone. The released version of OneWorld may have different numbers—though they will remain close.

The object librarian is a central repository for the definitions of all objects in OneWorld. It is comprised of five tables (F9860, F9861, F9862, F9863, and F9865). These tables maintain definitions and other required data to define the objects to the OneWorld system. The object librarian is shared between all environments and path codes under a normal setup of the OneWorld product. While you can create multiple copies of these tables, it requires quite a bit more administration and it is not recommended for most installations.

The object librarian is unique to each major release of the OneWorld product. This means upgrading your system adds a new set of object librarian tables. However, when you apply a cumulative update to B733.2 and earlier, you simply add records to an existing set of tables.

The F9860 Table (Object Librarian Master)

The F9860 table maintains a single entry for every object in the OneWorld system. Included in these definitions are the object IDs, its description, its object type (known as its function, such as BSFN, TBLE, APPL, and so on), the application ID (this is a holdover from earlier releases of the OneWorld product), the system code, and the parent DLL. In Figure 9-1, the top section is information from F9860. The grid information is from F9861.

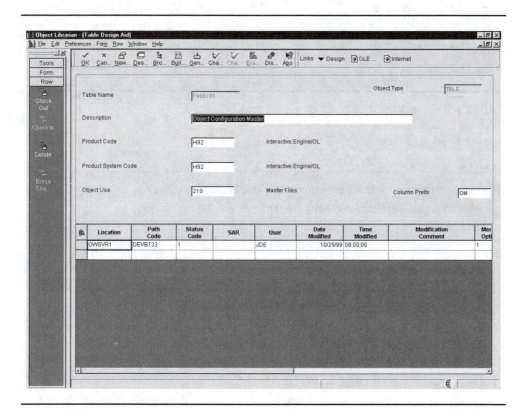

FIGURE 9-1. The object librarian

The F9861 Table (Object Librarian – Status Detail)

The F9861 table (see Table 9-2) maintains path code–specific entries of every object in the system. There can be more than one entry per object for a specific path code because this table maintains information such as object name, machine name where the object is located, path code name, the major release level, merge options, change status, who currently has the item checked out, and when they checked it out. The grid format in Figure 9-1 contains information from F9861.

Column Name	Description	Length	Type	Valid Values
SIOBNM	Object Name	10	String	The unique name associated with a specific object in OneWorld.
SIMKEY	Machine Key	15	String	The name of the workstation or server.
SIENHV	Environment Name	10	String	The name of the environment; this field is not used in the B733.2 version of OneWorld.
SIUSER	User ID	10	String	The identification associated with a specific OneWorld user.
SIDM	Date – Modified	6	Date	The date the object was modified.
SIJDEVERS	Version	10	String	The OneWorld primary release level (B732, B733, and so on).
SIMSAR	SAR Number – Modify	8	String	The SAR provided when the object was checked back into the primary system.
SISTCE	Status Code	1	Character	A code that identifies the status of an object in the development cycle. Valid values are maintained in the UDC product code 98 report code SE. 1: In production 2: In test 3: In development 4: Custom versions 5: In use by vocabulary overrides

TABLE 9-2. F9861 Table

Column Name	Description	Length	Type	Valid Values
SIDVP	Development Progress Code	1	Character	A code that identifies the type of modification performed. Valid values are maintained in the UDC product code 98 report code DP. Blank: No modifications performed 0: No modifications performed 1: CORE modifications performed 2: Tech modifications performed 3: CORE and tech modifications performed
SIMRGMOD	Flag – Modification	1	Character	A Y/N flag that indicates that an object has been changed. This flag is instrumental in determining items modified prior to an upgrade or update.
SIMGROPT	Option – Merge	1	Character	A flag indicating whether to merge objects. This can be set at the path code level. Valid options are maintained in the UDC product code 98 report code EO. Blank: Do not merge 1: Merge 2: Do not merge
SIRLS	Release Number	10	String	There are 28 valid release levels maintained in the UDE product code 98 report code RL.
SIPATHCD	Code – Path	10	String	This maintains the name of the path code maintaining the object.
SIMODCMT	Comment – Modification	20	String	A short comment on changes to the object.
SIPID	Program ID	10	String	The name of the program that changed the object record in F9861.
SIJOBN	Work Station ID	10	String	The name of the workstation that ran the application that modified the object record in F9861.
SIUPMJ	Date – Updated	6	Date	The date the object was modified.
SIUPMT	Time – Last Updated	6	Numeric	The time the object was modified.

TABLE 9-2. F9861 Table *(continued)*

The F9862 Table (Object Librarian – Function Detail)

You're probably wondering what other data you could possibly need in an object librarian. After all, you know what the objects are and where they reside. What else is there to define? The F9862 table (see Table 9-3) specifies every function in a business function. This table has more than 6,500 entries in the B733.2 version of OneWorld, while there are fewer than 5,000 actual business functions. Applications in OneWorld call actual functions instead of business functions directly.

Column Name	Description	Length	Type	Valid Values
SIOBNM	Object Name	10	String	The unique name associated with a specific object in OneWorld.
SIFCTNM	Name – Function	32	String	The standard name for the function. This must follow ANSI C naming conventions.
SIMD	Date – Modified	6	Date	The date the object was modified.
SIEVDSC1	Event Description ID	11	Identifier	The event description ID. 0 is used for all entries in B733.2.
SIFCTNID	ID – Business Function	11	Identifier	The unique identification associated with a OneWorld business function.
SIDSTMPLID	ID – Data Structure Template	11	Identifier	The unique data structure template identification.
SIJDEVERS	Version	10	String	The name for the release of OneWorld. This field is not used in B733.2.
SIMRGMOD	Flag – Modification	1	Character	A Y/N flag that indicates if an object has been changed. This flag is instrumental in determining items modified prior to an upgrade or update.
SIMRGOPT	Option – Merge	1	Character	A flag indicating whether to merge objects. This can be set at the path code level. Valid options are maintained in the UDC product code 98 report code EO. Blank: Do not merge 1: Merge 2: Do not merge

TABLE 9-3. F9862 Table

Column Name	Description	Length	Type	Valid Values
SIBUF1	Category – Business Function	3	String	The business function category as maintained in the UDE product code 98, report code V1. Blank: General APP: Application specification BAT: Batch processing CUR: Currency DTE: Date TAX: Tax TRG: Trigger
SIBUF2	Function – Business Function	3	String	The primary function that occurs in the business function as maintained in the UDC product code 98, report code V2 Blank: General CAL: Calculation DEL: Delete DFT: Default processing EDT: Edit FMT: Format GET: Data retrieval UPD: Add/Update
SIBUF3	Business Function Category 3	3	String	This field is used to segment business functions by type as determined by UDC product code 98, report code E1. Blank: Blank 1: Master business function 2: Major business function 3: Minor business function
SIBUF4	Business Function Category 4	3	String	This is for future use.

TABLE 9-3.   F9862 Table *(continued)*

Column Name	Description	Length	Type	Valid Values
SIBUF5	Business Function Category 5	3	String	This is for future use.
SIPID	Program ID	10	String	The name of the program that changed the object record in F9861.
SIUSER	User ID	10	String	The identification associated with a specific OneWorld user who modified F9862.
SIJOBN	Work Station ID	10	String	The name of the workstation that ran the application that modified the object record in F9862.
SIUPMJ	Date – Updated	6	Date	The date the object was modified.
SIUPMT	Time – Last Updated	6	Numeric	The time the object was modified.
SIDSTNM	Name – Data Structure Template	10	String	The name of the data structure template.
SIEVSK	Event Spec Key	36	String	The primary key used when generating the GBRSPEC TAM file.

TABLE 9-3.   F9862 Table *(continued)*

N O T E

When you are working with the OneWorld application (especially during troubleshooting), you may notice that a particular function will cause an issue. The logs almost never tell you what actual business function failed, simply the function in the business function that caused the issue. You can use the F9862 table to quickly cross-reference the offending function with the associated business function.

Inside and Out

The F9863 Table (Object Librarian – Object Relationships)

The F9863 table is exactly what it seems (refer to Table 9-4 for detailed column data on this table). It defines the connection between the business functions and other objects, primarily other business functions and tables. However, there are a few business functions that have direct relationships with UBEs and one that is even related to a data structure. This table has approximately 7,000 entries in the B733.2 version of OneWorld.

Column Name	Description	Length	Type	Valid Values
SIOBNM	Object Name	10	String	The unique name associated with a specific object in OneWorld.
SIFUNO	Object Type	4	String	The description of the use of the object as controlled by UDC product code 98, report code OF. APPL: Interactive application BL: Business function library BSFN: Business function module BSVW: Business view DSTR: Data structure GT: Media object data structure TBLE: Table definition UBE: Batch application
SIOBNMRL	Name – Object Related	10	String	Any related object.
SIJDEVERS	Version	10	String	The name for the release of OneWorld. This field is not used in B733.2.
SIMRGMOD	Flag – Modification	1	Character	A Y/N flag that indicates if an object has been changed. This flag is instrumental in determining items modified prior to an upgrade or update.

TABLE 9-4.   F9863 Table

Column Name	Description	Length	Type	Valid Values
SIMRGOPT	Option – Merge	1	Character	A flag indicating whether to merge objects. This can be set at the path code level. Valid options are maintained in the UDC product code 98 report code EO. Blank: Do not merge 1: Merge 2: Do not merge
SIPID	Program ID	10	String	The name of the program that changed the object record in F9861.
SIUSER	User ID	10	String	The identification associated with a specific OneWorld user who modified F9862.
SIJOBN	Work Station ID	10	String	The name of the workstation that ran the application that modified the object record in F9862.
SIUPMJ	Date – Updated	6	Date	The date the object was modified.
SIUPMT	Time – Last Updated	6	Numeric	The time the object was modified.

TABLE 9-4. F9863 Table *(continued)*

The F9865 Table (Object Librarian – Form Information)

The F9865 table defines each and every form in every application in the OneWorld system. Some of the information contained in this table includes the form name, its ID (where held over from earlier releases of OneWorld), the form description, the form type (parent/child, find/browse, and so on), the system code, the application, and the help file associated to it. There are more than 4,300 forms in the B733.2 version of OneWorld.

Inside and Out

Checked-Out Items

The F9861 table can be used to quickly identify items that are checked out by path code, machine, and user. By using a direct SQL statement against this table, you can determine who has what item checked out to what machine and when they did it. This can also be modified to run on a weekly basis to help identify when developers don't check items into the path code for the week. This will allow the CNC administrator to manage object development.

```
SELECT siobnm, sipathcd, simkey, siuser, siupmj FROM OBJB733.F9861
WHERE simkey<>'DEPLOYMENT SVR NAME'
ORDER BY sipathcd, siuser, siupmj
```

Another quick note on this is that it is a read-only select statement. Consequently, there is no way to damage your data or database by running the query above. This means you do not need to back up this table prior to using this method. It is both quick and efficient.

The Object Librarian and Copying a Path Code

If you are going to copy one path code to the other, you need to remember that the F9861 table defines the objects in each path code (especially if you want to check them out or build packages). Prior to copying the path code, run the SQL statement listed in the preceding Law of the West to ensure that no objects are checked out. Copy the central objects using R98403 or RDBMS. (Note: MS SQL Server 6.5 has been known to have issues with copying central objects.) Then copy the F9861 table to your local machine using R98403 (refer to Chapter 7 for more information on the R98403 Table Copy UBE). Run the following SQL statements against the object librarian F9861 table:

```
DELETE objb733.f9861 WHERE sipathcd='target path code'
```

In the access database (remember that you copied F9861 here in one of the steps above), run a make table query selecting records where the sipathcd equals the source path code. Call the table temp. Run an update statement against the resulting temp table to change the sipathcd field from the source to the target path code:

```
UPDATE temp SET sipathcd='target path code'
```

Change the name of the original F9861 table in your local access database to F9861_org. Rename the temp table to F9861 and use R98403 in append mode to add the new records. After that, the only remaining tasks would be to copy the appropriate directory structure, rename packages and INFs, copy F983051 from the version's data source, update the vrenhv field to equal your new path code, and use the new or refreshed path code.

Object Librarian Tools

We decided to offer a quick review of the tools associated with the object librarian but not go into an exhaustive explanation for a couple of different reasons. First, this book is not a developer's guide and since the tools associated with the object librarian are development tools, this isn't the proper forum for that type of discussion. Second, there is a developer's guide available from the J.D. Edwards Press that is the appropriate place for detailed instructions on this matter (*J.D. Edwards OneWorld: A Developer's Guide*).

Form Design Aid (FDA)

The FDA toolset (refer to Figure 9-2) is used to modify and create interactive applications for use in the OneWorld suite of applications. Using the FDA, you can create any of the seven form types in OneWorld (Find/Browse, Fix Inspect, Header Detail, Headerless Detail, Search & Select, Message Form, Parent/Child Browse).

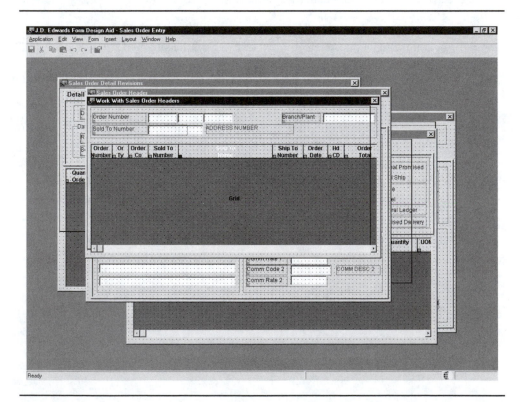

FIGURE 9-2. Form Design Aid development tool

Business Function Parent Library

Business functions are grouped into a series of libraries (DLL, sl, or applications, depending on the platform) for deployment throughout the ERP system. The object librarian controls which business functions are associated with which parent libraries (see Figure 9-3). J.D. Edwards recommends that custom business functions be placed into a company-specific parent library to safeguard it during upgrades and updates.

Business Function Design

This tool (refer to Figure 9-4), found in the object librarian, is able to add, create, or modify business functions. It also houses any attachments or other parameters (such as data structures, tables, and so on) used by the business function. To directly modify code in the business function, the toolset will automatically launch Microsoft Visual C++ on the local workstation.

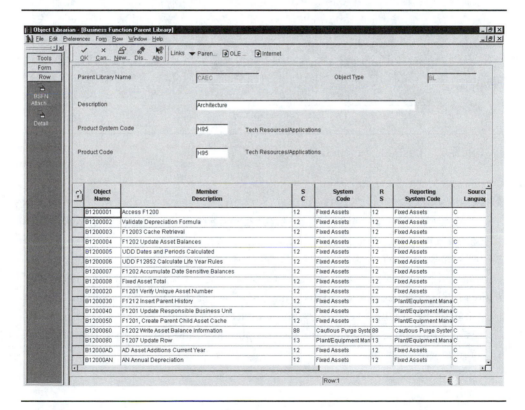

FIGURE 9-3. Business function parent library

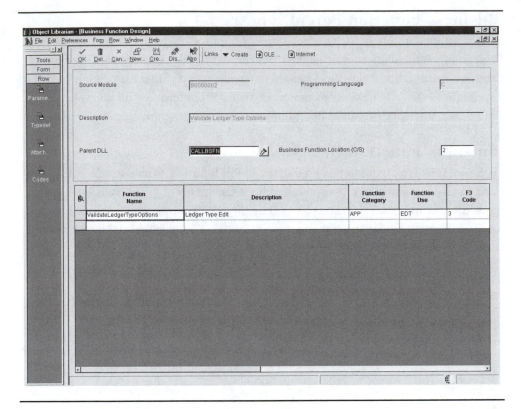

FIGURE 9-4. Business Function Design tool

Business View Design Aid

The Business View Design Aid is a tool accessed by the object librarian (see Figure 9-5). It is specifically designed to assist with the creation, modification, and maintenance of business views in the OneWorld suite of applications. Business views allow you to create custom definitions of how to view data in a table or between multiple tables. Because many of the tables in OneWorld have a huge number of associated tables, business views let you limit the number of columns you see or access in a table. Business views are used by business functions, interactive and batch applications, and named event rules on both servers and workstations.

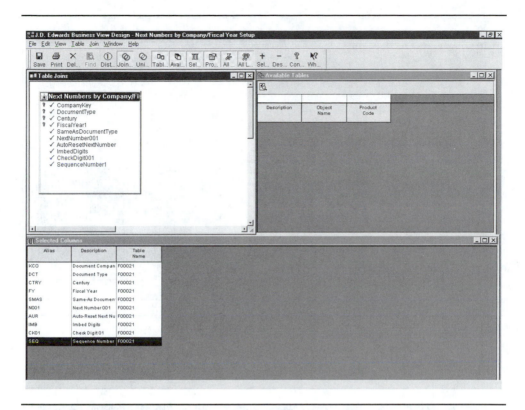

FIGURE 9-5.   Business View Design Aid

Data Structures

When you need to modify, create, or maintain data structures in OneWorld, the object librarian has a tool called Parameter Design specifically designed to assist in this development effort (refer to Figure 9-6). This tool is able to search the data dictionary, specify required fields, and link variable to specific data items.

Media Object Data Structure

Similar to the data structures listed above (and using the same toolset), media object data structures (see Figure 9-7) can be added, modified, and maintained from the object librarian.

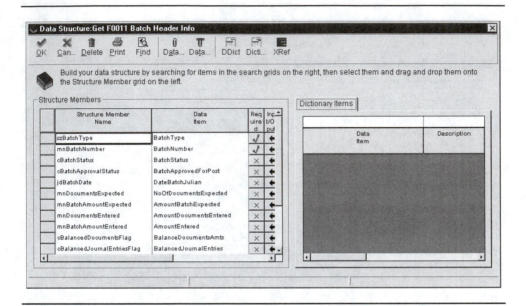

FIGURE 9-6. Data structures

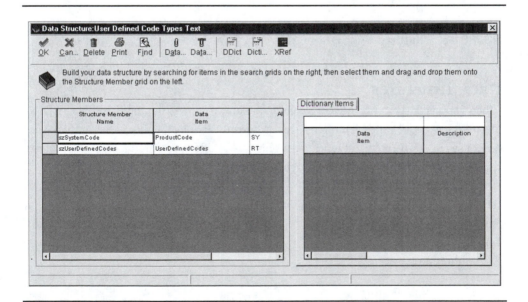

FIGURE 9-7. Media objects data structure

Table Design Aid (TDA)

As described in Chapter 7 of this book, the object librarian has a tool to define, create, and copy tables and their indexes in OneWorld (see Figure 9-8). All tables have to be defined to OneWorld prior to being used by the interactive and batch applications. The tool includes a data dictionary browser to find and then (in a drag-and-drop mode) add data items to tables and indexes of tables.

Batch Applications

The object librarian has a tool designed to add, modify, and maintain batch applications called the Report Design Aid (RDA). (See Figure 9-9.) This tool has the capability to create reports as well as manipulate data with reports, with a slew of custom tools using business functions, table IO, and such. This is the primary report aid for the OneWorld suite.

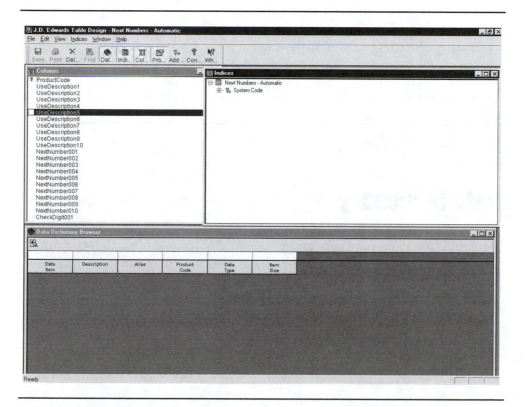

FIGURE 9-8. Table Design Aid

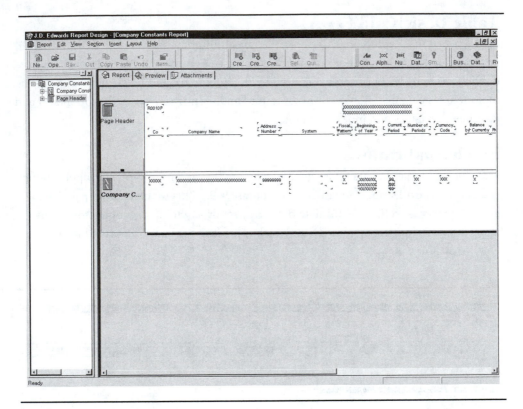

FIGURE 9-9.   Report Design Aid

Data Dictionary

What is the data dictionary and how does it qualify as part of the specialty applications group? It is one of the most important pieces of the OneWorld product. It is in every installation and implementation. If there is a problem with it, you will definitely hear about it. In this section, we will discuss in more detail what the data dictionary is and what considerations you need to have when you are working with it.

Data Dictionary Defined

The data dictionary is a central repository of data item information. Many of the elements in the data dictionary are immediately realized when changed without the requirements of recompiling the software. This is true of all components of the data dictionary except for row and column descriptions. The data dictionary performs the following functions in the OneWorld system:

- Defines every data item in the OneWorld system including column definitions and base text information. We will discuss this in more detail later in this section.

- Determines how data items appear on reports and interactive forms.

- Provides error messaging.

- Contains column and row descriptions. These may be used as default values when developing in OneWorld.

- Used in conjunction with UDC values to validate field data entry (when you enter information into a field and the field turns red indicating an error, the data dictionary was instrumental in determining the validity of the data entered).

- Provides field-level help messages.

- Determines the number of decimal places displayed in various interfaces and calculations throughout the system.

Data Dictionary Tables

The tables associated with the data dictionary include the following in the central repository:

- F00165 (Media Objects Storage)

- F9200 (Data Item Master)

- F9202 (Data Field Display Text)

- F9203 (Data Item Alpha Descriptions)

- F9207 (Data Dictionary – Error Message Information)

- F9210 (Data Field Specifications)

- F9211 (Data Dictionary Smart Fields)

We'll start with the F9200 table (Data Item Master), see Table 9-5, and work our way forward as we gain a better understanding of what is in the data dictionary. The F9200 table is the header information for each data item and includes the data item name, its system code, and its reporting code. It also contains some audit data, including the user identification of the user who either added or modified the data dictionary item last, the machine the change was issued from and when the change occurred.

Column Name	Description	Length	Type	Valid Values
FRDTAI	Data Item	10	String	Any alphanumeric combination up to 10 characters.
FRSY	Product Code	4	String	There are 276 valid values in the B733.2 product. More can be added to the UDC values where product code is 98 and record type is SY.
FRSYR	Product Code/Reporting	4	String	The same combination of valid values listed above. The difference is that this field is used for reporting and jargon purposes.
FRGG	Glossary Group	1	Character	C: Data item class D : Primary data elements K : Smart fields S : Secondary (dates, arrays, and so on) Or any additional value as validated against UDC product code H98, record type DI.
FRUSER	User ID	10	String	The user ID who last modified the data item. If the data item has never been modified, it will contain the name of the person who originally added the item.
FRPID	Program ID	10	String	The OneWorld batch or interactive application identification. These follow a standard naming convention.
FRUPMJ	Date – Updated	6	Date	The last date the data dictionary record was updated. This date is maintained in the following format: xxxyyy, where xxx is a three-digit number derived by taking the current system year and subtracting 1900 (for example, 2000 – 1900 = 100) and yyy is the three-digit Julian day (that is, January 1 is represented as 001).

TABLE 9-5.   F9200 Table

| FRJOBN | Work Station ID | 10 | String | This is the name of the workstation that made the entry or last modified the data dictionary record. |
| FRUPMT | Time – Last Updated | 6 | Numeric | The time the data dictionary was last updated or added. The format is hhmmss, where hh represents the hour (for example, 3:00P.M. is 15), mm represents the minutes, ss represents the seconds. |

TABLE 9-5. F9200 Table *(continued)*

There is a single index on the F9200 table called F9200_1. This index is on the FRDTAI column and is unique, ensuring that there are no duplications of data items (at least, there are no duplications of data item identifications). The next table we should discuss is F9202 (Data Field Display Text). (See Table 9-6 for more detailed information.) This table only has eight associated columns, but is one of the more widely used tables in OneWorld (especially for companies implementing OneWorld). It contains a language identifier and several different columns for descriptions and field-sensitive help.

The F9202 table contains a single unique index (F9202_1) based on the FRDTAI, FRLNGP and FRSYR (data item, language, and product code). The next table is F9203 (also known as the Data Field Display Text table). Table 9-7 contains a detailed look at this table. It maintains descriptions used in both the data dictionary searches and the object librarian records.

The F9203 table has two indexes (F9203_1 and F9203_2). F9203_1 contains FRDTAI, FRLNGP, FRSYR, and FRSCRN (data item, language, product code, and screen name) and is unique. F9203_2 has a single column associated (FRDSCA, alpha description); however, it is not unique. The next table up for discussion is the F9207 table (Data Dictionary – Error Message Information). It is important in that all error messages displayed in OneWorld originate from this table. Many organizations decided to modify these error messages to make more sense to their specific implementation of the product. There are only six columns that make up the F9207 table and they are explained in some detail in Table 9-8.

Inside and Out

Column Name	Description	Length	Type	Valid Values
FRDTAI	Data Item	10	String	Any alphanumeric combination up to 10 characters.
FRLNGP	Language	2	String	There are 25 languages identified with OneWorld as defined by the UDC system code of 01 and product code of LP.
FRSYR	Product Code/Reporting	4	String	The same combination of valid values listed above. The difference is that this field is used for reporting and jargon purposes.
FRCH1	Column Title 1 – XREF build	20	String	This is the first line of a column description for a report. When possible, it should not be longer than the data item itself; this will make writing reports easier.
FRCH2	Column Title 2 – XREF build	20	String	This is the second line of a column description for column headings on reports and forms. When possible, it should not be longer than the data item itself; this will make writing reports and developing applications easier.
FRCH3	Column Title 3 – XREF build	20	String	This is the third line of a column description for heading on reports and forms. It is always underlined for esthetic reasons.
FRDSCR	Description – Row	40	String	This is a row description for use with forms and reports. In an interactive application, the F1 will display this information as a description of the field itself. This is also known as field-sensitive helps.

TABLE 9-6.　F9202 Table

Column Name	Description	Length	Type	Valid Values
FRDTAI	Data Item	10	String	Any alphanumeric combination up to 10 characters.
FRLNGP	Language	2	String	There are 25 languages identified with OneWorld as defined by the UDC system code of 01 and product code of LP.
FRSYR	Product Code/Reporting	4	String	The same combination of valid values listed above. The difference is that this field is used for reporting and jargon purposes.
FRDSCA	Alpha Description	40	String	This field is used to help categorize data items and assists with identifying other like data items. When entering alpha descriptions, you should follow these rules: Date goes in front of a date data item. Amounts start each data item that holds amounts. Unit should be the first word for data items that contain units, quantities, or volumes. Name starts all 30 character description fields. Prompt begins yes/no prompting fields. Address Number starts all data items that contain address numbers.
FRDSCC	Description – Compressed	40	String	This is used in the data dictionary name search and is the alpha description without spaces, dashes, commas, or other punctuation.
FRSCRN	Screen/Report Name	10	String	The form or application name used in the object librarian tables.

TABLE 9-7. F9203 Table

Column Name	Description	Length	Type	Valid Values
FRDTAI	Data Item	10	String	Any alphanumeric combination up to 10 characters.
FRPGM	Program Name	10	String	The application/executable name.
FRERLV	Error Level	1	Character	Indicates the level of the error message. Valid values include the following: 1: Error message 2: Warning message 3: Informative message
FRTMID	Data Structure Template ID	11	Identifier	Identifies the data structure template.
FRDSON	Object Name – Data Structure	10	String	The name of the object used to identify the error message substitute variables.
FRDDID	Data Dictionary Identifier – Everest	11	Identifier	A unique number assigned to each data dictionary item.

TABLE 9-8.   F9207 Table

There is a single unique index on the F9207 table, labeled F9207_1, based on the FRDTAI column. The next table is the F9210 table (Data Field Specifications – refer to Table 9-9). This table has 46 columns and defines each data item in detail, including the type of field, the number of decimal places, and so on. This is the real information behind the data dictionary item definitions and can be considered the detail lines to F9200's header information.

Column Name	Description	Length	Type	Valid Values
FRDTAI	Data Item	10	String	Any alphanumeric combination up to 10 characters.
FRCLAS	Data Item Class	10	String	An information-only description of the attributes of a data item and its associated characteristics.

TABLE 9-9.   F9210 Table

Column Name	Description	Length	Type	Valid Values
FRDTAT	Data Item Type	1	Character	Defines the type of data to be maintained in the data field. A: Alphanumeric B: Binary O: Open P: Packed numeric S: Signed numeric
FRDTAD	Data File Decimals	2	Numeric	Indicates the number of decimal places right of the decimal point data is stored.
FRARRN	Number of Array Elements	3	Numeric	When specifying a data element in the data dictionary, you may specify the number of array elements associated with the data item. This will automatically add one data item per array.
FRDVAL	Value for Entry – Default	20	String	Used as an initial value automatically defaulted in on a data entry screen. The value should be no larger than the data item size.
FRLR	Reporting Code – Unit Master	3	String	A reporting code for the Unit Master File. The only valid value shipped with B733.2 is "Default." This is defined with a product code of 15 and a record type of RL.
FRCDEC	Display Decimals	1	Character	This is used to indicate the number of decimal places displayed to the user and used in various calculations throughout the system.

TABLE 9-9.   F9210 Table *(continued)*

Inside and Out

Column Name	Description	Length	Type	Valid Values
FRDRUL	Data Display Rules	6	String	A list of words describing how data items are displayed. Valid values shipped with B733.2 include: Blank: No formatting *PROC: Detail programming *RAB: Right adjust blank fill *RABN: Right adjust blank fill not CCtr *RAZ: Right adjust zero fill Code: Edit code formatting Mask: Edit mask/word formatting PGM: External formatting program
FRDRO1	Data Display Parameters	40	String	This field contains additional parameters for the data display rules above.
FRERUL	Data Edit Rules	6	String	A list of keywords indicating the type of editing and validation associated with a data item. These 17 values are listed in the UDC product code 98 record type ER. Blank: No editing *PROC: Detail programming CHKOBJ: Check object EQ: Equal FILE: Validation file GE: Greater or equal GT: Greater LE: Less than or equal LT: Less than NE: Not equal NRANGE: Not between NVALUE: Not in a list PGM: Validation program RANGE: Between SERVER: File server UDC: User-defined code VALUE: In a list

TABLE 9-9.   F9210 Table *(continued)*

Column Name	Description	Length	Type	Valid Values
FRERO1	Edit Rules Specification 1	40	String	The first of two parameters passed to the data edit rules. For example, if the data edit rule was UDC, the first value passed would be the product code.
FRERO2	Edit Rules Specification 2	40	String	The second parameter passed to the data edit rules. With the exception of RANGE and UDC, this value should be blank. For RANGE, the upper limit is provided. For UDCs, the record code is listed.
FRHLP1	Help Text Program	10	String	This field contains the name of a program to be executed when the F1 is pressed on the specific data field. If left blank, the glossary text will automatically display.
FRHLP2	Help List Program	10	String	This field is often used to display alternate language help text.
FRNNIX	Next Numbering Index Number	2	Numeric	The array element number pulled from the next-number revisions application.
FRNSY	System Code – Next Numbers	4	String	This is the system number from the next numbers as indicated with UDC product code 98 report code SY. There are 267 valid values shipped with the B733.2 version of OneWorld.
FRRLS	Release Number	10	String	The release version of OneWorld (such as B733).
FRUSER	User ID	10	String	The user ID who last modified the data item. If the data item has never been modified, it will contain the name of the person who originally added the item.

TABLE 9-9.   F9210 Table (*continued*)

Column Name	Description	Length	Type	Valid Values
FRUPMJ	Date – Updated	6	Date	The last date the data dictionary record was updated. This date is maintained in the following format: xxxyyy, where xxx is a three-digit number derived by taking the current system year and subtracting 1900 (for example, 2000 – 1900 = 100) and yyy is the three-digit Julian day (that is, January 1 is represented as 001).
FRPID	Program ID	10	String	The OneWorld batch or interactive application identification. These follow a standard naming convention.
FRJOBN	Work Station ID	10	String	This is the name of the workstation that made the entry or last modified the data dictionary record.
FRUPMT	Time – Last Updated	6	Numeric	This is the time the data dictionary was last updated or added. The format is hhmmss, where hh represents the hour (for example, 3:00 P.M. is 15), mm represents the minutes, ss represents the seconds.
FROWDI	Data Item – OneWorld	40	String	An identifier that forms the name of the C code data name used in business functions, data structures, and event rules. This identifier can't have blanks or special characters.

TABLE 9-9.   F9210 Table (*continued*)

Column Name	Description	Length	Type	Valid Values
FROWTP	Data Type – OneWorld	2	String	This identifies the type of data field and is used to generate tables. It is defined by UDC product code H98, report code DT, and has nine valid entries in B733.2. 1: Character 2: String 7: Identifier 9: Numeric 11: Date 15: Integer 17: Character (BLOB) 18: Binary 20: Variable string
FRCNTT	Control Type	1	Character	Defines the type of graphical user control associated with the data item (push button, check box, and so on).
FRSCFG	Flag – One World Security	1	Character	A flag indicating if row security can be applied to the data item. There are only 40 data items shipped by J.D. Edwards with this flag set to Y by default; however, you can change this variable when implementing row security.
FRUPER	Upper Case Only	1	Character	A Y in this field will ensure that the user enters uppercase only in the field.
FRALBK	Allow Blank Entry	1	Character	This will allow blank entries for specific data items. There are two conditions to this entry. If the data item is validated against a UDC and a blank value is in the UDC range, a blank value will be written to the data base regardless of this entry. The other condition is if the data item is mandatory, a blank will be allowed regardless of this entry.

TABLE 9-9. F9210 Table (*continued*)

Column Name	Description	Length	Type	Valid Values
FROWER	Data Edit Rules – OneWorld	6	String	Keywords describing editing techniques associated with the data item. There are 12 valid values as defined in the UDC product code H98 report code ER. EQ: Equal GE: Greater or equal GT: Greater HNDL: Table handle LE: Less than or equal LT: Less than NE: Not equal NRANGE: Not between RANGE: Between UDC: User-defined code VALUE: In a list ZLNGTH: Allocated length
FROER1	Edit Rules Specification 1 – OneWorld	40	String	The first of two parameters passed to the data edit rules.
FROER2	Edit Rules Specification 2 – OneWorld	40	String	The second of two parameters passed to the data edit rules.
FROWDR	Data Display Rules – OneWorld	6	String	A description of the formatting technique applied when data is displayed. This is controlled by the UDC product code H98 report code DR and has five valid values in B733.2. *RAB: Right adjust blank fill *RABN: Right adjust blank fill/not CCtr *RAZ: Right adjust zero fill CODE: Edit code formatting MASK: Edit mask/word formatting

TABLE 9-9.   F9210 Table (*continued*)

Column Name	Description	Length	Type	Valid Values
FRODR1	Data Display Parameters (OneWorld)	40	String	Additional information for display rules.
FRDBID	Display Business Function ID – OneWorld	11	Identifier	A OneWorld ID for a display rule.
FRBFDN	Object Name – Display Business Function	32	String	The object name of the business function used when displaying the data item.
FREBID	Edit Business Function ID – OneWorld	11	Identifier	An ID used for an edit rule behavior.
FRBFEN	Object Name – Edit Business Function	32	String	The object name of the business function used when displaying the data item.
FRSFID	Search Form ID – Everest	11	Identifier	The ID of the search form associated with a data item.
FRSFMN	Object Name – Search Form	10	String	The object name of the search form attached to the data item.
FRBVID	Business View ID – Everest	11	Identifier	The Everest ID that corresponds to a business view.
FRBVNM	Object Name – Business View	10	String	The object name of the business view associated with the data item.
FRPLFG	Flag – Platform (OneWorld/AS400)	1	Character	This indicates if the data item is valid for World, OneWorld, or both. 1: OneWorld only 2: World only Blank: Both development platforms
FRDDID	Data Dictionary Identifier – Everest	11	Identifier	A unique ID associated with every data item.
FRAUIN	Auto Include Flag (Y/N)	1	Character	This check box indicates that the data item should be fetched every time the table containing it is queried. Use sparingly.

TABLE 9-9. F9210 Table (*continued*)

There are two indexes associated with F9210 (F9210_1 and F9210_2) for the columns FRDTAI and FROWDI, respectively. F9210_1 is unique. The next table we'll discuss with regard to the data dictionary is F9211 (Data Dictionary Smart Fields) Refer to Table 9-10 for a more detailed explanation of what this table is and what functions the columns provide.

There is only one index associated with F9211 (F9211_1). It is unique and based on the single column, FRDTAI. In addition to the F92 series tables, the data dictionary also has an associated table for text and language data (F00165). This table is similar to many other F00165 tables used throughout the OneWorld system.

Column Name	Description	Length	Type	Valid Values
FRDTAI	Data Item	10	String	Any alphanumeric combination up to 10 characters.
FRSFCVBF	Smart Field Column Value BF	31	String	The name of the business function used to populate this field.
FRSFCVNM	Smart Field Column Value Mapping	10	String	The name of the Named Mapping associated with the Smart Field Business Function. This identifies the necessary information about the data items that allows the design tool to create the necessary Event Rule Logic.
FRSFCHBF	Smart Field Column Header BF	31	String	The name of the business function used to derive the column headers of the associated data item.
FRSFCHNM	Smart Field Column Header Map	10	String	The name of the Named Mapping Column Heading associated with the data item.

TABLE 9-10.   F9211 Table

Data Dictionary Locations

The data dictionary is maintained in several different locations throughout the enterprise. The recommendation is that you have a single data dictionary instance (there can be exceptions for development and co-existence) maintained in a central relational database repository. For speed considerations, OneWorld has been specifically designed to use locally replicated sets of data dictionary information. These are located in Table Access Management (TAM), a proprietary database file structure used exclusively with OneWorld, on each machine that has OneWorld code. This is similar to the central objects specifications in design.

Let's take the example of a typical customer configuration using a Sun/Oracle platform. The data dictionary tables reside on the enterprise server in the Oracle database. The same table data is also on the server in each OneWorld server path code on the server in the GLBLTBL, DDTEXT, and DDDICT files (there are a total of six files: each of the three files has a .DDB and .XDB file extension, such as GLBLTBL.DDB and GLBLTBL.XDB). Is that the only place the data dictionary information resides? No! Actually, clients also have the replicated files listed above on them as well. The original tables with all of the data dictionary files reside on the deployment server. When you now look at it, you have data dictionary information in four different primary locations.

The Data Dictionary and Development

Anyone who has worked with the OneWorld development toolset, either interactive or batch applications, knows that the column names for data fields are somewhat archaic – especially when you consider long filename support. You'll see column names like OMOBNM or VRPID and might have a difficult time understanding that these two columns actually contain the same data in two different tables. The actual data dictionary defined items are OBNM (object name) and PID (program identification).

Let's consider how the data dictionary helps with development. First, before any data item can be used in the system, it must be defined to the data dictionary. This is done using the data dictionary application (P92001; this will be discussed in more detail later in this section). When tables are designed, you use these data item definitions to describe your new table columns. The object librarian is then able to use these definitions when generating the table in the database.

Second, once you have a table to store the information in, you want to add, manipulate, and display the information for and to end users. The data dictionary allows you to control what type of data is entered into your tables, whether it is capitalized, what applications are used to validate the information entered, and even the number of decimals displayed to the end users. It controls every aspect of the data entered and displayed.

Finally, the data dictionary itself is integral to any OneWorld development. Each of the tools associated with OneWorld has and uses a data dictionary browser, allowing development to find, drag, and drop these definitions into the forms, reports, and tables they are creating and modifying. When a developer wants to add an index to a table through OneWorld, he can find the data item in the data dictionary browser and drag the definition of the data item into the index definition.

Working with the Data Dictionary Application

Now that you know what the data dictionary is and some of what it does, you need to know how to manipulate it and add to it as necessary. There is a disclaimer that needs to be put forward at this point. It is strongly recommended that you do not modify most of the data dictionary specifications as shipped by J.D. Edwards (one of the exceptions to this rule is the glossary text). Doing so could adversely affect any number of tables, interactive applications, or reports. Traditionally, it is only recommended that you add or modify items that have been added to the data dictionary. It is also recommended that you don't delete any data items shipped by J.D. Edwards.

Interactive Applications

To get to the data dictionary application, type **dd** in the Fast Path or go to the GH951 menu (refer to Figure 9-10) through the OneWorld Explorer.

You will notice that there is one primary application P92001, a secondary P92002 application containing several different versions based on what you are trying to accomplish, and several batch applications that are used to help administer data dictionary that can be accessed through this menu. The P92001 application is described in much greater detail in the J.D. Edwards OneWorld Developer's Guide; however, we wanted to go over what the application does and how the data dictionary works in general. As with most of the applications we describe, we will use an example so that you can gain a better understanding of the application itself. In this case, we are going to work with the alias ENHV and the environment field.

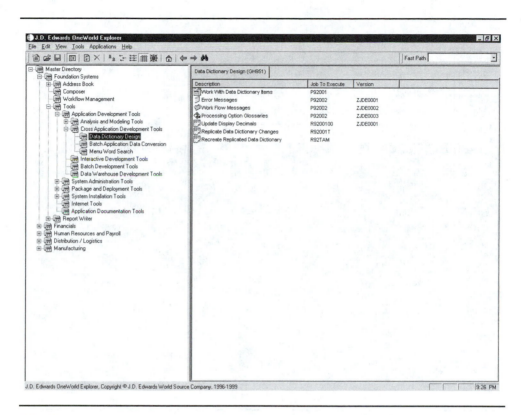

FIGURE 9-10. GH951 Data Dictionary Design

To start P92001, double-click it on the GH951 menu. You will see a basic search form allowing you to find your data dictionary item in different ways, including by data dictionary name, by alias, and by description. You can even find all of the data items by system code. All these options become useful when trying to find data items associated with a specific product or if you aren't quite sure what the data item is called. In the Alias QBE line, type **ENHV** and click the Find button (refer to Figure 9-11).

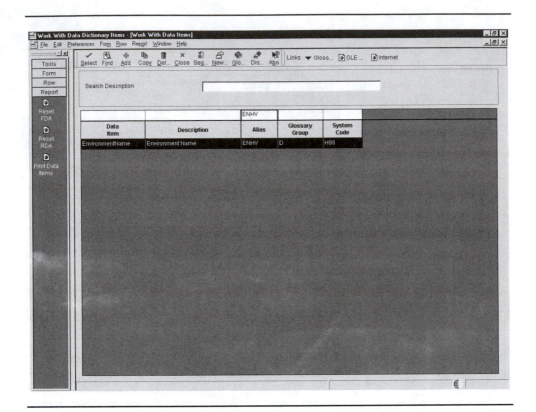

FIGURE 9-11.   EnvironmentName data item

Either click Select or double-click the grid row to access the EnvironmentName data item record (this can be seen in Figure 9-12). You will note that there are elements from several different tables displayed on this form; however, the majority of the information is from the F9200 and F9210 tables.

You will also note that this form contains a series of tabs that display most of the other data controlled by the data dictionary. Feel free to explore this application, but remember the warning provided earlier not to delete entries. If you accidentally modify something, click the Cancel button so you don't cause any harm to your OneWorld implementation.

P92002 – Messaging Application   This was a quick introduction to the P92001 application—as specified earlier, refer to the Developer's Guide for more information on

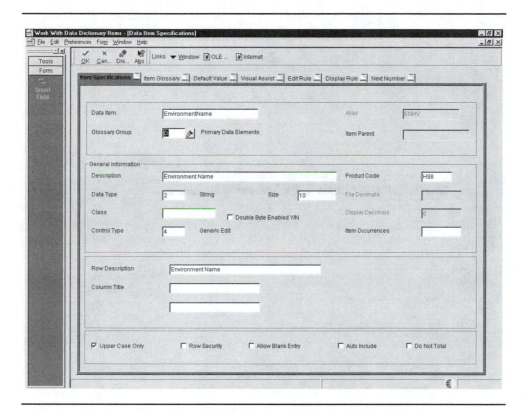

FIGURE 9-12. W9200C Data Item Specifications

this particular tool. The P92002 application primarily works with text information and error messaging (an example of this can be seen in Figure 9-13). One of the differences in this application as opposed to other applications in OneWorld is that you can specify particular languages as you modify these messages. This will allow you greater customization regarding the system itself—that is, it gives the look and feel of a custom application when you modify the error coding to make it more pertinent to your specific situation. One caveat to this process (and for that matter changing the glossary text of a data item using P92001): remember that the same message and data item can be used in multiple locations throughout OneWorld. Though making a change might make great sense to you for a specific application, it might be a very different story for another application.

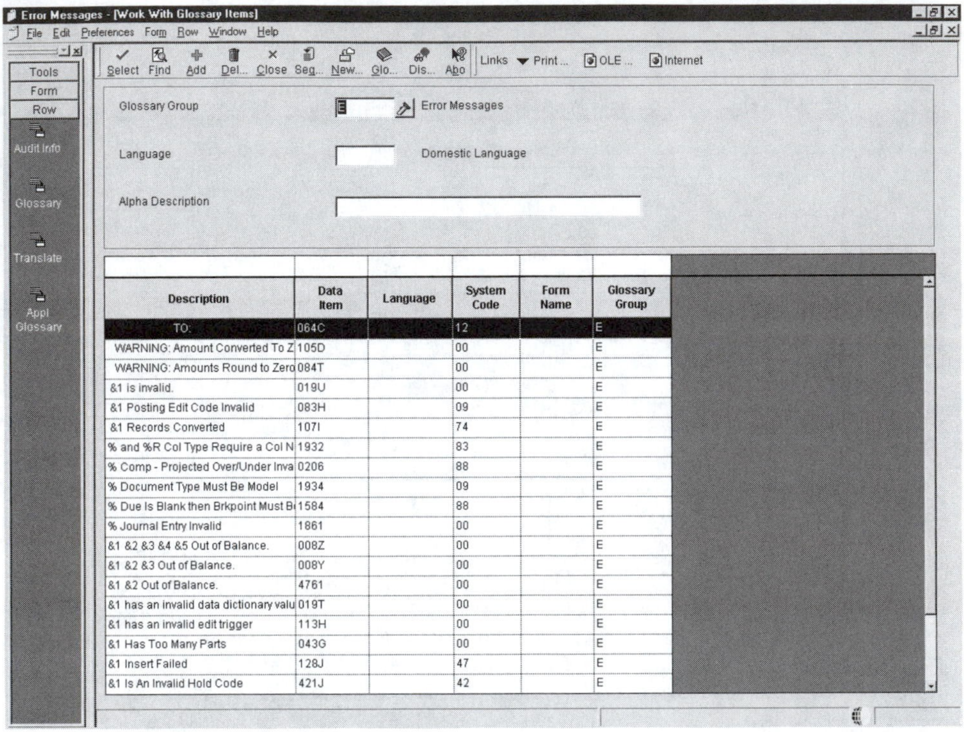

FIGURE 9-13. P92002 Error Messages

There are more than 7,900 error messages shipped with the B733.2 release (over 8,900 in the OneWorld Xe release, formerly B733.3) of the OneWorld product. There are more than 3,300 workflow messages and more than 2,200 glossary items shipped with the product. Each of these three types of messages use the same P92002 application but with different glossary group definitions.

- E   Error messages

- Y   Work flow messages

- H   Glossary items

Batch Applications

There are three batch applications associated with data dictionary maintenance; depending on how you use the data dictionary, you might use one or all them. J.D. Edwards recommends that you assign one or two users per functional area to be the data dictionary masters (primary and backup). These individuals should fully understand their functional area as well as have a solid understanding of how OneWorld is being used in those areas. Personally, however, we haven't found many organizations that want to provide that many individuals with the ability to manipulate the data dictionary. Instead, there are usually two or three people in the entire organization who have the ability to modify these records.

R9200100 – Update Display Decimals   Similar to this concept, the three data dictionary batch applications should also have tight security because they can definitely cause problems with your system. One of the most important of these batches is the R9200100 – Update Display Decimals UBE (refer to Figure 9-14). This UBE is designed to determine the number of display decimals used for display and calculations. If you are going to run this UBE, it is recommended that it be run prior to data entry. OneWorld stores numbers as integers in the database. The number of decimals you see is dependent on the number set in the data dictionary. If you have a substantial amount of data in your database and decide that inventory really should be calculated to four decimal places instead of two, you could quickly devalue your company's assets. There are no conversion programs in OneWorld to automatically add two zeros to every inventory field in the system.

What makes a mistake like this even worse is that the number of display decimals is used in every calculation from that point forward. We think you can see how quickly things could get messed up with this batch application. The only nice part is that you can always run the batch again and set the decimal places back to two if you've made this type of mistake. Our recommendation is that you determine the number of decimal places you want early in your implementation cycle, set it using the R9200100 batch application, and then place security to ensure that no one "accidentally" runs it.

Inside and Out

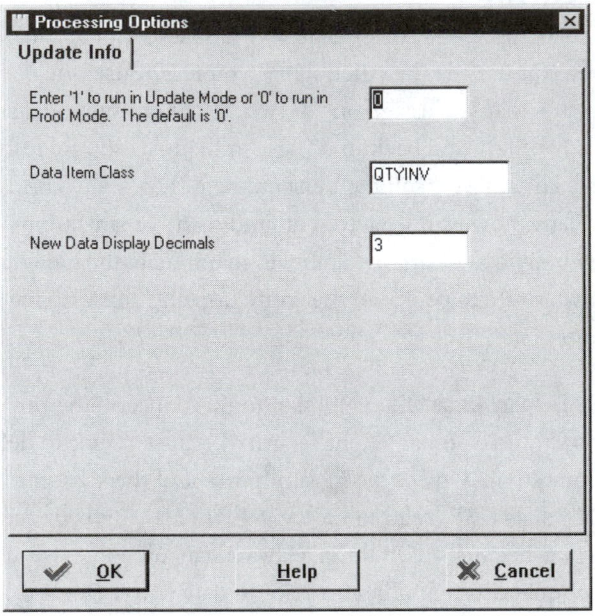

FIGURE 9-14.   R9200100 Update Display Decimals

Replicate Data Dictionary Changes   The next batch application on our list is the R92001T Replicate Data Dictionary Changes UBE (see Figure 9-15) located on the GH951 menu. This is a relatively harmless UBE designed to update local data dictionary TAM files with all changes from a specified date forward. It is relatively easy to use and is traditionally part of the data dictionary administration process (prior to making data dictionary changes, this can be run to ensure that the administrator's local TAM contains the latest data dictionary information).

When you launch the R92001T application, you will be prompted to select a version (XJDE0001 is shipped with the product). After selecting your version, check Data Selection and Override location. Run the UBE locally and validate that the Date Updated field has the date of your last full data dictionary TAM file build. When you run the UBE, your local TAM files will be updated with every change to the data dictionary since that date.

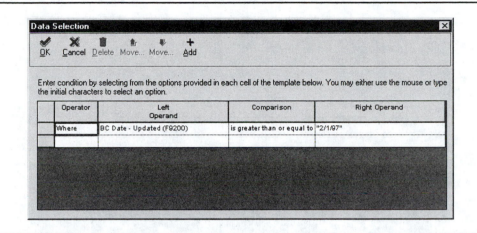

FIGURE 9-15. R92001T Replicate Data Dictionary Changes

Re-create Replicated Data Dictionary   The R92TAM application (refer to Figure 9-16) varies from R92001T in that rather than updating your existing TAM files located in the specifications directory of the path code you sign into, you create a new set of data dictionary TAM files located directly in the root of the B7 directory on the administrator's workstation. The amount of time necessary to re-create the data dictionary TAM files varies based on your local workstation. Once completed, these files can be copied to the deployment server for package builds or terminal servers to decrease required just-in-time-installation (JITI) on those machines. You also use these TAM files for the enterprise server. This is done through a process called TAMFTP (a special OneWorld application designed to convert workstation TAM into the server's platform specific file format).

Data Dictionary Administration

We've already described the tools at the data dictionary administrator's disposal. Now it is time to describe base data dictionary administration. As we mentioned earlier, you definitely don't want just anyone in the data dictionary applications. If something were to go drastically wrong with the data dictionary, it could easily cost someone his or her job. If you limit who has access to the menu and then add security beyond that, you can assume that your data dictionary will be kept relatively safe.

Inside and Out

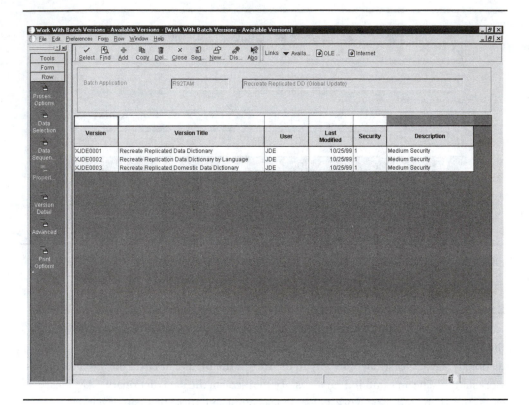

FIGURE 9-16.   R92TAM Re-create Replicated Data Dictionary

When an administrator begins working with the data dictionary application, he or she should be working from a fat client. This will allow the administrator to run some of the batch applications necessary to do this work. The administrator should work closely with functional leads to ensure that the glossary overrides necessary for that group are made. The administrator can also research where the data item is used to have a better understanding of what is being affected when changing the field-sensitive helps.

When you make changes to the data dictionary using a fat client, the changes are made to your local machine as well as to the tables in the relational database on the enterprise server (or data server if you have a distributed system). These changes can then either be pushed to clients through a new package build, be automatically updated on the clients (in the case of much of the data), or be replaced by copying over it with the new set (this is the usual method of updating the data dictionary TAM files on terminal servers).

Inside and Out

NOTE

Fat clients traditionally have very small data dictionary TAM files because they use JITI to grow the TAM as needed. This saves about 30MB on most fat clients. JITI is turned off on environments designed for thin clients so full data dictionary files need to be built and populated to ensure that any data dictionary requirements are on the terminal servers.

Other Data Dictionary Concerns

Many organizations set up data dictionary replication to their development machines to ensure that developers have the most recent set of data dictionary definitions (J.D. Edwards development does this as well). The goal behind data dictionary replication is to set up OneWorld in such a way as to automatically copy the relational database information to a TAM file. As such, this is a very interesting method of replication and is the only data replication that can be set up this way in OneWorld. Conceptually, you are still setting up a publisher (the relational tables on the enterprise or data server) and a subscriber (your workstation). The difference is that there is no data source that defines TAM files. Data sources set up through the installation and maintenance of OneWorld point to a relational database.

DEFINITION

TAM: *TAM is a J.D. Edwards proprietary flat file database format. TAM files are replicated relational data for local machines including OneWorld servers and workstations. They speed up overall processing because of their design (they react like a flat file with built in indexes, the .DDB and .XDB extensions respectively). They also vastly decrease network traffic because the files are local instead of residing in a relational database on the primary data server.*

In order to enable the replication of data dictionary information, you have to set up a specially defined data source (DATADICT) for each path code to which you want to replicate data dictionary records. The application to use is the P98DREP application found on the GH9011 menu. Because there are seven data dictionary tables in the relational database and only three sets of TAM files that contain data dictionary information, you set up a special publisher definition called DDDICT. All of this, including the step-by-step method can be found in Chapter 15.

Multiple Data Dictionary Concerns

Normally, J.D. Edwards recommends against having more than one data dictionary. However, there are two scenarios where this either is or could be appropriate. First, when you configure your system with coexistence in mind, you will have a data dictionary for World and another one for OneWorld.

DEFINITION

Coexistence: *Coexistence is when both the J.D. Edwards World and OneWorld products use the same database for most transactional data. There are several applications that cannot coexist including AR, HR, and the Reality Module. Most modules, however, can have data entry in either World or OneWorld.*

Second, there are certain situations where having a second data dictionary is required to enable development because of the close ties between development and the data dictionary. If either of these two situations occurs, there are certain administrative tasks necessary to ensure that the data dictionaries are synched up at the appropriate time.

Coexistence

The coexistence model has two separate data dictionaries, but because the transactional database is shared, it is important that these two sets of tables stay in sync. Because of the potential for problems, J.D. Edwards created an application in World that will compare the World and OneWorld data dictionaries. (Note: Use the P99800 XJDE0001 Dream Writer application in World.) There are a couple of things that this will do. First, if there are records in World that are not in OneWorld, the process will automatically add them to OneWorld. If the reverse is true, the differences will be printed in a report. You will then have to manually add the records to the World software. Second, all of the data item specifications from OneWorld are overwritten by the World definitions when there are discrepancies. This includes glossary information, row headings, column headings, data item size, system code, and decimal places (this is only if there are differences).

J.D. Edwards recommends that data dictionary changes be made at the same time in both areas. You would change the World data item first and then the OneWorld data item. If you follow this set of rules, it is relatively simple to keep the two in synch. However, as a safety precaution, it would be advisable to run this process in proof mode regularly to validate that you haven't missed anything.

Multiple Data Dictionaries for Development

Because the data dictionary is an active element in OneWorld—that is, does not require a code recompilation to enable the changes—it is possible that the development process (especially major rewrites of modules in OneWorld) could force you to support a data dictionary dedicated to the development process and another for production itself. Remember that there is no tool in OneWorld to compare these two data dictionaries. Consequently, you need to keep extremely good records of the changes made to the development side so they can be manually reconciled.

Wrapping Up the Data Dictionary

The data dictionary is essential in every installation of the OneWorld product defining data items and its specifications. You should try to limit the number of users who have access to the data dictionary application. Because the data dictionary defines all information in your system, it is possible to do significant damage using its tools. Although you can make safe changes to these tables, thought should be taken before doing so. It should then be done in a controlled atmosphere.

System Tables

Though system tables are unique enough to warrant a section in this chapter, we have discussed the majority of them in other sections in this book. When we talk about system tables, we are talking about tables that are shared across all environments and have the table owner sysb733. Some of the functions controlled by system tables include:

- Data sources (F98611 and F986115), discussed in Chapter 2

- Path codes (F00942), discussed in Chapter 2

- Environments (F0094 and F00941), discussed in Chapter 2

- OCM, the object configuration manager (F986101), discussed in Chapter 2

- Printers (F98616, F986161 to F986167), discussed in Chapter 17

- Users (F0092, F00921, F00922, F00924, F00925, and F0093), discussed in Chapter 13

- Security (F00950 and F98OWSEC), discussed in Chapter 13

- Servers and workstations (F9650 and F9651), discussed in Chapters 4 and 5

Because so much time and effort has already gone into describing the functionality and associated tools, system tables receive an honorable mention in this chapter. We will, however, tell you that there are 107 tables in the B733.2 release of OneWorld in the System – B733 data source (though some of them are maintained for backward compatibility only).

System Table Functionality

In Table 9-11 you will find a list of every table associated with the System – B733 data source for the B733.2 release of OneWorld. This provides a quick glance of various OneWorld system tables and their intended purpose.

Table Name	Description	Table Name	Description
F00085	Daylight Savings Rules	F9720511	AutoPilot Script/Release Compatibility Table
F0092	Library Lists – User	F972052	AutoPilot Include Scripts Table
F00921	User Display Preferences	F972053	AutoPilot Script Object Utilization Table
F00922	User Display Preferences Tag File	F97210	AutoPilot Playback Results Header Table
F00924	User Install Packages	F97211	AutoPilot Message Master Table
F0093	Library List Control	F97212	AutoPilot Next Numbers Table
F0094	Library List Master File	F97214	AutoPilot Playback Results Detail Table
F00941	Environment Detail – One World	F979860	AutoPilot B732 F9860 Conversion Table
F00942	Object Path Master File	F979865	AutoPilot B732 F9865 Conversion Table
F00945	Release Master	F98101	Imaging Constants
F00946	Release Compatibility Map	F9840	Installation Plan Master Table

TABLE 9-11.   System Tables and Their Descriptions

Table Name	Description	Table Name	Description
F00948	Release/Data Source Map	F98403	Environment Plan Detail Table
F00950	Security Workbench Table	F98405	Table Conversion Scheduler
F00960	Machine/Group Identification	F984052	Table Conversion – History Log
F83100	Date Title	F9843	Table Conversion – JDE Scheduler
F83110	Column Headings	F986101	Object Configuration Master
F91100	Favorites Relationships and Properties	F98611	Data Source Master
F91100D	Favorites – Alternative Description	F986115	Table and Data Source Sizing Table
F91300	Schedule Job Master	F986116	MVS Table and Data Source Sizing
F91310	Scheduled Job Parameters	F98613	Business View Environmental Server
F91320	Job Schedule	F986150	Server Transfer Package Contents
F91400	Report Director Templates	F986151	Server Package Transfer File
F91410	Report Director Templates Sequence Items	F986152	Server Package Master
F91420	Report Director Templates Smart Field Activation	F98616	Printer Definition
F91430	Smart Field Template Criteria	F986161	Default Printer Table
F91500	Application Header for Tip of the Day	F986162	Paper Definition
F91510	Tip Details for Tip of the Day	F986163	Printer Capability
F96021	Software Package Build Header	F986164	Output Conversions

TABLE 9-11. System Tables and Their Descriptions *(continued)*

Inside and Out

Table Name	Description	Table Name	Description
F9603	Software Package Header	F986165	Printer Security
F96215	Software Package Build Header – History	F986167	New Default Printer Table
F9622	Software Package Build Detail	F9882	Checkout Log Table
F96225	Software Package Build Detail – History	F98825	Package Deployment Scheduling
F9631	Software Package Detail	F98826	Package Deployment on Servers Information
F9640	CD Configuration Header File	F9883	OneWorld Network Locations Table
F9641	CD Configuration Detail File	F9888	Merge Log
F9642	Change Table Configuration Details	F98881	Specification Merge Logging File
F9643	CD Build Steps File	F988810	SpecMerge Tracking
F9644	CD Director Control File	F9889	Deployment Location Master
F9645	Software Mastering Update File	F98891	Deployment Location Path Code
F9650	Machine Master	F98892	Package Deployment Scheduling
F9651	Machine Detail	F98980	Font Override by Language
F9652	Deployment Group Header	F98CONST	Table of Constants
F9653	Deployment Group Detail Definitions	F98DRENV	Data Replication Environment Mapping Table
F9654	Deployment Locations Definition	F98DRLOG	Data Replication Change Log

TABLE 9-11.   System Tables and Their Descriptions (*continued*)

Table Name	Description	Table Name	Description
F9691100	Change Table – Favorites	F98DRPCN	Data Replication Pending Change Notifications
F9691400	Change Table – Report Director Template Header	F98DRPUB	Data Replication Publisher
F9691410	Change Table – Report Director Template Sequence	F98DRSUB	Data Replication Subscribers
F9691420	Change Table – Smart Field Activity	F98EVDTL	Event Detail File
F9691430	Change Table – Smart Field Criteria	F98EVHDR	Event Header File
F9691500	Change Table – Tips of the Day Header	F98MOQUE	Media Object Queues
F9691510	Change Table – Tips of the Day Detail	F98OWSEC	One World Security
F9720	AutoPilot Script Repository Table	F98TMPL	Templates
F972009	AutoPilot Constants Table	F98VAR	Table of Variables
F972051	AutoPilot Script Version Table		

TABLE 9-11.   System Tables and Their Descriptions (*continued*)

Server Map

In Chapter 2, we discussed data sources, including the one identified for each application (or logic) server. The questions to ask, however, are what tables are included in this data source, why they are needed, and what tools are available to help manipulate them. This section will be dedicated to answering these and other pertinent questions regarding the server map data source.

Inside and Out

Server Map Defined

Every application server (a server running OneWorld code and providing OneWorld services) must have an associated server map. Luckily, this doesn't mean that the servers can't share a server map (this will be detailed later in this section). To get a better feel for what the server map tables do and why you need them, let's examine what tables are a part of this data source. There are seven tables in the server map data source, including:

- F98611 (Data Source Master)

- F986101 (Object Configuration Master)

- F986110 (Job Control Status Master)

- F986111 (Job Number Master File)

- F986113 (Subsystem Job Master)

- F98DRLOG (Data Replication Change Log)

- F98DRPCN (Data Replication Pending Change Notifications)

Why would you need these tables to be segmented off from the tables used by workstations or other servers? Let's find out. The F98611 table (Data Source Master) contains a list of all defined data sources with pertinent information on how to access the data contained in them. Unfortunately, however, there are different applications used to access data from workstation to server platform. This is true with the single exception of NT workstations and servers. A prime example of this follows. Scenario: HP_UX/Oracle with a mixed architecture for workstations. The workstations would require the JDBOCI80.DLL (see Figure 9-17) defined in F98611 (located in the system data source) to read the Oracle database.

In the F98611 table located in the HP_UX server map, however, the appropriate DLL name would be libora80.sl (refer to Figure 9-18).

Because of the layout of the table, its indices, and required information, there is no way to have the same data source name listed twice, even if you did change the DLL names. If you manually changed the unique index to allow multiple entries, the foundation code is written in such a way as to take the first entry only. This would mean that either the server wouldn't get what it needed or the workstations wouldn't get what they needed to accurately connect to the data below. Could J.D. Edwards

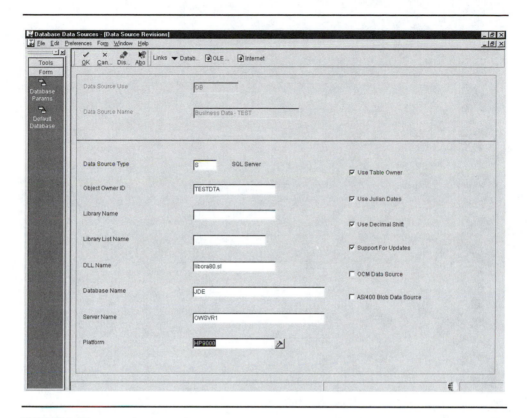

FIGURE 9-17.   Workstation data source

rewrite their foundation code to either have more fields available in the table (for example, a field for workstation DLL name, UNIX DLL name, and AS/400 application name)? Sure! But why would they go to this much trouble considering two sets of tables nicely answer the requirement and the tables are very small? Another option would be to provide different data source names for each different platform being supported. Although this is doable, we don't recommend it. It would confuse more than it would solve.

The F986101 table (Object Configuration Manager) is another table located in both the server map and system data sources. This table also differs between workstations and servers.

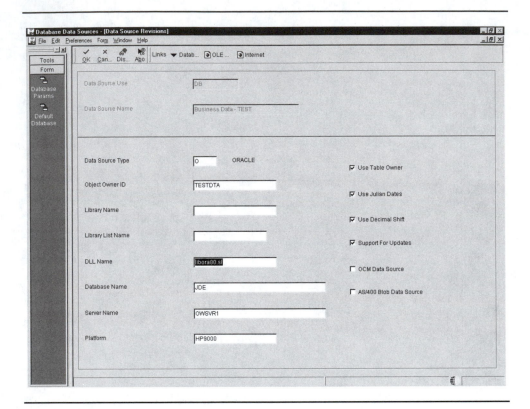

FIGURE 9-18.   Server map data source

The primary data source's difference, as called by the OCM, is OneWorld Local –
XXXB733 (where XXX represents the path code name; refer to Table 9-12 for an
example). This data source is defined as an access database and primarily used to
increase performance on the workstation. Unfortunately, neither UNIX nor the AS/400
platform supports Microsoft Access, making this mapping obsolete on any server with
the possible exception of NT.

OMDATP	OMSRVR	OMDLLNAME	OMDSTP	OMOCM1	OMOCMDSC
OneWorld Local – PRODB733	LOCAL	JDBODBC.DLL	A	DB	LOCAL

TABLE 9-12.   OneWorld Local for Workstations

There are also differences in mappings, including the translate/do not translate data sources associated with OneWorld implementations on AS/400. Because of these differences, separate tables are required.

The F986110, F986111, and F986113 tables are unique to the server map data source. These tables are used to track and maintain information on jobs submitted to the server. These tables can be shared between multiple servers because the information contained is server specific. As such, these tables could be moved to the system data source. However, there are three considerations we would recommend you think about prior to attempting this. First, it would require a foundation code change (only doable by J.D. Edwards) to make this work correctly. Second, the fact that many organizations choose to run in a distributed processing mode lends itself to having more than one table. Finally, raw performance is better when tables are smaller. It is possible to place millions of records in these tables (especially in high volume shops or shops that retain their UBE job history). Having different tables facilitates speed and maneuverability in the product.

The F98DRLOG and F98DRPCN tables relate to data replication. Each server has its own copy of these tables to facilitate two-way data replication. Each server having its own set also ensures that each application server can perform data replication functions. These tables do not contain data for workstations (those are maintained in the system data source).

Tools Associated with Server Maps

One of the primary tools associated with the server map data source is the Work With Server Jobs application (P986116). This application is accessible by several different methods, including the GH9011 menu, typing **WSJ** on the Fast Path, or clicking the Submitted Jobs button, located in either the User Options interface (accessed by choosing View | User Options on the main OneWorld Explorer interface – see Figure 9-19) or in the Form menu of the Batch Versions application (P98305).

(More information on the Work With Server Jobs and User Options applications can be found in Chapters 8 and 3, respectively.)

Inside and Out

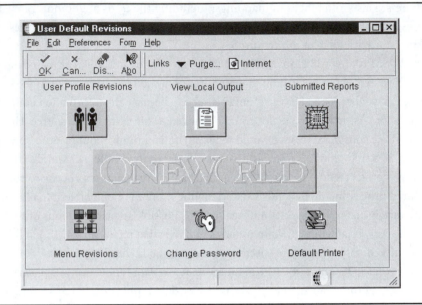

FIGURE 9-19. User options

This application (P986116) allows you to view, print, delete, terminate, change priority, put on hold, or release batch jobs submitted to various servers. OneWorld has built-in logic surrounding the entry point based on how you launch P986116. When you start using the menu, Fast Path, or user options routes, you are prompted to select which data source you want to use (refer to Figure 9-20).

You should choose the server that you submitted the job to. If, however, you launch P986116 from the Batch Versions application (P98305), it will automatically start with the server you launched against (see Figure 9-21).

Consequently, depending on your specific requirements, you should pick the launching method most appropriate to your own needs. When you've just launched a UBE, it is very convenient to use the P98305 launch point. It automatically goes to the server the UBE was launched against, automatically filters the output based on

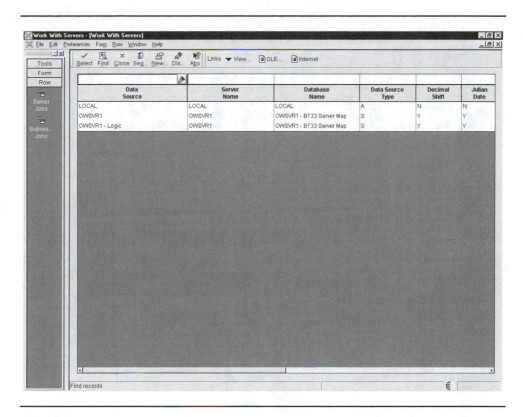

FIGURE 9-20.   Selecting servers

your user ID, and is easy to use. When you are more interested in viewing what jobs are active across the server, what jobs are currently in queue for either batch or subsystem processing, or what subsystems are currently active, you can either use the Fast Path or user options launch method. There is no right or wrong method of accessing the P986116 application; however, there are certain functions that are limited based on your access method.

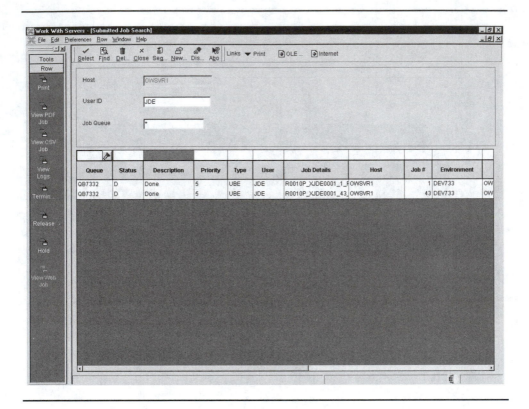

FIGURE 9-21.   Submitted batch information

Breaking the P986116 Down

For this section, we will assume that you either accessed P986116 using the Fast Path or the GH9011 menu. When you first launch this application, you are prompted (using the W986116A Work With Servers form) for the data source associated with the server you want to look at. This application queries the system F98611 data source master table for data sources with a SVR type. The results are presented in a grid format that allows the user to highlight and select the appropriate data source. If your OneWorld application server was called OWSVR1, you would either click to highlight or double-click to select this machine. If you click, you will be able to either select the submitted UBE batch jobs or subsystem jobs. These options will be explained in more detail shortly.

NOTE

You will see Local as an option in the W986116A form; however, if selected, there is no data behind it. This particular data source defines the local machines (workstations and servers) to them and does not have an associated server map data source or F986110 table. As such, you should not select this option.

Job Data and Detail   Once you have picked the server of your choice, the W986110BA form will launch, automatically finding all of the jobs in the F986110 table with your specific user identification. These will be displayed with the following information:

- **Queue**   The queue name the job was launched against
- **Status**   There are only a few valid entries

   E: Error

   D: Done

   S: Submitting

   W: Waiting

   H: On hold

- **Description**   The description of the status
- **Priority**   Indicates the priority of the job (the default is 5)
- **Type**   The type of job submitted (usually UBE)
- **User**   The user who launched the job
- **Job Details**   A combination of UBE name, version, job number, and output type
- **Host**   The server the job was submitted against
- **Job #**   The OneWorld job number associated with the specific job
- **Environment**   The environment the job was launched in
- **Origination Host**   The machine the job was launched from

- **Process ID**   The server process identification

- **Date Submitted**   The date the job was submitted

- **Time Submitted**   The time the job was submitted

- **Date Last Activity**   The date the job was last processed by the server

- **Time Job Activity**   The time the job was last processed by the server

The last two are pertinent because many jobs cross over dates and times. It is good to be able to determine when the server last updated the F986110 table.

Subsystem Jobs

One of the ways you can program a UBE to operate is in a continuous mode. These specially configured versions run on the server looking for specific records to work with. A prime example is the R42520 Pick Slip UBE. If you launch XJDE0006, this launches a UBE subsystem that then looks for records in the F986113 table in a waiting status. When the records populate the F986113 with a W status, the subsystem version of the R42520 UBE will automatically run the records and then delete each record once successfully completed. One of the things people want to be able to do is monitor their subsystems and the jobs that are in queue to run. The P986116 application has the capability to view both the subsystems and the jobs that are in the F986113.

Go to the GH9011 menu and double-click the Work With Server Jobs (P986116) application or type **wsj** in the Fast Path and then press Enter. This will launch the W986116A (Work With Servers) form. Click Subsystem Jobs on the Exit bar or choose Row – Subsystem Jobs from the menu selection on the W986116A form. This will launch the P986113 (Work With Subsystem Jobs) application. There are two Boolean options on this form (Processes and Waiting Jobs). By default, the Processes Boolean is checked. This will show you the subsystem jobs that are currently working on the server selected on the

W986116A form. If you have more than one of these UBEs running, it will show multiple entries and provides the following information. When you select the Waiting Jobs Boolean (refer to Figure 9-22), the P986113 application will automatically locate all of the records in the F986113 table (refer to Figure 9-23).

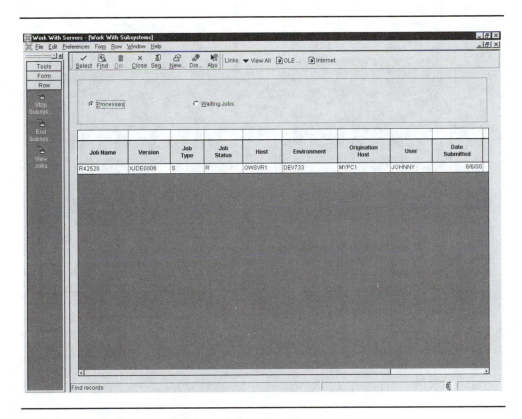

FIGURE 9-22. Waiting subsystem processes

Inside and Out

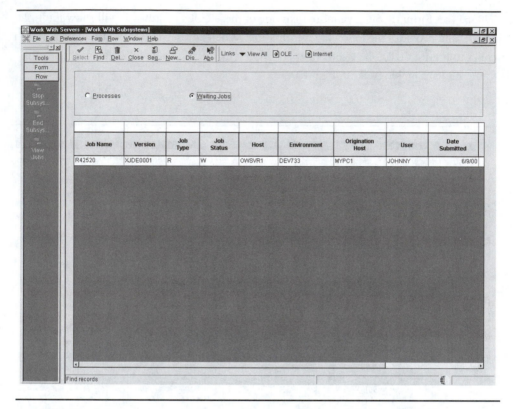

FIGURE 9-23. Waiting subsystem job

- **Job Name** The application name (such as R42520)

- **Version** The version of the application name (such as XJDE0006)

- **Job Type** The type of record

    R: Subsystem record

    S: Subsystem job

- **Job Status**   The status of the job

    E: Subsystem record to end job

    P: Subsystem record processing

    R: Subsystem job running

    W: Subsystem record waiting

- **Host**   The server running the subsystem service

- **Environment**   The OneWorld environment associated with a particular subsystem record or job

- **Origination Host**   The name of the workstation where the job or record was launched

- **User**   The OneWorld user ID that launched the record or job

- **Date Submitted**   The date the record or job was launched

- **Time Submitted**   The time the record or job was submitted

- **Job #**   The OneWorld number assigned to the specific record or job

UBE/Subsystem Counts

It is often handy to know how many UBEs have been launched per day and when your anticipated peak times are so you can work on the anticipated server response times. Additionally, especially during the modeling phase of your implementation, when you know that you've out-worked your server, it is nice to be able to determine the number of subsystem records currently waiting to be serviced. With these dynamics, you will have some of the empirical data you need to determine sizing requirements or new configurations for your system.

Using the information we've already provided, it is easy for you to create very simplistic queries against the server map data source for the information you need. We'll start by looking at the subsystems and then we'll move into the more difficult subject of UBEs. Subsystems use the F986113 table and once completed are erased from the system. Because of this, it is difficult to determine your peak usage times. Still, if you think you have a backup of subsystem jobs, this is relatively easy to validate. Go to the Work With Server Jobs application (P986113) and find the records. The only problem with this concept is that you would have to count the records you found. It is far easier to log on to the server, log on to the correct database (JDE for Oracle, JDEB733 for MS SQL Server, and B733MAP library for AS/400), and perform the query below:

```
select count(*) from svmb733.f986113 where sspid='R42520' and
ssvers='XJDE0001' and ssopcr='W' and ssenhv='CRP733'
```

This will return the number of pick slip records in the F986113 table that are currently in a waiting status in the CRP733 environment.

Now, to get the UBE count, you will find that you need to do a little more work. In particular, one of the decisions you need to make is whether to determine the number of UBEs launched per hour or every thirty minutes or even more often. You can use the select statement below and the one after that to produce even more information regarding the UBEs launched by your users. One nice thing about the F986110 table is that it won't automatically delete the UBE records after processing them like subsystems do.

```
select count(*) from svmb733.f986110 where jcenhv='PRD733' and
jcsbmdate='100xxx' and jcsbmtime<'080000'
```

This will provide the number of UBEs submitted prior to 8:00A.M. in the production environment. It is easy to modify this select statement to map out the number of UBEs submitted per hour. When looked at over a two-month period, you start to get a clear understanding of your end users' habits and system requirements. With a slight modification, you can actually pull out the names of the UBEs themselves.

select jcfndfuf2 from svmb733.f986110 where jcenhv='PRD733' and

jcsbmdate='100xxx' and jcsbmtime<'080000' order by jcfndfuf2 asc

Data Replication

The final two tables associated with the server map are F98DRLOG and F98DRPCN. These two tables are discussed in detail in Chapter 15. They are designed to enable server-to-server data replication and contain information on what the actual data change is and the subscriber machines (including other servers) that need the data change.

Control Tables

What are control tables and what do they do for you? There isn't as easy an answer as some of the other questions posed in this book, as there are a variety of different control tables that perform a variety of different functions throughout the system. This section is dedicated to explaining the functions performed by control tables and how they operate.

Control Tables Defined

Control tables are a group of 47 tables (refer to Table 9-13) that perform a series of background, non-transactional tasks, including next numbering, UDCs, menus, and workflow. The publisher (or primary) tables are maintained in a single data source with the nomenclature of Control Tables – Xyyy, where Xyyy represents the name of the environment (Prod, Test, CRP, and such). The control table's table owner (in databases that support table owners) is represented by xxxctl, where x represents the associated environment (prodctl, crpctl, testctl, and so on).

Table Name	Table Description	Table Name	Table Description
F0002	Next Numbers – Automatic	F9050	Rough Cut Answer Dependency
F00021	Next Numbers by Company/Fiscal Year – Automatic	F91011	Word Search Equivalence Table
F0004	User Defined Code Types	F91012	Word Search Ignore Word Table
F0004D	User Defined Codes – Alternate Language Descriptions	F91013	Menu Word Search Table
F0005	User Defined Codes	F9746	UDC Merge Table

TABLE 9-13.   Control Tables with Descriptions

Table Name	Table Description	Table Name	Table Description
F0005D	User Defined Codes – Alternate Language Descriptions	F9751	Menu Selection Changes by Release
F0082	Menu Master File	F9752	Menu Header Changes by Release
F00821	Menu Selections File	F9753	Menu Job to Exec Adds/Obsoletes by Release
F0083	Menu Text Override File	F9754	Menu Merge
F0084	Menu Path File	F98800	Process Master
F9000	Task Master	F98800D	Process Master Alternate Description
F9001	Task Relationships	F98800T	Process Master Supplemental Information
F9002	Task Descriptions	F98810	Activity Master
F9005	Variant Description	F98810D	Activity Master Alternate Description
F9005D	Variant Description Alternate Description	F98811	Activity Specifications
F9006	Variant Detail	F98830	Process Activity Associations
F9006D	Variant Detail Alternate Description	F98840	Organizational Structure Master
F9010	Environment Setup Answers	F98845	Organizational Structure Rule
F9020	ActivEra Qualifier Rules Header	F98860	Process Instance
F9021	ActivEra Qualifier Actions Detail	F98865	Activity Instance
F9022	ActivEra Qualifier Rules Detail	F98882	Composer Rough Cut Selections
F9023	Qualifier Actions Header Table – F9023	F98885	Composer Industry and Geographical Regions
F9025	Qualifier Rule Relationship Definitions	F98887	Composer Industry and Geographic Locations Xref
F9030	Documentation Cross Reference		

Inside and Out

TABLE 9-13. Control Tables with Descriptions *(continued)*

The Pristine Environment

There are many instances where the pristine environment is somewhat unique, and control tables are an excellent example of it. There is no control table data source associated with the pristine environment in a typical customer software configuration of OneWorld. (In Xe, there is a Control Tables – JDE data source.) Additionally, there is no table owner or database user called pristctl. Rather, the pristine environment keeps the tables traditionally defined as control tables in the business data data source with a pristdta table owner. Although this certainly poses no system level issues or instabilities, it is a consistent inconsistency to be aware of. The pristine environment maintains all the appropriate tables, just in a different location. Other examples of pristine's uniqueness include prepopulation of environmental business data, no object librarian records, and the tendency of companies to turn it off.

Next Numbers

You may have wondered how OneWorld assigns unique numbers to sales orders, the address book, accounts payable checks, and a whole slew of other items. The answer lies in two little tables: F0002 and F00021. These tables allow you several options for formatting and maintaining next numbers and are easily accessed through a simple interface. There are two next-number tables (F0002 and F00021) that maintain a list of numbers for the applications to use.

The F0002 Table (Next Numbers Automatic)

The F0002 table has 31 columns listing the system code, the elements in the system that contain next-number values, the next-number values for each element, and whether the next number uses check digit or not. The layout of the table is in four distinct sections (system code: 1 column; data item description: 10 columns; the next number itself: 10 columns; and a flag for check digit: 10 columns). Each system code can contain up to 10 data item elements. This is currently a limit on the number of items in a system code that can have next numbering due to a unique index on the F0002 table (F0002_1) based on the NNSY column.

The F00021 Table (Next Number by Company/Fiscal Year – Automatic)

The F00021 table has 10 columns (see Table 9-14 for more detailed information) and is designed to maintain specific next-number data for companies and fiscal year concerns.

Column Name	Description	Length	Type	Valid Values
NLKCO	Document Company	5	String	Used to retrieve the correct next number for a specific company.
NLDCT	Document Type	2	String	There are 259 rows shipped with the B733.2 version of OneWorld maintained in the UDC product code 00, report code DT.
NLCTRY	Century	2	Numeric	This is the two-character century qualifier (for example, 19 means items that have 19 for the century marker, such as 1998).
NLFY	Fiscal Year	2	Numeric	An identifier for the number of the fiscal year.
NLSMAS	Same-As Document Type	2	String	If you set up next numbers by company, you will have multiple document types that represent the same base value. This field links the two document types together.
NLN001	Next Number 001	8	Numeric	The actual next number to assign a specific document type.
NLAUR	Auto-Reset Next Numbers	8	Numeric	The number to use when resetting next numbers for a new fiscal year.
NLIMB	Imbed Digits	1	Character	This tells the next-number application how many characters to assign the fiscal year information in the next number itself. It imbeds this information in the beginning of the subsequent number.

TABLE 9-14. F00021 Table

Inside and Out

Column Name	Description	Length	Type	Valid Values
NLCK01	Check Digit 01	1	Character	This Yes or No field indicates whether a check digit is used for the next number.
NLSEQ	Sequence Number	6	Numeric	A number the system uses to sequence information.

TABLE 9-14.   F00021 Table (*continued*)

The combination of the F0002 and F00021 tables make up the next-number requirements for the OneWorld applications. Without custom coding, next numbers are used for voucher numbers, invoice numbers, journal entry numbers, employee numbers, address numbers, contract numbers, and sequential W-2s.

User-Defined Codes (UDCs)

In almost all implementations of OneWorld, companies quickly become aware of and then modify the UDC. But what are UDCs and what types of functions do they perform? The user-defined codes are one of the quickest methods of customizing the OneWorld suite of applications to meet the business needs of your organization. This customization can be performed easily and will not adversely affect upgrades and updates of the software itself. UDCs are used in OneWorld, in conjunction with the data dictionary mentioned earlier in this chapter, to validate data entry in interactive applications. They are also instrumental in many batch functions because they validate specific information in the OneWorld system.

Where UDCs Are Found

Because UDCs are used to validate information on interactive screens (sometimes multiple times per screen), J.D. Edwards has recommended that they be placed in the OneWorld Local – xxxB733 (where xxx represents the path code) data source. Having copies of the tables used for UDCs locally makes it substantially faster for validation. Unfortunately, having this data locally doesn't fulfill the requirements of an enterprise system. Because of this, they are also maintained in the Control Tables data source on a data server (this could be the enterprise server or another defined data server).

UDCs During CRP

As a general recommendation, during the prototype (or CRP) phase of an implementation, you should consider mapping users to the centrally located UDC tables. Because UDCs automatically get mapped to the OneWorld Local – xxxB733 data source, when they modify the UDCs they are only modifying their local copy—other users will not see the changes made. If you are able, mapping the UDC tables to the Control Tables data source will enable everyone to see and change the central copy of UDCs during the prototype phase. Prior to go-live, these mappings can be reversed.

To quickly make this change, let's assume you are working with the CRP733 environment as delivered with OneWorld. You will note that there are a series of tables mapped to the OneWorld Local – CRPB733 data source in the object configuration manager. Type in the following to determine the exact number of records you plan on modifying using the SQL script below:

```
select count(*) from sysb733.f986101 where omenhv='CRP733' and
      omdatp='OneWorld Local - CRPB733'
```

NOTE

The SQL scripts provided below are for the MS SQL database. Slight modifications will have to be made if you are using Oracle or DB2/400.

This should return an 8 count (F0004, F0004D, F0005, F0005D, F0082, F00821, F0083, F0084). During the prototype phase, all of these tables can be mapped to the Control Tables – CRP data source. Type in the following SQL script to change the records directly:

```
update sysb733.f986101
      set omdatp='Control Tables - CRP'
where omenhv='CRP733' and omdatp='OneWorld Local - CRPB733'
```

This should return eight rows affected. The next time someone logs on to the CRP733 environment, he or she will look to the master set of UDC tables.

UDCs are stored in the F0004 (User Defined Code Types) and F0005 (User Defined Codes) tables. The F0004 table acts as a header record defining the product codes and has more than 3,200 defined with the B733.2 version of OneWorld. The F0005 table acts as a detail record maintaining all of the actual values associated with each product code. There are almost 24,000 records in the F0005 table shipped with B733.2. If you are using multiple languages with OneWorld, alternate language information for UDCs are maintained in the F0004D and F0005D tables.

UDCs and Servers

You have probably already noticed a problem with the local UDCs in that many of the server platforms running OneWorld don't have the capability to run a Microsoft Access database (for example, SUN, HP9000, RS6000, and AS/400). Because of this, mapping the UDCs to the OneWorld Local – xxxB733 data source would not work. However, OneWorld servers have their own F986101 table (Object Configuration Manager). Because of this, you are able to map these tables to the relational, centrally maintained set of tables located in the Control Tables data source. By default, this is the way OneWorld is shipped.

Maintaining UDCs

During the production phase of your ERP project, you should have UDCs mapped locally for performance; however, the question is raised as to when and how you maintain the UDCs from that point forward. Most organizations select a controlled group of people to administer UDC changes. These UDC administrators are responsible for changing, adding, and deleting UDCs for the production environment. To make their job easier, we recommend setting up data replication with just-in-time replication (JITR) enabled (for more information on setting up data replication, refer to Chapter 15). The way that style of replication works is that any change made to the local machine is automatically replicated to the server as well. Although all of the users won't see these changes, the administrators and central tables will have the updates.

Updates should be pushed to normal user machines on a regular basis by rebuilding the JDEB7.MDB database deployed during a package deployment. If you don't want to deploy a new package, you can always replace the database through a simple batch file or other third-party product (such as SMS). Because of the mappings, servers will always have access to the latest UDC values.

The P0004A (User-Defined Codes) Application

We've mentioned changing the UDCs shipped with the release, but we haven't mentioned the tool used to effect these changes. The P0004A (User-Defined Codes) application, located on menu GH9011 and accessible through a whole series of different applications, is the primary tool used when modifying, adding, or deleting UDCs from any one specific environment (see Figure 9-24).

Using this application, you are able to add, modify, and delete specific values used for validation as defined with the data dictionary. In order to have a blank as an option (refer to Figure 9-25), you have to add a blank value in your UDCs.

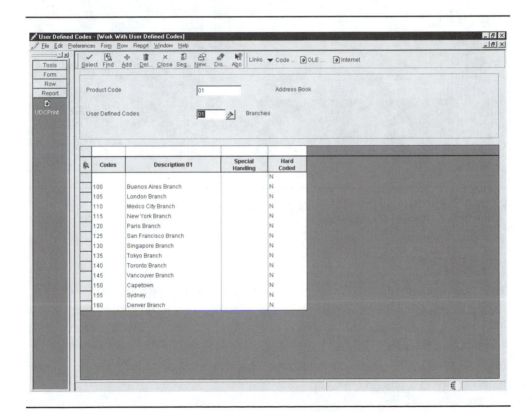

FIGURE 9-24. P0004A (User-Defined Codes) application

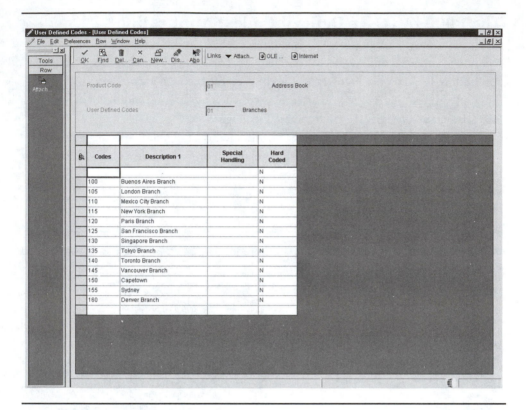

FIGURE 9-25.   Adding UDCs with the P0004A application

Summary

This chapter briefly describes a series of tables, data sources, and applications that are shared among all of the environments or are, minimally, not a part of the business data. They control your environment, define every object and data item in the system, show you information regarding batch versions and servers, and control the next numbers used by the business applications. This chapter easily represents some of the most important topics for OneWorld.

CHAPTER 10

Packages and Their Delivery

OneWorld Packages

Centralized versus Decentralized Strategy

Worksation Packages

Server Packages

Package Deployment

Troubleshooting Package Builds

Y ou cannot discuss OneWorld without talking about packages. Packages enable OneWorld to be a distributed solution. In this chapter, we are going to provide an understanding of the package build process and how this process affects your system's architecture. We'll cover the following topics:

- OneWorld packages

- Centralized versus decentralized package strategies

- Workstation packages

- Server packages

- Package deployment

- Troubleshooting packages

OneWorld Packages

A lot of people do not understand what OneWorld packages are and how they affect the system. Most people know only the high-level definition of a package, but in this chapter, we are going to provide more than just a high-level definition.

A package can be defined as a snapshot in time of your path code's central object tables and C components. Figure 10-1 illustrates this for you by giving you a high-level overview of package builds.

A path code, which is a J.D. Edwards' term used only in the context of OneWorld software, can be roughly defined as a set of central object tables and C functions. These central object tables are key to your OneWorld system, because these relational database tables contain information about your OneWorld objects.

A OneWorld object is a business function, data structure, business view, table, version, business library, UBE, or an application. These objects actually make up the software. When you enter a sales order, you are running an interactive application and business functions, which use a business view to access a table. When you perform a General Ledger post, you are running a UBE.

These objects "live" in a path code. The software comes with multiple path codes so that you can modify an object and one environment associated with that path code can see this change, while another does not see it until you move the modified object into that path code. The central object tables are relational database tables containing information about your objects that tells the system how the application will look—that is, what data the report will show.

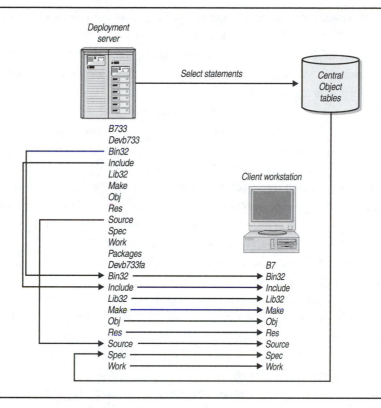

FIGURE 10-1. Package builds explained

N O T E

If you need more information on OneWorld environments and path codes, refer to Chapter 2.

One of the tables in the central objects contains over a million records in B733.2 and over two million records in OneWorld Xe (formerly B733.3). The reason that OneWorld uses relational database tables to store this information will become apparent in a moment. As stated previously, a package is a snapshot in time of these tables. When a package is built and this "snapshot" is taken, the information in the central object tables is read and converted into a new format, TAM (Table Access Manager). Your client workstations and OneWorld servers read TAM in order to run OneWorld. TAM is proprietary to the OneWorld software and is a miniature database.

TAM simply presents the information to your client workstations in a manner that can be accessed quickly. Just think how slow your system would be if all your machines had to make SELECT statements over the relational database tables in order to run OneWorld, and you will understand why converting the information in these tables into a TAM format is a good idea.

Speed is not the only advantage to TAM. Remember that a package, which is made up of TAM files and DLLs, is a snapshot in time of your central object tables. When you make a change to the software, you will probably want to test that change before just throwing it out to your end users. With TAM, you can do this. You can enable the majority of your workstations to continue running on a certain package, which means that they have an image of the application or report before your modification and are blissfully unaware of your change. You can then build a package with the change and move this change to some machines to test. As you can see, TAM gives you the ability to distribute objects around your system. It also brings up a need for change control management, which is discussed in Appendix A.

Now that you know about the central object tables and what they are used for in the package build process, let's discuss the C components. The OneWorld system uses business functions, which are pieces of C code and a OneWorld object. If you have done any programming, you know that in order to run, C code has to be compiled. When you perform a package build in OneWorld, you can tell the software to compile these objects. The compiler will then create a dynamic link library (DLL), which is called a "business function library" in OneWorld. These DLLs hold information that is required for the software to function correctly. In the following sections, we will discuss how the central object tables and the C components fit into the package build process.

Centralized versus Decentralized Strategy

Before we discuss the different types of packages, we first need to talk about the high-level architecture strategies as they relate to packages. OneWorld gives you the ability to be flexible with your system architecture so your system can grow as your business grows.

Standard Central Objects and Check-in Location

The OneWorld software is shipped with four path codes, which means that you have four different sets of central objects, header files, and source files. These standard path codes are:

- CRPB733 Conference Room Pilot path code

- DEVB733 Development path code

- PRODB733 Production path code

- PRISTB733 Pristine path code

The documentation that you receive with OneWorld shows you how to set up the standard configuration, including the path codes previously listed. The check-in location is a directory structure that contains the C component files for a path code. As you will see later in this section, you are not restricted to having the check-in location only on your deployment server.

The location where your central object tables are located depends on the type of platform you're running. For example, the standard configuration for an AS/400 system formerly was to place your central object tables on your deployment server in a SQL Server or an Oracle database. This meant that you had to purchase another database license and maintain it. Fortunately, J.D. Edwards came up with a solution to allow the central object tables to reside directly on AS400. (Consult the *J.D. Edwards AS400 Installation or Upgrade Guide* for more information.)

The standard is a little more straightforward if you are not installing the software on an AS/400. When you are installing a RS6000, HP9000, Sun Solaris, or Intel Windows NT machine, the standard is for your central object tables to reside on your enterprise server. You can separate the location of your central object tables when you configure the system.

Decentralized Strategy

You may need to create a custom or decentralized strategy for your path codes and check-in locations, for example, if your company is going to be developing in OneWorld. Most companies do not want their development objects on the same machine that acts as their production machine. After all, the nature of development means that the development environment will have some objects that are not fully stable.

To separate your development and production machines, you need to ask yourself what must reside on the development box and what must reside on the production machine. You should place your central object tables for the development path code on your development server. You also can place your conference room pilot path code on this server because this path code is normally associated with your testing environment. However, if you can afford it, it doesn't hurt to have a separate testing machine. Do you want an object that is not tested to be on your production system? We didn't think so. This concept is shown in Figure 10-2.

We also need to address the issue of where you would place your data. Let's start with the development machine, your most "unstable" machine. The developers are

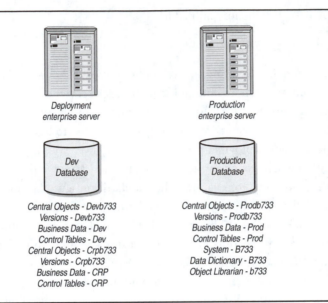

Deployment
enterprise server

Production
enterprise server

Dev
Database

Production
Database

Central Objects - Devb733
Versions - Devb733
Business Data - Dev
Control Tables - Dev
Central Objects - Crpb733
Versions - Crpb733
Business Data - CRP
Control Tables - CRP

Central Objects - Prodb733
Versions - Prodb733
Business Data - Prod
Control Tables - Prod
System - B733
Data Dictionary - B733
Object Librarian - b733

FIGURE 10-2. Separating your development and production machines

most likely going to need the machine cycled, logging turned on to isolate any problems, and in general, more maintenance tasks performed. This is why you place your development central objects, control tables, and business data on this machine.

You also probably want to place the Conference Room Pilot(CRP) central objects, control tables, business data, and host code on this machine, assuming you cannot afford a separate CRP machine because your testing environment is normally associated with your CRP path code.

Because J.D. Edwards supports multiple data dictionaries, it's difficult for us to specify where the data dictionary table should be placed. You can place these tables on the production machine, because that is your high-availability machine; however, that is not your only solution.

In OneWorld, the client machines normally have only a partial set of data dictionary TAM files. If they are attempting to run an object and they do not have the necessary data dictionary information in their TAM files, then these workstations will perform a just-in-time installation (JITI) of the data dictionary item. If you have only one data dictionary and your development staff changes something, it could be seen immediately on one of your production client workstations.

If you are going to run two data dictionaries, you need to understand that it is a tradeoff between taking on more maintenance tasks for your staff and having a more stable system. When you run two different data dictionaries, you will need to ensure that you move the data dictionary changes into your production data dictionary as you promote objects into your production path code. If you forget to do so, you will not be able to run any object that references a new or changed data dictionary item.

Finally, the authors recommend placing the system and object librarian tables on your production machine because it is your high-availability machine. If you lose the database with the system and object librarian tables, your OneWorld system will stop functioning. A little later in this chapter, we describe a configuration where you can have a separate system and object librarian for your production system. This configuration provides high availability, but it also adds a great deal of complexity to your system.

Advanced Distributed Strategies

You have a number of options in designing your architecture to ensure high availability. We have already discussed dividing up the central object tables and the data dictionary; we will now address separating the check-in location or setting up separate system and object librarian tables for your production system.

Advanced Check-in Location Configurations   OneWorld is so configurable that you do not need to keep your check-in location on the deployment server. You may be wondering why you would want to divide your check-in locations. Most companies will not want to do this; however, some organizations may have the need for such a configuration.

Hundreds of developers work in the J.D. Edwards development department, and each of them is working on a different project. Development has divided their check-in locations across different machines, which means that if they lose their deployment server and the check-in location is on a different machine, they can still check out their object and work with it, assuming that the database containing the system, object librarian, and central object tables is still up and running.

To expand on our example, we will add a new check-in location on a separate machine for the development path code. Keep in mind that this is an advanced CNC configuration so you must do additional work to set it up. When you install the deployment server, you must select the path codes that you wish to install. Once you have installed the deployment server, your directory structure will be similar to the one shown in Figure 10-3.

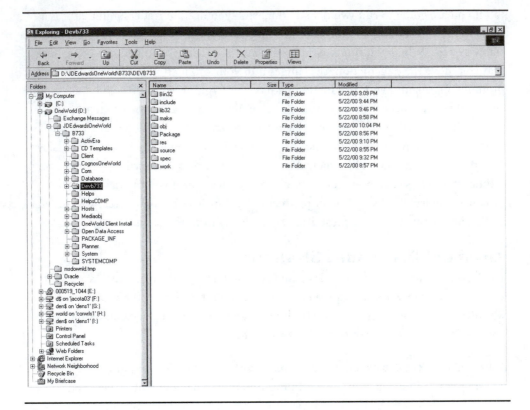

FIGURE 10-3. Standard deployment server directory structure

During the installation process, you are asked to set up your central object data source for each of your path codes. You would need to set up your development central object data source to point to a database on your development machine. Once you have done so, you need to change your development path codes check-in location before you execute your installation workbench.

To change your development path codes check-in location, first create a B733 directory structure on the server where your new check-in location will reside. Then copy the DEVB733 path code directory structure from your deployment server into this new location, which creates the necessary directory structure to point your development workstations to this check-in location. After you have copied this directory structure to your new machine and ensured that your new check-in location is functioning correctly, you can reclaim some disk space by deleting this path code from your deployment server.

Now that you have set up the directory structure, you must tell OneWorld about it—if possible, before you execute your installation workbench. If you have already executed your installation workbench, you can still move your check-in location; it just requires a little more setup.

If you have not executed your installation workbench yet, log on to OneWorld on the deployment server in the planner environment. Go to the Environments menu, GH9053. On this menu, select the Path Code Master application, P980042. In this application, select the Development Path code, which will take you into the Path Code Master Revisions screen, shown in Figure 10-4.

The information on this screen tells OneWorld where the check-in location resides on the system. This screen also tells the system where your central object tables reside. Table 10-1 describes the fields on the Path Code Master Revisions screen.

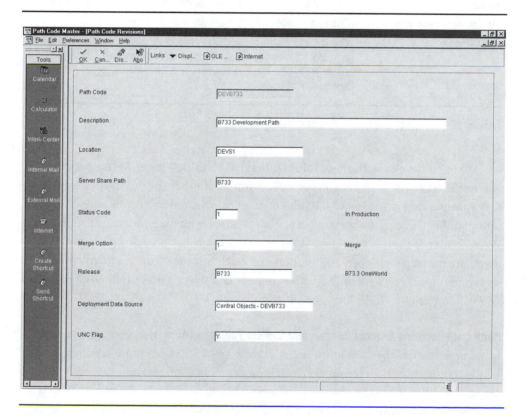

FIGURE 10-4. Path Code Master Revisions screen

Field	Description
Path Code	This is the name of your path code—in our example, DEVB733.
Description	A description of the path code.
Location	The J.D. Edwards standard is that this must be the same name as your deployment server, but since we are moving our check-in location onto a new machine, this field must contain the name of the machine where our check-in location resides. In our example, this is DEVS1.
Server Share Path	This is the name of a shared directory on the machine that contains the check-in location. The share name must match this field in case sensitivity and spaces included.
Status Code	This reporting code indicates the status of the path code. Accept the default.
Merge Option	Accept the default value for this field. This option tells the system that you can run specification merges into the path code.
Release	This is the release of OneWorld you are running—for example, B733.
Deployment Data Source	This data source points to your central object tables.
UNC Flag	This is the Universal Naming Convention flag. Ensure that this field is set to Y, since this setting enables the system to dynamically build a path statement to your check-in location using the location, server share path, and path code fields.

TABLE 10-1.   Path Code Master Revisions Screen Values

After you have entered these values into the Path Code Master Revisions screen, you can execute the workbench. The reason you want to set this up in advance is that your package deployment INF files contain path statements containing this information. These path statements are built when you finalize your installation plan. We will discuss these files in detail later in this chapter. For now, keep in mind that if you are moving your check-in location to a machine other than your deployment server, you must ensure that these files contain the correct path statements; otherwise, you will not be able to deploy your packages.

Setting up Separate Object Librarian and System Tables   Now that you know how to set up a custom check-in location, let's take a look at an even more advanced configuration. Like the custom check-in locations, this configuration should be set up only after thorough planning and only with the assistance of a person who is experienced in setting up advanced CNC configurations. Because this is an advanced configuration, more maintenance is required.

This configuration provides high availability. You may also want to use such a configuration if you need to develop objects in two separate locations, like the United States and Europe, and share them. When you set up this configuration, you will have two separate sets of system, object librarian, and data dictionary tables. Because you have two sets of object librarian tables, you must have strict naming convention procedures in place. You need strict naming conventions because it is possible to add an object with the same name in each instance of OneWorld. If you do so and transfer the object between the instances of OneWorld, the object in the target instance will be lost. The way to avoid this problem is by following strict naming conventions.

In our example of this configuration, one instance of the software is used for the production environment and the other for the development and testing of OneWorld objects. You may be wondering how to move new objects into the production instance of the software when you are running two separate instances of OneWorld. You have a couple of options. One option is that you can set up the software to allow an object transfer between the two systems, even though they are separate systems. Another option involves the use of product packaging. For more information on product packaging, please refer to J.D. Edwards' Web site at www.jdedwards.com.

You install the systems according to the J.D. Edwards' Installation manual, as if the systems were two totally separate installations that will never need to talk to each other. The only difference between the systems is that you are installing your production environments on one system and your development environments and path codes on the other system.

Once you have the systems installed, you must let them know about each other so that you can transfer objects between them. In our example, this entails installing a "dummy" production path code on the development server. In other words, when you install the development server, you install the production path code, but you point the check-in location and your central objects data source to the production instance of OneWorld.

When you perform an object transfer, you will move the object from the development instance of OneWorld into the production instance. You must set up the system so that your new object appears in the production instance's object librarian. You also need to ensure that you can move menus, user-defined codes, and data dictionary items.

In order to do so, you add custom data sources pointing to the production instance of OneWorld. For example, you create a new object librarian data source named Object Librarian—Production. You must create similar data sources for the data dictionary, versions, central objects, and control tables, which means that you must have network connectivity between the two sites. You also must ensure that the user who is transferring the objects has the appropriate permissions to the production instance's database.

TIP

In order for the record copy to function correctly, you must add definitions for the data dictionary, object librarian, and versions list data sources in the Release/Data Source Map application on menu GH9053.

TIP

For more detailed information on this topic, J.D. Edwards' advanced technology group has published a white paper, "Change Management: Two Distinct Installs with Network Connectivity." This white paper can be downloaded off the J.D. Edwards' web site at www.jdedwards.com.

Workstation Packages

We have discussed high-level strategies that you can use to assist you in setting up your system's architecture. Now let's talk about actually building a workstation package. As you work with OneWorld, you will learn that there are several different types of packages, which we will discuss in this chapter. These types of packages fall into two major categories: server or workstation packages. Workstation packages are deployed to your client workstations in order for OneWorld to run. You can choose from several different types of packages, each of which must be built.

NOTE

This chapter on package builds was written for the B733.1 and later releases of OneWorld. The package build process was rewritten as of B733.1.

The OneWorld system gives you several options for the types of packages that you can build. You must determine what type of package suits your business's needs.

Full Package

A full package is a complete snapshot in time of the specifications contained in your central object tables and the C components in your check-in location. When you build a full package, your package will include all of the objects checked into your path code at this time. When you deploy this package to a client workstation, that workstation will have the specifications for all of the objects in that path code.

This type of package takes up the most drive space and takes the longest time to build because of the amount of information that you are including in it. When you build a package, the system is performing SELECT statements over your central object tables and converting the information into TAM files.

This type of package, because of its simplicity, is the best one to build when you are just starting to work with OneWorld. You will always have all of the objects, which have been checked into your central objects, in the package.

Update Package

As you gain experience with the OneWorld software, you will discover that it is a real pain to build a full package, which takes six to eight hours, when you have changed only a handful of objects. For example, suppose you just applied an electronic software update (ESU), which modified only ten objects. If you are live and you need to roll this fix out as soon as possible, you won't want to wait for six to eight hours to build a full package.

DEFINITION

Electronic Software Update ESU: An ESU is the way that J.D. Edwards now delivers code changes. ESUs allow you to merge these fixes directly into your system so that you do not have to apply large code changes by hand.

When a limited number of objects have been modified, you should build an update package. When you build an update package, it builds the specifications only for the specific objects that you specify. When you deploy an update package, it will then "merge" these specifications into the existing package on the client workstation.

An update package is an ideal way of quickly deploying necessary changes to the system. In fact, these packages were specifically designed to deliver a few changes to the system in a relatively quick manner.

Partial Package

A partial package enables you to reduce the footprint on your client workstation. A partial package consists only of what is needed to run OneWorld and the applications that you specify. For example, if you know that some of your users are going to be using only a certain set of programs, you can build a partial package for them. Doing so will reduce the amount of disk space required on their systems.

Inside and Out

One note of caution in regard to partial packages: If the user tries to run an application that is not in the package specifications, the client will perform a JITI, installing the object directly out of the central object tables. If this object is not tested or has changed from the last time you built a package, the client workstation that performed a JITI on the object would have different specifications than your other client workstations. However, if you have implemented a proper set of security procedures, restricting your partial package users from accessing any applications that are not in their packages, your system will be safeguarded from this problem.

Partial packages can be a great way of installing OneWorld onto your workstations. You should use this type of package only after you have gained the necessary experience with OneWorld packages and are confident of your security solution.

Defining a Package

Let's discuss how you would actually define a package in the system. To start, you need to log on to a client workstation or on to the deployment server in the deployment environment. Once you have logged on to the system, you need to go to the Package and Deployment Tools menu GH8083 where you will notice several applications. In order to define a package, select Package Assembly (P9601). This application enables you to define your package. After you have double-clicked on this application, you will be taken into the Work With Packages screen. where you click the Add button to define a new package. Doing so will take you into a director that will guide you through defining a package. You will be initially presented with a welcome screen and then a Package Information screen, shown in Figure 10-5. This screen gathers key information about your package, which is listed in Table 10-2.

Once you have entered information for the fields on the Package Information screen, click the Next button to display the Package Type Selection screen, shown in Figure 10-6. On this screen, you are prompted to choose the type of package that you want to build. If you are not experienced with package builds, you should choose the full package.

The Package Type Selection screen has several radio buttons that you use to choose the type of package you want to build. If you want to assemble a full or a partial package, just click the corresponding button. However, if you choose to assemble an update package, the Include Object Specifications check box and the Parent Package field become accessible.

The Include Object Specification check box controls whether or not all the specifications of your objects are built into the update package. If you do not check this box, only a "shell" of the object is built into the update package. When you deploy

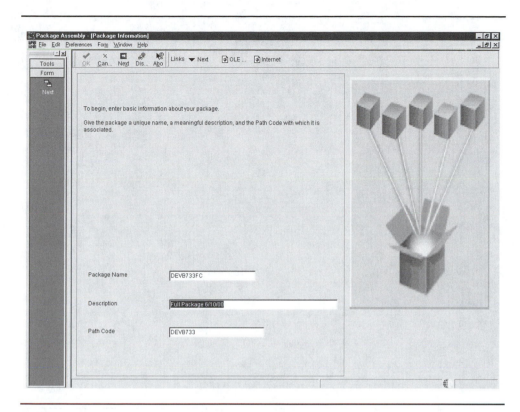

FIGURE 10-5. Package Information screen

Field	Description
Package Name	This is the name of your package. You should follow a standard naming convention so that you can easily determine the type of package from the package name. J.D. Edwards ends their full package name in "FA" or "FB." Do not name a package with the exact same name as a path code, nor should a package name begin with numbers.
Description	A description of your package. The authors recommend including a date or a meaningful description so that you can easily determine what the package was intended for.
Path Code	This is the path code that you are building the package over. Remember a package is a snapshot in time of the C components and central object tables of a path code.

TABLE 10-2. Package Information Screen Values

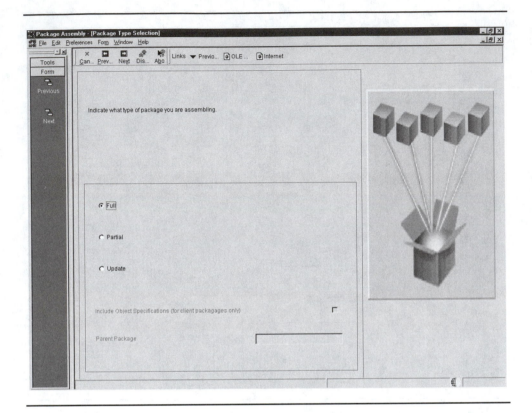

FIGURE 10-6.   Package Type Selection screen

the update package and a client workstation then tries to use this object, the system will perform a JITI on the object down to the client workstation directly out of the central objects. You must ensure that the copy of the object in the central objects is what you want on your client workstations.

The authors recommend checking the Include Object Specification check box to include all of the specifications for the objects that you define in your update package. That way, you do not have to worry about the client workstations installing the object directly out of central objects, which means that the object is easier to track and control.

CAUTION

The Include Object Specifications check box defaults as unchecked. You will want this check box checked most of the time, so be sure that it is set properly.

When you choose to assemble an update package, you must also fill in the Parent Package field. This field controls which full package is updated with the information from your update package. OneWorld will update the full package that you enter in this field with your changes from update packages. For example, when you hire a new employee, you do not have to deploy a full package and 25 update packages. You deploy only the parent package that you chose for your update package, and the new employee runs on the most current specifications of your OneWorld system.

After you have finished providing information in the Package Type Selection screen, click the Next button to display the Foundation Component screen. On this screen, you accept the default for your foundation, which is the system directory, or you can define a custom foundation. If you are new to OneWorld, accept the default. If you want more information on defining a custom foundation, refer to Chapter 11.

When you click Next on the Foundation Component screen, you will be prompted to choose your help component, the OneWorld help files. If you prefer, you can define a path to a custom set of help files, although most people will just accept the default and click Next.

The Database Component screen is displayed next. It tells OneWorld what access database to deploy to the client workstation. OneWorld software is normally shipped with the menu files and user-defined code files mapped to an access database located on the client machine; this screen controls which database is deployed. Unless your company is using store-and-forward functionality, a CNC consultant will usually map the menu and user-defined code tables directly to the database because the performance impact is minimal, and all your users can see a change as it happens.

When you click Next on the Database Component screen, the Object Component screen is displayed (see Figure 10-7). If you selected to build a full package earlier on the Package Type Selection screen, you can simply click Next on the Database

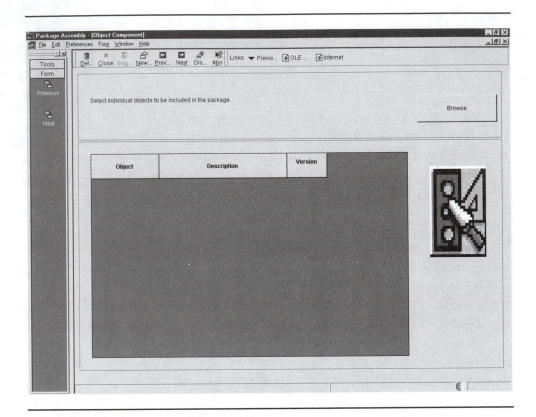

FIGURE 10-7.　Object Component screen

Component screen. If you selected to build a partial or an update package, you must tell the system what objects you want to include in the package.

Click the Browse button to select the objects you want to include. The Object Component Selection screen, shown in Figure 10-8, is displayed. This screen enables you to find the objects that you want to include in your update or partial package. You can find the objects by searching for the SAR number associated with them, the object name, the description, object type, status code, or the other fields on this screen with a Query by Example line.

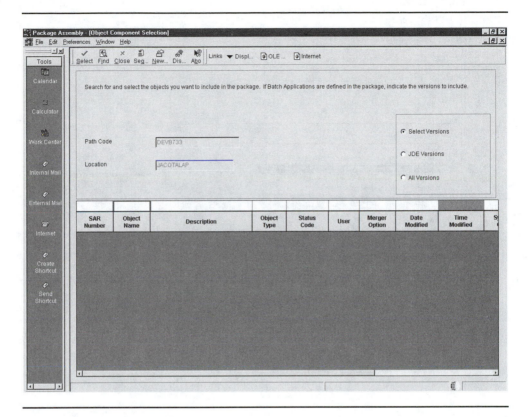

FIGURE 10-8.   Selecting objects for your update package

Once you find an object, you simply select it, and the screen will flash. You can choose multiple objects. If you want to add UBEs or interactive applications to your update package, you will need to pay attention to the three radio buttons on the Object Component Selection screen.

If you want to include all versions, select the All Versions radio button, which automatically selects all of the versions that are attached to the report. When you click the JDE versions button, only JDE versions will be included in the update package. If you choose the Select Versions button, you are prompted to select a version that you want to include in the update package. When you select a version, be sure that you see

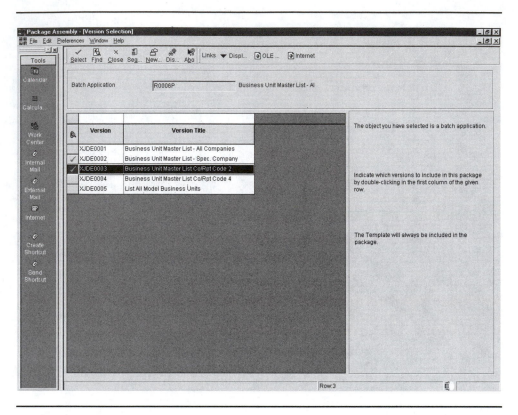

FIGURE 10-9.   Selecting versions

the pink check mark appear next to the version name (see Figure 10-9). Once you select your versions, you can close out of the Version Selection screen and select the next object to include in the package.

When you are defining an update or partial package and you finish selecting the objects that you want to include in the package, click Next to access the Language Component screen. On this screen, select a language that you want to deploy to your client workstations. English is always shipped with the OneWorld product, but if you want a different language, you must install the OneWorld Language CD, because the language records for OneWorld objects are stored in the central object tables.

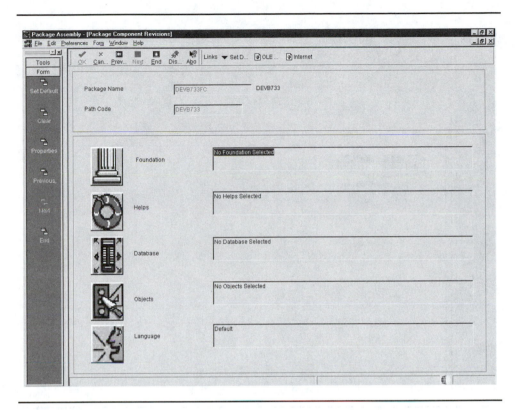

FIGURE 10-10.   Package Component Revisions screen

After you choose your language, click the Next button to access the Package
Component Revisions screen shown in Figure 10-10. On this screen, you will see
what you have selected for the foundation, help files, database, objects, and language.
To save your package assembly information, click the End button. If you click Cancel,
you will lose your changes.

NOTE

*If no foundation, help files, or database is selected, don't worry; the software will
use the default foundation, help files, or database.*

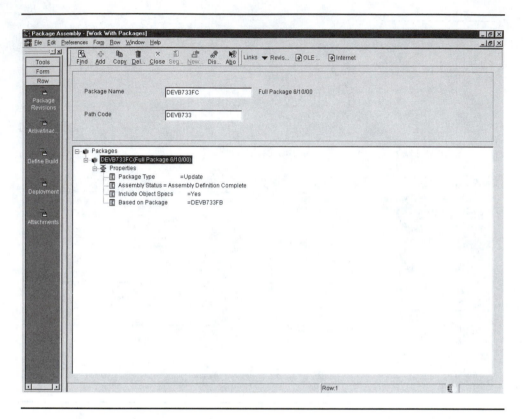

FIGURE 10-11. Activating a package in package assembly

When you click End, you are taken back to the Work With Packages screen (see Figure 10-11). The package that you have defined should be listed on this screen with an open box next to it, which means that the package is still in definition. You need to highlight the package name and select Row | Active/Inactive to display the package with the box closed. Now that you have defined the type of package that you want to build, you are ready to tell the software how to build the package.

In the Work With Packages screen, choose Row | Define Build to display the Package Build Definition director. This director will guide you through setting up your package build options. On the Package Build Location Screen, shown in Figure 10-12, tell the

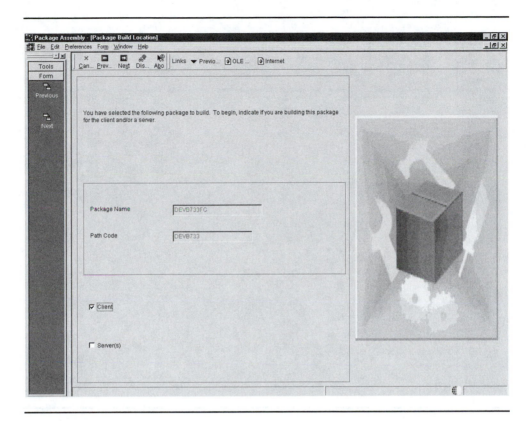

FIGURE 10-12. Package Build Location screen

software if you are going to be building a client workstation package, a server package, or both. You can build both types of packages, client and server, at the same time.

After selecting client, server, or both, click Next to display the Build Specification Options screen shown in Figure 10-13. This screen tells the OneWorld system to build the TAM specification files for a package. You are given this option so that if you have to go back later and rebuild part of a package due to errors, you won't have to build the entire package over again.

Notice that you have several different choices on the Build Specification Options screen. The All Specification Tables and the Individual Specification Table radio buttons

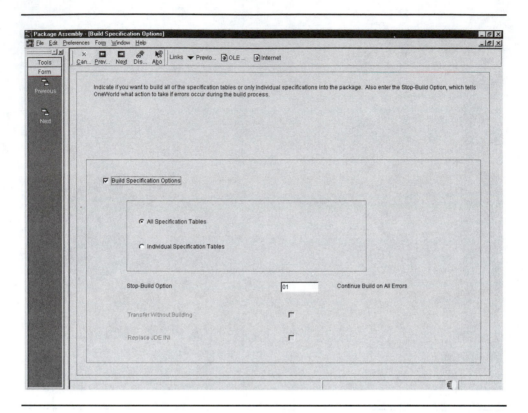

FIGURE 10-13.   Build Specifications Options screen

are available only if you are building a full package. They enable you to build all of the
TAM files or just one TAM file, which takes a lot less time. You might choose to build just
one TAM file, for example, if you were troubleshooting a package build. If you want to
build just one TAM file, select the Individual Specification Tables radio button and click
Next. This will take you into the Individual Specification Selection screen shown in
Figure 10-14 where you can indicate the specification tables you want to build.

   Let's return to the other options on the Build Specification Options screen, shown
earlier in Figure 10-13. The Stop Build option controls what happens when an error
occurs during the package build process. The valid values for this field are:

- 01—Continue Build On All Errors

- 02—Stop Build On Spec Failure

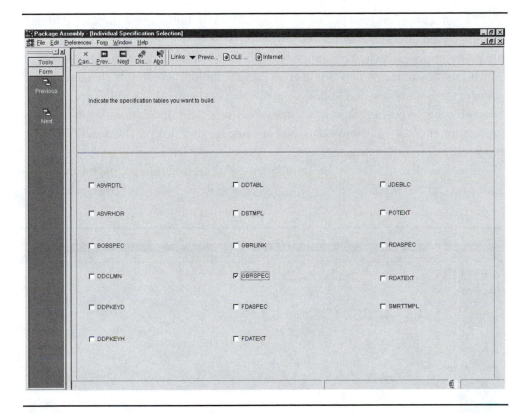

FIGURE 10-14. Individual Specification Selection screen

- 03—Stop Build On BSFN Failure

- 04—Do Not Compress If Errors

When you select Continue Build On All Errors, that package build will run to completion, even if a specification file does not build correctly. This is the most common value that you will select on this screen. A full package build can take six to eight hours so you will usually want the build to continue. If you allow the job to continue with errors, you can then just troubleshoot that error and may not have to rebuild the entire package. The Do Not Compress If Errors option tells the software not to compress the package if it has errors. OneWorld compresses your full and partial packages so that the software does not flood your network when you deploy the package to your workstations.

Two other options on this screen, Transfer Without Building and Replace JDE.INI, may be grayed out. The Transfer Without Building option is accessible only if you are creating a server package. This option tells the software to build the pack files, which we will discuss in the section "Full Server Package Build," later in this chapter, and transfer them to the server, but not to unpack them. The Replace JDE.INI option is accessible only if you are building an update package. This option allows you to replace the client workstation's JDE.INI file when the user accepts the package. This is a good way to roll out changes to the workstation JDE.INI files.

After you choose Next on the Build Specification Options screen, the Business Function Options screen, shown in Figure 10-15, is displayed. This screen controls

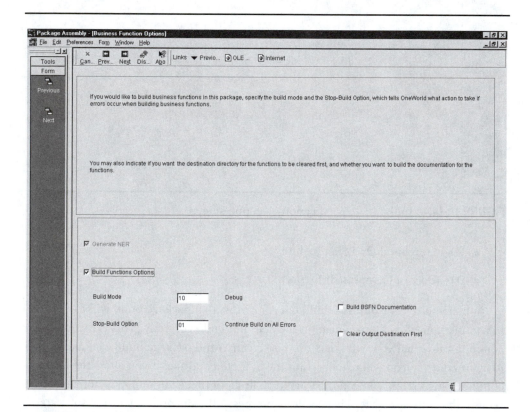

FIGURE 10-15. Business Function Options screen

whether the business functions are built. The specification TAM files for business functions are always built. However, if you are going to build the named event rules and DLLs, you will need to select the Build Business Functions check box. This option tells the system to call the Busbuild application in the back ground; this application will compile your business functions. This screen also has options that control the business function build (see Table 10-3).

After the Business Function Options screen, the Compression Options screen, shown in Figure 10-16, is displayed. This screen controls which directories are compressed during the package build process. The software will compress the packages so that when you deploy them to the workstations, you are moving only what is absolutely necessary. This option should be selected only for partial and full packages.

Option	Description
Generate NER	This option controls if the named event rules will be built.
Build Functions Option	This check box controls whether the Busbuild application will be called to build the business functions and named event rules.
Build Mode	This option determines how the business functions will be built. The valid values are: 10—Debug 20—Optimize 30—Performance 40—Instrumentation Normally you build the business functions in Optimize mode.
Stop Build Option	This option controls whether the build will stop when errors occur. The acceptable values for this field are: 01—Continue Build On All Errors 02—Stop Build On DLL Failure 03—Stop Build On First Error These options control the build process. Normally you use the Continue Build On All Errors option.
Build BSFN Documentation	This option builds the business function documentation.
Clear Output Destination First	This option clears the bin32, obj, and lib32 directories in the package before compiling the business functions.

TABLE 10-3. Business Function Options Screen Values

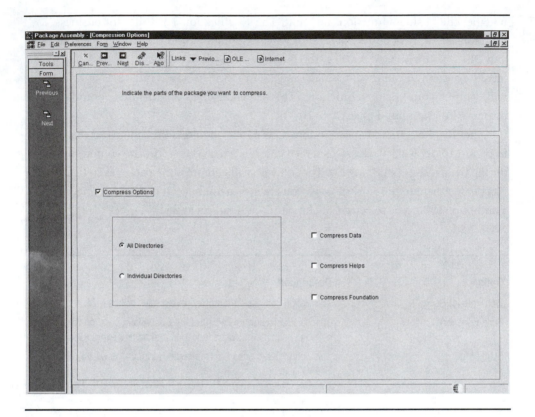

FIGURE 10-16.   Compression Options screen

If you compress the update packages, you will receive errors when you attempt to deploy them to the client workstations. The only time that you will need to compress an update package is when you are using the product packaging tools. Table 10-4 lists the options on the Compression Options screen.

After you click Next in the Compression Options screen, the Package Build Revisions screen, shown in Figure 10-17, is displayed. This is the final screen of the package build definition process. On this screen, you can review the definitions that you have set up for your specification build, business function build, and compression option build. If you are satisfied with the options you have chosen, click the End button, *not* the Cancel button. If you click the Cancel button, you will lose all your current definitions. When you click the End button, you are taken back to the Work With Packages screen.

On the Work With Packages screen, select your package name and click the Activate/Inactivate button.

Option	Description
Compress Option	This option controls whether or not the package will be compressed.
All Directories	When this option is selected, all directories in the package will be compressed.
Individual Directories	This option enables you to choose individual directories to compress.
Compress Data	When this option is selected, it will cause the access database to be compressed. You need to compress the data folder only if you have changed the access database.
Compress Helps	When this option is selected, it will compress the helps directory. You need to recompress the helps directory only if you have changed the help files.
Compress Foundation	When you choose this option, it will compress the system folder. You need to select this option only if you are installing a service pack; otherwise, the system folder will not have changed.

TABLE 10-4. Compression Options Screen Values

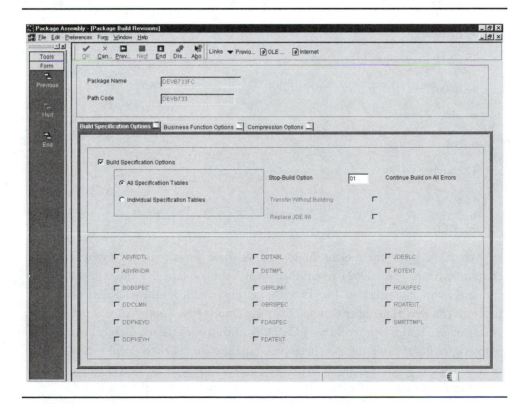

FIGURE 10-17. Package Build Revisions screen

What Happens During a Package Build

Now that you have activated the package, you are ready to begin the package build process. Go to the Row exit and click the Submit Build button. This will kick off a report, the R9621 Package Build report. In this section, we are going to cover what happens when this report runs.

R9621 for a Full Package Build

When a full package build is begun, the R9621 report will run. This report is the key to the package build process. If you understand what this report does, you will be able to debug most package build issues. First, this UBE creates the package directory structure on the deployment server under the path code directory that you are building the package for. This directory structure will have the same name as the package that you defined in OneWorld. Under this directory, you will find the following directories:

- bin32
- include
- lib32
- make
- obj
- res
- source
- spec
- work

When you begin the package build process, these directory structures will not contain anything. The R9621 report then creates the package INF file. This file contains pointers to the CAB files that will be generated from the package build process. You may remember that you defined compression options as you set up your package build. OneWorld uses CAB files during package deployment to reduce network traffic. We will discuss this topic in the section "Package Deployment," later in this chapter.

After the package INF file is created, the report then copies the .c and .h files, which are contained in the source and include directories, from the check-in location to the package name directory, as shown in Figure 10-18. These files are used in the definition of OneWorld for business functions and tables. The package build process also copies the contents of the make and work directories from the check-in location to the newly created package directory.

What about the lib32 and obj directories? They are created, but the contents of the check-in location are not be copied into these directories because they store information during the compiling of the business functions and named event rules.

NOTE

If you do not select to build business functions when you define your package, then the source, include, lib32 obj, make, and work directories are copied out of the check-in location. The software uses the contents of the check-in location and does not recompile the business functions and named event rules.

So far the package build process has only copied files and created directories. At this point, the package build process will read the central object tables and generate

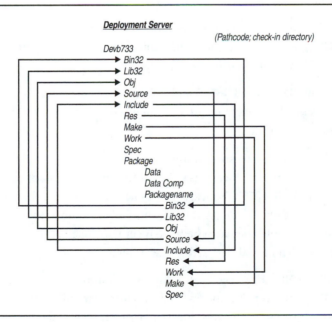

FIGURE 10-18.   Package build process

your TAM specification files in the spec directory under your package directory—for example, B733\Devb733\Package\ *package name* \spec, where package name is the name of the package you are building.

Let's discuss what this report reads from your central object tables in order to convert the information in these tables into the TAM file format. Each specification file that is built—for example, FDASPEC.DDB—has a corresponding central object table that contains information for this specification file.

- **DDTABL.DDB**   This specification file contains information on the tables within OneWorld. It is built from the F98710 table (Table Header).

- **DDCLM.DDB**   The information for this file comes from the F98711 table (Table Columns). It contains information on the columns in OneWorld tables.

- **DDPKEYH.DDB**   The information for this specification file comes from the F98712 table (Primary Index Header). This table and specification file contain information on each index.

- **DDPKEYD.DDB**   This TAM file contains information on the indexes for each column in the OneWorld tables, while the DDPKEYH file contains information on the table's indexes. This information is built from the F98713 table.

- **BOBSPEC.DDB**   This specification file gets its information from the F98720 table (Business View Specifications). This file contains a record for each business view in OneWorld.

- **GBRLINK.DDB**   The F98740 table (Event Rules Specifications) is read to build this file. It contains records for each event that has event rules attached to a OneWorld object.

- **GBRSPEC.DDB**   This specification file gets its information from the F98741 table (Event Rule Specifications). This is the largest file shipped with OneWorld. In the B733.2 release, this table contains more than one million records; in the OneWorld Xe release, this table contains over two million records. This table is so large because it contains one record for each line of event rules that are defined within the system.

- **DSTMPL.DDB**   This specification file gets its information from the F98743 table (Data Structure Templates). This file contains information on the business functions, processing options, form interconnection, and data structures.

- **FDATEXT.DDB**   The F98750 table (Form Design Aid Text) is used to build this specification file. This table and TAM file contain the text that is displayed on the applications within OneWorld.

- **FDASPEC.DDB**   This TAM file contains information on the columns, grids, buttons, and other controls displayed on the forms within OneWorld applications. It is built using information from the F98751 table (Forms Design Aid Specification).

- **ASVRHDR.DDB**   This specification file is built using information from the F98752 table (FDA/SVR Header Information). It contains a record for each application that has processing options attached to it.

- **ASVRDTL.DDB**   This file gets built using information from the F98753 table (FDA/SVR Detail Information). It contains information on all of the forms for each application contained within the system.

- **RDATEXT.DDB**   This file contains information on the text that is displayed on a OneWorld report. For example, the text descriptions for the columns on the one line per address report in OneWorld are built from information contained in the F98760 table (Report Design Aid Text).

- **RDASPEC.DDB**   This file is built with the information contained in the F98761 table (Report Design Aid Specifications). It contains information on the sections, columns, sort order, data selection, versions, and so on for the reports in the OneWorld system.

- **JDEBLC.DDB**   This file is built using information from the F98762 table (Business Function Source Information). It contains information on your business functions that are not stored in the c files.

- **CGTYPE.DDB**   This file is stored only in TAM file format. It contains code generated form types.

- **DDDICT.DDB**   This TAM file contains information on your OneWorld data dictionary items. The data dictionary is a light data dictionary, which means that this specification file contains only the information required to start OneWorld. As your end user uses the system, the software will read the data dictionary tables and perform a JITI on the data dictionary information that the user needs.

- **DDINDEX.DDB**   This file was used to contain the data dictionary indexes in the B732 release of OneWorld. However, as of B733 this file is no longer used.

- **DDTEXT.DDB**   This file contains the text information for the system's data dictionary items.

- **NEXTID.DDB**   This file became obsolete as of B733. As of B733, OneWorld keeps track of the objects in the system through unique names, instead of next IDs. When this file was used in previous releases, it got its information from the F98701 table (Next IDs).

- **GLBLTBL.DDB**   This table contains cache information on the data dictionary items that you have performed a JITI on. It also contains information on the tables within OneWorld. This information is cached to improve the performance of the system.

- **SMRTTMPL.DDB**   This file contains the required field information for data structures. It gets this information from the F98745 table (Smart Fields Named Mapping).

The package build process also creates files named the same as the previously described ones but with an XDB extension. These files are indexes over the DDB files. As stated previously, TAM files are really just a form of a database that is proprietary to J.D. Edwards' OneWorld software.

Busbuild   While the TAM specification files are being built, the business function build process is begun. The business function build process calls the C compiler that is required for your deployment server or development workstations. It uses this compiler to build your business functions and named event rules. This process occurs through the Busbuild application. This application is run on the machine that you kicked off the package build process from.

When Busbuild runs, it does several things in the background. For instance, the named event rules are generated. When you generate a named event rule through OneWorld, it creates a header and source file. Once these files are generated, they are placed in the source and include folders under your package directory.

Next the make files are generated, and the c source code is compiled into the obj files. Then Busbuild links the obj files into libraries that are placed in the lib32 directory under your package directory on the deployment server. The DLLs are generated from the libraries in the obj directory. These DLLs are then placed in the bin32 directory. Then the named event rule files are copied back into the check-in location.

At this point, if you chose package compression during the package definition process, the package is compressed. This generates a CAB file for each of the directories under your package directory. These CAB files contain all of the information in the directories they are named after; the only difference being that they are compressed. Thus, when you deploy a package, you are moving only what is necessary across the network.

Finally, the bin32, lib32, and obj directories are copied back into the check-in location so that if you build an update package, it will have the most current set of DLLs to add information into. If the directories were not copied back into the check-in location, information would be missing from these DLLs.

R9621 for an Update Package Build

Update packages are a great way to deliver a small number of changes to your end users in a small amount of time. You need to know how these packages are built in order to easily track down problems with them.

When you build an update package, it will kick off the R9621 report, which is used to build all packages. First, the package directory structure is created—for example B733\Devb733\Package\ *package name*, where *package name* is the name of the update package you are building.

Once this directory structure has been created, the PACKAGE.INF file is generated. This INF file is named the same as your package name and is used during the package deployment process.

After the INF file is generated, empty TAM specification files are generated under your package spec directory. Information is then added to these empty specification files. During a full package build, all of the information in your central object tables are placed into the specification files. However, during an update package build only information on the objects that you selected to be built into the package will be placed into the TAM specification files.

If you selected to build business functions for your update package, the software determines which business functions or named event rules you need to build. It will then copy the DLLs, which are listed in OneWorld as business function libraries, that are associated with these objects from the check-in location—for example, B733\Devb733\Bin32 into the bin32 directory under your package directory—because

Inside and Out

the update package needs to update the DLLs with the information from the objects you defined in your update package.

Once the DLLs have been copied, the include and source files will be copied from the check-in location to the package directories source and include folders. At this point, the Busbuild application executes in the background. It compiles any named event rules, table event rules, or business functions into the DLLs. So now your DLLs have all of the information they contained before they were copied into the package plus any new information that you have added through your update package definition.

So far the update package build process has been fairly similar to the full package build process. However, when this point is reached, the update package build process proceeds a little differently. A backup directory is created, and the CAB files from the parent package, which you defined during your package definition process, are backed up.

The obj, lib32, bin32, source, and include files are then copied from the update package to the corresponding directories in the parent package directory. Once this has been accomplished, these same directories are copied from the update package directory structure to the check-in location.

The process then moves on to merge the specification files from the update package with the specification files from the parent package. Then the update package build process is complete.

Why do we copy the information from the update package back into the check-in location? Remember that the DLL is updated with the new information contained in the update package, assuming you are building business functions, named event rules, or tables event rules with the update package build. If the software did not copy this DLL back into the check-in location, you would not have a good base DLL to add information to. So when you deployed this DLL to your client workstations, they would lose information that any other update package built into this DLL. This is why J.D. Edwards has the DLL copied back into the bin32 directory in the check-in location.

R9621 for a Partial Package

When a partial package is built, the R9621 report first generates the package directory structure, and then the package INF file is created. Then the specification files are generated.

With a partial package, the information contained in the specification files is sufficient only to log on to the system. The specification files also contain information on any applications that you defined for the partial package build. For example, if you defined the address book application to be built, all of the required information to log on to the system and the information needed to run the address book application would be built. With a partial package, you usually build in the applications that you want your end users to use and then restrict them from other applications through OneWorld security.

If they attempt to run an application that was not built into the partial package's TAM files, the system will then perform a JITI on that application directly out of the central objects. This process can be slow, and you may not want your end users to "grab" objects out of the central object files because they could then be running an application with different specifications than the ones that your other users have. Once the specification files are built, the Busbuild process begins, which builds the necessary business functions, named event rules, and table event rules.

Tables Used During a Package Build Definition and Build Process

Let's briefly discuss the tables that are used during the package build process. We are not referring to the central object tables; we are referring to the files that guide the build process. They contain various kinds of information, including the date you build your packages, the type of package you build, and what is contained in the package.

The F9603 table (Package Header) contains the following information on your packages:

- Name of the package

- Description of the package

- Path code that the package is being built over

- Type of package

- Package definition status

- Parent package name (for update packages only)

- Include Object Specs flag (for update packages only)

The F9631 table (Package Detail) contains the following information:

- Name of the package

- Path code that the package is being built over

- Package item type (when the package contains custom definitions for the OneWorld foundation, objects, data, or help files. Information will be listed in this column.)

- Object name (for update or partial packages)

- Version (the UBE version included in the partial or update packages)

You have probably noticed that the tables contain similar kinds of information. This is because these tables have to be linked so that the system can find the information to show you. The F96021 table (Software Package Build Header) contains the following information:

- Name of the package

- Path code that the package will be built over

- Whether the package is a client or server package

- Build status

- Whether the JDE.INI file will be replaced

- Date that the package was built

- Whether business functions were specified

- Build mode for the business functions

- Whether the output destination should be cleared when building business functions

- Amendments to the business function build log, if any

- What will stop the build (for example, Stop Build On Error or Continue Build On All Errors)

- Selection chosen to stop Busbuild on error

- Whether all of the specification files are being built

- Whether all of the specification files are being compressed

- Whether to transfer without building the specifications (for server packages only)

- Whether to build the business function documentation

The F9621 table (Package Build History) is an important table because it drives the Package Build History application. We will discuss the Package Build History application in the section "Troubleshooting Package Builds," later in this chapter. This table contains the following information:

- Name of the package

- Path code that the package is being built over

- Whether it is a client or server package

- Date and time the package was built

- Build status

- Whether the JDE.INI file is going to be replaced

- Whether specification files were built

- Whether business functions were built

- Build mode for business functions (for example, 20 Optimize)

- Whether to clear output destination during the business function build

- Amendments to the build log

- Selected stop Busbuild on error option

- Selected stop build on error for specifications option

- Whether all specification files were built

- Whether specification files were compressed

- Transfer without building the specifications (for server packages only)

- Whether you want to build business function documentation

The F9622 table (Package Build Detail) contains the following information:

- Name of the package

- Path code the package is being built over

- Whether it is a client or server package

- Which specification files to build

Inside and Out

- Which directories to compress

- Which business functions to build and their associated DLLs

The F96225 table (Package Build History Detail) contains a lot of the information that will be displayed on the Package Build History screen. It contains the following information:

- Name of the package

- Path code the package is being built over

- Whether it is a client or server package

- Build date and time

- Which TAM files were built

- Which business functions were built

- Which files were compressed

- Number of records read from the central object tables for each specification file

- Number of records written to each of the specification files that were built

- Status of each specification file (whether it built successfully or an error occurred)

- Number of pack records written and read (for server packages)

- Pack status (whether the pack operation was successful)

Figure 10-19 shows how all of this information is used during the package build process. This figure can help you understand how these tables drive the package build process.

Server Packages

Here's why server packages are necessary. When you run a report locally on a client workstation, you are using the TAM specification files on that client workstation to run this report. When you install your OneWorld host code onto an enterprise or application server, you are actually installing the necessary specification files to run reports on that server.

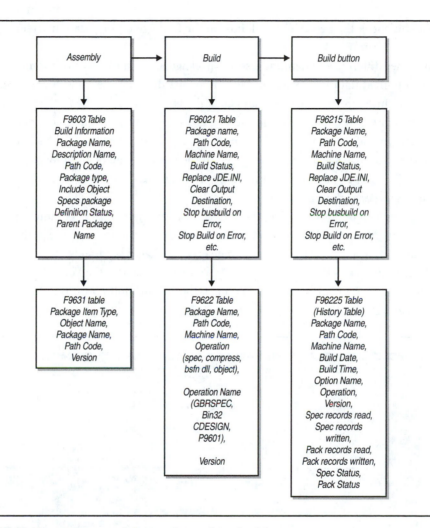

FIGURE 10-19.   Tables used during the package build process

Suppose you have developed a brandnew report. To move this report to your client workstations, you have to build a client package. The same is true for a server. If you have changed a report, business function, data structure, business view, or table definition, you will need to update the specification files on your enterprise or application server with this information. This process is completed via a server package.

When you define a server package, you follow a process similar to the one we discussed in the section "Workstation Packages," earlier in this chapter. One difference is that you check the Server(s) check box on the Package Build Location screen (shown earlier in Figure 10-12).

Another difference in defining a server package, instead of a workstation package, is that you must tell the system what server you are defining the package for. After you check the Server(s) check box and click the Next button on the Package Build Location screen, the Server Selection screen is displayed where you select a server.

When you select a server, a check mark is displayed to the left of the server name. Make sure that you see a check mark next to the server name before moving on from this screen. As you can see in Figure 10-20, you can build the same package on multiple servers at the same time.

You can also build the package as both a server and client package simultaneously. However, if you are having problems with the package build process, the authors recommend that you build your client and server packages separately.

After you have defined and activated your server package, the Work With Packages screen is displayed where you click the Submit Build button to kick off the server package build.

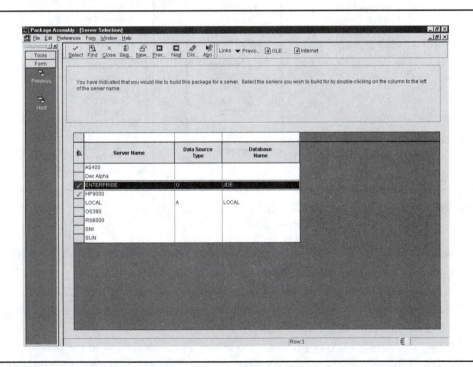

FIGURE 10-20. Server Selection screen

Full Server Package

When you build a server package, the R9621 report is run. First, the R9621 report builds the package directory structure under your path code on the deployment server. For example, if you built a package named DEVSVRFA over the DEVB733 path code, the B733\Devb733\Package\Devsvrfa directory is created. The Devsvrfa directory will contain the bin32, include, lib32, make, obj, res, source, spec, and work directories, just as it does when you build a client workstation package. The process then creates the package INF file, just as it does when a client workstation package is built.

After the package directory structure and the INF file are built, the R9621 report copies the source and include files from the check-in location to the package directory—in our example, Devsvrfa.

The report then builds the TAM specification files. If you are building only a server package, and not a server and client package, you will notice that the FDASPEC, FDATEXT, and SMRTTMPL specification files will not be built. They are not built because these files are related to interactive applications, which are never run on the enterprise or application servers. Interactive applications run only on client workstations. During a full client package build, 17 specification files are built; during a full server package build, 14 specification files are built.

The software knows which specification files are required to build a full server package by reading the F96225 table (Package Build Detail History). It reads the HDPKGOPER column in this table, looking for a value of 01, and the HDPACKSTS column, looking for a status of "Not Built" or "Error." This information tells the software to build a pack file for each TAM specification file listed in the table. These files are "compressed" TAM files that will be transferred to the enterprise or application server. After the process creates the pack files, it will then update the HDPACKSTS column to 03 successful for each specification record.

Then the process runs the Busbuild application in the background. This application runs only if you chose to build business functions when you defined your server package. When this application runs, it generates only the source and include files for the named and table event rules in the system. This is because most enterprise servers, except for Compaq Alpha and Intel Windows NT servers, do not use DLLs.

At this point, the R9621 UBE calls the R9622 Server Package Build report. This report will first create the server package INF file, which is placed in a directory on the deployment server under your package directory.

The server package INF file tells the system what information to transfer to the enterprise server. An example of this file follows:

```
[SERVER PACKAGE]
PackageName=DEVSVRFA;  Package name
Type=FULL    ; Type of Package
Platform=ALPHA4.0 ;Type of server Platform
BuildMachine=DEPLOYMENT  ;  The machine name of the server
BuildPort=6005    ; Port number
SPEC=1            ; Indicates Specs are included in the package.
SpecList= 0 , 1 , 10 , 13 , 14 , 15 , 16 , 17 , 18 , 2 , ; Indicates
which specs are included in this package
BSFN=1       ;Indicates what dlls are included in the package
BL007=1      ; Indicates this dll is included in the package

Dlls that are in the package
BLKTY3=1
BLRK001=1
BLRK009=1
BLRK11=1
C550MW66=1
CAEC=1
CALLBSFN=1
CAPS=1
CBUSPART=1
CCONVERT=1
CCORE=1
CCRIN=1
CCUSTOM=1
CDBASE=1
CDDICT=1
```

As you can see from this example, the package INF file ties into the server package build process, telling the system exactly what will be moved to the enterprise or application server. You may have noticed that the specification files have a series of numbers, each number corresponding to a specific specification file. The values for these numbers follow:

```
AVSRHDR = 0
AVSRDTL = 1
BOBSPEC = 2
DDTABL = 4
DDCLMN = 5
DDPKEYH = 6
DDPKEYD = 7
DSTMPL = 10
```

```
FDASPEC = 11
FDATEXT = 12
RDASPEC = 13
RDATEST =14
GBRLINK = 15
GBRSPEC = 16
POTEXT = 17
JDEBLC = 18
SMRTMPL = 19
```

This INF file also tells the system which DLLs are going to be transferred to the enterprise or application server. In building a server package, we need to build and move several DLLs including CCORE.

After the server package INF file is created, the R9622 then creates the directory structure on the enterprise server. As of release B733.1, J.D. Edwards has totally redesigned the server package build process, correcting a problem in previous releases. When a server package was built in release B732, it was built directly over the specification files used to run reports. This meant that if the package build process failed, it would bring down your enterprise or application server. To avoid this problem, release B733.1 has a new directory, the package directory, which is located under the DDP\B733 folder. The server packages are built under the package directory. The R9622 report creates a directory with the same name as your server package, containing the bin32, res, spec, lib32, obj, make, include, pack, and source directories. Thus, if you encounter an error, it will not affect your end users running reports on the enterprise server. The only time the directory structure that is used to run your reports on your enterprise server is affected is when you deploy a server package.

CAUTION

Since the software creates a package directory under the B733 folder, you should not use duplicate package names. If you named a package SVRFULL and you already had a SVRFULL package defined, even if it was under a different path code, this package would be written over and lost.

When the directory structure has been created, the R9622 report will transfer the pack files to the server under the pack directory. These files are transferred using JDENet, which is the same communication process that is used when you submit a UBE. Of course, this means that if you are performing a server package build, your host services must be up and running correctly.

The server package build process will then transfer the source and include files from your package directory on the deployment server to your enterprise or application server. These files are also transferred using JDENet. After all of these files are on the enterprise or application server, the R9622 report then unpacks the pack files from the pack directory. It then places the specification files into the spec directory under your package name directory on the server. Then the F96225 Software Package Build Detail History table is updated to show that your specification files have been successfully unpacked.

Then the business functions are compiled on the enterprise server. They must be compiled on the server so that they are in the correct format and because the AS400, RS6000, HP9000, and Sun Solaris systems do not use DLLs.

At this point, the server package build is complete, and you can access a report about the build. An example of a server package build report is shown in Figure 10-21.

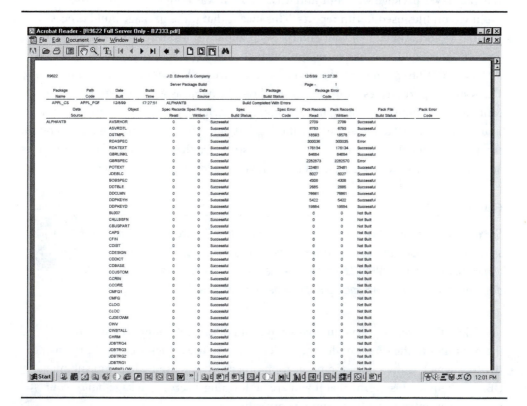

FIGURE 10-21. R9622 Server Package Build report

In the report shown in Figure 10-21, the Spec Records Read and Written columns contain zeros because the package built was a server package. In addition, a number of errors are listed under the Pack File Build Status column. This error status was received because one entry under the Pack Records Read column (300036) does not match the entry under the Pack Records Written column (300035). When you see an error like this on a report, you should review the log files to determine what went wrong. We will cover how to do this in the section "Troubleshooting Package Builds," later in this chapter.

Further down in the Pack File Build Status column, some "Not Built" messages are listed. These messages refer to the DLLs that you are moving over to the enterprise server. If you receive such messages on a Server Package Build report, don't worry about them. DLL files are not packed, so this "Not Built" message is not really an error message.

After you receive the R9622 report, you should look at your enterprise server's directory structure. You will want to ensure that it includes the package directory, that DLLs are under the bin32 directory (if you are building business functions), and that specification files are under the spec directory.

Update Server Package

You will use an update server package when you have only a few objects to move to your enterprise server. After all, a full server package can take up to eight hours! You can save a significant amount of time by building an update server package instead.

To define a server update package, you follow almost the same process as you do when defining a client workstation update package. You need to choose a parent package and tell the system what server you want to build the server package on. We discussed the process of selecting a server in the section "Server Packages," earlier in this chapter.

After you have defined your server package and clicked the Next button on the Server Selection screen (shown earlier in Figure 10-20), the Work With Packages screen is displayed. You can activate the package and submit the build by clicking the Submit Build button on the Work With Packages screen. This kicks off the now-familiar R9621 UBE.

First, the R9621 UBE creates the package directory structure on the deployment server. For example, if your package name is DEVUPD, and you are building the package over the DEVB733 path code, then the package directory will be created under the B733\Devb733\Devupd directory. This devupd directory contains the bin32, lib32, obj, res, make, source, include, and spec directories. The package INF file is created next. This file tells the system where to find information, such as the specification files.

Then the pack files are created by reading the relational database files. The R9621 UBE reads the required information in the central object files and places the information in the pack files. After these pack files are created, the Busbuild application is run in the background, generating the named and table event rules. This application will generate the source and include files necessary for the named and table event rules. These files will be placed in the source and include directories under your package name directory.

The R9621 UBE process then ends, and the R9622 UBE is started. This UBE will create the server package INF file under the server name directory on your deployment server. Then the R9622 UBE creates the directory structure on the enterprise server. The R9622 UBE transfers the pack files to the pack directory under the package directory on the enterprise or application server. These pack files, which are really just "compressed" TAM specification files, are moved to this directory through JDENet, the same process that is used to submit UBEs. These pack files are then unpacked and placed into the spec directory of your parent package on the enterprise or application server.

This parent package must be on the enterprise server; otherwise, your update server package will fail. J.D. Edwards ships the host code with a full package defined for each path code you install on the enterprise server. Don't delete these packages to reclaim disk space because you will need at least one per path code to perform update server packages. Since the update package updates the parent package's spec directory, the spec directory under the update package directory on the server will be empty.

Once the pack files are unpacked, the R9622 UBE then moves the source and include files from the deployment server to the enterprise server, under the update package directory. The DLLs that are going to be affected by the update package are then copied from the parent package, and the new source and include files are built into these DLLs. The DLLs are then copied back into the parent package.

This means that the parent package is updated with the specifications from the update package. If you lose or corrupt the spec directory under your path code directory on the enterprise server, which is used to run your reports, you can then copy the spec directory from the parent package into the path code directory after you stop your host services. This will bring your server back up to date, and you can simply start the host service again to run the reports. Keep this in mind as you run update server packages. We recommend that you build a full package on both the server and client side about once a month.

Package Deployment

The following sections will discuss how to deploy packages to your enterprise.

Deploying Client Packages

After you build a package, you need to get it to your client workstations in order for your end users to see the changes you have made to the software. You have several options for doing this.

Interactive Deployment

Interactive deployment, sometimes called pull package deployment, is one of the most common methods of deploying a package to your workstation. This method of package deployment should be the first that you will use on a OneWorld system. Once you have learned how to deploy workstation packages in this manner, you can move on to more complicated methods of package deployment.

You can deploy a package that you have built, or you can deploy a package that is shipped with the system. To start the deployment process, you need to log on to the client workstation as a user who has administrative rights. You need administrative rights because you will update the registry of your client workstation when you deploy a package. As of the OneWorld Xe release, this requirement is no longer in place.

After you log on to your client workstation, you need to start Windows Explorer. In Windows Explorer, you map a network drive to your deployment server. When you map the network drive, you should see the B733 directory that is shared during the installation process of OneWorld. Map your network drive to this directory. Then expand the B733 directory and double-click on the OneWorld client install directory where you will find the install manager.exe program. Double-click on this executable to start the Install Manager program.

From the first screen of the Install Manager program, click the Next button to access the Client Workstation Setup Package Selection screen, shown in Figure 10-22, which enables you to choose the package you want to deploy. Notice that the description of the package that you entered in the during the package build process is displayed for your end users. This description will help your end users choose the most current package. Select the package that you want to deploy and click the Next button.

The next screen enables you to choose the drive where you want the package to install. This screen also has two radio buttons that you can use to indicate whether you want to deploy development or production objects. If you choose the Development

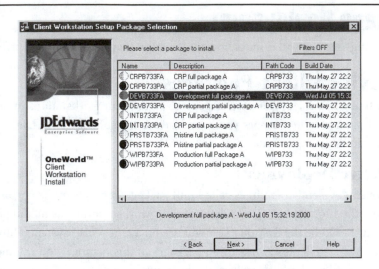

FIGURE 10-22.   Client Installation Package Selection screen

Objects radio button, you are telling the system to copy the source, include, work, make, and obj directories. These directories are required if you are going to perform development on this machine. If you choose to load the production objects, you will deploy only the bin32, spec, data, and res directories. These directories take up less of a footprint on your client workstation, and the end user will not need the other directories unless he or she is developing in OneWorld. After you have selected the drive letter you want to install the package to and have indicated whether you are installing development or production objects, click the Next button. The package will start to deploy to your workstation.

What Happens When a Package Is Deployed

A client workstation install is really only a fancy file copy. In B733, the client install process obtained information from the system tables. This meant that a connection had to be made to the database in order for a client workstation to be installed correctly. However, as of B733.1, you no longer have to have a connection to the database in order to deploy a client workstation. In B733.1 and later, the package deployment is handled strictly through INF files. These files tell the system where to copy data from for the package deployment process.

Suppose we are going to deploy a full client package that has been built under the DEVB733 path code. Once we begin the package deployment process, the system will connect to the deployment server and find the Install INF file under the OneWorld client install directory. The system will then read the file locations section of this file to determine where to find the package information. An example of the file location section follows:

```
[FileLocations]
PackageInfs=\\DPIS02\B733\package_inf
CurrentReleaseMasterPath=\\DPIS02\B733
ClientListener=\\DPIS02\B733\OneWorld Client Install\Push Install
Listener,Setup.exe,/s
```

The system reads the package INF's value in this file, which guides the system to find the package INF files. The package INF's path points to the deployment server's package_inf directory. If this path is incorrect, your package deployment will end before it begins.

N O T E

The release master path must be correct, or your package deployment will not function correctly. The values for this file are written during the installation process of OneWorld—specifically, when you release the plan.

Once the system finds the package_inf directory, it then finds your package INF file, in this case DEVB733FA. This file guides the system to the information that is needed to deploy a client workstation package. An example of this file follows:

```
[SrcDirs]
SDEVB733=\DEVB733\package\DEVB733FA
SSYS=\Systemcomp
SDEVB733DATA=\DEVB733\package\DATAcomp
SHELP=\HelpsCOMP
[DestDirs]
DDEVB733=%INSTALL\DEVB733
DSYS=%INSTALL\system
DDEVB733DATA=%INSTALL\DEVB733\data
DHELP=%INSTALL\helps
[FileSets]
DEVB7331=Y,$SDEVB733\bin32.CAB,$DDEVB733\bin32
DEVB7332=Y,$SDEVB733\spec.CAB,$DDEVB733\spec
```

Inside and Out

```
DEVB7333=Y,$SDEVB733\include.CAB,$DDEVB733\include
DEVB7334=Y,$SDEVB733\lib32.CAB,$DDEVB733\lib32
DEVB7335=Y,$SDEVB733\obj.CAB,$DDEVB733\obj
DEVB7336=Y,$SDEVB733\source.CAB,$DDEVB733\source
DEVB7337=Y,$SDEVB733\work.CAB,$DDEVB733\work
DEVB7338=Y,$SDEVB733\make.CAB,$DDEVB733\make
DEVB7339=Y,$SDEVB733\res.CAB,$DDEVB733\res
SYS=Y,$SSYS\System.CAB,$DSYS
DEVB733DATA=Y,$SDEVB733DATA\data.CAB,$DDEVB733DATA
HELP=Y,$SHELP\Helps.CAB,$DHELP
[Components]
ProdObj=DEVB7331,DEVB7332,DEVB7339
DevObj=DEVB7333,DEVB7334,DEVB7335,DEVB7336,DEVB7337,DEVB7338
Foundation=SYS
Data=DEVB733DATA
Help=HELP
[Typical]
Name=Development
Description=Install the development objects
Components=ProdObj,DevObj,Foundation,Data
1KB=1461761024
2KB=1469954048
4KB=1487040512
8KB=1523482624
16KB=1623457792
32KB=1852637184
64KB=2339307520
[Compact]
Name=Production
Description=Install the production objects only
Components=ProdObj,Foundation,Data
1KB=1191691264
2KB=1192681472
4KB=1194725376
8KB=1199259648
16KB=1208565760
32KB=1227358208
64KB=1266089984
[Attributes]
PackageName=DEVB733FA
PathCode=DEVB733
Built=Build Completed With Errors
PackageType=FULL
Release=B733
SystemBuildType=RELEASE
MFCVersion=6
SpecFilesAvailable=Y
DelGlblTbl=Y
```

```
ReplaceIni=Y
AppBuildDate=Thu May 27 22:27:40 1999
FoundationBuildDate=Thu May 27 22:27:40 1999
DataBuildDate=Thu May 27 22:27:40 1999
HelpBuildDate=Thu May 27 22:27:40 1999
DeploymentServerName=INTELNTC
Location=Corporate
DeploymentStatus=Approved
PackageDescription=Development full package A
IconDescription=JDEdwards OneWorld
DefaultEnvironment=DEV733
Spec=DEVB7333
ServerHelpPath=\Helps
[ODBC Data Sources]
OneWorld Local - DEVB733=Microsoft Access Driver (*.mdb)
[OneWorld Local - DEVB733]
Driver=odbcjt32.dll
DefaultDir=C:\ACCESS
DriverId=25
FIL=MS Access
JetIniPath=odbcddp.ini
UID=admin
Driver32=odbcjt32.dll
DBQ=$DDEVB733DATA\jdeb7.mdb
[START]
ProgramGroupName=OneWorld
Item1=SYSTEM\BIN32\Oexplore.exe,JDEdwards OneWorld
Explorer,SYSTEM\res\OneWorld.ico
[Desktop]
Item1=SYSTEM\BIN32\Oexplore.exe,JDEdwards
OneWorld,SYSTEM\res\OneWorld.ico
[Environment]
PathDEVB733=%INSTALL\DEVB733\bin32;
Pathsys=%INSTALL\system\bin32;
[Fonts]
Arial=Font\arial.ttf
```

First, the package deployment process reads the SDEVB733 variable under the [SrcDirs] section. This variable points to the package INF file under your deployment server's path code package INF file. This file contains path statements that are loaded into the SDEVB733 variable. This path statement is used in the [FileSets] section of the DEVB733FA.INF file to guide the system to the bin32, spec, include, lib32, obj, source, work, make, and res CAB files. These CAB files are what comprise the compressed OneWorld package. You deploy the package through compressed files to minimize the impact on the network.

Next the package deployment process reads the SSYS variable under the [SrcDirs] section. This variable caches a path statement that is then used in the [FileSets] section of the INF file to tell the system where to find the system CAB file. The same thing happens for the help directory.

The [Components] section of the DEVB733FA.INF file tells the system what to deploy. This section contains the beginning variable to the [FileSets] entries, which controls which directories will be deployed to the client workstation.

The typical and compact sections are read when you choose to install either the development or production version of the package. The only real difference in this type of package deployment is that fewer directories are copied when a compact or production package is deployed. This is because the source, include, and work directories are not required for a production package because you will not be developing from a production workstation.

The next section of the DEVB733FA.INF file is the attributes section. This section indicates the type of package that was built, its status, and the system build type. It also lists the date that the package was built, the name of the deployment server, the location that the package was built for, and if it is approved for deployment.

The ODBC data sources section sets up your access database ODBC in the Control Panel. This enables the OneWorld software to communicate with your local access database, which can contain menus and user-defined code tables.

The next two sections create shortcuts for the executable used to start a OneWorld client, and also to set the path statement on your local workstation to find the OneWorld software. The final entry in this file sets up the Arial font on your computer.

As you can see, the package INF files really are what controls the package deployment process. Without the entries in these files the software would not find the files that make up a OneWorld client package and thus would not be able to copy these files down to the client workstation. This is why it is so important to understand how the package INF files are used during a client package deployment.

How a Client INI File Is Created

When the client install process begins, it completes the process that we have described in the previous section. The JDE.INI file, which is contained under the B733\Oneworld Client Install\Misc directory, is copied from the deployment server. It is updated with information, such as path code, environment, and system settings, contained in the package INF file, which is located under the package_inf directory on your deployment server.

If you want to deploy changes to your client JDE.INI file, you must modify the JDE.INI file under the Oneworld Client Install\Misc directory. For example, when you want to deploy your security server settings to your client workstations, you modify the security section of the JDE.INI file under the Oneworld Client Install\Misc directory.

Silent and Verbose Deployment

A silent package deployment is basically the process of running a client installation from the command line. In order to run a silent package deployment, you pass the following command:

```
\\deploymentservername\B733\OneWorld Client install\setup.exe -S -U
username -P package name -D Install Path
```

This command begins package deployment in the background. The first part of this command is the path to the SETUP.EXE file on your deployment server. The other parameters tell the system how to install the package. The –S parameter tells the system that this deployment will be a silent package deployment. The –U parameter is the username, the –P parameter is the name of the package that you want to deploy. The –D parameter is the install path, which tells the system which drive you want to install the package onto on your client workstation. You can place this command in a bat file, if you like, and e-mail it to your end users.

A verbose package deployment is similar to a silent package deployment. The main difference is that the status of the deployment is displayed on your screen. You must modify the previously provided command line in order to run the deployment in verbose mode. Change the first parameter on the command line from –S to –V to indicate to the system that you want a verbose package deployment.

Assigning Packages to Workstations

When assigning packages to be deployed to the workstations, the Package Deployment application is used. This program can be accessed through the Deployment button in the Package Build application off the row exit, or it can be found on the Package And Deployment Tools menu GH9083.

After you start the work with Package Deployment application, click the Add button to access the Package Deployment director. This director can help you set up package deployments for your specific workstations, deployment servers, deployment groups, enterprise servers, and locations.

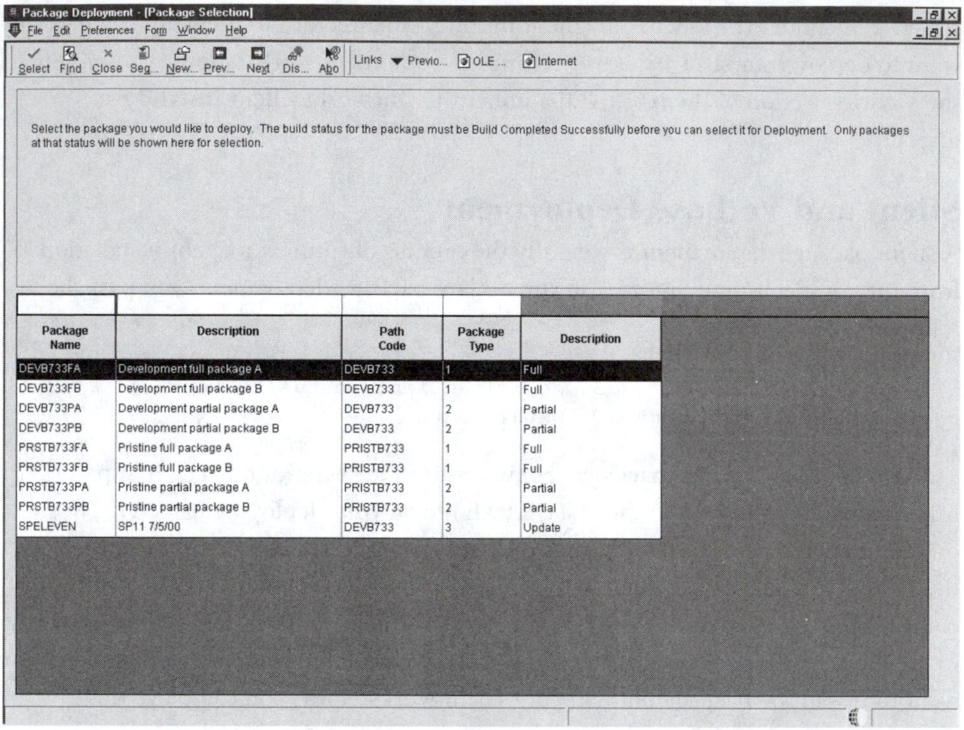

FIGURE 10-23. Package Selection screen

The Package Selection screen (see Figure 10-23) in the Package Deployment director, enables you to select the package that you want to assign to your client workstations. Only packages that have been successfully built will be displayed in this screen. Select the package that you want to deploy to your client workstations and then click the Next button.

Then the Package Deployment Targets screen, shown in Figure 10-24, is displayed. This screen enables you to specify the type of target you want to deploy your package to. Suppose we want to assign the package to specific workstations; on this screen, we check the Client Workstation check box and then click the Next button.

You can verify the name of the package that you are deploying and the path code that this package is associated with on the Package Deployment Attributes screen

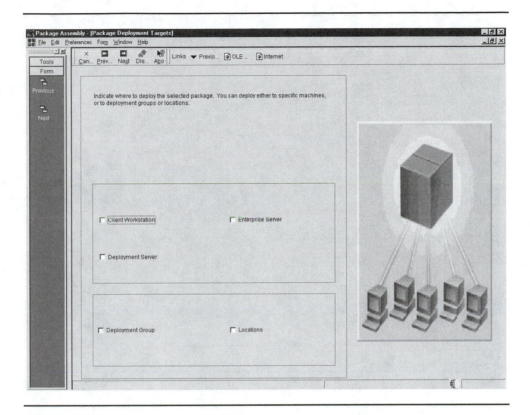

FIGURE 10-24. Package Deployment Targets screen

shown in Figure 10-25. It also enables you to make the package mandatory, which means that your end users will not be able to log on to the system until they accept the package. You can also set up a push installation from this screen; we will discuss push installation techniques in the section "Installing the Listener on Your Workstations," later in this chapter.

The Machine Selection screen enables you to choose the workstations that you want to assign the package to. You can select one or multiple workstations to deploy this package to. In order to select these machines, double-click on the first column of the grid so that a check mark is displayed. Once you have selected your workstations, click the Next button to access the last screen of this director. After you have saved

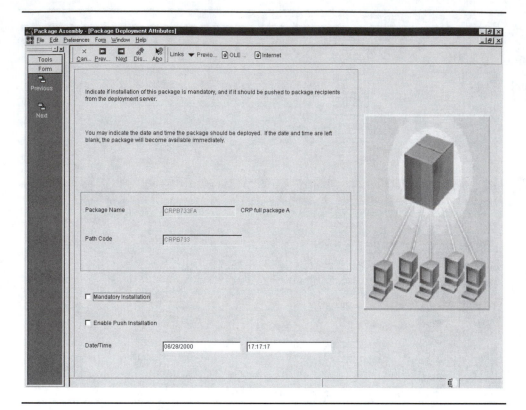

FIGURE 10-25.   Package Deployment Attributes screen

your changes on this final screen, you are ready to test the assignment of the package to your workstations.

Log on to one of the workstations that you have assigned the package to. You will then be prompted to select the package, as shown in Figure 10-26. If the package is mandatory, the end users will not be able to log on to the system unless they accept the package. You can deploy full and update packages in this manner.

Deploying Packages Using the Listener

After you have deployed a client workstation for the first time, a service will be installed on your client that, when set up, will listen for package installations. This means that you can schedule packages to be deployed to your workstations unattended.

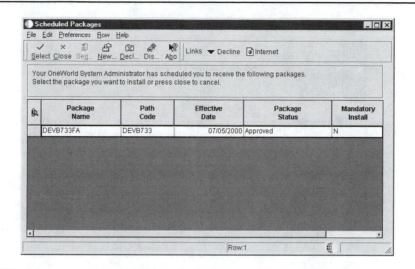

FIGURE 10-26. Scheduled Packages screen

Installing the Listener on Your Workstations   The OneWorld Listener is a service
that runs on your client workstation. This service can be set up as a local or network
service. When you install the Listener service, we recommend you set it up as a
network service. If the Listener is installed as a local service, the end user has to be
logged on to Windows NT in order to receive a package. If you set the service up as a
network service, the end user does not have to be logged on to Windows NT to receive
a package. This means that the client workstation just has to be turned on in order to
receive a package.

You can install the Listener service through a bat file, Microsoft Software
Management System(SMS), or manually by deploying the first package to the
workstation. Because this Listener service is installed by running a simple setup
executable, you could even deploy it through a Web page if you wanted to. This
executable and the other required files are located on your OneWorld deployment
server under the B733\Oneworld Client Install\Push Install Listener folder.

When you double-click on the setup executable file, a welcome screen is
displayed recommending that you close all other applications before you begin
the installation process. Click the Next button, which will take you into the OneWorld

Inside and Out

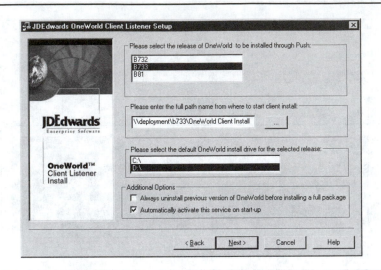

FIGURE 10-27.   OneWorld Client Listener Setup screen

Client Listener Setup screen shown in Figure 10-27. This screen enables you to set up your Listener service.

The screen shown in Figure 10-27 contains several fields. You must select the release of OneWorld software that will be installed through the service and enter the location where the service is to start the client install. This latter field must contain a network path statement to the client installation setup executable. The path statement consists of your deployment server's name and a path to the OneWorld client install directory. You enter the drive letter where you want the package installed on the client workstation in another field.

Two check boxes are available under Additional Options on the OneWorld Client Listener Setup screen. These options enable you to automatically start the OneWorld Listener service when the workstation starts up and to always uninstall the previous version of OneWorld before deploying a new full package. After you have made these choices, click the Next button.

On the OneWorld Client Listener Setup Type screen, shown in Figure 10-28, you select whether to set up your service as a local service or a network service. As stated previously, we recommend that you select the network service. Select the appropriate radio button, verify that you have enough space to install the service in the window at the bottom of the screen, and then click Next.

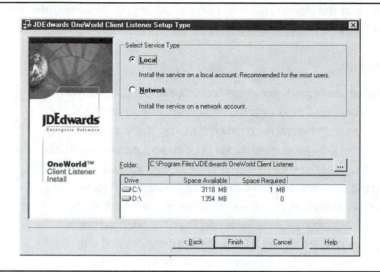

FIGURE 10-28. Setting up the Listener as a local or network service

If you have selected to set the Listener up as a network account, the OneWorld Client Listener Setup User Information screen (see Figure 10-29) is displayed and prompts you to enter a username, password, and domain. This username and password

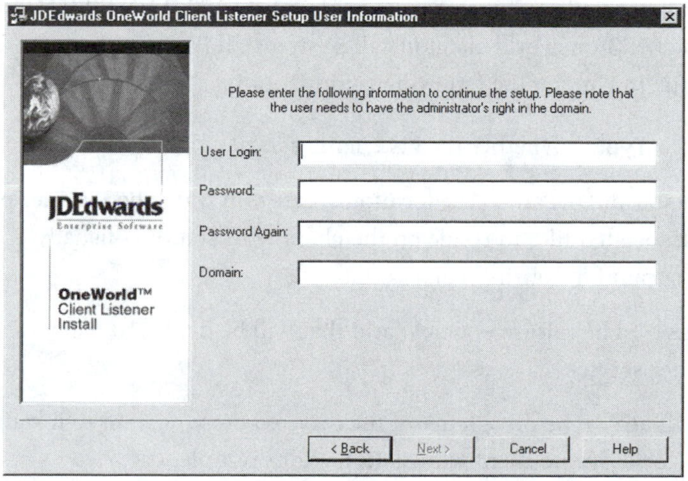

FIGURE 10-29. Setting up an account to log the Listener service into the network

are used to start the OneWorld client Listener. After you fill in this information and click Next, the Listener is installed.

CAUTION

If your end users use their own domain user accounts, they can get locked out of their client workstations. If the OneWorld Client Listener service is running, Windows NT considers that user logged on to the network. If your end users set up this service to start with their user and change their password, the service will pass the old, incorrect password to the domain controller. In most organizations, after three unsuccessful attempts to log on to the network, the account is usually locked out. To avoid this problem, we recommend you set up an account that is a member of the administrators group on your workstations. Then your OneWorld system administrators can use this account to troubleshoot problems or log on to the client workstations, if necessary. Because this account is a "secure" account, the password could be set up not to expire.

If you prefer that your end users not have to go through all of these screens and options, you can deploy the client Listener through a small bat file. Enter the necessary information into this bat file, which will install the client Listener in silent mode. This means that the end user is not prompted for input during the installation.

The options for the Listener silent install process are contained in an INF file that is located on your deployment server. This file, LISTEN_SILENT_SETUP.INF, is located in the b733\oneworld client install\push install listener directory. You can modify this file to contain the following information:

- **Service Type**   Whether the Listener is a local or network service.

- **WorkstationDirPath**   The location where you want the Listener program and associated files to reside on the client workstation—usually, C:\program files\ow listener.

- **Release**   The release of OneWorld that will be deployed using the Listener service.

- **InstallPath**   The drive letter of the drive where you want to install OneWorld on the client workstation—for example, C:\b7.

- **LaunchPath** The network path to the OneWorld client installation executable—for example, \\deploymentserver\b733\oneworld client install\setup.exe.

- **AutoStart** Whether the service will start automatically or manually. The valid values are 1 for automatic and 0 for manual.

- **UninstallPackage** Whether to uninstall the previous package if you are installing a full package.

After you set up this INF file, you then have to create a bat file for your end users. Simply open a blank Microsoft Word or Notepad document and enter the following command to call the Listener installation in silent mode:

```
Start \\deploymentservername\B733\OneWorld Client Install\Push Install
Listener\setup.exe /s listen_silent_setup.inf
```

Save the file as OWLISTENER.BAT or some other logical name. You can post this bat file on a Web site or server, or you can even e-mail it to your end users. All they have to do is double-click on the bat file, and the client Listener will be installed. Perhaps some of your users have different releases of the software or have the OneWorld software installed on different drives. If so, you can create a custom bat file for these users and specify a different INF file for the Listener install to use.

T I P

After you install the Listener service, if you want to change the options for it, you can simply right-click on the ear icon that is displayed on the right side of your Windows task bar. This accesses a screen that enables you to change the default parameters of the service.

Scheduling a Package to be Deployed Through the Listener Service After you set up your Listener service on your client workstations, you can set up push installations. This type of OneWorld installation uses the Listener service to install the OneWorld client workstation package. In order to set up a push installation, log on to the deployment server in the deployment environment or onto a client workstation

Inside and Out

in any environment. Then run the package deployment application, P9631, on the Package And Deployment Tools menu GH9083.

You set up your package for deployment in the same manner that we discussed in the section "Assigning Packages to Workstations," earlier in this chapter. The only difference is that when you get to the Package Deployment Attributes screen, shown in Figure 10-30, you check Enable Push Installation, specify a date and time, and click Next. The client package is pushed out to the workstation when this time and date have expired. You are then asked to select the client workstations that you want to deploy the package to.

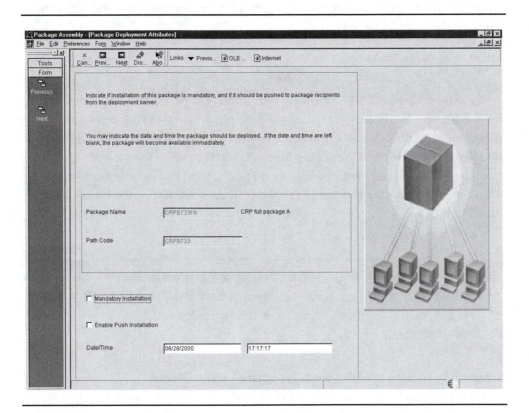

FIGURE 10-30. Package Deployment Attributes screen

When you set up the OneWorld scheduler application, the OneWorld Client Listener service interacts with the R98825 UBE that runs at specific times on your enterprise server. This application allows you to schedule reports to run at a specific time. The authors recommend that you set this report to run nightly, and then you can deploy packages during off hours if necessary.

Deploying Server Packages

To deploy a server package, double-click on the package deployment application, P9631, which is located on the Package And Deployment Tools menu GH9083. Then click the Add button on the Work With Package Deployment screen. The Package Selection screen, which was shown earlier in Figure 10-23, is displayed next. Select the package that you want to deploy to your enterprise server or servers on this screen and click the Next button.

On the Package Deployment Targets screen, indicate that you want to deploy a server package by checking the Enterprise Server check box. Because you are deploying an enterprise server package, everything will be grayed out on the Package Deployment Attributes screen, which is displayed next. Simply verify that your package name and path code information is correct and then click the Next button.

On the Enterprise Server Selection screen, choose the enterprise server that you want to deploy the server package to. When a server is selected, you will see a check box next to the enterprise server's name; then click Next.

What Happens When a Server Package Is Deployed

At this point, you are on the Work With Package Deployment screen; select the Machine radio button and click Find. You will then be presented with three directories: client workstation, deployment server, and enterprise server.

When you expand the enterprise server directory, you should see a directory named after the server that you set up to deploy the package to. Select this directory and click the Active/Inactivate button under the Row exit, which activates the package. Once you have activated the package, you can deploy it by selecting the package and clicking the Row exit Deploy button. This starts a UBE that will deploy the package to your enterprise server.

Inside and Out

When you click the Row | Deploy button for server packages, the R98825D UBE (Enterprise Server Deployment) is launched on the workstation or deployment server where you ran the package deployment application. The R98825D UBE is responsible for deploying your changes to the enterprise server. When this report is run, the files contained in the path code, for which you are deploying the server package, are locked. This means that no reports or business functions can run on the enterprise server while the report runs because the specification files are being updated with the information from your server package. This UBE also copies the bin32 directory, which contains your DLLs if you are on a Windows NT enterprise server, into your path code directory. Once this process is complete, the R98825D UBE will then release the path code directory, and any reports submitted will then be able to run.

CAUTION

You should always run server package deployments when your users are off the system. If your system runs 24 hours a day, however, you should run the server package deployments when the least number of users are on the system. This reduces the slight chance that a specification file will become corrupt due to a report attempting to access it at the same time as the R98825D UBE. Scheduling server package deployments like this is also a good idea because no reports will be able to run during the deployment of a server package.

If you are deploying an update package, you may think that the enterprise server deployment report will copy the specifications from the update package directory on your enterprise server. Although that is logical, it is quite incorrect. When you build an update server package, the package build process merges your update package changes with the parent package. So when you deploy an update package, the spec and bin32 directories are copied from the parent package directory into the path code directory. These directories are the only two needed to run the OneWorld host code. The include, source, lib32, work, and make directories are used only for the compiling of business functions and named event rules. This is why you will only find the spec and bin32 directories under your path code directory—for example, DEVB733, on your enterprise server.

Once the package deployment finishes, you should view when the dates and times were modified on your specification and DLL files on your enterprise server. If these

files contain a time stamp of when you deployed your package, and the R98825D
report shows "Success," you have successfully deployed your server package.

Troubleshooting Package Builds

If something goes wrong during a package build, you will want to have a few tricks of
the trade in your back pocket.

Troubleshooting Client Package Builds

When your package build completes, you should first check your build logs. For
a client package build, you will have two main log files: the BUILDERROR and
BUILDLOG logs.

The BUILDERROR file tells you if you have successfully built the specification
files for your package. This log file, which is located in your package directory on the
deployment server (for example, DEVB733FA) lists all of the specification files that
were built, like DDCLMN.DDB. You will want to review this log file to ensure that it
contains no errors. If you are building a full package, you will want to ensure that the
number of records read for each specification file match the number of records written.
Another quick and easy check, which can save time, is to ensure that the record count
that is listed in this log matches the number of records in the corresponding central
object table.

Suppose you are looking at the RDASPEC file in the BUILDERROR log. You should
make note of the number of records read and written. You then do a select count on
the F98761 table, which is the corresponding central object table for the RDASPEC
file. The number of records read and written should match the number of records in
the F98761 table for full packages.

You might also want to review the Build report, the NOTCHKDN file, and the
NOSOURCE file. The Build report gives you information on the size of the file
directories that were built for your package. It is handy to review in order to determine
if the package build was successful. The NOTCHKDN file shows you the objects that
were not checked in when the package was built. When you want to verify that an
object was checked in before the package was built, you should review this log file.
The NOSOURCE file tells you when a business function does not have a source file
associated with it.

Another quick and easy check is to compare the size of your new package to an old package. A full package should never be smaller than the shipped package. If you are building a partial or update package, you can still check to ensure that your file sizes are not zero and that your TAM specification files were created.

The BUILDLOG, which is located in the work directory under the package directory on the deployment server, tells you if your business function, named event rules, and table event rules built successfully. Because this file is rather large, scroll to the end of the log file, where you will find a summary of all of the DLLs that you are trying to build. Ensure that this summary contains no errors for any DLLs. If it does, you should investigate the errors because most of the time, you will build business functions with the option of Continue Build Upon Error. This means that everything, except the objects that encountered an error, will be in your DLL.

Nearer the beginning of the BUILDLOG file are headings for each DLL that was built and a list of all of the objects that were built into these DLL files. Suppose an error was logged on the CFIN DLL; you would want to look under the CFIN section of this log file to determine what object failed to compile and why.

Another common problem that you will want to look for is the message restored previous DLL. You will find this error message in the summary section of the log file. It means that no DLL was created, and thus the build completely failed for these DLL files. A number of circumstances may have caused this problem, including not having a C compiler installed on your build machine or not having the correct path statements in your build machine's JDE.INI file.

The JDE_CG section of the JDE.INI file is located at the beginning of the file. (The JDE.INI file can be found under the winnt directory on the build machine.) Make sure that the path statements in this section actually point to the location of your compiler. If they don't, you won't be able to build business functions, named event rules, or table event rules on that machine.

Troubleshooting Server Package Builds

When you build a server package, the log files on the deployment server are not the only things that you will need to review to ensure your server package was built successfully. Once you have reviewed the log files on your deployment server, you can move on to some more advanced log files.

You will want to ensure that the server INF file was created correctly. Remember that the server INF file is created during the server package build process. It tells the system exactly what to transfer to your server. If it is not created, you will get absolutely nowhere with your server package. The server INF file is located under a directory that is named the same as the server you built the package for in your package directory. For example, if your package was named DEVFC, your server was named ENTERPRISE, and your package was built over the DEVB733 path code, the server INF file would be located under the b733\devb733\package\devfc\enterprise directory.

As we mentioned earlier, the server INF file controls what is moved to your enterprise server with the server package. It is a detailed file that will tell you every specification file and DLL that will be built for your server. The following is an example of one of these files:

```
[SERVER PACKAGE]
PackageName=APPL;  Package name
Type=FULL       ; Type of Package
Platform=ALPHA4.0    ;Type of server Platform
BuildMachine=ALPHANTB  ;  The machine name of the server
BuildPort=6005      ; Port number
SPEC=1          ; Indicates Specs are included in the package.
SpecList= 0 , 1 , 10 , 13 , 14 , 15 , 16 , 17 , 18 , 2 , ; Indicates
which specs are included in this package
BSFN=1        ;Indicates what dlls are included in the package
BL007=1       ; Indicates this dll is included in the package
Dlls that are in the package
BLKTY3=1
BLRK001=1
BLRK009=1
BLRK11=1
C55OMW66=1
CAEC=1
```

From this example, you can see that the package being built is named APPL and that it is a full package. You can also see that this package was built for a server named ALPHANTB, which is a Compaq Alpha server. The software will use port 6005 to attempt to send the information to the enterprise server through JDENET. The next section of this file tells you the specification files that are being built for this package. Each specification file is associated with a number, which is why you see a list of numbers instead of the actual names of the specification files. The names of the specification files and their associated numbers follow. The file also lists the names of the DLLs that were built for this server package.

```
AVSRHDR = 0
AVSRDTL = 1
BOBSPEC = 2
DDTABL = 4
```

```
DDCLMN = 5
DDPKEYH = 6
DDPKEYD = 7
DSTMPL = 10
FDASPEC = 11
FDATEXT = 12
RDASPEC = 13
RDATEST =14
GBRLINK = 15
GBRSPEC =  16
POTEXT = 17
JDEBLC = 18
SMRTMPL = 19
```

Server Package Build Logs on the Server

The server itself also contains log files that can help you troubleshoot problems with a package build. To access these files, log on to your enterprise server, find the directory for packages, and select the name of your package. Under this directory, you will find a subdirectory called text, which contains a number of log files that end in STS or TXT. These log files provide vital information on your server package build. Before you read them, you should look at the sizes and dates modified of your server package's DLL files and specification files. This will assist you in determining if your package build was successful.

The STS files are status files that tell you the status of parts of your server package build. These files provide details on your TAM specification files and the DLLs that you are attempting to build. If the STS file is for a TAM specification, it lists the number of records read for this file and the number of records written into the TAM file. An example of this type of STS file follows:

```
OneWorld paktotam Status Log
----------------------------
process id:    302
copy status:   D (successful completion)
spec type:     asvrdtl

read count:    4313
write count:   4313
error count:   0
```

STS files are also available for the DLLs that you attempted to build. These files indicate the number of objects that did compile into the DLL and the number that failed. They can be useful when troubleshooting a server package build because a common problem is that the server cannot find the compiler on your enterprise server. This problem will show up in the STS log files for DLLs. The following is an example of a STS file for a DLL without errors:

```
OneWorld builddll Status Log
process id:     394
build status:   D (completion)
DLL name:       CALLBSFN
did compile count:       508
did not compile count:   0
module that is compiling:  LINK
modules that did not compile:
```

If the STS log file lists all of the objects as not compiling, this can be caused by bad JDE.INI file settings on your enterprise server. If you are experiencing a problem where the build process cannot find the compiler on your enterprise server, you should look at the JDE_CG section of the JDE.INI file. This section of the INI file points to key areas where your compiler exists. Ensure that these path statements are correct.

You will also want to ensure that the BSFN Builder section of your JDE.INI file is correct. When you build server packages, the Busbuild application will be run in the background. This application calls the C compiler and builds your DLLs for OneWorld. The BSFN Builder section of the INI file tells the software how to run Busbuild. The following is an example of this section of a server's INI file:

```
[BSFN Builder]
User=JDE
Pwd=JDE
PathCode=prod
BFDir=BSFNERR
BuildArea=z:\jdedwardsoneworld\ddp\B733  ; This is the area where the
package is located.
The rest are flags used in building the dlls:
DBSFNFlags=/Gz /Od /Zi /MDd /Yd /W4 /GX /Gy /Fp$(PRECOMPHDR) /D "WIN32"
/D "_DEBUG" /D "_WINDOWS" /D "IAMASERVER" /D "KERNEL" /nologo /c
RBSFNFlags=/Gz /O2 /MD /W4 /GX /Gy /Fp$(PRECOMPHDR) /D "WIN32" /D
"NDEBUG" /D "_WINDOWS" /D "IAMASERVER" /D "KERNEL" /nologo /c
DLinkFlags=/DLL /DEBUG /SUBSYSTEM:windows /out:$(DLLTARGET) /PDB:$(PDB)
/IMPLIB:$(LIBRARY) /FORCE:MULTIPLE /FORCE:UNRESOLVED /INCREMENTAL:YES
/VERBOSE /MAP
RLinkFlags=/DLL /DEBUG /SUBSYSTEM:windows /out:$(DLLTARGET) /PDB:$(PDB)
/IMPLIB:$(LIBRARY) /FORCE:MULTIPLE /FORCE:UNRESOLVED /VERBOSE
/MAP:$(MAPTARGET) /OPT:REF
```

Inside and Out

A problem in this section usually occurs because the username and password specified are not a valid OneWorld username and password. Another common problem is that a path code listed in this section does not exist on the enterprise server. Ensure that this setting is set to a valid path code because this setting determines the TAM specification files that will be used to run the Busbuild application. The most common problem with this section of the INI file is the build area being set incorrectly. This build area needs to reflect the drive letter where the host code software is installed and the path to the package and path code directories. If this is not set correctly, then the Busbuild application will not be able to run.

Another important aspect of this section of the server's JDE.INI file is that it indicates where the server's BSFNERR log file is located. This log file lists compiler errors and can be useful in tracking down issues. By default, this log file is located in the B733 directory. The rest of this section of the INI file consists of flags that tell the C compiler how to build the DLLs on your server. Do not change these flags without the direction of J.D. Edwards.

Another common problem on Windows NT platforms is the C compiler not being in the path statement for the machine. When you install the Microsoft C++ compiler, one of the prompts you will encounter is to register environmental variables. This selection is a check box that defaults to being unchecked. Make sure that this check box is checked so that the path statement for the compiler is placed into the user variable. You want to ensure that this path statement gets into the system path.

To ensure that you have this statement in your path on your enterprise or application server, choose Start | Settings | Control Panel. In the Control Panel, double-click on the system icon to access the System Properties screen. Select the Environment tab and then select the user variable. Then cut and paste the path of the C compiler into the value of the "path" variable. This will tell the system where to find your compiler.

If you need to add a variable and value into the system Environment tab, you can do so by selecting an existing variable and changing the name and value of the variable. Then click the Set button. This will not overwrite the existing variable and value; it adds a new variable to the Environment tab. The only way you can delete a variable is by using the Delete button on this screen.

Package Build History Application

The Package Build History application enables you to review what parts of your package build have failed; it even enables you to resubmit only the parts of your package that failed. This can save you a lot of time when you are dealing with full package builds.

The Package Build History application is located on the Package And Deployment Tools menu GH9083. When you double-click on the Package History application, the Work With Package Build History screen (see Figure 10-31) is displayed. You can view information on your client and server package builds on this screen.

You can review the build specification, build business functions, and compression options that you selected for your package. You can also review the objects that you defined for your package and whether the package is an update or partial package. Finally, you can review the status of your TAM specification files.

To review the status of your TAM specification files for your package, expand the Build Specification Options directory and select one of the TAM files. Information on the status of the TAM specification file build will then be shown in the grid on the right side of the screen. As you can see from Figure 10-31, this application provides a lot of information.

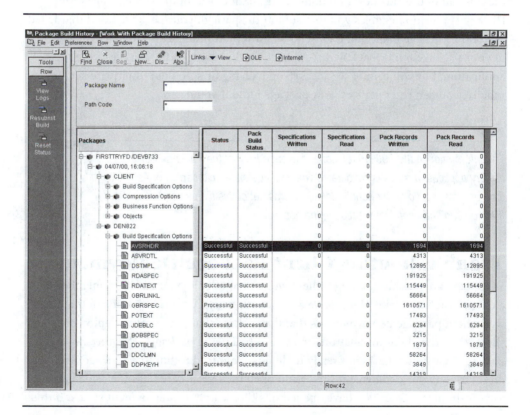

FIGURE 10-31. Work With Package Build History screen

When you use this application, you can tell at a glance if your TAM specification file was built, because the Status column indicates whether the build was successful or failed. The package shown in Figure 10-31 is a client and server package. The Pack Build Status column indicates whether the pack files, which are transferred to your enterprise server, were built correctly. The Specifications Written column shows how many records were written into each of your TAM files. This number should match the number in the Specifications Read column for a full package. The Pack Records Written and Pack Records Read columns are for server packages. These columns allow you to determine if your server package pack files were built correctly.

You can determine if your business functions were built correctly in much the same manner, by expanding the Business Function Options directory and selecting one of the business functions that you were attempting to build. Suppose an error was listed on this screen, and we subsequently fixed the problem. Half of our specification files and all of our business functions still have not been built. The Package Build History application enables you to resubmit the parts of your package build that failed. Select the package name and choose Row | Resubmit Build. This launches the parts of your package build that failed. You can also view some of the log files from this application, but you cannot see the STS or TXT log files on your enterprise server. Finally, you can reset parts of your package build if you desire.

TIP

The information in the F96215 relational database file that the Package Build History application reads is not deleted when you delete an old package. As time progresses, you may want to delete records out of this file by hand so that you can find useful information in the application.

Troubleshooting Client Package Deployment

When you are troubleshooting a client workstation deployment issue, remember that a client installation is nothing but a glorified file copy. A common problem that occurs with client package deployments is that the package that you want to deploy does not show up in the client installation director. Actually, the package's INF file shows the package in a status that is not ready to deploy. You need to find the package_inf directory on your deployment server and open the INF file that has the same name as your package. Once you have opened this file, search for deployment status. If this variable is not set to "approved," you will not see the package in the Client Installation Package director.

Another common problem that occurs with client package deployments is that the path statements in the package INF file are not correct. These path statements tell the software where to find the pieces of your package on the deployment server. The section of the package INF file, SrcDirs section variables, might not contain the machine name and path to the files. When this happens, the software will not be able to find the correct files to install the package, which means that once you select the package to deploy, the system will error out. An example of a valid SrcDirs package INF section follows. The authors recommend that you keep a copy of a valid package INF file for reference; it can be useful when you are troubleshooting a package deployment issue.

```
[SrcDirs]
SDEVB733=\\DEPLOYMENT\B733\DEVB733\package\DEVB733FA
SSYS=\\DEPLOYMENT\B733\Systemcomp
SDEVB733DATA=\\DEPLOYMENT\B733\DEVB733\package\DATAcomp
SHELP=\\DEPLOYMENT\B733\HelpsCOMP
```

Summary

In this chapter, we have covered a great deal of ground. We have defined what packages are and what types of packages are available. We have discussed the benefits and drawbacks of each type of package. We explained a centralized versus decentralized package strategy. This conversation on advanced CNC configuration will assist you in setting up your company's OneWorld solution.

We then discussed what happens when workstation packages are built. You learned how to define a workstation package and the choices that you have when setting up a client package build. The different options for the specification build, business function build, and compression options were discussed. The R9621 UBE was explained and discussed in detail. This UBE is the heart of the package build process.

The chapter then went on to discuss how you define server package builds. We talked about what the R9621 UBE does for server package builds. We also introduced the R9622 UBE and explained its importance. The reason you need to build server packages was also covered.

We then discussed the options you have in deploying your packages. We talked about deploying client workstation packages through an interactive session. We also talked about using silent and verbose installation methods. Finally, we discussed advanced deployment methods, such as assigning packages to your workstations so that they will be deployed when your users log on to the system, and push installation procedures. We also described what happens when you deploy server packages.

Finally, we spent some time discussing how to troubleshoot packages. We explained some common client and server package build issues. You were introduced to the Package Build History application and shown how it can assist you in troubleshooting your package builds. Finally, we also talked about common client workstation deployment problems. This information will assist you as you roll packages out to your end users.

CHAPTER 11

Service Packs

The longer you work with OneWorld, the more likely it is that you will find that a problem you are facing has been fixed in a service pack. These service packs are one way that J.D. Edwards delivers fixes to its clients. In this chapter, we are going to discuss service packs in detail and how they affect your system, including:

- Definition of a service pack

- When to apply a service pack

- Why to apply a service pack

- How to apply a service pack

- How to test and remove a service pack

Definition: What Is a Service Pack?

A service pack can be defined as the foundation code of OneWorld. In fact, as of B733.2, they are also called FSU (Foundation Software Updates). The foundation code of OneWorld is what allows OneWorld to run on multiple platforms. This foundation code is written by experts in multiple platforms such as UNIX, Windows NT, and DB2. The applications in OneWorld are then written using the tool set included in OneWorld. When an application programmer writes a program in OneWorld, they do not care if this program will attempt to access data on a UNIX machine, an AS400, or NT. Nor does the programmer care about what kind of database their program will be accessing. All of this is taken care of by the foundation or system code.

This is why a service pack can fix symptoms that are found in applications or reports. Since all applications are written to use this system code, an error in this foundation or system code can cause the errors to show up in applications or reports, even when these applications and reports are written correctly.

DEFINITION

FSU (Foundation Software Update): *This term is synonymous with service pack. As of B733.2, J.D. Edwards started using this term to describe service packs, so you may see the terms used interchangeably.*

The foundation code is contained in the system directory of your deployment server, enterprise server, and client workstations. You will notice that these folders do not contain source files. This is because the system code of OneWorld is considered a trade secret. This means that the only way that you can get changes into the foundation code is by getting a service pack from J.D. Edwards in Denver.

When to Apply a Service Pack

Now that you know what a service pack is, you might wonder when you should apply a service pack. You do not always need to take a service pack every time one is offered by J.D. Edwards. Service packs contain specific fixes for specific issues, which are tracked through SARs (Software Action Requests). If you are experiencing issues that have been fixed by a SAR in one of these service packs, you would then of course want to take that service pack.

DEFINITION

SAR (Software Action Request): *This is a term used by J.D. Edwards to track issues or enhancements within their software. If an issue or bug is found with the software, a SAR will be entered so that J.D. Edwards can assign programmers to fix the issue. Clients and business partners of the company can track the progress of these requests through J.D. Edwards' Web site.*

It is possible that these service packs will fix an issue that is not specifically in the J.D. Edwards' SAR list. Remember, a SAR is how J.D. Edwards tracks the bugs and enhancements in their software, so if you are absolutely stumped on an issue, a service pack may help you, but not always.

Why to Apply a Service Pack

The reason you would want to apply a service pack is simply to fix issues with the software. These service packs or fixes to the OneWorld foundation code resolve issues that manifest themselves in the applications or in the tool set that is supplied with OneWorld.

How to Apply a Service Pack

We have now discussed what a service pack is and when you would want to apply one. In this section, we will go over how to apply service packs to your OneWorld system. Although the procedure may sound complicated, it is not. What you need to keep in mind is that a service pack is the system directory on your deployment server, enterprise server, and client workstations. When you apply a service pack, all you are really doing is replacing the system directory on your machines.

In order to apply a service pack, you will need to follow certain basic procedures:

1. Back off your old Service Pack.

2. Run the Service Pack Setup disk.

3. Apply the new system code to your enterprise server.

4. Build and deploy an update package to your client workstations.

Backing Off Your Old Service Pack

Before you attempt to apply a new service pack, you will want to back off your old service pack. This is so that you can easily roll the service pack off in the event that it does not produce the desired results.

TIP

You should always have a backup before you attempt a major update or upgrade, or before applying a service pack to your system. To back up your system, you will need to back off certain directories on your enterprise server and deployment server.

Deployment Server

The first step to backing off your old service pack is to back up your deployment server. The easiest way to do this is to create backup directories and copy the contents of the directories affected by a service pack. The J.D. Edwards' documentation, states to only back off the system directory. Although this is correct, it is not complete. A service pack affects more than just your system directory on the deployment server.

When the setup disk for a service pack is executed, the system directory and the OneWorld client installation directory will be updated; a service pack updates DLLs in the OneWorld client installation directory

NOTE

Prior to B733.1 you would need to back off the client directory and the system directory. This is because the OneWorld client directory did not exist until B733.1 and the DLLs affected by a service pack were contained in the client directory.

TIP

Due to the fact that a service pack updating the OneWorld client installation directory is not currently documented in the J.D. Edwards' service pack instructions, you will need to create a temporary or backup directory and copy the contents of the OneWorld Client Installation directory into this new directory.

The next directory that you would need to back off on the deployment server is the system directory. To back off this directory, create a temporary directory and copy the contents of your current system directory into the temporary directory. This procedure allows easy recovery in the event of undesired results.

Enterprise Server NT or UNIX   Finally, you will need to back off the system directory on your enterprise server. If you are using Windows NT or a UNIX system, i.e., an HP9000, RS6000, or Sun Solaris, you can create a temporary directory and copy the contents of your current system directory into this temporary directory.

CAUTION

When you attempt this procedure, you must have your host services stopped or you could cause the corruption of your host code. On the Windows NT platform, you can bring your OneWorld services down through the Control Panel's services program. On UNIX machines, you can bring the host services down by using the EndOneWorld script.

Inside and Out

Enterprise Server AS400   If you are using an AS400 platform, you will need to back off the system library on your AS400. This system library is normally named after the release of OneWorld that you are running; for example, if you are running B733, the system library should be B733SYS. You can back off this library by using the `cpylib` command and copying the contents to a new library, e.g., B733SYSBAK. The B7331MAP and the Path Code libraries should also be backed off at this time, again using the `cpylib` command. This is because they are affected by a command that is run during the application of the service pack, `LNKBSFN`, and can become corrupt if this command fails. We will discuss the `LNKBSFN` command in the "Applying the New System Code to Your Enterprise Server" section.

Running the Service Pack Setup Disk

After you have backed off your system, you will want to run the service pack setup disk. Place the service pack setup disk in the deployment server's CD-ROM drive. You will be presented with a setup screen; select the option of installing the service pack. The service pack will install, updating the system and the OneWorld Client installation directory. Once the installation process finishes, you can apply the service pack to your enterprise server.

Applying the New System Code to Your Enterprise Server

In order to apply a service pack, you will need to move that service pack's system directory to the enterprise server. This process will be a little different for each of the platforms. Let's now take a look at how you would apply the service pack to the different platforms. Although this section gives you an overview of how to apply a service pack, keep in mind that each service pack comes with its own set of instructions. You will need to refer to these instruction to ensure that there are no special steps in applying a particular service pack.

TIP

Remember that when you apply a service pack to an enterprise server, you will need to stop your host services. This means that sign-on security, OneWorld replication, and the running of reports on your enterprise server will not be available during the installation of the service pack. The authors recommend that service packs be applied after hours or on the weekends, so as not to impact your production users.

AS/400

Let's start with applying the service pack to the AS/400 platform. Now that you have applied the service pack to the deployment server, you need to move your new system or J.D. Edwards' foundation code onto the AS/400.

Ending Host Services   To start this process, sign onto the AS/400 as the ONEWORLD user, is created during the installation program. Once you have logged onto the AS/400, you need to end your host services. This can be done by typing **ENDNET** on the command line; this command stops the OneWorld host services on the AS/400. Once this command completes, type the **CLRIPC** command. This cleans up any hanging processes on the AS/400 for the OneWorld services.

Rename System Library   Now that you have stopped your host services, you need to log off the AS/400 and log back on to the machine as a QSECOFR. Once you have signed on to the AS/400, you will have to rename the system library. This library is usually named after the release of OneWorld that you are on; for example, if you are on B733, the library is usually named SYSB733. To rename the library, type **RNMOBJ** on the command line and prompt the command by pressing F4. Set the object to SYSB733, leave the OBJTYPE as *LIB, and set the NEWOBJ to SYSB733BAK. You have now renamed the system library to SYSB733BAK.

At this point, you should also back off your Path Code Libraries and B7331MAP library by using the CPYLIB command. You can press F4 to prompt this command and fill in both the library you are copying and the name of your backup library.

Grant Authority   You must now grant your users more authority to the ONEWORLD user ID. To do this, enter the GRTOBJAUT command and prompt it by pressing F4. In the OBJ field, place ONEWORLD; in the OBJTYPE field, place *USRPRF; in the USER field, place *PUBLIC; and in the AUT field, type *USE. Now that you have granted the ONEWORLD user the correct authority, it is now time to copy the new foundation or system code onto your AS/400.

Create Temporary Directory   To copy your new foundation onto the AS/400, you first need to create a temporary library to copy the system files into.

NOTE

This temporary library is used to hold the files on the service pack CD. It is not used for a backup of the current system files.

In order to create this directory, type **CRTLIB JDETEMP**. This will create a temporary library on your AS/400 that will contain the new foundation code. Once your service pack is installed and tested, you can remove this library.

However, you are not done yet; you still need to create a save file. This file can be created by entering the CRTSAVF JDETEMP/SYSTEM command.

FTP process for the AS/400   The next step requires you to move to an NT computer where the service pack CD is in the CD-ROM drive. Normally, this machine would be the deployment server. Once you have logged in to this machine and placed the service pack CD in the CD-ROM drive, you need to perform the following steps:

1. Start a DOS session.

2. Type **FTP** and the name of your AS/400.

3. You will now be prompted for a user and password; enter the security officer user ID and password.

4. Type **cd** to change the AS/400 directory you are in to the jdetemp library.

5. You now need to change your local directory to find the necessary files off the service pack CD. To do this, type **lcd e:\hosts\AS400**, where E: is your CD-ROM drive containing your service pack CD.

6. Type **bin**; this will change the transfer mode to binary.

7. At the DOS prompt, type **put SYSTEM**; this will transfer the system files off the service pack disk onto your AS/400's temporary directory.

8. Type **quit**; this will disconnect you from the FTP session.

N O T E

The FTP session will time out if it is inactive for more than five minutes.

Restoring the System Library on the AS/400   You now need to log back on to your AS/400 and restore the system library. You should be logged on to the AS/400 as QSECOFR. Type

```
RSTLIB SAVLIB(B733XSYS) DEV(*SAVF) SAVF(JDETEMP/SYSTEM) RSTLIB(syslib)
```

You now have your new system library on the AS/400.

Recovering the Print Queue on the AS/400   The next step is to recover your print queue, which contains the reports that you have run. This print queue will exist in your old system library and will need to be moved into your current system library. Type the following:

```
CPYF FROMFILE(SYSB733BAK/PRINTQUEUE) TOFILE(SYSB733/PRINTQUEUE)
FROMMBR(*ALL) TOMBR(*FROMMBR) MBROPT(*REPLACE) CRTFILE(*YES).
```

DEFINITION

Printqueue: *The printqueue is a physical file that contains the PDG version of the reports that you have run on your AS/400 enterprise server. On other platforms, this is a directory that contains the PDF version of the reports that you have run.*

CAUTION

If you do not recover your print queue, you will not be able to see any of the reports that were run before the service pack was applied.

Restoring the INI File   When the new system library is restored onto the AS400, it does not contain your INI file. In order to copy your INI file, use the CRTDUPOBJ command. Press F4 to prompt this command. In the OBJ field, type **INI**; in the FROMLIB field, type **SYSB733BAK**; in the OBJTYPE field, type ***FILE**; in the TOLIB field, type **SYSB733**; in the DATA field, type ***YES**.

Relinking the Business Functions on the AS/400   The final step in this process is to relink all of the business functions located in each of the path code directories on the AS/400. To do this, type **LINKBSFN** and prompt the command with an F4. Enter the package name of the path code for which you are relinking business functions. This will normally be your path code's FA package; for example, CRP733FA. Once this step is complete for all path codes, log off the AS/400 and log back on as the ONEWORLD user.

   You should then run a porttest to ensure that everything is set up correctly. To run a porttest, you simply type **porttest** on the command line followed by a valid OneWorld user, password, and environment. The program will tell you if it succeeded or failed.

Inside and Out

Once you have run a successful porttest, start your host services again by typing in the STRNET command. Your AS/400 enterprise server is now on the new service pack.

HP9000, RS6000, or Sun Solaris

If you have an HP9000, RS6000, or Sun Solaris system, you will have to perform similar steps to apply a service pack. The first step is to move the new foundation code or system directory onto your UNIX system. To do this, you need to copy the system.Z file from the service pack CD to the hosts\HP9000,RS6000 or Sun directory on the deployment server. It is common to perform this procedure on the deployment server. All you need to do is place the service pack CD into the CD-ROM drive on the deployment server. The system.Z file will be located under a hosts directory on the service pack disk well; for example, E:\hosts\HP9000, where E: is the name of your CD-ROM drive.

Stopping Host Services   Once you have completed this step, log on to the enterprise server as the OneWorld user that starts your host services (for example, jdeb7331) and stop the host services. To stop the host services, type **CD $SYSTEM/bin32**. This is a short cut that should have been set up during the initial installation of the OneWorld software. If this shortcut is not set up, you will need to type

```
cd u03/JDEdwardsOneWorld/B733/system/bin32
```

where u03 is the drive on which OneWorld is installed on your enterprise server. Then type **EndOneWorld.sh**. When this command completes, type **rmics.sh**; this last command will clear up any hanging processes.

Backing Off the System Directory   Next, you must rename the system directory. To do this, change to the drive where OneWorld is installed on your enterprise server, for example, by typing

```
cd u03/JDEdwardsOneWorld/B733
```

Once you are on the correct drive, type **mv system systembak**. This will rename your current system directory to systembak. Once you have installed and tested the service pack, you can delete this directory; until then, it can be used to roll the service pack back.

Moving the Service Pack onto Your Enterprise Server   Now that you have renamed your current system directory, change your directory to a temporary directory; for example, cd u04/JDEdwardsOneWorld/B733/tmp. You will then need to move the system.Z file from the deployment server to your HP9000 enterprise server by using FTP. To do this:

1. Type **ftp** and your deployment server name. Enter JDE for the user (this user should have been set up during the installation process) and enter the appropriate password.

2. Now you need to change to the correct directory, the drive where OneWorld is installed; for example, Z:. Once you are on the correct drive, type;

   ```
   cd JDEdwardsOneWorld/B733/hosts/HP9000
   ```

   This is the directory to which you copied the system.Z file from the service pack disk; this file is your new foundation code for the HP9000 or other UNIX platform.

3. Once you are in the current directory, type **bin** to change the transfer mode to binary. Then type **get system.Z**. When typing this command, ensure that the Z is capitalized, since the zcat command, which is described below, will not recognize the file if the Z is not capitalized. This will copy the system.Z file into your temporary directory. Type **bye** to disconnect from the FTP session.

Checking Permissions on the System.Z File   You now need to ensure that the correct permissions are set on the system.Z file in your temporary directory on the HP9000. Type **chmod 777 system.Z**; this will set the appropriate permissions for this file. Then type

```
zcatg systmZ | (Cd /u04/JDEdwardsOneWorld/B733;tar xvf )
```

This will create the system directory for you on the HP9000.

Restoring Startup Scripts   Now that you have the new system directory, you need to restore the scripts that are used to start your host services. These are the RunOneWorld.sh and EndOneWorld.sh files. To copy these files, type **cp** and the directory from which you are copying the files followed by the directory to which you are copying the file. For example,

```
cp /u04/JDEdwardsOneWorld/B733/systembak/EndOneWorld.sh /u04/
JDEdwardsOneWorld/B733/system/EndOneWorld.sh.
```

Copy both the RunOneWorld and EndOneWorld files.

Inside and Out

Checking Permissions on the System Directory and Running a Porttest   Now that you have your new system directory and your scripts in the correct spot, you will need to ensure that your permissions are set correctly. To do this, go to the JDEdwardsOneWorld/B733 directory and type **chmod 775 system/lib/*system/libv32***. You have now installed the service pack on the HP9000, RS6000, or Sun Solaris system. Type **cd $SYSTEM/bin32** and run a porttest from this directory, which should be JDEdwardsOneWorld\B733\system\bin32. This shortcut should have been set up during the installation process. To run a porttest, enter the porttest command from the system/bin32 directory followed by a valid OneWorld user, password, and environment. Once you have run the porttest you can start your host services with the RunOneWorld.sh command.

TIP

When running a porttest, always type the environment, user, and password in uppercase. This is necessary because the porttest program passes these values exactly as typed to the database, and OneWorld stores the user names and environments in uppercase in the database. Passing an environment name in lowercase will cause your porttest to fail, and the logs will tell you that the environment could not be found.

NOTE

The installation process for the RS6000 and Sun Solaris system is almost identical. The only difference is that you get the system.Z file from the JDEdwardsOneWorld/hosts/RS6000 or Sun directory. Another minor difference is that the commands are slightly different on the RS6000—but anyone familiar with the RS6000 should be able to use the instructions above with ease.

Intel NT and Compaq Alpha

The final type of enterprise server that we will discuss installing a service pack on is the Intel NT and Compaq Alpha server. This is by far the easiest platform to apply a service pack to. The first step is to end your host services. You can do this from the Control Panel services program. In this application, you will see your JDE XXX Queue and JDE XXX

Network services, where XXX is the name of your OneWorld release (for example, B733). Stop the queue service first and then the network service.

N O T E

OneWorld does allow you to run update or cum levels in parallel as well as different releases. For example, a parallel release would be B732, a different release would be B733, and a cum level would be B733.1. If you are running a cum or update in parallel, the name of the update will follow the release level in the service name; for example, JDE B733 Update 1 Queue.

C A U T I O N

Microsoft has stopped its development work on the NT operating system for the Alpha platform. If you are on a Compaq Alpha machine, you should check Microsoft and Compaq's Web pages for information on this. It appears that J.D. Edwards will continue to support the Alpha until OneWorld requires an operating system or patch that is not available on the Alpha. The authors encourage you to plan moving to another platform so that this does not impact your business.

Backing Off the System Directory   Now that you have stopped your host services, open a Windows Explorer window. Go to Z:\JDEdwardsOneWorld\B733, where Z: is the drive on which OneWorld is installed on your enterprise server. Highlight the system directory, right-click, and rename the directory to systembak. Do not delete this directory, as you may need it if you have to roll back the service pack.

Moving the New System Directory to the Enterprise Server   Next, you will need to move the new system directory off the service pack disk to your enterprise server. Since your enterprise server is running Windows NT as an operating system, you can place the service pack disk directly into the CD-ROM drive on your enterprise server. The system folder will be under the Hosts folder and the appropriate host name on the service pack disk; for example, Intel NT. Using Windows Explorer, copy this directory and all of the files contained in the directory to Z:\JDEdwardsOneWorld\B733, where Z: is the drive that OneWorld is installed on your enterprise server.

Inside and Out

Permissions on the System Directory   When you copy a file from a CD, the permissions are set to read only on the files. So the next step is to set the permissions correctly on the files in your new system directory. To do this, open a DOS command window and change the directory to Z:\JDEdwardsOneWorld\B733, where Z: is the drive on which OneWorld is installed on your enterprise server. Type **attrib -r /s *.*.** to change the permissions for the system files. If you do not run this command, you will have problems starting your services.

T I P _____

One common problem that is encountered when the system directory files are set to read only is that the porttest program will hang. While this program hangs, your log files fill up quickly, assuming that you have logging turned on. If you see these symptoms, go to the system\bin32 directory on your enterprise server and check to see if the files are set to read only. If they are, run the attrib command detailed above.

Restoring the INI File   The last step in applying the service pack to an Intel NT or Compaq Alpha is to copy the INI file from your old system directory to your new system folder. Using Windows Explorer, copy this INI file from the systembak folder to the new system folder. If you do not do this, your host services will not run correctly. This is because certain values are set up in this file during the OneWorld installation process, and if you do not have these values in the file when you attempt to run your host services, you will have problems.

Once you have copied the INI file from your old system directory, you need to run a porttest and then start your host services from the Control Panel. To run a porttest, start a DOS session and change directory CD out to Z:\OneWorld\ddp\B733\System\Bin32, where Z: is the drive letter on which you have installed OneWorld. You then type the porttest command followed by a valid OneWorld user, password, and environment. It is a good idea to type the environment and user in uppercase, since the porttest program will pass whatever you type to the database, and the environment names are stored in uppercase in the database. If you pass an environment name in lowercase, your porttest will fail and the logs will say that the environment could not be found.

Building and Deploying an Update Package to Your Client Workstations

The next step in applying a service pack is to build an update package that contains the new system directory and deploy it to your workstations. Client update packages are the easiest and simplest ways to move the foundation code down to the client workstations. A full package would also move the foundation code to your client workstations, but these packages take a long time to build and install, which is why the update package is the preferred method of delivering a new service pack.

To build an update package that contains the foundation code, go to GH9083, the Package and Deployment Tools menu. Double-click on the Package Assembly Program P9601. You will now be on the package assembly screen. This screen is where you define your package assembly. Click on Add and this will take you to the Package Assembly Director. Click on the Next button and you will be taken to the Package Information screen. These screens are displayed in Figures 11-1 and 11-2. Table 11-1 explains the fields shown in these screens.

Click on the Next button and you will be taken to the Package Type Selection screen, shown in Figure 11-3. This screen allows you to choose what type of package

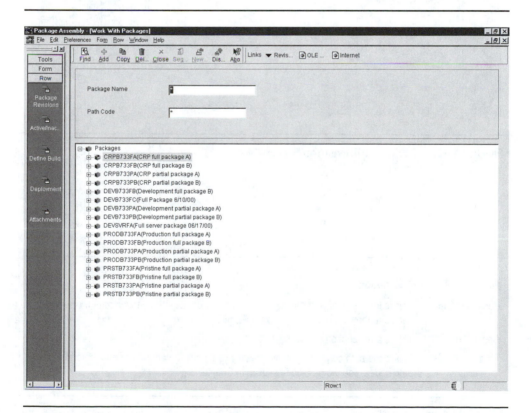

FIGURE 11-1. Package Assembly

Inside and Out

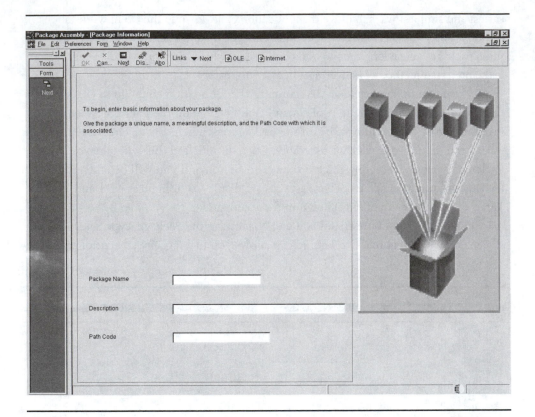

FIGURE 11-2. Package Information Screen

Field	Description
Package Name	This is the name of your package. The authors normally name these after the service pack that they are applying; for example, SP7.
Description	This is a description of your package.
Path Code	This is the path code that you are building your package under. For more information on path codes, see the path code section of Chapter 2.

TABLE 11-1. Values for the Package Information Screen

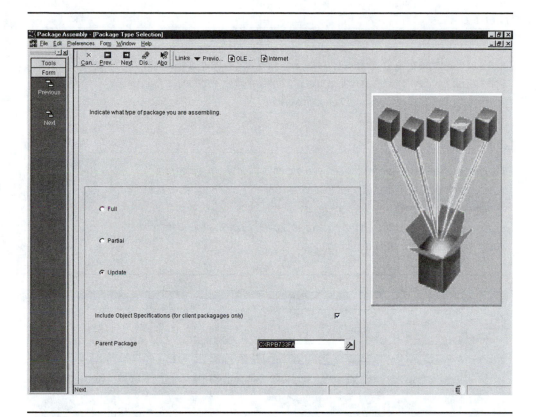

FIGURE 11-3.   Package Type Selection Screen

you are going to build. Select the radial button for an update package. You will need to also choose a parent package for your update package. This parent package needs to be a full package that exists in the path code that you are building your update package in. For example, if you were building an update package for the CRP path code, a good parent package to choose would be CRPB733FA. You do not have to check the Include Object Specifications box. See Chapter 10 for a further explanation on parent packages for update packages.

The next screen you will be prompted with is the Foundation Component screen. This screen allows you to choose where your foundation is pulled from. Remember that when we defined a service pack, we said that it was the foundation code of OneWorld and is contained in the system directory. Well, OneWorld allows you to point packages to different service packs! This way you can have one path code on one service pack level and another one on a different service pack level.

NOTE

You will only need a custom foundation when running two different service pack levels at the same time. If you applied one Service Pack to your development workstations and enterprise server, you could have another service pack on your production workstations and enterprise server.

CAUTION

It is important to remember that when you deploy a client from a different service pack level, you do not want to have an enterprise server and a client workstation on different service pack levels. This is because you could have issues when running UBEs on the enterprise server, since the foundation code, which the applications run on, has changed.

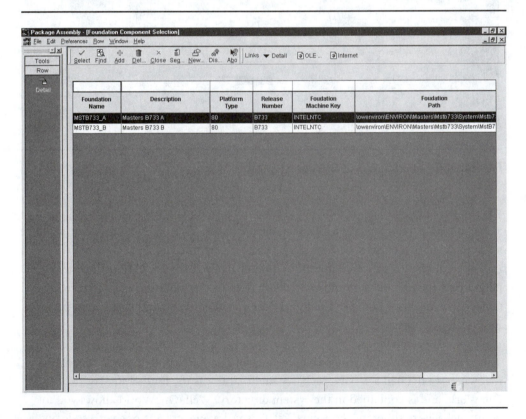

FIGURE 11-4. Foundation Component Selection Screen

If you want to add a custom foundation, click the Browse button. This will take you to the Foundation Component Selection screen (see Figure 11-4). From this screen, you can tell your package where to find its foundation or system folder. If you want to deploy one package with service pack X and another with service pack Y, you can do this by specifying a custom foundation.

In order to add a custom foundation, click Add from the Foundation Component Selection screen (see Figure 11-5). This will take you into the Foundation Item Revisions screen. The values on this screen tell OneWorld where to find its system directory. Table 11-2 describes the fields you will find on this screen.

Once you have selected a foundation or left it at the default (the default is usually appropriate), click Next. You will now be at the Help Components screen, which is almost identical to the Foundation Component Selection screen. The Help

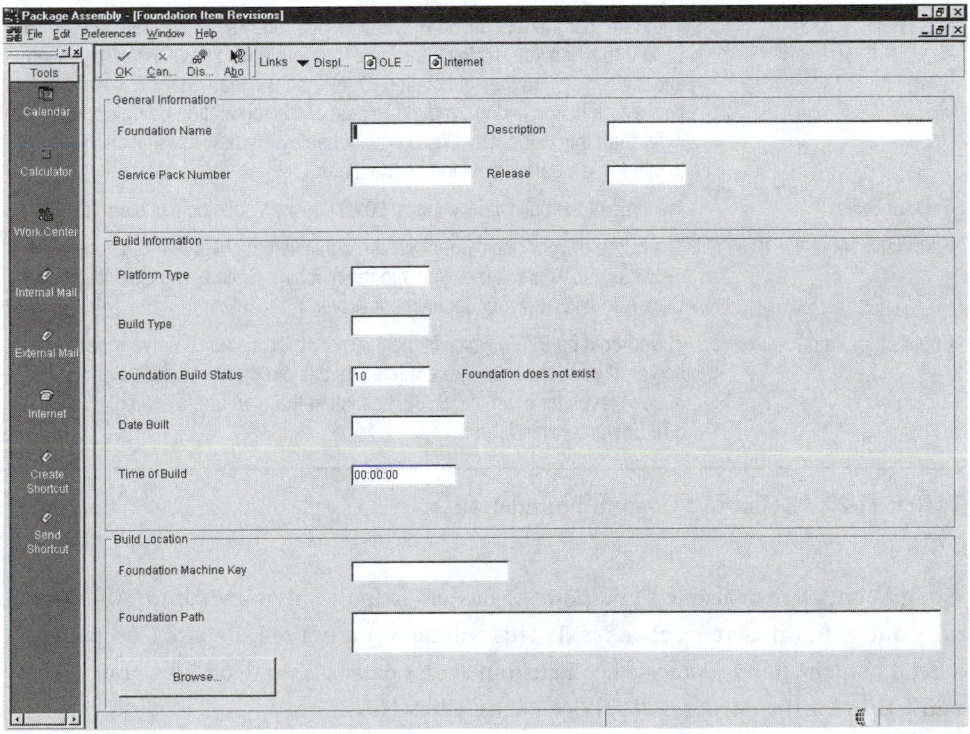

FIGURE 11-5. The Foundation Component Selection screen

Inside and Out

Field	Description
Foundation Name	The name of your custom foundation.
Description	A description of your foundation.
Service Pack Number	The level of the Service Pack.
Release	This is the release of OneWorld that you are running.
Platform Type	This value should be 80 for Intel NT, since workstations are required to be Intel machines. However, you could also use the value 90 - Client Win95, but the authors feel that this would cause more confusion then it is worth. The 80 value will work for both NT and Windows 95 workstations.
Build Type	This should be 20 for Optimize.

Foundation Build Status	The status of the foundation. This can be
	  10 - foundation does not exist
	  20 - foundation is built
	  30 - foundation is available
	(In our example, you should choose 30.)

Date Built	The date that the foundation was built. Place today's current date in this field. Similar to when you deploy a package, the foundation's build date is placed into the registry on the workstation. OneWorld will then check this date every time a foundation is deployed. If the date of the foundation being deployed is older than this value, OneWorld will not deploy the new foundation. Keep this in mind when defining custom foundations.
Time of Build	The time of the build. Leave this at 00:00:00 when defining a custom foundation.
Foundation Machine Key	The name of your deployment server. If this field highlights red, choose the visual assist. This will take you into the machine Search and Select screen. Click Add and add your deployment server.
Foundation Path	This should be B733, which is the directory that is shared on your deployment server. If your are on a different release, this directory should match your release level; for example, B732, assuming that you are following J.D. Edwards' standards.

TABLE 11-2.   Defining a Custom Foundation

Components screen also lets you point to custom help files if you want to. After you are done with this screen, click Next. This will take you to the Database Component screen, which allows you to select a custom access database that contains your menus and UDCs for the purposes of service packs. Click Next.

The next screen that you will see is the Object Component screen, as shown in Figure 11-6. From this screen, you can define the components of your package or objects that you wish to include in your package; for the purposes of a service pack, click Next. You will then be prompted to select a language. English is the default value, so press Next. This will take you to the Package Component Revisions screen; click End. You will now be back on the Work with Packages screen; press Find. You should now see your package, which will be represented with an open box beside it. Highlight your package and go to Row Activate; this will change the status of your package to Assembly Definition Complete.

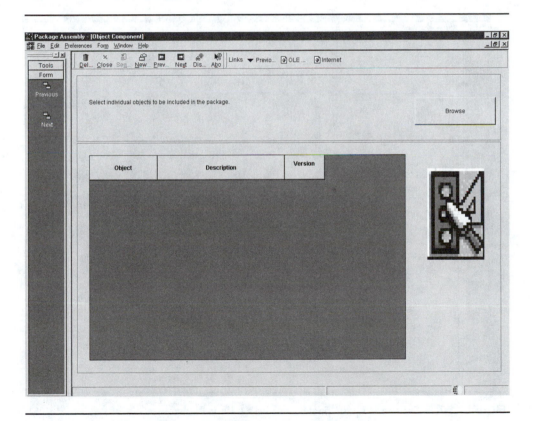

FIGURE 11-6. Package Component Selection Screen

Highlight the package name and go to Row Package Define Build. You will then be taken to the Package Build Definition director. Click Next to take you to the Package Build Location screen. Click in the Client box so that a checkmark appears, as shown in Figure 11-7. This tells OneWorld that you wish to build a package for your client workstations, which is the case, since you want to deploy the new foundation to the client workstations.

Click Next and you will be on the Build Specifications Options screen. Ensure that the Build Specifications Options box is *not* checked, as shown in Figure 11-8, and click Next.

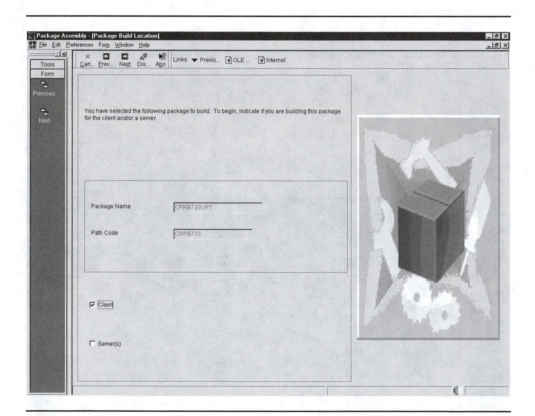

FIGURE 11-7.   Setting up your package to be a Client Package

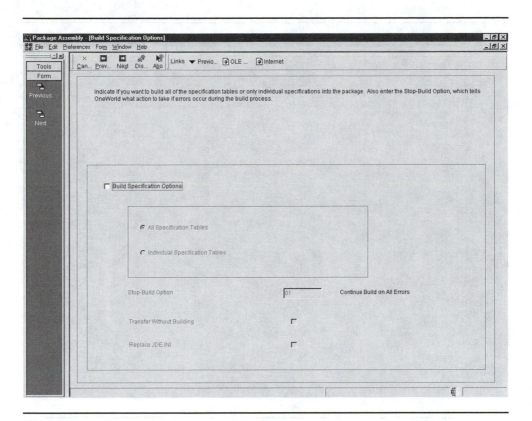

FIGURE 11-8. Build Specifications Options screen

The next screen is the Business Functions options. Ensure that the Build Function Options box is *not* checked, as shown in Figure 11-9, and click Next. These settings need to remain unchecked because you have not specified any objects to build. You do not need to build specifications or business functions since you are merely trying to deploy your new system folder.

Click Next and you will be taken to the Package Compression Options screen. On this screen, you will want to place a checkmark in the Compress Options and Compress Foundation boxes and click the Individual Directories button, as shown in Figure 11-10. You need to compress the foundation because this is what you are

Inside and Out

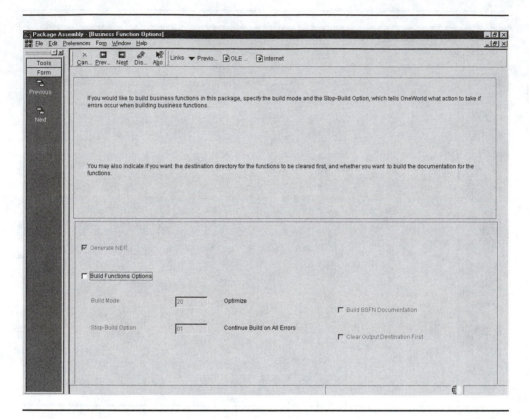

FIGURE 11-9.   Build Business Functions Option

deploying to the client workstations. The OneWorld client installation program looks for the CAB file in the systemcomp directory, not the system directory, to reduce traffic on your network. When you compress the foundation, an updated CAB file is created from the contents of your new system directory and placed in the systemcomp directory.

Click Next. You will then be presented with a screen asking to select the individual directories to compress, such as bin32, lib32, and others. Do not select any of these boxes and click Next. This will take you back to the Package Revisions screen; click End.

You will then be taken to the Work with Package Build Definition screen. From this screen, go to Row Active/Inactive and then Row Submit Build. Your new foundation will compress and the package status will be set to "build in progress". To deploy the update package, you will need to activate the package, from the package deployment application, and assign the update package to your workstations. See Chapter 10 for additional information.

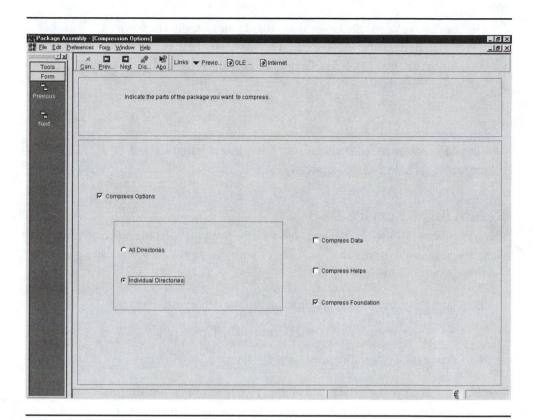

FIGURE 11-10.   Package Compression Option

How to Test and Remove a Service Pack

In this chapter, we have spent a lot of time discussing when you would want to apply a service pack and how to apply a service pack. However, we have only alluded to how to test and roll back a service pack when necessary. This may be necessary because, as anyone in the software industry knows, things do not always go as planned.

Testing a Service Pack

When testing a service pack, you need to test the service pack on both the workstation and the server. The easiest place to start is on the workstation. Once you have applied the service pack to your client workstations, you will need to test the issues that you applied the service pack to remedy. You will also want to test issue on your server, if applicable. To do this, you could run any UBEs on the server that were giving you problems.

Once you have tested the issues that caused you to apply the service pack in the first place, the authors also recommend a cursory test of other mission critical functionality. Although J.D. Edwards does test their service packs, sometimes issues surface with new service packs.

T I P

After applying a service pack, the authors recommend always testing row and column security, printing, and sign-on security.

Removing a Service Pack

If you do discover an issue or cannot meet a time line and need to roll off a service pack, there are some things that you need to keep in mind. You will need to complete the following procedures:

1. Restore the original system directory on the deployment server.

2. Restore the original OneWorldClientInstallation directory.

3. Restore the System directory on your enterprise server.

Restoring the Deployment Server　　The first step is to restore the original system directory on the deployment server. You should also restore the original OneWorldClientInstallation directory. You can do this through a Windows Explorer session on your deployment server. Remember, one of the first steps in this chapter was to back off this system directory. To restore the directory, ensure that you are logged out of OneWorld on the deployment server. Through a Windows Explorer window, rename the current system directory to systemservicepack. Once you have done this, you will need to rename the systembak directory to system. This directory should be under Z:/JDEdwardsOneWorld/B733, where Z: is the drive that OneWorld is installed on.

Restoring OneWorld Clients　　You will also have to recompress the system directory, as client installations will look for the CAB file contained in the systemcomp directory. Until you recompress your foundation, this CAB file will contain information from the service pack. To recompress the system directory, you need to go to menu GH9083, Package and Deployment Tools. Double-click on the P9621 package, Build Application, highlight your package, and go to Row Advanced. You will be prompted with a button to reset the package status, click Reset. Next, click Find from the Work with Package Definitions screen. Expand the package until you see the status under the Properties directory. Ensure that the build status is set to In Definition. If it is not, highlight the package name and go to Row Active/Inactive. Once you have done this, go to Row Build Revisions and ensure that only the Compress Options are set for foundation. Once you have done this, click OK and you will be back on the Work with Package Build Definition screen. Highlight your package and press Row Active/Inactive and then Row Submit Build. This will recompress your foundation or system code. You will then need to redeploy the package to your client workstations.

Restoring the Enterprise Server   The final step of this process is to restore the system directory on your enterprise server. This process will be a little different for each platform. We will go over restoring the system directory for the AS400, HP9000, Intel NT, and Compaq Alpha platform.

Let's start with the AS400 platform. First, log on to the AS400 as the ONEWORLD users and type **ENDNET**; this will end your host processes. Once this command is finished, log on to the system as QSECOFR. You will then need to use the RNOBJ; prompt this command by pressing F4. In the OBJ field, enter **SYSB733**; in the OCJTYPE field, enter ***LIB**; and in the NEWOBJ field, enter **SYSOLDSP**. This command will rename your system directory.

Now you will need to run the command again, except that you need to rename your systembak library sysb733. Once you have copied the system directory, you will need to grant other users authority to the ONEWORLD user profile. To do this, type **GRTOBJAUT** on the command line and press F4 to prompt the command. In the OBJ field, type **ONEWORLD**; in the OBJTYPE field, type ***USRPFFR**; in the USER field, type ***PUBLIC**; and in the AUT field, type ***USE**. This will give the ONEWORLD user the correct authority.

If you followed the instructions in this book, you should not have to copy your INI file again. If you didn't, you will need to copy your INI file and print queue directory. To copy the print queue directory, type the command

```
Type CPYF FROMFILE(SYSB733BAK/PRINTQUEUE) TOFILE(SYSB733/PRINTQUEUE)
FROMMBR(*ALL) TOMBR(*FROMMBR) MBROPT(*REPLACE) CRTFILE(*YES).
```

To copy your INI file, use the CRTDUPOBJ command. Press F4 to prompt this command. In the OBJ field, type **INI**; in the FROMLIB field, type **SYSB733BAK**; in the OBJTYPE field, type ***FILE**; in the TOLIB field, type **SYSB733**; and in the DATA field, type ***YES**.

Inside and Out

Now that you have your system directory restored, the only step left is to perform a LINKBSFN. Type this command and prompt it by pressing F4. Enter the package name for each path code; you will need to perform this for every path code. You have now successfully rolled a service pack off an AS400 enterprise server.

We will now discuss removing a service pack from a HP9000. To do this, you will need to copy the system directory on the HP9000. Since you copied the RunOneWorld.sh and EndOneWorld.sh scripts earlier, all you will need to do is end your host services and copy the system directory back. To end your host services, log on to the HP9000 as the user that starts your host services; for example, jdeb7331. Type **$SYSTEM/bin32**; this short cut should have been set up during the initial installation. Type **EndOneWorld.sh**; this will stop your host processes. Once this command has ended, rename your current system directory and rename your systembak file to system. You should then be able to run a porttest and start your host services.

N O T E

The steps to restore the system directory on the RS6000 and Sun Solaris systems are almost identical. An experienced administrator should be able to follow the instructions above and successfully roll a service pack off either of these platforms.

The Intel NT and Compaq Alpha platforms are by far the easiest platforms to restore a service pack on. Log on to your enterprise server and go to Start | Control Panel and double-click on the services program. You can start and stop the host services through this program. Highlight the JDE XXX queue service and click Stop, where XXX is the release level; for example, B733. Once this completes, highlight the JDE XXX Network service and click Stop.

Now that you have ended your host services, you need to open a Windows Explorer window and go to Z:/JDEdwardsOneWorld/ddp/B733, where Z: is the drive that you have installed OneWorld onto. Rename the existing system directory to systemold. Once you have done this, you need to rename the systembak directory to system. Copy your INI file out of the systemold/bin32 directory into your new system/bin32 directory. You should now be able to run a porrtest and then start your host services again.

Summary

This chapter should help you feel more comfortable with applying and administering service packs across your system. You should now have an understanding of what a service pack is, when to apply a service pack, how to apply a service pack, how to test a service pack, and how to roll a service pack off. As a OneWorld system administrator, you will find these skills invaluable, since J.D. Edwards delivers a lot of their fixes through services packs. The ability to effectively work with service packs separates average administrators from the good ones.

Inside and Out

CHAPTER 12

OneWorld Configuration Case Studies

When deciding what to write about for a comprehensive case study, we decided to look for some of the most interesting examples we could find. Each of the cases presented will have information detailing why they did what they did and where they went from there. Every company described in this chapter actually exists; however, we won't use names or actual businesses when describing them. In this chapter, we will discuss—from the technologist's point of view—the following cases:

- OneWorld and the Case of Two Separate Systems

- OneWorld and Truly Distributed Data

- OneWorld Continually Grows to Meet Expanding Needs

OneWorld and the Case of Two Separate Systems

It sounds like a badly written horror movie. As far as the writing goes, we'll let you decide, but there are certain horrors associated with separate systems. If you are brave enough, continue forward and see if you can figure out the ending before we reveal it to you.

The Company

There are several things to understand about this company—which we'll call Company A—that make its situation somewhat interesting if not unique. Company A is a start-up company heavily reliant on the Internet. Their business is based on emerging technologies and e-commerce.

Special OneWorld Requirements

In addition to the complexity that this type of implementation holds, there is added complexity based on the nature of this company's business. Company A is reliant on the Internet, which is its only source of sales. These sales come in through a proprietary Web site and are processed through OneWorld via direct API interfacing. Product delivery is dependent on suppliers. Customer financing goes through a third-party finance organization. This creates a business model similar to that shown in Figure 12-1.

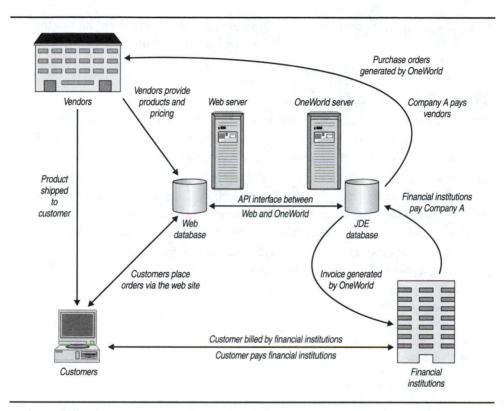

FIGURE 12-1. Company A's business model

Breaking the Business Down

Company A's business can be broken down into the following steps. Customers hit a Web site and apply for membership. Part of the membership includes being approved for financing through a third-party financial institution. Once approved, customers place orders on the Web. This data is converted for entry into OneWorld (the first opportunity for improved processes and processing). An invoice is generated for the financial institution that pays Company A and bills the customer. A purchase order is generated for the vendor. When product is shipped, Company A pays the vendor from the payment made on the invoice.

Additional complexity may be generated when multiple vendors are used to fill an order for the customer. If the customer's credit does not meet the product request, alternate forms of payment are accepted, including credit cards and prepayments.

Company A generates revenue by charging the customer more than the vendors charge. Their company's design is to leverage technology and ultimately own the entire niche industry.

Their OneWorld Needs

This company comes to the OneWorld family with no initial baggage. They do not own existing legacy systems, so their reliance on OneWorld is complete. Within their business they will ultimately implement most major modules that OneWorld has to offer, including finance (accounts receivable, accounts payable, general ledger), distribution (sales orders, inventory, purchase orders, and customer relations management), and personnel (payroll, human resources). There are pros and cons to this type of implementation. The biggest advantages are that the company will not require database conversions from existing systems nor will it require interfacing to existing systems. The single largest disadvantage is that the requirement to implement the project will, by necessity, be extremely fast, allowing for limited issue identification and problem resolution.

Pros:

- No data conversion

- No legacy interface

- Little preset "Here is how we do business," more "Here is how we want to do business"

- "Anything is better than nothing" philosophy

Cons:

- Requires rapid "Big Bang" approach

- Little time to implement

- Entire company will live or die based on this project

Initial OneWorld Configuration

Company A is an advanced technology organization, but with the costs of hardware, software, and systems administration, they chose an NT/Intel hardware platform powered by an Microsoft SQL Server database. Using this information and hoping to achieve high transaction volumes, the company chose to implement separate databases on OneWorld logic servers instead of a single enterprise server. Except for this, they began their implementation as a typical customer would. Figure 12-2 shows Company A's architecture at the beginning of their OneWorld implementation.

Notice that there are only fat clients (no thin or Web clients) and there are two different locations for this company. Can you figure out what the data sources for Company A would be? Review the information in Table 12-1 concerning this setup. The installation went smoothly and the solution seemed complete until development occurred.

Business Requirements

One of the specific requirements from a business standpoint was getting information from the databases that powered the Web into the databases that powered their ERP solution. There are several different ways of getting information into OneWorld. You can manually key data in, you can run conversion and batch process uploads, or you can directly interface your data using J.D. Edwards-supplied APIs. Each of these methods have advantages and disadvantages; however, the short-term pain of developing direct API interfaces promises the longest-term functionality and ease of use.

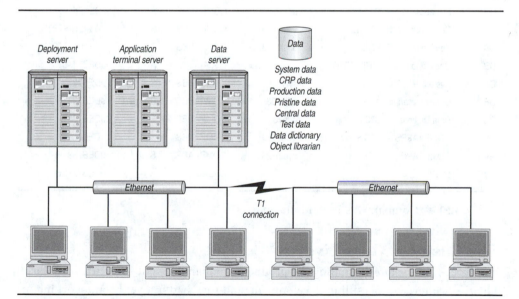

FIGURE 12-2. Company A's Initial OneWorld architecture

Data Source Type	Data Source Name	Table Owner	Server Name	Database Type	Database Name
DB	Business Data – PROD	proddta	COMPADBS	S	JDE_Production
DB	Control Tables – Prod	prodctl	COMPADBS	S	JDE_Production
DB	Central Objects – PRODB733	prodb733	COMPADBS	S	JDE_PRODB733
DB	Versions – PRODB733	prodb733	COMPADBS	S	JDE_PRODB733
DB	OneWorld Local – PRODB733		LOCAL	A	JDEB7.MDB
DB	Business Data – CRP	crpdta	COMPADBS	S	JDE_CRP
DB	Control Tables – CRP	crpctl	COMPADBS	S	JDE_CRP
DB	Central Objects – CRPB733	crpb733	COMPADBS	S	JDE_CRPB733
DB	Versions – CRPB733	crpb733	COMPADBS	S	JDE_CRPB733
DB	OneWorld Local – CRPB733		LOCAL	A	JDEB7.MDB
DB	Business Data – TEST	testdta	COMPADBS	S	JDE_Development
DB	Control Tables – Test	testctl	COMPADBS	S	JDE_Development
DB	Central Objects – DEVB733	devb733	COMPADBS	S	JDE_DEVB733
DB	Versions – DEVB733	devb733	COMPADBS	S	JDE_DEVB733
DB	OneWorld Local – DEVB733		LOCAL	A	JDEB7.MDB
DB	Business Data – JDE	pristdta	COMPADBS	S	JDE_Pristine
DB	Central Objects – PRISTB73	pristb733	COMPADBS	S	JDE_PRISTB733
DB	Versions – PRISTB733	pristb733	COMPADBS	S	JDE_PRISTB733
DB	OneWorld Local – PRISTB733		LOCAL	A	JDEB7.MDB
DB	System – B733	sysb733	COMPADBS	S	JDEB733
DB	Object Librarian – B733	objb733	COMPADBS	S	JDEB733
DB	Data Dictionary – B733	ddb733	COMPADBS	S	JDEB733
DB	COMPAAPPS – B733 Server Map	svmb733	COMPADBS	S	JDEB733
SVR	COMPAAPPS	svmb733	COMPAAPPS	S	JDEB733
SVR	LOCAL		LOCAL	A	JDEB7.MDB

TABLE 12-1. Company A's Initial Data Sources

The Business Goes Live

Just three months after installing the product, Company A went live with OneWorld. Their API interface was still in development, and they had not yet begun working on EDI interfaces with other companies. They manually keyed sales orders into OneWorld from printouts, and everything seemed to be moving along comfortably.

Then, shortly after going live with the system, Company A began experiencing problems surrounding database performance. During development, certain processes would run away, taking up all of the SQL Server's resources. When this occurred, the production system would go down with development. After the fourth or fifth such incident, Company A took drastic measures to ensure that their production environment was secured against problems arising from the development cycle.

Technology Activators Save the Day

Based on a J.D. Edwards white paper and recommendations from a branch of the J.D. Edwards World Wide Advanced Technologies, Company A decided to implement two totally separate systems. One system would be located at the corporate headquarters and would house the production system. The other site would house development, the conference room pilot, and pristine environments. Since two totally separate systems would need to be created, the hardware requirements for this company would double (two deployment servers, two application servers, and two data servers).

Questions and Answers

When Company A decided to pursue this configuration, the first question that had to be answered concerned the system's feasibility. After all, the changes required were significant. How would they move developed objects from one system to the next? What about data? How separate are these systems in reality?

Company A decided to provide a complete separation between these systems. For all intents and purposes, each system wouldn't even know the other system existed. This creates certain difficulties when sharing development, but these difficulties are easy to overcome using J.D. Edwards' technology activators. Using a set of specially configured data sources, path codes, and the record copy utility (found on menu GH9012), Company A can transfer developed code from one system to the next.

The Mechanics

Many products would take months to effect a massive change like this. For OneWorld, however, this transformation only takes a matter of days. The deployment server can be easily replicated using a third-party product designed to create system images for backup or mass production. Company A would need to reinitialize the OneWorld licenses, of course.

Implementing the application server, especially so early in the life cycle, involves nothing more than spinning the OneWorld disks again, copying the INI, and installing the services. Creating the database can either be accomplished by performing a backup of the existing database, restoring it to another server, or running a series of R98403 table copies. There would be some changes required for both OneWorld data sources (including a few new ones), and OCM remaps for UBE processing.

In all, the entire change, including system cleanup, would take less than one week. When the new development system came online (assuming Company A modified the client's ODBCs), the changes would be transparent to the users. A few might notice that the application server's name was different, but not enough to warrant concern. J.D. Edwards OneWorld is well equipped to handle situations like this one.

Final OneWorld System Configuration

The resulting OneWorld system configuration is shown in Figure 12-3, and the final data sources are listed in Table 12-2. Notice there is a complete duplication of the

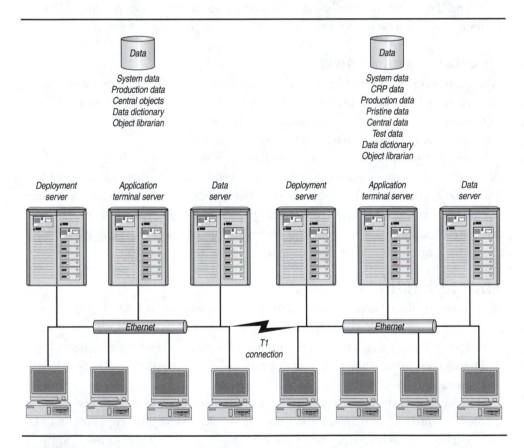

FIGURE 12-3. Final OneWorld configuration for Company A

Data Source Type	Data Source Name	Table Owner	Server Name	Database Type	Database Name	Function
DB	Business Data – PROD	proddta	COMPADBS	S	JDE_Production	Normal OW
DB	Control Tables – Prod	prodctl	COMPADBS	S	JDE_Production	Normal OW
DB	Central Objects – PRODB733	prodb733	COMPADBS	S	JDE_PRODB733	Normal OW
DB	Versions – PRODB733	prodb733	COMPADBS	S	JDE_PRODB733	Normal OW
DB	OneWorld Local – PRODB733		LOCAL	A	JDEB7.MDB	Normal OW
DB	System – B733	sysb733	COMPADBS	S	JDEB733	Normal OW
DB	Object Librarian – B733	objb733	COMPADBS	S	JDEB733	Normal OW
DB	Data Dictionary – B733	ddb733	COMPADBS	S	JDEB733	Normal OW
DB	COMPAAPPS – B733 Server Map	svmb733	COMPADBS	S	JDEB733	Normal OW
SVR	COMPAAPPS	svmb733	COMPAAPPS	S	JDEB733	Normal OW
SVR	LOCAL		LOCAL	A	JDEB7.MDB	Normal OW
DB	Business Data – TEST	testdta	COMPADB2S	S	JDE_TEST	Bridge Data Source
DB	Control Tables – Test	testctl	COMPADB2S	S	JDE_TEST	Bridge Data Source
DB	Central Objects – DEVB733	devb733	COMPADB2S	S	JDE_DEVB733	Bridge Data Source
DB	Versions – DEVB733	devb733	COMPADB2S	S	JDE_DEVB733	Bridge Data Source
DB	DEVObject Librarian – B733	objb733	COMPADB2S	S	JDEB733	Bridge Data Source
DB	DEVData Dictionary – B733	ddb733	COMPADB2S	S	JDEB733	Bridge Data Source
Development System Setup						
DB	Control Tables – CRP	crpctl	COMPADB2S	S	JDE_CRP	Normal OW
DB	Central Objects – CRPB733	crpb733	COMPADB2S	S	JDE_CRPB733	Normal OW
DB	Versions – CRPB733	crpb733	COMPADB2S	S	JDE_CRPB733	Normal OW
DB	OneWorld Local – CRPB733		LOCAL	A	JDEB7.MDB	Normal OW
DB	Business Data – TEST	testdta	COMPADB2S	S	JDE_Development	Normal OW
DB	Control Tables – Test	testctl	COMPADB2S	S	JDE_Development	Normal OW
DB	Central Objects – DEVB733	devb733	COMPADB2S	S	JDE_DEVB733	Normal OW
DB	Versions – DEVB733	devb733	COMPADB2S	S	JDE_DEVB733	Normal OW
DB	OneWorld Local – DEVB733		LOCAL	A	JDEB7.MDB	Normal OW

TABLE 12-2.   Company A's Final Data Sources

Inside and Out

Data Source Type	Data Source Name	Table Owner	Server Name	Database Type	Database Name	Function
DB	Business Data – JDE	pristdta	COMPADB2S	S	JDE_Pristine	Normal OW
DB	Central Objects – PRISTB73	pristb733	COMPADB2S	S	JDE_PRISTB733	Normal OW
DB	Versions – PRISTB733	pristb733	COMPADB2S	S	JDE_PRISTB733	Normal OW
DB	OneWorld Local – PRISTB733		LOCAL	A	JDEB7.MDB	Normal OW
DB	System – B733	sysb733	COMPADB2S	S	JDEB733	Normal OW
DB	Object Librarian – B733	objb733	COMPADB2S	S	JDEB733	Normal OW
DB	Data Dictionary – B733	ddb733	COMPADB2S	S	JDEB733	Normal OW
DB	COMPAAPPS – B733 Server Map	svmb733	COMPADB2S	S	JDEB733	Normal OW
SVR	COMPAAPPS	svmb733	COMPAAPP2S	S	JDEB733	Normal OW
SVR	LOCAL		LOCAL	A	JDEB7.MDB	Normal OW
DB	Business Data – PROD	proddta	COMPADBS	S	JDE_Production	Bridge Data Source
DB	Control Tables – Prod	prodctl	COMPADBS	S	JDE_Production	Bridge Data Source
DB	Central Objects – PRODB733	prodb733	COMPADBS	S	JDE_PRODB733	Bridge Data Source
DB	Versions – PRODB733	prodb733	COMPADBS	S	JDE_PRODB734	Bridge Data Source
DB	PRDObject Librarian – B733	objb733	COMPADBS	S	JDEB733	Bridge Data Source
DB	PRDData Dictionary – B733	ddb733	COMPADBS	S	JDEB733	Bridge Data Source

TABLE 12-2.   Company A's Final Data Sources (*continued*)

OneWorld system. The only connection these two systems will make is through the record copy utility.

How It Works

You can, especially on B733 and higher versions of OneWorld, migrate both data and objects at will between dissimilar systems with relative ease. To accomplish this particular task, you need to remember some of the basics of the associated applications and utilities, as described in Chapters 2 and 9. In addition to the bridge data sources set up in the preceding example, you also need to set up a bridge path code. This path code identifies the deployment server on the other system.

Let's take a quick look at the processes associated with this type of transfer. First, Company A can use the product packager to make this system work. Unfortunately, the product packager is not as robust as needed in this client's particular version of OneWorld. Since they need another method of transferring objects within their system, they are using the object transfer application (P9864) to move objects between their systems. (Refer to Figure 12-4 for a more detailed flowchart outlining their exact version control methodology.) This utility allows copying of data dictionary records, object librarian records, data source oriented records, including central objects and business data, and even menu records. For more information on this application, refer to Chapter 9.

Pros, Cons, and Lessons Learned

There are multiple lessons that can be learned from this case study. On the positive side, you will notice that the OneWorld system allowed Company A to completely restructure their system with a minimal amount of fuss. Second, where this configuration has additional maintenance requirements, there is a guarantee that one system will not affect the other. If production blows up, development will continue unabated (not that anyone would really care). If development blows up, production will not be affected. Third, the systems designed this way allow for superior performance with fewer system requirements per instance.

The biggest disadvantage to this system is the large quantity of system administration required to make both of these installations work. It is a much more complex configuration than average and requires a greater understanding of OneWorld to ensure it is properly maintained.

All users must be set up twice because the system tables are not being shared. Any data dictionary changes made to one system must be made to the other system as well. When Company A transfers objects between systems, there is no room for error. If they forget even a single object that's been modified, unpredictable results could occur. If it is a newly modified object, they have to remember to transfer the object definition first (remember, they're not sharing the object librarian) and the actual object between path codes second.

It goes without saying that this system will cost more than a typical OneWorld setup. This is, after all, double the hardware on a system that doubled the hardware in the beginning. When you consider that Company A's largest single complaint was runaway processes causing database performance degradation and system instability, what could they have done differently without the problems associated with two totally separate systems? Have you ever heard of the K.I.S. principal? Keep it simple! This concept goes a long way when providing a stable architecture for OneWorld (or any other ERP system).

Inside and Out

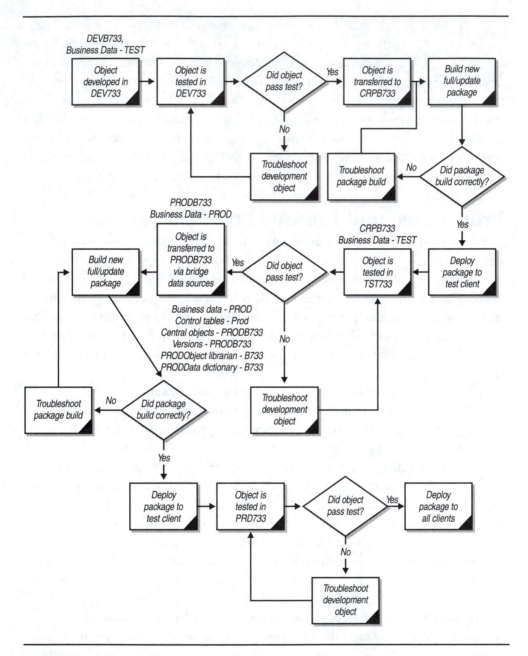

FIGURE 12-4. Company A's development cycle

Simple Solutions Pay

If the only difficulty is database performance due to development, Company A could have added a database server (refer to Chapter 5) for the CRP, development, and pristine databases. If a runaway process occurred, it would only affect those three environments, effectively secluding production. Company A would have benefited from this configuration by maintaining a single set of systems, object librarian, and data dictionary records.

Additional security could have been initiated to ensure production was further insulated from issues brought about by development. This solution would have been faster, less expensive, easier to maintain, and a better overall solution. Although the separate systems bought completely segregated installations, the question remains whether this was a necessary business requirement. Figure 12-5 details the alternative architecture.

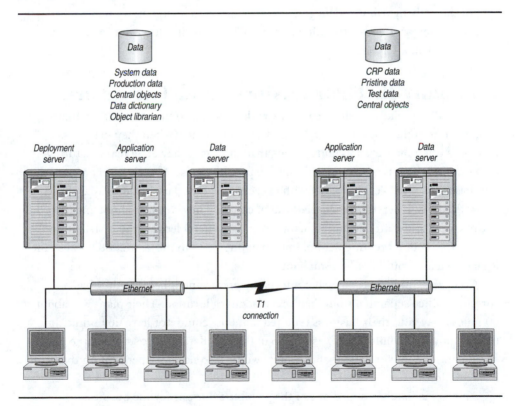

FIGURE 12-5.   Company A's alternate architecture

Where Are They Now?

Whether or not we agree with the philosophies associated with this particular solution, Company A continues to thrive with their two separate systems intact. The OneWorld technology activators allowed them to quickly provide a level of functionality not achievable with many ERP packages. This particular case study is definitely a glowing example of OneWorld configurability.

OneWorld and the Case of Truly Distributed Data

When you mention distributed data to most OneWorld practitioners, they immediately think about data replication, departmental servers, and WAN connectivity. But the case of the truly distributed data goes beyond this. In this section, we will go through Company B's reason for distributing their data between sites, their setup, and what became of them afterward.

Company B: Their Business and Their Needs

Company B is a relatively small company with around 150 million in annual sales generated from the production and sale of a bulk product (when they make a sale, it is more often measured in railroad cars than in bags). They are a manufacturing organization with a very low emphasis on computer systems. Yet their parent organization purchased the OneWorld product with expectations for its use. Company B chose NT with MS SQL Server as their platform of choice. They would be implementing the entire OneWorld suite, including manufacturing, general ledger, and distribution. They had the added requirement of implementing prior to the year 2000 because their legacy systems would not be compliant.

Company B was in a somewhat interesting predicament because they had a corporate office separated from their manufacturing location. Their plant was about 60 miles away, and their business required that they could not have downtime due to communication failures. It was the job of the installation to ensure that the plant could continue to work and that corporate would also not be dependent on the plant for operation.

This immediately stopped one of the possible solutions for the business requirement listed above—making the corporate office the remote location. If they housed the OneWorld servers at the plant and the communications lines failed, the corporate office would be offline until communications were re-established. This was no more desirable than having the plant offline. Due to the location of the plant, having redundant communication lines with different carriers was not an option— there was only one communication carrier in the area.

The Solution

The configuration discussed and ultimately implemented was distributing their database with appropriate tables located at each site. In anticipation of this requirement, they purchased a point-to-point T1 line.

Implementing B732.1 with approximately 1,200 business tables, they chose to separate 400 tables based on functionality on a server located at the plant. The other 800 tables remained at the corporate headquarters. But what if the line went down? How would they both work in the case of communication failure? The answer was data replication.

To facilitate this, they planned two enterprise servers, multitier locations, data replication, and multiple environments. Their OneWorld architecture is shown in Figure 12-6.

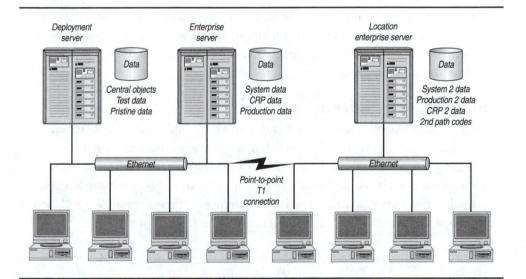

FIGURE 12-6. Company B's initial OneWorld configuration

The Particulars

There were two application/data servers with Microsoft SQL Server version 6.5, which we'll call CompB1 and CompB2. To support some replicated data and some data that resided in an offsite location, two production environments were designed. The first environment was PROD1 and had a base at the corporate headquarters. As such, the JDE.INI deployed to the fat clients looked to the local server for security services and system tables. In the case of PROD1, these system tables were also the set of published system tables. This environment also hosted 800 of the business data tables and had physical data replication set up for about 50 tables.

The second environment (called PROD2) contained an enterprise server, approximately 400 tables, and data replication for about 20 tables. The enterprise server acted as a security server and ran both UBEs and data replication. As clients logged on to the PROD2 environment, replicated tables on COMPB2 enterprise server supported their system requirements, cutting logon time from approximately 2 ½ minutes to 30 seconds.

In all, planning and configuring the system to accommodate this distributed system took about three weeks. During this time, the table maps were created, replication was set up, and the overall functionality of the system tested. The OCMs for PROD1 and PROD2 were modified to reflect both data-replicated tables and tables pointing to different locations. When the system went live, it was almost seamless to the users. Since tables were broken up by functionality and there was a definite separation of work between sites, the system's configuration allowed for maximum usage based on OneWorld technology activators.

The Hardware/Software

When Company B implemented this solution, it was early 1998 and several hardware configurations were not yet available, including NT/Intel machines with 1GB of RAM. This posed an issue for a client that wanted to implement a sophisticated architectural design. With what was available at the time, the systems listed in Table 12-3 were purchased.

The last two servers were designed to be enterprise servers running MS SQL Server version 6.5, OneWorld B732.1, and full replication for the two primary sites.

Deployment Server	Quantity	Description
	1	200MHz processor
		256MB RAM
	6	9GB hard drives
		2 drives in RAID 1 for a 9GB system partition
		4 drives in RAID 5 for a 27GB partition
COMPB1	Quantity	Description
	2	200MHz processor
		512MB RAM
	2	4GB hard drives in RAID 1 for a 4GB partition
	4	9GB hard drives in RAID 5 for a 27GB partition
COMPB2	Quantity	Description
	2	200MHz processor
		512MB RAM
	2	4GB hard drives in RAID 1 for a 4GB partition
	4	9GB hard drives in RAID 5 for a 27GB partition

TABLE 12-3.   Company B's Hardware Profile

Phase 1: Planning

There are three major phases that make a fully distributed data environment work within the OneWorld system. First, there is the planning phase. During this phase, the list of distributed tables was formulated by using system code and job functionality. Because this client had a clear delineation between activities that were corporate-based (sales, A/R, A/P, reporting) and those that were plant-based (inventory, manufacturing, shipping), system codes provided the road map to the distributed data model. Using the object librarian or a SQL statement, they could quickly identify most of the tables associated with a specific OneWorld module. (Don't forget that table names start with an F followed by system code.)

Inside and Out

Another list of tables needed to be generated for actual replication from corporate to the plant. Company B asked itself the question: If the lines of communication were broken, what information would we minimally require to continue operating offsite? They quickly came up with tables associated with logging on, control tables, object librarian tables, and any tables associated with specific applications that actually belong to other applications used by the applications they need (such as address book tables).

The final list of tables that needed to be compiled included those that are owned by the plant, but are required to allow the corporate applications to properly operate. Of course, both of these last two lists needed to be created and then analyzed taking basic data replication criteria into account. One of the considerations to keep in mind is that tables containing highly transactional data make very bad candidates for replication.

Why Did They Need Data Replication?　　If the T1 is fast enough, why not simply move the tables as required and use OCM to do the rest? It really is quite simple. The same business requirement that forced the distribution of the data in the first place forced the need to replicate some data. In the case of communication failure, both the plant and corporate needed to continue work as usual. Unlike most data replication strategies, this one was not based on improved performance requirements.

Phase 2: Setup

The second phase of this project was the actual setup of the data sources, path codes, environments, OCM, servers, and so on required to make this solution work. If you're going to set up an environment similar to the one described here, you need an in-depth understanding of OneWorld building blocks. Take a couple of minutes to review Chapter 2 and then see if you can determine all of the steps (not the click-the-button steps, but the big steps) to make the kinds of changes discussed for this company. Your list should be similar to the following:

1. Add a second enterprise server

   - Add two data sources to system and server map
   - Add new hardware and database software
   - Add server map tables to new database, modify F00053 and F000531 records
   - Add server software and OneWorld services
   - Start services and ensure servers are talking to each other

2. Migrate data tables

   - Create databases to house business data, system tables, and central objects

   - Copy identified tables for both CRP and production

   - Copy data dictionary

   - Copy central objects

   - Copy object librarian

3. Set up replication

   - Add four data sources

   - Set up publisher and subscriber records in both server maps and in the system data source

   - Synchronize tables

4. Update OCM and other system tables

   - Add nine data sources to both system and server map

   - Add manufacturing location specific path code

   - Add manufacturing location specific environments

   - Update OCM for replicated tables

   - Update OCM for remote tables

   - Update server map OCM for new environments

5. Set up multitier deployment

   - Define deployment server

   - Define deployment location

   - Push packages to deployment location

   - Modify remote INI to look at local path code, security server, and local system data

   - Deploy remote machines

So, did your list look like this one? If you've applied what you've learned working with the product and in this book so far, you should have been able to identify the major steps even if you didn't get some of the more detailed ones.

Data Source Name	Data Source Type	Owner	Target Data Base	Database Type
CompB2	SVR	svm2b732	JDE2	MS SQL v 6.5
CompB2 – Server Map	DB	svm2b732	JDE2	MS SQL v 6.5
Business Data – PROD2	DB	prod2dta	JDE2	MS SQL v 6.5
Control Tables – Production2	DB	prod2ctl	JDE2	MS SQL v 6.5
Central Objects – PROD2B732	DB	prod2b732	JDE2	MS SQL v 6.5
Versions – PROD2B732	DB	prod2b732	JDE2	MS SQL v 6.5
OneWorld Local – PROD2B732	DB	N/A	JDEB7.mdb	MS Access
Business Data – CRP2	DB	crp2dta	JDE2	MS SQL v 6.5
Control Tables – CRP2	DB	crp2ctl	JDE2	MS SQL v 6.5
Central Objects – CRP2B732	DB	crp2b732	JDE2	MS SQL v 6.5
Versions – CRP2B732	DB	crp2b732	JDE2	MS SQL v 6.5
OneWorld Local – CRP2B732	DB	N/A	JDEB7.mdb	MS Access
System – 2B732	DB	sys2b732	JDE2	MS SQL v 6.5
Data Dictionary – 2B732	DB	dd2b732	JDE2	MS SQL v 6.5
Object Librarian – 2B732	DB	obj2b732	JDE2	MS SQL v 6.5

TABLE 12-4.   Company B's Data Sources

Data Sources   In the steps above, we listed 15 new data sources. Refer to Table 12-4 for more information on them. Remember, in B732.1 many of the installation wizards used today did not exist. When you add this to the fact that the OneWorld technology consultant was from the old school, you will quickly realize that each of these 15 data sources were set up from scratch. Try to think your way through the required data sources for the changes required for this setup. Remember, you need to add two new path codes, two new environments, and have all the information necessary to run even when the system has lost communication between sites.

Phase 3: Test It and Turn it Loose

Phase 2 only took a few days to complete. Phase 3, however, should have taken longer. There were several different things immediately identified that needed to be tested, including the following:

- Test setup

- Test remote logon

- Test remote security services

- Test remote UBEs

- Test server package builds

- Stress-test the system

- Test both side functionality when the T1 line is down

- Test data replication

Though the number of items that needed to be thoroughly tested would make you think that weeks and even months should be dedicated to the testing process, the actual testing that was performed (due to time constraints) was approximately two days. This would turn out to be a critical flaw in this architectural implementation. The amount of work and the technical expertise necessary to maintain this system was never identified. The tests that were performed were surface tests. All passed without issue.

The System Goes Live

Without a sound, without external technology support, without real issues, the system went live approximately three months after being installed, upgraded, and configured. The client experienced issues surrounding the version of the software, but no real technology issues were raised.

Inside and Out

Determining Tables Opened at Login

There is a quick method of determining what tables are associated with logging on to the system. On any client machine, turn logging on (see the JDE.INI settings below). Double-click the OneWorld icon on your desktop. Enter your user ID and password and click OK or press the ENTER key on your keyboard. Once the OneWorld Explorer is open, use Windows Explorer to locate and open your JDEDEBUG.LOG located at the root of C:\. You can go through this log and locate where tables are opened and closed as well as what actions are being taken on each table (such as select, update, and so on).

```
[DEBUG]
TAMMultiUserOn=0
Output=file –*Note: This is not case sensitive
ServerLog=0
LEVEL=BSFN,EVENTS
DebugFile=c:\jdedebug.log
JobFile=c:\jde.log
Frequency=10000
RepTrace=0
```

Another way of knowing what tables are being opened when you log on is to refer to the list below. This list is for the B733.2 version of OneWorld.

OneWorld Tables Touched at Logon

Type of Table	Table Name	Description	Action
Business Data	F0006	Business Unit Master	Open/Close
Business Data	F0007	Workday Calendar	Open/Close
Business Data	F0008	Date Fiscal Patterns	Open/Close
Business Data	F0009	General Constants	Select - Read Only
Business Data	F0010	Company Constants	Select - Read Only
Business Data	F0012	Automatic Accounting Instructions Master	Open/Close

Law of the West

Type of Table	Table Name	Description	Action
Business Data	F0013	Currency Codes	Open/Close
Business Data	F0014	Payment Terms	Open/Close
Business Data	F0015	Currency Exchange Rates	Open/Close
Business Data	F0022	Tax Rules	Open/Close
Business Data	F0025	Ledger Type Master File	Open/Close
Business Data	F0026	Job Cost Constants	Open/Close
Business Data	F069116	Payroll Transaction Constants	Open/Close
Business Data	F08320	Benefits Plan Master	Open/Close
Business Data	F083202	Plan Additional Options	Open/Close
Business Data	F08320B	Plan/Plan Option Tag Table	Open/Close
Business Data	F08350	Categories within Benefit Groups	Open/Close
Business Data	F08351	Plans within Benefit Categories	Open/Close
Business Data	F0901	Account Master	Open/Close
Business Data	F1200	Fixed Asset Constants	Open/Close
Business Data	F3009	Job Shop Manufacturing Constants	Open/Close
Business Data	F40070	Preference Master File	Open/Close
Business Data	F40073	Preference Hierarchy File	Open/Close
Business Data	F4008	Tax Areas	Open/Close
Business Data	F4009	Distribution/Manufacturing Constants	Select - Read Only
Business Data	F40095	Default Locations/Printers	Open/Close
Business Data	F40203	Order Activity Rules	Open/Close
Business Data	F40205	Line Type Control Constants File	Open/Close
Business Data	F4070	Price Adjustment Schedule	Open/Close
Business Data	F4071	Price Adjustment Type	Open/Close
Business Data	F41001	Inventory Constants	Open/Close
Business Data	F41002	Item Units of Measure Conversion Factors	Open/Close
Business Data	F41003	Unit of Measure Standard Conversion	Open/Close
Business Data	F49002	Transportation Constants	Open/Close
Business Data	F49003	Load Type Constants	Open/Close
Business Data	F49004	Mode of Transport Constants	Open/Close
Business Data	F4950	Routing Entries	Open/Close
Business Data	F4951	Carrier Zone Definitions	Open/Close
Business Data	F4953	Routing Hierarchy	Open/Close
Business Data	F4970	Freight Rate Schedule	Open/Close
Business Data	F4971	Freight Rate Definition	Open/Close
Business Data	F4973	Rate Structure Definition	Open/Close

Type of Table	Table Name	Description	Action
Business Data	F4978	Charge Code Definitions	Open/Close
Business Data	F7306	Quantum Sales and Use Tax Constants	Select - Read Only
Business Data	F7308	Quantum Database Connection	Select - Read Only
Control Tables	F0004	User-Defined Code Types	Open/Close
Control Tables	F0005	User-Defined Codes	Open/Close
Control Tables	F0082	Menu Master File	Select - Read Only
Control Tables	F00821	Menu Selections File	Select - Read Only
Control Tables	F0083	Menu Text Override File	Select - Read Only
Control Tables	F0084	Menu Path File	Select - Read Only
System	F0092	Library Lists - User	Select - Read Only
System	F00921	User Display Preferences	Select - Read Only
System	F00925	User Access Definition	Select - Read Only
System	F0093	Library List Control	Select - Read Only
System	F00941	Environment Detail - One World	Select - Read Only
System	F00942	Object Path Master File	Select - Read Only
System	F00945	Release Master	Select - Read Only
System	F00950	Security Workbench Table	Select - Read Only
System	F00960	Machine/Group Identification	select/update
System	F91500	Application Header for Tip of the Day	Select - Read Only
System	F91510	Tip Details for Tip of the Day	Select - Read Only
System	F9650	Machine Master	select/update
System	F98101	Imaging Constants	Select - Read Only
System	F986101	Object Configuration Master	Select - Read Only
System	F98611	Data Source Master	Select - Read Only
System	F98613	Business View Environmental Server	Select - Read Only
System	F98825	Package Deployment Scheduling	Select - Read Only
System	F98950	User Overrides Table	Select - Read Only
System	F98980	Font Override by Language	Select - Read Only
System	F98DRENV	Data Replication Environment Mapping Table	Select - Read Only
System	F98DRLOG	Data Replication Change Log	Select - Read Only
System	F98DRPUB	Data Replication Publisher	Select - Read Only
System	F98DRSUB	Data Replication Subscribers	Select - Read Only

What Went Wrong?

The initial setup of the replicated tables went smoothly. Both servers talked to each other well, and data passed between them as designed in the B732.1 setup. The OCM modifications were also successful. Due to the speed of the T1 and the relatively small number of users (approximately 15 per site), users did not notice an appreciable difference between data located on their site server and data distributed to other sites. So what went wrong?

B732.1 data replication worked; however, it was not the most robust method of replicating data across a WAN architecture. Most of the sites using distributed data setups used the RDBMS to replicate between sites. Unfortunately, because of the client's desire to have a OneWorld solution, the fact that information technology (IT) was viewed as a necessary evil, and the fact that the IT staff consisted of one person who was not a database administrator (DBA), OneWorld data replication was the preferred replication methodology.

OneWorld data replication requires a large amount of administrative handling. While it is not difficult to set up, ensuring that all required messages are successfully delivered requires daily maintenance—especially when you are replicating a large number of tables. After six months of operation, Company B decided the speed of their T1 connection was great enough that they would reconsolidate their database, as shown in Figure 12-7.

What About the Business Needs?

What about the business requirement of allowing both sites continued OneWorld access even when communications were severed? Company B realized that manual processes could be used in place of OneWorld for shipping purposes, sales would continue and products could be created. In the case of a communication failure, life would go on and the business (although limping) would continue until communications were re-established.

Another factor involved with reconsolidating the databases was the decision to migrate from MS SQL Server version 6.5 to version 7.0. The two events could easily be tied into a single activity. OneWorld technology activators allowed the migration with relative ease. The resulting setup, along with increases in the OneWorld product, also allowed for the use of MS Windows Terminal Server Edition and Citrix Metaframe services. This provided another route into the OneWorld system in case of communication failure in the T1 line.

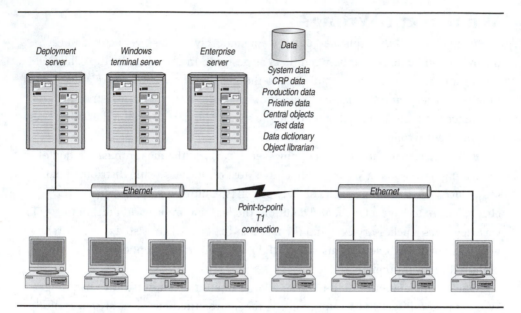

FIGURE 12-7.   Company B's final architecture

Simplicity Is Best

When asked what lessons were gleaned from this client's continued migration with the OneWorld product, we think that several very important items should be identified. First, extremely complicated solutions, even when workable, are not always the best solutions. In this case, the benefits associated with providing a difficult solution that performed exactly the way the client wanted were outweighed by the fact that the client did not have sufficient IT staff to maintain the solution.

Second, the flexibility of the OneWorld product, coupled with the fact that it is continually changing to embrace new technologies, allowed not only the original configuration, but also the rapid changes requested by the client. Many ERP packages would have trouble supporting the first configuration. Those other software packages would have had huge difficulties in allowing the changes to occur with the rapidity experienced with the OneWorld process. In all, less than two days were required to complete the changes, relocate the data files, and turn the replication off.

Third, quite a bit of time and effort were spent creating, implementing, administering, and finally undoing a solution that was not an actual business requirement. When push came to shove, the manufacturing plant did not need 24/7 access to OneWorld. Was it preferable? Yes, and it still is. However, it is not a fall-on-your-sword business requirement. If other options had been explored (such as manual ticketing), a substantial amount of time and resources could have been saved.

Finally, companies should never underestimate or skip the technology-modeling phase of a OneWorld implementation. One of the biggest problems faced by every OneWorld installation and rollout is the technology surrounding the product. Too often, the technology is ignored until it is too late. Proper planning for technology, including modeling architectural designs, is a requirement for implementing the product. Had the design been modeled prior to go-live, it would have quickly become apparent that the T1 was efficient enough to handle their speed concerns. Even deployments of the OneWorld product rarely lasted more 30 minutes across the WAN. Where testing a solution isn't a hard requirement for implementing OneWorld, it is something that greatly enhances the probability of the implementation's success.

Where Are They Now?

During the last year, Company B has seen signification development surrounding specific OneWorld functionality. They have also recently upgraded their version of OneWorld to B733.1 for both functionality and performance gain. They have migrated most of their business operations to OneWorld and continue to work aggressively with the product. Their IT staff has grown to two.

OneWorld Continually Grows to Meet Expanding Needs

The following case study is a good indication of OneWorld's ability to continually change, effectively merging both technology and the business needs of companies over time. Let's take a look at Company C and see where they started and where they've ended up. There have been hiccups along the way, but it is a classic example of how you can take advantage of these changes to improve performance, reliability, and functionality within your own solution. The OneWorld product can be a highly fluid architectural product, and this versatility is one of the powers of the solution it provides.

How It All Started

When Company C first began its search for a new ERP solution, they dedicated approximately 20 people as a functional core team to find and implement this solution. The search began in 1997 because of known Y2K deficiencies in their existing homegrown mainframe software. There were a series of goals in the search, including a desire for client/server architecture, capability within the software to be both modifiable and upgradeable as new releases became available, the requirement that the software be able to meet their business needs, and the requirement of the software to interface with certain third-party software (FormScape and Vertex, to name two).

Company C

Company C is a retail organization with branches in North America. They have multiple retail outlets that get tied into their single software solution. As a primary retailer with multiple warehouses, this organization required the ability to service these multiple decentralized outlets while centrally managing and controlling inventory and reporting sales. As with most retail organizations, they have different types of customers, including customers who walk in off the street as well as established corporate accounts. This provides additional requirements for sales orders, inventory management, A/R, and invoicing.

Because of the centrally managed logic, they also had unique printing requirements, including printing the same document on three different printers in three different locations. This requirement would add additional third-party software interface requirements to their overall solution. Still, their business requirements were not beyond the functional specifications of the OneWorld product.

Personnel

Most companies, when first starting a project such as implementing OneWorld, look at exactly how they are going to staff these projects, both in the short and long term. Company C decided to keep most of their IT department, to be retooled into OneWorld specialists. They would further augment these specialists with experienced consultants from both J.D. Edwards and other third-party consulting agencies as appropriate.

Although this isn't the only method of getting people for a project like this one, it is a viable option if you understand the pros and cons associated. Their two systems analysts would become OneWorld systems analysts with special emphasis on data conversions, business customization, and process design. Their mainframe DBA would become an Oracle DBA. The team put together for software selection would become the core team of functional experts for both the implementation and training.

Third-party consulting from J.D. Edwards and other agencies would not only provide technical and technology expertise, but would also assist with the implementation itself, a knowledge transfer from consultant to functional expert and support after go-live.

Their Chosen Solution

As you can already guess, Company C picked OneWorld as their software of choice. For reliability, scalability, and raw business capability, they went with the HP9000 series of server and Oracle 7.2. Their first installation of the software was in the first quarter of 1998 and was very simplistic. They were at version B731.2 of the OneWorld product with a proposed architecture like the one shown in Figure 12-8.

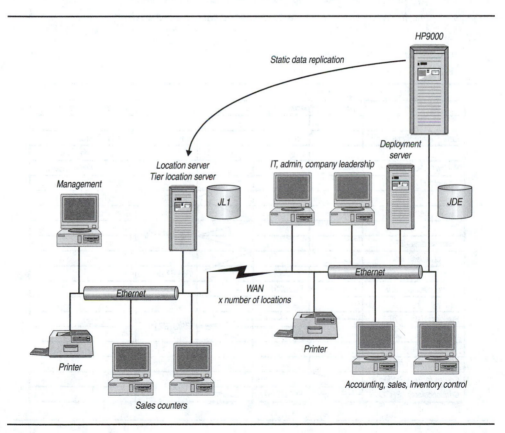

FIGURE 12-8. Company C's planned architecture

You will notice that they have a single K-class server as an enterprise server tied to a simple 2-tier basic architecture. The only complication to the original plan was the location servers. These were planned, but were not scheduled for implementation until early 1999. Their data sources are represented in Figure 12-9, as are their environments and path codes for the installation itself. None of the CNC work proposed by the planned architecture is represented here.

NOTE

If you have already read Chapter 2, you will notice several discrepancies between data sources defined for B731.2 and data sources in B733.2. In particular, they hadn't started separating the version tables from the central objects yet, and there weren't as many release-specific data sources as there are today.

Environment Specific Data Sources			Shared Data Sources
Data Source Name	**Path Code**	**Environment**	OneWorld local
			Machine name
Business data - CRP			Machine name - Server map
Control tables - CRP			System
		CRPB731	Object librarian
Central objects - CRP	CRPB731		Data dictionary
		TESTB731	Local
Business data - TEST			
Control tables - Test			
		DEVB731	
Central objects - DEV	DEVB731		
Business data - JDE		PRISTB731	
Central objects - JDE	PRISTB731		
Business data - PROD			
Control tables - Production		PRODB731	
Central objects - PROD	PRODB731		

FIGURE 12-9. Initial Architecture

The Second Chapter

The installation went well. There were no major issues due to the software or hardware. Services worked on the server, and workstations could be deployed. Packages could be built, and objects could be modified. For the next two months, Company C worked with the software, becoming more familiar with what it could and could not do. They identified gaps in the solution and worked with various methods of bridging those gaps.

In the second quarter of 1998, Company C decided to take advantage of an upgrade provided by J.D. Edwards to the B732 base version of the software. The newer version added quite a bit more functionality to the base software. Only two months into the implementation, there were no modifications or even real data in OneWorld. Consequently, Company C could have opted to completely reinstall the latest OneWorld product. However, in this particular case, they chose to upgrade the system. This upgrade had some initial issues; however, the client was up and running on their new software within three weeks.

When B732.1 came out in the third quarter of 1998, Company C again decided that the 4,000 application changes from the base release to the cumulative one were worth the effort of doing it. That, in addition to the wisdom of not going live on a base release, caused them to invest in yet another update. In addition to the OneWorld update, they opted to put in place Oracle 7.3 and a new HP9000. The new machine contained significantly more storage space as well as more processors, more RAM, and the capability to grow as the company grew. They made a base decision that the information they had to date was not pertinent to their implementation. Their third-party consulting company preferred to set up applications and reports again and re-enter data. No real data conversions had occurred at this point.

So, in the third quarter of 1998, they reinstalled the OneWorld product using the new database and enterprise server. Their base architectural design remained the same, though they were now discussing changes based on an upcoming service pack release of the OneWorld product which would support Windows Terminal Server Edition. Their IT staff recognized this technology as a must-have advantage, allowing central administration and control, use of WinTerm devices, decrease in communication requirements, and overall money savings.

The System Goes Live

In the fourth quarter of 1998, Company C went live with financials after nine months, an installation, an upgrade, and a second installation on a new set of hardware. They were implementing a base two-tier architecture. The financials were only in their corporate offices. The go-live itself was relatively uneventful, with data loads going as planned and the transition as anticipated. As they started 1999, Company C planned on upgrading to B733 to take advantage of OneWorld development tool enhancements integrated in that release. However, their current *real* environment looked like the one shown in Figure 12-10.

Since Company C was a live client with reports and other minor modifications, they couldn't choose a data-only upgrade or even a reinstallation like the one they had done in the past. Instead, they were forced to perform a full upgrade. Still, migrating to B733 base was a business requirement to accommodate modifications needed to go live with sales order management, inventory control, and distribution.

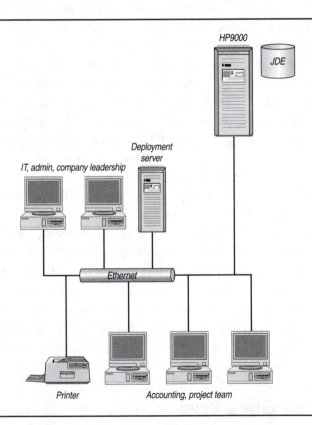

FIGURE 12-10. Company C's actual go-live architecture

The upgrade was painful; however, after a month, the base environments seemed somewhat stable. With B733 base, not only did they plan to do offsite development, they also changed their overall CNC architectural design to accommodate Windows Terminal Servers. This new design is shown in Figure 12-11.

The Development Effort

Since the majority of the development effort was being performed offsite and out of state, Company C chose to implement location database servers and allow the developers access to their site remotely. The cost of a six-month development project

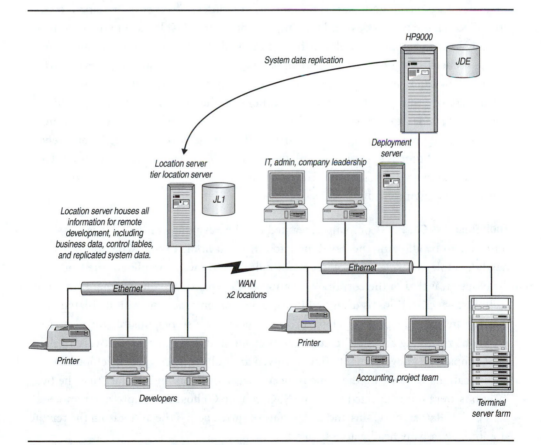

FIGURE 12-11. Company C's B733 architecture with development and WTSE servers

in travel alone for more than 30 people would be staggering. By allowing the developers to stay in their own offices, Company C realized a significant savings. The problem that most developers point out with this type of project however, is the speed with which they can modify and test the resulting product.

To properly plan for this, Company C took several factors about the underlying J.D. Edwards OneWorld architecture into account. First, all real development is performed on the workstation. The deployment server acts as a central repository for the objects themselves, but you don't do development on that server. You check C code out of the deployment server, modify it locally, and then check it back into the server when complete or for backup purposes. Second, if check-out/check-in times are a factor, you can configure path codes to reside on different servers. These path codes are called remote path codes, and the only real difference besides where the C code is actually located is that any packages being built will also reside on the remote servers. Third, if check-out/check-in times are not a major player, or if multiple sites require access to the same set of code (this is an example where you might have two or more developers working in different remote locations on the same development project), remote path codes are not a viable option. Finally, for raw performance considerations, the amount of time necessary to check items into and out of a path code is relatively small. The real time is spent modifying the objects and testing the modifications. To this end, Company C chose to implement location servers with specially designed development environments.

Their Business Case   Company C wanted to take advantage of the cost savings represented by allowing the developers to remain at home except when delivering newly completed projects. As each major modification was completed, the lead developer traveled to the corporate location of Company C to ensure that it met the technical specifications as designed in the development documentation created at the beginning of the project. These project leads were also responsible for resolving problems revolving around the creation, transfer, and design of the software itself.

Company C's development effort revolved around two sites with developers at both locations working on the same projects. Because of this and the fact that the two locations were not connected via a WAN, Company C chose not to provide remote path codes. Rather, check-ins and check-outs occurred across the WAN from the remote site to the company headquarters.

NOTE

*Depending on the applications being modified, the size of the WAN connection,
and the development rules in place, significant amounts of time can be wasted
in this cycle checking items out of and into a remote deployment server.*

The Mechanics of Making Development Happen   NT/Intel servers (really nothing
more than large PCs) allowed Company C to create environments specifically designed
for the remote locations. These servers had an Oracle database and very little else.
They did not have the OneWorld server software installed, but they did double as tier
location servers. On the database itself, very simple databases provided business data,
control tables, and specific system tables designed to speed up logons and provide all
the necessary data to test the application customizations. If your company is going to
perform something similar to this, follow these guidelines:

- Be sure the location servers meet the minimal specifications as outlined on the
  J.D. Edwards Web site, including OS level, MDAC level, and database level.

- Remember that having external databases doesn't mean that someone on the far
  side will take care of them. Clearly define roles necessary to make this happen,
  including backup procedures and regular database administration.

- Remote development by third parties requires additional management, including
  clearly communicating your development rules. Some examples include:
  check-ins must occur on Friday by midnight; if you are checking an item to look
  at it, be sure to erase the check-out when completed; all object transfers will be
  performed by project leads; and so on. Additional management will also be
  required to ensure that the rules outlined for the project are adhered to. Irreparable
  harm can come if you don't properly manage large development projects.

Now, can you determine the steps necessary to actually add a development
environment for this company? Take a few minutes to do this, and then see if you
came up with the following steps:

1. Install OS, database, and any other third-party software required (such as
   the backup software).

2. Define new OneWorld data sources for business data, control tables, and
   system tables.

Inside and Out

3. Create database and table spaces (if required) for the copied data. Create new ODBC or connect strings as required for the database connection.

4. Copy Business Data – TEST and Control Tables – Test from the enterprise server to the new location (database) server. You can either use the R98403 UBE or database imports/exports to accomplish this.

5. Decide which system tables you want to copy—you can use the list of tables hit at logon earlier in this chapter for a starting point. Logically decide if you want to do each of these tables or some subset of them. Once you have your list of system tables, decide the proper method of replicating data: database, third party, or OneWorld replication. Set this up and ensure that the tables get correctly copied.

6. In the OneWorld Environment Master application (P0094), copy the DEV733 environment (refer to Chapter 2 for more information on this application). Be sure you give it a new name and description, but do not change the path code. Remember, in this particular scenario, the client decided against providing additional path codes. Consequently, all of the development will use the DEVB733 path code located on the deployment server.

7. In OCM, modify the new environment so the default for tables uses the new business data control tables defined in step 1. You will also need to modify the OCM to reflect the tables you chose to replicate. In this scenario, Company C did not replicate all the system tables. Consequently, some of the information still resides across the WAN—not all system table mappings should be changed.

8. Set up users and groups to access the new environment.

9. Set up multitier deployment and copy current DEVB733 packages to the location server.

10. Test the new environment and the deployment capabilities of the new server prior to shipping it to the remote site. Make sure the remote location is able to connect the new server and their existing workstations into the WAN connection provided.

NOTE

Since the topic is development and packages are required to deploy developmental changes, you should keep in mind that all packages (both server and client) should be built at the corporate location—the one with the deployment server. If you are implementing remote path codes, the packages should be built on the same LAN where the path code and central objects reside.

So, did your list look anything like this? If you are missing a large number of steps, we recommend that you review Chapters 2, 5, and 13. Though we understand this is somewhat complicated, the majority of the work necessary to accomplish this involves basic CNC modifications. The testing becomes a little more complicated, but creating a new location server is relatively simple.

Windows Terminal Servers

Though Company C began some initial explorations into the capabilities of Windows Terminal Server in conjunction with OneWorld on B732.1 service pack9, the real testing and implementation didn't begin until after their upgrade to B733. They set up several terminal servers and installed the OneWorld product. As they increased their reliance on this technology, they noted both favorable and unfavorable results. On their particular version of OneWorld, there were specific issues that have since been changed in how the product works with the OS itself.

First, they noted that two people launching the same version of the same report from the same server could get the same information even after changing data selection or processing options. This was a result of shared TAM files and the timing of the report submissions and was first identified in October of 1998. J.D. Edwards fixed this in B733.2.

Second, Company C received an inordinate number of RDA and FDA "TAM files in use" errors. Again, this issue was related to more than one person trying to launch applications and reports on the same machine using the same TAM files. J.D. Edwards fixed this in service pack 3 of the B733 product.

Third, there were a series of memory violations received when certain applications were used in Terminal Server that did not manifest when run on a client workstation. Service Pack 3 contains five or six different software action requests (SARs) to improve memory management of the OneWorld application on Terminal Server.

Fourth, they often experienced the splash screen error. The splash screen error is where the OneWorld login screen comes up, you punch in your user ID and password, the OneWorld splash screen shows up, and then OneWorld aborts with no visible indication to the user that an error has occurred (of course, in a couple of minutes, most users realize that OneWorld has failed). This error is actually a Terminal Server error where the OS is not completely cleaning up the TEMP directory when users log off. As new users log on to the server, they are assigned a temporary directory that already existed—unfortunately, they don't have rights to that directory because it was created for the earlier user. When OneWorld tries to populate information into the temporary directory, it aborts due to the permissions issue. The resolution for this particular issue is to ensure that the temporary directory is cleared every night and to clear it during the day if you see the problem. By creating a very simple CMD file, you can automate clearing out the TEMP directory.

Finally, even though Company C was implementing a Terminal Server Farm and roaming NT user profiles, Windows Terminal Server wasn't particularly good at cleaning out the PROFILES directory. There were a couple of times when this directory grew so large that the C drive ran out of room. In the same script that cleaned up the TEMP directory, you can put in commands to clean up the PROFILES directory as well.

What Terminal Server Bought Them   From the paragraph above, you might think that implementing Terminal Server was more trouble than it was worth. Still, implementing this solution did provide a series of advantages for Company C. One of the biggest wins associated with this implementation was the fact that it allowed central hardware and software administration. By using Terminal Servers, Company C did not have to put data servers at each of their retail locations. This saved support personnel necessary to service and maintain these servers. It also allowed a simpler OneWorld architecture to be put into place.

Another win was realized when Company C decided to implement WinTerm devices instead of fat client workstations. The WinTerm devices only cost about $300 each. This was a substantial savings over a workstation with 128MB of RAM, a 400MHz processor, and 8GB of hard drive (approximately $1,800 at the time).

Terminal Servers also decreased their WAN requirements. Although 8 to12KB per user is a rule of thumb with Terminal Server, using a remote client costs substantially more in raw bandwidth. By implementing Terminal Server, there was substantially less information being passed between remote locations.

Finally, Terminal Servers run substantially faster than client workstations across a WAN. The logon is faster, and the applications are closer to the enterprise server, so there is less latency, causing everything to run faster. And yes, on the occasion that you are alone with the Terminal Server, you have 2GB of RAM and four processors at your disposal.

The Average Terminal Server and What Company C Learned   Company C started out with only a few of these machines; they ended up with more than 20 in a server farm. The average Terminal Server was a quad 550MHz processor, with 2GB of RAM and 27GB (three 9GB drives) of hard drive space. These machines were set up with RAID 0. Why would Company C choose this particular type of RAID, which doesn't provide any redundancy? The reasons are simple. First, on timed trials, RAID 0 was substantially faster than either RAID 1 or RAID 5. Second, with more than 20 servers in the farm and roaming menus in use, no one really cares if you lose a drive. The systems administrators take the server out of the farm, the user logs back on to different servers, and away you go. You can easily buy the loss of a machine or two and the time it takes to bring them back online.

Another huge advantage to working with Terminal Servers is that Company C opted to implement Citrix Metaframe. This product allows you, among other things, to shadow other desktop sessions. Since Company C opted to deploy the entire desktop to its users, this allowed them to provide a superior helpdesk functionality. When users ran into OneWorld issues, they could be shadowed, allowing the helpdesk to see and control the session as required.

N O T E

This particular feature also allows the Big Brother of IT to observe people as they play on the Internet. Though some people think this is a violation of privacy, company equipment is designed for company business and companies do have a right to ensure that their equipment is being properly used.

Windows Terminal Server Architecture   Although J.D. Edwards usually recommends that companies employing the Windows Terminal Server solution with OneWorld use a three-tier architecture, Company C went against this conventional wisdom. Through exhaustive testing (illustrated in Figure 12-12), they decided that the best overall solution for their organization was a basic two-tier architecture strictly using the terminal servers as fat clients in place of traditional workstations. The rationale behind this decision was based on tests using a true three-tier architecture, a virtual three-tier architecture, and a two-tier architecture. The three-tier architecture, although it did offload processing requirements from the terminal servers, wasn't as fast as the two-tier

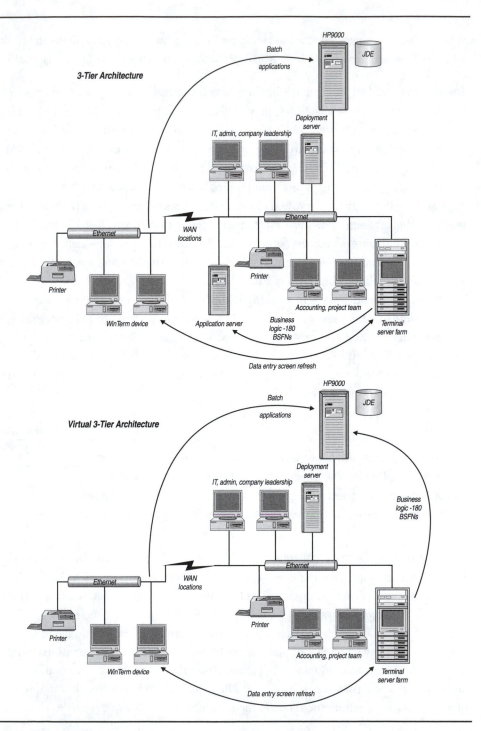

FIGURE 12-12.   Company C's tested configurations

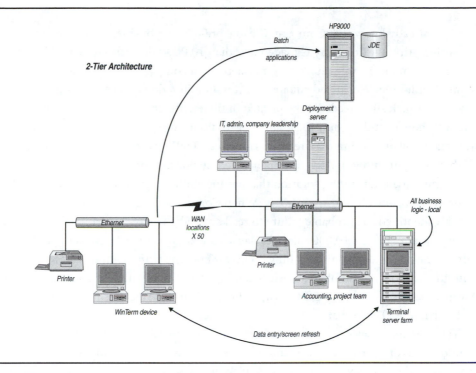

FIGURE 12-12.   Company C's tested configurations (*continued*)

architecture. The virtual three-tier architecture, though significantly faster than the two-tier architecture, was too much for the enterprise server. Processes on the enterprise server would go into an infinite loop when stressed. The two-tier architecture, however, supported 25 users comfortably per Terminal Server and was simple to maintain and relatively fast.

Printing

As mentioned earlier in this case study, Company C had some interesting printing challenges, including the raw number of sales orders created daily. With centralized processing, the first OneWorld version Company C began with would have printed all the sales to the same printer without direct user intervention. Of course, considering that Company C has stores all over North America, this would have made business difficult at best. To further complicate matters, this earlier version of OneWorld only supported PostScript printers without a series of modifications to the server's JDE.INI. Although it wouldn't have been impossible, it would have been difficult to support the business's printing requirements.

You already know that Company C had a pre-existing business requirement regarding printing. Company C made more than 10,000 sales per day. Though that may not seem like a large number of transactions in comparison to Wal-Mart, it is significant for OneWorld and equates to several million dollars in sales daily. The sales order pick slips needed to be printed in three different locations (the counter, the warehouse, and accounting). OneWorld has absolutely no functionality to automate such a printing requirement. However, OneWorld does work with a series of third-party printing options. Company C chose FormScape.

FormScape is a printing solution that has the ability to read the PDF format and redirect the print solution accordingly. When Company C tested this solution, they quickly identified the probable failure to read and redistribute the print quickly enough. Company C's 10,000 sales per day averaged more than 1,200 sales per hour, with some peak sales hours reaching 3,000 orders. The print solution simply couldn't support the number of orders coming in at any one time. Fortunately, FormScape also supports ASCII format, and in particular, it runs this format substantially faster than the PDF format.

The volume of sales orders forced Company C to re-evaluate their printing solution. Could OneWorld print ASCII instead of PDF? Yes, for the UNIX platform, there was a special script developed to change PDF to ASCII. When evoked, it would initially create a PDF file and then generate an ASCII equivalent. Because of this capability within OneWorld, and with a minor modification of the script, a significant performance increase could be realized.

How Does It Work?   Most printing solutions like FormScape read the output and determine the printer or printers to submit to based on predesigned, configurable jobs. Company C was able to meet their printing requirements and have enough flexibility to allow future growth within the system. FormScape provides OneWorld with a virtual printer. In the UNIX script that converts the PDF to ASCII, Company C inserted a simple command to print to that virtual printer, as shown in Figure 12-13. This automated the printing policies required by Company C's business needs. In fact, this solution worked so well that Company C was also able to add their invoice procedures to the FormScape solution.

Bar Coding

Well, you might have guessed that an organization that has sales and warehouses would have bar coding requirements as part of their overall OneWorld solution. What

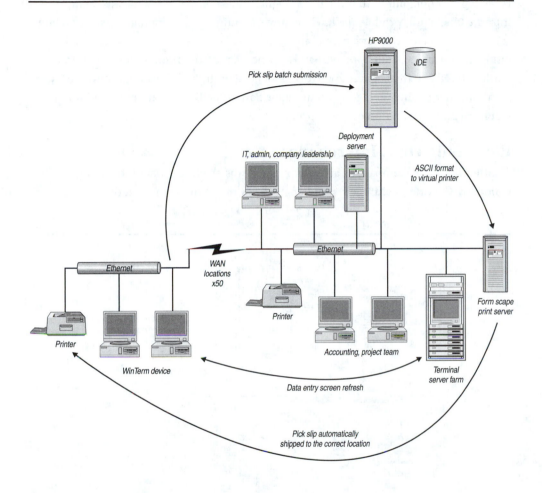

FIGURE 12-13. Printing process flow

should a warehouse do to fulfill this requirement within the OneWorld ERP solution?
Company C began working with an organization called Data Systems International
(DSI) during the B732.1 phase of their implementation to accommodate their bar coding
requirements. DSI wrote the bar coding solution in the B733 product. Some of that
work was pioneered at Company C. In essence, the bar coding solution provided by
DSI is relatively straightforward. It does use remote devices for data entry (both

receiving and outgoing). After the B733 upgrade, most of the DSI work was incorporated into the OneWorld product itself. Company C continued developing their bar coding solution, and a bar code server (refer to Figure 12-14) was added to the overall solution. Other than the fact that approximately 25 percent of the remote devices didn't work correctly in the beginning (errors associated with the hardware, not the software solution), bar coding worked without major flaws. The DSI solution allowed for receiving and distribution of inventory.

Electronic Data Interchange

Another initiative Company C actively pursued was electronic data interchange (EDI). Company C worked with their suppliers to allow direct invoicing and ordering of

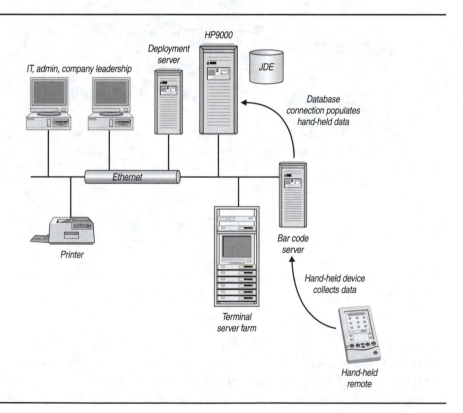

FIGURE 12-14. Bar coding process flow

products. This process was arranged using existing OneWorld functionality for EDI (system code 47) with Harbinger's EDI software. Although this effort did bring out a series of issues, the overall process worked with some diligence on the part of the organization. Company C installed EDI servers and automated much of the overall process by using scripted NT commands. The EDI functionality of OneWorld and Harbinger was exhaustively tested until it adequately performed as required to meet the business needs. The basic work flow of an EDI transaction can be seen in Figure 12-15.

Half the Company Goes Live

Although Company C continued testing functionality, performance, and scalability, they went live with half their organization in the third quarter of 1999. The modules included sales, inventory, and distribution. At this point, the company's future rested on the OneWorld product. No significant issues were raised and both stress and

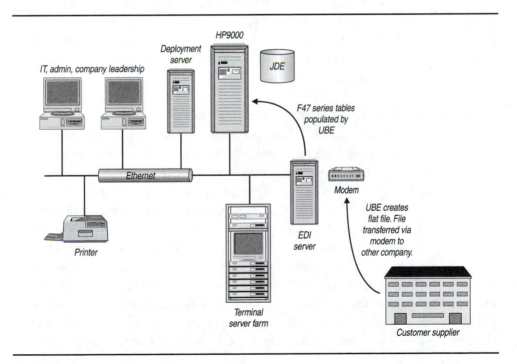

FIGURE 12-15. EDI work flow

performance testing continued. With half the company live on a day-to-day basis and the other half of the organization's go-live pending, Company C began stress-testing the system with more than 500 people on the system and 3,000 sales orders produced per hour. This tested both the hardware's ability to maintain speed and reliability and all of the software's various solutions.

When repeatedly tested, neither the hardware nor the software could maintain the performance required of the production system. Let's take a quick look at the hardware in use. The enterprise server was an HP9000, now supporting ten 240MHz processors and 8GB of RAM. The deployment server was a quad 450MHz processor with 2GB of RAM and 56GB of available hard drive. The basic terminal server was a quad 550MHz processor with 2GB of RAM and 27GB hard drive. It looked grim for Company C.

During high peak testing, a pick slip could take as much as one and a half hours to print. There were times when processes on the server itself would run completely out of control and remain out of control until forcibly ended. Approximately two times a week, a process would corrupt the TAM files on the enterprise server, requiring a restore of all the associated files. When added to other problems with enterprise server processing that could take an estimated 62 hours a day (if there were that many hours in a day)—printing issues, EDI, bar coding, and platform-related issues—Company C was in a serious situation.

OneWorld Optimization Saves the Day

Many of the problems associated with the performance issues seen by Company C ended up being effectively solved by optimizing the OneWorld product to perform the work required by the business and getting the required developmental support of J.D. Edwards itself. When Company C began optimizing the product, the speed that pick slips ran increased by three times. Using optimization techniques of both the product and its process flow, Company C was able to decrease the end-of-day processing requirements to about seven hours. J.D. Edwards personnel assisted by providing a couple of one-off software modifications to enhance the overall OneWorld product. These one-off software modifications were planned for future releases of OneWorld itself. Because of Company C's willingness to act as a beta site for the modifications, the business need, and the cooperation between the two companies, these changes were made available to Company C before they were released in a general availability release.

While optimizing the various operating systems and hardware, Company C came to the realization that optimizing HP_UX for an enterprise server is a very difficult task. This is related to the two applications running on the OS itself. Oracle, while liking RAM, does not require a huge amount of processor time. Because of this, the time hack associated with an Oracle database server similar to the one Company C used could have been as low as three. OneWorld, on the other hand, likes both RAM and processor. If you are using a lot of interactive application logic on the enterprise server, OneWorld would optimally like a processor time hack around 17 or 18. Because the two software requirements are diametrically opposed on this one system variable, most companies will find they have to configure their systems somewhere in between the two. Because of this, the server performs neither of the jobs optimally. Most companies are able to more than adequately get by with what they have. However, if they get to a point of growth where they are trying to optimize their systems for the maximum use, they may find they have problems reconciling these two requirements.

The Rest of the Organization Goes Live

With the optimizations in place, with the code installed and tested, with the hardware in place and the software positioned to take maximum advantage of the overall architectural configurations, Company C took the remaining half of the company live on sales, inventory, and distribution. There were a series of issues almost immediately realized due to their hardware. The entire system had to be shut down some days, but the problem was eventually identified as a hardware issue. Once HP became involved, they were able to replace the defective parts quickly and get Company C back on the road to success.

Where Are They Now?

Company C continues to grow. They have recently added another HP9000 server to their system to allow them to physically separate the database from the OneWorld application server. They are looking at upgrading from B733 to B733.2 and are aggressively pursuing various options within the OneWorld arena. Through their implementation, they have changed their architecture multiple times (refer to Figure 12-16) with relative ease, taking advantage of emerging technologies as they became available through the power of ActivEra. Theirs is definitely a story of success.

Inside and Out

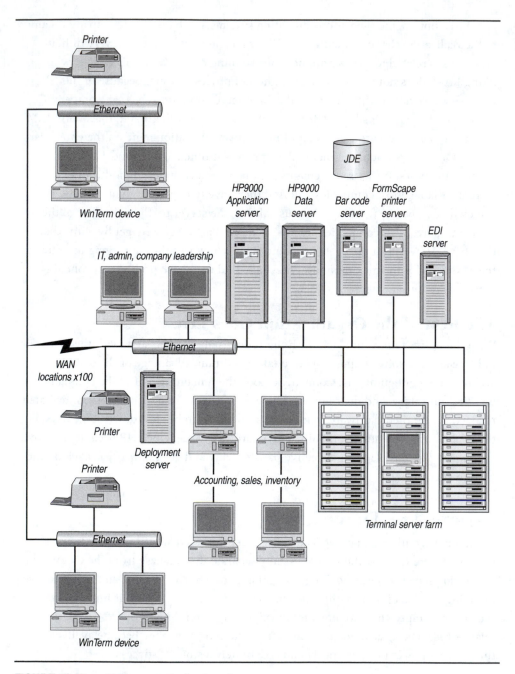

FIGURE 12-16.   Company C's final architecture

Summary

In the case studies presented in this chapter, different architectural designs, modifications, and options were presented. These do not encompass the whole range of possible architectural possibilities or the only ways to meet the various business requirements illustrated. Still, this chapter provided you and your organization with some insight into the power and flexibility of the OneWorld product. We showed how you can meet your own business needs through the use of OneWorld technology activators in their ActivEra offering. As for OneWorld, it will quickly prove one of the most versatile products on the market.

PART II

System Administration and Troubleshooting

CHAPTER 13

OneWorld Integrated Security

anagers and implementers of OneWorld need to feel confident about the security of their new ERP package. This chapter describes how to ensure your company's data is protected from intentional and unintentional damage. We will cover the following:

- Menus

- Users and groups

- OneWorld application security

- Integrated security

- License security

Menus: The Doorways to OneWorld

Menus are entry points for users to the OneWorld suite of applications. Because they are gatekeepers, they have an integral part to play in OneWorld security and in how you customize the product to maximize user productivity.

OneWorld Menus Defined

Menus can point to interactive applications, batch applications, other OneWorld menus, WorldVision links, MS Windows applications, and Web subheadings. Interactive applications are OneWorld programs that use an interface to directly interact with users for collecting and manipulating data—for example, the P01012 application (Work with Addresses). Batch applications are UBEs that run without continued interaction from users. Once a UBE is launched, no further interaction takes place between users and the application itself. (By the way, there are over 2,100 UBEs with over 5,000 total versions.) OneWorld menus can also contain other OneWorld menus linking the user to even more menu options. If you are in a coexistence mode and have WorldVision, you can link WorldVision applications into OneWorld. MS Windows applications, including Word, Excel, and PowerPoint, can be launched from the OneWorld explorer. Finally, Web subheadings (a text line used to describe the applications listed underneath) are visible only when you choose the Web view for OneWorld Explorer. They act as titles to group various applications.

Menus Mean Different Things to Different People

Most OneWorld users rarely even know that they are using a menu. They simply understand that they double-click on an icon and an application starts up. When they get through with that application, they might navigate through the OneWorld screens and double-click on the next application that they need to work with. They usually don't think about the fact that menus completely control what they can run.

To the application leads, menus are a method of tightly controlling how work flows for their divisions. If all of the applications that their people need to use are easily accessible and centrally located, it's easier to accomplish day-to-day activities. Most of the applications that a user requires to perform any given job are centrally located.

A department manager or project lead (and CFOs, CIOs, and CEOs) may not even know what a menu is—or care—for that matter. They are vaguely aware of that OneWorld thingy that their business depends on and is costing an arm and a leg. Finally, for systems administrators, menus are something that can be used to facilitate customer work flow and enable users to access applications within OneWorld. From systems administrators' viewpoint, menus have to be maintained and can provide security to the lawless OneWorld user/hacker—And let's face it, all users are hackers; some are just better than others.

For the Techies

The following four tables are associated with menus:

- **F0082 Menu Master file**   Contains the menu name, the system code, and the level of display.

- **F00821 Menu Selections file**   Contains the menu name, associated menus or applications, and associated versions.

- **F0083 Menu Text Override file**   Contains the menu name, the selection number, and what the override text should be.

- **F0084 Menu Path file**   Contains the menu name, the selection number, and where to find the associated icon.

Troubleshooting

Menus and Security

Menus can be more than mere access points into applications in the OneWorld ERP solution. An administrator can secure menus (and we highly recommend it) in such a way that very few users are able to modify them. They are powerful tools that enable the OneWorld physical environment to be customized. However, menus can cause harm if not properly controlled.

Because of the menus' ability to launch Windows applications and WorldVision in addition to OneWorld applications, you could, if you chose, make OneWorld the single desktop application by directly adding other Windows applications, such as MS Word, Excel, and Project, to the OneWorld Explorer. These applications can be launched from the OneWorld Explorer rather than from the Start button or the Office Shortcut Bar.

Menus enhance security by providing menu filtering. Before menu selections are displayed, they automatically undergo a filtering process. Menus are be filtered based on both country code and security. If a menu selection is defined for a specific country (for example, Canada), a user outside of Canada won't see that menu selection. If you apply application security to a specific user for an application on the menu, the user does not see that menu selection. You cannot lock users out of menus themselves, but still they play an important roll in OneWorld system security.

How Menus Work

Menus provide the user with the ability to launch various applications using both OneWorld technologies and basic command-line capabilities. When you launch a OneWorld application (either interactive or batch), OneWorld looks the program up in the object librarian (described in Chapter 9) and uses the appropriate programs (either DLLs or EXEs) to run the application. These applications run in windows separate from the OneWorld Explorer, but the Explorer is aware of them. Users quickly learn that when they try to close the Explorer with an application still open, they receive an error message indicating that all applications must be closed prior to exiting OneWorld.

For non-OneWorld applications, the exact path to the executable must be provided to launch the application. If it is a program that can be launched using a Windows shortcut, odds are it can be launched using the OneWorld Explorer. Later in this chapter, we will see how menus can be integrated into your overall OneWorld enterprise security plan.

Menus: Adding and Customizing

The four menu tables mentioned earlier reside in the Control Tables data source. As such, they are unique to most environments. Menus are maintained using the Menu Design application P0082, which can be accessed through the following:

- Systems Administrator menu GH9011

- OneWorld Dialogs application P0085

- Cross Application Development Tools menu GH902

Menu Naming Conventions

Similar to all of the objects within OneWorld, names of menus should follow naming conventions. All menus start with the letter "G." "Why 'G,'" you ask? Well, we've never really gotten a good explanation for this, but we can give you a reason that is as likely as not.

In earlier versions of the World product both 'A' and 'M' were used for menus in different releases. When the A7 series came along, they needed a new menu identifier that was unique. After thinking about it, they came up with 'G' which is also the seventh letter of the alphabet. Seventh letter, seventh major release level. What do you think? Well, true or not, all menus start (by convention) with the letter 'G.'

Following this letter, the next two (or sometimes three) characters represent the system code. For example, the Address Book menu is "G01," starting with the letter "G" and followed by "01," the system code assigned to the address book. The next character is for the display level or skill level, and the remaining characters, if there are any, are used to further identify the menu, making the name unique. We often refer to menus such as "GH961" or "GH9011," with the system codes of "H96" and "H90," respectively. You can see how the remaining characters further differentiate the menu name.

If your company is planning on adding custom menus, you should try to use the system codes 55 through 59. These system codes are reserved for customer use, and J.D. Edwards guarantees not to use them, ensuring they are maintained during upgrades or updates.

The Anatomy of the Menu Application

The menu design application is designed to easily allow you to modify or add menus and menu elements to OneWorld. Before you get to those type modifications, however, let's look at some of the information in this first form.

Menu Select Form (W0082B)   The Menu Select form (see Figure 13-1) is the first entry point when using the Menu Design application; on this form, you can find, add, and ultimately access any menu defined to your specific OneWorld environment. The form contains information including menu identification, menu title, system code, level of detail, and language. Additionally, using the exit bar or menu options, you can view F0082, (Menu Header detail) or Menu Print UBE.

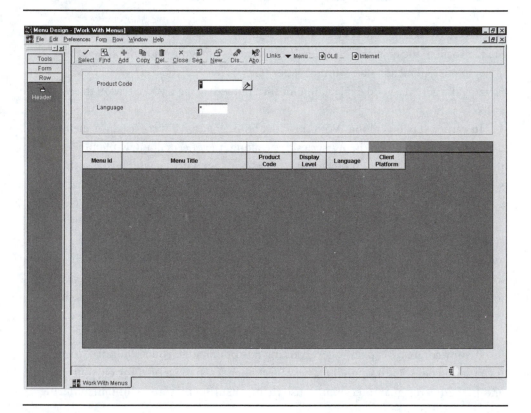

FIGURE 13-1.   Work With Menus screen

NOTE

If your OCM is set to access the menu tables locally and data replication is not turned on, you will be doing all of your work on your local database, not to the centrally maintained tables in the Control Tables data source. If you want to modify the master tables, you should either override your own OCM or log on to an environment set up for this purpose. Contact OneWorld OCM administrator or security officer to access the OCM application.

Menu Header Revisions Form (W0082M)   Information in the W0082M form (see Figure 13-2) includes the menu header information, such as the menu identification, menu title, product code, menu classification, level of display, advanced_technical operations and setup menus. This form also has an associated Form menu (which is also in the exit bar) with options including Selections (which automatically takes you to the Work With Menu Selections form) and Titles Override (used for entering menu titles for multiple languages). In this form, you can add or modify the previously mentioned menu header information.

As mentioned earlier, menu identification should follow the OneWorld standard naming conventions and must be unique. The menu description is displayed on the OneWorld Explorer tab. Whatever you enter for this description is displayed to anyone who can access the menu.

You can choose several different levels of detail; however, this has no bearing on who can access the menu or what they will see. This is a holdover from the World product. The levels include display all, daily operations, periodic operations, adv/tech operations, setup operations, programmers, sr. programmers, in development, major product directories, product groups, and display—no changes allowed. Regardless of what you put in this field, your menus will look the same, can be accessed the same—by the same people—and will contain the same options.

After a menu header is created, they are used to access various OneWorld and external applications. In addition, when you set up a menu header, a Fast Path is automatically added to that environment's control tables, which enables you to quickly access your new menu.

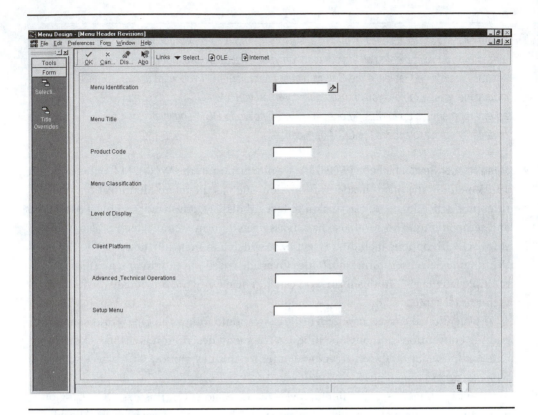

FIGURE 13-2. Menu Header Revisions form

An Example

To illustrate the mechanisms behind menus, start OneWorld and click View | User Options | Menu Design (refer to Figure 13-3). If a security message is displayed, your security manager is doing his or her job; if not, either you are supposed to have access, or security isn't fully set up.

On the Work With Menus form, click the Add button and the Menu Header form launches. Enter the following information:

1. **G550199** (Company specific address book menu)

2. **Test Menu**

3. **Daily** and then click OK.

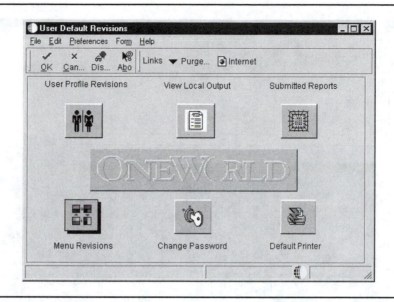

FIGURE 13-3.   Menu Design application

N O T E

If you want to add menus to the Advanced and Setup fields of the custom menu, do so before clicking OK. These defined menus will always be at the bottom of normally defined applications and menus (that is, if you add 100 items to the menu, these defined menus come in as 101 and 102, respectively).

After clicking OK on the Menu Header Revisions form (W0082M), the Menu Select form (W0082B) is displayed. You should enter the name of your newly defined menu (G550199) in the QBE (Query by Example) field Menu Identification and click Find. Your new menu header will appear in the grid at the bottom of the form as shown in Figure 13-4.

When you select the new menu header, you launch the Work With Menu Selections form (W0082L). This form shows every object (interactive application, batch application, menu, or third-party product) listed on this menu. Notice that no

Troubleshooting

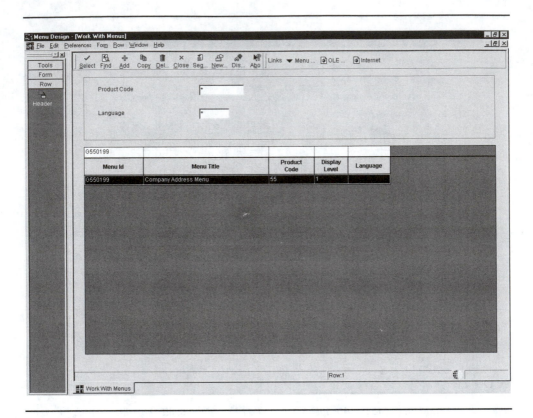

FIGURE 13-4.   Work With Menus screen

associated objects are displayed. To add objects, click the Add button, which launches the Menu Selection Revisions form (W0082A) shown in Figure 13-5.

As you can see in Figure 13-5, several fields must be filled out to ensure that the object is properly defined. At the bottom of this form, you indicate what type of object you are defining. You can also choose the icon you want associated with this menu item.

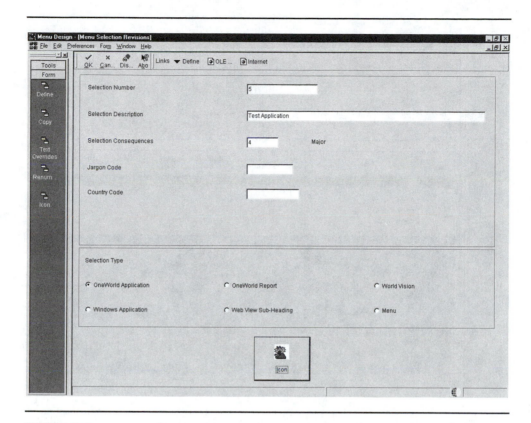

FIGURE 13-5. Menu Selection Revisions form

For a complete list of all of the fields within the various menu options, refer to Table 13-1. As part of our example, you might want to add at least one selection from each of the menu options (refer to Figure 13-6). For more information regarding the type of data in each of the forms associated with the P0082 Menu application, review Table 13-1.

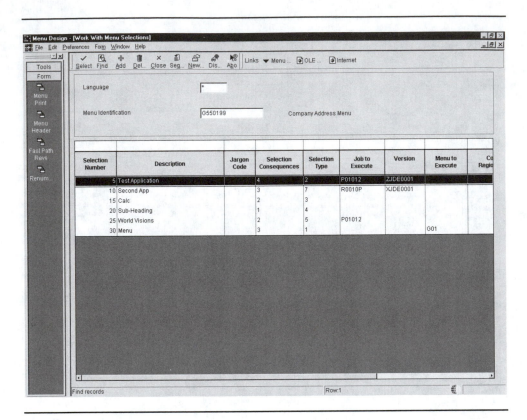

FIGURE 13-6. A complete menu

NOTE

A little-known and totally undocumented aspect of the OneWorld product links users with menus. When you add a new user using the P0082 application, an entry is actually added to the F0084 table. The record holds each user's name with a selection number of 0 and a path type of active menu. This table is environment specific where users are system wide; this means that this link is good only in the environment it is added into. As far as we can tell, however, the record really isn't needed or used in OneWorld.

Form	Title	Fields	Form Escapes
W0082A	Menu Selection Revisions	Selection Number Selection Description Selection Consequences Jargon Code Country Code OneWorld Application Windows Application OneWorld Report Web View Sub-Heading WorldVision Menu Icon	Define Copy Text Overrides Renumber Icon
W0082B	Work With Menus	Product Code Language Menu ID Menu Title System Code Display Level	Header Menu Print
W0082C	OneWorld Report	Batch Application Option Code Version	Report Version
W0082D	WorldVision	Fast Path Run Minimized	
W0082F	Windows Application	Command Line Working Directory Run Minimized	Browse
W0082G	OneWorld Application	Object Name Form Name Option Code Version Application Type	Application Version
W0082H	Menu Execution	Menu to Execute	

TABLE 13-1. P0082 Menu Form Description

Troubleshooting

Form	Title	Fields	Form Escapes
W0082M	Menu Header Revisions	Menu Identification Menu Title Product Code Menu Classification Level of Display Advanced_Tech Operations	Selections Title Overrides
W0082L	Work with Menu Selections	Language Menu Identification Selection Number Description Jargon Code Selection Consequences Selection Type Job to Execute Version Menu to Execute Country Region Code Language Menu ID	Menu Print Menu Header Fast Path Rev. Renumber

TABLE 13-1.   P0082 Menu Form Description *(continued)*

Users and Groups

If you have just installed the OneWorld system without adding security, your users
have total access. It is up to you as a system administrator to decide how you want to
limit access to the system. This leaves you in an interesting dilemma. You will probably
ask yourself: "What kind of security do I need? What types of security are built into
OneWorld? Do I need to worry about setting up security on the database itself?" In this
section, we cover essential information on how to secure your OneWorld system,
including how to define, maintain, manage, and secure your users and groups.

Defining Users/Groups

In order to secure a system from users, users must be defined in the system. When OneWorld is set up out of the box, the only users that are defined are the users shipped by J.D. Edwards. These users usually are JDE, APPLEAD, CNCADMIN, DEVUSER, and PRODUSER. These users are shipped to provide examples of how you should set up your users. The JDE user is an all-around user profile that is used during the installation process. The APPLEAD user is the manager or supervisor who is responsible for the personnel using the various OneWorld modules. The CNCADMIN user is a recommended user ID for your system administrator. DEVUSER is an example of a development user profile. PRODUSER is an example of a production user on your system. The real benefit to these example users are that they show you how J.D. Edwards recommends you assign environments to your user profiles, which we will cover later in this chapter. Until the installation is complete, you must log on as the JDE user.

To add user profiles, log on to a client workstation into any environment. The table that holds your OneWorld user profiles (F0092, the Library Lists—User table) is called a "system table," which means that no matter what client machine you log on to (in any environment), you will be hitting the same table. Log on to the workstation as JDE. Type **GH9011** into the Fast Path (this is located at the top-right side of your screen). The System Administration Tools menu appears on the right side of the OneWorld Explorer. This menu contains many useful applications that assist an administrator in maintaining a OneWorld system. Double-click on the User Profile application P0092. The Work With User Profiles screen, shown in Figure 13-7, is the main screen you use when adding users and groups. Click Find, and all of the users and groups that are shipped with the system are displayed.

You can add and delete users, assign environments to them, and set up security from this screen. It enables you to easily manage your users and security from one location. To add a new user to your system, click the Add button on the Work With

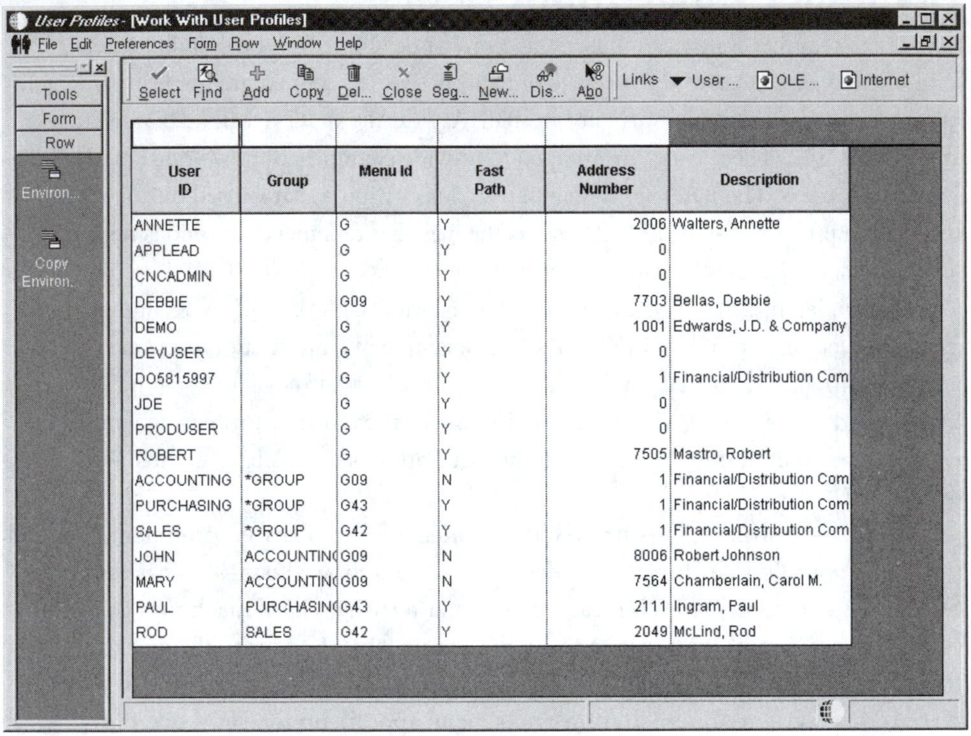

User ID	Group	Menu Id	Fast Path	Address Number	Description
ANNETTE		G	Y	2006	Walters, Annette
APPLEAD		G	Y	0	
CNCADMIN		G	Y	0	
DEBBIE		G09	Y	7703	Bellas, Debbie
DEMO		G	Y	1001	Edwards, J.D. & Company
DEVUSER		G	Y	0	
DO5815997		G	Y	1	Financial/Distribution Com
JDE		G	Y	0	
PRODUSER		G	Y	0	
ROBERT		G	Y	7505	Mastro, Robert
ACCOUNTING	*GROUP	G09	N	1	Financial/Distribution Com
PURCHASING	*GROUP	G43	Y	1	Financial/Distribution Com
SALES	*GROUP	G42	Y	1	Financial/Distribution Com
JOHN	ACCOUNTING	G09	N	8006	Robert Johnson
MARY	ACCOUNTING	G09	N	7564	Chamberlain, Carol M.
PAUL	PURCHASING	G43	Y	2111	Ingram, Paul
ROD	SALES	G42	Y	2049	McLind, Rod

FIGURE 13-7. P0092 application

User Profiles. The User Profile Revisions screen, which is shown in Figure 13-8, contains the following fields:

User ID	Enter the name of the user that you are adding. Until you set up sign-on security (which is covered later in this chapter), this user has to exist in your database. This feature is an administrator's friend because it reduces your workload and is a required part of securing any ERP system.
User Class/Group	An optional field where you can enter the group your OneWorld user belongs to. These groups allow users to inherit their settings, such as assigned environments, similar to groups in Windows NT systems. When you are adding a group, you need *GROUP in this field. Assigning a group greatly reduces your security setup.
Allow Fast Path (Y/N)	This is a field in which you enter Y or N, which will either allow users to use the Fast Path, which we have consistently referred to in this book and is in greater detail in Chapter 3, or locks them out of this functionality. If this is set to a N then your user will not see the Fast Path field.
Address Number	A number that is assigned when you add users, customers, or suppliers into the Address Book program. Workflow uses this information for OneWorld messaging. We recommend that you set your users up in the address book prior to setting up actual users and groups. Don't assign a valid address number to a group.
Menu Identification (also know as initial menu)	The menu that your user sees on the left side of OneWorld Explorer.
Default Icon File	A path field that points to a directory where applications reside. This field is used, for example, when you are calling WorldVision programs from OneWorld.
Language	Specifies the language that the user wants displayed when he or she logs on to the system. The default is the domestic language (for example, English).
Date Format	Enables a user to specify a date format. If this field is left blank, the date format defaults from the computer's regional settings in the Control Panel.
Date Separator Character	Specifies the date separator. If this field is left blank, the system value is used.
Decimal Format Character	Specifies the character that is used as a decimal separator.
Localization Country Code	Contains a country code that enables OneWorld to recognize localization changes.
View Style Type	Controls how the user sees the program icons when logging into OneWorld, enabling the system to be personalized. You can specify small icons, large icons, details, or a Web view of the programs.

Troubleshooting

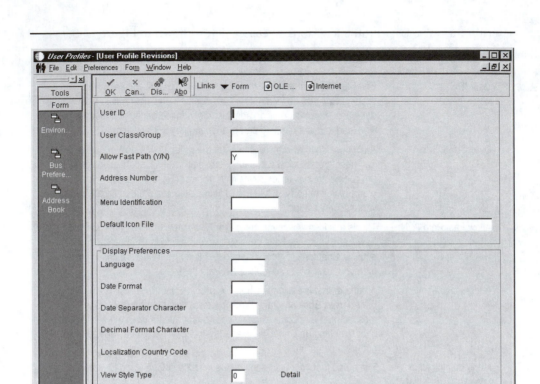

FIGURE 13-8. User Profiles application

After you have filled in the fields on the User Profile Revisions screen, you are still not finished adding your users. As you see in Figure 13-8, you have several exits to other programs that enable you to configure user profiles just the way you want them to be. The Environment exit allows you to assign environments to your users. This means that when your users sign on to the system, they see only the environments that you assign them. So if you want Frank in accounting to see the production environment, you can specify this in the Environment exit. You can also assign environments to groups, so when a user is assigned to a group, he or she inherits the rights to these environments and can log on to them. This is the best method of setting up environmental access because it requires the least amount of work for the systems administrator. You set up one environment for the group and simply make exceptions beyond that.

You can assign environments either through the Work With User Profiles screen or the User Profile Revisions screen (both shown earlier). After you choose the Environments exit, you are taken into the User Environments Revision screen (see Figure 13-9) where you can add environments on the grid. You can also determine in what order the environments are presented to users when they log on to the system by setting the Display Sequence Number. Setting this option is not required, but it can make users' lives easier by listing the most commonly used environments first. The process is virtually the same for assigning environments for users and groups. The only difference is that when assigning environments to groups, you have the ability to set up an environment list once for multiple users. You then set up the user profile to be associated with that group. In the User Profile Revisions screen, you enter the name of the group (for example, FINANCE) in the User Class/Group field. The user then inherits the environments that you assigned to the group.

NOTE

Remember that user profiles are system variables, but that the address book is environmental information. This can make a significant difference if your users have different address book numbers in different environments. In this case, user workflow won't work correctly, and you might see errors when you submit UBEs to the server. These errors won't stop the UBE process; however, they occasionally cause questions and concerns on the part of users. Because we usually recommend that environments be updated regularly, most organizations don't have this particular issue.

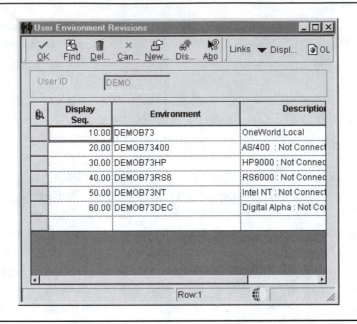

FIGURE 13-9.　User Environment list

Dueling Environments

You may be wondering which set of environments a user sees if you have environments assigned to both the user and to the group. This depends on how the application looks for environments when you initially log on to OneWorld. OneWorld determines environments by using a search hierarchy. The search hierarchy for environments is users and then groups. As soon as the system receives a return on this search, it quits looking. So if environments are listed for the user and other ones are listed for the group, the user gets the ones listed for their specific ID.

The Business Preferences screen contains three options: Industry Code, Business Partner Code, and Customer Code. These options enable the user to define codes that trigger specific functionality.

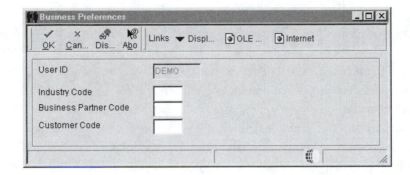

Another option in the User Profile Revisions screen is the Address Book exit, which accesses the Address Book screen. This screen enables you to add address book entries in the Address Book program. On the User Profile Revisions screen, an Address Number field is used by workflow to send messages to users informing them of the status of jobs.

When you are finished adding your user in the User Profile Revisions screen, click OK. This takes you back to the Work With User Profiles screen. Click Find, and your new user will be listed in the grid. This screen has several Form and Row exits that assist you in administering the OneWorld system. The options available under the Row exit are discussed in the next section.

The Real Meat

Let's start by describing what is under the row exit. Under the Row exit on the Work With User Profiles screen are the Environments and Copy Environments options. The Environments option is the same as the one described previously on the User Profile Revisions screen (refer to the section "Be Advised," earlier in this chapter). The Copy Environments option is a handy tool that enables you to copy environments that have been assigned to one user to another user or group. In the Work With User Profiles screen, select the user whose environment list you wish to copy and then click Copy Environment. The Copy Environment screen is launched, and it enables you to specify a user or group you wish to copy the environment to. The name you enter is assigned all of the environments listed in the grid form on the user profile application, as shown in Figure 13-10. If that user already has environments assigned that you forgot about, you will receive a warning message telling you that the user already has environments assigned to it. You can then click OK to replace the environments with the ones you are copying, or you can click Cancel and check to see if you really want to overwrite those environments. This will ensure that you don't accidentally overwrite the environment selections already available to a user or group.

Troubleshooting

Law of the West

Creating Custom Library Lists

Users are able to access various environments based on entries in the F0093 table. You can set up special tables that quickly and efficiently limit user access. This oftentimes proves beneficial when you are trying to get everyone into a single environment for testing purposes (for example, you want everyone in the test environment and no one in production). The F0093 table can be put in place quickly using the R98403 UBE or the object librarian table copy utility (Object Management Workshop in Xe). The steps required to use a custom F0093 are as follows:

1. Using the R98403 (Environment Database Creation UBE), copy the F0093 table from the System – B733 OneWorld data source to your OneWorld Local – XXXB733 OneWorld data source (where *XXX* represents a path code on the administrator's machine).

2. Using MS Access, open the JDEB7.MDB database corresponding to the OneWorld data source. This database is located in *x*:\b7\xxxb733 (where *x* represents the drive OneWorld is installed on and *xxx* is path code specific).

3. Make a copy of the F0093 table (we usually name it F0093_org).

4. Using MS Access, open the F0093 and modify it appropriately. In the case of testing above, you would limit the entries to groups only and a single environment for each. This will ensure that users logging in will only have the single option listed.

5. Using the R98403, copy the F0093 table from your OneWorld Local – XXXB733 OneWorld data source (use the same data source as the first step above) to the System – B733 data source.

6. Conduct the testing. When completed, use MS Access to rename the F0093 located in the local JDEB7.MDB database to F0093_test. Rename the F0093_org to F0093 and repeat the step above replacing the system table. This will grant all users their original environmental options.

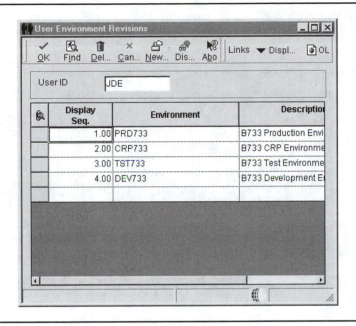

FIGURE 13-10. User Environment Revisions screen

Under the Form exit are three options: User Overrides, Sign On Security, and Security Workbench. User Overrides call the User Overrides program P98950. This program can also be found on the Systems Administration Tools menu GH9011. It enables an administrator to monitor the overrides that end users have set up on the system. The administrator can also copy and delete overrides. This means if a user has set up a number of helpful overrides, your other users do not have to go through the pain of setting them up. You can just copy the override and set the user to *PUBLIC, which means that every user sees this override when using the system. Refer to Figure 13-11 for an example of the User Profiles application.

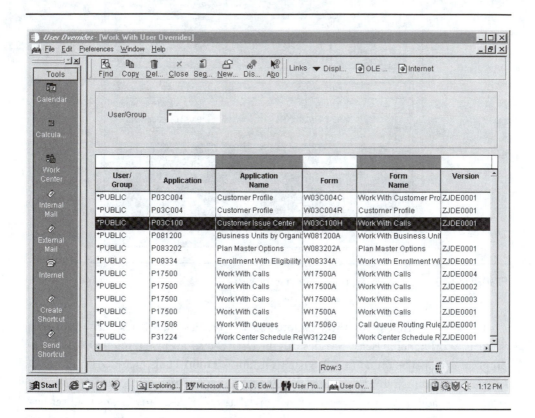

FIGURE 13-11. User Overrides screen

After you click the Copy button, you will see a screen similar to Figure 13-12.

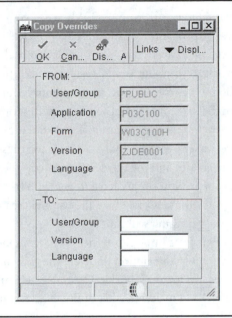

FIGURE 13-12. Copying User Overrides

User Override Considerations

Sometimes a User Overrides table can cause you problems. The F98950 table is contained in the Central Objects data source. When a service pack is applied, this table has been known to cause problems. When these records are created, they are created in a certain manner, and this manner changes from service pack to service pack. So when you apply a service pack to your OneWorld system, five out of a hundred users may start complaining about OneWorld applications memory violations. But when you sign in as the user on the same machine, the program functions correctly. The reason some users are experiencing these program memory violations is because of the HC (hypertext control) user overrides that are set up for these users. (For more information on user overrides and the types represented, refer to Chapter 16.)

To correct this problem, you simply have to get rid of the records that are causing the memory violations for those users. Once the users recreate the overrides on the new service pack level, everything will function correctly.

There are two options for getting rid of these records. One is to use the User Overrides application. To use this option to delete these records, run application P98950, User Overrides, on menu GH9011. Then place **HC** in the QBE (Query by Example) line and click Find to access a list of the user override records that are causing problems. Select each of these records and click Delete. If you have a large number of these records, there is a more efficient option for deleting these records.

An easier way to delete these records is through an SQL statement directly against the F98950 table. Before you perform this statement, the authors recommend that you back up the table . Then run a SELECT statement before you run a DELETE statement. Here are the SQL statements that you should run:

Select * from CRPB733.F98950 where UOUOTY = 'HC';

This statement shows you the records that you are going to delete; note the number of records returned. You should see the exact same number of records affected by the following DELETE statement. Run the DELETE statement using the following SQL statement:

Delete CRPB733.F98950 where UOUOTY = 'HC'; Commit;

The COMMIT statement is necessary only if you are running Oracle. After you have deleted the records, you can have your users log on and test the application again. As stated previously, you will encounter this problem most likely when you apply a service pack. However, on some occasions, some of these records get corrupted and cause problems. When this is the case, one user will experience problems with a specific application, but you can log on as another user, and everything works fine. If this is the problem that you face, we recommend backing up the table and deleting all the overrides for that user for that specific application.

Sign-on Security

The next option under the Form exit on the Work With User Profiles screen is the Sign On Security exit. This option calls the program P98OWSEC, User Security, which is also found on the Security Maintenance menu GH9052. The program P98OWSEC, User Security, enables you to set up your OneWorld users to pass a database user and password under the covers. This means that you do not have to maintain two different users in two different systems (the database and the OneWorld system tables). It also means that your users won't know what the system user is so that they cannot perform manual SQL statements against your database. A user who can manually manipulate your database through SQL statements can cause all sorts of damage to the system and frustration for you and the end users. This situation can also cause severe business problems. The user who can perform SQL statements against the database can get into confidential files (for example, the payroll files) or can directly manipulate financial records.

Sign-on Security Concepts

With an understanding of the concepts behind sign-on security, setting it up will make much more sense. You should first understand that you will be setting up entries in a relational database table. This table contains your OneWorld and database users and encrypted OneWorld and database passwords. This system table is read (but not by the client machines) when sign-on security is set up. The table (and in fact, the entire sign-on security process) is controlled by a kernel process on the enterprise server.

The sign-on security kernel polls the F98OWSEC table and controls sign-on security. It is important to note this because the client machines are not directly reading the F98OWSEC table. Instead, they are communicating with the server through JDENET to validate the users' OneWorld passwords and to obtain the system user and password that will be passed to the database. This means that most of the problems with sign-on security are database related or are caused by client machines communicating with the enterprise server. We explain how to set up a server as a security server and how client machines know which server is their security server later in this chapter.

To populate the F98OWSEC table, use the P98OWSEC program on the Security Maintenance menu GH9052. Double-clicking on this program takes you into the Work With User Security screen shown in Figure 13-13. (A Form exit on the User Profiles program takes you to the same application.) The Work With User Security screen is where you set up and maintain your OneWorld passwords and where you specify what system

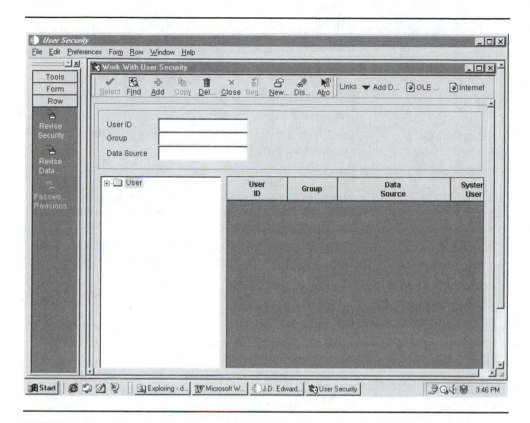

FIGURE 13-13. Work with User Security (P98OWSEC)

user ID is passed to the database. However, these database users need to be set up in your database by your database administrator. This program enables the OneWorld system administrator to specify different database users for different OneWorld data sources, or a single database user for all datasources.

The Work With User Security screen enables you to easily see what security has been set up for individual users or groups. It contains a data source field where you can specify a specific database user and password to be passed when a certain data source is used by that user or group. By working with your database administrator, you can secure your system so that your end users have only the access that they truly need and not the access that they think they need. How this all comes into play will become clearer after we go over adding and modifying security for users.

To set up a user through the User Security application, click Add on the Work With User Security screen. This takes you into the Security Revisions screen shown in Figure 13-14. The options on this screen are the following:

User ID	Enter a valid OneWorld user, or if you are revising a user's security, the username is displayed in this field.
User Class/Group	Specify a group. If your user is part of a group, he or she inherits the security setup of that group.
Data Source	Specify a data source so that the system user and password specified will be passed for this data source. For example, if the data source is Business Data—CRP, the system user is crpdta, and the password is crpjde, these users and password are passed every time this data source is used by the user specified in the User ID field.
System User	This is the database user that is passed to the database "under the covers." This user must exist in the database in order for sign-on security to function correctly.
System Password	The password that is passed to the database "under the covers." It must be a valid database password.
OneWorld Password	The password that the user enters during the OneWorld sign-on process. If you permit it, your users can change this password. This password is not related to the database user or password.
Allowed Password Attempts	This setting is similar to a feature in Windows NT. If this number of attempts to log on to the system for a user with the incorrect password is exceeded, the account is disabled.
Invalid Password Attempts	The number of attempts to log onto the system with an invalid password.
User Status	Use these radio buttons to enable or disable a user account. If an account is disabled, the user cannot log on to the system.
Password Change Frequency	Specifies, in days, how often a user must change his or her OneWorld password.
Security Changed	The number of times the password of that user has been changed. This field is blank when you add a user.

TIP

If records already exist for a user, OneWorld does not stop you from adding security revisions. This means that you can specify different users and passwords to be passed to the database for different data sources.

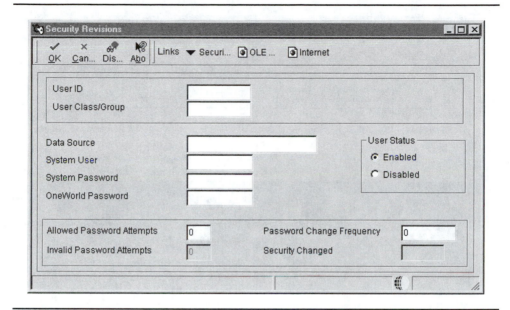

FIGURE 13-14.   Security Revisions form

A Form exit on the Security Revisions screen shows you the security history of a user (see Figure 13-15). It is basically an audit log that shows you the activity of a user's account. You can easily see when a user has changed his or her password and when a user's sign-on security profile was set up. The information on this screen is similar to the security logging in Windows NT.

If you cancel out of the Security History screen, you will be back at the Security Revisions screen. Click OK to finish setting up the security profile for your user or group. This takes you back to the Work With User Security screen. This screen contains several Form exits: Add Data Source, Revise All, Security History, and Required/Not Required. The Data Source exit takes you to the Data Source Revisions screen (described in Chapter 2). The Revise All exit enables you to change all of the users' settings. If you wish to enable *all* of your user accounts, you can do so, or if you want to change the password frequency or the incorrect log on attempts before disabling the accounts, you can do so from the Revise All screen.

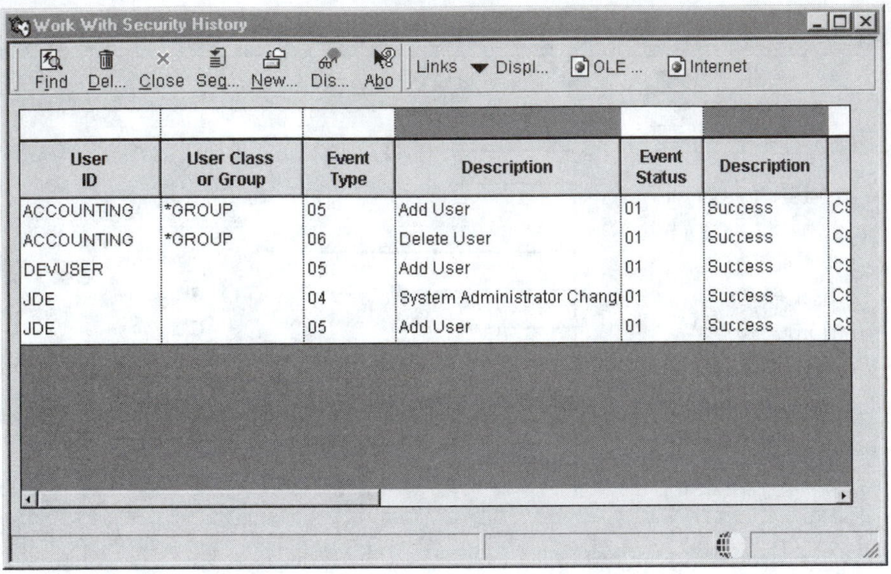

User ID	User Class or Group	Event Type	Description	Event Status	Description	
ACCOUNTING	*GROUP	05	Add User	01	Success	C$
ACCOUNTING	*GROUP	06	Delete User	01	Success	C$
DEVUSER		05	Add User	01	Success	C$
JDE		04	System Administrator Chang	01	Success	C$
JDE		05	Add User	01	Success	C$

FIGURE 13-15.   Working with Security History form

Security History is also available as a Form exit. The Security History screen shows you the changes that have been made to your sign-on security profiles, as described previously. The Required/Not Required option is important because it requires the user to connect to a security server and have his or her OneWorld password validated before the user is allowed to log on to the system. The way in which the system checks for whether sign-on security is required isn't all that complicated. When you choose the Required/Not Required option, it sets a flag under the RMRLS01 column in F00945, the Release Master file. When the client workstation logs in, it reads this flag even if sign-on security is not turned on in the client workstation's INI file. (We discuss these INI settings later in this chapter.)

Law of the West

Steps Prior to Forcing Sign-on Security

Do not set sign-on security to be required unless you are sure that sign-on security is configured correctly. If your security kernel does not come up correctly on your enterprise server, your users will not be able to log on to the system (including the system administrator's user account). What do you do now? Panic? All you need to do is remove the flag from the F00945 table that tells your OneWorld client workstations that sign-on security is required. In order to do this, you can use a SQL statement after first backing up the table. You should always pass a SELECT statement before an UPDATE or DELETE statement. The following are the SELECT and UPDATE statements that you should use:

Select * from sysb733.f00945 where RMRLS01 = 'SEC';

Once you have confirmed that the record returned is the one the you want to update, use the following SQL statement to make sign-on security not required:

Update sysb733.f00945 where RMRLS01 = 'SEC' set RMRLS01 = ' ';
Commit;

The COMMIT statement is necessary only if you are running Oracle. Once you have completed this step, you still need to turn off sign-on security in your client machines' INI file under the Security section. You can then log on to the system as a user that exists in the database and OneWorld. If you do not have a user that exists in both, you are prompted with database sign-on screens during the log-in process. Sign through these screens with a valid database user. This logs you on to OneWorld so you can troubleshoot sign-on security.

Other Application Options

Several other options are available under Row exit on the Work With User Security screen: Revise Security, Revise Data Source, and Password Revisions. These options may be grayed out when you initialize this form. You have to find user and data source security records before you can modify them. On the Revise Security screen, enter a user ID in the User field and click Find. You can then click the User Revisions option, which takes you to the Security Detail Revisions screen shown in Figure 13-16. The fields on this screen are as follows:

User ID	This field is grayed out and shows the name of the user whose sign-on security profile you are modifying.
User Status	This is the status of your user account. It is either enabled or disabled. This field is where you enable user accounts that have been disabled due to invalid sign-on attempts. The valid values are: 01—Enabled 02—Disabled
Password Change Frequency	This field specifies, in days, how often your OneWorld users have to change their passwords.
Allowed Password Attempts	The number of incorrect sign-on attempts that the system allows before disabling the user account.
Invalid Password Attempts	The number of invalid password attempts on the account.
Security Last Changed	The last date that the security was changed.
Change	The checkboxes in this field are grayed out and correspond to the previously listed fields.

The Data Source Revisions exit enables you to change the system user and passwords that are used for a specific data source. This option is grayed out unless you fill in the data source that has been set up for a sign-on security profile. You can also find records associated with a data source by filling in the name of the data source and clicking Find. This enables you to enter a new system user and password for use with this data source. For example, if you wanted database user TEST1 to be passed every time the Business Data–PROD data source was used, you enter **TEST1** and the appropriate password as the system user and password as shown next.

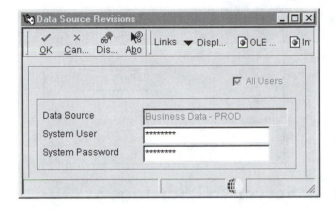

The Password Revisions exit is fairly self-explanatory. It enables you to change your OneWorld users' passwords. When users tell you that they changed their passwords and cannot remember them, you can reset them. This option is grayed out until you find a user that has been set up with sign-on security.

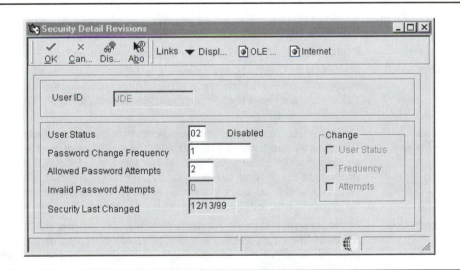

FIGURE 13-16. Security Detail Revisions form

Troubleshooting

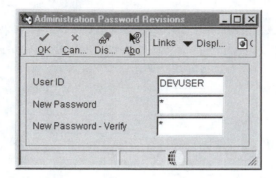

Enterprise Server INI Settings

Let's look at how sign-on security applies to your enterprise server. When working with sign-on security, you must remember that the work takes place on the enterprise server. In order to set up sign-on security on your enterprise server, open up the INI file on that enterprise server. The settings in the Security section of the INI file follow:

Security Server	The name of the server that handles your sign-on security.
User	A database user who is passed to the database for SELECT statements over the F98OWSEC table.
Password	A database password associated with the previously described user.
Data Source	The name of the OneWorld data source where the F98OWSEC table resides. This is usually the System—B733 data source. NOTE: This setting is case sensitive. It must match in case and spaces used the OneWorld data source in F98611 (the Data Source Master table).
Default Environment	This setting should equal the name of the environment that is associated with a path code where the specifications for the F98OWSEC table exist. These specifications are contained in the DDCLMN.DDB and XDB TAM files. Since F98OWSEC is a standard J.D. Edwards table, this setting can be almost any environment, as long as the associated path code exists on the enterprise server. It is important to note that the replication kernel and TP Monitor use this environment setting as well.
Security Mode	This setting controls whether or not standard logons (unified logons or both) are accepted by the system. A unified logon is where OneWorld validates the user and password using Windows NT account validation. All you have to do is set your users up in Windows NT. The accepted values are 0—Standard OneWorld logons only (the default) 1—Unified logon only 2—Both logon modes

Allowed Users	The user list/group for the authentication of OneWorld users using unified logon. By default, this setting is blank. If you choose to use unified logons, you can specify users or groups for logon. If you choose unified logons and leave this setting blank, all users who attempt to log on are validated by the unified logon server.
NumServer	The number of security servers that you have running in your system. The default is 1. If this value is higher than 1, the system attempts to authenticate users by sending a message to each security server in the order the servers appear until a server validates the user or no more security servers are listed.
History	This setting writes security access history to the F9312 table.

By filling in these INI settings and setting up your users' sign-on security profiles in the P98OWSEC program, you are securing the system from users who do not know what they are doing—and from users who do and are attempting to use the system in a malicious manner.

Setting up sign-on security should be done during the first part of the conference room pilot phase of your implementation. By performing sign-on security at this early phase, the system administrator and users are accustomed to regarding sign-on security as a part of the system. It also provides more time to test the system and ensure that no loopholes exist that someone can exploit.

T I P

Even if you choose not to implement sign-on security, do not comment out all of the Security section in the INI file. UBEs sometimes do not function correctly when this section is completed blocked out. The end users receive errors telling them that their jobs could not be run on the enterprise server. The log on the client workstation will also show an error stating that auto install of specs failed. When you check the log on the enterprise server, you will see that it is failing on an environment that is not even defined on your system. This is a hard-coded value that is used when the Security section is commented out. To correct this problem, uncomment everything in the Security section and leave the Security Server= value blank if you are not using sign-on security.

Client Workstation INI Settings

The INI file on the OneWorld client workstations contains a Security section; the settings are as follows:

SecurityServer	The name of the security server.
DataSource	The name of the OneWorld data source where the F98OWSEC table exists. This setting is case sensitive. It must match the entry in F98611, the Data Source Master table, in case and spaces used.
DefaultEnvironment	This setting should be a valid environment for that workstation.
RowSecurity	No_Default
UnifiedLogon	The TRUE or FALSE values for this setting specify whether or not a unified logon server will be used to authenticate logons. The default value is FALSE. It is also important to note that this is a hidden INI file setting, which means that you have to add it in order to use the unified logon functionality. Remember when adding settings to INI files that they are case sensitive.
Try_If_Unified_Failed	This setting tells OneWorld whether or not to use the standard logon process if the unified logon fails. The default is FALSE, which means in the case of a login failure, do not try to use the standard logon process. If this setting is set to TRUE, the standard logon process is used if the unified logon fails.

To secure a system, you must control the database users' privileges. This means that if you are using TEST as your database user for production, TEST does not need rights, at the database level, to the development environment's tables, including the Business Data tables and the Central Object tables.

Another option is to assign specific database users to certain groups with appropriate privileges. Your database administrator can then track these users through the database and ensure that they have only the necessary privileges. It also provides an audit trail to track which users are updating or deleting records. If you suspect users of tampering with the system, you can assign a specific database user to their profiles and track the tables that they access in the database. With this type of database security, your system will truly be secured. This ensures you won't be surprised by an end user publishing your payroll files on the Internet!

Troubleshooting

NOTE

OneWorld uses the F98OWSEC table to house user IDs, passwords, and system users. We highly recommend that you secure this table using the RDBMS so that only the appropriate system user can access the data. Although the passwords are encrypted, the IDs themselves are not. This situation provides a would-be hacker with half the code necessary to gain complete access to your system.

Security Workbench

Limiting the type of database IDs that your OneWorld users pass to the database should only be part of your security solution. Although it is true that when sign-on security is set up correctly, a user who is passed to the database does not have the privileges to perform SELECTs over the financial tables, for example, you should take every precaution to make sure your system is secure. If you limit the security solution to only sign-on security and the user passed to the database does not have the proper permissions to the tables, all sorts of errors will be displayed on users' screens and in the client workstation's logs. This means that you (as a system administrator) will be receiving calls from your end users saying that the system doesn't work! To avoid spending a lot of time explaining what applications the end users can and cannot run, you should probably set up application security. It will save you a lot of headaches.

You can set up application security by going to the Security Maintenance menu GH9052 where you can find the Security Workbench application P00950. This application enables you to set up a variety of different security options. From this application you can set up the following:

- Application security

- Action security

- Row security

- Column security

- Processing options security

- Tab security

- Exit security

- Exclusive application security

- External calls security

As you can see, this application can be a powerful tool in assisting you in securing your OneWorld system. The task for you, as a system administrator, is to use this tool for the good of your end users! Although your company may not need all of these different types of security, it is a good idea to be aware of the functionality that OneWorld offers. Although your business may not need some of these features today, they might tomorrow.

To start setting up application security, double-click on the Security Workbench program P00950. This takes you into the Work With User/Group Security screen. When you click Find, the types of security that are set up for each user or group are listed in the Security Type column in the grid as shown in Figure 13-17. The valid values for this field are:

- Action Security

- Column Security

- Application Security

- Row Security

- Processing Option Security

- Hyper Exit Security

- External Calls Security

- Tab Exit Security

- Exclusive Application Security

Not only can you see what type of security is set up for each user and group at a glance, but you can review the entries in detail by selecting the desired entry and clicking the Select button. This takes you into the appropriate screen, depending on the type of security set up for that user or group. For example, if the user you selected had row

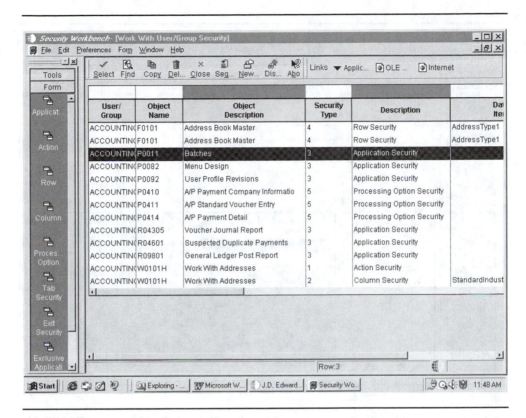

FIGURE 13-17. Work with User/Group Security screen

security set up, selecting the record takes you into the Row Security application, where you can modify the security profile. Just as you can copy environments and overrides, you can copy security profiles. You select the record or records that you wish to copy and click the Copy button. This launches the Work With Security Revisions screen where you can specify the user to whom you want to give a copy of the existing security records. You can also specify whether you want to add these new security records to the user's security profile or you want to replace the existing records in the user's security profile. You cannot automatically overwrite any existing records unless you choose to.

Application Security

Now, let's go over each type of security that you can setup through the security workbench program. We will start by going over Application Security, which is the

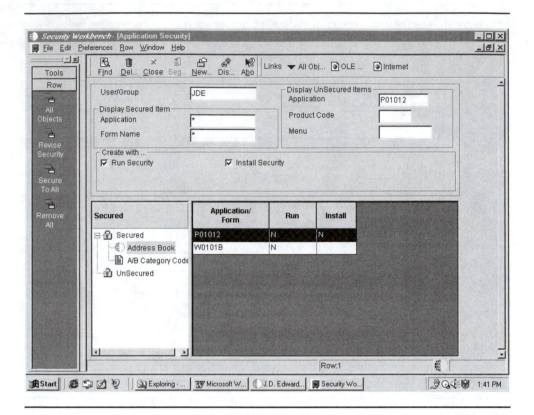

FIGURE 13-18. Application Security for the Address Book

first option listed under the Form exit on the Work With User/Group Security screen. The Application Security screen (see Figure 13-18) enables you to lock users out of running applications and/or installing applications. This prevents your users who are using partial packages from installing the application through just-in-time installations (JITIs). The fields and the options on this screen are the following:

User/Group	The name of the user or group that you are applying application security to.
Application (Display Secured Item)	This is where you enter the name of a secured application, so that you can review and/or revise the type of security that is set up on that application.
Form Name (Display Secured Item)	This field enables you to search for a specific form of an application that is secured. This means that you can enable your users to run the application but not certain forms of that application.

Application (Display UnSecured Items)	This field is used to find applications that are not secured for the user/group specified in the User/Group field.
Product Code (Display UnSecured Items)	This field enables you to search for unsecured items by product code. If you want to lock a user or group out of all applications in certain system code, you can easily do so.
Menu (Under UnSecured Items)	This field enables you to search for applications by using menus.
Run Security	When this check box is checked, it indicates that you want to prevent people from running the application.
Install Secutiry	This check box locks users out of installing the application.
Secured	This grid column shows two folders: Secured and Unsecured. When you enter a user and programs in the previously described fields, you see secured applications or unsecured applications by expanding these directory trees.
Application/Form	This grid column contains the application or form name, showing the secured and unsecured applications and forms.
Run	This grid column indicates whether the user or group specified has the ability to run the application. Valid values are Y and N.
Install	This grid column indicates whether the group or user has the authority to install the application. Valid values include Y and N.

To secure a user from running or installing an application, you enter the username or group name in the User/Group field.

For this example, let's use the JDE user. Because we will also secure P01012, the Address Book Revisions application, you need to enter the application number, **P01012**, under the Application field in the Display Unsecured Items area. When you click Find, two directories are displayed in the grid: the Secured and Unsecured directories. When you expand the Unsecured directory, the P01012 application is displayed. Drag this application from the Unsecured folder to the Secured folder. The application is now secured. The user will not be able to run or install the application depending on how the check boxes for run and install are checked.

It is important to note that this application security setup is cached. To see it, you have to log the user out and back on to OneWorld. After logging back on to OneWorld, use the Fast Path to get to the G01 menu. Notice that you can't see the P01012 application. This is because of menu security filtering.

Going back to P00950, the Security Revisions application, several Row exits are on this form. The options available from these Row exits can save you time and prevent frustration. The first option, All Objects, enables you to secure all the objects in the system from that user or group. This places an entry in the Secured folder for all objects, which means that the user cannot run any of the applications in the system. Many system administrators prefer to start setting up their application security in this manner and then grant permissions for specific applications as the need arises. This means that end users have less opportunity to get themselves into trouble.

You may be wondering how any of the applications can be used if they are all locked down. You can grant the permissions back to the users by placing the application name in the Application field under Display Unsecured Items. Click Find, expand the Unsecured directory, and the application name is displayed there. Ensure that the Run and Install check boxes are unchecked and drag the application under the Secured directory to grant the user the ability to run and install this application.

If you make a mistake, don't panic. You can revise the security once it has been set. Suppose you accidentally left the Run and Install check boxes checked, locking the user out of the application. All you have to do is uncheck the Run and Install check boxes. Then expand the Secured directory and select the entry for the application. The Run and Install fields will be set to N; in order to change these settings, ensure the Run and Install check boxes are not selected and then click Revise Security on the Row exit. This sets the Run and Install options to Y, granting your user permission to run and install the application. If only one box is checked, the user will be locked out of either installing or running the application, but not both. If you no longer need the entry, you can select the grid record and click Delete to eliminate the entry from the Security Workbench application.

The Secure To All option, under the Row exit on the Security Revision screen, creates an entry, for the application specified, with all of the check boxes or restrictions turned on. This is different from all object security in that it is application specific. You do not have to check all of the check boxes if you want to enforce all of the restrictions. The Remove All option under the Row exit removes all of the security that you have set up for the user in the User/Group field.

In the next section, we discuss action security. If you are on the Application Security screen, you click Close to take you back to the Work With User/Group Security screen.

Action Security

Action security gives you more flexibility. You can enable users to run an application that may be required for them to perform their job duties. However, you can limit the functions that users can perform in the application. Figure 13-19 shows the Action

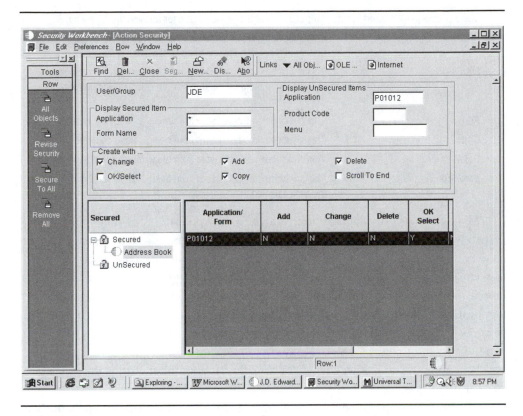

FIGURE 13-19. Action Security form

Security Application screen. The options and fields available on this screen are the following:

User/Group	Enter the name of your user or group.
Application Name (Display Secured Item)	Enter an application name in this field to see if it was secured for a specific user or group
Form Name (Display Secured Item)	This field can be used to see if a specific form has security set up for the user or group in the User/Group field.
Application (Display UnSecured Items)	Enter the name of the application that you want to place security on in this field—for example, P01012.
Product Code (Display UnSecured Items)	This field enables you to search for applications by product code. It is useful when you are attempting to lock down certain types of applications, like financial applications.

Menu (Display UnSecured Items)	This option enables you to search for applications by menu.
Change	This check box, when checked, tells OneWorld to prevent users from changing records in the specified application.
OK/Select	This check box, when checked, prevents users from committing records through the OK button, or from selecting records with the Select button.
Add	This check box restricts users from being able to add records.
Copy	This check box restricts users from being able to copy records.
Delete	This check box restricts users from being able to delete records.
Scroll To End	This check box restricts users from being able to scroll to the end of the data selected in an application.

The Action Security application is similar to the Application Security application. When you place a username in the User/Group field and the application name, product code, or menu in the fields under Display UnSecured Applications and click Find, two directories are displayed: Secured and Unsecured. When you wish to secure an application, you check the Desired Restrictions Exchange check box and drag the application from the Unsecured to the Secured directory displayed in the left grid. This secures that application for that user or group. When this security is in effect, the OK, Add, Copy, and Delete buttons are grayed out based on which action security you're implementing. If you restrict change functionality, users cannot change the existing records in the system.

The exact exits that are on the Application Security screen (discussed previously in the section "Application Security") are also on the Action Security screen. The following quick reference chart lists the Row exits:

All Objects	This Row exit enables you to secure all objects from the user or group specified in the User/Group field. This exit is useful when you want to lock everything down and then grant permissions back as needed to your users.
Revise Security	This exit enables you to revise existing security records. You find the record for the desired applications under the Secured directory, select it, click the appropriate check boxes, and take the Revise Security exit. This changes the security on the application for that user.
Secure to All	This exit enables you to create a security entry for the user/group and application specified with all of the restrictions turned on. This means you do not have to check all check boxes by hand.
Remove All	This exit enables you to remove all of the security set up for the user in the User/Group field.

Row and Column Security

Row and column security are absolutely critical to most businesses. For many businesses to fully operate, their users must be able to run applications that contain data the company does not want them to see. Row and column security enables you to restrict your users from seeing records in the tables of your choice. In order for row and column security to make sense, think of database tables or an Excel spreadsheet. These examples have rows of data along a horizontal plane and columns of data along a vertical plane. The ability to hide entire rows of data or just certain columns enables your end users to do their jobs while still securing them from obtaining restricted data.

Row Security

The Row Security exit is available from the Security Workbench program. The Row Security application (see Figure 13-20) enables you to hide entire rows of data from your end users. For example, you can hide all of your employees' names and addresses in the address book. You can set up row security on F0101, the Address Book Master table, to accomplish this. You can also restrict users from seeing certain ranges of address book numbers. You can access the Row Security application by clicking the Row exit for Row Security in the Work With User/Group Security application. The options and fields available in this application are the following:

User/Group	The name of the user or group that you are setting up row security entries for.
Table	The table that you want to restrict users from seeing rows of data in.
Data Item	The data dictionary data item that enables you to secure rows in tables from users. The data dictionary is used to control the data displayed in OneWorld applications.
From Value	This field is used to determine the lower range of the data item in the table.
Thru Value	This field is used to determine the upper range of the data item in the table.
Add	This field is used to restrict users from being able to add records in the From Value to Thru Value range. The acceptable values for this field are Y to allow users to add records and N to restrict users from adding records.
Change	This field enables you to restrict users from being able to change records in the From Value to Thru Value range. The acceptable values for this field are Y and N.
Delete	This field enables you restrict users from being able to delete records. The acceptable values for this field are Y to allow users to delete records and N to restrict users from delecting records in the defined range.
View	This field enables you to restrict users from being able to view records in the From Value to Thru Value range. The acceptable values for this field are Y to allow users to view records and N to restrict users from viewing records in this range.

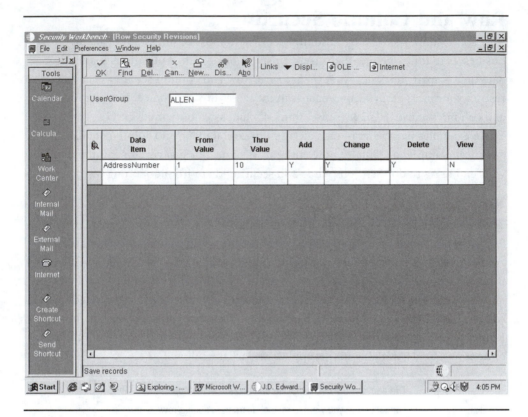

FIGURE 13-20. Row Security Revisions form

TIP

When you enable your users to see records, but not change them, they will not receive a nice neat error. When they press Display Errors they will see "error file cannot be accessed." If they inquire about this error, they will see a description asking them to increase the IBM authority on AS/400, regardless of what platform they are on. Keep this in mind when setting up row security so that you do not produce more calls from your end users than necessary. It is also important to note that when you secure users from seeing certain rows within a table, this security shows up in the Universal Table browser as well as in the OneWorld interactive applications that access the table.

Column Security

Column security enables you to secure entire columns in tables from your users. When you choose Column Security, the Column Security Revisions screen is displayed (see Figure 13-21). The options and fields available from this screen are the following:

User/Group	Enter the user or group that you wish to set column security for.
Table	Specify the name of a table whose columns you want to restrict.
Application	Lock down an application by specifying a data item for that application.
Form Name	Specify a specific form to which you want to apply column security.
Data Item	Enter the data item from the OneWorld data dictionary that is used to describe the column in the table, application, or form that you want to lock down.

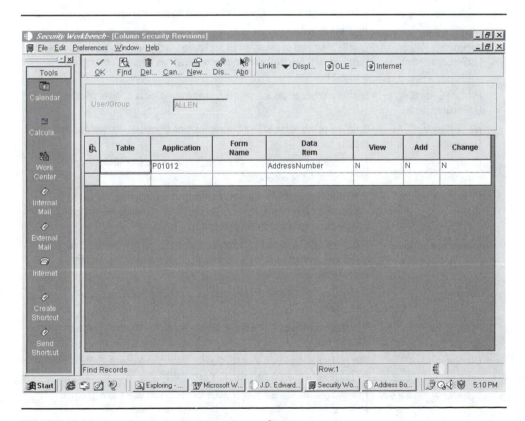

FIGURE 13-21. Column Security Revisions form

View	Specify Y to allow your users to see this column and N to hide the column from their view.
Add	Specify Y to allow users to add records to this column or N to restrict users from adding entries into this column.
Change	Specify Y to allow users to change records in the column specified or N to restrict users from changing data in this column.

Processing Option Security

Application processing options can be locked down with the Security Workbench by using (you guessed it) Processing Option Security! When you take the Processing Options exit from the Work With User/Group Security screen, you see the screen shown in Figure 13-22. The options and fields are the following:

User/Group	Specify the user or group that you want to set up processing option security for.
Application (Display Secured Item)	Enter the application or report name in this field for the secured application that you want to find.
Application (Display UnSecured Items)	Specify the name of the report or application that you want to set up processing option security for. (Not all reports or applications have processing options attached to them.)
Product Code (Display UnSecured Items)	Specify product codes to assist you in searching for specific applications.
Menu (Display UnSecured Items)	Specify a menu name to limit the applications or reports you want to assign security for.
Change	This check box restricts users from changing processing options for the specified report or application.
Prompt For Values	This check box restricts users from prompting an application or report for values. *Note:* When security is not set up, users normally can prompt for values by right-clicking on a program or report.
Prompt For Versions	This check box restricts users from prompting for versions on an application or report. *Note:* When security is not set up, users normally can prompt for versions by right-clicking on a program or report.
Secured	This grid column shows the applications or reports that have security set up on them.
Application/Form	This grid column shows the name of the application or report that security is set up on.
Change	This grid column takes a Y or N value for restricting a user's ability to change the processing options on a report or application.
Prompt For Versions	This grid column takes a Y or N value for restricting users from prompting for versions.

Prompt For Values	This column takes a Y or N value for restricting users from prompting applications or reports for values.

The Processing Options Security application is similar to the Action and Application Security applications in that when you want to set up security on a specific report or application, you enter the usernames or group names in the User/Group field and the application or report name into the Application field under the Display Unsecured Items area. Click Find, and two directories are listed in the Secured column: Unsecured and Secured. Expand the Secured directory and drag the application from the Unsecured directory to the Secured directory. Ensure that the check boxes that you want are checked to restrict access to the application's or report's processing options. This secures the

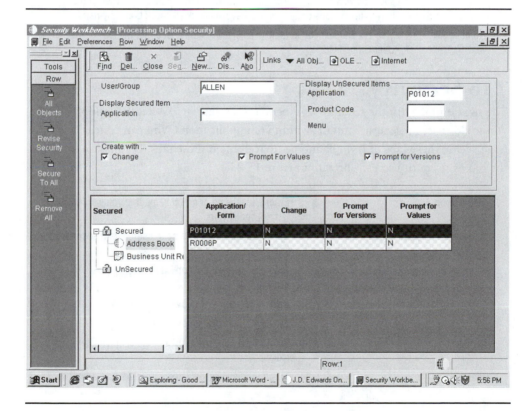

FIGURE 13-22. Processing Option Security screen

application or report from the user or group specified. Notice that the Row exits from this application also match the Row exits for the Application and Action Security programs. The following table has been provided for your convenience; it lists the Row exits for the Processing Options Security application:

All Objects	This Row exit enables you to secure all objects from the user or group specified in the User/Group field.
Revise Security	This exit enables you to revise existing security records. You can find the record for the desired application under the Secured directory. Select the record, check the appropriate check boxes, and take the Revise Security exit. This changes the security on the application for that user.
Secure To All	This exit enables you to create a security entry for the user/group and application specified with all of the restrictions turned on. This means that when you want to turn all the options on, you do not have to check all check boxes by hand.
Remove All	This exit enables you to remove all of the security set up for the user in the User/Group field.

Tab Security

The next option with the security workbench is tab security. What this option allows you to do is set up security on tabs within your applications. You can restrict users from seeing these tabs or from changing the values on these tabs. Let's take a look at the tab exit security screen shown in Figure 13-23.

User/Group	Enter a username or group name that you want to set up tab exit security on.
Application (Display Secured Item)	Specify an application name to search for a secured application.
Application (Display UnSecured Items)	Enter the name of the application that you want to place tab exit security on.
Product Code (Display UnSecured Items)	Search for applications by product codes.
Menu (Display UnSecured Items)	Search for applications by using menus.
Change	This check box restricts users from changing items on a exit tab.
View	This check box restricts users from viewing exit tabs.

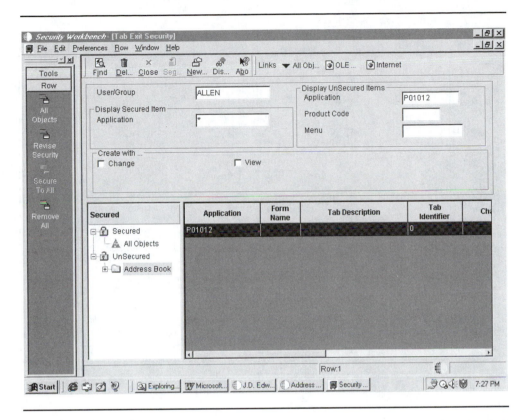

FIGURE 13-23.   Tab Exit Security screen

Figure 13-24 is a screen shot of the Address Book Revisions application. When a record is selected, everything on the screen is grayed out.

Exit Security

Exit security enables you to secure the menu bar exits from your end users. These exits enable users to call applications that you may not want them to access. To run exit security, choose the Exit Security program from the Work With User/Group Security form. This takes you into the Hyper Exit Security program, shown in Figure 13-25.

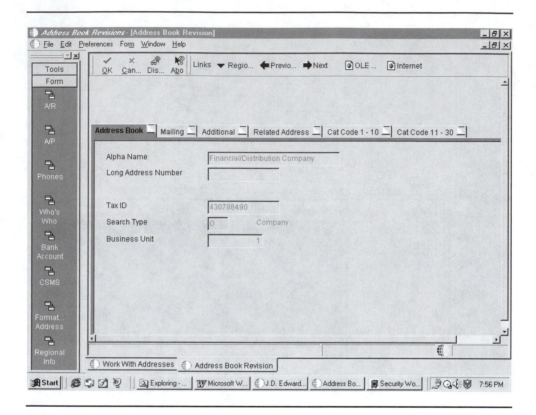

FIGURE 13-24. Address Book Revisions form

This type of security is absolutely vital to securing your OneWorld system. Without this type of security, your end users could get into trouble. The options and fields available from the Hyper Exit Security screen are the following:

User/Group	Enter the user or group that you wish to set security up for. *PUBLIC is allowed, but wildcards are not.
Application (Display Secured Item)	Enter the name of an application that is secured.
Application (Display UnSecured Items)	Enter the name of the application that you want to set security up for.
Product Code (Display UnSecured Items)	Enter product codes to assist you in finding applications.
Menu (Display UnSecured Items)	Enter the name of a menu; this field enables you to easily find applications.
Run Security	This check box restricts users from running or using the exits.

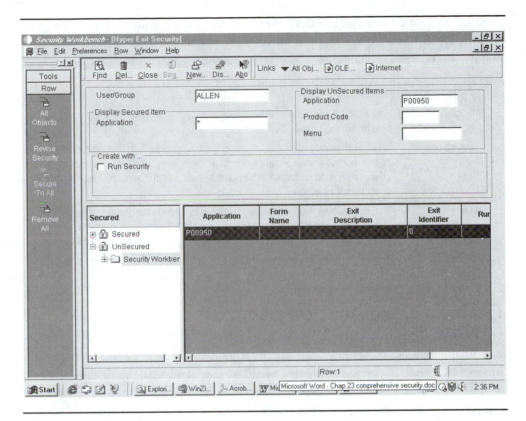

FIGURE 13-25. Hyper Exit Security form

Securing users from hyper exits is very similar to the other types of security. You place the application name in the Application field under the Display Unsecured Items area, click Find, expand the Unsecured directory, and you then see a directory with the application name. You can expand the application directory, and the exits for that application are displayed. To secure exits, you drag the desired one to the Secured directory with the Run Security check box checked. This secures the exits from your users. It is frustrating for users to see an error after they have attempted to run the Form exit. When the exits are grayed out, users know that they cannot run the application called by the exit.

To remove security from an application, you can highlight the secured record and click the Delete button on the menu bar. If you want to temporarily shut off exit security, you can find the secured application by entering the application in the

Application field and selecting the record for the exit. You then uncheck the Run Security check box and click revise security on the row menu. This turns off the security for that exit. The Row exits available from the Hyper Exit Security form are the following:

All Objects	This Row exit enables you to secure all objects from the user or group specified in the User/Group field.
Revise Security	This exit enables you to revise existing security records. You find the record for the desired applications under the Secured directory, select it, check the appropriate check boxes, and click the Revise Security exit. This changes the security on the application for that user.
Secure To All	This exit enables you to create a security entry for the user/group and application specified with all of the restrictions turned on. This means that when you want to turn all the options on, you do not have to check all the check boxes by hand.
Remove All	This exit enables you to remove all of the security set up for the user in the User/Group field.

Exclusive Application Security

The Exclusive Application Security application enables you to grant privileges to users on specific applications. This means that you can accommodate business needs. For example, suppose you have a user who you want to be able to see confidential information about your vendors; however, as part of that user's job, the employee needs to run a report that contains some of this information about the vendors that you don't want the users to see. In this situation, you can use exclusive application security to grant the user access to the information needed to run the report, but you can secure the user out of that information through other applications and reports. To set up exclusive application security, you click the Exclusive Application exit on the Work With User/Group Security form. This takes you to the Exclusive Application Security form (see Figure 13-26), which enables you to grant your users specific privileges for an application or report. The options available on this form are as follows:

User/Group	Enter the name of the user or group that you want to set up security for. Wildcards are not allowed, but *PUBLIC is.
Object Name	Enter the name of the object that you want to give the user rights to.
Object Description	The value for this field is the default; it contains a description of the application or report.
Run Application	Enter **Y** to grant the user or group the right to run the report or application. Enter **N** to restrict the user from running the application or report.

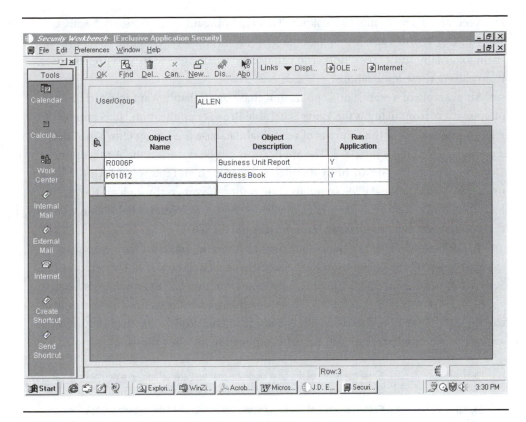

FIGURE 13-26. Exclusive Application Security form

To add an application or report, you simply enter the name of the application or report in the Object Name field, tab through the Description field, and enter **Y** in the Run Application field. When you have completed entering all of the applications or reports that you want to allow your user to run, click OK to save the records. If you want to remove an entry for exclusive application security, enter the user or group in the User/Group field, click Find, select the desired record, click the Delete button, and then click OK to save the changes. This completes the set up of exclusive application security for your user or group.

External Calls Security

The external calls security is used to lock down applications that can be called externally—for example, any applications that can be launched by double-clicking on an executable from Windows Explorer. This type of security is necessary because some of OneWorld's applications are standalone executables, enabling users to call them externally from OneWorld. You can use external calls security to prevent users from calling these applications.

An example of a standalone application that you probably want to restrict most of your users from using is the Universal Table Browser application. This application enables users to view the contents of relational database files using OneWorld data sources in a graphical interface. The application can be run from the Applications Development menu GH902 or by double-clicking on the UTBROWSE.EXE file located under the workstations' B7/System/bin32 directory. If you go through all the effort to lock the users out of using the program within OneWorld, you probably don't want them to be able to access the program outside of OneWorld either.

To lock users out of programs such as the Universal Table Browser, you take the External Calls Row exit from the Security Workbench program, located on the Security Maintenance menu GH9052. This takes you into the External Calls Security application shown in Figure 13-27. This form enables you to secure your users from calling standalone OneWorld programs outside of OneWorld. The fields and options available from the External Calls Security application are the following:

User/Group	Enter the name of the user or group that you are setting up external calls security for. This cannot be a wild card, but it can be the group *PUBLIC.
Executable (Display Secured Item)	Enter the name of the executable that is secured from the user. Click Find, and you should see the application under the Secured directory.
Menu (Display UnSecured Items)	Enter the name of the menu from which the application that you want to restrict users from is called. In our example of restricting users from the Universal Table Browser application, you would enter **GH902**. When you click Find, all of the unsecured applications are listed under the Unsecured directory.

To set up external calls security, you drag the name of the application that you found by entering the name of the menu the application is on from the Unsecured to the Secured directory in the grid. This locks down that application so that end users cannot run the application outside of OneWorld. If you want to remove security from the user or group, you find the application by using the menu or executable field. You

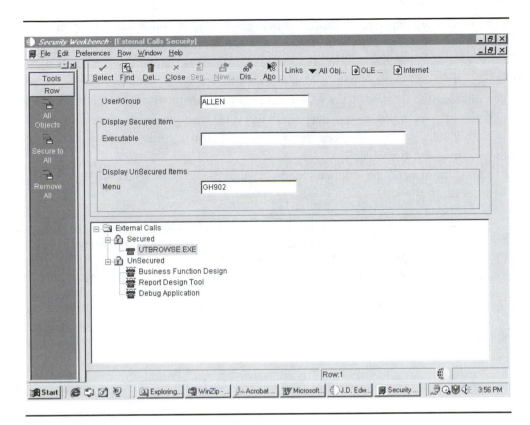

FIGURE 13-27. External Calls Security form

then expand the Secured directory, select the application, and click Delete. This removes the security on this application for this user.

Differences Between Releases B733.1 and B733.2

The security application illustrated in this chapter is on the B733.1 release. In B733.2, the application has changed slightly. The only real difference in the application between the two release levels is that a Run check box is included on the screen in release B733.X.

Just as is the case in previously described areas of security, you must check this check box before dragging the application name to the Secured directory. In release B733.2, you also can copy an existing user's or group's security profile for external calls. When you copy the security profile, you have the option to specify the user/group. You can specify that you can copy the setup and replace the existing setup on that user, or you can add the new records, which you are copying from the specified user, to your target user profile. With this ability, you do not overwrite any existing security records; you simply amend them to the security profile.

The Row exits on the External Calls Security application are similar to the other security applications:

All Objects	This exit enables you to secure the user or group specified from all of the applications that are standalone in OneWorld. You may want to restrict the majority of your users and then grant the privileges back as necessary.
Secure To All	This exit enables you to secure any applications listed in the Unsecured directory. Thus, if you search on menu GH902 and click the Secure To All exit, all of the standalone applications that appeared on that menu are secured from your user or group.
Remove All	This exit enables you to remove all of the security that has been set up for that user.

Law of the West

Adding OneWorld Security Without OneWorld

We've described the various methods of setting up your OneWorld application security; however, because this security is maintained in the F00950 table, you can download this table to your local workstation using the R98403 Table Copy UBE. Once the application is on your local machine, you can use MS Access to directly enter security without having to go through the bothersome OneWorld Explorer format used by the P00950 application. When you've entered all of the security you want, you can use the R98403 UBE to copy the table back into place. You can also use this method to copy security from one group to another. This is useful if you are not using the P00950 application's copy function.

Some people will find they can quickly modify the F00950 security table while initially setting up security during the implementation stage. It is important to understand security inside and out before choosing to use this type of setup, but the tools will allow your organization to rapidly set up security without having to switch from one type of security to another. All of the application security setups use the same table. This method gives the security administrator a single format for all of the different security types.

Integrated Security

In order to ensure that your organization's system is completely secure, you must integrate what you've learned in the previous sections of this chapter into a single concept that is easy to implement and fulfills the needs of the business in the most cost-effective manner possible.

Security Levels

You must consider four basic levels of security when planning an integrated security strategy:

- Physical security

- Operating system security

- Database security

- OneWorld (or application) security

Physical Security

Most people don't think about physical security when implementing a new ERP. They are much more interested in what type of application security can be implemented, but implementing a new enterprise plan provides the opportunity to ensure that the best business practices are being used throughout the organization. Physical security deals with the physical security of the servers and workstations that administer or access your system. Most IT personnel understand what should be done regarding physical security. However, understanding and taking the time to actually do physical security are two different things. Even though securing servers and workstations can be a hassle, can cost lots of money, isn't any fun, it's important to implement.

Recommendations   First, ensure that your servers are behind locked doors. We are amazed at the number of times we've walked unimpeded into a server room, and no one has asked who we were or what we were doing with the computers.

Second, the environment that you maintain in your computer room is also a part of security. When the temperature gets too hot, you are running cables all over the place, or you've attached power strips to power strips to extension cords, you are adversely affecting your physical security, and your company is at risk. As an IT professional, part of your job is to make sure that this doesn't happen.

Third, a large part of your physical security includes user policies that are actually enforced. It rarely takes much effort to walk into a company and sit down at a computer that is already logged onto the network and is ready to access data that shouldn't be available to someone outside that department and certainly not to someone from outside the company.

Fourth, part of physical security includes having documented procedures and policies. Documenting your security measures helps point out potential flaws and loopholes.

Third-Party Physical Security Specialists   Many firms actually make a living from simply agreeing to hack into another company, testing that company's security. It takes less than 30 seconds to introduce a program onto a system that can extract all of the system logins and passwords. A simple policy of locking your computer if you're leaving your desk minimizes this risk. An alternative is setting screen savers with passwords to provide additional physical security.

Almost all of the big five consulting companies have entire organizations that can assist you with computer security including the Internet, computer policies, and physical security itself. As part of their consulting operations, they can assist your company by providing years of experience and substantial resources.

OS Security

Your operating system, for both servers and the network, should be properly secured utilizing the native OS. When you add OneWorld, the deployment server, database servers, and application servers should have security in place to ensure that unauthorized personnel don't access them. Don't secure the file system share placed on the deployment machine. Don't try to outguess or over-secure this system. Rather, use the security recommendations from J.D. Edwards. At times, overly enthusiastic security managers (especially the ones who truly don't understand the product, the OS, or security in general) actually harm the system by placing too much security on this server. The results have been a loss of productivity, developed objects, and time during upgrades.

The majority of OS security should be based on the needs of each organization. Different basic concepts are associated with each of these security policies. The security the J.D. Edwards OneWorld product requires on each system is outlined in the appropriate installation manuals.

NOTE

When performing electronic data interchange (EDI) operations, many companies access files from and write files to servers other than the enterprise or application server. If you choose to do this, the network user who has started the OneWorld services must have change access to the target machine. If not, you cannot delete the inbound or create the outbound files as appropriate.

Database Security

When you use either Oracle or MS SQL Server with OneWorld, you set up a series of users in the RDBMS that should be closely guarded. Most people conversant with OneWorld know the users and their default passwords. It is highly recommended that you change these passwords at your earliest convenience and that you maintain these passwords for the life of the product. Try this test. Depending on your database, attempt to log into your JDE tables directly using the following information. The users and associated passwords are the same regardless of the database type:

Database Type	Connection Tool	User ID	User Password
Oracle	SQL Plus	proddta	Proddta
MS SQL Server	MS Access—link table via ODBC data source	prodctl	Prodctl
DB2/400	MS Access—link table via ODBC data source	prodb733	prodb733

If you managed to see a list of available tables using the information above, you have serious security problems within your database that need to be addressed as quickly as possible. All of the database owners can be changed after the installation except for the JDE user. Many organizations use the JDE database user for multiple purposes. Prior to changing this user, make sure your CNC administrator and DBA work together to change the password in all of the appropriate locations (there are a series of different places including INIs and INFs on the system).

System User   We have discussed a security method within OneWorld called sign-on security, in which OneWorld users are given database user IDs and passwords behind the scenes and unbeknownst to them. This methodology gives the system administrator another opportunity to control the users' ability to access data. Most organizations simply create a single user for accessing all database tables. However, this practice provides little security. We recommend you create several database users that have varying degrees of access to ensure that you are able to perform the following:

- Identify problems with performance.

- Properly control OneWorld users by data source.

- Provide a tool to determine database use by functional group.

Providing a tool to determine database use by functional group can be accomplished by creating a different business data system user for each functional group. Most databases have the ability to determine which users are accessing the system and to what degree. This might lead you to decide to implement departmental data servers (refer to Chapter 5 for information about database servers).

Application Security

You already understand the mechanics of application security, but it now becomes a question of implementation. There are three methods of using OneWorld application security to fully integrate OneWorld security: security by inclusion, security by exclusion, and OneWorld application integrated security.

As discussed previously, OneWorld uses a security mind set similar to MS Windows in that it gives users access to every application, form, and UBE within the system until security is set up. This ideology differs from other networking applications (such as NetWare) where no access is provided until it is specifically given to the user.

Security by Inclusion   It only takes the following single line of OneWorld application security (refer to Figure 13-28) to switch from the "include everything unless I exclude it" policy to one in which you "include nothing unless I include it":

*PUBLIC   *ALL   RUN='NO'

This effectively stops every user on the system from running any application.

NOTE
_____

We strongly recommend that you immediately create a user with the following security line:

*User ID   *ALL   RUN='YES'*

Companies have locked themselves out of important tools and programs

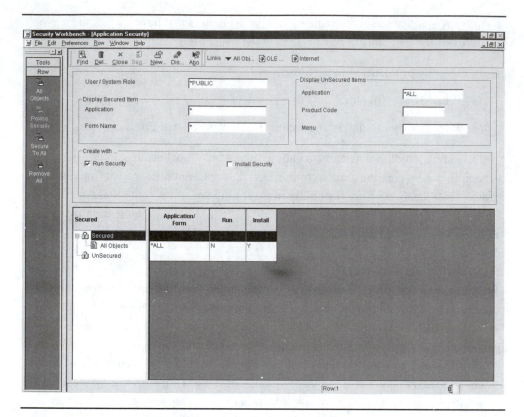

FIGURE 13-28.   Inclusive OneWorld application security

because they didn't follow this recommendation. Although it is simple to recover from this type of error, there is no reason to if you take the proper precautions. Refer to Figure 13-29 for an example of backdoor security.

Once you've made this entry, you've effectively ensured that the user is unable to run any of the OneWorld programs. From this point forward, the system's security manager is able to add security to the ERP system including all of the applications that the users or groups need. If the program isn't on the users' or groups' list of approved applications, they cannot see or use them. Hence, we refer to this as "inclusive security."

Although many security managers are comfortable with the basic concepts provided by inclusive security, it is easy to not provide enough access and to subsequently hamper the user and organization as a whole. Any security provided

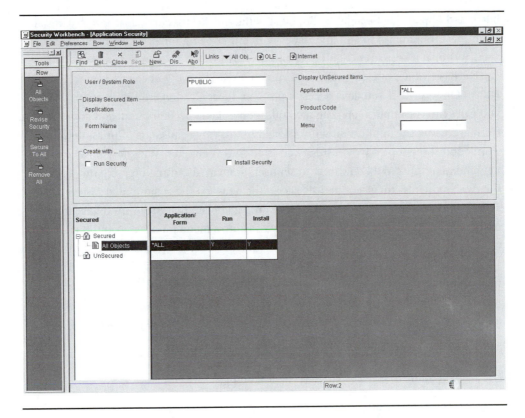

FIGURE 13-29. Backdoor for total security

needs to be leveraged against your current and ultimate goals for the software.
We do not recommend implementing inclusive security during the pilot phase of an
implementation because it is too restrictive. If your organization chooses inclusive
security, it must be set up during the modeling phase of the implementation (that is,
after the majority of setting up and testing have been accomplished).

Exclusive Security   Implementing exclusive security means OneWorld security
manager excludes users from using a specific object and/or application. The greatest
advantage to this type of security is that it is relatively easy to set up and maintain. You
never have to worry about being too restrictive. In fact, it is the exact opposite that you
need to concern yourself with. If you are not careful, your users can get into all sorts of
trouble that they expect you to save them from.

Integrated Application Security   So, what is the quickest security method that won't open the company up to possible issues with either being too secure (Inclusive Security) or not secure enough (Exclusive Security)?

Here is a quick question. Can you run an application if you can't get to it? Answer: No! In OneWorld, if you don't access a program through a hyperlink, shortcut, or menu, you can't run the application. The next question quickly becomes how do I stop someone from accessing the application without having to apply thousands of lines of security? Think about the topics we've already covered in this chapter. We know how to create new menus, right? We know how to set users up with an initial menu. Now, combine the two. Suddenly, the user can only access the items on the custom menu we've created.

From this point, most administrators would complain that they would have to set up menus for each user, right? Wrong! If you set up a menu for a group and then add OneWorld application security to it, you can quickly limit users to exactly what they need.

A quick example of this method includes "layering security." Create organized menus for a group, and you will quickly identify specific programs that only one member of the group needs to access. To accommodate this situation, you create a new menu for this one user (usually a manager). Or you could do the following:

1. Put the one application into the same menu as the rest of the group.

2. Add a line of security such as the following:

   Group, Application, RUN=NO.

3. Add a second line of security allowing the manager access to the application:

   Manager, Application, RUN=YES.

The users will see a menu without the application (remember, menus filter based on user access). The manager, however, will be able to see the item and consequently run it. Because of the security search hierarchy, the same menu looks different depending on who logged in, the security is layered, and the security was set up quickly without extensive effort.

Why It Isn't the Only Method   By combining menus, users/groups, and security, OneWorld application security can be quickly deployed and modified. You may be wondering why everyone doesn't implement this kind of security. Many organizations do choose this particular form of security, but it is not without its drawbacks. Using this integrated form of security does not alleviate the requirement of securing particular actions, columns, rows, processing options, or hyperlinks within the various applications.

Many applications link to other applications or menus. Unless you research this interconnectivity, you might not be providing the level of security necessary to your system.

Another consideration when setting up this type of security is that custom menus have to be manually updated when you update your version of OneWorld. If either the program or version changes from one release to the next, you have to manually update every place that calls the older version.

A good example of this situation is the OneWorld B732 version and the B733 version of the address book. In the older version, the application for the address book was P0101. Under the current release, it is P01012. With a custom menu, you have to change every time you put the address book on a menu.

Why Use Integrated Security?   If you have concerns about integrated security being too much effort to maintain, you will want to know why we chose to include it as an option. If you used either inclusive or exclusive security to secure your system, you would have the same difficulty you experience with integrated security. Every user and group you had secured from the address book would be able to use it when you upgraded because you would have secured the wrong application.

The primary benefit to using integrated security is that it is much faster to set up than exclusive security (after all, there are over 1,700 applications and over 2,100 UBEs that you need to secure), and it is less likely to allow for errors caused by not providing access to a required object. An added benefit is that you are able to provide superior workflow for your users by providing a custom menu designed just for them. This change makes the users' lives easier; it is faster with less actual security setup; it is less prone to mistakes; it requires less thought and is not difficult to maintain.

Troubleshooting

Security by Environment

Many of our clients have complained that OneWorld lacks a means to secure a user in one environment from using a particular application but allowing access in another. OneWorld application security is, you remember, a system table shared across all environments. We considered several different options including setting up two user IDs per person, setting up different instances of OneWorld, and setting up procedural methods of controlling people. All of these methods have limitations. Then we began wondering when security was actually cached to the users' workstations. We know that it is cached to memory during startup, but exactly when became both a question and the answer to unlocking this riddle.

Certain information is stored in the memory cache on each workstation. This information includes data sources (F98611), OCM (F986101), and security (both F98OWSEC and F00950), along with a series of other tables. OneWorld uses the default database information provided in each workstation's JDE.INI file to read specific information when you initially start OneWorld Explorer. The information cached includes data sources and OCM. Security isn't cached until after the user provides a user ID for logging into OneWorld. By using P986115, the Object Configuration Manager program, you can redirect where security is found for each environment.

If this is of interest to your organization, do the following:

1. Using the R98403, copy the F00950 table from the system data source (System – B733) to the appropriate environment-associated business data (that is, Business Data – PROD).

2. Use P986115, the OCM application, to map the F00950 table to this business data. Your entry would have these elements:

Environment	**PRD733**
Object Name	F00950
Data Source	Business Data – PROD
Object Type	TBLE
User ID	*PUBLIC

3. Once you are finished with the preceding steps, click OK, click Cancel, and then find the entry that you just made in the OCM application. Notice that the entry is not active. Activate the entry, log out of OneWorld, and log back on to the environment you just modified.

4. Use the P00950 application to set up the specific security for this environment.

When users log on to OneWorld, they look to this new table caching at startup. As a caveat to using this particular method of securing OneWorld, you have to set security for each environment you separate. We usually recommend setting up base security before you copy the tables. This decreases the amount of redundant work you have to perform. Remember, with any change you choose to make to the normal configuration of OneWorld, you may have additional work in day-to-day maintenance and when migrating from one release of the product to another. Still, the advantages often outweigh the additional work.

OneWorld License Security

In this short, sweet, poignant section, we go into detail about the license and security files used by OneWorld and where they reside. We won't go into how you can modify them (after all, that would be illegal, immoral, and totally reprehensible).

Security Files on the Workstation

Have you ever wondered how OneWorld knows when your security license has expired? How about why you can't just copy the B7 directory from one client to another and have it work? Heck, even if you do a registry hack, it still fails. What is the secret? Well, we will give you a hint. Have you ever wondered why you have to have a C drive (even if it is only a mapped network drive used as the C drive) on a Windows Terminal Server?

That's right! OneWorld writes files to the root of the C drive of every client installed (including FAT clients and Terminal Servers). The J.D. Edwards security files are JDEAUTH.DDA, JDEAUTH.XDA, JDESEC.DDS, JDESEC.XDS. Let's think about what information J.D. Edwards' OneWorld needs for each client. The license security takes machine name, date stamp, and the basic applications you're authorized to run.

Although OneWorld does maintain a list of authorized files, it does not actually restrict users based on these files. When you install the OneWorld product, you have installed all modules, and this is reflected in the files delivered to each workstation. Consequently, if you purchased licenses for the GL module only, once it's installed, you have access to all other modules including manufacturing, distribution, human resources, and payroll. At the workstation level, the machine name and the date are the most important pieces of information you have.

Why J.D. Edwards Licensing Is Date Specific

From a software developer's point of view, date-specific licensing makes great sense. If we license your company to use our software for a specific amount of time, we don't want you to be able to simply set the system date back and continue using the software. There is a simple way to test this statement. On a OneWorld client, set the OS date back one day. Now try to start OneWorld. Oops! It looked like you were going to get in for a minute there, didn't it? But now you have a Security Violation (see Figure 13-30). All you have to do is cancel out, set the date back, and restart OneWorld.

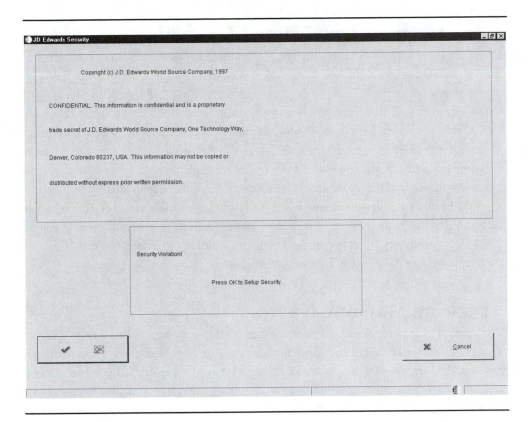

FIGURE 13-30. Security Violation

MS Windows Terminal Servers

Here is another interesting test that you can perform that will tell you more
J.D. Edwards OneWorld secrets. Find the security files on a Windows Terminal Server.
How many sets are there? Now change the system date and have two people log on to
and start OneWorld. Did they both have security errors? If you think about what this
tells you about security on this machine, you will come up with some interesting
information. Only a single set of security files are on this server. This single set is
used by all users who log onto the server.

Concurrent versus Named Licensing

Under the current OneWorld security setup, the number of machines you can install is the exact same as the total license count. There is no difference in security itself. If you purchase 30 concurrent licenses for 60 people, understanding that only 30 can be on OneWorld at any one time, you will find that you can install only 30 machines. The OneWorld product tracks licenses by machine name. So either your 60 people are going to share the same 30 PCs, or you are going to have to put in a Terminal Server to ensure everyone has access to the OneWorld software. If you implement the latter of the two options, you will find that more than 30 people can access the system at any one time.

J.D. Edwards is accommodating when it comes to the problems associated with not being able to install as many machines as you want for your concurrency requirements. The J.D. Edwards' contracts department provides additional licenses as required to ensure that you will be able to fulfill your business needs.

Tracking Machine Names

The machine name resides on the security files on the workstation. But where is the master list of all machines OneWorld has been deployed to? How does it know when it has deployed the thirtieth machine in the example provided earlier? If you had clicked OK on the security errors you received earlier during the test, you would have seen a screen that allowed you to get security authorization from the deployment server. A special table on this server contains all of the names of the installed machines. If you had logged on when you clicked Get Authorization, you would see the application access the JDECLNT.MDD file. If you read this file, you will see that every machine deployed is listed in this TAM file.

Renaming a Machine

You now know that the OneWorld product allows you to install only the number of physical client machines corresponding to the total number of licenses you've purchased. If you rename a machine or the machine crashes, you've just lost a license. You can recover this license by either renaming the machine back and then uninstalling the client using the MS Windows Uninstall utility in the Windows Control Panel, or by building a new machine with the same name as the original, redeploying OneWorld to it, and then uninstalling it. Almost every client we've ever been to has lost licenses because of this situation. The good news is that you now know about it so you won't make this mistake.

Viewing Licensing Information Through OneWorld

One of the tools that can be used to view licensing information about OneWorld is the P98538 (License Usage application). This program enables you to see what machines currently take up a security license. This program is view only and physically reads the JDECLNT file on the deployment server (see Figure 13-31). You cannot change this information using this application.

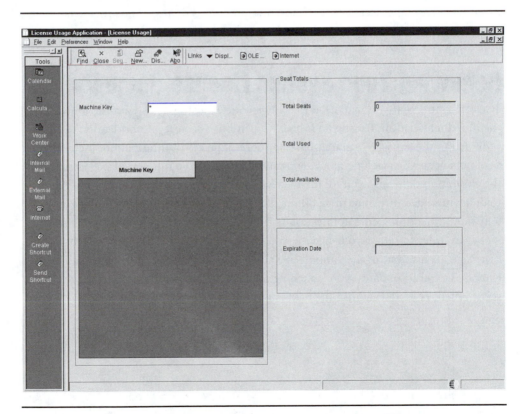

FIGURE 13-31.   License Usage Application

Changing or Renewing Your OneWorld Workstation License

Two different events may cause you to renew your OneWorld license. We've already talked about when the workstation receives a security violation. Simply click the OK button, and the License Security application starts up. Click Get Authorization on the form menu to automatically connect with the JDECLNT file on the deployment server. If the workstation is on the list of machines, a security authorization code is generated. If the machine is not on that list, and a usable license is available (that is, you haven't reached your license limit), the machine name is added to the list, and a security code is generated. If the machine name is not on the list and no license is available, you receive an error, and access to the OneWorld product is denied. The other event that may cause you to renew your OneWorld license is discussed in the next section.

Renewing Your System License Security

The other time that you may need to change your licensing deals with the limit set by the initial installation. During an initial installation, a security authorization code is provided to the software installer based on several pieces of information, including deployment server machine name, expiration date, and the number of licenses. When the expiration date has expired, the OneWorld application denies you access. Rather than having the entire enterprise offline, however, you can run P98SRV, the Reset Software Protection Codes application (see Figure 13-32) located on the GH9052 menu. In order to renew your license, you have to call J.D. Edwards (either the contracts department or the support line) to get a new authorization code with an extended expiration date. After punching the code in, simply click OK, and your security will be renewed until the next expiration time.

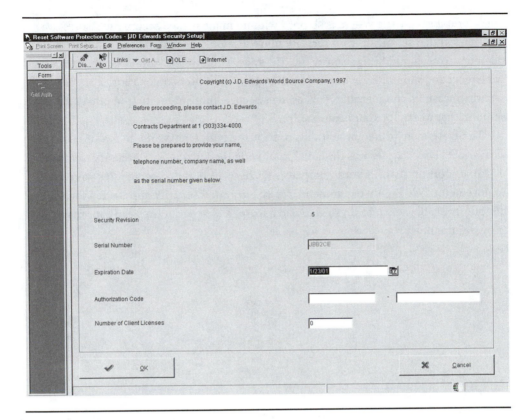

FIGURE 13-32. Server Security

Summary

This chapter began with a discussion of how menus can be used to implement security measures in OneWorld. We described how to set up security for your applications in

OneWorld. Because the system is shipped with no implemented security measures, we recommend that setting up your security solution should be part of your implementation planning. You should bring security into the system in the early or middle phase of your conference room pilot. Early implementation gives your users time to adjust to the security measures and it enables you, as the system administrator, to iron out a security solution that works for your business.

There are many different methods of securing both OneWorld and your enterprise as a whole. This chapter was designed to provide the knowledge necessary to creatively design a solution that fits your company's needs as well as accommodates your users' requirements. We highly recommend a fully integrated security approach addressing all four levels of security (physical, OS, database, and application). This approach provides the most robust security available.

CHAPTER 14

Operating System and Database Security

PYP (Protect Your Platform)

Operating Systems and File Security

Databases

The JDE User

You have invested a considerable sum of money on your hardware platform and on the implementation of OneWorld. To protect your ERP environment from within OneWorld, you created groups and then users, assigned the users to the groups, and applied OneWorld application security to custom menus accessed by those groups (refer to Chapter 13, which details OneWorld application-based security). After all, you do not want your sales clerks reviewing year-end data or the part-time employees viewing your VP's annual salaries. Have you covered your real vulnerability, though? To really protect yourself, it is crucial that you follow best PYP—Protect Your Platform—practices.

Because of the various options and configurations, this chapter cannot provide thorough, specific recommendations for securing your site. However, it will examine topics and recommendations for securing your OS and databases within a PYP framework, including the following areas of concern:

- Operating systems and file security

- Database security

- The JDE user and related profiles

PYP (Protect Your Platform)

The OneWorld platform has many points of entry (or attack) that need to be considered for appropriate defense. On an aggregate level, the operating system (server and network) and database are primary targets once OneWorld application security is established (refer to Chapter 13). On a granular level, the difficulties in securing your platform can be challenging because of OneWorld's flexibility. Imagine an implementation that has Windows NT deployment servers, a mix of UNIX and Windows NT application servers—some of which double as remote data servers—and a coexistent AS/400 enterprise server with a campus of Windows Terminal Server thin clients, a Web-based zero client, and numerous fat clients.

Can someone with network access map a drive to your Windows NT deployment server's B733 share, point, and delete files? Can someone with some knowledge of SQL7.0 gain access to your SQL server by creating an ODBC data source with the system administrator (SA) user ID and view personnel records? Or worse yet, can they stop SQL services and manually delete the physical SQL data files? Can World users initiate the WRKLNK command, drill down to OneWorld path code specification files and delete specifications? Remember, your OneWorld application needs security implemented both from within and from without. What good is runtime security on a UBE if the specs for it have been completely deleted along with the specifications for the other 5,000 UBEs?

PYP: Areas of Concern

Key areas of concern at the infrastructure level include the following:

- Operating system security

- File security

- Database security

OneWorld sign-on security provides a quick means to achieve a basic level of comfort in securing these three areas. After all, you can apply a single system user to all of your users in OneWorld. However, this simplicity has its faults in that it does not allow any flexibility in assigning security to any of these three key elements.

In your approach to creating a security model for your implementation, your first step would be to consider the degree of applicability to each touch point (node) in your infrastructure. Table 14-1 illustrates this point.

OneWorld installations require that a number of system users be created within both the operating system and databases on which OneWorld will be installed. We strongly recommend that one of the first security PYP steps you take is to change the passwords for each of these users. When the time comes to perform an update or an upgrade, you can either modify the J.D. Edwards scripts to reflect these new passwords

Node Type	User Group	OS Security	DB Security	File Security
	Production User	No access	No direct access	No access
Ent Server	CNC Admin	Full access	Full access	Full access
	DEV User	No access	No direct access	Access
App Server	Production User	No access	No direct access	No access
	CNC Admin	Full access	Full access	Full access
	DEV User	No access	No direct access	Access
Data Server	Production User	No access	No direct access	No access
	CNC Admin	Full access	Full access	Full access
	DEV User	No access	No direct access	Access
Dep Server	Production User	Limited access	No direct access	Limited access
	CNC Admin	Full access	Full access	Full access
	DEV User	Limited access	Limited access	Limited access
Workstation	Production User	Sign-on	Client connect tools	
	CNC Admin	Admin	Full suite	
	DEV User	Admin	Development tools	
Thin Client	Production User	Sign-on	Client connect tools	OS off limits
	CNC Admin	Full	Client connect tools	Full access
	DEV User	Sign-on	Client connect tools	OS off limits

TABLE 14-1.   Security by Group and Machine Type

or you can reset the passwords within the operating system and database to
J.D. Edwards expected defaults. We list these users and passwords in Table 14-2.

In addition to changing these OneWorld-required operating system users and
database logons, we also recommend changing the database default passwords for
MS SQL and Oracle.

Upon installation of MS SQL, many times we find that the system administrator
password (SA) is left blank. Create a password for SA, but make sure that the password
is secure and known by a very small group in your organization (but by more than
one individual).

Oracle requires the creation of an Oracle OS user and also installs a system
manager, whose logon is System with a password of Manager. We recommend you
change this password. Additionally, Oracle installs a user called Internal. Disable or
change the password for this user as well.

	User	Password
Unix	JDEB7332	JDEB7332
	Oracle	Oracle
AS/400	OneWorld	OneWorld
	JDE	JDE
MS SQL & Oracle	JDE	JDE
	OBJB733	OBJB733
	DDB733	DDB733
	CRPDTA	CRPDTA
	DEVDTA	DEVDTA
	PRISTDTA	PRISTDTA
	PRODDTA	PRODDTA
	CRPCTL	CRPCTL
	TSTCTL	TSTCTL
	PRDCTL	PRDCTL
	CRPB733	CRPB733
	DEVB733	DEVB733
	PRDB733	PRDB733
	PRISTB733	PRISTB733

TABLE 14-2.   User IDs/Passwords for OneWorld

Operating Systems and File Security

OneWorld servers and clients exist on a myriad of operating systems, including Windows NT Server 4.0, a variety of UNIX flavors, OS/400, Windows Terminal Server, IIS, Windows NT Workstation 4.0, and Windows 98 and 95. We will first look at server-side security exposures and OneWorld, and then we will look at client-side exposures.

We will examine servers by role and then by type within role. Not all server operating systems can play the same functional role. For instance, a Sun Solaris box cannot operate as a deployment server although it can host Oracle-based Central Object specification data.

Deployment Servers

J.D. Edwards requires that OneWorld deployment servers be Windows NT 4.0 servers (OneWorld Xe, formerly B733.3, allows Windows 2000 to be used) with Pentium chips. Security within Windows NT is very lax by default—full access is granted to everyone, requiring manual intervention to create a secure environment.

Clearly, the deployment server is wide open to hacking and cracking. However, in order to develop an adequate security model for the deployment server, it is important to understand the function fulfilled by this particular server.

The deployment server is basically a file server housing OneWorld code. It also acts as an authentication server, and in some cases, the server also hosts a database to maintain Central Object specifications. In certain circumstances, the deployment server will require different care than mere file security.

N O T E

J.D. Edwards publishes recommended file security for the deployment server. Rather than applying security during the installation of OneWorld, you can be assured a smoother installation if you wait until after the installation is complete to apply this security. In the interim, the B733 share necessary during the installation procedure can be restricted to an installation user or group to protect the share from network access. J.D. Edwards published recommendations for the deployment server are readily found in the installation manuals.

The files maintained on this server have a specific purpose: development and package creation. Users who primarily need access are developers and package administrators, and then limited access goes to production users.

The B733 Share   One of the first things that J.D. Edwards insists occur after the initial load of the OneWorld product to the deployment server (even before creating and installing a plan) is adding a share to the deployment server's file structure (see Figure 14-1). This share is release specific—that is, if you are running the B732.1 release of OneWorld, your deployment server share is B732; if you are running B733.2, the share is B733. All application code (both foundation and path code specific) resides in subdirectories of the B733 directory structure.

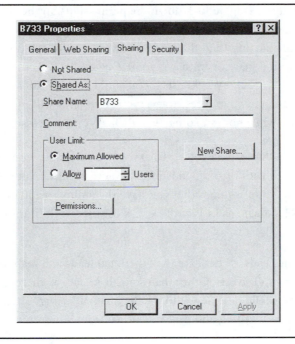

FIGURE 14-1. B733 Windows NT share

Troubleshooting

NOTE

Because this is a Windows NT share, networked users have two very quick methods of establishing connectivity to it. They can browse the Windows NT network neighborhood and open the deployment server. B733 will appear as a shared directory they can then open. They can also map this directory using Windows Explorer and the UNC \\depsvrname\b733 (where depsvrname is the name of the deployment server).

Unfortunately, the B733 share provides top-level access to virtually all of the OneWorld files on the deployment server. If you lock down the B733 share to OneWorld production users, you will get an error message when the OneWorld program fails to update the authorization files. Normal users do need access to these authorization files.

So what do you do? Do you lock down the permissions on the shares and risk not providing the proper access to required files? Or do you lock down the file structure itself? Our recommendation (and that of J.D. Edwards) is to lock down the file structure and leave the share open to everyone. As a minimal security measure, if you created a global group of OneWorld users, you could provide full access for the share to that group and then remove access to everyone else. This will provide some share-level security while not impeding overall OneWorld processes.

Locking Down the Deployment Server   To assist you with this, we have created a multigroup/user grid with recommended OS file access permissions, shown in Table 14-3. This security setup assumes that you have the ability to add global groups to your Windows NT domain as in Figure 14-2. Most users will fit into one of the four groups listed:

- **Application Leads**   These are the functional leads and managers (AR, AP, distribution, and so on). Other than some base access, there is very little that these users should be doing with the deployment server. The possible exception to this is report writing and base functional troubleshooting.

- **CNC Admin**   These are the people who administer the OneWorld system. Because the CNC Admin group will build packages, they have greater system access requirements than normal users. Additionally, there are times when these users might modify objects. Consequently, they must have full access.

- **DEV Users**   These are people who modify the OneWorld system, including report writing and application development. Because of the OneWorld requirement to check in modified objects, these users must have change access to the various path codes.

N O T E

If a user checks in an object and receives a message indicating that the check-in was unable to copy a file, this is often a result of incorrect access to the deployment server. During the check-in process, OneWorld attempts to copy files (.h and .c header and code files) from the developer's workstation to the deployment location. If they have insufficient rights (that is, read only or no access), OneWorld is unable to copy the file. The object check-in, however, will continue and appear to have worked. There have been many instances of customer's losing their custom development during an upgrade because of this issue.

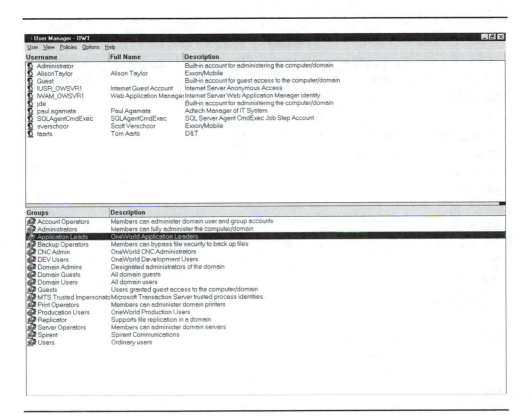

FIGURE 14-2. OneWorld global groups

- **Production Users** These are the day-to-day users of the OneWorld package. They have the least access requirements of any of the defined users.

Deployment Server File Structure Security In Table 14-3, we have provided recommended Windows NT security for the deployment server's OneWorld file structure. Unless otherwise noted, all subdirectories and files should have the same security. Table 14-3 is by directory name and group (this assumes you have named your global groups using the methods recommended earlier in this chapter). These directories are found under the B733 (or B732) of the JDEdwardsOneWorld (or OneWorld) directory, based on the release level of OneWorld your organization is using.

- **C** Change
- **R** Read only
- **NA** No access

	Windows NT Group/User Names				
	Application Leads	CNC Admin	DEV User	JDE	Production Users
Directory Name					
ActivEra	C	R	C	C	NA
CD Templates	NA	C	NA	C	NA
Client	R	R	R	C	R
filename jdeclnt.ddc	C	C	C	C	C
filename jdeclnt.xdc	C	C	C	C	C
CognosOneWorld	R	R	C	C	R
COM	NA	NA	NA	C	NA
CRPB733	C	C	C	C	C
subdirectory name Package	R	C	R	C	R
Database	NA	NA	NA	C	NA
DEVB733	same as CRPB733				
Helps	R	R	R	C	R
HelpsCOMP	R	C	R	C	R
Hosts	NA	NA	NA	C	NA
Interoperability	NA	NA	NA	C	NA
Mediaobj	C	C	R	C	R
OneWorld Client Install	R	C	R	C	R
Open Data Access	C	R	C	C	R
PACKAGE_INF	R	C	R	C	R
Planner	NA	NA	NA	C	NA
PrintQueue	NA	NA	NA	C	NA
PRISTB733	same as CRPB733				

TABLE 14-3.   Deployment Server File Security Grid

	Windows NT Group/User Names				
Directory Name	**Application Leads**	**CNC Admin**	**DEV User**	**JDE**	**Production Users**
PRODB733	same as CRPB733				
System	R	C	R	C	R
SYSTEMCOMP	R	C	R	C	R

TABLE 14-4. Deployment Server File Security Grid *(continued)*

Application Servers

Application servers host OneWorld logic. Sometimes they run a database containing server map data, but an RDBMS is not required: the required server tables can be contained on the enterprise server.

NOTE

When an application server also hosts a database with business data, it is considered an enterprise server. These servers provide database table hosting services in addition to logic, security, replication, and data transaction processing services.

OneWorld application code (also known as logic) resides within a path code. The application servers contain path codes with replicated runtime objects, and from a security viewpoint, are considered file servers. Even though the logic is managed by OneWorld services, the application server is basically a server with files that should be protected.

Security for logic servers is relatively easy. OneWorld users do not need a direct sign-on to the application server. Other than the JDE user mentioned earlier (or other designated network user), no network account needs full rights to the application server. Basically, only the CNC admin needs access to the server for package updates, maintenance, and troubleshooting purposes. There are no required directory shares associated with the application server, so this file system can be closely controlled.

UNIX Servers and Their Users   OneWorld users do not need access to the UNIX OS. Usually, there is a single release-specific user ID created to start and stop services in the UNIX platform. This user will need full read and write access to the logical volumes containing the J.D. Edwards OneWorld software (if you have used symbolic links to spread the disk IO among several different logicals, be sure you have given the OneWorld user ID access to all of them).

If you have several different users who have access to the UNIX OS for either maintenance or other development-related activities, you should ensure that they can't access the JDE.INI file located in the INI directory off the root of B733.2. This file often contains database-specific user and password information.

The AS/400   Because of the integrated nature of OS/400 and DB2/400, the same user ID used for sign-on security (explained in Chapter 13) is also able to directly access the AS/400 itself. Though the identity of this system user can be guarded, if it does get out (because of an all object authority requirement), there is a substantial amount of destructive capability to be had. For this reason, we recommend that this user ID's first command be **sign off**. A user set up in this configuration can make a database connection but cannot actually access the OS itself.

An example of this would be where your system administrator allows users to watch as they add new user IDs to OneWorld. During this process, the user could observe the administrator putting in the system user ID and password and then take this information back to his workstation. Using Client Access, the user is able to set up a logon screen for the AS/400. If the ID is set up correctly, as soon as the user signs on to the AS/400, he is immediately signed back off. This provides very nice OS/database security for the 400.

Database Servers

Database servers are used in distributed data environments. These servers host an RDBMS, but do not host OneWorld files related to logic—in other words, they do not provide OneWorld services except for database-oriented services. OS user IDs are not required for any user other than the DBA or system administrator. However, database logons are required. These logons will correspond to the sign-on security system user/ password, as well as relevant table owners. We highly recommend that you implement multiple database logons to simplify problem identification and resolutions. We are not advocating the use of hundreds of logons, however; one per group would be beneficial in determining who or what kicked off a process that is crushing the server. (Trust us, there is nothing worse than not knowing which one of the 300 JDE database users kicked off a query that is thrashing the database.)

Sign-on Security OneWorld assists you in securing your database by allowing sign-on security. This is explained in detail in Chapter 13; however, a quick description of the process follows. User A signs on to OneWorld using her OneWorld identification (UserA) and password (coolbeans). Based on JDE.INI settings and database parameters, the Oexplore application automatically contacts the security server (OWSVR1 in our example below), verifies the OneWorld user ID and password in the F98OWSEC table, and returns the data source specific system user ID and password to cache on the workstation. From that point forward, the OneWorld applications are "aware" of the OneWorld user ID, but the database only sees the system user.

```
[SECURITY]
SecurityServer=OWSVR1
DataSource=System - B733
DefaultEnvironment=PRD733
Row Security = NO_DEFAULT
```

The actual OneWorld user ID doesn't exist in the database. Even if you allow the users access to a database management tool, because they don't have a valid database logon, they still won't be able to crack your system. The problem with this particular method is that it doesn't provide many opportunities for the DBA to determine exactly who is running finds without QBE selection criteria (especially if everyone has the same system user and you're using either thin or zero client architectures). Again, there is nothing worse than having 600 JDE logons and trying to identify the guilty party.

This is why we recommend a small, controlled series of database users so you can minimally identify the group with the offending user.

N O T E

You will not want to change the passwords of the system user often. This information is stored in the F98OWSEC for each user in an encrypted format. As such, you can't use the SQL language to change the values in the field and must change each and every one instead. This can be very costly in time and effort for the security administrator.

Data File Structures   Databases are created on data files. These files are physical file structures in the OS file system and are subject to malicious attack. In order to ensure that these files are not "accidentally" deleted, we recommend that the DBA system user be the only ID able to manipulate them. One way you can secure these files is by not providing normal user access to the database servers. Because of the capability of OneWorld to sign on users, there is no need for these users to have access to the database servers at all.

N O T E

This is true except in the case of the OneWorld run in a coexistence mode with single logon capabilities. Under this scenario, the World user IDs often have access to libraries containing the data files. To control this, take command-line capabilities away from World users and apply the SECAUT program as referenced in Chapter 6.

Databases

Throughout this chapter, we have provided hints on database security. One of the keys (as mentioned earlier) is to change the default database passwords for database IDs used during the installation. In particular, this should be one of the first things done after the installation is completed and audited. All of the database users can be modified without hesitation, with the possible exception of the JDE user (be sure you have a complete understanding of what this user is doing prior to changing its password).

C A U T I O N

Do not use JDE or one of the table owners as the system user ID used in sign-on security. These IDs are known to anyone who has worked with OneWorld for any amount of time and can be read in various logs. Rather, create a new set of IDs for sign-on security.

When you change these passwords, maintain a list of all of them in a secure location. For the most part, you won't need to access these passwords regularly. However, there are scenarios where there might be a need to use them. This is particularly true when undergoing a particularly intense development effort. In this case, rather than providing access to the password list, provide the individual developers with the passwords they need to get their job done. Think of each password as need-to-know information.

Each of the database users have access to a schema within the database that provides them with the ability to change and create data and tables at will. Considering the power of the SQL language, this is not something you want everyone to have. Going a step further, once the development effort is over, change the passwords of compromised database IDs. However, because this does impact OneWorld itself, it should be done in a coordinated manner between the CNC administrator and the database administrator.

The JDE User

The JDE user ID is used in all of the installations and upgrades of the OneWorld system. It maintains full rights to the entire deployment server. It is also often used to start services on the OneWorld Windows NT application server. In this scenario, the JDE user needs to be a local administrator to each of the application servers and any other server directly affected by the OneWorld process. One of the best methods of securing JDE is to not assign it as a domain administrator, but rather, to add it to the local administrator group of each server needed. You can further control this user ID by restricting it to only logging on specific machines (see Figure 14-3). This ensures that the ID is not used throughout the enterprise.

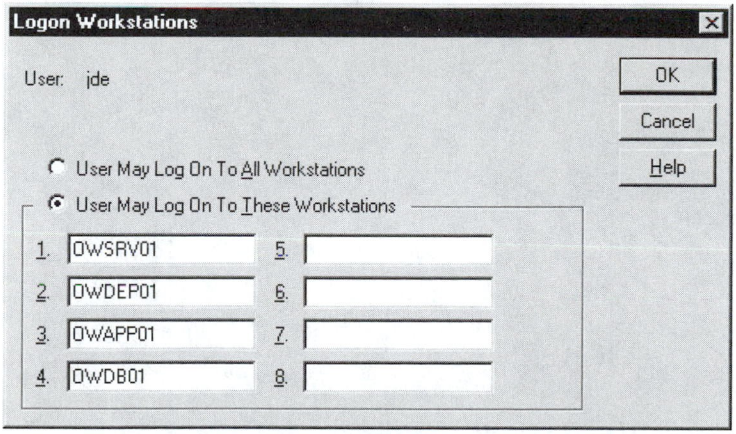

Troubleshooting

FIGURE 14-3. Machine security on the JDE user

Summary

This chapter has provided several methods and considerations that are imperative to your ability to properly secure both the operating system and the database of the OneWorld servers. Although this is one of the easier securities to forget, the necessity of PYP (Protect Your Platform) can't be overstated. In combination with Chapter 13, this chapter allows you to more completely secure your OneWorld implementation (and subsequently your job). Plan your security strategies in advance, implement them, try to break them, and learn to rest easier at night. On a final note, anyone can crack any security if they have the inclination, time, and knowledge. Though you can't guarantee that your system will be foolproof, you can make it more difficult to break into by implementing the recommendations listed here.

Data Replication

In today's fast-paced industry, your clients expect you to have the information they need right at your fingertips. They want answers and they want them fast. This adds some difficulty to implementing and maintaining a system because you want to put your data close to your users. This is not always an easy thing to do since many companies have sites and, thus, end users around the country or even the world. Data replication can assist you in keeping your data close to your end users. In this chapter, we will cover:

- What replication is

- When to use replication

- Types of OneWorld replication

- Reports for replication

- Host services for replication

- Third-party replication

What Replication Is

Replication is the process of moving data from one location to another, thus keeping the data in sync between multiple databases, machines, and/or sites. This allows you to keep your data close to your end users, and as many of you know, if the data is close to your end users, performance is generally better! If you have multiple sites around the country or the world that all need to view the same data, you can use replication to keep these sites' data in sync. You can also use replication to ensure you have the ability to recover your data in the event of a disaster. You can set this up so that every time a user makes a change it is replicated to another machine. That way, if you lose one machine you just bring the other machine online. There are countless permutations of replication, and it will mean something a little different to each company.

Replication Terms

When you start thinking about data replication, you will need to keep the terminology straight. This will be important as you plan your data replication strategy.

Publisher

When you are thinking about replication, a *publisher* is what describes the table and machine that move or publish changes to other machines. This table can be thought of as a master table. It might be helpful to imagine these machines and tables as a newspaper publisher. When there is news, these machines publish this news for their subscribers. When this table changes on the publisher machine, the change is then given to other machines. It is important to note that a publisher machine can also be a subscriber to another machine, as long as it is the subscriber to a different table than the one for which it is a publisher.

Subscriber

This term describes a machine and relational database table that receives changes from another machine. So if that other machine—which is a publisher—has the table updated, the *subscriber* will receive these changes. It is important to understand the concept of a subscriber because these machines are going to be of strategic importance to your business. These are going to be the machines at your field offices. Every time users in one of these offices log on to the system, their machines will be updated with information, such as a price list for your products.

Data Replication Publishers Table

This is a relational database table, which is in the OneWorld System data source that contains information on the machine and tables that are your data replication publishers. This table, F98DRPUB, will contain information on your publisher machine names, the table being published, and what OneWorld data source this table exists in. It is this information that OneWorld uses to keep track of your published tables. So when a specific table on a specific machine in a specific data source changes, the system will then know to move changes out to the subscribers of this table.

Data Replication Subscriber Table

This is a relational database table in the OneWorld System data source which contains information on the machines and tables that are subscribers. This table, F98DRSUB, is basically a list of all of the machines and tables that have subscribed to publisher machines and tables. OneWorld uses this list to determine where to deliver the changes when a publisher table changes.

Troubleshooting

In Sync Flag

This is a flag that is contained in the data replication subscriber table F98DRSUB. This flag will be either Y or N. This value is contained in the DRSUBSNC field of the F98DRSUB table. This setting tells OneWorld if the subscriber table is synchronized or contains the same data as the publisher table. If this is set to N, the client knows that it has to sync up with the publisher table. We will cover exactly how this is accomplished later in this chapter.

Synchronization

This is the process of making the data in a subscriber table, located on a subscriber machine, match the data in a publisher table on a publisher machine. This process can happen automatically through the replication software or you can force your subscriber machines to synchronize. This will be covered in detail later in the chapter.

Pending Change Table

This is a relational database table that tracks the changes to publisher tables. This table will contain an entry for each change to a publisher table, until a subscriber machine reads the table and moves this change down to that machine. This table, unlike the data replication publisher and subscriber tables, is populated in the server map data source. This is because replication is driven by a kernel process on a OneWorld enterprise or application server. It is this replication kernel that populates the pending change table. We will discuss how this happens from start to finish a little later in the chapter.

Overview of OneWorld Replication

To fully understand OneWorld replication, you need to first understand the logic behind how it was designed to function. OneWorld replication was designed to follow a specific logical approach. It is this logic that allows one application to be able to set up many different types of replication.

Tables Used by OneWorld Replication

OneWorld data replication uses several tables to administer the replication functionality. It is important to note that these tables exist in the system data source as well as the server map data source within OneWorld. However, most of these tables are not used in the server map data source. We will cover the few exceptions.

F98DRENV (Data Replication Environment Mapping Table)   This table contains information on the path codes in your system. It is mainly used for data dictionary replication. The entries in this file tell OneWorld what path code to replicate data dictionary changes to. How this works will be covered in the "Data Dictionary Replication" section later in this chapter.

F98DRLOG (Data Replication Change Log)   This table contains logging information on your data replication: what table was changed, the publisher data source, the user who changed the table, pending deliveries, and the change identifier. This information is very useful once you have set up data replication. With this logging information you can tell what publisher tables have been changed, what OneWorld data source they reside in, and the user who made the change. This is key since, if the change is incorrect, you can then track that person down and ensure that the mistake does not happen again. The number of pending deliveries tells you how many changes have not been delivered to the subscriber machine for this object. The change identifier is just a unique number OneWorld uses to track changes made to the publisher tables. This number provides a "hook" for OneWorld between the F98DRLOG and F98DRPCN files. It is important to note that although this table exists in the system data source, it will only be used and populated in the server map data source of your replication server.

F98DRPCN (Data Replication Pending Change Notifications)   This file contains information on changes that have been made to a published table. It contains the name of the published table, the publisher data source, the subscriber data source, the subscriber, the date changed, and a change identifier. The important thing to remember about this table is that it controls the changes for data replication. When a change is made, a record will be inserted into this table and will remain in the table until the subscriber logs on to the system and accepts the change. This is why this table contains the name of the subscriber as well as the subscriber data source. The table also has a column for a change identifier. This is how this table "hooks" into the F98DRLOG table. So when a subscriber logs on to the system and takes a change, the F98DRLOG will be updated by reducing the pending deliveries by one. It is important to note that although this table exists in the system data source, it will only be used and populated in the server map data source of your replication server.

F98DRPUB (Data Replication Publisher)   This table contains information on what tables are being published through data replication and on what machines these tables reside. This is your list of newspaper publishers and what type of information they will publish.

F98DRSUB (Data Replication Subscribers)   This table contains information on the tables that are being subscribed to. It also contains the names of the subscriber machines. If you think of this in the context of our newspaper publisher example, these are the houses that subscribe to the different newspapers or types of information.

What Happens When a Published Table Is Changed

In this section, we are going to walk through what happens on a system with replication set up when a publisher table is changed. This will familiarize you with the concept of how data replication flows through a OneWorld system. This concept will be important to keep in mind when we get to how you actually set up data replication in the OneWorld system. If you refer to Figure 15-1, you can start to see how the replication process flows.

In the example, a workstation has updated a publisher table. This published table resides on our enterprise server, which is also our data replication server. The kernel process on this machine receives a message that a published table has been changed. It then writes the change to the F98DRPCN and F98DRLOG tables in the Server Map data source.

There is also a work group server. A work group server is normally used to move data closer to the end user. This *work group server* is our subscriber in this example. If this machine is on the network, the change will immediately be sent to the work group server. If it is not on the network, it will read the change out of the F98DRPCN when it comes online. This change is then written to the subscriber table located on this machine. Now the workstations that get their data off of the work group server are seeing the same data as the workstations that are looking at the enterprise server for this data.

Work group servers contain information for your departments or remote sites. Replication can ensure that the users of these servers are seeing the same data as your local users. Work group servers used to be a popular WAN solution. These servers should serve a business need, however, because setting up a work group server with replication can be complicated and costly. You will then need a trained staff to maintain that server. A simpler and less expensive WAN solution is a Web server or Windows Terminal Servers. It is important to mention that you can also set up replication to move tables down to your local workstations' Access database.

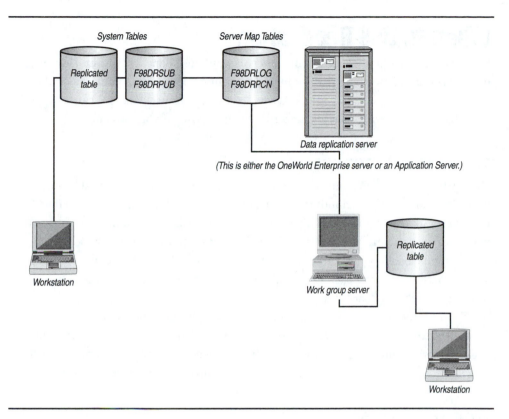

FIGURE 15-1.   Data replication flow

Normally these Access databases will contain your user-defined code and menu tables. However, if you are on a LAN this will not provide a performance boost for you. So there really are very few circumstances where you would replicate tables down to a workstation.

One exception would be if you were going to use store-and-forward functionality. This is where you replicate enough information that a user can disconnect a machine from the network, enter information, connect back onto the network, and upload their information into the system. At the same time they are uploading information they would also need to ensure that their replicated tables were up to date. This type of functionality can be handy if some of your users are traveling salespeople.

When to Use Replication

We have already briefly touched on when you would use data replication. However, in this section we are going to dig a little deeper into what business needs would cause you to need data replication. After all, you do not want to use data replication if you don't have to, as it adds overhead and maintenance costs to your system.

Disaster Recovery

One instance when you might want to use some type of replication would be for disaster recovery. If you cannot risk losing data out of a table, you can set up data replication to keep another machine in sync with your data. If you lose your primary machine, your backup machine has all information up to the last transaction. If you only had tape backup you could possibly lose up to a day's worth of data, assuming you are performing tape backups nightly. For organizations that enter thousands of orders a day, this is unacceptable.

Not to discourage you from using OneWorld replication, but if you are using replication to mirror your system for disaster recovery there are some third-party software packages specifically designed to accomplish this. OneWorld replication was designed more for moving data closer to your users than for mirroring your entire enterprise.

Remote Sites

Another business reason that may drive the use of replication is having remote sites. If you have seven branch offices across the country that need to see the same data as the users in your corporate office, you can use data replication to move this data close to your users at these remote sites. This might be a time when you might look at the possibility of using a work group server. However, you should look at all WAN solutions before deciding on a work group server, as Windows Terminal Server and Web server solutions are also available.

Store and Forward

If you have users who travel and will be disconnected from the network, you will need to use data replication to accommodate these users. You can set up OneWorld to replicate all the necessary tables so a user can disconnect his or her machine from the network, perform work, and reconnect to the network. You might use store-and-forward functionality if you have a traveling sales force. This sales force will need to enter their orders while being disconnected from the network. To do this, you could replicate the necessary data and system tables to these salespeople's laptops. They would then be able to enter their orders while they are on the road. When they connect their laptops back to the network, they will receive any changes to the tables to which they are subscribing. The store-and-forward functionality also provides a batch job to upload the data entered when offline. This really is not a part of replication. You would just need replication to ensure that the tables necessary to run OneWorld were up to date on each of these laptops.

Data Dictionary Changes

As OneWorld evolves, data dictionary changes will probably be one of the main reasons you set up replication. This is because Windows Terminal Servers and Web clients are replacing work group servers. These solutions are easier to set up and easier to maintain. In OneWorld, the data dictionary controls how things are displayed, such as column names in applications or reports. Why would you need to set up replication for data dictionary changes? OneWorld stores data dictionary information in two different formats: a relational database format and a TAM format. When data dictionary changes are made, the relational database tables are updated. An example of how OneWorld data dictionary functions is shown in Figure 15-2. Once you understand how the OneWorld data dictionary works, you will better understand the need for data dictionary replication.

When a user on a workstation logs on to the system and uses an application, the system will look at the local GBLTBL TAM file to see if the data dictionary item has been copied down. If it has not, the workstation will read the data dictionary relational database files and copy the item down to the DDDICT and DDTEXT specification files. These are the files that OneWorld uses to determine items such as column names when an application or report is run. This same logic holds true on the enterprise servers or application servers for when a report is run on the server. It will first look in the GBLTBL specification files to see if the item exists on the server. If it does not, it will JITI it down to the server's DDDICT and DDTEXT files. This means if the item has changed, and you do not have data dictionary replication setup, your server or workstation will not see the change if it has already copied that data dictionary item down. This is why it is so important that you keep the data dictionary in sync, to have consistent results when you run reports on your enterprise server as well as locally.

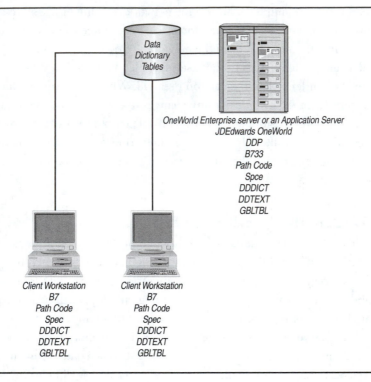

Data
Dictionary
Tables

OneWorld Enterprise server or an Application Server
JDEdwards OneWorld
DDP
B733
Path Code
Spce
DDDICT
DDTEXT
GBLTBL

Client Workstation
B7
Path Code
Spec
DDDICT
DDTEXT
GBLTBL

Client Workstation
B7
Path Code
Spec
DDDICT
DDTEXT
GBLTBL

FIGURE 15-2.   Example of OneWorld data dictionary

N O T E

When you enter new data dictionary items into the OneWorld system, two things will happen. One is that the relational database data dictionary tables will be updated. The other is that the TAM DDDICT and DDTEXT files will be updated on the workstation where you are making your data dictionary changes.

Types of Replication

With the different types of replication offered by OneWorld, you can come up with a simple solution or a fairly complex one. What you do should be determined by your business's needs.

Pull Replication

This type of replication occurs when the subscriber polls a server and, when a change is detected, pulls the change down, as shown in Figure 15-3. Pull replication is one of the easier forms of replication to set up. This type of replication is commonly used to move menu tables and user-defined code tables to the end user's workstations. Although OneWorld is shipped with these tables mapped to the Access database on the local client workstation, we have found this does not buy you much in the way of performance on a local area network. We recommend that you map these tables directly against your enterprise server. When this is done, your users will see their changes immediately after they have been made.

When a workstation, Workstation B in Figure 15-3, updates a published table, OneWorld replication will place a record in the F98DRPCN and F98DRLOG file. When Workstation A logs on to the system it will cache all of the entries in the F98DRSUB and F98DRPUB table. This is how it knows which tables the workstation

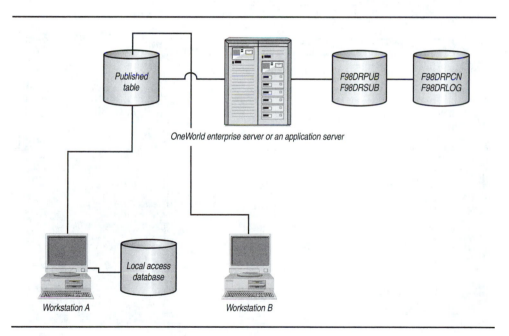

FIGURE 15-3. Example of pull replication

subscribes to and which tables are publishers. The workstation will also read the F98DRPCN file to determine if there are any changes for it. In this case, there would be, and the change would be pulled down to Workstation A and placed in the access database on the workstation. Now, if this was the first time that Workstation A had logged on to the system since replication was set up, it would be flagged as out of sync. What this means is that the entire table would be copied down to Workstation A, not just the change. This is normally only done once to get the subscriber in sync with the publisher table. After that, only changes will be pulled down.

Setting up pull replication in OneWorld is actually easier than you might think. The Data Replication program located on menu GH9011 (System Administration) controls all replication for OneWorld. Double-click on this application and you will be taken to the Work With Publishers screen, shown in Figure 15-4.

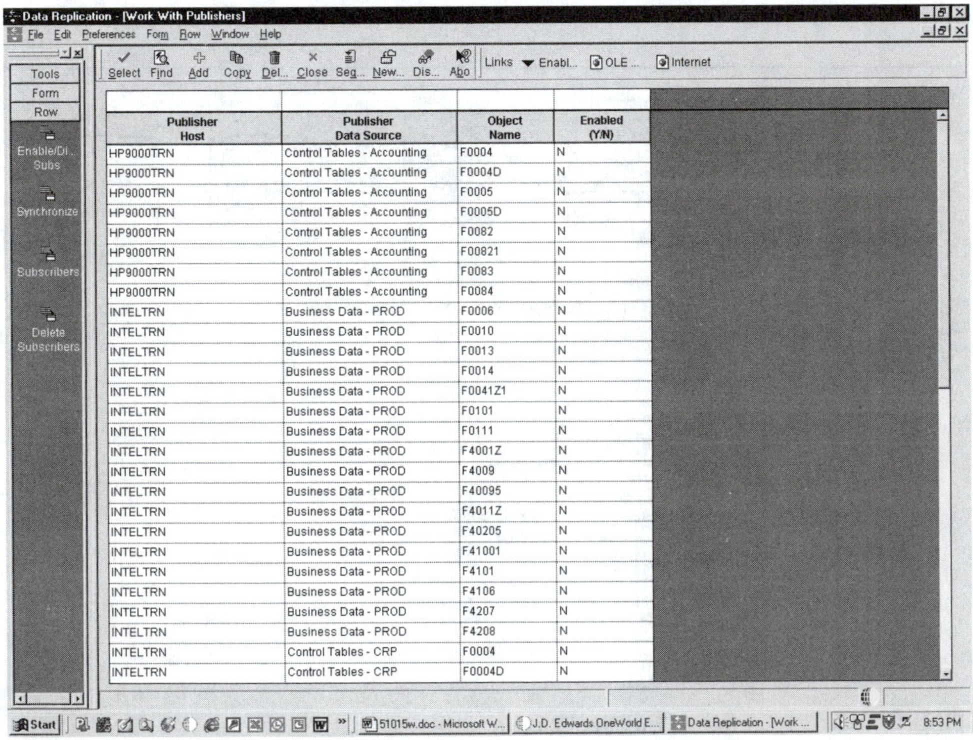
Data Replication - [Work With Publishers]
File Edit Preferences Form Row Window Help
Select Find Add Copy Del... Close Seq... New... Dis... Abo
Links Enabl... OLE ... Internet
Tools
Form
Row
Enable/Di... Subs
Synchronize
Subscribers
Delete Subscribers
Publisher Host | Publisher Data Source | Object Name | Enabled (Y/N)
HP9000TRN | Control Tables - Accounting | F0004 | N
HP9000TRN | Control Tables - Accounting | F0004D | N
HP9000TRN | Control Tables - Accounting | F0005 | N
HP9000TRN | Control Tables - Accounting | F0005D | N
HP9000TRN | Control Tables - Accounting | F0082 | N
HP9000TRN | Control Tables - Accounting | F00821 | N
HP9000TRN | Control Tables - Accounting | F0083 | N
HP9000TRN | Control Tables - Accounting | F0084 | N
INTELTRN | Business Data - PROD | F0006 | N
INTELTRN | Business Data - PROD | F0010 | N
INTELTRN | Business Data - PROD | F0013 | N
INTELTRN | Business Data - PROD | F0014 | N
INTELTRN | Business Data - PROD | F0041Z1 | N
INTELTRN | Business Data - PROD | F0101 | N
INTELTRN | Business Data - PROD | F0111 | N
INTELTRN | Business Data - PROD | F4001Z | N
INTELTRN | Business Data - PROD | F4009 | N
INTELTRN | Business Data - PROD | F40095 | N
INTELTRN | Business Data - PROD | F4011Z | N
INTELTRN | Business Data - PROD | F40205 | N
INTELTRN | Business Data - PROD | F41001 | N
INTELTRN | Business Data - PROD | F4101 | N
INTELTRN | Business Data - PROD | F4106 | N
INTELTRN | Business Data - PROD | F4207 | N
INTELTRN | Business Data - PROD | F4208 | N
INTELTRN | Control Tables - CRP | F0004 | N
INTELTRN | Control Tables - CRP | F0004D | N
Start
51015w.doc - Microsoft W...
J.D. Edwards OneWorld E...
Data Replication - [Work ...
8:53 PM

FIGURE 15-4. Work With Publishers screen

This is where you would have added all your entries for pull replication. This screen contains some important information. It tells you the publisher host name, which is the machine that is publishing the table. This screen also shows you the publisher host data source. This is the data source where the table, which is shown in Figure 15-4 under Object Name, resides on the publisher machine. The final piece of information this screen shows you is if the replication is enabled for each entry. If replication is disabled, subscribers will not receive changes made to this table. You will want to keep all this in mind as we go through setting up pull replication.

To set up pull replication, click the Add button on the Work With Publishers screen. This will take you to the Publisher Revisions screen, shown in Figure 15-5. OneWorld uses the information on this screen to determine the type of replication

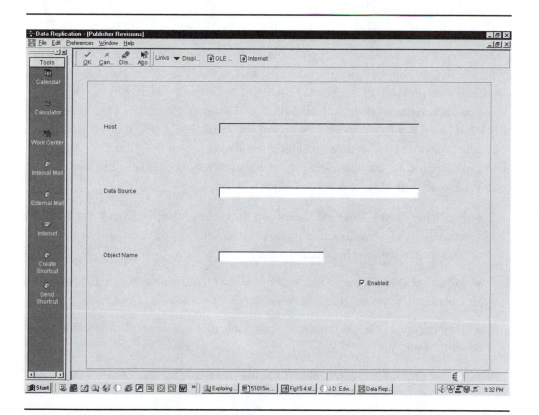

FIGURE 15-5. Publisher Revisions screen

you are setting up. How OneWorld does this will become apparent as we go through each type of replication. The fields on this screen are:

- **Host**   This is the name of the publisher host machine. This value will default in when you enter the data source. You cannot change this field; it is derived from the machine name in the data source you chose.

- **Data Source**   This field needs to be the OneWorld data source that contains the replicated or published table.

- **Object Name**   This is the name of the published table.

- **Enabled**   This check box determines if replication is turned on or not. If this box is unchecked, this record is disabled. When an entry is disabled, subscribers will not receive any changes.

Once you have set up your publisher entries, you will need to set up your subscriber entries. Remember, the subscribers are the machines that OneWorld replication keeps in sync. We will go over the exact process a little later in the "Example of Pull Replication" section. To set up subscribers, click Cancel on the Publisher Revisions screen. This will take you back to the Work With Publishers screen, shown previously in Figure 15-4. Click Find on this screen, highlight the record you just added, and go to Row Subscribers. This will take you to the Work With Subscribers screen, shown in Figure 15-6. This is where you specify the machines that will have any changes made to the publisher table pulled down to them. The fields are as follows:

- **Publisher Host**   This field shows you the name of the publisher host. This value will default in from the publisher data source. You must also have an SVR data source with the host machine name.

- **Publisher Data Source**   This is the OneWorld data source where the published table resides on your publisher host. This value will default in.

- **Object Name**   This is the name of the table that is being replicated. This value will default in.

- **Subscriber**   This column shows the machines that are subscribers to the table listed in the Object Name field.

- **Data Source**   This is the OneWorld data source where the replicated table exists on the subscriber machine.

- **Subscription Type**   This is the type of replication used. The values for this field are:

  - **JTR**   Just-in-time replication
  - **NON**   Third-party replication
  - **PSH**   Push replication
  - **PUL**   Pull replication

- **Enabled Y/N**   This field is a Y or N value that determines if your replication is enabled for the subscriber record.

- **Synchronized**   This column shows if the subscriber table is synchronized with the publisher table. If this is set to N, the subscriber table is out of sync. When

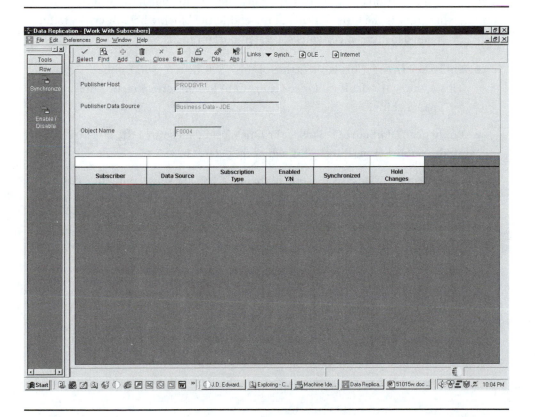

FIGURE 15-6.   Work With Subscribers screen

this is set to N, the user will be prompted to synchronize the table upon logon. What this means is that the table is copied down in its entirety. When it is in sync, changes are pulled down on an individual basis.

- **Hold Changes**   When this is set to True, all the changes for the subscriber will be held and not delivered until this setting is turned off.

The Row exits for this screen are:

- **Synchronize**   This Row exit will set your subscriber record to synchronized.

- **Enable/Disable**   This Row exit will enable and disable the subscriber records.

To add a subscriber machine into the system, click Add on this screen. This will take you to the Subscriber Revisions screen, shown in Figure 15-7. This is where you enter all the information on your subscriber machine. Using our newspaper publisher example, this entry is the little old lady at the end of the block who subscribes to the *New York Times*. This screen contains several important fields:

- **Publisher Host**   This is the name of the machine that will publish the table. This value will default in. Once again, an SVR data source record must exist for this machine.

- **Publisher Data Source**   This is the OneWorld data source the table resides in on the publisher machine. This value will default in.

- **Object Name**   This is the name of the table you are subscribing to. This value will default in.

- **Subscriber Machine**   This is the name of the machine you are setting up as a subscriber. You should be able to see a record for this machine in the Machine Identification application.

- **Subscriber Data Source**   This is the name of the OneWorld data source where the object will reside on the subscriber machine.

- **Subscription Type**   This is the type of replication you are setting up for this subscriber machine. The valid values are:

  - **JTR**   Just-in-time replication
  - **NON**   Third-party replication

- **PSH**   Push replication
- **PUL**   Pull replication

- **Enabled**   This check box tells OneWorld if replication is turned on for this subscriber record.

- **Synchronize**   This check box tells OneWorld if the table is in sync with the publisher table or not. The default is unchecked, which means the table is not synchronized and thus the end user will be prompted to synchronize the table upon logon. If they say Yes to synchronize, the table will be copied in its entirety.

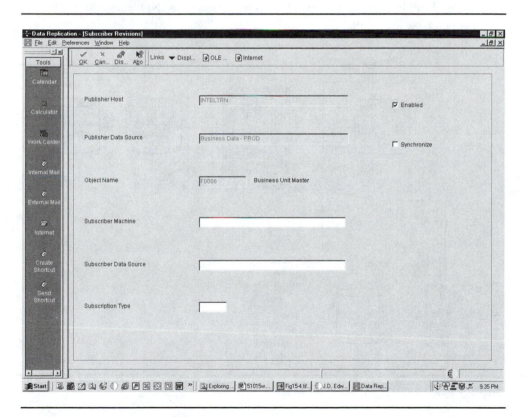

FIGURE 15-7.   Subscribers Revisions screen

Example of Pull Replication

All these screens are used again and again when you set up data replication. Now let's actually bring some of this into focus with an example of pull replication. In this example, we have set up all your menu and user-defined code tables to replicate down to your local client workstations. This process is shown in Figure 15-8.

When a workstation logs into the system it will read the F98DRPUB and F98DRSUB tables. This information is then cached or stored in the workstation's memory. The system checks the subscriber record to see if it is in sync or not. If it is not in sync, the system will copy down the published table from the publisher machine in its entirety. In this example, this table is the F0004. This is a hit to the network so you should only need to sync these tables up once. You can force the system to sync the tables up upon login each time, by adding the [REPLICATION] section to the client workstations INI file and placing the variable ForcedSync=0/1 off/on.

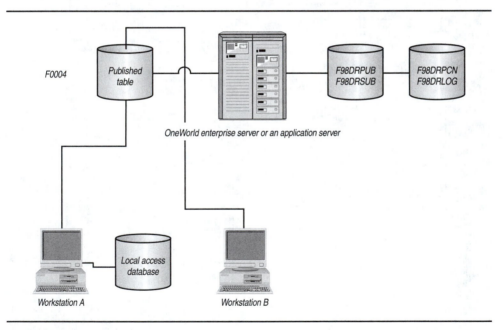

FIGURE 15-8.   Pull replication example

Push Replication

Push replication is also known as server-to-server replication. This type of replication is used to move data from one server onto another server. It is used to keep the data close to your end users. This is the type of replication that is most often used when you set up work group servers. An example is shown in Figure 15-9. We want to show you all of the options available with replication. However, in general, Windows Terminal

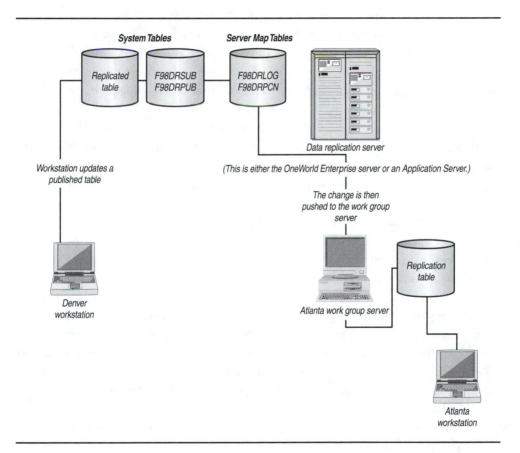

FIGURE 15-9. Server-to-server replication

Server and Web clients are a better WAN solution than setting up work group servers. Work group servers are expensive to maintain and add complexity to the system.

In our example, a workstation in Denver has changed a published table. The work group server in Atlanta is a subscriber to this table. Since the work group server is already logged on to the network, it will receive the change immediately. If the work group server is not available, an entry will be written to the F98DRPCN table. The work group server would then pull this change down when the OneWorld host services on this machine come online again.

As you can see, this solution brings the data closer to the end user in Atlanta. To set up server-to-server replication, you need to first add a server as a publisher. Go to menu GH9011 (System Administration) and double-click P98DREP. This will take you back to the Work With Publishers screen you are already familiar with. From this screen, click the Add button. On the Publisher Revisions screen, highlight the OneWorld data source that points to your publisher server.

Once you have added the publisher entry, you will need to add your subscriber entry. Highlight the publisher record you just added and go to Row Subscribers. This will take you to the Work With Subscribers screen. From this screen, click Add, which will take you to the Subscribers Revisions screen. On this screen, enter the name of your subscriber machine, the subscriber data source, and the subscription type. The subscription type will be PSH for push replication. This tells OneWorld that you want to have replication push changes out to a database on another server. How this happens was illustrated earlier in Figure 15-9.

Although this type of replication is in OneWorld's base functionality, you will need to use it with some caution. Remember that replication is controlled by a kernel process on your enterprise server. This means that every time you make a change to a replicated table, you will have overhead added to your system. After all, you just asked the OneWorld system to move your change from one database on a machine to a different database on a different machine. So when you set up server-to-server replication, you will not want to replicate high volume tables. If you are entering 10,000 sales orders a day, you may not want to use OneWorld server-to-server replication, as this will definitely affect your system performance. With that in mind, let's move on to a different type of replication.

Data Dictionary Replication

This type of replication is the most commonly used. This replication moves your data dictionary changes through your OneWorld system. Your data dictionary is contained in two different formats: relational database tables and TAM files. These TAM files are what OneWorld applications and reports use when they run on the local client workstations and enterprise server. The TAM files are not shipped complete, so if the data dictionary item that the report or application is calling is not found in the data dictionary TAM files, the system will go to the relational database tables. Once the system finds this entry, it will copy the data dictionary item from the relational database into the TAM files. By adding entries to the GBLTBL specification files, the system then keeps track of what changes were made to the local TAM files.

Now imagine that you changed a data dictionary item so that a column name appears differently. If you want the workstation or server to see this change to the data dictionary item, you will need to tell that workstation or server to go get the change from the data dictionary relational database tables. How do you do this? You guessed it: data dictionary replication. Is this the only way to get the client or server to see your changes to the data dictionary? Well, not exactly.

Other Ways to Move Data Dictionary Changes Around the System

Although data dictionary replication is the best way to move your changes around the system, it is not the only way. You can also move data dictionary changes by removing certain specification files. If you are a system administrator, you really do not want your average user to delete specification files on your system's workstation and servers. However, if you need to move a data dictionary change down to a server or a workstation when data dictionary replication is not set up or functioning correctly, you can.

Manually Moving Data Dictionary Changes to a Workstation   If you need to manually force a change to be just-in-time installed to a workstation, you can do this through a few easy steps. First, log the workstation off OneWorld. Open Windows Explorer and find the OneWorld B7 directory. In this directory, find the path code you are interested in—for example, CRPB733. In this path code directory, you will find a SPEC directory. Open this directory and find the GBLTBL, DDDICT, and DDTEXT specification files. Move these files to your recycle bin. If you want to see the change in multiple path codes, you will need to perform this procedure for each path code on your workstations.

Now that you have moved the GBLTBL, DDICT, and DDTEXT specification files off, you need to log on to OneWorld. When you next log on, you will see some just-in-time installation. This is the system rebuilding the GBLTBL, DDICT, and DDTEXT files on your workstation. The workstation will now see your changes to the data dictionary items. As you can see, although this procedure works, it is not one you want your end users practicing.

Manually Moving Data Dictionary Changes to an Enterprise or Application Server   To do this with an enterprise server, you follow the same procedure that was described for workstations. The only difference is that instead of logging off OneWorld, you stop your host services. On NT/Intel, RS6000, and HP9000 platforms, you will simply find the specification files in the OneWorld\DDP\B7332\PATHCODE\Spec directory. Move the files off and restart your host services. The data dictionary and global table files will be created again when you start your host services and run a report.

The AS/400 platform is a little different than the other platforms. On the AS/400, you need to perform a WRKLNK command. This will show you the specification files on the AS/400. You then stop your host services and move off the affected files. Again, these files will be re-created when you start your host services and run a report.

Data Dictionary Replication Flow

Before we go into the specifics on setting up data dictionary replication, you need to first understand the concept. As we have already discussed, the GBLTBL specification files contain information on what data dictionary items are contained in the DDICT and DDTEX specification files on your workstation or enterprise server.

When you set up data dictionary replication, an interesting process takes place. When a change is made to the data dictionary relational database tables, OneWorld senses this. It then places an entry into the F98DRPCN (pending change notification) table. If the subscriber is on the system, they will immediately receive the change. If they are not on the system, they will get the change when they log on to the system the next time.

When the change is actually pushed out, it is not a relational database change. OneWorld updates the global tables on the client workstation. The system will delete the entry, if it exists, for the changed data dictionary item. The next time the client workstation or enterprise server uses an application that needs this data item, it will not find the entry in the GBLTBL specification files. This tells the system to go out and pull the change down from the data dictionary relational database tables, through just-in time installation.

Setting Up Data Dictionary Replication

Setting up data dictionary replication for your workstations and enterprise servers is not that difficult. The logic that is followed by the system for this type of replication is shown in Figure 15-10. It can be accomplished through the Work With Publishers screen. From this screen, click the Add button. This will take you to the Publisher Revisions screen, shown in Figure 15-11. In the Data Source field, enter **Data Dictionary – BXXX**, where XXX is the release of OneWorld you are running. In the Object Name field, enter **DDICT**. This is a special value that tells OneWorld you are

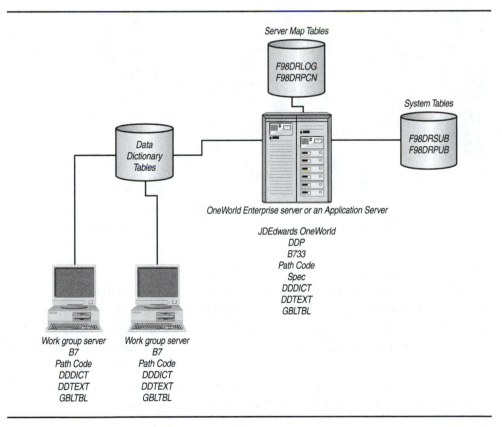

FIGURE 15-10.   Data Dictionary Flow

Server Map Tables

F98DRLOG
F98DRPCN

System Tables

F98DRSUB
F98DRPUB

Data
Dictionary
Tables

OneWorld Enterprise server or an Application Server

JDEdwards OneWorld
DDP
B733
Path Code
Spec
DDDICT
DDTEXT
GBLTBL

Work group server
B7
Path Code
DDDICT
DDTEXT
GBLTBL

Work group server
B7
Path Code
DDDICT
DDTEXT
GBLTBL

Troubleshooting

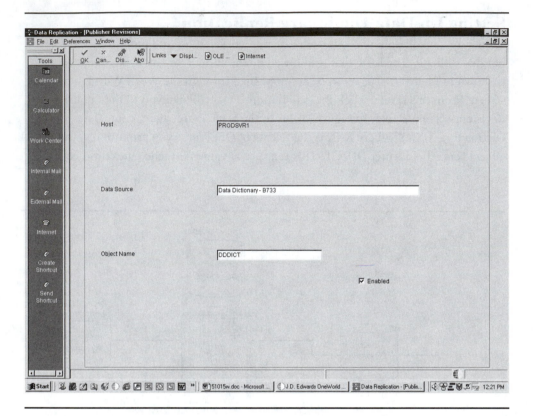

FIGURE 15-11.   Adding a publisher record for data dictionary replication

going to replicate the data dictionary. If you click the visual assist, you will not find
this value, so you will need to type it in. This sets OneWorld up so that any changes
to any of the data dictionary tables will be replicated. Remember, with this type of
replication you are really replicating from a relational database table to a set of TAM
files. Be sure the Enabled check box is checked and click OK. This will clear the screen
so you can add another publisher if you want. When you are finished adding publisher
records, click Cancel. However, for data dictionary replication you only need one
publisher entry for each set of data dictionary tables.

T I P

As of B733.1, you can have multiple data dictionaries. If you are a large development shop, you may want to consider this option. If you make a change to the data dictionary, a production client can just-in-time install this change down. This can have an effect on your applications in the production environment if they use the changed data dictionary item. This is why you may want to consider two data dictionaries. However, if you do have one data dictionary for your development environment and another for your production environment, you will need to promote the data dictionary changes as you promote custom objects into the production path code. This will add an extra bit of maintenance to your system.

When you use data dictionary replication, you set up a record in the Work With Publishers application that tells the system to monitor for changes to the Data Dictionary tables. When a data dictionary table is changed, a record will be written to the F98DRPCN. This will cause the system to delete an entry in GBLTBL specification records on the client workstation. This means that when the client workstation uses an application, it will read the GBLTBL specification files to see if the data item has been installed. Since this entry has been deleted from the GBLTBL specification files, the new data item will be brought down.

Setting Up Data Dictionary Subscriber Records   To set up subscriber records, choose the Subscriber option under the Row exit. This will take you to the Work With Subscriber Records screen, where you are going to add your subscriber servers and workstations. To do this, click the Add button, which will take you to the Subscriber Revisions screen. On this screen, enter the name of your subscriber machine, your subscriber data source, and your subscription type. In the Subscriber Machine field, enter the name of the machine you want to replicate the data dictionary down to. You will need to know what path codes are installed on this machine and which ones you want to set up data dictionary replication for—why you need to note this will become clear in a minute. In the Subscriber Data Source field, type **DATADICT**; again, this is a special value. Why you need to use this specific value will be discussed in the next section. Finally, enter the subscription type of **JTR** for just-in-time replication. You may notice that the Synchronize check box grays out with a checked value. This is because OneWorld knows you are setting up data dictionary replication and with this type of replication, you are not going to need to copy the entire contents of your data dictionary tables.

Setting up this subscriber record is shown in Figure 15-12; when you have completed this, click OK. This will clear the screen, allowing you to add another subscriber machine if you want. Click Cancel when you are finished to take you back out to the Work With Subscribers screen. Verify that your subscriber records are enabled and then close this screen, which will take you back to the Work With Publishers screen.

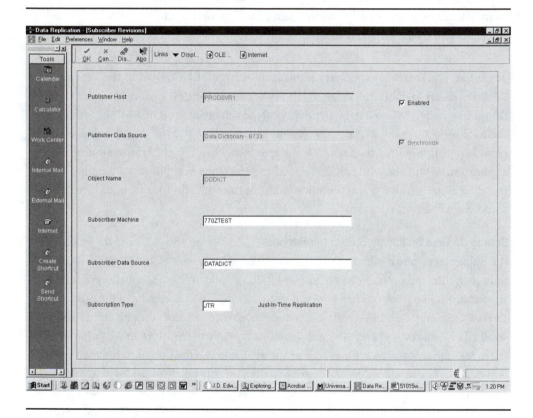

FIGURE 15-12.   Setting up a subscriber record for data dictionary replication

Setting Up the Environment Map for Data Dictionary Replication   You have one more step in setting up data dictionary replication. To do this, go to Form and select the Environment Map option from the Work With Publishers screen. This will take you to the Work With Data Dictionary Environments screen. The name of this screen is a little misleading. Remember how you had to use a specific name for your data source (DATADICT) when you set up your subscriber records? The reason is that this screen gives that value meaning. This data source is not a true OneWorld data source. It tells OneWorld how to find the path code on your workstation or server to replicate the data dictionary changes to.

How does the system do this? When you add a record in the Work With Data Dictionary Environments screen, it writes a record to the F98DRENV table, which is contained in the system data source. When your subscriber machine logs on the system, it will cache this information, which tells it what path code uses the DATADICT data source.

To make this a little clearer, we will quickly walk through adding an entry in the Work With Data Dictionary Environments screen. From this screen, click the Add button. This will take you to the Data Dictionary Environments Revisions screen. In this screen you will specify a path code and the DATADICT data source. This is how OneWorld knows what path code to update the data dictionary TAM files for. In Figure 15-13, you can see an example of the CRPB733 path code setup for data dictionary replication. Once you have entered your information, click OK. You can set up an entry for each of the path codes on your system.

Just-in-Time Replication

The next type of OneWorld replication we will discuss is just-in-time replication (JTR). This is a special type of replication. It acts differently than the other types of replication we have covered to this point. With just-in-time replication, the system will look for the object on the local workstation first. It will then look to a secondary location, which is normally your enterprise server or work group server. This is what makes just-in-time replication so special; you will not get any extra network traffic unless the object does not exist on the workstation (see Figure 15-14).

Troubleshooting

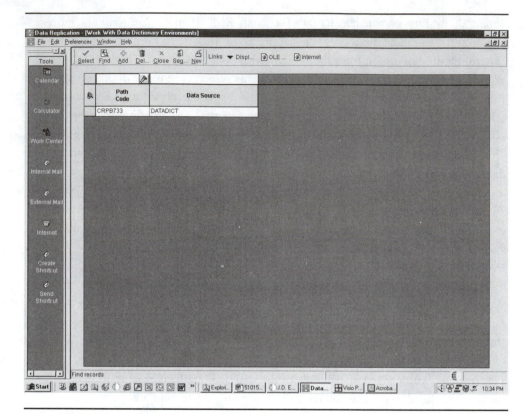

FIGURE 15-13.   Setting up data dictionary environments

You can have just-in-time replication set up for different circumstances. The major examples of when just-in-time replication works well with OneWorld are:

- Validating a user-defined code (UDC) field

- Using a visual assist

- Data dictionary replication

Validating a User-Defined Code (UDC) Field

When you tab out of a UDC field, OneWorld will validate that user-defined code automatically. This prevents you from using bad codes. If, for example, you enter

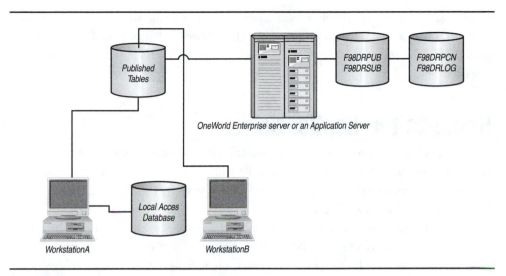

Published Tables

F98DRPUB
F98DRSUB

F98DRPCN
F98DRLOG

OneWorld Enterprise server or an Application Server

Local Acces Database

WorkstationA

WorkstationB

FIGURE 15-14.   Example of how just-in-time replication functions

an invalid search type in the address book, you do not want that search type entered into your data. OneWorld will let you know that the search type you entered is not in your user-defined code table. When OneWorld is shipped, your user-defined code tables are mapped locally to the workstations. This means, if you keep this configuration, OneWorld will attempt to validate the value from the user-defined code table on the local workstation first. If the value is not in the local table, OneWorld will then look at the publisher data source.

When the system looks at the publisher data source, it will again attempt to find the value specified in this table. If the system finds this value, it will validate the user-defined code value and at the same time replicate this value down to the local workstation. If the system does not find the value in the publisher data source, it will cause the system to return an error letting you know the value specified is not a valid user-defined code.

Using a Visual Assist

OneWorld will also use just-in-time replication when you use a visual assist in the systems applications. When you click a visual assist button, the system will automatically look at the publisher data source and display the user defined code values contained there. Not all of these values may exist in the subscriber data source, so if you select a value that does not exist in the subscriber data source from the list provided by the visual assist, the system will replicate this value down to your local workstations.

Reports for Replication

Setting up a large number of publishers and subscribers seems like a daunting process. However, the software provides tools to assist you in setting up your publisher and subscriber records. One option is to just copy records using the copy button in the Work With Publishers application.

Another option, which is the main focus of this section, is the Create Publisher And Subscriber Records Report R00960. This report is located on the Advanced Operations menu (GH9012). This report reads the machine identification table (F00960), which stores information about your OneWorld workstations and servers. With information from this table, the R00960 report can create publisher and subscriber records.

This report can make your life either a whole lot easier or a whole lot harder. If you use this report correctly, it will help you. If you just use this report blindly, it can cause great difficulty in your replication configuration. With that in mind, let's take a look at how to correctly use the R00960 report.

First, you will need to decide if you are going to set up subscriber records, publisher records, or both. You can specify this through the processing options on this report. Double-click the report on menu GH9012 (Advanced Operations) or you can go to the batch version and find this report. When you do, go to Row Processing Options. This will take you to the Processing Options window for this report. The Create Publisher And Subscriber Records report has two processing option tabs: Process and Process Continued. These tabs are shown in Figures 15-15 and 15-16.

As you can see in Figure 15-15, the first processing options allow you to run the report in proof mode and specify the values used when creating a publisher data source. These options are:

- **Enter a "1" to run in Proof mode…** This field controls whether the report will be run in proof or final mode. A value of 1 will run the report in proof mode. A blank will run the report in final mode.

- **Publisher Data Source** This is the data source that will be used for your publisher records.

- **Object Name** This is the name of the object you are going to publish (for example, F0004).

- **Enabled** This field controls whether the publisher data source is enabled or disabled.

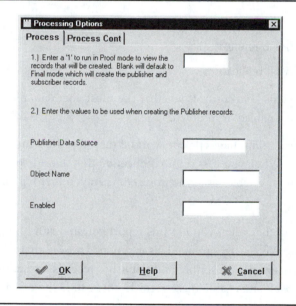

FIGURE 15-15. Processing options for the Create Publisher And Subscriber Records report

When you use this report to create publisher records, you should run it so that the records are disabled first and then go back and enable them one at a time. This ensures that you know what tables are being published, and which machines are subscribing to these tables, so you will spend less time troubleshooting your replication configuration if you have a problem.

The remaining options, shown in Figure 15-16, are as follows:

- **Subscriber Data Source**   This is the data source that will be used for the subscriber records you are creating.

- **Subscription Type**   This is the type of replication you are going to use. This can be:

  - **JTR**   Just-in-time replication

  - **NON**   Third-party replication

  - **PSH**   Push replication

  - **PUL**   Pull replication

- **Enabled**   This field controls whether the subscriber data records you are creating are enabled or disabled.

- **Synchronize**   This flag tells one world if the subscriber and publisher table are in sync. When you first set up replication this should be set to N. This will ensure that your tables are synchronized when you first log on to the subscriber machine.

We recommend that when you use this report you first run it in proof mode and review the results. We also recommend, as mentioned above, that when you run this report you specify that the subscriber and publisher records are set up as disabled. You can then go back and enable these records; this will help you to keep control of your system.

Another neat thing about this report is that you can place data selection on it. This means you can limit the number of records the report creates. After all, do you really want this report to pick up all of your workstations and enterprise servers if you have something like 300 workstation installations? Probably not, so keep data selection in mind when you use this report.

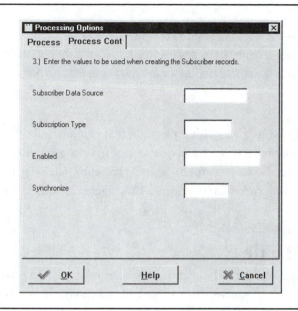

FIGURE 15-16. More processing options for the Create Publisher And Subscriber
Records report

Host Services for Replication

As we have mentioned throughout this chapter, the replication process is handled by
a kernel process on the enterprise server. In this section, we are going to dig a little
deeper into how replication really works.

NOTE

*How replication works on the enterprise server is similar to how it works on
the client. When you start the host services, all the information contained in the
F98DRPUB and F98DRSUB files is cached. If you have changed anything after
you started your host services, you will need to either restart your host services or
use the Refresh Hosts Form exit in the Work With Publishers application. This will
cause your host services to read the F98DRSUB and F98DRPUB files again.*

CAUTION

It is important to note that if you are using server-to-server replication, the publisher server needs to come up first and then the subscriber server. If you start these machines in any other order, server-to-server replication will not function correctly.

There is a lot that happens with replication that you normally do not see. So how do you troubleshoot replication if you believe you have your publisher and subscriber records set up correctly and you are still having problems? The system has the capability to log the replication process as it happens. This logging is controlled through INI file settings.

Server INI File

Let's start by going over the INI file entries for your server. As you have seen throughout this book, the server INI file controls several functions. It is what sets up the kernel processes for security, UBEs, JDENet, and even replication. If you have opened the server INI file and looked at it, you will probably say that you can see the area of INI that starts the kernel process for security and some others, but you do not see one that controls the replication.

As of B733.1, the section in the INI file for replication is hidden. This is because the replication kernel process uses information from the kernel process that controls the security server. You will see exactly how this takes place in a minute.

Kernel Process Entries

If you open your enterprise server's INI file, you can find a section titled [SECURITY]. When the replication kernel starts, it will use the information under the security section of the server's INI file. The entries in this section are as follows:

- **User**   This is the name of a database user and password. This is used to read the F98OWSEC file, which starts the security kernel.

- **Password**   This is the password for the database user.

- **DefaultEnvironment**   This is the name of a valid OneWorld environment that will be used to start the kernel process for security.

We will go over each of these entries and how they affect replication.

The replication kernel will use the *DefaultEnvironment* value to start. The replication kernel needs to reference a valid OneWorld environment to start up correctly. This kernel process will control how replication is handled through your system. You will need to be using sign-on security or enter a default environment for the replication kernel to start correctly. The *user* is a database user that is used to perform select statements over database tables. The *password* entry is the password that will be passed to the database.. We recommend that you set up sign-on security first and then replication. How to set up sign-on security is covered in Chapter 13.

Logging for Replication   The OneWorld system allows you to log the replication process. This is controlled through an INI setting. This INI setting is under the [DEBUG] section of the INI file. You will need to add an entry of RepTrace under the [DEBUG] section. This value is either a 1 for logging turned on or a 0 for logging turned off. When you turn logging on, you will be able to see entries in the JDEDEBUG.LOG on your enterprise server. If you just turn on replication logging, it will not be enough; you will also need to turn on the normal debug logging on your enterprise server.

Remember, the logging information is cached, so if you turn on replication logging you will need to cycle your host services to see the logging. When this logging is turned on, you will see messages like "Rep Message 512 sent to BULLS1 successfully" in your log files on the enterprise server. What this message tells you is that the replication kernel has successfully sent a change or rep message to the machine BULLS1. A replication message is a message from one server or client machine to another telling it that there is a message for the machine.

Client INI File

For replication to work correctly, you will need to ensure that your client INI file is set up correctly as well as your server INI files. You can do this by manually changing every client INI file entry, which would be an incredible amount of work and is not recommended. To push the changes out to your client workstations, change the INI file on your deployment server under the J.D. Edwards OneWorld\ B733\OneWorld Client\Mics directory. In this INI file, make sure the DefaultEnvironment setting under the [SECURITY] section contains a valid OneWorld environment.

You also want to ensure that you can easily turn on replication logging on your client workstations. To do this, add the entry **RepTrace** under the [DEBUG] section of this INI file. You should set this to zero, which is turned off. These settings will be copied down to your client workstations when they install a package.

With this logging turned on, you can perform complete tests of your replication solution. As we discussed earlier, when replication logging is turned on, an entry will be written to the log files saying that a rep message was either successfully received by your workstation or sent to your enterprise server.

Now that you understand the replication process, you should be able to troubleshoot almost any replication problem. However, before we move on, we'd like to leave you with a tip if you are experiencing problems with replication. When you call J.D. Edwards customer support, you should have the following items in hand and ready to send to them:

- The F98DRPUB file contained in the system data source

- The F98DRSUB file contained in the system data source

- The JDE.INI file from the enterprise server

- The JDE.INI file from the client workstation

- The JDE.LOG and JDEDEBUG.LOG from the client workstation and the enterprise server after you have turned replication logging on and attempted to update a replicated table

This information will help J.D. Edwards customer support resolve your issue faster. With this information they will be able to see exactly how you have set up your replication configuration.

Third-Party Replication

Our discussion of replication would not be complete if we did not touch on third-party replication. OneWorld replication does not need to be the only solution you use. In fact, if you are setting up a large amount of replication, you probably will want to use a product from a vendor that specializes in replication. This can be either a specialized type of software or the replication functionality built into your database.

If you use a third-party software to replicate some of your tables, keep a few things in mind. One is that you will not be able to set up data dictionary replication through a third-party application. You also will not be able to track any of your replication changes through the OneWorld software.

So if you are going to use a third-party replication solution, we recommend that you plan how you are going to track your changes and how you are going to implement this solution for OneWorld. We also recommend that you determine what type of replication needs you have. If you are using data replication to mirror your system, you will need to make sure your replication solution can handle this and that you have the ability to roll transactions back if you lose power in the middle of a transaction.

Summary

In this chapter, we have gone over replication and what it can mean to your business. Replication can be a great asset to you. It can assist you in moving your data closer to your end users. However, it can also complicate your overall system solution.

The important thing to remember when thinking about replication is what your business needs are. Why do you need to replicate information across your system? Is it for wide area network performance? If so, there may be a better solution to your issue than replication.

We went on to discuss the different types of replication OneWorld offers. We discussed pull replication, push replication, data dictionary replication, just-in-time replication, and third-party replication. These different types of replication allow you to implement a variety of replication solutions throughout your enterprise. We covered how to set up replication through the Work With Publishers application in OneWorld.

We then moved on to how the replication process flows. We covered how the kernel process handles replication. This chapter also talked about how to turn on logging for your replication solution. This type of troubleshooting will aid you in solving any replication issues you might have. Finally, we talked about what to have in hand if you need to contact J.D. Edwards customer support on a OneWorld replication issue.

Troubleshooting

CHAPTER 16

OneWorld Administrative Tasks

I n this chapter, we are going to cover several of the administrative tasks that you face as a OneWorld administrator. In this arduous position, you have to wear many different hats (version control specialist, network architect, systems analyst, quality assurance manager, systems administrator, and the list goes on). It is your responsibility to keep the system up and running smoothly.

We are going to go discuss the following topics in this chapter:

- Multitier deployment

- Server Administration workbench

- OneWorld server code

- User overrides

- Scheduler

Multitier Deployment

In Chapter 5, you learned that a deployment server is used to deploy the software throughout your enterprise. Multitier deployment is a Configurable Network Computing (CNC) concept that assists you in deploying your client packages (especially to remote sites or to large numbers of fat clients). The concept of packages is discussed in Chapter 10. In this section, we are going to discuss system administration activities that can enhance the delivery of your packages to end users.

Definition

Multitier deployment enables you to deploy packages with the least amount of impact on your network and primary deployment server. When you deploy a package, it takes up bandwidth on your network and resources on your deployment server. If you are deploying to only a few users, this is not an issue. However, some organizations need to deploy a package to 300 workstations in one day, and some workstations may be across a wide area network.

J.D. Edwards developed multitier deployment as a tool for deploying hundreds of client workstations at the same time without crushing the network or the deployment server.

A typical OneWorld installation includes a deployment server, client workstations, and at least one enterprise server. In order to deploy 300 client workstations in one day, you have to add more deployment servers! OneWorld enables you to add deployment servers to your architecture. These deployment servers are called *tier 2 deployment servers*. The original deployment server is your primary deployment server where package builds write Table Access Manager (TAM) files to. The tier 2 deployment servers receive that package information from the primary deployment server. These tier 2 deployment servers then service a set of workstations. This means that your primary deployment server does not become overwhelmed.

Multitier Deployment in the OneWorld Architecture

OneWorld software is highly configurable and scalable. Multitier deployment enables you to scale the software to meet your needs.

A good rule of thumb when thinking about multitier deployment is that if you have more than 50 users who will be deploying a package on the same day, you should add another deployment server. For example, suppose you have 300 OneWorld users who are using fat client machines. You want to ensure that end users receive the most recent package in a timely manner. In order to provide this service, you add five tier 2 deployment servers. (Remember our rule of thumb that each deployment server can deploy a package to only 50 users in the same day.) Even though your company has all of their OneWorld end users at the same facility, you still need to set up multitier deployment.

Your company must carefully examine its end users' job functions as they relate to OneWorld. This helps you assign these users to deployment servers. For example, you can group your financial department on to one deployment server because the personnel in this department work in similar applications. Figure 16-1 shows how you can set up your servers to meet your end users' needs.

As you can see from Figure 16-1, multitier deployment can save you from overloading your deployment server. It can also save you from overloading a network segment because each deployment server can be on a different segment. You can talk to a network specialist on how to get the most out of your network.

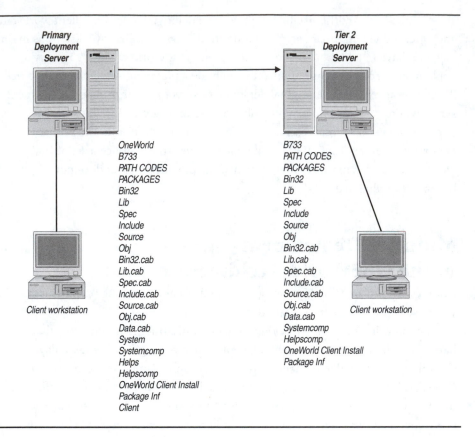

FIGURE 16-1.   Simple example of multitier deployment

Multitier Deployment with a WAN

Suppose your company has added another site with 50 employees who are going to use a fat client solution with a workgroup server. Thus, you have to deploy 50 more workstations over a wide area network. You obviously do not want a lot of traffic going across that wire during peak hours. That kind of traffic would cause your network administrator's blood pressure to rise!

To handle this situation, you simply add another tier 2 deployment server at your remote site. Then you can deploy your packages out to this second-tier deployment server during off hours. When this deployment server has received these packages, it can then service the 50 end users at the remote site. When you deploy a package, to these end users, you are deploying the package across the LAN instead of the WAN, which makes a difference. This configuration is shown in Figure 16-2.

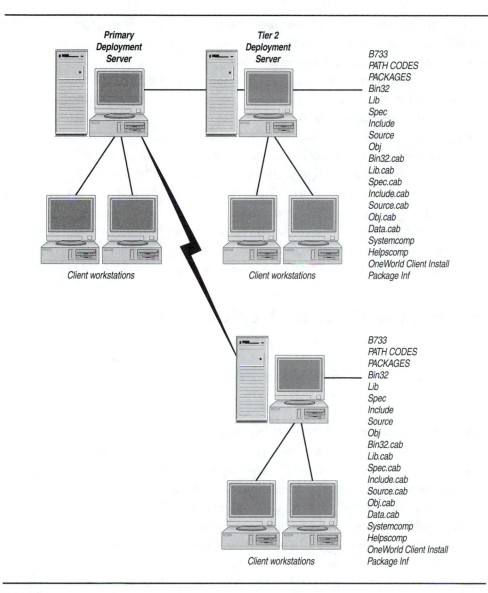

FIGURE 16-2.   Example of multitier deployment over a WAN

N-Tier Deployment

Suppose your company acquires another company and now has another 150 end users who reside at the same remote site as the original 50. Remembering our rule of thumb, you do not have enough deployment servers at this site to handle the demand. You also do not want to add additional traffic to the WAN by adding more tier 2 deployment servers. So you add a tier 3 deployment server.

A tier 3 deployment server receives its packages from a tier 2 deployment server. This means that your primary deployment server gives the tier 2 deployment server the information it needs across the WAN at off peak hours. This tier 2 deployment server then gives this information to the tier 3 deployment servers. The tier 2 deployment server and the tier 3 deployment servers are on the same network, which means that you are going over a LAN instead of the expensive and usually slow WAN. Figure 16-3 shows the configuration of the tier 3 deployment servers.

As you can see in Figure 16-3, tier 3 deployment servers become necessary as your company grows, and OneWorld software enables you to accommodate your company's growth by allowing you to add an N-tier deployment server. This means you can add as many levels of tiered deployment servers as your company requires.

Setting Up Multitier Deployment

You need to perform several steps in order to set up OneWorld multitier deployment. These steps give the system the information that it needs to find the primary deployment server, tier 2 deployment server, or the records for CD deployment. With this information, the system enables you to push the necessary information out to your servers.

Deployment Server Share Name

When you set up multitier deployment, you first need to ensure that your share name is set up correctly on your deployment server. This share name is the key to multitier deployment being able to find package information. When you use multitier deployment, the system looks at F00942, the Path Code Master table to determine where to find the package you want to deploy (we discuss how to set up the Path Code Master table later in this section). The system gets the deployment server name, share path, and path code name. With this information, it tries to find the deployment server on the network by name. The system then attempts to connect to the share path, an example of which is B733. If this directory is not shared, multitier deployment fails.

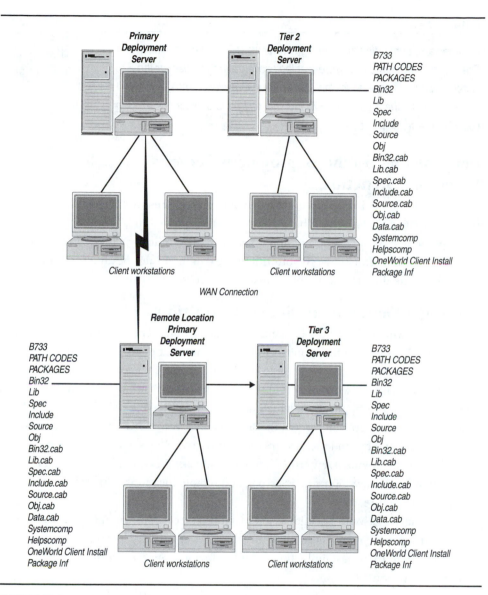

FIGURE 16-3. Example of tier 3 deployment servers

CAUTION

It is important to mention that although Windows NT is not case sensitive, the OneWorld share name is. Ensure that the capitalization you use for the B733 directory is the same used for the share path in OneWorld. Thus, if you told the system that the share path was B733, do not share the directory as b733, or you will experience issues.

Permissions on the Deployment Server's Directory Structure

The next step in setting up a multitier deployment is to ensure that you have both read and write permissions on both your primary deployment server and your tier 2 deployment server. This permission is set through Windows NT. If you do not have the proper permissions, the multitier program might not be able to create the appropriate directory structure, causing the process to fail.

Adding a Deployment Server Definition

At this point, you add your deployment server definitions. These definitions give the system vital information that it needs to perform multitier deployment. To add your deployment server definition, log on to OneWorld, go to the Package And Deployment Tools menu, GH9083, where you find the Machine Identification program, P9654A. Double-click on this application, which takes you into the Work With Locations And Machines screen where you can tell the system about your tier 2 deployment server.

Press Find and expand the directory structure tree. This screen shows you your workstations, deployment, enterprise, and data servers, JAVA application servers (Web server), Windows Terminal Servers, and remote locations. This information is depicted in Figure 16-4.

From the Work With Locations And Machines screen, shown in Figure 16-4, highlight the Deployment Server directory under your primary location and click the Add button. In our example, this is the Deployment Server directory under the Corporate location.

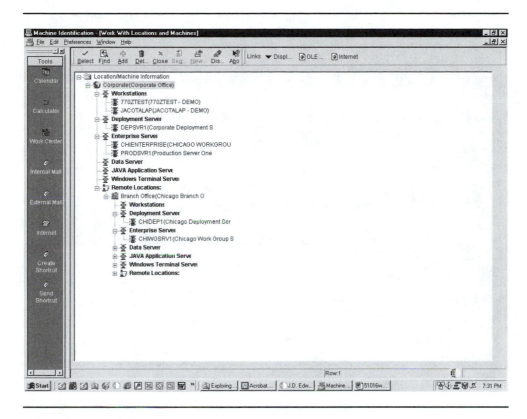

FIGURE 16-4. Work With Locations And Machines screen

The Deployment Server Revisions screen (shown in Figure 16-5) is displayed; this is where you enter data that tells the system how to find your tier 2 deployment server. You must ensure that all of the proper data is entered on this screen, or you will experience issues later on in your multitier deployment activities. The fields on the Deployment Server Revisions screen are described in Table 16-1.

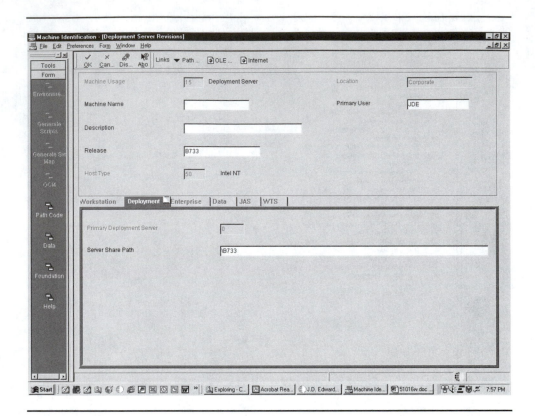

FIGURE 16-5. Deployment Server Revisions screen

Field	Description
Machine Usage	This field should default to 15 for the deployment server and be grayed out. If it is not, click Cancel, highlight the Deployment Server directory, and click Add on the toolbar.
Location	This field is grayed out and shows the location that the deployment server is associated with. In OneWorld, a location is where you define machines and environments. The software is first installed at one primary location (for example, Denver), and you can then set up as many remote locations as necessary.

TABLE 16-1. Fields on the Deployment Server Revisions Screen

Field	Description
Machine Name	The name of the deployment server you are setting up. You need to be able to ping this machine by this name on the network.
Description	A description of your deployment server.
Release	The release number of OneWorld software that you will be placing on the deployment server.
Host Type	This defaults at 50 for Windows/Intel NT. The tier 2 deployment servers must be Windows/Intel NT, because they are simply file servers that contain the system's package files.
Primary User	The primary user of the machine. If you aren't sure of what to enter in this field, use **JDE**.
Primary Deployment Server	This field indicates whether this deployment server is the primary deployment server for the location. (Remember you can have multiple locations. This is what allows you to implement a tier 3 solution.)
Server Share Path	This is the name of a directory that you will need to share on your deployment server. It normally is B733. You need to list this directory so that the software knows where to copy the files onto the tier 2 deployment server.

TABLE 16-1.   Fields on the Deployment Server Revisions Screen *(continued)*

After you have entered information on the Deployment Server Revisions screen, click OK to save it. This takes you back to the Work With Locations And Machines screen. Click Find on this screen and expand the Deployment Server directory, under your primary location (which in our example is Corporate). The new deployment server definition is displayed. You have now told the system that you have a tier 2 deployment server for your primary location, the server's name, and the share path where the system will copy information.

For a Remote Location

Suppose your company has acquired an office in Atlanta. You need to deploy packages to client machines at this location. You need to tell the system about the remote location in Atlanta. To do this, you click Find on the Work With Locations And Machines application. Then expand the directory structure, highlight the Remote Locations directory, and click Add on the toolbar. This takes you into the Location Revisions screen shown in Figure 16-6. On this screen, you tell the system about your remote location and its parent location. The parent location is responsible for pushing information out; basically, the parent location feeds your remote location information. Table 16-2 describes the fields in the Location Revisions screen.

Troubleshooting

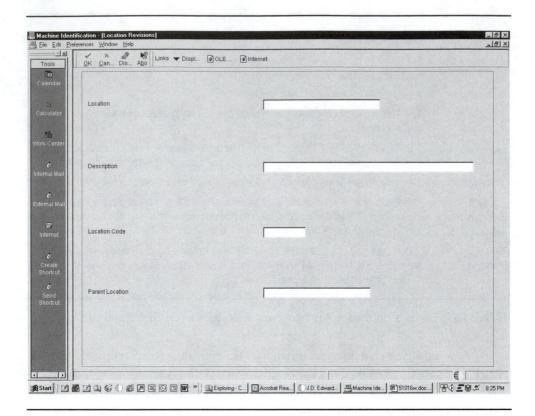

FIGURE 16-6.   Location Revisions screen

Field	Location
Location	Enter the name of your location.
Description	Describe your location. Be sure to enter information in this field that enables you to easily identify the location and how it ties into your business.
Location Code	If the location is your parent or master location, this field is blank. If the location is a remote location, you must enter a three-letter code to describe the location. If you set up environments for this remote location, OneWorld enters the code at the beginning of the environment names, which enables you to easily see what environments are used where.
Parent Location	The location that the remote location depends upon to receive information. If you are adding a parent location, this field is blank.

TABLE 16-2.   Fields on the Location Revisions Screen

After you fill in the necessary information on the Location Revisions screen, click the OK button to save your information. This takes you back to the Work With Locations And Machines screen. Click Find on this screen and expand the directory structure. Under the Remote Locations directory, you should see the location you just added.

Under the remote location in Figure 16-7, are displayed directories for workstations, deployment, enterprise, and data servers, JAVA application servers, Windows Terminal Servers, and the remote location for this location. This means that you have the option of setting up servers that service this site on the remote site's LAN, which used to be a popular solution, using replication to keep the servers in sync. It's more practical to use multitier deployment to offload client installations from your main site rather than setting up multitier deployment with workgroup servers as a

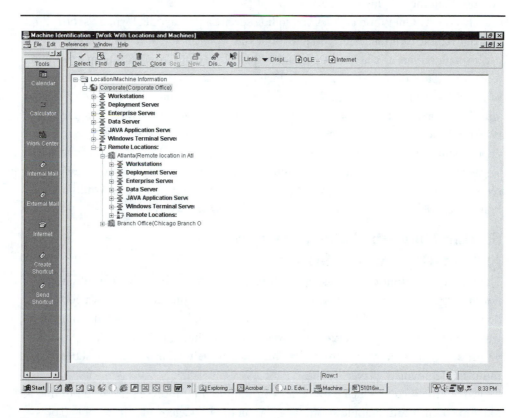

FIGURE 16-7. Example of a remote location (Atlanta)

WAN solution. This is because a Windows Terminal Server or Web server solution usually is less expensive and can adequately meet the needs of your business.

Highlight the Deployment Server directory under your remote location and click the Add button to access the Deployment Server Revisions screen. The location field now shows Atlanta (in our example) instead of Corporate. You can refer back to Figure 16-5 to see what this screen looks like. After you have entered your deployment server information, click OK, which takes you back to the Work With Locations And Machines screen.

As previously mentioned, you can add multiple tier 2 deployment servers to the primary location. If you are pushing a package across the WAN for your users in Atlanta, you do not want to have to push that package across the WAN more than once. If you have more than 50 users in Atlanta that deploy a package in one day, you need another deployment server.

This is why OneWorld enables you to first specify a primary deployment server for your remote location. Once you have done this, you can add as many secondary deployment servers as you like. A package is then pushed out from your primary location to your remote location. This package, which is going across the WAN, is placed on your primary deployment server for the remote location. Once the package has made it that far, you can run a job at the remote location to move this package from the remote location's primary deployment server to the location's secondary deployment servers, (your tier 3 deployment servers). This means that this copy goes across the LAN instead of the WAN.

You can add as many remote locations and deployment servers as your business requires. You must be sure that you have the resources to support your configuration. Remember each added location increases complexity and overhead.

Setting Up Path Codes to Deploy to Your Deployment Servers

The path code definition defines which directory structure should be placed on your new server. If the users that this server services use only the CRPB733 path code, you do not need to have the PRDB733 path code on this deployment server. It would be a waste of disk space on the server and a waste of your time. (This is another reason why you should plan where your end users go and what their needs are before setting up multitier deployment servers.)

To tell the system which path codes you want to put on these servers, go to the Machine Identification application, P9654A, on the Package And Deployment Tools menu, GH9083. This application drives multitier deployment. The Work With Locations And Machines screen, as shown earlier in Figure 16-4, is displayed.

Expand the directory structure until you see the Deployment Server directory structure for the location you are interested in. For example, if you want to work with a tier 2 deployment server located at your primary location, you expand the primary location and then the Deployment Server directory. The deployment server that you want to work with is listed. If you want to work with a deployment server at a remote location, you expand your primary location first, then the Remote Location directory, and then the remote location you are interested in. Finally, expand the Deployment Server directory structure.

When you finally get to the deployment server that you want to work with, the procedure for adding a path code or multiple path codes to the deployment server is the same. Once you have found the record you are interested in, highlight it and click the Select button. This takes you into the Deployment Server Revisions screen shown earlier in Figure 16-5. This screen displays information, such as the deployment server name and share path, on the deployment server that you have defined. OneWorld requires additional information to successfully implement a multitier deployment.

Click the Path Code exit on the Deployment Server Revisions screen to access the Machine Path Code Revisions screen shown in Figure 16-8. You may be wondering why you couldn't set up the path code when you defined the deployment server record. You can define the path code at that time; we have chosen to present the information in this manner because we want you to understand how multitier deployment functions before you get caught up in the details of how to set it up in OneWorld.

Now that you understand how the multitier deployment process flows from one site to the next, let's return to the Machine Path Code Revision screen, which tells OneWorld which directory structure to copy to your tier 2 deployment server. Remember, each path code has its own directory structure on the deployment server. (For more information on path codes, refer to Chapter 2. For more information on how the directory structure fits into packages and package builds, refer to Chapter 10.)

In our example, we are defining the path codes that reside on our tier 2 deployment server. Our end users, who are using this deployment server to receive their packages, need to work in both the production and conference room pilot path codes. This is why we are defining the production path code and the CRP path code in our example. After you have defined the path codes to reside on your new deployment server, click OK; this takes you back to the Deployment Server Revisions screen.

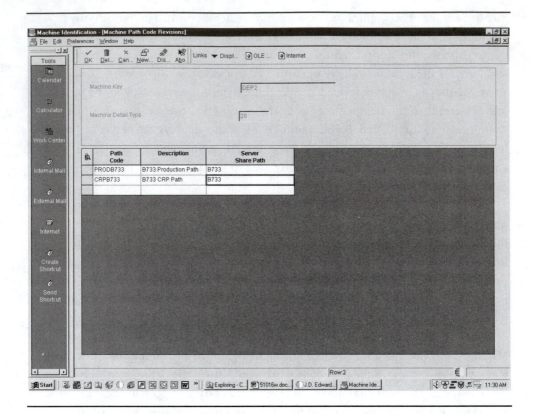

FIGURE 16-8. Machine Path Code Revisions screen

T I P

You notice that the development path code is not mentioned or shown in our example. This is because you shouldn't move your development path code to remote locations. J.D. Edwards recommends that all development work take place at one site. If you have 300 developers, like J.D. Edwards, you should define tier 2 deployment servers, but they should reside at your primary location, not at a remote location.

Defining the Access Databases That Are Moved to Your New Deployment Server

At this point, you still have to tell the system whether you want to move other pieces of data out to your new deployment server. One of these pieces of information is telling the system what "data" to move out to your new deployment server. You need to tell the system what Access database you wish to move out to your new deployment server. As mentioned previously, OneWorld is shipped with the menu and user-defined code tables mapped to an Access database. This Access database is held on the deployment server and moved down during a client installation (for more information on client installations, refer to Chapter 10). This means that you should move this Access database to your new deployment server. Now each path code has its own Access database. To tell the system how to move this Access database, go to the Form exit and select Data on the Deployment Server Revisions screen. This takes you into the Deployment Server Data screen shown in Figure 16-9.

If you have not added a custom database—that is, a path to an Access database—you can leave this screen blank. When the system does not find a path, it uses the default path, which is shipped with the software. For example, if the system were looking for the CRP path code's Access database, it would look on the deployment server under B733\CRPB733\Datacomp. On the Deployment Server Data screen, you tell the system where the Access database that you are looking for is located. Enter your cursor in the Data column and then click the visual assist button. This takes you into the Database Items Search And Select screen.

If you do not have a record in this screen, which points to your Access database, you can easily add one to the system. Click the Add button to access the Data Items Revisions screen shown in Figure 16-10. Table 16-3 lists the fields in this screen.

Troubleshooting

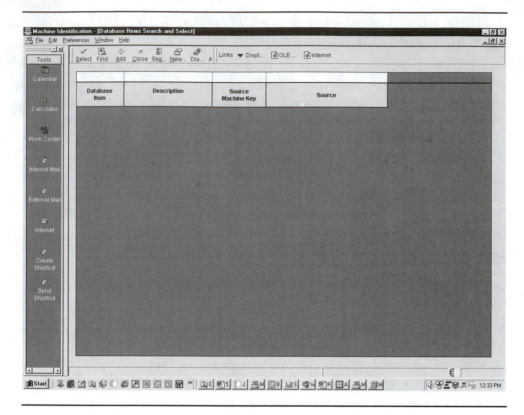

FIGURE 16-9.   Deployment Server Data screen

T I P

When you set up your Database Revisions screen values, you need network connectivity to the deployment server you specify in the Source Machine Key field. When you enter this record and the directory structure in the Source field, the system verifies that it can connect to the deployment server and find this directory structure. If it cannot, you receive an error.

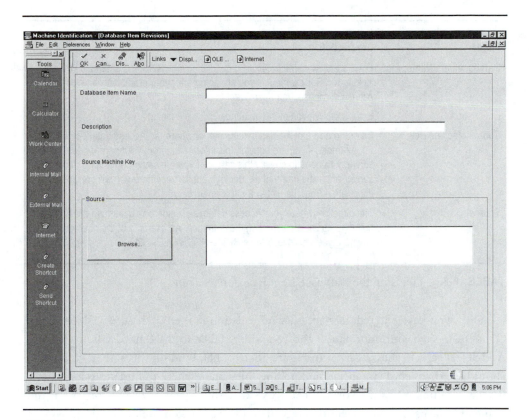

FIGURE 16-10. Database Item Revisions screen

T I P

When you tell the system where to find the database, do not point the system directly to the database. Instead, point the system to the compressed database, which is located in the Datacomp directory. You can save time and bandwidth by moving the compressed file.

Field	Description
Database Item Name	Enter a logical name in this field describing which Access database you are looking for. For example, if you are going after your production environment's Access database, you might want to use DPRODB733.
Description	Enter a description of the database you are defining.
Source Machine Key	Enter the name of the deployment server where the Access database resides. For example, if you are copying this information from your primary deployment server, you need to specify this server. If you are setting up a tier 3 deployment server, enter the name of the deployment server where you will copy this information from, i.e., a tier 2 deployment server.
Source	The directory where your Access database resides. You can use the Browse button to assist you in finding the database. An example of the directory structure you would look for is B733\PRODB733\DATA.

TABLE 16-3.   Fields on the Database Item Revisions Screen

Once you have entered the necessary information in the Database Revisions screen, click OK to save your information and you will be taken to the Database Items Search And Select screen, shown earlier in Figure 16-10. Click Find on this screen, and you should see the record you just added, telling the system where to find your access database, which your OneWorld Local—XXX data source points to (where XXX is the name of your path code). Select this record and you are taken back to the Deployment Server Data screen, shown earlier in Figure 16-9. Tab through the Description field, and the server share path information should default in. Remember that the server share path needs to match your share name in Windows NT in case and spaces used; after you have verified that this information is correct, click OK. This takes you back to the Deployment Server Revisions screen shown earlier in Figure 16-5.

Defining Your Foundation Information for Multitier Deployment

If you remember in Chapter 11, we told you that in OneWorld the term *foundation* means the system directory, which is the foundation that OneWorld applications rest on. Every client workstation has a system directory, which is required for the software to function correctly. Because you are setting up a new deployment server so that your client workstations can deploy packages from it, you need to have a system directory on this new deployment server for the client installation process to copy down to your workstations.

Thus, the next step in setting up multitier deployment is telling the system where the foundation or system directory is located. This record tells the system to copy this directory from the primary deployment server to your new deployment server. Go to the Form exit on the Deployment Server Revisions screen and take the Foundation exit to access the Deployment Server Foundation screen shown in Figure 16-11.

If you don't want to have a custom foundation, you can simply leave this screen blank. If the system does not see an entry in this screen, it uses the default location, which is where the system directory resides when the software is shipped. OneWorld also enables you to specify a custom foundation. You can simply point the software to the location where you have placed your system directory.

To define the foundation for your new deployment server, enter the cursor in the field under the Foundation column and click the visual assist button to access the

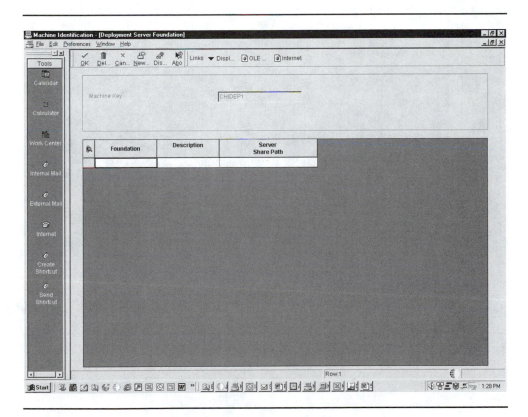

FIGURE 16-11. Deployment Server Foundation screen

Foundation Item Search And Select screen shown in Figure 16-12. Click Find on this screen to display all previously defined records. If some records are listed, select the appropriate record and verify that it does in fact point to the foundation or system directory on the machine that you desire.

If no records are listed in the Foundation Item Search And Select screen or the entries do not point to the correct location, click the Add button. This takes you to the Foundation Item Revisions screen, shown in Figure 16-13, where you tell the system on which machine the foundation or system directory that you want to move to your new deployment server resides. Table 16-4 describes the fields in this screen.

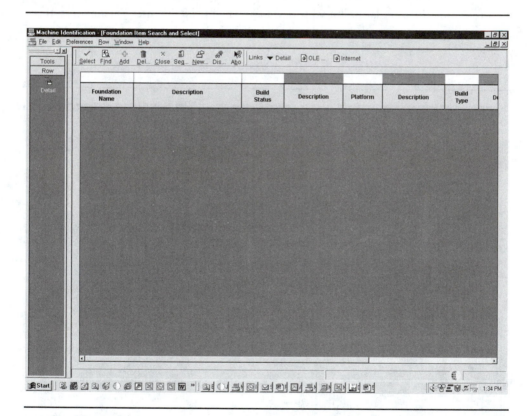

FIGURE 16-12. Foundation Item Search And Select screen

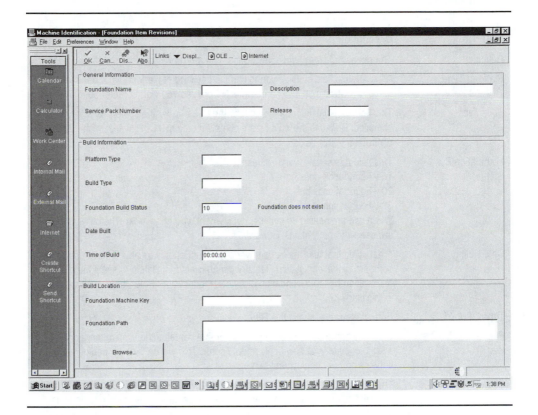

FIGURE 16-13.   Foundation Item Revisions screen

Troubleshooting

Field	Description
Foundation Name	Enter a logical name for your foundation. This name should make sense to you, and you should be able to figure out where this system resides by looking at this name.
Description	Enter a description of this foundation in this field.
Service Pack Number	This field contains the service pack that you are running on—for example, SP9 is Service Pack 9.

TABLE 16-4.   Fields in the Foundation Item Revisions Screen

Field	Description
Release	The release of OneWorld software that you are running on.
Platform Type	Although this field enables you to choose any kind of platform, your deployment server will always be a Windows/Intel NT box, so you want to enter **50** in this field.
Build Type	This field contains information on how the DLLs under the system directory were compiled. Because these DLLs are compiled only at J.D. Edwards, enter **20 optimized** in this field.
Foundation Build Status	This field has several valid values: 10—Foundation does not exist 20—Foundation is built 30—Foundation is available When you are setting up multitier deployment, you choose 30. The other values are used internally at J.D. Edwards.
Date Built	A date field that tells the system when the foundation was built. This is used to compare to the workstation Registry during client installation to see if the client workstation has this foundation or a newer foundation. Enter the current date in this field.
Time Of Build	Enter the current time in this field.
Foundation Machine Key	Enter the name of the deployment server that contains the system directory you wish to copy to your new deployment server. This will be the new deployment server's primary deployment server.
Foundation Path	The directory structure path, on the machine specified in the Foundation Machine Key field, where the system directory exists. Use the Browse button to find this information.

TABLE 16-4.   Fields in the Foundation Item Revisions Screen (*continued*)

T I P

When you choose a foundation path, you must have network connectivity because the system will try to connect to this directory structure to verify its existence. If the system cannot connect to the machine and directory structure that you defined, you receive an error.

T I P

When you tell the system where to find the foundation, do not point the system directly to the foundation. Instead, point the system to the compressed files, which is located in the systemcomp directory. Moving a compressed file saves on time and bandwidth.

After you finish defining your information, click OK. This takes you back to the Foundation Item Search And Select screen, shown earlier in Figure 16-12. Click Find on this screen and select the foundation record that you just defined. This takes you back to the Deployment Server Foundation screen, shown earlier in Figure 16-11. Tab through the Description field, and the server share path will be displayed. Ensure that this share path name exactly matches the share name in case and spaces used. An incorrect entry here is one of the most common problems with multitier deployment setups. Once you have verified your deployment server foundation record, click OK to save your definition.

Defining Help Information for Multitier Deployment

At this point, you should consider whether you need to move your help files onto your new deployment server. You can set up your workstations so that they do not have the help files on them and they are located somewhere else on the network. If you are deploying the help files to your new deployment server, you need to tell the system where to find the help information. If you are unsure about what to do for this step, go ahead and define the helps for your new deployment server.

Suppose you have customized your help files for your end users, and you do not want to move all of them because this site uses only the manufacturing suite. The system enables you to specify a path to a set of custom help files.

To tell the system how to find your help files, go to the Form exit and select help on the Deployment Server Revisions screen. This takes you to the Deployment Server Helps screen. Place your cursor in the Helps column and click the visual assist to access the Helps Items Search And Select screen shown in Figure 16-14.

Troubleshooting

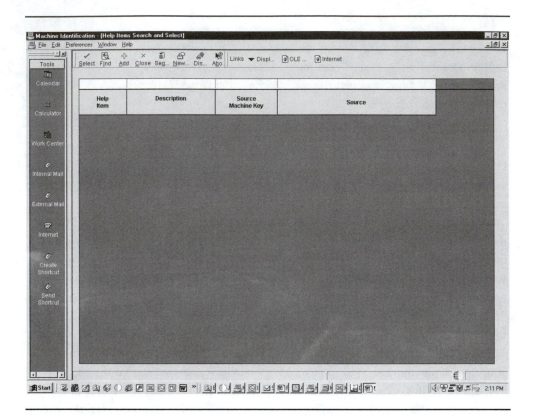

FIGURE 16-14. Help Items Search And Select screen

On the Help Items Search And Select screen, click Find to see if you have already set up records to point to your help files. If you have, select this record and confirm that it points to the help directory on your new deployment server's primary deployment server. Remember, this is the deployment server that will push information to your new N tier deployment server. If you do not find any records or if you do not have a record pointing to the correct machine, click the Add button. This takes you to the Help Item Revisions screen, shown in Figure 16-15, where you tell the system how to find the help files that you want to move to your new deployment server. This screen is almost identical

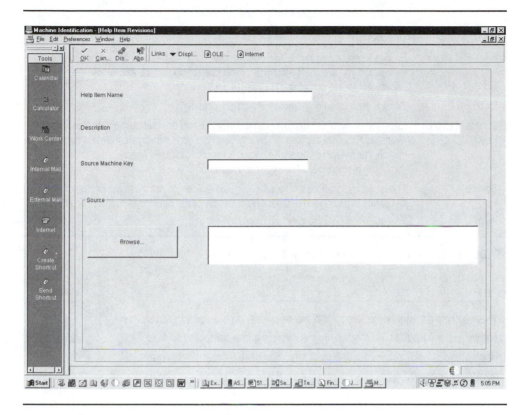

FIGURE 16-15. Help Item Revisions screen

to the Data Item Revisions screen. The fields on the Help Item Revisions screen are described in Table 16-5.

T I P

Again, when you enter a machine and a directory structure definition in the Source Machine Key and Source fields, the system tries to connect to that directory structure to confirm its existence. If you do not have network connectivity to this machine or if the directory structure does not exist, you receive an error.

Field	Description
Help Item Name	Enter a logical name in this field describing which help files you are looking for. For example, if you are going after your production environment's Access database, you might want to use something like HPRODB733.
Description	Enter a description of the help files you are defining.
Source Machine Key	Enter the name of the deployment server where you are getting the help files from. For example, if you are copying this information from your primary deployment server, specify this server. If you are setting up a tier 3 deployment server, enter the name of the deployment server where you copy this information from.
Source	The directory structure where your help files reside. You can use the Browse button to assist you in finding the database. An example of the directory structure you look for is B733\HelpComp.

TABLE 16-5.   Fields on the Help Item Revisions Screen

T I P

When you tell the system where to find the help files, do not point the system directly to the help files. Instead, point the system to the compressed help files, which are located in the Helpcomp directory. You save time and bandwidth by moving compressed files.

After you have entered the necessary information in the Help Item Revisions screen, click OK to save the record. This takes you back to the Help Items Search And Select screen. Click Find on this screen, highlight the helps record that you have defined, and click Select to access the Deployment Server Helps screen. Tab through the Description field, and the server share path will default in. Verify that this server share path matches the share name you have defined in Windows NT exactly. If it does not, you will have issues with your multitier deployment setup. Click OK to save the information; this takes you back to the Deployment Server Revisions screen.

Congratulations, you have now told the system about your new deployment server and the files that reside on it. However, you are not finished setting everything up yet.

You have not copied any information from the primary deployment server to the new deployment server.

Moving Directories to Your New Deployment Server

Any deployment server added through multitier deployment does not really run the OneWorld software, which means that you cannot log on to OneWorld on these machines. These machines act as file servers so that they can take some of the workload off of the original deployment server. These servers can also help move your package information closer to your end users if you have a WAN in your configuration.

To start the process of copying the directory structure to your new deployment server, log on to your network as a Windows NT user who has read and write privileges to the directory structure on your new deployment server (or servers) as well as your primary deployment server. You can be on the primary deployment server or a client machine, as long as you have the correct permissions to the deployment servers' directory structures.

Double-click on P9631, the Package Deployment application on the Package And Deployment Tools menu GH9083. This takes you to the Work With Package Deployment screen shown in Figure 16-16.

Click the radio button that displays the information in the manner you desire and click Find. You can review information by machines, deployment groups, locations, or packages. We recommend that you display your information by locations when setting up multitier deployment. This helps you keep things straight when you are defining your deployment information for your new deployment servers. Click the Add button on this screen to access the Package Deployment director.

Defining a Deployment Record for Your Multitier Deployment Server   Click the Next button on the introductory screen to the Package Deployment director. This takes you into the Package Selection Screen. This screen prompts you for the name of the package you wish to deploy or move to your new deployment server. For our example, let's select the CRPB733FA package and click Next.

This takes you into the Package Deployment Targets screen. (This screen was also covered in Chapter 10.) Check the Deployment Server check box and then the Next

Troubleshooting

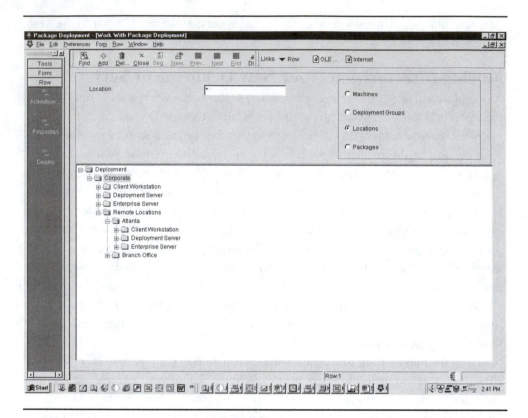

FIGURE 16-16.   Work With Package Deployment screen

button. This takes you into the Package Deployment Attributes screen shown in Figure 16-17, where you tell the system when your package can be moved to your new deployment server.

When the deployment process runs, it reads the date and time stamp that you set on the Package Deployment Attributes screen. You can define all of your package deployments at once and set them to run at different times, when they will have the least impact on network traffic and when the source and target deployment servers are

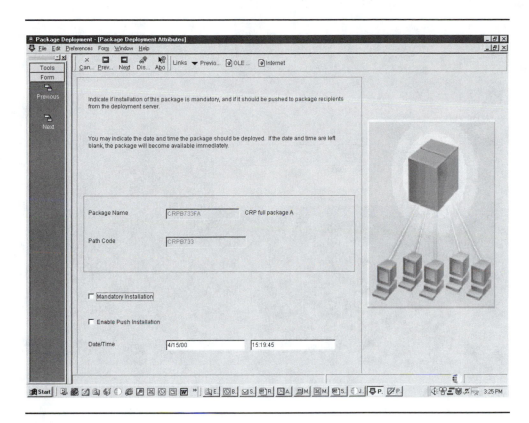

FIGURE 16-17.   Package Deployment Attributes screen

available. Do not check the Mandatory Installation or the Enable Push Installation check boxes. You use these options to deploy packages to your client workstations (for more information on package deployment, refer to Chapter 10). After you entered the date and time when you want your package to move from your primary deployment server to your new deployment server, click the Next button to access the Deployment Server Selection screen shown in Figure 16-18.

This screen displays all of the deployment servers that you have defined in the system. Select the deployment server that you wish to move your package to. After you

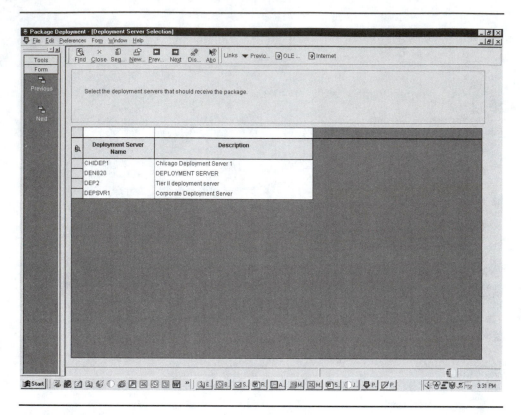

FIGURE 16-18.   Deployment Server Selection screen

have selected the deployment server that you desire, click the Next button. This takes
you to the Work With Package Deployment screen, where you click the End button.

CAUTION

*When you get to the Work With Package Deployment screen, click the End
button. It is easy to accidentally click the Cancel button. If you do click the
Cancel button, you will lose your package deployment definition information
and have to start over.*

At this point, you can tell the system to copy the packages to your deployment server. You can use the Package Deployment application or run a report that moves your packages to your deployment server.

C A U T I O N

As we mentioned earlier in this chapter, you need to manually create a B733 share name through Windows Explorer on your new deployment server. This directory must be created and shared before you can tell the system to copy the packages from one deployment server to the next.

You can move your package to your deployment server by finding the deployment server listing in the Work With Package Deployment screen. Highlight your deployment server and click the Deploy button located under the Row exit in this application. This launches the R98825C report. As it launches, you are prompted for the report output destination. You export the report to your screen, a printer, or to CSV.

The report moves your package from your primary deployment server to your new deployment server. The report reads the records that you have set up in the Machine Identification application. The R98825C report looks for the location of the foundation, and the Access database and help files to copy. It also looks for the path codes you want on your new deployment server. When this report finishes, you should have a path code directory structure on your new deployment server.

T I P

A common reason for this report to fail is because the Windows NT user you are signed on to the network as does not have sufficient read/write privileges to the directory structure. Another common cause of failure is that the name of the B733 directory is not defined using the same case as you used when you defined the directory within the OneWorld applications. This inconsistent use of capitalization can cause the R98825C report to fail.

Moving the Client Installation Programs to Your New Deployment Server   You can't deploy a client from your new deployment server until you complete one last step. The good news is that this step must be done only once, for each release and/or service pack level of the software. You must move the client installation software onto your new deployment server.

If you know how to copy directory structures within Windows Explorer, you are set because in this last step, all you are doing is moving a directory structure that contains the client installation programs.

First, you need to map a drive, using Windows Explorer, to your primary deployment server as well as to your new deployment server. Then simply copy the OneWorld client installation directory from your original deployment server to your new deployment server. This directory contains the client workstation installation programs that are required to deploy the OneWorld software to your client workstations. However, you need to perform this process only once, unless you have changed to a different release of the OneWorld software.

At this point, you need to modify the INSTALL.INF file located under the OneWorld Client Install directory. This file tells the client installation software where to find the package INF files (for more information on package INF files, refer to Chapter 10).

After you have opened the INF file, you need to change two entries in this file: the PackageInfs and the ClientListenter entries. These entries contain the name of your primary deployment server. You need to change these entries to the name of your new deployment server. This tells the client installation software to look on your new deployment server for your package INF files, which in turn tells the installation software to pull the packages from your new deployment server. You change the client listener entry because the system enables you to push unattended packages out to your workstations (for more information on push installation, refer to Chapter 10). In order for this to take place, you need to deploy the client listener software to your workstation. This path tells the installation software where to copy the client listener program from. The following is an example of the entries in the CLIENT.INF file:

```
[FileLocations]
PackageInfs=\\DPIS02\B733\package_inf
CurrentReleaseMasterPath=\\DPIS02\B733
ClientListener=\\DPIS02\B733\OneWorld Client Install\Push Install
Listener,Setup.exe,/s
```

Do not change the current release master path because it should point to your primary deployment server. After you have changed these entries and deployed your packages out to your new deployment server, you are ready to install a client workstation from this deployment server. An example of the directory structure that you should have on your new deployment server is shown in Figure 16-19.

CD Multitier Deployment

This section takes you deeper into an advanced CNC concept of multitier deployment. You can also place packages and the OneWorld client installation software onto a CD, which means that if you have only a small bandwidth between remote sites and you do not want to tie up your network pushing packages across this small pipe, you don't have to. You can burn a CD with the package you wish to deploy to your remote site and drop it into the mail. Figure 16-20 provides an example of CD deployment.

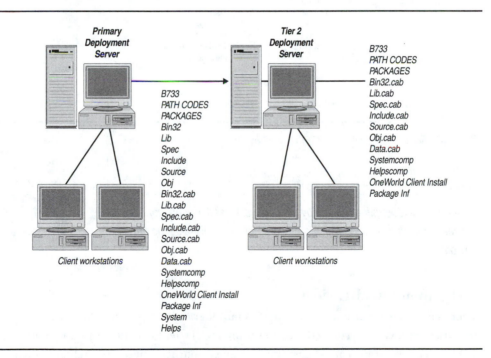

FIGURE 16-19.   Example of tier 2 deployment server's directory structure

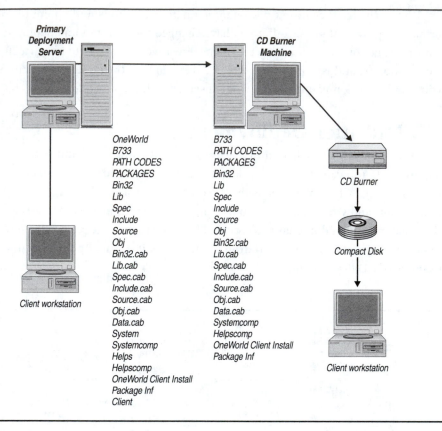

OneWorld	B733
B733	PATH CODES
PATH CODES	PACKAGES
PACKAGES	Bin32
Bin32	Lib
Lib	Spec
Spec	Include
Include	Source
Source	Obj
Obj	Bin32.cab
Bin32.cab	Lib.cab
Lib.cab	Spec.cab
Spec.cab	Include.cab
Include.cab	Source.cab
Source.cab	Obj.cab
Obj.cab	Data.cab
Data.cab	Systemcomp
System	Helpscomp
Systemcomp	OneWorld Client Install
Helps	Package Inf
Helpscomp	
OneWorld Client Install	
Package Inf	
Client	

FIGURE 16-20.   Example of CD deployment

CAUTION

When you are attempting CD deployment, you still need network connectivity between your sites for licensing information. However, this takes up hardly any bandwidth.

CD Burner Definition

There's a lot of similarity in setting up CD multitier deployment and "normal" multitier deployment. The first step in setting up CD deployment is to set up your CD burner definition. You can use any type of CD burner you desire. Actually, the term *CD burner definition* is kind of a misnomer. It describes an actual file server, basically a tier 2 deployment server. After you move your packages onto this deployment server, you then copy this information to your CD. This is normally done through a drag-and-drop procedure, but it depends on the CD burner software you are using. The important thing to keep in mind is that the system is just moving the directories to another machine. You have to manually burn your own CD.

J.D. Edwards developed the system like this for a specific reason. If they had written the software to connect directly to a CD burner, most of which can be placed on a network, they would have tied the software to a specific brand of CD burner and a specific release of software for the CD burner, which is not very configurable. This is why the CD burner definition is truly just a "holding area" for the directories before you move them onto your CD burner.

To tell the system about this "holding area" you need to define the CD burner in the Machine Identification application located on the Package And Deployment Tools menu GH9083. You simply double-click on this application, which takes you into the Work With Locations And Machines screen shown in Figure 16-21. Adding this definition to your system is going to be exactly like adding a "normal" tier deployment server.

Highlight the Deployment Server directory under the location you desire and click Add to access the Deployment Server Revisions screen. You need to enter the same information that you did for a "normal" tier deployment server, including the deployment server name, share path, release, and primary user. Then take the Path Code Form exit. Define the path codes you want to move to this "holding area" for your CD deployment and the data, foundation, and helps for this record as well. We described how to accomplish this in the earlier sections, such as "Defining Your Foundation Information for Multitier Deployment." Follow the exact same procedure for adding your CD burner definition.

After you define your CD burner or "holding area," you need to deploy your packages to this machine. You follow the same procedure that we went over previously. Then copy the client installation programs to the CD burner machine and modify the CLIENT.INF file as previously described.

Setting up the INF Files

After you have moved all of the required directory structure across to your CD burner location, you need to modify some of the files on this CD burner machine to tell OneWorld that you are placing the packages on a CD. To start this procedure, find the CLIENT.INF file located under the OneWorld Client Install directory on the CD burner machine. Open this file and go to the PackageInfs and ClientListener values in

Troubleshooting

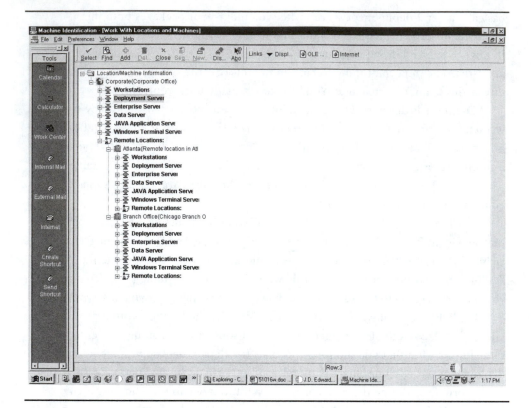

FIGURE 16-21.   Work With Locations And Machines screen

the File Locations section. These values are currently set to paths to your primary deployment server. You need to tell OneWorld to move up one directory instead of going across the network to find another machine. To do so, you would replace the name of your primary deployment server with ".." (two periods without the quotes). This tells the client installation software to look one directory level up for the client listener and package INF files. The following is an example of how we changed the PackageInfs and ClientListener values:

```
[FileLocations]
PackageInfs=..\package_inf
CurrentReleaseMasterPath=\\DPIS02\B733
ClientListener=..\OneWorld Client Install\Push Install Listener,Setup.exe,/s
```

At this point, you modify the package INF files to tell the system to look on the CD rather than across the network for the information that it needs. Go to the package INF directory on your CD burner machine and find the INF files for the packages that you are moving to your CD. You then modify these files to reflect the correct location of your information. In the package INF file, which is *PACKAGENAME*.INF, you modify the source directory area of the INF file. This section of the INF file contains your primary deployment server's name and share path. Remove the deployment server name and share path. Replace this information with ".." (two periods without the quotes), which tells the software to look one directory level up for the information. An example of the source directories area of a package INF file follows:

```
[SrcDirs]
SDEVB733=..\CRPB733\package\CRPB733FA
SSYS=..\systemcomp
SDEVB733DATA=..\CRPB733\package\datacomp
SHELP=..\helpscomp
```

After you are finished modifying the INF files, you are ready to burn your CD. Simply use the CD burner and CD burner software of your choice and move the following directory structure to your CD:

```
B733
    Path code Directory
Package Name
Package INF Directory
Datacomp Directory
    Helpscomp Directory
    Systemcomp directory
    OneWorld Client install directory
```

We recommend that you test the CD before you drop it in the mail to your remote site because it is easy for a typo to creep into one of the INF files, which will give you headaches.

CD Deployment and Update Packages

We have discussed burning a CD to deploy packages to your workstations. Bear in mind that once you use a CD to deploy a package to a client workstation, you need to perform a manual step on the machine to deploy update packages to that machine. This is because the client workstations keep track of where they deployed their package from in the registry. If you deploy to this workstation through CD deployment, the registry entry refers to the workstation's CD-ROM.

If you schedule an update package to a workstation that was deployed through a CD, the system looks for the OneWorld client installation software on the workstation's CD-ROM. Unless you are going to burn an update CD for every user and ensure that each one has this CD in his or her machine, you need to change the workstation's registry entry. Change the workstation's registry entry to point to a valid deployment server that contains the update packages you wish to deploy. This registry entry can be found under HKEY_LOCAL_MACHINE\SOFTWARE\ JDEdwars\OneWorld\Install.INI\B733. Under this path, you will find the launch path registry value, which points to the workstation's CD-ROM drive. If you wish to deploy update packages to this machine, you need to change this launch path value to a valid deployment server, which contains your update packages. An example of what this registry setting looks like is shown next.

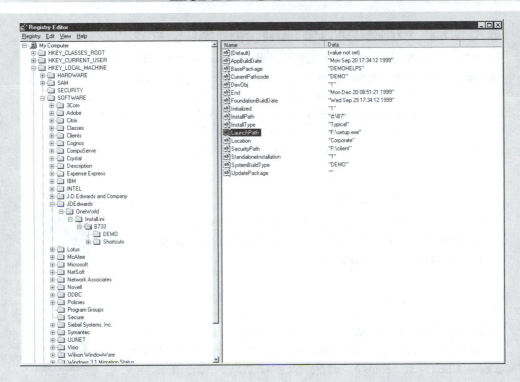

You need network connectivity between the client workstation you are installing with a CD and your primary deployment server so that your workstation has access to the licensing files.

Server Administration Workbench

J.D. Edwards provides a tool, the Server Administration workbench (SAW), to assist you in maintaining and monitoring your application and enterprise servers. You can set up this tool to provide logging information and to e-mail or page you if a problem arises.

One of the primary uses of SAW is to monitor the host code on your enterprise servers. You can easily track the two most important processes, JDENet and JDEQUEUE, which enable your host code to function correctly.

DEFINITION

JDENet: *JDENet handles communication between the client machines and the enterprise server. It is also responsible for starting processes, such as the replication kernel, on the enterprise server.*

DEFINITION

JDEQUEUE: *JDEQUEUE polls a relational database, the F986110 table, to see if a report or UBE is waiting to be processed. When JDEQUEUE finds a job or UBE to run, it starts a child process to run the job (Runbatch). Once that process completes, JDEQUEUE looks for the next job in the F986110 table. This process is set up to poll for a specific batch name. You can also set up multiple JDEQUEUE processes so that you can run several jobs at the same time in one queue.*

In order to monitor these processes, you can use SAW in several different ways. Not only does SAW enable you to monitor the server processes from a client workstation, it also enables you to monitor the processes on the enterprise servers themselves. This tool enables you to change your INI file, view your logs, start and end your host services, view the list of users connected to a process, turn logging on or off, and even print your logs.

Monitoring Servers

As system administrator, you can set up SAW to run on your own workstation. This application can run in the background and monitor the servers on the system.

Using SAW on NT Servers and Workstations

You can start SAW in several ways. However, for the sake of our discussion we will start the server administration workbench by typing SAW in the Fast Path. This takes you into the SAW application; the SAW interface is shown in Figure 16-22.

In order to tell the application about your server, you click the red plus icon on the menu bar, which brings up a list of servers (in the Server Selection/Configuration screen shown next) that the software can "see" by monitoring for JDENet messages. If your server's host services are not up and running, you won't be able to see the machine listed when you click the plus icon. If the server is over a router, you may not be able to see the machine in this list. Fortunately, you can enter the name of the machine in the field above the list of machines and hit enter to add the machine name into the list.

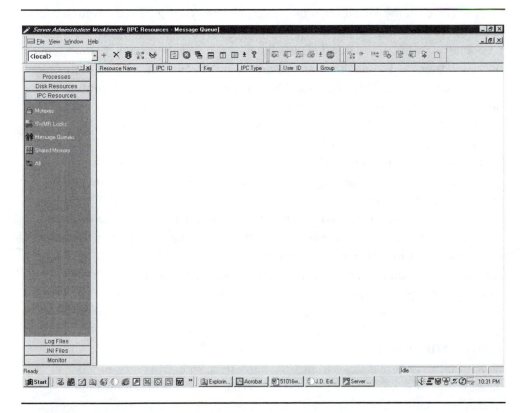

FIGURE 16-22. SAW screen

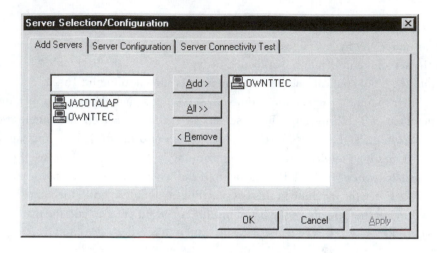

You can click the All button in the Server Selection/Configuration screen to select all of the servers in the list on the left and move them into the box on the right, telling SAW that you wish to monitor these machines. If you make a mistake, you can remove the server from the box on the right, telling SAW not to monitor it anymore.

The Server Selection/Configuration screen also contains the Server Configuration tab, where you have to fill in the correct information before the SAW application functions. The first field in this tab is a drop-down box that enables you to specify the server you are interested in. The port numbers in the Connection and Listen Port fields tell OneWorld what port to listen and connect to the OneWorld host services software on. The final field enables you to tell the system what kind of enterprise server you are using.

On the Server Connectivity Test tab, you enter the name of the server you are interested in and click the Start button. This executes a ping over JDENet. This tab shows the number of attempts and the number of successes. If the ping fails, be sure that your server name and port numbers are correct and that your host services on that enterprise or application server are up and running. Remember SAW uses JDENet to communicate so if these services are not up and running, you will not see the server.

Removing a Server

If you want to remove a server from SAW, you can do so in two different ways: the delete button (the X icon) and the add button (the red plus icon) on the toolbar. First select the sever you wish to remove from the drop-down box and click the X icon to remove the server definition from SAW.

You can also click the add button, which looks like a red plus symbol, on the toolbar, which takes you into the Server Selection/Configuration screen. The Add Servers tab contains a Remove button, which you click to remove the selected server.

Displaying Processes Running on a Server

Now that you have defined your server, you are going to use the server definition to find out what is really happening on your enterprise or application server. Start by taking a look at the processes that are running on your server. Select the Processes tab on the Server Administration Workbench screen. This tab contains icons for all the processes, including the kernel processes, network processes, and queue processes.

Kernel Processes   The Kernel Process exit enables you to monitor only your kernel processes, which are JDENet_k processes on your enterprise server. Different kernel types perform different functions for your OneWorld system. For example, the security kernel provides validation for your users who are using sign-on security, and the call object kernel runs business functions on the enterprise or application server.

To monitor kernel processes, select the server that you wish to monitor from the drop-down box in the upper-left corner of the Server Administration Workbench screen. Then click the kernel icon under the Processes tab to see a list of all of the kernel processes running on your enterprise server.

Network Processes   You follow similar steps (similar to the ones described in the preceding section) to display network processes. The list of network processes shows you the JDENet processes, which handle the communication between your enterprise or application servers and your client workstations. You can see if these processes are running, when they started, and the name they use to access the process.

Queue Processes   The queue processes poll F986110, the Job Control Status Master file for a specific batch queue, which you specify when you set up the kernel process. Once this process finds an entry, it starts a RUNBATCH process, which actually runs the UBE. If these processes are not functioning correctly, your UBEs will sit in a wait status until you bring them back online.

Information Provided about Processes   When you click any of the icons on the Processes tab, the right side of the Server Administration Workbench screen displays a series of columns, as shown in Figure 16-23. Table 16-6 describes the fields on the Processes tab.

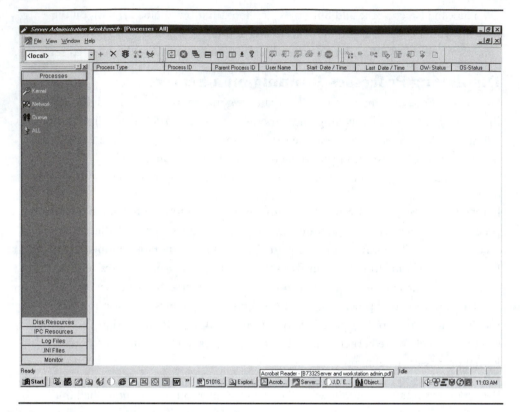

FIGURE 16-23.   Information that SAW Provides about server processes

For information on specific processes, highlight the process that you are interested in and select View | Process Information.

To display the log files related to a specific process, highlight the process and choose View | Process JDE.LOG or View | Process JDEDEBUG.LOG.

Logging Processes   Using SAW, you can turn on logging for a specific process, which does not affect performance as adversely as turning on logging through the INI file on the enterprise server. To log a specific process, highlight the process, right-click, and select to turn logging on.

Column	Description
Process Type	The type of process that you are viewing: kernel, network, or queue process.
Process ID	The process ID number that is assigned by the operating system, which is valuable information when you are attempting to debug your server. For example, all the server logs are preceded by the process ID, such as JDE_123.LOG, where 123 is the process ID. You can use this information to see which log files match up to which process on your server. You can also see which process you may need to attach a compiler to if you are going to debug a business function on your server.
Parent Process ID	The parent process ID number (if the selected process is a child to another process). You can use this information to track problems to the parent process.
User Name	The name of the OneWorld user who is using the process that you are monitoring.
Start Date/Time	When the process was started so you can determine how long your process has been up and running.
Last Date/Time	The last time that the process was accessed or used by the system.
OW Status	The status of the process in OneWorld.
OS Status	The status of the process as the operating system sees it.

TABLE 16-6.   Information that SAW Provides about Server Processes

N O T E

You can also view the users of a process. Highlight the process that you are interested in and choose View | Process Users. A list of the users who are using the selected process is displayed.

T I P

You can view the log files and print them by clicking the appropriate icon on the toolbar.

Stopping Your Processes   Sometimes you want to stop a process that is causing problems, but you do not want to bring down your host services. Highlight the process and choose File | Stop Process. This stops that specific process. When you stop a specific OneWorld kernel process, the system reads the INI file the next time a JDENet process requests the kernel, and the system starts that kernel process up again. Before you begin using this functionality, be sure that you understand when a process will start up again without cycling your host services.

Monitoring Your Server's Disk Resources

When you select the Disk Resources tab, two options are available: you can view the disk space for OneWorld or for all of your disks on the enterprise server. It's helpful to be able to quickly and easily check your disk space through SAW. Because OneWorld is highly configurable, your server might be located on the other side of town, of the country, or even of the world! SAW enables you to monitor disk space on your enterprise server no matter where it is located.

To monitor the disk space on your server, simply choose the server you wish to monitor from the drop-down box at the top right of the Server Administration Workbench screen shown in Figure 16-24. Then choose to monitor either the OneWorld disk space, which shows you only the disk space on the drive where the OneWorld host code is installed, or all disk space. Table 16-7 describes the columns on the Disk Space screen of SAW.

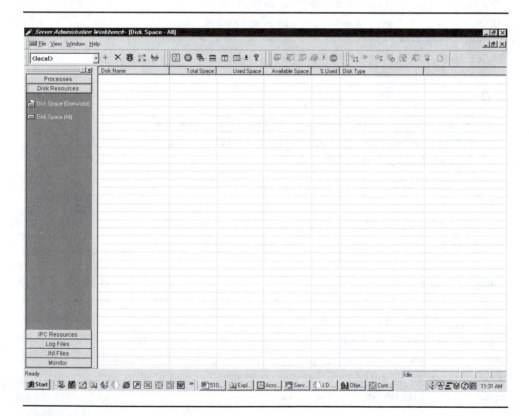

FIGURE 16-24.   Monitoring disk space with SAW

Column	Description
Disk Name	The name of the disk drive
Total Space	The amount of total space the disk contains
Used Space	The amount of disk space in use
Available Space	The amount of free disk space
% Used	The percentage of disk space used
Disk Type	The type of disk: a fixed hard disk, remote disk, or CD ROM

TABLE 16-7. Disk Information that SAW Provides

IPC Resources

The IPC Resources tab on the Server Administration Workbench screen provides information on interprocess communication (IPC).

Mutexes A mutex (which is short for "mutual exclusion locks") performs locking for processes. Only one process can hold the mutex at any one time. This type of locking is relatively simple, but it also provides good performance for almost all locking needs for processes on your servers.

SWMR Locks SWMR stands for "single writer multiple reabder lock." With SWMR locking multiple processes can read, but only one process at a time can write. SWMR locks are used for the specification or TAM files on your enterprise or application servers. Many processes can read these files, but only one at a time can update them. When the writer process takes control, all of the readers are locked out. When the readers have control, the write process is locked out. This type of locking has more overhead, and thus is slower than mutexes.

Message Queues Message queues are used to pass the data contained in packets from one process to another. A message queue automatically buffers a certain amount of data so that the sending process can continue to work. The amount of data that can be buffered is not unlimited and can run out.

J.D. Edwards uses the native operating system on UNIX and AS/400 platforms. For Windows NT, J.D. Edwards uses JDEIPC to handle message queues. Let's look at a simple example of how a message queue works in the context of OneWorld host services.

For example, a message queue is used when a JDENet process hands work off to a kernel process. A kernel process is the JDENet_k process running on your enterprise server. When the JDENet process hands off work to a kernel process, the sending process enters data in a message queue. The receiving process then reads the data out of the message queue and uses it to perform work.

Shared Memory   Shared memory is when two processes use information in a specific location in the server's memory. When the first process places information in the server's memory, the size of the memory is fixed. The second process can then obtain information out of this memory location.

Under most circumstances, an associated mutex or a SWMR lock processes access to the shared memory segment, which stops the software from stepping on itself.

Information Provided about IPC Resources   Table 16-8 describes the columns in the IPC Resources tab, as shown in Figure 16-25.

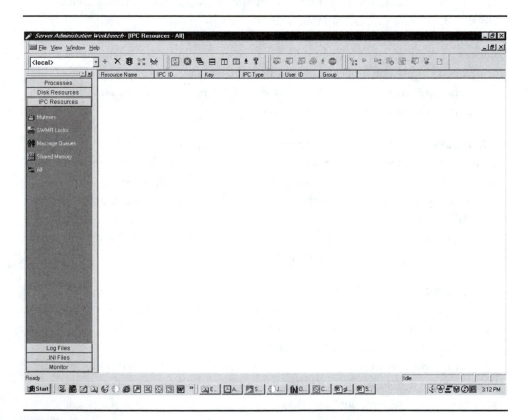

FIGURE 16-25.   Information that SAW Gives You on IPC Resources

Field	Description
Resource Name	The name of the IPC resource.
IPC ID	The ID number of the IPC resource.
Key	When the process you are monitoring is an MSGQueue process, this column shows the memory address the process is using based on the StartIPC value in the INI file. If you are monitoring a mutex process, this column always shows the value 1.
IPC Type	The type of IPC resource (for example, a message queue).
User ID	This column shows you the user ID that is using the IPC resource.
Group	A reference for the group that is using the IPC resource.

TABLE 16-8.   Information Provided about IPC Resources

Using this information may be difficult at first. Keep in mind the following:

- What resource are you viewing?

- Is it a data dictionary specification or TAM file?

- What type of lock is on it?

Log Files

You can view information about the server and print queue logs in SAW. When you click on either of these options, the left side of the Server Administration Workbench screen displays the name and size of the log files and when they were last modified.

SAW also enables you to view these log files. Highlight the log file and then select View. Be sure to check the size of the log file before you attempt to open it or you could be waiting a while!

You can also view your print queue log files from this application, which means that you don't have to go to your enterprise or application server to view them. When you are attempting to debug a problem within a UBE, you turn on UBE logging and run the report. This logging process creates a log file for your UBE in the print queue directory, which you can easily view in SAW.

INI File

SAW enables you to display and modify your INI file. To view your INI file, simply click the Display INI File button on the INI Files tab. This brings up your INI file for you to review and/or modify.

Troubleshooting

N O T E

SAW enables you to view and modify only the INI file for the local server and not for remote servers. You have to be running SAW on the local server in order to modify its INI file.

Monitor

The Monitor tab on the Server Administration Workbench screen enables you to monitor processes on your servers across the system, as long as their host services are up and running. This screen provides such information as the names of the servers you have on the network, the date and time when their host services were started, and the status of the server as it pertains to OneWorld.

Configuring SAW to Monitor Servers   You can configure SAW to make it possible to monitor OneWorld servers on your network. Click on the server monitor icon on the Monitor tab and go to File | Settings. This takes you to the OneWorld Server Monitor Settings screen shown in Figure 16-26. You will find the following tabs, which we will discuss next:

- General tab

- Port/Server Selection tab

- Notification Configuration tab

The General tab enables you to set up general test parameters. The fields on the General tab are described in Table 16-9.

The Port/Server Selection tab tells the monitoring functionality in SAW which servers and ports to monitor for OneWorld processes. You can monitor multiple servers using the same port number. You can also enter a different port number to monitor processes on a server with a nonstandard port number, like 6001.

T I P

The port numbers that your OneWorld host code runs on are defined in the JDE.INI file on your servers. You need to ensure that the port you are defining in your JDE.INI file and the one that you are defining in SAW are the same.

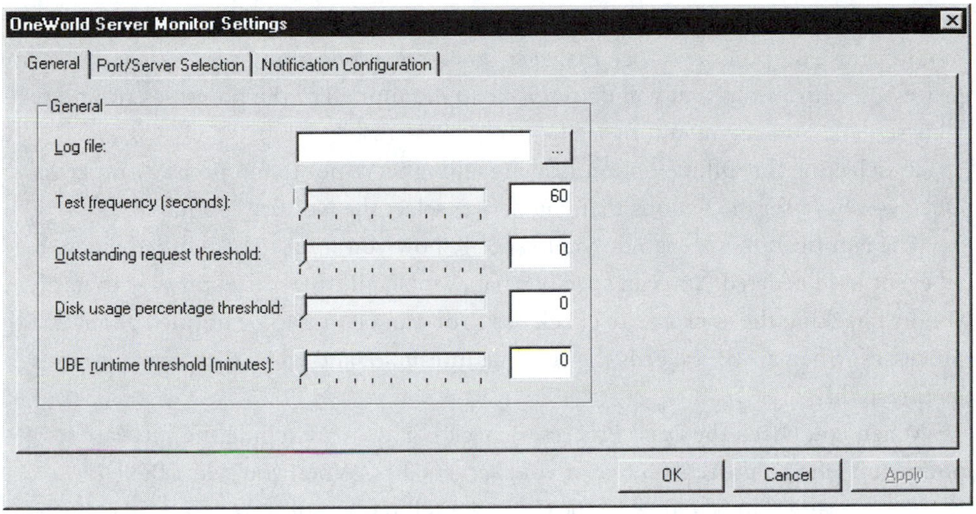

FIGURE 16-26. Server Monitor Settings screen

Field	Description
Log File	Enter a path to tell SAW where to write the OWMON.LOG file, which contains information on the servers you are monitoring.
Test Frequency (Seconds)	This field tells SAW how often, in seconds, to test or monitor your servers.
Outstanding Request Threshold	This field tells SAW how many requests for a certain process, like the call object kernel process, should be received before sending a message to the system administrator.
Disk Usage Percentage Threshold	This setting tells SAW to notify the system administrator when a certain percentage of a server disk is used.
UBE (Runtime Threshold)	This field specifies, in minutes, how long a report can run before a message is sent to the system administrator. This setting enables you to be notified when a job is taking too long and backing up your system.

TABLE 16-9. Fields on the General Tab

Troubleshooting

After you have specified the servers and their port numbers on this tab, you then need to tell the software what you are going to monitor for. You can tell SAW to monitor for UBE processes, lock manager processes, replication processes, and security processes. This means that you do not have to monitor all of the processes running on your servers. You can monitor specific ones.

By selecting the Offline option, you are telling SAW not to monitor any process. Once you have set the options that you desire, select the Notification tab.

The Notification tab enables you to specify how you want to be notified when an event has occurred. You can specify what events will trigger the software to notify you by checking the appropriate check box. You can choose to be notified about dead processes, when a UBE exceeds the runtime threshold, and when disk usage exceeds its threshold.

When you check the Dead Processes check box, you are telling the software to notify you when a process on one of your servers dies. When you select the UBE Exceed Runtime Threshold check box, you are telling the software to notify you when a UBE exceeds the threshold you set on the General tab of the Server Administration Workbench screen. For example, suppose you set this threshold at 60 minutes. If someone starts a large job that takes over 60 minutes, you are notified and can stop this job, preventing other jobs from having to wait. Some jobs should be run only at night. This tool also lets you know if you have a runaway job, so that you can take the appropriate action.

When you check the Disk Usage Exceeds Threshold check box, you are notified when you are running out of disk space on a server that you are monitoring. Common reasons for running out of disk space are leaving logging turned on for the servers and your database extending or expanding dynamically as you enter data (both Oracle and SQL Sever 7.0 have this functionality). If you don't monitor your disks, these databases can outgrow your disk space.

You can enter your e-mail address in the E-mail box or a pager's e-mail address in the Pager Address box. You can be notified through an e-mail, a page, or both.

N O T E

You need to set up your JDE.INI file on the machine that is monitoring your servers to tell OneWorld about your e-mail, which you can do by entering your default exchange or Outlook profile in the JDE.INI file under the JDEMAIL section. You also need to ensure that you can send e-mail from this machine—that is, you must set up your e-mail program correctly.

You need to set up the e-mail frequency and the pager message size. Most pagers have a limit on the size of the text that they can receive, which is why the SAW application enables you to specify the number of lines of text to send to the pager. You can also specify, in seconds, the e-mail frequency—how often SAW sends out another e-mail on server problems. We recommend that you set this setting to a reasonable level, or you could end up sending out a lot of e-mail or pages!

Once you have finished entering this information, click the Apply button. This commits the information. You can also click the OK button to apply your setup and close the window.

Server Monitor   Select the Server Monitor exit on the Server Administration Workbench screen to access the Server Monitor screen shown in Figure 16-27.

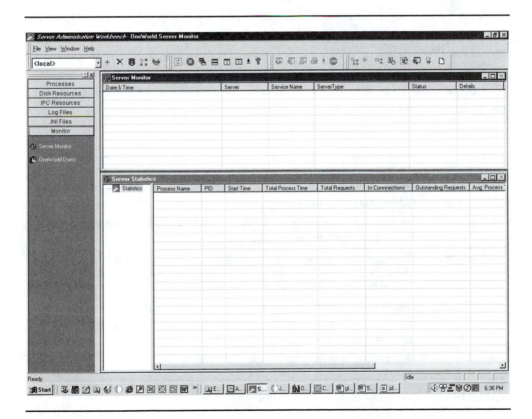

FIGURE 16-27.   Server Monitor screen

It displays the server you are monitoring, the date and time of tests SAW has performed on the server, the server type, and the status of the server. You can quickly review this information to determine the last time that your host services were cycled on your servers. Table 16-10 describes the columns in the Server Monitor screen.

The Server Monitor screen tells you about your processes at a glance. For example, if you need to quickly determine whether your processes are up or down, use the Server Monitor screen. If you need more information, check the Server Statistics screen.

Server Statistics   There is a parent-child relationship between the Server Monitor screen and the Server Statistics screen. Think of the Server Monitor screen as showing header records and the Server Statistics screen showing detailed records. This screen provides a lot of information on the processes that are listed in the Server Monitor screen. Table 16-11 lists the values of this screen.

This screen does not show any information unless you expand the directory on the left side of the screen. You can then drill down to look at the process information for the server of your choice. SAW tests the servers at specific intervals, meaning that SAW then displays this information to you by breaking it up into time segments.

You can view more detailed information on processes by highlighting a process in the Server Statistics window, choosing View | Processes | Selection Information.

Field	Description
Date & Time	When SAW performed tests on the server.
Server	The name of the enterprise or application server. If SAW is in between tests on the server, this column displays the value Sleep.
Service Name	The port number specified for the server. If Sleep is displayed in this column, it means that SAW is in between tests on the server. Remember, when you set up SAW, you specify how often you will test the server.
Server Type	The type of process that you are monitoring—for example, UBE.
Status	The status of the process specified in the Server Type column. For example, if the process is offline, it will show up in this column.
Details	Provides details on the processes SAW is monitoring.

TABLE 16-10.   Columns in the Server Monitor Screen

Field	Description
Process Name	The name of the process being monitored.
PID	The process ID that the operating system has assigned this process. Remember that the server log files relate directly to these process IDs—for example, JDE_123.LOG where 123 is the process ID. NOTE: The name of this column is displayed as "Job Number" for AS/400s.
Start Time	The date and time the process started.
Total Process Time	Total processing time for the process.
Total Request	The number of requests made to the process.
In Connections	The number of workstations currently connected.
Outstanding Requests	The number of requests that are waiting to be serviced by the process. If this number exceeds a threshold that you set, you, as system administrator, will be paged. You can then increase the number of kernel processes that start for that type of kernel. For example, if you do not have enough call object kernels, and requests are being queued up. The number of kernel processes that are started are controlled by an INI setting.
Average Process Time	The average process time for the process, which is computed by dividing the total process time by the total number of requests serviced.
Average Process Time—Last Period	The average process time for the last period or test. You can compare this value to the overall average process time to determine how your processes are performing on the server.
Lock Collision	The number of processes that have "bumped heads," that is, attempting to perform the same task at the same time.

TABLE 16-11. Columns on the Server Statistics Screen

Keep in mind that you are looking at information that is stored in memory on your server. To flush the buffer of the information that is being displayed in the Server Monitor screen or the Server Statistics screen, select Clear Screen under the View menu. This flushes the buffer of the information contained in the screen you selected. New information is then displayed in the screen as SAW continues to monitor your servers.

If you want to stop monitoring your server processes, you can do so by clicking the close icon (the round red button with an "x") on the toolbar. This closes the screen and tells SAW to stop monitoring. However, it does not erase the data contained in these screens.

Troubleshooting

Monitoring OneWorld Users   When you select the OneWorld Users option under the Monitor tab, SAW displays the users that are connected and their machine names. This functionality enables you to track what your users are doing on the system. To determine which users are attached to a process, double-click on the process that you are interested in.

By clicking the OneWorld Users button on the Monitor tab, you display a list of the users that are on the server, not the specific processes that they are using. This can be useful when you would like to send a user a message. Simply highlight the user you wish to send a message to and then select User Message under the File menu. A popup box is displayed; you can enter the message that you wish to send to your user in this box. No matter how tempting, we suggest you not send your CIO a get-back-to-work message.

Starting and Stopping Host Services

SAW enables you to start and stop the host services on your servers. This is why only system administrators should have access to this application. To start and stop your host services, select the traffic light icon on the toolbar to access the Available Services screen. You can then stop your host services.

N O T E

Stopping host services from a client workstation through SAW can only be done for Windows NT enterprise/application servers.

Using SAW on AS/400

SAW runs on any of the supported OneWorld platforms, including the including AS/400 itself!

Because we have already covered the functionality provided by SAW, we will concentrate on the differences of running SAW on AS/400.

Accessing SAW

Accessing SAW on AS/400 is simple: just log on as the ONEWORLD user and type SAW on the command line. This starts the Server Administration workbench. (The ONEWORLD user, or any users who have the OneWorld software's system library in their library list, is created during the initial installation of the software. The SAW program resides in this library on the AS/400.)

The AS/400 Server Administration Workbench screen, shown in Figure 16-28, lists options for running SAW on the AS/400 platform. It also displays the port number that OneWorld is running on.

Monitoring Servers

The Work With Servers screen enables you to monitor AS/400 and Windows NT servers. After you select the servers you want to monitor, the name of the server is displayed in the upper-left side of your screen.

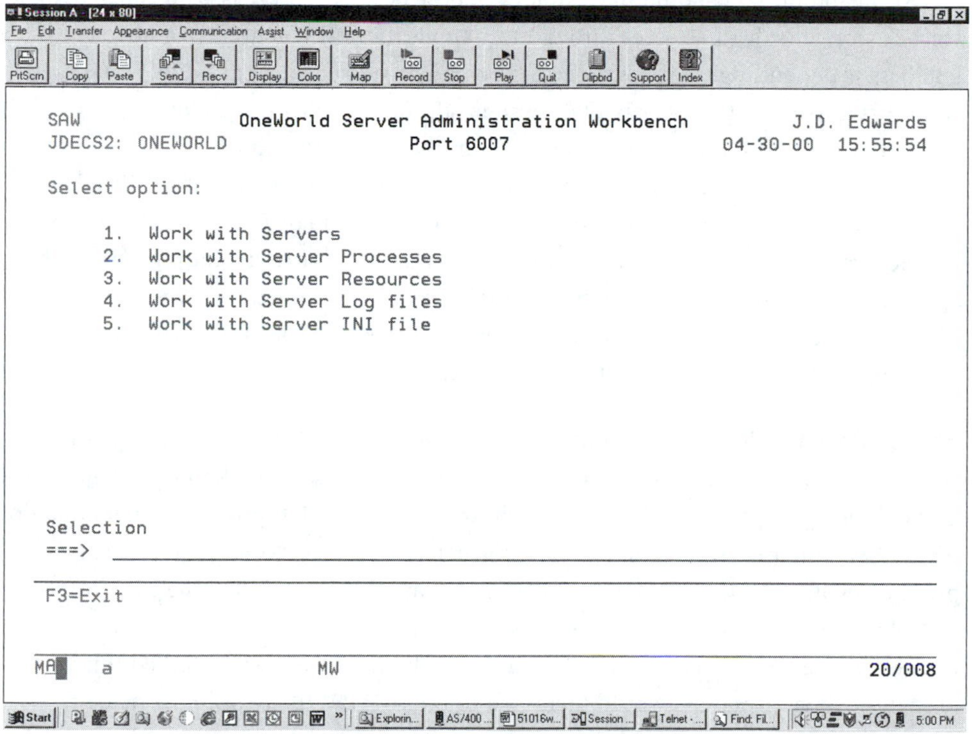

FIGURE 16-28.   AS/400 Server Administration Workbench screen

C A U T I O N

When you choose a remote server to monitor, the OneWorld host code must be running on the same port as it is on the AS/400 where you are setting up SAW. If it is not on the same port, you will not be able to access the server through SAW.

Monitoring Server Processes

What you see on the Work With Server Processes screen depends on what state the host processes are in on your server. If the OneWorld host processes are not started, you have only one choice: Start OneWorld Host Processes. If the host processes are already running, you have more options. You can either stop your host processes or monitor the server processes.

At this point, you should have an idea of how powerful SAW is. You can actually start or stop your host services through this application. If you are live and your business is depending on these processes being up and running smoothly, you don't want just anyone in this screen. Only system administrators should have sign-on access to the AS/400 that has the ability to run the SAW application.

On the Display OneWorld Server Processes screen, several options are listed at the top. You can display a job, end a job, and display JDE.LOG or JDEDEBUG.LOG for the job. Several more options are listed at the bottom of the screen, including exiting the application, refreshing your screen, viewing all processes, viewing only kernel processes, viewing only NET processes, viewing queue processes, and you can change your view and cancel out of or resequence a screen.

End Job Option   The End Job option tells the system to kill the process or job that you select. When you select a kernel process, such as the security kernel, place 3 in the Opt column, and press ENTER, you are telling SAW to kill that process. You should do this only if you are sure you understand the consequences of killing the process. Some processes will restart after they are killed. For example, if you killed the call object kernel process due to it hanging, the next time a job requested a business function, the host processes would look for the call object kernel. Because you killed this kernel, the host processes would then look to the JDE.INI file to see how many processes it should start up. The code then starts another call object kernel.

C A U T I O N

If you kill a kernel job that is hanging, understand the consequences. Some business functions, such as when you run a post job, are responsible for committing records. If you just killed that business function's call object kernel, do you now have a header record, but no detail record? As you gain experience with OneWorld kernel processes, you will be better able to determine the consequences of killing kernel processes.

Display Job   This option simply displays details on the job that you selected. For example, if you wanted to know when a process was started, use this option.

Display Log   This option enables you to view the JDE.LOG files on AS/400. Instead of having to sort through all of your logs, you can simply choose the process you are interested in and tell the system to retrieve just those JDE.LOG files. This can save you a lot of time because the only other way to find the log is to either open the log files one by one or find the job number the process is associated with and then find the JDE.LOG that has this job number in its name.

Display Debug   This option enables you to display the JDEDEBUG.LOG files that are associated with a specific processes. For example, if you are attempting to debug a sign-on security problem, you can use SAW to display the JDEDEBUG log for the security kernel process.

Delete Log   Suppose you are running some tests and you want to clean up your old log files before running the test again. You can do so through SAW. Simply place 9 in the Opt column next to the process whose logs you want to remove and press ENTER. This deletes all of the log files associated with that process.

Help   This option calls the help files. If you need more information about an item on this screen, use the help option to assist you.

Exit   This option is fairly self-explanatory. It takes you out of SAW.

Troubleshooting

Refresh   Again, this option is a fairly self-explanatory one. It refreshes the information on your screen. When you have been in the screen for a while and want to ensure all your kernel processes are still running, click the Refresh button.

All Processes   This option enables you to display all of the different types of processes running on your machine at the same time. When you are not sure what you are looking for at first, you most likely will want to view all of the processes running on your server.

Kernel Processes Only   This option enables you to restrict your view to only kernel processes. It is basically a filter that filters out any other process types.

Net Processes Only   This option is also a filter. It tells the software to display only JDENet processes. It is handy when you are troubleshooting a communication problem.

Queue Processes   This option enables you to apply a filter so that you see only your queue processes. These processes are your OneWorld job queues.

Change View   This option enables you to display the information in a different manner. Each system administrator has preferences as to how he or she wants information displayed, and this option enables you to indulge that preference.

Cancel   The Cancel button simply takes you back one screen so that you end up on the main menu of the SAW application. When you want to back up and take a different option within the SAW program, click the Cancel button.

Resequence   This option enables you to resequence the data on the screen. This means you can display your data in a different manner.

Server Resources

If you press F12 or click the Cancel button, you are taken from the Display OneWorld Process screen back to the main screen for SAW. Select the option Working With Server Resources. This option enables you to work with the interprocess communication and disk resources.

Working with IPC Resources   After you select the Work With Server Resources option from SAW's main menu, you are prompted to display either OneWorld resources or disk space resources. Choose the OneWorld Resources option, and you are taken into the Display OneWorld Resources screen shown in Figure 16-29 where you can monitor your message queues (MSG), single write multiple read (SWMR), shared memory (SHM), and mutual exclusion (MTX) resources. For more information on these resources, see the section "Monitoring Servers with SAW" earlier in this chapter.

Displaying Disk Space Resources   When you press F12 on the Display OneWorld Resources screen, you are taken back to the Work With Server Resources screen, which contains the Display Disk Resources option. This option enables you to see the disk resources available on your machine. As many AS/400 administrators can tell you, this type box does not react well to running out of disk space! This is why SAW can save your bacon.

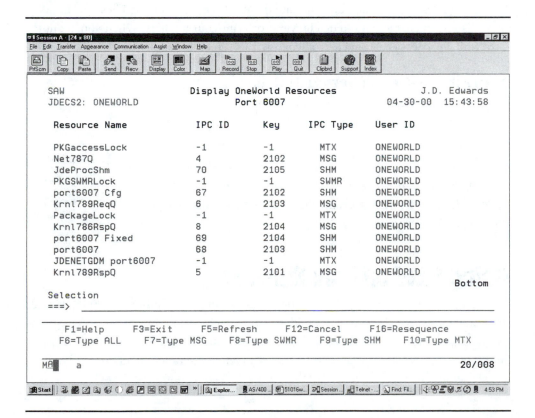

FIGURE 16-29.   Display OneWorld Resources screen

Troubleshooting

When you select the Display Disk Resources option, you are taken into the Display System Status screen, which displays your systems resources. You can monitor your system on this screen because you can see a percentage of CPU usage, as well as other important information.

TIP

You can see different information, such as pool data, by pressing the F11 *button.*

Working with Server Log Files

In addition to using SAW to display the log files for specific processes, you can also view all of the server logs. On the main menu of the SAW application, select the Work With Server Log Files option. This takes you into the Work With Server Log Files screen.

This screen enables you to delete, view, or print your log files. When you are not sure which process is causing a problem, use this screen to assist you.

Working with the Server INI File

From the main menu of the SAW application, select the Work With Server INI File option. This automatically loads the JDE.INI file into an editor.

NOTE

You may have noticed that we did not cover how to set up notification for system administrators. That is because that functionality is available only on Windows NT machines.

Using SAW on Unix Servers

You can also use the SAW application on UNIX machines, including RS6000, HP9000, and Sun Solaris. In this section, we will give you a quick run down of the SAW options available for UNIX machines. We will not go into as much detail as we did previously in the section covering Windows NT because much of the functionality is similar.

Starting SAW

In order to start the SAW program on a UNIX server, enter the following command-line entry:

saw.sh

This command starts the SAW application for UNIX servers and takes you to the main menu. This menu is almost identical to the main menu for AS/400, which we discussed previously.

Monitoring Other Servers

Selecting the Work With Servers option from the main menu takes you into the Work With Servers screen where you are prompted to enter the name of the server that you wish to monitor. Enter the name of the server and click OK.

You need to be able to ping that server by name in order for SAW to function correctly. Also, the OneWorld host services on that machine need to use the same port as the OneWorld host services on the machine you are on. If the system cannot find the server or the services on the same port number, it times out.

Working with OneWorld Processes

When you select the Work With Server Processes option, you are prompted with another menu. This screen will seem familiar to those who read the previous sections about using SAW on AS/400. This screen enables you to start and stop your OneWorld host services and display the OneWorld processes running on your server by selecting the Display OneWorld Host Processes option.

NOTE

Because you can start and stop your host services from this menu, only system administrators should be allowed access to this application. After all, when your business depends on this server running smoothly, you do not want an end user to bring it down.

When you select the Display OneWorld Host Processes option, you are taken into the Display OneWorld Host Processes screen. Isn't that neat how that works? You can monitor the processes running on your system. This screen also enables you to view the JDE.LOG and JDEDEBUG.LOG files for specific processes. Simply highlight the process that you are interested in and select 7 to view the JDE.LOG file and 8 to view the JDEDEBUG.LOG file.

You can remove the logs for a specific process. Simply highlight the process and press 9, the Remove Log option, which removes all of the log files associated with that kernel process.

As with SAW on the AS/400 platform, SAW on UNIX platforms also enables you to get detailed information on a process. Simply highlight the process that you are interested in and enter 5. This shows you the type of process that you are looking at, the last time it was active, the total kernel process time, the total requests to the kernel, and other information. When you want to see which users are waiting on a kernel process, this is a good place to start, along with the log files associated with that kernel process.

Displaying IPC and Disk Space Resources

On the main menu, select the Interprocess Communication (IPC) And Disk Space Resources option. You will be prompted with another menu in which you indicate whether you want to work with IPC resources or disk space resources.

Working with IPC Resources   Select the option to work with IPC resources and you'll be taken into the Display OneWorld Resources screen, which enables you to display only certain resources, such as kernel resources. You can also easily see if you are looking at shared memory, a message queue, a mutual exclusion, or a SWMR lock. This information can be useful when you are debugging issues on the server.

Working with Disk Resources   Back on the screen that prompts whether you want to work with IPC resources or disk resources, choose the Disk Resources option. You are taken into the Display Disk Space Resources screen, which enables you to see the disks you have on the system, the total space on the disks, the used and available space, and the percentage of used space. You can easily tell if you are running out of disk space.

A UNIX system running OneWorld can crash because the system administrator left the server logging turned on and was not monitoring disk space utilization. The box runs out of disk space so the OneWorld system can no longer write to the database or the log file, and thus, the services come down. You can easily avoid this problem by monitoring your disk space utilization through SAW. You can even set this application up on a Windows NT workstation to page you when you pass a specified point of disk space utilization. This topic was covered earlier when we discussed SAW on Windows NT machines. You cannot set up a notification service through SAW on a UNIX platform. Unfortunately, this service is available only on Windows NT machines.

Displaying Server Log Files

This option enables you to view, print, or delete your server's log files.

Working with the JDE.INI File

The Work With Server INI file option can save you the hassle of trying to find the INI file through conventional means. When you select this option, you are taken to a screen that displays the different parts of the JDE.INI file. You can then select the part of the JDE.INI file that you wish to modify and press the F6 button to change the variables in this section of the JDE.INI file.

To edit the JDE.INI file as a whole, press F8 to open the vi editor.

How OneWorld Server Code Really Works

In this section, we teach you the OneWorld host code functions. We will describe how the server communicates with other machines on the system and how work is accomplished on OneWorld servers.

UBEs and some business functions usually run on an enterprise or application server. An interactive application never runs on an enterprise server or application server. Interactive applications run only on the OneWorld client code.

Now that we have that straight, let's go through how the host code functions. A UBE first is launched from a client workstation, which uses JDENet to tell the enterprise server about the job. This is how the users' data selections and processing options are moved to the server when a report is run.

Once this request gets to the server, a JDENet_n process, which we go into more depth on later, becomes aware of the job. It then determines what type of request the client workstation is making—for example, a request to run a UBE. It then hands this job off to the proper kernel process. A record is written to F986110, the Job Master Control file. The queue process then finds this record and launches a runbatch job, which actually runs the UBE.

When runbatch starts, it finds the table access manager (TAM) specification files that it needs to run. TAM is a snapshot of your central objects at a point in time. So if you developed the report that you are running, checked this report in, and built a server package, you would then have the necessary records in TAM format.

This is why server packages are necessary. Reports run on the enterprise server do not look to your database to get the specification information they need to run. All of the information about the report itself is contained in TAM specification files and DLLs for business functions. As mentioned previously, the runbatch process uses TAM specification files run UBEs. Specifically, runbatch looks at your path code on the enterprise server. It then goes down this path code until it finds the Spec directory. It uses information in the RDATXT and RDASPEC files to run your report.

At this point, your UBE is running, but it needs to get data from the database. The system then calls upon JDEBASE, which is the functionality that enables OneWorld to communicate with different types of databases. It is the code that the applications coded in OneWorld sit on. An application developer does not have to worry if his or her report gets data from an Oracle, SQL Server, or DB400 database because the JDEBASE code provides a means to call data on these platforms. All the developer has to do is use a standard call and not worry about the details. JDEBASE handles this process.

The system reads the OCM mappings for the table it is looking for and finds a data source for this table. The system then reads F98611, the Data Source Master table, which tells the system which machine and what type of database the data resides on, who the owner is, and how to get to the data. To determine how to get to the data, the system reads the DLL name from the data source. If the DLL refers it to Oracle, the system is coded to make calls directly to an Oracle database. If the DLL tells the system that the database is DB400, SQL Server, or Access, then the system looks for an ODBC data source and uses it to connect to the database (assuming you are on a Windows NT server). If you are running a job on AS/400, JDEBASE can make calls for data directly on AS/400 as well.

Once the job is complete, the runbatch process updates F986110, Job Master Control file to show that the job is complete. This process also produces a PDF file, which contains the results of your report. When you view a completed job from a client workstation within OneWorld, the system copies this file to the client through JDENet. You can then view the results of your report.

JDENet

This piece of the system does a lot more than just make UBEs work. JDENet can be defined as middleware that uses TCP/IP sockets-based messaging, which enables the system to be highly configurable and distributed. With JDENet, you can run processes on several different platforms. Finally, this middleware supports both synchronous and asynchronous messages. JDENet enables the system to submit requests to the OneWorld host code on many different platforms. It is basically the phone line the system uses to communicate.

JDENet is used on the system in multiple places. It is used any time a client workstation sends a request to an enterprise or application server, which means if your client workstation needs to be validated for sign-on security, it sends a request via JDENet. JDENet is also used for Lock Manager, running business functions on the server (call object), running UBEs, and OneWorld replication.

Not only is JDENet used on client workstations, it also provides two-way communication. This means that the client workstations can communicate with the enterprise and application servers and vice versa.

JDENet is used by every kernel process on the enterprise or application server. The security kernel uses JDENet to validate OneWorld users and passwords when they sign on. The call object kernel uses JDENet to receive requests to run a business function on the enterprise server and return data. The replication kernel uses JDENet to keep workstations and servers in sync with published tables. As you can see, JDENet is a key piece of the OneWorld software.

Under the Covers of JDENet

JDENet sends packets of data, each of which is identified by a number that is assigned by the caller. If a client workstation sends a message to an enterprise server or application server, it tags the message with a number so that it knows this message was sent by that workstation.

This middleware contains two different types of logic: JDENet_n and JDENet_k. The JDENet_n processes handle the messages coming in from different machines, including other enterprise or application servers. These processes handle sending and receiving messages at the same time.

This is where the JDENet_n process's responsibility ends, and the JDENet_k processes come into play. These processes determine where to send the message that was accepted by the JDENet_n process. The JDENet_k process looks at the message and determines what is being requested. Let's say, for example, that the request is to run a business function on the enterprise server. The JDENet_k process hands this work off to the call object kernel process, which handles running business functions on the server. If this process is not currently running, JDENet_k starts a new call object process. (We cover how this works in the section "Kernel Processes" later in this chapter.) Once this kernel process is finished with the work, it sends a message back to the requester, if needed, via JDENet.

Ports   The software listens and communicates on a specific port that it specified in the JDE.INI file. The first JDENet_n process listens and communicates on the port specified in the JDE.INI file. This port is used only by the JDENet_n process, which defines an instance of OneWorld. As other JDENet_n processes are started, they listen on system allocated ports. If you are going to use the Web server functionality of OneWorld behind a firewall, it can be a real headache! So J.D. Edwards has responded to this problem by placing a hidden JDE.INI file setting in the software. This setting enables you to specify a range of predefined ports, which will be used by the JDENet_n processes. This functionality is available as of B733.2 Service Pack 10.

A client workstation connects to the enterprise server using JDENet (connecting to the first JDENet_n process) and sends a request to an enterprise or application server. The request is received on the server. The JDENet_n process then decides which NET process should handle the request. After deciding which NET process will handle the connection, it sends the client a message that contains an IP address and the port to connect to. Remember, only the first JDENet_n process is listening on the port number specified in the JDE.INI file. So our client has now been given a new port number and NET process to communicate with.

The client workstation then establishes a stream socket connection to the new NET process. Once this connection is established, the JDENet_n process determines which kernel process needs to be contacted. The JDENet_n process then contacts the JDENet_k process and places a request into a request queue. The JDENet_k processes then calls a dispatch function, which performs the necessary work. The information is then sent back to the JDENet_k processes, which in turn send this message to an out queue associated with the JDENet_n process. The JDENet_n process takes this message to the out queue and sends the information back to the client workstation. Figure 16-30 depicts this process.

N O T E

J.D. Edwards publishes JDENet APIs so that you can use third-party software to call a JDENet function. This is what J.D. Edwards calls interoperability.

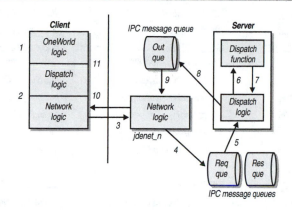

FIGURE 16-30. The internal design of JDENet

Kernel Processes

Kernel processes are the JDENet_k processes on your enterprise or application servers. They perform some of the work on the enterprise server. In this section, we are going to cover how these processes tie into the system.

Each OneWorld kernel type performs a specific function, which are listed in the JDE.INI file and are shown in Figure 16-31. The JDENet_n process hands off a request to the JDENet_k kernel process, and this process performs work, getting data from a database, using TAM to run a UBE, or calling a business function to perform work.

The type of work that is performed depends on which type of kernel process is called. In our discussion of the Server Administration workbench earlier in this chapter, we explained how to monitor your specific kernel processes. Let's see how these processes are started and controlled by the JDE.INI file.

Tweaking Server Kernel Processes

Suppose you have a lot of end users who are running business functions on the enterprise server. In this section, we cover how to set up your server kernel processes to handle this work.

As mentioned previously, each different type of kernel process performs a different function. Table 16-12 describes the kernel definitions.

[JDENET_KERNEL_DEF1]
dispatchDLLName=jdenet.dll
dispatchDLLFunction=_JDENET_
DispatchMessage@28
maxNumberOfProcesses=1
beginningMsgTypeRange=0
endingMsgTypeRange=255
newProcessThresholdRequests=2
numberOfAutoStartProcesses=0

[JDENET_KERNEL_DEF2]
dispatchDLLName=jdekrnl.dll
dispatchDLLFunction=_JDEK_Dispatch
UBEMessage@28
maxNumberOfProcesses=3
beginningMsgTypeRange=256
endingMsgTypeRange=511
newProcessThresholdRequests=0
numberOfAutoStartProcesses=0

[JDENET_KERNEL_DEF3]
dispatchDLLName=jdekrnl.dll
dispatchDLLFunction=_DispatchRep
Message@28
maxNumberOfProcesses=1
beginningMsgTypeRange=512
endingMsgTypeRange=550
newProcessThresholdRequests=0
numberOfAutoStartProcesses=0

[JDENET_KERNEL_DEF4]
dispatchDLLName=jdekrnl.dll
dispatchDLLFunction=_JDEK_Dispatch
Security@28
maxNumberOfProcesses=2
beginningMsgTypeRange=551
endingMsgTypeRange=580
newProcessThresholdRequests=0
numberOfAutoStartProcesses=0

[JDENET_KERNEL_DEF5]
dispatchDLLName=jdekrnl.dll
dispatchDLLFunction=_TM_Dispatch
TransactionManager@28
maxNumberOfProcesses=1
beginningMsgTypeRange=601
endingMsgTypeRange=650
newProcessThresholdRequests=0
numberOfAutoStartProcesses=0

[JDENET_KERNEL_DEF6]
dispatchDLLName=jdekrnl.dll
dispatchDLLFunction=_JDEK_Dispatch
CallObjectMessage@28
maxNumberOfProcesses=10
beginningMsgTypeRange=901
endingMsgTypeRange=1156
newProcessThresholdRequests=0
numberOfAutoStartProcesses=0

[JDENET_KERNEL_DEF7]
dispatchDLLName=jdekrnl.dll
dispatchDLLFunction=_JDEK_Dispatch
JDBNETMessage@28
maxNumberOfProcesses=1
beginningMsgTypeRange=1201
endingMsgTypeRange=1456
newProcessThresholdRequests=0
numberOfAutoStartProcesses=0

[JDENET_KERNEL_DEF8]
dispatchDLLName=jdekrnl.dll
dispatchDLLFunction=_JDEK_Dispatch
PkgInstallMessage@28
maxNumberOfProcesses=1
beginningMsgTypeRange=1501
endingMsgTypeRange=1756
newProcessThresholdRequests=0
numberOfAutoStartProcesses=0

[JDENET_KERNEL_DEF9]
dispatchDLLName=jdesaw.dll
dispatchDLLFunction=_JDEK_Dispatch
SAWMessage@28
maxNumberOfProcesses=1
beginningMsgTypeRange=2001
endingMsgTypeRange=2256
newProcessThresholdRequests=0
numberOfAutoStartProcesses=0

[JDENET_KERNEL_DEF10]
dispatchDLLName=jdekrnl.dll
dispatchDLLFunction=_JDEK_Dispatch
Scheduler@28
maxNumberOfProcesses=1
beginningMsgTypeRange=2501
endingMsgTypeRange=2756
newProcessThresholdRequests=0
numberOfAutoStartProcesses=1

[JDENET_KERNEL_DEF11]
dispatchDLLName=jdekrnl.dll
dispatchDLLFunction=_JDEK_Dispatch
PkgBuildMessage@28
maxNumberOfProcesses=1
beginningMsgTypeRange=3001
endingMsgTypeRange=3256
newProcessThresholdRequests=0
numberOfAutoStartProcesses=0

[JDENET_KERNEL_DEF12]
dispatchDLLName=jdekrnl.dll
dispatchDLLFunction=_JDEK_Dispatch
UBESBSMessage@28
maxNumberOfProcesses=1
beginningMsgTypeRange=3501
endingMsgTypeRange=3756
newProcessThresholdRequests=0
numberOfAutoStartProcesses=0

FIGURE 16-31.   Example kernel settings in server JDE.INI files

Kernel Definition	Description
JDENET_KERNEL_DEF1	This kernel is used for internal testing and echo routines.
JDENET_KERNEL_DEF2	This kernel process handles UBE requests.
JDENET_KERNEL_DEF3	This kernel definition starts kernel processes that handle OneWorld replication.
JDENET_KERNEL_DEF4	This kernel definition starts security server processes that validate OneWorld user accounts and passwords.
JDENET_KERNEL_DEF5	This kernel definition starts transaction monitor kernel processes. These kernel processes handle monitoring transactions and record locking.
JDENET_KERNEL_DEF6	This kernel starts OneWorld Web kernel processes, which are used for OneWorld Web servers.
JDENET_KERNEL_DEF7	This starts kernel definition starts processes that handle call object requests. Call object requests are requests for logic processing.
JDENET_KERNEL_DEF8	This kernel definition starts kernel processes that handle JDBNet.
JDENET_KERNEL_DEF9	This starts kernel processes that handle server package installs.
JDENET_KERNEL_DEF10	This kernel definition starts kernel processes that enable the server administration workbench to function. This allows SAW to monitor the kernel processes on the enterprise server, since it has memory allocated on the server, which the other processes write information into.
JDENET_KERNEL_DEF11	This kernel definition starts kernel processes that enable the Scheduler application to function. These kernel processes enable you to schedule a report to run unattended at a certain time.

TABLE 16-12.   Kernel Definitions in the JDE.INI File

Tweaking the Call Object Kernel Definition

Let's run through an example of how you set up the JDE.INI file to provide the correct number of kernel processes. As an example, we will describe setting up the call object kernel to handle users running business functions on enterprise or application servers.

First open your JDE.INI file on your enterprise server. This file controls how your server kernel process acts. Scroll down to the call object kernel definition, kernel definition number 6.

A rule of thumb is to have one call object kernel process per six end users. The following is the kernel definition for the call object kernel (also see Table 16-13):

```
[JDENET_KERNEL_DEF6]
dispatchDLLName=jdekrnl.dll
dispatchDLLFunction=_JDEK_DispatchCallObjectMessage@28
```

```
maxNumberOfProcesses=10
beginningMsgTypeRange=901
endingMsgTypeRange=1156
newProcessThresholdRequests=0
numberOfAutoStartProcesses=0
```

Suppose you have 120 users who are going to be on the system running business functions against the enterprise server. First you must increase the maximum number of kernel processes to at least 20. We recommend you pad this number a little because you do not have to start these processes unless there is demand for them. In our example, we recommend setting the maximum number of kernel processes to 25.

Then you should consider the new threshold request variable setting. As stated previously, this variable controls how many outstanding requests against a kernel process there should be before the system starts a new kernel process. You need to take a look at your system and your business needs before setting this variable. In our example, you have 120 users, but you have to ask yourself if they are "hard" users. Do they all sign on to the system at the same time?

For our example, let's set this variable to 2, which means if two outstanding requests against the call object kernel processes are queued up, then a new kernel process starts up until the maximum number of kernel processes are reached.

Variable	Description
DispatchDLLName	JDENet function that handles JDENet messages.
maxNumberOfProceses	Maximum number of kernel processes that can be run on your servers for this kernel type. In the preceding example of a kernel definition for the call object kernel, the server could run only 10 call object kernel processes.
beginningMsgTypeRange	The beginning message range for each kernel type.
endingMsgTypeRange	The ending message range for each message type.
newProcessThresholdRequests	This setting checks to ensure that a certain number of requests for this kernel have queued before starting a new call object kernel process.
numberOfAutoStartProcesses	This setting tells the system how many call object kernel processes to start when you start the host processes.

TABLE 16-13.   Kernel Definition Variable Values

As stated previously, the number of auto start processes variable controls the number of processes that start up when you start your host services. This number can never be higher than the value for the max number of kernel processes setting in the JDE.INI file. Because kernel processes take up system resources when they are running, you also must consider the demand on the system when you are setting this variable. Ensure that you don't start up too many kernel processes upon starting your host services. In our example, we set this number to 15, which means that 15 kernel processes start up when you start your host processes. Because we set the new process threshold request variable to 2, a new kernel process starts every time two outstanding requests are queued against this kernel process, until the maximum number of kernel processes is reached, which we set at 25.

At this point, you still need to modify the JDENet section of the JDE.INI file. The following is the JDENet section of the JDE.INI file:

```
[JDENET]
maxNetProcesses=
maxNetConnections=
maxKernelProcesses=
```

TIP

It is a good idea to have a backup of your JDE.INI file before you make too many changes to it.

The max net processes setting controls the number of JDENet_n processes that start. This variable should normally be set to 1 per every 30 users. Because we have 120 users in our example, we would set this variable to at least 4.

The max net connections setting controls the number of connections each NET process can handle. Set this variable to the number of users divided by 1.2. This allows your system to meet your business needs.

The max kernel processes setting controls the number of kernel processes that can start on the server at one time, which means that this number cannot be less than all of the maximum kernel processes that you defined under each kernel definition. (See Table 16-14.)

At this point, you are ready to cycle your host services, and your changes will not take effect until you do.

Troubleshooting

Kernel Setting	Recommended Setting
UBE Kernel	One process for each 50 users
Security Kernel	90:1 ratio of users to available processes
Call Object Kernel	One call object kernel process per 6 users
JDBNet Kernel	One kernel process per 90 users
Workflow Kernel	One kernel process per 40 users

TABLE 16-14. Rules of Thumb for Kernel Settings

User Overrides

A user override can be any of several different events that make each user's OneWorld Explorer unique. For example, say a user wants to modify the column order in a grid format. The OneWorld Explorer is designed to enable this customization with ease and efficiency by adding a new format. When the user goes back into the application after making this change, the format is automatically displayed with the columns in the order the user specified.

User overrides are application definitions that modify the presentation of data to the end user. They don't modify the table, the SELECT/UPDATE/INSERT/DELETE statements being generated by an application, or any actual code in the system. User overrides change the way data is presented on a per application, version, and user level.

The F98950 table (see Table 16-15) maintains user override data. It is part of the Central Objects data source (that is, it is different for each path code) but does not load during LOADALL. This table is loaded during the Environment workbench and is populated with 235 records in the Pristine environment. There are 11 columns in this table, and it contains binary data.

Column Name	Description	Length	Type	Valid Values
UOUOTY	User override types	2	String	GD, GF, HC, PC.
UOUSER	User ID	10	String	Any valid user ID including *PUBLIC and any groups.
UOOBNM	Object name	10	String	Any application name including batch and interactive applications.
UOFMNM	Form name	10	String	Any form name associated with an application.
UOCTRLID	Event rules control ID	11	Identifier	A numeric identifier assigned by the system.
UOVERS	Version history	10	String	Any valid version of an interactive or a batch application.
UOLNGP	Language	2	String	Any of 25 possible language codes. See the Note that follows for more information.
UOSEQ	Sequence number	6	Number	This number is assigned by the system to sequence connected records. The number itself can't have commas, zero balances, or signs. If you have 15 records for a single user, application, and version, the first record would have a 0.0 sequence, and the last would have 14.0 in this field.
UOBINDTA	Binary data	30000	Binary	Binary information listing the exact specification modification.
UOOVF1	Flag—Future use 1	1	Character	Y. Currently used in the upgrade/update process to indicate successful conversion from release to release.
UOOVF2	Flag—Future use 2	1	Character	Currently not used.

TABLE 16-15. F98950 Table

NOTE

These codes are found in the F0005 table with a system code of 01 and a code type of LP and can represent any of the tier-one languages including B—Flemish, C—Czech, CS—Chinese Simplified, CT—Chinese Traditional, DN or K—Danish, DU—Dutch, E—English, F—French, FN—Finnish, G—German, HU—Hungarian, I—Italian, J—Japanese, KO—Korean, NO—Norwegian, P—Portuguese, PO—Polish, RU—Russian, S—Spanish, TH—Thai, and W—Swedish. You cannot modify this information. It is pulled directly from F00921, the User Display Preferences table.

Types of User Overrides

Table 16-15 identifies user override types, which include GF, GD, HC, and PC. But this information, in and of itself, probably doesn't go far enough to provide the information that the hidden computer geek inside of you really wants to hear. Maybe the following will quell the hunger:

- GF—Grid Format

- GD—Grid Definition

- HC—Hypertext Control

- PC—Portal

How User Overrides are Created

For the most part, the entries in the F98950 table are automatically entered by OneWorld Explorer without assistance from a systems administrator. Because of this and because of the automatically shipped entries, the F98950 table can become large.

Adding New Formats

Customizing your formats enables you to speed up certain repetitive jobs and streamline what you are asking your computer operators to do. In this section, we are going to modify the sales order entry screen (P4210, W4210A—Sales Order Detail Revisions) to enter just the data needed prior to moving to the next detail line. This change will enable your users to speed up the sales order process, which your customers will appreciate. You can do similar modifications to any other process.

1. Prior to adding a custom grid format, save the original format by naming it JDE. This can be done in a couple of different ways. First, while at the application you want to modify, right-click in the grid and select Format from the pop-up menu, shown in Figure 16-32. The first selection is New Format. A prompt appears where you can name the format. Enter **JDE** and click OK.

   A second method of performing this step is by clicking the Preferences menu on the menu bar. Then choose Grid | New Format. The same prompt is displayed as described earlier, and you can enter **JDE** and click OK. This results in a standard JDE format being created for this application.

2. Now that you have an original copy of the grid format, you can add another new format. For this example, we will create one called SOE.

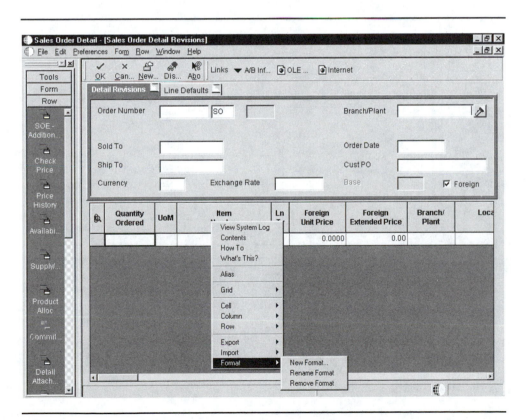

FIGURE 16-32. Mechanics of saving a format

3. On the tab for the SOE format, move the columns to the order you want by using drag and drop. In Figure 16-33, we moved the Item Number column next to the Quantity Ordered column.

4. Exit the application in the usual way.

5. Now go back and verify that the formats you created are still there. Exit all the way out of the OneWorld Explorer (which writes the changes to the F98950 table) and then restart it. This step, although not strictly necessary, is a prudent measure. If the format is not listed, the F98950 table wasn't revised, and you need to try again. If the record is listed, the database underneath has two new entries that look something like the ones in Table 16-16. As you add additional formats to various applications, you get an additional GD record per format, but

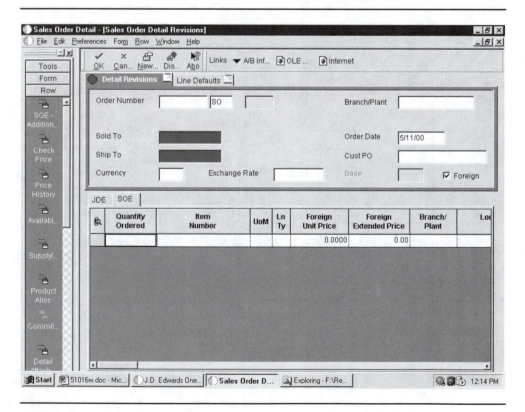

FIGURE 16-33.   Rearranging columns

UOUOTY	UOUSER	UOOBNM	UOFMNM	UOCTRLID	UOVERS	UOLNGP	UOSEQ	UOBINDTA	UOOVF1	UOOVF2
GF	JDE	P4210	W4210A	5001	ZJDE0001		0			Y
GD	JDE	P4210	W4210A	5001	ZJDE0001		1			Y

TABLE 16-16.   Example F98950

no additional GF records are generated (that is, if you have four formats on a single application, five entries (one GF and four GD) will be listed in the F98950 table.

Here are some helpful hints that you should read prior to creating hundreds of new formats:

- Assign one or two people in each functional group to create the formats that help streamline the work you do on a day-to-day process prior to training your personnel. It's easier for you to teach a few people as part of the core team; they have the best understanding of what modifications will speed up their work the most. By doing this prior to training everyone else, you ensure that your trainees all use the same method, which decreases confusion and retraining.

- When you are teaching these format masters, ensure the trainees know to research each form they want to change prior to making the change. This decreases your work in the next step (that is, you won't have to work with multiple changes as they rethink how they are getting their work done).

- Use the P98950 application to push the newly created formats to the functional group or to everyone in the organization (described later in this section). This ensures a uniform look-and-feel across the enterprise.

- Always test your new formats to ensure that they don't adversely affect the performance of the users or the application (see the section that follows).

What Could Go Wrong

The following information is taken from an actual incident that we troubleshot. Although we never directly identified the source of the issue, we did find a resolution.

We've seen similar issues multiple times and fixed the problem exactly the same way each time, so we feel relatively comfortable providing this solution.

Especially after service pack releases and upgrade/updates, you may experience issues with specific user overrides you've created. One of the telltale signs occurs when a single user can't do his or her work: the user continually gets memory error messages. For example, a single user who worked for a client we assisted couldn't launch a UBE. Every time this user tried to launch the UBE, a memory violation kicked the user out of OneWorld. By the time we learned about this issue, it had been going on for nearly four weeks.

Basic troubleshooting took over. We logged on to the user's machine and attempted to launch a UBE. It launched with no problem and ran to completion on the server (we immediately gave the user a skeptical look). Then we asked the user to launch while logged on as us. Still, no problem. We had the user log on to OneWorld as himself and try again. It blew up. At this point, we logically determined that it related to the user's profile. We created a new profile for the user and had him try it again. No problem, which confirmed that the problem was related to the user's profile. Unfortunately, this didn't really give us much to work with.

We turned logging on and had the user log on using his original profile. We got him ready to launch and marked the logs to identify what was happening. Boom! The last table hit was F98950. Finally, we were getting somewhere. When we performed a direct SQL statement (which follows) against the table, we realized that it contained several entries for this user:

Select uouser, uoobnm, uoctrlid, uovers from crpb733.f98950 where uouser='ES94969' and uoobnm='P4210'

This statement returned two entries. Unfortunately, since the override data itself was in binary format, we weren't able to determine what the actual problem was. So we decided to try deleting the two entries and had the user log out of OneWorld and try again. That fixed the issue.

Delete from crpb733.f98950 where uouser='ES94969' and uoobnm='P4210'

This is not a first-line troubleshooting measure; it is something that you want to watch very closely. Only delete entries as a last resort or when instructed to by the JDE support line. We have found other similar issues surrounding this particular table, and they are often associated with service packs, updates, and upgrades. The specifications that the applications anticipate and that are actually entered in the F98950 table vary from release to release. If the table isn't upgraded successfully, or if the expected specifications change during a service pack release, it can cause issues.

The other potential issue is that moving columns around can cause problems with various business functions. One line of reasoning is that some business functions anticipate data in certain areas; when they either don't find it or aren't able to populate it the way they expect, it can cause issues. We are somewhat skeptical of this particular line of reasoning because of the nature of a user override. Remember, user overrides don't actually move data or modify tables. They strictly change the presentation of data to the end user.

The best defense when working with user overrides is to discourage individual users from making customizations. As recommended earlier, have one or two people per functional area perform the modifications, test them, and then push these changes to the entire group or to the entire organization. As the CNC administrator, you can run an application that copies individual records for groups or everyone.

Deleting a Grid Format

You can quickly and easily delete a single format through the normal application interface. Go to the application that has the associated format you want to delete. In this section, we are going to use the P4210 application as we did earlier. Choose the tab corresponding to the format you want to delete and do one of the following: Either right-click the grid, select Format from the pop-up menu, and then click on Remove Format (the least amount of work) or click the Preferences menu, select Grid, and then Remove Format. Either method deletes the offending format.

User Override Administration

One of the ways that you can make life easier for the user is to copy useful user overrides.

The P98950 User Overrides application (shown in Figure 16-34), accessible from the System Administration Tools menu, GH9011, is a relatively simple application that manipulates records in the F98950 table. This is the preferred method of modifying OneWorld records.

About the Application

P98950, the User Override application, has two forms designed to assist the administrator with managing these records. One of these forms (W98950E —Work with User Overrides) is designed as a primary interface where you can display, copy,

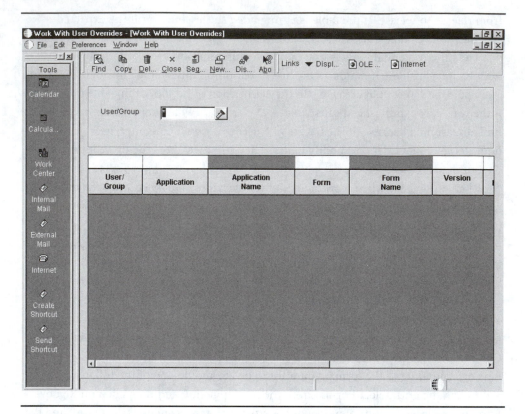

FIGURE 16-34.   P98950 application

and delete records. The second form (W98950D – Copy Overrides) is used to actually copy the records themselves.

W98950E—Work with User Overrides Form   The W98950E form is designed with a single entry field and a grid format. The User/Group field has a visual assist associated with it to help you find records associated with the specific user or group. When used, it adds a WHERE clause, limiting the returned records to the ones associated with the user or group. The information presented in the grid format can't be modified. Table 16-17 contains this information.

Field Name	Alias	QBE*	Information Presented
User/Group	USER	Y	The user or group including *PUBLIC
Application	OBNM	Y	The application name as provided in the Object Librarian
Application Name	DL01	N	The application description
Form	FMNM	Y	The specific form the override is on
Form Name	DL01	N	The form description taken from the Object Librarian
Version	VERS	Y	The specific version of the application with the override
Language	LNGP	Y	The language
Type	UOTY	Y	The type of user override (GF, GD, PC, or HC)

*Indicates QBE field when OCM is set with a 3 (query on indexed fields only)

TABLE 16-17.   W98950E Grid Format

N O T E

GD records are not displayed. Instead, the GF master record is displayable. There is a direct relationship between the GF and GD records. If you copy a GF record, all of the associated GD records are copied as well.

W98950D—Copy Overrides Form   The W98950D form has two distinct sections displaying and allowing information to be added, but it contains no grid formats. It displays information regarding the record that you are copying, including user/group, application, form, version, and language. All of the fields in the upper half of this form are grayed out indicating that you cannot modify this information. The lower half of the form displays information regarding the user you are copying the records for. Only three fields are in this section: User/Group, Version, and Language. Obviously, you can enter information into this part of the W98950D form.

Finding a Specific Record   To find a specific record using the P98950 application, start the application as described earlier. If you are looking for all records for a specific user or for groups of users, enter the username or group's name in the User/Group field. You can enter the name in the standalone field on the W98950E form or in the

QBE line entry. We usually use the QBE line because if we have to find other items, it must be done from the QBE line.

Figure 16-35 shows three entries. When you look at them closely, you will notice that there is only a single entry per application/version combination. And yet, we know that we added two grid formats (remember, one for the JDE tab and one for our customized SOE tab). As stated previously, each GF record is associated with a single GD record, and the GD record is the record that is found using this application. If you want to delete a single format and you've created several, you need to follow the preceding instructions for deleting a grid format.

Finding a Record for a Specific Application   It is often useful to locate a record based on the application and version you want to copy or delete. This is done in a similar

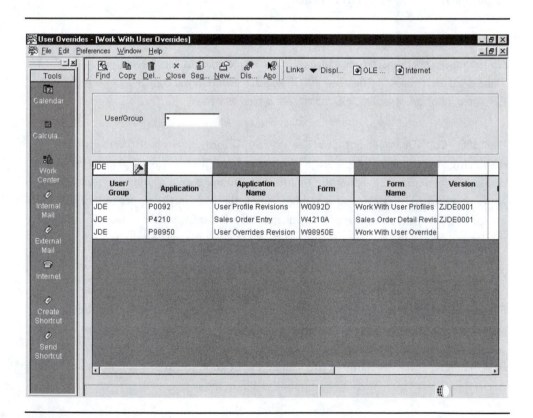

FIGURE 16-35.   Finding records for a specific user

manner to the method described previously. The only difference is that the only choice you have is using the QBE find functionality. Enter the name of the application by itself, or the name of the application with the specific version, and click Find on P98950, the User Overrides application, as shown in Figure 16-36.

You can mix and match your selection criteria to help in finding the exact record that you need to either copy or delete. The most useful combinations include User/Application and User/Application/Version. The QBE lines automatically force uppercase on letters and accept the asterisk (*) as a wild card character when you're not quite sure of the exact version.

Copying a Record   The process for copying a record is relatively simple. Find the record that you want to push out to a group or the entire user community. Be sure that you have picked the correct record (that is, if different versions of the same application

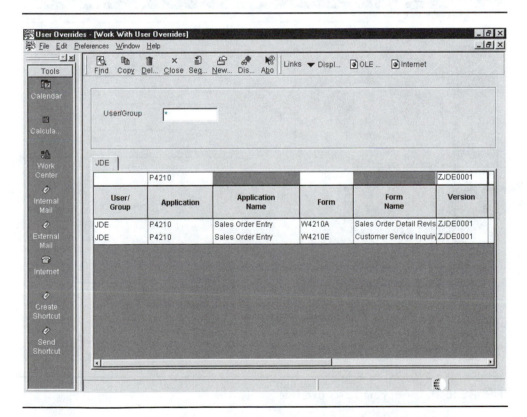

FIGURE 16-36.   Finding a record using the application and version QBE lines

have been modified, you would want to pick the correct one). Highlight the record and click the Copy button on the W98950E form. This launches the W98950D form with the header information already filled in. Enter information in these columns: User/Group (*PUBLIC is an acceptable entry that creates an entry for the entire user community), Version, and Language (see Figure 16-37). Click the OK button, and the record is added to the F98950 table.

You are not required to make entries in the Version and Language fields. If you don't choose to enter this data, the information from the copied record is used instead, which enables a very quick copy. (Find and highlight record, click Copy, enter the new user/group, click OK, and you're finished.) If you copy a record and enter a different version, the new format may not work. This depends on the version of the application

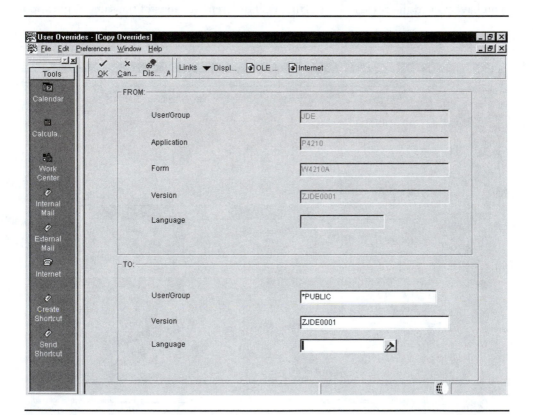

FIGURE 16-37.   Copying a user override

that you selected. If both versions are using the same forms, the copy will work. However, if both versions are using different forms within the same application, you won't see the desired effects.

Deleting a Record Using the P98950 Application   When you use the P98950 application to delete an entry, remember that you delete all of the associated records. This application does not lend itself to deleting a single format if there are multiple formats for the same form, application, and version. On W98950E, the Work With User Overrides form, find the record that you want to delete, highlight it, and click the Delete button. You are prompted to confirm the deletion. Click the OK button and all associated records are deleted from the F98950 table.

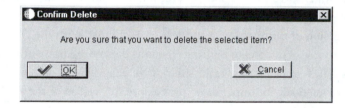

When a User Modifies a Format Pushed to a Group

A user who modifies a format that is pushed to a group is always a concern when you are administering the system. When you push a format to everyone and you have no way of stopping users from modifying their local machines, what can you do to maintain the standard? The solution, although certainly not perfect, is simple. When users modify a format from the CNC administrator, they create new formats that are specific to them without modifying the base template created, tested, and copied to the user community. If you have written policies discouraging this particular activity, you can occasionally query the database and find those users who have violated these rules. You can then use the P98950 application to quickly delete these modifications, and the users can't stop you. At some point in this type of game, they give up trying to create these new formats.

On the other hand, if you don't mind your users creating their own customized views that could cause other issues—time—and troubleshooting, you can still push out a recommended override as a base product and allow your user community to branch out from there. Most end users use the formats that they've been trained on and given as a standard.

Troubleshooting

Wrapping Up User Overrides

This topic deals with your ability to automate many of the redundant tasks necessary on a daily basis in the OneWorld system.

The OneWorld Scheduler

The OneWorld Scheduler is actually P91300, the Schedule Jobs application found on the GH9015 menu. Components of this application are on the enterprise/application server (a schedule service), and an interactive interface designed for adding, deleting, and modifying the job schedules and actual tables (F91300, F91310, and F91320) located in the System – B733 data source. (We'll talk about these tables in more detail in a couple of paragraphs.)

A single version of the interactive application is shipped with the OneWorld product; however, you can create multiple versions depending on your organizational requirements. These versions can be added to the menu, or you can have the single menu entry automatically prompt you to pick a specific version of the application. The Schedule product can accommodate your requirements from a local, national, and global organization based on your individual needs.

F91300, the Schedule Job Master Table

F91300 is the master table for the job scheduling interactive application and services and is their starting point (see Table 16-18). This table is part of the System – B733 data source, a change in the B733.2 version of the OneWorld software.

Nine indexes are associated with the F91300 table, and the F91300_1 is unique.

You need a location to store the parameters associated with the jobs you want to schedule. To accommodate these parameters, the OneWorld developers added F91310, the Scheduler Parameter table.

The F91310 table, the values of which are shown in Table 16-19, has only a single index, and it is unique—F91310_1. F91320, the Job Schedule Table, houses the schedule of jobs to be run.

Column Name	Description	Length	Type	Valid Values
SJSCHJBTYP	Scheduled job type	2	String	01 (batch applications) or 02 (workflow process).
SJSCHJBNM	Scheduled job name	30	String	Any name up to 30 characters in length that uniquely defines the job. We recommend that the name be meaningful to the CNC or schedule administrator.
SJSCHRPTNM	Scheduled report name	10	String	The name of the batch job or workflow process that is being scheduled on the server.
SJSCHVER	Scheduled version	10	String	Indicates the version of the job scheduled.
SJPROCNAME	Process ID	10	String	A unique numeric identifier for a specifically scheduled job. The next number is automatically entered when no value is assigned by the user.
SJSCHSTTIME	Scheduled start ANSI C UTC time	15	Numeric	The time in a modified universal time coordinate (UTC), shown in minutes instead of seconds, that the job is scheduled to launch.
SJSCHENTIME	Scheduled end ANSI C UTC time	15	Numeric	Specifies (in modified UTC) when a specific job can be launched.
SJNUMJOBOCC	Number of job occurrences	9	Numeric	The maximum number of times a job can be submitted. The scheduled entry is updated to Not Active after the last submission.
SJCURRUNCNT	Number of runs	9	Numeric	The number of times a scheduled job has run.
SJMAXRESUB	Maximum number of job resubmissions	9	Integer	Tells the schedule service the maximum number of times to resubmit a job before ending in error.

TABLE 16-18. The F91300 Scheduler Master Table

Troubleshooting

Column Name	Description	Length	Type	Valid Values
SJSCHJBSTAT	Scheduled job status	2	String	Specifies whether a job is active (that is, should be considered for submission) or inactive. Valid values are 01 (active) or 02 (inactive).
SJSCHENHV	Environment job will be launched in	10	String	When you specify the environment, the batch engine knows what set of data and server code to run against.
SJSCHJOBSVR	Server scheduled job will be launched on	30	String	Indicates the server the UBE job will run on.
SJSCHUSER	User the job will be launched by	10	String	Specifies a specific user to launch the job. The results populate the users work center.
SJSCHPSWD	Password to be used to launch job	10	String	The user's OneWorld password.
SJJDELOG	Logging (JDE.LOG)	1	Character	Enables you to turn UBE logging on for this specific job. If UBE logging is already enabled on the server, this flag is ignored.
SJTRACING	Tracing	1	Character	Similar to the SJJDELOG column, this column enables UBE tracing on the server. If UBE tracing is already enabled, the flag is ignored.
SJUBELOGLVL	UBE logging level	1	Character	Valid values include: 0—Error messages 1—Informative messages and log entry 2—Section-level messages 3—Object-level messages 4—Event rule messages 5—Database mapping messages 6—UBE internal function calls, textout values
SJPNTR	Printer name	30	String	The name of the OneWorld-defined printer. The printer definition includes orientation and paper type used in formatting the UBE.

TABLE 16-18.   The F91300 Scheduler Master Table (*continued*)

Column Name	Description	Length	Type	Valid Values
SJJOBQUE	Job queue	10	String	The name of the OneWorld-defined job queue on the server where the UBE will run. Out of the box, valid values include QBATCH, RBATCH, TBATCH, and QB7332. If you add additional job queues, be sure to add entries into the F0005 table.
SJRESBONERR	Policy to resubmit on job error	2	String	Valid values include: 01—Do not resubmit 02—Resubmit immediately—all errors 03—Resubmit after *n* minutes—all errors 12—Resubmit immediately—connection errors only 13—Resubmit after *n* minutes—connection errors only 22—Resubmit immediately—runtime errors only 23—Resubmit after *n* minutes—runtime errors only
SJRESBTIME	Time delay before resubmitting error job	15	Numeric	The time in minutes the schedule server waits before resubmitting a job that ended in error.
SJINPRTMOTPY	In process timeout policy	2	String	Tells the server what to do when a job has run too long. Valid values include: 01—Do nothing, let the job continue until completion 02—End Job automatically 03—End and resubmit the job 04—End the job and resubmit it after a delay
SJINPRMAX	Maximum time a job should be in process	15	Numeric	Specifies the maximum number of minutes a job can run. The default value is 1 minute; the number must be greater than 0.
SJINPRTMOUT	Delay until resubmitting a timeout job	15	Numeric	Instructs the schedule server the amount of time to wait before resubmitting a job terminated for processing too long.

TABLE 16-18. The F91300 Scheduler Master Table (*continued*)

Troubleshooting

Column Name	Description	Length	Type	Valid Values
SJJOBEXPIRE	Job expires this many minutes after start	15	Numeric	Tells the server when a job has expired. Once expired, a job won't be run again. The default value is 1; the value must be greater than 0.
SJSCHRCRTYP	Recurrence type	2	String	There are 15 valid entries (two each for daily, monthly, period, and by time, four for yearly, one for custom, one for one-time only, and one for weekly).
SJCO	Company	5	String	Any code that identifies specific organizational entities on your system as defined in F0010, the Company Constants table.
SJSCHNUMMNS	Scheduled minutes	5	Numeric	The time in minutes between each job submission.
SJSCHNUMHRS	Scheduled hours	5	Numeric	The number of hours between each job submission.
SJSCHNUMDY	Scheduled days	9	Numeric	The number of days between each job submission.
SJSCHNUMWKS	Scheduled weeks	5	Numeric	How often (measured in weeks) the job is submitted.
SJSCHNUMMN	Scheduled month	5	Numeric	The number of months between each job submission.
SJSCHDAY	Day	1	Character	Indicates that the job will be submitted by the server on the day specified.
SJWEEKDAY	Weekday	1	Character	Indicates to the server that the job should be submitted every weekday.
SJWEEKEND	Weekend	1	Character	Forces the server to submit the job on days during the weekend.
SJMONDAY	Monday	1	Character	Indicates that the job will be submitted on a Monday.
SJTUESDAY	Tuesday	1	Character	Indicates that the job will be submitted on a Tuesday.
SJWEDNESDAY	Wednesday	1	Character	Indicates that the job will be submitted on a Wednesday.
SJTHURSDAY	Thursday	1	Character	Indicates that the job will be submitted on a Thursday.

TABLE 16-18.   The F91300 Scheduler Master Table (*continued*)

Column Name	Description	Length	Type	Valid Values
SJFRIDAY	Friday	1	Character	Indicates that the job will be submitted on a Friday.
SJSATURDAY	Saturday	1	Character	Indicates that the job will be submitted on a Saturday.
SJSUNDAY	Sunday	1	Character	Indicates that the job will be submitted on a Sunday.
SJTIMEZONES	Time zone list	2	String	Lists UDC values for 51 different time zones starting at UTC (listed as 0) through + and −12.
SJDAYLIGHTSV	Adjust local time for daylight savings	1	Character	Tells the server whether it should adjust for daylight savings time.
SJDSAVNAME	Daylight savings rule name	10	String	A unique name for different daylight savings rules (these rules change from country to country).
SJSCHCTCD01	Scheduler category code 1	6	String	A specific code for categorizing a scheduled job.
SJSCHCTCD02	Scheduler category code 2	6	String	A second code for categorizing a scheduled job.
SJSCHCTCD03	Scheduler category code 3	6	String	Categorizes a scheduled job.
SJSCHCTCD04	Scheduler category code 4	6	String	Categorizes a scheduled job.
SJSCHCbTCD05	Scheduler category code 5	6	String	Categorizes scheduled jobs.
SJSCHFU1	Numeric—Future use 1	15	Numeric	A numeric field set aside for future use.
SJSCHFU2	Numeric—Future Use 2	15	Numeric	Another numeric field set aside for future use.
SJSCHFU3	String—Future Use 3	30	String	A string field set aside for future use.
SJSCHFU4	String—Future Use 4	30	String	A string field set aside for future use.
SJUSER	User ID	10	String	A code used to provide end users with a unique identification—the user who last updated the record.
SJPID	Program ID	10	String	The identity of either batch or interactive OneWorld applications that updated the record.

TABLE 16-18. The F91300 Scheduler Master Table (*continued*)

Troubleshooting

Column Name	Description	Length	Type	Valid Values
SJJOBN	Workstation ID	10	String	The workstation that performed the PID.
SJUPMJ	Date—Updated	6	Date	The six-digit date indicates the last time the record was updated.
SJUPMT	Time—Last Updated	6	Numeric	The time HHMMSS that the record was last updated.

TABLE 16-18.   The F91300 Scheduler Master Table (*continued*)

Column Name	Description	Length	Type	Valid Values
SPDSTRTYPE	Parameter data structure type	2	String	Lists the parameter data structure type for the job.
SPJOBN	Workstation ID	10	String	The workstation that performed the PID.
SPPARMCHAR	Character Parameter	1	Character	Stores the value for a scheduled job when that value is a character.
SPPARMDATE	Date parameter	6	Date	Stores the date to be passed for a scheduled job.
SPPARMSCHNUM	Numeric parameter	15	Numeric	This field stores a numeric parameter that needs to be passed with a scheduled job.
SPPARMSEQ	Parameter sequence	5	Numeric	Specifies the order that the parameters will be passed in when submitting a scheduled job.
SPPARMSTRG	String parameter	256	String	Stores a string parameter to be passed for a scheduled job.
SPPARMTYP	Parameter type	2	String	Indicates the type of field that the parameter is.
SPPID	Program ID	10	String	Holds the name of the OneWorld application that added or modified the record in the F91310 table.
SPSCHDTAS	Parameter size	5	Numeric	Indicates the size of the parameter value stored on a record-by-record basis.
SPSCHJBNM	Scheduled job name	30	String	A unique name for each scheduled job.

TABLE 16-19.   The F91310 Scheduler Parameter Table

Column Name	Description	Length	Type	Valid Values
SPUPMJ	Date updated	6	Date	The six-character date the record was last updated.
SPUPMT	Time last updated	6	Numeric	The six-character time (HHMMSS) the record was last updated.
SPUSER	User ID	10	String	The OneWorld user ID who logged on and made the change to the record.

TABLE 16-19. The F91310 Scheduler Parameter Table *(continued)*

The F91320 table, values of which are shown in Table 16-20, has five indexes. The first one (F91320_1) is unique.

Column Name	Description	Length	Type	Valid Values
JSDONOTEXPR	Job does not expire	1	Character	Specifies that the current record job schedule will not expire; overrides a set job expiration.
JSJOBN	Workstation ID	10	String	The server designated to run a particular job.
JSJOBNBR	Workstation ID	15	Numeric	A unique number assigned to a specific job.
JSLNCDATP	Launch location	30	String	The logic data source the job will run on.
JSLNCENVH	Launch environment name	10	String	The environment the job will run against.
JSPID	Program ID	10	String	The program ID.
JSPROCIST	Process instance	8	Numeric	Specifies the instance of the workflow process.
JSPROCVER	Process version	5	Numeric	A number from 1 to 99999, identifying a unique version of a workflow process.
JSRESUBCT	Number of resubmissions	8	Numeric	A number between 1 and 99999999, indicating the number of times a job should be resubmitted if it ends in error.

TABLE 16-20. The F91320 Job Schedule Table

Column Name	Description	Length	Type	Valid Values
JSSCHJBNM	Scheduled job name	30	String	A unique name associated with a specifically scheduled job.
JSSCHLNCSTAT	Scheduled launch status	2	String	The status of the scheduled job launch.
JSSCHLNCTIME	Scheduled launch ANSI C UTC time	15	Numeric	The time, in UTC, when the schedule server should launch the job.
JSSCHSTTIME	Scheduled start ANSI C UTC time	15	Numeric	The time the job started as measured in UTC.
JSSCHUSER	User who will launch the job	10	String	The OneWorld user identification used to start the job. This user must have rights to the job and associated tables to perform the job.
JSUPMJ	Date updated	6	Date	Captures the last date the record in the F91320 table was updated.
JSUPMT	Time last updated	6	Date	Maintains the last time the record was updated.
JSUSER	User ID	10	String	Houses the ID of the last user who updated the record in the F91320.

TABLE 16-20. The F91320 Job Schedule Table (*continued*)

Setting Up the Scheduler

After the initial installation of the enterprise and/or application server, the services won't work until you've completed the very simple process of setting them up.

Processing Options Associated with P91300

P91300, the Job Scheduler application, has an associated T91300 processing options template. (For more information on processing option templates, refer to *J.D. Edwards OneWorld: A Developer's Guide* (Osborne/McGraw-Hill, J.D. Edwards Press, 2000.) This template contains a few primary pieces of information that are vital to the operation of the Scheduler itself. The first tab associated with the template is the Display tab (see Figure 16-38), whose values are shown in Table 16-21.

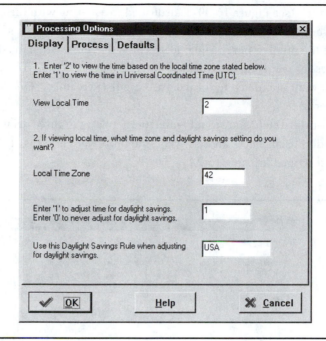

FIGURE 16-38. Display Tab on T91300

Field	Description	Valid Values
Number 1	View local time	1—UTC 2—View local time (default)
Number 2 A	Local time zone	A visual assist associated with this field provides valid values (based on the UDC values with system code H91 and UDC TZ).
Number 2 B	Daylight savings time	1—Adjust for daylight savings (default) 2—Never adjust for daylight savings
Number 2 C	Daylight savings rule	A visual assist associated with this field provides valid values (based on daylight savings rules defined to your system). USA is shipped by JDE.

TABLE 16-21. Display Tab Information

The second tab (see Figure 16-39) is dedicated to assisting with the overall processing of the Scheduler. When you've set a single job to recur at a specified rate, you can define the number of scheduler job records that are written in advance in the scheduler tables for recurring jobs that have no end date (see Table 16-22). How many records do you want populated in the database itself? (Remember, OneWorld has to write each record.)

The final (or third) tab, shown in Figure 16-40, relates to three defaults available for the application itself. These are relatively straightforward and easy to set. The Default tab is described in Table 16-23.

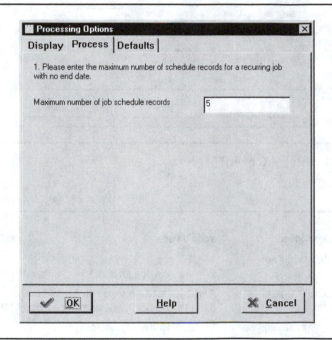

FIGURE 16-39. Process tab on the T91300 table

Field	Description	Valid Values
Maximum number of jobs	Maximum number of scheduled jobs for jobs with no end date.	Numeric value

TABLE 16-22. Process Tab

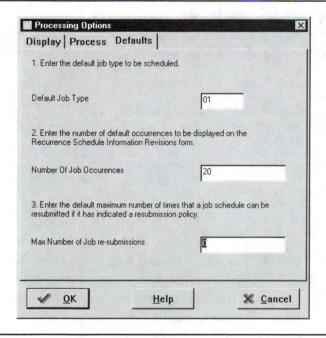

FIGURE 16-40. Default tab on the T91300 table

Field	Description	Valid Values
Default Job Type	Tells the scheduler to default in either UBEs or workflow jobs	01—UBE (default) 2—Workflow
Number of Job Occurrences	Number of occurrences that you want displayed for recurring jobs	Numeric value (20 is default)
Max number of resubmissions	Default number of times a job is resubmitted	0 is the default

TABLE 16-23.   Default Tab

Activating the Schedule Service Server

If you look at the logs associated with starting OneWorld on the enterprise server when you first install OneWorld, the following logs are associated with the schedule server.

```
243/155     Mon May 22 08:39:13 2000              IPCPUB1915
    process 243 <jdenet_k> registered in entry 1
243/155     Mon May 22 08:39:14 2000              sc_dsptc140
    INITIALIZING SCHEDULER SERVER KERNEL
243/155     Mon May 22 08:39:14 2000              sc_dsptc163
    Attempting to auto-start the Scheduler.
243/155     Mon May 22 08:39:14 2000              sc_dsptc823
    Failed to fetch the control record from the F91300. Could not validate the Scheduler Name.
243/155     Mon May 22 08:39:14 2000              sc_dsptc860
    Scheduler does not run on this machine. The real Scheduler Server is .
243/155     Mon May 22 08:39:14 2000              sc_dsptc195
    This server will not start the Scheduler.
```

Why do you think that you get this type of error? Is there something wrong with your installation on that server? Actually, the only thing wrong with the services is that the JDE.INI file on the server is specifying that a single scheduler kernel be started, and the F91300 table doesn't contain an entry for a default schedule server. Because of this, when the server's services are launched, they automatically try to start the schedule services and can't validate the server's name.

```
[JDENET_KERNEL_DEF10]
dispatchDLLName=jdekrnl.dll
dispatchDLLFunction=_JDEK_DispatchScheduler@28
maxNumberOfProcesses=1
beginningMsgTypeRange=2501
endingMsgTypeRange=2756
newProcessThresholdRequests=0
numberOfAutoStartProcesses=1
```

To fix this particular issue is actually the first step in setting up the schedule server's services.

Adding a Schedule Server   The process is very straightforward and easy to accomplish. Just follow along with these step-by-step instructions:

1. Log on to OneWorld as a user who is able to run and modify P91300, the Job Schedule application.

2. Fast-path (or menu-travel) to the Job Scheduler menu GH9015.

3. Start the P91300 application by double-clicking the application icon. If your menu has not been altered, it prompts you for a specific version to launch. J.D. Edwards ships only a single version, as shown in Figure 16-41. Launch it

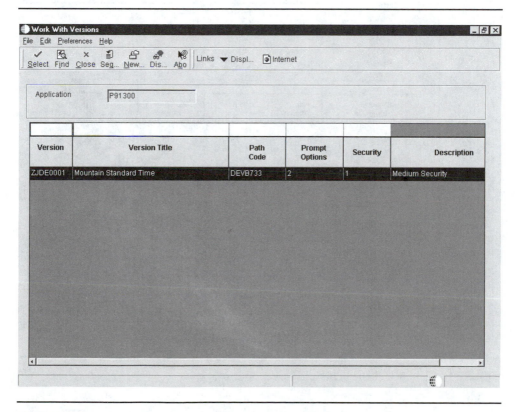

FIGURE 16-41.   Select the version you want to work with

by either clicking the Select button or by double-clicking the row entry. If more than one version is listed, launch the version associated with the time zone your schedule server is running in.

4. Choose Schedule Server under the Forms menu, as shown in Figure 16-42 (you can alternately use the exit bar to toggle to this function).

Notice that the W91300G form launches and that many of the fields represented on the form contain no information. If you open OneWorld's universal table browser (UTB—it can be started either by entering **UTB** at the Fast Path or by launching the UTBrowse executable located in the x:\b7\system\

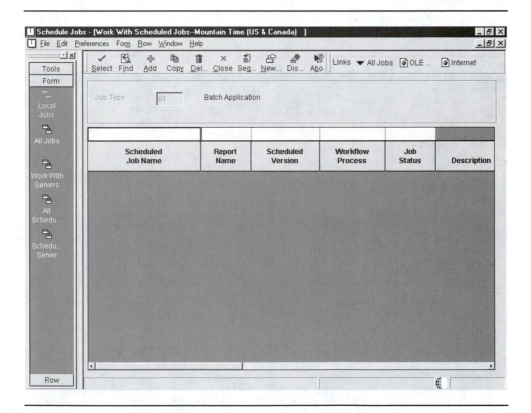

FIGURE 16-42. Select the Schedule Server option

bin32 directory), you see that the F91300 table contains no information. This is the reason that the schedule server could not start its service, as shown in Figure 16-43.

5. Select Change Server, shown in Figure 16-44, from the exit bar or from the Form drop-down menu, launching the W91300N form. On this form, enter the name of the enterprise or application server that you want to run the schedule service and enter the service port (if you don't know what service port you are using, look in the JDE.INI file on the server in the [JDENET] section). Then click the OK button to save the changed data.

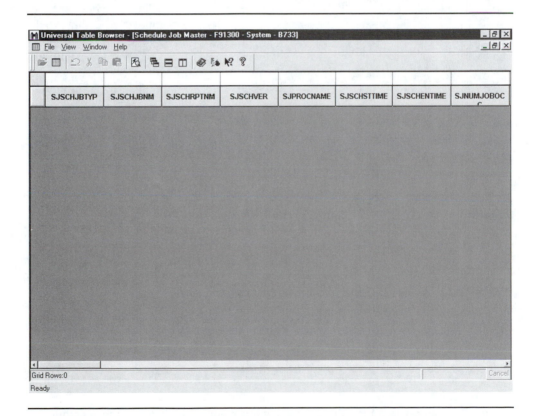

FIGURE 16-43. UTB and the F91300 table

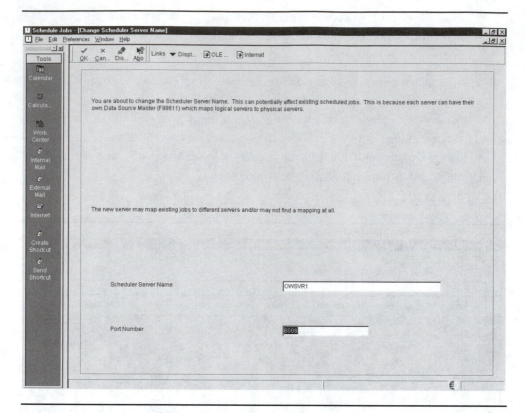

FIGURE 16-44. W91300N Change Scheduler Server Name form

N O T E

You can either use the visual assist or enter the server's name; however, you need to understand that the entry is actually the server's associated SVM (or logic) data source. If you do decide to simply enter the entry, remember that it is case sensitive. If you don't remember exactly how you entered the name for the data source, use the visual assist to avoid making a mistake.

6. You can see that there are quite a few more populated fields in the Scheduler Server Control (W91300G) form. These entries represent the information that you entered in step 5. You can update two fields on this form: Scheduler Sleep Time and Job Monitor Sleep Time.

The following fields are in the W91300G form, shown in Figure 16-45:

- **Scheduler Server Name**   This field (JSSRVR) contains the logic data source associated with the server running the schedule services.

- **Port Number**   The Wins Socket port address (JSSAWPORTNUM) associated with OneWorld network communication on your specific version. The port number is different for each version of OneWorld to allow parallel release support.

- **Scheduler Sleep Time**   (JSSCHRSLEEP) The amount of time in seconds that the server waits between active searches of the F91320 table for new jobs to submit. The server queries the F91320 table at regular intervals looking for jobs that are scheduled to be submitted. This time indicates how long the server waits between queries.

- **Next Submit Date**   (JSNXTSBDT and JSNXTSBTMSTR) The time and date that the schedule server will query the database next.

- **Next Job Monitoring Date**   When the schedule server will next check the status of a submitted job (JSNXTJMDT and JSNXTJMTMSTR).

- **Job Monitor Sleep Time**   The amount of time in minutes (JSJMSLEEP) that the server will wait between checking on jobs submitted previously.

The default values for the Scheduler Sleep Time and the Job Monitor Sleep Time are automatically set to 60 seconds and 15 minutes, respectively. The Scheduler Sleep Time field tells the server how long to wait between queries. This is an essential function of the schedule service to decrease the overhead associated with continual queries against the database. This entry basically tells the server to look for jobs that need to be submitted once a minute. If you are administering this system, it may seem to you that the scheduler is off somewhat; we'll explain why in just a moment.

The Job Monitor Sleep Time field indicates the time interval between queries against F986110, the Job Control Status Master table. The job schedule server keeps track of each job it launches in order to determine if it needs to resubmit it, stop it, or update the status of the job itself (these statuses include scheduled, launched, and completed). Consequently, by setting this variable, you are telling the server how often it should validate the progress of the submitted jobs in their overall job process.

7. Click OK twice to get out of the P91300 schedule utility. Then stop and restart the services on your enterprise and/or application server. When you start your

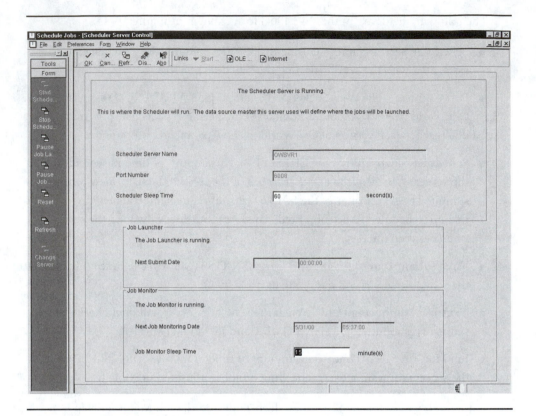

FIGURE 16-45.   W91300G Scheduler Server Control form

network service and if you have logging on the server, you can browse your directory containing your server logs, and you will find one similar to the following:

```
106/363      Wed May 31 06:21:59 2000              IPCPUB1915
      process 106 <jdenet_k> registered in entry 1
106/363      Wed May 31 06:22:00 2000              sc_dsptc140
      INITIALIZING SCHEDULER SERVER KERNEL
106/363      Wed May 31 06:22:00 2000              sc_dsptc163
      Attempting to auto-start the Scheduler.
106/363      Wed May 31 06:22:01 2000              sc_dsptc207
      Auto-starting the Scheduler Server
106/363      Wed May 31 06:22:01 2000              sc_dsptc246
      Scheduler is now started.
```

If you go back into the P91300 table, pick the version of the application that you've been working with, and then select Scheduler Server from the Form menu, the screen shown in Figure 16-46 is displayed. Note that not only does the log indicate that the services have successfully started, but the application now indicates that the Scheduler Server, Job Launcher, and Job Monitor are all running.

Things to Know about Time

If you are using the server's system time, it might seem as if the server isn't launching the jobs in a timely manner. You might see a discrepancy in the launch time because the scheduler job launch and job monitor sleep times are based on when the service first started and then every 60 seconds (for the scheduler job launch) and 15 minutes (for the job monitor sleep time) thereafter. If the service started at 4:35:35 p.m., the schedule server looks for new jobs to launch at 35 seconds after each minute—not at the turn of every minute. Although this is a minor concern to those who are used to administering the OneWorld schedule services, it can be disconcerting to those who are first testing this system.

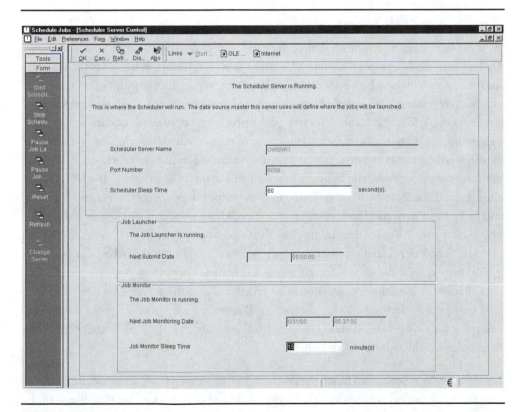

FIGURE 16-46. Job scheduler running

In addition, time can be somewhat confusing. Remember, when you enter any time for submission of a job or sleep status, it is using the server's time stamp in conjunction with the indicated job time zone (e.g., Central Standard Time). If there is a disparity between the time on your watch or computer and the server, the schedule server always uses its own time (like it is going to be able to read the time on your watch). This has been known to cause administrators to think that the schedule utility isn't working properly. Not to worry. Synchronize your system times and the system will work the way you expect.

Scheduling Batch Applications

J.D. Edwards has done a very creditable job in documenting the scheduling of batch application with the scheduler in the "OneWorld Systems Administration Guide" provided on the technical documentation CD. This section will cover some of the things you need to consider beyond the actual "how to" of implementing the scheduler.

Custom Batch Versions

As you begin creating your own end-of-day/scheduler usage, keep in mind that the OneWorld Scheduler does not submit UBEs to the server. Rather, it launches the UBE on the server. You may be wondering what the difference is. Simply put, during the UBE submission process, UBE specifications are packed and transferred from the workstation to the server. UBE specifications are things like processing options, data selections, and printer information. Consequently, if you were to change your data selection so that you saw only sales activity over the last 30 days, this information itself is generated by the end user on the workstation. When the user clicks the final OK to submit the UBE to the server, the information is transferred to the enterprise/application server and is then merged into its own path code-specific TAM files. After this occurs, the server is then able to run your specific UBE and produce the results that you need.

The Scheduler doesn't have this submission process. When the Scheduler launches a UBE on a server, the server doesn't merge a specification package into its own TAM files. Rather, it uses the specifications that are already on the server to run the UBE. You may be wondering how this affects you. If someone were to change the data selection on a UBE version that you were launching nightly, the UBE launched by the Scheduler would also reflect this change.

Create Your Own Scheduled Batch Versions   The way that a CNC administrator gets around this situation is by creating a custom version of the UBE for exclusive use with the scheduler. We usually recommend putting an "S" at the end of the version name so that

you can quickly determine that it is a scheduler version. Then you can apply application security to the version to keep people from accidentally changing or submitting the UBE. In this section, we are not going to go over the how-to of adding or copying versions of UBEs. If you want more information regarding this, refer to Chapter 8.

The Trouble with Unattended UBEs

You should keep in mind a couple of considerations to effectively utilize the OneWorld Scheduler as a corporate solution. One of these considerations is the intrinsic nature of the UBEs themselves. Once you begin working with the OneWorld product (or if you already have experience with UBEs), you quickly learn that some UBEs need to run before others. They feed information forward that is required to complete a process.

Refer to Chapter 19 to gain a better understanding of queues on the server. After you have read this information, you will understand that you can define several different (or identical) batch queues. To ensure that the sequential UBEs run sequentially, it is recommended that they be launched (one after the other) into what is commonly referred to as a *single-threaded queue* (this is actually a singly defined queue to the OneWorld enterprise/application server).

At the same time, however, you learn that some UBEs can be run simultaneously. (Refer to the examples provided throughout this manual, referencing the R42800 Sales Update UBE. To gain an appreciable benefit, you need to run more than one version at a time.) If you create several queues with the same name/identification, you can point the versions to the multithreaded/defined queue. This can be done, as described in Chapter 19, using the version details.

Notice in Figure 16-47 that there is a field in the upper-right corner of the W98305E Version Detail form where you can specify what job queue to use. This can also be done using the Scheduler utility itself as part of its Advanced Functions—Batch Applications Overrides. When you are adding or revising a specifically scheduled job, click the Advanced Functions button located on the exit bar. Then select the Batch Applications Overrides tab, as shown in Figure 16-48. The Job Queue is the last option on that form. It pulls up a User Assist button based on defined UDCs with the names of the queues.

We recommend that you set what queue the batch is run in using the version detail itself. We recommend this primarily because you can't accidentally change this field. To make a change via batch version, you have to check the version out, then go into Version Details, then check the version back, and finally, create a server package with these new version specifications (this can also be done by submitting the version via a workstation with the new specifications). Because of this, any change made is probably intentional.

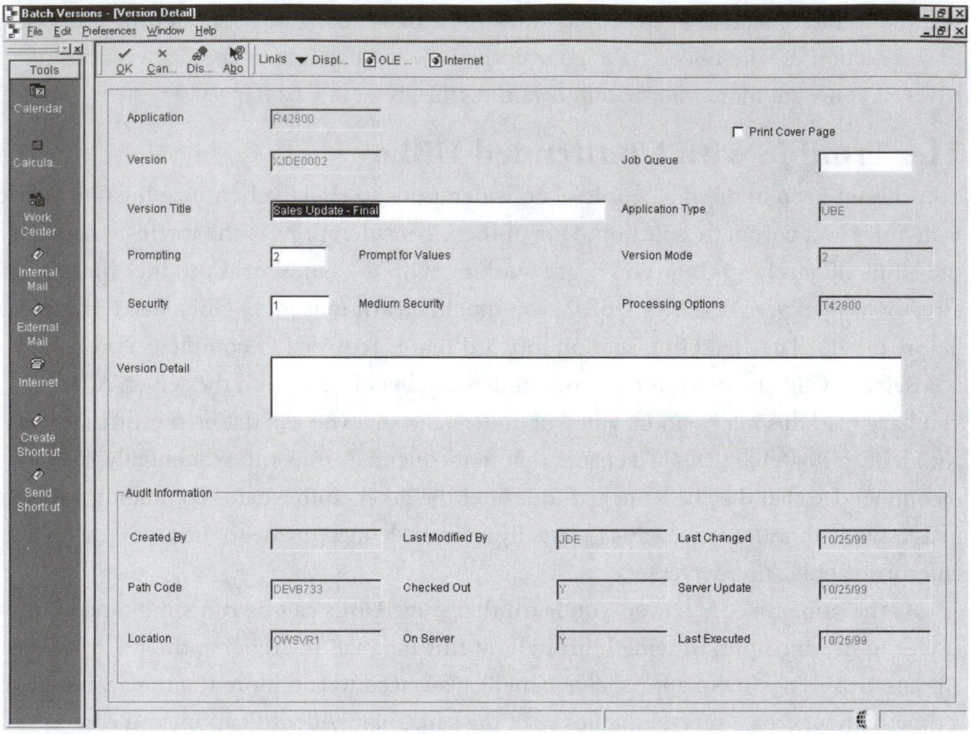

FIGURE 16-47.   Batch version job queues

If you use the Scheduler Batch Applications Overrides to make this change, it can be done accidentally when you are viewing other pieces of information dealing with the specific job. It doesn't need to be as deliberate a procedure. The advantage, of course, in choosing the Scheduler functionality is that it is much faster, but it is a double-edged sword. That is why we recommend the safer route.

Another Consideration

When deciding to run UBEs with the OneWorld Scheduler, you should also consider posting jobs. Most posting jobs cannot be done when other posting jobs are running. Although we would like to offer a good solution for this (and there isn't one), our solution isn't a physical tool in OneWorld. This comes down to a procedural method similar to the one listed for UBEs that requires one being run before the other. In essence, all of these posting jobs should be launched sequentially

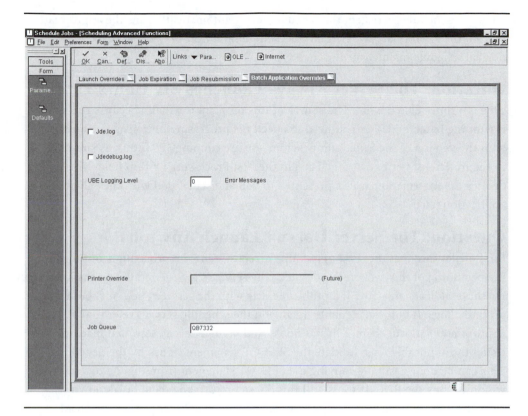

FIGURE 16-48. Batch applications overrides

against a queue that has only a single instance defined to the server the jobs are being launched against.

Trouble Resolution

Not many problems are associated with the Scheduler application once it is set up and working. In this section, we provide a series of situations and possible resolutions or appropriate troubleshooting methodologies. These questions have come from actual clients.

Question: The Workstation Is Offline

Once the schedule is set up, the workstation is no longer part of the schedule system. The three tables associated with the Scheduler traditionally reside on the enterprise server. Additionally, the schedule server is running the service that launches UBEs.

Once the schedule is created, the schedule server automatically runs the appropriate jobs on the appropriate server. The workstation no longer plays a part except in normal schedule maintenance.

Question: The Server Always Launches Six Hours Late

This is a time-related issue. The source of this problem is usually because the server is running based on UTC. You need to check the processing options associated with the version of the Scheduler program you are running (P91300), as shown in Figure 16-49. Verify that 2 is listed in the first Processing Option field. This defines the information as it is presented to you and scheduled with the Scheduler application itself.

Question: The Server Doesn't Launch Any Jobs

First, make sure that the server is set up correctly using the procedures outlined in the beginning of this section. Next, check the service's logs generated on the server. Do these indicate an error? If a problem exists with the service itself, it should show up in the logs. If it doesn't, enable tracing on the schedule server (refer to the appropriate platform chapter in this book) and bounce services on that machine. Using the applicable logs, validate the SELECT statement in use by the Scheduler. This can be done easily by copying the SELECT statement from the log to a query window using the RDBMS toolset. If this doesn't return any data, break down why. Does it call for information using the wrong table owner? If so, either the OCM or the data source definition is wrong. Do the tables exist? Is there data in all three associated with the Scheduler? If not, what is missing? These are the kinds of questions required to troubleshoot the data component of the Scheduler.

Question: The Scheduler Is Hit or Miss

This is probably related to older (pre-B733.2) versions of OneWorld. When the OneWorld Scheduler was released in B733 base, the three tables associated with the Scheduler were a part of business data, which meant that you had multiple sets of scheduler tables. This didn't work well for clients that set up and tested in one environment and had a production server in another environment.

When the schedule server launches the Scheduler service, it reads the default environment from the JDE.INI file. On the older versions of OneWorld, this meant that it would read only from one of the five sets of tables initially deployed during the installation. If you, on a workstation, logged on to an environment other than the one the server logged on to, your jobs would not be read because you would have populated a different set of tables. In the B733.2 product, OneWorld moved the tables to the System –

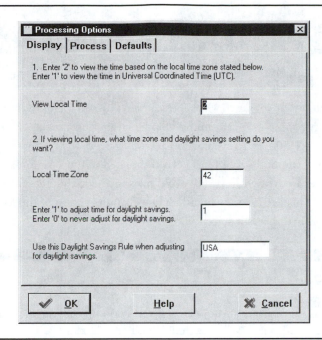

FIGURE 16-49.   Using UTC with processing options

B733 data source, which is used by all of the environments. This nicely solves the issue for the clients on B733.2 or better. If your organization is on either B733 or B733.1, your options are as follows.

1. Copy the tables to the System – B733 data source. Modify both server and workstation OCM to look for the new data source. See the "Law of the West" that follows.

2. Remember which environment your server uses as a default and always log on to this environment when adding or modifying the schedule.

Question: The Reports Generated Aren't Consistent

This problem is usually a result of not having custom UBEs for the schedule server or not having them secured. If a user is accidentally launching these UBEs and modifying either the data selection or processing options, you can easily see issues surrounding the UBE output. Make sure that you have custom versions scheduled and the appropriate security for the version.

B733 and B733.1 Scheduler Solutions

If you want to modify your B733 or B733.1 Scheduler to enable administration from any of the environments, perform the following functions:

Copy the F91300, F91310, and F91320 tables from the business data, data source where the majority of the work has been completed to the system data source. Always copy the tables in their entirety and avoid mixing and matching tables from different data sources. This can be done by utilizing a custom version of the R98403 UBE where you have modified the data selection.

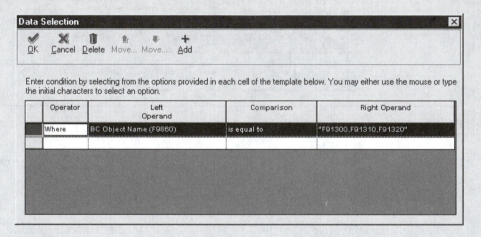

Once you have set your object name equals clause, you also need to modify the processing options associated with this UBE. Notice that we have set processing options 2, 3, and 4 but not 1 or 5. For processing option 2, enter **System – B733** as the target data source for the table copy. On processing option 3, enter **2** to create the table and copy all of the data to the new tables. Processing option 5 tells the UBE where to find the source set of tables you want to copy.

Law of the West

Processing Options

Environment | Update | Print | Licensing

1. Enter the Environment for the database to be created for. (If this report is called from another process, the Environment will be passed in)

2. or Enter the Data Source for the database to be created for.
`System - B733`

3. Enter a '1' to load Production Data or a '2' to load Demonstration Data. The default is to load production data. (If this report is called from another process, this flag will be passed in)
`2`

4. Enter the source Data Source for Loading of Data. (If this report is called from another process, the source Data Source will be passed in)
`Business Data - PROD`

5. or Enter the Source Environment for the database to be copied from. (If this report is called from another process, the Source Environment will be passed in)

OK   Help   Cancel

The other method of copying these tables through OneWorld is using the table design aid (TDA) in the object librarian. This is described in more detail in Chapter 7.

Change the server and workstation OCM using the following SQL statements. The first statement always verifies the number of records that you need to change. The second statement actually modifies the system. If you have an Oracle database, don't forget to follow the UPDATE statement with a COMMIT statement. Additionally, since OneWorld does support four different database formats (DB2/400, Oracle, MS SQL Server, and MS Access), you may have to change the following format to support your specific database. These format differences have been mentioned in several different chapters. If you have any questions concerning your specific format, consult your system DBA. The following example is for MS SQL Server.

select count(*) from sysb733.f986101 where omobnm='F91300'

NOTE

Be sure you are comfortable making direct database changes before performing this procedure. If you are not comfortable, refer to Chapter 2 for more information on the OCM tool.

Repeat this for each table, and make a note of the number returned. It should equal the number of environments you have.

update sysb733.f986101 set omdatp='System – B733' where omobnm='F91300'

Repeat this for each table, and make a note of the number returned. It should equal the number noted previously.

Summary

Over the last hundred pages we have detailed five functions that you as the system administrator will need to know how to support. We have discussed how multitier deployment can assist you in implementing package deployments across a wide area network, and how this functionality can help you to deploy packages to hundreds of users. How the server administration workbench can assist you in supporting your OneWorld implementation was also covered. You learned how to monitor all of your server's kernel processes, disk resources, IPC resources, and the users who are logged onto the system. You also learned how to turn logging on and view log files using SAW. We even showed you how to set this software up to page or e-mail you in the event of a problem. This will significantly reduce the time it takes to resolve issues on your system.

The OneWorld server host code was also discussed in detail as to how it affects your system and what services it provides. The chapter then went on to discuss how you can personalize the appearance of the grid format in your applications and how to maintain these changes with the user overrides application. Finally, we told you how you can schedule your OneWorld reports to run at night using the scheduler application. With this knowledge in hand, your job as a OneWorld system administrator just got a little easier.

Troubleshooting

CHAPTER 17

Printing in OneWorld

The OneWorld Printing Application

Importing and Exporting from OneWorld
  Grid Forms

Printing with Third-Party Products

Third-Party Printing Case Study

Y ou've done all the work, entered all the data, even run the reports. Now it's time to finally see the results of your efforts. All you have to do is print it all out, right? Sure, no problem. Of course, from a system process point of view, more difficult questions immediately pop up—for example, what type of printer do you have (line, PostScript, etc.)? Do you want to print it to a Microsoft Excel file? What about a comma-delimited file that would allow you to do a whole series of different things, including importing it to different data manipulators? Do you want the form printed on legal or letter-sized paper, or maybe your company uses an odd-sized paper that you need to custom define?

Actually, the questions above are only the tip of the iceberg. Printing in OneWorld becomes even more complicated with centralized processing in a decentralized system. How do you print to different locations automatically? This chapter will help answer some of those questions and point to other options in your OneWorld system. We will cover the following:

- Basic OneWorld printing in B7332 and higher versions of OneWorld

- Troubleshooting

- Third-party product integration

The printing application received a complete redesign in version B733.2 of the OneWorld product, and we think this is all for the best. In this chapter, we will address printing in OneWorld for versions B733.2 and higher, and also cover topics such as exporting data from OneWorld into and out of the OneWorld grids. You will often want to print certain data that is not in a report. When this occurs, you could go to a third-party product and use a SQL statement to extract the data. Or you could spend the time necessary to create a report in the OneWorld system. Both of these often generate more work than a one-time request should muster. By contrast, exporting the data directly from the grid to one of the office suites is a fast method of creating and ultimately printing the data (and you can also make some very nice ad hoc reports using this method of printing).

The OneWorld Printing Application

One of the first changes that most people noticed in OneWorld printing from version B733 to B7332 is that there is now a single menu entry point into the printing application (P98616) located on the GH9013 Printers menu. This is a significant change from the five menu entry points in earlier versions of OneWorld and even more significant over the largely INI-driven printer setup required prior to B732. When you actually start the P98616 Printers application, however, you will quickly realize that this program has undergone a complete overhaul, with a new, easy look and feel designed to take much of the pain out of defining printers.

A Quick History Lesson

Before B732, printing various reports in OneWorld was a hit or miss proposition. UBEs generated .PDF formatted files. The only supported printers were those that supported PostScript. You could make a line printer work with the OneWorld product, but this required additional setup and JDE.INI modifications. If you really wanted to have your reports look great, you had to modify the UBE itself to ensure it looked right printed on whichever printer you usually printed it on.

Then came the first of the OneWorld printing applications. It represented a quantum leap from what was available before, particularly in functionality. There were its detractors; people claimed that it was difficult to set up and to use. However, most of these people missed what the printer application provided them. No longer did you have to redesign UBE output to accommodate the printer. You no longer had to worry that shipping your print job to a different printer would result in ugly output.

N O T E

This is with the possible exception of line printers. The number of different line printers and their associated drivers and specialty fonts can still cause issues with printer output.

With this enhancement, you could define the printer (including remote printers), its conversion driver, and even set up specific printers for users, groups, or servers. This application used the F98616 series of tables (F98616, F986161, F986162, F986163, F986164, and F986165). It also added direct line printer conversions without requiring JDE.INI changes and eventually even PCL support. For an application many complained about, it really made significant improvements to the overall OneWorld printing solution.

Finally, with the release of the B733.2 version of OneWorld, we see yet another quantum leap in OneWorld printing. We will concentrate on these changes for the remainder of the chapter. For those of you who are still on older versions of the OneWorld product, this will give you an extra incentive to migrate to the latest version of OneWorld.

P98616 – OneWorld Printers

Now comes a very important question: what has changed in this release over what had become tried and true? In order to fully understand the changes, it is good to know how it works underneath. There are now eight tables in the F98616 series (see Table 17-1). Many of these are only being shipped for backward compatibility. The tables actually used in the B733.2 version of the OneWorld product include the F986162, F986163, F986166, and F986167 tables.

This new application is wizard driven and walks the OneWorld systems administrator through printer setup. All the tasks necessary to define printers, paper,

Table Name	Description	Information
F98616	Printer Definitions	This was the master of the older system, containing printer name, conversion program, line printer space specifications, printer type, and paper type.
F986161	Default Printer Table	This table defined default printers for users and groups and contained user/group name, environment, host, printer name, and active status.
F986162	Paper Definitions	There were three defined printer types in older versions of OneWorld. This table maintains information on paper type, height, width, and unit of measure.
F986163	Printer Capability	This table defines printer definitions to include printer physical device name, paper orientation (landscape or portrait), and paper type (letter, legal, and so on).
F986164	Output Conversion	This table defines output conversions programs, including program name, host, and conversion program specifications.
F986165	Printer Security	This table only contains fields for physical device name and user.
F986166	Bar Code Font Support	This table includes font name, environment, host, status, version, program ID, job number, and update information.
F986167	New Default Printer Table	This table includes physical device name, report ID, version, user, group, environment, host, and status.

TABLE 17-1.   Tables Associated with the P98616 Printers Application

and user defaults can be accessed through the same application providing a common interface that is easy to use. We will quickly look at each of these tasks in the remainder of this section.

Adding New Printer Definitions

As you might guess, you have to add a printer definition to the system before it is available for use. The newest P98616 application wizard makes this easy and quick. You start by using Fast Path to go to the GH9013 Printers menu. Double-click on the P98616 Printers application, starting the printer director (shown in Figure 17-1). Notice that you have options for adding a printer, modifying a printer definition, and defining default printers. Click the Add Printer button.

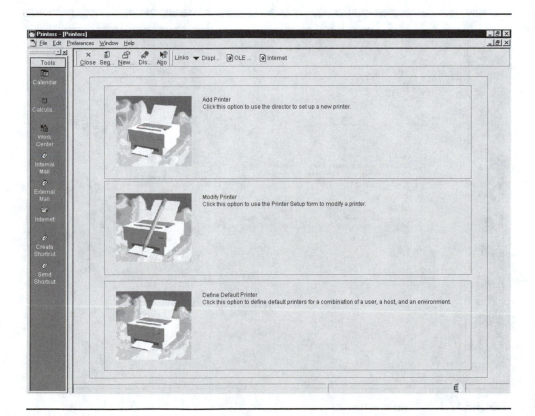

FIGURE 17-1. P98616 Printers Application

This takes you to the printer setup director (see Figure 17-2). Notice that this director is designed to do the following:

- Define platform type and information necessary for the printer

- Define the printer model and its location

- Define paper types supported by the printer and the default paper type for that printer

- Choose the printer definition language (PDL) supported by the printer and its default PDL

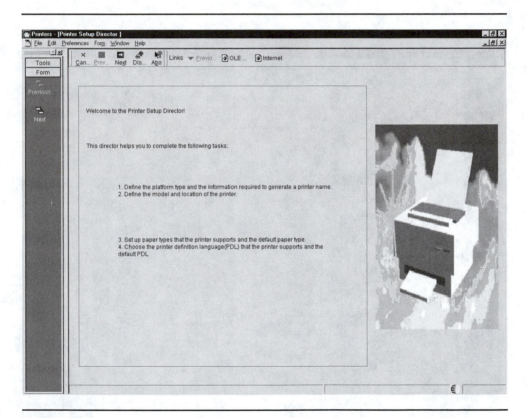

FIGURE 17-2.   Printer setup director

By clicking the next button, you will see Figure 17-3. On this form, you need to choose the platform of the server you're defining to the system.

The valid platform types are defined by UDCs (Product Code H93, Report Code PL) and include ALPHA, AS400, HP9000, LOCAL, NTSVR, RS6000, and SUN. Once you have entered a hardware/OS platform (see Figure 17-3), click the Next button.

N O T E

If you choose either LOCAL or ALPHA, it will automatically default to NTSVR. NTSVR is used for all NT hardware platform types. If you choose either SUN or RS6000, it will automatically default to HP9000. HP9000 is used for all UNIX platforms.

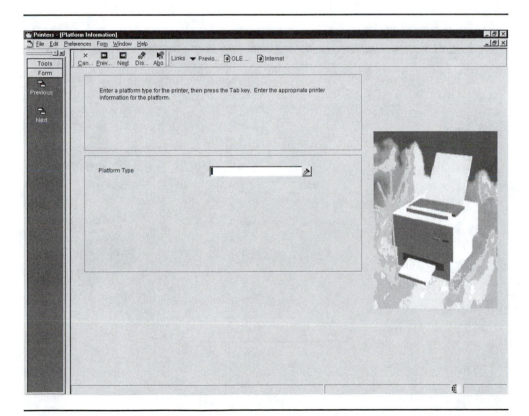

FIGURE 17-3. Printer setup director

You will be prompted to enter the print server name and the printer's shared name if you are defining an NT platform (see Figure 17-4). When defining a UNIX platform, you will only be prompted for the printer name (in UNIX, the lpstat command is useful for determining the name of the printer as it is defined to the UNIX server). Defining an AS400 platform prompts you for the library name and the output queue name. Once you have entered this information, click the Next button.

NOTE

Any of the information entered for either the NT or UNIX platforms will automatically be entered in lower case. For the AS400 platform, the library and output queues are automatically in upper case.

FIGURE 17-4. Platform information

You will need to enter the model of the printer and its location. There are two options for printer model: Laser or Line Printers. Select the paper types supported by this printer by double-clicking the header grid of each supported paper type and indicating the default paper for that specific printer (refer to Figure 17-5). Make sure the green check mark is visible. The types of paper predefined by J.D. Edwards include legal, letter, and A4. You will also need to define the default paper type by typing a 1 in the Default Type column in the paper grid. If you don't, you will receive an error in the application.

Before clicking the End button, you should fill in the supported paper details. This can be done by clicking the Details tab on this form (shown in Figure 17-6).

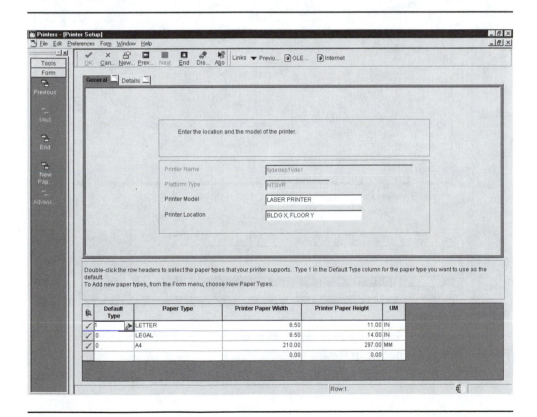

FIGURE 17-5. Printer definition and paper types

NOTE

*If you are defining a line printer, you need to also indicate the paper dimensions.
If you are defining a printer servicing an AS/400, you will need to choose
EBCDIC encoding for non-AS/400 printers.*

When you are done filling in this information, click the End button on the printer director.

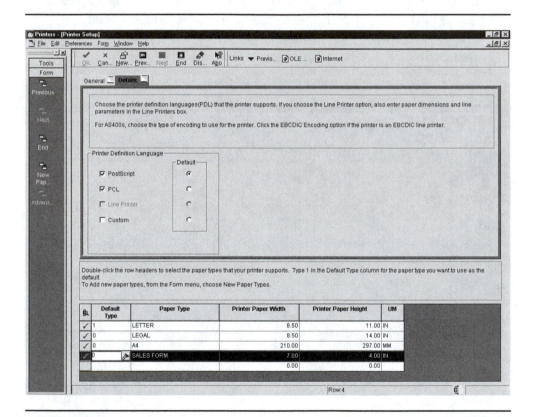

FIGURE 17-6.   Printer setup Details tab

Adding New Paper Types If you want to add additional paper types, you can do this by clicking the New Paper Types button on the Form escape menu (see Figure 17-7) or Exit bar when you are defining the printer-supported paper types (form W98616AE).

When you click this button, the W98616C form launches (Work With Paper Types). Click the Add button (W98616D) and fill in the appropriate information for your custom paper type (see Figure 17-8).

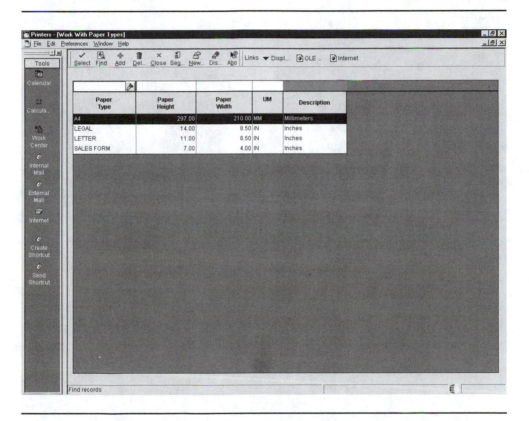

FIGURE 17-7. Click the New Paper Types button on the Form menu

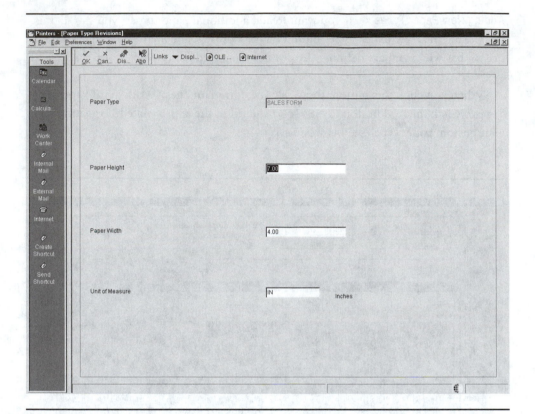

FIGURE 17-8.   Paper information

What You Should Know   If you are interested in what has happened underneath the application, you have just added multiple records to two of the F98616 series tables, including one into the F986162 table and eleven into the F986163 table (see Table 17-2).

PDPAPT	PDPHT	PDPWD	PDUOM
SALES FORM	4	7	IN
PCPHYD	**PCPTOC**	**PCPCAP**	
\\jdedep1\jde1	C	*JDE PCL	
\\jdedep1\jde1	DC	*JDE PS	
\\jdedep1\jde1	DP	LETTER	
\\jdedep1\jde1	H	ALPHA	
\\jdedep1\jde1	H	LOCAL	
\\jdedep1\jde1	H	NTSVR	
\\jdedep1\jde1	P	A4	
\\jdedep1\jde1	P	LEGAL	
\\jdedep1\jde1	P	SALES FORM	
\\jdedep1\jde1	T	LASER PRINTER	
\\jdedep1\jde1	W	3RD FLOOR - X BUILDING	

TABLE 17-2.   Printer Information

Modifying Printer Definitions

You may be wondering, with all of that information automatically generated, how are you going to successfully make changes without a serious understanding of the SQL language? Have no fear. When the printer director was designed, this was taken into consideration. As you can see in several preceding figures, there is an option on the first form entry point on the P98616 Printers application to add printers, modify printers, and define default printers.

Troubleshooting

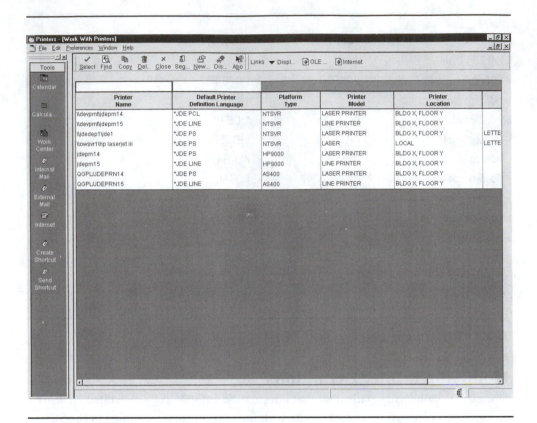

FIGURE 17-9.   Printer items that are changeable

Why would you need to modify a printer? First, modifying a printer is quicker than deleting and re-adding it. Second, you might have forgotten something when entering some of the printer information. Third, you may need to define new paper types for special forms created to fit your specific business needs. Finally, where the application allows you to modify some of the printer definition data, you are not able to modify everything. Consequently, you probably want to know what can and can't be modified. These items are shown in Figures 17-9 and 17-10.

Items that can be changed include:

- Printer model

- Printer location

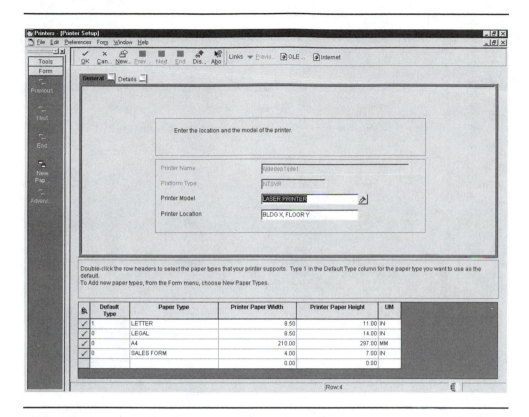

FIGURE 17-10. More printer items that are changeable

- Paper types

- Supported printer definition languages (PDL)

Items that cannot be changed include:

- Printer name

- Printer type

So, what should you do if you need to change something that is on the "do not modify" list? The official OneWorld answer is that you have to delete the printer entry and then re-add it. However, depending on what the item is, there may be another solution. For more information, see the Law of the West section below.

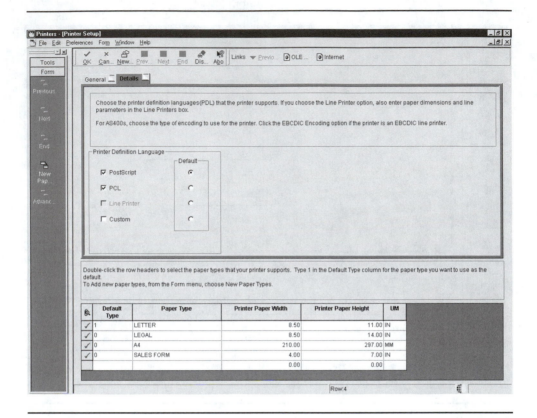

FIGURE 17-11. Printer Setup form

Modifying a Printer

Modifying a printer is easy and straightforward. Start the P98616 Printer application located on the GH9013 menu. Click the Modify Printer button—this will launch the W98616Y (Work With Printers) form. On this form, you will need to select the printer you want to modify. You can do this by either double-clicking it or highlighting it and then clicking the Select button. This will launch the W98616AE (Printer Setup) form (see Figure 17-11). On this form you can change or add additional paper types as required.

Law of the West

Updating Printer Definitions Through SQL

Almost any data in OneWorld can be modified by directly changing it in the tables themselves using the host database tools and the SQL language. However, prior to making any changes to tables directly, we urge you to do the following. First, make sure that you fully understand the table(s) that contain the data you are going to modify. Does this data also have a direct correlation to data in other tables or is it a standalone table? Do you understand the application repercussions associated with directly modifying the data? Should you be making the changes you are about to make? Second, we highly recommend that you back up the tables containing the data you will be modifying. Although you may think you understand the data, there is nothing safer than having a readily available backup, which does not require point in time recovery.

With all of this in mind, you can modify the actual name and host type used by directly modifying the F986163 table. The key to this is that we've already provided you with the tables associated with the printer utilities. If the printer name is wrong, and it is the key to actually printing on the right printer, you can quickly change it with a simple update SQL statement like the one below. Don't forget to commit the change if you are using Oracle.

```
update sysb733.f986163 set pcphyd='\\erpent\ntprnt1' where
pcphyd='\\jdedep1\ntprnt1'
```

Defining Default Printers

To better administrate which printers are used for what and to make life easier for users, you can define default printers for users based on environment and logic host. If a user attempts to run a UBE without having a default printer, there will be an error indicating that no printer has been selected. If there are printers defined in OneWorld, the user can continue launching the UBE by clicking the Change Printer button on the Form menu (W986162B). This will launch the Printer Search & Select form (W98616F), shown in Figure 17-12, where the user can select any printers currently defined in OneWorld.

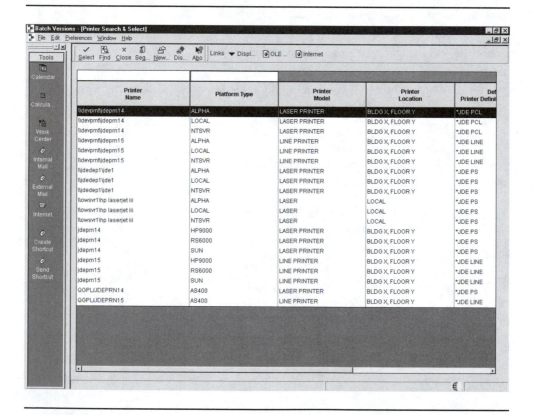

FIGURE 17-12.   Printer Search and Select

NOTE

Default printers can be set up for OneWorld users but not groups. You can use the *PUBLIC to define a default printer for everyone for *ALL environment or specific environments and specific hosts. You are then able to make exceptions to the rules for specific user requirements.

Default Printers   On the P98616 Printers application (launched by going to the GH9013 menu and double-clicking the Printers application), click Define Default Printers. This will launch the W98616O form, which lists all the default printers currently defined on the system (see Figure 17-13). The grid form pulls data from

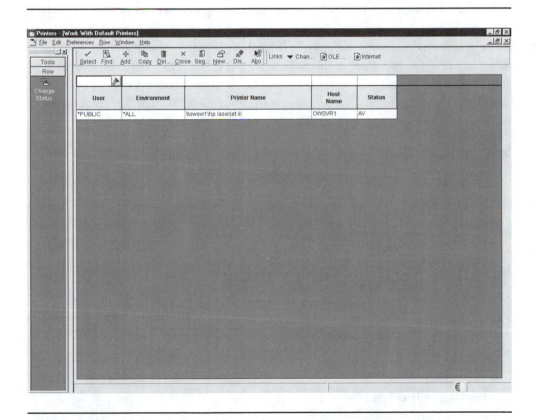

FIGURE 17-13.   Printer Search & Select form showing default printers

the F986167 table in the system data source. Although you can add several different records for a single user, environment, and host, only one of these can be active at any one time.

NOTE

There is a unique index on the F986167 table (F986167_1) for user, environment, host, and physical printer name. Active or inactive, the application will not allow you to set up two printers that are identical for these four values. You cannot have two records for a single user or host, and two different physical printers that are both active. Remember, you are setting up a default, and you can't have two.

To add a new default printer, click the Add button. This will launch the W98616M form where you can enter the following information: User, Environment, Printer, Host, and Status, as shown in Figure 17-14. All of these are self-explanatory with the possible exception of Status. In this field, you enter either AV or NA. This is what allows multiple printer records for the same user/host/environment to exist in the database. After entering the appropriate information, click OK. The form stays open with the assumption that you will be adding additional default entries.

What You Should Know   Under the covers, this will add a single record to the F986167 table that looks something like this.

DPPHYD	DPREPORTID	DPVERS	DPUSER	DPENHV	DPEXEHOST	DPSTSO	DPJOBN	DPUPMT	DPUPMJ
\\jdedep1\jde1	0		JOE	PRD733	LOCAL	AV	CHIJMILER9	53014	2/28/2000

JDE.INI Settings for Printing

We have mentioned several times that in earlier versions of OneWorld, much of the printer setup and definitions were completed in the JDE.INI. Indeed, some settings remain in today's INI for printing:

[NETWORK QUEUE SETTINGS]

PrintImmediate=FALSE

SaveOutput=TRUE

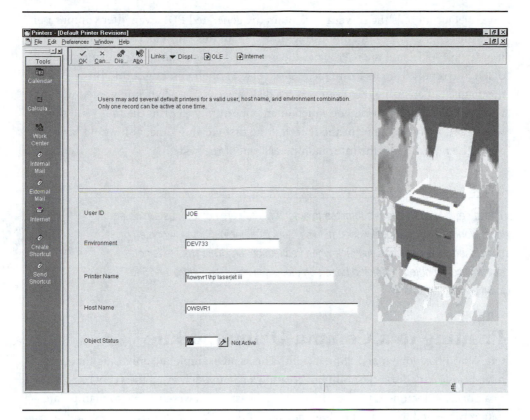

FIGURE 17-14. Adding default printers

These are settings that are put in the workstation's JDE.INI to override application settings in OneWorld. Prior to making changes to this INI, you should understand that the changes will be in effect for the length of that workstation's OneWorld session. This is not something that you should change on the fly and then change back.

PrintImmediate tells the server to automatically print the submitted UBE to the printer selected at launch time. Every time you launch a UBE, there is an associated printer. If PrintImmediate is set to TRUE, the UBE will automatically print the report output to that printer. OneWorld ships with this setting set to FALSE. The reason is that every UBE submitted by the workstation would automatically print, which would be a huge waste of paper.

SaveOutput tells the server to maintain the generated PDF even after you print or view the report. One of the interesting things about this particular setting is that when it is set to FALSE and the user views the generated report, the server will automatically delete the report from its PrintQueue directory. Though you might find this a good mechanism of ensuring that your server's disk space is not needlessly wasted with old reports, it does not provide you much of an opportunity to print the job. With this setting set, if you didn't print the report at the first viewing time, you would have to rerun the report to get the information back out of the system.

NOTE

These settings are for jobs submitted to a server. They are not for jobs run on a local workstation. The local workstation's output is either immediately printed or not, based on the settings you pick when you launch the UBE. The file is not automatically printed or deleted based on these settings. See Figure 17-15 for local printing options.

Printing to a Comma-Delimited File

OneWorld has done it and done it right! This is an example of something that users have been asking for—the ability of creating a comma-delimited file (CSV) as opposed to a portable document format (PDF). In the past, users were unable to manipulate data represented in a report unless they used Adobe Writer. A PDF is presented as a picture to most office products, including word editors and spreadsheets. Because of this, users have been unable to do anything but print the information. If they wanted to directly manipulate data, they either created UBEs that generated flat files, exported from an application grid format, or were forced to rekey the data into the format of their choice.

With the advances made in the B7332 version of OneWorld, this is a thing of the past. One of the options when submitting a UBE is Export To CSV (refer to Figure 17-15). This does not mean no PDF is generated and that OneWorld only creates a comma-delimited file. First, the UBE engine creates the PDF-formatted output and then it exports the data to a comma-delimited file (this file is located in the PrintQueue directory next to the PDF file itself). On our local machine, OneWorld even automatically launches Microsoft Excel to read and manipulate the data at the user's discretion.

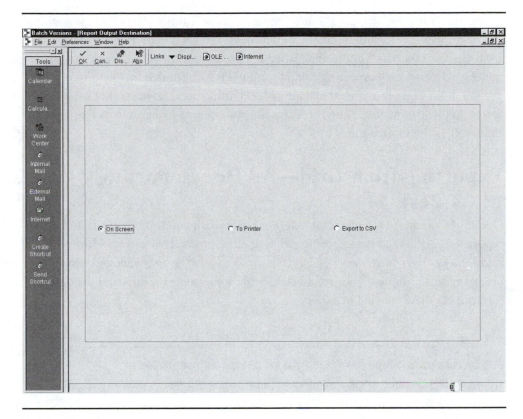

FIGURE 17-15. Local UBE printing choices

Importing and Exporting from OneWorld Grid Forms

Although the ability to import and export data far outreaches mere printing capability in OneWorld, it does provide another method of doing just that. Since it does significantly more, however, this next section deals with all of its aspects, not just printing. If you're interested in the technology, application, and power of OneWorld, we think you will find this section highly informative.

The first set of questions you should be asking is what can and can't be imported and exported out of the OneWorld suite of products. Luckily, you do not have to memorize a huge list of applications for either of these utilities. To verify if something can be imported or exported out of OneWorld, all you need to do is right-click the form (grid or otherwise) of the application itself. OneWorld will automatically provide you with the option of exporting and importing if it is supported by the form type. In general, most grid forms are compliant with exporting data. However, the list of grid forms that will allow importing is very small. (An example of a grid form that allows importing is the Journal Entry form.)

Exporting from Grid—Ad Hoc Reporting at Its Best

OneWorld exporting is a powerful tool, especially when you want to create ad hoc reports on the fly. You can export to different office products at will from almost any grid form in OneWorld. Depending on what you have on your system and what you are trying to accomplish, you should choose the appropriate product and the range of information that you want to export.

N O T E

Just because you can export data from a grid format does not mean that you can import into the same format. If you want to use exporting and importing data to modify OneWorld data, be sure to verify that the application supports both prior to export.

OneWorld has the ability to export to the following applications: Microsoft Excel and Word, Lotus 1-2-3 and WordPro, and Corel QuattroPro and Word Perfect. Though both spreadsheets and word applications are supported, you should consider the reason you are exporting the data. The output varies based on what you are exporting. Products like Word, WordPro, and Word Perfect automatically wrap text that is too long. They also handle spacing differently than other applications. This can make the output extremely ugly. Spreadsheet applications, however, tend to maintain figures and associated spacing very well. If you are limiting the amount of data you are exporting, word processors can allow you to quickly put data into reports or documents that you are creating. However, products like Excel and Lotus 1-2-3 are generally used for export purposes. From there, the information is often brought into associated word processing applications.

Exporting

During both installation and upgrades, it is a very useful thing to be able to quickly document where you left the system. For the purpose of this demonstration, we are going to use the P986115 Database Data Source application. Start that application (found on the GH9011 menu) and select the system data source. Click Find and then right-click in the grid form. Choose Export from the menu (see Figure 17-16) and select the application of your choice. The Export Assistant will launch, providing you with choices based on your application selection.

For a spreadsheet, you will have the opportunity to create a new spreadsheet or open an old one. If you choose to open an existing workbook, you will have to indicate

Troubleshooting

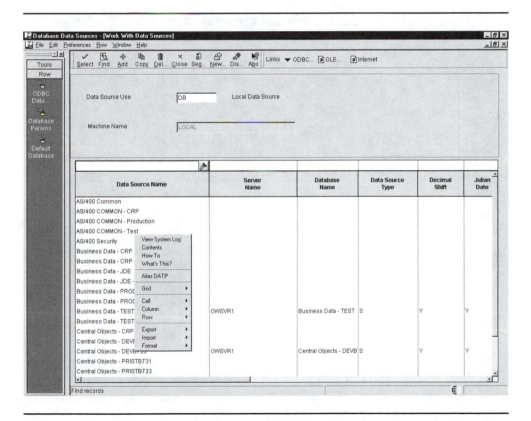

FIGURE 17-16. Starting the export

the worksheet you want to export to (see Figure 17-17). If you choose to start a new workbook, the OneWorld export utility will put the data on sheet 2. If you choose to export to a word processing application, the Export Assistant (see Figure 17-18) does not give you a choice of opening an existing document. Rather, it immediately requires you to select the range of data that you want to export prior to continuing.

Once you have filled out the selections on the Export Assistant, you will need to select the actual range of data in the grid form that you want to export. You make this selection for both the worksheet or the word processor by clicking on the first row you want to export and dragging the cursor to the bottom row that you

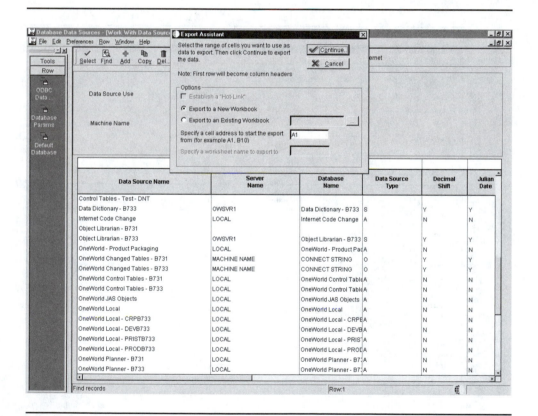

FIGURE 17-17.   Exporting to a Spreadsheet

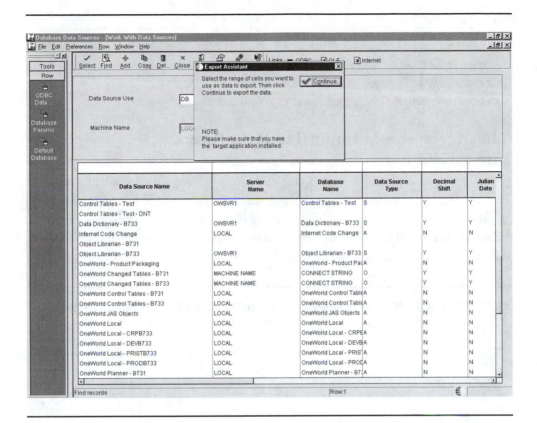

FIGURE 17-18.   Exporting to a Word Processor

Troubleshooting

want. After highlighting the data, click the Continue button on the Export Assistant and watch it work.

Importing to Grid—A OneWorld Powerhouse

There are a small number of applications that allow you to import data directly into the grid form. Still, this is a powerful feature for the OneWorld application suite. When importing, OneWorld limits the number of applications that you can use to Microsoft Excel, Lotus 1-2-3, and Corel QuattroPro. Importing follows simple rules. The information in the spreadsheet obviously needs to be correct, in the proper format and layout.

TIP

You can quickly create documents to use as a template for import spreadsheets by exporting the data first. This method will create an example of exactly how your data should be formatted, the order of the data itself, what elements of data need to be included, and a good description of the data elements required.

The Mechanics of Importing Data Directly into a Grid Form

The first step in importing directly to the grid form is setting up a spreadsheet with the data you want to import and understanding the application you will be manipulating in this way. For this example, we will be using the P0911 Journal Entry application found on menu G0911. We will be adding in several rows of a journal entry. Start by double-clicking on the application, then click Add (refer to Figure 17-19).

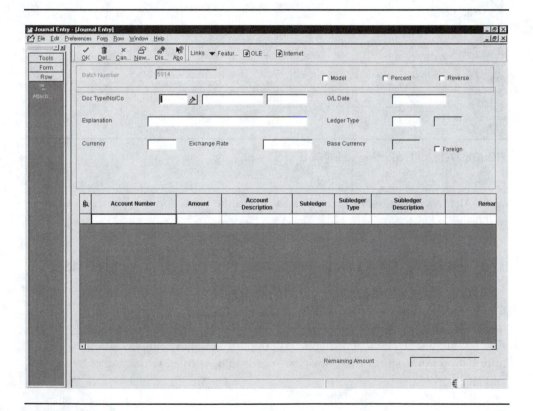

FIGURE 17-19. The W0911A form, pre-import

Right-click on the grid form itself, then choose Import and the supported spreadsheet application of your choice. A form titled Open launches (shown in Figure 17-20). This form is importing's equivalent of the Export Assistant. On this form, you will need to specify the actual file containing the data, the range of data you want to import, and the worksheet that contains the data.

You also have the choice of establishing a hot-link between the P0911 application and the spreadsheet itself. We'll talk more about that in a minute. Other things to note about the Open form is that it automatically chooses the file types for the application you chose in the step above. If you picked Microsoft Excel, it automatically looks for Excel files. The same goes for Lotus and Corel. Click the Open button to continue.

The information is imported into the Journal Entry form and certain business functions automatically start to validate and complete the entry.

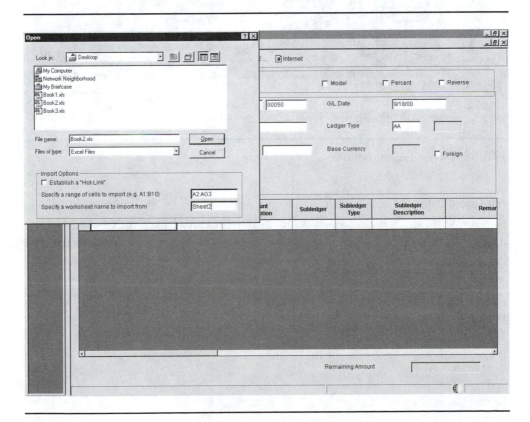

FIGURE 17-20. Import data selection

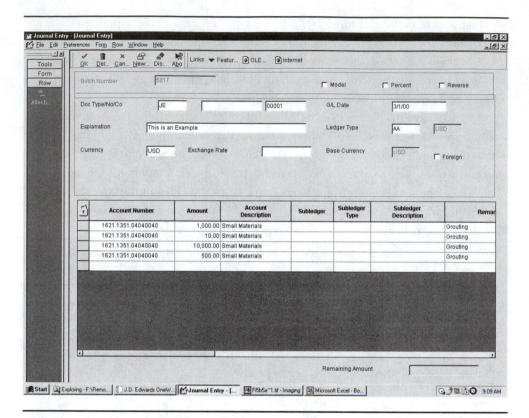

FIGURE 17-21.   Import options

Hot-Linked Data   The Hot-Link option creates a link between the spreadsheet and the OneWorld application. As data is modified in the spreadsheet, the OneWorld application is automatically updated and vice versa. This allows a tremendous amount of flexibility in how the two products interact. Additionally, the Hot-Link option is available when you export data out of a OneWorld grid form, but only on grid forms that support importing data and only if you choose a spreadsheet export. During a hot-link session, both the spreadsheet and the OneWorld application remain open. If you close either of the applications, the link is temporarily broken. Starting up the spreadsheet will not reestablish the link.

Troubleshooting Printing in OneWorld

With the P98616 Printers application being run with a built-in printer director, what could go wrong with printing as it is defined in the OneWorld product? In truth, we have had very little problem printing in OneWorld when it is set up properly. Of course, we can't guarantee that you or your CNC administrator will set it up correctly. Consequently, this section will cover some common mistakes and how you can fix them in OneWorld. One of the topics we won't cover, however, is how to set printers up on each of the hardware platforms. We are working under the assumption that your systems administrator knows how to set up printers, verify that they are working with the servers, and perform basic troubleshooting for the printers themselves.

Printer Problems

Some of the most common problems with printing in OneWorld are really the easiest to fix. There are two types of printing in OneWorld: printing from a workstation and printing from a server. Both of these machines have to have printers set up and working correctly in order to ensure that you can print from OneWorld. If you can print from other applications, odds are that you can print from OneWorld as well.

Workstation Printing

There are almost no OneWorld-related problems associated with printing from a workstation. In order to print, be sure you set up Adobe Acrobat and a default printer. There are also two ways to print from OneWorld on a workstation. First, if you launched a job on a server, you can view the output of the UBE on the workstation by clicking the View PDF Job or View CSV Job on the Work With Server Jobs application (P986110B). This will transfer the .PDF or .CSV to your local PrintQueue directory located under the workstation's B7 directory and then launch the appropriate application to view it. From these applications, you can print to any printer defined on the workstation. This type of printing is very straightforward and is not prone to error.

The second way you can print on the workstation is also from the Work With Server Jobs application. On the Form menu bar, you will see an option to print. This will automatically launch the Printer Search And Select form. You can either keep the default printer or select a new printer. Click OK and the job will print directly from the server itself (refer to Figure 17-22). It will not copy the output to your local machine and you will not be able to view the product first.

N O T E

If you pick a different printer type, the output may not look as good as it would have using the original printer type. This is especially true if you change the output printer to a line printer format.

The most common issue when printing on the workstation is OneWorld's inability to correctly pull up the associated program for viewing the report output. If you attempt to view a .PDF, for example, OneWorld will automatically attempt to launch

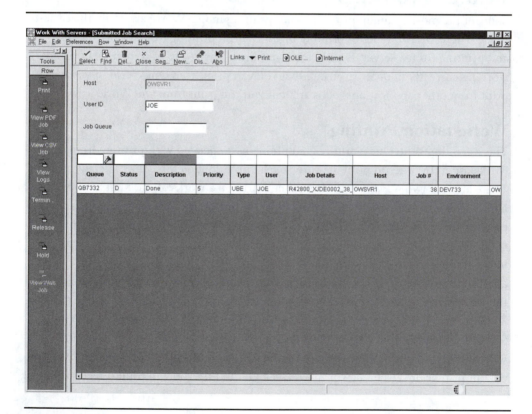

FIGURE 17-22.   Printing from Work With Server Jobs

the Adobe Acrobat Reader. If your workstation system environment variables do not have the location of the Adobe Reader, OneWorld will prompt you with an error stating that it cannot find the Acrobat Reader and ask if you want to find it yourself. If you click Yes, a computer browser will launch and locate ACRORD32.EXE on your system. This, however, will not update your system with the proper location. The next time you attempt to view another job, you will have to go through this ritual again. The easiest way to fix this problem is to reinstall the Adobe Acrobat Reader as a user with administrative rights on the workstation. This will ensure that the environment and registry variables are properly updated so OneWorld can launch the reader.

Another problem with printing from the workstation occurs if the user chooses to view the document prior to printing and receives an error stating that the .PDF file does not start with %pdf. One of the possible causes of this is that the file is not correctly copying to the local workstation. We've seen instances of this when the workstation does not have enough free space on its hard drive to hold the .PDF file. Creating additional room on the workstation will quickly solve this problem. There are two other reasons that the file might not copy correctly to the workstation. If there are network issues, this could cause problems. The other reason would be if the actual .PDF file on the server is either corrupt or has been deleted. In either case, running the report again might be required to make sure you can access the file.

Another problem with printing reports from the workstation occurs when the user specifies direct server printing to a printer that is not defined on the server. This rarely meets with good results; however, the user is almost powerless to determine why his or her job won't print. The systems administrator should be able to quickly identify this type of issue and resolve it by telling the user to select a different printer or by actually setting the printer up on the server itself.

Printing from the Server

To remain consistent, we will still be working under the assumption that your system administrator knows how to set up, verify printing capabilities, and troubleshoot printing on the various platforms. There are several issues users can run into when trying to print directly from the server. (We described one of these issues in the preceding paragraph.)

Other issues include the printer or the print queue being offline on the server itself. We've seen UNIX systems where a print queue will go offline and collect literally hundreds of print requests. Once the OS reestablishes communication with the printer, the print jobs will process. The first troubleshooting step you should perform is

Troubleshooting

verifying that the printer is set up correctly on the server and is online. The printer conversion programs are automatically chosen for you by the printer director in OneWorld B733.2. You should check the line printer settings to ensure that you have the correct information listed, including characters per inch, columns per page, lines per inch, and lines per page. In versions prior to this, however, you should also carefully verify that the conversion program is set correctly for the type of printer you are defining.

Printing with Third-Party Products

OneWorld cannot do everything with regard to printing. One situation might be if you want to print a particular form in multiple locations simultaneously (for example, in a retail operation). You use OneWorld P4210 to enter a sales order. You have a pick slip automatically print for the customer, but you might also want one printed in a warehouse so that someone can actually get the product off the rack. You might want a third copy printed in the back room for your records. In the normal setup of OneWorld, the only way to do this is to print the ticket and then reprint the ticket, selecting a different printer each time. To further complicate matters, what if you wanted to do this with centralized logic processing for hundreds of locations? As an organization, you would probably want to streamline this process.

OneWorld has the capability to use third-party products with good results that will allow you to perform a series of functions you would not be able to do using just OneWorld native printing. The majority of these products take data directly from OneWorld out queues and perform the printing job defined in their own systems.

Table 17-3 shows a list of printing solution companies and products that have working partnerships with J.D. Edwards and their OneWorld product. For a complete, up-to-date listing of business partnerships between J.D. Edwards and other third-party organizations that provide printing solutions, check their Web site (http://www.jdedwards.com/).

Third-Party Printing Case Study

The following is a brief case study consisting of third-party printing solutions and OneWorld. Although we will not go into detail on the OneWorld implementation itself, we will quickly outline the company's business requirements, the implementation of

Company	Product
AFP Technology	FormScape
Bottomline Technologies	Paybase
	Laser CheckWrite
	MICR Encoded Checks
Create!print International	Create!print for J.D. Edwards OneWorld
	Create!fax
Lexmark Solution Services	OptraForms
JetForm	Central
	Intempo
	Filler
	JetForm Design
	JetForm Central
Optio	OptioDCS
	OptioFAX
	OptioCheckBook
	e.comPresent
	Optio DesignStudio
Western Business Systems	Business Forms

TABLE 17-3.   Printing Business Partners

the printing solution, and how their requirements were met. The case study is not designed to provide a step-by-step solution, but rather the general methods and processes used during integration and implementation of the printing solution.

The Business and Its Requirements

A retail organization with multiple remote sites, although they had a mainframe, was implementing OneWorld rather than remediating their legacy systems. As such, they opted to migrate to an HP9000 backend with terminal servers as the primary user interface. They had several specific printing requirements, including secured check printing, multiple printer locations in remote locations, impact line printing (dot matrix) and fax printing. This solution was on B733 base, not on the B733.2 OneWorld product.

The Printing Solution

This organization opted to use FormScape for its printing solution in OneWorld. A FormScape server was installed and configured with a print queue (this was actually a directory in the NT file system). A printer definition in OneWorld was set up using a modified conversion script on the UNIX box that automatically converted the PDF to ASCII text and then printed the output to the FormScape server.

In FormScape, specific jobs were created identifying several pieces of information. Particularly, the FormScape jobs searched for specific data in specific locations in the output file to determine the appropriate printer in the enterprise. This provided most of the printing requirements for the organization, including printing to multiple remote printers automatically while still having centralized processing.

To solve the fax problem, this company opted to implement RightFax. Although RightFax is not one of the supported fax solutions provided by J.D. Edwards, nevertheless, when it comes right down to it, printing from a workstation is traditional Windows printing. If RightFax works on a Windows Terminal Server (and it does), it will adequately meet the faxing requirements of most companies.

Summary

In this chapter, we detailed multiple printing solutions in the OneWorld suite of products, including how to set up printers in OneWorld, print from both servers and workstations, troubleshoot various issues, and integrate third-party products. Printing in OneWorld has undergone drastic changes—all for the better—and it represents a mature solution that is able to change to meet your company's needs.

CHAPTER 18

Upgrade Tools and Rules

Differences Between Upgrades and Updates

Upgrades

Updates

Application Software Updates (ASUs)

Electronic Software Updates (ESUs)

Retrofitting Modifications

Running in Parallel

A s with most things, software packages change. Companies must expand their software's functionality to keep up in the marketplace. This rule also applies to OneWorld. This is why J.D. Edwards has built tools into their software to allow their clients to upgrade their software. This means you do not have to scrap all your custom modifications to the software to take advantage of new functionality.

In this chapter, we will go over how the upgrade process flows and some of the rules that apply to the process. We will discuss the differences between upgrades and updates. We will also touch on some of the new developments in the technology used to upgrade or update OneWorld systems. This new technology is application software updates (ASU) and electronic software updates (ESU). Finally, we will include some real-world experiences with upgrades that the authors have performed. This chapter will cover:

- Differences between upgrades and updates

- Upgrades

- Updates

- Application software updates

- Electronic software updates

- Retrofitting modifications

- Running in parallel

Differences Between Upgrades and Updates

To truly understand the upgrade process, you must first understand the difference between upgrades and updates. J.D. Edwards has produced several different releases of OneWorld software (B733 is an example of a release). An update does not contain quite as many objects as a release. An example of an update would be B733.1. Currently both updates and upgrades can contain new functionality. The main difference between updates and upgrades is in how they are applied.

While talking about the differences between upgrades and updates, we will talk about how these processes affect objects on your system. Some examples of these objects are reports, tables, and applications. The OneWorld software allows you to keep your modifications to these objects when you upgrade or update the software, as long as you follow J.D. Edwards' rules when you develop your custom objects or modify existing J.D. Edwards' objects.

J.D. Edwards Methodology for Updates and Upgrades

J.D. Edwards assumes certain things will always be done for updates and upgrades. Although this is addressed in their manuals, we feel it is necessary to explain this methodology here as well.

Standard Methodology for Updates and Upgrades

When you perform an update or an upgrade, you should follow the following guidelines. These guidelines are fairly simple and will help keep you out of trouble. They include applying the update/upgrade to an environment other than your production environment. J.D. Edwards recommends that you use the CRP environment, as this environment was designed for you to set up your business processes. Before the update/upgrade is applied, you should ensure that the CRP environment's business data, control tables, and central objects match those of your production environment. Once you have done this, you will need to freeze all development work in the production environment, including the addition of new interactive or batch versions. This is done so that once you have performed the upgrade to the CRP environment you can then copy the central objects over from the CRP path code to the production path code. This allows you to quickly upgrade your production environment with minimal risk, since you do not have to run the specification merge for the production environment. Following this methodology also gives you a good feel as to how long the upgrade/update table conversions will take. This will help you to plan the upgrade/update of your production environment.

Following the above procedures, you will also need to copy your path code directory structure on your deployment server and your enterprise server from one path code to another. (Path codes are explained in Chapter 2.) Normally, this would entail copying the production path code to the CRP path code. You need to back up several of your relational database tables. We will touch upon these relational database tables later in the chapter. Backing up these tables allows you to recover the system if you experience problems during an update or upgrade. Once you have completed these steps, which are documented in greater detail in the J.D. Edwards upgrade guides, you will be prepared to update/upgrade your system.

Troubleshooting

You are probably thinking this is an awful amount of work to perform for an update. True, it is a lot of work, but if you follow this methodology you will be successful in your updates. If you do not follow the above methodology, and try to apply an update/upgrade directly into your production environment, you will most likely have problems. For these reasons, J.D. Edwards asks all of their clients to follow this methodology.

Updates

Let's start by describing how the update process flows. With an update prior to OneWorld Xe (formerly B733.3), J.D. Edwards leaves your objects, which are stored in your central object data source, in place. J.D. Edwards stores the information that the applications and reports in OneWorld use in relational database tables. These tables, called TAM or table access manager, are contained in your central objects data sources. OneWorld uses these tables to create the files that workstations use to run OneWorld. This concept is addressed in more detail in the Chapter 10. When you apply an update to the system, J.D. Edwards leaves your objects where they are and either adds or merges its changes into the central object tables. So if the update includes 25 new applications, the specifications for these applications will be added directly into your central object tables. This concept is shown in Figure 18-1.

So what happens if J.D. Edwards has added functionality to an existing application that you have customized? The new changes are added, and your customizations may

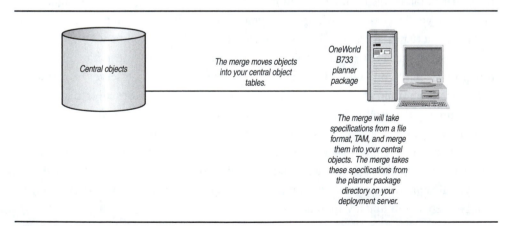

FIGURE 18-1.   How an update moves objects into your system

be disabled. One example of this is event rules. Your custom event rules would be disabled, and the new event rules from the update would be added. The programmers at your site would need to go back and retrofit the modification. This would mean checking out the application or report and deciding whether to use their custom event rules or just keep the new J.D. Edwards event rules. The thing to remember is that you may not always want to keep your modifications, or your modifications may need to be changed to produce the functionality you want.

DEFINITION

Event rule: *An event rule is a type of code that performs certain functions at specific points in an application or report's execution. This code is set up through the OneWorld design tools (that is, it is native to OneWorld).*

Upgrades

When you perform an upgrade, you are actually moving to a newer release of the software. In a perfect world, a new release would mean new functionality and an update would mean bug fixes. However, this is not a perfect world. Currently, J.D. Edwards ships new functionality in both updates and upgrades. One prime example of this is how new functionality was added to the package-build process in B733.1, which is release B733 update or cumulative update level 1. The company is moving to try and ship new functionality only in upgrades and concentrate on bug fixes in updates. This should start around release B733 update level 3, which is now referred to as OneWorld Xe. Saying you will receive new functionality only with upgrades would not currently be accurate.

So what is the real story about upgrades? The real difference is that with an upgrade you basically install a new system first. That's right, you install a brand new OneWorld system. The only thing you do not reinstall is your business data tables. In Figure 18-2, you can see the types of tables that are loaded fresh with an upgrade.

As you can see from Figure 18-2, the tables in the system, object librarian, data dictionary, and central objects data sources are reloaded with upgrades. This means they are totally independent of your earlier release. So, if you upgraded from B732 to B733, you would have two sets of the tables contained in these data sources. Your B733 system would look at the new tables, and your B732 system would look at the older tables.

How do you get the modifications from one release level to the next? Remember, you have reloaded your object librarian and your central object tables. The central

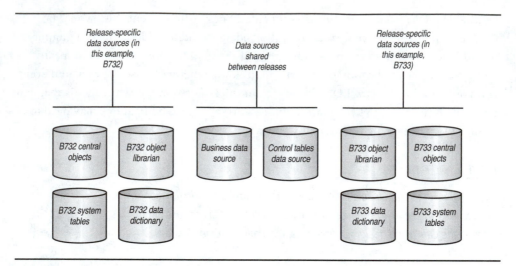

FIGURE 18-2. Tables that reload during an upgrade

object tables contain your custom modifications to the OneWorld applications and reports. The upgrade process, through a specification merge report, moves your modifications from the older release level's central objects to your new release level's central object tables; this is shown in Figure 18-3. It also adds the entries into the new object librarian data source. This is important, as the object librarian is responsible for keeping track of the objects on the system, and the object librarian application provides the means for users to use the design tools.

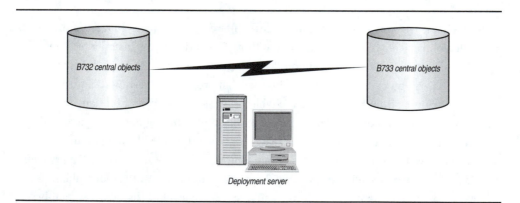

FIGURE 18-3. Upgrade process at a high level

An important thing to note here is that the merge report, which moves your objects, usually takes less time to run for an upgrade than for an update. The reason for this is that most clients will have fewer modifications than J.D. Edwards. In an update, you are merging J.D. Edwards' changes into the central objects, and in an upgrade, you are merging your changes into the shipped central object tables. Most of the time you will have fewer objects, keeping in mind that the update from B733 to B733.1 contained around 8,000 changed objects. This is why J.D. Edwards is changing their approach to updates. As of OneWorld Xe, the update and upgrade process will be the same. This is because the process is cleaner, easier to understand, and easier to set up.

That probably answers your general questions on the differences between upgrades and updates, but are you wondering what happens to your business data during an upgrade? When an upgrade is performed, sometimes the format of the existing relational database tables change. An example of this would be if you upgrade from the OneWorld release B732 to B733 and several business data tables in the B733 have changed—there are additional columns or the columns have changed size. This means the tables need to be changed, or the applications in the new release of OneWorld will not function correctly. When the applications make calls to tables, they expect certain column sizes. If these do not match, the application will not be able to access the table. This is why the upgrade process converts your business data tables in place. Otherwise, you would need to reload all of your business data tables every time you wanted to perform an upgrade. This would not be acceptable, as some clients have more than a million records in some of their business data tables. This is why table conversions are run in place. If any new tables need to be added, they will be generated during the upgrade processes in the appropriate data source.

NOTE

As of B733.1, table conversions can be required for an update as well. However, these conversions will be limited to only ones that are absolutely necessary.

Platforms

The question may come up when setting up an upgrade or update: Will the process differ greatly from platform to platform? The answer is, not very much. Most of your setup for an upgrade or an update is done on the deployment server. The only time the platform specifics come into play is when you set up the host code for your enterprise servers or when you perform database-specific functions. The specification merges, table conversions, and workbenches are all run from the deployment server, and no matter what platform your enterprise server is, your deployment server will be an NT/Intel machine.

Upgrades

As we have already discussed, upgrades are the process of moving your software from one release level to another. This procedure is normally done to take advantage of new functionality or to resolve problems with the software. In this book, we are not going to go over all of the points of an upgrade. However, after reading this chapter you should have a good idea of what happens during an upgrade, and when an object will be added, replaced, or merged. You will also learn the common problems encountered during an upgrade, and how to manually confirm that your upgrade was successful.

Basic Parts of an Upgrade

The first part of any successful upgrade is planning, planning, and a little more planning. If there is anything you should fight to avoid in an upgrade it is being surprised and running out of time. However, if you take the time to plan the upgrade up front, it will pay for itself many times over in the long run. There are several things you should look at when planning an upgrade:

- Disk space requirements
- Required software levels
- Backup procedures
- When to roll back
- Impact on your end users

Disk Space Requirements

We cannot tell you how painful it is to have an expensive consultant fly out to your site only to sit and wait for you to install more hard drive space. Unfortunately, this does happen sometimes. This is why it is so important to ensure that your system has the necessary free drive space before that consultant even thinks about hopping on a plane or before you dedicate one of your people to the project. An upgrade is a project and should have a project plan.

How do you ensure that you do not get into this situation of not having enough disk space? Visiting J.D. Edwards' Web site is good start. This Web site contains all the manuals for upgrading the OneWorld software and is updated as new releases come out. These documents have listings of what is called minimum disk space requirements. You need at least this much free drive space and possibly more, depending on the number of custom objects you have on your system. If you have developed 5,000 custom reports, J.D. Edwards' minimum space requirements probably will not be enough for you. These are based on a "standard" upgrade, and they are meant to be just that—a baseline. If you know that you have more custom objects, take that into account when you look at disk space requirements. You also do not really want to go with the bare minimum. Don't leave yourself with little room for additional business data, new custom objects, new environments, or other changing business needs.

N O T E

The recommended upgrade procedure is to run two releases in parallel: your production environment running on the old release while you test the new release in another environment and path code. This means that you need the space required for your old production environment as well as additional space for the new release.

Required Software Levels

Another factor that needs to be considered when you are looking to upgrade your system is what levels your third-party software needs to be at in order for the new release of OneWorld to function correctly. Again, this is listed on the J.D. Edwards Web site. These minimum technical requirements documents list the required levels for *most* of your third-party software. These documents will tell you what release of the database, operating system, PTF levels, and compiler to run. However, they will not tell you the details on what level of MDAC to run on your client machines. This information currently can only be obtained by calling customer support. So before you apply the latest service pack to the Windows NT operating system, you should log a call to ensure you are not going to cause your OneWorld users problems. However, in the future this information should be available either on J.D. Edwards' Web site or on

Troubleshooting

Microsoft's Web site. We have been told that J.D. Edwards is currently working with Microsoft to find the best way of publishing this type of information.

DEFINITION

Microsoft Data Access Component (MDAC): *This is software, provided by Microsoft, that allows you to communicate with other software packages, such as databases. The MDACs accomplish this by delivering drivers, which work with your operating system.*

It may also turn out that you need to upgrade some of your third-party software—for example, a database or operating system—to perform the OneWorld upgrade. This will need to be reflected in your upgrade's time line. If you do not plan this activity ahead of time, you will run into problems at the eleventh hour.

The following section covers an example of J.D. Edwards' minimum technical requirements, which will tell you if you need to upgrade your database or operating system in order for your new release of OneWorld to function properly.

OneWorld B733.2 Minimum Technical Requirements for Windows NT Enterprise Servers

The following tables in this section, taken from the J.D. Edwards Web site, list the minimum hardware and software technical requirements for OneWorld Windows NT enterprise servers. We will use this as an example of what information a J.D. Edwards' minimum technical requirements document will give you. For current information on the requirements on all platforms, please refer to J.D. Edwards' Web site (www.jdedwards.com) or to the "Hardware and Software Requirements" section of your OneWorld Installation, Upgrade, or Update Guide.

Hardware Requirements

This table lists the minimum hardware requirements for OneWorld Windows NT enterprise servers.

Hardware	Requirements	Notes
CPU	200MHz (minimum)	Compaq AlphaServer or Intel Pentium
RAM, hard drive	Contact your system representative for optimal system hardware specifications	Review "OneWorld Disk Space Requirements." This document can be found at www.jdedwards.com.
CD-ROM	Required	
Printer Support	PostScript, PCL, or line	

Software Requirements

This table lists the minimum software requirements for OneWorld Windows NT enterprise servers.

Software	Requirements	Notes
Operating system	Windows NT 4.0 server with SP4 or higher	Windows NT SP5, SP6, or SP6a is strongly recommended
ANSI C compiler	Microsoft Visual C++ 6.0 SP1 or higher	RISC Edition (Compaq Alpha) Professional Edition (Intel)
Database	Microsoft SQL 7.0, Microsoft SQL 7.0 SP1, or Oracle 8.0.5 or higher, including Oracle 8.1.5 (Oracle 8I)	See the section "Additional Requirements (Database Systems)." SQL 7.0 SP1 requires Windows NT SP5 or higher. Oracle has not released a version of Oracle 8.1.5 (Oracle 8I) for the Compaq AlphaServer. For more information, see the section "Informational Web Sites."
Cluster support (optional)	Microsoft Cluster Server	For more information see "OneWorld B733.2 Technical Requirements for Microsoft Cluster Services," which can be found at www.jdedwards.com

NOTE

(Compaq Alpha and Intel Processors) The Windows NT Server operating system and other listed software components come in both Compaq Alpha and Intel versions. Compaq AlphaServer customers must be sure to purchase software for the Compaq Alpha version, and Intel server customers should purchase software for the Intel version.

NOTE

J.D. Edwards requires all new OneWorld installations using Microsoft Windows NT to upgrade to Windows NT SP5 or higher.

CAUTION

B733.2 is the last release of OneWorld where the Compaq Alpha is a supported platform. If you are on a Compaq Alpha, you will need to plan on moving off this platform.

Additional Requirements (Database Systems)

Depending on the database used, OneWorld Windows NT enterprise servers may require additional database components. This table lists additional database requirements.

Database	Additional Requirements	Notes
Microsoft SQL Server 7.0 (base)	MDAC 2.1 SP1 (file version 2.1.1.3711.11) with ODBC Jet 3.51 fallback	Use of an incorrect version may result in data corruption. All driver versions are available on MDAC 2.1. For MDAC download information, see the section "Informational Web Sites."
Microsoft SQL Server 7.0 SP1	MDAC 2.1 SP2 (file version 2.1.2.4202.3)	SQL 7.0 SP1 requires Windows NT SP5 or higher. Use of the incorrect version may result in data corruption. MDAC 2.1 is available from Microsoft. For download information, see the section "Informational Web Sites."

Database	Additional Requirements	Notes
Oracle 8.0.5 or higher, including Oracle 8.1.5 (Oracle 8I)	Networking: Oracle Client Software CD Database administration: Oracle SQL*Plus 8.0.5 or higher	Your Oracle Client CD must match your specific version of Oracle. Oracle SQL*Plus is on the database CD, but is licensed separately. Your version of Oracle SQL*Plus must match your release version of Oracle.

Informational Web Sites

This table lists informational Web sites for J.D. Edwards OneWorld software technical requirements and Microsoft products. Clients are advised to frequently use these URLs to acquire the most current information.

Subject	Web Site
Microsoft Web site	http://www.microsoft.com From Microsoft's home page, select either the Downloads or the Search option, then browse to the required product information.
OneWorld technical requirements	https://knowledge.jdedwards.com/JDEContent/TechMarketingCU/information/bjtechreqs.htm

N O T E

The OneWorld technical requirements web page will require you to sign onto the J.D. Edwards Knowledge Garden. If you are a customer or business partner of J.D. Edwards, you should have a user and password assigned to you. If you do not, contact J.D. Edwards' customer support.

Backup Procedures

This planning step is one of the most critical for an upgrade. This is your safety valve. This step ensures that if everything goes wrong you will still be able to conduct business. If you do not perform this step, you run the possibility of losing business data or objects. After all, let's be realistic—you could have the best installer in the world, but that will not do you much good if the disk drive crashes.

Let's go over some of the important steps that should be taken before an upgrade starts.

Backing Up Your Database

Although this sounds obvious, you would be amazed at how many companies do not have a disaster recovery plan. We are discussing backing up your database in the

Troubleshooting

context of preparing for an upgrade, however, you should have a procedure to do this nightly for changes and weekly full backups. This is not something that should be left to chance, as you may be the one who has to tell your CEO that your luck has run out.

With that in mind, the first thing to consider is what environments and path codes are going to be upgraded. This will help you determine what tables will need to be backed up. Let's go through an example. Say you are going to upgrade your system from B732 to B733. Since you are following the recommended upgrade procedure, you will be upgrading the CRP and development environments, while leaving your production environment at the B732 release level.

You will need to back up all your database tables. This means you will need to back up your database tables for all of your environments. This is because when you perform an upgrade you will be touching your business data tables, control tables, and, of course, your central objects tables. At a minimum, you will want to ensure that you have a good backup of these tables for the environments you are upgrading and that you have tested that backup. It is very important to test your tape backup periodically, so you do not receive any unpleasant surprises. Once you have backed up these tables, you will need to also back up the directory structure and registry of the deployment server.

Backing Up Your Deployment Server's Directory Structure

The next step is to back up your deployment server's directory structure. With an upgrade, the old directory structure will be left in place and a new directory structure will be created for the new release of the software. So if you are upgrading from B732 to B733, you will have one folder for B732 and one for B733, shown in Figure 18-4. This is because you are moving from one release to the next. However, the thing to keep in mind is that your deployment server would not be on B732. When you log in to the deployment server, the registry and your desktop shortcut will point to the new directory structure, B733. This means you will need to maintain your old system using a client workstation from the time you install the new release's setup CD.

What do you need to back up on your directory structure? If you are doing an upgrade, you should back up the path codes' directory structure that you are upgrading. This would mean backing up the CRPB732 and/or DEVB732 directory. The reason is

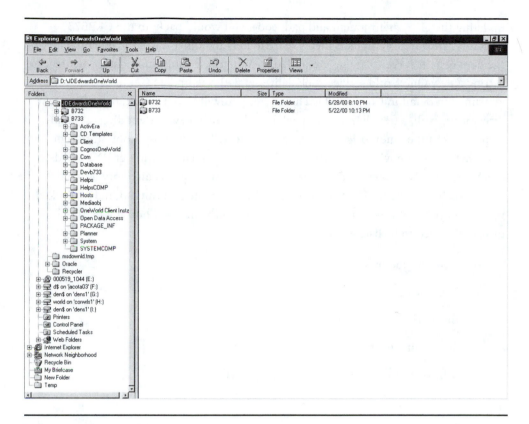

FIGURE 18-4. Directory structure for an upgrade

when you upgrade to B733, the specification merge (which we will discuss later in this chapter) copies files out of this directory into a path code directory under B733. This is so your source and header files are moved when you upgrade.

During an update, backing up your directory structure becomes even more vital. This is because you will not have two different directories, as described above. You will be copying files directly into your existing structure—for example, B733. Again, you are going to want to back up the path code directory you are updating. So if you are updating the CRP environment and path code, you would back up the CRPB733 directory. However, an update affects more folders than just the path code directory on the deployment server that you are updating. When you apply an update, you are also getting a new OneWorld service pack delivered with the update (service packs are explained in detail in Chapter 11). This means you will have to back up your system directory as well. After all, a service pack is really only a new system directory and some DLLs in the OneWorld client install directory. Finally, it is important to note here that an update will replace the JDEB7.MDB access database under JDEdwards\ OneWorld\B733\Planner\Data, so you will want to back up this directory as well. Below is a list of directories that are affected by an update and thus should be backed up. The purpose of this section was to take some of the mystery out of why these directories need to be backed up:

- Planner\Data directory

- Client directory

- OneWorld Client Install directory

- System directory

- Path code directories that are being updated

T I P

As of OneWorld Xe, J.D. Edwards will make the update and upgrade processes the same. This is because of J.D. Edwards' desire to make the process easier on the customer and to reduce merge times. Normally, J.D. Edwards modifies or enhances more objects than their clients. This is why an update merge sometimes takes longer than an upgrade merge (remember, in an upgrade merge, you are only moving the objects you changed). The reason is, while J.D. Edwards may have enhanced thousands of objects, most clients will only have modified or added several hundred custom objects.

Placing an Up-to-Date Full Package on a Client Machine

The next step—building a full package on your old release and deploying it to a workstation that will not be used prior to the upgrade—should be considered a safety stop. If you have a problem with an object, you can then recover the object by checking it in from this client workstation, which is a lot easier than recovering a full set of central object tables from tape for one object! To do this, you would need to do a forced check-out and then simply check the object in. The object would now be back to the same state it was in before you started the update. Again, this last step is a valuable safety check, and we would not recommend skipping it.

DEFINITION

Forced check-out: *This is the process of manually entering a check-out record into the object librarian so that it appears the object was checked out. This allows you to check in the object from that workstation. This procedure should only be used when necessary, as you are replacing what is in your central objects with what is on the client workstation.*

Restoring an Object Through a Forced Check-out

We have been discussing how a forced check-out may become necessary to restore an object into your OneWorld system. Let's briefly cover how this would be accomplished. It is important to note that a forced check-out should only be done when necessary, because whatever is checked in last wins. To perform a forced check-out, from your client workstation running the package you built prior to the update or upgrade, access the object librarian application. This application is located on menu GH902 (Cross Application Development Tools).

Once you are in the object librarian, find the report, application, business function, business view, or data structure you are interested in. You can find this object by placing the object name in the Query By Example line. Once you have found the object you are after, highlight the object, and select it. This will take you into the design aid program. You will see an entry in the screen for your deployment server and the path codes the object exists in. What you will then need to do is type in the name of your client workstation under the location column. Enter the path code you are interested in—in this example, we are using the CRPB733 path code. Once you have entered this information, you will need to enter a status code of 3, for in development; you may also have to enter a SAR number. Then enter the name of the user who is making the change and a merge option of 1.

Once you have entered this information, click OK to save the record. This will take you out to the Work With Object Librarian screen. Select your object again, and you will see the forced check-out record you created. An example of this is illustrated below. Now all you have to do is check the object in.

Law of the West

By checking the object in, you are having OneWorld replace the records for this object, in the central object tables, with the records contained in the TAM files on the client workstation. This means that if you are on a client with the latest package, before the upgrade or update, you have just restored the object back to its original state prior to the upgrade or update.

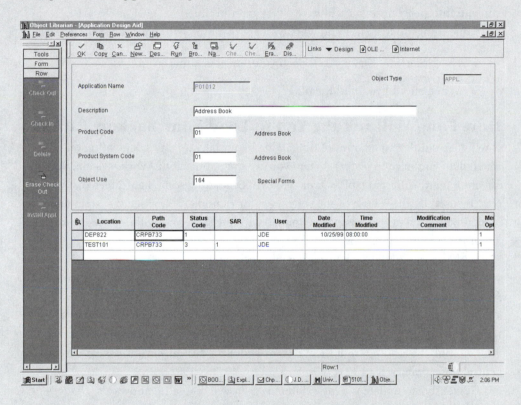

When to Roll Back

The question always comes up, what if everything goes wrong? Can we get back or will our end users be down the next day? The answer to that question will depend on you. If you plan correctly, you will be able to roll back to your previous release and not affect your users. However, if you do not plan for the possibility of rolling back and you run into problems, you will have a very painful time.

Some things to keep in mind when you are planning your rollback strategy are:

- How long will it take you to load your tape backups?

- When should you pull the plug?

How Long Will It Take You to Load Your Backup Tapes?

It will take a different amount of time to load your backup tapes depending on how much data you have to restore. When you are upgrading a OneWorld system, you are affecting many different tables. True, you will be loading some new tables that will only be used by the release of the software—for example, a new set of system tables are loaded with each new release. So if you have to roll back, you will not need to worry about these tables right away.

However, you will also be running table conversions over your business data. If you need to restore this data, you will need to estimate how long it will take you to restore these affected tables. You can get a list of the business data tables that will have a table conversion run over them from the OneWorld upgrade guide. Another set of tables you will need to worry about is your central object tables. During an upgrade, you will only be reading from them to move your modifications into a new release's central object tables.

Currently, an update is a little different. You will merge J.D. Edwards' changes directly into your central object tables, so if something goes wrong you will need to restore these tables from tape. Some of these tables are quite large—the F98741, for example, has more than a million records in release B733.1. You should have a good idea of what these tables are before you start your upgrade or update The time it will take to restore these tables not only depends on what tables you need to restore. It will also depend on how you backed your data up. With Oracle and SQL Server, you can back up the entire database at once. Many clients will adopt this type of backup strategy. If you follow this strategy, you will need to restore the entire database and then move the tables you need back into your system, so it is very difficult to restore just a single table. This is not a bad thing unless you need to restore one table to rerun a table conversion!

The final point we will leave you with is this: if you roll back, do you roll your deployment server back as well? It would not really be necessary for upgrades since you would still be able to deploy the older release to workstations. You would just need to maintain the system from a workstation instead of the deployment server, since the deployment server is now on the next release. However, if you are performing an update prior to OneWorld Xe, you will need to roll your deployment server back. This is because there is no separate directory structure for an update at this level. That means your directory structure on the deployment server has been affected. So if you rolled back all your data but not this directory structure, you would have problems. At a minimum, you would be deploying a different service pack level and possibly a different set of specifications. If you are applying an update prior to OneWorld Xe, you will need to restore your deployment server's directory structure. You will also need to restore the registry of this machine or you will have problems running OneWorld on the deployment server. Build this into your estimate of how long it will take you to roll the system back.

When Should You Pull the Plug?

At this point, you should have an estimate of the amount of time it will take to roll your system back. When you are working on the production environment, this time estimate is critical. If you are working over a weekend and you think it will take you ten hours to roll the system back, you do not want to start the rollback at midnight on Sunday. This time estimate will give you a point where you know if you do not throw the towel in you are risking bringing your end users down. We have seen people so desperate to get the system up that it costs them more money and frustration than if they had just rolled the system back and attempted the upgrade again the next weekend.

Impact on Your End Users

If an upgrade or an update is planned and executed correctly, there will be minimal impact on your end users. This means you will have a controlled rollout to your end users. The only real impact on them should be the possibility of the need for training on new functionality contained in the new release or update. However, if the update or upgrade is not planned correctly and you do not have a good timeline, the impact on end users can be severe. We don't want to scare you to death, we just want to drive the

Troubleshooting

point home that an upgrade or an update is a project and needs to be planned as one. It is also a project that affects mission-critical applications, which means you should have contingency plans in place so that your upgrade or update is not even an event for your end users.

Nuts and Bolts of an Upgrade

In this section, we will not give you step-by-step instructions on the upgrade process, since the J.D. Edwards manuals cover this. However, what we do hope to leave you with is a better understanding of what is happening when you run the major steps of the upgrade. This knowledge should assist you in performing successful upgrades and help you determine where to start troubleshooting.

NOTE

This section is written with the assumption that you have reviewed the OneWorld upgrade manual. If you have not, please review it as it will greatly enhance your understanding of this section.

Installation Planner

Let's start where everything is based from, the OneWorld installation planner. At this point you would have already backed up your system and prepared your environments for an upgrade—making the CRP environment and path code match the production environment and path code. One of the first steps in an upgrade, installation, or update is to set up your OneWorld installation planner. This program assists you in planning your OneWorld configuration. The program can be found on menu GH961 (System Installation Tools), shown in Figure 18-5.

You will notice there are two different types of OneWorld installation planners. These are the typical installation planner and the custom installation planner. The difference is that the typical installation planner assumes you are going to set up the

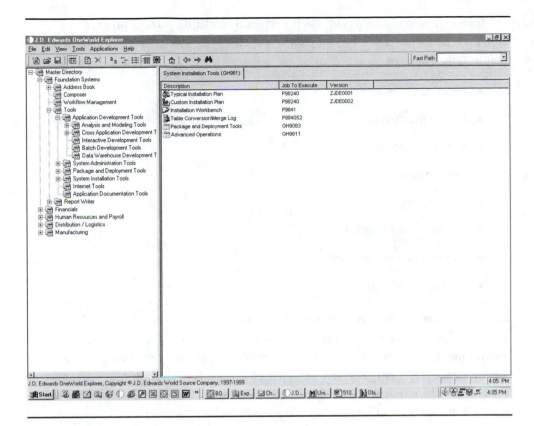

FIGURE 18-5. System installation tools menu

standard J.D. Edwards environments and data sources. This planner will set up most of these for you almost automatically. All you will need to enter is a few values. The custom installation planner gives you the option of taking the standard defaults for environments and data sources or you can customize the plan.

If you are new to OneWorld, use the typical installation planner program. However, no matter which type of plan you choose, you will still go through the same major steps. These are:

- Locations planner

- Data source planner

- Environments planner

- Hosts planner

- Table conversions planner

- Control tables planner

- Specification merge planner

- Package build planner

Location Planner   The first step is to plan your install locations. This area of the planner allows you to plan which sites you are going to have. You can set up environments for each site or location. When you set up a location, you give it a location code if it is not your base or starting location. This location code will appear at the end of the environments you set up for your location. Say, for example, that you have a branch office in Chicago that you want to set up. If you set up a location for this office, you can also set up environments for this office, so they can view their own business data. These environments' names would contain the location code you gave them, so if your location code was CHI, your Chicago production environment would appear as PRD733CHI. This allows your administrators to keep track of your environments with greater easy. You will not need to worry about setting this up for an upgrade; your locations would already have been set up during the installation process.

Data Source Planner   This area of the planner allows you to plan your data sources. We covered what data sources are and how they are used in Chapter 2. Basically, this area of the planner is asking you how you want to organize your data for each of your environments. During an upgrade, you will be prompted to verify the settings of your data sources. However, unless your tables for your new release are going to be on a new enterprise server, you will not need to change the data sources.

Environments Planner   This is the area of the planner that allows you to select the environment you want to upgrade. So, for example, if you are upgrading the CRP environment, you will want to select this environment. Since each environment is associated with a path code, this will tell the software that you are upgrading that path code. When you perform an upgrade, you will need to pay attention to planning your environments. The environment workbench, which we will discuss a little later, creates new tables during an upgrade, which are needed for the new release. This is why you want to ensure that you select the environment you're upgrading.

Upgrading a Custom Environment and Path Code

Many companies use only the standard J.D. Edwards environments. As we have discussed above, these environments are easy to select for upgrading. However, some clients have created their own custom environments and path codes. This means the software will not know about them unless you tell it they exist.

So how do you tell the software that you want to upgrade a custom environment? Actually, it is not as difficult as you might think. What you can do is go through your upgrade plan and select all of the standard environments you want to upgrade (for example, CRPB732). Once you have selected your standard environments and completed the defining the plan, you can then go back and add your custom environment to your plan. To do this, go to menu GH961 and run the installation planner. Once you are in this program, click Find and expand your upgrade plan. Highlight and select the Environments folder.

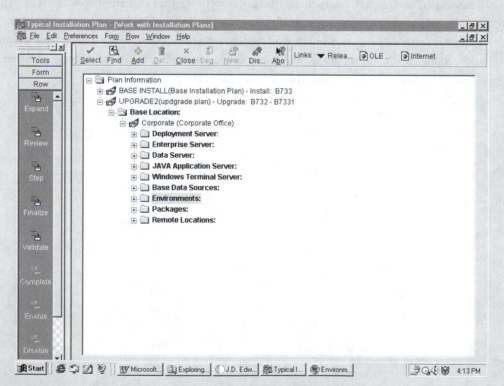

Law of the West

This will take you to the Environment Planner screen. On this screen you should see the standard J.D. Edwards environment you selected to upgrade. In the case of our example, we are upgrading CRPB732 to CRP733. However, we also want to upgrade our custom environment and path code. To do this, place your cursor in the blank line under the Environment Name column header. This will give you a visual assist button; click this button and select your custom environment. You will then need to set up the load data, table conversion, control table merge, and specification merge flags for your custom environment. These flags control whether a merge will be run for that environment. Since you have an existing example, you should copy the flags for your standard J.D. Edwards environment.

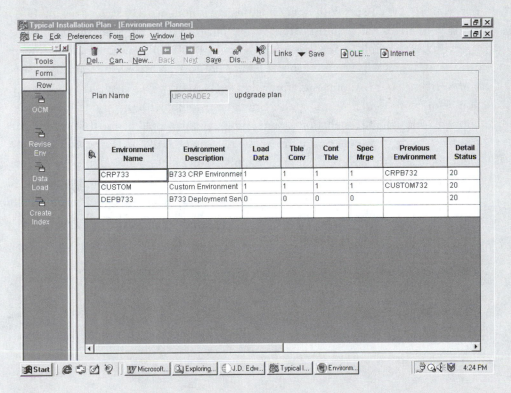

	Environment Name	Environment Description	Load Data	Tble Conv	Cont Tble	Spec Mrge	Previous Environment	Detail Status
	CRP733	B733 CRP Environmen	1	1	1	1	CRPB732	20
	CUSTOM	Custom Environment	1	1	1	1	CUSTOM732	20
	DEPB733	B733 Deployment Ser	0	0	0	0		20

Plan Name: UPGRADE2   updgrade plan

You will also have to list the name of your custom environment in the previous release. In our example, the name of our previous environment was CUSTOM732. In the rest of the fields you would enter the same values as your standard J.D. Edwards environment, except for the parent environment field (you cannot see in the previous illustration as it is too far to the right). In this field, you would enter the name of your custom environment—for our example, CUSTOM. (This is the far right field in Environment Planner.) You have now told the software that you have a custom environment, which is to be upgraded.

However, you are not done yet. Before you proceed, you will need to verify values in your planner environment for your custom environment and path code. If you do not, you will have issues with upgrading this environment and path code. You need to verify your environment information, verify your path code information, and verify that you have records for this environment in the P98DREP data replication program.

We will cover why you need entries in the P98DREP program in a moment; let's start with verifying your environment information in OneWorld. This is just a safety check for you before you attempt your upgrade. However, if your environment does not appear correctly through the installation planner program, this would be the first spot to start troubleshooting. To verify this information, go to menu GH9053 (Environments). Double-click on the environment master application, P0094. This will take you to the Work With Environments screen. Enter the name of your custom environment in the Query By Example line, above Environment Name, and click Find. Once you have found your custom environment, highlight the records and click Select. This will take you to the Environment Revisions screen, shown next.

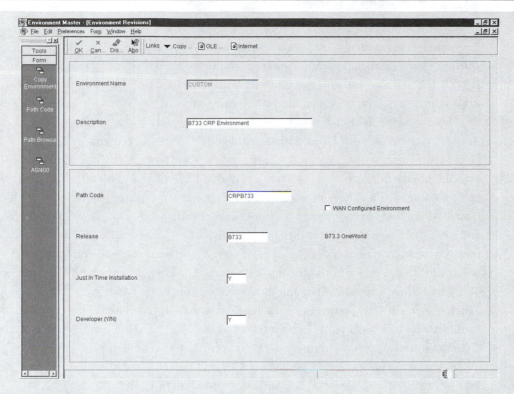

On this screen, you will want to verify that your environment name is correct and that the path code the environment is associated with is correct. While you are on this screen, you will also want to ensure that the release specified is correct, that just-in-time installation is set to Y, and that the developer flag is set to Y. Once you have verified this information, you can move on to verifying your path code information. It is important that this information is correct, because this is what the installation planner is using to execute your plan.

To verify your path code information, go to the Form Path Code exit from the Environment Revisions screen. This will take you to the path code master application. It will also show you the information for your custom path code. This information must be absolutely correct or you will have problems with your upgrade. The specification merge reads this information and uses it during the merge process.

Once you take the Form Path Code exit you will be taken into the Path Code Revisions screen for your environment's path code. On this screen you will need to verify some information. First, make sure the path code name is correct. Next, make sure the Location field shows the name of your DEPLOYMENT server. If this is not the correct name, you will have problems with the specification merge, as this name tells OneWorld to find source and header files on the specified machine. The next field you will need to ensure is correct is the Server Share Path field. This field will need to match your share name on the deployment server. The status code of your path code will normally be a 1, for in production. The Merge Option field must be a 1, for merge. The Release field should be the same as the release you specified for your environment. The Deployment Data Source field is a key field as well. It contains the OneWorld data source name, which contains your central object tables. When the merge process reads this data source, it can determine where your central object tables reside (on what database and machine). The UNC flag must be set to Y. This allows OneWorld to take advantage of the universal naming convention functionality.

The last thing you will need to verify before proceeding with your upgrade or update is that you have entries in your P98DREP data replication program. This is how some of the control table merges determine where your tables reside. Some tables, like menus, are shipped with Object Configuration Manager mapping pointing them to the local access database on the client workstations. The developers of OneWorld know this and thus they know they cannot trust this mapping, since they want to merge against the control tables in your relational database.

How do you solve this problem? Have control table merges read the F98DRPUB table, looking for specific records. This is how the merge determines where your tables reside. (In case you were wondering, the P98DRPUB application uses the F98DRPUB table.)

To verify you have the correct records, double-click on the P98DRPUB application on menu GH9011 (System Administration). This will take you to the Work With Publishers screen, shown here. On this screen, you will see some entries with SERVER

Law of the West

NAME listed as the publisher host. These are bogus entries; they are not used for replication. Instead they are used to tell the control table merge where to find its data. In the example illustrated below, F0004 resides in the data source Control Tables – CRP. You will notice that this record is not enabled, because it is only used for the control table merge to find its data. If you have a custom environment, you will need to copy these records and use the correct data source for your environment.

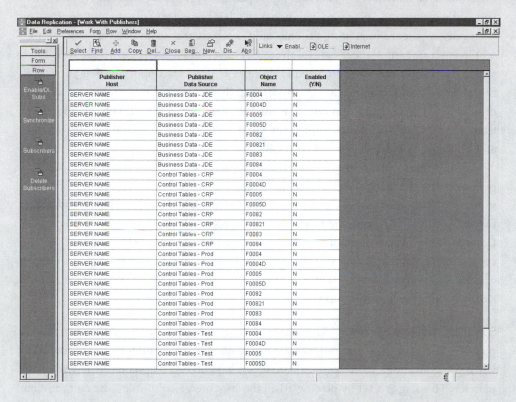

If, for example, your custom environment's name is CUSTOM and the F0004 table for this environment resides in the OneWorld data source Custom Control Tables, you would need to ensure that you had a record pointing to this data source in the Work With Publishers application. Once you have done all this, you are now ready to continue upgrading or updating your custom environment and/or path code.

Hosts Planner　This planner allows you to set up your enterprise, data, Windows Terminal, and JAS servers. These different server types are discussed in detail in Chapter 5. When you add your plan, the software allows you to set up new hosts or you can just accept the old ones. So this area of the planner will normally be set up almost automatically for you.

Table Conversion Planner　This area of the planner is set up behind the scenes. When you add your upgrade plan, you will be asked what release you are upgrading from and what release you are upgrading to. This and the table conversion flag that you set up on the environment planner control the table conversion merge. Shown below is the screen where you specify the To and From release. It is very important that you specify the correct To and From release, as this is what drives the control merges. We will discuss how the To and From release is used later in this section. If you are upgrading from B732.1 to B733.2, for example, you will need to specify this in the From Release and To Release fields, shown in Figure 18-6.

If you want to ensure that the control table planner is set up correctly, you can review it after the fact by running the installation planner program on menu GH961 (System Installation Tools). Once you are in the installation planner, click Find and expand your plan. Expand the Environments directory. Highlight and select the Control Table Merges directory, shown in Figure 18-7. This will take you into the control table planner, where you can verify that your To and From release is set up correctly. The actual reports that run, which are listed in this screen, are populated automatically when you set up your plan.

Specification Merge Planner　The next area of importance is the specification merge planner. This area, like the control table merge planner, is set up for you automatically when you go through your upgrade plan. It also keys off of a flag set in the environment planner. This flag is a set by placing a 1 in the spec merge column on the environment planner screen. This should be set to 1 to run the specification merge. If you accept the defaults when setting up your upgrade plan, this will default in. This area of the plan controls what version of the specification merge, R98700, is run. During an upgrade you will run version ZJDE0001; this is normal processing for an upgrade. However, you also may need to run version ZJDE0003, which is the restart version. We will discuss this in more detail later in this section.

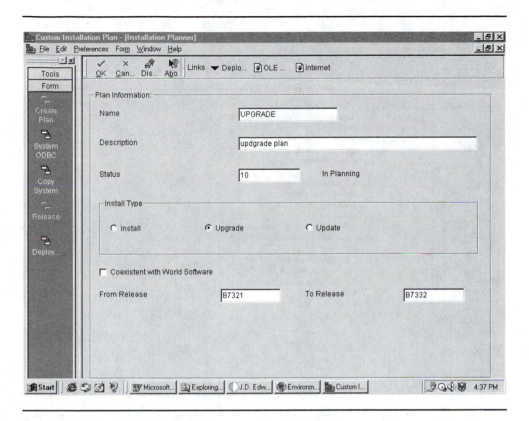

FIGURE 18-6. Setting From/To release levels in the Planner

Package Build Planner   Again, OneWorld sets this up for you behind the scenes. This planner sets up the records so that OneWorld will know about the shipped J.D. Edwards packages. These packages are shipped so that you can immediately deploy a client workstation after an installation or upgrade.

Installation Planner Summary   We have now covered the high points of the installation planner. The next step in the processes is actually executing your plan through the installation workbench. However, before we move on to that section, it is important to cover a job the installation planner does: creating the system tables that most of your installation workbenches insert data into. These tables are created when

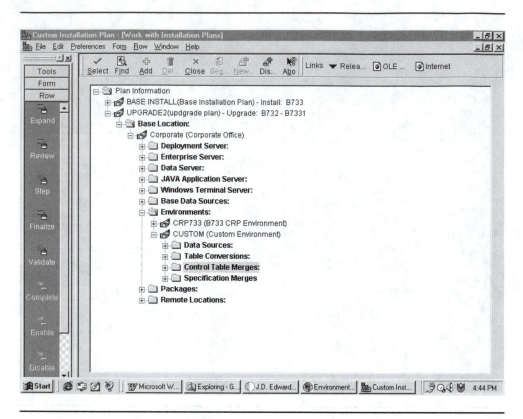

FIGURE 18-7.   Selecting the Control Table Merge planner

you release your plan. These tables are owned by the SYSXXX, where XXX is the release of OneWorld you are running.

Installation Workbench

You have set up your upgrade plan; now you have to execute it. To do this, you need to use the installation workbench, which is located on the GH961 menu (System Installation Tools). This program takes all the information you set up in the planner and runs the merges you planned. We will go through every screen on the installation workbench and touch on what really happens when you run each of these workbenches. Let's start by going over the workbenches you will see:

- Locations workbench

- Data source workbench

- Environments workbench

- Hosts workbench

- Table conversions workbench

- Control tables workbench

- Specification merge workbench

- Package build workbench

Locations Workbench   This workbench lists all the deployment locations you set up in the planner. Remember, you can specify multiple locations within OneWorld, which makes the system easier to maintain if you have multiple sites running OneWorld, each with their own set of environments. When you execute this workbench, it takes the information in the F9654 deployment locations definitions tables from the JDEPLAN.MDB file on the deployment server. It then populates the F9654 table in the System – B*xxx* data source, where *xxx* is the release of OneWorld you are running, since the system tables for OneWorld are release specific.

N O T E

During an upgrade, key information is copied from your previous release's system tables into your planner for the new release. This means you will be able to see the locations you set up in the prior release of OneWorld when you upgrade, so you do not have to set them up again and again. When you execute the workbench, this information will then be written to your new release's system tables.

Data Source Workbench   This workbench sets up your data sources for the new release, using the information you specified in the installation planner. Again, since new releases have their own set of system tables, you would run this workbench. When this workbench is executed, it populates the F98611 table (Data Source Master) in your system data source. It gets this information from the F98611 table in the JDEPLAN.MDB file on your deployment server. This is where all your information is stored when you set up your plan. This process also copies information from the

F986115 table and Data Source Sizing table. Again, it copies this information from JDEPLAN.MDB. This table contains information on your data sources. If you are running OneWorld against an Oracle database, this table would contain the Oracle table space and index space that each data source would use. Normally each data source, except for the versions data source, would have its own table space and index space. This is so that your database administrator can administer the database with greater ease.

Environment Workbench   This workbench is vital to your installation or upgrade. The environment workbench does two major jobs. It populates a set of tables, which we will go over in this section, and it calls a batch job that populates and creates your database tables. As you can see, a lot goes on behind the scenes when you kick off this workbench.

Let's start with the tables this workbench populates. These tables are all system tables:

- **F0093, Library List Control**   This table controls the environments your users are allowed to see when they log on to the system.

- **F0094, Library List Master**   This file contains your environments and their descriptions.

- **F00941, Environment Detail**   This table holds your environments' names, release levels, and associated path codes, and shows if just-in-time installation is enabled.

- **F00942, Path Code Master**   This table contains information on your path codes. It contains the name of the path code, your deployment server, your share path, if you are using universal naming convention (UNC), and the data source that contains your path code's central object tables.

- **F986101, Object Configuration Manager**   This table holds all of the object configuration mappings for your environments. The purpose of these mappings was covered in Chapter 2.

This workbench also kicks off a universal batch engine (UBE), R98403, when necessary. This UBE is what creates and populates your business data tables during an installation. If you have selected to load production data, the UBE will create your business data tables empty. The R98403 engine is also smart enough to not do anything if the table already exists. The only tables it will create are ones required for

OneWorld to function. An example of these would be the menus and user-defined code tables. This is so that you can load your business data into the system. If you choose to load demonstration data, the business data tables would be loaded with example data shipped from J.D. Edwards.

When you are performing an upgrade, you will *only* load production data. This is because you do not want to overlay your existing business data tables. However, you do want to allow the workbench to create any new tables for your new release of OneWorld.

Hosts Workbench   This workbench is now called the machine workbench. It populates the host configuration files from JDEPLAN.MDB. These files are:

- **F9650, Machine Master**   This table contains information on your deployment, enterprise, workstations, data servers, Windows Terminal Servers, and JAS servers. This file contains a data source for the machine, when it is an enterprise server, the machine type, database type (if machine is an enterprise server), machine name, release level, and where the machine is located. This location is set up during the location workbench.

- **F9651, Machine Detail**   This table contains some details on the machines. It contains the names of the machines, the path codes for those machines, the share path (when appropriate), and the port that is used.

- **F98402, Host Plan Detail**   This table just holds the status of the machines for the planner. It will say their status is at 60, for complete, once the workbench is done executing.

This workbench also updates tables other than system tables. It creates your server map tables. These tables are used for your enterprise servers to run UBEs. The tables that are populated are:

- **F986101, Object Configuration Manager**   This table stores the mappings for the enterprise server. These mappings are used when a UBE is run on the enterprise server.

- **F98611, Data Source Master**   This table contains the OneWorld data sources that are used when a UBE is run on the enterprise server.

- **F986115, Table and Data Source Sizing**   This table is exactly like the system table and data source-sizing table. It contains information on what Oracle table spaces and index spaces your data sources use, if you are using Oracle.

Troubleshooting

Adding a New Environment to Your Server Map

Not all environments will automatically be created in your server map. The host/machine workbench will create server map entries for all environments listed in the environment workbench. However, if you want to add a new environment later, you will need to do so manually from the machine identification program, located on menu GH9611 (Advance Operations). Double-click on this program, click Find, expand the Enterprise Server directory, highlight your enterprise server, and click Select.

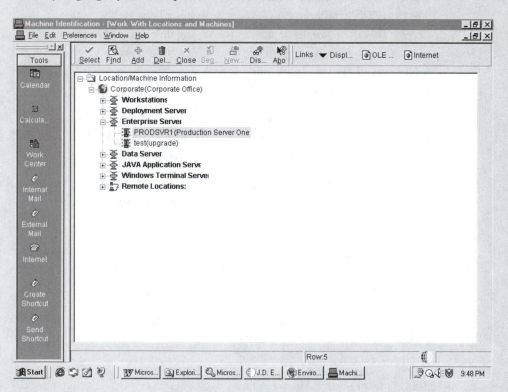

Law of the West

This will take you to the Enterprise Server Revisions screen, shown here. It is from this screen that you can add new environments into your enterprise server's server map.

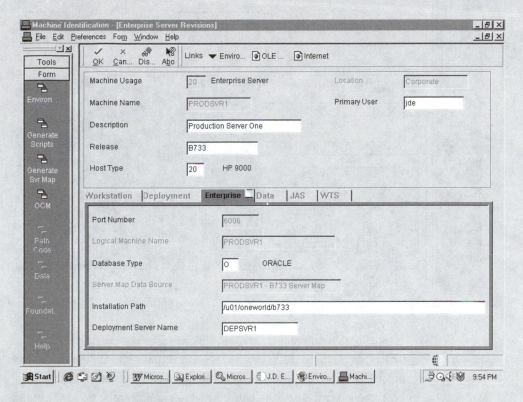

To do this, go to Form Environments and add a new environment by placing your cursor in the blank line under the Environments column header. You will be prompted with a visual assist, which will allow you to choose your environment.

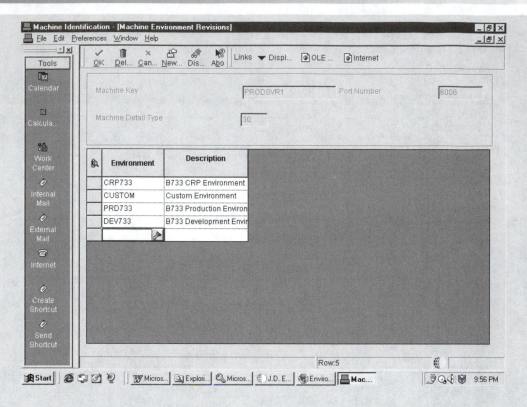

After you choose your environment, click OK; this will take you back to the Enterprise Server Revisions screen. Now you will need to actually create the new mappings in your server map. To do this, go to Form Generate Server Map. This will connect to your server map data source, which is listed in the Enterprise Server Revisions screen, and create the new entries in the server map F986101 table (Object Configuration Manager) and the F98611 table (Data Source Master). This procedure should be done when your users are off the system, since you are creating your mapping tables again. You should also start and stop your host services once you have generated the server map. This is because the object configuration mappings are cached by the host services upon startup.

Package Workbench   The package workbench is the process that sets up OneWorld so that you can deploy some shipped packages from J.D. Edwards. These packages allow you to start testing without having to build a full package, which can take up to eight hours. In the context of an upgrade, you would want to deploy the shipped J.D. Edwards package and then check out a few of your custom objects to ensure that all of your code is there.

That being said, let's go over exactly what this workbench does behind the scenes. The package workbench populates the F9885 (Install Package Header), F9886 (Install Package Detail), and F9887 (Install Package Build History) files. These files are the relational database files OneWorld uses when you are working with the package applications. (For more information on packages, refer to Chapter 10.)

N O T E

The shipped packages ending with FA or PA are already built for you, however the package names ending with FB or PB will need to be built before they can be deployed.

Table Conversion Workbench   As OneWorld progresses from release to release, some tables change format. How does the software accomplish this since these are business data tables? The answer is table conversions! OneWorld uses these conversions to change the format of tables during an upgrade. These table conversions will be supplied by J.D. Edwards. In this section, we are going to take away the mystery of the table conversion process, as it relates to an upgrade.

Let's start with how things flow when you go into the table conversion workbench. The first thing the software does is read the change table and populate the table conversion workbench screen with the table conversion you need to run. The way this application finds the records to show you is not as complex as you might think. It reads the F9843 table (Table Conversion Scheduler), polling for the To release and From release you specified in your upgrade plan. Since J.D. Edwards ships this table with every upgrade, it will contain entries for the appropriate conversions to upgrade from different releases.

Troubleshooting

If you want to see how this works, there is an application that will tell you what table conversions are scheduled to run. This application also reads F9843, *table conversion scheduler* table. This application is located on the GH9611 menu (Advanced Operations). The program is named Table Conversion Scheduler P98430. When you run this program you can see what table conversions will be run. An example of what this application looks like is shown in Figure 18-8.

Now that you have seen how the table conversion workbench is populated, let's move on to covering what information this screen really gives you. By reading the information on this screen, you can determine the order the table conversions will run in and which table conversion must complete prior to the next one being launched.

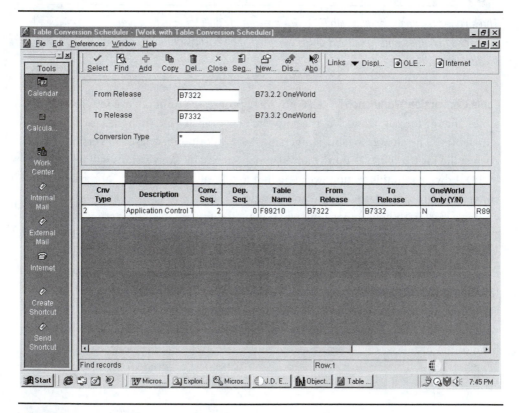

FIGURE 18-8. Table conversion scheduler application

This is shown in Figure 18-9. The fields on this screen give you a vast amount of information:

- **Plan Name** This field will default in with your plan name.

- **New Status** This is the status the workbench will set the table conversion to upon completion.

- **Synch** This radio button tells OneWorld to run the table conversions synchronously (one after the other).

- **Asynch** This radio button, when selected, tells OneWorld to run the table conversions asynchronously. This means if the conversions are not dependent

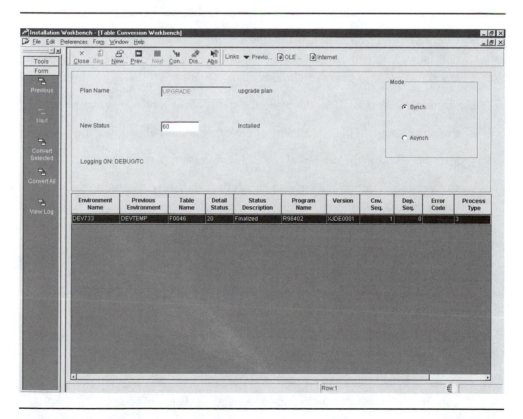

FIGURE 18-9. Table conversion workbench

on any other conversion they will run at the same time. As of B733.1 and B733.2, you will not want to run your table conversion merges asynchronously, as this option is not quite ready yet. You will not see a real performance gain by running the table conversion asynchronously on the deployment server. However, you will see a gain when these table conversions are allowed to run on the enterprise server, which is why J.D. Edwards is offering asynchronous table conversions.

- **Environment Name**   This field lists the name of the environment you are upgrading to.

- **Previous Environment**   This is the previous release's environment. If you are upgrading from B732, this will be a temporary environment.

- **Table Name**   This lists the name of the table that will be converted.

- **Detail Status**   This field lists the status of the table conversions. This will normally be 30 (validated), 50 (failed), or (60 complete). Any table conversion at a status of 30 or lower can be executed.

- **Status Description**   This describes the status of the table conversion.

- **Program Name**   This is the name of the conversion that will be run.

- **Version**   This is the version of the table conversion that will be run.

- **Conversion Sequence**   This field shows the order of sequence in which the table conversions will be run. Any conversion sequence under 100 is a technical table conversion.

- **Dependency Sequence**   This field shows you if the table conversion is dependent upon the successful completion of another table conversion. If a table conversion is dependent upon another conversion and that conversion fails, the conversion will not execute.

- **Error Code**   This column will show you if the conversion has started, finished normally, or finished abnormally.

- **Process Type**   This will tell you the type of process that is being executed to convert your table. Normally, this will be a 3 for batch process.

- **Process Description**   This is a text description of the process type.

These table conversions can run a while, so we recommend that you monitor your table conversions through the Table Conversion/Merge Log application, P984052 (see Figure 18-10). This application reads a logging table, F984052 (Table Conversion History). The application can then tell you what conversion is running, the start, completed date, and the conversion status. Not only can you tell if your table conversions are running, but you can also see if the conversion finished normally or failed. This application is located on menu GH961 (System Installation Tools).

When you go into the Table Conversion/Merge Log program, you will notice several things. The first is that this application allows you to search for conversions that were started and/or finished between certain dates and times. This functionality comes in handy when you are troubleshooting your table conversions and have run them multiple times. It allows you to filter out the garbage and concentrate on the

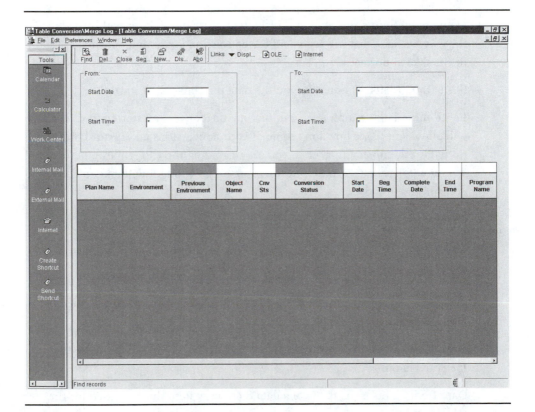

FIGURE 18-10. Table conversion/merge log application

records you need. The application will also show quite a bit of information on each conversion:

- **Plan Name**   This is the name of the plan the conversion was run from.

- **Environment**   This shows you the environment the conversion was run against.

- **Previous Environment**   This is the name of the existing environment, which will be used to create your new upgraded environment. An example would be CRPB732.

- **Object Name**   This is the name of the table that the table conversion affects.

- **Cnv Sts**   This column shows the status of the table conversion. This will be 1 for conversion started, 2 for conversion finished normally, or 3 for conversion finished abnormally.

- **Conversion Status**   This field is just a text description, keyed off the value of the Cnv Sts field, that will tell you if the conversion is running, finished normally, or finished abnormally.

- **Start Date**   This column tells you the date the conversion started.

- **Beg Time**   This column tells you the time the conversion started to run. This will allow you to see how long some of your conversions take. You should probably take note of this when you are upgrading the CRP environment, so you will have an accurate time estimate on how long it will take to convert your production data.

- **Complete Date**   This is the date the table conversion finished on.

- **End Time**   This is the time the table conversion ended.

- **Program Name**   This is the name of the table conversion that was run.

- **Version**   This is the version of the table conversion that was run. Remember, table conversions are basically reports.

- **User ID**   This is the identification code for the OneWorld user profile that ran the conversion.

- **Data Item**   This is the name of a data dictionary item that was used for the table conversion.

When your table conversions finish, you will have a series of reports in your PRINTQUEUE directory on the deployment server. These reports will tell you if the table conversions completed successfully or not. However, you should not rely solely on these reports to determine if your table conversions ran successfully. So how do you determine if they ran successfully?

Let's start by going over how to turn your logging on for table conversions. This logging is what is really going to help you track down any issues you may have with a table conversion. To take advantage of this logging, have the following setting set up in your JDE.INI file on the deployment server, which will be located under the WinNT directory, before you run your table conversion workbench. The values you need to change are listed below.

N O T E

Once you change these settings, you will need to log out and back into OneWorld as some of the settings are cached upon logon.

```
[DEBUG]
Output=FILE
ServerLog=1
[TCENGINE]
TraceLevel=1
;(This setting can be 0-10, 10 providing the most information)
[UBE]
UbeSaveLogFile=1
```

This setting saves a log file under your PRINTQUEUE directory for some of your table conversions. Since each table conversion is basically a UBE, this setting will allow you to see the logs from that report running.

The [TCENGINE] section may not be in your JDE.INI file. If this is the case, you will need to manually add this section. Remember that case matters in this file so the section should be entered exactly as shown above.

N O T E

Not all of your table conversions will produce a PDF file or report. Refer to the J.D. Edwards upgrade manual for the ones that will generate a PDF file.

Troubleshooting

Law of the West

Running an Upgrade After You Have Changed Database User Passwords

It is important to note here that you may have changed some of your table owner passwords in your database. Can OneWorld handle this? The answer is yes, but this is handled in a different way than you might think. Most people will think this will be handled through sign-on security, which was covered in Chapter 13. However, this is incorrect. When you are performing any kind of upgrade or update, you can leave the sign-on security running for your client workstations, but since your deployment server is on a new realease of OneWorld, sign-on security will not be set up for that release of OneWorld. This is because sign-on security requires host code to be running on an enterprise or application server for that release of OneWorld, and you are not to the point where you would lead this host code in your upgrade. To disable this functionality, open the JDE.INI file located under the winnt directory. Find the security sections and blank out the SecurityServer entry's value. This will disable sign-on security for your deployment server.

Don't panic—this does not mean you need to change all your database users' passwords to match the database user. OneWorld handles changing these passwords during an update or upgrade through the JDE.INI file. What you will need to do is add a section to this file. The section is described here; remember that case matters in this file!

```
[DSPWD]
dsowner=dspassword
```

The dsowner will be the database table owner—for example, prddta—and dspassword will be the database password you set up for this owner. Once this is set up, OneWorld will read these owners and passwords and pass them to your database when the table conversions or your merges are run. Remember to log off and back on to OneWorld once you make this change, as it may be cached.

858

After you have run your table conversion workbench you will need to go back to determine if your table conversion ran correctly or had a problem. We will then cover what to look for in your log files. In the upgrade/update manuals, there is a section named "Verifying Your table Table Conversions." You will want to look at this section, as it contains information on specific tables that were converted. However, we will go over the process here so that you are comfortable with confirming your table conversions.

The first report that always gets launched in any workbench is R98405. This report really is just a driver report that launches each report or conversion listed in the workbench. The report will then tell you whether the workbench process ran to completion or had a catastrophic error. If your conversion report tells you that it completed normally you still may have errors with that conversion, but looking at this report gives you a good cursory check to verify that your conversions at least ran to completion. When you review this report you should not see any failures or errors on it. If you do see errors, the next step would be to start checking your logs.

Let's say you have a failure on the R98405 report. What do you do? Even in the worst case scenario, you would be able to restore that table from backup and run the conversion again. However, most of the time this not necessary. The first thing to do is review your log files to see what may have caused the error.

A good log file to start with is the JDE.LOG file. This file is located under the C root on your deployment server. It will show you if you lost connection to the database or if you do not have permissions to the table. If this is the case, you will see errors in this log such as "unable to connect to Business Data – Prod." If you see this, start working backward, asking why can't the table conversion connect to this data source? Did all of the conversions fail or just the ones that affect tables in this data source? You can also look at JDEDEBUG.LOG, which is located under the C root on your deployment server, for more detail. This log shows you some of the SQL commands that are being passed to your database. What we recommend is to match the time stamp from the error you find in JDE.LOG. That way you can see what the software is doing at that moment. This will help you isolate the issue.

What happens if the JDE.LOG and JDEDEBUG.LOG do not show you the error? You're not out of luck. There is some additional logging that you turned on. Remember that [TCENGINE] section you added to your JDE.INI file? This provides you with logging that is very specific to the table conversion process. These logs are located in the PRINTQUEUE directory on your deployment server. They will be named after the table conversion, but these logs will be a text file instead of a PDF report.

System Administration and
Troubleshooting

Types of Table Conversions That Are Run During an Upgrade/Update

To fully understand the log files you are looking at, you should understand the types of conversions that happen during an upgrade. These types are technical conversions, application conversions, and special conversions.

Technical table conversions are run against technical tables, which are used to run OneWorld. This type of table conversion is written using the Report Design Aid tool in OneWorld. These conversions do not have input and output. This type of conversion is typically used to change a BLOB field in a table; it cannot change the format of a relational database table. An example of this is that table conversions are run against central object tables during an upgrade from B732 to B733. This would be considered a technical table conversion, which is a process type of 1. You can see what kind of process type a table conversion is by going into the Table Conversion Scheduler program on menu GH9611 and selecting the table conversion. This type of table conversion will produce a PDF report for each conversion run and log files in the PRINTQUEUE, if you have table conversion logging turned on.

Application table conversions are written using the Table Conversion design tool. This type of conversion does have table input and output (I/O). This type of conversion can change the format of a relational database table. Application table conversion can be run in place or across data sources.

An in-place conversion means the table is not moved, it is converted right where it is. This is done by the conversion program creating a temporary table. The data is then copied from the original table into this temporary table, which has been created in the new format. The conversion re-creates the original table in the new format, copies the data from the temporary table into this new table, and drops the temporary table.

A cross data source table conversion means the table is going to move from one OneWorld data source to another. For this type of conversion to take place, the input table has to exist in the source data source in the old format and the target table has to exist in the target data source in the new format. After all, this conversion is really just moving the data from the input table to the output table. How does the target table get there? When you perform an upgrade, the environment workbench will create any new tables for that release. This is how the table is created with a new format, or a cross table conversion will create the table. The table conversion uses the TAM specifications of the new path code to create the table.

A special table conversion is the first type of technical table conversion that runs. In releases prior to OneWorld Xe, the R98402 report is the special table conversion that is run. This table conversion will regenerate indices and table formats for new tables and for worktables. In the release OneWorld Xe and beyond, a different report will run. This is R98407, which will handle all database changes that do not require a table conversion, so new tables and worktables will be generated here. This conversion will generate a PDF report.

DEFINITION

Worktable: *This is a table used as a temporary workspace for applications. This allows them to manipulate data in an area outside of the production table.*

Keep this information in mind as we cover how to read these log files and how to verify your table conversions using these log files.

TIP

Not all table conversions will produce a PDF report. Application table conversions will only produce log files, even when they are successful. This is by design, so don't panic if you see conversion programs in your workbench, but do not have a matching PDF report for that conversion.

The table conversion log files contain a lot of information on the table conversions. These files are actually what you need to use to verify that the conversions completed successfully. We are going to go over several samples of table conversion logs in this section. The things to look for are the conversion type, data sources, number of columns in the table before and after conversion, environments, and the records read/inserted. You will also notice that there are several different types of table conversions that will take place—technical, cross data source, and in-place table conversion logs.

Let's start with an example of a technical table conversion log. This type of table conversion is normally used to change BLOB (Binary Large Object) fields in tables. These conversions will have a conversion sequence of 100 or less. Following is an example of a technical table conversion.

NOTE

All technical table conversions must finish before any application table conversions having a conversion sequence of greater than 100 will run.

```
Opening UBE Log for Report R8998743, version XJDE0001
--UBE--[0]-- 136/216  Start Time : 22:03:42
--UBE--[0]-- 136/216  Entering K2ResetObjectHeight.
--UBE--[0]-- 136/216  Leaving K2ResetObjectHeight.
--UBE--[0]-- 136/216  Beginning expansion of VarLen in F98743: user JDE
--UBE--[0]-- 136/216  F98743 opened: data source Central Objects - CRPTEMP, environment CRPTEMP
--UBE--[0]-- 136/216  Ending DSTMPL expansion in F98743:
--UBE--[0]-- 136/216           6975 F98743 Records processed.
--UBE--[0]-- 136/216           6975 F98743 Records were successfully expanded.
--UBE--[0]-- 136/216           0 F98743 VarLen expansions failed.
--UBE--[0]-- 136/216        End Time : 8:53:23
UBE job finished successfully.
```

If you know how to read this log, it shows you a lot of vital information. The first thing it shows you is the table conversion report name, R8998743, and the version that was executed, XJDE0001. This log also tells you what the conversion was attempting to do—in this case, it is expanding the VarLen column in the F98743 table. Moving down this log you will also notice that the environment and the data source that is being used are listed. This is very useful in troubleshooting, since sometimes the table is mapped to the wrong place. You would notice this in the log because a data source you did not expect would appear. This line also tells you the conversion opened the table; if the conversion was unable to open the table, you would see that as well. At the bottom of the log are the real meat and potatoes. This area tells you how many records were read and how many were successfully converted. If this number does not match, you may have a problem.

T I P

If you are running with an Oracle database and your rollback segments are not large enough, the table conversion will only process x amount of records each time it is run, since it goes beyond the rollback segment's limit before committing the records. This has been a common problem in B732 to B733 upgrades. To avoid this problem create an 800 megabyte to 1 gigabyte rollback segment called RBSBIGONE. Take your other rollback segments offline and place this rollback segment online before you attempt to run your table conversions and specification merge.

N O T E

You will almost always see a message at the end of these logs saying "UBE job finished successfully." This does not necessarily mean your conversion actually ran successfully. This only means the batch process ended successfully; the work it was attempting to do may or may not have been done. This is why you need to read each one of the table conversion logs to verify your table conversions. Yes, it is a pain, but much less of one than finding out you have a data corruption problem three months later because you did not check the logs.

Let's now move on to look at a table conversion log that runs across data sources. Remember, a cross data source table conversion moves data from a table in one OneWorld data source to a new table in another OneWorld data source. Below is an example of what one of these logs would look like.

```
TCEngine Level 1 D:\B7\system\TCEngine\tcinit.c(1669) : VersionFromEnv property CRPTEMP
TCEngine Level 1 D:\B7\system\TCEngine\tcinit.c(1672) : VersionToEnv property CRP733
TCEngine Level 1 D:\B7\system\TCEngine\tcinit.c(319) : Initializing environments and user handles
TCEngine Level 1 D:\B7\system\TCEngine\tcinit.c(383) : Done initializing environments and user handles
TCEngine Level 1 D:\B7\system\TCEngine\tcinit.c(976) : Opening table F98306, for input.
TCEngine Level 1 D:\B7\system\TCEngine\tcinit.c(1150) : Input F98306 is using data source Versions - CRPB732.
TCEngine Level 1 D:\B7\system\TCEngine\tcinit.c(976) : Opening table F98306, for output.
TCEngine Level 1 D:\B7\system\TCEngine\tcinit.c(1069) : Output F98306 is using data source Central Objects - CRPTEMP.
TCEngine Level 1 D:\B7\system\TCEngine\tcinit.c(214) : Inside TCDetermineConvMode
TCEngine Level 1 D:\B7\system\TCEngine\tcinit.c(244) : Data sources aren't the same, check if we can use Insert from Select.
TCEngine Level 1 D:\B7\system\TCEngine\tcinit.c(247) : Insert from Select is ok.
TCEngine Level 1 D:\B7\system\TCEngine\tcinit.c(301) : ForceRowByRow option is set.
TCEngine Level 1 D:\B7\system\TCEngine\tcinit.c(308) : Conversion method is Row by Row.
TCEngine Level 1 D:\B7\system\TCEngine\tcinit.c(1331) : Inside TCInitJDBConvBuffers
TCEngine Level 1 D:\B7\system\TCEngine\tcinit.c(976) : Opening table F98306, for input.
TCEngine Level 1 D:\B7\system\TCEngine\tcinit.c(764) : Inside TCInitTableColBuffers
TCEngine Level 1 D:\B7\system\TCEngine\tcinit.c(764) : Inside TCInitTableColBuffers
TCEngine Level 1 D:\B7\system\TCEngine\tcinit.c(1171) : Inside TCSetupBufferSharing
TCEngine Level 1 D:\B7\system\TCEngine\tcinit.c(1252) : Column OBNM and OBNM will share buffers
TCEngine Level 1 D:\B7\system\TCEngine\tcinit.c(1252) : Column POTP and POTP will share buffers
TCEngine Level 1 D:\B7\system\TCEngine\tcinit.c(1252) : Column ITNUM and ITNUM will share buffers
TCEngine Level 1 D:\B7\system\TCEngine\tcinit.c(1252) : Column SQNUM and SQNUM will share buffers
TCEngine Level 1 D:\B7\system\TCEngine\tcinit.c(1252) : Column LNGP and LNGP will share buffers
TCEngine Level 1 D:\B7\system\TCEngine\tcinit.c(1252) : Column CRIU and CRIU will share buffers
TCEngine Level 1 D:\B7\system\TCEngine\tcinit.c(1252) : Column UPMJ and UPMJ will share buffers
TCEngine Level 1 D:\B7\system\TCEngine\tcinit.c(1252) : Column TDAY and TDAY will share buffers
TCEngine Level 1 D:\B7\system\TCEngine\tcinit.c(1252) : Column POTX and POTX will share buffers
TCEngine Level 1 D:\B7\system\TCEngine\tcinit.c(1252) : Column PGIX and PGIX will share buffers
TCEngine Level 1 D:\B7\system\TCEngine\tcinit.c(1372) : Inside TCInitLevelBreaks
TCEngine Level 1 D:\B7\system\TCEngine\tcinit.c(1377) : Checking input table F98306
TCEngine Level 1 D:\B7\system\TCEngine\tcinit.c(1498) : Inside TCInitFormatChecks
TCEngine Level 1 D:\B7\system\TCEngine\tcinit.c(1537) : No eTCOnFormatFetched event found for format F98306
TCEngine Level 1 D:\B7\system\TCEngine\tcinit.c(1762) : Conversion R8998306 version XJDE0001, Spec Version 1.1
TCEngine Level 1 D:\B7\system\TCEngine\tcinit.c(1762) : Will clear output tables before conversion
TCEngine Level 1 D:\B7\system\TCEngine\tcinit.c(1762) : Conversion from environment CRPTEMP to CRP733
TCEngine Level 1 D:\B7\system\TCEngine\tcinit.c(1762) : Input F98306 is a OneWorld Table
TCEngine Level 1 D:\B7\system\TCEngine\tcinit.c(1762) : F98306 contains 1 format(s) 'F98306'
TCEngine Level 1 D:\B7\system\TCEngine\tcinit.c(1762) : Output F98306 is a OneWorld table and will be cleared
TCEngine Level 1 D:\B7\system\TCEngine\tcinit.c(1762) : F98306 contains 1 format(s) 'F98306'
TCEngine Level 1 D:\B7\system\TCEngine\tcinit.c(1762) : The conversion contains the following 13 properties:
TCEngine Level 1 D:\B7\system\TCEngine\tcinit.c(1762) : DesignTimeInputEnv=P733CIA
TCEngine Level 1 D:\B7\system\TCEngine\tcinit.c(1762) : DesignTimeOutputEnv=A733CIA
TCEngine Level 1 D:\B7\system\TCEngine\tcinit.c(1762) : TCType=0
TCEngine Level 1 D:\B7\system\TCEngine\tcinit.c(1762) : LogAllErrors=1
TCEngine Level 1 D:\B7\system\TCEngine\tcinit.c(1762) : LogInputRecs=0
TCEngine Level 1 D:\B7\system\TCEngine\tcinit.c(1762) : LogOutputs=0
TCEngine Level 1 D:\B7\system\TCEngine\tcinit.c(1762) : LogDeletes=0
TCEngine Level 1 D:\B7\system\TCEngine\tcinit.c(1762) : LogUpdates=0
TCEngine Level 1 D:\B7\system\TCEngine\tcinit.c(1762) : LogCTActions=0
```

```
TCEngine Level 1 D:\B7\system\TCEngine\tcinit.c(1762) : LogCTDetails=0
TCEngine Level 1 D:\B7\system\TCEngine\tcinit.c(1762) : ForceRowByRow=0
TCEngine Level 1 D:\B7\system\TCEngine\tcinit.c(1762) : ProofMode=0
TCEngine Level 1 D:\B7\system\TCEngine\tcinit.c(1762) : CurrencyTriggers=0
TCEngine Level 1 D:\B7\system\TCEngine\tcinit.c(1762) : Format F98306 contains 10 column(s)
TCEngine Level 1 D:\B7\system\TCEngine\tcinit.c(1762) : Format F98306 contains 13 column(s)
TCEngine Level 1 D:\B7\system\TCEngine\tcinit.c(1762) : There is ER logic associated with the event Row Fetched from F98306
TCEngine Level 1 D:\B7\system\TCEngine\tcinit.c(1762) : System function Insert Row into format F98306
TCEngine Level 1 D:\B7\system\TCEngine\tcrun.c(747) : Conversion R8998306 XJDE0001 done successfully. Elapsed time - 329.343000 seconds.
TCEngine Level 1 D:\B7\system\TCEngine\tcrun.c(755) : Fetched 10689 rows from F98306
TCEngine Level 1 D:\B7\system\TCEngine\tcrun.c(763) : Inserted 10689 rows, failed to insert 0 rows into F98306
```

You will notice several things about this log. The first is that the conversion initializes the environments used. It then attempts to open the input table and target tables. If it cannot open one of these tables, you will see the error at this point in the log. You can also see what OneWorld data source the conversion is attempting to use to find the input and output tables. This is very useful in troubleshooting; if the conversion cannot open the table, you can start by looking at the data source to ensure it is set up correctly. Since the conversion is a cross data source conversion, it will be done row by row; you can see this stated in the log file. The log file then continues on to show you all the columns that are being used. After this is done the conversion moves on to checking the input table. The log tells you what conversion program and version are being run—in this case, R8998306 is being run as well as the environments being used for the conversion. Remember, we are going across data sources so we have two different environments mapped to different data sources. The log checks the formats of the input and output tables before showing you if the output table will be cleared (in this case, it will be). You will see the number of columns that were in the input and output tables. In this case, the number changed from 10 to 13. Finally, the log will show you the number of rows inserted and the number of rows that failed to be inserted.

This information can be used to verify that your table conversion did run successfully. In this case, you would look at your new table to ensure that it has 13 columns and that it contains 10,689 rows of data. This is called verifying a table conversion. We know it is very tedious, but sometimes the report will be fooled into thinking that the conversion finished successfully when the log shows that it actually failed on a number of rows.

An in-place table conversion log will look very similar to a cross data source table conversion log. However, with an in-place table conversion, the log files would show the input and output data sources as the same. The only other differences would be

Troubleshooting

that the conversion would check to see if it could alter the table. The log will tell you this is an in-place conversion and assign the table a temporary name.

The fact that this temporary name is shown in the log file is very important. If the table conversion fails, it will normally not have overlaid your current table, and you have a temporary table hanging out there in your database. You need to manually drop this table before running the table conversion again, so it is important to note the temporary table name.

If there is a table format change, you will see the number of old columns and the number of new columns listed. This is an easy way to verify your table conversion. Finally, you will see the number of records or rows copied, which again can be used to verify your table conversion.

In this section, we have discussed the ins and outs of what really happens when you run the table conversion workbench. We have discussed the different types of table conversions: technical table conversions, in-place table conversions, and cross data source table conversions. We have also covered how to verify your table conversions so you are not surprised later! It is our hope that this information, although a little dry, will keep your system out of trouble.

Control Table Workbench   The next workbench you will be presented with during an upgrade is the control table workbench. This workbench is what moves J.D. Edwards' changes into the system's control tables. The control table workbench affects the data dictionary, user-defined codes, menus, and user overrides tables. These tables are ones that you as a client can modify or customize.

Let's start by briefly defining each of these items. The data dictionary is what tells OneWorld about all of the table formats for the columns used in the relational database tables and how to display column descriptions for all applications. The user-defined codes are codes the applications use which your users can define. An example of a user-defined code is a search type in the address book application. In this application, you can limit your search by telling the application to look only for employees or vendors, for example. This is a user-defined code, so you could add a code to keep track of contractors. The menu tables contain information on the menus for OneWorld. The software allows you to modify existing menus or add your own custom menus. The user overrides table contains information on how your users' OneWorld interface is set up. An example would be specific column order or data sequencing in applications. Users can set up the address book, for example, to show them the records in descending order. All of these changes take time, and you do not want to lose them when you upgrade the software.

This is why the control table workbench exists. It handles adding the new entries for your new J.D. Edwards release. This workbench will be executed for both updates and upgrades. In this section, we are going to dig into what really happens when this workbench is executed. This information should assist you in isolating and solving problems you may encounter during an upgrade. We will cover all of the merges that are kicked off from this workbench. These are the data dictionary, user defined code, and menu merge.

The data dictionary merge moves the new data dictionary changes from J.D. Edwards into your system. This merge is automatically kicked off when you run the control table workbench. We will take a look at what happens "under the covers" when this merge is run.

The first thing you must grasp when you look at this merge is that you will have two data dictionary data sources after an upgrade. So if you are upgrading from B732 to B733, you will have a Data Dictionary – B732 and a Data Dictionary – B733 data source. When you perform the upgrade, your B732 data dictionary files are copied into the B733 data dictionary data source; this is a manual process performed during the upgrade. After this is done, the changes for the B733 release are merged into the data dictionary tables. These tables are as follows:

- F9200 – Data Item Master

- F9202 – Data Field Display Text

- F9203 – Data Item Alpha Descriptions

- F9207 – Data Dictionary – Error Message Information

- F9210 – Data Field Specifications

- F9211 – Smart Fields

- F00165 – Media Objects

These are what you can consider the target tables or the tables that will be updated. The way OneWorld knows what to add into these tables is by reading the change tables. These change tables contain all the changes between releases and update levels. The merge reads these tables looking for the To and From release you specified in your upgrade plan. So if your plan had From release B732 and To release B733, the merge would poll the change tables for these values to determine what changes took place between those two releases for the data dictionary. These change tables are shipped on the upgrade or update disk from J.D. Edwards. Once the merge finds the records that have changed between the two releases, it merges these records into your new release's data dictionary tables. The change tables that are used during this process are as follows:

- F9755 – Data Item Master Changes by Release

- F9757– Data Item Alpha Description Changes by Release

- F9759 – Error Message Pgm Call Changes by Release

- F9760 – OneWorld Data Field Specification Changes

The next merge that is executed during the control table workbench is the user-defined code merge. This merge adds new user-defined codes into your system. Again, this process uses a change table to determine what has changed between releases. The merge will read the F9746 table (UDC Merge). It reads this table looking for what has changed from your specified To and From release, which you specified in the planner. It then moves these changes into your user-defined code tables. The user-defined code tables are as follows:

- F0004 – UDC Type

- F0004D – Alternate Language

- F0005 – User-defined Codes

- F0005D – Alternate Language

TIP

You may want to spot-check a few records listed in the user-defined code and data dictionary merge report to ensure that the changes were added to all of the affected tables.

The menu merge moves the changes from J.D. Edwards into your current menu tables. This merge, like the others we have discussed, also uses change tables to determine what to merge into the menu tables. Let's start by going over the menu tables. These are as follows:

- F0082 – Menu Master

- F00821 – Menu Selections

- F0083 – Menu Text Override

- F0084 – Menu Path

The menu merge will update these tables after polling the menu change tables to determine what has changed between your releases. Again, these change tables are shipped from J.D. Edwards and will reside in the JDEB7.MDB access database located under the planner\data directory on your deployment server. The change tables that are read during this merge are as follows:

- F9751

- F9752

- F9753

- F9754

Specification Merge   The specification merge is very important to an upgrade or an update, as this is the process that actually moves or updates your OneWorld objects specification files. So if you created a custom report in release B732 and you are upgrading to release B733, this is the process that moves your custom report into the new release of OneWorld.

If you understand the logic behind the specification merge, it takes a lot of the mystery out of the process. In this section, we will go over the following:

- The files involved

- What happens when the specification merge is run

The best place to start when trying to understand the specification merge is what files are affected. When you know what the specification merge is touching, the merge process makes a lot more sense. There are data sources that contain files the merge updates. These are as follows:

- Object librarian

- Versions list

- Central objects

The object librarian tables are responsible for keeping track of what objects are on the system. This is a shared data source, meaning that every environment uses the same tables. This is how OneWorld ensures that you do not add two reports with the exact same name. It is also how it keeps track of what objects actually exist. These tables are used for check-in/check-out, object transfer, package builds, and, of course, during the specification merge.

When you are performing an upgrade, you will have two object librarian data sources. You may be thinking, if this data source is shared by all environments, how can I have two of them? The tables in this data source are shared by all OneWorld environments, but the data source is also release specific. That means that you will have an Object Librarian – B732, which your system on the B732 release will use, and you will have a new object librarian data source for B733. The planner has asked you repeatedly for a previous environment. This is so that the merges can find the required data from the previous release to perform their functions. In the case of the specification merge, it will need to find the names of the new objects you added into the OneWorld system. It can then move them into the new release of OneWorld. The specification merge will also move any objects you have modified into your new release. The tables that are read from the previous release and updated in the new release during this merge are as follows:

- F9860 – Object Librarian Master Table

- F9861 – Object Librarian Status Detail

- F9862 – Object Librarian Function Detail

- F9863 – Object Librarian – Object Relationships

- F9865 – Form Information File

The next data source that is hit during the specification merge is the versions list data source. This data source contains the header records for all of your report and application versions. A version of a OneWorld report allows you to have different data selection or processing options without having to create a new report to do this. So you can give Fred in accounting his own version and Sally in sales her own version of the report. They then see only the data that is relevant to their needs. With applications, the versions allow you to set up different processing options. This data source also contains your processing options text. This file shows you the text descriptions on all of your processing options. The tables that are read and updated in this data source are as follows:

- F983051 – Versions List

- F98306 – Processing Option Text

The specification merge will move versions from one release to the other. This is so your users do not have to set up their data selection and processing options all over again, which can take a great deal of time.

T I P

Before you run the specification merge you should verify that your versions are checked in. If the versions are not checked in, the specification merge will not move them to the new release of OneWorld. Produce a list of versions that are not checked in by executing the following select statement over the F983051.

```
Select * from XXX.F983051 where vrvrsavail='N';
Where XXX is the owner for the table, CRPB733, for example.
```

The final data source that is hit during the specification merge is your central objects data source. You will have a specific central objects data source for each path code (for more information on path codes, see Chapter 2). These tables contain the specifications for all of your objects in that path code. So if you wrote a custom report, the specifications for that report will be held in these central object tables. These tables are also related directly to the TAM files on your workstations. Each of these tables stores information on a specific type of OneWorld object and are read during a package build. For more information on package builds, see Chapter 10. During an upgrade, you need to keep in mind for troubleshooting what kind of information these tables store, so if a report does not come across, you will be able to investigate why. We will cover this in detail in a little later. The tables in your central object data sources are shown in Table 18-1.

As you can see, the central object tables contain a lot of information. Keep this in mind as we go over exactly what happens when the specification merge is run.

Now that we have covered the tables that are updated during the specification merge, we will go over what the merge does. Reading this chapter, you probably feel like you are drinking from a fire hose, but you will be prepared to troubleshoot an upgrade, including the specification merge process. When you kick off the specification merge from the workbench, this process entails the tables the specification merge uses to run, the object librarian merge, the version list merge, and the spec merge processes. We will cover each of these topics in this section.

The specification merge follows a logical process to move your objects from one release to the next, using some very specific tables. These tables allow the merge to keep a log file and to keep track of what objects have been merged. These tables are as follows:

F98881 – Specification Merge Logging File

F988810 – SpecMerge Tracking File

When the specification merge is kicked off, the first thing that the merge does is read the old release's object librarian F9860 table (Object Librarian Master) and the

Table	Table Name	TAM File
F98710	Table Header	DDTABL.DDB
F98711	Table Columns	DDCLMN.DDB
F98712	Primary Index Header	DDPKEY.DDB
F98713	Primary Index Detail	DDPKEYD.DDB
F98720	Business View Specifications	BOBSPEC.DDB
F98740	Event Rules – Link Table	GBRLNK.DDB
F98741	Event Rules Specification Table	GBRSPEC.DDXB
F98743	Data Structure Templates	DSTMPL.DDB
F98745	Smart Field Named Mappings	SMRTTMPL.DDB
F98750	Forms Design Aid Text Information	FDATEXT.DDB
F98751	Forms Design Aid Specification Information	FDASPEC.DDB
F98752	Forms Design Aid/Software Versions Repository Header Information	ASVRHDR.DDB
F98753	Forms Design Aid/Software Versions Repository Detail Information	ASVRDTL.DDB
F98760	Report Design Aid Text Information	RDATEXT.DDB
F98761	Report Design Aid Specification Information	RDASPEC.DDB
F98762	JDEBLC – Behavior Information	JDEBLC.DDB
F98306	Processing Option Text	POTEXT.DDB

TABLE 18-1. Central Object Tables and Their Correlating TAM Files

F9861 table (Object Librarian Detail) for objects that have been marked as modified and have a merge option set to a 1. The merge takes this information and then populates the F988810 table, setting all the objects to a not processed status. As you will see, this is a very important part of the specification merge.

Merge Modification Flag

Let's take minute to go over how the objects in your system get their modification flag set to C and the merge option set to 1. This is an actual step in the upgrade process. This is where you choose what objects you are going to bring forward into the new release of OneWorld. This step is accomplished through the specification merge selection program (P98401) on menu GH9611. This application is shown here. You can see several objects shown in this screen have a modification flag of C. When you create a new object in OneWorld, it will tag that object as changed. OneWorld does this by setting the modification flag, in the F9861 table, to C. It will also set this flag to C if you check an object in. In our example, we have two standard J.D. Edwards' reports that show as being modified, R0006P and R0008P.

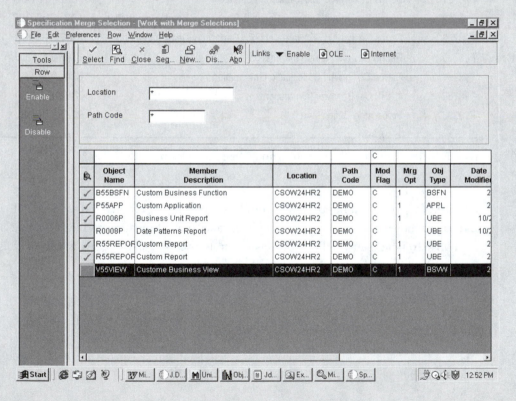

Law of the West

Just because a report was checked in does not mean it should be merged across. You should review this screen carefully and ensure that you only mark the correct items to merge across. You do this by highlighting the item and clicking Select. This will set the merge option to 1, which tells OneWorld to merge the item. If the merge option is blank or 2, this tells OneWorld not to merge the item.

This process is how you tell OneWorld what objects you want to merge across. However, you will also need to make sure, during this process, that all of your objects are checked in. You can do this by running a SQL query over your database. Remember, this query will be run over your older release of OneWorld's object librarian table; in our example, our old release is B732.

```
select * from B732obj.f9861 where SIMKEY != "YOURDEPLOYMENT SERVER'S NAME";
```

This query will show all objects, except for UBE and interactive versions, that are still checked out to a client workstation. Verify that the most current changes, which you want to move, are checked in. You now know what objects are checked in, but remember, we mentioned earlier that versions are merged as well. So you will need to ensure that the versions your users want to move into the new system are also checked in. If a version is not checked in, the merge cannot move the version, since the specifications for that version only exist on the client machine where it was created. To be sure your versions are checked in, you can run this SQL statement. You will have to run the statement once for each path code you are upgrading.

```
select * from cprb732.F983051 where VRVRSAVAIL = 'N';
```

This select statement will show you the names of the versions that have never been checked in. The specification merge will look for this flag to ensure that it is set to Y. If you have checked a version in and then back out again, this flag will be Y. If you changed anything since you checked the version out, those changes will not be moved into the new release. During an upgrade, one of the most common mistakes is not having versions checked in. This is why it is so important to understand the logic of how the specification merge works.

CAUTION

*Currently, as of B733.2, there is no way to check in interactive versions. If you have added interactive versions, you will need to change the VRVRSAVAIL value for these versions to **Y**. Otherwise these versions will not be moved into your new release. You can do this through a SQL statement:*

```
update crpb732.F983051 set VRVERSAVAIL='Y' where VRPID ='NAME OF YOUR APPLICATION'
and VRVERS = 'NAME OF YOUR CUSTOM VERISON';
```

This will tell OneWorld to move your interactive versions from the old release to your new release. Remember to use a commit statement if you are using Oracle, otherwise your changes will not be committed to the database.

Now that you know why the specification merge looks at the object librarian F9860 and F9861, and how the modification flag gets set, let's move on to what it does with this information. Once the merge reads all the records that have a modification flag of C and a merge option of 1, it populates the F988810 file (SpecMerge Tracking) with this information. This file is what gives you the capability to restart your merge if it fails, as of release B733. Before B733, if your merge failed, you needed to completely restore your central object tables and start the merge all over again. Considering that some of these merges ran up to 16 hours, this was a major rollback. Many installers would run the merge only to have a database connectivity issue at hour 15. This is why the merge now has a restart capability, provided by F988810, which keeps track of the object being merged. The process also now checks all the data sources used first to ensure it can connect to them.

The merge will populate the F988810 table with entries for each object that had a modification flag of C and a merge option of 1. You can see the contents of this table through an interactive application: the specification merge status application. This application truly is the window that shows you what the merge is doing. We are going to go over this application very carefully, explaining how the merge uses this table to complete its work.

Before we go into details on the specification merge status application, it is important to note that in early releases of OneWorld, there used to be a separate object librarian and version list merge. This caused some problems. The specification merge is dependent upon the successful completion of the object librarian and version list merge. What used to happen is that people would not realize that their object librarian or version list merge had failed, when these were separate processes. They would then move on to the specification merge, which would attempt to use the records these merges were supposed to place in the new release's files. However, since these failed, the specification merge would not find the records it needed. Thus, this merge would fall over. J.D. Edwards reacted to this situation by incorporating the object librarian merge and the specification merge into one report. Now, if one of these merges fails, the report will know and will not attempt the specification merge.

With all of this information in mind, if that's possible, let's continue our discussion of how the specification merge works. The merge has read the object librarian from your old release and populated the F988810 table with the objects that have a modification flag of C and a merge option of 1. This is where things start to get interesting. The merge will read this table and execute several steps based on what it finds in the table.

We will go over how this table is used for the merge during "normal" merge and what happens if you have to restart your merge.

How are you going to be able to tell if you need to restart the merge? How are you going to track the merge's progress? Take heart—there is an easy-to-use application, the specification merge status program (P98700), that is designed to do nothing but assist you in tracking your specification merge's progress. This application reads F988810, which is the table the merge just populated. This application is located on menu GH9611 (Advanced Operations). When you double-click on this application, you will be taken into the SpecMerge Status screen. This screen, shown in Figure 18-11, will tell you exactly what the specification or spec merge is doing.

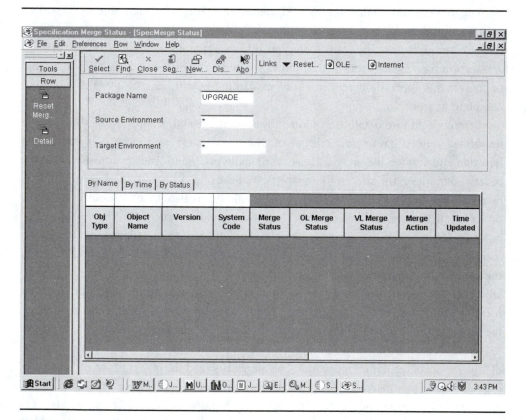

FIGURE 18-11. Specification merge status application

We are going to go over this application from top to bottom. We realize this will be a little tedious, but this is the heart of the specification merge process. This is what controls the merge. Below are listed each of the important fields in this application and a brief description of what each does. Some of these fields cannot be seen in the figure, as they are off to the right.

N O T E

If you are merging a lot of objects, you can use the Query By Example (QBE) line to help you find the object you are looking for faster. This is helpful when you are troubleshooting a specific object.

- **Package Name**   During upgrades, this will be the name of your plan. This is what the merge uses as a key when it populates F988810.

- **Source Environment**   This is the name of the environment you are upgrading.

- **Target Environment**   This is the name of the environment you are upgrading to.

- **Object Type**   This is the type of the object that is being merged. This could be a UBE, APPL, BSFN, and so on.

- **Object Name**   This is the name of the object you are merging.

- **Version**   This field will contain the name of a version for a report or interactive application. You may see multiple instances of the report name, but the version column will list different versions to move across.

- **System Code**   This is the OneWorld system code. 55-59 are reserved for client use.

- **Merge Status**   This description field tells what the merge status is. This field will contain one of several descriptions:

  - Not Processed

  - In Process

  - No Action

  - Success

  - Error

Troubleshooting

- Warning

- Warning SY88

- PO Changed

- **OL Merge Status** This description field shows whether the object librarian merge result was successful, not processed, warning, warning SY88, or error.

- **Version Merge Status** This description field shows whether the version merge was successful, not processed, or encountered an error.

- **Merge Action** This description field tells if the object was added, replaced, or merged.

- **Time Updated** This field shows the time when the object was updated.

- **Date Completed** This field shows the day the object was merged.

- **OL Merge Status** This description field tells what the merge status is. This field will contain one of several descriptions:

  - 0 Not Processed

  - 1 In Process

  - 2 No Action

  - 3 Success

  - 4 Error

  - 5 Warning

  - 6 Warning SY88

  - 7 PO Changed

- **VL Merge Status** This field shows the status of the version list merge using numbers. The QBE line can be used to quickly find errors or objects that have not merged yet. This column uses the same values as the OL Merge Status column.

- **Merge Status** This column shows the status of your spec merge. This is the merge that moves the specifications from one release to the next. It uses the same values as the OL Merge Status column. However, you really will only see success, not processed, warning, no action, or error in this column.

- **Plan Name**   This will be the name of your upgrade plan.

- **Source Environment**   This is the environment you are upgrading from.

- **Target Environment**   This is the environment you are upgrading to.

This list should have given you an idea of the kind of information that is stored in the F988810. Now let's walk through how a record would be processed by the specification merge when it reads this table.

If you remember, we stated that when the merge is run for the first time, F988810 is populated with all the records that were marked in the previous release's object librarian with a modification flag of C and a merge option of 1. When this table is populated, it sets the records in the following columns to not processed for each object in the tables. These columns are:

- OL Merge Status

- VL Merge Status

- Merge Status

The reason these columns are all set to not processed is so that the merge can start working on them one by one. It will run through the object librarian and version list merge first and pick up every record set to not processed. If the record encounters an error, the merge will either stop or mark the record as errored. Once these merges are complete, the report then attempts to merge your specifications from your previous release's central objects to your new release's central objects. This merge will update the central object tables for each type of object that is merged. We went over these tables earlier, and we will touch on them again when we go through auditing the merge.

So what happens if you lose your database connectivity right in the middle of the merge or you run out of disk space? Well, in the past you would probably use some extreme language, since prior to B733 this would have meant resorting to all of your central object tables and running the merge over again. Because of the F988810 table, this is no longer necessary. Remember that everything in this table is originally set to being not processed. If your merge falls over, you can find the records that are marked as error and in process. These are the ones you would need to troubleshoot.

Let's say you ran out of disk space so you couldn't add any more records to your database. We now know why the merge failed, but how do you get it going again? Actually, this process is very simple. What you would do is go into your upgrade plan through the custom installation plan program (P98240) (see Figure 18-12). This application is located on menu GH961 (System Installation Tools). Once you are in this application, expand your plan out. Under the Environments directory, there will be a Specification Merges directory. Highlight this and click Select.

This will take you into the specification table merge planner. This is the part of the planner that contains information on your specification merge. Since you have run the merge once and encountered problems, you will want to restart the merge. To do this you need to change the version of the merge that is executed by the workbench (see Figure 18-13).

Scroll to the right in the Specification Table Merge Planner screen and you will see the program name that is being run (R98700) and the version. Highlight the column in

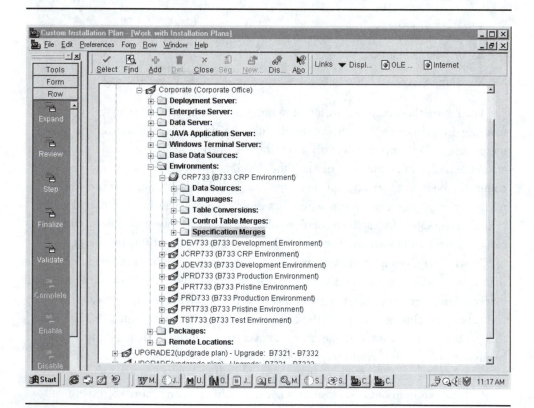

FIGURE 18-12.   Installation planner

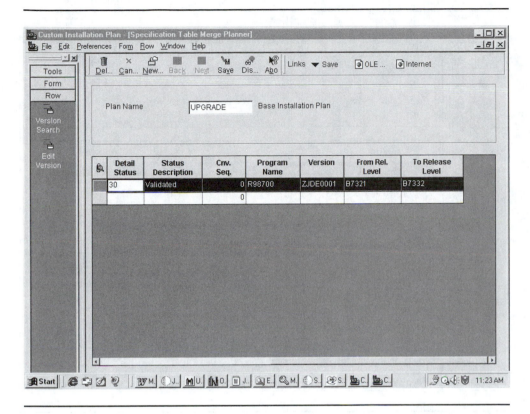

FIGURE 18-13.   Changing the specification merge version in the planner

the grid and go to Row Version Search. This will take you to the Batch Versions screen (see Figure 18-14). On this screen, you will see several different versions:

- **ZJDE0001**   This version is used for the upgrade normal processing.

- **ZJDE0002**   This version is used for the update normal processing.

- **ZJDE0003**   This version is the upgrade restart. This is the version you need to use when restarting your upgrade specification merge. This version only reads F988810 for records that have not been processed, whereas the normal processing version (ZJDE0001) will repopulate this table and thus can merge items twice.

- **ZJDE0004**   This version is used to restart an update's specification merge.

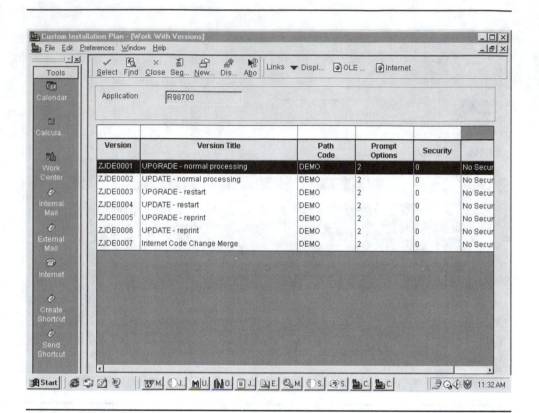

FIGURE 18-14. Specification merge versions

- **ZJDE0005** This version is used to reprint the results of an upgrade specification merge. Everything that is printed on the specification merge report is stored in the F98881 table. This is so that you can go back and reprint the results of your merge any time you need to.

- **ZJDE0006** This version reprints the results of an update specification merge.

- **ZJDE0007** This merge is run for electronic software updates. These are replacing code changes as of B733.2. We will discuss these in more detail later.

In this case, you are restarting the upgrade specification merge, so you would select version ZJDE0003. When you select this version, you will be prompted with the processing options for the version. Let's take a minute to go through these so that you really understand the specification merge.

The first thing you will see is the Options tab, shown here. This tab has four values, which we will discuss.

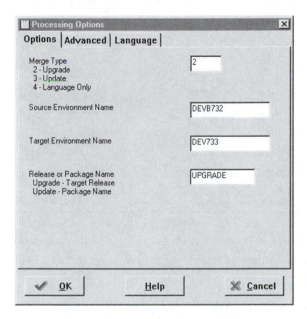

- **Merge Type**   You should not change this value; this is why J.D. Edwards ships the different versions, as they set these to either upgrade or update as necessary.

- **Source Environment Name**   This value indicates the source environment for your merge. This value is passed when the merge is executed from the workbench, so if it is not correct here don't worry about it.

- **Target Environment Name**   The value is the environment to which you are upgrading. This environment name is also passed in by the workbench.

- **Release or Package Name**   This field contains your plan name for an upgrade. For an update, this field will contain the package name.

The next tab is the Advanced tab; the fields are discussed here.

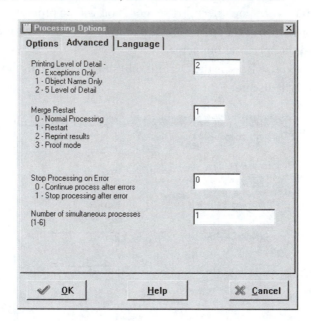

- **Printing Level of Detail**   This field controls how much detail you will see on the specification merge report. We normally set this to 5, which will show the most detail.

- **Merge Restart**   This field should be set to 1, since you are restarting the upgrade specification merge.

- **Stop Processing on Error**   This field allows you to have the merge stop when it encounters an error. Since the merges are normally fairly large jobs, we recommend you set this to 0, so that the merge will continue to process even if it encounters an error. You can then go back and troubleshoot those errors.

- **Number of Simultaneous Processes**   This option allows you to set up multiple threads of the specification merge to run at the same time. This can reduce the amount of time needed for the merge to run. Since you now have three reports merging your objects, each thread will merge a set of objects. When they finish, you will have a report for each thread as well as a master spec merge report. Once thing to remember, though, is that the more threads you run the more memory will be required.

The final tab in the processing options for the R98700 is Language.

Processing Options	☒

Options | **Advanced** | **Language**

Update translated text (Updates Only)
  0 - Do not replace translated text
  1 - Replace translated text   `0`

Source data source for translated text

| ✓ OK | Help | ✗ Cancel |

You only need to be concerned with this tab if you are applying languages other than English. If this is the case, please consult the J.D. Edwards upgrade guide for specific instructions on languages. Once you click OK on the Processing Options screen, you will be taken back to the Specification Table Merge Planner screen. Be sure to set the detail status for your merge to 30 (validated), as it will either be 60 (complete) or 50 (failed), since we are restarting the merge.

CAUTION

Once you have finished making your changes on the Specification Table Merge Planner screen, be sure to click the Save button before clicking Cancel or your changes will not be saved.

Now that you have set up your merge to run again, double-click on the installation workbench program, on menu GH961. Then click Next until you get to the specification merge. Click the Merge button to kick off your restart of the specification merge.

We have covered a lot of ground on how the specification merge runs. We have talked about what tables it uses to run and what tables it updates. However, for this section to be complete, we need to explain what the different merge actions are and why they are used. These merge actions are:

- Add

- Replace

- Merge

If the merge is going to add an item, this means the item does not exist in the new release. In the context of an upgrade, this would be your custom objects. Remember, during an upgrade you load the new release's central objects out of the box, so the only objects that are in these tables are shipped J.D. Edwards' objects. When you run the specification merge, it finds your custom object in the old release, and when it moves the object to the new release, it looks to see if the object exists. If it does not, the merge will add it.

The replace is more for updates than upgrades. If you are moving an object into the system during an update and it is not marked as a modification of C and a merge option of 1, the object will be replaced. It is deleted and then added back into the system by the specification merge. So in the case of an update, J.D. Edwards is merging changes into your existing central objects. If the R0006P was included in the update or ESU (as they follow the same standard), for example, and this object was not marked to merge, it would be replaced with the specifications of the object that were included in the update or ESU.

The final merge action you will see is merge. This is an important action. What this tells you is that the object exists on both the old release and the new release. However, since you marked this object to come across, you have told OneWorld this is an object you have customized and you want to save your customizations. Your changes will be brought across and added to the object in the new release—however, your changes will be disabled. This is so that you can go back into the program and see if you want the changes from J.D. Edwards, which could include new functionality, or your changes. It also forces you to review your code to ensure that it will work with the changes J.D. Edwards has made to the object. This process is called retrofitting, and you should allow time in your upgrade plan to perform this activity.

Law of the West

How the Specification Merge Affects Source and Header Files

Before we move on, it's important to note how some other objects move during the specification merge. Not all of your objects are stored in the central objects data source. This is because OneWorld uses C code for its business functions. It also uses header records for its tables. How do these files move from one release to the next?

When you run the specification merge, it reads the path code master record for your path code (for more information on path codes, see Chapter 2). These records tell OneWorld what central objects data source to use. However, they also tell OneWorld where your source and header files are stored. This is because the path code master records contain the name of your deployment server and the share path that you have set up (for example, B733).

With this information, the merge actually finds these files by using the deployment servers name and the B733 share. It is then hard-coded to look for the source directory and the include directory under your path code directory. We have been using the example of the CRP environment and path code. So when the merge is run, it will look under the CRPB732\source or CPRB732\include folders. These folders are called the check-in location for the CRP path code. The merge then copies these files into your new environment's path code. In our example, this would be CRPB733.

If your merge tells you "unable to copy file" for business functions or tables, this normally means that one of your path codes is set up incorrectly in the path code master program. This program is located on menu GH9053; for more information, see Chapter 2.

When the specification merge finishes, the really good installers don't stop. They go under the covers to audit the specification merge. This helps to limit any surprises later. To pass this skill along to you, we have included an appendix on the subject. This appendix goes over how to audit the specification merge by using the universal table browser. You can find Appendix E at the back of this book.

Updates

You have already learned most of what is involved in an update by reading the "Upgrades" section. In this section, we will cover the differences and how these will affect you during an update.

Let's start by reviewing how the process of an update is different from the process of an upgrade. In an upgrade, you load the central objects out of the box for your new release. In an update, you add objects to your existing central objects by merging them from TAM specifications sent by J.D. Edwards. This is shown in Figure 18-15.

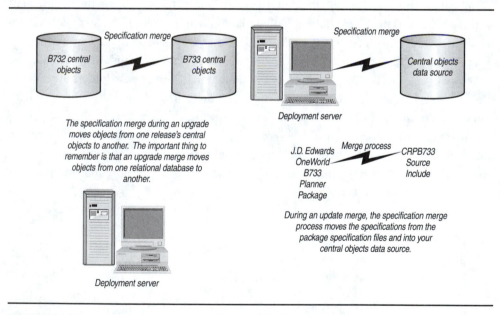

FIGURE 18-15. The difference between upgrade and update

Law of the West

The Update Process After OneWorld Xe

Now that you can clearly see the difference between an upgrade and an update, we are going to throw you for a complete loop. As of OneWorld Xe, J.D. Edwards is going to make the upgrade and update processes match exactly. This means that when you perform an update at this level, you will completely reload the central object tables. You will have a new set of system tables, a new set of object librarian tables, and a new directory structure.

Is this madness? Not really. It is actually J.D. Edwards responding to their clients' suggestions. During an update, the specification merge can take a large amount of time. This is because of the large number of objects that J.D. Edwards is modifying. Using the current method of an update, you have to merge every single object J.D. Edwards has touched. This takes a lot of time. They are changing the processes so that they load all their changes into the system and then merge the client's changes in. Most clients will not be modifying 8,000 objects, which is roughly the number of objects that were touched between B733 and B733.1.

This process will make the updates faster and easier to understand, since now you only need to understand one process. However, it will also dramatically increase the amount of disk space required for an update.

Table Conversions

As of release B733, table conversions can be included in an update. In the past, table conversion were not allowed during updates; only worktables were allowed to be changed, which was accomplished through the environment workbench. So what does this mean for you? It means you will need to go through the same table conversion verification process that we covered in the "Upgrades" section of this chapter, only you will have fewer table conversions to verify. It also means that once you convert a table, only a client machine on the correct update or cumulative level can access that data. The reason is that the format of the table has now changed, so if you attempt to access the table with a lower cumulative level of the software, you could corrupt the data in this table.

Control Table Merges

The control table merges for an update run in exactly the same manner as the upgrade control table merges. They use the exact same control tables to merge the changes, shipped by J.D. Edwards, to the user-defined codes, menus, and data dictionary.

Environment Workbench

The environment workbench also does the same thing during an update as during an upgrade. It will add only new tables into the system. The report you get after the environment workbench, R98403, will show "existing table no action" for any tables that already existed in your system.

Specification Merge Workbench

This is where some of the differences between an upgrade and an update really start to show. During an upgrade, you are merging from one set of central objects to another. During an update, you are merging from a package—TAM files—into your relational database. This package is located under the planner\package directory. The package will be named after the update. This means you will have to tell the specification merge, R98700, that it should be looking for a package, for example, CUMB733-1. You do this through the processing options on the R98700 report. To view the processing options, go to batch versions and find this report. Highlight version ZJDE0002 and go to Row Processing Options. This will take you to the processing options of this version.

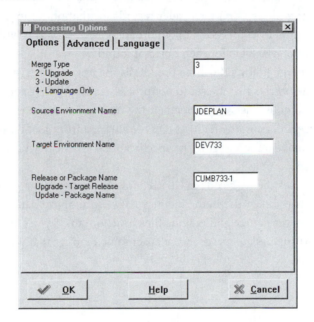

The Release Or Package Name field will need to be set to the name of your update package. There is a visual assist here, but the update package name will not be in the values the visual assist shows. If you are unsure of what the proper value for this field should be, look under the planner\package directory on your deployment server.

What Happens When You Run an Update Specification Merge

When you run the specification merge for an update, it follows almost exactly the same logic as an upgrade specification merge. In this section, we will cover what differences there are and why. This will help you understand the update procedure.

Troubleshooting

F988810 and F98881   During an upgrade, the specification merge will read the previous release's object librarian tables for objects with a modification flag of C and a merge flag of 1. In an update, you do not have two separate object librarian data sources. So how does the merge process know what to merge? It reads the TAM specifications of the update package, under planner\packages on your deployment server. The merge will then find the header records for that object in the local JDEB7.MDB file, under planner\data, on your deployment server. It will then add entries into the F988810 table for each object it found.

The update merge follows the same process as the upgrade merge. It will poll this table selecting the objects that are set to not processed. It will first perform the object librarian and version list merges. Remember, the records for the object librarian and version list merge will be in the JDEB7.MDB file shipped from J.D. Edwards. The merge will then move on to merging the specifications for the objects from the TAM files into your central objects.

This process uses the path code master records in your planner, just like the upgrade merge. These records tell the merge what central object data source to update and where to copy the source and include files from and to. If you encounter errors in the merge, restart the update merge in the exact same manner that we just covered for the upgrade merge.

Law of the West

Merge Flags for an Update

An important fact to keep in mind here is how the modification and merge option flags are used during an update. During an upgrade, they tell the merge what to bring across into your new release. During an update, they are used in a slightly different manner.

During an update, only J.D. Edwards' objects will be merged into your system. You really only have to worry about the modification and merge option flags if you have modified a J.D. Edwards object. If you have, you will want to mark these objects as changed and set their merge option to 1. Do this in the exact same manner as you would for an upgrade, through the specification merge selection program on menu GH9611.

The only difference here is that you are telling OneWorld not to replace these objects. If the object is not marked with a modification flag of C and a merge option of 1, the update process will drop this object out of your system and add it back in. This is what happens when the specification merge shows a merge action of replace. If the object is a new object, it will just add it into your system.

However, if the object already exists and you have marked this object with a modification flag of C and merge option of 1, your changes will be preserved. The merge will disable your changes and add in all of the changes from J.D. Edwards. You will then have to retrofit these modifications.

T I P

Once the specification merge is finished, you will need to build a package and deploy it to your client workstations. Otherwise, they will not be able to use any of the new objects or see the modifications to objects without checking those objects out.

Server Packages

You are shipped new host CDs with both updates and upgrades. When you load these CDs, you will have all the necessary specifications to run the objects included in the update. However, you will not have any of your custom modifications on the enterprise server. To move these modifications across, you will have to perform a server package build. This is described in more detail in Chapter 10.

Application Software Updates (ASUs)

An application software update (ASU) is very similar to a regular update. The only real difference is that ASUs do not include table conversions. So why even have an ASU? Because when J.D. Edwards makes the update process and upgrade process the same, they will still need a way to deliver certain changes between update levels.

An example of these changes would be a tax ASU. If you are going to produce your W-2s and 1099s through OneWorld, you will need to apply a special ASU every year. This is because the government changes the rules a little bit every year, and you will need to incorporate these new rules into the software to be compliant. J.D. Edwards delivers these changes through an ASU. So you cannot totally get away from merging from TAM specifications into your central objects. However, this process will be used for a lot fewer objects, since ASUs are very small in size. Unlike updates, they do not include thousands of changes.

Electronic Software Updates (ESUs)

If you have worked with OneWorld for a while, you probably know what a code change is. A code change is a set of instructions J.D. Edwards sends to clients to resolve specific issues addressed in software action requests (SARs). These code changes basically tell you what code to change in the OneWorld objects in order for them to work correctly. This process requires someone skilled in using the OneWorld tool set. It also can be a fairly long and difficult process; we have seen code changes as long as 100 pages!

Fortunately, J.D. Edwards has responded to this issue by developing an entirely new way to apply code changes. This is what they now call an electronic software update (ESU). An ESU really is a very small update. Instead of having you manually change everything in OneWorld, you would apply an ESU. This functionality is included in the OneWorld software as of B733.2.

These ESUs can be downloaded off the J.D. Edwards Web page. They are applied to the system in the exact same way as an application software update or a cumulative update. The difference is that because an ESU is so small, it only affects certain objects, thus it can be applied quickly. However, like any other update, you first want to apply the ESU into a non-production environment and test it.

Sounds great, right? Well, like all things in life, there is a trade-off. The trade-off comes when you have modified an object that is included in an ESU. What this means is that you would mark your object as being changed and set the merge option to 1. This would tell the specification merge to merge your changes into the object shipped from J.D. Edwards. However, this means the exact same thing as it did for an update. Your code will be disabled—for example, with event rules, you will have to go back into the object and retrofit your modifications. So don't take an ESU just to take it, or you could be in store for more work than you counted on.

Retrofitting Modifications

We have briefly referred to retrofitting modifications many times in this chapter. In this section, we will try to give you an idea of what this means and why you must include some time for retrofitting your modifications into your upgrade plan. If you don't, you will not make it through your upgrade in the time you have allotted.

Retrofitting modifications is really not that horrible. It just takes some time and a specific skill set. This is why you need to plan for retrofitting your modifications. The first thing to do is get a rough idea of how many objects you will need to retrofit. During an update, upgrade, application software update, or electronic software update, the only time you will need to retrofit an object is if both you and J.D. Edwards have changed the object. Therefore, this will not affect any of your custom objects, only the shipped objects you modify.

With this in mind, when you prepare to upgrade you should collect a list of all the J.D. Edwards objects you have changed. You will also want to find out if the reason these objects were changed was only for code change. If it was, do not bring these changes forward. Unless this problem was discovered right before the update was released, the fix for that object should be included in the update. You can verify this by looking at the software action requests numbers included in each update, or you can look at the specific SAR and it will tell you the release and update that the issue is fixed in.

Once you have a list of the objects changed and what was changed for these objects, you can then determine what type of resources you will need to dedicate. Normally, whenever possible, the programmer who made the change should retrofit the modification. If this is not possible, the person who is retrofitting the modification needs to understand what the modification was trying to accomplish and the importance of the modification. This will help him or her incorporate your changes into the J.D. Edwards objects without losing your functionality or the added functionality from J.D. Edwards.

T I P

Currently, you may have to look at a large number of objects to retrofit. This is because OneWorld will only look at the modification flags to see if it needs to bring this object forward. In OneWorld Xe the software gets a little smarter: J.D. Edwards will be shipping a change table for the specification merge process. The software will be able to tell if J.D. Edwards has changed that object. If they have not changed the object between releases or update levels, and you have marked the objects with a modification flag of C and a merge option of 1, it will not merge. That is right—it will not merge. What the specification merge will do is perform a replace of the object in the new release. Since J.D. Edwards did not change anything on the object, all of your changes are copied across, replacing the existing object. This means this object would not need to be retrofitted.

Running in Parallel

This is a topic that really throws a lot of people for a loop. What it means is the ability to run two different releases or update levels of OneWorld at the same time. This is so that you can thoroughly test the new release or update before bringing it into your production environment.

Running Two Separate Releases of OneWorld in Parallel

Let's start by describing how you would run two separate releases of OneWorld in parallel. The first thing you would do is follow the J.D. Edwards standard upgrade procedure. This is where you should first make your CRP environment match the production environment as closely as possible. You will want to move some production data so you can test against it, your user-defined codes, and menus. You will also need to ensure that the specifications for the CRP path code match those of your production path code. After all, it would not really be an accurate test if you upgraded different objects. To do this, J.D. Edwards has shipped several versions of the R98403 to assist you in copying this data from your production environment into your CRP environment. Details on how this is accomplished can be found in every J.D. Edwards' upgrade manual.

Once the production environment and path code match the CRP environment and path code, you are ready to start your upgrade. However, the second you start to upgrade the CRP environment, that environment belongs to the person performing the upgrade. You also should freeze your development in the production path code. This means you will not add any new objects, including versions, or they will not be brought forward. This occurs because when you upgrade your production environment, you do not run a specification merge. All you do is copy the CRP path code into your production path code, and run your control table merges and your table conversions. This upgrades your production environment with less risk and in a lot less time. You can upgrade the production environment over a weekend.

However, before you upgrade the production environment, you will want to test your applications in the CRP environment. Since you cannot shut down your business while you are doing this, you will need to run in parallel. In the example we have been using throughout this chapter, we are upgrading the CRP environment from B732 to B733. Once we have run through the upgrade procedures, which were touched upon earlier in this chapter, we are ready to run in parallel.

Deployment Server

For an upgrade, you will have two different directory structures on your deployment server: one for the old release and one for the new release of OneWorld (in our example, B732 and B733). Then what release is your deployment server really running? It is going to be running the newest release of OneWorld, so in our example this would be B733. This does not mean you can no longer build packages in your old release or you cannot add users or other administrative functions. What it does mean is that these processes will need to be done from a client workstation on the old release (in our example, B732).

You can also still deploy packages to workstations running the old release. You will just need to ensure that you either assign the package to the workstation from a client running the old release of OneWorld or that you use the installation programs under the old releases directory structure on the deployment server. In our example, this would be the setup program located in the Client directory under the B732 share on your deployment server.

Enterprise Server

If you want to run in parallel, you will need to address some specific setup issues. We have already touched on the setup issues for the deployment server, so let's talk about the ones on the enterprise server. When you install your host CDs, you will be able to create two different instances of OneWorld on your enterprise server. This is really only a different directory structure for all platforms except the AS/400. When you run in parallel with the AS/400, you will specify different library names. The libraries used for your AS/400 enterprise server to run OneWorld are:

- B733SYS (network and kernel code).

- Path code libraries, for example, PRODB733. These libraries contain modules necessary to recompile and execute business functions.

- Integrated file structure (IFS); this will have your path code names as well. These are contained in the structure path code/specfile, which contain your specification files. Also in the IFS is the JDEB7XX directory, in which there will be logging information.

On all of the other platforms, the host code will install a new directory structure. So if you were running B732 and B733, you would have a B732 and a B733 directory on the enterprise server. This means you will need enough disk space on your enterprise server to hold the host code for both of your release levels. However, this is not the only thing you will need to watch out for. There are specific settings in the JDE.INI file that you will need to ensure are correct so you can run two releases in parallel.

These settings control the port number OneWorld uses to communicate. You cannot have two different releases of OneWorld attempting to use the same port. What happens is much like two people trying to talk at the same time on a telephone line; all they do is drown each other out and you hear only gibberish. To avoid this, you simply tell OneWorld what port to use in the JDE.INI file. This information is contained under the [JDENET] section. Below is an example of this section. You would need to ensure that your B732 release's INI file and your B733 release's INI file specify different port numbers or they will talk over each other.

NOTE

*Each new release or update level of OneWorld host code will have its own INI
file. This is so that it is truly separate from your old release. It is also because
INI settings may change from release to release.*

```
[JDENET]
serviceNameListen=6009
serviceNameConnect=6009
```

There is one other section of the INI file that will need to be modified if you
are going to run in parallel. This is under the [JDEIPC] section of the INI file. The
abbreviation IPC stands for interprocess communication. This is how processes
running in the background share information. If you have two releases of OneWorld,
you will need to ensure that they both do not try to communicate using the same area
of memory for their interprocess communication. To do this, you simply need to
modify the [JDEIPC] section of the INI file for each release. Below is an example
of this section from an INI file:

```
[JDEIPC]
ipcTrace=0
maxNumberOfSemaphores=200
startIPCKeyValue=
```

The ipcTrace value is a logging feature. Do not turn this on unless instructed
by J.D. Edwards' support, as it will affect your system's performance. The real value
you will need to worry about here is the startIPCKeyValue. This value cannot match
between the two releases of the software, running on the same enterprise server. This
starting value will need to be different by at least 1,000 between your releases. So if
your B732 release's INI file had a starting value of 6000, your B733 release's INI file
should have a minimum starting value of 7000. This will stop the two releases from
using the same area of memory.

If you are running on a Windows NT platform, you will have to worry about one
other setting: the CLSID value. This value is a universally unique identifier (UUID),
which identifies a COM component. Each COM component has its CLSID in the
Windows registry so it can be loaded by other applications. You can generate this
UUID by using the Uuidgen program, which is contained in Microsoft's Visual C++
compiler program.

Troubleshooting

Running in Parallel on an Intel/NT platform

J.D. Edwards has done a pretty good job of allowing you to run two different releases in parallel. However, there are a few places where you might run into a snag. Two of the current known snags are that any release or update level prior to B733.1 uses the Visual C compiler level of 5.0, and that release B733.1 and beyond uses the Visual C compiler level of 6.0.

What does this mean to you? Some users have had issues when running these two compilers on the same machine. So that means that you would not be able to have a development machine run both B732 and B733.1 releases. It also means you cannot have visual C 5.0 and 6.0 on the same enterprise server. Why is this important? Because the J.D. Edwards host code requires you to have a compiler loaded. What will probably be recommended to get around this problem is that you load an application server to run your newer release. Yes, that means you now have two servers running OneWorld. This really is the safest solution.

However, there is a solution that may get you out of this without having to use two different machines. We have not tested this solution, but feel we need to include it in this book. The solution is to copy certain DLLs into the system directory of your pre-B733.1 host code. Once you have done this, you could uninstall the visual C 5.0 compiler and install the visual C 6.0 compiler. What you are really doing is giving the B732 release of OneWorld the DLLs it needs from the compiler without having the compiler loaded on your machine. The steps you would take are:

1. Create two batch files to swap out some DLLs. To do this, open a Notepad session and enter **REM**. This file will handle copying the DLL used by the compilers back into the winnt\System32 directory.

2. Copy c:\winnt\system32\vc50-mfc*c:\winnt\system32.

3. Save this file as something referencing your old compiler, for example, VCVERSION5.BAT.

4. Open another file in Notepad and enter **REM**. This file copies the VC60 DLLs.

5. Copy c:\winnt\system32\vc60-mfc*c:\winnt\system32.

6. Save this file as VCVERSION 6.BAT.

7. If you have MSVC 5.0 installed on your machine, create a directory for each version of the compiler's DLLs under your winnt\system32 directory:

   - C:\winnt\system32\vc50-mfc

   - C:\winnt\system32\vc60-mfc

8. Copy the following DLL files from your winnt\system32 directory into the vc50-mfc directory. (This is assuming you have VC 5.0 currently installed.)

   - mfc42d.dll

   - mfc42d.pdb

   - mfcd42d.dll

   - mfcd42.pdb

   - mfcn42d.dll

   - mfcn42d.pbd

   - mfco42d.dll

   - mfco42d.pdb

9. You would then uninstall MSVC 5.0 and install MSVC 6.0.

10. Copy the following changed DLL files from c:\winnt\system32 into the vc60-mfc directory you created:

    - mfc42d.dll

    - mfc42d.pdb

    - mfcd42d.dll

    - mfcd42d.pdb

    - mfcn42d.dll

    - mfcn42d.pdb

- mfco42.dll

- mfco42d.pdb

11. If you have already installed MSVC 6.0, just copy the MSVC 5.0 DLLs from the installation disk into your vc50-mfc directory.

12. Before building a server package, you would need to ensure that you ran the VCVERSION6.BAT file before running a server package on B733.1 and above. If you need to perform a server package for release B733 and below, run the VCVERSION5.BAT file before performing the server package.

Client Workstations

You only have one more step before you are done. You need to ensure that your client machine INI files are using the correct port number as well. These settings are held in the [JDENET] section of the INI file, just like on the enterprise server. If you have already deployed your client workstation, you can just go to the winnt directory for Windows NT clients, or the Windows directory for Window 95/98 clients. In this directory, you will find your INI file. Open the INI file and ensure that the port numbers under the [JDENET] section match those you set up for your enterprise server. In our example, these would be 6009 for the serviceNameListen and serviceNameConnect. Since your old release is already running, if you have not deployed any client workstations you will just need to ensure that when they are deployed the correct port number is placed in the JDE.INI file. To do this, you would confirm the port number in the JDE.INI file located in the OneWorld Client Installs\Mics directory on your deployment server. Once you find this file, search for the [JDENET] section and ensure that your serviceNameListen and serviceNameConnect are set to the correct port number.

T I P

Although it is always a good idea to ensure the two releases you are running are using different ports, you really will not have to worry about this if you did not change the port number after your initial installation of OneWorld. This is because J.D. Edwards ships each release and update level of their software coded to use a different port. However, checking to make sure they are different will not hurt either!

C A U T I O N

Although you can run a system in parallel this does not mean you can have clients on two different releases running in the same environment. In this chapter, we have discussed how an upgrade can change the format of a table. Once you change the format of the table, only a client on the correct release can access the table. If you attempt to access a table on a client on a different release, OneWorld will experience problems. It is also possible for you to corrupt the table. So the moral of the story is, once an environment is upgraded, only access that environment with client workstations on the correct release.

Troubleshooting

Summary

Congratulations, you made it through one of the most difficult parts of OneWorld to understand! We wanted to ensure you had the information needed to not only survive, but to excel at an upgrade. After all, whenever you are upgrading a live system, it affects mission-critical applications. So the more information you have, the better!

In this chapter, we have covered the differences between upgrades and updates. We stressed that currently the difference is that an upgrade will merge from one set of central object tables to another. The important thing to remember is that the upgrade merge is moving objects from one set of relational database tables to another. During an update, prior to OneWorld Xe, the specification merge will read TAM files on your deployment server and merge the specifications in these files into your central object tables. We also covered the fact that as of OneWorld Xe, the update and upgrade process will be the same, meaning you will merge from one set of central objects to another. This makes the update processes easier, but it will also require a lot more disk space.

We covered the pieces of the installation planner program. This chapter showed you how the planner sets up your workbench. We provided some insight on how the pieces of OneWorld tie together. This information should assist you in planning an upgrade, update, or an electronic software update. It will also help you troubleshoot any problems with these processes.

We also discussed what the temporary environment is used for during upgrade. This environment provides a placeholder for the J.D. Edwards software to perform table conversions over the central objects, specifically for upgrades from B732. These table conversions remove the next ID numbers.

This chapter also covered the entire upgrade process and how to troubleshoot the upgrade. It is nice to know how to perform an upgrade, but to have the skill set to troubleshoot an upgrade is even more valuable. When things go right, life is good, but when things go badly, a person with the ability to troubleshoot an upgrade will really show his or her worth. That is why we included a section in this chapter on how to troubleshoot table conversions, as well as the specification merge process. These skills are vital to the upgrade process. It is our hope that this chapter has helped equip you with the skill set needed to troubleshoot any update, upgrade, or electronic software update.

This chapter went on to tell you about application software updates and electronic software updates. An application software update is how J.D. Edwards delivers things like updates for you to run your 1099s or W-2s from within OneWorld. Since the government changes tax rules every year, the timing probably will not match up to J.D. Edwards' release schedule. So J.D. Edwards delivers application software updates, which are just very small updates. These small updates merge objects from TAM files into your central objects database.

The electronic software updates are replacing code changes (SARs) as of B733.2, so you will not have to manually apply these code changes anymore. Now you can just download an electronic software update and merge the fixes into your system. However, you will need to go back and retrofit any modifications you made to affected J.D. Edwards' objects.

Finally, we covered what retrofitting your modifications entailed. This is where the merge process used for updates and upgrades will disable your changes. You then need to go into these objects and enable your changes. This forces you to see what changes J.D. Edwards has added and to ensure that your changes will work with what has been added by the merge.

It is our hope that this chapter, although long, was informative. Our experience has shown that the problems you cannot figure out until three in the morning are often small ones that could have been avoided if you had only known about them. The entire purpose of this chapter was to give you enough information so you do not get tripped up—or if you do, you can quickly get back on your feet.

Troubleshooting

## CHAPTER 19

Optimizing OneWorld to Fit Your Business Needs

When to Optimize

The Five-Step Optimization Methodology

Creating Multiple Queues on a Server

Optimization is one of our favorite topics. The OneWorld product, by definition, treats every company and every platform the same. Yet anyone who knows anything about AS/400, UNIX, Windows NT, Oracle, or MS SQL Server will tell you that these products are definitely not created equal. Further, we can tell you from personal experience (with over 35 implementations of the OneWorld product) that no two companies are the same. So, how do you create a product that is universally right for each platform and each client? The answer is that you don't! Instead, you create a software suite that generates a best of breed for various industries. The question that you must now ask yourself is how you can tune the product to work the best in your specific environment doing what you do as opposed to being a general all-purpose product. Tuning OneWorld is what this chapter is dedicated to discussing. We will talk about the following:

- How do you know when to optimize OneWorld?

- A five-step method of optimizing the product

- Adding multiple queues to an application server

When to Optimize

Let's start with a full understanding of what optimizing OneWorld actually means. When we talk about optimizing this product, we are talking about making changes to the product, the process, or even the entire system in order to realize a performance gain in the system itself. Let's take a specific example of a company that needed to optimize the OneWorld system to perform their specific business. If you run a large number of sales orders through OneWorld—either manually inserting them, using EDI functionality, or even using a direct interface between a POS (point of sale) system and OneWorld APIs—you will need to run the sales update UBE (R42800) and the pick slip UBE (R42520). In our example client, the Sales Order entry application (P4210) is also populating information used for invoicing clients. How much processing time will it take to do this? It depends on the number of sales orders and the number of lines of detail generated to make an accurate assessment. For the purpose of this example, let's assume that the client is running 20,000 sales per day with an average of five lines of detail per sales, producing approximately 100,000 lines of detail per day. In the B733.1 product (assuming that application servers haven't been added to off-load the processing), it would take approximately 32 hours of processing per day to run the Sales Update UBE alone. When you add the other required processing, the client is looking at over 60 hours of processing per day.

Stop! There Simply Isn't Enough Time in the Day to Process it All

Do you have 60 hours to process everything daily? And even if you did, do you really think your customers will be willing to wait two hours for a receipt? If they are, cool; our recommendation is that you increase the size of your waiting room, put in some good cable channels, and provide culinary experiences that make the wait worthwhile. Suppose you go to Wal-Mart to buy a pack of gum and the clerk indicates that you have to wait for two hours for a receipt. We understand that the sales order example is far-fetched. Nevertheless, are your clients willing to wait indefinitely for OneWorld to work? Of course not; this is a clear example of when you should optimize the product.

You should not wait until you're confronted with extreme circumstances before you optimize OneWorld. Once your company has completed its initial setup, you should begin evaluating OneWorld optimization opportunities. The OneWorld system will respond only as well as it's configured. Although J.D. Edwards doesn't have a phase of their technology implementation methodology specifically set aside for optimizing the product, we think that this step is so important that you shouldn't hesitate to perform it. We have seen several implementations suffer because both end-of-day processing and optimization were left until after go-live. You shouldn't let your organization run into a similar situation.

The Five-Step Optimization Methodology

This methodology is not patented, but it should be. After all, if you follow these five steps, your OneWorld system is guaranteed to run faster and more efficiently. And we've never had a client complain when we've increased system performance. The real goal behind this process is to look at what you're trying to do from an application's perspective and then apply the technology to get the job done.

Step 1: Optimize the OS

In truth, we want to go beyond just the operating system to the enterprise server(s) as a whole. This includes the hardware, its configuration, and the software (the OS). Think about what you can do with your particular server that will increase its performance. First, you'll want to evaluate several system parameters. Although these parameters differ according to your platform, there are quite a few options in each.

If you don't have the in-house skill sets necessary to make this evaluation, it is worth the money to hire someone who does. Our usual recommendation is that you enter into a service agreement with an organization that has specific experience working with the J.D. Edwards OneWorld suite of products. This is advantageous for two reasons.

First, these consulting firms already know the product and have experience tuning the hardware and software. Few things are worse than paying an expensive consultant to learn your software and system. Second, because these consultants have already done the exact same task multiple times at other companies, they are able to transfer this knowledge to your in-house IT staff more readily. This is always advantageous unless you've entered into a long-term services outsourcing agreement with the consulting firm.

OS Factors of Performance

On any platform, you need to identify if you are suffering a performance bottleneck and if so, where it is located. Some of the platform-independent parameters that should be watched during peak and trough times include disk IO, memory use, processor use, virtual memory use, and NIC card use and performance. Additionally, you should pay close attention to nice and negative nice on the UNIX platform. During these evaluations, you should also pay close attention to which processes are requiring the majority of the systems' resources and which resources in particular they are depleting. With this information, you can begin creating a plan to optimize the hardware and OS.

Let's take the example provided earlier of a company suffering slow performance during peak sales times. They are using the HP9000 and feel that their system should be able to handle the workload of the subsystem. Following the first step of optimization, they evaluated their system and determined a disk IO bottleneck. What options do they have (without spending more money) to decrease the disk IO on this specific drive? A couple of things were done to decrease this system's requirements. The company was running with logging on the enterprise server. However, when we suggested turning logging off, they were adamant that it should stay on. So, by using basic J.D. Edwards OneWorld CNC, we moved the logs to a different logical drive located on a different disk controller. Notice in the JDE.INI settings that follow how the OneWorld install location is on /u17 and the logs are on /u20:

```
[DEBUG]
Output=FILE
Trace=TRUE
ClientLog=1
```

```
DebugFile=/u20/jdedwardsoneworld/b7332/log/jdedebug.log
JobFile=/u20/jdedwardsoneworld/b7332/log/jde.log
LogErrors=1
JDETSFile=/u01/jdedwardsoneworld/b7332/log/JDETS.log
RepTrace=0

[INSTALL]
DefaultSystem=system
ClientPath=client
PackagePath=package
DataPath=data
B733=/u17/jdedwardsoneworld/b7332
Double_Byte=0
LocalCodeSet=WE_ISO88591
```

This got us part of the way there, but the performance was still unacceptable, and the disk IO was still too high. We continued looking at the problem and thought our way through the issue. Although the company was live (in a production mode), they were also still in a CRP mode for some functionality and development (this was the reason behind their wanting to keep the logging on). Consequently, the disks had to service all three environments and were having difficulty because of the high volume. We recommended setting up another enterprise server to satisfy CRP and development. But, remember the limitation set earlier: They didn't want to spend more money.

DEFINITION

CRP: CRP stands for Conference Room Pilot and is a phase of the implementation where the software is initially configured and tested for OneWorld. In OneWorld Xe (formerly B733.3), the name has been changed from CRP to Prototype to be more descriptive of what you actually do during this phase of the implementation.

This time, the OS itself came to the rescue. Using HP_UX, we moved the server code for Pristine, CRP, and development to different drives available on the server. We then linked the path codes back to the B733 directory. As far as OneWorld was concerned, those directories were still in the same directory structure provided by J.D. Edwards. However, disk IO was reduced substantially because of this system optimization.

Other OS Considerations

Sometimes you simply won't get by with what you've got. OS tuning can certainly go a long way toward fixing many of the problems you may be experiencing. It may even be the ultimate solution, but you might have to increase what you have to get there.

Let's consider a different company as an example of what to look for. This company decided on an AS/400 solution with a single S30 two-way and 1GB of RAM. They implemented financials and began preparations for bringing manufacturing on line, but their systems were too slow. Using the first step of optimization, they determined that AS/400 was the fault line. They didn't have enough RAM or enough processing power to run OneWorld with their existing workload. We recommended that they off-load some of their system requirements to another server, and they accepted this solution. They purchased an S30 four-way with 4GB of RAM, moved production to the new box, and kept their first box as a development machine and a backup of the production box. This wasn't a cheap solution, but it did alleviate the issue and provided business-critical redundancy.

Is Step 1 the Solution?

Step 1 (optimize the OS) isn't necessarily the entire solution. Through proper maintenance and careful evaluation, however, it can be a vital part of the solution. But before you spend another half million on hardware, you need to carefully evaluate the other steps in optimizing OneWorld to fit your business needs.

Step 2: Optimize the Database

Once your hardware is optimally configured, the next step is to ensure that the backend of the OneWorld product, the database, is optimized. In other chapters, we've indicated that the data is the single most important component in this (or any) ERP product. Without proper maintenance and planning (both up front and during periodic reviews), your RDBMS can cost your company valuable time and system performance. A finely tuned database is one of the requirements for optimizing OneWorld.

Optimizing Databases

Some of the steps for optimizing your database should be performed before you install the OneWorld product. First, we highly recommend you search the J.D. Edwards Knowledge Garden Web site (https://knowledge.jdedwards.com/; you will need to obtain a username and password for this site), which includes a couple of tuning guides located in the WWAT (World Wide Advance Technology) section that are downloadable. They contain database tuning parameters for specific databases. These guides also make general recommendations that are applicable to any database.

One of these recommendations includes separating your indexes, logs, and data files and putting them on different physical drives. Let's think about why you would want to do this. When you write data to the database, you actually write to several locations at the same time. If the data files, logging files, and indexes are located on the same drive, you write the data multiple times and can run into a disk constraint. If you separate these files, you will not only speed up the actual processing, but also decrease potential disk contention.

Distributing Your Data Files

Different RDBMSs favor different size data files. Consequently, you will often get substantial benefits from maintaining multiple smaller, more efficient data files. For example, with Oracle, an 800 to 1,000MB data file is very efficient. However, in a large organization, many of these files would be required. Depending on the hardware configuration, these data files can also be distributed so as to achieve a better performance ratio.

An Example

We will illustrate an example of distributing the data files, using the following information:

- The production data and index space is 50GB.

- CRP is a duplicate of production.

- Test and development are subsets of production data at approximately 10GB of data/index.

- The hardware is an HP9000 with 1080GB, in 120 disks each with a 9GB drive. This server has six disk controllers and has hardware RAID 1/0 (each disk is individually mirrored and then striped into logical drives) with four disks combined into each logical pairing. There are five logical drives per disk controller, similar to the diagram in Table 19-1.

Controller 1

Disk 1	Disk 2		Disk 5	Disk 6
Disk 3	Disk 4		Disk 7	Disk 8
	U01			U02

Disk 9	Disk 10		Disk 13	Disk 14
Disk 11	Disk 12		Disk 15	Disk 16
	U03			U04

Disk 17	Disk 18
Disk 19	Disk 20
	U05

Controller 2

Disk 21	Disk 22		Disk 33	Disk 34
Disk 23	Disk 24		Disk 35	Disk 36
	U06			U07

Disk 25	Disk 26		Disk 37	Disk 38
Disk 27	Disk 28		Disk 39	Disk 40
	U08			U09

Disk 29	Disk 30
Disk 31	Disk 32
	U10

Controller 3

Disk 41	Disk 42		Disk 45	Disk 46
Disk 43	Disk 44		Disk 47	Disk 48
	U11			U12

Disk 49	Disk 50		Disk 53	Disk 54
Disk 51	Disk 52		Disk 55	Disk 56
	U13			U14

Disk 57	Disk 58
Disk 59	Disk 60
	U15

Controller 4

Disk 61	Disk 62		Disk 65	Disk 66
Disk 63	Disk 64		Disk 67	Disk 68
	U16			U17

Disk 69	Disk 70		Disk 73	Disk 74
Disk 71	Disk 72		Disk 75	Disk 76
	U18			U19

Disk 77	Disk 78
Disk 79	Disk 80
	U20

Controller 5

Disk 81	Disk 82		Disk 85	Disk 86
Disk 83	Disk 84		Disk 87	Disk 88
	U21			U22

Disk 89	Disk 90		Disk 93	Disk 94
Disk 91	Disk 92		Disk 95	Disk 96
	U23			U24

Disk 97	Disk 98
Disk 99	Disk 100
	U25

Controller 6

Disk 101	Disk 102		Disk 105	Disk 106
Disk 103	Disk 104		Disk 107	Disk 108
	U26			U27

Disk 109	Disk 110		Disk 113	Disk 114
Disk 111	Disk 112		Disk 115	Disk 116
	U28			U29

Disk 117	Disk 118
Disk 119	Disk 120
	U30

TABLE 19-1.   Disk/Logic Drive Configuration

System Administration and Troubleshooting

NOTE

Table 19-1 represents a single approach to the disk configurations available. It is what we had to work with on this particular client; however, even this was not optimal for Oracle. To maximize read and write operations within Oracle, you would normally want to configure some hard drive logicals with a minimum of six read and write spindles. On the UNIX platform, it is not a requirement that all of the logicals be identically configured. This provides additional flexibility in configuring the hardware.

The goal is to optimally configure the Oracle data files in this environment. If we have 50GB in indexes and data, we will see approximately 25GB of actual data files and 25GB of index data files with the OneWorld product. Remember, we want to separate the indexes and the actual data to maximize performance. Running some quick numbers for production, we need approximately 32 data files if we maintain a 800MB size. We need an additional 32 index data files for production. CRP has the same size requirements as production. The test data, however, has seven index and seven data files. Development uses test data, which means no additional requirements, and Pristine requires one of each.

We also need approximately 2GB of space per path code (the typical installation has four path codes). In this, however, we will use what we know about OneWorld to both save space and reduce complexity. In a production system with minimal amounts of custom development, the central objects are not used as much as the production data. Consequently, we can get by with larger data files. We will use two data files (one data and one index) of 1.5GB each.

NOTE

We also need to plan for control-table table space; however, we're not including it in this example because of its small relative size.

Our final count (excluding system, server maps, object librarian, and data dictionary table spaces) comes to a total of 152 data files (see Table 19-2).

Three data files should be spread out to each logical drive providing a nice distribution of data; however, some other considerations should be taken into account prior to making this move. First, since this is an enterprise server, we need to have actual OneWorld server code on this machine. We can either dedicate an entire logical drive to it or spread out the code and mount the drives so that OneWorld doesn't know

	Data Data Files		Index Data Files		
	Data	Path Code	Data	Path Code	
PRD733	32	1	32	1	
CRP733	32	1	32	1	
TST733	7	0	7	0	
DEV733	0	1	0	1	
PRT733	1	1	1	1	
Total	72	4	72	4	152

TABLE 19-2.   Data File Count

the difference. Second, since we are obviously using Oracle in this example (MS SQL Server and DB2/400 won't work on an HP9000), we also have redo logs and archive logs to accommodate. Just like the data and indexes, performance gains can be achieved if they are separated. Third, to speed up backup and recovery, it might be beneficial to save one or two logical drives for data dumps, OneWorld logging, and so on. Finally, you also have to accommodate the OS itself.

Taking all of these factors into consideration, we really have 25 logical devices to work with. Drives U05, U10, U15, U20, and U25 are being reserved for these other requirements. Still, simple math indicates that six data files per remaining logical drive adequately fulfill the dispersal requirements for database optimization.

But it's not that simple! Remember, we want to separate the data files and the index files. Does this mean that we should provide 12 logical drives for data and 12 for indexes? We could do this, but the name of the game is optimization. By spreading files, we are limiting disk contention. By separating data and indexes, we are further limiting disks as potential bottlenecks. But, does this mean that we should separate production indexes from CRP data? No! These are totally different environments, and by mixing these types of data files, we can further improve performance. With this in mind, we come up with a data design like the one shown in Table 19-3. (Use proddtat01…32.dbf and proddtai01…32.dbf.)

CONTROLLER 1

U01	U02	U03	U04
proddtat01.dbf	proddtat02.dbf	proddtat03.dbf	proddtat04.dbf
proddtat13.dbf	proddtat14.dbf	proddtat15.dbf	proddtat16.dbf
proddtat26.dbf	proddtat27.dbf	proddtat28.dbf	proddtat29.dbf
crpdtai06.dbf	crpdtai07.dbf	crpdtai08.dbf	crpdtai09.dbf
crpdtai19.dbf	crpdtai20.dbf	crpdtai21.dbf	crpdtai22.dbf
crpdtai32.dbf	devb733t01.dbf	testdtai01.dbf	testdtai02.dbf

CONTROLLER 2

U06	U07	U08	U09
proddtat05.dbf	proddtat06.dbf	proddtat07.dbf	proddtat08.dbf
proddtat17.dbf	proddtat18.dbf	proddtat19.dbf	proddtat20.dbf
proddtat30.dbf	proddtat31.dbf	proddtat32.dbf	crpdtai01.dbf
crpdtai10.dbf	crpdtai11.dbf	crpdtai12.dbf	crpdtai13.dbf
crpdtai23.dbf	crpdtai24.dbf	crpdtai25.dbf	crpdtai26.dbf
testdtai03.dbf	testdtai04.dbf	testdtai05.dbf	testdtai06.dbf

CONTROLLER 3

U11	U12	U13	U14
proddtat09.dbf	proddtat10.dbf	proddtat11.dbf	proddtat11.dbf
proddtat21.dbf	proddtat22.dbf	proddtat23.dbf	proddtat24.dbf
crpdtai02.dbf	crpdtai03.dbf	crpdtai04.dbf	crpdtai04.dbf
crpdtai14.dbf	crpdtai15.dbf	crpdtai16.dbf	crpdtai17.dbf
crpdtai27.dbf	crpdtai28.dbf	crpdtai29.dbf	crpdtai30.dbf
testdtai07.dbf	testdtat07.dbf	pristb733t01.dbf	pristb733i01.dbf

CONTROLLER 4

U16	U17	U18	U19
proddtat12.dbf	proddtai01.dbf	proddtai02.dbf	proddtai03.dbf
proddtat25.dbf	proddtai12.dbf	proddtai13.dbf	proddtai14.dbf
crpdtai05.dbf	proddtai24.dbf	proddtai25.dbf	proddtai26.dbf
crpdtai18.dbf	crpdtat04.dbf	crpdtat05.dbf	crpdtat06.dbf
crpdtai31.dbf	crpdtat16.dbf	crpdtat17.dbf	crpdtat18.dbf
pristdtat01.dbf	crpdtat28.dbf	crpdtat29.dbf	crpdtat30.dbf
	pristdtai01.dbf		

TABLE 19-3. Oracle Data File Breakout

CONTROLLER 5

U21	U22	U23	U24	
proddtai04.dbf	proddtai05.dbf	proddtai06.dbf	proddtai07.dbf	
proddtai15.dbf	proddtai16.dbf	proddtai17.dbf	proddtai18.dbf	
proddtai27.dbf	proddtai28.dbf	proddtai29.dbf	proddtai30.dbf	
crpdtat07.dbf	crpdtat08.dbf	crpdtat09.dbf	crpdtat10.dbf	
crpdtat19.dbf	crpdtat20.dbf	crpdtat21.dbf	crpdtat22.dbf	
crpdtat31.dbf	crpdtat32.dbf	devb733i01.dbf	testdtat01.dbf	

CONTROLLER 6

U26	U27	U28	U29	U30
proddtai08.dbf	proddtai09.dbf	proddtai10.dbf	proddtai11.dbf	proddtai11.dbf
proddtai19.dbf	proddtai20.dbf	proddtai21.dbf	proddtai22.dbf	proddtai23.dbf
proddtai31.dbf	proddtai32.dbf	crpdtat01.dbf	crpdtat02.dbf	crpdtat03.dbf
crpdtat11.dbf	crpdtat12.dbf	crpdtat13.dbf	crpdtat14.dbf	crpdtat15.dbf
crpdtat23.dbf	crpdtat24.dbf	crpdtat25.dbf	crpdtat26.dbf	crpdtat27.dbf
testdtat02.dbf	testdtat03.dbf	testdtat04.dbf	testdtat05.dbf	testdtat06.dbf

TABLE 19-3.   Oracle Data File Breakout (*continued*)

Our Apology After the Fact

That was a lengthy example of database optimization. An experienced DBA will take care of most of this optimization, but even after your database is optimized, you should do additional tasks regularly to ensure that the database is not the weak link in your project. Indexes and tables can become fragmented, which is especially true for tables that are highly transactional in nature. Databases like Oracle and MS SQL Server assign a certain amount of space to a table or index. As data is entered by employees, the table will reach its limit and request additional space from the RDBMS. Although the table will automatically expand to the required space, it usually won't be contiguous space. Because of this, the database will have to work harder, searching form data. We've seen some databases with up to 3,000 extents on a single table. Needless to say, this is not effective. Although you can ask different DBAs and get different answers as to how many extents you should have before you begin loosing performance, we say you should begin evaluating a table when it reaches 10 or more extents. This doesn't necessarily mean you should fix it if your table has that many extents, but you should start watching it closely. Some of the tables prone to fragmentation include F0911, F4201, F4211, F4101, F4111, F4301, and F4311.

So, how do you fix a fragmented table or index? If you dump the data via export, you can drop the indexes and table. Then you can re-create the table with a large single extent and increase its next extent size. We recommend looking at this data as part of your weekly database maintenance. If you are using Oracle 8i, you will find that the database does a significantly better job of optimizing the database. Although it doesn't eliminate the need for a DBA to monitor system performance, it does do a better job of managing the file structure.

Step 3: Optimize the Process

One of the fastest methods of optimizing a OneWorld process is evaluating the SQL statements being produced by the application itself. Luckily, J.D. Edwards gives you a perfect tool for doing this—the JDEDEBUG.LOG. Unless your RDBMS has a built-in SQL analyzer with the ability to look at SQL statements from specific machines or a specific process or unless you have purchased a third-party application with the ability to evaluate SQL statements (and a slew of applications are able to do this), the JDEDEBUG.LOG will quickly become your best friend. Even if you do have the ability to analyze your SQL database traffic, you might still find the JDEDEBUG.LOG simpler to work with and understand. Every direct SQL call made by a specific process is captured in this log. It also captures every BSFN (business functions) called by the system. (These BSFNs may also have specific database calls that have hidden potential.)

Using the JDEDEBUG.LOG, you can make an evaluation of the statement itself. These statements have three different points of opportunity. It is up to your DBA and custom developer to determine which of the three you have (if any) and what the best method of solving the issues are.

SQL Opportunities

First, check the SQL statement to identify if it is performing a full table scan. Do you see code like "SELECT * FROM PRODDTA.F4211?" That statement means select all rows and all columns from a specific table. If the table has 205 columns and several hundred thousand records, you can imagine how long it will take to return the results. This issue is generally resolved through educating the end user to use the QBE line (this will add a WHERE statement to the SQL statement generated) or through application redesign. Do you really need all of the columns and all of the rows of the table you are hitting? If you need only 25 of the columns, you could substantially decrease your database activity. Another potential at this juncture occurs if the statement reads "SELECT SDDOCO, SDLINID, SDAN8, SDNXTR FROM PRODDTA.F4211." Your DBA, OneWorld developer, or CNC administrator can verify if the PRODDTA.F4211 has an index with the same columns in that order. If it doesn't, you might be able to increase your application performance by adding a new index that corresponds to the statement.

Second, if the SQL statement contains a WHERE clause, check the columns in the clause itself. Do these columns have a corresponding index? If not, you can often substantially increase the performance of this statement by adding an appropriate index to the database. One thing to note, however: it is possible to slow performance on the database by adding too many indexes. To validate the addition of a specific index, add it to the database directly before modifying a OneWorld table definition. If it increases your overall performance, go ahead and modify the OneWorld table definition itself. This will ensure that you are able to regenerate this change and migrate it to future releases of the product.

Third, and this one is similar to the second opportunity, see if your SQL statement has an ORDER BY statement. If it does, you might be able to increase the speed of your process' SELECT, UPDATE, and DELETE statements even more by adding indexes. You want to add these indexes by following the same procedure that is described in the preceding paragraph. We often refer to this type of optimization as *low hanging fruit*. It is easy to identify, test, and implement.

Step 4: Apply Process Redesign

We can best illustrate the meaning of "applying process redesigns" with another example. Let's take the end-of-day processing requirements of the sales update UBE (R42800). The more records you have to process in this particular UBE, the slower it will go. To decrease the number of records, you could sell less, but we don't think management would approve of that solution. However, if you apply data selections based on the sales order type and location, you can quickly break it into multiple processes. Each of them will run faster than the single UBE. Even their combined time will be significantly less than that of the one UBE.

Certain batch jobs, primarily posting jobs, can't be run simultaneously. However, in this case, R42800 (sales update) is not a posting job, and several can be run at the same time. This saves even more time. If your batch engine server can run multiple processes simultaneously (seven, eight, or more), you can see significant time savings. You can also schedule these UBEs using the OneWorld scheduler. This will automate much of the overall process and will decrease the additional burdens associated with splitting up the process in the first place. You can redesign the process to be easy to administer and time efficient.

Are There Other Process Redesigns?

Some of the other opportunities provided by the OneWorld suite include processing various application functions asynchronously or in batch. Let's take the example of the P4210 table (Sales Order Entry application). As you add rows of detail to this application, BSFNs populate information throughout the grid form including item cost, description, and unit of measure, in addition to other columns. If you add multiple lines (5 widgets, 3 thingamabobs, and 25 whatnots), you can decide if the BSFN should immediately begin processing the line upon exit or wait until all items have been entered to process. Several applications allow this and other modifications to data selections and processing options. We recommend that you closely evaluate what process (batch or interactive) is considered too slow and then evaluate the options provided by the product itself.

Other items of consideration are a little more ambiguous. Let's take the example of nightly processing. Exactly when you process some functions will either adversely or positively affect the overall process design—for example, running a large report during your peak sales time or doing end-of-month processing during the middle of the day. Depending on your business requirements, you need to intelligently balance system resources with time and business requirements. This balance completely depends on your company's requirements for reporting, their type and volume of work, and the ability of their architectural design. Don't forget that one of the goals behind optimization is improving performance without the requirement of adding hardware. If your organization doesn't care about effectively using what they have and they have large sums of money at their disposal, you can always scale the OneWorld product to fit your needs.

Let's provide one more example of the process redesign. The process for performing a B733.1 EDI outbound 850 transaction has three steps. Step 1 is a batch version submission of R43500 (see Figure 19-1). When submitted, this batch automatically extracts records from the F4301 and F4311 tables and populates the designated F47 series tables. It also advances the record statuses in the F43 series tables so that the UBE will not grab the same record twice.

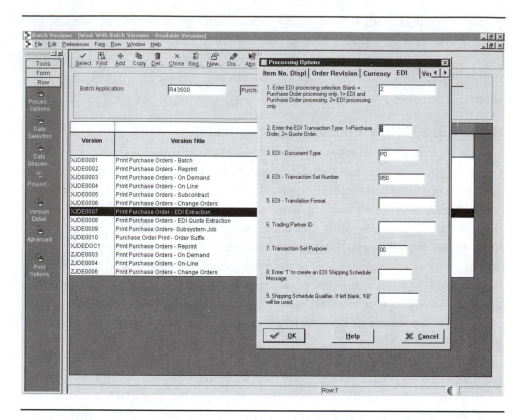

FIGURE 19-1. Processing Options associated with the R43500

Step 2 is a batch version submission of the R47012C application (see Figure 19-2). This batch extracts unprocessed records from the F47 series tables and creates a flat file in a specific location (this is determined by processing options).

Step 3 is a batch version submission of R47017 (see Figure 19-3). This UBE updates a column in the F47 series tables to Y for the update as sent flag. This flag is used when extracting records from the F47 series tables for the flat file. The R47012C specifically queries for records that don't have a Y in this field. This step ensures that the next flat file won't contain the same records as the previous one.

If you want to automate this process, you can launch these UBEs using the batch scheduler in OneWorld. But what happens when one of the processes takes longer than

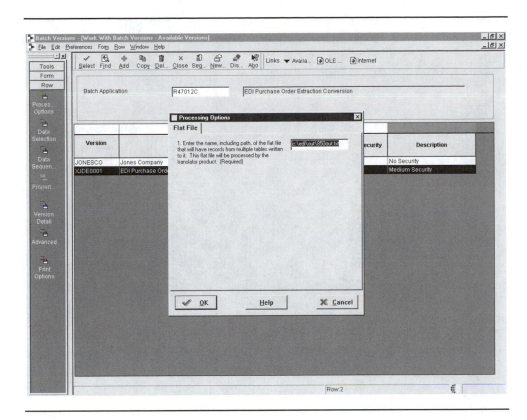

FIGURE 19-2. R47012C application

Troubleshooting

normal? If you've scheduled the processes to occur many times a day, UBEs running into other scheduled jobs would be an issue. Even if all of the UBEs are launched into a single instance queue, they would back up, causing consternation if not an actual problem.

Redesigning This Process

Using the RDA (report design aid), you can link each UBE to automatically call the next one before exiting. This will allow you to launch a single UBE, which won't stop until all of it is completed. It is an easy redesign that makes scheduling this overall process much easier. Notice in Figure 19-4, the second to the last line of code calls another UBE prior to the final "end if."

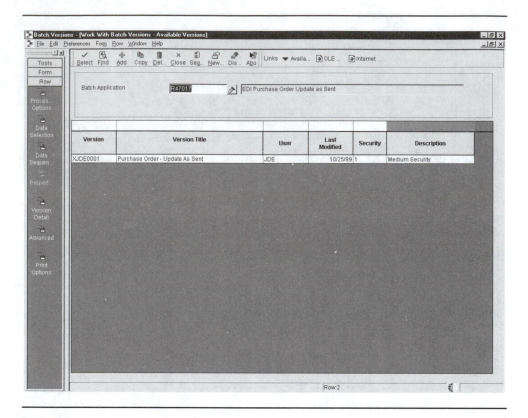

FIGURE 19-3.   R47017

Step 5: Apply CNC Concepts Where Available

When possible, you should apply whatever CNC options are available. If you can segment certain people to separate application servers, do it. It will increase your systems complexity, but it will also streamline your system's resource requirements. It might even be the difference between having a solution that works and one that doesn't.

Let's take the first example and see how applying CNC concepts could have helped that organization. We know they didn't want to add additional hardware to the mix, but what if, because of the number of sales people they had, their system simply couldn't process all of the pick slips necessary? They would first optimize the hardware and OS and then optimize the database, followed by optimizing the OneWorld process. After that, they would attempt to redesign the process. Finally, they would be forced to apply CNC solutions. Many organizations start with this solution; however, we feel that the other options should be tried first.

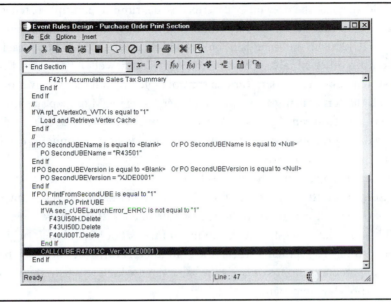

```
Event Rules Design - Purchase Order Print Section                    _ □ ×
File  Edit  Options  Insert
✓ | ✗ ⮹ 🗎 ⛉ | 🖫 | ♀ ⊘ | 📱 | 🖨 | ✗ | 🔍
· End Section                    ▾ | x= | ? | f(o) | f(s) | ⁙ | ⁍≣ | ⛁ | 🖺
        F4211 Accumulate Sales Tax Summary                                  ▲
      End If
   End If
   //
   If VA rpt_cVertexOn_WTX is equal to "1"
      Load and Retrieve Vertex Cache
   End If
   //
   If PO SecondUBEName is equal to <Blank>     Or PO SecondUBEName is equal to <Null>
      PO SecondUBEName = "R43501"
   End If
   If PO SecondUBEVersion is equal to <Blank>   Or PO SecondUBEVersion is equal to <Null>
      PO SecondUBEVersion = "XJDE0001"
   End If
   If PO PrintFromSecondUBE is equal to "1"
      Launch PO Print UBE
      If VA sec_cUBELaunchError_ERRC is not equal to "1"
         F43UI50H.Delete
         F43UI50D.Delete
         F40UI00T.Delete
      End If
      CALL( UBE:R47012C , Ver: XJDE0001 )
   End If
   End If                                                                   ▼
Ready                                    Line : 47                    ⧉
```

FIGURE 19-4.   UBE calling another UBE

In the previously described situation, they could add several small application servers or another larger one. We'll start with adding several small ones because the normal PC today (with processing speeds over 700 MHz and available RAM up to 512MB) could make reasonable (albeit small) application servers. If this company had 100 retail sites, they could add 25 to 100 small servers (depending on the sales volume) to their CNC design. These machines would be located wherever the database or enterprise server was located. Their CNC administrator would then remap specific users or groups to the other servers, which would allow the power of the OneWorld design to accomplish their specific business requirements.

Let's consider other CNC opportunities. In the B733 base product, the R42800 Sales Update Batch uses the F42UI800 table as a temporary workspace. Based on data selection, records are written to this table and crunched, and the results are written back to the F42 series tables. Once properly processed, these records are then deleted from the F42UI800. The only problem with this process is that data corruption could (and often would) occur if the table had more than 1,200 records.

Previously, we split this UBE into several different versions based on data selection and then decided to run several at the same time. Unfortunately, although splitting the batch would alleviate the previously described issue, running multiple batches at the same time would cause it again. CNC can help this situation. We could create several different F42UI800s in different data sources and then use OCM to direct each batch version to use a different table. This solution works quite well. By copying this table into the system, object librarian, various control tables, data dictionary, various central objects, and the server map data sources and then using OCM to map specific users to these other tables, we can effectively decrease the number of records in the table. This ensures no data corruption and speeds up overall processing by running seven, eight, or nine batches simultaneously.

If they still wanted to use the batch scheduler in this scenario, they would set up custom users to run the batches (refer to Chapter 13). They can then schedule these custom users to run the batches in the appropriate queues. If they have the ability (through historic data) to estimate the number of transactions per batch (using the data selections placed on them earlier), they can intelligently load these batch files to bring them to an end at approximately the same time, which will help their overall efforts in end-of-day processing.

Summarizing the Five-Step Optimization Process

The following is a summary of the five-step optimization process. We thought that it might be handy if there was a single, quick list for reference purposes.

1. Optimize the OS (and don't forget the hardware).

2. Optimize the RDBMS.

3. Optimize the process (you might have development associated with this step).

4. Apply process redesign (think outside of the box for clever solutions).

5. Apply CNC techniques (this step could include additional hardware but doesn't have to).

Creating Multiple Queues on a Server

Previously, we have referred to having more than one UBE running at a time so in this section, we will describe setting up multiple queues. Using queues enables you to manage your batch processing requirements. To accommodate UBEs that must be run sequentially, you can create a single queue and then run these UBEs through this queue. Launching these UBEs one by one will simply enter them in a queue where they will be run in the order launched. To facilitate UBEs that can be run simultaneously, you create multiple queues with the same name. The only real limit to the number of queues you create is the number your server can handle. We've seen one server handle over 25 queues (albeit, it was a big server).

We often hear people refer to "multithreaded queues." In truth, the UBE queue is single threaded. A multithreaded queue is a queue that uses multiple processors simultaneously to perform work. In place of this, OneWorld can be configured to have multiple queues with the same name allowing multiple UBEs to be run simultaneously. This is different than multithreaded queues. Consequently, when someone asks you if you can make the UBE queues multithreaded, you now know enough to further qualify what the person really means before you undertake a multimillion dollar rewrite of the OneWorld foundation code—code that, by the way, you can't even access.

Multiple Queues

There are several reasons for creating multiple queues. Multiple queues are, after all, a simple optimization that rapidly returns the investment of time and effort. To better understand UBE versions, you should refer to Chapter 8. In addition, we will go into some detail on the UBE process itself.

UBE Process

The batch process is relatively straightforward. A UBE is submitted to a server through the P98305 table (Batch Version application). Most users access this by simply double-clicking on the appropriate menu icon. They rarely realize that by doing so, they have actually launched the P98305 application. The second most common way UBEs are launched is by clicking a button in an application—for example, the sales order process. By completing the sales order, a batch job is automatically launched to print a pick slip. These batches are often launched against a subsystem. (A subsystem is a specially configured UBE that continually checks for certain conditions to occur. When these predefined conditions do occur, the subsystem automatically performs another step. In the preceding example, a particular version of the R42520 Pick Slip batch version, when launched, looks for other specific versions of R42520 populating the F986113 table, Subsystem Job Master, with a W status ("W" stands for waiting). When this occurs, the subsystem automatically grabs the record, processes it, and then deletes it from the F986113 table.)

Another way that batch versions are submitted is through a linked process. Many batch versions call other batch versions during their execution—for example, printing checks. The R07231 Print Checks UBE is called by another process within the AP process. It does not have to be launched separately. There are many other examples of these types of processing dependencies.

UBE Submission   UBEs are processed through the OneWorld system in a couple of different ways; however, we'll provide a quick overview of just one of them. A user submits a UBE to an application server (this could also be an enterprise server), which populates the F986110 table with a record including a BLOB (binary large object) containing information specific to the submitted version (including processing options, data selection, and printer definitions). When the application server's batch queue services start, each JDEQUEUE service begins continually querying the F986110 table for records that are in a waiting status for that particular server. When the new record is inserted into that table, the JDEQUEUE process initiates a call reading the record and processing it with the RUNUBE application. Part of the process includes merging the UBE specifications (information contained in the BLOB) into the existing server files (RDASPEC, RDATEXT, GBRSPEC, GBRTEXT, and POTEXT). Once merged, the job is performed, and the results are generated in a PDF format (and, optionally, a comma-delimited format). The F986110 table is updated with an "S," then a "P," and ultimately a "D" (which stand for submitting, processing, and done, respectively).

Why Add Queues

Going into that much detail when explaining UBEs in the previous section was necessary to show the area of weakness in the process and why you might want to optimize your system by adding additional batch queues. If your organization launches multiple batch jobs of varying lengths, you can see (through the process) that your server could easily fall behind. By adding additional queues, you are able to perform more work in the same amount of time. As mentioned earlier, you can run as many of these queues as your server can handle.

CAUTION

If you set up the queues, they can be run simultaneously. If you set up too many, you can slow down your system instead of speeding it up.

Setting up multiple queues will allow you to speed up your overall processing by two, five, or nine times, or more. This is also particularly helpful when you have users who insist on running large UBEs during the middle of the day. These UBEs won't stop the rest of your business.

The Required Steps

Let's get down to how we add batch queues to servers. Unfortunately, each of the platforms has its own method. In the following sections, we'll go into detail concerning each of the three major platforms (Windows NT, UNIX, and AS/400). In this section, however, we will cover a part that all three platforms have in common.

Increasing the Number of JDEQUEUE Processes

Increasing the number of JDEQUEUE processes is not the same as increasing the number of queues. In the previously described UBE process, remember that the JDEQUEUE simply looks at the F986110 table and identifies when an unprocessed record is in a waiting status. Once identified, it passes the UBE to the actual queue. Although there is often a one-to-one relationship between the JDEQUEUE and the queue itself, this is not a requirement. As you increase the number of available queues, you will be more likely to see a difference in these numbers.

Adding more of the JDEQUEUE services is almost as easy as pointing and clicking. Each of the servers' JDE.INIs contains a dispatch UBE function _2 that defines the number of JDEQUEUE services.

```
[JDENET_KERNEL_DEF2]
dispatchDLLName=jdekrnl.dll
dispatchDLLFunction=_JDEK_DispatchUBEMessage@28
maxNumberOfProcesses=1
beginningMsgTypeRange=256
endingMsgTypeRange=511
newProcessThresholdRequests=0
numberOfAutoStartProcesses=0
```

There is a relationship between all of the kernel services and the maximum number of kernels. When you increase the dispatch UBE kernels, be sure to increase the maximum number of kernels as well.

Troubleshooting

```
[JDENET]
netPgmName=jdenet_n
krnlPgmName=jdenet_k
serviceNameListen=6008
serviceNameConnect=6008
maxNetProcesses=5
maxNetConnections=1250
maxKernelProcesses=50
maxKernelRanges=12
```

Once you've made the change to the server's JDE.INI, save the change and reboot the OneWorld services. You don't have to reboot the entire machine (that was for your AS/400 and UNIX devotees who firmly believe that you shouldn't have to IPL (reboot the server) more than once every three years). Instead, follow whatever steps are necessary for stopping and starting OneWorld processes.

N O T E

On Windows NT, use the work with services application located in the Control Panel. Locate the JDE B733 Update 2 Queue (or other release equivalent) and click the Stop button (refer to Figure 19-5).

Services			
Service	Status	Startup	
DHCP Client		Disabled	**Close**
Directory Replicator		Manual	Start
EventLog	Started	Automatic	
FTP Publishing Service	Started	Automatic	**Stop**
IIS Admin Service	Started	Manual	
JDE Update 2 B733 Network	Started	Automatic	**Pause**
JDE Update 2 B733 Queue	Started	Automatic	Continue
License Logging Service	Started	Automatic	
Messenger	Started	Automatic	Startup...
MSDTC	Started	Automatic	
			HW Profiles...
Startup Parameters:			Help

FIGURE 19-5.   Windows NT services

Once these processes have stopped running, highlight the JDE B733 Update 2 Network service and click Stop. Ensure that all JDE-related processes actually stopped using the Windows NT Task Manager. Then start them back up in the reverse order (start the network services first).

On UNIX, run the EndOneWorld.sh script located in the B733/system/bin32 directory after logging on as jde (or the appropriate UNIX user—for example, jdeb7332). Run the rmics.sh script located in the same directory to clean up any existing semaphores. Run a **ps – ef|grep jde** (or the appropriate UNIX user) to ensure that no processes are hanging. If any are hanging, use the **kill –9** command to stop them. Once all processes have ended, run the RunOneWorld.sh script to restart the services.

On AS/400, log on to the server as the OneWorld user and enter the ENDNET command. Follow this with WRKACTJOB and verify that the OneWorld services came down. Type in CLRIPC to clean up the OneWorld environment and enter STARTNET to restart the OneWorld processes.

Before we outline how to add queues, remember that prior to making a modification to any J.D. Edwards OneWorld delivered script or JDE.INI, you should make a copy of the original. Just because you have decided to use the information in this book does not excuse you from taking the usual recovery precautions.

Increasing the Number of Queues on Windows NT

Since each platform has its own method of increasing the number of queues available, we arbitrarily decided to start with Windows NT. Similar to the JDEQUEUE process, you increase the number of actual queue processes through the application server's (this could also be the enterprise server's) JDE.INI. Open the JDE.INI located in the directory x:\jdewardsoneworld\ddp\b7332\system\bin32.

N O T E

On B733.1 or earlier, the path would look like this: x:\oneworld\ddp\b7331\system\bin32. Replace the "x" with the drive letter where the OneWorld application code is located.

Find the section of the JDE.INI with [NETWORK QUEUE SETTINGS] as its header. Two items must be modified in this section. First, the number of queues (UBEQueues=x) needs to be increased. Second, you need to identify the queues by name (for example, UBEQueue1=QB7332, UBEQueue2=QB7332, UBEQueue3=QB7332, UBEQueue4=PBATCH).

```
[NETWORK QUEUE SETTINGS]
QEnv=PRD733
QUser=JDE
QPassword=JDE
QueueDelay=30
UBEPriority=5
JDENETTimeout=60
UBEQueues=1
UBEQueue1=QB7332
PackageQueues=1
PKGQueue1=QB7332
SpecInstallQueues=1
SpcQueue1=QB7332
KillImmediate=1
```

This second part enables you to decide the number of simultaneous runs. Let's take the example requirement of running five UBEs simultaneously: one accounting queue and three end-of-day processing queues. You would have 11 total queues. We didn't explain (although you can see it in the JDE.INI excerpt previously shown) that there is a package queue and a specification installation queue in addition to the UBE queues, which accounts for the total of 11. For the example just provided, your [NETWORK QUEUE SETTINGS] would look like the following:

```
[NETWORK QUEUE SETTINGS]
QEnv=PRD733
QUser=JDE
QPassword=JDE
QueueDelay=30
UBEPriority=5
JDENETTimeout=60
UBEQueues=9
UBEQueue1=QB7332
```

```
UBEQueue2=QB7332
UBEQueue3=QB7332
UBEQueue4=QB7332
UBEQueue5=QB7332
UBEQueue6=ACTB7332
UBEQueue7=EODB7332
UBEQueue8=EODB7332
UBEQueue9=EODB7332
PackageQueues=1
PKGQueue1=QB7332
SpecInstallQueues=1
SpcQueue1=QB7332
KillImmediate=1
```

NOTE

Again, although you don't have to have a one-to-one ratio of JDEQUEUEs to queues, it would be beneficial to increase the number in this scenario. We would recommend at least three for this configuration:
[JDENET_KERNEL_DEF2]
dispatchDLLName=jdekrnl.dll
dispatchDLLFunction=_JDEK_DispatchUBEMessage@28
maxNumberOfProcesses=3
beginningMsgTypeRange=256
endingMsgTypeRange=511
newProcessThresholdRequests=0
numberOfAutoStartProcesses=0

The next time you start your OneWorld services, you automatically launch these new queues.

Increasing the Number of UBE Queues on UNIX

UNIX does not use the JDE.INI to control the number and names of active queues on the server. Rather, it uses the script designed for starting OneWorld services to launch the UBE queues and the script for ending services to kill the queues (RunOneWorld.sh and

EndOneWorld.sh, respectively). The RunOneWorld.sh script is where you would add additional queue applications, including multiple numbers of a queue with identical names and queues with different names (that is, if you wanted to create a queue where you were guaranteed only one UBE would process at any given time, you would add a single entry with a unique name in the RunOneWorld.sh script).

The easiest method of adding additional queues to a UNIX server is by copying an existing queue entry using a text editor (VI or another text editor). If you want to create a queue with the same name, simply change the log number to a sequential, unused number. If you want to change the name of the queue, change both the queue name and the log number. This will ensure that any logging done will be to a unique log file making it easier to troubleshoot potential problems.

NOTE

Be sure to copy the ampersand (&) at the end of each UBE line. It tells UNIX to run the runque.sh script in the background.

Killing the UNIX Queues   You don't need to add killques to the EndOneWorld.sh script if the only modification you've made is adding additional queues with the JDE delivered name. However, if you have added queues with different names, you need to add a line calling a killque process with the specific name of the queue you added.

An Example   All of this OneWorld/UNIX mumbo-jumbo may confuse you, but there is nothing like a good example to bring it back into focus. Consider this example the doctor's prescribed eyewear for understanding UNIX queues. In the following, we will work with a company that we've discussed before. They are a retailer (their actual system is Windows NT, but we'll pretend they have UNIX), and they have certain processing requirements including single process capability for multiple batch posting jobs, multiple end-of-day processing requirements, separate requirements for processing up to five UBEs simultaneously (we will use the same examples provided in the NT example: QB7332, ACTB7332, and EODB7332).

Their initial RunOneWorld.sh and EndOneWorld.sh scripts had the following
sections listed. (This is for the B733.2 version of OneWorld. If your version is different,
your scripts may vary widely from the following.)

Original RunOneWorld.sh

```
OWUSR="JDEB7332"
OWPWD="JDEB7332"
OWENV="PRD733"
OWQUE1="QB7332"
OWQUE2="QB7332"


echo "     Starting OneWorld spec install queue..." >> $LOGFILE
$SYSTEM/bin32/runque.sh $OWUSR $OWPWD $OWENV $OWQUE1 001 5 >
$SYSTEM/bin32/specque.log 2>&1 &
echo "     Starting OneWorld batch queues..." >> $LOGFILE
$SYSTEM/bin32/runque.sh $OWUSR $OWPWD $OWENV $OWQUE1 UBE 5 >
$SYSTEM/bin32/ubeque1.log 2>&1 &
$SYSTEM/bin32/runque.sh $OWUSR $OWPWD $OWENV $OWQUE2 UBE 5 >
$SYSTEM/bin32/ubeque2.log 2>&1 &
echo "     Starting OneWorld package queue..." >> $LOGFILE
$SYSTEM/bin32/runque.sh $OWUSR $OWPWD $OWENV $OWQUE1 PKG 5 >
$SYSTEM/bin32/pkgque.log 2>&1 &
```

Original EndOneWorld.sh

```
OWUSR="JDEB7332"
OWPWD="JDEB7332"
OWENV="PRD733"
OWQUE1="QB7332"
OWQUE2="QB7332"


echo $(date) "   Stopping Spec Install queue..." >> $LOGFILE
    $SYSTEM/bin32/killque.sh $OWUSR $OWPWD $OWENV $OWQUE1 001 >> $LOGFILE 2>& 1
    echo $(date) "   Stopping Batch queues..." >> $LOGFILE
    $SYSTEM/bin32/killque.sh $OWUSR $OWPWD $OWENV $OWQUE1 UBE >> $LOGFILE 2>& 1
    if [ ! "$OWQUE1" = "$OWQUE2" ] ; then
        $SYSTEM/bin32/killque.sh $OWUSR $OWPWD $OWENV $OWQUE1 UBE >> $LOGFILE 2>& 1
fi
    echo $(date) "   Stopping Package queue..." >> $LOGFILE
    $SYSTEM/bin32/killque.sh $OWUSR $OWPWD $OWENV $OWQUE1 PKG >> $LOGFILE 2>& 1
```

After their CNC administrator modified their scripts, the pertinent sections looked like the following:

CAUTION

We have not added the scripts in their entirety in the original or revised versions due to space constraints. We have simply added the pertinent sections of them for the examples provided.

Revised RunOneWorld.sh

```
OWUSR="JDEB7332"
OWPWD="JDEB7332"
OWENV="PRD733"
OWQUE1="QB7332"
OWQUE2="QB7332"
OWQUE3="QB7332"
OWQUE4="QB7332"
OWQUE5="QB7332"
OWQUE6="ACTB7332"
OWQUE7="EODB7332"
OWQUE8="EODB7332"
OWQUE9="EODB7332"


echo "    Starting OneWorld spec install queue..." >> $LOGFILE
$SYSTEM/bin32/runque.sh $OWUSR $OWPWD $OWENV $OWQUE1 001 5 > $SYSTEM/bin32/specque.log 2>&1 &
echo "    Starting OneWorld batch queues..." >> $LOGFILE
$SYSTEM/bin32/runque.sh $OWUSR $OWPWD $OWENV $OWQUE1 UBE 5 > $SYSTEM/bin32/ubeque1.log 2>&1 &
$SYSTEM/bin32/runque.sh $OWUSR $OWPWD $OWENV $OWQUE2 UBE 5 > $SYSTEM/bin32/ubeque2.log 2>&1 &
$SYSTEM/bin32/runque.sh $OWUSR $OWPWD $OWENV $OWQUE3 UBE 5 > $SYSTEM/bin32/ubeque3.log 2>&1 &
$SYSTEM/bin32/runque.sh $OWUSR $OWPWD $OWENV $OWQUE4 UBE 5 > $SYSTEM/bin32/ubeque4.log 2>&1 &
$SYSTEM/bin32/runque.sh $OWUSR $OWPWD $OWENV $OWQUE5 UBE 5 > $SYSTEM/bin32/ubeque5.log 2>&1 &
$SYSTEM/bin32/runque.sh $OWUSR $OWPWD $OWENV $OWQUE6 UBE 5 > $SYSTEM/bin32/ubeque6.log 2>&1 &
$SYSTEM/bin32/runque.sh $OWUSR $OWPWD $OWENV $OWQUE7 UBE 5 > $SYSTEM/bin32/ubeque7.log 2>&1 &
$SYSTEM/bin32/runque.sh $OWUSR $OWPWD $OWENV $OWQUE8 UBE 5 > $SYSTEM/bin32/ubeque8.log 2>&1 &
$SYSTEM/bin32/runque.sh $OWUSR $OWPWD $OWENV $OWQUE9 UBE 5 > $SYSTEM/bin32/ubeque9.log 2>&1 &
echo "    Starting OneWorld package queue..." >> $LOGFILE
$SYSTEM/bin32/runque.sh $OWUSR $OWPWD $OWENV $OWQUE1 PKG 5 >
$SYSTEM/bin32/pkgque.log 2>&1 &
```

Revised EndOneWorld.sh

```
OWUSR="JDEB7332"
OWPWD="JDEB7332"
OWENV="PRD733"
OWQUE1="QB7332"
OWQUE2="QB7332"
OWQUE3="QB7332"
OWQUE4="QB7332"
OWQUE5="QB7332"
OWQUE6="ACTB7332"
OWQUE7="EODB7332"
OWQUE8="EODB7332"
OWQUE9="EODB7332"

echo $(date) "   Stopping Spec Install queue..." >> $LOGFILE
    $SYSTEM/bin32/killque.sh $OWUSR $OWPWD $OWENV $OWQUE1 001 >> $LOGFILE 2>& 1
    echo $(date) "   Stopping Batch queues..." >> $LOGFILE
        $SYSTEM/bin32/killque.sh $OWUSR $OWPWD $OWENV $OWQUE1 UBE >> $LOGFILE 2>& 1
        $SYSTEM/bin32/killque.sh $OWUSR $OWPWD $OWENV $OWQUE2 UBE >> $LOGFILE 2>& 1
        $SYSTEM/bin32/killque.sh $OWUSR $OWPWD $OWENV $OWQUE3 UBE >> $LOGFILE 2>& 1
        $SYSTEM/bin32/killque.sh $OWUSR $OWPWD $OWENV $OWQUE4 UBE >> $LOGFILE 2>& 1
      $SYSTEM/bin32/killque.sh $OWUSR $OWPWD $OWENV $OWQUE5 UBE >> $LOGFILE 2>& 1
      $SYSTEM/bin32/killque.sh $OWUSR $OWPWD $OWENV $OWQUE6 UBE >> $LOGFILE 2>& 1
      $SYSTEM/bin32/killque.sh $OWUSR $OWPWD $OWENV $OWQUE7 UBE >> $LOGFILE 2>& 1
      $SYSTEM/bin32/killque.sh $OWUSR $OWPWD $OWENV $OWQUE8 UBE >> $LOGFILE 2>& 1
      $SYSTEM/bin32/killque.sh $OWUSR $OWPWD $OWENV $OWQUE9 UBE >> $LOGFILE 2>& 1
echo $(date) "   Stopping Package queue..." >> $LOGFILE
    $SYSTEM/bin32/killque.sh $OWUSR $OWPWD $OWENV $OWQUE1 PKG >> $LOGFILE 2>& 1
```

We hope it is clearer now, but if not, keep the following warning in mind. Prior to modifying any provided J.D. Edwards OneWorld script, you should make a copy of the original. This enables you to recover from any mistakes you might make during this process. If you (as the CNC administrator) have questions concerning the modification of these scripts, consult with your UNIX administrator. If this doesn't resolve your issues (or if you are the UNIX administrator), contact the company you are working with on CNC-related issues. If you are not actively working with a company to ensure your CNC setup, you can call the J.D. Edwards OneWorld Response Line (800 289-2999) for assistance or contact your J.D. Edwards OneWorld Account Manager who can get you in touch with someone who can assist you in this matter.

Troubleshooting

Starting Queues on the Fly

If you have a backlog of UBEs that you need to quickly complete, you can launch additional queues by entering the same command seen in the RunOneWorld.sh script with a minor modification. Simply use the command exactly as follows (and include the ampersand at the end) at a UNIX command prompt and hit ENTER. This can be done as many times as necessary to help alleviate the back log.

1. Log on to UNIX as the appropriate OneWorld account (for example, JDEB7332).

2. Run the following command. The JDE JDE can be replaced with any legitimate OneWorld user and password. PRD733 can be replaced with any valid environment on the server (obviously, you want to pick the environment where the backlog exists). QB7332 can be replaced by whichever queue is backlogged. UbequeX.log should be replaced with the sequential number of the queue you are starting.

   ```
   $SYSTEM/bin32/runque.sh JDE JDE PRD733 QB7332 UBE 5 >
   $SYSTEM/bin32/ubequeX.log 2>&1 &
   ```

3. Repeat step 2 as many times as you want to launch the number of queues you want.

4. Log out of UNIX when complete.

Be careful when using this process; if you add more than your server is able to handle, you could slow the process. In addition, if adding more queues causes a system instability, these queues could crash. If they do, you might have problems on your hands, especially if they crash at the wrong time during the UBE's processing. This could cause data corruption, among other problems.

Increasing the Queues on the AS/400

As indicated earlier, each platform has its own method of increasing the number of queues for processing batch files. The AS/400 is certainly no exception to this rule. In particular, OneWorld on the AS/400 uses the actual subsystem shipped with the OS/400: QBATCH. During a OneWorld installation, you add a job queue called QBAT733 to the QBATCH subsystem. You have two options at this point. You can either change the job queue specifications on QBAT733 to allow multiple jobs to run simultaneously, or add another job queue that you then specify to run multiple processes. We recommend you make the QBAT733 job queue able to handle more than one job simultaneously. You should then add another job queue that can process only a single job at a time, which will enable you to run some batches one at a time. All of this is done strictly using the OS/400 instead of JDE.INIs or scripts.

This process of increasing the queues on the AS/400 is one of the major differences between the other two platforms and the AS/400. Because subsystems and job queues are an integral part of the operating system, rather than simply adding additional job queues, you enable one of the queues to run multiple jobs simultaneously. The subsystem itself is multithreaded even though the individual processes within the queue still run against a single processor. In this case, the AS/400 is like the other platforms.

Adding a Job Queue to QBATCH   This process allows you to add multiple job queues to the QBATCH subsystem. You can configure them as multiple queues with a single job name or with multiple job queue names to fit your specific requirements. Remember, certain jobs within OneWorld require being run sequentially. These jobs need a queue that can have only a single active job at any one time. From the OS/400 command line, enter the following:

1. CRTJOBQ JOBQ(QGPL/JASTEST). Refer to Figure 19-6.

2. ADDJOBQE SBSD(QBATCH) JOBQ(JASTEST) SEQNBR(60) (You need to modify the sequence number to ensure that there is no contention with existing job queues.) See Figure 19-7.

3. VERIFY - WRKSBSD SBSD(QBATCH). This is shown in Figure 19-8.

4. 5=DISPLAY, as shown in Figure 19-9.

5. CHOOSE 6. Job queue entries (as represented in Figure 19-10).

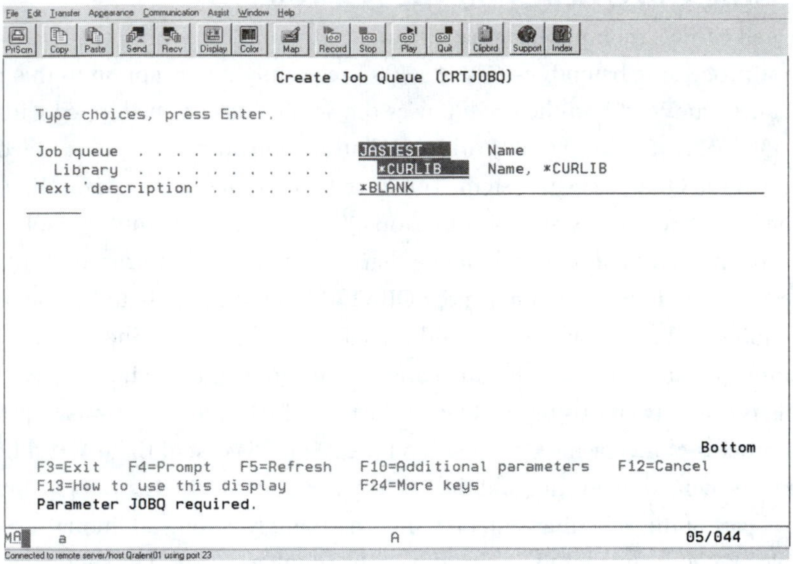

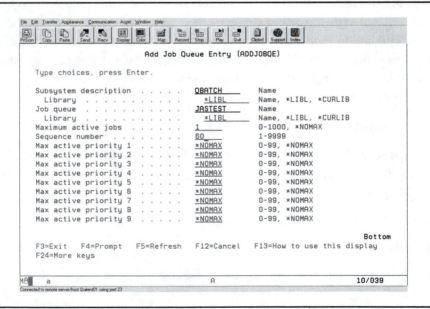

FIGURE 19-6.   Creating a job queue

FIGURE 19-7.   Modifying the sequence number

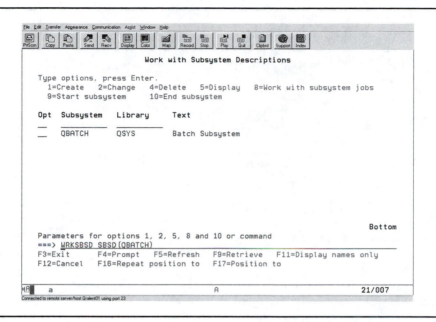

FIGURE 19-8.   Verify the job queue you just created

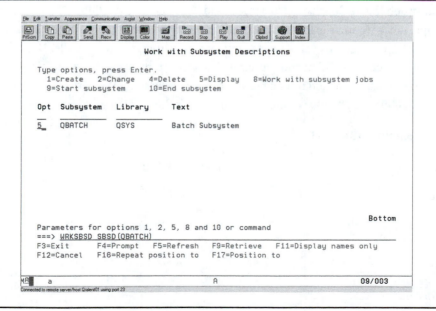

FIGURE 19-9.   Display QBATCH

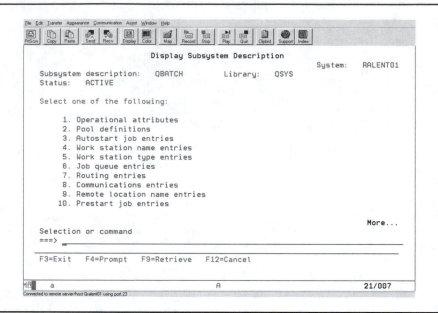

FIGURE 19-10.   Job queue entries

Making a Job Queue Capable of Multiprocessing   To change the QBAT733 queue to run multiple jobs , we use the following OS/400 command. One of the variables is Maximum Active Jobs. Change this value to as many jobs as your server can handle. Don't forget to monitor processor and memory utilization when you increase the number of concurrent jobs. If you add too many, you can adversely affect the performance of the server itself. At the OS/400 command prompt, enter the following:

WRKJOBQ QBAT733

Press ENTER. Select #2 for change and then press ENTER.

Enter the number of jobs you want to run simultaneously in the Maximum Active Jobs field and choose Save. The changes are instantaneous and do not require re-IPLing the system.

Changing Your UBE Version to Take Advantage of New Queues

The good news is that there is nothing you need to do to enable batch applications to use multiple queues (if you add additional QB7332 queues, the UBEs submitted will automatically use them). When you add queues with different names, you must direct the batch application to use these new queues instead of the default queues. To push certain UBEs to certain queues, you make a change to the UBE itself with the P98305 table (Batch Versions application). If you highlight a specific version, you can check the version out to your local fat client as shown in Figure 19-11 (refer to Chapter 8 for more detail).

Once you've checked the version out (doesn't the power to modify objects feel good?), you can click the Detail button on the W98305A form to view the version details form (W98305E). Notice that the following example shows that the Job Queue (alias jobque) field is blank (see Figure 19-12). This tells the system to use the default job queue. If, however, you put a specific name of a batch queue in this field, save it, and then check the version back into the server, you will have changed where the batch is submitted by default.

Under the Covers   The reason that the previously described process works is that the queue will process records in the F986110 only for a specific server in a W status with a specific queue name. If you change the batch version queue submission previously listed but do not add the queue name, the version goes into the F986110 but never actually processes.

Troubleshooting

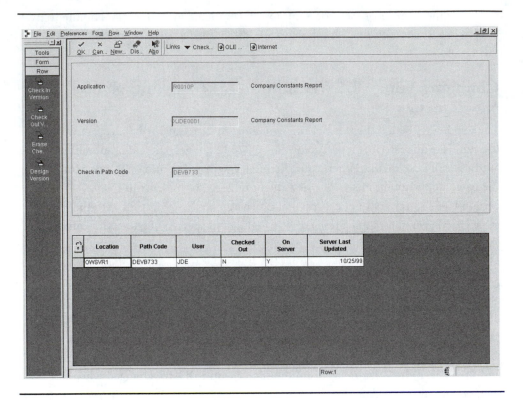

FIGURE 19-11. Checking out versions to the fat client

Summary

This chapter has been dedicated to optimizing the OneWorld product to best suit your organization's needs. Most of this optimization or tuning can be done without requiring additional hardware or software. Our recommendation is that you identify each potential bottleneck in your system and run it through the unpatented five-step process outlined in the preceding pages. The odds are that you will be pleasantly surprised by the outcome.

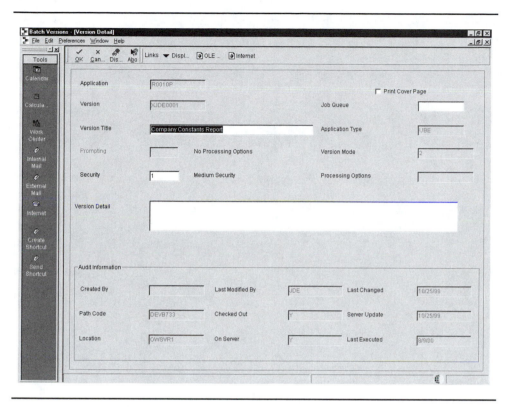

FIGURE 19-12.   The Version Detail form (W98305E)

CHAPTER 20

Log Files

Log Files Available

Logging Settings in the JDE.INI File

What is one thing that a system administrator needs to review, but hates to look at? Log files! When you are a system administrator, looking at log files usually means you have a problem. However, when you know what to look for in these log files, you can troubleshoot system problems faster so you are not at work at 4:00 A.M. working on an issue.

In this chapter, we are going to cover some of the common logging techniques, and some that are not so common. We will talk about:

- Log files available

- Logging settings in the JDE.INI

Log Files Available

When you start working on OneWorld systems, one of the first things you need to know is where to look for errors. This is what truly defines a good OneWorld system administrator from an average system administrator. To become a good OneWorld system administrator, you will first need to know what log files are available to you on your enterprise server. We will cover the more common log files first and then move on to more advanced log files.

Server JDE.LOG files

Let's start with the JDE.LOG file on the enterprise server, one of the simplest log files to read. This log file contains the high-level errors that have occurred on a system and is a good place to start when troubleshooting problems on your enterprise server. Understanding how these files are created and named will help you read them. When you look at your enterprise server, you will notice that you have more then one JDE.LOG file at a time. This is another reason why you need to understand how logging works.

The JDE.LOG on your enterprise server and application server is named JDE_<Process ID>.LOG. The process ID number is assigned by the operating system. You will also get a log for each type of kernel process that you start on your enterprise server. You can turn this logging on in your JDE.INI file (we will cover how to do this later in the chapter).

When you open a JDE.LOG file on your enterprise server, you will see a statement at the beginning of the log file. This statement tells you what kernel process this log file is logging for; for example, the security kernel.

```
219/265     Mon May 15 16:56:12 2000            IPCPUB1915
    process 219 <jdenet_k> registered in entry 7

219/265     Mon May 15 16:56:12 2000            jdeksec2068
    INITIALIZING SECURITY SERVER KERNEL
```

You will also be able to find entries in the server JDE.LOG files for the replication, scheduler, call object, and JDENET kernel processes. When you start up your host services for the first time, you should check these log files to be sure the kernel processes came up correctly. You will see another entry when the RUNUBE process starts up. This log file will show you the process ID, the thread, the user who submitted the UBE, the name of the UBE, and the version submitted. This log entry can be useful in troubleshooting problems while running UBEs on your enterprise server.

As we mentioned before, the JDE.LOG delivers some of the high-level error messages. For example, if the server could not connect to the database, a connection error would show up in the JDE.LOG file. However, this connection error would not show you the exact statement that was passed to the database. You would need the JDEDEBUG.LOG to find this statement. This can be done by matching up the time of the error in the JDE.LOG to the JDEDEBUG.LOG.

We will show you exactly how to do this, but first let's actually step through some error messages in the JDE.LOG and make sure you realize how much information is contained in this log file. Even if you have been using OneWorld for a while, we might be able to let you in on something new on the log files! In the example JDE.LOG, shown in Figure 20-1, you can see what information you can get from the simplest log file in OneWorld.

Process ID and Thread Number

In our example log file, shown in Figure 20-1, we have a sign-on security problem. When you read this log file, it is important to understand all the information it is giving you. Starting from the left side, the first thing shown is the Process ID and thread number. When a developer is designing a process, he can tell the process to run either single- or multithreaded. When a process is run in a single-threaded fashion, only one request to the CPU is placed at a time. Say the process needs to have three

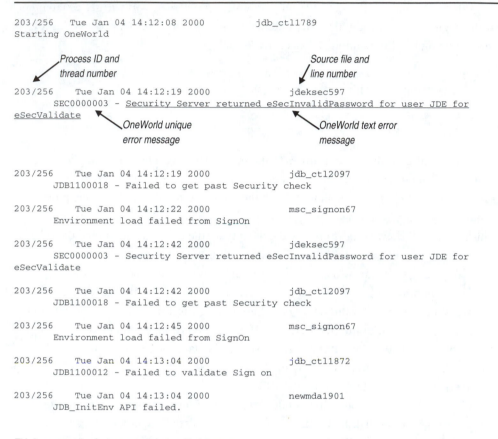

```
203/256   Tue Jan 04 14:12:08 2000          jdb_ctl1789
Starting OneWorld
```

Process ID and
thread number

Source file and
line number

```
203/256    Tue Jan 04 14:12:19 2000              jdeksec597
    SEC0000003 - Security Server returned eSecInvalidPassword for user JDE for
eSecValidate
```

OneWorld unique
error message

OneWorld text error
message

```
203/256    Tue Jan 04 14:12:19 2000          jdb_ctl2097
    JDB1100018 - Failed to get past Security check

203/256    Tue Jan 04 14:12:22 2000          msc_signon67
    Environment load failed from SignOn

203/256    Tue Jan 04 14:12:42 2000              jdeksec597
    SEC0000003 - Security Server returned eSecInvalidPassword for user JDE for
eSecValidate

203/256    Tue Jan 04 14:12:42 2000          jdb_ctl2097
    JDB1100018 - Failed to get past Security check

203/256    Tue Jan 04 14:12:45 2000          msc_signon67
    Environment load failed from SignOn

203/256    Tue Jan 04 14:13:04 2000          jdb_ctl1872
    JDB1100012 - Failed to validate Sign on

203/256    Tue Jan 04 14:13:04 2000          newmda1901
    JDB_InitEnv API failed.
```

This is an example of a compounded error. Each process has failed because of a single sub-process causing cascading error messages.

FIGURE 20-1. Reading a JDE.LOG file

different pieces of work completed. The first request will have to finish processing before the second request can be processed.

Multithreaded processes can take better advantage of the CPU by placing simultaneous, independent requests for CPU processing time. This is generally more efficient.

When you read a server JDE.LOG file, you will need to be aware that some processes may have multiple threads and several process IDs can be tracked through the log file. This information will allow you to determine in what process ID and thread you are having a problem. In the example in Figure 20-1, all of the messages share the same process ID and thread.

Source File and Line Number

Moving to the right on the log file you will see a time stamp—in our example, Tue Jan 04 14:12:19 2000. This time stamp can help you by matching the time of the error you find in a JDE.LOG file with a JDEDEBUG.LOG file, which can provide you with additional information.

However, if you go a little further to the right in an error line, you will see the name of the source file and on what line this error message is located. Unfortunately, most of the errors you find in the JDE.LOG will refer to a system or foundation source file. J.D. Edwards does not ship the foundation source code for OneWorld. So normally, all this will give you is what member is failing. However, if an error is ever escalated to J.D. Edwards development, this information allows them to easily find the line of code that is returning the error. This is why it is so important that you provide J.D. Edwards with the log files when they are attempting to assist you in troubleshooting an error. The log file may not give you much information, but it will help them as they step through the C code to determine what is causing your problem.

OneWorld Unique Error Message

Currently, this unique error message is not of as much use to you as it could be. J.D. Edwards was originally going to create a repository of all these errors and possible solutions. Although some of this is in place now, error messaging is another area in which the company is working to provide its customers with a more robust solution.

OneWorld Text Error Messages

This is a brief text description of the problem. In our example, the text tells us that the security server returned an invalid password for the user JDE. Some of these error messages, like this one, are very useful and specific. However, others have to be generic, since several different things could have caused the error message to be invoked. We recommend that you keep track of the issues and resolutions seen at your site. That way, when you encounter an error, you may not have to reinvent the wheel to solve the error.

Troubleshooting

NOTE

What commonly happens in OneWorld is that the first error encountered causes others to compound after it. Our example shows this. The true error was that an invalid password was passed to the sign-on security kernel, but as you can see, many other errors where spawned due to the original error.

Server JDEDEBUG.LOG Files

The first time you look at the JDEDEBUG.LOG file, you will probably think, what language was this written in? Don't worry, we are going to help you decipher this log file, which can appear intimidating. When you know what you are looking for, this file can be your best ally in debugging a OneWorld issue. Figure 20-2 shows an example of a JDEDEBUG.LOG.

```
jdedebug_203.log - Notepad                                                  _ 8 X
File  Edit  Search  Help
May 15 16:45:07 ** 203/319    ****   jdeDebugInit -- output to file.
May 15 16:45:07 ** 203/319    ONEWORLD Session started in ENV PRD733 for JDE
May 15 16:45:07 ** 203/319    Entering JDB_InitEnv
May 15 16:45:07 ** 203/319    Entering JDB_SetEnv
May 15 16:45:09 ** 203/319    Entering JDB_InitUser with commit mode 0.
May 15 16:45:09 ** 203/319    Entering JDB_BeginTransaction
May 15 16:45:09 ** 203/319    Entering JDB_InitUser with commit mode 0.
May 15 16:45:09 ** 203/319    Entering JDB_BeginTransaction
May 15 16:45:09 ** 203/319    Entering JDB_FreeUser
May 15 16:45:09 ** 203/319    Entering JDB_InitUser with commit mode 0.
May 15 16:45:09 ** 203/319    Entering JDB_BeginTransaction
May 15 16:45:09 ** 203/319    Entering JDB_OpenTable( Table = F986101)
May 15 16:45:11 ** 203/319    ORACLE DBInitDrv envr=01143DE0
May 15 16:45:13 ** 203/319    ORACLE DBInitCon envr=01143DE0 conn=01143530 DEN822 A (jde@JDE) V81 (srvrusers=1) 1
May 15 16:45:13 ** 203/319    Entering JDB_SetSelection
May 15 16:45:13 ** 203/319    Entering JDB_SelectKeyed
May 15 16:45:13 ** 203/319    ORACLE DBInitReq conn=01143530 requ=01B1CDB8 DEN822 (JDE) new
May 15 16:45:13 ** 203/319    SELECT OMENHV, OMAPPLID, OMOBNM, OMDATP, OMDATS, OMUGRP, OMOAPP, OMDATM, OMOVRE, OMSY,
OMSTSO, OMFUND, OMOCM2 FROM SVMB733.F986101  WHERE  ( OMENHV = 'PRD733' AND OMSTSO = 'AV' )  ORDER BY OMSTSO ASC,OMAPPLID ASC
May 15 16:45:13 ** 203/319    Entering JDB_Fetch
May 15 16:45:13 ** 203/319    Entering JDB_Fetch
May 15 16:45:13 ** 203/319    Entering JDB_Fetch
May 15 16:45:13 ** 203/319    Entering JDB_Fetch
May 15 16:45:13 ** 203/319    Entering JDB_Fetch
May 15 16:45:13 ** 203/319    Entering JDB_Fetch
May 15 16:45:13 ** 203/319    Entering JDB_Fetch
May 15 16:45:13 ** 203/319    Entering JDB_Fetch
May 15 16:45:13 ** 203/319    Entering JDB_Fetch
May 15 16:45:13 ** 203/319    Entering JDB_Fetch
May 15 16:45:13 ** 203/319    Entering JDB_Fetch
May 15 16:45:13 ** 203/319    Entering JDB_Fetch
May 15 16:45:13 ** 203/319    Entering JDB_Fetch
May 15 16:45:13 ** 203/319    Entering JDB_Fetch
May 15 16:45:13 ** 203/319    Entering JDB_Fetch
May 15 16:45:13 ** 203/319    Entering JDB_Fetch
May 15 16:45:13 ** 203/319    Entering JDB_Fetch
May 15 16:45:13 ** 203/319    Entering JDB_Fetch
May 15 16:45:13 ** 203/319    Entering JDB_Fetch
May 15 16:45:13 ** 203/319    Entering JDB_Fetch
May 15 16:45:13 ** 203/319    Entering JDB_Fetch
May 15 16:45:13 ** 203/319    Entering JDB_Fetch
May 15 16:45:13 ** 203/319    Entering JDB_Fetch
May 15 16:45:13 ** 203/319    Entering JDB_Fetch
May 15 16:45:13 ** 203/319    Entering JDB_Fetch
```

FIGURE 20-2.   Example of JDEDEBUG.LOG

When you look at a JDEDEBUG.LOG, the first thing to determine is what you are looking for. Do you know from the JDE.LOG that you have encountered an error at some point in time? That time frame on the JDEDEBUG.LOG file is where you should start looking. As experienced OneWorld system administrators can tell you, if you are having a low-level problem you may or may not receive an error in the JDE.LOG. So knowing how to read the JDEDEBUG.LOG, is a very valuable skill.

In our example of the JDEDEBUG.LOG, you can see that the software is creating an environment handle. The next statement shows you the machine and connect string the system is attempting to connect to. This can be useful information—if you are seeing data you did not expect, you can make sure you are actually looking at the database and machine you think you are looking at!

The JDEDEBUG.LOG has some similarities to the JDE.LOG. It will start with a date and time stamp. Then moving to the left, you will see a process ID and task number. Remember when we discussed the JDE.LOG we mentioned that some processes will have multiple threads? You can track these processes and threads through the JDEDEBUG.LOG as well. Moving further to the right you will now see a message, such as Entering JDB_InitEnv or a select statement.

Tracking the exact select statements passed to the database when you are experiencing a problem can be very helpful in troubleshooting. We cannot tell you how many times a select statement out of the JDEDEBUG.LOG has shown us what is causing the problem. An easy example would be if you were connecting to an Oracle database, but the select statement was not passing an owner. The OneWorld data source, which is contained in the F98611 Data Source Master table, tells OneWorld what user to pass to the database. If this field is blank or if the Use Table Owner flag is not set in the OneWorld data source, the system would not pass a table owner to the database.

Another trick that will assist you in debugging is to use your database administrator when necessary. If you think you are failing on a select statement being passed through OneWorld, pass the exact select statement outside of OneWorld. It might be a database setup issue instead of a OneWorld issue.

What this log file will also tell you is the tables you are hitting for a process. The software will tell you when it opens a table or closes a table. An example would be the JDEDEBUG.LOG statement:

```
May 14 17:02:07 ** 289/287 Entering JDB_CloseTable( Table = F98611)
```

This statement tells you that the F98611 table was closed. You will also see statements like JDB_Fetch. This tells you that OneWorld is fetching information from

Troubleshooting

a table. You will need to page up in the log file to determine what table the system is getting this information from.

Let's take another look at some of the select statements in the JDEDEBUG.LOG. You will notice that the values in some of these select statements have "?" in them instead of true values. An example would be:

```
SELECT SISY FROM F9860  WHERE  ( SIOBNM = ? )
```

What this means is that this value has already been shown once somewhere in the log file above that point, and the statement is being passed again. This may change in the future, but for now you will need to just page up until you find the statement you are looking for.

The next area a JDEDEBUG.LOG gives you information on, with standard tracing set up, is business function calls. This log file shows you when it calls a business function. It will also show you if this business function returned success, failure, or a warning. An example of the system calling a business function would be:

```
May 14 17:02:35 ** 289/287   Return value is 0 for DetermineIfVertexIsActive.
(BSFNLevel = 2).
```

This statement tells you that the business function returned success (a return value of 0 means success). If this return value is a 1, the business function has returned a warning. If the return value is anything other than a 0 or 1, you have an error. So if you are troubleshooting an issue on your enterprise server or on your client workstations, you can verify that the business functions finished correctly.

This troubleshooting technique comes in handy when you have master business functions running on the enterprise server. Say, for example, you have mapped all of your sales order master business functions to the enterprise server. If you are having a problem, you can turn on your logging, re-create the error, and determine if a business function is failing.

Up to this point, we have only covered basic logging information. We are now going to move on to describe a few different log files and the types of tracing available to you when you use OneWorld.

UBEDEBUG.LOG

When you have used OneWorld for a while, you will notice that JDEDEBUG.LOG and JDE.LOG don't log very much information on a UBE while it is running. They will show you when the UBE started and if it finished, but these logs will not give you any real detail on what the UBE is doing as it runs. Unfortunately, just because a UBE finishes does not mean that it did what you wanted. So how do you troubleshoot a UBE that is not performing as it should?

You will need to log what that UBE is doing as it runs. To do this, you can turn on UBEDEBUG logging. This type of logging produces a special log file that will tell you what the report was doing as it ran. To turn this type of logging on, open your JDE.INI file and find the UBE section. Under this section, find the UBEDebugLevel setting. This setting controls whether you will log what happens when a UBE runs. The valid values for this setting are 0 through 6. Zero means the logging is turned off, and 6 is the highest level of logging available.

Now that you have set this value to 6, you are ready to go, right? Not quite. You have told OneWorld to log the activities of your UBEs, but you have not told the system to keep these logs. The system will only keep the log files if it thinks that the UBE process itself has failed. As we mentioned, this may not be the case. So what you will want to do is find the DEBUG section of your JDE.INI file and set the KeepLogs setting to 1. This value tells the system to keep the UBEDEBUG log files. If this is set to 0, the log file will only be kept if the UBE process itself fails.

N O T E

In newer releases of the software, B733.2, the KeepLogs setting has been replaced by the UBESaveLogFile under the UBE section of the JDE.INI file. The functionality is the same, the variable name and location have just changed. If you have both in the INI file, it will not cause problems.

Now you are ready to save your JDE.INI file and run your UBE. Once you have run your UBE, you will want to look in the PRINTQUEUE directory on the machine you ran the report on. If you ran the report locally, look in the PRINTQUEUE directory on your workstation, and if you ran the report on the enterprise server, look in the PRINTQUEUE directory on that server. The log file will be the same name as your report followed by an underscore and the version of the report that you ran. Basically, it will match the name of your PDF file, but it will be a text file.

T I P

When you change an entry under the UBE section in your JDE.INI file, you will not need to log out of OneWorld and back in to have the change take effect. This section of the JDE.INI file is read each time you run a UBE job.

As you can see in Figure 20-3, this log file can give you critical information on your UBE. This file is similar to JDEDEBUG.LOG, except that it shows you specifically what your UBE is doing. This means you can see the select statements that are performed. If you are seeing a performance problem when a certain report is run, you can actually go through this log file to see if the report is doing something it shouldn't, such as passing open select statements across a large table when it doesn't have to.

This log file will also show you what business functions are being called by your report, so if one is failing, this is where you would find the error. Again, you can search

```
Opening UBE Log for report R0010P, version XJDE0001
--UBE--[6]-- 289/249    ubeReport_EntryPoint START
--UBE--[0]-- 289/249    Start Time : 19:53:54
--UBE--[6]-- 289/249    UBEReport_LoadSpecifications Start
--UBE--[1]-- 289/249    Currency Flag is Z
--UBE--[4]-- 289/249    SELECT SISY FROM F9860  WHERE  ( SIOBNM = ? )
--UBE--[4]-- 289/249    SELECT SISY FROM F9860  WHERE  ( SIOBNM = 'R0010P' )
--UBE--[1]-- 289/249    Report Title is Company Constants Report, Company Title is
J.D. Edwards & Company, System Code is 00
--UBE--[6]-- 289/249    K2Print START
--UBE--[4]-- 289/249    SELECT  *  FROM F986167  WHERE  ( DPUSER = ? AND DPENHV = ?
AND DPEXEHOST = ? AND DPSTSO = ? )   ORDER BY DPUSER ASC,DPENHV ASC,DPEXEHOST
ASC,DPSTSO ASC
--UBE--[4]-- 289/249    SELECT  *  FROM F986167  WHERE  ( DPUSER = 'DEMO' AND DPENHV =
'DEMOB73' AND DPEXEHOST = 'WinClient' AND DPSTSO = 'AV' )   ORDER BY DPUSER ASC,DPENHV
ASC,DPEXEHOST ASC,DPSTSO ASC
--UBE--[6]-- 289/249    K2PRINT END
--UBE--[6]-- 289/249    UBEReport_StartProcessing Start
--UBE--[2]-- 289/249    Pre-initializing Page Header Section
--UBE--[2]-- 289/249    InitSection for Page Header
--UBE--[2]-- 289/249    Done Pre-initializing Page Header Section.
--UBE--[2]-- 289/249    Starting UBE Message Loop
--UBE--[2]-- 289/249    Process Init Report Header Section
--UBE--[2]-- 289/249    Process Init Section
--UBE--[2]-- 289/249    InitSection for Company Constants Detail
--UBE--[4]-- 289/249    SELECT  *  FROM F0010  ORDER BY CCCO ASC
--UBE--[4]-- 289/249    SELECT  *  FROM F0010  ORDER BY CCCO ASC
--UBE--[2]-- 289/249    Process Adv Section
--UBE--[2]-- 289/249    Processing Adv Section for Company Constants Detail
--UBE--[2]-- 289/249    Process Init Page Header Section
--UBE--[2]-- 289/249    Process Adv Section
--UBE--[2]-- 289/249    Processing Adv Section for Page Header
--UBE--[2]-- 289/249    Process Do Section
--UBE--[2]-- 289/249    Processing Do Section for Page Header
--UBE--[4]-- 289/249    --ER: Line(1): Loading Data Structure for BSFN
```

FIGURE 20-3.   Example of UBEDEBUG.LOG

for the return code of a business function. Not all reports use a lot of business functions, however, this is still a very handy debugging technique.

This log file will also tell you what columns are being used or hit when a report is run. You will see statements similar to:

```
UBE--[3]-- 289/249     Processing Do Object CCARFJ in Section Company Constants
Detail
```

This tells you the report has looked at the column CCARFJ. What this really shows is a data dictionary item, ARFJ, but these data dictionary items are used to specify columns for tables. This is why the value has a CC table prefix on it. If you look above this statement, you can determine what table this report was looking at. In this example the table is F0010 Company Constants.

If you combine this information with the select statements in the log file, you can look for areas where the report is causing performance problems. Say the report was doing an open select statement over a table when it only needed to perform a select statement over a single column that had an index on it. If you catch something like this, you can reduce your reports' runtime. If you are creating custom reports, we recommend that you design and test them for performance as well as functionality.

Transaction Processing Log

Now let's move on to another type of log file that can assist you in your troubleshooting techniques. We'll start by describing transaction services. A transaction is a piece of work comprised of SQL statements. For example, if you enter a sales order into a OneWorld system, the sales order header and detail files need to be updated with the correct information. Otherwise you would have a header record without any child records or vise versa. This means multiple SQL statements. How do you ensure that all of these statements have completed successfully?

That is what the OneWorld transaction processing service does for you. It ensures that these statements are both made, and it will roll one back if necessary so that it commits either both SQL statements or nothing. If you are having problems with transaction processing, turning on transaction processing logging might be a good start.

To turn on transaction processing logging, open your JDE.INI file on the server and find the JDETSFile variable in the DEBUG section. This variable is what tells the system where to write the transaction processing logging file, so a valid value for this

Troubleshooting

variable would be JDETS.LOG. This log file will give you information about your transaction processing service. Where this log file is located will be determined by the INSTALL section of the JDE.INI; there will be a variable for the release of OneWorld you are running. So if you were running B733, for example, the directory structure this variable is set to equal would be where you would find your JDETS.LOG file

Now that you know where the log file will exist, you still need to turn on the logging. To do this, find the LOCK MANAGER section of your JDE.INI file. Under this section, you will find the LogServices entry. This entry controls the logging for your transaction processing. You can set this to 1 to turn the logging on or 0 to turn it off. Figure 20-4 shows an example of this type of logging.

To understand this log file, you need to understand what happens during transaction processing. Transaction processing in OneWorld uses a two-phase commit coordinator. This coordinator will write the logs for each data source to the hard drive. These log files contain all of the SQL statements that were carried out. If any of the data sources that are being hit fail to have the record committed, you can return all of your data to a consistent state by reviewing the contents of this log file.

Once this step is successful, the software moves on to the second phase. In this step, the software will commit the transactions to each of the data sources. If one of these commits fails, a commit log report will be generated, based upon the log files that were created in phase one. This log file is the JDETS.LOG file.

If all of the commit statements function correctly, the log files generated in phase one will be deleted. In our example, notice the garbage collection interval. This shows the interval at which all expired records are removed from the transaction manager service record registry. You will also see the time stamp record life span; this is also a period of time that a record will exist before being cleaned from the record registry.

```
22597 Garbage Collection Interval = 5400
    Timestamp Record LifeSpan = 3600
22597 Entering jdeGetTMEnv...
22597 Getting TM Environment ...
22597 Initializing JDB environment ...
```

FIGURE 20-4. Example of transaction processing log

IPC Tracing

When you are implementing a system like OneWorld, you need to know how to read all of the log files and tracing options within those log files. This is why good system administrators are always looking for new logging tricks and procedures.

One trick of the trade is interprocess communication (IPC) logging. Normally, you would not turn on an IPC trace unless the J.D. Edwards development staff instructed you to do so or unless you had a really good understanding of how interprocess communications are used with OneWorld software.

To turn on IPC tracing, open your JDE.INI file, then find the JDEIPC section. Under this section, find the ipcTrace variable. If you do not find this variable, you can add it to the JDEIPC section of the JDE.INI file. However, it is important to remember that this variable, like so many others in the JDE.INI file, is case sensitive, so be careful when you type it in. This variable can be set to a value of 0 to 3. A setting of 0 means IPC tracing is turned off. A setting of 1 means you have turned the IPC tracing on and general IPC trace messages will be logged. If you set this variable to 2, you will get the IPC handle state trace messages. When this variable is set to 3, you will get general IPC errors and IPC handle state trace messages. These last two settings are only available in OneWorld Xe (formerly B733.3).

All of this logging information will be written to the JDEDEBUG.LOG. This means you will need to have the JDEDEBUG logging turned on before you turn on the IPC tracing. To turn on the JDEDEBUG logging, find the DEBUG section of your JDE.INI file. Change the Output variable to FILE and the LogErrors variable to 1. When you turn on the JDEDEBUG.LOG for an enterprise or application server, you will need to cycle your host services.

TIP

This type of logging is only used on enterprise and application servers. You will not need to attempt to set up interprocess communication logging on the client workstation.

Once you have turned this tracing on, start your host services again. When your services have come up you will want to get to a point, right before you experience your problem. Say that your problem occurs when you enter a sales order, with your master business functions running on the enterprise server, and J.D. Edwards has asked you to get an IPC trace. You would ensure that logging is set up on your enterprise/application server, get logged onto your client machine and up to the point where you can re-create the error, and then move off the log files on your enterprise server. This is so you don't have to sort through a ton of information that does not apply to your problem. After you have moved your log files, you would re-create your error. Once you have the error, you will need to capture the log files off your enterprise server so that you have an accurate picture of what happened at the point of your error.

Remember, these log files can grow very quickly, especially when you have additional tracing or detailed logging turned on. Once you have captured the log files you need, turn off the logging in your JDE.INI file and bounce your host services again. If you leave this logging turned on, you will affect your system performance and you can fill up your hard disk with log files. We have seen this done to large systems when the system administrator forgot to turn off logging and it happened to be around the holidays. After a week or two, the hard drive filled up and the OneWorld host services came down, since they could no longer write to the disk. Don't learn this lesson the hard way. Before you leave for the weekend, you should always make sure the logging is turned off on your system.

TIP

If you are live and this error only occurs at what seems like random times, you may have to bite the bullet and take a performance hit by turning on logging. However, you can take steps to minimize this uncomfortable time. If you are monitoring for failed process on the server, set up the server administration workbench on a client machine and configure the software to page you when a process dies. (The server administration workbench is covered in Chapter 16.) That way you will know exactly when the error occurred, you can capture the log files, turn logging off, and be a hero to your end users!

This is all good to know, but you're probably wondering, what does tracing information look like? In a word, confusing, unless you are really familiar with this type of logging. If this looks like gibberish to you, don't panic. This is a very low-level type of tracing. Normally when you turn this type of tracing on you will be sending this log file to a J.D. Edwards developer who has the OneWorld source code to refer to as well and can determine what might be going wrong. With that said, below is an example of interprocess communication (IPC) tracing statements.

```
Jun 21 13:37:47 ** 22796   IPC1200006 - lockIPCInit lock semop succeeded.
Jun 21 13:37:47 ** 22796   IPC2100021 - createResource 1 for eIPCMutex ~~JDERes~ successful, use=6.
Jun 21 13:37:47 ** 22796   IPC2100020 - createAssocLock for ~JDERes~ successful.
Jun 21 13:37:47 ** 22796   IPC1100005 - ipcInit completed successfully, Use count=6.
```

As you can see, this log will not be useful to the standard user. However, if you have some programming experience it may provide you with some useful information. In this example, you can see that a semaphore is being locked and a mutex is being created for a resource. Mutexes are covered in Chapter 16 under the server administration workbench section.

To give you a brief rundown of what is happening here, the semaphore is used to control a pool of identical resources on your enterprise/application server. The mutex is a mutual exclusion lock, which means that only one process can hold the mutex, and thus the resource, at a time. So in our example, a process has been granted a lock on some resource. If you know what is happening at the time of this lock and have the source code for OneWorld, you can debug a problem with interprocess communication.

DEFINITION

Interprocess communication (IPC): *Interprocess communication, as it relates to OneWorld, is used by the J.D. Edwards host code to communicate between processes and create new processes when necessary. The software also uses IPC to hide platform-specific details from the higher-level OneWorld code.*

Troubleshooting

A Little More Information on Log Files

Now that we have told you how complicated reading an IPC trace can be, let's see if we can give you a little more information to clear this log file up. If you are a person who likes to dig for information on what the errors in a log file mean, you will want to know how to find additional information on the errors you will find in a IPC trace log file.

The first thing to do is set up IPC tracing and capture your log file, as we discussed above. Once you have this information, wouldn't it be nice to have some more information on what the statement in the log file means? You can find all of the return codes and a brief description of each in a file that is shipped with the software. This is a header file called JDEIPC.H located under the B7\System\Include directory on your client workstation. It contains all the return codes that will be used in the IPC trace messages. The following table lists these error messages and a description of each, taken directly from the JDEIPC.H file. We encourage you to review this file as it contains a lot of useful information.

TIP

There are other header files that contain valuable information located in the B7\System\Include directory. Browse through this directory and look at these files, but do not change any of them since it can have a negative affect on the software.

EIPCNoError	No error has occurred
EIPCInvalidParm	One or more parameters was invalid
EIPCInvalidHandle	The IPCHANDLE was invalid
EIPCInvalidName	The name of the resource is not valid
EIPCAlreadyExists	The resource already existed
EIPCNameExists	The name of the resource has already been used

EIPCNotFound	The resource was not found
EIPCNotLockable	Can't WaitLock or Unlock the resource
EIPCInvalidLockState	Already or not locked
EIPCMallocFailed	Memory allocation failed
EIPCQueueError	A system error occurred on a MsgQueue operation
EIPCNoMoreSemaphores	All the system semaphores have been used
EIPCNoMoreIPCResources	The IPC Resource array is full
EIPCNoMoreOSResources	Operating System resources exhausted (ENOSPC)
EIPCCantChangeDir	Can't CD to a different directory
EIPCCantChangeDisk	Can't CD to a different disk
EIPCCantStopProcess	OS Kill of child process failed
EIPCCantCreateComSharedMem	Can't create IPC's Common Resource Shm
EIPCInternalHashError	IPC Hash table corrupted
EIPCCantLockForInit	Can't lock IPC initialization lock
EIPCCantCloseOSResource	Can't close kernel IPC resource
EIPCCantCreateOrAttMem	Can't create or attach to shared memory
EIPCProcessExitError	Can't get exit status for child process
EIPCMutexError	A system error occurred on a mutex operation
EIPCSemInitError	System error while initializing semaphore
EIPCCantSpawnProcess	System error spawning new process
EIPCMessageQueueCapacity	NT message queue is full or empty
EIPCNotInitialized	IPC subsystem not initialized before use
EIPCInvalidOSParam	OS returned EINVAL
EIPCOSError	Unrecognized OS error
EIPCTimedOut	Timed out on lock or message queue
EIPCNotImplemented	Tried to use a facility that isn't there yet

JDENet Tracing

JDENet is what OneWorld uses to communicate between machines. Wouldn't it be nice to be able to set up a trace that would tell you what is happening when you experience a problem with JDENet? Better yet, wouldn't it be great if you knew what the error codes that JDENet returns meant? In this section, we'll take a look at the high-level JDENet return codes, and cover how to set up JDENet tracing.

Definition of JDENet

It is important to have a clear understanding of what JDENet is and how it will apply to you, because JDENet affects almost all areas of the OneWorld system. It becomes important when you are attempting to troubleshoot problems in OneWorld.

JDENet is middleware that is TCP/IP sockets-based. This middleware is what gives OneWorld the capability of being a distributed solution. Without JDENet, you could not run some processes on one machine and others on another. JDENet allows the software to communicate across machines. To give you a practical example, this allows you to distribute where you run such things as business functions and UBEs. You don't have to run these locally on your client workstation; with JDENet you can communicate with an application/enterprise server and run in a distributed architecture.

This doesn't mean that every time you do something in OneWorld you will use JDENet. When you submit a UBE or run a business function that is mapped to an enterprise server, you will use JDENet to communicate with that server. You won't be using JDENet when you perform a database operation. Most network database operations use a driver that employs transport mechanisms supplied by that specific database vendor. This does not involve JDENet. Say for example that you go into your address book and click Find. This will make a database call asking for records out of the F0101 Address Book Master file. This call will go through Microsoft's ODBC middleware, if you are running against an AS400 SQL server database or Microsoft Access database. The ODBC middleware will actually get the information from the database, not JDENet. It is important that you understand this so that you know when to look at JDENet tracing.

Troubleshooting

N O T E

The only time JDENet will act as the middleware in a database operation is if you are using JDBNet.

D E F I N I T I O N

JDBNet: *JDBNet is a piece of software that J.D. Edwards wrote to allow the OneWorld software to access data on a database not supported by certain platforms. An example of this is the OneWorld host code on an AS400 making a call to an Oracle database. There is currently no software on the market to meet this need, so J.D. Edwards wrote JDBNet. The call to the Oracle database would be communicated between the two machines via JDENet.*
So both machines would need to be running the OneWorld host code.

High-Level JDENet Return Codes

The most common situations in which you will receive a JDENet return code are when you submit a UBE from a client workstation or when you are attempting to run a master business function on an enterprise/application server from a client workstation. If you have been working with OneWorld for a while, we are sure you are familiar with a communications error or a remote job error. An example of this error is shown in Figure 20-5.

When you get this error, open the JDE.LOG on the client workstation. Scroll to the bottom, where you will see an error like this:

```
JDENET_CreateAssocMsg failed. Error = 5
```

This shows you that JDENet was attempting to perform a specific function and ran into an error. JDENet then gave you a return code from this error. In this example, the return code is 5.

Finding the High-Level JDENet Return Codes on Your System   How do you determine what this return code means? Table 20-1 gives you all the high-level JDENet return

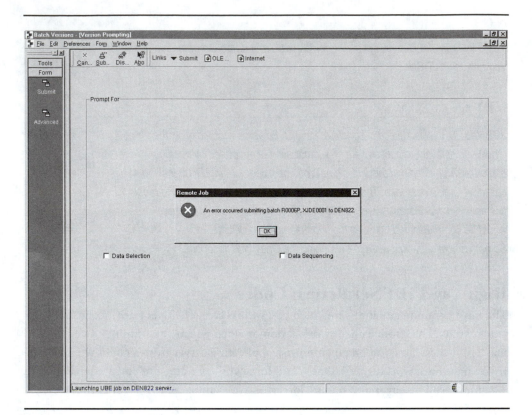

FIGURE 20-5. Remote job error example

codes in a nice, neat chart. But you should also know how to find these return codes yourself, just in case you don't have this book handy when you run into a problem.

To do this, open Windows Explorer on any OneWorld client workstation and find the B7\system\include directory. Under this directory, find the JDENET.H file. This is a public header file that will give you information on JDENet. Open this file and search on "error," which will take you to the area of the header file that contains the JDENet error return codes. An example of this section of the JDENET.H file is shown in Figure 20-6.

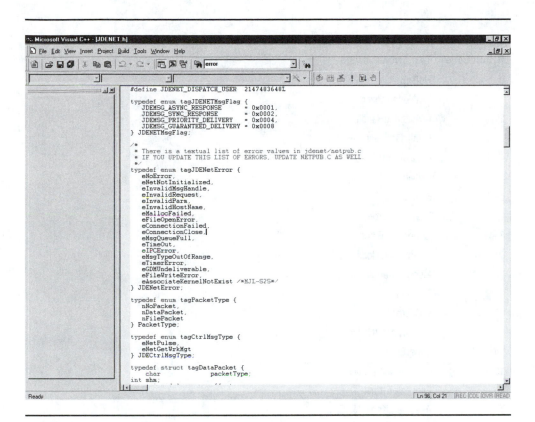

FIGURE 20-6. JDENET.H file showing JDENet return codes

As you can see, this file shows you a lot of JDENet return codes. However, you don't see a return code of 5. The error codes aren't numbered in this file, so you'll need to count, starting just under the tag JDENetError definition. Starting with 0 for the return NoError and counting down the list, you can see that the JDENet return code InvalidHostName would be number 5.

Since you may not want to go through this include file to determine what each and every return code for JDENet means, Table 20-1 offers a list of these return codes. This should save you some time and frustration.

JDENet Return Code	Text Error Message
0	NoError
1	NetNotInitialized
2	InvalidMsgHandle
3	InvalidRequest
4	InvalidParm
5	InvalidHostName
6	MallocFailed
7	FileOpenError
8	ConnectionFailed
9	ConnectionClose
10	MsgQueueFull
11	TimeOut
12	IPCError
13	MsgTypeOutOfRange
14	TimerError
15	GDMUndeliverable
16	FileWriteError
17	AssociateKernalNotExist

TABLE 20-1. JDENet Return Codes

Once you know what a return code means, it is much more useful to you! Let's cover a few examples very quickly. If you get a return code of 11, you are experiencing a time out. The first thing to do is make sure your enterprise/application server's host services are running. If they are and you are only experiencing this error from time to time, you might want to increase the JDENETTimeout variable under the NETWORK QUEUE SETTINGS section of your workstation's JDE.INI file. This can help if you are running on a bottlenecked network.

With this type of information, you can start to troubleshoot even complex issues on your system. If, for example, you get the JDENet return code of 12, you know you have an interprocess communication error. Your next step should be running an IPC trace on your enterprise/application server.

Setting Up JDENet Tracing

Now that you know what high-level return codes you can expect from JDENet, let's dig a little deeper. You do not have to depend just upon these return codes to assist you in troubleshooting a JDENet issue; you can also set up JDENet tracing. This type of tracing will give you detailed information on what the OneWorld JDENet middleware is doing.

To turn on this type of tracing, open your JDE.INI file and find the JDENet section. This section of the INI file controls the JDENet tracing. Under this section, you will find a NetTrace variable. You can set this variable to either 0 or 1. A setting of 0 tells the software not to perform JDENet tracing. A setting of 1 turns this tracing on. As with IPC tracing, you will need to have JDEDEBUG logging turned on to see this type of tracing information. That means you will need to cycle your host services for this type of tracing to work. We know it's a pain, but what is worse, the issue you are experiencing or a temporary performance degradation due to turning on logging?

Once you have turned this tracing on, look for the trace messages in the JDEDEBUG.LOG file. Again, when your host services come up, you will want to get your client machine setup to reproduce the error, clear out the server's log files, reproduce the error, and then capture the log files.

You may recall that JDENet is a sockets-based messaging middleware. This is why you will see messages relating to specific sockets in the log file containing JDENet trace messages. For most people, this will not give you a lot of information to go on, so you will probably only be capturing a log file like this for J.D. Edwards' development organization to look at. An example of this type of tracing is shown below.

```
Jun 21 13:41:12 ** 22821    Socket 8 is in state SocketConnected
Jun 21 13:41:12 ** 22821    Socket 8,event-FD_READ,error-0

Jun 21 13:41:12 ** 22821    Socket 8,recv-36,rc-(36),err-0
```

Replication Tracing

If you are using OneWorld replication, you will probably want to know that the replication messages are actually getting through to the machines you have set replication up on. This is why there is replication tracing.

Turning On Replication Tracing

Let's say you have set up OneWorld replication and it does not seem to be working correctly. What do you do? Well, you can bring in an expensive consultant to help you or you can take advantage of the functionality available in OneWorld and try to fix the problem yourself before calling in the cavalry.

The first thing to do is to make sure you have replication set up. Since this chapter is about logging, not replication, we are going to assume that all of the entries are in the OneWorld data replication application. After you confirm that these entries are correct, turn on replication logging by opening the JDE.INI file and locating the RepTrace value under the DEBUG section of the INI file. This can be set to either 1 or 0. If you set this value to 1, you are telling the software to perform replication tracing. If it is set to 0, no tracing will be performed.

Like so many of the other types of tracing we have discussed, these replication trace messages will also be written to the JDEDEBUG.LOG log file. This means that you will want to turn on your JDEDEBUG logging before you close that JDE.INI file. Up to this point, the tracing that we have discussed is only on enterprise or application servers. You can set up OneWorld replication to replicate to client workstations. This is why you can set up replication tracing on a client workstation as well as on enterprise servers. In both cases, you turn replication tracing on in the same manner.

Replication Trace Messages

Once you have turned on your replication trace, you will want to log back into OneWorld on the client workstation and start your server's host services. Get to a point where you are about to change a publisher table. When you are at this point, you will want to either clear out or mark your JDEDEBUG logs on both the client and the server. This is so that you can easily find the messages you are looking for.

When you make a change to a publisher table, a message gets sent to your server saying that this table has changed and that all the subscribers need to be notified. When you turn on replication tracing, you will be able to see this notification as it takes place. This will help you determine where you are experiencing a problem with OneWorld replication and correct the issue.

Below is an example that shows a replication trace on a client workstation. In this example, the client workstation has successfully sent a replication message to an enterprise server, HP9000A. This example also shows that this client workstation has received a subscriber notification from the enterprise server. So you would know from this message that this workstation is functioning correctly in the context of data replication.

```
Jul 15 10:03:12 ** 194/106    Rep Message 512 sent to HP9000A successfully
Jul 15 10:12:18 ** 194/106    Received SUBNOTIFY from HP9000A
```

When you are looking into a replication problem, you will also want to look at the enterprise server's logs. After all, just because the client sent a replication message doesn't mean the enterprise server actually received it. Below is an example of replication tracing on your enterprise server. As you can see in this example, the enterprise serve did actually receive a message. It then sent a message to another machine. This type of tracing information will help ensure that your replication solution is acting in the manner that you expect.

```
Jul 15 10:14:52 ** 194/106    Received PUBNOTIFY from U10SLAB8
Jul 15 10:14:54 ** 194/106    Rep Message 513 sent to JDEOW1 successfully
```

TAM Trace

The next area of tracing available to you can really get interesting, as this is a fairly low-level type of logging. As you learn to use this type of logging, your understanding of how OneWorld really works will increase. In this section, we are going to cover what TAM is, how to set up a TAM trace, and what the results of a TAM trace look like.

What Is TAM?

If you are new to OneWorld, you may have never heard the term TAM before. This is because TAM, which stands for Table Access Manager, is proprietary to J.D. Edwards OneWorld software. These files are located under the SPEC folder contained in your path code directory on your client workstations and enterprise servers and will end in a .DDB or .XDB extension. TAM can be described as a snapshot of your central object tables at some point, and was designed to allow OneWorld to run in an acceptable amount of time.

When you log on to a client workstation, the OneWorld software determines the path code to run and finds these TAM files on your local workstation. It then reads these TAM files to run applications and reports. The .DDB files contain the actual information, and the .XDB files are an index over the .DDB files. This is why you can have one workstation running a different version of an application than another workstation.

You may ask, what about the enterprise and application servers, don't they have files with the .DDB and .XDB extensions? You are absolutely correct. OneWorld application and enterprise servers also look at these files to determine the specifications for the reports they run. If your workstations and servers had to make select statements across your central object files every time you wanted to run something in OneWorld, you would be waiting a while! After all, just one of the files in the central object tables contains more than two million records in the Xe release of OneWorld.

N O T E

You will never run an interactive application on a OneWorld enterprise or application server. These servers are used to run business functions and UBEs. All interactive applications execute on the client workstations.

To keep TAM straight in your mind, you might want to think of it as a miniature database. When you do a package build, OneWorld will take the information out of your central object relational database tables and place it into a TAM format. This database supports multiple field indexing, both ascending and descending. This helps keep the response time of running OneWorld objects in an acceptable range.

Setting Up a TAM Trace

Earlier we mentioned that you have TAM files on both the enterprise servers and client workstations. This also means that it would be logical for you to be able to run a TAM trace on these servers and workstations. J.D. Edwards agrees with this logic, which is why you can set up a TAM trace on both.

To set up a TAM trace, you will need to modify your JDE.INI file. Open this file and find the DEBUG section. Under this section, find the TAMTrace level entry. This entry may or may not exist in your INI file. If you need to add it, be sure you enter it correctly, as this entry is case sensitive. This type of tracing can be set up to give you different levels of detail. The software allows you to set this entry from 0 to 9. When this entry is set at 9, it will give you the most detail. A setting of 0 turns this type of tracing off.

When you set up a TAM trace, you will need to know where these trace messages are written to. Again, these trace messages will appear in the JDEDEBUG.LOG file. This means you will need to turn on JDEDEBUG logging to see these messages.

If you are having a problem running an application on all client workstations that are running a certain package, you may want to run a TAM trace. What this tells you is that this object probably has changed between the two packages, assuming you did not have a package build issue.

Results of a TAM Trace

When you run a TAM trace, you will notice how quickly it fills up your log file. Once you have turned this tracing on, you will want to get to the point right before you are about to duplicate the error, mark or clear your log file, re-create the error, and capture the log files. This will give you information on what is happening as the application runs. Figure 20-7 shows an example of what a TAM trace will look like.

This information may be a little daunting at first glance, but don't worry—you will be able to pull vital information out of TAM trace results. In this example, we had the tracing set to as much detail as possible. When you look at this log file, the first thing to do is locate the problem. If you have marked your log file before re-creating the error, you will have a good place to start.

As you read this file, you are looking for what is being read up to the error. In this example, you can clearly see which TAM files are being read. You can also determine what values the software is looking for. If you look at the top of Figure 20-7, you can see that the software is looking in the GBRLINK.XDB file for a value of F986101.

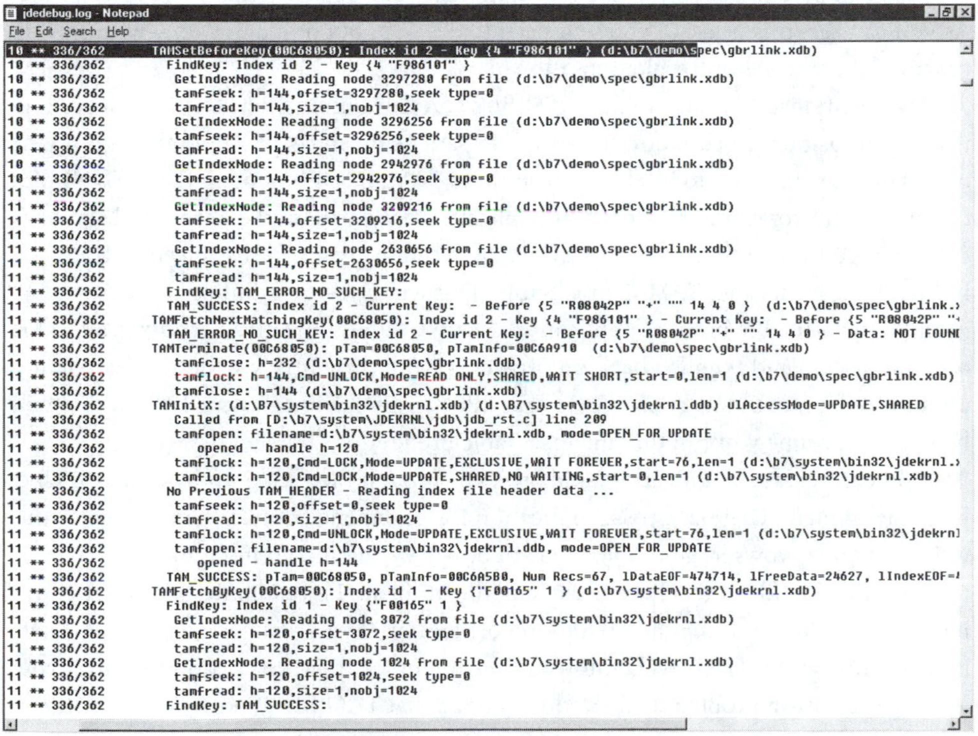

```
jdedebug.log - Notepad
File Edit Search Help
10 ** 336/362        TAMSetBeforeKey(00C68050): Index id 2 - Key {4 "F986101" } (d:\b7\demo\spec\gbrlink.xdb)
10 ** 336/362          FindKey: Index id 2 - Key {4 "F986101" }
10 ** 336/362            GetIndexNode: Reading node 3297280 from file (d:\b7\demo\spec\gbrlink.xdb)
10 ** 336/362            tamfseek: h=144,offset=3297280,seek type=0
10 ** 336/362            tamfread: h=144,size=1,nobj=1024
10 ** 336/362            GetIndexNode: Reading node 3296256 from file (d:\b7\demo\spec\gbrlink.xdb)
10 ** 336/362            tamfseek: h=144,offset=3296256,seek type=0
10 ** 336/362            tamfread: h=144,size=1,nobj=1024
10 ** 336/362            GetIndexNode: Reading node 2942976 from file (d:\b7\demo\spec\gbrlink.xdb)
10 ** 336/362            tamfseek: h=144,offset=2942976,seek type=0
11 ** 336/362            tamfread: h=144,size=1,nobj=1024
11 ** 336/362            GetIndexNode: Reading node 3209216 from file (d:\b7\demo\spec\gbrlink.xdb)
11 ** 336/362            tamfseek: h=144,offset=3209216,seek type=0
11 ** 336/362            tamfread: h=144,size=1,nobj=1024
11 ** 336/362            GetIndexNode: Reading node 2630656 from file (d:\b7\demo\spec\gbrlink.xdb)
11 ** 336/362            tamfseek: h=144,offset=2630656,seek type=0
11 ** 336/362            tamfread: h=144,size=1,nobj=1024
11 ** 336/362          FindKey: TAM_ERROR_NO_SUCH_KEY:
11 ** 336/362          TAM_SUCCESS: Index id 2 - Current Key:  - Before {5 "R08042P" "+" "" 14 4 0 }  (d:\b7\demo\spec\gbrlink.x
11 ** 336/362        TAMFetchNextMatchingKey(00C68050): Index id 2 - Key {4 "F986101" } - Current Key:  - Before {5 "R08042P" "
11 ** 336/362          TAM_ERROR_NO_SUCH_KEY: Index id 2 - Current Key:  - Before {5 "R08042P" "+" "" 14 4 0 } - Data: NOT FOUN
11 ** 336/362        TAMTerminate(00C68050): pTam=00C68050, pTamInfo=00C6A910  (d:\b7\demo\spec\gbrlink.xdb)
11 ** 336/362            tamfclose: h=232 (d:\b7\demo\spec\gbrlink.ddb)
11 ** 336/362            tamflock: h=144,Cmd=UNLOCK,Mode=READ ONLY,SHARED,WAIT SHORT,start=0,len=1 (d:\b7\demo\spec\gbrlink.xdb)
11 ** 336/362            tamfclose: h=144 (d:\b7\demo\spec\gbrlink.xdb)
11 ** 336/362        TAMInitX: (d:\B7\system\bin32\jdekrnl.xdb) (d:\B7\system\bin32\jdekrnl.ddb) ulAccessMode=UPDATE,SHARED
11 ** 336/362            Called from [D:\b7\system\JDEKRNL\jdb\jdb_rst.c] line 209
11 ** 336/362            tamfopen: filename=d:\b7\system\bin32\jdekrnl.xdb, mode=OPEN_FOR_UPDATE
11 ** 336/362               opened - handle h=120
11 ** 336/362            tamflock: h=120,Cmd=LOCK,Mode=UPDATE,EXCLUSIVE,WAIT FOREVER,start=76,len=1 (d:\b7\system\bin32\jdekrnl.x
11 ** 336/362            tamflock: h=120,Cmd=LOCK,Mode=UPDATE,SHARED,NO WAITING,start=0,len=1 (d:\b7\system\bin32\jdekrnl.xdb)
11 ** 336/362          No Previous TAM_HEADER - Reading index file header data ...
11 ** 336/362            tamfseek: h=120,offset=0,seek type=0
11 ** 336/362            tamfread: h=120,size=1,nobj=1024
11 ** 336/362            tamflock: h=120,Cmd=UNLOCK,Mode=UPDATE,EXCLUSIVE,WAIT FOREVER,start=76,len=1 (d:\b7\system\bin32\jdekrn
11 ** 336/362            tamfopen: filename=d:\b7\system\bin32\jdekrnl.ddb, mode=OPEN_FOR_UPDATE
11 ** 336/362               opened - handle h=144
11 ** 336/362          TAM_SUCCESS: pTam=00C68050, pTamInfo=00C6A5B0, Num Recs=67, lDataEOF=474714, lFreeData=24627, lIndexEOF=
11 ** 336/362        TAMFetchByKey(00C68050): Index id 1 - Key {"F00165" 1 } (d:\b7\system\bin32\jdekrnl.xdb)
11 ** 336/362          FindKey: Index id 1 - Key {"F00165" 1 }
11 ** 336/362            GetIndexNode: Reading node 3072 from file (d:\b7\system\bin32\jdekrnl.xdb)
11 ** 336/362            tamfseek: h=120,offset=3072,seek type=0
11 ** 336/362            tamfread: h=120,size=1,nobj=1024
11 ** 336/362            GetIndexNode: Reading node 1024 from file (d:\b7\system\bin32\jdekrnl.xdb)
11 ** 336/362            tamfseek: h=120,offset=1024,seek type=0
11 ** 336/362            tamfread: h=120,size=1,nobj=1024
11 ** 336/362          FindKey: TAM_SUCCESS:
```

FIGURE 20-7. Example of TAM trace

Remember, the XDB value is the index for TAM files. So basically the software is looking at the index, trying to find the value it needs.

As you continue reading these trace messages, you will notice you can also see what types of locks are being placed on the TAM files. With a little practice, you will be able to use this information to help track down the problems with your application or report. This is a lot easier if you have a baseline to compare against. To get such a baseline, you can perform a TAM trace on a machine that is functioning correctly and then perform another TAM trace on a machine that is having a problem.

This comparison will help you in isolating where you are having a problem. Let's say you have isolated the issue down to a statement that is attempting to find a record in the RDASPEC file. Now what? First, see if this TAM file even has this entry. If it does, you can then compare the entry to a working client workstation. If you believe that one of your central object data sources contains a good copy of this object, you can also compare the entry for this object in these tables to the entry in your TAM files. As you can see, this is a skill you will need to develop, but don't give up—with some practice, these traces will make sense to you.

We mentioned looking at your TAM files and determining if a record exists or if it is the same as on a workstation that is not experiencing an issue. To do this, set up the universal table browser to be able to read these TAM files. First, open the JDE.INI file on your client workstation (interactive applications only run on the client workstations).

Next, go to the INTERACTIVE RUNTIME section. You will then need to add a hidden JDE.INI setting: TAMMenus=Show. This will give you additional functionality in the universal table browser application. Many JDE.INI file entries require you to log off your system and then log back on. However, with this entry you do not have to log off and back on to OneWorld for it to take effect. This section of your JDE.INI file will be read every time you run the universal table browser.

You can access the universal table browser through the Fast Path by typing **UTB** or by going to menu GH902, Cross Application Development Tools. When you enter the universal table browser, go to File | Open Local TAM, as shown in Figure 20-8. Open the specification file you believe is causing the problem. For example, say you are having a problem running the R0006P report locally. If you really need to know what is happening at the TAM level, you would turn on your TAM trace, find the entry you are experiencing a problem with, and then open that TAM file looking for the entry.

For this example, choose the RDASPEC file. Once the TAM file opens, you will notice it has columns and records contained in these columns. These columns have a

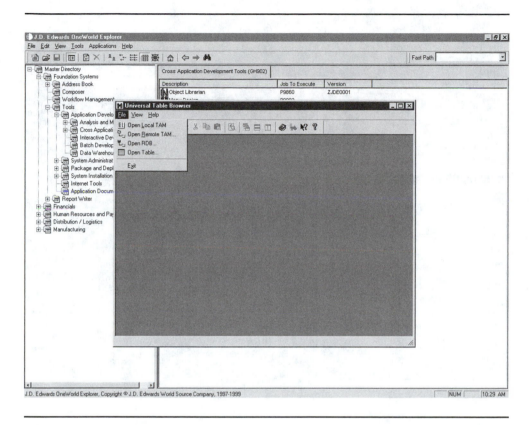

FIGURE 20-8. TAM browse through the UTB

Query by Example line above them so you can easily search for the record you are looking for. Search for the R0006P report. The results of this search are shown in Figure 20-9.

T I P

*The Query by Example line in the universal table browser is case sensitive. Keep this in mind when you are searching for records. In our example, you would need to enter **R0006P** in uppercase as shown or you would not find your records.*

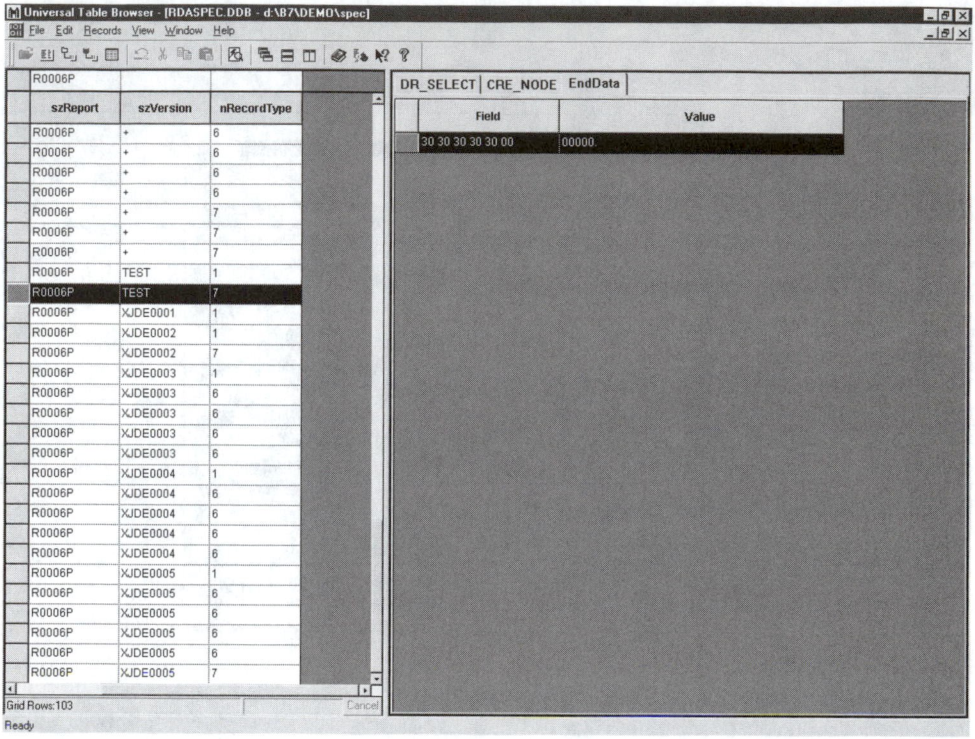

FIGURE 20-9. TAM browse example

Now that you have found the report, you can attempt to find the entry that was causing an issue. The neat thing about the universal table browser is that it allows you to read BLOB (binary large object) fields. The values of these BLOBs will appear to the right as tabs. This information may assist you in troubleshooting an issue, as you can compare what is on one client machine to another through the UTB, and you can also use the UTB to compare your TAM file entries to the central object tables. We have used this functionality to determine such things as when a business view is missing from a package and central objects and why data selection is not functioning correctly. In fact, in the example shown in Figure 20-9, you can see the data selections for the TEST version of the R0006P report. This is the value 000000; if you wanted to see the column the report was looking for this value in, you can find it under the CRE_NODE tab.

With a little practice, using TAM trace and TAM browse can greatly assist you in isolating problems with your system. Although this tracing can look intimidating, always keep in mind what you are looking for. When you find the line that is different from the working version of an application, you know that is a good place to start.

ODBC Trace

The final type of tracing we are going to discuss in this chapter is an ODBC trace. ODBC stands for Open Database Connectivity, and it is a functionality provided by Microsoft. What this really means is that it is middleware, which allows you to communicate with different types of databases. In the context of OneWorld, these databases will be on AS400, SQL Server, and Access.

Microsoft included some logging with this code, so you have yet another tool to assist you in troubleshooting an issue on your system. If you have problems making calls to your database, setting up an ODBC trace may help.

Setting Up an ODBC Trace

Let's say you are having a database problem. Your call to the database is not getting there or you are getting unexpected results. For example, if you created an application and you expect it to write records containing data within 12 columns in a table. However, as you are testing this application you notice that only 10 columns are being populated with data.

What do you do? The first step would be to look at your JDEDEBUG.LOG file to see what type of SQL statement is being passed to the database. If the statement itself only contains 10 columns, you know that something is wrong with how this statement is being constructed. That would indicate a problem within the OneWorld software. You would then need to go back and look at your code for this application to make sure it is set up correctly.

If that is not the problem or you want more information on what the database is being passed, you can set up an ODBC trace. To do this, you need to be on the workstation or enterprise server that is making the call to the database. Go to the Control Panel on this machine and double-click on the 32-bit ODBC Data Sources icon. This will open the ODBC Data Source Administrator dialog box, shown in Figure 20-10. In this dialog box, select the Tracing tab. This is where you will be setting up your ODBC trace.

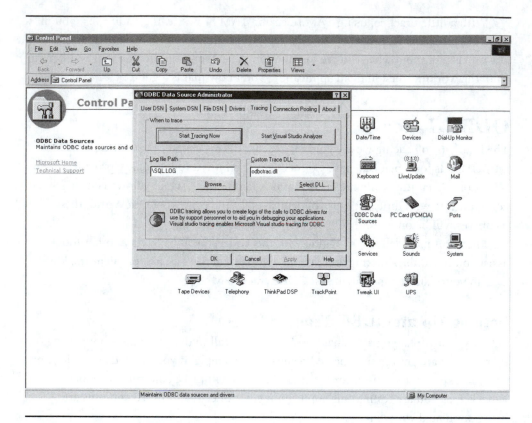

FIGURE 20-10. Setting up an ODBC trace

On this tab, you will need to specify your log file path. This field will default to \SQL.LOG. You will want this log file to generate somewhere you can easily find it; for example, C:\SQL.LOG. Once you have chosen where your log file is going to be placed, you can set up your workstation to re-create the error. Do this before you start your ODBC trace, as this log file will grow quite large very quickly. When you are ready, click Start Tracing Now, then re-create your error.

After you have re-created your error, you will need to turn the ODBC tracing off. To do this, go back to the Tracing tab, shown in Figure 20-10. You will notice that the When To Trace button now says Stop Tracing Now. Click this button to stop the ODBC trace.

CAUTION

Do not forget to stop your ODBC trace. If you don't, you will see a performance degradation on the machine and you will fill up the hard drive very quickly.

Example of an ODBC Trace Log

You now know how to set up an ODBC trace, but what does the SQL log file look like? What is it really going to tell you? In this section, we are going to touch on these topics. Below is an example of what an ODBC trace log file looks like. If you use the default naming convention, this log file will be named SQL.LOG.

```
oexplore      e7:76    ENTER SQLPrepare
          HSTMT               0x020f2920
          UCHAR *             0x0eb374b0 [     684] "UPDATE F0101   SET
ABALKY=?,ABTAX=?,ABALPH=?,ABDC=?,ABMCU=?,ABSIC=?,ABLNGP=?,ABAT1=?,ABCM=?,ABTAXC=
?,ABAT2=?,ABAT3=?,ABAT4=?,ABAT5=?,ABATP=?,ABATR=?,ABATPR=?,ABAB3=?,ABATE=?,ABSBL
I=?,ABAN81=?,ABAN82=?,ABAN83=?,ABAN84=?,ABAN86=?,ABAN85=?,ABAC01=?,ABAC02=?,ABAC
03=?,ABAC04=?,ABAC05=?,ABAC06=?,ABAC07=?,ABAC08=?,ABAC09=?,ABAC10=?,ABAC11=?,ABA
C12=?,ABAC13=?,ABAC14=?,ABAC15=?,ABAC16=?,ABAC17=?,ABAC18=?,ABAC19=?,ABAC20=?,AB
AC21=?,ABAC22=?,ABAC23=?,ABAC24=?,ABAC25=?,ABAC26=?,ABAC27=?,ABAC28=?,ABAC29=?,A
BAC30=?,ABGLBA=?,ABPTI=?,ABPDI=?,ABMSGA=?,ABRMK=?,ABTXCT=?,ABTX2=?,ABALP1=?,ABUR
CD=?,ABURDT=?,ABURAT=?,ABURAB=?,ABURRF=?,ABUSER=?,ABPID=?,ABUPMJ=?,ABJOBN=?,ABUP
MT=? WHERE  ( ABAN8 = ? ) "
          SDWORD                    684
oexplore      e7:76    ENTER SQLExecute
          HSTMT               0x020f2920
oexplore      e7:76    EXIT  SQLExecute  with return code 0 (SQL_SUCCESS)
          HSTMT               0x020f2920
```

The ODBC trace information shown above is from a client workstation. As you can see, this type of tracing gives you very detailed information. One of the nice things about this log file is that it tells you what executed the ODBC call. In this example, this is oexplore. What this log file will also tell you is the return code from ODBC. In this case, we did receive a return code of success from this log file.

As you will see from the log excerpt below, there is not much difference between an ODBC trace log file on the client workstation or on your enterprise server. The only real difference is that the oexplore is no longer making the ODBC call. Since you are on an enterprise server, the ODBC call will now be made by the jdenet_k process. These log files should assist you in determining if the problem lies in your database calls or elsewhere.

```
jdenet_k 6003   d6:15f   ENTER  SQLAllocConnect
          HENV                  0x00cccf60
          HDBC *                0x018b66e4
jdenet_k 6003   d6:15f   EXIT   SQLAllocConnect   with return code 0 (SQL_SUCCESS)
          HENV                  0x00cccf60
          HDBC *                0x018b66e4 ( 0x00ccd200)
```

Logging Settings in the JDE.INI File

To wrap this chapter up, we will very briefly review the JDE.INI file settings for setting up logging. However, don't leave with the impression that these are the only settings you should worry about. There are several "hidden" JDE.INI file settings, which we will not cover here. Check the Osborne/McGraw-Hill Web site at www.osborne.com for a white paper on this subject.

In this chapter, we have covered several different types of logging. Below is a summary of the JDE.INI settings that are needed to set up this type of logging.

```
[DEBUG] Section
LogErrors=0|1
      1 = Create JDE.LOG and JDEDEBUG.LOG.
KeepLogs=0|1
      1 = Save UBE logs.
RepTrace=0|1
      1 = Generate Replication tracing log messages in JDEDEBUG.LOG
TAMTraceLevel=0-9
      0 = No TAM messages in JDEDEBUG.LOG.
      9 = Highest level of TAM messages in JDEDEBUG.LOG
Output=NONE|AUX|FILE|BOTH
      NONE = Only JDE.LOG created.
      AUX = Messages to standard output.
      FILE = Messages to JDEDEBUG.LOG.
      BOTH = Messages to standard output and JDEDEBUG.LOG.
[UBE] Section
UBEDebugLevel=0-6
      0 = No UBE messages.
      6 = Highest level of UBE messages.
```

The example above shows JDE.INI file entries that apply to both workstations and enterprise/application servers. We have listed next the entries that only apply to enterprise or application servers. In the DEBUG section, this example shows entries for a UNIX machine. However, if we were discussing an Intel machine, it would show the drive letter and path where you would like your log files to be created. It is important that this directory exists, since the software will not create it. If the directory does not exist, the log files will not be created. If there is no path in this section—in other words, if the DebugFile or JobFile is set to equal the name of the log—the log files will be created in the system\bin32 directory.

```
[DEBUG] Section (cont'd)
     DebugFile=/u17/b732/log/JDEDEBUG.LOG
     JobFile=/u17/b732/log/JDE.LOG
     JDETSFile=JDETS.log
[INSTALL] section
     B733=/u01/oneworld/B733     ; Location of JDETS.log
[JDENET] Section
     netTrace=[0|1]
     [JDEIPC] Section
     ipcTrace=[0|1]
```

Summary

In this chapter, we have covered the options available to you when you are setting up logging. You may not have to use all of these options, but it is nice to know they exist. As you learn more about OneWorld, your skill at setting up and reading log files will increase.

We have discussed the gambit of OneWorld log files, starting with the simplest log file, JDE.LOG. We then went on to explain what information is contained in JDDEBUG.LOG. Once we covered these basics, we explained the tracing options available to you through OneWorld. This tracing information can truly make all the difference between resolving an issue quickly or having the issue drag out.

Troubleshooting

## CHAPTER 21

OneWorld on the AS/400

Troubleshooting Basics for the AS/400

From Processing to Data

OneWorld Troubleshooting Toolset

Client Access Express

System Integrity

AS/400 Commands

Though the AS/400 platform is a very popular platform within the J.D. Edwards OneWorld community. Many clients migrating from World to OneWorld choose to stay on the AS/400 platform because they already have the platform maintenance and troubleshooting skill set in-house. World, the predecessor to OneWorld, is an AS/400-dedicated application. In fact, you can even see the influence of the AS/400 within certain OneWorld naming conventions and administration applications.

Another common reason for the AS/400's popularity is the stability of the platform. OneWorld users want to make sure that their ERP system (the central nervous system of their business) will be consistently and constantly available and, clearly, the AS/400 has proven itself strong on both points.

Troubleshooting Basics for the AS/400

Given the popularity of the AS/400 within the OneWorld community, it is important that we cover troubleshooting basics for the AS/400, especially as they relate to OneWorld on this platform.

Physics

A truth of physics is that the natural tendency in the universe is toward disorder. This holds true even for the otherwise super-stable AS/400 platform when an ERP system enters the picture. As stable as AS/400 is, you will still have the need for troubleshooting.

Troubleshooting is as much about preventative maintenance and best practices as it is about resolving issues that arise. Most of this book has been geared toward providing a better understanding of best practices when it comes to OneWorld. However, as soon as users enter the system, or system changes are made, problems can arise. Identifying and resolving those issues can be one of the most challenging (and dare I say it?) fun activities related to OneWorld CNC.

Mind-set

In order to troubleshoot OneWorld, a CNC administrator must be the sort of person who enjoys methodically searching for a needle in a haystack. This person must temper the thrill of the hunt with a scientific approach to eliminating hay until the needle is found. This person must also know the difference between the needle and the hay and have quite a bit of experience at working with needles and hay. Such people are not easy to find, but then, neither is the needle. One typo, one misplaced byte, can send a portion of an ERP system awry. OneWorld is no exception.

Rules and Tools

In addition to applying a methodical approach, you must have the right tools and be thoroughly familiar with their use. We will address the following topics in this chapter to provide a more structured approach to finding the needle in the haystack:

- AS/400 OS and DB tools

- OneWorld tools on AS/400

We discuss these topics within a framework of identifying common problems and describing their resolutions. At the end of this chapter, we provide a list of the minimal AS/400 skills required of a OneWorld CNC practitioner to support OneWorld on the AS/400 platform.

AS/400 OS and DB Tools

AS/400 has a multitude of utilities that can be used to effectively support CNC troubleshooting efforts. Joblogs and database tools are the foremost.

Joblogs As the name entails, joblogs are logs that track actions, events, and errors related to processes on AS/400. OneWorld processes on AS/400 are controlled via services: Network, JDENET_K, and Sentinel. Network is controlled by JDENET_N in the B73XSYS library. This OneWorld service is responsible for handling network calls. All client requests for OneWorld logic are filtered through this service. Other dedicated processes are managed via the JDENET_K processes. On service startup, the JDE member of the INI file is read from the B733XSYS library. The JDE member sections should contain 12 sections defining various OneWorld dedicated server-side processes managed by the Network, JDENET_K, and Sentinel processes.

Following a OneWorld installation, you start OneWorld services by issuing the STRNET command. You can monitor startup processes by doing a WRKACTJOB. As these services start, they run through a series of statuses listed in Table 21-1.

Service	Begin Status	Ready Status
Sentinel	SIGW (Signal Wait—initial thread of job waiting for signal).	SIGW
Network	SIGW	SELW (Select Wait—initial thread of job in select wait status)
JDENET_K	RUN	DEQW (Initial thread waiting for completion of a dequeue operation)

TABLE 21-1.   OneWorld Services and Status on the AS/400

To help troubleshoot problems with service startups, you can review the associated joblogs (we will talk about reviewing the J.D. Edwards–provided logs later in this chapter) with WRKUSRJOB for OneWorld. You will then see the joblogs for the associated service jobs as follows:

1. Type **WRKUSRJOB ONEWORLD** and then press ENTER.

2. Identify the job, as in JDENET_K, SENTINEL, or NETWORK.

3. Choose the 8=WORK WITH SPOOLED FILE option.

4. Choose the 5=DISPLAY option.

If you need to send this spool file to somebody such as the J.D. Edwards Support Line (800 289-2999), you can do the following:

1. Create a datafile using CRTPF.

2. Run the CPYSPLF command with the output target pointing to the new datafile.

3. FTP the file to your workstation.

We recommend that whenever you start services, you review any associated logs. Even though the services might appear to be running without problems based on their status, the logs can reveal problems beneath the surface.

Joblogs and BSFN Build   In addition to service logging, joblogs are excellent tools to help troubleshoot the compilation of the J.D. Edwards' business functions on AS/400. Business functions are ANSI C programs compiled on AS/400. These C programs are translated from Microsoft C++ on the deployment server to ANSI C, which is then compiled by the ILE/C engine. Problems commonly associated with the business function build process include the following:

- System Openness Includes (QSYSINC) not installed

- ILE/C not installed

- Erroneous characters in the C++ base code

- Missing headers or source

The first two issues should be addressed via the Preinstallation audit (see Appendix A), but installation of System Openness Includes is often overlooked. In order to determine whether System Openness Includes is installed, you can run WRKLIB QSYSINC. If the QSYSINC library is not there, then ILE/C is not installed properly. Furthermore, if the H file does not exist within the QSYSINC library, OneWorld business function builds will not operate. To install the QSYSINC library, your organization must be licensed for it. If you are, you can run WRKLICPGM and, with the appropriate CD, choose option 13 to install the library and necessary programs. If the QSYSINC library is not installed, you will get errors such as the following in the joblog:

```
CZM0504 Unable to find #include file *LIBL/SYS(TYPES.h
CZM0504 Unable to find #include file *LIBL/H(MILIB).
CZM0504 Unable to find #include file *LIBL/H(QCAPCMD).
```

ILE/C is the required C compiler version for OneWorld on AS/400. In order to verify that ILE/C is installed, you can run DSPSFRSC. The display should return with version ILE/C.

Erroneous characters in the C files are more difficult to troubleshoot. C++ can recognize certain characters and certain commenting conventions that ILE/C does not recognize. It pays to be aware of acceptable ANSI C characters in case your OneWorld implementation on AS/400 will include custom business function coding.

Even if you are not aware of ANSI C characters, you can still troubleshoot business function builds by using JDE AS/400 logging. These logs provide specific information as to where an unacceptable character was reached. Or, if there is some other problem, the logging specifies that as well.

For example, suppose you are building an update package that includes the XT4311Z2 business function and two other objects. Within the object librarian, you will notice that it belongs to the CDIST dynamically linked library. R9622 reports that the server build completes with errors, but you will not find much more information on the deployment server. You need to examine the JDE AS/400 logs to troubleshoot the problem. The following steps will help you understand this process better:

1. Display the stream file generated on the server by the build process with the following command:

   ===> dspstmf stmf('/oneworld/packages/*packagename*/text/cdist.sts')

   Alternatively, you can open the file through Windows Explorer because this location is an IFS directory structure. The stream file will appear as the following:

   ```
   Display Stream File
   Stream file. . . : /oneworld/packages/packagename/text/cdist.sts
    Offset . . . . . :          0           Size :         378
    Control. . . . . :
    Find . . . . . . :
    ...+....1....+....2....+....3....+....4....+....5....+....6....+.
   OneWorld builddll Status Log
   ---------------------------
   process id:    181897
   build status:  P (building DLL)
   DLL name:      CDIST
   did compile count:    2
   did not compile count: 1
   module that is compiling:  LINK
   modules that did not compile:
   xt4311z2
   ```

2. Review the log files created in the package library created on AS/400 with the package name. DSPLIB will reveal the following objects:

   ```
   Display Library
    Library  . . . . . . :    packagename    Number of objects  . :   8
    Type . . . . . . . . :    PROD           ASP of library . . . :   1
   Create authority . . :    *SYSVAL
    Type options, press Enter.
      5=Display full attributes   8=Display service attributes
    Opt  Object           Type         Attribute            Size
      Text
        MSACCESFBA         *SQLPKG                           69632
   ```

```
XT4311Z1              *MODULE    CLE                    4632576
CDIST                 *FILE      PF                     8949760
BSFN SOURCE
   FAILED             *FILE      PF                     3694592
   H                  *FILE      PF                     1183744
BSFN SOURCE
   HXX                *FILE      PF                        8192
BSFN SOURCE
   LINKLOG            *FILE      PF                        8192
   LOG                *FILE      PF                        8192
```

You can then do a DSPPFM against the FAILED physical file and go to the end
of the file where the AS/400 compiler provides specific information on the lines
where the failures occurred:

MSG ID   SEV   Text
                (<SEQNBR>-<FILE NO>:<FILE LINE NO>)
CZM0041   30   Identifier must be declared before it is used.
                (10763-0:10743, 10974-0:10951, 10975-0:10952, 11005-0:10
CZM0347   30   Syntax error: possible missing or .
                (10739-0:10719, 10967-0:10944, 11172-0:11149)
                     * * * * * E N D   O F   M E S S A G E

3. At the referenced line, you can see even more detailed error information that
   enables you to troubleshoot the problem:

```
10742        |
10743   10 |              dsAgreementSearch.cDueTo = 'C';
===========> ............a....................................................
*=ERROR===========> a - CZM0041 Identifier dsAgreementSearch must be declared
10744   11 |              dsAgreementSearch.cCurrencyToConvert = '1';

10719    1 |    DSD3800050A1 dsAgreementSearch = {0};
===========> ...............a.................................................
*=ERROR===========> a - CZM0347 Syntax error: possible missing ';' or ','.
10720        |
```

Object Locks and Locked Objects   In order to maintain messaging and data integrity,
OneWorld processes "lock" data files for updates or even copies. These object locks
can prevent good backups, data copies, and file access.

Law of the West

Services, Object Locks, and Backups

We recommend that you bring down the OneWorld services on AS/400 prior to running your backups to remove any OneWorld process-based object locks. We strongly recommend that you verify your backups using the backup logs and by periodically restoring backups.

As part of the backup routine, we recommend that you delete all *SQLPKG packages other than IBM-supplied *SQL packages as described in Chapter 6.

In order to see how OneWorld locks objects, you can do the following:

1. Enter WRKACTJOB on the command line.

2. Enter 5 next to a OneWorld process.

3. Choose Work With Object Locks.

A list of the objects locked by a OneWorld process is displayed. After you end services, do a WRKOBJLCK on some of the same objects, and the locks should be gone. If the locks remain, try issuing a manual kill. If the manual kill does not work, either your sign-on does not have sufficient permission to kill the process or a full system shutdown with an initial program load (IPL) is required. Prior to performing an IPL, try killing the process after logging on to AS/400 as QSECOFR.

QZDASOINIT Processes   In addition to AS/400-based OneWorld services, AS/400 network management services, called QZDASOINIT processes, can also lock objects and become locked in the process. QZDASOINIT processes manage ODBC connections from the networked OneWorld clients. If you are having problems with OneWorld services and with network connections, we recommend verifying whether any QZDASOINITs are hung. Admittedly, this occurrence is rare, but we have visited clients who were down due to such an issue. We recommend the following steps in such a situation:

1. End OneWorld services with ENDNET.

2. Enter CLRIPC on the command line.

3. Enter WRKACTJOB on the command line.

4. Scroll down to verify whether any QZDASOINITs are available.

5. Manually try to force any remaining QZDASOINITs to end.

6. If manual shutdown fails, an IPL is in order.

In addition to object locks, you can verify tables that OneWorld processes are accessing by choosing Work With Open Files rather than Work With Object Locks. This information can be useful for troubleshooting at the data level.

Display Object Description (DSPOBJD)   AS/400 treats files as objects. Display Object Description (DSPOBJD) is a useful tool for displaying object size, creation date, last used date, and owner. This tool also can be helpful in comparing changes in objects. For instance, if you apply a OneWorld service pack and begin to have issues, you can do a DSPOBJD against the JDEKRNL in B73XXSYS (where XX represents the version release of OneWorld) library versus the saved system library to see if there is a noticeable difference in object size. If the new object is significantly smaller, you might want to consider investigating whether the service pack was applied correctly.

Qbatch   We would be remiss if we did not address batch processing on AS/400. There are several key points we need to discuss:

- Single-threaded jobqueues

- Adding jobqueues

- Troubleshooting batch jobs

Single-Threaded Jobqueues

AS/400 presents a series of utilities that make batch processing extremely accessible from an administration and troubleshooting standpoint. With the initial installation of OneWorld, you will find a single-threaded jobqueue called QB7332 within the Qbatch subsystem. Perform the following steps to verify:

1. Type **WRKSBSD SBSD(QBATCH)** and press ENTER.

2. Choose the 5=DISPLAY option.

3. Choose the "6. Job queue entries" option.

At this point, you can review whether the jobqueue is single threaded (that is, whether it allows only one job at a time to process). *Do not change this setting!* Many administrators notice that because only one jobqueue is defined for OneWorld and because the jobqueue is single threaded, OneWorld batch jobs begin to pile up. Depending on the nature and number of jobs, it can literally be hours for the jobs to process through. So the AS/400-savvy administrator changes the jobqueue setting to make it multithreaded. *Again, do not change this setting!*

J.D. Edwards created the default jobqueue to be single threaded for a reason. The reason is that there are a series of batch jobs that *must* run in single-threaded mode. These jobs call other jobs at the outset of processing, but the called jobs must wait for the initial job to complete. If these jobs are run in a multithreaded jobqueue, the jobs run simultaneously (the outcome is not pretty). We provide a summary of these batch jobs in Table 21-2 but strongly advise that you check the J.D. Edwards Knowledge Garden for updates (https://knowledge.jdedwards.com).

System Code	System Name	UBE	UBE Name	Comments
42	Sales	R49700	Cycle Billing	*Caution:* Although single-threaded processing is highly recommended, processing options and data selection should be used to prevent selection of the same records in case it is to be run in a multithreaded jobqueue.

TABLE 21-2.   UBEs requiring Single-Threaded Jobqueus

System Code	System Name	UBE	UBE Name	Comments
		R42800	Sales Update	Same as above
		R42520	Pick Slips	Same as above
		R42500	Batch Ship Confirmation	Same as above
		R42565	Invoice Print	Same as above
		R42118	Batch Backorder Release	Same as above
		R42997	Commitment	Same as above
37	Quality Management	R37900	Certificate of Analysis Extract	Must run before R37460.
		R37901	Product Test Report Extract	Must run before R37450 Produce Test Report.
		R31410	Order Processing	Must run before R37470 Tests Results Worksheet.
30A	Product Costing	R30812	Cost Rollup	Caution: Although single-threaded processing is highly recommended, processing options and data selection should be used to prevent selection of the same records in case it is to be run in a multithreaded jobqueue. This includes both parent items and components added through the Bill of Materials (BOM) explosion.
		R30835	Frozen Cost Update	Same as above

TABLE 21-2.   UBEs requiring Single-Threaded Jobqueus (*continued*)

Troubleshooting

System Code	System Name	UBE	UBE Name	Comments
31	Shop Floor Management	R31410	Work Order Processing	Caution: Although single-threaded processing is highly recommended, processing options and data selection should be used to prevent selection of the same records in case it is to be run in a multithreaded jobqueue.
31A	Manufacturing Accounting	R31802	WIP and Completion J/Es	Should not run while Shop Floor transaction and work order processing and/or attachments are running for the same work orders.
		R31804	Work Order Variances	Should run after R31802 is processed in final mode.
49	Transportation	R4981	Freight Update	Caution: Although single-threaded processing is highly recommended, data selection should be used to prevent selection of the same records in case it is to be run in a multithreaded jobqueue.

TABLE 21-2.   UBEs requiring Single-Threaded Jobqueus (*continued*)

System Code	System Name	UBE	UBE Name	Comments
7	Payroll	R052901	Generate Timecard Entries	*Caution:* Although single-threaded processing is highly recommended, processing options and data selection should be used to prevent selection of the same records in case it is to be run in a multithreaded jobqueue.
		R07200	PrePayroll	*Caution:* Although single-threaded processing is highly recommended, use data selection to select employees into only one version in case of multithreaded processing.
		R07230	Payroll Print Driver	*Caution:* Although single-threaded processing is highly recommended, this report can be run in multithreaded jobqueues.
		R072902	Generate Payroll Journal Entries	Same as above
		R07250	Final Update	Same as above

TABLE 21-2.   UBEs requiring Single-Threaded Jobqueus (*continued*)

Troubleshooting

System Code	System Name	UBE	UBE Name	Comments
9	G/L	R093021	Indexed Allocations	*Caution:* Although single-threaded processing is highly recommended, the computation should be reviewed to verify that no dependencies exist for multithreaded processing.
		R09130	Refresh Reconcilation	*Caution:* Although single-threaded processing is highly recommended, each job must select a separate account in data selection to be run in a multithreaded queue.
		R097011	Intercompany Accounts in Balance	This integrity should be run with no data selection.
		R097031	Account Balance Without Account Master	This integrity should be run with no data selection.
		R097041	Accounts Without Business Units	This integrity should be run with no data selection.
11	Multi-Currency	R11411	Detailed Currency Restatement	UBE has no data selection. All or nothing.
13	Equipment Maintenance	R12807	PM Schedule Update	Data selection must be set to ensure the same schedules are not being processed simultaneously.

TABLE 21-2.   UBEs requiring Single-Threaded Jobqueus *(continued)*

System Code	System Name	UBE	UBE Name	Comments
48S	Service Billing	R48120	Billing Workfile Generation	*Caution:* Although single-threaded processing is highly recommended, processing options and data selection should be used to prevent selection of the same records in case they are run in a multithreaded jobqueue.
		R481202	Billing Detail Transaction Re-Extend	Same as above
		R48121	Invoice Generation	Same as above
		R48122	Voucher Generation	Same as above
		R48131	Journal Generation	Same as above
		R48132	G/L Journal Generation	Same as above
		R48197	Billing Vouchers A/P-G/L Journal Generation	Same as above
		R48198	Create G/L Entries	Same as above
		R48199	Billing Invoice A/R-G/L Journal Generation	Same as above
		R48300	Journal Edit Register	Same as above
52	Contract Billing	R52121	Contract Billing Invoice Generation	Same as above

TABLE 21-2.   UBEs requiring Single-Threaded Jobqueus *(continued)*

Troubleshooting

System Code	System Name	UBE	UBE Name	Comments
03B	Accounts Receivable	R03B500X	Statement Processing	*Caution:* Although single-threaded processing is highly recommended, can be multithreaded after applying a code change and other instructions provided by J.D.Edwards.
		R03B525	Credit Analysis Refresh	Same as above
		R03B16	Statistical History Refresh	*Caution:* Although single-threaded processing is highly recommended, if data selection can be determined by parent/child trees (which is difficult to do), then multithreaded processing is acceptable.
		P03B11Z1I	Batch Input Processor	*Caution:* Although single-threaded processing is highly recommended, can be multithreaded with user data selection on UBE.
4	Accounts Payable	R04570	Create Payment Control Groups	Cannot run multithreaded. Duplicate payment control numbers might be assigned if multiple UBEs are run simultaneously.

TABLE 21-2.   UBEs requiring Single-Threaded Jobqueus *(continued)*

System Code	System Name	UBE	UBE Name	Comments
4	Accounts Payable	R04571	A/P Auto Payments - Print Driver	Cannot run multithreaded. Duplicate check numbers might be assigned because sequential numbers from a table are used. This is also a limitation of all the other payment formats.
4	Accounts Payable	R04575	A/P Auto Payments - Update Driver	Cannot run multithreaded. Duplicate internal payment number might be assigned because sequential numbers from a table are used.

TABLE 21-2.   UBEs requiring Single-Threaded Jobqueus *(continued)*

Adding jobqueues   If you decide you need a multithreaded jobqueue (or just another single-threaded jobqueue in addition to QB7332), you can create one by first creating the jobqueue and then adding it to the Qbatch (or other) subsystem with the following steps:

1. Enter the command CRTJOBQ JOBQ(QGPL/JASTEST).

2. Enter the command ADDJOBQE SBSD(QBATCH) JOBQ(JASTEST) SEQNBR(60).

When you add the jobqueue to the subsystem, you can define how many jobs can be run in the queue concurrently with the Maximum Active Jobs line by simply entering the number. Then, to direct users to that jobqueue, take the following steps:

1. Enter the name of the jobqueue as a valid UDC value in 98/JQ.

2. Add (not copy) a version of the report(s) to be run in the jobqueue. In the Job Queue field on the Version Add screen, you can assign your new queue to the version. Note: Unfortunately, the VersionListAdd business function converts

Troubleshooting

this value to binary large object format (BLOB) in the F983051 table, so you cannot manipulate it with SQL after entering it in OneWorld.

Following these two steps, you can either add the version to a menu and assign the menu to a user or group (which we recommend), or you can notify your user base which version should be used and hope they listen to you (we do not recommend this approach).

Troubleshooting Batch Jobs   You can troubleshoot batch jobs by reviewing the associated joblogs. For instance, let's say that user Kstern is having some problem with the R0010P report. Using either WRKACTJOB or WRKUSRJOB, you can drill down to the joblog review as follows:

1. Enter the command WRKUSRJOB KStern <ENTER>.

2. Identify the job, for instance R0010P.

3. Choose selection 8=WORK WITH SPOOLED FILE.

4. Choose selection 5=DISPLAY.

Then you can review the log to discover any errors as in the following example:

```
*..+..1..+..2..+..3..+..4..+..5..+..6..+..7..+..8..+..9..+..0..+..1..+..2..+..3
  5769SS1 V4R3M0 980729    Job Log    ENTERPRISE    8/16/00 18:48:11    Page  1
 Job name . . . : R0010P  User  . . . : KSTERN  Number . . .: 138775
  Job description . . . . . . :    JDE    Library . . . . . : QGPL
```

This joblog header indicates that you have the correct joblog. The correct server (Enterprise), date and time, job name (R0010P), and user (KSTERN) are listed. Scan to the bottom of the log to see if any error descriptions are included. In this case, we have used bold to emphasize the error message:

```
MCH1001   Escape  40   8/16/00  18:48:10  #auexcpt             000B24   DBDR        B7332SYS    *STMT
To module . . . . . . . . :    DBDRV_CP
To procedure . . . . . . . :    CallAGConnectPgm
Statement . . . . . . . . :    27
Message . . . . . :   Attempt to use permanent system object DB_ROUTER without  authority.
Cause . . . . . :   You tried to use the permanent system object DB_ROUTER without having the correct authority.
```

At this point, the job ended with a status of 40, which means that the job ended without becoming active. The reason is provided in the message, and the Cause section provides further explanation. Clearly the next step is to review DB_ROUTER object authorities for user Kstern. In this case, authority on the DB_ROUTER object was set to *EXCLUDE for all users. In other words, all users would have had issues submitting jobs on AS/400. Correcting this exclusion allowed Kstern and others to successfully submit and run jobs.

The job ending codes and their descriptions are as follows:

0	The job completed normally.
10	The job completed normally during controlled ending or controlled subsystem ending.
20	The job exceeded end severity (ENDSEV job attribute).
30	The job ended abnormally.
40	The job ended before becoming active.
50	The job ended while the job was active.
60	The subsystem ended abnormally while the job was active.
70	The system ended abnormally while the job was active.
80	The job ended (ENDJOBABN command).
90	The job was forced to end after the time limit ended (ENDJOBABN command).

From Processing to Data

Up to this point we have addressed troubleshooting OneWorld processing on the AS/400. Now we will turn our focus to troubleshooting data related issues.

Displaying Open Files

As a bridge from OneWorld services to data, the AS/400 Display Open File utility is helpful at revealing files accessed by OneWorld processes. You can access this utility by doing the following:

1. Enter WRKACTJOB on the command line.

2. Select Work With Process.

3. Select Display Open Files.

Working with this utility after an issue arises is helpful in that you can pinpoint which files are being accessed. You can then use database tools to examine the content of these files, as well as OS tools to examine the structure and description of the files.

However, if your organization has the bandwidth, we recommend documenting open files for key processes before issues arise. You can then determine whether any changes have occurred within OCM or in overall file availability, which might cause some issues.

As we mentioned, object locks can prevent data copies from occurring in a clean manner. When you refresh the OneWorld CRP or development environments with production business data, some files might not carry over to the library. Or even if the files carry over, the data might not.

By displaying open files you will quickly be able to identify the files in question. Using a host of tools and methods, you can then compare these files to files of the same name in the other OneWorld environments and/or in restored backup data.

Comparing Files

After tracing object locks and open files, a prime technique for troubleshooting OneWorld on AS/400 is to compare the same files between environments. Typically, OneWorld has five environments, but one, TST733, is actually a combination of CRP733 and DEV733. This leaves you with four main data sets to review when troubleshooting.

Some key AS/400 tools to use in comparing files are Display File Description, Interactive SQL, Program Development Manager, and Display Database Relations. Let's look at each one of these tools in turn.

Displaying File Description (DSPFD)

This utility enables you to determine some of the following key information (and is particularly useful when troubleshooting coexistence issues—see Chapter 6):

- Whether the file is SQL defined or based on data description specification (DDS)

- Coded character set identifier (important for multilanguage implementations)

- Data space size

- Physical file open/close access counts

- Write, update, and delete operations

- Logical and physical reads

- Records rejected by key selection

- Last changed, saved, and restored date/time

- Last used date

- Format

- Total records (including the total deleted records)

Clearly this utility is powerful and informative. You can use this information to determine if a file is getting hit and how often, and whether it is the original or a restored file.

Reorganizing Physical Files

The AS/400 deleted records remain in file storage even though the data has been removed. File sizes grow with each addition and deletion. If you are experiencing performance issues, you should reorganize the physical files (RGZPFM). This command cleans up deleted record space for faster file parsing. The following program can be useful to automate this process:

1. Run the Display File Description (DSPFD) command for all files within a library.

```
File . . . . . . . . . . . . . . > *ALL           Name, generic*, *ALL
Library . . . . . . . . . . . > SDGCRPDTA        Name, *LIBL, *CURLIB...
Type of information . . . . . . > *MBRLIST        *ALL, *BASATR, *ATR...
                                + for more values
 Output . . . . . . . . . . . . > *OUTFILE        *, *PRINT, *OUTFILE
 File attributes . . . . . . . .    *ALL          *ALL, *DSPF, *PRTF, *DKTF...
                                + for more values
 File to receive output . . . . > CRPFILE         Name
 Library . . . . . . . . . . >    JASSAV          Name, *LIBL, *CURLIB
 Output member options:
   Member to receive output . . .   *FIRST        Name, *FIRST
   Replace or add records . . . .   *REPLACE      *REPLACE, *ADD
```

2. Create and run the following Command Language (CL) program.

```
FMT **  ...+... 1 ...+... 2 ...+... 3 ...+... 4 ...+... 5 ...+... 6 ...+... 7
        *************** Beginning of data ********************************
0001.00       PGM         PARM(&LIB)
0002.00       DCL         VAR(&LIB) TYPE(*CHAR) LEN(10)
0003.00       DCLF        FILE(JASSAV/FILOUT)
0004.00       DSPFD       FILE(&LIB/*ALL) TYPE(*MBRLIST) +
0005.00                     OUTPUT(*OUTFILE) OUTFILE(JASSAV/FILOUT)
0006.00 READ:     RCVF      DEV(*FILE)
0007.00       MONMSG      MSGID(CPF0864) EXEC(GOTO CMDLBL(END))
0008.00       IF          COND((&MLNDTR *EQ 0) *OR (&MLFTYP *NE 'P')) +
0009.00         THEN(GOTO CMDLBL(READ))
0010.00       RGZPFM      FILE(&LIB/&MLFILE)
0011.00       MONMSG      MSGID(CPF2981)
```

```
0012.00                  GOTO      CMDLBL(READ)
0013.00  END:            ENDPGM
         ****************** End of data ********************************
```

Optionally, you can set the default on the files to *YES for Reuse Deleted Records. This can be done with the following command:

CHGPF FILE(CRPDTA/F0911) REUSEDLT(*YES)

The system then automatically cleans up deleted records.

Interactive SQL (STRSQL)

AS/400 has numerous database utilities, and one of our favorites is Interactive SQL, which you initiate with the STRSQL command. This utility enables you to do the following:

1. Manually enter SQL statements as found in JDEDEBUG logs

2. Review data within files

3. Review file structure for column headings and tuple length

STRSQL is a highly versatile data manipulation tool. With this utility, you can perform SELECTs, INSERTs, UPDATEs, and DELETEs. You can perform complex joins as well. Prior to actually performing INSERTs, UPDATEs, or DELETEs, we recommend that you back up the data files to a save library. The Interactive SQL tool even enables you to create the save file by simply changing the output parameters to be output to a file rather than displayed on a screen.

N O T E

*For coexistence clients, we do not recommend that you use Interactive SQL to back up files prior to performing data manipulation queries because the files will be created with type *SQL rather than DDS. CRTDUPOBJ is a better method for maintaining the proper file type.*

Even after backing up the data, you probably want to bring down the OneWorld services for certain types of data manipulation queries, especially for queries run against OneWorld system data files.

One of the best uses for STRSQL is to run the exact query as found in the JDEDEBUG logs. Queries that fail help you focus your troubleshooting on the data itself. Queries that succeed point to problems other than data.

Program Development Manager (PDM)

The Program Development Manager is an excellent tool for manipulating OneWorld AS/400 physical files and the content of members, especially the INI member of the JDE file. In fact, the PDM tool is called when you select Edit INI from the A98OWMNU menu found within JDEOW. To start this tool, you execute STRPDM. The screen that results enables you to work with object, file, or member-level objects.

Editing the INI File

Prior to editing the INI member to enable logging, make changes in kernel services for performance, or enable/disable other functions such as security or transaction processing, we strongly recommend that you make a copy of the file in a save library. We also strongly recommend that you bring down OneWorld services prior to editing the member. In some cases, certain edits can confuse the AS/400 IPC functions forcing you to bring down communication services. Error messages on CLRIPC following ENDNET are a clear indicator that you must bring down communication services or even possibly IPL the system.

At any rate, to edit the INI file, perform the following:

1. Enter the command **STRPDM**.

2. For member, type in **INI**.

3. For file, type in **JDE**.

4. For library, type in **B73XSYS** (where *X* refers to your particular OneWorld version).

You are then presented with a screen that enables you to copy, view, or edit the member. We recommend you choose to edit it only if you truly need to edit the member. If you are digging for information, viewing the member is preferable.

After opening the INI file to make changes, you can enter **F** *Keywork* to perform a find for a section or keyword. Pressing ENTER moves the cursor to that section of the INI, where you can easily enter your changes. Pressing F3 takes you out of the edit mode and into a prompt screen for either saving your changes or discarding and closing the member.

When you start services, any changes you have made to the INI file are read by OneWorld. You can then go through the process of verifying whether the changes you have made are valid and desired.

N O T E

You can FTP the INI file to your workstation for safekeeping. However, we do not recommend that you FTP the INI back to AS/400. Even if the INI is FTPed to the server during the installation process, it is far better to make your edits using STRPDM on AS/400 to avoid entering erroneous characters with a PC-based editor.

NOTE

The WRKLIBPDM command, related to STRPDM, can be used in cases where
you are having trouble with backups or data refreshes. For instance, using
WRKLIBPDM, you can attempt to change a particular library name. If you
cannot do so, then you possibly have journaling within the library, or a
process has a lock on an open table. If you can change the name of the library
successfully, it is highly likely that the backup or data refresh will be successful.

Database Relations

In Chapter 6, we discussed a method to get a listing for all of the logical files that exist
in a library along with a join query that enables you to compare lists. However, you
also need to be able to quickly view the definition for logicals relevant to a particular
table. Running the AS/400 Display Database Relations (DSPDBDR) command is an
excellent way to view definitions of a file's associated logicals.

Using DSPDBDR, you can validate the logicals defined on AS/400 for a data file
and then compare that definition against the definition found in OneWorld's object
librarian. Any discrepancies can be dealt with by backing up the file, then deleting
the logicals and regenerating them.

If the regeneration of logicals fails, the most likely reason is that duplicate records
entered into the file during the period in which the discrepancy arose between actual
logicals and defined database relations. The index generation then fails because the
definitions maintain a unique constraint and so cannot be generated over a file that
has duplicate records.

At this point, you can delete the file altogether, regenerate it, and then do a CPYF
with drop duplicate/ignore error parameters from the backed up file to the new file.
The records are copied, and the unique constraint maintained by the logicals force
any duplicate records to drop.

OneWorld Troubleshooting Toolset

In addition to the AS/400 tools we have reviewed, J.D. Edwards also provides a
powerful troubleshooting toolset on AS/400, including:

JDE logging and DSPSTMF
Porttest
RUNUBE

JDE Logging and DSPSTMF

Learning to read the JDE and JDEDEBUG logs is valuable. We suggest you review Chapter 20 in addition to reading this section. For the most part, the logs are similar across platforms. However, activating, finding, and reviewing the logs are, to some degree, platform dependent.

Activating the Logs

In order to activate OneWorld logging on AS/400 from AS/400 (UBE logging can be activated from the client GUI), you can use the Program Development Manager to edit the JDE member of the INI file. The steps to take are the following:

1. First issue the ENDNET command

2. Then issue the CLRIPC command

3. Open the INI file with the Program Development Manager using either the A98OWMNU selection or with STRPDM, and then make the following changes:

```
[DEBUG]
Output=FILE
Trace=TRUE
DebugFile=JDEB7332/jdedebug.log
JobFile=JDEB7332/jde.log
JDETSFile=/JDEB7332/JDETS.LOG
ClientLog=1
LogErrors=1
KeepLogs=1
RunBatchDelay=0
TAMTraceLevel=1
RepTrace=1
```

Locating the Logs   JDE logs are written to the IFS directory structure, which is a hierarchical file structure available on AS/400. IFS objects can be accessed via Windows Explorer. The JDE member contains the definition of the folder destination for the logs. To access this directory, you can execute a Work Link command (WRKLNK) to get to the root of this file structure. The logs are typically stored in the JDEB7332 directory. Enter 5 for Next Level to go into the directory where you can view a listing of the JDE and JDEDEBUG logs.

NOTE

OneWorld logging can take up large amounts of disk space and can diminish processing efficiencies on AS/400. JDE and JDEDEBUG logging should be turned off for day-to-day operations. The logs reside in the IFS directory structure and are not automatically cleaned up; if you do have logging turned on, it is recommended that you frequently delete old logs to manage your disk space usage.

Viewing the Logs   To view the JDE log and JDEDEBUG files on AS/400 without resorting to a PC, J.D. Edwards provides the Display Stream File command, which is installed during the OneWorld installation. The command syntax is the following:

```
DSPSTMF STMF('/JDEB7332/JDE_XXX.LOG)
```

Porttest

This test is particularly useful to verify that OneWorld IPC calls on AS/400 can communicate over the assigned port number (as defined per files F9650 and F9654) and that OneWorld can access data. Porttest is available on each OneWorld platform, but like logging, running porttest differs per platform.

To run porttest, you must have both the B733SYS and QGPL libraries in your library list. After verifying your library list, and without services running, you then issue the following command:

```
porttest [OneWorld User Name] [OneWorld Password] [Environment]
```

If the porttest fails, basic configuration issues need to be resolved. If porttest succeeds but you are still having problems, you can begin to examine areas other than sign-on user access, porttest definitions, and service functionality. The JDE and JDEDEBUG logs are helpful in determining errors surrounding porttest.

RUNUBE

Another tool within the troubleshooting toolset is the RUNUBE command. RUNUBE is the step that follows a successful porttest and startup of OneWorld services. Reviewing the JDE and JDEDEBUG logs during RUNUBE is helpful in determining error resolution.

RUNUBE is the command you use to launch a batch from the command line. After initializing OneWorld services, you can run the RUNUBE command as follows:

```
runube [JDE User Name] [JDE Password] [Environment] [Report Name] [Version]
[Batch/Interactive] [Save/Delete] [Print/Hold] [Printer Name]
```

If the UBE does not run locally, services and authorities are suspect. The logs contained within the JDEB7332 file will be useful once again. Also, the AS/400 communication services should be verified at this juncture.

What Else?

If you can log on to AS/400, run porttest, start OneWorld services, and launch a UBE via the command line, then your OneWorld base operations are more than likely sound. Issues at this point would revolve around network connectivity, including TCP/IP and client access issues. Other than client access issues, traditional OneWorld troubleshooting techniques applicable to all platforms are relevant.

Client Access Express

OneWorld clients communicate with the host via a process of translation from J.D. Edwards middleware—JDENET and JDEBASE—to host-specific client communication programs, such as Client Access Express in the case of AS/400 servers. (See Figure 21-1.)

Client Access Express is a 32-bit Windows client providing TCP/IP only connections to AS/400 host servers. OneWorld accesses the DB2 database on AS/400 using the Client Access Express ODBC DLL (with enhanced multithreaded capabilities) and sends client requests for server-based services using Client Access Express' TCP/IP sockets.

Documentation on Client Access Express is thorough and voluminous. We cover only some of the more OneWorld-relevant troubleshooting aspects.

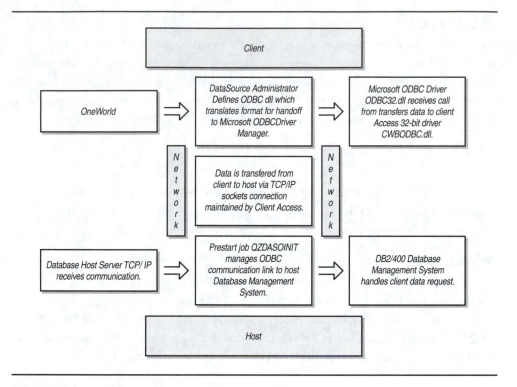

FIGURE 21-1.   Client-to-host communication channel

When It Doesn't Work

When the OneWorld client fails to connect to the AS/400 enterprise server, you should verify several important conditions:

- Can you connect to the Enterprise Server via Client Access Express?

- Does CWBPING return successfully?

- Does ping return successfully?

If the answer is "no" to the preceding questions *and* you have Client Access Express installed, you can use a variety of network trace tools available with OneWorld and with Client Access Express.

System Integrity

Although AS/400 may seem indestructible, various troubleshooting touchpoints, and system administration touchpoints as well, fall within preventive troubleshooting measures. It is important that AS/400 system integrity be well guarded. We describe two concepts for consideration in the sections that follow.

Security

Via password changes for OneWorld installation profiles, OneWorld sign-on security, and properly applied operating system security, you can prevent many issues that are a result of direct user access to the OneWorld system database.

Disk Maintenance

WRKDSKSTS provides utilization measures. Run this command often. It is important to remember that disk performance begins to degrade around 72 percent capacity, so keep this number in mind as a maximum limit not to be exceeded. You can minimize disk utilization with the activities described in the sections that follow.

Delete Old Reports

UBE reports are stored on AS/400 as members in the PRINTQUEUE file in the system library (for example, B733SYS). Old report output should be deleted or archived to reduce disk space usage. The frequency of deletion or archiving depends on usage patterns within each organization. However, there is an upper limit of approximately 32,000 members per file in AS/400. If you reach this limit, you will not be able to run UBEs successfully on AS/400 and will see the following error message in the JDEDEBUG logs:

At the start of the log:

```
810830 Thu Oct 7 02:04:04 1999 JDEKRNL_A/C/RUNBATCH1044
Processing PrintUBE request failed - see previous messages
```

Further down in the log :

```
-UBE--[0] dwDBPrinterType is 4
Oct 7 02:24:31 ** Locking /DEVB732/specfile/rdatext.ddb in READ mode.
Oct 7 02:24:31 ** Unlocking TAM file /DEVB732/specfile/rdatext.ddb
Oct 7 02:24:31 ** Unlocking TAM file /DEVB732/specfile/rdaspec.ddb
Oct 7 02:24:31 ** Locking /DEVB732/specfile/rdaspec.ddb in READ mode.
Oct 7 02:24:31 ** Unlocking TAM file /DEVB732/specfile/rdaspec.ddb
--UBE--[0] SS:Unable to Start Print Job
--UBE--[6] K2PRINT END
```

You can clear out members from the PRINTQUEUE file by executing WRKMBRPDM FILE(B733XSYS/PRINTQUEUE)* and then selecting option 4 next to each member you want to delete.

Delete Old Packages

Packages are stored in the integrated file system on AS/400 under the OneWorld directory. You can execute WRKLNK OneWorld and then drill down from there.

Backups

Even though your enterprise server is an AS/400, you must still perform full backups and verify them on a regular basis. Although backup strategies differ, it is important that OneWorld services are not running over the data set during backups. If you have only one AS/400, we suggest you stop OneWorld services as previously mentioned to avoid object locks. Having a second AS/400 with third-party data replication tools pushing the data from your production box to the second server enables you to run a 24x7 shop, still get your backups, and have a failover box if necessary.

We recommend you back up the OneWorld specification files in addition to libraries. These specification files are stored in the integrated file system on AS/400. These objects must be specifically saved using the OS/400 SAV command. Performing this save is critical in having a complete backup of your OneWorld installation on AS/400.

Clean Up Unused Space

As we discussed previously, remember to reorganize your physical file members periodically to remove deleted record space. Also, examine your libraries from time to time. During the life of a OneWorld implementation and given the ease of doing CPYLIBs, you might find that a number of libraries were created on a temporary basis and are no longer needed. After verifying they are no longer needed, delete them with DLTLIB.

AS/400 Commands

Finally, we would like to leave you with a chart of commands to master for troubleshooting OneWorld on AS/400 (see Table 21-3). While there are literally thousands of additional commands, the commands in this table provide a solid base for troubleshooting OneWorld on AS/400.

System Management Sign-on

Sign-on	System Values	PTFs	Hardware	Software
WRKUSRPRF	WRKSYSVAL	DSPPTF	WRKCFGSTS	GO LICPGM
		LODPTF	PWRDWNSYS	
		APYPTF	DSPHDWRSC	

Disk Usage	History Logs	System Information	Cleanup
DSPDSKSTS	DSPLOG	PRTSYSINF	GO CLEANUP
RCLSTG			

Work Management

Job Control	Output Queues
DSPSBSD	WRKOUTQ
WRKACTJOB	WRKSPLF
WRKJOB	WRKWTR
DSPJOBLOG	STRPRTWTR

Object Management

Object Mgt.	File CMDs	Library CMD	IFS
DSPOBJD	WRKF	DSPLIB	WRKLNK
WRKOBJ	CPYF	WRKLIB	DSPSTMF
WRKOBJLCK	DLTF		
EDTOBJAUT	CLRPFM		
	DSPFD		
	DSPFFD		
	DSPDBR		
	RGZPFM		

TABLE 21-3. Useful AS/400 Commands

Troubleshooting

Security		
Users	**System**	**Objects**
CRTUSRPRF		DSPOBJAUT
WRKUSRPRF		WRKOBJAUT

Misc			
Backup	**Programming**	**Networking**	**Utilities**
SAVSYS	STRSEU	CFGTCP	STRQRY
SAV			STRSQL
SAVCHGOBJ			STRDFU
INZTAP			
DSPTAP			

TABLE 21-3.　Useful AS/400 Commands (*continued*)

Summary

In this chapter, we discussed troubleshooting OneWorld on the AS/400 platform and focused on the intersection of OneWorld and OS/400. (Chapters 22 and 23 present troubleshooting specific issues, the resolution of many of which are relevant to the AS/400.) With a firm grasp of the use of the tools described in this chapter, you will be prepared to troubleshoot your way through most issues that will arise (feel free to call us if you get a really tough one).

CHAPTER 22

Troubleshooting NT

MDAC Levels

Windows NT Service Packs

Microsoft Access ODBC Driver Level

File Permissions on OneWorld
    Directory Structure

Windows NT Compression

Starting Host Services Automatically

This book would not be complete if we did not go over some of the specific issues that have been seen with the Windows NT operating system. The good news is that there are not many of these issues and they are fairly easy to work with, so this will be a relatively short chapter. However, we will cover the major issues that have been seen with OneWorld and the Windows NT operating system:

- MDAC levels

- Windows NT Service Packs

- Microsoft Access ODBC driver level

- File permissions on the OneWorld directory structure

- Windows NT compression

- Starting host services automatically

MDAC Levels

A question that seems to always come up is, "What level of MDAC should I be on for OneWorld?" This depends on what release of OneWorld you are on. The current breakdown at the time this chapter was written, taken from the J.D. Edwards Web site, is described in the following sections.

DEFINITION

MDAC: MDAC stands for Microsoft Database Access Component. MDAC is a way in which Microsoft delivers windows DLLs, which are used for communication purposes. These DLLs affect the driver levels of your ODBCs in the Control Panel.

CAUTION

You will need to apply MDACs to your system no matter what database you are running. So if you are using Oracle, for example, you will still need to apply the required MDAC level to your workstations. If you do not, you can run into problems.

B732

With OneWorld B732 there are different levels of MDAC that you will need to be on. If you are running B732 with OneWorld Service Pack 11.3.1 or higher, you should be on MDAC 2.1 SP2 (this is file version 2.1.2.4202.3). If you are running on an earlier release of OneWorld, you can be on a lower level of MDAC.

CAUTION

You cannot run on MDAC 2.0, as this has caused problems with OneWorld.

B733

If you are the OneWorld release of B733, your choice is simple. You will need to run MDAC 2.1 SP2. It is also important to note that at this release the minimum driver level for your SQL Server ODBC is 3.70.07.90. If you use a lower driver level, you can run into possible problems.

Windows NT Service Packs

Most businesses that are using the OneWorld applications are also using some other vendor's applications, such as Microsoft. This means they need to maintain the system for these applications as well as for OneWorld. Often Microsoft will require service packs to use a certain functionality or fix some issues with their software. This should cause any OneWorld system administrator to pause, since OneWorld is running on the Windows NT operating system and if you change the operating system you can affect the OneWorld system. J.D. Edwards does try to keep up with Microsoft on their service packs. When a service pack is offered, J.D. Edwards will test that service pack against OneWorld and certify it for certain releases. Since this information is constantly changing, you will want to check with J.D. Edwards customer support to see if the service pack you want or need is supported with your release of OneWorld. However, this book would not be complete if we did not cover the information that was current at the time this book was written.

Troubleshooting

Windows NT 4.0

Most companies today are running either a workstation or a server on the Windows NT 4.0 operating system. So these companies will need to maintain their systems, which means taking service packs from Microsoft to keep their systems running correctly. The trick is to not cause even more damage when trying to apply a fix. With this in mind, let's cover the release and service pack levels of OneWorld that have been tested against Microsoft's service packs.

NT Service Pack 4.0

The releases that have been tested with this service pack are B732.X and the OneWorld Service Pack level of 11 or higher. This means you can run this Microsoft service pack against any OneWorld release that is higher than this, for both the workstation and the server. If you implement this service pack on a lower OneWorld release or service pack level, the results are unpredictable.

NT Service Pack 5.0

The recommendation of J.D. Edwards is that all new implementations of OneWorld upgrade to Windows NT Service Pack 5.0 or higher. This recommendation applies to both workstations and servers. The releases of OneWorld that have been tested against this configuration are B732 Service Pack 11 and higher. Any new implementation that is above this release level should implement NT service Service Pack 5.0.

NT Service Pack 6.0a

The recommendations for this service pack applies to both workstations and servers. This service pack has been tested against OneWorld release levels B732, with a OneWorld Service Pack level of 12.2 or higher. This information should assist your system administrator in maintaining your business's NT systems.

Microsoft Access ODBC Driver Level

There has been a problem, on some systems, with a certain driver level of Microsoft Access. You will see this driver level problem when you apply MDAC 2.1 SP1, which is file version 2.1.13711.11. What can happen is that client installations will get to about 80 percent complete and then just disappear. We have seen this more often when installing deployment servers on Windows NT machines with MDAC 2.1 SP1 installed on them. To avoid this problem, you need to roll your ODBC Jet driver back to the 3.51 level or apply MDAC 2.1 SP2.

File Permissions on OneWorld Directory Structure

Some of the most common problems with OneWorld and the NT operating system boil down to one thing: file permissions. In order for package builds, checking objects in, and client installations to work correctly, the permissions on the file directory structure must be sufficient for your users. In this section, we will go over the permissions for the deployment and enterprise servers. This should give your system administrator enough information to lock down the OneWorld directory structures without running into some unpleasant surprises.

The Deployment Server

This section discusses which permissions you need to set on the B733 directory for your deployment server. Some of these permission recommendations were taken from a J.D. Edwards installation manual while others have been developed through the authors' experiences. They should give you a good idea of how you can lock down the directory structure and why. We will go over the different folders contained in the B733 directory and the permissions that should be set for them for the different types of users of a OneWorld implementation. When we say different types of users, we mean your OneWorld users' NT accounts; for example, a developer will need more accesses, through windows NT permissions, than a user in accounting. We will cover some "standard" types of users in order to explain this concept. The types of users are:

- **JDE** This is a power user that normally has more privileges on the system and thus will need a higher level of privileges for your deployment server's directory structure.

- **Production users** These are your normal end users. These are the users that enter your data day to day and keep your business running.

- **Developer users**   These are programmers who would be responsible for modifying your OneWorld system. They will need a higher level of permissions than other users.

- **CNC administrators**   This type of user describes your supervisors. They are not going to need all permissions, but they will need more than the production users.

T I P

Your system administrator should have full permissions to all of the OneWorld files on the deployment server because this person is responsible for maintaining, updating, and upgrading the system.

ActivEra

This directory is needed for the ActivEra console. This means that any users who will be using the AvtivEra console will need change permissions to this directory. Any user who is not using this console can be locked out of this directory, prior to OneWorld Xe (formerly B733.3). The system administrator and the JDE user should have full control over this directory.

CD Templates

This directory is new as of B733.2. This directory contains the CD templates for product packaging. Product packaging is a new application that allows you to take development off of one instance or install of OneWorld and move the object to another instance of OneWorld; for example, if your company had one install of OneWorld in the United States and another in Australia. These instances are totally separate OneWorld systems. However, your company has just spent thousands of dollars to develop applications that are needed at both sites. Do you redo all of the applications over again? With product packaging, you can create your own Electronic Software Update ESU CD and move your changes onto the system in Australia.

This is a very powerful tool that should only be used by the system administrator. So all other users, besides the JDE user, should have only list permissions to this directory. This will restrict them from affecting the files contained in this directory. However, you will also want to set up OneWorld security on the product packaging application.

CognosOneWorld

This directory contains file for Cognos. Users who are using Cognos will need change permissions to this directory. The system administrator's account and JDE user should have full control over this directory. All other users should only have list permission to this directory.

Com

This directory contains files that are used for Com. Com allows you to "hook" other applications into your OneWorld system. It is a part of the J.D. Edwards' interoperability solution. Only the developers who are using Com should have change permission to this directory. The JDE user and the system administrator's account should have full control permissions on this directory. All other users should have only list permissions.

Client Directory

The client directory contains a couple of files that all users need change privileges on. These files are JDECLNT.DDC and JDECLNT.XDC. The reason your users need change privileges is that these files contain the names of workstations that have installed OneWorld. That's right, these are the system's licensing files. When your workstations perform client installations, they will read these files to see if you have a license available. If you do have a license available, the workstation will update these files with the name of the machine. This is why, when you set up your file security through windows explorer, all your users need change privileges to the JDECLNT files. In Windows NT, when you set up file permissions you will see No Access, List, Read, Add, Add & Read, Change, Full Control, Special Directory Access, and Special File Access. When you give a user change permissions, this user will be able to read, write, execute, and delete these files.

All the other files in this directory can be locked down to different levels for each type of user. Let's start with the JDE user, which is shipped with OneWorld. If you are using this OneWorld user, you should have change privileges on the client directory. Remember, the JDE user is a powerful user in OneWorld. Your production, development, CNC administrators, and application lead users only need to have read permissions to this directory.

Path Code Directory

The path code directory means the directories that are named after your path codes. Some examples of these names are CRPB733, PRODB733, DEVB733, and PLANNER.

These directories contain the source files and include files. This is why certain users are going to need more permissions than others to check on modifications on the OneWorld system. The people on the system using the JDE user will need more permissions than other users since this a power user in OneWorld.

NOTE

Typically, the JDE NT user account, which is set up during installation time, is used by only your system administrators.

Your production users, on the other hand, will not need as much authority. After all, your normal data entry clerk better not be coding on your system! If they are, we can almost guarantee you are going to have problems. This type of user would need his or her NT permissions set to read-only on all subdirectories of the path code directory. This is so that these users will have enough rights to install packages to their workstations, but not enough rights to damage the system.

Your developer users are going to need the ability to change all files within the path code directory. This is because these are your programmers, the people who are going to modify files on your system, such as the source and include files. The CNC administrative users are going to need change privileges on all the subdirectories and files under the path code directory.

Database Directory

This directory is really only used during the installation, update, or upgrade process. It contains BAT files that load your central object tables. If a user who does not know what he is doing executes one of these BAT files, your central object tables would be overlaid or corrupted. This is why the only type of user that needs access to this directory would be the JDE user. The people who are using this user would be applying your update and upgrades. The production, development, and CNC administrative user types should be locked out of this directory. Another reason to lock all other users out of this directory is that the JDESET.BAT file contains database users and passwords. These include the JDEDBA user who is a very powerful user set up during the installation of the system in your database.

Helps Directory

This directory contains the help files for OneWorld. These files can be deployed to the client workstations, but since they take up a fairly large footprint, most sites will leave them on the deployment server and allow their users access to them. You can modify the existing help files or add custom help files to address your business needs. However, unless you want some interesting documentation, you probably do not want the normal user to have the ability to change these files. This is why we recommend that all user types except for JDE and any user responsible for customizing your help files, only have read permissions to this directory. Since JDE is your power user, they would need the ability to change files in this directory.

N O T E

If you install the help files to the client workstations, these files are not copied directly out of the Helps directory. Instead, to lessen the impact on the network, a compressed file is copied out of the HelpsCOMP directory. If you modify the help files, you will need to recompress them, thus recreating the compressed file in the HelpsCOMP directory, through the package build application.

Hosts Directory

This directory is used during the installation, update, or upgrade process to hold information on your enterprise server. In fact, when you install your system it will create an INI file for each of your enterprise server machines in a directory named the same name as your enterprise server, under the Hosts directory. Again, since the files contained in this directory are only used during an installation, all user types—except for JDE, who would need change privileges—should be locked out of this directory.

MediaObj Directory

This directory contains the Media Objects that are linked into OneWorld. So if, for example, you attach an Excel spreadsheet to an address book record, this is where the actual spreadsheet would be saved. This is so that all users on the system who need the information in the spreadsheet can access it. J.D. Edwards recommends that your CNC administrator and JDE user types have change permission, while your production and development users only have read permissions. This is a directory where administrators should take the permissions one user at a time, since a production user may need change permissions to perform their job duties.

OneWorld Client Install

This directory contains the programs and files necessary to run a client installation. This means that you will have to grant your users enough permissions to deploy packages, but not enough to damage the system. As usual, the system administrator

Troubleshooting

and the JDE account will need full control over this directory. Your other users will need a different level of permissions. You will want to grant these users permission to read, write, and execute files and programs in this directory. To do this, you will need to use the special directory access option in Windows Explorer security.

Like most things in life, however, there is an exception. Under the OneWorld Client Install directory is the font and the mics directories. The font directory contains the Arial font, which will be installed on the users' workstations during a client workstation install. Your users will only need read permission to this directory. The mics directory is a little more important. Under this directory are the CLIENT_INI.INF and JDE.INI files. The JDE.INI file contains entries that are deployed to the client workstations. This file controls entries in the workstations' JDE.INI file. An example would be when turn on sign on security you will want to define a security server in your workstation INI files. If you change the JDE.INI file under the OneWorld Client Install\Mics directory your client workstations will have this entry placed into their INI files when they accept a package.

As you can see, you do not want your normal end user to have a lot of permissions to these files. That is why your normal users should only have read permissions. This will help reduce the deployment of incorrect JDE.INI file changes.

Open Data Access Directory

This directory contains files that are used to Open Data Access functionality. This is primarily a development activity, so developers who are working on Open Data Access will need change permissions to this directory. The system administrator's account and the JDE account will need full control permission to these files. All other users will only need list permission to this directory.

Printqueue Directory

This directory contains all the PDF versions of reports run locally on the deployment server. These reports are normally related to the installation and package build process, so your normal end users should not need to view them. This is why you should lock all users out of this directory except for your JDE or system administrator users who will need change permissions.

Package_INF Directory

This directory contains the INF files that control the client and server package installation process. This means that you will need to grant users enough permission to deploy packages, but not enough to cause damage. In order to do this, all users, except for the system administrator and the JDE user, only need read permissions to this directory and all files contained in the directory. The system administrator's account and the JDE account will need full control permission to this directory.

TIP

If you are having a user other than your system administrator build your OneWorld packages, they will need change access to the package_inf, path code, and printqueue directories. At most sites, the system administrator is responsible for building packages.

System Directory

In Chapter 11 we covered service packs, which are basically a replacement of the System directory. This directory contains the foundation of the OneWorld system. It contains all the DLLs and files that make it possible for OneWorld to connect to different databases and platforms. The JDE user will need to have change permissions on this directory and the files contained within the directory. The administrative users will need to have full control over this directory. As for all other users, they will only need read only access. An important note here is that when a client workstation is deployed, it gets the system directory by copying down a compressed, CAB, file from the SYSTEMCOMP directory. The permissions for this directory would be the same as for the system directory.

The Intel NT and Compaq Alpha Enterprise Server

The enterprise server also has a directory structure that your system administrator is not going to want to leave wide open. The administrators who do leave the directory structure open are normally the same people who say, "Who changed the INI file!" Enterprise servers running Windows NT have a similar directory structure to the deployment server. However, you can have much greater latitude on locking this directory structure down than you do with the deployment server. The important thing to keep in mind is that you want to allow enough permissions for your end users to view their jobs, run their jobs, and still not be able to change any files that would bring the enterprise server down. The following information should help your administrator lock down the OneWorld directory structure in Windows NT.

CAUTION

Because Microsoft is no longer supporting new development of the Windows NT operating system on the Compaq Alpha platform, the last release of OneWorld that will be supported on this platform is OneWorld Xe. Any release higher than this will not be able to run on the Compaq Alpha platform.

OneWorld\DDP Directories

Your users will need access to these directories to view their jobs. The neat thing here is that you do not have to grant all of your users permissions to this directory structure. Your OneWorld host services on NT need to be started by a user who has had administrative rights to the enterprise server. When a user submits a job or tries to view a job, their NT account is not used to access this directory structure; the account that is starting your host services is used. This means that if the end user deletes a UBE using the OneWorld applications, the job will be removed, unless you implemented OneWorld action security restricting the user from doing this. The JDE user type and the NT user account that starts your host services will need full control over all these directories and all subdirectories. This is so that your host services have the necessary permissions to run correctly, and your administrator can administer the system.

NOTE

The DDP directory is a default setup from J.D. Edwards; this may or may not appear at client sites.

Path Code Directories

These directories are named after the path codes on your system, such as CRPB733, PRODB733, DEVB733, and PRISTB733. These path codes contain the specifications necessary to run reports and business functions on the enterprise server. However, your normal end users will not be accessing these files. When a report is run, it is processed through a program started by your host services so that the program can access these files using the NT account that started the service. Except for this account, your administrator's account, and the JDE user type, all other users will only need read permissions.

System Directory

The System directory is the foundation code of OneWorld. This code is what gives OneWorld the ability to access different databases and run on different platforms. Again, you will want to give the JDE user, your administrator's user, and the NT account that starts up the host services full control over this directory. All other users will only need read permissions.

INI File   System administrators need to remember that the JDE.INI file needs to be locked down from their end users. Since this file is read by the host services, if a user changes the file, you could run into problems. The fact that this file is read mostly upon startup of your host services can cause no end of frustration for your system administrator. By the time the administrator realizes something has changed, there will be no way to track down who has changed the JDE.INI file. This file is contained in the OneWorld\DDP\System\Bin32 directory on the enterprise server for NT platforms. All users, except for the system administrator and the user who starts your host services, should only have the list permission to this file. The Services program in the Control Panel controls the OneWorld host services. Windows NT allows your system administrator to specify an account to start the services, or it will allow them to start the services with a system user. With OneWorld, you will want to always start the host services as a user with administrative privileges on the enterprise server. The Service dialog box is shown here.

Troubleshooting

N O T E

When you change an NT password, you will need to change this password for the user starting the OneWorld host services as well. If you don't, the service will not start correctly. Also, the service should not be running at the time you change the NT password. If it is, NT will deactivate the user ID, and you will have to drop the services and then reactivate the ID. This is why the authors recommend that you create an NT account specifically for starting your OneWorld host services. When you do this, you will not have to worry about locking someone out of the network.

Windows NT Compression

It always seems that no matter how much disk space we have on systems, we use it up, and then we have to start figuring out how to stretch our existing amount of hard drive space. A question that always seems to come up is, "Can I use the compression feature of NT and not blow the system out of the water?" If you call customer support and ask them this question, they will only tell you this is not a supported configuration. We are here to tell you that this *will* work on the deployment server. However, it will slow things way down. The reason is that NT will have to deal with the compression every time you try to access something on the deployment server's directory structure. So if you are going to compress directories, you may not want to do a full bore compression. The best approach would be to compress a directory and then work with the system to see if the performance is up to what you need. The directories you could get away with compressing with the least impact to the system are:

- ActivEra

- CognosOneWorld

- Database

- Helps

- Hosts

- Media Objects

- Open Data Access

- Planner

- System

By compressing these directories you will save on disk space, but you will also pay for this savings with performance. The next logical question would be, "Can I compress my client workstation directories to save on the footprint placed on my machines?" Because of possible performance implications, we do not recommend using NT compression on the workstations. If your hard disk space is such an issue, you may want to look at a Windows Terminal Server or Web client solution. Of course, you could also break down and buy some additional hard drive space.

CAUTION

Do not use third-party compression software, because this could produce unpredictable results. The authors have not tested third-party software and feel that using such software would be an unnecessary risk.

Starting Host Services Automatically

Another interesting feature of the NT operating system is that it allows you to start your host services automatically, through the Control Panel. However, like everything else in life, there is a catch. These host services are dependent on the database being up and running, and NT has a habit of saying the database is up and running when it is not actually up and running. We will go over how to start your host services automatically and all the fun catches that come with it.

Control Panel Autostart

To start your host services automatically, go into the Control Panel and set up the B733 Network and B733 Queue service to start automatically. However, to do this you should place a dependency on your host services. Use the following procedure:

1. If you already have your host services installed, stop them using the Control Panel.

2. Open a DOS session and change to the drive where OneWorld is installed on your enterprise server. Type:

```
cd OneWorld\B733\System\Bin32
```

3. Once in that directory, the first thing to do is uninstall the host services. You can do this by using the following commands:

To uninstall the queue service:

```
-u jdesququ
```

To uninstall the network service:

```
-u jdesnet
```

4. The next step is to install the host services with dependencies. Through the same DOS window, type:

```
-i jdesnet -d "NAME OF YOUR DATABASE SERVICE"
-i jdesque -d "Name of your J.D. Edwards network service"
```

You have set your network service to be dependent upon the database service and your queue service to be dependent upon your network service. Now you can set your host services to start automatically through the Control Panel. This means that every time you start your machine, your host services will come up. You will also want to ensure that the services are being started as a user who has administrative authority on the server.

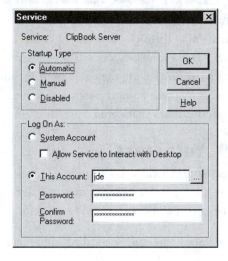

Starting Host Services Automatically with a Script

If you are performing nightly backups, which you should be doing, and need to take the host services down and back up automatically when no one is around to check on them, you will want to set up a script that will start your database service and the host services with a delay between them. The Windows NT operating system does allow you to set the services up automatically, but as described earlier, sometimes NT lies to you and the database is not truly up and running. When this occurs, the host services will not function correctly. To avoid this, you need to set up a script to start your database and host services with a delay between them. Below is an example of the startup and shutdown script. You can then place these scripts in the AT scheduler, which is in Windows NT. This will bring your services up and down so that you can perform backups of your system, and avoid the risk of the host services starting incorrectly.

NOTE

To use these scripts, you will need to have the sleep and kill executable out of the NT Resource Kit on your server.

Example of a startup script:

```
Net Start 'Database Service
C:\ntreskit\sleep 60
Net Start 'OneWorld Net Service'
C:\ntreskit\sleep 30
Net Start 'OneWorld Queue Service'
```

Example of a shutdown script:

```
Net stop 'OneWorld Queue Service'
C:\ntreskit\sleep 30
Net stop 'OneWorld Network Service'
C:\ntreskit\sleep 60
```

```
kill jdequeue.exe
kill jdenet_n
kill runprint.exe
kill jdenet_k
```

(This will kill any hanging processes. If you have a hanging process and try to start your host services again, they will not come up correctly.)

```
Net stop 'Database service'
```

Summary

In this chapter, we went over some of the specific issues that apply to the Windows NT operating system. We discussed the required MDAC levels and the NT service pack levels for OneWorld implementations. We also covered some of the options with NT compression and issues with host services on the NT operating systems. This information should help you avoid potential problems with your system.

## CHAPTER 23

UNIX Configuration, Troubleshooting, and More

UNIX, UNIX, UNIX

UNIX System Configurations

Oracle Implementation Considerations

Explaining the UNIX/OneWorld Server

Troubleshooting the UNIX Platform

O f all of the platforms, UNIX is the most stable, reliable, and configurable. It is truly a world-class system that runs OneWorld better than any of the other platforms. J.D. Edwards must agree. After all, why else would J.D. Edwards support three different flavors of UNIX? Of course, other OneWorld technologists, feel the same way about the AS/400 and Windows NT/Intel platforms.

NOTE
_____

This chapter assumes you know something about the UNIX O/S and how to manipulate your specific version of UNIX (Solaris, HP_UX, or AIX). This chapter is designed as a supplement to the Server and Workstation Administration guide shipped on the technical documentation CD with the J.D. Edwards OneWorld software.

In this chapter, we'll discuss:

- UNIX, UNIX, UNIX

- UNIX system configurations

- Oracle implementation considerations

- The OneWorld/UNIX server

- Troubleshooting the UNIX platform

UNIX, UNIX, UNIX

As mentioned in the introduction, there are three different flavors of UNIX (HP_UX, AIX, and Solaris) supported by the J.D. Edwards OneWorld product. They correspond to HP9000, RS6000, and Sun, and each has its own requirements, recommendations, and software. In the sections that follow, you will find a list of the minimal requirements for the B733.2 and OneWorld Xe (formerly B733.3) releases of the product. We highly recommend that you closely adhere to these requirements.

NOTE

Although many flavors of UNIX come with a built-in version of a C compiler, the supplied version does not fulfill your C code compiler requirements. These compilers do not have all of the tools necessary to perform the required OneWorld code generation tasks. Unfortunately, these recommended C compilers carry an additional cost that needs to be factored into your overall plan and budget.

UNIX Requirements for OneWorld B733.2

The hardware requirements for UNIX systems are dependent on your customers' specific needs. Each of the primary hardware (Sun, HP, and IBM) vendors (and most of their VAR resellers) employs people dedicated to determining the hardware size requirements for their clients. Find the minimum requirements listed below.

- Database Oracle 8.0.5 or higher, including Oracle 8.1.5 (Oracle 8i).

- Database CD Oracle 8.0.5 Server, Enterprise Edition.

- Database administration software.

- Oracle SQL*Plus 8.0.5. SQL*Plus is on the database CD but requires a separate license.

- Oracle Client Software CD networking software. (The CD must match your release of Oracle.)

- Sun Clustering, High Availability 2.2 required for cluster support.

- Support is available for the standard Oracle 8.0.5 or higher. OneWorld no longer supports the 7.x versions of the Oracle database.

- Oracle Parallel Server is not supported by J.D. Edwards for OneWorld.

UNIX Requirements for OneWorld Xe

Below you will find the UNIX requirements for OneWorld Xe. You will note that there are only minor discrepancies. When you are ready to install or upgrade to the OneWorld Xe version, however, we strongly recommend that you verify the minimum requirements list on the J.D. Edwards Knowledge Garden (https://knowledge.jdedwards.com). As of the time of publication for this book, the list below indicates the specific software necessary for the Sun OS.

- ANSI C compiler—workshop version 5.0

- Database Oracle 8.0.6 or 8.1.5 (8i)

- Oracle SQL*Plus 8.0.6 database administration

- High Availability 2.2 cluster support

Platform Preferences

There are pros and cons to each of the platforms. For a series of reasons, the Sun platform wins our support. The Sun box is highly scalable, and its OS is very configurable. The RS600 is the least deployed of any OneWorld-supported platform. It's not that there are any specific problems with it; it's simply that very few accounts actually use it. As such, it is suspect. The HP9000, one of the oldest OneWorld enterprise systems, is a proven platform; however, its OS is not flexible enough to run Oracle and OneWorld optimally on the same system. Oracle, by nature, wants a small processor time slice. OneWorld logic, on the other hand, likes a very large processor time slice. Because HP_UX v10 and v11 have a single kernel parameter for the time slice, you end up setting it somewhere in the middle, a setting that doesn't run either application well.

Sun, on the other hand, can easily handle both applications by allocating specific processors and memory to specific processes. This ability, coupled with the expert service provided by Sun, makes this UNIX platform our favorite. The only real disadvantage to the Sun platform is that it has only been a certified platform since May of 1999. As such, it is relatively new to the OneWorld enterprise scene. It may not be a good fit for all organizations; however, we definitely recommend it for medium to large implementations.

UNIX System Configurations

Although this subject has been addressed in other chapters (for example, Chapter 19), we thought that no chapter on UNIX would be complete without a detailed section describing how to set up and properly configure your UNIX box to adequately handle Oracle and OneWorld. Although some considerations (such as money, performance requirements, and so on) simply have to be taken into account, there is an optional method of configuring your system to ensure it runs at peak performance. In this section, we will discuss an example company with the following characteristics:

- Approximately $500 million in sales

- Five sites connected via a WAN

- Approximately 400 users (due to location, assume there are 240 concurrent users)

- Approximately 100GB in legacy data

We will walk through the process for optimally sizing and configuring a system for this client. Many clients have a difficult time identifying the volume of transactions on their legacy systems, which makes it difficult to determine how to size their new system. Some of the questions that can be asked to make this process simpler are:

- Across all of your sites, how many sales orders do you perform daily and how many actual lines of detail are generated?

- How many reports are run daily?

- How many EDI transactions get posted daily? Hourly?

- How many invoices are generated daily?

- How many account payable checks are cut daily, weekly, or monthly?

- How many journal entries are posted into the general ledger monthly?

All of these questions directly relate to the volume of transactions that affect a system and give a general idea of how hard a company will stress its new software solution. The next question concerns the organization's anticipated growth rate: Is the industry undergoing explosive growth, or is there a slow steady increase in the market?

Is the organization going through a seasonal slump? What about pending acquisitions? Maybe they are implementing OneWorld to enable continued organizational growth. This makes determining system requirements much more difficult, but it's a factor that helps determine the platform selection (for example, a highly scalable system is necessary for an organization that's growing).

The final question usually asked is the amount of legacy data on the current systems. In our example company, we indicated that this client maintained 100GB of legacy data. The fact that a company has 100BG of legacy data does not require that all of this information be housed in OneWorld. The reality of the OneWorld implementation is that only some of the legacy data will require conversion into a new ERP system.

Although we often use the amount of legacy data as a good indication of the amount of data generated regularly by an organization, it is not a reliable indicator. Most companies use OneWorld substantially more than their old systems. This observation, coupled with the fact that OneWorld has a completely different architecture than a legacy system (unless the legacy system is J.D. Edwards' World product), also makes the amount of legacy data a poor tool for determining disk space requirements. For many organizations, however, it is one of the few tools available.

Providing the Answer

With the information provided in the answers to the questions listed in the previous section, we are ready to engage J.D. Edwards and our hardware vendor to determine the size and type of machines necessary to run the example company's business. You may be thinking, "Why should we engage J.D. Edwards and a hardware vendor instead of an implementation provider?" Quite simply, J.D. Edwards and their hardware vendor alliances have performance labs in Denver where these variables have quantifiable matrixes to properly scope the size, memory, and CPU requirements and then return with the number and type of servers, amount of RAM, number of processors, and amount of and recommended RAID configurations for these servers. When these hardware vendors size the primary data server, the question of exact RAID configuration should be addressed. The most costly is also the best (RAID 1/0), but there are multiple ways of creating this RAID array. Each of the vendors should be able to discuss the company's options and help guide them through the decisions they need to make.

For example, for 400 users with a moderate volume, a ten-write spindle configuration is optimal. This is done in a RAID 1/0 by mirroring ten sets of drives and then stripping across the sets. Some systems can't accommodate this type of RAID, so be sure you discuss it with your hardware vendor prior to moving forward.

Sun Sizing

To create this section, we've asked for the assistance of our local Sun supplier in creating a solution for our example company. The Sun Sizing questionnaire is shown in Figure 23-1.

J.D. Edwards OneWorld Technical Documentation Series
Sun Microsystems JDE Global Technology Center

JDE OneWorld on Solaris

Configuration Worksheet

Instructions

E-mail the complete questionnaire to the address included. Please type or print clearly and concisely.

This document is intended to provide the Sun Microsystems J.D. Edwards competence center with appropriate information to estimate the proper hardware configuration to support a J.D. Edwards OneWorld implementation.

Important Contact Information

It is often necessary during the sizing of a system to contact the customer or reseller for further information. If these details are not completed, it could lead to delays in the processing of the sizing request. Without this information, no sizing will be performed.

FIGURE 23-1. Sun Sizing questionnaire

Customer Information

Company Name:	J2's OneWorld Book Company	
Company Address: Include Street, City, State, Province, Country	180 N. Stetson Ave. Chicago, IL 60601 USA	
Industry:	Book Developers	
Contact:	*Primary*	*Secondary*
Name:	Joe Miller	John Stern
Contact Title:	Associate Author	Associate Author
Telephone Number:	(312) 946-2987	(312) 946-2777
Contact Fax Number:	(312) 297-2987	(312) 297-2777
E-mail Address:	josmiller@dttus.com	jstern@dttus.com
Configuration required by (date)?	ASAP	ASAP

Other Information

Please provide any contacts for resellers, sales representatives, and integrators that have been identified for the project.

Integration Partner

Name:	Deloitte & Touche, LLP
Phone:	(800) DTT-SALE
Fax:	(312) DTT-FAXX
E-mail:	

Sun or Reseller Systems Engineer

Name:	
Phone:	
Fax:	
E-mail:	

FIGURE 23-1.   Sun Sizing questionnaire *(continued)*

Sun or Reseller Sales Representative

Name:

Phone:

Fax:

E-mail:

J.D. Edwards Account Manager

Name:	Ima Manager
Phone:	(555) 555-1234
Fax:	(555) 555-9876
E-mail:	Ima_manager@jdedwards.com

Sizing Methodology

To accurately create a Pre-Sales Sizing of a OneWorld system, detailed information is required. The CPU and memory requirements are derived from the peak transaction volume and concurrent user populations per application. The quality of the configuration produced from the questionnaire is only as good as the quality of the data supplied.

In the early stages of a OneWorld project, customers are not always able to accurately estimate the Transaction loads asked for in this questionnaire, especially if they have yet to determine the exact OneWorld business process specifications. To accommodate this situation, sizings can be done in several ways:

1. **Sizing Based on Concurrent Users counts only.** *Can be valuable for budgetary planning.*

The least accurate sizing scenario is that no transaction volumes or business data can be supplied, only user numbers are available. In this case, a server sizing can be performed using default (interactive-only) transaction rates. The basis for calculating default transaction rates is a user working continuously on the system, processing one screen every 30 seconds. This equates to the following default transaction rates, per user per hour:

FIGURE 23-1. Sun Sizing questionnaire *(continued)*

Module	Default Transaction Rate
Financials	60
Distribution/Logistics	30
Manufacturing	15
Equipment Management	30
Human Resources	15
Arch/Eng/Cont/RE (AEC)	15
Energy and Chemical	24

2. **Sizing based on Yearly Transaction counts, but without "interface and batch transaction" data.**

If the customer is able to estimate yearly transaction data for all modules, it is possible to perform an initial server sizing based on several rules of thumb about operational procedures, batch reporting, and OneWorld database size. This sizing process can be more accurate than method #1 above, but ignores the potentially significant impact of "interfaces and large batch transaction" loads.

3. **Sizing based on Peak Hourly Transaction counts, major interfaces, and batch transaction data.**

If the customer is able to accurately complete this questionnaire, along with the J.D. Edwards Database Sizing questionnaire, one is able to get a close approximation of OneWorld system requirements.

Estimated Disk Storage Requirements[1] (Required)			
	Pilot	Phase 1	Production
Total Storage (GB)	150 gb	200 gb	300 gb
Deployment Server – Development/Testing/Training Systems			
		# Users (Peak)	Require Separate System? (Y/N)
Development		25	Y
Prototyping (Configuration Acceptance CRP)		35	Y

FIGURE 23-1. Sun Sizing questionnaire (*continued*)

Testing		50	N	
Training		50	N	
OneWorld Environment CNC		**Database Servers**	**Application Servers**	**Development Environment**
Number of development, test production servers:				
Number in each site		1	1	1
OneWorld Application Users (Required)				
OneWorld Application Areas	**Total Users (Licensed)**		**Maximum No. of Concurrent (Active) Users[2]**	
Do not double count users of applications. Allocate users across modules.	**All Applications Total**	**Pilot**	**Production Phase 1**	**Production Final**
Financials	100	10	40	60
Distribution/Logistics	150	15	0	90
Manufacturing	150	15	0	90
Equipment Management	0	0	0	0
Human Resources	0	0	0	0
Arch/Eng/Cont/RE (AEC)	0	0	0	0
Energy and Chemical	0	0	0	0
Other				
Total	400	40	40	240
System Availability (Required)				
Require 24 hours per day, 7 days per week System Availability? (Y/N)			Y	
High Availability required (Automatic Failover & Startup)? (Y/N)			Y	
If yes, what is the required Recovery time? (In minutes or hours as appropriate)			8 hrs recovery	

[1] Please supply an estimate for the disk storage required for each phase. The J.D. Edwards Disk Sizing Worksheet contains very detailed questions and may be obtained from a OneWorld functional specialist

[2] The definition of a "Concurrent (Active) User" is a user who is both logged on to the system and actively engaged in using an OneWorld Application.

FIGURE 23-1. Sun Sizing questionnaire *(continued)*

Troubleshooting

Glossary

Client   A desktop personal computer running Windows 95 or Windows NT Workstation or thin client via a Web browser.

Document Retention Period   Indicates the period of time that documents are held from creation to deletion or archival.

Inquiries   A OneWorld user submitting a management report or doing an inquiry on module of J.D. Edwards OneWorld such as Customer Service Order Inquiry, Open Order Inquiry, Vendor Ledger Inquiry.

Transaction   A business transaction is an action carried out by the user at the OneWorld Menu, such as entering a sales order or purchase order or checking on the status of a customer order.

Transactions per peak hour   Describes the total volume of transactions in a peak workload hour per application for both On-line transactions and batch transactions. Batch transactions may also include data feeds from other applications such as EDI. Indicates Batch-Of-On and Offline mode transactions. A transaction is defined as an operational business event, such as the entering of a sales order.

Users   Indicates the peak (allow for special business cycle or seasonal processing) number of J.D. Edwards OneWorld application users. This will be a primary factor used to determine the CPU requirements.

- logged on active (concurrent): logged on users *doing work*

- logged on inactive: logged on users *not doing work during the peak period*

- Query only: logged on active users *performing queries, no update*

FIGURE 23-1.   Sun Sizing questionnaire *(continued)*

After being e-mailed to Sun, this document was used to create the sizing recommendations shown in Figure 23-2. Once we receive the recommended sizing from the Sun/J.D. Edwards team, we take it to our applications integrator for a sanity check. Remember, the listed hardware configuration is a recommendation based on the information submitted by the client (in this case, the authors). The systems integrator has a better understanding of an organization's specific needs and can consequently provide recommendations.

Customer: Fictional Company No. 1

Sizing based on

	Concurrent	Active
Financial	100	60
Distribution	150	90
Manufacturing	150	90
Chemical/Gas	0	0
Engineering	0	0
Other	0	0

Batch reserve: 35%
Spooling reserve: 15%

Required Software

Operating system: Solaris 7 or later

Recommended patches: HW 5/99 Maintenance Update 2

Please check http://www.sun.com for the latest in Solaris support information.

SPARCcompiler C 5.0

Recommended patches: 106748-02, 107058-02, 107357-04

FIGURE 23-2. Sun sizing recommendations

JDE OneWorld: B733.2 Service Pack 10 or higher

Recommended patches: none

Please check http://www.jdedwards.com for the latest OneWorld support information.

Database: Oracle 8.0.6 or higher Enterprise Edition Server

Recommended patches: none

Please check http://www.oracle.com for the latest Oracle support information.

Recommended Software

BMC Patrol

Patrol Console

Knowledge module for Solaris

Knowledge module for Oracle

Knowledge module for JDE OneWorld (under development)

Solaris Enterprise Volume Manager 3.0

Solaris Enterprise Backup

Oracle hot backup module recommended

Hardware Configuration

Production System configuration (required)

CPU: 2 database, 4 application

Memory: 2GB database, 4GB application

FIGURE 23-2. Sun sizing recommendations (*continued*)

Suggested database server configuration (required)

    E450 or E420R Workgroup server

    2 processors (336MHz with 2MB cache or faster)

    2GB memory (8GB would provide optimal interleave)

    36GB of internal disk for OS, applications, and swap (72GB mirrored)

Note: Enterprise server internal storage increased above standard profile to accommodate multiple (4) path codes.

    Database storage: Estimated 100GB (200GB mirrored) based on standard user profiles. For a more complete storage estimate, please contact your local J.D. Edwards technical marketing representative. The performance estimates are based on logical volume mirroring. Use of RAID-5 can affect the overall system performance and is not recommended. Please refer to Tuning Oracle on UNIX Platforms (v. 7.x, 8.0.x, 8.1.x), part of the J.D. Edwards @ Work technical documentation series, for more information on RAID-5.

Note: The preferred storage device is A3500/A1000 configured with write cache enable and host based volume management.

Note: For optimal database performance, at least 8 (16 if mirrored) disk spindles are required for the database.

Suggested application server(s) configuration (required)

    2 × E450 or E420R Workgroup server

    2 processors (336MHz with 2MB cache or faster)

    2GB memory (8GB would provide optimal interleave)

    36GB of internal disk for OS, applications, and swap (72GB mirrored)

FIGURE 23-2. Sun sizing recommendations *(continued)*

Troubleshooting

Deployment Server (required)

1 CPU Pentium 200MHz or faster

256MB memory

NT 4.0 plus Service Pack 3, 4, or 5

Oracle 8.0.6 SQL client (to match Enterprise server)

MS Access 97

Visual C 6.0 Standard Edition Service Pack 1

60GB disk

Note: Deployment server storage estimate increased above standard profile to accommodate multiple (4) path codes.

Windows Terminal Server (optional)

Note: Estimate 10 to 40 users per Windows Terminal Server depending on application mix (OneWorld client, MSoffice apps, etc.).

Windows terminal server configuration

2 × Pentium Xeon 400MHz or faster

2GB memory

30GB disk

Note: Estimate 30 users per WTS system for the purposes of this sizing.

Training System Configuration (optional)

E250 or E220R Workgroup server

2 processors (336MHz with 2MB cache or faster)

FIGURE 23-2.   Sun sizing recommendations (*continued*)

2GB memory

36GB of internal disk for OS, applications, and swap (72GB mirrored)

Database storage: Estimated 50GB of raw storage (100GB mirrored).

Development System Configuration (optional, recommended)

E250 or E220R Workgroup server

2 processors (336MHz with 2MB cache or faster)

2GB memory

36GB of internal disk for OS, applications, and swap (72GB mirrored)

Database storage: Estimated 50GB of raw storage (100GB mirrored).

Test System (QA) (optional, very highly recommended)

2 × E450 or E420R Enterprise server

2 processors (336MHz with 2MB cache or faster)

2GB memory

36GB of internal disk for OS, applications, and swap (72GB mirrored)

Database storage: Estimated 100GB of raw storage (200GB mirrored).

Note: This server does not require an additional deployment server although it is highly recommended.

FIGURE 23-2.   Sun sizing recommendations *(continued)*

As you can see from the preceding information, the hardware vendors are providing a substantial amount of knowledge support during the sizing exercises. For many new organizations, the concept of separate testing and training systems from their production systems is a foreign concept. While these systems are certainly not required, they are recommended as part of a total solution.

When analyzing the returned recommendation, many organizations quickly add up and identify that seven Sun servers are listed. Do they actually have to put in seven separate servers? No, whether they break out the application, production, and database servers into separate servers or they combine them into a single server is completely up to them. In this case, for ease of administration, we recommend a single six-by-six system (six processors and 6GB of RAM) for the production box and use the ability of the Sun O/S to partition the appropriate parts of the system for their various functionalities.

Oracle Implementation Considerations

The only supported database platform for OneWorld on a UNIX system is Oracle—in particular, Oracle 8.0.5 or Oracle 8i (8.1.5) and their subsequent releases. (With the addition of B733, the Oracle 7 series is no longer supported.) As most Oracle DBAs will tell you, the ability of this database to perform is directly proportional to how it is configured. J.D. Edwards proposes certain guidelines for their OneWorld platform on the best configurations for Oracle itself. We highly recommend that you read through the guidelines prior to actually installing the Oracle instance on your UNIX server. However, these recommendations are guidelines and should not be viewed as the definitive tuning guide.

Oracle DBAs

We've talked with many clients new to OneWorld, UNIX, and Oracle that, for one reason or another, have decided that they wanted to grow an Oracle DBA as opposed to hiring one. In this section, we discuss the advantages and disadvantages of this strategy. Then we provide a means of making this strategy work.

First, when you grow a DBA, there is an associated cost of training, which can easily reach $10,000 or more. The time required for taking the classes necessary to bring the prospective DBA up to speed should be taken into consideration. Second, most Oracle DBAs need a minimum of two years to become skilled at working with the product. All of the training in the world won't replace good old-fashioned experience. Third, the process of implementing a system is not necessarily the best time to train someone. OneWorld can't be installed until Oracle is installed. It is much better to correctly install the database that is housing OneWorld the first time.

NOTE

Many of the changes necessary for the database's initial configuration need to be performed when the database is installed. These changes can be retrofitted; however, a substantial amount of work has to be done to accommodate this methodology.

Finally, you have to ask yourself if you are willing to bet your company on the skills of someone who really doesn't know the product. Are you willing to put financials, manufacturing, inventory, sales, and HR on the line in case the new DBA misses something that a more experienced DBA would recognize and fix?

Pros and Cons

Something that might help you with this decision is to understand the motivations for growing the skill set as opposed to hiring the skill set. One of the main motivations for growing a DBA is that it is cheaper than hiring a skilled one. We can make a couple of arguments in response to this motivation. First, although it is initially true that growing a DBA is cheaper, once the grown DBA becomes skilled, you will either have to pay the additional cost, or he or she will go elsewhere. Second, although you will save on the cost of the employee's compensation, you will incur additional training costs associated with bringing him or her to the required skill level. Finally, although growing a DBA may be cheaper, how much money will you lose to problems related to inexperience?

Another motivating factor for growing a DBA is that you will earn the lasting appreciation of the employee, which will in turn create a positive working environment where your staff will understand that you want them to grow as individuals and to continue to develop as employees. This positive factor does provide a solid reason for the growing a DBA. Unfortunately, it doesn't always work (especially for larger companies where the employee will go through the training in order to find a better job with another company). To offset this possibility, many organizations put training contracts in place for their employees. These contracts state that the employee will work for the company for a certain amount of time in exchange for the training. If the employee leaves before the time has expired, he or she is obligated to pay a prorated amount of the training back to the company. Sometimes this scare tactic works to keep people within the organization, but if the employee wants to leave, the hiring company may be willing to pay the difference to be able to hire the trained DBA.

How to Make It Work

If you decide that growing a DBA is the route you want to take, you need to have a plan to maximize the benefits of this approach while simultaneously minimizing the associated risks. We recommend that you contract the services of a consultant during your employee's training period. This way, your employee gets to draft off of the experience of the consultant, and the system is still configured correctly. A consultant is a costly alternative that eventually pays off. By using a consultant, you are able to increase the learning curve of your own employee, enjoy the services of a well-trained consultant who is familiar with your system (which also prevents you from being held hostage in a salary dispute), and buy some insurance in case something does go wrong. In all, augmenting the growing DBA with the services of a consultant is an effective combination.

Setting up Oracle to Work for OneWorld

One of our first recommendations for making Oracle work with OneWorld on the UNIX platform is to obtain the Oracle on UNIX tuning guide created by J.D. Edwards' World Wide Advanced Technology team (any J.D. Edwards employee, including your client manager, can provide this guide). This guide, mentioned earlier in this chapter, provides a series of recommendations for Oracle- and UNIX-specific parameters designed to assist in running OneWorld. You should have anyone preparing your system validate the system setup against the recommendations in this guide.

In-house UNIX or Oracle Skills

Our recommendations vary if the personnel in your IT department have existing UNIX and, in particular, Oracle on UNIX skills. Because J.D. Edwards does provide a series of tuning suggestions that can be tempered with your personnel's experience, your next best step is to get this person (or people) into a OneWorld installation class or a special workshop provided by your implementation partner, which will educate them on how this ERP package works both on the server and with Oracle. People who have years of experience on these platforms quickly come up to speed with the skills necessary to effectively tune, monitor, and support OneWorld. Your company will still need assistance in planning and designing the architecture and implementation of the product, but it will also have come a long way toward being self-sufficient.

No In-house UNIX or Oracle Skills

Even if your organization lacks individuals with in-house UNIX or Oracle skills, you aren't so far behind that you should give up all hope of completing the implementation. Your first steps include mapping out a comprehensive plan for the implementation of the technology, identifying how you are going to get someone in house to support this application, starting Oracle training for those individuals, and identifying a skilled third-party implementation partner who can help you in the interim. With proper planning, your implementation will be every bit as successful and expeditious as one owned by the company that has the in-house skills necessary to implement OneWorld.

UNIX, Oracle, and OneWorld Data File Configuration

While the J.D. Edwards Oracle tuning parameters nicely explain a series of different tuning options, they do not go into enough information regarding the placement of various data files within OneWorld. One of the biggest bottlenecks your organization is likely to encounter is disk IO. We've seen this in multiple companies of various sizes. To proactively deal with this issue, you need to carefully plan where data files will exist on your new system. First, let's explore the various data files or logs that get generated by Oracle and what they are used for to gain a better understanding of what we need to plan for.

The elements to consider include data files for Oracle table spaces (both index and actual data), redo logs, Rollback segments, archive logs, OneWorld error logs, OneWorld output, and OneWorld specification files. In the case of a batch application running on the server and updating the database, you could have all of these files being written simultaneously on the UNIX system (this is especially the case when you are running the pick slip subsystem and hundreds or thousands of pick slips are generated per hour). If all of these files types are on the same logical disk array, we promise that you are in for a bad time. To help with this situation, we highly recommend that you distribute these files on different logical disks on the system itself. To perform this distribution, however, requires different steps and planning in OneWorld and Oracle. It is also helpful to understand Oracle data files when initially designing the Oracle instance created to support the OneWorld project.

First, we recommend data files between 800 and 1,000MB in size. Oracle is not as efficient with larger data files. Second, since you determine where these files exist when you create the OneWorld table spaces, we recommend you spread them out among available logical drives. Third, ensure that index data files are on different logical drives than their corresponding data, data files. Because both index and data, data files are used simultaneously, separating these files decreases disk IO contention. Fourth, separate your redo logs from both data and index data files. These redo logs are also written at the same time as the other files. Fifth, separate the archive logs (archive logs are backed up redo logs) on separate disks.

For a more detailed example of the data file breakout on a UNIX box, refer to Chapter 19.

Explaining the UNIX/OneWorld Server

The UNIX/OneWorld server plays a key role in the overall implementation of the OneWorld system. Whether your organization has chosen to implement OneWorld using two UNIX servers (one for the database and one for the OneWorld applications) or a single enterprise server isn't relevant to this discussion. Rather, we will describe the OneWorld applications that run on the UNIX server, how they physically work, and how to start and stop these services.

NOTE

For more detailed explanations on how to start and stop services (and other related topics), refer to the J.D. Edwards documentation: Server and Workstation Administration.

OneWorld Server Services

The OneWorld UNIX server performs the same basic functionality as any other OneWorld application server. It is instrumental in a OneWorld implementation and provides a number of services including:

- Batch application services

- Security services

- Server package build services

- Data replication services

- Remote called procedure services

Service Interaction

In this section, we provide a brief explanation of how services work on the OneWorld application server; a more detailed explanation is in Chapter 16. The OneWorld application server runs multiple types of kernels, including network, queue, call object, scheduler, replication, and security kernels. Although most of these kernels are relatively self-explanatory (for example, security kernels run requests for security services, replication kernels monitor and provide replication service requests, and so on), let's look at how the various kernels work together with the server and the workstations.

When the service JDENet is launched via the RunOneWorld.sh script, it launches a "master" JDENet process. This process then launches additional jdenet_n kernels as required by the system and defined by JDE.INI. These kernels are responsible for facilitating the communication between the workstation and the server. The jdenet_n kernels take the incoming service message and ship it to the appropriate jdenet_k based on the message type as defined in JDE.INI. Once the service has been performed, jdenet_k ships the results back to jdenet_n, which, in turn, ships it back to the workstation.

All of the queues and net services are launched via the RunOneWorld.sh script. When you need to stop these services, you can do so using the EndOneWorld.sh script. Both of these scripts are located in the $SYSTEM/bin32 directory. These scripts are described in the sections that follow.

RunOneWorld.sh

OneWorld services on the UNIX application server have come a long way. In particular, they are more stable, and the scripts required to start them have been significantly enhanced, making their administration much simpler. These scripts start the services cleanly, validating that all previous services have stopped and then launching one jdenet_n master net service and three queue services (one for batch jobs, one for specification package builds, and one for object package builds). These services can be clearly seen by entering the following UNIX command:

```
ps –ef|grep jdeb7332
```

where jdeb7332 is the UNIX server user that is launching the services. This UNIX server user must have the proper rights on the system and to certain Oracle files.

NOTE

If you have modified your RunOneWorld.sh script to activate additional queues or modified JDE.INI to enable a virtual three-tier architecture (or additional call object kernels to enable various interfaces), you might need to place "Imore" at the end of the previously listed command to view the processes a page at a time.

Prior to actually launching RunOneWorld.sh, you should run rmics.sh, a OneWorld utility. This utility cleans up the OneWorld environment on the server, ensuring that the environment starts cleanly. Entering the following commands can perform this service:

```
cd $SYSTEM/bin32   *This command calls the bin32 directory to focus
rmics.sh           *This command cleans the OneWorld environment up.
cd ../log          *This command changes to the log directory.
rm -f jde*log*     *This command deletes all of the files starting with jde or log.
RunOneWorld.sh     *This command launches the OneWorld services.
```

The RunOneWorld.sh script that is shipped with the OneWorld Xeversion is shown in this section. You will notice that we have not modified this particular script with the required variables as described in the *J.D. Edwards OneWorld Technical Documentation Installation Guide* (UNIX-based systems). We have added command descriptions in **bold** next to the various commands.

- OWUSR="JDESVR"—Change this to the OneWorld user you want to start services. This user must be set up in OneWorld and have valid entries in the F0092, F00921, and F0093 tables.

- OWPWD="JDESVR"—Change this to this user's OneWorld password as maintained in the F98OWSEC table.

- OWENV="PDEVHP01"—Change this to a valid OneWorld environment name as maintained in the F0094 table for this specific user. The list of valid environments for each user is maintained in the F0093 system table.

- OWQUE1="QBATCH"—Change this to a valid queue name used in your release. In OneWorld Xe, the default queue is QB7332.

- OWQUE2="QBATCH"—Change this to a valid queue name used in your release.

```ksh
#!/bin/ksh
#                              RunOneWorld.sh
## Set START_NEW_LOGFILE=1 if you want to rewrite the logfile at each startup
START_NEW_LOGFILE=0

OWUSR="JDESVR"
OWPWD="JDESVR"
OWENV="PDEVHPO1"
OWQUE1="QBATCH"
OWQUE2="QBATCH"

## Set MULTI_INSTANCE=1 if you are running multiple instances of OneWorld
## under the same Unix user id.
MULTI_INSTANCE=0

#----------------------------------------------------------------------- #
# VARIABLE DEFINITIONS THAT YOU SHOULD NOT HAVE TO CHANGE...
#----------------------------------------------------------------------- #
set +u
USER=$(whoami)    *This determines the user id who launched the RunOneWorld.sh script.

HOST=$(hostname)*This determines the machine name.
OSTYPE=$(uname) *This determines the operating system (Solaris, HP_UX, or AIX)

## On AIX, process id shows up in column 2, it's column 1 on others...
if [ $OSTYPE = "AIX" ]
  then
    COLUMN=2
  else
    COLUMN=1
fi

unset SILENT_MODE
if [ "$1" = "-s" ] ; then
    SILENT_MODE=1
fi

## In MULTI_INSTANCE mode, we need to be able to find the INI file to get
## certain settings.  If we can't, then exit with an error.
if [ "$MULTI_INSTANCE" = "1" ] ; then
    MFLAG="-m"
    if [ -f ./JDE.INI ] ; then
      PORT_NBR=$(grep "^serviceNameListen" ./JDE.INI | sed 's/.*=//')
    elif [ -f $JDE_BASE/JDE.INI ] ; then
      PORT_NBR=$(grep "^serviceNameListen" $JDE_BASE/JDE.INI | sed 's/.*=//')
    else
      if [ -z "$SILENT_MODE" ] ; then
        echo "    This script cannot support multiple instances of"
        echo "    OneWorld without access to a JDE.INI file."
        echo "    You must either set the $JDE_BASE environment"
        echo "    variable correctly, or turn off MULTI_INSTANCE"
        echo "    mode in the RunOneWorld.sh script."
```

```
        echo "       exiting..."
      fi
      echo "    This script cannot support multiple instances of" >> $LOGFILE
      echo "    OneWorld without access to a JDE.INI file." >> $LOGFILE
      echo "    You must either set the $JDE_BASE environment" >> $LOGFILE
      echo "    variable correctly, or turn off MULTI_INSTANCE" >> $LOGFILE
      echo "    mode in the RunOneWorld.sh script." >> $LOGFILE
      echo "       exiting..."  >> $LOGFILE
      exit 1
    fi
fi


#---------------------------------------------------------------------- #
# FUNCTION DEFINITIONS...
#---------------------------------------------------------------------- #
function GetPIDS
{
  if [ "$MULTI_INSTANCE" = "1" ]
    then
      PIDS=$(ps -ef | grep $USER | grep $PORT_NBR | grep -v grep | awk '{print $2}')
      PIDS="$(ps -ef | grep $USER | grep $SYSTEM | grep -v grep | awk '{print $2}') $PIDS"
    else
      PIDS=$(ps -u $USER | grep jdenet | awk '{print $'$COLUMN'}')
      PIDS="$(ps -u $USER | grep jdequeue | awk '{print $'$COLUMN'}') $PIDS"
  fi
  if [ "$PIDS" = " " ] ; then
      PIDS=""
  fi
}


function CheckForProcesses
{
  GetPIDS
  if [ -n "$PIDS" ] ; then
      if [ -z "$SILENT_MODE" ] ; then
          echo "    There are already OneWorld processes"
          echo "    running for this user / instance..."
          echo "       exiting..."
      fi
      echo "    There are already OneWorld processes" >> $LOGFILE
      echo "    running for this user / instance..." >> $LOGFILE
      echo "       exiting..."  >> $LOGFILE
      exit 1
  fi
}


function CheckIPC
{
  $SYSTEM/bin32/rmics.sh $MFLAG >> $LOGFILE
  if [ ! $? = 0 ] ; then
      if [ -z "$SILENT_MODE" ] ; then
          echo "    IPC resource conflict -"
```

```
            echo "  You may need to change the startIPCKeyValue in your INI file,"
            echo "  or your JDE_BASE environment variable may be set incorrectly."
            echo "         exiting..."
        fi
        ## (error message already written to $LOGFILE by rmics.sh)
        exit 1
    fi
}


#---------------------------------------------------------------------- #
# MAIN PROCESSING...
#---------------------------------------------------------------------- #

## First, let's make sure the log file directory is valid - otherwise, all
## of the log messages will disappear.

LOGDIR=$(dirname $LOGFILE)
if [ ! -d $LOGDIR ] ; then
    echo " Invalid directory name for LOGFILE - "
    echo "  $LOGDIR"
    echo " You must correct RunOneWorld.sh and retry."
    exit 1
fi


if [ "$START_NEW_LOGFILE" = "1" ] ; then
    rm $LOGFILE
fi

echo "***********************************************************" >> $LOGFILE
if [ ! $? = 0 ] ; then
    echo " Unable to write to the logfile - "
    echo "  $LOGFILE"
    echo " You might not have permission to write to this file or directory."
    echo " Make sure file permissions are set correctly and retry."
    exit 1
fi


if [ -z "$SILENT_MODE" ] ; then
    echo $(date) "  Starting JD Edwards OneWorld on $HOST"
fi
echo $(date) "  Starting JD Edwards OneWorld on $HOST" >> $LOGFILE

CheckForProcesses

CheckIPC

echo "     Starting jdenet_n..." >> $LOGFILE
$SYSTEM/bin32/jdenet_n > $SYSTEM/bin32/jdenet_n.log 2>&1 &

sleep 2
GetPIDS
```

```
if [ -z "$PIDS" ] ; then
    if [ -z "$SILENT_MODE" ] ; then
        echo "     The jdenet_n process did not start..."
        echo "        Check the jdenet_n.log, or the log file associated"
        echo "          with the jdenet_n process id."
    fi
    echo "     The jdenet_n process did not start..." >> $LOGFILE
    echo "        Check the jdenet_n.log, or the log file associated" >> $LOGFILE
    echo "          with the jdenet_n process id." >> $LOGFILE
    exit 1
fi

echo "    Running cleanup to check for unfinished jobs..." >> $LOGFILE
$SYSTEM/bin32/cleanup $OWUSR $OWPWD $OWENV $OWQUE1 > $SYSTEM/bin32/cleanup.log 2>&1 &
if [ ! "$OWQUE1" = "$OWQUE2" ] ; then
    $SYSTEM/bin32/cleanup $OWUSR $OWPWD $OWENV $OWQUE2 > $SYSTEM/bin32/cleanup.log 2>&1 &
fi

echo "    Starting OneWorld spec install queue..." >> $LOGFILE
$SYSTEM/bin32/runque.sh $OWUSR $OWPWD $OWENV $OWQUE1 001 5 > $SYSTEM/bin32/specque.log 2>&1 &

echo "    Starting OneWorld batch queues..." >> $LOGFILE   *This is where you would add additional queues
as described in Chapter 19.
$SYSTEM/bin32/runque.sh $OWUSR $OWPWD $OWENV $OWQUE1 UBE 5 > $SYSTEM/bin32/ubeque1.log 2>&1 &
$SYSTEM/bin32/runque.sh $OWUSR $OWPWD $OWENV $OWQUE2 UBE 5 > $SYSTEM/bin32/ubeque2.log 2>&1 &

echo "    Starting OneWorld package queue..." >> $LOGFILE
$SYSTEM/bin32/runque.sh $OWUSR $OWPWD $OWENV $OWQUE1 PKG 5 > $SYSTEM/bin32/pkgque.log 2>&1 &

if [ -z "$SILENT_MODE" ] ; then
    echo "\n$(date)    JD Edwards OneWorld startup complete.\n"
fi
echo "\n$(date)    JD Edwards OneWorld startup complete.\n" >> $LOGFILE

exit 0
```

EndOneWorld.sh

Similar to the RunOneWorld.sh script, the EndOneWorld.sh script is designed to stop all OneWorld services associated with a specific instance of the OneWorld product. This script has also been changed significantly over the last few releases, producing a quicker, more efficient shutdown process. The same variable definitions are used in EndOneWorld.sh as in the RunOneWorld.sh script.

```
#!/bin/ksh
#                          EndOneWorld.sh
#----------------------------------------------------------------- #
# VARIABLE DEFINITIONS...
#----------------------------------------------------------------- #
```

```
LOGFILE="$SYSTEM/bin32/startstop.log"

OWUSR="JDESVR"
OWPWD="JDESVR"
OWENV="PDEVHPO1"
OWQUE1="QBATCH"
OWQUE2="QBATCH"

## Set MULTI_INSTANCE=1 if you are running multiple instances of OneWorld
## under the same Unix user id.
MULTI_INSTANCE=0

PORT="*INI"

#---------------------------------------------------------------------- #
# VARIABLE DEFINITIONS THAT YOU SHOULD NOT HAVE TO CHANGE...
#---------------------------------------------------------------------- #
set +u
USER=$(whoami)

HOST=$(hostname)
OSTYPE=$(uname)

## On AIX, process id shows up in column 2, it's column 1 on others...
if [ $OSTYPE = "AIX" ]
  then
    COLUMN=2
  else
    COLUMN=1
fi

unset SILENT_MODE
if [[ "$1" = "-s" || "$2" = "-s" ]] ; then
    SILENT_MODE=1
fi

unset FAST_MODE
if [[ "$1" = "now" || "$2" = "now" ]] ; then
    FAST_MODE=1
fi

## In MULTI_INSTANCE mode, we need to be able to find the INI file to get
## certain settings.  If we can't, then exit with an error.
if [ "$MULTI_INSTANCE" = "1" ] ; then
    MFLAG="-m"
    if [ -f ./JDE.INI ] ; then
      PORT_NBR=$(grep "^serviceNameListen" ./JDE.INI | sed 's/.*=//')
    elif [ -f $JDE_BASE/JDE.INI ] ; then
      PORT_NBR=$(grep "^serviceNameListen" $JDE_BASE/JDE.INI | sed 's/.*=//')
    else
      if [ -z "$SILENT_MODE" ] ; then
```

```
              echo "      This script cannot support multiple instances of"
              echo "      OneWorld without access to a JDE.INI file."
              echo "      You must either set the $JDE_BASE environment"
              echo "      variable correctly, or turn off MULTI_INSTANCE"
              echo "      mode in the EndOneWorld.sh script."
              echo "       exiting..."
          fi
          echo "      This script cannot support multiple instances of" >> $LOGFILE
          echo "      OneWorld without access to a JDE.INI file." >> $LOGFILE
          echo "      You must either set the $JDE_BASE environment" >> $LOGFILE
          echo "      variable correctly, or turn off MULTI_INSTANCE" >> $LOGFILE
          echo "      mode in the EndOneWorld.sh script." >> $LOGFILE
          echo "       exiting..."  >> $LOGFILE
          exit 1
      fi
fi


#------------------------------------------------------------------- #
# FUNCTION DEFINITIONS...
#------------------------------------------------------------------- #
function GetPIDS
{
  if [ "$MULTI_INSTANCE" = "1" ] ; then
      PIDS=$(ps -ef | grep $USER | grep $1 | grep $PORT_NBR | awk '{print $2}')
      PIDS="$(ps -ef | grep $USER | grep $1 | grep $SYSTEM | awk '{print $2}') $PIDS"
      if [ "$PIDS" = " " ] ; then
          PIDS=""
      fi
  else
      PIDS=$(ps -u $USER | grep $1 | awk '{print $'$COLUMN'}')
  fi
}


function KillProcess
{
  for signal in 2 9
    do
      GetPIDS $1
      if [ -z "$PIDS" ] ; then
          return
      else
          echo "      sending signal $signal to all $1 processes..." >> $LOGFILE
          kill -$signal $PIDS
          sleep 1
      fi
    done
}


function RestoreAndExit
{
  ## This is executed by Check_runbatch if the user aborts the script
```

```
    stty $SAVE_stty
    echo "\n$(date)    Shutdown process halted by user intervention.\n " >> $LOGFILE
    exit 1
}

function Check_runbatch
{
    ## This function will warn the user if runbatch processes are still
    ## running and - if not in "silent" or "fast" mode - allow them the
    ## opportunity to abort the shutdown.  We don't want to just do a read
    ## for input in case this script is being run from another script, or
    ## being automated, and no command line options are passed.
    GetPIDS runbatch
    if [ -n "$PIDS" ] ; then
        echo "  ***** One or more runbatch processes is still executing!" >> $LOGFILE
        if [[ -z "$SILENT_MODE" && -z "$FAST_MODE" ]] ; then
            SAVE_stty=$(stty -g)
            trap 'RestoreAndExit' INT
            stty intr ^[
            echo "    ***** One or more runbatch processes is still executing!"
            echo "    ***** These will be killed if you do not act now!!"
            echo "\n      Hit escape within 10 seconds to end this script...\n"
            sleep 10
            stty $SAVE_stty
        fi
        echo "  ***** These processes will be terminated abnormally!" >> $LOGFILE
        $SYSTEM/bin32/endnet $PORT >> $LOGFILE 2>&1
        KillProcess runbatch
    fi
}

function Check_misc
{
    ## Add to this list if there are other JDE processes
    ## that we want this script to end.
    GetPIDS porttest
    if [ -n "$PIDS" ] ; then
        echo "    Found porttest... It will be stopped..." >> $LOGFILE
        KillProcess porttest
    fi
    GetPIDS killque
    if [ -n "$PIDS" ] ; then
        echo "    Found killque... It will be stopped..." >> $LOGFILE
        KillProcess killque
    fi
    GetPIDS runube
    if [ -n "$PIDS" ] ; then
        echo "    Found runube... It will be stopped..." >> $LOGFILE
        KillProcess runube
    fi
}
```

```
function StopQueues
{
  ## Don't try to stop queue processes if there aren't any...
  GetPIDS jdequeue
  if [ -z "$PIDS" ] ; then
      echo "      No jdequeue processes were found." >> $LOGFILE
  else
      ## If we're in "fast" mode, we'll skip running the killque scripts...
      if [ -z "$FAST_MODE" ] ; then
          echo $(date) "   Stopping Spec Install queue..." >> $LOGFILE
          $SYSTEM/bin32/killque.sh $OWUSR $OWPWD $OWENV $OWQUE1 001 >> $LOGFILE 2>& 1
          echo $(date) "   Stopping Batch queues..." >> $LOGFILE
          $SYSTEM/bin32/killque.sh $OWUSR $OWPWD $OWENV $OWQUE1 UBE >> $LOGFILE 2>& 1
          if [ ! "$OWQUE1" = "$OWQUE2" ] ; then
              $SYSTEM/bin32/killque.sh $OWUSR $OWPWD $OWENV $OWQUE1 UBE >> $LOGFILE 2>& 1
          fi
          echo $(date) "   Stopping Package queue..." >> $LOGFILE
          $SYSTEM/bin32/killque.sh $OWUSR $OWPWD $OWENV $OWQUE1 PKG >> $LOGFILE 2>& 1
      else
          echo "      Forcing immediate shutdown of jdequeue processes..." >> $LOGFILE
      fi
      ## Make sure the jdequeue processes are gone...
      KillProcess jdequeue
  fi
}

function Check_jdenet
{
  GetPIDS jdenet
  if [ -z "$PIDS" ] ; then
      echo "      No jdenet processes were found." >> $LOGFILE
  else
      echo "      Ending jdenet processes..." >> $LOGFILE
      $SYSTEM/bin32/endnet $PORT >> $LOGFILE 2>&1
      ## endnet can sometimes take a few seconds to get rid of everything.
      ## Adjust the sleep time depending on how patient you are...
      sleep 3
      ## Make sure all jdenet processes are gone...
      KillProcess jdenet
  fi
}

function CheckIPC
{
  $SYSTEM/bin32/rmics.sh $MFLAG >> $LOGFILE
  if [ ! $? = 0 ] ; then
      if [ -z "$SILENT_MODE" ] ; then
          echo "      IPC resource conflict -"
          echo "  You may need to change the startIPCKeyValue in your INI file,"
          echo "  or your JDE_BASE environment variable may be set incorrectly."
```

```
           echo "          exiting..."
       fi
       ## (error message already written to $LOGFILE by rmics.sh)
       exit 1
   fi
}


#-------------------------------------------------------------------- #
# MAIN PROCESSING...
#-------------------------------------------------------------------- #

## First, let's make sure the log file directory is valid - otherwise, all
## of the log messages will disappear.

LOGDIR=$(dirname $LOGFILE)
if [ ! -d $LOGDIR ]
   then
     echo " Invalid directory name for LOGFILE - "
     echo "   $LOGDIR"
     echo " You must correct EndOneWorld.sh and retry."
     exit 1
       fi

       echo "------------------------------------------------------------" >> $LOGFILE
       if [ ! $? = 0 ]
         then
            echo " Unable to write to logfile - "
            echo "   $LOGFILE"
            echo " You might not have permission to write to the directory or file."
            echo " Make sure file permissions are set correctly and retry."
            exit 1
       fi


       if [ -z "$SILENT_MODE" ] ; then
            echo $(date) "  Stopping JD Edwards OneWorld - This may take a minute..."
       fi
       echo $(date) "  Stopping JD Edwards OneWorld on $HOST" >> $LOGFILE

       Check_runbatch

       Check_misc

       StopQueues

       Check_jdenet

       CheckIPC

       if [ -z "$SILENT_MODE" ] ; then
            echo "\n$(date)   JD Edwards OneWorld shutdown complete.\n"
       fi
```

```
echo "\n$(date)   JD Edwards OneWorld shutdown complete.\n " >> $LOGFILE

exit 0
```

Cleaning up the UNIX Environment   You can run a couple of UNIX commands to ensure that all of the associated OneWorld processes have stopped. First, enter the following command:

> ps –ef|grep jdeb7332

where "jdeb7332" is the user that started the OneWorld services . This command will return a list of every process currently running for that specific user. If jdeque, jdenet, jdequeue, jdenet_n, jdenet_k, or killque process is in the resulting list, you must manually clean it up by entering the following command:

> kill –2 *yyyyy*

where *yyyyy* represents the process ID for the specific process you want to stop. If this command does not stop the offending OneWorld process (you can determine this by rerunning the previously listed **ps –ef|grep** command), you can enter the following command that will:

> kill –9 *yyyyy*

where *yyyyy* represents the process ID for the specific process you want to stop.

rmics.sh

After validating that all of the user ID–associated OneWorld processes have stopped (by rerunning the previously listed **ps –ef|grep** command), you need to run rmics.sh, a OneWorld utility. This command is found in the $system/bin32 directory and was briefly mentioned previously as a step to take prior to starting the OneWorld services on the UNIX platform. Similar to the startup procedure, this command should be used after stopping services. The details of this command for the OneWorld Xe version follow:

```
#!/bin/ksh

USER=`whoami`
OSTYPE=`uname`

if [ $OSTYPE = "SunOS" ]
```

```
then
AWK=nawk
USER=`whoami`
else
AWK=awk
USER=`id -u -n`
fi


######################################################################
##  Don't allow this script to run if there are jde processes   ##
##  still running.  If "-m" is passed, there may be multiple     ##
##  instances of OneWorld for this user, so bypass this step.    ##
######################################################################
if [ ! "$1" = "-m" ]
then

  ps -u $USER | egrep
"jdequeue|runbatch|jdenet_k|jdenet_n|clearloc|endnet|killque|pdf_conv|porttest|runprint|runube|
builddll|buildpkg|linkpkg|unpackal|verifyoc" | grep -v egrep

  if [ $? = 0 ]
  then
    echo " OneWorld processes are still running!!"
    echo " This script should not be run until all OneWorld processes have ended."
    echo " "
    exit 1
  fi

fi

ipcs | grep $USER

STARTIPC=
MAXNUMRES=
if [ -f ./JDE.INI ] ; then
  STARTIPC=`grep "^startIPCKeyValue" ./JDE.INI | sed 's/.*=//'`
  MAXNUMRES=`grep "^maxNumberOfResources" ./JDE.INI | sed 's/.*=//'`
elif [ -f $JDE_BASE/JDE.INI ] ; then
  STARTIPC=`grep "^startIPCKeyValue" $JDE_BASE/JDE.INI | sed 's/.*=//'`
  MAXNUMRES=`grep "^maxNumberOfResources" $JDE_BASE/JDE.INI | sed 's/.*=//'`
fi

if [[ ! $STARTIPC = *([0-9]) ]] ; then
    echo " The startIPCKeyValue in your INI file must be a numeric value!"
    exit 1
fi

if [ "$STARTIPC" = "" ] ; then
  STARTIPC="5000"
fi
if [ "$MAXNUMRES" = "" ] ; then
```

```
  MAXNUMRES="1000"
fi
ipcs | grep $USER | $AWK \
'BEGIN \
{ \
  USER = "'`echo $USER`'"; \
  STARTIPC = "'`echo $STARTIPC`'"; \
  MAXNUMRES =  "'`echo $MAXNUMRES`'"; \
  IPCMIN = STARTIPC; \
  IPCMAX = STARTIPC + MAXNUMRES - 1; \
  HEXMIN = sprintf( "0x%8.8x", IPCMIN); \
  HEXMAX = sprintf( "0x%8.8x", IPCMAX); \
  print "echo delete all MessageQueues, Shared Memories, and Semaphores, range:"; \
  print "echo", HEXMIN, "to", HEXMAX, "[" IPCMIN, "to", IPCMAX"], owned by", USER; \
} \
{ \
  TYPE = substr( $0, 1, 1); \
  STRING = substr( $0, 2); \
  split( STRING, VALUE); \
  ID = VALUE[1]; \
  KEY = substr( VALUE[2], 3); \
  gsub( ".", "& ", KEY); \
  gsub( "a", "10", KEY); \
  gsub( "b", "11", KEY); \
  gsub( "c", "12", KEY); \
  gsub( "d", "13", KEY); \
  gsub( "e", "14", KEY); \
  gsub( "f", "15", KEY); \
  KEYLEN = split( KEY, HEX); \
  KEYVAL = HEX[1]; \
  for ( Z = 2; Z <= KEYLEN; Z++) { \
    KEYVAL = ((16 * KEYVAL) + HEX[Z]); \
  } \
  if (((0 + IPCMIN) <= (0 + KEYVAL)) && ((0 + KEYVAL) <= (0 + IPCMAX))) { \
    printf "ipcrm -%s %d\n", TYPE, ID; \
  } \
}' | sh


ipcs | grep $USER

## if the ipcs return value is 1 (i.e. nothing returned), this is good.
## if the ipcs return value is 0 (i.e. something returned), there are
##   leftover IPC resources, so print a warning.
if [ $? = 0 ]
  then
    echo " "
    echo " There are leftover IPC resources for this user."
    echo "   If you are not running another OneWorld instance under this"
    echo "   user id, you may need to remove these resources manually."
    echo " "
fi
```

```
## This next bit determines the exit status.  If there are any
## IPC resources within the range, (regardless of user)
## this will return the number.
function GetIPCInRange
{
  ipcs | $AWK \
  'BEGIN \
  { \
    USER = "'`echo $USER`'"; \
    STARTIPC = "'`echo $STARTIPC`'"; \
    MAXNUMRES =  "'`echo $MAXNUMRES`'"; \
    IPCMIN = STARTIPC; \
    IPCMAX = STARTIPC + MAXNUMRES - 1; \
    HEXMIN = sprintf( "0x%8.8x", IPCMIN); \
    HEXMAX = sprintf( "0x%8.8x", IPCMAX); \
  }  \
  { \
    TYPE = substr( $0, 1, 1); \
    STRING = substr( $0, 2); \
    split( STRING, VALUE); \
    ID = VALUE[1]; \
    KEY = substr( VALUE[2], 3); \
    gsub( ".", "& ", KEY); \
    gsub( "a", "10", KEY); \
    gsub( "b", "11", KEY); \
    gsub( "c", "12", KEY); \
    gsub( "d", "13", KEY); \
    gsub( "e", "14", KEY); \
    gsub( "f", "15", KEY); \
    KEYLEN = split( KEY, HEX); \
    KEYVAL = HEX[1]; \
    for ( Z = 2; Z <= KEYLEN; Z++) { \
      KEYVAL = ((16 * KEYVAL) + HEX[Z]); \
    } \
    if (((0 + IPCMIN) <= (0 + KEYVAL)) && ((0 + KEYVAL) <= (0 + IPCMAX))) { \
      printf "%s\n", $0; \
    } \
  }' | cat
}


GetIPCInRange

EXIT=$(GetIPCInRange | wc -l)

if [ $EXIT != 0 ]
  then
    echo " "
    echo " Not all IPC resources were removed - OR - "
    echo " Another user has IPC resources in your range"
    echo "   You may need to change the startIPCKeyValue in your INI file,"
```

```
       echo "   or your JDE_BASE environment variable may be set incorrectly."
       echo " "
fi

exit $EXIT
```

Troubleshooting the UNIX Platform

A series of issues affect the UNIX application server in addition to the other platforms. This section will cover some of the issues with the UNIX platform. In particular, we will concentrate on the more common issues seen by the user or by the UNIX administrator and their likely causes and resolutions.

General Troubleshooting Tools

One of the tools you are most likely to use on the UNIX platform (or any other for that matter) is the jde_*processid*.log (where *processid* represents the actual process ID assigned by UNIX to the particular kernel and/or process) and jdedebug_*processid*.log (where the *processid* represents the actual process ID assigned by UNIX to the specific kernel and/or process). The server's JDE.INI, located in the INI directory on the UNIX server, controls these logs. A series of different logging options are available as indicated in Table 23-1.

JDE.INI Setting	Values/Definitions
[DEBUG]	
Output=NONE	Determines the output of the jdedebug log generated on the server. Valid values include: NONE—The jdedebug file is disabled. FILE—The jdedebug file is enabled for database and runtime trace information. EXCFILE—The jdedebug file is enabled for runtime trace information. BOTH—The runtime trace information is written to both the jde and jdedebug logs.
Trace=FALSE	TRUE or FALSE—This value writes additional runtime trace information to the server.

TABLE 23-1.   JDE.INI Log Settings

JDE.INI Setting	Values/Definitions
ClientLog=0	This setting tells the server to write business function data to both the server and workstation logs. This increases network traffic substantially and should be done only when directed to by the JDE Response line. Valid values are: 0—Disable 1—Enable
DebugFile=/u01/jdedwardsoneworld/ b7332/log/jdedebug.log	This setting tells the server where to write the JDEDEBUG.log.
JobFile=/u01/jdedwardsoneworld/ b7332/log/jde.log	This setting tells the server where to write the JDE.logs.
GlobalCompactSizeInit=1024	
GlobalCompactSizeDestroy=0	
LogErrors=0	This setting tells the server to log any errors in the JDE.LOG. Valid values are: 0—Don't log errors. 1—Log errors.
JDETSFile=JDETS.log	This setting specifies the location and name of the lock manager trace file.
KeepLogs=0	This setting tells the server to keep logs after services have ended. Valid values are: 0—Don't keep logs. 1—Keep logs.
RepTrace=0	This setting enables log message replication.
[TAM]	
TAMTraceLevel=0	This setting indicates the level to trace the server's table access management files.
[MEMORY DEBUG]	
Frequency=10000	This setting instructs the server in the frequency of logging associated with memory debugging.
Full=1	This setting tells the server to conduct full debugging.
[JDEIPC]	
ipcTrace=0	This setting enables interprocess communication (IPC) tracing on the server. IPC tracing data is written to the JDEDEBUG.LOG. Valid values are: 0—IPC tracing is off. 1—IPC tracing is on.

TABLE 23-1. JDE.INI Log Settings *(continued)*

JDE.INI Setting	Values/Definitions
[JDENET]	
netTrace=0	This enables JDENET tracing on the server. JDENET is one of two pieces of the OneWorld middleware and works with network communications.
krnlCoreDump=1	This setting instructs the UNIX server to produce a kernel core dump if the kernel is terminated incorrectly.
netCoreDump=1	This setting instructs the UNIX server to produce a kernel core dump if the net service terminates in error.
[UBE]	
UBEDebugLevel=0	This indicates the amount of data written to the UBE logs located in the PrintQueue directory on the UNIX server. Each level includes all of the information in the previous level in addition to the new messaging. Many of these messages are not error messages but contain data on how the UBE process ran. Valid values are: 0—Error messages only 1—Informative messages 2—Section-level messages 3—Object-level messages 4—Event rule messages 5—SQL statements 6—UBE function messages

TABLE 23-1.　JDE.INI Log Settings (*continued*)

When You Can't Find the Security Server

Not being able to find the security server is one of the more annoying server-based errors that has several different causes. Some of the causes are self-explanatory (for example, the server does not have network connectivity), and some are related to OneWorld. Let's quickly review the process of determining the cause and what you need to do to fix the problem.

Users will report that when they attempted to log into OneWorld, they received a message box that specified, "Unable to connect to security server." This problem is the result of several different causes.

Questions to Ask

When you find out that users are seeing the "Unable to connect to security server" message, you should ask the following questions:

- Are you receiving a series of these calls or is this a single instance/user?

- Can you log off and log back on to OneWorld with a normal user ID? (Be sure you don't try this using the JDE ID; this is a valid database user ID.)

- Is this a time when a large number of users are signing on to OneWorld?

Possible Causes

Here is a list of reasons why users may be experiencing this problem:

- Check the services on the server itself by running the command **ps –ef|grep** *xxx* (where *xxx* represents the user who starts the OneWorld services). It is possible that the security services are not running on the security server. They either have not been started or have abnormally aborted. If no OneWorld services are returned, the services need to be started using the RunOneWorld.sh script. If services are present, you probably have a situation where the kernel is either too busy to respond (see the following bullet) or it has ended abnormally. If the kernel has ended abnormally, you should stop the OneWorld services using the EndOneWorld.sh script, ensure that all of the processes ended correctly by using the **ps –ef|grep xxx** command, clean up the UNIX environment using the OneWorld utility rmics.sh, and then start the services again by using RunOneWorld.sh. If the services ended abnormally, there is the possibility that a core dump file was created. Dump files can be found in the $SYSTEM/bin32 directory under the name core.dmp.

- If a lot of security-related activities are on the system (a lot of users are initially logging on to OneWorld), it is possible that the security kernel(s) are simply too busy to service the security request and that request timed out. When this happens, you need to increase the number of security service kernels launched by the OneWorld security server by modifying the security server's JDE.INI as follows:

```
[JDENET_KERNEL_DEF4]
dispatchDLLName=libjdeknet.so
dispatchDLLFunction=JDEK_DispatchSecurity
maxNumberOfProcesses=1 (increase this number as appropriate)
beginningMsgTypeRange=551
endingMsgTypeRange=580
newProcessThresholdRequests=0
numberOfAutoStartProcesses=0
```

- It is possible that the server is actually offline or is having network difficulties and the workstation legitimately can't connect with it. To test network connectivity, enter the following command at a command prompt on the workstation: **ping** *servername* (where *servername* is the name of the server). Because UNIX is case sensitive, ensure that you use uppercase or lowercase letters where appropriate.

When Users Can't Launch UBEs

At times, users will attempt to launch UBEs on the server and will not be able to. Not a lot of information is available from their machines, and although they might be able to override the location to a different location (that is, another application server or locally), they might be on a terminal server, and additional application servers may not be available. The causes of this problem are similar to the causes of the "Can't connect to the security server" problem described earlier.

Questions to Ask

Ask the same kinds of questions that were listed previously. Is it that no one can launch any UBEs or is it a specific person or machine that can't? Can you launch a UBE as a normal user from your workstation? Are the services on the server running? (Use "ps –ef|grep *xxx*," where *xxx* represents the user that launched the OneWorld services on the server.) If the services are running, use the UNIX tool top (we recommend you enter **–s2** after the **top** command to increase the refresh interval from every five seconds to every two seconds) to validate that the processes are getting time and are not defunct.

Try launching a UBE on the UNIX server using the following command-line UBE submission process:

cd $SYSTEM/bin32
runube USER PWD ENV UBE VERSION QUEUE INTERACTIVE/BATCH
PRINT/HOLD SAVE/DELETE [PRINTER NAME]

- **runube** The OneWorld UNIX command that launches the universal batch engine. This can't be in uppercase letters.

- **USER** The name of the OneWorld user identification, in uppercase letters.

- **PWD** The OneWorld password, in uppercase letters, as identified in the F98OWSEC table.

- **ENV** The name of the environment in uppercase letters.

- **UBE** The name, in uppercase letters, for the UBE you want to launch.

- **VERSION** The version of the UBE, in uppercase letters, that you want launch.

- **QUEUE** The name of the queue, in uppercase letters, that you want the UBE to run in (for example, QB7332 for the OneWorld Xe release; other more notable batch names include QBATCH).

Can you run the UBE locally? Validate that the issue is the submission process to the server.

Possible Causes and Resolutions
Do the following to resolve this particular problem:

- Validate that there is room in the svmb733t and svmb733i table spaces. These table spaces are used by the server map, and they often have a 1GB growth restriction. Validate that there is room to add to the F986110 table. In the case of a runaway UBE process, the submission process may have launched several hundred UBEs and filled up the allocated database space.

- Validate network connectivity from the workstation to the server by using NETTEST.EXE, a OneWorld utility that is located in the b7\system\bin32 directory of the client machine. This utility will check for OneWorld port-specific communications between the server and the workstation itself.

Troubleshooting

To use this utility, double-click on the application. You will see the interface shown in Figure 23-3.

Using this program, you need to delete the data in the file selection and then click the Send button.

- Validate that you can launch a UBE on the server using the previously described method .

Tons of UBEs Are in Wait Status

This problem is experienced by most users once they have submitted a UBE. They will go to the Work with Servers application by using either the batch submission entry or the User Options entry. By changing the selection criteria to * for user and today's date, users will often check to see why their UBE hasn't processed yet. Many other

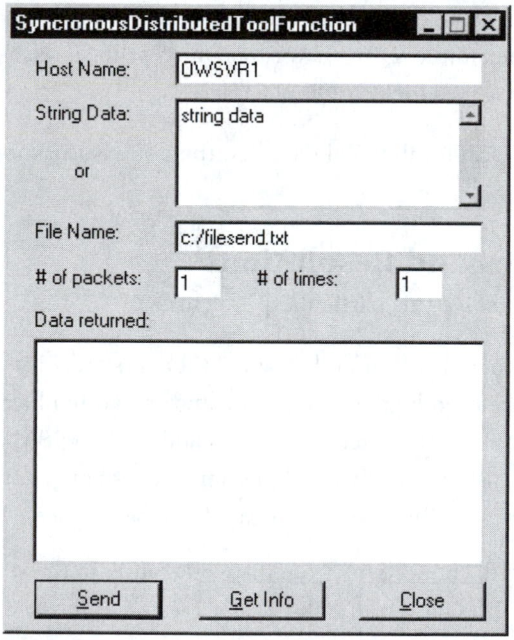

FIGURE 23-3. The Nettest interface

users, not seeing the output they expect, will launch additional UBEs exacerbating the problem. There are several reasons that UBEs might be in a Wait status.

Questions to Ask

You should ask the following questions:

- What UBEs are currently running?

- Identify the number of UBEs in a Wait status. Are there ten, a hundred, or thousands?

- Do all of the UBEs with a Wait status have a legitimate or the same queue name?

- Were they all launched today?

- Is a peak time in the sales or accounting cycle causing abnormally high system use?

- Have you seen this problem before?

- Were all of the UBEs launched in the same OneWorld environment?

Possible Causes and Resolutions

UBEs begin backing up for any of several reasons, and your CNC/system administrator should be able to quickly identify why this problem is occurring. First, because UBEs are entered into the F986110 table, there is a record of each UBE. The W or Wait status indicates that the UBE has not been picked up by the jdequeue services on the UNIX server. If you have thousands of UBEs in a Wait status, you might have a runaway UBE process that submitted the same UBE over and over. We have seen one UBE actually launch 120,000 UBEs. Although it is certainly not a common occurrence, it is a possible explanation. Check to make sure that the UBEs aren't all the same UBE.

If you are seeing an abnormally high volume of UBE activity, it is distinctly possible that the server is simply not servicing all of the UBE requests in a timely manner. You should validate that services are running and that UBE queues are actively running UBEs. You should also look at Chapter 19 to optimize your instance of OneWorld. It is possible, based on the particular UBE running, that a single UBE has locked the server's Table Access Manager (TAM) files, keeping other UBEs from running in the same environment. Over time, you will be able to identify if any UBEs are locking files (they will be the one or two UBEs running when other UBEs begin to back up).

Law of the West

Starting Additional UBE Queues on the Fly

If you have run into a scenario in which, for one reason or another, you simply have an abnormally high UBE volume on the server, the CNC administrator can start additional UBE queues on the fly if the server is able to handle the additional processing requirements. You should look at your overall server resource management prior to adding additional queues to ensure that you will not be creating more work than is worthwhile. If you do determine that your server has enough system resources (including memory, processor, and a disk IO situation that is not too high), log on to the UNIX server as the same user that normally launches the OneWorld services and enter the following command:

```
$SYSTEM/bin32/runque.sh USR PWD ENV QUEUE UBE 5 > $SYSTEM/bin32/ubequeX.log 2>&1 &
```

- USR—A valid OneWorld user identification.

- PWD—The password associated with the OneWorld user.

- ENV—A valid environment for the OneWorld user.

- QUEUE—The name of the normal or requested queue (for example, QB7332).

- UBE—Tells the runque.sh script the type of queue to launch. In this case, it is a UBE queue.

- ubequex.log—*x* represents the number of UBE queues on your system.

This command will launch another UBE queue on your system. If you have the available UNIX system resources, you can launch four or more to assist with cleaning up the UBE backlog. These queues will continue to run until you stop services using the EndOneWorld.sh script. You do not need to identify the associated process IDs to terminate them, and in fact, you would not want to abnormally terminate these processes. Provided you used a valid queue name when starting the additional services, the EndOneWorld.sh script will automatically stop the new queues. If you added a new queue name (one not already identified in the EndOneWorld.sh script), you must manually kill the processes using the **kill –2** or **kill –9** commands in UNIX.

When All of the UBEs End in Error

If all of the UBEs, both custom and shipped versions, are suddenly ending in error, but services like security continue to run unabated (you are able to log out of OneWorld on a workstation and log back in), you could be facing a single problem: TAM file corruption on the server. (This problem is more likely than a database connection loss because logging back on to OneWorld forces the security server to read the F98OWSEC and F0092 tables. Another way you know that it isn't a database issue is the fact that the UBEs end in error. For them to have been read, run, and updated with an E status means that database connectivity does exist, at least on some level.)

TAM files on the server are a proprietary J.D. Edwards file structure located in the path code/spec directory (for example, /u01/jdedwardsoneworld/b7332/PRODB733/ spec) that contains the data in the Central Object Specifications tables. Another clear indication of TAM corruption is the inability to restart OneWorld services on the UNIX server. You will see this when the path code used in the server's JDE.INI is the same as the path code with the corrupted TAM, and you've bounced OneWorld services.

Five sets of TAM files are associated with UBEs. If a UBE ends abnormally (for example, a queue has a memory violation and terminates), it is possible that the universal batch engine had one or more of these TAM files in a locked state. When the queue stopped, the TAMs remain locked, and consequently, no other queues could access them. When this occurs, you need to refresh your TAM files (we recommend refreshing all of them to ensure your path code remains in synch) from your nightly backup. Because refreshing these from tape could take an abnormally long time, it is often useful to have a relatively recent set in a backup directory on the UNIX box. Follow these steps:

1. Stop OneWorld services on the server using the EndOneWorld.sh script.

   cd $SYSTEM/bin32/EndOneWorld.sh

2. Ensure that all of the OneWorld processes (jdenet_n, jdenet_k, jdequeue, killque, and so on) have stopped.

   ps –ef|grep *xxx*

   where *xxx* represents the user ID that launched the OneWorld services.

3. Manually kill any hanging processes.

   kill –2 12345

where 12345 represents the UNIX assigned process ID.
kill −9 12345

where 12345 represents the UNIX assigned process ID.

4. Clean up the OneWorld environment by using the rmics.sh script.

cd $SYSTEM/bin32/rmics.sh

5. Delete the spec directory in the specific path code having the problem (if all of the UBEs in production fail, delete the PRODB733/spec directory).

cd $SYSTEM/../PRODB733
rm −r spec

6. Move the backed up spec directory into place.

mv bkup/spec ./spec

NOTE

*This will use the one backup spec directory. If you'd rather, copy it using a **cp** command.*

7. Restart the OneWorld services.

cd $SYSTEM/bin32/RunOneWorld.sh

When Services Won't Start

You usually encounter this problem during the installation process and not during implementation or after go-live. If you do encounter this problem during installation, make sure that you've updated all of the correct fields in JDE.INI. Also ensure that your UNIX user can perform a tnsping (an Oracle utility ensuring you have database connectivity). If those both prove okay (you know that Oracle isn't an issue, and you have permissions on the TNSNAMES.ORA file), check the file permissions to the directories and files for OneWorld on the UNIX server. Make sure that your OneWorld user ID has full read, write, and execute permissions on these files (this is a step during the installation of the UNIX server itself where you use the **chmod** 777 command on the associated files and file structures). Verify that you've made the appropriate changes (as outlined in the *J.D. Edwards OneWorld Installation Manual for UNIX*) to the .profile and .oneworld files. If this also proves okay, you need to run the rmics.sh script, modify JDE.INI so that full logging is on as described previously, and restart the OneWorld services. Odds are that one of the JDE logs will contain enough information that you will be able to determine what the problem is.

If you do see this scenario after the services are running, you probably have corrupted TAM files in the code/spec directory listed in the [DB System Settings] section of the server's JDE.INI. Rather than deleting the existing spec directory, you can rename this directory using the **mv** command and copy in the backup directory using the **cp** command. Rerun the rmics.sh script and try starting the OneWorld services again. If they come up, you know that it was a TAM corruption issue.

When Users Have Lost Connection with the Server

This problem is the last troubleshooting issue we will discuss in this chapter, and it deals with a three-tier architecture (or a virtual three-tier architecture) where the application server is a UNIX box. Three-tier architectures map interactive application business functions from the workstation to the server for either speed or offloading processing purposes. When you run this type of logic on the server, call object kernels are used to actually perform the calculations. When a OneWorld user first launches one of these service calls to the server (by actually using an application), he or she is assigned to a specific call object kernel for the duration of the time the user is on OneWorld. (This is true in B733.2; however, in OneWorld Xe, the architecture is supposed to support a better load balancing plan where you might be running in several different kernels based on when your calls were made, as opposed to when other user's calls were made.) Because of this assignment, when a call object kernel unexpectedly terminates, the user's OneWorld session reverts back to running these business functions locally. New connections to other call object kernels are not made until the user logs out of OneWorld and then logs back on.

Anyone who works with UNIX understands that processes will occasionally terminate (this will happen even though J.D. Edwards has spent a considerable amount of time making these processes as stable as possible). Because processes occasionally terminate, the best method of handling this rare event is educating users so that when they receive a message indicating that they have lost communication with the server, they know automatically to log off of OneWorld and then log back on. It is OneWorld's client version of rebooting the system.

Final Hints for Troubleshooting

The best method of learning how to troubleshoot the UNIX/OneWorld system is by doing it, calling the J.D. Edwards Support Line when necessary, and learning the peculiarities of your system. One of the hints we like to use is the **tail** command on some of the logs, and in particular, a **tail –f** is useful when troubleshooting because it will provide a real-time end of the log. As the log continues to build, you will continue to see the screen presentation of the real-time end of the file. If you have chosen to grow a UNIX administrator instead of already having the skill sets in house or purchasing the skill sets, be sure that you provide that administrator with the appropriate classes for the flavor of UNIX you are supporting. In addition, as we suggested earlier, be sure that you bring in an experienced consultant who can decrease the overall learning curve for your administrator.

Overall, the OneWorld/UNIX/Oracle combination is relatively straightforward and trouble free. Once properly configured, this system will provide a robust platform with the ability to grow.

Summary

The UNIX chapter was intentionally designed as a chapter that augments existing J.D. Edwards' material with undiscussed topics or provides additional breadth to the topics covered by both the J.D. Edwards material and this book. It is essential to the platform that it be sized, configured, and architecturally designed up front in order to maximize performance while minimizing downtime and hardware bottlenecks. OneWorld has special tools designed for the UNIX platform, and while there are differences between the three supported UNIX flavors, there are significant similarities as well. We hope this chapter has taken a slightly different approach to the platform question and answers many of the questions you had and questions you didn't know to ask. You've made an excellent choice of platform, and you will be able to continue with this system in the future.

CHAPTER 24

Workstations

Specific Workstation Issues and Resolutions

95/98/NT Issues and Resolutions

Workflow

e have talked a lot in this book about advanced OneWorld topics. Now let's take a minute and step back to look at a subject that is just as important as any advanced Configurable Network Computing (CNC) configuration. It is the one thing all end users must use: a OneWorld workstation. If the workstations are not functioning correctly, your users will not be able to do their jobs. But do we need an entire chapter on this? Yes! There are several different types of workstations and specific issues with workstations depending on the operating system you choose. In this chapter, we will cover:

- Specific workstation issues and resolutions

- Known problems for FAT, Thin, Zero, and Developer's Workstations

- 95/98/NT issues and resolutions

Specific Workstation Issues and Resolutions

Almost everyone agrees that if they could avoid a problem they would. This section should help you to avoid some common issues.

Logon Issues

There are several issues that come up again and again when users try to log on to their workstations. This list is by no means all-inclusive, but it should give you an idea of where to start looking when you run into logon issues on your client workstations. These issues are presented in an issue/resolution format.

Issue/Resolution

Issue: When I attempt to log on to a client workstation, I am presented with a database window asking for a user and password. What causes OneWorld to give me this sign-on window?

Resolution: This database sign-on screen will be presented to your end users when the system is unable to connect to the database or does not have the correct permissions to a table. One problem that will cause you to see a database sign-on screen every time is that you do not have an Open Database Connectivity (ODBC) defined for that data source. If this is the cause, you will see an error similar to the ones listed below in your JDE.LOG, which is located on the C root of the client workstation:

```
Sun Jan 02 09:43:16 2000                        JDBODBC638
ODB0000045 - SQLDriverConnect failed. DSN: System - B733
Sun Jan 02 09:43:16 2000                        JDBODBC639
[Microsoft][ODBC Driver Manager] Data source name not found and no default
driver specified - SQLSTATE: IM002
Sun Jan 02 09:45:30 2000                        jdb_drvm608
JDB9900164 - Failed to connect to System - B733
Sun Jan 02 09:45:32 2000                        JTP_CM286
JDB9909003 - Could not init connect.
```

What this log is telling us is that no ODBC drive is defined for the System – B733 data source. You can even see the exact ODBC data source name that OneWorld is trying to find after the DSN section in this log. This means you will need to define or correct the ODBC definition in the workstation's Control Panel. When you go into the Control Panel, you will see ODBC Data Sources, as shown here. Double-click on this icon.

This will take you into the ODBC Data Source Administrator. In this application, add a system ODBC data source. A system ODBC is needed so that all of your NT or Windows 95/98 users can see this ODBC definition. If you add a user ODBC, only that specific user will be able to see the ODBC definition.

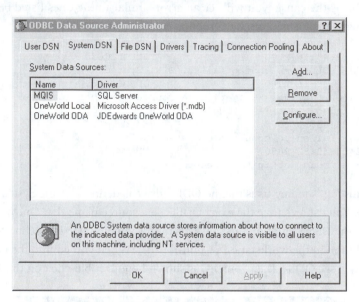

OneWorld data sources will look for ODBC data sources to connect to all supported databases, except for Oracle. OneWorld gets the ODBC data source name from the Database Name field in the OneWorld data source. If this ODBC does not exist or does not match in case and space, the user will get a database sign-on screen. If you are using Oracle, the connect string will be listed in the OneWorld data source's Database Name field and you will see errors in your log saying you were unable to connect to the instance. This is normally due to a faulty TNSNAMES file configuration in your Oracle client software (for more information on OneWorld data sources, refer to Chapter 2). The important thing to remember when you see a database sign-on screen is that you are not making a connection to the database or you do not have permissions to the database. Don't panic, just start with the JDE.LOG on the client workstation and ask yourself why this workstation or user would have a connection problem with the database. It could be your TNSNAMES file or a database permissions problem. Looking at the JDE.LOG should help cut your troubleshooting time down.

Issue/Resolution

Issue: OneWorld should set up all of my ODBC data sources automatically when I install a client workstation. However, my workstations are missing some of my ODBC data sources. The installation did create some of them, but not all of them. Why?

Resolution: Currently, there is a limitation in OneWorld as to the number of ODBC data source entries you can have in the ODBCDATASOURCE.INF, which is read when you install a client workstation so that OneWorld can automatically set up all of your ODBCs. If you have more then 32 entries or different ODBC data sources defined, OneWorld will ignore some of these definitions, thus, not creating the ODBC data sources on the client workstation.

Another resolution to this issue may be the fact that the ODBCDATASOURCE.INF file does not contain all of your ODBC data sources or was not created at all. This file resides in the B733\client directory and should be verified to ensure it has been created properly. In release B733.1 and higher, every time you add a new OneWorld data source (other than a data source that points to an Oracle database), you will be prompted to create an ODBC. When you complete this ODBC definition, the information will be written to the ODBCDATASOURCE.INF file. So if you see "ODBC definition failed" when you add a OneWorld data source, you could not update the ODBCDATASOURCE.INF file for some reason.

N O T E

There is a software action request (SAR) on the ODBCs being created. A SAR is how J.D. Edwards tracks fixes to their software. When a SAR is entered, development resources are assigned to fix the problem or enhance the software, and clients can monitor the status of these SARs through J.D. Edwards' Web page. This SAR number is 3967356.

Issue/Resolution

Issue: I am running against an AS/400 as an enterprise server. My users can log on to three workstations without a problem, but the fourth workstation gets a database sign-on screen. This happens on both Windows 95 and Windows NT workstations.

Resolution: This problem is normally caused due to the user profile on the AS/400. The AS/400 will allow the system administrator to limit the number of sessions a user can have open on the AS/400 at any one time. What happens is that everyone uses

Troubleshooting

that user by signing on to OneWorld directly as this user or having this user passed through sign security. The maximum number of connects, however, is exceeded on the AS/400, thus the fourth client workstation gets a database sign-on screen. To fix this issue, set the user profile on the AS/400 to an unlimited number of sessions.

Issue/Resolution

Issue: When I sign on to my client workstation, I get the error "unable to connect to security server." When I click OK through this error, I get a database sign-on screen. **Resolution:** What this error means is that you are attempting to use sign-on security and your workstation cannot connect to your security server. Since the actual work for sign-on security is taking place on your security server, that is where you need to start troubleshooting. The first thing is to check the logs on the security server. For more details on how to set up and troubleshoot sign-on security, see Chapter 13.

Issue/Resolution

Issue: When I log on to my workstation, I cannot see any of my menus. **Resolution:** This is normally caused by either a mapping issue or a user profile setting. What can happen is you set up an incorrect mapping telling OneWorld to look for your menus in a location where they do not exist. To see if this is the case, check your Object Configuration Manager mappings and also check your JDEDEBUG.LOG. This log will normally be located on the C root of the client workstation. This log lists the select statements being passed to the database, so you can easily see if OneWorld is passing an incorrect user. The other common problem is that the OneWorld user profile is set to default the user's initial menu to a blank menu. Initial menus and other user profile functionality are covered in Chapter 13.

Known Problems for FAT, Thin, Zero, and Developer's Workstations

Issue/Resolution

Issue: I am using a Windows Terminal Server, which was working; however, now I am getting FDASPEC locking errors when my users are attempting to access applications. **Resolution:** Windows Terminal Server is a great wide area network (WAN) solution for your users. This software allows multiple users to connect to a machine over the WAN and use applications on that machine with minimal network traffic. When this is set up for OneWorld, multiple users are using the same client installation to perform their work. J.D. Edwards had to come up with a way for multiple users to access their specification files. This is done through an INI setting. In your Windows Terminal Server INI file, you will need to have the entry: MultiUserTAM=1. If this is set to 0, OneWorld thinks that only one user can access the specification files, which is why you get a locking error.

Issue/Resolution

Issue: When I attempt to log on to OneWorld on my Windows Terminal Server, I get the splash screen and then the program just disappears. If I attempt to run the application again, it does the same thing, although the machine was working at one time.

Resolution: When you log on to a Windows Terminal Server, it creates a temporary directory for each user, normally under C:\TEMP. When the session is ended, this temporary directory should be cleaned up by the operating system—however, this does not always happen. This temporary directory is found by an ID number, and if you reboot the Windows Terminal Server, the IDs will be set back to 1. So when a user logs on, he would then be pointed to another user's folder under the TEMP directory, which he would not have permissions to. This causes the OneWorld application to disappear. The solution to this problem is to get rid of the TEMP directories; this is normally done through a script that is read upon startup.

Issue/Resolution

Issue: I am getting the error "obsolete JDE.INI file" when I attempt to run OneWorld on my Windows Terminal Server session. However, when I log on to the server itself, as the administrator, it works fine.

Resolution: When you install OneWorld on a Windows Terminal Server machine, you will need to install the application through the Control Panel's Add/Remove Programs application. Otherwise, it will not be installed to allow Windows Terminal Server to copy an INI file for each user. This is why you get the "obsolete JDE.INI file" error.

Issue/Resolution

Issue: When I attempt to connect to my OneWorld JAS server, I get an error saying "server cannot handle parameters."

Resolution: This is an indication that WebSphere is not set up correctly. You will need to review settings for WebSphere.

T I P

J.D. Edwards is putting a lot of effort into their Web product, so it is changing quickly. Check their Web page for the latest changes.

Troubleshooting

Issue/Resolution

Issue: I am running OneWorld against an Oracle database. Do I still need to be on the current MDAC level for my workstations?

Resolution: Currently, it is J.D. Edwards customer support's recommendation that all workstations be on the current MDAC level, even if you are running Oracle. The current required MDAC level can be found on J.D. Edwards' Web page.

Issue/Resolution

Issue: I have installed a developer's workstation, but this workstation does not have any files in the source and include folders under the path code that was installed—for example, DEVB733\source.

Resolution: When client workstations are installed, OneWorld automatically checks to see if the required compiler is installed. If it is not, OneWorld assumes this will be a production workstation and does not allow you to install a client with development objects, such as the source and include files. To remedy this, you just need to have the compiler installed on the machine before attempting to install OneWorld on that workstation.

> *N O T E*
>
>
>
> *Only developer's workstations need the source and include files. If you are only installing production workstations, they do not need to have a compiler installed on them. It is important to understand this, as you can drive the price of your implementation up in hard drive space and licensing costs.*

Issue/Resolution

Issue: When my users are in certain applications, they get the error "unable to connect to [my enterprise server's name]." Sometimes logging off OneWorld and back onto the system seems to clear the error up for a little while. Since interactive applications only run on the client workstations, why are they receiving this error?

Resolution: It is true that interactive applications only run on the workstations. However, business functions can run on the enterprise server as well as on the client workstations. Normally when you see an error like this, you have mapped business functions to run on your enterprise server, and this is where your problem really lies. To solve this problem, check your mapping and your server's INI file configuration to ensure that it can run business functions on the server.

TIP

The INI settings are necessary to run business functions on an enterprise server change from time to time, so it is a good idea to check J.D. Edwards' Web site for information on this subject every couple of months.

Issue/Resolution

Issue: My client workstation was running fine last week, but it has been slowing down as I use it from day to day.

Resolution: This may be a symptom of a deeper problem, but one thing you can check is the size of your GBLTBL.DDB and GBLTBL.XDB files. These files contain cached information to increase performance. However, if they get too big, they can slow the system down—we have seen these files at sizes over 9MB. This should not normally be the case. You can delete these files and they will automatically be re-created. To do this, log off OneWorld. On the workstation, find the GBLTBL files under B7\PATHCODE\spec, where PATHCODE is the path code you have installed on the client (such as PRODB733). Find the GBLTBL.DDB and GBLTBL.XDB files and move these to your recycle bin. When you log back on to OneWorld, you will see a lot of just-in-time installation (JITI). This is because the GBLTBL spec files contain information on what data dictionary items have been JITIed onto the client workstation. Since they are now being created, you will JITI all required data dictionary items to log on to OneWorld. If this solves your problem, but you need to perform this procedure again and again, this could be a symptom of a larger problem and should be looked into.

Issue/Resolution

Issue: I have made some data dictionary changes on my system administrator's machine, but I only see these changes on a couple of client workstations. Why?

Resolution: The data dictionary information is held in the DDTXT, DDDICT, and GBLTBL specification files on the client workstations. The information in these files is passed through just-in-time installation. If you make a data dictionary change on one workstation, it will update that workstation's local specification files and the relational database tables for the data dictionary. To get these changes out to your workstations, you need to either set up data dictionary replication (this type of replication is covered in Chapter 15) or for a temporary workaround, you can delete the DDTXT, DDDICT, and GBLTBL specification files on your workstation. To do this, log off OneWorld, open a Windows Explorer session, and go to B7\PATHCODE\spec, where PATHCODE is the name of the path code installed on your workstation (for example, PRODB733). Highlight the DDDICT, DDTXT, and GBLTBL files and send them to the recycle bin. There will be a DDB and XDB version of each file; the DDB is the actual file, and the XDB is the index over the file—be sure to move both to the recycle bin. When you log back on to OneWorld and use the desired application, your new data dictionary changes will be installed through just-in-time installation.

Issue/Resolution

Issue: When I attempt to check an object in from the object librarian application, I get the error "unable to copy file." I can click OK through this error and the object seems to be checked in. Is this a problem?

Resolution: The answer is yes, this is a problem! What this error means is that OneWorld was unable to copy a file from your client workstation to your check-in location. This is because OneWorld does not just use a relational database to store objects. OneWorld also uses source and include files for tables and business functions. These files are needed for a successful package and business function build. The most common problem is permissions to your check-in location—that is, your developer's network user does not have read/write privileges to the B733\PATHCODE\ include or source directory on your deployment server, where PATHCODE is the path code you are attempting to check the object into (for example, CRPB733). A full listing of the required permissions is listed in Chapter 22. Another common problem is that your path code definition is incorrect; see Chapter 2 for details on path code definitions.

Issue/Resolution

Issue: When I log on to my client workstation, I get the error "JITI (Just In Time Installation) has been disabled for this environment."

Resolution: The JITI feature can be turned on or off in the environment master program P0094. This program can be found on the Environments menu (GH9053). Double-click on this application, click Find, and select the environment where the error is occurring for your user. You will now be in the Environment Revisions screen, shown in Figure 24-1. At the bottom of this screen is a field named Just In Time Installation. If this is set to N, your end users will not be able to JITI any applications. This should normally be set to Y. The only time J.D. Edwards recommends that you set this to N is when you have transferred objects into the production path code and you are testing them—you do not want to have any users JITI the application until you are done with your tests. In our experience, you should do your testing in the CRP path

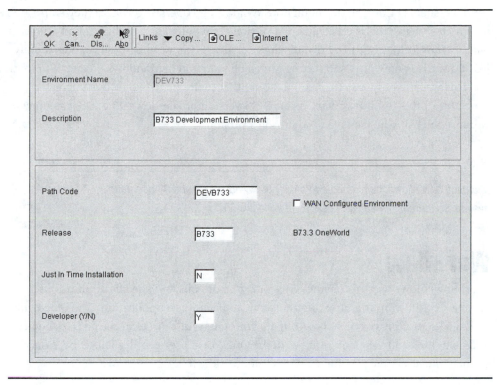

FIGURE 24-1. Turning JITI on or off in the environment revisions screen

code, against data similar to your production data, and leave the JITI set to Y at all times. It just causes your end users too much pain, and there really is no risk if you test objects in the CRP path code against a copy of the production data.

95/98/NT Issues and Resolutions

Issue/Resolution

Issue: My Windows NT workstations are working fine. However, when my users attempt to use a Windows 95 workstation, they have problems in the applications. All of these machines are running on the same OneWorld package; the only difference is the operating system.

Resolution: J.D. Edwards does support Windows 95 and 98. However, they have had nothing but problems with OEM versions of this software. Microsoft allows some of its vendors, such as Compaq, to modify the Windows 95 operating system they ship with their systems; this is called an OEM version of the software. This has caused problems within OneWorld, since J.D. Edwards does not always know what these vendors modify. J.D. Edwards is now only supporting Microsoft's version of Windows 95 and Windows 98. This was the only way they could ensure that their clients would not encounter problems of this kind. If you are on an OEM version of Windows 95 or 98, customer support will ask you to move to Microsoft's version.

NOTE

Microsoft only allows their vendors to modify the Windows 95 and 98 operating system, so there is not an OEM version of Windows NT.

Workflow

Workflow allows users to see messages or errors on jobs and specific applications. Setting workflow up is a little different from application to application. The only really technical setup for workflow is setting up your OneWorld users in the address book and using this address book number in the OneWorld user profile. This is necessary so that your users receive the messages from workflow.

Summary

In this chapter, we have gone over some of the common problems system administrators will face. We have attempted to touch on all of the different configurations you may use. Although this list of issues and resolutions is by no means complete, it should give the administrator an idea of where to start looking for a solution, and as many experienced computer professionals can tell you, that is half the battle.

PART III

Appendix

Appendix A

APPENDIX A

The OneWorld Implementation

The Software Selection Process

Things to Know About the Contract

Phases of the Technology Implementation

The OneWorld Installation

Modeling Your Solution

Training

Development and Version Control
    Methodolgy

Go-Live Activities

Globalization

Interoperability and OneWorld

Although this is one of the more important topics of this book, many of you may be wondering why we haven't gone into more detail about how you implement the OneWorld product and why this information is in an appendix instead of in several chapters. The reason is that this topic could quite easily fill a book on its own. It is a huge topic that deserves its own forum. Although we can't dedicate the next 900 pages to it, we still felt it was necessary to hit on many of the points you need to know when preparing to implement this product. In this appendix, we're going to cover the topics listed below in varying degrees of scrutiny—and none of them as well as we'd like or they deserve. As a final note, if this is a subject you want to see a book dedicated to, let your voice be heard. Contact the publishers and tell them you want more.

- The software selection process

- Things to know about the contract

- Phases of the technology implementation

- The installation

- Modeling your solution

- Training

- Development and version control

- Go-live

- Globalization

- Interoperability and OneWorld

The Software Selection Process

We've been asked more than once why we needed to write about how you select your organization's package in a book about a specific suite of products. Our answer is usually short, sweet, and only a little glib. It is our firm belief that all software packages were not created equal. When compared side by side with other packages, the OneWorld product will fare significantly better. Additionally, although the hardcore market value of this book is with clients who have either purchased, implemented, or will soon implement the product, we also feel that this guide will serve those organizations as yet undecided as to what to implement. This is not required reading. Feel free to skip around as necessary to glean the information you need.

Preparing to Make the Move of a Lifetime

Are we being over-dramatic? Not really. Regardless of the size of your organization, when you choose to implement an enterprise resource planning (ERP) product, you have just decided to turn your entire world upside down. In so many ways, however, this can be a very positive thing. So much so, in fact, that you will survive it and come out substantially better—or be crushed by it and leave (by choice or not) bitter and angry.

It all comes back to a basic premise, a premise that dramatically changes everything taught in business school. Regardless of whether you call it information technology (IT), information systems (IS), or data processing (DP), this function has moved beyond the nicety, the necessary evil, or the business advantage. It is the business (period). Information technology is the reason you have a product to sell. Information systems are the reason you're able to anticipate your customer's requirements. Data processing is the reason you beat your competition to market, gained the required momentum and name recognition, and ultimately own 70 percent of the market share. But it goes beyond a single software package that manages your manufacturing, distribution, inventory, sales reporting, accounts receivable, accounts payable, general ledger, human resources, and payroll. For many companies that create first-class IS operations, there are market openings to farm out that talent and truly make IT a profit center. And companies are making that move.

Let's get back to the basics of what you need to keep in mind when choosing your new software package. These questions are generic in nature and can lead you to many different solutions including (but not limited to) the OneWorld product. One of the first questions that must be asked when looking at new software is, why? It's a simple question and yet most organizations have problems answering it. If you want to implement a new product because of a perceived return on investment (ROI), okay. If it is because you need this new system to gain or maintain market share, fine. If it is because your current system is on its last leg and needs to be replaced before you are, all right. If it is because you read about it in a magazine and the ad used industry catch-words like GUI, client/server, ERP, interoperability, Java, or e-anything—hold on, stop!

You see, unless you have a good reason that has solid foundations in tried business practices, you really need to think about it. You'd better do your research and all signs should point to yes. A small organization will spend 2 to 3 million dollars implementing an ERP product. The middle tier will spend 10 to 20 million. Large companies can easily spend in excess of 50 million dollars over a two- or three-year implementation. Before you commit your organization to this type of capital expenditure, you'd better understand why you're doing it.

Do You Understand Your System Requirements?

This question isn't being directed to the system administrators who'll quickly stand up and spout out the fact that you have 26 UNIX servers seamlessly integrated with 150 Windows NT servers. Rather, this is more a question for your business or systems analysts. Can you break down your business processes and identify the key components of your business? If so, can your people work in such a way as to think beyond what is, ignore what could be, and arrive at what should be? Business processes can be redesigned and streamlined, and technology can be used to your advantage. Understanding what your organization truly needs versus what they want or already have is key to understanding your system requirements.

Are There Any Existing Products that Already Fit the Bill?

What software products are on the market today that address even 50 percent of the functionality you're looking for? Add these together and create a long list of potential options. Now, look closer. How many of these products fit 70 percent of your systems' requirements? Create the short list.

You might be wondering how you know what your company's needs are. Is there any one person who knows enough to make a decision of this nature? This is probably related to the size of your organization. The larger the company; the less likely any one person will know enough to make an intelligent decision in this matter. Instead, your organization would be wise to invest in a group of people (specialists from each functional group) who not only understand their area, but are also open to looking beyond the procedures currently in place.

You should either flow-chart your current procedures and create a list of requirements for each functional area or hire a professional consulting organization to assist you in this endeavor (firms like Deloitte & Touche [D&T] do a tremendous job in this area). The reason that we highly recommend this initial effort is that most organizations cannot provide a comprehensive list of current (much less future) requirements. The forward-thinking organization will create this group of functional specialists as a group responsible for identifying requirements, as well as selecting and ultimately implementing the software. This group, with the appropriate IS assistance, will be able to intelligently create long and short requirements lists.

Create the Request for Proposal

As you begin researching the long and short lists of software packages, you should use the list created from your functional requirements and as many foreseeable requirements as possible. Take these requirements and format a request for proposal (RFP). But don't stop with just functional requirements. Add questions about the company's history, the number of industry-specific implementations pending, in progress and completed, the availability of consulting and troubleshooting support, and the business partnerships and interfaces. You should also find out the number of failed implementations, the number of pending lawsuits or forced arbitrations, and what their actual licensing looks like. Have your IS personnel put forth very specific questions concerning security, hardware and software support, application support, vision of the technology supporting the product, and its future trends. Also make sure your IS staff includes upgradability, customization, architecture, scalability, and true technology. Word these questions to glean past, present, and future technology trends.

As you create the RFP, ensure that your questions are both detailed enough to provide each vendor with an objective set of questions, and specific enough to ensure that the returned answers address the questions themselves and aren't redirected by the sales and marketing people actually answering the RFP.

Use the information derived from the RFP process to research the potential vendors list. You can never do too much research on these vendors. Remember, whichever organization you ultimately choose, their software is going to redefine your current and future ability to create and distribute your products and services. What do industry leaders think about the particular software and software company? What about financial analysts? How long has the company been in business—and will they still be tomorrow?

What Are Your Current Technology Skill Sets?

We would never suggest that something as trivial as IT skill sets drive a decision of this nature. But it is one of the factors that should be taken into consideration when looking at new software packages. As you choose a new software package, difficult questions must be answered. Can your current IS team support the new software at the same time they're supporting the existing systems? Do they have the appropriate skill sets for the new hardware, software, and infrastructure? If not, are you going to hire experienced people, retrain existing personnel, or hire new personnel and train them? As discussed in some of the chapters in this book, hiring experienced personnel with unique skill sets can be a costly undertaking.

Can You Afford this Move at this Time or Can You Afford Not To?

There is a huge question looming here that we really can't answer for you. Remember, the cost of implementing an ERP in actual money and in human effort, disruptions, and quality of life is staggering when done on a large scale. It is important to factor this information into your overall decision. You must also weigh the wisdom of implementing a large-scale software package at this particular time in your company's business cycle and what the consequences of not doing it would be. In many situations, now is the right time to make new foundations that will enable your company's future growth. This also relates to how easy the software is to upgrade. Because a full ERP implementation can easily last three to five years, you can often begin the implementation factoring in future development. If you do pick this route and the vendor is responsible for this future development, be sure you get the software/functional deliverable in writing prior to signing a contract. It should include a date of completion, the functionality description (for example, CRP interface with company X's ABC product), and (especially if this is critical to your business) appropriate penalties for failure to perform.

Things to Know About the Contract

If you are reading this book, your organization is in one of two scenarios with regards to a software contract with J.D. Edwards—you either have one or you don't. This next section is dedicated to providing insight into the software contract (some clauses that are common to almost every one of them) and will hopefully point out some features you already know if your organization has a contract and things for you to look for if it does not. Ultimately, our goal is to provide a clear explanation to what you either have or will agree to.

It's a License—You Didn't Purchase It

J.D. Edwards does not sell you the OneWorld suite of applications. Rather, they license the right to use the software to your organization. If you purchased the software, you would not have to call in every year and acquire an authorization code. What does that mean to you? First, there are parts of the code they won't provide to you. In particular, J.D. Edwards will not provide their foundation code (the architectural code that controls processes like communications and the batch engine). Another way of looking at it is that J.D. Edwards will allow you to decorate the OneWorld software however you want but not let you look at the frame of the structure.

Second, J.D. Edwards does have the right to take their software back (especially if they find violations to the contract). This happens more often, however, when the client and J.D. Edwards find that they have reached an impasse on some functionality or relationship issue. In this situation, there are a series of different steps that can occur. Although these issues are often worked out, when they aren't, J.D. Edwards has been known to return the cost of the software to the client and take their software back.

Finally, while the default authorization code is provided for three months, the contracts department at J.D. Edwards often provides a security authorization code for one year. However, this still means that you have to call in once a year to continue using the software. We've never seen an authorization code provided over two years. If you owned the software, you would be able to use it indefinitely without having to maintain contact with the vendor. Do you have to call Sears every year to continue using your refrigerator?

Microsoft also licenses their software. They don't sell it. In fact, if you begin reading the licenses of the software you "purchase," you will see that there are actually very few you really bought. This is a change that occurred early in the software consumption cycle to help save the intellectual property of the software authors themselves.

The Covenant Not to Sue

When you agree to license the OneWorld software, you've entered into a relationship with J.D. Edwards in which both parties agree not to sue the other. Rather, they agree to an impartial arbitration process. Is it still legally binding? Yes. Can either party still be forced to pay for damages? Yes. So what is the difference?

One of the primary differences between the arbitration process and lawsuit process is that arbitration is significantly quicker. You don't have to wait on the currently backlogged judicial system (instead, you have to wait for the backlogged arbitration system). There is no jury to be swayed by inspirational speeches delivered by professional orators. Instead, you get a panel of legal and industry experts who can facilitate the two opposing sides in coming to a consensus on how to move forward efficiently and to the mutual satisfaction of all parties involved.

Prior to going into a relationship with such a vendor, make sure you have everything you want, are concerned about, or can think of in writing first. If you need a certain software functionality in the product that is planned by the vendor but not currently available, get this written into the contract with hard deliverable dates. If they are not willing to commit to this, you need to consider if they are your vendor of choice. The goal isn't to create a situation where you have to sue or go into arbitration, but you should remember that this software will totally redefine how you do business. Clearly outline the roles and responsibilities of both parties. Expectations should be realistically set early in this process so everyone involved has a clear understanding of what they have to do.

Hiring Consultants

Several times in this book we've talked about the requirement of staffing the right people to ensure that your project is a success. We've also mentioned that you can hire experience, grow experience, or die by the experience. On the other hand, many clients have slyly approached the issue by making statements like the following to J.D. Edwards consultants on-site: "How much would someone like you cost this company?" or "But we probably couldn't afford you," or "You probably wouldn't be interested in a job like this." Well, we are here to tell you that almost anyone is for hire at the right price, job, and performance package. However, J.D. Edwards has intentionally placed several clauses into their software contract to discourage this practice.

In the contract itself, you will find verbiage specifying that neither they nor you will hire or contract through a third party a current or previous employee for a period of six months after termination from the company. It also states that if they or you violate this clause, the offending party will owe the other party the equivalent of six months salary (calculated from the annual salary) of said employee. Although it is certainly not the rule, we have seen the cross-pollination of employees going in both directions, though our personal experience has a 3:1 ratio going to the client.

Quick Calculations

Let's use a quick example. Company X decides to hire one of the J.D. Edwards OneWorld application developers. This developer's salary at J.D. Edwards is $75,000 per year with the opportunity of another $75,000 in bonus. Company X agrees to hire this employee at $150,000 per year with a three-year minimum contract protecting the consultant and their investment in them. Company X approaches J.D. Edwards management about the arrangement and they decide to hold Company X to its contractual obligations instead of releasing them. (Not holding the company would of course be a great gesture toward ensuring good relations between J.D. Edwards and the client; however, 90 percent of the time J.D. Edwards will charge the client anyway.) Company X would owe J.D. Edwards $37,500 for hiring the developer. The reason for this is that the developer's salary was $75,000 while he was at J.D. Edwards. The bonus potential (though certainly a factor in the salary that Company X had to pay the consultant) doesn't factor into the equation. The only way that Company X would get by with $0 is if they decided not to hire the developer after all—and this is exactly what J.D. Edwards is hoping will occur. Of course, the contract the consultant cleverly had signed prior to Company X approaching J.D. Edwards protects the consultant in this scenario.

System Audits

The actual licensing of the OneWorld product is relatively lax from strict IS standards. There are multiple methods of cheating the software itself and getting more people on the system than you should, as we've pointed out earlier. However, you should also be aware of J.D. Edwards' right to audit your computer system. If they find that you are in violation of the software agreement signed earlier, it could cost you licensing fees, penalties, or a loss of the software itself.

Our best advice to you is to follow the letter of your licensing agreement. Can you cheat the system? Sure. But if you get caught, it could include fines, your company firing you, and even jail time. Is saving your organization some money up front worth this to you?

Phases of the Technology Implementation

One of the biggest differentiators in today's implementation marketplace is the methodology to get the job done. In this section, we will outline a tried and true OneWorld technology implementation methodology. We hope it will assist those of you who are contemplating your implementation. For those of you who have already completed this process and are reading this section, you may find a point or two that will make it easier for you the next time you go through this type of project.

- **Phase 1**   Initial planning
- **Phase 2**   Software installation
- **Phase 3**   OneWorld technology training

- **Phase 4**   OneWorld architecture modeling

- **Phase 5**   Pre-go-live activities

- **Phase 6**   Go-live support

- **Phase 7**   Continuing technology support

Events Associated with a Technology Implementation

Table A-1 gives you a concise look at the events associated with each phase of technology implementation and a description of each. The phases are described in detail in the following sections.

Phase 1: Initial Planning

It all comes down to planning, planning, and more planning. The number one thing that will either make or break your implementation is how well you have planned both the technology and the application implementation. Have you adequately considered the effect of the changes you are facing? Is your company ready for this type of change? What about a detailed listing of the tasks that need to be completed?

During Phase 1 of the technology implementation, you are primarily focused on creating the plan and beginning the initial steps for the technology implementation. You have to make decisions regarding hardware and software, size your equipment, and create the detailed architecture and technology plan, ensuring that you haven't left out critical steps. This technology plan is what leads your organization throughout the remaining phases of the technology implementation.

One of the primary milestones (and this can change based on the plan you put together) is having hardware and software in house and configured for the installation. Once this occurs, you are ready to move to the next phase of the technology implementation. And don't forget, you have to complete this first phase before the application team needs the OneWorld environment. As always, the technology is a slave to the application requirements. Another possible milestone that many organizations select is the installation of a prototype environment. This is usually a

Events	Notes
Phase 1: Initial Planning	
Initial planning session	Designed to create a detailed plan regarding OneWorld Technology Implementation. Includes a series of assessments and strategies following the basic principle of AS-IS, To Be, Gap Analysis, Gap Mitigation, and final strategy.
Hardware/software acquisition	Completed by the client.
Third-party hardware/software installation	Completed by client, third party, and D&T Technology Consultant.
NT/Intel Systems	
Enterprise Systems	
RDBMS	
Third-party software (C compiler, ODBC, connectivity, etc.)	
Pre-installation audit	Tests the setup and configuration of hardware and software one week prior to OneWorld installation. This allows time to correct any deficiencies found.
Systems ready for OneWorld installation	Milestone.
Phase 2: Software Installation	
OneWorld installation	Normally five days are booked in case unforeseen issues arise. Under normal conditions the installation should take approximately three days.
Post-installation audit	Completed immediately after installation.
OneWorld Client/Server Package Build	
UBE launch local and server	
AB/User Profile/Environment Assignment	
Activate sign on security, change JDE	
Test backup capabilities	
Initial installation complete	Milestone.

TABLE A-1.   Technology Implementation Events

Appendix

Events	Notes
Phase 3: Technology Training	
OneWorld application security	Workshop regarding OneWorld security options in addition to setting up technical application security.
DB/OS security	Usually done in conjunction with prior step.
OneWorld systems administration workshop	Includes Data Dictionary, User Overrides, OneWorld Troubleshooting, Systems Administration Workbench, etc.
Package build and version control workshop	Includes how to, under the covers, and OneWorld object migration.
Phase 4: OneWorld Architecture Modeling	
CNC architecture review	Review includes detailed outlines of OneWorld Architectural design.
CNC implementation	Includes implementing and testing OneWorld CNC design.
Nightly operations/scheduler	Set up, train, and implement nightly operation requirements and the OneWorld scheduler.
Stress testing/performance tuning	Creates a base line and then provides a stress test for the hardware, software, and OneWorld application to ensure that current systems will provide necessary performance levels for the client. Milestone.
General troubleshooting	Where this is oftentimes not required, we include time for technology assistance in the application and architectural troubleshooting arena.
Application security implementation	Application security implementation should be accomplished by the client after the OneWorld Application Security workshop. If required, a D&T trained Technology Consultant can provide assistance.
Phase 5: Pre-'Go-Live' Activities	
General troubleshooting	While this is oftentimes not required, we include time for technology assistance in the application and architectural troubleshooting arena.
Technology readiness assessment	Designed to ensure that all aspects of the OneWorld technology implementation are ready to fully support the Go-Live environment. Milestone.
Final package builds/deployment	All final software modifications are tested, packages built and deployed. Deployment is tested.

TABLE A-1.   Technology Implementation Events (*continued*)

Events	Notes
Operations hand-off	One-on-one time ensuring knowledge transfer between D&T Technology consultants and General Growth Properties IS personnel.
Phase 6: Go-Live Support	
General assistance	If required or desired, includes troubleshooting, setup and maintenance.
OneWorld application "go-live"	Milestone.
Phase 7: Continuing Technology Support	
CNC review/tuning	Completed over time. Analyzing new technology and architectures to identify opportunities for ROI.
Upgrade/update assistance	Provides for planning and upgrading/updating OneWorld software from initial software release to "current" releases.
Other support as requested	Provide assistance as required in the area of OneWorld technology.

TABLE A-1. Technology Implementation Events (*continued*)

quickly thrown together NT/Intel configuration of the OneWorld product to assist with application's core team training efforts.

Phase 2 and 3: Technology Implementation Considerations

In addition to understanding the overall process of events associated with implementing OneWorld from the technology point of view, you also need to understand what the technology considerations are and must be during an implementation of this type. To help with this, the following sections go into some detail concerning these considerations. The base methodology employed includes determining base hardware and software, then desired architecture, then any additional hardware or software required by the architecture, then personnel requirements, then communication requirements, and finally backup and recovery requirements.

Base Hardware Considerations

There are several different pieces of hardware required for any OneWorld implementation. These include a database server, a logic or application server, a deployment server, and workstations. Based on your specific implementation, the database and logic server might be the same machine. If so, this machine is known as an enterprise server. We have seen clients combine the enterprise server with the deployment server, providing a single machine solution. However, J.D. Edwards has considered programmatically disabling this capability. Consequently, we don't recommend combining them.

OneWorld currently supports the following hardware platforms for database and application servers: Sun, HP9000, WinTel solutions (including Compaq), the RS6000, and the AS/400. The deployment server must be a Microsoft Windows NT server running on an Intel chipset. The clients can be any Windows 95/98/NT/2000 solution, including the Terminal Server edition. Clients can also be comprised of what are termed zero clients. Basically, these clients are Web-based machines that access OneWorld's Java or HTML clients.

Base Software Considerations

Once you have decided what your hardware platforms are, you need to decide on your software requirements. The first piece of software that we can promise all OneWorld clients have is OneWorld itself. After that, you need to consider Window NT, MS C++, a C compiler for the hardware selection of your choice, a database platform (either Oracle, MS SQL Server, or DB2/400), backup software, Citrix Metaframe, data warehousing software, data mining tools, and development tools for conversions and interfaces.

To assist you with this process, we highly recommend you spend some time on the J.D. Edwards Knowledge Garden determining your minimal system requirements. This does not mean we're recommending that you go with minimal configurations. Rather, this is an excellent area to determine what the software requirements are for OS and other third-party products. Make sure that you follow their recommendations carefully. If you choose to install a newer version of some of the products than what is recommended by J.D. Edwards, it can cause serious issues, including an inability to install or create packages and data corruption. Worse still, you might not be able to identify these issues until weeks or even months have passed. A good example of this is MS Visual C++ required for building packages. When version 6 came out, OneWorld still required version 5. This caused problems for clients because they had to contact Microsoft directly to get the required version. Version 6 uses a different compiler engine. If clients attempted to use 6, the packages would not build correctly.

Architectural Considerations

Now that you have picked your base hardware and software, you are able to make decisions as to the OneWorld architecture best suited to fit your organizational needs. When you begin considering what your architecture should be, we highly recommend you revisit Chapter 1 for a quick refresher course on the available architectures:

- 2-tier

- 3-tier

- Virtual 3-tier

- N-tier

- Fat clients

- Thin clients

- Zero clients

Our experience indicates that there is no single right solution for most organizations. Rather, most clients deploy a combination approach utilizing the power of the OneWorld product to meet their business requirements. After all, saying that there is only one right architecture for everyone is like saying everyone should wear blue shirts. Your implementation partner and J.D. Edwards can help you determine what is the best for your particular situation.

Revisit Your Hardware and Software Considerations

Now that you have decided on the architectural design for your organization, it is time to revisit the requirements of your overall implementation. If you are implementing the Web client, what type of servers are you going to use as Web servers? What about terminal servers? Do you have enough WinTel boxes to accommodate your organization? If, on the other hand, you have decided to implement a virtual 3-tier architecture, are your original specifications for the enterprise server robust enough to handle the configuration? It is something that you need to evaluate.

You also need to determine additional software requirements. Are you using a thin client architecture, and if so, are you going to use Citrix's Metaframe with it? How many licenses will you need? If you are going to have a zero client configuration, you need to determine what additional applications are required. At the end of these considerations, you should have a very good understanding of your requirements from both the hardware and software side. You should also have worked with your implementation partner, your hardware vendor, and J.D. Edwards to determine the actual size requirements for what your company needs.

Determine Your Personnel Requirements

The next major step in the planning process includes evaluating your personnel from the human resource point of view as well as the technology point of view. Some of the human resource points include having the right number of people with the right skill sets in place to support existing legacy systems and the new ERP solution. Does your IS organization already have the necessary bandwidth to accomplish this or do you need to augment them by adding additional skills and personnel? Are you going to add to their existing force through hiring or are you going to augment them with contract or consulting support? If you do hire the skills necessary to accomplish both jobs, what is your plan for the support staff when the legacy system is shut down? Are they going to be re-tooled within the organization, subbed out to other consulting organizations, or just let go? These considerations should be evaluated.

Work with your implementation partner to determine the number of support personnel required to accomplish this new project. If you are going to have to augment your personnel, are you going to hire or train the skills you need? There are pros and cons to both methods (as described several times in this book). It is important to create these strategies early in the process.

Rework What You Can

Senior management within your organization has bought off on this new ERP implementation with the understanding that it will cost millions but that it is also a business imperative. Although we certainly don't recommend that you gouge them for everything you've ever wanted, the reality is that you have one chance to redesign your systems, either fixing them if they are broken or bringing them current with existing technologies. The odds of you ever getting this opportunity again are slim. Seize the opportunity to make it happen. If you need a hot redundant site and if you can create a business case validation for this argument, you should do it.

Backup/Redundancy   With the new system comes new opportunity. We highly recommend that your organization do the right thing up front and often with their backup and recovery scheme. Having a spare drive is no good unless it is tested. Redundant systems don't buy the organization anything other than additional costs if they don't work when you need them to. RAID, though always recommended, doesn't provide your company with redundancy if you don't know how to break the RAID. You have to test your systems, the backup, and the built-in redundancy to make sure it is worth the money spent and provides your company with the security you need.

As any good IT person will tell you, you can spend as much as you want or as little as you can afford when creating your backup procedure. There are, however, some things that should be taken into consideration when deciding what to backup and how often. If you are backing up your central objects (refer to Chapter 2 for more information on central objects), you should also back up the appropriate path code directories on the deployment server itself. Remember that the database and the directory structure containing C code must stay in sequence. If you need to restore the database portion of a path code, we strongly recommend that you also restore the associated C code. You are only able to do this when you back them both up.

There are some sets of data—and yes, some path codes—that really don't need to be backed up regularly or even at all. Pristine data and path code data never need to be backed up because J.D. Edwards ships this information on the original installation CDs. If you lose this or it becomes corrupted, you can always restore it from the CDs. Depending on where you are in the implementation cycle, you can also decide whether you need to back up CRP data, test data, or CRP and DEV path codes. If you don't need to back up this data or path codes, you can literally save hours of downtime in the backup process.

Phase 4: OneWorld Architecture Modeling

As you might be able to guess, it isn't simply enough to install OneWorld and have it magically fit your organizational requirements. Most companies are not single site, fully wired locations with PCs situated where you need them to get work done. However, even if you do work for that type of company, you will still need to perform OneWorld architectural modeling. Most organizations that are evaluating, purchasing, or implementing OneWorld are sizable enough that they need to carefully determine an architecture that will support their business requirements. In Chapter 1, we discussed the various architectures available, and earlier in this appendix, we stated that you would require assistance determining the best architecture for your particular needs. Now we are also going to recommend that you get assistance with your modeling phase.

What Is the Modeling Phase Used For?

The modeling phase is more than simply setting up the pre-designed OneWorld architecture. It is more than simply testing your architecture. It is more than simply stress-testing your system and its software solution. The first step of the modeling phase includes validating the architecture designed in the pre-installation phase of your implementation. Because of the time required to implement OneWorld, especially on big accounts, the likelihood that new technologies will be introduced is significant. These technologies or architectures might be of interest and use in your specific situation and should be evaluated.

Once you have finalized the go-live architectural design of your enterprise solution, it is necessary to actually put this architecture in place. This usually includes adding application servers, deployment locations, MS Windows terminal servers, database servers, redundant or clustered systems, Java application servers, or other hardware and software. Depending on the complexity of your situation, this could take anywhere from a couple of days to several weeks. This can also be done in a phased approach, especially if it fits your rollout plan. Although the first few additions will be more difficult, as you continue installing servers in your architectural design, the process will become easier and easier.

The next step in the modeling phase has you base line, technically test, stress test, and finally perform a fully integrated stress test on the architecture in place. The initial testing that needs to be accomplished determines bandwidth usage and reliability of your overall architecture without the addition of OneWorld itself. One of the items that needs to be determined is whether your existing systems adequately perform your day-to-day activities without the addition of the new ERP system. You should include in these tests basic server and workstation utilization, as well as memory usage, hard disk capacity and usage, and overall CPU usage evaluated against daily loads, including office suites, e-mail, and other normal software communications. (Many of the network operating systems tend to be chatty—how is your network holding up under a normal load?)

Once you have determined base system utilization, you are ready to go to the next two levels of system testing. You need to determine the overall performance of your technical solution beginning with one OneWorld user and going forward. Although the first user provides you with an understanding of the requirements for a single user, you will often find that there is not a linear association that allows you to extrapolate what 50 or 100 users will require. Just because user A uses 10K WAN bandwidth, has the workstation CPU usage go from 5 to 40 percent and the RAM drop from 50MB available to 10MB, it doesn't mean that user B will have the same system requirements. Additionally, when you get both user A and user B working in tandem, it doesn't mean that you can double user A's results to extrapolate their combined usage. Generally, we recommend that you test 1, 2, 5, 10, 50, 100, 200, 500, and then 1,000 users to come to some type of understanding on how volume of users will affect your system and how the architecture supports it. In addition, we have seen an organization put more than 700 users live on the system as a test. The results were not only interesting but also highly informative. If you anticipate your concurrent users to exceed this number, it would be well worth the effort of coordination, time, and effort to perform a few of these tests.

N O T E

J.D. Edwards provides clients with the ability to use products like Auto Pilot (a scripting tool often used in system stress testing), but we find that there are few substitutes for having real people perform the test. Scripts rarely mess up by hitting the wrong button or sneezing or answering a phone call during the middle of the test, resulting in a quick Internet lookup. They are the perfect world and we will recommend scripts for testing when the human race becomes perfect.

The final step, and we recommend that it actually be done in conjunction with the tests listed above, includes a fully integrated stress test. Many organizations stress test their systems by having people perform what we call heads-down keyboard entry. In essence, they get users, or scripts, to enter the simplest of transactions as quickly as possible for a prolonged period. The problem with this type of test is that it is unrealistic and consequently produces unrealistic results (often these results are worse than more realistic testing would provide). A fully integrated stress test has users performing their normal, daily duties at the level they would at their peak month-end (traditionally the period with the highest system utilization).

Phase 5: Pre-Go-Live Activities

For the well-planned, superbly executed implementation, these are relatively few in number. Actually, they go down to one: you need to perform a pre-go-live assessment. This includes both a technology assessment and an application assessment. Prior to betting your organization's livelihood on a single product (an ERP system), you need to ensure that it will adequately meet the business needs of your company. If you have performed the fully integrated stress tests mentioned in the paragraphs above, your work is relatively quick and easy. Your implementation partner will work with you to create a comprehensive list of tests (really a checks and balances system) that will fully explore the proposed business solution. If your system meets these criteria, you can go live. If not, you need to consider going live or postponing go-live pending additional functionality, further testing, or some type of fallback position. Don't take your company live if the solution isn't ready. We have seen several organizations financially suffer because of their eagerness to hit a deadline instead of providing the proper solution.

If you've encountered significant issues in the base implementation, pre-go-live activities include additional training, troubleshooting technical and application issues, completion of required modifications and then additional training, increased phased implementations (such as taking a lesser number of users or sites live on less of the software at a single time), or changing the architecture to a less aggressive stance. Remember that the OneWorld architecture is specifically designed to enable rapid changes in architectural models. If what you're doing fails your fully integrated stress tests, look for alternative solutions.

Pre-Go-Live Activities

Specific pre-go-live activites include the following:

1. Final testing of standard J.D. Edwards applications.

2. Final training of go-live personnel.

3. Final preparation/coordination of the competency center.

4. Final validation of customizations.

5. Final validation of technology architecture.

Phase 6: Go-Live Activities

There are a series of go-live activities that must be carefully planned, coordinated, and carried out prior to go-live. Chief among these is the requirement to complete data transfers from legacy systems to the production environment. Other than that, if everything is planned and executed properly, go-live becomes the anticlimax of the implementation. One of the items we want to stress, however, is that go-live is not the purpose behind the ERP implementation. Rather, it is a by-product of the implementation. ERP solutions fail because organizations become fixated with the concept of go-live and fail to provide a solution that will provide their companies with their base requirements. A company gains nothing from an ERP solution if it can't buy and sell products or services. If the solution doesn't meet these minimum goals, it is a waste of time, money, and resources.

Properly planned, going live is a flip of a switch, nothing more.

Phase 7: Continuing Technology Support

A client once told us that the reality of an ERP project is that it never ends. Most organizations, even if they suspend modifications and alterations to the OneWorld product, will ultimately decide to modify, interface, or in some other way change their system. One of the most common changes includes upgrading the OneWorld version your organization is on to a later version of the software. Many companies actually do this during the initial implementation. After go-live, based on business need, many companies decide that they need to go through an upgrade. An upgrade is, in effect, another implementation. Often there are tens of thousands of changes to the applications and database structure associated with an upgrade.

Any organization that installs and implements OneWorld version B733 or later has the ability to skip two major releases of the OneWorld product (that is, if you are on B733, you can skip all of the B733 series and go directly to whatever comes after the B9.1 series). This provides companies with the ability to stabilize on a particular set of OneWorld; however, when they do move to the next release, there are likely to be significant changes to their systems. These upgrades should then be treated as new implementations with CRPs and other associated activities.

Post-Go-Live Activities

When we talk about post-go-live activities, we are talking about work that continues after your company has gone live with the product. Where certainly not limited to the activities listed below, many companies include events like the following:

- Custom modifications

- Custom interfaces

- Service packs

- Electronic software updates (ESUs)

- Updates/upgrades

The OneWorld Installation

The installation process is significantly better than once upon a time. Most installations are completed within two or three days. But even with the advances posted since we first started performing them (1996), there are things that you should be aware of from an implementation process point of view. The next section of this appendix is dedicated to assisting you in preparing for and successfully completing this very important step in the implementation process.

Before You Install

What types of activities need to occur prior to you installing the OneWorld suite of software? What should not only your company, but your implementation partner be doing in advance? What about your hardware vendor? Finally, what options do you have in the installation itself? So many questions, so many options. It is hard to know where to start, so we'll start at the beginning.

Scoping and Planning

There are a series of events that occur prior to the installation, but after signing the contract. Although we will briefly mention these events, we simply don't have the room necessary to complete them in the confines of this manual.

The primary phase that occurs prior to the installation itself is referred to by some as scoping and planning. Scoping and planning is all about creating a detailed plan before you embark on the implementation. It includes gaining a full understanding of where you are in your current systems (also known as the as-is state), what the OneWorld product will bring you (also known as the to-be state), and what you need to do to mitigate the difference (gap and mitigation strategies). Although the net change activity may start in this phase, depending on the size of your organization, it may not be completed during this phase.

Net change is where you determine if the new functionality being implemented fits your business needs. If it doesn't, your organization has to decide whether to make changes to OneWorld, interface with another software vendor, or do something else to get the functionality you are looking for. There are many different options to consider, and it is helpful to have a seasoned implementing team help you navigate through them.

Some of the other activities that must be done prior to installation include deciding which business center will house the hardware and software. Are you going with a single installation of the product or multiple? What type of architecture do you want to implement? Are you going to implement the product geographically, by product, or both? You also need to evaluate your current staff and their skill sets, and decide on a hardware and software platform to support the product. Make a choice regarding who will help you implement the software. We have never seen a successful implementation where the client attempted to be its own implementation specialist. You absolutely must include either J.D. Edwards or another implementation partner if you want the implementation to be a success.

There are other factors that need to be put in place prior to the implementation proper. These include:

- How you are going to train your users on the product?

- Will it require additional hardware or environments? What about support?

- How are you going to support the product during the implementation itself?

- What about after go-live, version control, system/software stress testing, integrated function testing?

- What type of architecture do you plan to use for the majority of your clients?

And the list goes on.

Pre-installation Planning

You've selected your hardware and software for the installation itself. How do you know what to order, how much to order, and what software is required to support it all? Once you have decided what your platform is and given some thought to when you are going to perform your installation and implementation, one of the first things you need to do is visit the J.D. Edwards Knowledge Garden Web site. This Web site is designed as a central repository that allows data mining as well as a method of communication between J.D. Edwards and their clients. On the Knowledge Garden, you are able to view the minimal technical requirements for each platform. These are minimal configurations, not production recommendations. If you follow the hardware minimal requirements, the product will work; however, we won't promise you any speed or a robust system. This section is, on the other hand, an excellent location to find the software requirements for the third-party and OS products themselves.

TIP

Occasionally you will see that OneWorld supports version x and higher of the third-party product. View this type of statement with caution. Your organization needs to stay with tested and approved versions. An example of this is where J.D. Edwards states in their minimum technical requirements that they support version 2.0.1 and higher of IBM's WebSphere for their JAS servers. This is not the case for B733.2. They support version 2.0.1 but do not support version 3.0.1. This can get you in trouble. If you have questions as to exactly what versions are or are not supported, call the J.D. Edwards support line at (800) 289-2999.

Sizing Your Hardware

Many clients start with a miniature of their final hardware configuration. This allows them to intelligently decide the appropriate hardware and software based on their own experience as opposed to J.D. Edwards and the hardware vendors' recommendations. Using a pre-production system does not have to be a waste of time and effort. Several benefits can offset the additional hardware costs associated with this type of activity.

If you want to use a Sun/Oracle solution with J.D. Edwards, you could purchase a smaller Sun box to start. This provides your users with the ability to start working with the product quicker; the system can be used for development and testing upgrades throughout the life cycle of the product. Additionally, it allows you to see what it takes to manage the system (including OneWorld) and to learn some of the best business practices to implement in the final production solution. Finally, it allows you to postpone the immediate expenditure of funds on hardware and software. Wait until tomorrow and you will be able to purchase a more powerful system, with more memory and functionality, for less. This truism produces a powerful incentive to postpone hardware purchases. Starting with a smaller system allows an organization (especially one that has a longer implementation cycle) to take advantage of this opportunity.

Hardware Vendors, J.D. Edwards, Third-Party Implementers, and You

When it is time to finally size your production system, the best method of determining your organization's requirements is actually a four-group conglomerate. You should feed information regarding number of users, amount of legacy data, the number of transactions per hour, up-time requirements, and any noticed growth during the conference room pilot (this last assumes you implemented a mini-solution during the scoping and planning phase) to the hardware vendor and J.D. Edwards client support personnel. They will bang their heads together and come up with a recommended hardware sizing solution for your company based on a requested life cycle. As a good rule of thumb, you should then take those recommendations to whoever is helping you implement the OneWorld product (assuming that it isn't J.D. Edwards or the hardware vendor). They will be able to give it a good once-over based on the number of implementations that they have already assisted. When all of this is done, you will have a good hardware recommendation for your production environment.

Purchasing the Hardware and Software

There is no special trick to this trade. Make sure that you not only get three different quotes from three dissimilar sources, but also make sure that what you are quoted is identical. As an example, we have certain opinions about refurbished hardware. However, if your organization has decided that refurbs are okay, make sure you know which quotes include refurbished goods and which parts are refurbs and which are new. Make this disclaimer part of the quote. If your organization frowns on refurbs, be sure that all of the vendors quoting fully understand that the equipment must be new. It is a minor issue, but it is one that we've seen catch people before.

Pre-installation Audit

You should have mapped out your overall technology implementation plan prior to purchasing and installing the system. This can be a single day or a multi-day event with your implementer, your IT staff, and your CNC implementation team. Most of the timetables associated with this are planned in a backward mode based on the timetables created by the application implementation team. From these meetings, there will be a clear understanding of the support team's roles and responsibilities. You would then acquire your hardware and software based on the OneWorld technology plan created in the earlier session. When you get this equipment in house, you should install the base system, including any third-party software (including the database) based on any recommendations provided by J.D. Edwards itself. J.D. Edwards has some posted recommendations on the Knowledge Garden for setting up various third-party products.

Once this is done, most installation consultants will require a one-day event where they verify the pre-setup. This is done to ensure that everything is in place prior to the installation itself. The exact content of these audits varies from service team to service team, but they deal primarily with making sure all the hardware is in place, functioning properly, can communicate with each other, and that all required third-party software is installed correctly. This is done a week prior to the install to allow you enough time to correct any deficiencies found.

The Installation

The OneWorld system installation is relatively straightforward but still requires an experienced installation person. Can one of your own IT staff perform the simplest of installations? Sure, they can, provided they have attended the class and tried it once or twice. If you have a complicated installation, however, we highly recommend that you get a truly experienced installer to do the initial installation and configuration. If you want to watch over their shoulder so one of your people can take over this operation in the future, do so.

The installation itself generally takes between two and five days based on the complexity of the installation and unforeseeable issues that could arise during the installation. The overall process goes something like this: perform pre-installation procedures, install the deployment server, create a plan on the deployment server, implement the created plan, install the application server, install a workstation, test the functionality of the installation itself. It's just that easy. The installation itself might include JAS servers, Windows terminal servers, data servers, and application servers. It can also include multiple deployment servers based on the plan created earlier.

The Post-installation Audit

If the implementer is experienced, they will also have, as part of the plan, time set aside to verify the installation itself. After all, it is one thing to say that the installation went well and another thing to prove that it went well. The audit can take one to two days to complete, but at a minimum, it should include package builds for workstations and server (also a JAS server if it is part of the overall implementation), UBE submission from the server and workstation, appropriate counts on tables and table records, and so on. Once completed, you will have a document proving the veracity of the installation and configuration itself.

Wrapping Up the Installation

The installation is always seen as a milestone in an implementation. Unfortunately, it isn't as simple as clicking SETUP.EXE. With the proper prior planning, the right resources, and a little bit of luck, these can be completed with few problems and fewer headaches. For more information on the specific steps of the installation itself, refer to the appropriate J.D. Edwards installation manual shipped with their software or download the most recent copy from their Web site.

Modeling Your Solution

There have been many different names for this particular activity within the OneWorld arena; however, the best known is the conference room pilot (CRP). CRP is a path code (that is, it is integral to the J.D. Edwards-defined software version control methodology), an environment (including its own business data and control tables), and, as the conference room pilot, is actually a phase within the implementation. Today, this phase is more commonly referred to as the prototype or modeling phase. Still, because of the existence of the path code and environment, the name CRP has not gone out of vogue. This section will detail some of the activities and considerations of modeling your solution and will hopefully provide you with a guideline for this particular phase of your implementation.

From the Application Point of View

The modeling phase of the application's implementation is a rigorous set of decisions, modifications, documentation, and testing of the various settings of the applications themselves. With your implementation partner, you will go through each and every application that makes up your overall solution in detail with exactly how it will be used (and by whom), what processing options will be set, what versions of what applications will be used by what people, and how the software will address your business specifications.

Although J.D. Edwards intentionally designed OneWorld to be able to handle changes in business processes after implementation (this is known as part of the ActivEra solution), this phase is still the most important part of the implementation cycle. Though you could change many of the processing options with relative ease, there would be a whole series of changes you simply don't want to have to change after the fact.

The P4210

Let's take the P4210 Sales Order as an example of some of the considerations necessary to properly implement the OneWorld product. The P4210 is the largest application in OneWorld and also has the distinction of being the most heavily modified by the largest number of clients. This is because there are almost as many ways of selling something as there are things to sell. This application also touches nearly every other module within OneWorld (including the address book, customer master, accounts receivable, accounts payable, inventory, purchase orders, taxes, payroll and work flow), and it is how your company makes and records its profitability. In short, there is no other application within the product itself that is as complicated or as important to get right than the P4210 (this, of course, assumes that your organization is using the Sales Order module within OneWorld).

There are 106 processing options associated with the P4210 application. Your company probably won't use all of them, however, they do determine information like starting status and next status. These statuses tell other applications what function is required next (such as purchase orders, updating end-of-day sales, and so on) and then they update the sales statuses. Some of these processing options also call other application versions (if you are using the R42520 subsystem to process pick slips), they determine how the sale is handled, including how it checks inventory, whether it checks the customer's account, what purchase order version to run, how to process inventory transfers, and so on.

Because of the complicated and integrated nature of the product, it is important to set up the application the way that best suits your business requirements and then test the solution. Often, you will set up more than a single version of this application for use by different groups within your organization. Some might use the pick-slip subsystem; others may not and could treat every sale as an order to be fulfilled rather than having the stock readily available. These differences also need to be addressed within the application. During the modeling phase of the OneWorld implementation, you, along with your implementation provider, will determine how to set up and test this application for use with the client. This setup and testing is what the modeling phase is designed to answer.

Other Modeling Phase Activities

Other than setting up and testing the various applications for speed, reliability, and data integrity, the modeling phase is often used for end-user training and integrated testing. In the example above, we indicated that the P4210 is integrated with a whole series of other applications. As part of the modeling phase, with the processing options you chose as part of your implementation, you would want to test that the data accurately hit and updated all of the other modules within OneWorld.

When you tried to sell product to a client who was on credit hold, were you notified that they were on credit hold? When you sold the product, did it decrement your inventory? When you attempted to sell more of the product than you physically had, did it sell your remaining inventory and back order the appropriate amount of goods? When your salesperson made a large sale, were they credited for commission payroll purposes? Did the sales properly add up at the end of the day and month? Did the cash, credit, and check report the proper amounts of each, with proper currency conversions, at the end of the day and month? Did the inventory module automatically place orders to replenish minimum order quantities of products sold? How fast did the system work and was it adequate for your clients?

These are just a few of the questions that need to be tracked and answered before you sign off on the OneWorld solution for your organization. You should also verify that there weren't orphaned records (records where there were sales details without headers) or other data corruption (such as the address number for the client on all of the lines of the sales order and the header record being the same). Any instances of this type of problem would indicate a serious issue with the application or the implementation setup that would need to be addressed prior to go-live. Obviously, the integrated test is used to track data throughout the system as opposed to a single application (the results of a modular or functional test).

From the Technologist's Point of View

The modeling phase, from the technologist's point of view, is really quite simple. It is comprised of implementing the various technology solutions, testing those solutions, modifying any deficiencies or taking additional opportunities provided, testing the final solution, and having all of this culminate prior to the rollout of the solution itself. We usually use the Quarter Rule with large-scale implementations.

The Quarter Rule

When implementing the product itself, our goal is to have the required technologies in place three months prior to the application implementation team's arrival. As an example, say we wanted to have a phased regional/application go-live starting with North America and financials (refer to Table A-2). Our plan would push financials across the globe prior to implementing the distribution module. Finally, we would complete the ERP package by implementing manufacturing and then HR/payroll in the same manner as the prior two modules. Table A-2 shows a graphic representation of the proposed application rollout schedule.

Now, as we begin our backward planning to implement the technology necessary for this implementation, not only would we take into consideration the proposed

Application Rollout Schedule

Module	FYQ1 2001 Jan Feb Mar	FYQ2 2001 Apr May Jun	FYQ3 2001 Jul Aug Sep	FYQ4 2001 Oct Nov Dec	FYQ1 2002 Jan Feb Mar	FYQ2 2002 Apr May Jun	FYQ3 2002 Jul Aug Sep	FYQ4 2002 Oct Nov Dec
Financials	North America	South America	Europe	Japan	China			
Distribution		North America	South America	Europe	Japan	China		
Manufacturing			North America	South America	Europe	Japan	China	
HR/Payroll				North America	South America	Europe	Japan	China

TABLE A-2.   Application Rollout Schedul

timeline for the application rollout (our business imperative for implementing the technology), but we could also add various phases to the technology implementation. One of the most important things to remember in this overall cycle is that the technology has to come in advance of the implementation itself. You can't model the applications without the OneWorld product being installed in the first place (unless, of course, you opt to model the product in your implementation partner's solution center).

In this example, we decided to start with a prototype instance of the OneWorld product, then moved to the actual production system hardware using the knowledge gained from the prototype for implementation purposes. The prototype equipment was then used as both development equipment and testing equipment for future upgrades and version control testing. As a final phase of the technology, our implementation included the addition of the Web client. You will also note that the overall communications pipe required for each phase increased with the increased number of modules actively used.

Also note in Table A-3 that the equipment necessary for production rollout was implemented, completed, and tested the quarter prior to the actual rollout of the applications. If you want your overall implementation to be a success, we highly recommend that you complete the technology enough in advance that you can fully test it prior to the application team actually needing it. Clients that wait to implement the technology in a JIT (just-in-time) scenario tend to run afoul of equipment shortages, unexpected system outages, and other technology-oriented issues slowing their application rollout.

Fully Integrated Stress Tests

As mentioned earlier in this appendix regarding the requirement of testing your solution, it is not enough to simply perform the traditional stress test on your technology system. Does the hardware and software solution provided support the business objectives of the project? This question needs to be ensured with the proposed technology solution. Unfortunately, each client is so different that there can be no guarantee without adequate testing of the solution against their organization's data and software use pattern. The best method of ensuring that the software and hardware solution does fit their business requirements is to perform the fully integrated stress test. This test can be performed using emulation software; however, it is more realistic when performed with real people reacting under normal day-to-day, month-end pressures.

Technology Rollout Schedule

Technology	FYQ1 2001 Jan Feb Mar	FYQ2 2001 Apr May Jun	FYQ3 2001 Jul Aug Sep	FYQ4 2001 Oct Nov Dec	FYQ1 2002 Jan Feb Mar	FYQ2 2002 Apr May Jun	FYQ3 2002 Jul Aug Sep	FYQ4 2002 Oct Nov Dec
Prototype Hardware & Software	North America							
	South America							
	Europe							
Citrix Client		Japan						
Connectivity		China						
Initial Go-Live Hardware Connectivity at 8K/Person				North America	South America	Europe	Japan	China
Implement Web-Based Design Connectivity at 10K/Person					North America	South America	Europe	Japan

TABLE A-3.   Technology Implementation Rollout Schedule

This test should be performed during the modeling phase. Once completed, the results need to be analyzed and if the system is found to be deficient, additional planning needs to occur to bring in a solution that will solve the business objectives. As such, and because of the critical nature of this series of tests, we normally recommend that this type of testing be started early in the second half of the modeling phase and continue until the client is satisfied with their results. If the solution fails, you have an opportunity to bring in technology (hardware and software) experts as well as J.D. Edwards to find an acceptable solution without having to postpone go-live. Unfortunately, many clients end up performing this series of tests at the very end of the modeling phase. If the test shows severe deficiencies, the client has no option other than postponing go-live and consequently costing their company additional money as well as possibly jeopardizing the project itself.

Security Considerations

During the modeling phase, you would also want to implement your security plan, including all four layers of security as discussed in Chapter 13 (physical security, OS security, database security, and application security). Since the application security is designed by group with exceptions for specific users beyond that, you would want to test that the groups have access to applications required by their jobs but are secured against doing anything they shouldn't have the ability to modify or see. This process, designed by both application lead and CNC resources, is implemented by the CNC administrator and tested by the application lead or their designated representative. (Although CNC resources intimately understand how the security application works, they are not versed enough in each module to fully understand who should have access to what and to what degree. Because of this, the CNC resources are able to train the application lead on what security options are available and to implement the final solution though they normally do not test that solution.) Any discrepancy in the security plan should be tweaked and corrected to ensure the new product is adequately protected from intentional and accidental damage on the part of the end user and the occasional corporate raider.

Training

With any ERP implementation, one of the most important elements is training your organization on the new systems and software. To this end, there are several different strategies from which to choose. This section is dedicated to describing some of these methodologies and providing additional recommendations regarding your training strategy. While the majority of this section will detail training strategies for end-user training, we first wanted to take a couple of minutes to discuss training the core implementation team.

Pre-Implementation Training

One of the considerations many companies face when starting this type of implementation is that their core team does not know the new software. Even if, as recommended earlier, they were part of the software selection process, they really don't know how to install, configure, and implement this new solution. They will have an understanding of what the system is capable of, but this understanding will be tainted by the sales process. (We can all agree that the software is presented in its best light during the sales process—and that there is a yet-undetermined number of possible issues that will need to be resolved prior to creating the final solution.) To this end, not only does training need to occur, but also an overall education. It is not enough to learn how to set up a system a particular way. This team needs to understand all of the available options of their new software solution and what the ramifications of each possible option are.

Though we can make some basic recommendations on courses that provide a general understanding of the various software modules, the real training comes in when your core implementation team begins working on a daily basis with the implementation provider of your choice (such as Deloitte & Touche, IBM Global Services, and so on). These providers, during the course of evaluating your current system, will begin making strategies designed to ensure the software is optimally configured for your implementation. By the end of the implementation, your original core team will have enough experience that you could subcontract them to implement other companies' projects.

If your organization has allocated internal resources prior to choosing an implementation partner, we do recommend that you attend some of the foundation courses during your selection process. This will enable some transfer of knowledge and will provide a positive direction during this interim period.

J.D. Edwards Training Strategies

Obviously, you can pay to have your employees go to J.D. Edwards' training locations to receive functional and technical training. This is a good solution for initial training;

still, there are some distinct downsides to using this method as the sole solution for most organizations. J.D. Edwards has the most comprehensive OneWorld training program in the world. However, their training staff consists of professional trainers who often don't have as much real-world experience as you would want or need. Although many of their trainers are able to answer clients' questions, many others are less able to field the more difficult questions regarding specific client scenarios. When this does occur, the trainers are very good about capturing the questions and getting answers for them. Still, most organizations would prefer their training staff to be able to answer these questions in the first place.

Because J.D. Edwards doesn't have training locations in every city in every state, having to fly your people to established training sites can become an expensive proposition. This expense is added to the expense of the class itself. If your organization were to do this for its entire staff, the costs could be prohibitive.

J.D. Edwards training classes are designed for what they feel is the common client. This, of course, is not optimal for your organization. Each client tends to set up its own set of procedures and processes for how they use OneWorld. This may or may not be the same set of procedures taught in the J.D. Edwards class. Finally, unless you time the training exactly right, your users will lose a substantial amount of the education obtained. This often happens because users receive the training but then don't use the product (because it is still in the modeling phase) for one or two months. In this scenario (which by the way can occur with any training strategy), the end user shouldn't have gone at all. They would have a base understanding of the applications themselves and nothing more.

OneWorld Computer-Based Training

J.D. Edwards recently developed and introduced a configurable software package of computer-based training (CBT). This currently provides functional modules including foundation, financial, distribution, and manufacturing. If your organization is not heavily customizing the OneWorld product, you will be able to effectively add this to your overall training strategy as either a refresher course or to augment training (this is especially useful for remote site training). These courses can be ordered through your J.D. Edwards Client Manager.

J.D. Edwards On-Site Training

This was particularly popular a couple of years ago. However, in fiscal year 1999, J.D. Edwards changed directions with this particular model. J.D. Edwards on-site training was a very good option bringing together experienced instructors (usually field consultants) and the client at the client site. This allowed a customized version of the traditional class to be taught providing far superior training to the end user. This concept, however, also had its problems. First, the client often did not have an operational system to provide the class. Even when OneWorld's Stand-Alone product was used, often the client didn't have adequate hardware in place to show the software. Second, it is harder to support consultants when you can't control the overall environment. Customized classes didn't necessarily cover all of the material that the regular class would. Because the class was being taught at the client site, the instructors often provided longer client-specific discussions which ultimately used up the available time. Finally, there was no recourse when a client decided that they didn't want to pay for the services of the instructor. The client would complain (after the fact) that the class didn't cover all of the material and that they were dissatisfied with training. At that point, it quickly became a no-win scenario for J.D. Edwards.

Because of these issues, J.D. Edwards increased the cost of their on-site training to the point that it discourages the practice all together. There are, however, factions within the J.D. Edwards camp that disguise on-site training as workshops. These workshops (while a little less formal) serve the same function as the on-site training course for the cost of the consulting time alone.

The Decentralized Training Model

Depending on the size of your site(s), this may be an appropriate strategy. Although we would never recommend an organization put together on-site training for a small site with only a couple of users, it is a cost-effective, user-friendly method for sites with ten or more users. Most implementations are of a size that no one trainer will know all of the modules well enough to be the only on-site trainer. Consequently, based on the number of modules being implemented at any one site, more than one trainer is required. Depending on your organization training support plans (discussed in greater detail later in this section), it becomes an economic strain to support small, on-site training. When you couple the two reasons and then do the math, ten or more users becomes a nice rule of thumb.

Advantages of On-Site Training

On-site training can provide an organization with several advantages, not the least of which are validating connectivity, throughput, system performance, and support services. It allows an organization to "test" their architecture and CNC model (especially when supported remotely). It allows the organization's competency center (the regional/organizational system support group) to validate their plans, including multilingual support, time support, and application/system support. On-site training can easily be tied into stress testing and fully integrated stress testing.

It also provides an organization with the opportunity to customize their training for each site. Why would you want to customize your training? Well, other than the obvious reason—making the most out of the necessary monetary expenditure—many organizations choose not to customize their OneWorld training. We, however, are of the opinion that customized training is more efficient, more personal, and easily worth the time and effort of doing it. It shows the common end user that this isn't just an initiative being forced down from corporate and that their day-to-day jobs are taken into consideration during the implementation itself.

On-site training also allows change management to take the temperature of the organization as it begins rolling out this new solution. We have seen several implementations fail because the users in the field did not support the solution. This provides your management infrastructure the opportunity to identify and head off issues before they explode.

Disadvantages of On-Site Training

One of the main disadvantages of on-site training is time. Depending on the number of sites, the implementation approach (phased, big-bang, regional/functional phased), and your organization's internal resources, you may not have the time or people to adequately perform on-site training. As with any other training, the longer the time period from actual class work to hands-on application, the less the end user will retain. After just a couple of weeks, the training could have been skipped altogether.

Another possible disadvantage of on-site training is resources. Much of this relates to the requirements of the organization for training in hardware, software, and personnel. Can your organization support current legacy systems, the system modeling effort, any currently "live" sites, and multiple training sites? Something to keep in mind during training is that it is the first exposure many of the end users will have to the new software. If it is poorly set up or supported, you can expect the user base to begin undermining the entire project.

Regional Training Centers

Depending on your overall structure, many organizations find a happy medium between off-site and on-site training by creating regional training centers. These can easily be positioned in a geographically advantageous location minimizing travel while still not providing a complete on-site training strategy. Organizations usually create these centers of excellence in previously established regional headquarters using as much of pre-existing equipment and support personnel as possible.

Advantages of Regional Training

Regional training centers allow for more customized training while still decreasing the overall costs associated with providing training at each individual site. It still allows your change management team to keep their fingers on the pulse of the common user while making the time requirements significantly less. It also decreases the number of experts required to train the area, especially when balanced against training at each site. Regional centers are more professionally run and present a better overall image to the end user. More effort can be placed in creating effective, eye-catching training presentations. It also allows for significantly improved equipment and connectivity. This improves end user first impressions and overall attitudes.

Disadvantages of Regional Training

There is a higher cost of travel and facilities associated with regional training centers. For whatever it is worth, it is still much simpler to have a few people travel to each site than each site traveling to a central area. There is also a higher cost associated with regional centers because they tend to be larger and better equipped than individual site training.

Train the Trainer

This training model works well for many organizations, and can be used in conjunction with regional training centers, on-site training, and J.D. Edwards training. Conceptually, your goal is to create one or two functional experts at each site who then conduct local training. An added benefit is that these trainers can then be used as the first tier in the support (or helpdesk) arena. These "power" users need to be carefully picked and managed. They need to establish close working relationships with your organization's competency center. Under normal conditions, the trainers would be trained regionally, nationally, or globally. After this initial training, they would spend some time with the competency center fielding calls or working on the applications during the modeling phase. These two events will provide them with an in-depth understanding of the product.

Their final steps toward becoming a trainer would be either assisting the professional trainers create course outlines and materials or taking a class designed to train them on the dos and don'ts of training. We really can't stress enough the need for the right people in this position, both for their ability to provide and receive knowledge transfers and for their attitudes toward the software and the project as a whole. Remember that these trainers will now directly interface with and help shape the opinions of the end-user community. With the wrong people in place, irreparable damage may occur to the project as a whole. One of the ways your organization will be able to measure their success with this strategy is the amount of support an area receives during and after go-live. The higher the level of required support, the less effective the trainer.

Advantages of Training the Trainer

Training the trainer provides site-specific functional leads able to provide training to the remaining site staff. It also lowers costs in training and support, increases area feedback, and enhances knowledge networking throughout the organization (trust us, the trainers will work among themselves and with the competency center—many of your more creative solutions will come out of this type of synergy). This strategy can be used in conjunction with any of the other strategies available for training, making it extremely versatile and a good overall solution.

Disadvantages of Training the Trainer

There are only two real disadvantages to this method, and they revolve around the people themselves. First, if you pick the wrong people, they have the ability to harm the entire project. It doesn't take many comments like "this thing is always so slow" or "I really prefer the old system" to spread the seeds of discontent. In a recent study of failed ERP projects (ERP's Second Wave conducted by Deloitte & Touche), 62 percent were due to people considerations and issues. The highest of these issues was change management—this relates to overall end-user acceptance. Only 12 percent were due to technology considerations.

Second, areas may develop an undesirable dependency on just a few people. This could result in human resources issues later in the software cycle. Area offices can be held hostage if key personnel insist on certain pay raises or shortened workweeks and they are the only "experts" on the system. Although most companies won't support the employee trying to make this type of ploy, it can cause tension and difficult times when or if those one or two employees are no longer with the organization.

How Will You Support Training?

This is an extremely important question regardless of which overall training strategy you choose to utilize. The support we are talking about relates to hardware, software, communications, systems hosting, and environment control. How you choose to do this directly affects the end users' first perceptions of this new system. Could this cost your organization additional funding? Of course it could. Is it worth the time and effort of doing it right? 100 percent.

Stand-Alone Supporting Training

If you have been to a J.D. Edwards class, you know that each student's PC has its own version of OneWorld installed running off separate databases. This is similar to the Stand-Alone version of OneWorld used in many demonstrations with the only true difference being a database designed to support the training material rather than the demonstration data. Although we have seen companies use this same product in their training strategy, we recommend that you create your own training version of Stand-Alone. This has many advantages, such as having the latest copy of your applications (including processing options) set up the way you plan on working and customized reports and applications as well as having actual company data to work with.

Technical Considerations for *Stand-Alone Training* There are a couple of technical considerations to keep in mind if you are supporting Stand-Alone training. First, when users are going through the training, they will not be able to see the changes or additions that other students made. This is both good and bad. It is good in that each student can perform the same class exercise without worrying about adding the version that has already been added or changing the address that has already been changed. It is bad in that there is no interaction, so you miss many of the potential day-to-day conflicts that can occur. Additionally, because the different software isn't actually networked, you can't effectively set up and demonstrate workflow. This may be a very important part of your overall solution and this training strategy doesn't support it.

Second, the applications, both interactive and batch, are only going to work as well or as fast as the individual hardware. Keeping in mind the earlier concept of first software impressions, the individual workstations should be beefed up to provide that positive first look. Third, your organization will want to maintain very positive control on the hardware installed with this particular version of OneWorld. It may contain company data, which could then easily walk out the door.

T I P

When you are refreshing your environments in a stand-alone scenario, you do not need to refresh the entire machine starting with the OS. Rather, all you need to refresh is the B7 directory on each client workstation. The stand-alone database (traditionally the JDEB7.MDB database) is located in the x:\b7\data directory (where x represents the drive where OneWorld was originally installed). By replacing the entire B7 directory, you not only refresh the data, but you also refresh the path code associated with training. The backup can be from a hidden directory on each machine (this makes the overall solution simpler because you can write a simple batch REFRESH.CMD file and then use AT, a Windows NT scheduling command, to automatically refresh the required information weekly).

T I P

Use the policy editor with your specific OS to ensure that users can't add or modify the OS system itself. Many end users will change desktop parameters (including background, colors, and screen savers, some with passwords) during the course of the training cycle. By locking this down, many potential conflicts will be avoided.

Appendix

Creating a Stand-Alone Version of OneWorld for Training

When you consider what the J.D. Edwards Stand-Alone version actually is, it becomes relatively simple to re-create it using your code and your business data. This special version is a complete set of client code reading from the OneWorld Local data source. This MS Access data source points to the same local database that all environments initially point to (the JDEB7.MDB located in the x:\B7\path code name\data directory). To create your own special version of the Stand-Alone product, you need to make a couple of decisions.

First, do you want to create a custom path code to support this endeavor? There are pros and cons to making a custom path code, primarily related to version control and additional space and memory resources on the server. For the purposes of this example, we are not going to create a new path code, rather we are going to use the CRPB733 path code. During the implementation process, this is the path code that most closely represents what the production path code will look like.

Second, do you want to add a special training user or to enable individual users to access the training environment? The advantage of creating a custom user is that it is easy to administer and set up the training. The advantage of letting everyone have access to the training environment is that it ensures that you have properly set up each user in advance to go live. For the purpose of this demonstration, we are not going to set up everyone. Instead, we will go the easier route.

Follow the relatively simple logic listed below for more detail on the "how to" of this strategy. Remember that this would be done during the implementation cycle. Additionally, if you choose to do this, you need to consider the support necessary to update this environment regularly.

1. Create a full package build for the CRPB733 path code (for example, CRPB733FB).

2. Create a new training environment (for example, TRN733) using CRPB733 as the path code. When you create this environment, be sure that you add instead of copy it. When you add an environment, no records are populated in the F986101 (Object Configuration Manager) table. You can then add a single entry for DEFAULT, TBLE, OneWorld Local – CRPB733, *PUBLIC (shown here).

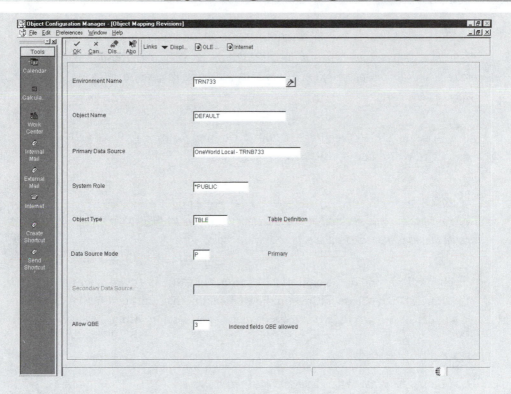

3. Create complete global table records with the R98CRTGL UBE.
   Copy the resulting TAM files to the deployment server (for example,
   \\depsvr\b733\CRPB733\package\CRPB733FB\spec). Replace existing files.

4. Create complete data dictionary records using the R92TAM UBE.
   Copy the resulting TAM (located in the B7 root directory on the
   client that ran the R92TAM) to the deployment server (for example,
   \\depsvr\b733\CRPB733\package\CRPB733FB\spec). Replace existing files.

5. Use the R98403 version XJDE0021. Go from data source Business Data – CRP
   to OneWorld Local – CRPB733. This will copy all of the business data from the
   CRP733 environment to the JDEB7.MDB database located on the workstation
   that ran the R98403. Compress the database using the MS Access database
   compression utility.

6. Use the R98403 version XJDE0012. Go from Control Tables – CRP to OneWorld Local – CRPB733.

This will copy all of the control tables from the CRP733 environment to the JDEB7.MDB database located on the workstation that ran the R98403. Compress the database using the MS Access database compression utility.

7. Use the R98403 version XJDE0023. Go from System – B733 to OneWorld Local – CRPB733. This will copy all of the system tables to the JDEB7.MDB located on the workstation that ran the R98403. Some of the information in these tables needs to be modified for security reasons. If you only have a single OneWorld user ID for this environment, you can clean up the F0092 and F00921 tables. You can also clean up the OCM, data sources, and other similar tables. Compress the database using the MS Access database compression utility.

8. Use the R98403 version XJDE0502. Go from Data Dictionary – B733 to OneWorld Local – CRPB733. This will copy all of the data dictionary tables to the JDEB7.MDB located on the workstation that ran the R98403. Compress the database using the MS Access database compression utility.

9. Use the R98403 version XJDE0503. Go from Object Librarian – B733 to OneWorld Local – CRPB733. This will copy the five object librarian tables

to the JDEB7.MDB located on the workstation that ran the R98403. Compress the database using the MS Access database compression utility.

10. Use the R98403 version XJDE0019. Go from Central Objects – CRPB733 to OneWorld Local – CRPB733. Make sure that processing option #3 is 1 (we don't want to copy the data—simply create the tables). This will copy the central objects to the JDEB7.MDB database located on the workstation that ran the R98403.

11. Using the Object Librarian copy table utility, copy the following tables.

Table Name	Source Data Source	Target Data Source
F98306	Central Objects - CRPB733	OneWorld Local - CRPB733
F983051	Versions - CRPB733	OneWorld Local - CRPB733

12. Recompress the JDEB7.MDB database using the MS Access database compression utility. Copy this database to the deployment server (for example, \\depsvr\b733\CRPB733\package\data). Using the package build application within OneWorld (P9621 located on the GH9083 menu), recompress the CRPB733FB package. This will create new .CAB files with the updated TAM and database.

13. Modify the JDE.INI located in the B733\OneWorld Client Install\Misc directory with the following information.

```
[DB SYSTEM SETTINGS - SECONDARY]
Base Datasource=OneWorld Local – CRPB733
Object Owner=
Server=LOCAL
Database=OneWorld Local – CRPB733
Load Library=JDBODBC.DLL
Decimal Shift =N
Julian Dates=N
Use Owner=N
Secured=N
Type=A
Library List=
Library=
```

14. Optional: Set up multitier deployment using a CD-ROM. This will allow you to install the training Stand-Alone version you have just created with a CD as opposed to across the network.

Dedicated Training Centers

Many organizations, regardless of their size, find creating a training lab beneficial for end-user training. A dedicated training center truly has many different advantages. Primary among the advantages is that it separates end users from their day-to-day activities. It is difficult to be interrupted by the phone when you are not at your desk. When you remove your employees from their familiar surroundings, they will be able to concentrate on learning. Another advantage of a dedicated training facility is that it allows for a standardization of equipment and software. It also allows better control and consequently more professional training.

The chief disadvantage to dedicated training centers is having the staff and equipment available to support them. Unless you budget accordingly, one center often bears the brunt of everyone's training. The costs of training are large enough to affect the bottom line and no site will want to pay for it all.

Centralized Support

It is very easy to add a training environment to the development, CRP, or production system. The question is whether your organization wants to support training in this manner. By adding an environment designated for training, your organization will benefit from the ability to test run your systems. They will also benefit from the fact that the people who are ultimately responsible for supporting the ERP solution get an advanced look at some of the support requirements. The disadvantages are that there will be times when you will have to decide if you want to support the project team or the training team. Training can also adversely affect the project team by inappropriately stressing the system.

Decentralized Support

Your organization can also choose to set up a series of instances of the OneWorld product located closer to the user base. The advantages of using decentralized systems are that the project team continues unaffected by training and the support is spread among multiple areas and personnel. The disadvantages of this are maintaining version control and a good set of company specific training data. When you add that to an increase in hardware, setup, and system training costs, this may not be the best choice for your organization.

Continued Training

The majority of this section talks about the training necessary to implement the product itself for both the project team and end users; however, there is also a continuing education element to having and maintaining an ERP product of this type. Although many companies stop training after go-live, larger organizations will need to maintain a training program for both refresher courses and new employees. While the continuing training requirement is not as intense as the initial implementation training effort, it is still an important part of maintaining your new ERP investment and shouldn't be overlooked.

Development and Version Control Methodology

Contrary to what you might expect, J.D. Edwards recommends that the CNC administrator, rather than a developer, should dictate the version control policy during a OneWorld implementation instead of a developer. Yet, when you think about it, it really does make sense. Creating and deploying packages is the responsibility of the CNC specialist. The problem you might face, however, is that neither your CNC nor your developers have ever worked with a product similar to this one. Because of this, we decided to provide a detailed version control scheme, including flow-charting, decision-making bodies, some definitions of forms that need to be created, and some examples. All of these can be used and customized to create a version control policy that would work for you.

How to Use this Material

When we created this material, we intentionally attempted to create a product that would work for a large company instead of a smaller organization. Our rationale for this was that a smaller company could remove elements of the provided process and streamline the methodology to fit their specific needs. Because this methodology may not fit your specific needs, you should feel free to use part, all, or none of this information when creating your own development and version control methodology.

Can You Separate Development and Version Control?

Not really! This section really doesn't address the "how to" of development; rather, we go into detail about the procedures necessary to develop safely, protecting your development investment. There are some relatively simple rules to developing in OneWorld. There are a similar series of rules for version control. These rules are incorporated into the flowcharts that follow at the end of this section.

Development

As you decide to modify your system, there are several things you should keep in mind. One is that the J.D. Edwards upgrade methodology will not carry over all modified objects. Because objects that you may have modified may also have been modified by the OneWorld developers in Denver, the upgrade methodology had to be developed in such a way that it combines both your changes and J.D. Edwards'. Part of this methodology maintains your changes. Other parts, however, take the J.D. Edwards modification over your own. When this happens, you have to retrofit (or reapply) your modifications. This pulls up two very basic development rules to work with. First, perform all development with upgrades in mind. J.D. Edwards has manuals describing development rules; if you follow these rules, you will be in good stead. If you need more guidance concerning development dos and don'ts, the J.D. Edwards Press has a book on the topic for any company going in this direction that is a must have.

The second rule about development is that you should copy J.D. Edwards' objects when you want to modify them instead of modifying the originals. Although this is not the case with development done at the directions of the J.D. Edwards support line, this is a good rule of thumb when your organization has chosen to modify existing OneWorld functionality. When you copy the objects you want to modify, you're ensuring that your modifications will be preserved during upgrade without needing to retrofit the changes. It will also give you some time to evaluate the new J.D. Edwards code before deciding if you need or want their new functionality. If you want both their new functionality and your modifications, there is very little difference between retrofitting and remodifying the object.

Other Development Rules and Explanations

When you copy a version of a OneWorld report (see Figure A-1), provide it with a new name, and change its processing options or data selections, you are performing development. This is one of the biggest areas of development that your organization will undertake, but you won't even be aware that it is happening most of the time. During most OneWorld application classes, the instructors are extremely quick to demonstrate to the class how easy it is to copy and add versions of UBEs that they can then modify (for example, change the data selection or processing options). To do this, users don't have to have access to the object librarian or the RDA (Report Design Aid) formally. Instead, rather than launching the UBE using the P98305 batch application, they can highlight the version they want and then click the Copy or Add button.

Presto, they were just involved in the development process. Unfortunately, however, these instructors rarely teach their students how to check these new versions into the deployment server. What usually results is hundreds of versions that can't be used on more than one machine. This is especially confusing for people on Windows Terminal Server. It works one day, is gone for a week, and suddenly comes back—actually, the user

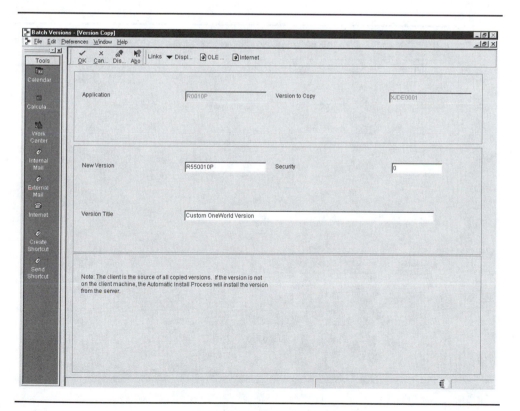

FIGURE A-1.   Copying batch versions

just logged on to different terminal servers on the days it disappeared. This adds days or even weeks to the upgrade process as versions are identified and checked in or deleted. Finally, it represents a huge loss of time and effort.

Training your users to check-in their new version (see Figure A-2) or restricting the users who can add or copy versions is a good development rule to adopt. We prefer limiting who can perform these functions for several reasons. First, UBEs have the potential to be very powerful pieces of software. Because of this, you might not want everyone to be able to create custom versions of them. Second, limiting the number of people who can do this allows your CNC administrators to ensure they are trained in how to check-in and check-out (as well as create and copy) custom versions. Finally, by throwing security on the P98305 application, you will decrease the total number of these versions created. Trust us, having to upgrade 400 versions is bad enough. Having to upgrade 4,000 or 40,000 would be unacceptable.

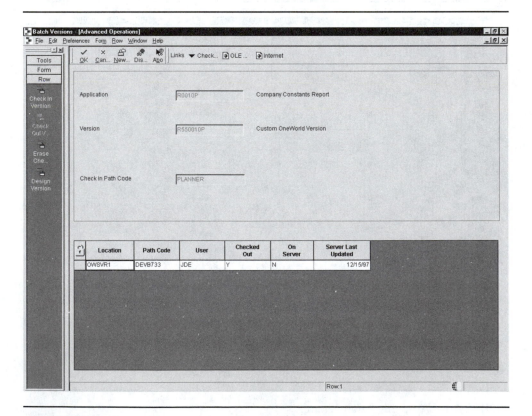

FIGURE A-2.   Checking batch versions in

Checking Items In

Although each organization tends to have their own rules regarding check-ins on objects, every company should insist it be done and done regularly. As a minimal rule of thumb, we recommend that objects under development be checked in at least once a week. Depending on the organization, we've recommended daily. This is because all development is done on the client workstation, yet most client workstations aren't backed up or on a UPS.

Let's take a worst-case scenario. Your company needs a modification to base J.D. Edwards OneWorld functionality. The developers have been feverishly working to complete the modification so that it can be tested prior to going live. One developer, after two months of work, is finally ready to check his key part into the deployment server. Just then, boom—lightning strikes, and his machine takes a fatal surge of electricity. This developer, because he chose not to check his work in, just lost two months (320 man-hours times $300/hour = $96,000) of work. Your go-live will have to be pushed off, and you will have to explain to the CEO why and how this could happen. Do you have your résumé polished up?

By forcing regular check-ins via documented procedure and double-checking the database, you can salvage the situation described above. You should regularly back up your deployment server (especially during CRP and development cycles) and database. If you have a nightly check-in policy, you would only lose a couple of hours in this scenario. Your go-live would occur on schedule, and though no one will sing your praises, you won't need to look for a new way to put your children through college, pay your mortgage, or eat.

Validating Items Checked Out

To quickly verify if any objects are checked out, perform the following SQL statements using the appropriate database tool.

Oracle (SQL Plus or SQL Worksheet)

SELECT simkey, siobnm, sipathcd, siuser, siupmj FROM objb733.f9861 WHERE simkey <> 'deployment machine name' ORDER BY simkey, sipathcd, siuser;

SELECT vrmkey, vrpid, vrvers, vrusr0, vrchkoutdat, vrvrsavail FROM "path code table owner".f983051 WHERE vrchkoutsts='Y' ORDER BY vrmkey, vrusr0, vrpid, vrchkoutdat;

N O T E

The second SELECT statement must be repeated for each path code using the appropriate path code table owner name (prodb733, crpb733, devb733, and so on).

MS SQL Server (Query Analyzer)

SELECT simkey, siobnm, sipathcd, siuser, siupmj FROM objb733.f9861 WHERE simkey <> 'deployment machine name' ORDER BY simkey, sipathcd, siuser

SELECT vrmkey, vrpid, vrvers, vrusr0, vrchkoutdat, vrvrsavail FROM "path code table owner".f983051 WHERE vrchkoutsts='Y' ORDER BY vrmkey, vrusr0, vrpid, vrchkoutdat

---

N O T E

The second SELECT statement must be repeated for each path code using the appropriate path code table owner name (prodb733, crpb733, devb733, and so on).

DB2/400 (Use the Command STRSQL)

SELECT simkey, siobnm, sipathcd, siuser, siupmj FROM jdeb733/f9861 WHERE simkey <> *'deployment machine name'* ORDER BY simkey, sipathcd, siuser

SELECT vrmkey, vrpid, vrvers, vrusr0, vrchkoutdat, vrvrsavail FROM *"path code table owner"*/f983051 WHERE vrchkoutsts='Y' ORDER BY vrmkey, vrusr0, vrpid, vrchkoutdat

N O T E

The second SELECT statement must be repeated for each path code using the appropriate path code table owner name (prodb733, crpb733, devb733, and so on).

Limit the Number of Checkouts

Another development gem is limiting the number of checkouts per object. This is done by modifying a processing option on the F9860 (Object Librarian) application (see Figure A-3).

The rational for this is really quite simple. It is too easy for multiple developers to work on the exact same object simultaneously. The mechanics behind this usually has multiple development projects running concurrently. Remember, the actual development occurs on the individual client workstation. Until the object is checked back into the deployment server, the changes only reside on that workstation (see Figure A-4).

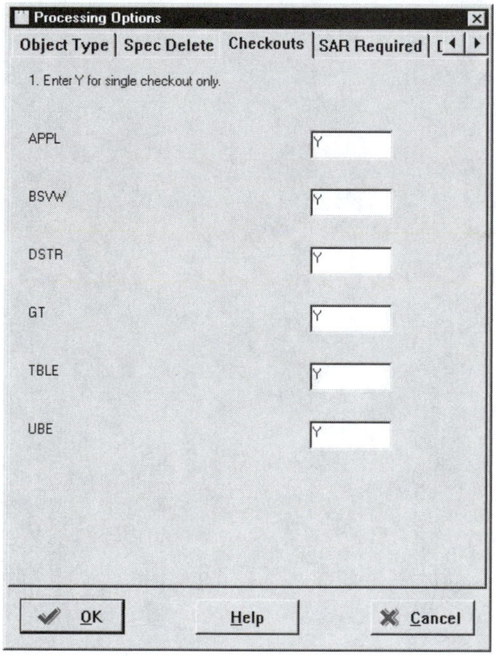

FIGURE A-3.   Object librarian processing options

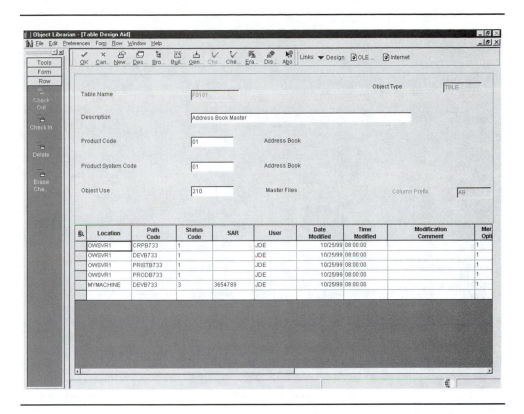

FIGURE A-4. Checked-out object

Developers will work around someone else having already checked the object out by manually changing the check-out status from a 3 to a 4 (refer to Figure A-5). This doesn't affect the user who already has the item checked out and does allow an additional checkout.

Why would you discourage this practice? If multiple people have the same object checked out, you have a huge risk associated. How do you plan to combine their individual development efforts? What happens if someone checks in a previous copy overwriting a newer version of the code? How can you recover from this type of incident? Answer: you may not be able to.

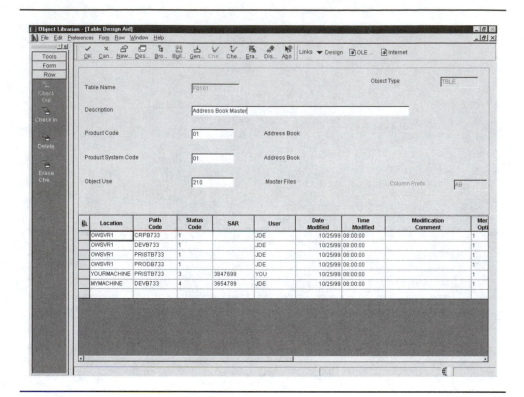

FIGURE A-5.   Two items checked out

A little security goes a long way. You can secure your users from making these changes by applying action security on the STCE field (see Figure A-6). This will effectively stop your development users from changing this field.

Encourage Developers

Encourage your developers to use good development practices. Do this by publishing your OneWorld development rules, training each one on the dos and don'ts of the situation, and sacrificing the first offender. Though the last is a little harsh, we're quite sure it will get everyone else's attention. Here are some things to remember:

- If you've checked an item out just to look at its code, erase your checkout when you're done. You might be stopping someone else from doing his or her job.

- Always check out an object you want to work with rather than doing a fake or forced checkout. You don't know if your deployed package has the latest changes.

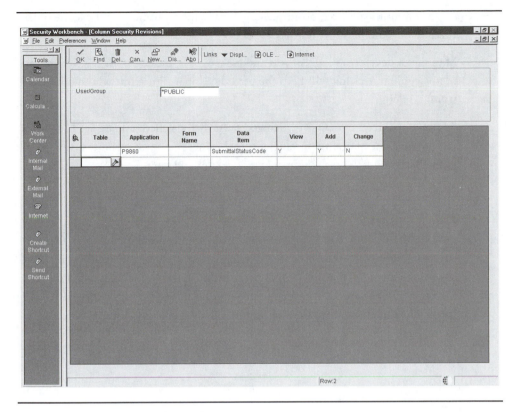

FIGURE A-6. Object librarian security

DEFINITION

Fake/forced checkout: *A fake (also known as forced) checkout is when a user manually enters a checkout line into the F9861 (Object Librarian) grid using the P9860 application instead of clicking the checkout button. This ensures that the object's specifications and C code are not copied from their respective locations.*

- Contact the owner of a checked-out object prior to erasing or deleting the checkout. You certainly will appreciate the same consideration from them.

- Prior to performing a fake or forced checkout, notify your development project lead and CNC administrator. These individuals should have a good understanding of what objects are in what current state.

- Over-communicate when multiple developers are set to modify the same object. It really does help.

- Maintain a developers log. As you make changes, annotate your log. In the case of an accident, this log will help the next developer figure out what you were trying to do.

- As functional requirements are changed or further clarified, update the functional requirements, technical requirements, and business case test scenarios immediately. It is too easy to say you'll do it later and later never comes.

- Don't wait and try to fix something. If it's messed up, notify the project team lead immediately. It will be easier to fix if the right people know about it.

- Own up to mistakes made. Everyone will make them and knowing them in advance might save valuable recovery time. For example, if you accidentally checked in an older object on top of a newer one when you had intended on erasing your checkout, the proper people may be able to immediately fix it. If you allow the issue to go unnoticed until the next package build, it may be too late.

Law of the West

Recovering Overwritten Objects

If you find yourself in the uncomfortable situation where someone checked in an older version of software on top of a modified object, you may be able to salvage the situation, depending on where you are in your development cycle. To determine if you will be the hero of the hour, follow the flowchart shown here. *Scenario:* Developer A checks in an older version of an object on top of a newer version.

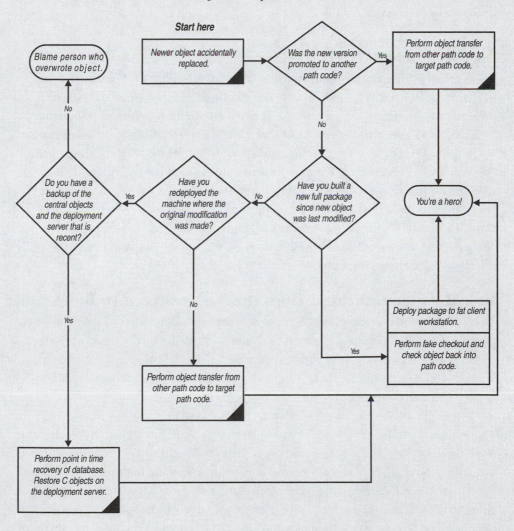

Create a Developing Path Code

Although J.D. Edwards OneWorld ships with a development path code, add an additional one if your company plans on doing major development. This will provide your developers with a location where they can work without feeling the cumulative effects of all of their projects. It will also provide them with a place where they can try new things and even make mistakes without adversely affecting other phases of the implementation. When code is nearing completion, it can be transferred into the DEVB733 path code and then follow the traditional development cycle.

Version Control

Up to this point, we've only addressed development. For those CNC administrators out there, do not fear. You need to have some basic development dos and don'ts prior to thinking about version control. The first question that many of you might be asking is what exactly version control entails. Does it mean controlling versions of OneWorld throughout the development cycle? Is it involved with ensuring tested OneWorld code is deployed in a timely manner throughout the enterprise? Is it managing third-party products introduced into the enterprise? What about deciding (or helping to decide) when to do a new upgrade or service pack? Maybe version control is about helping the developers do their work. The reality is that it is about all of these things—they all affect how OneWorld works and all of them must be carefully orchestrated to ensure the system runs properly.

Just How Complicated Does the System Need to Be?

To be effective, the system doesn't have to be complicated. However, if the system you put into place is complicated, it doesn't necessarily mean it won't be effective. Rather, it is important to try to put the appropriate measures in place that will ensure your organization has the control that facilitate their personal success. What works for Company A may not work for Company B.

You might ask if you can get by without a formal version control process. Theoretically, yes. However, we've never seen an organization successfully fly this one by the seats of their pants. Rather, they start their OneWorld implementation with little to no thought about version control and end up changing their philosophy after the first or second stumble. Is version control easy to manage? It can be. In fact, we're going to make it even easier for you by providing a series of tools you can use as a template. If it is more cumbersome than you want to deal with, you have the option of trimming it down. But remember, what we're providing is something that does work. Modifying it might decrease its effectiveness.

Definitions Used in the Tools

The following are some acronyms that require a brief description prior to your being turned loose on these flowcharts. Once you've mastered these, we're sure you will find them very useful.

- **CCB (change control board)** A board of business functional group leads whose primary responsibility is in allocating resources for making software modifications to the enterprise system.

- **SMRB (software modification review board)** A board of technically oriented people whose job includes verifying software modifications (both proposed and completed) prior to introduction to the enterprise production packages. Makes recommendations on third-party product introduction, assigns appropriate resources to assist systems analysts (SA) in the creation of functional requirement requests (FRR), technical requirement requests (TRR), and business case test scenarios (BCTS).

- **JDERL (J.D. Edwards Response Line)** The support line established as part of the J.D. Edwards support offering.

- **SA (systems analyst)** Technically oriented business expert whose responsibilities include assisting in the development of the FRR, TRR, BCTS, researching issues revolving the use of the OneWorld system, creating business solutions for rapid ROI, and functioning as the second line of internal software support.

- **ITPM (information technology project manager)** A liaison between the OneWorld development team, the SA, and the IT department assigned to a particular software modification request.

- **FTs (functionality testers)** End users used to assist with testing modifications from a functional/functionality perspective. Skills range from power user to system novice.

- **TM (technology manager)** A person designated to manage the technology portion of a project.

- **RCA (release control manager)** Individual or group of individuals responsible for maintaining release level control in the enterprise. Release control should maintain accepted release versions of third-party products (including OS releases) as well as OneWorld release levels. The RCA works closely with version control.

- **DEPSVR (deployment server)** A server used as a central repository for C code in a central deployment strategy OneWorld implementation. Refer to Chapter 5 for more information on the deployment server.

- **APPSVR (application server)** A server containing OneWorld server code used for various services in the OneWorld enterprise solution. For more information regarding application servers, see Chapter 5.

- **VC (version control)** The appropriate version control representative.

- **JDEKG (J.D. Edwards Knowledge Garden)** https://knowledge.jdewards.com/

- **WIPB733 (work in progress path code)** A custom path code designed to allow developers to begin working on modifications without being concerned with package build interruptions. Initial modifications are done to this path code and then migrated to DEVB733 to begin formal version control procedures.

- **SMT (software modification test)** A complete test of the OneWorld software to ensure changes have not adversely affected other non-modified areas. This differs from the BCTS in that it looks at all modules instead of modules directly modified.

- **SP (service pack)** Refers to a OneWorld service pack. When J.D. Edwards makes changes to the foundation code, they bundle these changes as a service pack. Service packs are release-specific and should only be applied when the client is suffering from an issue directly addressed by the service pack.

- **MNGT (management)** Any of a number of individuals responsible for people, functional areas, projects, or a combination thereof.

- **BCTS (business case testing script)** A test script designed to ensure that modifications meet the business requirements for the modification itself. This script should be created prior to the modification itself and should be under version control.

- **JDESAR (J.D. Edwards Software Action Request)** Traditionally known as a SAR, this should be differentiated from ISAR.

- **PMO (project management office)** A group of individuals designated to administrate the project. They handle the paperwork, the signed documentation, and project timelines ensuring the smooth flow of the project itself.

- **ESOW (executive statement of work)**   A single-page document outlining a request for system modification. Included elements: business issue, proposed modification, estimated cost, and approval routing.

- **FRR (functional request requirements)**   A standardized form outlining the detailed functional requirements surrounding a proposed change to the OneWorld system.

- **TRR (technical request requirements)**   A standardized form outlining the detailed technical requirements of a proposed change to the OneWorld system. This form would include all of the necessary detail to perform the requested modification with a detailed cost estimate, including time, required resources, and capital.

- **FTRR (functional/technical request requirements)**   The combined output of a revised ESOW, FRR, and TRR. This form provides all of the necessary information for the CCB to review and either approve or reject proposed changes to the OneWorld system.

- **NCA (net change analysis)**   A review of base OneWorld functionality against functional system requirements. The difference defines a software gap that must either be programmed around, interfaced with another product, or process re-engineered to accommodate.

- **ISAR (internal software action request)**   An alphanumeric tracking number for client modifications. J.D. Edwards uses the SAR tracking system for changes made to objects within the system. We highly recommend that companies create their own ISAR system for tracking company-specific changes.

How to Use the Flowcharts

Now that you have a few new abbreviations to work with, you will find the following flowcharts relatively easy to use. Each chart has an identifier in the upper-right corner consisting of alpha and numeric characters (for example, A1). Each block also has a number assigned. Combined, these allow users to go between forms as required. (For example, if you were on A2 box 5 and it instructed you to go to A1 box 14, you would pull up the A1 form and locate box 14. From there you would continue on form A1 until completion or until instructed to go to a different form.) Each flowchart maintains a similar feel and read and was designed to accommodate most of what a company needs for version control.

- Flowchart A1 (see Figure A-7) is designed to address OneWorld enhancements originating at the user level (for example, a user identifies a system change to either increase productivity or to actually accomplish daily, monthly, or yearly work).

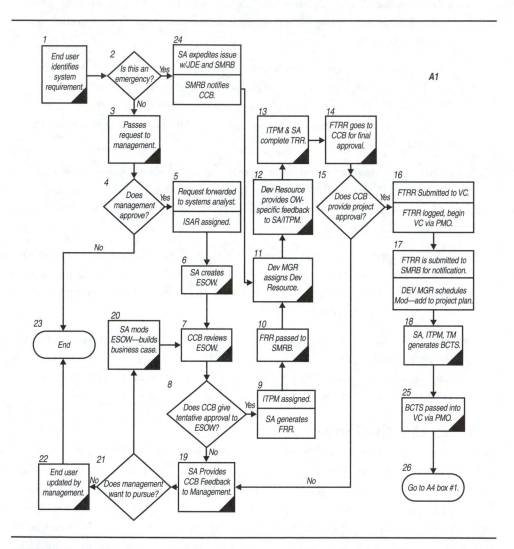

FIGURE A-7. A1 – OneWorld Enhancement

- Flowchart A2 (see to Figure A-8) is designed to address software troubleshooting resulting in a OneWorld modification (for example, a OneWorld issue that requires a system or code modification either identified by the J.D. Edwards Support Line or internally recognized).

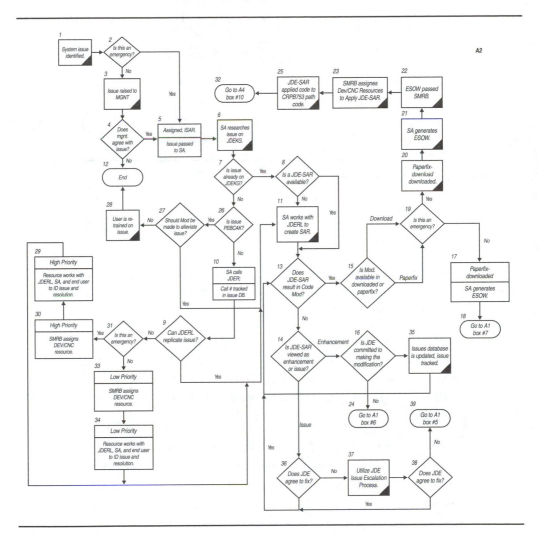

FIGURE A-8.   A2 – OneWorld Software Troubleshooting

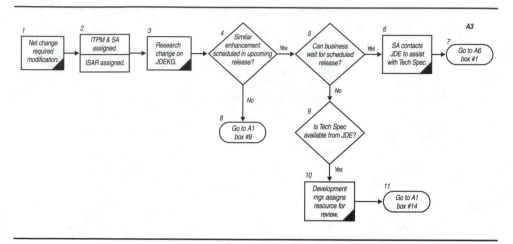

FIGURE A-9.   A3 – OneWorld Net Change

- Flowchart A3 (see Figure A-9) is designed to address Net Change Analysis identified issues.

- Flowchart A4 (see to Figure A-10) is designed to address the physical activities surrounding the actual modification of the OneWorld system itself and how it ties into development and version control.

- Flowchart A5 (see Figure A-11) is designed to address third-party version control (for example, if a user updates software on their system, they could adversely affect the operation of the OneWorld software itself—modifying the MDAC level by downloading the latest edition of Internet Explorer could cause data corruption).

- Flowchart A6 (see Figure A-14) is designed to address OneWorld service pack, cumulative, and major release upgrade version control procedures (for example, when to apply, when not to apply, why you should or shouldn't apply, and so on).

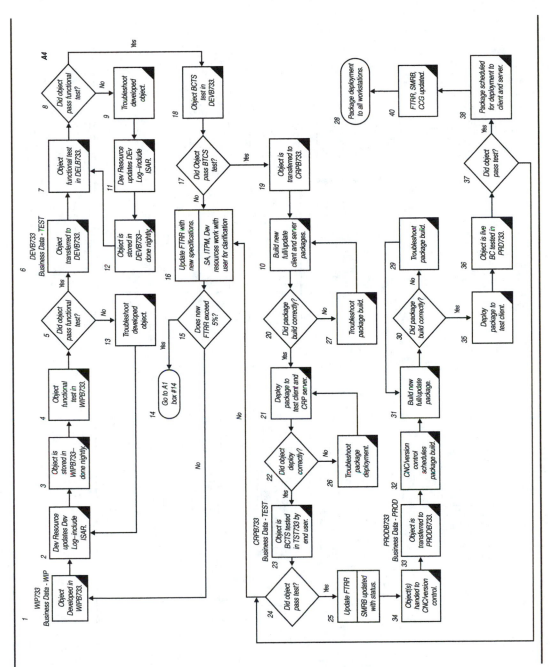

FIGURE A-10. A4 – OneWorld Development

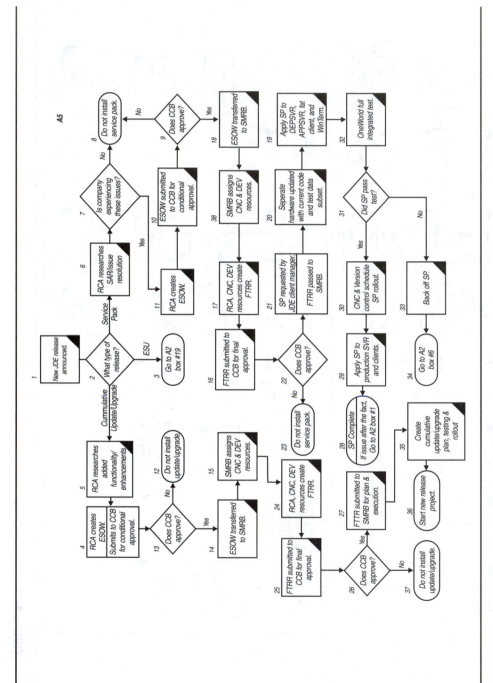

FIGURE A-11. A5 – Third-party Software Version Control

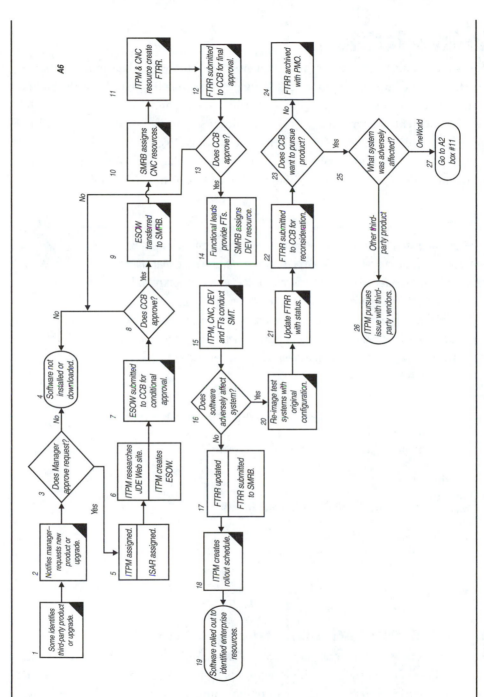

FIGURE A-12. A6 – OneWorld Release Version Control

Go-Live Activities

This is the culmination of all of the implementation activities to date and a significant milestone in the implementation itself. Many organizations feel that this is the end of their ERP implementation experience, and although we won't necessarily agree with the last statement, we agree that this is a significant step in the ownership of an ERP suite of applications. Properly planned and executed, go-live is a non-event. Some organizations split the following steps into two distinct phases: pre-go-live and go-live. For the purpose of this discussion, however, we will treat these as a set of activities.

NOTE

In the following few pages, we'll discuss some of the steps and considerations necessary for going live with the OneWorld product. Keep in mind that different companies have different required steps (some included, some not) based on business and application decisions made during the implementation itself. Because of the huge number of potential differences, it is impossible to make a clear determination on exactly what steps your particular company may need. As such, we will discuss the most prominent steps that you need to consider prior to going live with the OneWorld product.

Still, this section should give you some things to talk about, including:

- Technical and application audits
- Final user training
- Software package builds and deployments
- Final testing
- Real-time data conversions
- Flipping the switch

Application and Technical Audits

Application and technical audits are a time to have another person validate what you've completed is done correctly and that your company is ready to go live with OneWorld. The timing is critical to receiving a go or no-go rating on the audit itself. A OneWorld go-live audit needs to be performed about one month prior to go-live. This provides the auditor with a good example of what is completed and what is still left to complete, while simultaneously giving the client time to correct any deficiencies. The importance of the audits should not be overlooked. This is especially true for the OneWorld client. If you choose to go live after failing an audit, you can pretty much guarantee that your company will have no legal recourse against the software vendor or the implementation partner.

Application Audits

There are application audits that deal primarily with individual modules within this ERP package and how those products interact with each other. They also look at training and the company's overall readiness to complete go-live successfully. The importance of the application audit is that it is able to point to weaknesses within your organization's plans to go live. We have seen application audits fail and those accounts that choose to go live anyway invariably suffer from their decision. Some of the items that they will look for include:

- Application setup (processing options, versions, and so on)
- Batch version setup
- Custom menu design
- Application security
- End-user training
- Documentation

Technology Audits

On the flip side of the application audit is the OneWorld technology audit. Many organizations feel that the technology will take care of itself, and even though it isn't the number one reason that ERP projects fail, it does represent 12 percent of all failures. With this large a risk, it is always prudent to validate that what has come before is ready to go. Although we rarely specify differences, if your organization has undergone substantial customization to the OneWorld product, a technical software audit should be performed at the same time as the technology audit. This will ensure the integrity of the developed and modified applications. Some of the items looked at include:

- OneWorld architecture
- Security plan

Appendix

- Modifications and version control

- Hardware and software release levels

- The results of system stress tests (performance oriented)

- IS personnel training

- Any customizations to the product

- Interfaces with other software packages

Final User Training

This should be more than just completing the training cycle for the end user. It is also the time your organization needs to complete the knowledge transfer from your implementation partner to your staff members.

End-User Training

Training at the beginning of the implementation, or even in the middle of an implementation, is wasted on the user who returns to his or her normal job and doesn't touch OneWorld again for several months. Additionally, there is no advantage to training end users on unmodified modules (if you're customizing modules) or on software missing a large number of custom UBEs or defined business processes. Consequently, most organizations will find that they are performing the majority of their end-user training toward the end of their implementation. This allows users to be trained just prior to go-live on the software and with a copy of the data that they will use in the production environment. For more information on training strategies, see "Training" in this appendix.

Technical and Application Knowledge Transfer

Most organizations attempting to implement a product like OneWorld use implementation partners (for example, J.D. Edwards consultants, Deloitte & Touche, and so on) to augment their own staff during the initial installation and setup of the product through go-live. Once they go live, however, most organizations anticipate the required third-party consulting to diminish and ultimately stop altogether. In order to ensure that your organization is ready for the consultants to go home, there needs to be a knowledge transfer between the implementation partners and your staff. This knowledge transfer is application and technology driven and is an important part of this process.

During the course of the implementation, there will be a substantial transfer of experience due to working together day in and day out. Part of your go-live process should ensure that everything is properly documented and trained beyond the normal knowledge transfer. Depending on your implementation design, you may also have functional areas where the consultants performed the majority of the setup and testing. In these functional areas, you need to ensure that there has been an adequate transfer of knowledge.

Software Package Builds and Deployments

It is safe to say that 100 percent of companies that implement OneWorld will modify the OneWorld product in one way or another. These modifications may be nothing more than placing your company's data on the top of a UBE version. Then again, they could involve millions of dollars of coding and systems integration. Regardless of the amount of modifications performed, you need to build and test your final go-live software packages.

A mistake that many organizations make is that they continue making code changes (applying SARs, completing coding, creating new reports, and so on) up to go-live. We don't recommend this strategy for a couple of reasons. An organization needs to set in stone a timeline with completed go-live software. This should minimally be one week (but preferably several weeks) prior to go-live. This artificial constraint allows the system's administration to build and then application experts test the software being delivered to the end user. The longer the time period in advance when no new modifications are performed, the more stable the product tends to be. Remember, as you take this new multimillion dollar system live, your end-user acceptance of it is a key factor to its success. With this in mind, failure to stop modifications provides an unstable environment for go-live and sets the stage for the implementation to fail.

Final Testing

If you haven't finished your integrated, stress, and functional testing, now is your last opportunity, and oh, by the way, you're late. If you aren't comfortable with the final software and procedural solution, you'd better rethink go-live and do so quickly. One of the final tests that needs to be conducted revolves around your software solution for J.D. Edwards' OneWorld product. Validate that all of the reports and modifications to various modules within the system work as anticipated or are removed from the production set of code.

Real-Time Data Conversions

The final conversions that need to be performed relate to what systems are going live at any one time. If you are implementing inventory within OneWorld for multiple sites, you need time to convert existing quantities on hand from your legacy system to your OneWorld system. Now, based on your overall plan, you might perform this conversion by conducting a full inventory at each site and then having people enter the quantities into OneWorld (obviously the items themselves should already be in the database and only missing the quantities by site). Then again, your conversion process could be a program (either built externally or within OneWorld) or another data population method. If you are implementing accounts receivable, you need to enter outstanding debts. Accounts payable needs to come up to speed with what you owe other organizations. And the list goes on.

The fact that you need to convert data from a legacy system to your new OneWorld suite means that you need to plan some time when you aren't changing your legacy information. Does this mean that you have to work manually during this time period? Maybe, but this is ultimately decided as a strategy for your organization. At some point in the process, however, you will need to actually get the data from your existing system into the one you are implementing. This is yet another process that should be planned in the beginning of the implementation process. Work closely with your integration partner when planning this important part of implementation. We really can't overemphasize the importance of this phase. Remember, the data that you start with is as important (if not more so) than the applications themselves.

Flipping the Switch

As we stated at the beginning of this section, going live should be a non-issue. With all of the planning and execution required to successfully implement the product, the end users should come in on Monday and start using their new OneWorld product. Some organizations do feel pain associated with go-live, but these organizations are typically the ones that didn't fully plan, implement, test, and train for the product effectively. If everything is planned and executed accordingly, the end users can start right in using their new business software interface for the betterment of your company.

Globalization

The process of globalization is more than just having business locations in multiple countries, it is more than just supporting several languages, and it is more than just tax and currency. Globalization is the process of integrating your multicountry sites with a single business solution. This section will detail some of the considerations that you need to keep in mind as you integrate and globalize your company.

Language Considerations

This section will outline some considerations revolving around languages on a global implementation. This language support concern is exacerbated by the addition of double-byte languages.

DEFINITION

Double-byte language: *A double-byte language is one whose alpha characters are so complicated that a single byte (8 bits) of information is insufficient to maintain the entire set of possible characters. An example of a double-byte language is Japanese.*

Although J.D. Edwards OneWorld can support English and Japanese, it cannot support English, Japanese, and Chinese on the same server. Another issue would be supporting English, Japanese, and German on the same server because of special character sets required by the German language. But, before we go there, let's look at J.D. Edwards' supported languages.

OneWorld Tier-1/2/3 Languages

The following languages are tier-1 languages as defined by J.D. Edwards. This means that the language component represented is fully functional and fully supported by J.D. Edwards and their development staff. There are also tier-2 and tier-3 languages that are supported by J.D. Edwards. The language tiers within OneWorld indicated the order in which the languages are moved into a general available status and the quantity of support as well as who provides the software translations.

- **Tier 1**   Subset of documentation and software translation

- **Tier 2**   Software only

- **Tier 3**   Software only, translated by business partners

Traditionally, additional languages are available between 30 and 90 days after the general availability of the OneWorld release. OneWorld Xe (formerly B733.3) is no exception to the rule. They have additional cumulative releases available for the

OneWorld product (B733.4, 5, and 6); however, these should only contain code fixes and would be supported accordingly.

NOTE

Language support varies from release to release. For an up-to-date list of languages and their Tier for support, refer to the J.D. Edwards Knowledge Garden (https://knowledge.jdedwards.com).

OneWorld Tier-1 Languages

English (base language)
Chinese (simplified)
French
German
Italian
Japanese
Portuguese
Spanish

OneWorld Tier-2 Languages

Chinese (traditional)
Danish
Dutch
Finnish
Korean
Norwegian
Swedish

OneWorld Tier-3 Languages

Arabic
Czech
Greek
Hungarian
Polish
Russian

Base Language

OneWorld's base language is the invariant character code set. This set is composed of the English characters A-Z, the numerical characters 0-9, and most common punctuation marks. This base language acts as a common denominator, in effect, as it is present in each of the character code sets required for the various languages supported by OneWorld. The invariant code set as a base language enables multiple instances and third-party solutions to meet county-specific reporting requirements in complex environments.

Multiple Character Code Sets and Reports

Currently, OneWorld enables multiple language support via distinct character code sets at the OS and database level. Support for multiple languages via multiple character code sets can prevent global/multinational organizations from installing OneWorld as a single instance in cases where reporting requirements extend beyond a single double-byte and English requirement, or beyond a single Western European code set and English reporting requirement.

Rather, multiple instances of OneWorld are required for such organizations to meet country-specific reporting requirements via OneWorld. Third-party solutions can possibly be employed to meet these needs as well and can be used to supplement OneWorld.

Unicode

Although J.D. Edwards' OneWorld does support numerous single-byte and double-byte languages, it does not yet support these languages via Unicode. Support for Unicode is expected with Development Release B10 (release date still to be determined). It should be noted that Unicode is not a translator—Japanese characters entered in Japanese will not be viewed as English to the English-reading end user. However, Unicode will enable single database and operating level OneWorld instances for multiple double-byte and western European languages and English.

Until Unicode is supported by the J.D. Edwards OneWorld product, it is very possible that you will have to have multiple instances of the product (with a very good possibility that your implementation will have multiple sets of hardware) within the organization. Does this spell the short-term doom of your globalization efforts? Maybe yes, maybe no. On the short term (for example, through 2001) the odds are that you will not be able to get to a single instance of the product on a single set of hardware for all of your sites using a solution that J.D. Edwards will approve of. However, this is definitely not the end of the road.

Planning the Language Rollout   Many organizations choose to implement in what are called phases (for example, they spread the implementation across the company for both modular implementation and regional locations). This buys the organization the ability to leverage time, training, and the core implementation team while simultaneously providing some insurance in the case of failure of the product to adequately support the business (even if one region suffers sales losses due to the software implementation, it doesn't take the entire company down). This also allows the organization to spread the cost of the implementation over a longer time period while simultaneously benefiting from the ever-decreasing cost of hardware (in other words, you don't even purchase the required regional hardware until it is time to implement those sites).

Planned correctly, you will be able to postpone the sites that will cause you to create multiple instances of the product. If not, you might be able to plan so that the hardware used for the first couple of sites is rolled into your ultimate redundancy plans. This will mean that an upgrade of the OneWorld product would need to be incorporated into your implementation plan, but it would also allow you to leverage a short-term technical inadequacy to create a long-term solution.

Finally, even if all of the above fails to fit your organization's requirements, it still won't stop the overall globalization of the company. Multiple instances of the product, even on multiple sets of hardware, doesn't necessitate decentralized systems. All of the systems can, if you so choose, be co-located at a central location leveraging the skills and support necessary to maintain it. You are also able, regardless of the number of instances of the product, to keep the entire company on a single version of a single product. This is a significant improvement over what many large organizations currently deploy (for example, multiple solutions on multiple platforms with multiple issues rolling all of the information into a single reporting entity).

Languages and Their Support

A final note concerning languages and what your organizations will support. You do not need to support every native language for sites that will operate the OneWorld product. Many organizations limit the languages support to major languages and major implementations of the product. This means that some locations are either using English or one of the other supported languages instead of their native language. Because of the prevalence of English in business today, it can become a common denominator in the overall language strategy of your organization. Simply support the languages that have enough significance that you realistically need to support them. If you have an office of five salespeople responsible for less than 1 percent of your overall sales in Malaysia, don't feel that you need to support all of the languages in that country. There is a very good chance that the people responsible for the sales will also understand English (especially since it is a language that is taught in their school system).

It is up to the implementation team to accurately determine the languages that need to be supported during and after the implementation. This should occur during the scoping and planning phase as part of a language strategy. We use the base format for all major implementation strategies: as-is, to-be, gap analysis, and mitigation strategy. Many implementations try to provide everything to everyone. When considering languages, however, this isn't always the best solution for the organization. We've seen one company who in their as-is supported two languages for more than 26 countries. In their to-be, they wanted to support 26 languages. They had to make some hard decisions concerning languages. Although implementations of this type do allow you the opportunity to put in place everything you want, there are costs associated with doing it. In this case, they decided to keep all of the new languages. Because they decided this up front, they were able to plan the hardware and software necessary to accomplish this goal.

Global Development Requirements

Although this is related to the language issues listed above, there are distinct issues surrounding customization of J.D. Edwards' OneWorld code in multiple languages. If you are going to support double-byte development, you should install the database that houses the central objects with the appropriate language code set in the beginning. If you don't, you will need to add another deployment server to house the custom development for that language with its central objects. While this doesn't sound like a huge issue, this is the first step for a decentralized system. If your goal is to go for a single instance of the product, you will begin seeing that goal crumble.

This development also extends to custom reports. Remember, if you actually type information into the report or version template via the RDA (Report Design Aid) toolset, you've done so in a particular language. There is no code translator available for this. You would need to redevelop this report in all of the languages you wanted to support. Obviously this could pose a problem, or at least additional work. If you use the field description provided with the data dictionary when creating the custom report, this would be translated via the data dictionary itself into any supported language.

This is significant for several reasons. First, it indicates that much of your customized code is savable. Second, because much of the customization is saved, it means that your localization efforts are decreased when you support multiple languages on a single instance of the OneWorld product. Finally, it allows you to understand how they perform a huge amount of the language customization. By translating the data dictionary, much (although not all) of the effort of language customization is complete. This could be significant if your company has a requirement to contract for a language not currently supported by J.D. Edwards. We would usually recommend that you contract with a professional organization to develop multiple languages for the OneWorld product. The product is complicated enough without the requirements of a language translation.

Currency and Taxation

J.D. Edwards' OneWorld definitely supports multiple currencies; however, many organizations might have an issue revolving around when the conversion is applied in various suites of the software. Our recommendation surrounding currency is that you research the possible issues early in the implementation. If you do have an issue, this will provide more time for you to determine the best route of addressing it. Your implementation partner should be able to provide assistance with these assessments.

Along with currency, we have to add taxation (after all, you can't have one without the other). Various countries have various taxation regulations that might, or might not, be addressed in the OneWorld product. As with the currency issues, you need to address possible considerations up front. The earlier you can identify possible issues, the quicker you can resolve them. You will also want to ensure that OneWorld either has (or you can develop) the appropriate forms for audit and reporting income in the various countries you have holdings in.

Application and Technical Support

Now, say that none of the issues listed above actually affect your organization. You're home free, right? Not necessarily. If you have a centralized organizational structure with the entire operation located in one or two locations, you need to address how you plan on supporting this organization. If someone calls your internal support line at three in the morning speaking in traditional Chinese, are you prepared to:

1. Have someone actually answer the phone?

2. Have that person understand the language and the subsequent question posed?

3. Have the right skill sets available to fix the issue presented?

It is more than a little question and one that needs to be addressed as early as possible. Are your personnel able to provide the translation of application and technology issues that could beset them at all hours of the night? Most nonglobally aligned organizations don't have this particular issue because each country has its own system and subsequent support, or the support is still regionally located so that there are not large discrepancies in time zones. Globalization tries to centralize the company based on business processes but adds additional complexity in areas like this.

Many organizations choose to implement a follow-the-sun support organizational structure. This is where there are two or three primary support locations with the centralized support occurring and rolling over to the next site based on time. With this type of support structure, if someone in North America had an issue at 2:00A.M., they would still receive their support from overseas instead of the North American competency center. Follow-the-sun provides a couple of benefits in that your organization is not trying for 24-7 support architectures. However, there are additional complexities in that you now need multiple sites where all of the pertinent languages are spoken and that have access to the remote control tools necessary to provide both application and technical support.

Interoperability and OneWorld

Many companies are interested in OneWorld interoperability. The first question that needs to be addressed with regard to this topic is exactly what is meant by interoperability. Is it the ability of a hardware platform to talk to another? Yes! Is it the ability to share information between one OS and other? Yes! Is it the ability to share data between one application and another? Yes! Actually, interoperability is all of the above and can be easily defined as the following: the ability of an application to share and communicate data between differing applications, regardless of hardware platform. This can occur intra-company (different applications run by the same company) or inter-company (between two different companies).

Electronic Data Interchange (EDI)

Is EDI dead? Within the industry, EDI is the longest running and most widely accepted attempt at intra-company interoperability, and it is still a viable option, especially when properly configured. However, it definitely isn't the latest or coolest attempt on the block to communicate electronic data between sites. So why doesn't everyone do it? Simply, no one within the industry could create a universally accepted set of rules regarding what data elements, in what order, with what characteristics comprised a transaction set. The complexity of getting two dissimilar systems from two different organizations to talk to each other is hard enough. It becomes significantly worse when you use different rules for each organization.

J.D. Edwards' OneWorld supports many of the more common EDI transaction sets and the following sections will explain how this process works. As is often the case, it is helpful when working with OneWorld to have a concrete example illustrating how something is done, and this is certainly true with EDI transactions. Consequently, we are going to illustrate the 850 Purchase Orders on the following pages. Due to space constraints, we will not cover every possible EDI transaction within OneWorld.

The 850 Outbound

To create the 850 outbound transactions with the OneWorld product, it is helpful to understand a little bit about the OneWorld product as a whole and which tables are used based on system code. For more information on this type of data, you can refer to Chapter 7. Purchase orders are used to request products from an internal or external vendor. They are typically generated from sales orders or from stock re-supply criteria and often have a series of lines of detail (for example, most organizations don't create new purchase orders for each individual item, rather they order all of the goods from a specific vendor on the same order). Within OneWorld, the purchase order information resides in the F43 series of tables. The question that needs to be asked is how does OneWorld get the information from the relational database into a format that can be easily shipped to other organizations.

OneWorld EDI uses a series of tables (the F47 series) as an in-between buffer zone. The problem is getting information from the F43 series tables to the F47 series tables and from the F47 series tables into a format that is easily transferable between dissimilar systems. Once you have a process for this, you can work a reverse process for bringing information back in the system. Still, before we move on, let's make sure that we have fully addressed the issues and determined logical resolutions for them. If you take records out of the F43 series tables and copy them into the F47 series tables, how do you determine which records to copy? What about records that have already been copied? Once you have these records in the F47 series tables, how do you get them into a format that can easily be transferred from one company to the next? How do you know which records you've already shipped from the F47 series tables?

Extracting EDI Purchase Orders   When you set up purchase orders within OneWorld, you will run across the Purchase Order Print UBE (R43500). One of the shipped versions of this UBE is specifically designed to copy records from the F4301 and F4311 (purchase order header and detail tables) to the F47016, F470161, F47017, F470171, and F4706 tables. This UBE (refer to Figure A-13) selects records from the 43 series tables based on various selection criteria, including purchase order status and vendor.

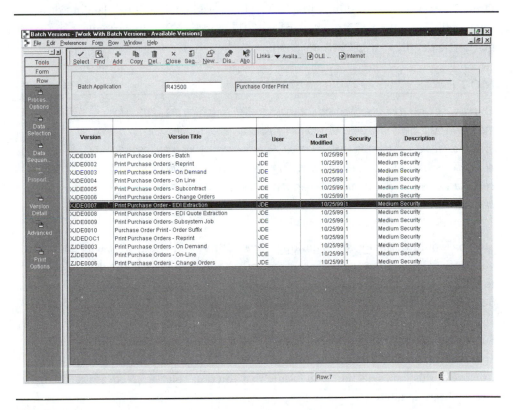

FIGURE A-13.   R43500

This allows you to customize your particular solution. Some clients want all of their purchase orders to run via EDI, although others only have EDI agreements with specific vendors. You have the ability (using the R43500) to specify which records are extracted. It also gives you the ability to set it up to automatically advance the line status. Using this technique, you can ensure that you don't order the same thing twice.

EDI Purchase Order Extraction Conversion   Once you have populated the F47016 and F47017 tables, you are ready to convert the information from your relational database to a flat file (this is the file format normally used to transfer EDI data from one organization to the next). To do this, you should run the R47012C (EDI Purchase Order Extraction Conversion) UBE. This UBE is designed to pull the data out of your relational tables (the F47016, F470161, F47017, and F470171 in particular) and generate a flat file in a specified location.

N O T E

You can use UNC (Universal Naming Convention) when specifying the location for the flat file placement. This provides you with significant flexibility within your own system to create a solution that works for you. As an example, your enterprise and application servers may have enough disk IO that you wouldn't want to have to continually create flat files on them. As part of your solution, you could have these files automatically pushed to a server designated for this purpose.

You would normally create multiple copies of this UBE—one for each vendor that you worked with either regularly or irregularly—and then change the data selections to only pick records associated with that vendor (see Figure A-14). This can be easily done by using the vendor's address number as part of the selection criteria. You will also note that there is a selection pulling records that do not contain a Y in the Successfully Sent field (SYEDSP column). When records are extracted from the F43 series tables, no value is entered into the EDSP (EDI – Successfully Processed) field. Because of this data selection, you ensure that you don't pick up records that have already been updated.

The PDF output shows a blank page instead of readable output; however, the generated flat file contains EDI purchase order information in an EDI X.12 format like the records below.

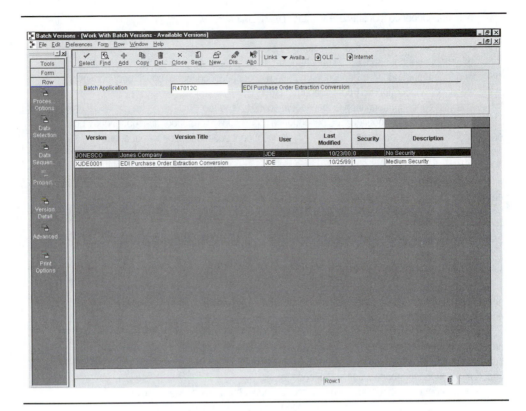

FIGURE A-14.   R47012C

"H","00000000000000000001.0000000000","00001","0000000000000000100000.0000000000
","PO","000000000000000000000000000000000","850   ","
 ","0/0/00","S","000000000000000000000000000000000"," ","9000   "," "
 ","00","00001","0000000000000000004700.0000000000","OZ","000","   30"," "," "
" "," "   " "   " "
","0000000000000000004341.0000000000","0000000000000000006031.0000000000","6/15/05",
"6/1/05","6/15/05","6/15/05","0/0/00","0/0/00","0/0/00","0/0/00","0/0/00","   "," "
    " "   "   "   "   "   " "
" "   " "   " " " "   " "
","," "," ","000000000000000000000000000000000"," "," "   " "," "
 ","000000000000000000000000000000000","000000000000000000000000000000000"," "," "
" "   " "," "," "
","000000000000000000000000009000.00","000000000000000000000000000000000","
","KG","M3"," "," "," "," "," "," ","N"," "," "," "   " "
 ","000000000000000000000000000000000","F","FRF","0000000000000000000000.1751000000

"," ","00000000000000000000000051399.20","DEMODATA "," "," "

","0/0/00","000000000000000000000000000000","000000000000000000000000000000","

"," ","DEMO ","ER43500 ","TN06DN12

","5/7/97","00000000000000161034.0000000000"

"D","000000000000000000001.0000000000","00001","000000000000000100000.0000000000",

"PO","000000000000000000001.0000000000","850 ","

","0/0/00","S","00000000000000000000000000000000"," ","9000 ","

","00001","000000000000000004700.0000000000","OZ","000","000000000000000000001.00

00000000"," 30","00001"," "," "," "," ","000000000000000000000000000000","

"," "," "," ","000000000000000000000000000000","

","000000000000000000000000000000000","00000000000000004341.00000000

00","000000000000000006031.0000000000","7/15/05","6/1/05","7/15/05","7/15/05","0/0/00","0/0/00","0/0/

00","0/0/00","0/0/00","0/0/00","6/1/05","000000000000000000000000000000000","

"," ","000000000000000060062.0000000000","2001 ","2001

"," "," "," "," "," "

","000000000000000000000000000000000","000000000000000000000000000000000","Cro-

Moly Frame, Red "," "," ","S ","230","220"," "," "," "," "," "

"," "," "," ","200","

","EA","000000000000000000030.0000000000","000000000000000000000000000000","00

00000000000000030.0000000000","000000000000000000000000000000","00000000000

00000000000000000000000","000000000000000000000000000000","

","000000000000000000200.0000000000","0000000000000000000000006000.00","00000000

00000000000000000000000000","0000000000000000000000006000.00","00000000000000000

0000000000000","000000000000000000000000000000","00000000000000000000000000

000000","000000000000000000000000000000","

","000000000000000000200.0000000000","0000000000000000000000006000.00"," "," "," "

"," "," "," "," "," ","000000000000000000001.0000000000"," "," ","N"," "," "," "

"," "," "," "," "," ","N"," "," "," "

","000000000000000000000000000000","000000000000000000000000000000000"," "," "

"," "," "

","EA","000000000000000000030.0000000000","EA","000000000000000000030.0000000000

","EA","000000000000000000000000000000","OZ","000000000000000000000000000000

0","

","IN30","000000000000000000000000000000","000000000000000000000000000000","

"," "," "," "," ","000000000000000000000000000000"," "," "," " "," " "

"," " "," " "," " "," ","000000000000000000000000000000","

"," "," "," "," "," "," "," "," "," "," "," ","N"," "," "," "," "," "

","000000000000000000000000000000","

","000000000000000000000000000000","000000000000000000000000000000","FRF","0

00000000000000000000.1751000000","000000000000000001142.2045000000","00000000000

000000000000000000000","000000000000000000000000000000","0000000000000000000

000034266.14","000000000000000000000000000000","000000000000000000000034266.

14","000000000000000000000000000000","

","0/0/00","000000000000000000000000000000","000000000000000000000000000000",

" ","DEMODATA ","DEMO ","ER43500 ","TN06DN12

","5/7/97","00000000000000161034.0000000000"

Although this may not mean much to you, it contains a single header line with a single detail line from a purchase order in the EDI X.12 format. With this output and the EDI translator of your choice (for example, Sterling, Harbingers, and so on), you are able to map your purchase order to your vendor's data mapping. Once picked up and translated by the EDI translation software, the resulting file is automatically transmitted to the vendor. The OneWorld process for outbound 850 transactions, however, is not complete.

Updating Files as Sent　The final step (after flat file conversion) that needs to occur from the OneWorld side is updating the records in the F47016 and F47017 tables as sent. This needs to be done to ensure that the next time the R47012C is run it doesn't pick up records already shipped. You can choose to update all records in these tables or you can add a data selection corresponding to the flat file creation process. We've seen either of these strategies work. As for what would be best for you, this is based on the regularity of the process and how much control your company needs.

You should run the R47017 (EDI Purchase Order Update as Sent) UBE to update the records in the F47016 and F47017 tables. By default, the UBE automatically updates all records in the EDI purchase order tables that have a blank in the EDSP column to a Y. The next time that the R47012C is run, it will automatically skip the marked records.

Automating the EDI Process

In an outbound EDI scenario with OneWorld, your organization will need to run three separate UBEs per EDI pass. On the inbound, there are two more UBEs required. If you choose to perform this every 15 minutes, you can quickly see the complexity required to successfully complete it—especially considering timing. Although you can automate the submission of UBEs on the enterprise or application server (see more on the OneWorld Scheduler in Chapter 16), you will still have issues surrounding processes that don't complete on time or that end in error. To help automate this process, we recommend that you customize the UBEs themselves by linking them with the report interconnect option in the RDA Event Rules End Section (see the following illustration).

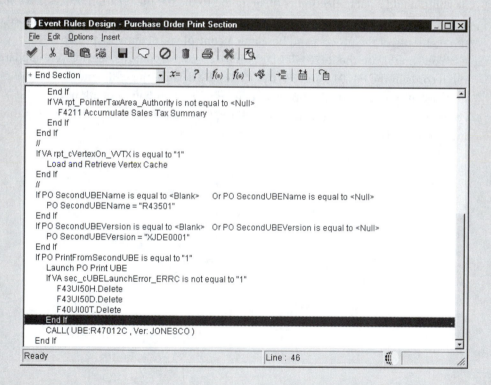

Notice the modification allowing the reports interconnect is performed using event rules and is able to specify the exact versions to call. This allows you to perform vendor-specific version setup within your EDI strategies (this is a must for most organizations). Also, note that we chose to put the UBE call prior to the last End If of the End section and that we decided to only allow asynchronous processing. This will ensure that the last function of the prior UBE is launching the next UBE and that the entire process will complete simultaneously. (For more information on modifying UBEs, refer to the J.D. Edwards OneWorld Developer's Guide published by the J.D. Edwards Press.) Another option with the UBE processes is to make the R43500 a subsystem (continually running on the server in the background looking for appropriate records to process), and then link and schedule the EDI specific UBEs on a more regular pattern. Although both of these are options (and yes, you could perform a combination of the two), you can leverage your implementation partner in helping you decide which option is best for your specific business needs.

Interfaces and Integration

J.D. Edwards provides several robust interfaces and integration points to numerous third-party products, including Siebel, Numetrix, Cognos, Maximo, SynQuest, and so on. There is a variety of different mechanisms available for developing interfaces (both two-way and one-way data interchanges) within the product. There are also methods of interfacing products to J.D. Edwards that are not supported by J.D. Edwards itself and consequently should be performed with caution. Regardless of the mechanism you've chosen to implement with regards to interfacing and third-party integrations, a key to successful implementation is the testing process associated with the project itself. Any time data is either brought into or copied from OneWorld, a robust testing process should be put in place to ensure bytes in equal bytes out and vice versa.

- Batch interfaces/Z file integration

- API calls (also known as master business functions)

- Flat file conversions

- Database triggers

- External programming with the programming tools of your choice

Batch Interfaces/Z File Integration

What is a Z file and why does it intrude upon the implementation process? Initial loads of data or interfacing your new, bright, shiny ERP open architecture system to your old legacy system is part of 95 percent of all OneWorld implementations. The data conversions might be nothing more than transferring inventories and accounts receivables to the newly implemented modules. Then again, it might be an interface able to read data directly from the legacy system into OneWorld. Regardless of your business dictated scope of project, the odds are that you will either work with or at least contemplate working with the J.D. Edwards Z files. These are specially designed tables for loading data from external sources. J.D. Edwards has created batch processes to take data from the Z files and populate all of the appropriate OneWorld tables. In addition to mere population, the information is also validated and posted correctly within the OneWorld system itself during this process.

API Calls

OneWorld provides a series of published APIs (application program interfaces) available for direct connections. The advantage to using OneWorld APIs (as opposed to non-OneWorld methodologies) is that these APIs use the same MBFs (master business functions) as normal OneWorld applications. This ensures that the data coming in conforms to OneWorld standards, formats and is run through all of the appropriate checks, and modifies all of the appropriate tables for whichever function you are trying to perform. When, however, inexperienced programmers call OneWorld APIs, we have seen issues revolving data loops that ultimately bring the database to its knees. This is not so much a concern for the experienced programmer, and even the inexperienced quickly learn the tricks necessary to ensure that this doesn't occur often. Still, it is something worth mentioning. The only other concern to using published APIs is where J.D. Edwards decides to modify the MBFs (this occurs with updates, upgrades, and possibly with ESUs). When this occurs, your organization will need to test your interface designs (to include data integrity) prior to rolling the change out to the production environment. Though this is a common practice for update and upgrades, the introduction of the ESU in 1999 added an additional point where this might be needed.

Flat File Conversions

OneWorld has also long held the capability to pull information from comma-delimited files maintained on workstations. However, in B733.2 the majority of this functionality is built into batch applications. In this release, the object librarian contains a tool (P47002 – Flat File Cross Reference) that details the majority of built-in flat file functionality. From the name of this application alone, you can deduce that it is related to EDI (now the primary use for flat files; see Figure A-15). For those of you expecting to use the old table conversion tools, these too have been marked with system code 88 indicating that they are obsolete.

Database Triggers

Database triggers are a very quick method of achieving OneWorld interoperability (especially when used between dissimilar applications). However, the speed of achieving this solution carries with it certain opportunities that need to be taken into consideration prior to your complete reliance on this methodology. First, database triggers do not use the J.D. Edwards middleware. Although, on the database level, going from Oracle to Oracle is very simplistic, going from Oracle to DB2/400 will require substantial programming or the introduction of a third-party middleware product to facilitate. Obviously, this introduces additional complexity to the solution.

Second, OneWorld does not use database triggers from an application standpoint. The rationale behind this programmatic solution is that each of the three primarily

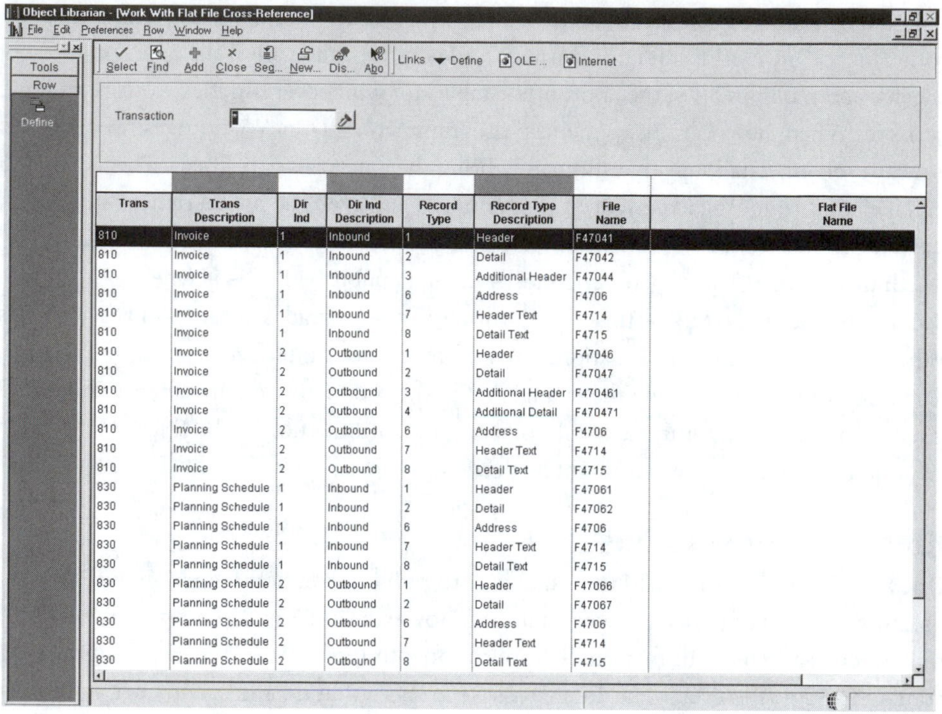

Trans	Trans Description	Dir Ind	Dir Ind Description	Record Type	Record Type Description	File Name	Flat File Name
810	Invoice	1	Inbound	1	Header	F47041	
810	Invoice	1	Inbound	2	Detail	F47042	
810	Invoice	1	Inbound	3	Additional Header	F47044	
810	Invoice	1	Inbound	6	Address	F4706	
810	Invoice	1	Inbound	7	Header Text	F4714	
810	Invoice	1	Inbound	8	Detail Text	F4715	
810	Invoice	2	Outbound	1	Header	F47046	
810	Invoice	2	Outbound	2	Detail	F47047	
810	Invoice	2	Outbound	3	Additional Header	F470461	
810	Invoice	2	Outbound	4	Additional Detail	F470471	
810	Invoice	2	Outbound	6	Address	F4706	
810	Invoice	2	Outbound	7	Header Text	F4714	
810	Invoice	2	Outbound	8	Detail Text	F4715	
830	Planning Schedule	1	Inbound	1	Header	F47061	
830	Planning Schedule	1	Inbound	2	Detail	F47062	
830	Planning Schedule	1	Inbound	6	Address	F4706	
830	Planning Schedule	1	Inbound	7	Header Text	F4714	
830	Planning Schedule	1	Inbound	8	Detail Text	F4715	
830	Planning Schedule	2	Outbound	1	Header	F47066	
830	Planning Schedule	2	Outbound	2	Detail	F47067	
830	Planning Schedule	2	Outbound	6	Address	F4706	
830	Planning Schedule	2	Outbound	7	Header Text	F4714	
830	Planning Schedule	2	Outbound	8	Detail Text	F4715	

FIGURE A-15. P47002 flat file cross reference

supported databases (MS SQL, Oracle, DB2/400) use triggers differently. Because J.D. Edwards uses all three database platforms, they had to also support the lowest common denominator. This affects your interoperability operations in that you can't update a single table within the OneWorld suite and have the associated tables automatically update. If you are going to use triggers to assist with interfacing different applications, you need to have a robust understanding of every associated OneWorld table and other associated application.

Finally, J.D. Edwards traditionally will not support interface data integrity when the interface is done via database triggers. The triggers themselves don't go through APIs/MBF and there is no validation from the J.D. Edwards OneWorld standpoint. OneWorld doesn't even know that the additional data is in the database tables (obviously it will find the data, but it didn't go through any of the business logic or design applied to the OneWorld suite of products).

External Programming

This is another non-OneWorld method of either initially loading data or interfacing different applications with the same pros and cons associated with database triggers. The differential is the tool used to make the work happen. Many organizations, however, insist that external programming is a quick, efficient method of completing this type of work. Our recommendation is that you pick the method best suited to your particular business requirements and know the associated risks with that decision.

e-Opportunities

One of the largest developmental growth areas within the OneWorld product is its e-business capabilities. What is nice about the way J.D. Edwards handles its e-offering is that it is based on the same specifications as its normal C code. This means that there is no additional coding necessary to complete this offering. Rather, the Java or HTML code is based on the existing and modified code in your system. As with any other e-product, the Web-based OneWorld uses servers instead of fat clients to do all of the work. As of OneWorld Xe (B733 cumulative 3), the OneWorld Web offering is 100 percent and is designed for speed and scalability.

Earlier versions of the OneWorld Web product contained deficiencies in the manner it handled certain form types (there are seven form types defined in the OneWorld suite of products—for more information on them, refer to J.D. Edwards OneWorld Developer's Guide published by the J.D. Edwards Press). The OneWorld Xe product contains redesigns that greatly improve the ability of the product to return information in a timely manner.

The completion of the OneWorld Web offering provides additional benefits to the company that is striving to increase the interoperability of their systems. Not only does it provide easy access to a host of published APIs, it also provides direct access for any client on the Web based on the agreement of the two organizations.

Index

U